COST ACCOUNTING
A Managerial Emphasis

Charles T. Horngren Series in Accounting

Charles T. Horngren, Consulting Editor

Auditing and Assurance Services: An Integrated Approach, 10th ed. ■ ARENS/ELDER/BEASLEY

Advanced Accounting, 8th ed. ■ BEAMS/ANTHONY/CLEMENT/LOWENSOHN

Governmental and Nonprofit Accounting: Theory and Practice, 7th ed. ■ FREEMAN/SHOULDERS

Financial Accounting, 5th ed. ■ HARRISON/HORNGREN

Cases in Financial Reporting, 4th ed. ■ HIRST/MCANALLY

Cost Accounting: A Managerial Emphasis, 12th ed. ■ HORNGREN/DATAR/FOSTER

Accounting, 6th ed. ■ HORNGREN/HARRISON/BAMBER

Introduction to Financial Accounting, 9th ed. ■ HORNGREN/SUNDEM/ELLIOTT

Introduction to Management Accounting, 13th ed. ■ HORNGREN/SUNDEM/STRATTON

COST ACCOUNTING
A Managerial Emphasis

Twelfth Edition

Charles T. Horngren
Stanford University

Srikant M. Datar
Harvard University

George Foster
Stanford University

PEARSON
Prentice Hall

Upper Saddle River, NJ 07458

Library of Congress Cataloging-in-Publication Data

Horngren, Charles T.
Cost accounting: a managerial emphasis/Charles T. Horngren, Srikant M. Datar, George Foster.—12th ed.
p. cm.
Includes bibliographical references and index.
ISBN 0-13-149538-0
1. Cost accounting. I. Datar, Srikant M. II. Foster, George. III. Title.
HF5686.C8H59 2005
658.15'11—dc22 2004061743

Senior Acquisitions Editor: Wendy Craven
Editorial Director: Jeff Shelstad
Project Manager (Editorial): Kerri Tomasso
Editorial Assistant: Joanna Doxey
Developmental Editor: Erika Rusnak
Director of Development: Steve Deitmer
Media Project Manager: Caroline Kasterine
Director of Marketing: Eric Frank
Senior Managing Editor (Production): Cynthia Regan
Senior Production Editor: Anne Graydon
Permissions Supervisor: Charles Morris
Production Manager (Manufacturing): Arnold Vila
Associate Director Manufacturing: Vincent Scelta
Design Director: Maria Lange
Interior Design: John Romer/Jill Little
Cover Design: John Romer
Cover Illustration/Photo: Donovan Reese/Photodisc Green/Getty Images, Inc.
Illustrator (Interior): GGS Book Services, Atlantic Highlands
Director, Image Resource Center: Melinda Reo
Manager, Rights and Permissions: Zina Arabia
Manager, Visual Research: Beth Brenzel
Manager, Cover Visual Research & Permissions: Karen Sanatar
Image Permission Coordinator: Robert Farrell
Photo Researcher: Elaine Soares
Manager, Print Production: Christy Mahon
Composition/Full-Service Project Management: GGS Book Services, Atlantic Highlands
Printer/Binder: Courier-Kendallville
Typeface: 10/12 Giovanni Book

Photo Credits: **page 1** Getty Images, Inc.–Taxi; **page 8** Federal Express Corporation; **page 26** Michael Newman/PhotoEdit; **page 33** Charles Gupton/CORBIS–NY; **page 60** AP Wide World Photos; **page 75** Gail Albert Halaban/Corbis/SABA Press Photos, Inc.; **page 97** Philip Gould/Corbis/Bettmann; **page 106** U.S. Air Force; **page 138** Corbis Digital Stock; **page 160** Ariel Skelley/Corbis/Stock Market; **page 180** Jim Commentucci/The Image Works; **page 194** Rusty Jarrett/Getty Images; Inc. **page 221** William Taufic/CORBIS–NY; **page 232** Bill Aron/PhotoEdit; **page 256** David Young-Wolff/PhotoEdit; **page 268** Robert Maass/CORBIS–NY; **page 294** Frank Zullo/Photo Researchers, Inc.; **page 306** Brownie Harris/Corbis/Stock Market; **page 332** Woodfin Camp & Associates; **page 348** AP Wide World Photos; **page 378** Michael Newman/PhotoEdit; **page 390** Mark Wagner/aviation-images.com; **page 419** Mark Richards/PhotoEdit; **page 427** Michael Newman/PhotoEdit; **page 455** David Parker/Photo Researchers, Inc.; **page 473** Peapod, Inc.; **page 492** Keith Dannemiller/Corbis/SABA Press Photos, Inc.; **page 506** Jeff Greenberg/PhotoEdit; **page 531** Ki Ho Park/Kistone Photography; **page 548** Andre Jenny/Alamy Images; **page 565** Najlah Feanny/CORBIS–NY; **page 580** Peter Frischmuth/Argus/Peter Arnold, Inc.; **page 594** Ron Sherman/Creative Eye/MIRA.com; **page 618** Adidas—Salomon AG; **page 632** Will & Deni McIntyre/Getty Images Inc.—Stone Allstock; **page 647** Lucas Schifres/Corbis/Stock Market; **page 659** Kevin Wilton/Corbis/Bettmann; **page 672** Jochen Tack/DAS FOTOARCHIV/Peter Arnold, Inc.; **page 691** Bill Aron/PhotoEdit; **page 705** Harry How/Getty Images; **page 724** MASON MORFIT/Getty Images, Inc.—Taxi; **page 742** Mason Morfit/Getty Images, Inc.—Taxi; **page 759** Satushek, Steve/Getty Images, Inc.—Image Bank; **page 777** Bruce Hands/Getty Images, Inc.—Stone Allstock; **page 791** Getty Images, Inc.—Taxi; **page 810** Laura Rauch/AP Wide World Photos.

Credits and acknowledgments borrowed from other sources and reproduced, with permission, in this textbook appear on appropriate page within text.

Pearson Education LTD.
Pearson Education Singapore, Pte. Ltd
Pearson Education, Canada, Ltd
Pearson Education–Japan
Pearson Education Australia PTY, Limited
Pearson Education North Asia Ltd
Pearson Educación de Mexico, S.A. de C.V.
Pearson Education Malaysia, Pte. Ltd

PEARSON
Prentice Hall

10 9 8 7 6 5
ISBN 0-13-149538-0

To Our Families

Joan, Scott, Mary, Susie, Cathy (CH)
Swati, Radhika, Gayatri, Sidharth (SD)
The Foster Family (GF)

ABOUT THE AUTHORS

Charles T. Horngren is the Edmund W. Littlefield Professor of Accounting, Emeritus, at Stanford University. A Graduate of Marquette University, he received his MBA from Harvard University and his Ph.D. from the University of Chicago. He is also the recipient of honorary doctorates from Marquette University and DePaul University.

A Certified Public Accountant, Horngren served on the Accounting Principles Board for six years, the Financial Accounting Standards Board Advisory Council for five years, and the Council of the American Institute of Certified Public Accountants for three years. For six years, he served as a trustee of the Financial Accounting Foundation, which oversees the Financial Accounting Standards Board and the Government Accounting Standards Board.

Horngren is a member of the Accounting Hall of Fame.

A member of the American Accounting Association, he has been its President and its Director of Research. He received its first annual Outstanding Accounting Educator Award.

The California Certified Public Accountants Foundation gave Horngren its Faculty Excellence Award and its Distinguished Professor Award. He is the first person to have received both awards.

The American Institute of Certified Public Accountants presented its first Outstanding Educator Award to Horngren.

Horngren was named Accountant of the Year, Education, by the national professional accounting fraternity, Beta Alpha Psi.

Professor Horngren is also a member of the Institute of Management Accountants, from whom he received its Distinguished Service Award. He was also a member of the Institutes' Board of Regents, which administers the Certified Management Accountant examinations.

Horngren is the author of other accounting books published by Prentice Hall: *Introduction to Management Accounting*, 13th ed. (2005, with Sundem and Stratton); *Introduction to Financial Accounting*, 9th ed. (2005, with Sundem and Elliott); *Accounting*, 6th ed. (2005, with Harrison and Bamber); and *Financial Accounting*, 6th ed. (2005, with Harrison).

Horngren is the Consulting Editor for the Charles T. Horngren Series in Accounting.

Srikant M. Datar is the Arthur Lowes Dickinson Professor of Business Administration at Harvard University. A graduate with distinction from the University of Bombay, he received gold medals upon graduation from the Indian Institute of Management, Ahmedabad, and the Institute of Cost and Works Accountants of India. A Chartered Accountant, he holds two masters degrees and a Ph.D. from Stanford University.

Cited by his students as a dedicated and innovative teacher, Datar received the George Leland Bach Award for Excellence in the Classroom at Carnegie Mellon University and the Distinguished Teaching Award at Stanford University.

Datar has published his research in various journals, including *The Accounting Review, Contemporary Accounting Research, Journal of Accounting, Auditing and Finance, Journal of Accounting and Economics, Journal of Accounting Research*, and *Management Science*. He has also served on the editorial board of several journals and presented his research to corporate executives and academic audiences in North America, South America, Asia, Africa, and Europe.

Datar is a member of the Board of Directors of Novartis A.G. and has worked with many organizations, including Apple Computer, AT&T, Boeing, British Columbia Telecommunications, The Cooperative Bank, Du Pont, Ford, General Motors, Hewlett-Packard, Kodak, Mellon Bank, PepsiCo, Solectron, Store 24, Stryker, TRW, Visa, and the World Bank. He is a member of the American Accounting Association and the Institute of Management Accountants.

George Foster is the Paul L. and Phyllis Wattis Professor of Management at Stanford University. He graduated with a university medal from the University of Sydney and has a Ph.D. from Stanford University. He has been awarded honorary doctorates from the University of Ghent, Belgium, and from the University of Vaasa, Finland. He has received the Outstanding Educator Award from the American Accounting Association.

Foster has received the Distinguished Teaching Award at Stanford University and the Faculty Excellence Award from the California Society of Certified Public Accountants. He has been a Visiting Professor to Mexico for the American Accounting Association.

Research awards Foster has received include the Competitive Manuscript Competition Award of the American Accounting Association, the Notable Contribution to Accounting Literature Award of the American Institute of Certified Public Accountants, and the Citation for Meritorious Contribution to Accounting Literature Award of the Australian Society of Accountants.

He is the author of *Financial Statement Analysis*, published by Prentice Hall. He is co-author of *Activity-Based Management Consortium Study (APQC and CAM-I)* and *Marketing, Cost Management and Management Accounting (CAM-I)*. He is also co-author of two monographs published by the American Accounting Association-*Security Analyst Multi-Year Earnings Forecasts and The Capital Market and Market Microstructure and Capital Market Information Content Research*. Journals publishing his articles include *Abacus, The Accounting Review, Harvard Business Review, Journal of Accounting and Economics, Journal of Accounting Research, Journal of Cost Management, Journal of Management Accounting Research, Management Accounting,* and *Review of Accounting Studies*.

Foster works actively with many companies, including Apple Computer, ARCO, BHP, Digital Equipment Corp., Exxon, Frito-Lay Corp., Hewlett-Packard, McDonalds Corp., Octel Communications, PepsiCo, Santa Fe Corp., and Wells Fargo. He also has worked closely with Computer Aided Manufacturing-International (CAM-I) in the development of a framework for modern cost management practices. Foster has presented seminars on new developments in cost accounting in North and South America, Asia, Australia, and Europe.

BRIEF CONTENTS

CONTENTS

PREFACE

Studying Cost Accounting is one of the best business investments a student can make. Why? Because success in any organization—from the smallest corner store to the largest multinational corporation—requires the use of cost accounting concepts and practices. Cost accounting provides key data to managers for planning and controlling, as well as costing products, services, and customers. The central focus of this book is how cost accounting helps managers make better decisions. Cost accountants are increasingly becoming integral members of decision-making teams instead of just data providers. To link to this decision-making emphasis, the "different costs for different purposes" theme is used throughout this book. By focusing on basic concepts, analyses, uses, and procedures instead of procedures alone, we recognize cost accounting as a managerial tool for business strategy and implementation. We also prepare students for the rewards and challenges facing them in the professional cost accounting world both today and tomorrow. In this edition, for example, we emphasize both the development of analytical skills such as Excel to leverage available information technology and also the values and behaviors that make cost accountants effective in the workplace.

Hallmark Features of Horngren/Datar/Foster: *Cost Accounting*

- Exceptionally strong emphasis on managerial uses of cost information
- Clarity and understandability of the text
- Excellent balance in integrating modern topics with existing content
- Emphasis on human behavior aspects
- Extensive use of real-world examples
- Ability to teach chapters in different sequences
- Excellent quantity, quality, and range of assignment material

The first thirteen chapters provide the essence of a one-term (quarter or semester) course. There is ample text and assignment material in the book's twenty-three chapters for a two-term course. This book can be used immediately after the student has had an introductory course in financial accounting. Alternatively, this book can build on an introductory course in managerial accounting.

Deciding on the sequence of chapters in a textbook is a challenge. Every instructor has a favorite way of organizing his or her course. Hence, we present a modular, flexible organization that permits a course to be custom tailored. *This organization facilitates diverse approaches to teaching and learning.*

As an example of the book's flexibility, consider our treatment of process costing. Process costing is described in Chapters 17 and 18. Instructors interested in filling out a student's perspective of costing systems can move directly from job-order costing described in Chapter 4 to Chapter 17 without interruption in the flow of material. Other instructors may want their students to delve into activity-based costing and budgeting and more decision-oriented topics early in the course. These instructors may prefer to postpone discussion of process costing.

Enriched Content and Pedagogy in the Twelfth Edition

The pace of change in organizations continues to be rapid. The Twelfth edition of *Cost Accounting* reflects changes occurring in the role of cost accounting in organizations and in research on cost accounting. Examples of key additions and changes in the topic areas of the twelfth edition are:

1. **Increased coverage of strategy and strategic uses of cost information.** Chapter 13, entitled "Strategy, Balanced Scorecard, and Strategic Profitability Analysis," has been revised and simplified. In addition, Chapter 1 describes strategy and strategy implementation; Chapter 3 presents the application of cost-volume-profit analysis to strategic decisions as in pricing, product promotion, and choosing cost structures; Chapter 5 describes how activity-based cost information helps companies choose strategies and design products and how it helps manage costs; Chapters 6, 7, and 8 discuss how budgets and variances provide managers with feedback about the validity of their strategies; Chapter 9 describes how managers make strategic decisions regarding capacity; Chapters 11 and 12 show the application of relevant costs and relevant revenues to strategic decisions such as opening and closing divisions and pricing of products; Chapters 19 and 20 address the strategic benefits of quality and just-in-time inventory systems. Chapter 21 shows how capital budgeting techniques help in strategic decisions.
2. **A framework for cost accounting and cost management introduced in Chapter 2** to provide a bridge between the concepts introduced in Chapters 1 and 2 and the topics presented in Chapters 3 through 12. The framework emphasizes three key ideas for the study of cost accounting and cost management: (1) calculating the cost of products, services, and other cost objects, (2) obtaining information for planning and control and performance evaluation, and (3) identifying relevant information for decision making. The framework provides a structure for discussing topics in later chapters, such as strategy, evaluation, quality and just-in-time systems, that invariably have product-costing, planning and control, and decision-making perspectives.
3. **Increased coverage of the balanced scorecard in Chapter 13** describing how the balanced scorecard can help companies determine whether the problems they are facing are the result of poor strategy or poor implementation. The balanced scorecard and its four perspectives serve as an organizing framework for topics such as quality and time in Chapter 19, management control in Chapter 22, and performance evaluation in Chapter 23.
4. **Activity-based costing (ABC) presented in a single chapter (Chapter 5)** with links to simpler job-costing systems (presented in Chapter 4). New ABC-related material has been added on activity-based management and nonvalue-added costs (Chapter 5), activity-based budgeting (Chapter 6), and customer-profitability analysis (Chapter 14). Activity-based costing and activity-based management material is also included in Chapters 7 and 8 on variance analysis; Chapter 10 on cost estimation; Chapter 11 on outsourcing and adding or dropping business segments; Chapter 12 on design decisions; Chapter 13 on reengineering and downsizing; Chapter 19 on quality costs and quality improvements; and Chapter 20 on supplier analysis.
5. **Increased discussion of decision uses of cost accounting information.** This increase occurs in many topic areas, such as activity-based costing (Chapter 5), variance analysis (Chapters 7 and 8), capacity analysis (Chapter 9), cost estimation (Chapter 10), relevant costs and prices (Chapters 11 and 12), process costing (Chapter 17), quality management (Chapter 19), and transfer pricing (Chapter 20).
6. **Systematic incorporation of new and evolving management thinking** including activity-based management (Chapter 5), integrated approach to variance analysis (Chapter 8), and levers of control (Chapter 23).
7. **Incorporating advances in technology** into coverage of topics. Many of the Concepts in Action boxes focus on technology, information systems, and the Internet—for example, e-business strategies and the management accountant (Chapter 1); influence of application service providers (ASPs) on cost structures (Chapter 2); cost structures and

the risk-return trade-off at Amazon.com (Chapter 3); using activity-based costing to measure and manage e-banking (Chapter 5); budgeting using web-based technology (Chapter 6); growth versus profitability choices of dot.com companies (Chapter 13); making custom fit Adidas sneakers (Chapter 17); overcoming bottlenecks on the Internet (Chapter 19); printing concert CDs on demand (Chapter 20).

New to This Edition

NEW! Excel Labs

- *For Professors:* Key Tables and Exhibits from the text are reproduced online in Excel. Instructors can access the Excel worksheets to support in-class discussion, to demonstrate key concepts, to explain difficult points, or to perform what-if (sensitivity) analysis. The Excel Labs can be found on the Instructor's Resource Center (IRC) and inside OneKey.
- *For Students:* Excel templates for selected end-of-chapter exercises and problems (marked with an icon) are available online at **www.prenhall.com/horngren/cost12e**. These templates allow students to complete selected exercises and problems using Excel. The focus is on having students use Excel to understand and apply chapter content. This Excel-based learning is completely optional; therefore, students may choose to solve these exercises and problems manually.

Excel Lab
www.prenhall.com/horngren/cost12e

NEW! Focus on Values and Behaviors Boxes

As a result of a series of corporate scandals, companies are paying increasing attention to values and ethics. The twelfth edition adds a new feature on values and behaviors that explores the behavioral aspects of the management accountant's job and the ethical challenges management accountants face. The boxes describe the values and behaviors that make management accountants effective. Examples of behaviors and values are:

- *Working in cross-functional teams and as business partners of managers*—Krispy Kreme on p.15, Enron on p. 107, Johnson & Johnson on p. 238, and Toyota, p. 429
- *Promoting fact-based analysis and making tough-minded, critical judgments without being adversarial*—Enron on p. 15, Fidelity Investments on p. 505, and Bridgestone/Firestone on p. 668
- *Leading and motivating people to change and be innovative*—Kanthal on p. 15, and USAA Federal Savings Bank on p. 159
- *Communicating clearly, openly, and candidly*—Pitney Bowes on p. 15, Boeing on p. 201, McDonald's on p. 238, Starbucks on p. 238, and Boeing on p. 345
- *Having a strong sense of integrity and doing the right things*—Worldcom on pp. 15 and 74, Halliburton KBR on p. 29, Bristol-Myers/Squibb on p. 303, Boeing on p. 536, Royal Dutch/Shell on p. 599, and Enron on p. 741.

Note: Behavioral issues are also included in many other chapters such as building a culture for learning and support and trade-offs between setting attainable versus ideal standards (Chapter 7), effect of joint-cost allocations on performance measurement and managerial behavior (Chapter 16), effect of management control and transfer pricing on managers' behavior (Chapter 22), and the role of organization culture, values, and intrinsic motivation in motivating managers (Chapter 23)

NEW! Opening Vignettes

Each chapter opens with a vignette that focuses on the chapter's example company. The vignettes engage the reader in a business situation, conversation, or dilemma, illustrating why and how the concepts in the chapter are relevant in business.

NEW! Prentice Hall Grade Assist (PHGA)

PH Grade Assist

PHGA is an online homework and quizzing program. Selected end-of-chapter exercises and problems from the text (marked with an icon) are available in PHGA. Instructors can post assignments and receive grades. All questions are algorithmically generated so each student session generates different problems and answers while providing immediate feedback and scoring for instructors and their students. A comprehensive list of exercises and problems in PHGA is available in the Instructor's Resource Manual.

Special Section for Current Adopters

Thank you for your continued support of Cost Accounting. To ease your transition from the eleventh edition, here are selected highlights of chapter changes for the twelfth edition.

Chapter 3 has been reorganized to first present cost-volume-profit analysis concepts and then the formulae and breakeven calculations. These changes focus students more on the chapter's key concepts and framework and less on memorization. There is also more discussion of operating leverage.

Chapter 4 features more straightforward exhibits. A summary income statement has also been added to show how all the transactions fit together.

Chapter 5 includes a more systematic incorporation of new and evolving management thinking, including discussion of activity-based management, unused capacity, and implementation of activity-based costing systems.

Chapter 7 has been reorganized so that the discussion on static and flexible budgets are tied together, providing a more integrative and managerial chapter.

Chapter 8 offers a new discussion that links the production-volume variance to the sales-volume variance and describes what each variance attempts to explain. New material has also been added regarding disposing of the production-volume variance.

Chapter 9 strengthens the link between the two parts of the chapter by discussing how under absorption costing operating income increases as a result of either producing more units or increasing the cost per unit produced. More material has also been added on managerial issues such as management control and performance evaluation.

The *Chapter 12* discussion on target costing and target pricing has been strengthened by focusing on the implementation of target costing. The chapter also uses one common example to compare short-run and long-run pricing decisions.

Chapter 13 illustrates how companies can use the balanced scorecard to determine whether the problems they are facing are the result of poor strategy or poor implementation. The presentation of strategic profitability analysis has also been simplified by showing separate calculations for variable costs and for fixed costs.

Chapters 17 and 18 exhibits have been significantly simplified making it easier for the student to focus on the core material.

Chapter 19 uses the balanced scorecard as an organizing framework for discussing issues of quality and congestion.

Chapter 20 has been reorganized using the framework for management accounting presented in Chapter 2.

The *Chapter 21* discussion on strategic considerations in capital budgeting has been rewritten to include a discussion of R&D investment decisions.

Chapter 22 offers an enhanced discussion on using the balanced scorecard for management control.

Chapter 23 applies the balanced scorecard concepts to discuss nonfinancial performance measures and the links to strategy. It adds new material on the levers of control arguing that reward systems must be balanced with boundary systems (to prevent bad behavior), belief systems (that inspire and motivate managers), and interactive control systems (to monitor future strategic uncertainties).

Assignment Material

The twelfth edition continues the widely applauded close connection between text and assignment material forged in previous editions.

Questions require students to understand basic concepts and the meaning of key terms.

NEW EXCEL TEMPLATES! Excel templates for selected end-of-chapter exercises and problems (marked with an icon) are available online at **www.prenhall.com/horngren/cost12e**. These templates allow students to complete selected exercises and problems using Excel. The focus is on having students use Excel to understand and apply chapter content. This Excel-based learning is completely optional; therefore, students may choose to solve these exercises and problems manually.

Exercises are short, structured assignments that test basic issues presented in the chapter.

Problems are longer and more difficult assignments.

Collaborative Learning Problems require students to think critically about a particular problem or specific business situation.

Get Connected Internet Exercises lead students to a Web site related to the material presented in the chapter.

Cases offer an in-depth description of a particular company and accompanying case questions that challenge students to apply the concepts in the chapter to a specific business situation. Some cases are accompanied by a video.

Content that Motivates: Real Business Examples

Students become highly motivated to learn cost accounting if they can relate the subject matter to the real world. We have spent considerable time interacting with the business community, investigating new uses of cost accounting information, and gaining insight into how changes in technology are affecting the roles of cost accounting information.

Concepts in Action Boxes. Found in every chapter, these boxes cover a diverse set of industries including airline transportation, automobiles, banking, defense contracting, electronics, entertainment, Internet services, manufacturing, and retailing. Examples are drawn from many different companies, including Amazon.com on p. 75, Northrup Grumman on p. 106, Hendrick Motorsports on p. 194, Sandoz on p. 232, The Cooperative Bank on p. 348, Delta Airlines on p. 389, IKEA on p. 427, Web Van and Peapod on p. 473, Nextel on p. 506, Adidas on p. 618, Toyota on p. 647, Clear Channel Entertainment on p. 705, AES Corporation on p. 762, and CEO Compensation on p. 810.

Global Surveys of Company Practice Boxes. Results from surveys in more than two dozen countries are cited in the many Global Surveys of Company Practice boxes found in almost every chapter throughout the book. This extensive survey evidence enables students to see that many of the concepts they are learning are widely used around the globe. Selected Examples include:

- *Activity-based cost information (p. 153)*—cites evidence from United States, Holland, India, Ireland, New Zealand, Singapore, and United Kingdom.
- *Budgeting (p. 185)*—cites evidence from United States, Australia, Finland, Greece, India, Japan, New Zealand, Singapore, Sweden, and United Kingdom.
- *Variable costing (p. 304)*—cites evidence from United States, China, Estonia, Finland, India, Malaysia, and Norway.
- *Pricing (p. 435)*—cites evidence from United States, Australia, Canada, China, Denmark, Hong Kong, India, Ireland, New Zealand, and United Kingdom.
- *Balanced scorecard (p. 464)*—cites evidence from United States, Austria, Finland, Germany, Hong Kong, Portugal, and Scandinavia.

Teaching and Learning Support

For Instructors

- *Instructor's Resource Center*
  www.prenhall.com/accounting
  This password-protected site is accessible from the catalog page for *Cost Accounting*, 12th ed., and hosts the following resources:
  - Instructor's Manual
  - Test Item File
  - TestGen EQ for PC
  - Image Library—Access to most of the images and illustrations featured in the text.
  - Excel Labs
  - NEW PowerPoint Presentation
  - Solutions to Spreadsheet Templates provide instructors with answers to selected exercises and problems.
- *Instructor's Resource Manual* by Jay Law of Central Washington University offers helpful classroom suggestions and teaching tips.
- *Test Item File* by John Haverty of St. Joseph's University offers an array of questions ranging from easy to difficult. An electronic version of these questions is also available.
- *Solutions Manual* by Charles T. Horngren, Srikant M. Datar, George Foster, and Ratna Sarkar provides instructors with answers to all end-of-chapter material.
- *Solutions Transparencies* are also available to instructors.
- *Cost Accounting Video Library* produced by Beverly Amer of Northern Arizona University and Aspenleaf Productions provide real-company scenarios. Three (3) new clips are available to add to your *Cost Accounting* library. These brief videos take students "on location" to real companies where real accounting situations are discussed and explained. These clips are available on video or online at **www.prenhall.com/horngren/cost12e**
- *PowerPoint Presentation* created by Michael Flores of Wichita State University provides you with a slide show ready for classroom use! Use the slides as they are, or edit them to meet your classroom needs.
- *PH Accounting Excel Tips* covers basic tasks, navigation keys, shortcuts, productivity tips, and new features of Microsoft Excel 2003.
- *Instructor Resource Center on CD-ROM* contains every print and technology ancillary. This makes it extremely easy for faculty to (1) customize any supplement, (2) access any supplement while using a computer, and (3) transport "the entire package" from home, to class, to office.

For Students

- *Prentice Hall Companion Website* offers access to:
  - Online quizzes
  - *Cost Accounting*, 12th ed., Video Library segments
  - Three (3) chapters of the *Student Guide*
  - Spreadsheet templates for select end-of-chapter exercises and problems
- *Student Guide* by John K. Harris helps reinforce key concepts
- *Student Solutions Manual* by Charles T. Horngren, Srikant M. Datar, George Foster, and Ratna Sarkar assists with solutions for all even-numbered end-of-chapter problems.

ACKNOWLEDGMENTS

We are indebted to many people for their ideas and assistance. Our primary thanks go to the many academics and practitioners who have advanced our knowledge of cost accounting. The package of teaching materials we present is the work of skillful and valued team members. John K. Harris aided us immensely at all stages in the development and production of this book. He critiqued the eleventh edition and gave a detailed review of the manuscript for the twelfth edition. Ratna Sarkar reviewed the manuscript, created Excel worksheets, and gave suggestions for improvement in addition to developing some excellent end-of-chapter assignment material. Beverly Amer proved to be an invaluable resource in researching and writing the video cases. Tommy Goodwin provided outstanding research assistance on technical issues and current developments. We would also like to thank the dedicated and hard working supplement author team of Jay Law, John Haverty, and Michael Flores. The book is much better because of the efforts of these colleagues.

Professors providing detailed written reviews or comments on our drafts include:

Robyn Alcock
Central Queensland University

David S. Baglia
Grove City College

Charles Bailey
University of Central Florida

Robert Bauman
Allan Hancock Joint Community College

David Bilker
University of Maryland, University College

Marvin Bouillon
Iowa State University

Dennis Caplan
Columbia University

Donald W. Gribbin
Southern Illinois University

Rosalie Hallbauer
Florida International University

John Haverty
St. Joseph's University

Jean Hawkins
William Jewell College

Jiunn C. Huang
San Francisco State University

Zafar U. Khan
Eastern Michigan University

Larry N. Killough
Virginia Polytechnic Inst. & State Univ.

Keith Kramer
Southern Oregon University

Jay Law
Central Washington University

Sandra Lazzarini
University of Queensland

Gary J. Mann
University of Texas at El Paso

Ronald Marshall
Michigan State University

Maureen Mascha
Marquette University

Pam Meyer
University of Louisiana at Lafayette

Marjorie Platt
Northeastern University

Roy W. Regel
University of Montana

Pradyot K. Sen
University of Cincinnati

Gim S. Seow
University of Connecticut

Rebekah A. Sheely
Northeastern University

Robert J. Shepherd
University of California, Santa Cruz

Kenneth Sinclair
Lehigh University

Vic Stanton
California State University, Hayward

Carolyn Streuly
Marquette University

Gerald Thalmann
North Central College

Peter D. Woodlock
Youngstown State University

James Williamson
San Diego State University

Sung-Soo Yoon
UCLA at Los Angeles

Our association with CAM-I has been a source of much stimulation as well as enjoyment. CAM-I has played a pivotal role in extending the frontiers of knowledge on cost management. We appreciate our extended and continued interaction with Jim Brimson, Callie Berliner, Charles Marx, R. Steven Player, Tom Pryor, Mike Roberts, and Pete Zampino.

We thank the people at Prentice Hall for their hard work and dedication, including Steve Deitmer, Anne Graydon, Wendy Craven, Kerri Tomasso, Joanna Doxey, Arnold Vila, and Heidi Allgair at GGS Book Services. We must extend special thanks to Erika Rusnak, the development editor on this edition, who took charge of this project from the beginning and directed it across the finish line. This book would not have been possible without her dedication and skill.

Rebecca Rowell and Lisa Van Hazinga expertly managed the production aspects of all the manuscript preparation with superb skill, tremendous dedication, and much grace.

We are deeply appreciative of their good spirits, loyalty, and ability to stay calm in the most hectic of times. The constant support of Bianca Baggio, Niesha Bryant, Katie Haskin, Chris Lion, Luz Velasquez, Carla West, and Debbie Wheeler is greatly appreciated.

Appreciation also goes to the American Institute of Certified Public Accountants, the Institute of Management Accountants, the Society of Management Accountants of Canada, the Certified General Accountants Association of Canada, the Financial Executive Institute of America, and many other publishers and companies for their generous permission to quote from their publications. Problems from the Uniform CPA examinations are designated (CPA); problems from the Certified Management Accountant examination are designated (CMA); problems from the Canadian examinations administered by the Society of Management Accountants are designated (SMA); problems from the Certified General Accountants Association are designated (CGA). Many of these problems are adapted to highlight particular points.

We are grateful to the professors who contributed assignment material for this edition. Their names are indicated in parentheses at the start of their specific problems.

Comments from users are welcome.

CHARLES T. HORNGREN
SRIKANT M. DATAR
GEORGE FOSTER

CHAPTER 1

THE ACCOUNTANT'S ROLE IN THE ORGANIZATION

LEARNING OBJECTIVES

1. **Describe how cost accounting supports management accounting and financial accounting**
2. **Understand how management accountants affect strategic decisions**
3. **Describe the set of business functions in the value chain**
4. **Identify the dimensions of performance that customers are expecting of companies**
5. **Distinguish between the planning and control decisions of managers**
6. **Distinguish among the problem-solving, scorekeeping, and attention-directing roles of management accountants**
7. **Describe three guidelines management accountants follow in supporting managers**
8. **Understand how management accounting fits into an organization's structure**
9. **Understand what professional ethics mean to management accountants**

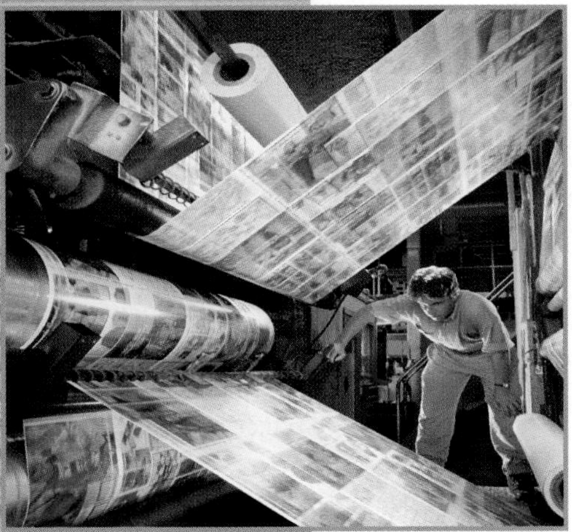

Lord of the Rings. Pirates of the Caribbean. Finding Nemo. What do these movies have in common? Each was a major box office hit, generating hundreds of millions of dollars in revenue. What we saw on the big screen, however, did not come without cost. Behind the scenes, studio accountants weren't just watching the action on the set; they used modern cost accounting techniques to carefully track where the money was spent and why. At the end of each movie's run, the studios could tell just how successful the project had been.

The entertainment industry isn't the only one concerned about costs. Whether their products are automobiles, restaurants, or the latest designer fashions, managers must understand the cost behaviors of their operations or risk losing control. Cost accounting information is used for strategy formulation, research and development, budgeting, production planning, pricing, and more. Consider Naomi Crawford, manager of the *Daily News*, a newspaper in Denver, Colorado. Her desk is regularly papered with more than just the morning news. For example, she receives monthly performance reports containing strategic cost information that helps direct her attention to critical issues facing the newspaper operation. During one morning's report review, she hears a knock at her door from Ramon Sandoval, the management accountant.

Ramon: Hi, Naomi. Got a minute? I'd like to discuss some new initiatives I'm undertaking that you might find useful.

Naomi: Sure. I was just reviewing the latest round of performance reports, so your timing is perfect. You've certainly done a good job of streamlining the reports so that I can see how well we are doing relative to our strategic plans. The way the reports direct my attention to critical areas is a real time-saver.

Ramon: Glad you like them. I've recently started collecting data on how we spend money in the different business functions here at the paper—design and layout, production, marketing, distribution, and customer service—to get a better idea of how each function adds value to the company. I'm also trying to measure how well we're doing with our cost-reduction program and with the initiatives dealing with efficiency, quality, and innovation.

Naomi: That's great. Would you be able to add in a survey of the functional line managers you're working with to get their reactions? I'm guessing they'll be as excited as I am with the information you uncover.

This vignette illustrates how modern cost accounting provides the information managers need to make decisions that can lead to outstanding performances. The study of modern cost accounting yields insights into how managers and accountants contribute to operations, and it also prepares them for leadership roles. Many large companies, such as Teva Sport Sandals, Sony Pictures, and Nike, have senior executives with accounting backgrounds. Managers use management accounting information to choose a strategy, communicate it, and determine how best to implement it. This chapter describes how management accounting provides the financial and nonfinancial information that helps managers deal with these challenges.

Management Accounting, Financial Accounting, and Cost Accounting

The "Margin Notes" aid your understanding of cost accounting. They consist of key points to think about, examples, questions with answers, and study tips.

Study Tip: The *Student Guide* that accompanies this book has several valuable features. One is the "Highlights" for each chapter, which you can use as a *preview* before you read the chapter or as a *quick review* after you read it. Go to **www.prenhall.com/harris** and print Chapter 1. Use the Highlights (pp.1–3) to preview the chapter.

Accounting systems take economic events and transactions, such as sales and materials purchases, and process the data into information helpful to managers, sales representatives, production supervisors, and others. Processing any economic transaction means collecting, categorizing, summarizing, and analyzing. For example, costs are collected by category, such as materials, labor, and shipping. These costs are then summarized to determine total costs by month, quarter, or year. The results are analyzed to evaluate, say, how costs have changed relative to revenues from one period to the next. Accounting systems provide the information found in the income statement, the balance sheet, and the statement of cash flow and in performance reports, such as an investigation into the cost of operating a plant or of providing a service. Managers use accounting information to administer the activities or functional areas they oversee and to coordinate those activities or functions within the framework of the organization. This book focuses on how accounting assists managers in these tasks.

Unlike the remainder of the book, Chapter 1 has no "number crunching." It emphasizes the accountant's role in providing information for managers.

Individual managers often require the information in an accounting system to be presented or reported differently. Consider, for example, sales order information. A sales manager may be interested in the total dollar amount of sales to determine the commissions to be paid. A distribution manager may be interested in the sales order quantities by geographic region and by customer-requested delivery dates to ensure timely deliveries. A manufacturing manager, to schedule production, may be interested in the quantities of various products and their desired delivery dates. An ideal database—sometimes called a data warehouse or infobarn—consists of small, detailed bits of information that can be used for multiple purposes. For instance, the sales order database will contain detailed information about product, quantity ordered, selling price, and delivery details (place and date) for each sales order. The database stores information in a way that allows each manager to access the information that he needs. Many companies are building their own Enterprise Resource Planning (ERP) systems, single databases that collect data and feed it into applications that support each company's business activities, such as purchasing, production, distribution, and sales.

1

Describe how cost accounting supports management accounting and financial accounting

. . . cost accounting measures costs of acquiring or using resources

Management accounting and financial accounting have different goals. **Management accounting** measures, analyzes, and reports financial and nonfinancial information that helps managers make decisions to fulfill the goals of an organization. Managers use management accounting information to choose, communicate, and implement strategy. They also use management accounting information to coordinate product design, production, and marketing decisions. Management accounting focuses on internal reporting.

Financial accounting focuses on reporting to external parties such as investors, government agencies, banks, and suppliers. It measures and records business transactions and provides financial statements that are based on generally accepted accounting principles (GAAP). Managers' compensation is often directly affected by the numbers in these financial statements. Consequently, managers are interested in both management accounting and financial accounting.

Exhibit 1-1 summarizes the major differences between management accounting and financial accounting. Note, however, that reports such as balance sheets, income statements, and statements of cash flows are common to both management accounting and financial accounting.

In financial accounting courses, the product costs used to calculate cost of goods sold are given. In this book you will learn how to calculate these product costs.

Cost accounting provides information for management accounting and financial accounting. **Cost accounting** measures, analyzes, and reports financial and nonfinancial information relating to the costs of acquiring or using resources in an organization. For example, calculating the cost of a product is a cost accounting function that answers financial accounting's inventory-valuation needs and management accounting's decision-making needs (such as choosing products to offer). Modern cost accounting takes the perspective that collecting cost information is a function of the management decisions being made. Thus, the distinction between management accounting and cost accounting is not so clear-cut, and we often use these terms interchangeably in the book.

Managers use cost-management information (for example, product costs and number and type of customer complaints) for decision making.

We frequently hear business people use the term *cost management*. Unfortunately, that term has no uniform definition. We use **cost management** to describe the approaches and activities of managers in short-run and long-run planning and control decisions that

EXHIBIT 1-1

Major Differences Between Management Accounting and Financial Accounting

	Management Accounting	Financial Accounting
Purpose of information	Help managers make decisions to fulfill an organization's goals	Communicate organization's financial position to investors, banks, regulators, and other outside parties
Primary users	Managers of the organization	External users such as investors, banks, regulators, and suppliers
Focus and emphasis	Future-oriented (budget for 2006 prepared in 2005)	Past-oriented (reports on 2005 performance prepared in 2006)
Rules of measurement and reporting	Internal measures and reports do not have to follow GAAP but are based on cost-benefit analysis	Financial statements must be prepared in accordance with GAAP and be certified by external, independent auditors
Time span and type of reports	Varies from hourly information to 15 to 20 years, with financial and nonfinancial reports on products, departments, territories, and strategies	Annual and quarterly financial reports, primarily on the company as a whole
Behavioral implications	Designed to influence the behavior of managers and other employees	Primarily reports economic events but also influences behavior because manager's compensation is often based on reported financial results

increase value for customers and lower the costs of products and services. For example, managers make decisions regarding the amounts and kinds of materials being used, changes in plant processes, and changes in product designs. Information from accounting systems helps managers to manage costs, but the information and the accounting systems themselves are not cost management.

Cost management has a broad focus and should not be interpreted to mean only continuous reduction in costs. Planning and control of costs are usually inextricably linked with revenue and profit planning. As part of cost management, managers often deliberately incur additional costs, for example in advertising and product modifications, to enhance revenues and profits.

Cost management is not practiced in isolation. It's an integral part of general management strategies and their implementation. Examples include programs that enhance customer satisfaction and quality, as well as research and development (R&D) and marketing programs to promote "blockbuster" new products.

Strategic Decisions and the Management Accountant

2

Understand how management accountants affect strategic decisions

. . . they provide information about competitive advantages and resources

The key to a company's success lies in creating value for customers while distinguishing itself from competitors. Identifying how a company will get this done is what strategy is all about. However, a chosen strategy (such as lowering the costs of a company's major products) is only as good as its implementation (for example, training workers to improve quality and reduce waste). The management accountant provides input that aids in developing and implementing strategy. To understand the management accountant's role, we must first understand these tasks in more detail.

Surveys cite strategic planning as a critical success factor for management accountants. See Global Surveys of Company Practice, p. 12.

Strategy specifies how an organization matches its own capabilities with the opportunities in the marketplace to accomplish its objectives. In other words, strategy describes how an organization will compete and the opportunities its employees should seek and pursue. Businesses follow one of two broad strategies. Some companies, such as Southwest Airlines and Vanguard (the mutual fund company), have been profitable and have grown over the years on the basis of providing quality products or services at low prices. Other companies such as EMC Corporation, the manufacturer of data-storage equipment, and Pfizer, the pharmaceutical giant, generate their profits and growth on the basis of their ability to offer unique products or services that are often priced higher than the products or services of their competitors.

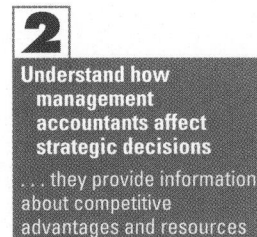

Deciding between these strategies is a critical part of what managers do. Management accountants work closely with managers in formulating strategy by providing information about the sources of competitive advantage—for example, the cost, productivity, or efficiency advantage of their company relative to competitors or the premium prices a company can charge relative to the costs of adding features that make its products or services distinctive. Management accountants also help formulate strategy by helping managers answer questions such as:

- Who are our most important customers, and how do we deliver value to them? How sensitive are their purchases to price, quality, and service?
- What substitute products exist in the marketplace, and how do they differ from our product in terms of price and quality?
- What is our most critical resource? Is it technology, production, or marketing? What demands will be made on this critical resource by the new strategic initiatives?
- Will adequate cash be available to fund the strategy, or will additional funds need to be raised?

Strategic cost management describes cost management that specifically focuses on strategic issues.

In designing its strategy, a company must match the opportunities and threats it sees in the marketplace with its resources and capabilities. Sometimes a company may see opportunities and threats that require it to build capabilities. For example, after Amazon.com's success in selling books online, Barnes and Noble also developed capabilities to sell online by building its information and technology infrastructure. Toyota has built flexible computer-integrated manufacturing (CIM) plants that enable it to use the same equipment to produce a variety of cars, in response to changing customer tastes. Companies can also use their existing capabilities to create new opportunities. For example, Kellogg Company uses the reputation of its brand to introduce new types of cereal. However, the best-designed strategies and the best-developed capabilities are useless unless they are effectively executed.

The Management Accountant's Role in Implementing Strategy

Managers implement strategy by translating it into actions. In building action plans, managers seek input from customers and evaluate and assess how competitors will react. They ask questions such as, "Are the right executives in place to execute the plans? Do the executives have the necessary cash and human and physical resources to implement the plans? Should the company sell more products to existing customers or find new customers? What can go wrong? What contingency plans does the company have if things do go wrong?" Generating an open forum in which questions such as these can be freely debated is essential for good strategic planning and implementation. Creating value for customers is also an important part of planning and implementing strategy. Value is the usefulness a customer gains from a company's product or service. We now discuss how a company goes about creating this value.

3

Describe the set of business functions in the value chain

. . . R&D, design, production, marketing, distribution, and customer service

Value-Chain Analysis

Value chain refers to the sequence of business functions in which customer usefulness is added to products or services. Exhibit 1-2 shows six business functions: R&D, design, production, marketing, distribution, and customer service. We illustrate these business functions using SONY Corporation's television division.

1. **Research and development**—Generating and experimenting with ideas related to new products, services, or processes. At SONY, this function includes research on alternative television signal transmission (analog, digital, high-definition) and on the clarity of different shapes and thicknesses of television screens.
2. **Design of products, services, or processes**—Detailed planning and engineering of products, services, or processes. Design at Sony includes determining the number of component parts in a television set and the effect of alternative product designs on quality and manufacturing costs.
3. **Production**—Acquiring, coordinating, and assembling resources to produce a product or deliver a service. Production of a SONY television set includes the acquisition and assembly of the electronic parts, the cabinet, and the packaging used for shipping.

Understand the distinctions between R&D and design. R&D is basic research and idea generation. Design turns research and ideas into reality. It encompasses prototype development and specifications of the manufacturing process.

EXHIBIT 1-2 **Managers in Different Parts of the Value Chain**

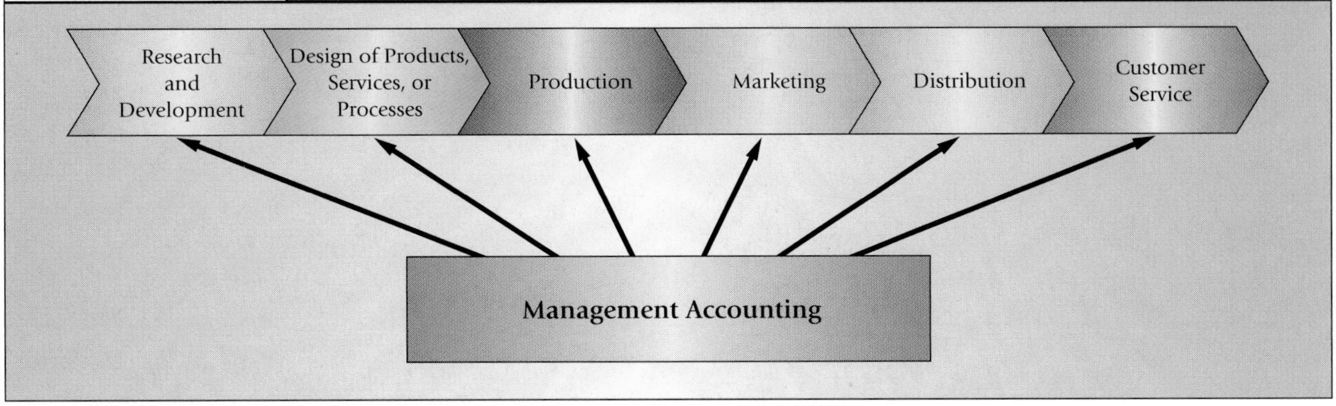

4. **Marketing**—Promoting and selling products or services to customers or prospective customers. SONY markets its televisions through trade shows, advertisements in newspapers and magazines, and on the Internet.
5. **Distribution**—Delivering products or services to customers. Distribution for SONY includes shipping to retail outlets, catalog vendors, direct sales via the Internet, and other channels through which customers purchase televisions.
6. **Customer service**—Providing after-sale support to customers. SONY provides customer service on its televisions in the form of customer-help telephone lines, support on the Internet, and warranty repair work.

Each of these business functions is essential to SONY satisfying its customers and keeping them satisfied (and loyal) over time. Companies use the term *customer relationship management (CRM)* to describe a strategy that integrates people and technology in all business functions to enhance relationships with customers, partners, and distributors. CRM initiatives use technology to coordinate all customer-facing activities (such as marketing, sales calls, distribution, and post-sales support) and the design and production activities necessary to get products to customers.

Exhibit 1-2 depicts the usual order in which different business-function activities physically occur. Do not, however, interpret Exhibit 1-2 as implying that managers should proceed sequentially through the value chain when planning and managing their activities. Companies gain (in terms of cost, quality, and the speed with which new products are developed) if two or more of the individual business functions of the value chain work concurrently as a team. For example, inputs into design decisions by production, marketing, distribution, and customer service managers often lead to design choices that reduce total costs of the company.

Management accountants track the costs incurred in each value-chain category. Their goal is to reduce costs in each category and to improve efficiency. Cost information also helps managers make cost-benefit tradeoffs. For example, is it cheaper to buy products from outside vendors or to do manufacturing in-house? Is it worthwhile to invest more resources in design and manufacturing if it reduces costs in marketing and customer service?

Supply-Chain Analysis

Companies can also implement strategy, cut costs, and create value by enhancing their supply chain. The term **supply chain** describes the flow of goods, services, and information from the initial sources of materials and services to the delivery of products to consumers, regardless of whether those activities occur in the same organization or in other organizations. Consider the soft drinks, Coke and Pepsi. Many companies play a role in bringing these products to consumers. Exhibit 1-3 presents an overview of the supply chain. Cost management emphasizes integrating and coordinating activities across all companies in the supply chain, as well as across each business function in an individual company's value

The value chain in Exhibit 1-2 could be expanded to highlight costs implicitly included in each business function. Examples include administrative costs and future cash outlays for environmental cleanup costs associated with actions of the current period.

Accounting helps managers coordinate the business functions of the value chain—for example, by analyzing whether more money spent on R&D and design will reduce subsequent production and customer-service costs.

Study Tip: The *Student Guide* includes at least one "Featured Exercise" and accompanying solution for each chapter. To check your understanding of the business functions in the value chain, see the Featured Exercise on p. 4 of the *Student Guide*. The solution is on p. 5.

Some companies subcontract one or more of the six business functions. For example, Nike subcontracts its production (manufacturing) function. Even with subcontracting, the challenge of coordinating all of the business functions remains.

EXHIBIT 1-3 Supply Chain for a Cola Bottling Company

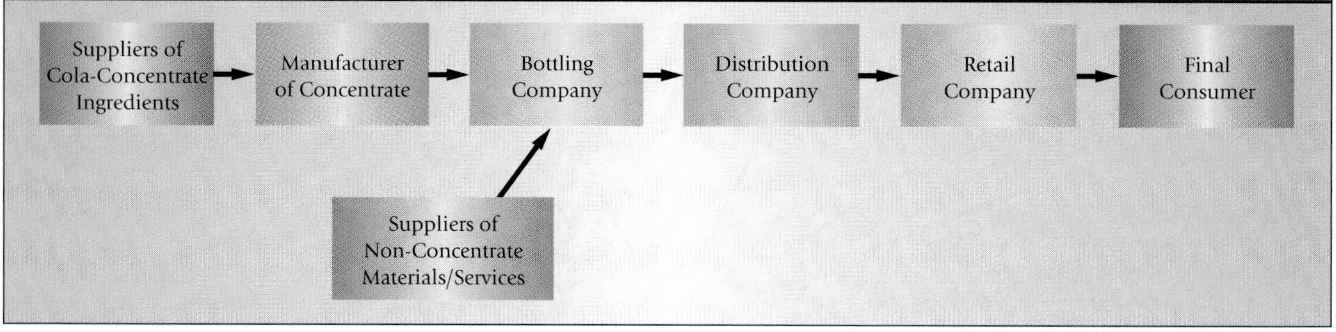

chain, to reduce costs. For example, both Coca-Cola Company and Pepsi Bottling Group contract with their suppliers (such as plastic and aluminum companies and sugar refiners) to frequently deliver small quantities of materials directly to the production floor to reduce materials-handling costs. Consider another example: To reduce inventory levels in the supply chain, Wal-Mart is asking its suppliers such as Coca-Cola to be responsible for and to manage inventory at both the Coca-Cola warehouse and Wal-Mart.

4

Identify the dimensions of performance that customers are expecting of companies

. . . cost and efficiency, quality, time, and innovation

Toyota often "loans" its engineers to suppliers to help suppliers streamline their production processes. In return, Toyota expects to receive a share of the suppliers' cost savings in the form of reduced prices.

Key Success Factors

Customers want companies to use the value chain and supply chain to deliver ever-improving levels of performance regarding several (or even all) of the following:

- **Cost and efficiency**—Companies face continuous pressure to reduce the cost of the products or services they sell. To calculate and manage the cost of products, the management accountant tries to understand the tasks or activities (such as setting up machines or distributing products) that cause costs to arise. Managers monitor the marketplace to determine prices that customers are willing to pay for products or services. Management accountants calculate a target cost for a product by subtracting the operating income per unit of product that the company thinks it can earn from the "target price." Managers work with management accountants to achieve the target cost by eliminating some activities (such as rework) and by reducing the costs of performing activities in all value-chain functions—from initial R&D to customer service.

  Increased global competition is placing even more pressure on companies to lower costs. U.S. companies are cutting costs by outsourcing some of their business functions. Nike, for example, has moved its manufacturing operations to China and Mexico. Citigroup and America Online are increasingly doing their software development in Spain, Eastern Europe, and India.
- **Quality**—Customers expect high levels of quality. Total quality management (TQM) is a philosophy in which management improves operations throughout the value chain to deliver products and services that exceed customer expectations. TQM encompasses designing the product or service to meet the needs and wants of customers, as well as making products with zero (or minimal) defects and waste and with low inventories. Management accountants evaluate the costs and revenue benefits of TQM initiatives.
- **Time**—Time has many components. New-product development time is the time it takes for new products to be created and brought to market. The increasing pace of technological innovation has led to shorter product life cycles and the need for companies to bring new products to market more rapidly. The management accountant measures the costs and benefits of a product over its life cycle.

  Customer-response time describes the speed at which an organization responds to customer requests. To increase customer satisfaction, organizations must complete activities faster and meet promised delivery dates reliably. Delays or bottlenecks occur when the work to be performed exceeds the available capacity. To increase output in these situations, managers need to increase the capacity of the bottleneck operation. The management accountant's role is to quantify the costs and benefits of relieving the bottleneck constraints.

- **Innovation**—A constant flow of innovative products or services is the basis for ongoing company success. The management accountant helps managers evaluate alternative investment decisions and R&D decisions.

Management accountants help managers track performance on the chosen key success factors vis-à-vis the performance of competitors on the same factors. Tracking what is happening in other companies serves as a *benchmark* and alerts managers to the changes their own customers are observing and evaluating. The goal is for a company to *continuously improve* its critical operations—for example, on-time arrival for Southwest Airlines, customer access for online auctions at eBay, and cost reduction at Sumitomo Electric. Sometimes more-fundamental changes in operations—such as redesigning a manufacturing process to reduce costs—may be necessary. The Concepts in Action (p. 8) describes how companies choose their e-business strategies to reduce costs, improve quality, innovate, and grow. However, successful strategy implementation requires more than value-chain and supply-chain analysis and execution of key success factors. Companies must also look to planning and control systems to help them to fully integrate, develop, and implement their strategies.

Planning and Control Systems

5

Distinguish between the planning decisions

. . . planning decisions help managers achieve the organization's goals

and the control decisions of managers

. . . control decisions aid managers in implementing decisions and using feedback

Planning comprises selecting organization goals, predicting results under various alternative ways of achieving those goals, deciding how to attain the desired goals, and communicating the goals and how to attain them to the entire organization. Management accountants serve as business partners in these planning activities by helping to develop strategies, improve business processes, and build teamwork and commitment. Because of their understanding of what creates value and the key success factors, management accountants help managers make better decisions and improve performance.

The most important planning tool is a budget. A **budget** is the quantitative expression of a proposed plan of action by management and is an aid to coordinating what needs to be done to implement that plan. The information used to project budgeted amounts includes past financial and nonfinancial information routinely recorded in accounting systems. The budget expresses the strategy by describing the sales goals; the production, distribution and customer-service costs that would be needed to achieve sales goals; the anticipated cash flows; and the potential financing needs. Because the process of preparing a budget crosses business functions, it forces coordination and communication throughout the company, as well as with the company's suppliers and customers. Management accountants play a valuable role in the budgeting process because they have an overview of the organization as a whole and understand the financial consequences of different actions.

Excellent implementation requires follow-through on how well the plans are materializing. This is the role of control. **Control** comprises taking actions that implement the planning decisions, deciding how to evaluate performance, and providing feedback that will help future decision making.

When taking actions, individuals pay attention to how they are measured. Performance measures tell managers how well they and their subunits are doing. Linking rewards to performance helps motivate managers. These rewards are both intrinsic (self-satisfaction for a job well done) and extrinsic (salary, bonuses, and promotions linked to performance). A budget serves as much as a control tool as a planning tool. Why? Because a budget is a benchmark against which actual performance can be compared.

Planning and control are distinct activities, but they go hand in hand. Managers maximize the benefit of a plan when they use it for control. It is difficult to control a cost without a plan.

Although budgets are primarily financial, managers use both financial and nonfinancial information in planning and control systems to help implement their strategies. For example, action plans often include targets for market share, quality, new-product development, and employee satisfaction. When exercising control, managers compare actual and targeted nonfinancial measures and take corrective actions.

Feedback: Linking Planning and Control

Planning and control are linked by feedback: **Feedback** involves managers examining past performance (the control function) and systematically exploring alternative ways to make better-informed decisions and plans in the future. Feedback can lead to changes in goals,

CONCEPTS IN ACTION

E-Business Strategies and the Management Accountant

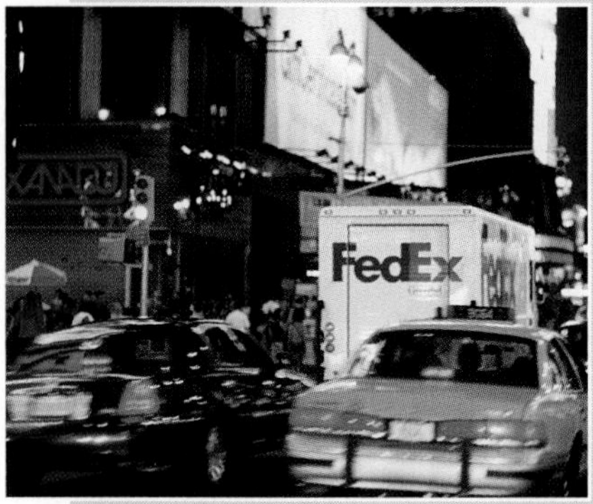

How should a company choose its e-business strategy? Should it focus on initiatives that reduce costs, make the company more responsive to customers, or integrate the value chain and the supply chain? One way to think about strategic choices is the E-Business Value Matrix, which is organized into four quadrants along the dimensions of business criticality and practice innovation.

New Fundamentals include such e-business applications as creating an employee directory or putting information about employee benefits on a company's internal Web site so that employees can access information easily. These applications are not critical to the success of the business nor do they create new markets. But they will probably reduce costs and require only a small investment.

Rational Experimentation refers to strategies such as those pursued by pharmaceutical companies, including Merck, Novartis, and Pfizer, to provide information and literature about their products to doctors and insurers. Such practices are innovative but not critical to business success because the companies' sales representatives can also provide the doctors with this information. Such initiatives can be justified on the basis of their revenue potential and lower costs.

Federal Express also uses rational experimentation by offering customers a wide range of shipping information (including options and package tracking), account management tools, and sales and promotional opportunities on its Web site. Like the pharmaceutical companies, this information is available elsewhere, but the Internet allows for greater customer control and operating efficiency.

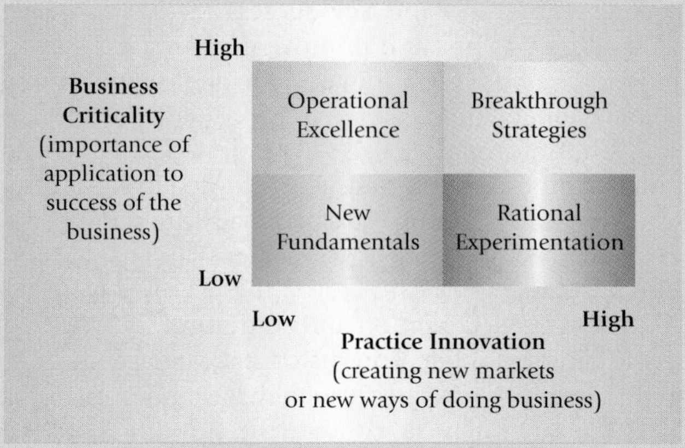

Breakthrough Strategies are strategies like those pursued by eBay, the auction site that enables individuals to buy and sell goods online, or Google, which uses complex algorithms to provide the most accurate online content searches. These strategies are innovative, critical, and risky and are motivated by opportunities for rapid revenue growth.

Operational Excellence includes strategies pursued by companies such as Dell Computer. Dell uses the Internet to sell computers directly to customers and to efficiently acquire materials and components from suppliers. Managing customer relationships and the supply chain are critical to Dell's business, and the use of the Internet is now standard practice at Dell. Dell's operational excellence leads to lower costs and, consequently, more sales, and is central to sustaining competitive advantage.

Most successful companies have tried to populate all four quadrants with their e-business initiatives. Management accountants have helped identify the costs and benefits of these alternative investment strategies. As a broad generalization, the benefits of e-business initiatives on the left side of the matrix have emphasized cost reductions; the benefits on the right side have emphasized revenue growth from distinctive product offerings.

Source: Hartman, A., J. Sifonis, and J. Kador, *Net Ready* (New York: McGraw Hill, 2000). Copyright © 2000. Reprinted by permission of The McGraw-Hill Companies; Google, Inc. April 29, 2004, S-1: Registration Statement. Mountain View, CA: Google, Inc., 2004, and various company financial reports.

changes in the ways decision alternatives are identified, changes in the range of information collected when making predictions, and changes in managers. In their role as business partners, management accountants play an active role in linking control to future planning.

An Example: Planning and Control and the Management Accountant

The *Daily News* has a strategy to differentiate itself from its competitors by focusing on in-depth analyses of news by its highly rated journalists, using color to enhance attractiveness to readers and advertisers, and developing its Web site to deliver up-to-the-minute news, interviews, and analyses. It has substantial capabilities to deliver on this strategy. It owns an automated, computer-integrated, state-of-the-art printing facility and has developed a Web-based information technology infrastructure. Its distribution network is one of the best in the newspaper industry. As part of its strategy, the *Daily News* wants to increase its revenues. Let's see how the *Daily News* will implement its strategy.

Consider first the planning decisions. To increase revenues and be consistent with its strategy, two main alternatives were evaluated:

1. Increase the selling price per newspaper
2. Increase the rate per page charged to advertisers

After consulting with potential advertisers and Ramon Sandoval, the management accountant, the *Daily News*'s manager, Naomi Crawford, decided to increase advertising rates by 4%, to $5,200 per page in March 2007. She then communicated the new advertising rate schedule to the sales representatives and advertisers. Ramon budgeted advertising revenues to be $4,160,000 ($5,200 per page × 800 pages predicted to be sold in March 2007).

The left side of Exhibit 1-4 provides an overview of the planning and control decisions at the *Daily News*. The right side of the exhibit highlights how the management accounting system aids in decision making.

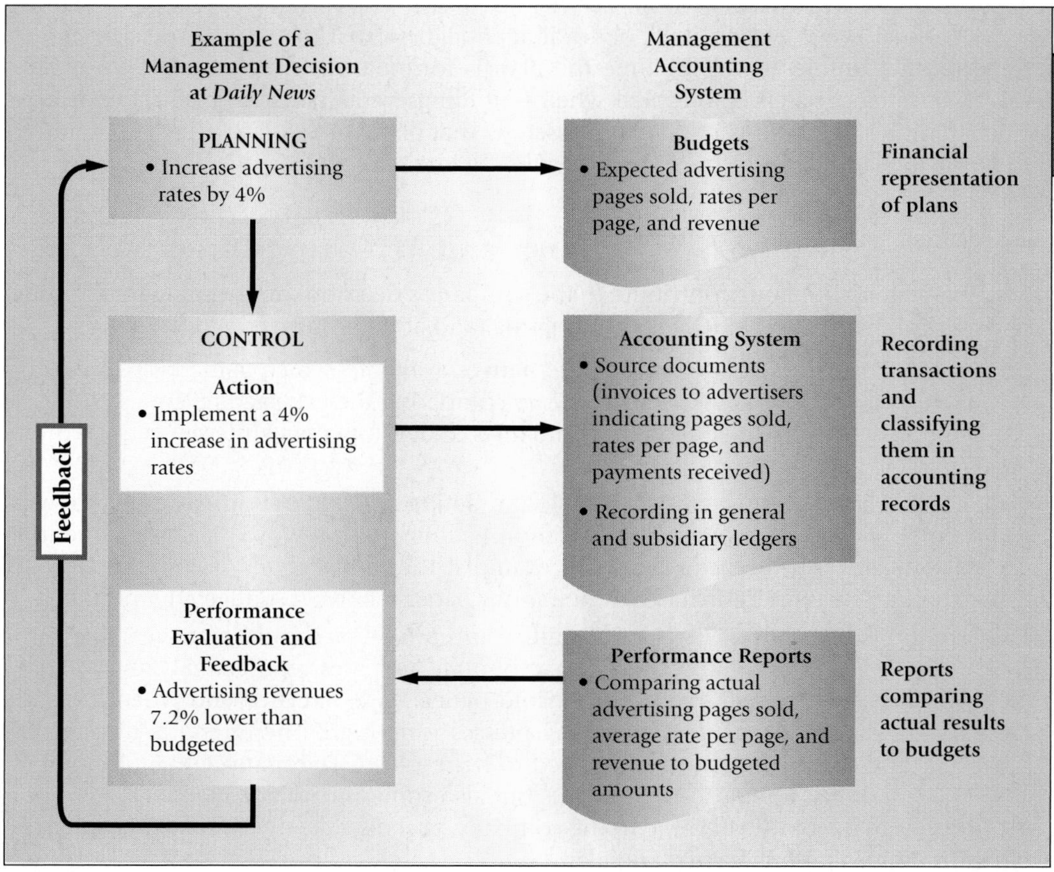

EXHIBIT 1-4
How Accounting Aids Planning and Control at the *Daily News*

EXHIBIT 1-5

Performance Report of Advertising Revenues at the *Daily News* for March 2007

	Actual Result (1)	Budgeted Amount (2)	Difference: (Actual Result – Budgeted Amount) (3) = (1) – (2)	Difference as a Percentage of Budgeted Amount (4) = (3) ÷ (2)
Advertising pages sold	760 pages	800 pages	40 pages Unfavorable	5.0% Unfavorable
Average rate per page	$5,080	$5,200	$120 Unfavorable	2.3% Unfavorable
Advertising revenues	$3,860,800	$4,160,000	$299,200 Unfavorable	7.2% Unfavorable

Consider the *Daily News*'s control decisions. One control decision is performance evaluation, such as a monthly performance report in which Ramon compares actual results for a period with amounts budgeted for that period. During March 2007, the newspaper sold advertising, issued invoices, and received payments. These invoices and receipts were recorded in the accounting system. Advertising revenues for March are the aggregate of the advertising done that month for the individual accounts. Exhibit 1-5 shows the *Daily News*'s performance report of advertising revenues for March 2007. This report indicates that 760 pages of advertising (40 pages fewer than the budgeted 800 pages) were sold. The average rate per page was $5,080, compared with the budgeted $5,200 rate, yielding actual advertising revenues of $3,860,800. The actual advertising revenues were $299,200 less than the budgeted $4,160,000.

The performance report in Exhibit 1-5 spurs investigation and more decisions. For example, did the marketing and sales department make sufficient efforts to convince advertisers that, even with the new higher rate of $5,200 per page, advertising in the *Daily News* was a good buy? Why was the actual average rate per page $5,080 instead of the budgeted rate of $5,200? Did some sales representatives offer discounted rates? Did economic conditions cause the decline in advertising revenues? Are revenues falling because editorial and production standards have declined? Answers to these questions could prompt the newspaper's publisher to take subsequent actions, including, for example, adding more sales personnel or making changes in editorial policy. Good implementation requires the marketing, editorial, and production departments to coordinate their actions.

One final point: A plan must be flexible enough so that managers can seize sudden opportunities unforeseen at the time the plan is formulated. In no case should control mean that managers cling to a plan when unfolding events (such as a sensational news story) indicate that actions not encompassed by that plan (such as spending more money to cover the story) would offer better results for the company (from higher newspaper sales).

6

Distinguish among the problem-solving,

... analyzing for making decisions

scorekeeping,

... reporting results

and attention-directing

... focusing managers on issues

roles of management accountants

Problem-Solving, Scorekeeping, and Attention-Directing Roles

Management accountants contribute to the company's decisions about strategy, planning, and control, by problem solving, scorekeeping, and attention directing.

- **Problem solving**—Of the several alternatives available, which is the best? An example of problem solving is the *Daily News* comparing the expected revenues and costs of proposals from three different companies to develop a new Internet version of the *Daily News*.
- **Scorekeeping**—How are we doing? Accumulating data and reporting results to management describing how the organization is doing and how well it is implementing its strategies. At the *Daily News*, for example, the management accountant records actual revenues and purchases of newsprint paper relative to budgeted amounts.
- **Attention directing**—What opportunities and problems should managers focus on? At the *Daily News*, the management accountant prepares reports analyzing the days on which an excessive number of unsold papers were returned and when the daily utility costs of operating the printing presses were high. These reports direct managers' attention to situations that need to be resolved. The management accountant not only directs attention to problems but also sometimes alerts managers to opportunities that would add value to the company, such as a creative newspaper subscription policy that might increase sales.

Different decisions place different emphases on these three roles. For strategic decisions and planning decisions, the problem-solving role is most prominent. Consider the *Daily News*'s strategic decision to try to increase revenues by increasing advertising rates per page (Exhibit 1-4). The newspaper's management accountant serves as a problem-solver to help make this strategic decision by providing information about past increases or decreases in advertising rates and the subsequent changes in advertising revenues, as well as by collecting and analyzing information on advertising rates charged by competing media outlets (including other newspapers). The manager and the management accountant work together to make a better decision about whether to increase the advertising rate per page, and, if so, the magnitude of the increase.

For control decisions at the *Daily News* (which include both actions to implement planning decisions and decisions about performance evaluation), the management accountant's scorekeeping and attention-directing roles are most prominent because they provide feedback to managers. For example, recording the details of advertising revenues and writing up a summary in the monthly income statement show how scorekeeping aids control. An example of control via attention directing is a report highlighting the reduced March 2007 advertising revenues, with details of the specific advertisers that cut back or stopped advertising after the rate increase went into effect. This feedback helps managers decide which advertisers to target for intensive follow-up by sales representatives.

Feedback from scorekeeping and attention directing often leads managers to revise planning decisions and sometimes to make new strategic decisions. Information that prompts a planning decision is frequently reanalyzed and supplemented by the management accountant in the problem-solving and business-partner roles. The ongoing interaction among strategic decisions, planning decisions, and control decisions means that management accountants often are simultaneously doing problem-solving, scorekeeping, and attention-directing activities. The Global Surveys of Company Practice (p. 12) indicate the increasingly important roles management accountants are playing in helping managers develop and implement strategy.

Key Management Accounting Guidelines

7

Describe three guidelines management accountants follow in supporting managers

. . . employing a cost-benefit approach, recognizing behavioral as well as technical considerations, and calculating different costs for different purposes

Three guidelines help management accountants provide the most value to their companies in planning and control activities: Employ a cost-benefit approach, give full recognition to behavioral considerations as well as technical considerations, and use different costs for different purposes.

Cost-Benefit Approach

Management accountants continually face resource-allocation decisions, such as whether to purchase a new software package or hire a new employee. The **cost-benefit approach** should be used in making these decisions: Resources should be spent if they are expected to better attain company goals in relation to the expected costs of those resources. The expected benefits from spending should exceed the expected costs. The expected benefits and costs may not be easy to quantify. Nevertheless, the cost-benefit approach is useful for making resource-allocation decisions.

Consider the installation of a company's first budgeting system. Previously, the company used historical recordkeeping and little formal planning. A major benefit of installing a budgeting system is that it compels managers to plan ahead, compare actual to budgeted information, and take corrective action. These actions lead to different decisions that create more profits than the decisions that would have been made using the historical system. The expected benefits exceed the expected costs of the new budgeting system. These costs include investments in physical assets, in training managers and others, and in ongoing operations.

Although it is difficult to quantify the costs and benefits of a budgeting system, the question is, Will costs and benefits be considered implicitly (as part of a "gut feeling") or examined explicitly (as estimated amounts)? It is better to be as explicit as feasible, but using some gut feeling may be unavoidable.

Behavioral and Technical Considerations

The cost-benefit approach is the criterion that assists managers in deciding whether, say, to install a proposed budgeting system instead of continuing to use an existing historical system. Consider the human (the behavioral) side of why budgeting is used. Budgets

GLOBAL SURVEYS OF COMPANY PRACTICE

Today's Management Accountant

What do management accountants do? The following table, based on a survey of U.S. certified management accountants,[a] shows the percentage of respondents who named a particular work activity in their top five work activities (out of 29 activities identified to them) in terms of time devoted to the activity.

Accounting systems and financial reporting	62%	Computer systems and operations	21%
Managing the accounting/ finance function	42%	Process improvement	20%
Internal consulting	42%	Performance evaluation	17%
Short-term budgeting	37%	Tax compliance	14%
Long-term strategic planning	25%	Accounting policy	13%
Financial and economic analysis	24%	Consolidations	11%

But to what end are management accountants using their time and skills? In recent years, management accounting has reached a critical juncture. Shifts in perceptions have caused management accountants to be increasingly seen as business partners focusing more and more on key strategic issues, well beyond the boundaries of the traditional finance functions. A recent survey of 2,000 Institute of Management Accountants members identified the following seven priorities facing today's management accountants.[b]

1. Generating cost information
2. Cost reduction
3. Improving processes
4. Contributing to core strategy
5. Setting standards
6. Reducing risk
7. Automating processes

Similar changes are also occurring globally within the profession. One survey of United Kingdom accounting professionals predicted the following tasks would be the most vital to the management accountant's job in the next five years: [c]

1. Business performance evaluation
2. Cost/financial control
3. Interpreting/presenting management accounts
4. Profit improvement
5. Planning/managing budgets
6. Strategic planning and decision making
7. Implementing business strategy

Another survey of Irish accountants noted several trends within management accounting practice.[d] Among these were management reliance on traditional accounting techniques (with only supplemental use of new methods) and movement toward accountants as business partners. Similarly, U.S. respondents identified the demand for "actionable" cost information and continued use of traditional management accounting tools.

---

[a]Siegel, G., and J. Sorensen, "The Practice Analysis of Management Accounting."

[b]Ernst & Young, *2003 Survey of Management Accounting.*

[c]Burns, J., and H. Yazdifar, "Tricks or Treats?"

[d]Pierce, B., "Management Accounting Without Accountants?"

Full citations are in Appendix A at the end of the book.

induce a different set of decisions within an organization because of better collaboration, planning, and motivation. A management accounting system has two simultaneous missions, one technical and one behavioral. The technical considerations help managers make wise economic decisions by providing them with the desired information (for example, costs in various value-chain categories) in an appropriate format (for example, actual results versus budgeted amounts) and at the preferred frequency (for example, weekly versus monthly). The behavioral considerations motivate managers and other employees to aim for goals of the organization.

Both accountants and managers should always remember that management is not confined exclusively to technical matters. Management is primarily a human activity that should focus on how to help individuals do their jobs better—for example, by helping them to understand the activities that add value and those that do not. Moreover, when workers underperform, behavioral considerations suggest that managers should personally discuss with workers ways to improve performance and not just send them a report highlighting their underperformance.

Different Costs for Different Purposes

This book examines alternative ways to compute costs. That's because there are different costs for different purposes. This theme is the management accountant's version of the "one size does not fit all" notion. A cost concept used for the external-reporting purpose of accounting may not be an appropriate concept for internal, routine reporting to managers.

Consider the advertising costs associated with Microsoft Corporation launching a major new product. The product is expected to have a useful life of two years or more. For external reporting to shareholders, television advertising costs for this product are fully expensed in the income statement in the year they are incurred. GAAP requires this immediate expensing for external reporting. In contrast, for internal purposes of evaluating management performance, the television advertising costs could be capitalized and then amortized, or written off as expenses over several years. Microsoft could capitalize these advertising costs if it believes doing so results in a more accurate and fairer measure of the performance of the managers that launched the new product.

We now discuss how organization structure affects the reporting responsibilities of the management accountant.

Organization Structure and the Management Accountant

We focus first on broad management functions and then look at the accounting and finance functions in more detail.

Line and Staff Relationships

8

Understand how management accounting fits into an organization's structure

. . . for example, the responsibilities of the controller

Most organizations distinguish between line management and staff management. **Line management**, such as production, marketing, and distribution management, is directly responsible for attaining the goals of the organization. For example, managers of manufacturing divisions may target particular levels of budgeted operating income, certain levels of product quality and safety, and compliance with environmental laws. Similarly, the pediatrics department in a hospital is responsible for patient billings, costs, and quality of service. **Staff management**, such as management accountants and information technology and human-resources management, exists to provide advice and assistance to line management. A plant manager (a line function) may be responsible for investing in new equipment. A management accountant (a staff function) works as a business partner of the plant manager by preparing detailed operating-cost comparisons of alternative pieces of equipment.

Increasingly, organizations such as Toyota and Dell are using teams to achieve their objectives. These teams include both line and staff management so that all inputs into a decision are available simultaneously. As a result, the traditional distinctions between line and staff have become less clear-cut than they were a decade ago.

The Chief Financial Officer and the Controller

The **chief financial officer (CFO)**—also called the **finance director** in many countries—is the executive responsible for overseeing the financial operations of an organization. The responsibilities of the CFO vary among organizations, but they usually include the following areas:

- **Controllership**—includes providing financial information for reports to managers and shareholders, and overseeing the overall operations of the accounting system
- **Treasury**—includes banking and short- and long-term financing, investments, and cash management

- **Risk management**—includes managing the financial risk of interest-rate and exchange-rate changes and derivatives management
- **Taxation**—includes income taxes, sales taxes, and international tax planning
- **Investor relations**—responding to and interacting with shareholders
- **Internal audit**—includes reviewing and analyzing financial and other records to attest to the integrity of the organization's financial reports and to adherence to its policies and procedures

The **controller** (also called the *chief accounting officer*) is the financial executive primarily responsible for management accounting and financial accounting. This book focuses on the controller as the chief management accounting executive. Modern controllers do not do any controlling in terms of line authority except over their own departments. Yet, the modern concept of controllership maintains that the controller does control in a special sense. That is, by reporting and interpreting relevant data (problem-solving and attention-directing roles), the controller exerts a force or influence that impels line managers toward making better-informed decisions as they implement their strategies.

You may not be aware of the variety of jobs available to accountants. Exhibit 1-6 illustrates the diverse areas that report to the CFO. An understanding of accounting is essential in many of those areas.

Exhibit 1-6 is an organization chart of the CFO and the corporate controller at Nike, the leading footwear and apparel company. The CFO is a staff manager who reports to the chief operating officer (COO), who reports to the chief executive officer (CEO). As in most organizations, the corporate controller at Nike reports to the CFO. Nike also has regional controllers for the major geographic regions in which it operates, such as the United States, Asia Pacific, Latin America, and Europe. Individual countries sometimes have a country controller. Organization charts such as the one in Exhibit 1-6 show formal reporting relationships. In most organizations, there also are informal relationships that must be understood when managers attempt to implement their decisions. Examples of informal relationships are friendships among managers (friendships of a professional or personal kind) and the personal preferences of top management about the type of managers they choose to rely on in decision making.

Ponder what managers do to design and implement strategies and the organization structures within which they operate. Then think about the management accountants' and controllers' roles. It should be clear that the successful management accountant must have technical and analytical competence *as well as* behavioral and interpersonal skills. The Focus box on p. 15 lists some desirable values and behaviors. We will elaborate on these values and behaviors as we discuss different topics in subsequent chapters of this book.

At no time has the focus on ethical conduct been sharper than it is today. Corporate scandals at Enron, WorldCom, Arthur Andersen, Ahold, Health South, and Tyco have seri-

EXHIBIT 1-6

Nike: Reporting Relationships for the CFO and the Corporate Controller

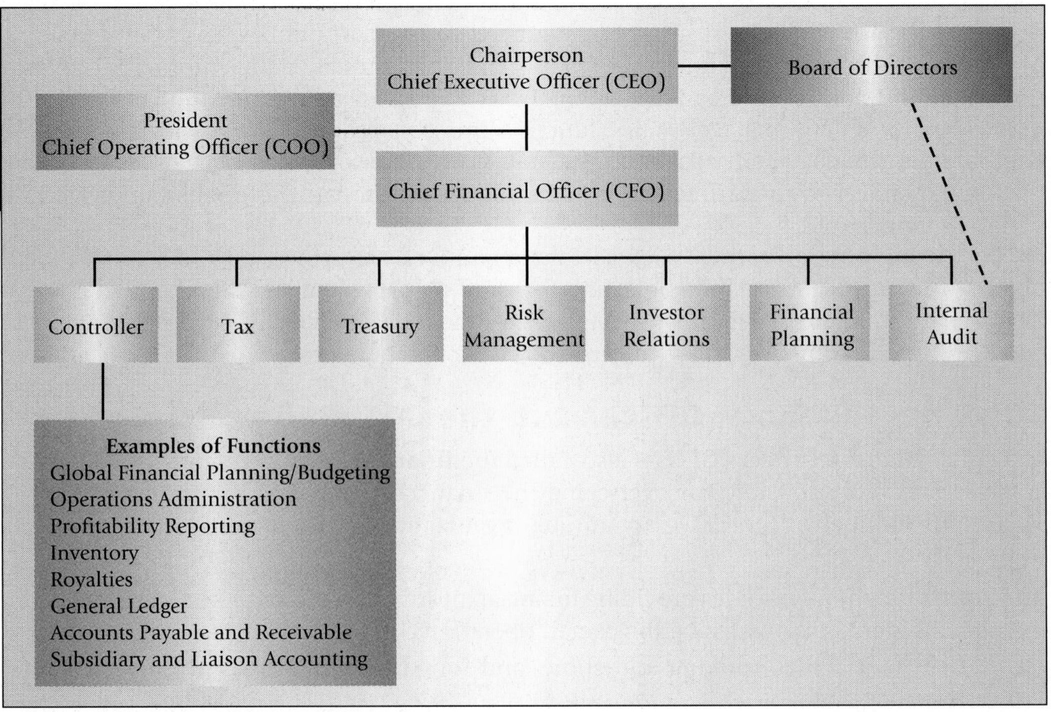

FOCUS ON VALUES AND BEHAVIORS

MANAGEMENT ACCOUNTING BEYOND THE NUMBERS

When you hear the job title "accountant," what comes to mind? The CPA who does your tax return each year? High-level managers at Enron or Tyco? To people outside the profession, it may seem like accountants are just "numbers people." It's true that most accountants are adept financial managers, yet their skills don't stop there. To be successful in the accounting profession, management accountants must possess certain values and behaviors that reach well beyond basic analytical abilities.

Working in cross-functional teams and as a business partner of managers. It is not enough that management accountants simply be technically competent about management accounting. They need to be able to work in teams, to learn about business issues, to understand the motivations of different individuals, to respect the views of their colleagues, and to show empathy and trust. At Krispy Kreme, the North Carolina–based doughnut franchise, management accountants exhibit these values and behaviors when working on teams that make product pricing, store location and design, and cost management decisions. When the company chooses a new franchise out of hundreds of applicants who inquire each week, it doesn't just take the $2 million in store start-up fees and turn the new owners loose. Krispy Kreme management teams up with the new owners to be sure that each franchise is on the path to success.

Promoting fact-based analysis and making tough-minded, critical judgments without being adversarial. Management accountants must raise tough questions for managers to consider, especially when preparing budgets. They must do so thoughtfully and with the intent of improving plans and decisions. Sometimes, as in the case of Enron, the once-thriving energy company that went bankrupt, management accountants apparently did not raise the questions they should have about the company's complex business model. In Enron's energy services division, executives were compensated based on internal estimates of company worth, so executives were motivated to inflate contract values even though no actual cash flow was generated. The company also took on longer-term, high-risk contracts with lower liquidity and set up "related party" entities run by senior Enron officials to hide much of its financial manipulation. When the company finally started to come clean about its financial statements, nearly five years' worth of consolidated financial reports were restated, reducing earnings by almost $600 million. Enron eventually filed for bankruptcy, costing many people their jobs and retirement savings and causing its stock price to plummet.

Leading and motivating people to change and be innovative. Implementing new ideas, however good they may be, is seldom easy. When Kanthal, the Swedish manufacturer of heating elements, introduced its innovative product-costing system, the controller and his team of management accountants made sure that the vision for the change was well understood and that all managers were educated and trained in the new methods. The managers who achieved short-term successes served as champions for the new system.

Communicating clearly, openly, and candidly. Communicating information is a large part of what management accountants do. Consider Pitney Bowes, Inc. (PBI), a $4 billion global provider of integrated mail and document management solutions and a leader in the communications industry for over 10 years. In 1993, the company's Mailing Systems president championed a reporting initiative to give managers feedback in key areas. The initiative succeeded because it was clearly designed and openly communicated by PBI's team of management accountants. By 2000, the initiative was used across all of Pitney Bowes and is still in wide use today.

Having a strong sense of integrity and of doing the right things. Management accountants must never succumb to pressure from managers to manipulate financial information. They must always remember that their primary commitment is to the organization and its shareholders. At WorldCom, under pressure from senior managers, members of the accounting staff concealed billions of dollars in costs. Because the accounting staff lacked the integrity and courage to do what was right, WorldCom landed in bankruptcy. Members of the accounting staff now face prison terms for their actions.

Source: *Andy Serwer, "The Hole Story."* Fortune, *July 7, 2003.; Mark Green, Jeannine Garrity, Andrea Gumbus and Bridget Lyons, "Pitney Bowes Calls for New Metrics,"* Strategic Finance, *May 2002.*

ously eroded the public's confidence in corporations. All employees in a company, whether in line management or staff management, must comply with the organization's—and more broadly, society's—expectations of ethical standards.

Professional Ethics

9 **Understand what professional ethics mean to management accountants**

. . . for example, management accountants must maintain integrity and objectivity in every aspect of their jobs

Accountants have special obligations regarding ethics, given that they are responsible for the integrity of the financial information provided to internal and external parties. The Sarbanes–Oxley legislation in the United States, passed in 2002 in response to a series of corporate scandals, focuses on improving internal control, corporate governance, monitoring of managers, and disclosure practices of public corporations. These regulations legislate tough ethical standards on managers and accountants and provide a process for employees to report violations of illegal and unethical acts.

Ethical Guidelines

Professional accounting organizations promote high ethical standards. Professional accounting organizations representing management accountants exist in many countries. Appendix D at the end of the book discusses professional organizations in the United States, Canada, Australia, Japan, and the United Kingdom. Each of these organizations provides certification programs. For example, the **Institute of Management Accountants (IMA)**—the largest association of management accountants in the United States—provides programs leading to the **Certified Management Accountant (CMA)** certificate and the **Certified in Financial Management (CFM)** certificate. These certificates indicate that

EXHIBIT 1-7

Standards of Ethical Conduct for Management Accountants

Practitioners of management accounting and financial management have an obligation to the public, their profession, the organization they serve, and themselves to maintain the highest standards of ethical conduct. In recognition of this obligation, the Institute of Management Accountants has promulgated the following standards of ethical conduct for practitioners of management accounting and financial management. Adherence to these standards, both domestically and internationally, is integral to achieving the Objectives of Management Accounting. Practitioners of management accounting and financial management shall not commit acts contrary to these standards, nor shall they condone the commission of such acts by others within their organizations.

Competence

Practitioners of management accounting and financial management have a responsibility to:

- Maintain an appropriate level of professional competence by ongoing development of their knowledge and skills.
- Perform their professional duties in accordance with relevant laws, regulations, and technical standards.
- Prepare complete and clear reports and recommendations after appropriate analysis of relevant and reliable information.

Confidentiality

Practitioners of management accounting and financial management have a responsibility to:

- Refrain from disclosing confidential information acquired in the course of their work except when authorized, unless legally obligated to do so.
- Inform subordinates as appropriate regarding the confidentiality of information acquired in the course of their work and monitor their activities to assure the maintenance of that confidentiality.
- Refrain from using or appearing to use confidential information acquired in the course of their work for unethical or illegal advantage either personally or through third parties.

Integrity

Practitioners of management accounting and financial management have a responsibility to:

- Avoid actual or apparent conflicts of interest and advise all appropriate parties of any potential conflict.
- Refrain from engaging in any activity that would prejudice their ability to carry out their duties ethically.
- Refuse any gift, favor, or hospitality that would influence or would appear to influence their actions.
- Refrain from either actively or passively subverting the attainment of the organization's legitimate and ethical objectives.
- Recognize and communicate professional limitations or other constraints that would preclude responsible judgment or successful performance of an activity.
- Communicate unfavorable as well as favorable information and professional judgments or opinions.
- Refrain from engaging in or supporting any activity that would discredit the profession.

Objectivity

Practitioners of management accounting and financial management have a responsibility to:

- Communicate information fairly and objectively.
- Disclose fully all relevant information that could reasonably be expected to influence an intended user's understanding of the reports, comments, and recommendations presented.

Source: Statement on Management Accounting Number 1-C, *Standards of Ethical Conduct for Practitioners of Management Accounting and Financial Management* (Montvale, NJ: Institute of Management Accountants, 2000). Reprinted with permission from the Institute of Management Accountants, Montvale, NJ, www.imanet.org.

the holder has demonstrated the competency of technical knowledge required by the IMA in management accounting and financial management, respectively.

The IMA has issued a *Standards of Ethical Conduct for Management Accountants*. Exhibit 1-7 presents the IMA's guidance on issues relating to competence, confidentiality, integrity, and objectivity. The IMA provides its members with an ethics hotline service. Members can call professional counselors at the IMA's Ethics Counseling Service to discuss their ethical dilemmas. The counselors help identify the key ethical issues and possible alternative ways of resolving them, and confidentiality is guaranteed.

Details of the IMA's guidance on ethical issues, including its ethics hotline service, are available at **www.imanet.org**.

Typical Ethical Challenges

Ethical issues can confront management accountants in many ways. Here are two examples:

- **Case A:** A management accountant, knowing that reporting a loss for a software division will result in yet another "rightsizing initiative" (a gentler term than "layoffs"), has concerns about the commercial potential of a software product for which development costs are currently being capitalized as an asset rather than being shown as an expense for internal reporting purposes. The division manager argues that showing development costs as an asset is justified because the new product will generate profits. However, he presents little evidence to support his argument. The last two products from this division have been unsuccessful. The management accountant has many friends in the division and wants to avoid a personal confrontation with the division manager.
- **Case B:** A packaging supplier, bidding for a new contract, offers the management accountant of the purchasing company an all-expenses-paid weekend to the Super Bowl. The supplier does not mention the new contract when giving the invitation. The accountant is not a personal friend of the supplier. He knows cost issues are critical in approving the new contract and is concerned that the supplier will ask for details about bids by competing packaging companies.

In each case the management accountant is faced with an ethical dilemma. Case A involves competence, objectivity, and integrity. The management accountant should request that the division manager provide credible evidence that the new product is commercially viable. If the manager does not provide such evidence, expensing development costs in the current period is appropriate. Case B involves confidentiality and integrity.

EXHIBIT 1-8

Resolution of Ethical Conflict

In applying the standards of ethical conduct, practitioners of management accounting and financial management may encounter problems in identifying unethical behavior or in resolving an ethical conflict. When faced with significant ethical issues, practitioners of management accounting and financial management should follow the established policies of the organization bearing on the resolution of such conflict. If these policies do not resolve the ethical conflict, such practitioners should consider the following courses of action:

- Discuss such problems with the immediate superior except when it appears that the superior is involved, in which case the problem should be presented initially to the next higher managerial level. If satisfactory resolution cannot be achieved when the problem is initially presented, submit the issues to the next higher managerial level.

  If the immediate superior is the chief executive officer, or equivalent, the acceptable reviewing authority may be a group such as the audit committee, executive committee, board of directors, board of trustees, or owners. Contact with levels above the immediate superior should be initiated only with the superior's knowledge, assuming the superior is not involved. Except where legally prescribed, communication of such problems to authorities or individuals not employed or engaged by the organization is not considered appropriate.
- Clarify relevant ethical issues by confidential discussion with an objective advisor (e.g., IMA Ethics Counseling Service) to obtain a better understanding of possible courses of action.
- Consult your own attorney as to legal obligations and rights concerning the ethical conflict.
- If the ethical conflict still exists after exhausting all levels of internal review, there may be no other recourse on significant matters than to resign from the organization and to submit an informative memorandum to an appropriate representative of the organization. After resignation, depending on the nature of the ethical conflict, it may also be appropriate to notify other parties.

Source: Statement on Management Accounting Number 1-C, *Standards of Ethical Conduct for Practitioners of Management Accounting and Financial Management* (Montvale, NJ: Institute of Management Accountants, 2000). Reprinted with permission from the Institute of Management Accountants, Montvale, NJ, www.imanet.org.

Ethical issues are not always clear-cut. The supplier in Case B may have no intention of raising issues associated with the bid. However, the appearance of a conflict of interest in Case B is sufficient for many companies to prohibit employees from accepting "favors" from suppliers. Exhibit 1-8 on page 19 presents the IMA's guidance on "Resolution of Ethical Conflict." The accountant in Case B should discuss the invitation with his immediate supervisor. If the visit is approved, the supplier should be informed that the invitation has been officially approved subject to his following corporate policy (which includes the confidentiality of information).

Most professional accounting organizations around the globe issue statements about professional ethics. These statements include many of the same issues discussed by the IMA in Exhibits 1-7 and 1-8. For example, the Chartered Institute of Management Accountants (CIMA) in the United Kingdom identifies the same four fundamental principles as in Exhibit 1-7: competency, confidentiality, integrity, and objectivity.

PROBLEM FOR SELF-STUDY

Campbell Soup Company incurs the following costs:

a. Purchase of tomatoes by a canning plant for Campbell's tomato-soup products
b. Materials purchased for redesigning Pepperidge Farm biscuit containers to make biscuits stay fresh longer
c. Payment to Backer, Spielvogel, Bates, the advertising agency, for advertising work on Healthy Request line of soup products
d. Salaries of food technologists researching feasibility of a Prego pizza sauce that has minimal calories
e. Payment to Safeway for redeeming coupons on Campbell's food products
f. Cost of a toll-free telephone line used for customer inquiries about using Campbell's soup products
g. Cost of gloves used by line operators on the Swanson Fiesta breakfast-food production line
h. Cost of handheld computers used by Pepperidge Farm delivery staff serving major supermarket accounts

Required

Classify each cost item (**a–h**) as one of the business functions in the value chain shown in Exhibit 1-2 (p. 5).

SOLUTION

a. Production
b. Design of products, services, or processes
c. Marketing
d. Research and development
e. Marketing
f. Customer service
g. Production
h. Distribution

DECISION POINTS

The following question-and-answer format summarizes the chapter's learning objectives. Each decision presents a key question related to a learning objective. The guidelines are the answer to that question.

Decision	Guidelines
1. What information does cost accounting provide?	Cost accounting measures, analyzes, and reports financial and nonfinancial information relating to the cost of acquiring or using resources in an organization. Cost accounting provides information to both management accounting and financial accounting.

2. How do management accountants support strategic decisions?	Management accountants contribute to strategic decisions by providing information about the sources of competitive advantage.
3. How do companies add value?	Companies add value through R&D; design of products, services, or processes; production; marketing; distribution; and customer service. Managers in all of these value-chain business functions are customers of management accounting information.
4. What are the dimensions of performance that customers are expecting of companies?	Customers are expecting that companies deliver performance through cost and efficiency, quality, time, and innovation.
5. How do managers implement strategy?	Managers implement strategy by making planning decisions and control decisions. Planning decisions include deciding on organization goals, predicting results under various alternative ways of achieving those goals, and then deciding how to attain the desired goals. Control decisions include taking actions to implement the planning decisions and deciding on performance evaluation and feedback that will help future decision making.
6. What roles do management accountants perform?	In most organizations, management accountants perform multiple roles to implement strategies: problem solving (comparative analyses for decision making and planning), scorekeeping (accumulating data and reporting reliable results), and attention directing (helping managers properly focus on problems and opportunities).
7. What guidelines do management accountants use?	Three guidelines that help management accountants increase their value to managers are (a) employ a cost-benefit approach, (b) recognize behavioral as well as technical considerations, and (c) identify different costs for different purposes.
8. Where does the management accounting function fit into an organization's structure?	Management accounting is an integral part of the controller's function in an organization. In most organizations, the controller reports to the chief financial officer, who is a key member of the top management team.
9. What are the ethical responsibilities of management accountants?	Management accountants have ethical responsibilities that are related to competence, confidentiality, integrity, and objectivity.

TERMS TO LEARN

Each chapter will include this section. Like all technical terms, accounting terms have precise meanings. Learn the definitions of new terms when you initially encounter them. The meaning of each of the following terms is given in this chapter and in the Glossary at the end of this book.

attention directing (p. 10)
budget (p. 7)
Certified in Financial Management (CFM) (p. 16)
Certified Management Accountant (CMA) (p. 16)
chief financial officer (CFO) (p. 13)
control (p. 7)
controller (p. 14)
cost accounting (p. 2)
cost-benefit approach (p. 11)
cost management (p. 2)
customer service (p. 5)
design of products, services, or processes (p. 4)
distribution (p. 5)
feedback (p. 7)
finance director (p. 13)
financial accounting (p. 2)
Institute of Management Accountants (IMA) (p. 16)
line management (p. 13)
management accounting (p. 2)
marketing (p. 5)
planning (p. 7)
problem solving (p. 10)
production (p. 4)
research and development (p. 4)
scorekeeping (p. 10)
staff management (p. 13)
strategic cost management (p. 4)
strategy (p. 3)
supply chain (p. 5)
value chain (p. 4)

PH Grade Assist

Prentice Hall Grade Assist (PHGA)
Your professor may ask you to complete selected exercises and problems in Prentice Hall Grade Assist (PHGA). PHGA is an online tool that can help you master the chapter's topics. It provides you with multiple variations of exercises and problems designated by the PHGA icon. You can rework these exercises and problems—each time with new data—as many times as you need. You also receive immediate feedback and grading.

ASSIGNMENT MATERIAL

Questions

1-1 How does management accounting differ from financial accounting?

1-2 "Management accounting should not fit the straitjacket of financial accounting." Explain and give an example.

1-3 How can a management accountant help formulate a strategy?

1-4 Describe the business functions in the value chain.

1-5 Explain the term "supply chain" and its importance to cost management.

1-6 "Management accounting deals only with costs." Do you agree? Explain.

1-7 How can management accountants help improve quality and achieve timely product deliveries?

1-8 Distinguish planning decisions from control decisions.

1-9 What are three roles that management accountants perform?

1-10 What three guidelines help management accountants provide the most value to managers?

1-11 "Knowledge of technical issues such as computer technology is a necessary but not sufficient condition to becoming a successful management accountant." Do you agree? Why?

1-12 As a new controller, reply to this comment by a plant manager: "As I see it, our accountants may be needed to keep records for shareholders and Uncle Sam, but I don't want them sticking their noses in my day-to-day operations. I do the best I know how. No bean counter knows enough about my responsibilities to be of any use to me."

1-13 As used in accounting, what do IMA and CMA stand for?

1-14 Name the four areas in which standards of ethical conduct exist for management accountants in the United States. What organization sets forth these standards?

1-15 What steps should a management accountant take if established written policies provide insufficient guidance on how to handle an ethical conflict?

Exercises

PH Grade Assist

1-16 Value chain and classification of costs, computer company. Compaq Computer incurs the following costs:

- **a.** Electricity costs for the plant assembling the Presario computer line of products
- **b.** Transportation costs for shipping the Presario line of products to a retail chain
- **c.** Payment to David Kelley Designs for design of the Armada Notebook
- **d.** Salary of computer scientist working on the next generation of minicomputers
- **e.** Cost of Compaq employees' visit to a major customer to demonstrate Compaq's ability to interconnect with other computers
- **f.** Purchase of competitors' products for testing against potential Compaq products
- **g.** Payment to television network for running Compaq advertisements
- **h.** Cost of cables purchased from outside supplier to be used with Compaq printers

Required Classify each of the cost items (**a–h**) into one of the business functions of the value chain shown in Exhibit 1-2 (p. 5).

1-17 Value chain and classification of costs, pharmaceutical company. Merck, a pharmaceutical company, incurs the following costs:

- **a.** Cost of redesigning blister packs to make drug containers more tamperproof
- **b.** Cost of videos sent to doctors to promote sales of a new drug
- **c.** Cost of a toll-free telephone line used for customer inquiries about drug usage, side effects of drugs, and so on
- **d.** Equipment purchased to conduct experiments on drugs yet to be approved by the government
- **e.** Payment to actors for a television infomercial promoting a new hair-growth product for balding men
- **f.** Labor costs of workers in the packaging area of a production facility
- **g.** Bonus paid to a salesperson for exceeding a monthly sales quota
- **h.** Cost of Federal Express courier service to deliver drugs to hospitals

Required Classify each of the cost items (**a–h**) as one of the business functions of the value chain shown in Exhibit 1-2 (p. 5).

1-18 Management accounting system and its customers. A recent annual report of Ford Motor Company included the following comments:

- "Delivering great value to our customers. That's our passion."
- "Throughout Ford Motor Company, we're focused on improving the quality and value of our products and speeding delivery to market."

Required

1. Who are the customers of management accounting?
2. How may the value of management accounting systems to the customers of management accounting systems be enhanced?

PH Grade Assist

1-19 Value chain, supply chain, and key success factors. A survey on the ways organizations are changing their management accounting systems reported the following:

- **a.** Company A now prepares a value-chain income statement for each brand it sells.

b. Company B now presents in a single report all costs related to achieving high quality levels in its products.

c. Company C now presents in its performance reports estimates of the manufacturing costs of its two most important competitors, in addition to its own manufacturing costs.

d. Company D now contracts with its suppliers to frequently deliver small quantities of materials directly to the production floor.

e. Company E now reports the percentage of times it fails to meet delivery dates that it has promised to customers.

Required

Link each of these changes to value-chain or supply-chain analysis or to the key success factors that are important to managers.

1-20 Planning and control decisions. Barnes & Noble is a book retailing company. Most of its sales are made at its own stores, which are located in shopping malls or in central business districts. A small but increasing percentage of sales is made via BarnesandNoble.com, whose major competitor is Amazon.com.

The following five reports were recently prepared by the management accounting group at Barnes & Noble:

1. Annual financial statements
2. Weekly report to vice president of operations for each Barnes & Noble store (includes revenues and operating costs)
3. Study for vice president of new business development of the expected revenues and costs of BarnesandNoble.com, selling music products (CDs, cassettes, etc.) as well as books
4. Weekly report to book publishers and trade magazines on the sales of the 10 top-selling fiction and nonfiction books at both its own stores and BarnesandNoble.com
5. Report to insurance company on losses Barnes & Noble suffered at three of its North Carolina stores due to a hurricane

Required

For each report, identify both a planning decision and a control decision used by a Barnes & Noble manager.

1-21 Problem solving, scorekeeping, and attention directing. For each of the following activities, identify the main role the accountant is performing—problem solving, scorekeeping, or attention directing.

PH Grade Assist

a. Preparing a statement of the past year's monthly sales for the vice president of marketing at IBM

b. Preparing a statement indicating products for which sales declined relative to the past year for the vice president of marketing at IBM

c. Identifying alternative strategies to reduce warranty costs for the manager of the Lighting Division at GE

d. Preparing a report for the manager of the Lighting Division at GE regarding the warranty policies and estimated warranty costs of leading lighting companies

e. Analyzing the impact on product costs of design changes in the headlights used in Subaru cars

f. Preparing a report recording actual costs incurred during the first year of production (actual costs can then be compared to the planned or budgeted costs)

g. Preparing a report about how the unit costs of a new product are anticipated to decline over time as the plant gains experience in producing it

h. Preparing a performance report for the shipping department at Xerox Corporation

i. Developing alternative strategies to reduce costs for the shipping department at Xerox Corporation

j. Analyzing for the manager of global business development at General Motors the costs and benefits of having some parts made in Korea

1-22 Problem solving, scorekeeping, and attention directing. For each of the following activities, identify the main role the accountant is performing—problem solving, scorekeeping, or attention directing.

1. Interpreting differences between actual results and budgeted amounts in a shipping manager's performance report at a Daewoo distribution center
2. Preparing a report showing the benefits of leasing motor vehicles rather than owning them
3. Preparing journal entries for depreciation on the personnel manager's office equipment at Citibank
4. Preparing a customer's monthly statement for a Sears store
5. Processing the weekly payroll for the Harvard University Maintenance Department
6. Explaining the product-design manager's performance report at a Chrysler division
7. Analyzing the costs of different ways to blend materials in the foundry of a General Electric plant
8. Tallying sales, by branches, for the sales vice president of Unilever
9. Analyzing for the president of Microsoft the impact of a contemplated new product on net income
10. Interpreting why an IBM sales district did not meet its sales quota

1-23 Professional ethics and reporting division performance. Marcia Miller is division controller and Tom Maloney is division manager of the Ramses Shoe Company. Miller has line responsibility to Maloney, but she also has staff responsibility to the company controller.

Maloney is under severe pressure to achieve the budgeted division income for the year. He has asked Miller to book $200,000 of revenues on December 31. The customers' orders are firm, but the shoes are still in the production process. They will be shipped on or about January 4. Maloney says to Miller, "The key event is getting the sales order, not shipping the shoes. You should support me, not obstruct my reaching division goals."

Required

1. Describe Miller's ethical responsibilities.
2. What should Miller do if Maloney gives her a direct order to book the sales?

Problems

PH Grade Assist

1-24 Planning and control decisions, Internet company. WebNews.com offers its subscribers several services, such as an annotated TV guide and local-area information on weather, restaurants, and movie theaters. Its main revenue sources are fees for banner advertisements and fees from subscribers. Recent data are:

Month/Year	Advertising Revenues	Actual Number of Subscribers	Monthly Fee per Subscriber
June 2004	$ 400,988	28,642	$14.95
December 2004	833,158	54,813	19.95
June 2005	861,034	58,178	19.95
December 2005	1,478,072	86,437	19.95
June 2006	2,916,962	146,581	19.95

The following decisions were made from June through October 2006:

a. June 2006: Raised subscription fee to $24.95 per month from July 2006 onward. The budgeted number of subscribers for this monthly fee is shown in the following table.
b. June 2006: Informed existing subscribers that from July onward, monthly fee would be $24.95.
c. July 2006: Offered e-mail service to subscribers and upgraded other online services.
d. October 2006: Dismissed the vice president of marketing after significant slowdown in subscribers and subscription revenues, based on July through September 2006 data in table.
e. October 2006: Reduced subscription fee to $21.95 per month from November 2006 onward.

Results for July–September 2006 are:

Month/Year	Budgeted Number of Subscribers	Actual Number of Subscribers	Monthly Fee per Subscriber
July 2006	140,000	128,933	$24.95
August 2006	150,000	139,419	24.95
September 2006	160,000	143,131	24.95

Required

1. Classify each of the decisions (**a**) to (**e**) as a planning or a control decision.
2. Give two examples of other planning decisions and two examples of other control decisions that may be made at WebNews.com.

1-25 Problem solving, scorekeeping, attention directing, and feedback, Internet company (continuation of 1-24). Consider the five decisions made in Problem 1-24.

Required

1. For each of the five decisions (**a–e**), provide an example of pertinent information that an accountant could provide, and indicate whether the accountant would be acting in a problem-solving, scorekeeping, or attention-directing role.
2. Identify one decision that WebNews.com made as a result of feedback from the control system.
3. What further action might WebNews.com take based on the feedback from the July through September 2006 subscriber information?

PH Grade Assist

1-26 Management accounting guidelines. For each of the following items, identify which of the management accounting guidelines applies: cost-benefit approach, behavioral and technical considerations, or different costs for different purposes.

1. Analyzing whether to keep the billing function within an organization or outsource it
2. Deciding to give bonuses for superior performance to the employees in a Japanese subsidiary and extra vacation time to the employees in a Swedish subsidiary
3. Including costs of all the value-chain functions before deciding to launch a new product, but including only its manufacturing costs in determining its inventory valuation
4. Considering the desirability of hiring one more salesperson
5. Giving each salesperson the compensation option of choosing either a low salary and a high-percentage sales commission or a high salary and a low-percentage sales commission
6. Selecting the costlier computer system after considering two systems
7. Installing a participatory budgeting system in which managers set their own performance targets, instead of top management imposing performance targets on managers
8. Recording research costs as an expense for financial reporting purposes (as required by U.S. GAAP) but capitalizing and expensing them over a longer period for management performance-evaluation purposes
9. Introducing a profit-sharing plan for employees

1-27 Role of controller, role of chief financial officer. George Perez is the controller at Allied Electronics, a manufacturer of devices for the computer industry. He is being considered for a promotion to chief financial officer.

Required

1. In this table, indicate which executive is *primarily* responsible for each activity.

Activity	Controller	CFO
Managing accounts payable		
Communicating with investors		
Strategic review of different lines of businesses		
Budgeting funds for a plant upgrade		
Managing the company's short-term investments		
Negotiating fees with auditors		
Assessing profitability of various products		
Evaluating the costs and benefits of a new product design		

2. Based on this table and your understanding of the two roles, what types of training or experiences will George find most useful for the CFO position?

1-28 Software-procurement decision, ethics. Jorge Michaels is the Chicago-based controller of Fiesta Foods, a rapidly growing manufacturer and marketer of Mexican food products. Michaels is currently considering the purchase of a new cost-management package for use by each of the company's six manufacturing plants and its many marketing personnel. Four major, competing products are being considered by Michaels.

Horizon 1-2-3 is an aggressive software developer. It views Fiesta as a target of opportunity. Every six months, Horizon has a three-day users' conference in a Caribbean location. Each conference has substantial time allowed for "rest and recreation." Horizon offers Michaels an all-expenses-paid visit to the upcoming conference in Cancun, Mexico. Michaels accepts the offer, believing it will be very useful to talk to other users of Horizon software. He is especially looking forward to the visit because he has close relatives in the Cancun area.

Prior to leaving, Michaels receives a visit from the president of Fiesta. She shows him an anonymous letter sent to her. It argues that Horizon is receiving unfair favorable treatment in Fiesta's software decision-making process. The letter specifically mentions Michaels' upcoming "all-expenses-paid package to Cancun during Chicago's cold winter." Michaels is deeply offended. He says he has made no decision, and he believes he is very capable of making a software choice on the merits of each product. Fiesta currently does not have a formal, written code of ethics.

Required

1. Do you think Michaels faces an ethical problem in regard to his forthcoming visit to the Horizon users' group meeting? Refer to Exhibit 1-7 (p. 16). Explain.
2. Should Fiesta allow executives to attend user meetings while negotiating with other vendors about a purchase decision? Explain. If yes, what conditions on attending should apply?
3. Would you recommend that Fiesta develop its own code of ethics to handle situations such as this? What are the pros and cons of having such a written code?

1-29 Professional ethics and end-of-year actions. Janet Taylor is the new division controller of the snack-foods division of Gourmet Foods. Gourmet Foods has reported a minimum 15% growth in annual earnings for each of the past five years. The snack-foods division has reported annual earnings growth of more than 20% each year in this same period. During the current year, the economy went into a recession. The corporate controller estimates a 10% annual earnings growth rate for Gourmet Foods this year. One month before the December 31 fiscal year-end of the current year, Taylor estimates the snack-foods division will report an annual earnings growth of only 8%. Warren Ryan, the snack-foods division president, is not happy, but he notes that "the end-of-year actions" still need to be taken.

Taylor makes some inquiries and is able to compile the following list of end-of-year actions that were more or less accepted by the previous division controller:

a. Deferring December's routine monthly maintenance on packaging equipment by an independent contractor until January of next year
b. Extending the close of the current fiscal year beyond December 31 so that some sales of next year are included in the current year
c. Altering dates of shipping documents of next January's sales to record them as sales in December of the current year
d. Giving salespeople a double bonus to exceed December sales targets
e. Deferring the current period's advertising by reducing the number of television spots run in December and running more than planned in January of next year
f. Deferring the current period's reported advertising costs by having Gourmet Foods' outside advertising agency delay billing December advertisements until January of next year or by having the agency alter invoices to conceal the December date
g. Persuading carriers to accept merchandise for shipment in December of the current year although they normally would not have done so

Required

1. Why might the snack-foods division president want to take these end-of-year actions?
2. The division controller is deeply troubled and reads the "Standards of Ethical Conduct for Management Accountants" in Exhibit 1-7 (p. 16). Classify each of the end-of-year actions (**a–g**) as acceptable or unacceptable according to that document.
3. What should Taylor do if Ryan suggests that these end-of-year actions are taken in every division of Gourmet Foods and that she will greatly harm the snack-foods division if she does not cooperate and paint the rosiest picture possible of the division's results?

Collaborative Learning Problem

1-30 Global company, ethical challenges. In June 2006, the government of Vartan invited bids for the construction of a cellular telephone network. ZenTel, an experienced communications company, was eager to enter the growing field of cellular telephone networks in countries with poor infrastructures for land lines. If ZenTel won a few of these early contracts, it would be sought after for its field experience and expertise. After careful analysis, it prepared a detailed bid for the Communications Ministry of Vartan, building in only half of its usual profit margin and providing a contractual guarantee that the project would be completed in two years or less. The multimillion-dollar bid was submitted before the deadline, and ZenTel received notification that it had reached the Vartan government. Then, despite repeated faxes, e-mails, and phone calls to the ministry, there was no news on the bids or the project from the Vartan government.

Steve Cheng, VP of Global Operations for ZenTel, contacted the U.S. commercial attaché in Vartan, who told him that his best chance was to go to Vartan and try to meet the deputy minister of communications in person. Cheng prepared thoroughly for the trip, rereading the proposal and making sure that he understood the details.

At the commercial attaché's office in Vartan's capital, Cheng waited nervously for the deputy minister and his assistant. Cheng had come to Vartan with a clear negotiating strategy to try to win the bid. Soon the deputy minister and his staff arrived, introductions were made, and pleasantries were exchanged. The deputy minister asked a few questions about ZenTel and the bid and then excused himself, leaving his assistant to talk to Cheng. After clearly indicating that many other compelling bids had been made by firms from around the world, the assistant said, "Mr. Cheng, I guarantee that ZenTel's bid will be accepted if you pay a $1 million commission. Of course, your excellent proposal doesn't have to be altered in any way." It was clear to Cheng that the "commission" was, in fact, a bribe. Tactfully, he pointed out that U.S. laws and ZenTel's corporate policy prohibited such a payment. The assistant wished him a good day and a pleasant flight home and left.

Required

1. As a shareholder in ZenTel, would you prefer that ZenTel executives agree to the payment of the "commission"?
2. When Cheng described his experience to his friend Hank Shorn, who managed international business development for another company, Hank said that his own "personal philosophy" was to make such payments if they were typical in the local culture. Can you argue for Hank's point of view?
3. Why would ZenTel have a corporate policy against such payments?
4. What should Steve Cheng do next?

Get Connected: Cost Accounting in the News

Go to www.prenhall.com/horngren/cost12e for additional online exercise(s) that explore issues affecting the accounting world today. These exercises offer you the opportunity to analyze and reflect on how cost accounting helps managers to make better decisions and handle the challenges of strategic planning and implementation.

CHAPTER 1 Video Case

REGAL MARINE: The Accountant's Role

Regal Marine is one of the United States' leading luxury performance-boat manufacturers. Sales of all models in a recent year topped $100 million, with their biggest customer, Boat Tree, buying close to 90% of all boats produced by Regal Marine. Headquartered in Orlando, Florida, Regal Marine currently makes 22 different models, ranging from a 14-foot runabout sport boat to the 40-foot Commodore yacht. The product life cycle for each of Regal Marine's boats is three to five years, depending on the size of the boat, with smaller boats having shorter life cycles. These short life cycles result in a continuing stream of new products that work their way through the company's value chain.

Cross-functional design teams with representatives from R&D, production, purchasing, design, accounting, marketing, customer service, upholstery, and cabinetry work together to fine-tune prototype designs. Customer feedback is gathered at boat shows, and suppliers regularly present their new product innovations to the company for potential use in future boat models. To streamline manufacturing, each team attempts to use existing components and production processes, when feasible. Computer-aided design (CAD) systems are used for all designs. When the design of a new model is finished, Regal Marine makes a prototype of it before producing the new models.

To make a new boat model, a foam-based carving called a *plug* is created. CAD system specifications are used to drive the automated carving of plugs. The plug becomes the basis for making the molds for fiberglass hulls and decks. The finished molds are then used to make thousands of fiberglass hulls and decks. Regal Marine has several hundred molds, representing their largest capital investment. Molds are kept even after production of outdated models is stopped.

At the Orlando factory, production begins with coating the molds with gelcoat and then spraying the dried gelcoat with chopped fiberglass and resin. Then the fiberglass hulls and decks are popped off the molds and wheeled into assembly stations that move in synch each day. While hulls and decks are being crested, other manufacturing departments—such as upholstery, cabinetry, electrical, and small-part fabrication—prepare the components that will be installed in each boat during assembly. Trained workers install required components—fasteners, electrical parts, upholstered seats, and cabinets, for example—according to a strict schedule that assures that each assembly station's work is done each day so the lines keep moving. It takes anywhere from 2 to 20 days to complete production, depending on the boat size. In the smaller sport-boat category, for example, 10 boats a day roll off the assembly line. As soon as boats are quality-checked and approved for delivery, they are loaded onto trucks for delivery to customers such as Boat Tree. No boats are kept in finished-goods inventory.

QUESTIONS

1. For each of the following activities, identify the main role the accountant is performing: problem solving (P), scorekeeping (S), or attention directing (A).
   a. Preparing a schedule of depreciation for boat hull and deck molds
   b. Analyzing the desirability of using standard Volvo-Penta boat engines in a new boat model
   c. Preparing the daily report of the number of hull defects found during the quality check on the Sport Boat assembly line
   d. Explaining the Commodore Yacht Division's monthly performance report
   e. Interpreting differences between actual results and budgeted amounts on the Prototyping Department's monthly performance report
   f. Preparing a monthly statement of boat sales, by model and customer, for the company's vice president of sales
   g. Analyzing for the Design Team the impact on product costs of a new dashboard-odometer display
   h. Preparing a cost comparison of two plywood manufacturers for use by the purchasing manager
2. Classify each of the cost items (**a–h**) into one of the business functions of the value chain.
   a. Cost of a toll-free telephone line used for customer inquiries about product specifications, performance, and warranty coverage
   b. Cost of sales and promotional materials for use at boat shows
   c. Labor costs of workers in the Cabinetry Department of the production facility
   d. Cost of an industry research report on boat industry trends
   e. Equipment and trucks purchased for transporting finished boats to retail outlets such as Boat Tree
   f. Boat hull and deck mold-fabrication costs
   g. Cost of a new CAD design station used by the Design Department
   h. Costs of upholstered seats for Commodore yachts

CHAPTER 2

AN INTRODUCTION TO COST TERMS AND PURPOSES

LEARNING OBJECTIVES

1. Define and illustrate a cost object
2. Distinguish between direct costs and indirect costs
3. Explain variable costs and fixed costs
4. Interpret unit costs cautiously
5. Distinguish among manufacturing companies, merchandising companies, and service-sector companies
6. Describe the three categories of inventories commonly found in manufacturing companies
7. Distinguish inventoriable costs from period costs
8. Explain why product costs are computed in different ways for different purposes
9. Describe a framework for cost accounting and cost management

What does the word *cost* mean to you? Is it the price you pay for something of value? A cash outflow? Something that affects profitability? There are many different types of costs, and at different times, organizations place more or less emphasis on them. When times are good, companies often focus on selling as much as they can, with costs taking a backseat. But when times get tough, the emphasis usually shifts to costs. Tennessee Products, a manufacturer of different types of speaker systems, is facing this unpleasant situation. For the first time in its five-year history, the company has sustained a quarterly loss, and it's a significant one.

Julia Morgenthal, CFO, is concerned that the company's success and profitability up to this point has led to complacency among its managers in controlling operations. She has called in Jonathan Berg, the controller, to discuss the problem.

Julia: Jonathan, with our most recent quarter's dismal performance, we need to examine every aspect of our operation. I'm afraid our success to this point has led to a lack of concern for managing costs.

Jonathan: Agreed. What do you have in mind?

Julia: I want to hold a short meeting for our managers to redirect our attention to costs—you know, direct versus indirect, variable versus fixed, and inventoriable versus product costs. I want our management team to deeply understand the distinctions among these costs, so that we can expect to turn this situation around.

Jonathan: Sounds good. I think our managers have a better handle on direct costs representing items such as materials and labor that can be easily identified with each of our products. But they may be more fuzzy about the other costs and how to manage them.

Julia: Great. Put together a summary of cost terminology as it relates to our operations for our next management meeting. I'll make this review the basis of my discussion of returning to profitability this quarter.

As this conversation indicates, managers need to understand costs in order to interpret and act on accounting reports. Organizations such as United Way, Stanford University Hospital, and Nokia generate reports containing a variety of cost concepts and terms that managers need to run their operations. Managers who understand these concepts and terms are best able to use the information provided and can avoid misusing it. A common understanding of cost concepts and terms helps communication among managers and management accountants. This chapter discusses cost concepts and terms that are the basis of accounting information used for internal and external reporting.

Costs and Cost Terminology

Accountants define **cost** as a resource sacrificed or forgone to achieve a specific objective. A cost (such as direct materials or advertising) is usually measured as the monetary amount that must be paid to acquire goods or services. An **actual cost** is the cost incurred (a historical or past cost), as distinguished from a **budgeted cost**, which is a predicted or forecasted cost (a future cost).

To guide their decisions, managers want to know how much a particular thing (such as a product, machine, service, or process) costs. We call this thing a **cost object**, which is anything for which a measurement of costs is desired. Exhibit 2-1 lists examples of different types of cost objects for which Procter & Gamble, the consumer-products company, wants to know the costs.

A costing system typically accounts for costs in two basic stages: accumulation followed by assignment. **Cost accumulation** is the collection of cost data in some organized way by means of an accounting system. For example, a publishing company that purchases rolls of paper for printing magazines collects (accumulates) the costs of individual rolls used in any one month to obtain the total monthly cost of paper. Beyond accumulating costs, managers with the help of management accountants assign costs to designated cost objects (such as the different magazines the company publishes) to help them make strategic decisions (such as the pricing of different magazines and which magazines to emphasize). Managers also assign costs to cost objects to implement strategy. For example, costs assigned to a department aid in decision making about department efficiency. Costs assigned to customers help managers understand the profit earned from different customers and help them make decisions about how to allocate resources to support different customers. **Cost assignment** is a general term that encompasses both (1) tracing accumulated costs that have a direct relationship to a cost object and (2) allocating accumulated costs that have an indirect relationship to a cost object.

An understanding of this chapter's cost terms and concepts provides the foundation for the remaining chapters.

Study Tip: Go to **www.prenhall.com/harris** and print Chapter 2 of the *Student Guide*. Use the Highlights (pp. 9–12) to preview the chapter.

In the definition of *cost*, "sacrificed" refers to a resource that is consumed—for example, a company paying $3,000 to lease a warehouse. "Forgone" refers to giving up an opportunity to use a resource—for example, after spending the $3,000 to lease a warehouse, the company could not use that $3,000 for another purpose.

1

Define and illustrate a cost object

. . . examples of cost objects are products, services, activities, processes, parts of the organization, and customers

In each of the following questions, the cost object is in italics: What selling price should be charged for a *product*? Which *machine* is the least expensive to operate?

Direct Costs and Indirect Costs

We now describe how costs are classified as direct and indirect costs and the methods used to assign these costs to cost objects.

2

Distinguish between direct costs

. . . costs that are traced directly to the cost object

and indirect costs

. . . costs that are allocated to the cost object

Cost Tracing and Cost Allocation

- **Direct costs of a cost object** are related to the particular cost object and can be traced to it in an economically feasible (cost-effective) way. For example, the cost of cans or bottles is a direct cost of Pepsi-Colas. The cost of the cans or bottles can be easily traced to or identified with the drink. The term **cost tracing** is used to describe the assignment of direct costs to a particular cost object.
- **Indirect costs of a cost object** are related to the particular cost object but cannot be traced to it in an economically feasible (cost-effective) way. For example, the salaries of supervisors who oversee production of the many different soft drink products bottled at a Pepsi plant are an indirect cost of Pepsi-Colas. Supervision costs are related to the cost object (Pepsi-Colas) because supervision is necessary for managing the production and sale of Pepsi-Colas. Supervision costs are indirect costs because supervisors also oversee the production of other products, such as 7-Up. Unlike the cost of cans or bottles, it is impossible to trace supervision costs to the Pepsi-Cola line. The term **cost allocation** is used to describe the assignment of indirect costs to a particular cost object.

Consider the audits performed by a public accounting firm. The firm traces direct professional labor costs to each audit using time records. Indirect costs, such as rent on the firm's office space and depreciation on its computers, cannot be traced to individual audits, so these costs must be allocated to the audits.

Exhibit 2-2 depicts direct costs and indirect costs and both forms of cost assignment—cost tracing and cost allocation—using the example of *Sports Illustrated* magazine, which is published by Time Warner. The cost object is the *Sports Illustrated* magazine. The paper on which the magazine is printed is a direct cost. The cost of the paper can be traced in a cost-effective way to *Sports Illustrated* magazine. Consider the cost of leasing the building

EXHIBIT 2-1

Examples of Cost Objects at Procter & Gamble

Cost Object	Illustration
Product	*Crest Tartar Control: Original Flavor* toothpaste product
Service	Telephone hotline providing information and assistance to users of *Pampers Diapers* products
Project	R&D project on alternative scent-free formulations of *Tide* detergent products
Customer	Safeway, the retailer, which purchases a broad range of Procter & Gamble products
Brand category	*Vidal Sassoon* range of hairstyle products
Activity	Development and updating Web site on the Internet or setting up machines for production
Department	Environmental, Health, and Safety Department

that houses the editorial staffs of magazines published by Time Warner, such as *Time, People,* and *Sports Illustrated.* This leasing cost is an indirect cost of *Sports Illustrated.* The company can *trace* the lease amount paid to the building, but there is no separate lease agreement for the space used solely by the editorial staff of *Sports Illustrated.* Therefore, the company cannot trace the lease cost to *Sports Illustrated.* Time Warner can, however, *allocate* to *Sports Illustrated* a part of the lease cost of the building, for example, on the basis of an estimate of the relative percentage of the building's total floor space occupied by the *Sports Illustrated* editorial staff.

Managers want to assign costs accurately to cost objects. Inaccurate product costs will mislead managers about the profitability of different products; as a result, managers might unknowingly promote unprofitable products while deemphasizing profitable products. Generally, managers are more confident about the accuracy of direct costs of cost objects, such as the paper cost of *Sports Illustrated* magazine.

Indirect costs pose more problems. Consider the lease. Allocating the cost of the lease on the basis of the total floor space occupied by the staff of each magazine makes sense. This approach measures the building resources used by each magazine reasonably accurately. The more floor space a department occupies, the more lease costs that should be assigned to it. This allocation assumes that the quality of the space (such as the layout and the number of windows offering a good view) used by the different magazines is fairly similar. Accurately allocating other indirect costs, such as the cost of Time Warner's top management, to *Sports Illustrated* magazine is more difficult. Should these costs be allocated on the basis of the size of the editorial staff? The number of magazines sold? Some other measure? It is not so clear how to measure the share of top management's time used by each magazine. The Focus on Values and Behaviors feature (p. 29) describes some additional issues managers might face when allocating costs.

EXHIBIT 2-2

Cost Assignment to a Cost Object

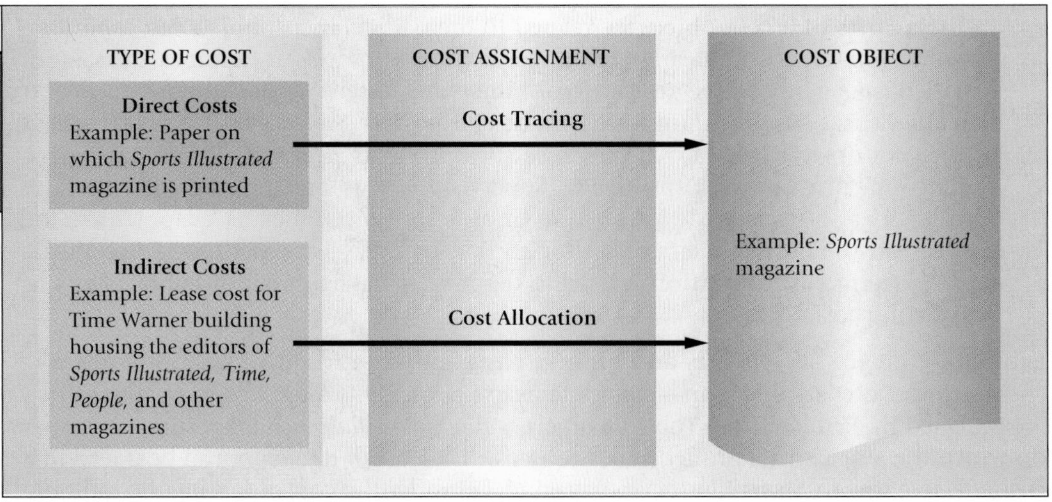

FOCUS ON VALUES AND BEHAVIORS

OVERCHARGING THE U.S. GOVERNMENT

Distinguishing direct costs from indirect costs and deciding how to allocate indirect costs to products requires management accountants to work closely with managers. Sometimes, however, managers may have a personal financial incentive to propose a cost allocation method that will allocate fewer costs to some products and higher costs to others. For example, General Electric (GE), a top Fortune 500 company with multimillion-dollar government aerospace contracts, was found to have overcharged employee direct labor hours on projects. Top management responded by developing the company's ethics and integrity policy, which all employees must now sign when hired. In addition, the company posts its policy publicly on the Web and includes a section urging employees to be on the lookout for improper, incomplete, or unauthorized cost charging on contracts.

Consider another example. The U.S. Department of Defense (DoD) has contracts with private companies such as Lockheed Martin, General Dynamics, and Boeing to supply military equipment such as fighter jets, submarines, and tanks. Through its own internal Defense Contract Audit Agency (DCAA), the DoD discovered that some of its equipment suppliers had overallocated indirect costs to the DoD products and underallocated indirect costs to their other commercial products. The reason: The DoD paid suppliers on the basis of a cost-plus profit margin. The higher the costs the supplier allocated to the DoD business, the higher the revenues the supplier earned. In a recent case, the DCAA, through its normal audit process, found that Halliburton KBR overcharged the U.S. government as much as $61 million for fuel sold to Iraq as part of the government's rebuilding contract.

Management accountants must always make careful and professional judgments when choosing among alternative cost-allocation methods. The failure of the defense contractors' management accountants to properly allocate costs to the DoD led to severe penalties and fines for their companies and, in some cases, criminal prosecution.

Sources: *For Halliburton and DCAA; Lawrence DiRita, Acting ASD (Public Affairs) Thursday, December 11, 2003;* **www.defenselink.mil/transcripts/2003/tr20031211-0985.html**. *For General Electric:* **www.ge.com/en/commitment/social/integrity/workwith_govt.htm**.

Factors Affecting Direct/Indirect Cost Classifications

Several factors affect the classification of a cost as direct or indirect:

- **The materiality of the cost in question.** The smaller the amount of a cost—that is, the more immaterial the cost is—the less likely that it is economically feasible to trace that cost to a particular cost object. Consider a mail-order catalog company like Lands' End. It would be economically feasible to trace the courier charge for delivering a package to an individual customer as a direct cost. In contrast, the cost of the invoice paper included in the package would be classified as an indirect cost. Why? Because although the cost of the paper can be traced to each customer, it is not cost-effective to do so. The benefits of knowing that exactly, say, 0.5 cent worth of paper is included in each package do not exceed the data processing and administrative costs of tracing the cost to each package.
- **Available information-gathering technology.** Improvements in information-gathering technology make it possible to consider more and more costs as direct costs. Bar codes, for example, allow manufacturing plants to treat certain low-cost materials such as clips and screws, which were previously classified as indirect costs, as direct costs of products. At Dell, component parts such as the computer chip and the CD-ROM drive display a bar code that can be scanned at every point in the production process. Bar codes can be read into a manufacturing cost file by waving a "wand" in the same quick and efficient way supermarket checkout clerks enter the cost of each item purchased by a customer.
- **Design of operations.** Classifying a cost as direct is easier if a company's facility (or some part of it) is used exclusively for a specific cost object, such as a specific product or a particular customer. For example, the cost of the General Chemicals facility that is dedicated to manufacturing soda ash is a direct cost of soda ash.

Be aware that a specific cost may be both a direct cost of one cost object and an indirect cost of another cost object. *That is, the direct/indirect classification depends on the choice of the cost object.* For example, the salary of an Assembly Department supervisor at BMW is a direct cost if the cost object is the Assembly Department, but it is an indirect cost if the cost object is a product such as the BMW X5 sport-utility vehicle (SUV) because the Assembly Department assembles many different models. A useful rule of thumb is that the broader the definition of the cost object—the Assembly Department rather than the X5 SUV—the higher the proportion of total costs that are direct costs and the more confidence management has in the accuracy of the resulting cost amounts.

Cost-Behavior Patterns: Variable Costs and Fixed Costs

3
Explain variable costs and fixed costs
. . . the two basic ways in which costs behave

The distinction between variable costs and fixed costs is necessary to address key questions. For example, how much would manufacturing costs change if the output level increased by 5%?

Costing systems record the cost of resources acquired, such as materials, labor, and equipment, and track how those resources are used to produce and sell products or services. Recording the costs of resources acquired and used allows managers to see how costs behave. Consider two basic types of cost-behavior patterns found in many accounting systems. A **variable cost** changes *in total* in proportion to changes in the related level of total activity or volume. A **fixed cost** remains unchanged *in total* for a given time period, despite wide changes in the related level of total activity or volume. Costs are defined as variable or fixed with respect to *a specific activity* and for *a given time period*. The Global Surveys of Company Practice on page 31 indicate that identifying a cost as variable or fixed helps in making many management decisions. To illustrate these two basic types of costs, consider costs at the Spartanburg, South Carolina, plant of BMW.

1. **Variable Costs:** If BMW buys a steering wheel at $60 for each of its BMW X5 vehicles, then the total cost of steering wheels should be $60 times the number of vehicles produced, as the following table illustrates.

Number of X5s Produced (1)	Variable Cost per Steering Wheel (2)	Total Variable Cost of Steering Wheels (3) = (1) × (2)
1	$60	$ 60
1,000	60	60,000
3,000	60	180,000

The steering wheel cost is an example of a variable cost because *total cost* changes in proportion to changes in the number of vehicles produced. The cost per unit of a variable cost is the same. Focus on the table. It is precisely because the variable cost per steering wheel in column 2 is the same that the total variable cost of steering wheels in column 3 changes proportionately with the number of X5s produced in column 1. When considering how variable costs behave, always focus on total costs.

Exhibit 2-3, Panel A, graphically illustrates the total variable cost of steering wheels. The cost is represented by a straight line that climbs from left to right. The phrases "strictly variable" and "proportionately variable" are sometimes used to describe the variable cost in Panel A.

EXHIBIT 2-3
Graphs of Variable and Fixed Costs

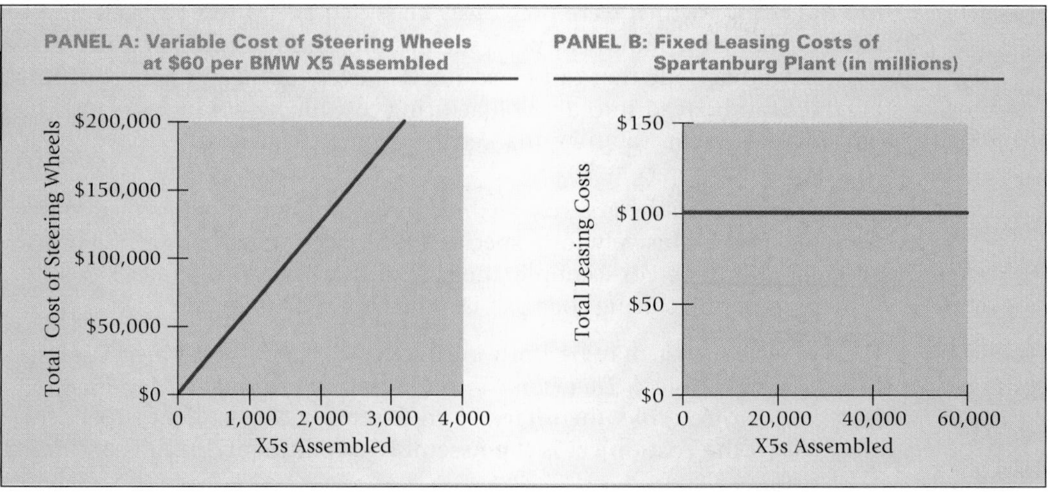

GLOBAL SURVEYS OF COMPANY PRACTICE

Distinguishing Between Variable Costs and Fixed Costs

Many chapters in this book illustrate the insights gained from distinguishing fixed costs from variable costs. A recent survey of management accounting practice in the United States identified several tools used by more than 40% of respondents that rely on the distinction between fixed and variable costs.[a]

Planning and Budgeting Tools	Chapter(s) in the Book Discussing the Tool in Detail
Budgeting and variance analysis	6, 7, and 8
Activity-based management	5
Capital budgeting	21
Decision-Support Tools	
Profitability and breakeven analysis	3, 4, 5, 11, 12, and 13
Transfer pricing	22
Product-Costing Analysis Tools	
Traditional costing	4
Overhead allocations	14, 15, and 16

Global surveys of company practice provide additional evidence that a large percentage of firms use systems that distinguish fixed costs from variable costs.

New Zealand[b] = 84%
United Kingdom[b] = 90%
Estonia[c] = 80%

When companies were asked to describe how they identify fixed and variable costs, "classification on a subjective basis based on managerial experience" and "treating all overheads as fixed and all direct costs as variable" were selected as the two most popular methods used in the United Kingdom and New Zealand.

[a]A. Garg et al., "Roles and Practices in Management Accounting Today."
[b]C. Guilding, D. Lamminmaki, and C. Drury, "Budgeting and Standard Costing Practices in New Zealand and the United Kingdom."
[c]T. Haldma, and K. Lääts, "Contingencies Influencing the Management Accounting Practices of Estonian Manufacturing Companies."
Full citations are in Appendix A at the end of the book.

Consider an example of a variable cost with respect to a different activity—the $20 hourly wage paid to each worker to set up machines at the Spartanburg plant. Setup labor cost is a variable cost with respect to setup hours because setup cost changes in total in proportion to the number of setup hours used.

2. **Fixed Costs:** Suppose BMW incurs a total of $100,000,000 in leasing costs per year for its Spartanburg plant. These costs are unchanged in total over a designated range of the number of vehicles produced during a given time span (see Exhibit 2-3, Panel B). Fixed costs become smaller and smaller on a per unit basis as the number of vehicles assembled increases, as the following table shows.

Annual Total Fixed Leasing Costs (1)	Number of X5s Produced (2)	Fixed Leasing Cost per X5 (3) = (1) ÷ (2)
$100,000,000	10,000	$10,000
100,000,000	25,000	4,000
100,000,000	50,000	2,000

Again examine the table. It is precisely because *total* leasing costs are fixed at $100,000,000 that fixed leasing cost per X5 decreases as the number of X5s produced increases; the same fixed cost is spread over a larger number of X5s. Do not be misled by the change in fixed cost per unit. When considering fixed costs, always focus on total costs. Costs are fixed when total costs remain unchanged despite significant changes in the level of total activity or volume.

Example: Suppose you make belts using leather that costs $5/belt (a variable cost) in a workshop rented for $450/month (a fixed cost). Calculate total costs and per unit costs for 1 Belt and 10 Belts:

	1 Belt		10 Belts	
	Total	Per Unit	Total	Per Unit
Leather	$ 5	$ 5	$ 50	$ 5
Rent	450	450	450	45
Total	$455	$455	$500	$50

Total VC vary with the number of belts produced (from $5 to $50 as volume increases from 1 to 10 belts), but *per unit VC are constant* at $5/belt (for both 1 and 10 belts). *Total FC are constant* at $450 (for both 1 and 10 belts), but *per unit FC vary* with the number of belts produced (from $450 to $45 as volume increases from 1 to 10 belts). Therefore, total cost per belt depends on the number of belts produced.

Why are some costs variable and other costs fixed? Recall that a cost is usually measured as the amount of money that must be paid to acquire goods and services. Total cost of steering wheels is a variable cost because BMW buys the steering wheels only when they are needed. As more X5s are produced, proportionately more steering wheels are acquired and proportionately more costs are incurred.

Contrast the description of variable costs with the $100,000,000 of fixed costs incurred by BMW to lease its Spartanburg plant for a year. This plant capacity is acquired well before BMW uses it to produce X5s and before BMW even knows how much of the capacity it will use. Suppose the plant has the capacity to produce 50,000 X5s each year. If the demand is for only 45,000 X5s, there will be idle capacity. However, BMW must pay for the unused capacity. If demand is even lower, say only 40,000 X5s, plant leasing costs will not change; they will continue to be $100,000,000. However, idle capacity will increase. Unlike variable costs, fixed costs pay for resources (such as for plant capacity) that cannot be quickly and easily changed to match the resources needed or used. Over time, managers can take actions to reduce fixed costs. For example, BMW may choose to sublease part of the plant to other companies.

Do not assume that individual cost items are inherently variable or fixed. Consider labor costs. Labor costs can be purely variable with respect to units produced when workers are paid on a piece-unit (piece-rate) basis. Some garment workers are paid on a per-shirt-sewed basis. In contrast, labor costs at a plant in the coming year are sometimes appropriately classified as fixed. For instance, a labor union agreement might set annual salaries and conditions, contain a no-layoff clause, and severely restrict a company's flexibility to assign workers to any other plant that has demand for labor. Japanese companies have for a long time had a policy of lifetime employment for their workers. Although such a policy entails higher labor costs, particularly in economic downturns, the benefits are increased loyalty and dedication to the company and higher productivity. The Concepts in Action on page 33 describes how the Internet offers companies the opportunity to convert fixed costs of application software into variable costs by renting software applications on an as-needed basis.

A particular cost item could be variable with respect to one level of activity and fixed with respect to another. Consider annual registration and license costs for a fleet of planes owned by an airline company. Registration and license costs would be a variable cost with respect to the number of planes owned. But registration and license costs for a particular plane are fixed with respect to the miles flown by that plane during a year.

To focus on key concepts, we have classified the behavior of costs as variable or fixed. Some costs have both fixed and variable elements and are called *mixed* or *semivariable* costs. For example, a company's telephone costs may have a fixed monthly payment and a charge per phone-minute used. We discuss mixed costs and techniques to separate out their fixed and variable components in Chapter 10.

Cost Drivers

A **cost driver** is a variable, such as the level of activity or volume, that causally affects costs over a given time span. That is, there is a cause-and-effect relationship between a change in the level of activity or volume and a change in the level of total costs. For example, if product-design costs change with the number of parts in a product, the number of parts is a cost driver of product-design costs. Similarly, miles driven is often a cost driver of distribution costs.

The cost driver of a variable cost is the level of activity or volume whose change causes proportionate changes in the variable cost. For example, the number of vehicles assembled is the cost driver of the cost of steering wheels. If setup workers are paid an hourly wage, the number of setup hours is the cost driver of (variable) setup costs.

CONCEPTS IN ACTION

How Application Service Providers (ASPs) Influence Cost Structures

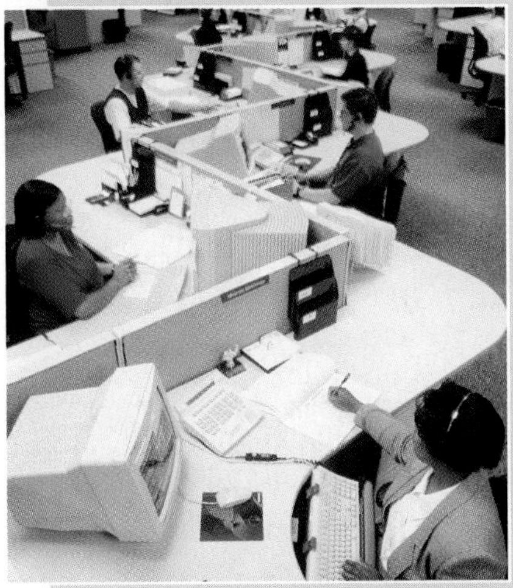

The growing complexity of applications software, coupled with the demand for information technology departments to operate in a leaner way, has caused many organizations to turn to application service providers (ASPs). ASPs allow companies to rent software online from service providers by accessing applications software from a remote server via a Web browser. Some companies prefer ASPs to buying software because they can access the applications and features they need, on demand, from online providers while paying only for the time the software is used. As companies further streamline information technology (IT) costs, ASPs become a more attractive, less capital-intensive option. Zach Nelson, CEO of NetSuite, a leading ASP, recently told *ASPnews.com*, an online newsletter, that "Customers don't want to give all the money up front; they want to buy it for as much as they're using, they want to buy it on a subscription."

Let's think about what this development means. Consider application software, such as e-mail and messaging, supply-chain and procurement planning, human resources management, customer-relationship management, and budgeting, required by a small- to medium-sized company of 250 employees. What options does the company have? It could (1) choose to build its own proprietary systems at a very high cost; or (2) purchase packaged software, recruit and retain in-house IT resources to install and maintain the software, and build and maintain the IT infrastructure necessary to support the applications. Both solutions entail high fixed costs, so many small businesses choose not to automate basic processes such as financial reporting and human resources.

ASPs such as Corio, Microsoft, Salesforce.com, Surebridge, and USinternetworking design, develop, maintain, and upgrade application packages and then charge companies a price for using each package. From the perspective of their customers, ASPs convert the fixed costs of applications software to variable costs. If business declines, ASP customers are not saddled with the fixed costs of the applications software. Of course, if customers use a lot of the applications software, they can end up paying more overall than they would have paid if they had developed the applications themselves.

The nonfinancial reasons why companies may not use ASPs are concerns about (1) security of data sent over the Internet, (2) losing control over important applications, and (3) lack of reliability of the network. (This is why ASPs offer service agreements that guarantee 99.9% uptime.)

Sources: T. Eisenmann and S. Pothen, *Application Service Providers*, Harvard Business School Note, 2001. R. Lavery, "The ABCs of ASPs," *Strategic Finance*, May 2001; D. Clark, "Renting Software Online: The Next Big Idea," *The Wall Street Journal*, June 3, 2003, B1; T. Bajarin, "ASPs Gain Ground," *Asia Computer Weekly*, July 21, 2003. K. Newcomb, "The Second Coming of ASPs?" *ASPnews.com*, May 5, 2004.

Costs that are fixed in the short run have no cost driver in the short run but may have a cost driver in the long run. Consider the costs of testing color printers at Hewlett-Packard. These costs consist of Testing Department equipment and staff costs that are difficult to change and, hence, are fixed in the short run with respect to changes in the volume of production. In this case, volume of production is not a cost driver of testing costs in the short run. But in the long run, Hewlett-Packard will increase or decrease the Testing Department's equipment and staff to the levels needed to support future production volumes. In the long run, volume of production is a cost driver of testing costs.

Relevant Range

Relevant range is the band of normal activity level or volume in which there is a specific relationship between the level of activity or volume and the cost in question. For example, a fixed cost is fixed only in relation to a given wide range of total activity or volume (at which the company is expected to operate) and only for a given time span (usually a particular budget period). Consider Thomas Transport Company (TTC), which rents two refrigerated

EXHIBIT 2-4

Fixed-Cost Behavior at Thomas Transport Company

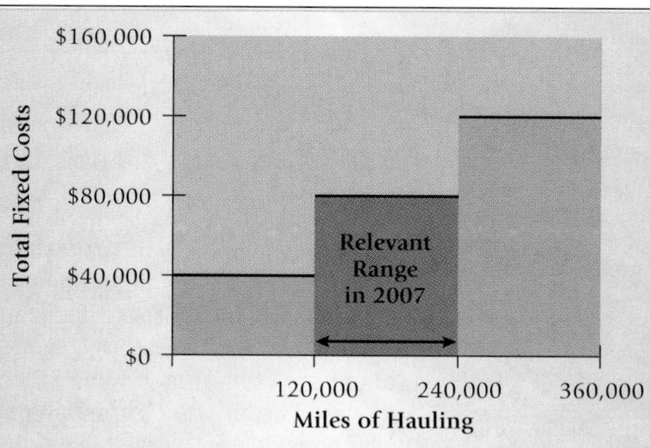

trucks that carry agricultural produce to market. Each truck has annual fixed rental costs of $40,000. The maximum annual usage of each truck is 120,000 miles. In the current year (2007), the predicted combined total hauling of the two trucks is 170,000 miles.

Exhibit 2-4 shows how annual fixed costs behave at different levels of miles of hauling. Up to 120,000 miles, TTC can operate with one truck; from 120,001 to 240,000 miles, it operates with two trucks; from 240,001 to 360,000 miles, it operates with three trucks. This pattern will continue as TTC adds trucks to its fleet to provide more miles of hauling. Given the predicted 170,000-mile usage for 2007, the range from 120,001 to 240,000 miles hauled is the range in which TTC expects to operate, resulting in fixed rental costs of $80,000. Within this relevant range, changes in miles hauled will not affect the annual fixed costs.

Fixed costs may change from one year to the next. For example, if the total rental fees of the two refrigerated trucks is increased by $2,000 for 2008, the total level of fixed costs will increase to $82,000 (all else remaining the same). If that increase occurs, total rental costs will be fixed at this new level of $82,000 for 2008 for miles hauled in the 120,001 to 240,000 range.

The basic assumption of the relevant range also applies to variable costs. That is, outside the relevant range, variable costs, such as direct materials, may not change proportionately with changes in production volume. For example, above a certain volume, direct material costs may increase at a lower rate because of price discounts on purchases greater than a certain quantity.

Relationships of Types of Costs

We have introduced two major classifications of costs: direct/indirect and variable/fixed. Costs may simultaneously be:

- Direct and variable
- Direct and fixed
- Indirect and variable
- Indirect and fixed

Exhibit 2-5 shows examples of costs in each of these four cost classifications for the BMW X5.

4

Interpret unit costs cautiously

. . . for many decisions, managers should use total costs, not unit costs

Total Costs and Unit Costs

The preceding section concentrated on the behavior patterns of total costs in relation to activity or volume levels. We now consider unit costs.

Unit Costs

Generally, the decision maker should think in terms of total costs rather than unit costs. In many decision contexts, however, calculating a unit cost is essential. Consider the chairman of the social committee of a fraternity, who is trying to decide whether to hire a musical group for an upcoming party. He estimates the cost of hiring the group to be $1,000. This knowledge is helpful for the decision, but it is not enough.

EXHIBIT 2-5

Examples of Inventoriable Costs in Combinations of the Direct/Indirect and Variable/Fixed Cost Classifications for a Car Manufacturer

		Assignment of Costs to Cost Object	
		Direct Costs	**Indirect Costs**
Cost-Behavior Pattern	**Variable Costs**	• Cost object: BMW X5s produced Example: Tires used in assembly of automobile	• Cost object: BMW X5s produced Example: Power costs at Spartanburg plant. Power usage is metered only to the plant, where multiple products are assembled.
	Fixed Costs	• Cost object: BMW X5s produced Example: Salary of supervisor on BMW X5 assembly line	• Cost object: BMW X5s produced Example: Annual lease costs at Spartanburg plant. Lease is for whole plant, where multiple products are produced.

Before a decision can be reached, the chairman must also predict the number of people who will attend. Without knowledge of both total cost and number of attendees, he cannot make an informed decision on a possible admission price to recover the cost of the party or even on whether to have a party at all. So he computes the unit cost by dividing the total cost ($1,000) by the expected number of people who will attend. If 1,000 people attend, the unit cost is $1 per person; if 100 attend, the unit cost soars to $10.

Unless the total cost is "unitized" (that is, averaged with respect to the level of activity or volume), the $1,000 cost is difficult to interpret. The unit cost combines the total cost and the number of people in a handy, communicative way.

Accounting systems typically report both total-cost amounts and average-cost-per-unit amounts. A **unit cost**, also called an **average cost**, is computed by dividing total cost by the number of units. The units might be expressed in various ways. Examples are automobiles assembled, packages delivered, or hours worked. Suppose that, in 2007, its first year of operations, $40,000,000 of manufacturing costs are incurred to produce 500,000 speaker systems at the Memphis plant of Tennessee Products. Then the unit cost is $80:

$$\frac{\text{Total manufacturing costs}}{\text{Number of units manufactured}} = \frac{\$40{,}000{,}000}{500{,}000 \text{ units}} = \$80 \text{ per unit}$$

If 480,000 units are sold and 20,000 units remain in ending inventory, the unit-cost concept helps in the determination of total costs in the income statement and balance sheet and, hence, the financial results reported by Tennessee Products to shareholders, banks, and the government.

Cost of goods sold in the income statement, 480,000 units × $80 per unit	$38,400,000
Ending inventory in the balance sheet, 20,000 units × $80 per unit	1,600,000
Total manufacturing costs of 500,000 units	$40,000,000

Unit costs are found in all areas of the value chain—for example, unit cost of product design, of sales visits, and of customer-service calls. By summing unit costs throughout the value chain, managers calculate the unit cost of the different products or services they deliver and determine the profitability of each product or service. Managers use this information, for example, to decide which products they should emphasize and the prices they should charge.

Use Unit Costs Cautiously

Although unit costs are regularly used in financial reports and for making product mix and pricing decisions, *managers should think in terms of total costs rather than unit costs for many decisions*. Consider the manager of the Memphis plant of Tennessee Products. Assume the $40,000,000 in costs in 2007 consist of $10,000,000 of fixed costs and $30,000,000 of variable costs (at $60 variable cost per speaker system produced). Suppose the total fixed cost and the variable cost per speaker system in 2008 are expected to be unchanged from 2007. The budgeted costs for 2008 at different production levels, calculated on the basis of total variable costs, total fixed costs, and total costs, are:

Study Tip: Practice is helpful if you want to master cost accounting concepts and techniques. To check your understanding of cost behavior, see Featured Exercise 1 (*Student Guide*, p. 12) and Review Exercise 2 (p. 16). The fully explained solutions are on pages 12 and 20, respectively.

Units Produced (1)	Variable Cost per Unit (2)	Total Variable Costs (3) = (1) × (2)	Total Fixed Costs (4)	Total Costs (5) = (3) + (4)	Unit Cost (6) = (5) ÷ (1)
100,000	$60	$ 6,000,000	$10,000,000	$16,000,000	$160.00
200,000	$60	$12,000,000	$10,000,000	$22,000,000	$110.00
500,000	$60	$30,000,000	$10,000,000	$40,000,000	$ 80.00
800,000	$60	$48,000,000	$10,000,000	$58,000,000	$ 72.50
1,000,000	$60	$60,000,000	$10,000,000	$70,000,000	$ 70.00

For many decisions, managers should use total costs rather than unit costs because fixed cost per unit changes when the related level of total volume changes. Consequently, unit costs should be interpreted with caution when they include a fixed-cost component.

A plant manager who uses the 2007 unit cost of $80 per unit will underestimate actual total costs if 2008 output is below the 2007 level of 500,000 units. If actual volume is 200,000 units due to, say, the presence of a new competitor, actual costs would be $22,000,000. Using the unit cost of $80 times 200,000 units predicts $16,000,000, which underestimates the actual total costs by $6,000,000 ($22,000,000 − $16,000,000). *The unit cost of $80 only applies when 500,000 units are produced.* An overreliance on unit cost in this situation could lead to insufficient cash being available to pay costs if volume declines to 200,000 units. As this table indicates, for decision making, managers should think in terms of total variable costs, total fixed costs, and total costs rather than unit cost.

We now discuss cost concepts used in different sectors of the economy.

Manufacturing-, Merchandising-, and Service-Sector Companies

5

Distinguish among manufacturing companies, merchandising companies, and service-sector companies

. . . different types of companies face different accounting issues

We first define three different sectors and provide examples of companies in each sector.

1. **Manufacturing-sector companies** purchase materials and components and convert them into various finished goods. Examples are automotive companies, food-processing companies, and textile companies.
2. **Merchandising-sector companies** purchase and then sell tangible products without changing their basic form. This sector includes companies engaged in retailing (such as bookstores or department stores), distribution, or wholesaling.
3. **Service-sector companies** provide services (intangible products)—for example, legal advice or audits—to their customers. Examples are law firms, accounting firms, banks, mutual fund companies, insurance companies, transportation companies, advertising agencies, radio and television stations, and Internet-based companies such as Internet service providers, travel agencies, and brokerage firms.

Financial Statements, Inventoriable Costs, and Period Costs

The distinction between inventoriable costs and period costs, described later in this section, is necessary for financial reporting in both the manufacturing and merchandising sectors of the economy. Service-sector companies provide only services or intangible products. Because they do not hold inventories of tangible products for sale, the concepts of inventoriable costs and period costs do not apply to service-sector companies. As background, we will first look at the different types of inventory that companies hold and some commonly used classifications of manufacturing costs.

Types of Inventory

Manufacturing-sector companies purchase materials and components and convert them into various finished goods. These companies typically have one or more of the following three types of inventory:

1. **Direct materials inventory.** Direct materials in stock and awaiting use in the manufacturing process (for example, computer chips and components needed to manufacture cellular phones).
2. **Work-in-process inventory.** Goods partially worked on but not yet completed (for example, cellular phones at various stages of completion in the manufacturing process). Also called **work in progress**.
3. **Finished goods inventory.** Goods (for example, cellular phones) completed but not yet sold.

Merchandising-sector companies purchase tangible products and then sell them without changing their basic form. They hold only one type of inventory, which is products in their original purchased form, called *merchandise inventory*.

6

Describe the three categories of inventories commonly found in manufacturing companies

. . . the categories are direct materials, work in process, and finished goods

Commonly Used Classifications of Manufacturing Costs

Three terms commonly used when describing manufacturing costs are direct material costs, direct manufacturing labor costs, and indirect manufacturing costs.

1. **Direct material costs** are the acquisition costs of all materials that eventually become part of the cost object (work in process and then finished goods) and that can be traced to the cost object in an economically feasible way. Acquisition costs of direct materials include freight-in (inward delivery) charges, sales taxes, and custom duties. Examples of direct material costs are the aluminum used to make Pepsi cans and the paper used to print *Sports Illustrated*.
2. **Direct manufacturing labor costs** include the compensation of all manufacturing labor that can be traced to the cost object (work in process and then finished goods) in an economically feasible way. Examples include wages and fringe benefits paid to machine operators and assembly-line workers who convert direct materials purchased to finished goods.
3. **Indirect manufacturing costs** are all manufacturing costs that are related to the cost object (work in process and then finished goods) but that cannot be traced to that cost object in an economically feasible way. Examples include supplies, indirect materials such as lubricants, indirect manufacturing labor such as plant maintenance and cleaning labor, plant rent, plant insurance, property taxes on the plant, plant depreciation, and the compensation of plant managers. This cost category is also referred to as **manufacturing overhead costs** or **factory overhead costs**. We use *indirect manufacturing costs* and *manufacturing overhead costs* interchangeably in this book.

This book uses the term *direct manufacturing labor* because labor used in other business functions of the value chain can also be traced directly to cost objects. For example, in some cases salespersons' salaries can be traced directly to specific customers and called *direct marketing labor.*

We now describe the distinction between inventoriable costs and period costs.

Inventoriable Costs

Inventoriable costs are all costs of a product that are considered as assets in the balance sheet when they are incurred and that become cost of goods sold only when the product is sold. For manufacturing-sector companies, all manufacturing costs are inventoriable costs. Consider again BMW and its X5 SUV. Costs of direct materials issued to production (from direct material inventory), direct manufacturing labor costs, and manufacturing overhead costs create new assets, starting as work in process and becoming finished goods (the X5s). Hence manufacturing costs are included in work-in-process inventory and in finished goods inventory (they are "inventoried") to accumulate the costs of creating these assets. When the X5s are sold, the cost of manufacturing them is matched against the revenues from the sale. The cost of goods sold includes all manufacturing costs (direct materials, direct manufacturing labor, and manufacturing overhead costs) incurred to produce them. The X5s may be sold during a different accounting period than the period in which they were manufactured. Thus, inventorying manufacturing costs in the balance sheet during the accounting period when goods are manufactured and expensing the manufacturing costs when the goods are sold and revenues are recognized in a later income statement achieves matching of revenues and expenses.

7

Distinguish inventoriable costs

. . . assets when incurred, then cost of goods sold

from period costs

. . . expenses of the period when incurred

Inventoriable costs are assets because they have value as long as the company owns them. When the inventory (finished goods) is sold, its cost is transferred from the balance sheet to the income statement as cost of goods sold.

EXHIBIT 2-6

Examples of Period Costs in Combinations of the Direct/Indirect and Variable/Fixed Cost Classifications at a Bank

		Assignment of Costs to Cost Object: Direct Costs	Assignment of Costs to Cost Object: Indirect Costs
Cost-Behavior Pattern	Variable Costs	• Cost object: Number of mortgage loans Example: Fees paid to property appraisal company for each mortgage loan	• Cost object: Number of mortgage loans Example: Postage paid to deliver mortgage-loan documents to lawyers/homeowners
	Fixed Costs	• Cost object: Number of mortgage loans Example: Salary paid to executives in mortgage loan department to develop new mortgage-loan products	• Cost object: Number of mortgage loans Example: Cost to the bank of sponsoring annual golf tournament

For merchandising-sector companies such as Wal-Mart, inventoriable costs are the costs of purchasing the goods that are resold in their same form. These costs comprise the costs of the goods themselves plus any incoming freight, insurance, and handling costs for those goods. For service-sector companies, the absence of inventories means there are no inventoriable costs.

Period Costs

Period costs are all costs in the income statement other than cost of goods sold. Period costs are treated as expenses of the accounting period in which they are incurred because they are expected to benefit revenues in that period and are not expected to benefit revenues in future periods (because there is not sufficient evidence to conclude that such future benefit exists). Expensing these costs in the period they are incurred matches expenses to revenues.

For manufacturing-sector companies, period costs in the income statement are all nonmanufacturing costs (for example, design costs and distribution costs). For merchandising-sector companies, period costs in the income statement are all costs not related to the cost of goods purchased for resale. Examples of these period costs are labor costs of sales floor personnel and advertising costs. Because there are no inventoriable costs for service-sector companies, all their costs in the income statement are period costs.

Exhibit 2-5 showed examples of inventoriable costs in direct/indirect and variable/fixed cost classifications. Exhibit 2-6 shows examples of period costs in direct/indirect and variable/fixed cost classifications at a bank.

Illustrating the Flow of Inventoriable Costs and Period Costs

Inventoriable costs and period costs flow through the income statement at a merchandising company analogous to the flow of costs at a manufacturing company. At a merchandising company, however, the flow of costs is much simpler to understand and track. After mastering this manufacturing example, you will have no difficulty with a merchandising scenario.

We illustrate the flow of inventoriable costs and period costs through the income statement for a manufacturing company, for which the distinction between inventoriable costs and period costs is most detailed.

Manufacturing-Sector Example

The income statement of a manufacturer, Cellular Products, is shown in Exhibit 2-7. Revenues of Cellular Products are (in thousands) $210,000. **Revenues** are inflows of assets (usually cash or accounts receivable) received for products or services provided to

EXHIBIT 2-7

Income Statement and Schedule of Cost of Goods Manufactured of a Manufacturing-Sector Company, Cellular Products

	A	B	C	D
1	**PANEL A: INCOME STATEMENT**			
2	**Cellular Products**			
3	**Income Statement**			
4	**For the Year Ended December 31, 2007 (in thousands)**			
5	Revenues		$210,000	
6	Cost of goods sold:			
7	Beginning finished goods, January 1, 2007	$ 22,000		
8	Cost of goods manufactured (see Panel B)	104,000		
9	Cost of goods available for sale	126,000		
10	Ending finished goods, December 31, 2007	18,000		
11	Cost of goods sold		108,000	
12	Gross margin (or gross profit)		102,000	
13	Operating costs:			
14	Marketing, distribution, and customer-service costs	70,000		
15	Total operating costs		70,000	
16	Operating income		$ 32,000	
17				
18	**PANEL B: COST OF GOODS MANUFACTURED**			
19	**Cellular Products**			
20	**Schedule of Cost of Goods Manufactured**[a]			
21	**For the Year Ended December 31, 2007 (in thousands)**			
22	Direct materials:			
23	Beginning inventory, January 1, 2007	$ 11,000		
24	Purchases of direct materials	73,000		
25	Cost of direct materials available for use	84,000		
26	Ending inventory, December 31, 2007	8,000		
27	Direct materials used		$ 76,000	
28	Direct mаufacturing labor		9,000	
29	Manufacturing overhead costs:			
30	Indirect manufacturing labor	$ 7,000		
31	Supplies	2,000		
32	Heat, light and power	5,000		
33	Depreciation—plant building	2,000		
34	Depreciation—plant equipment	3,000		
35	Miscellaneous	1,000		
36	Total manufacturing overhead costs		20,000	
37	Manufacturing costs incurred during 2007		105,000	
38	Beginning work-in-progress inventory, January 1, 2007		6,000	
39	Total manufacturing costs to acccount for		111,000	
40	Ending work-in-progress inventory, December 31, 2007		7,000	
41	Cost of goods manufactured (to Income Statement)		$104,000	
42	[a]Note that this schedule can become a Schedule of Cost of Goods Manufactured and Sold simply by including the beginning and ending finished goods inventory figures in the supporting schedule rather than in the body of the income statement.			

customers. Cost of goods sold for Cellular Products is computed as (see Exhibit 2-7, Panel A):

Beginning inventory of finished goods, January 1, 2007	$ 22,000
+ Cost of goods manufactured in 2007	104,000
− Ending inventory of finished goods, December 31, 2007	18,000
= Cost of goods sold in 2007	$108,000

Gross margin = Revenues − Cost of goods sold = $210,000 − $108,000 = $102,000

Cost of goods manufactured refers to the cost of goods brought to completion, whether they were started before or during the current accounting period. Cellular Products calculates the cost of goods manufactured in three steps (see Exhibit 2-7, Panel B):

Step 1: Cost of direct materials used (light blue shaded area)

Beginning inventory of direct materials, January 1, 2007	$11,000
+ Purchases of direct materials in 2007	73,000
− Ending inventory of direct materials, December 31, 2007	8,000
= Direct materials used in 2007	$76,000

Step 2: Total manufacturing costs incurred in 2007

Total manufacturing costs refers to all direct manufacturing costs and manufacturing overhead costs incurred during 2007 for all goods worked on during the year. Cellular Products classifies its manufacturing costs into the three categories described earlier.

(i) Direct materials used in 2007 (shaded light blue)	$ 76,000
(ii) Direct manufacturing labor in 2007 (shaded light green)	9,000
(iii) Manufacturing overhead costs (shaded blue)	20,000
Total manufacturing costs incurred in 2007	$105,000

Step 3: Cost of goods manufactured in 2007

The cost of goods manufactured during 2007 includes the cost of beginning work in process and costs incurred during the year. Also note that some of the manufacturing costs incurred during 2007 are held back as the cost of the ending work-in-process inventory. The cost of goods manufactured in 2007 is calculated as (shaded teal):

Beginning work-in-process inventory, January 1, 2007	$ 6,000
+ Total manufacturing costs incurred in 2007	105,000
= Total manufacturing costs to account for	111,000
– Ending work-in-process inventory, December 31, 2007	7,000
= Cost of goods manufactured in 2007	$104,000

Study Tip: To check your understanding of the income statement for manufacturing companies, see Featured Exercise 2, true–false statement 8, and multiple-choice question 7 (*Student Guide*, beginning p.13). Fully explained solutions begin on p. 19.

Exhibit 2-8 shows related general-ledger T-accounts for Cellular Products' manufacturing cost flow. Note how the cost of goods manufactured ($104,000) is the cost of all goods completed during the accounting period. These costs are all inventoriable costs. Goods completed during the period are transferred to finished goods inventory. These costs become cost of goods sold in the accounting period when the goods are sold. Also note that the direct materials, direct manufacturing labor, and manufacturing overhead costs of the units in work-in-process inventory ($7,000) and finished goods inventory ($18,000) as of December 31, 2007, will appear as an asset in the balance sheet. These costs will become expenses next year, when these units are sold.

The $70,000 comprising marketing costs, distribution costs, and customer-service costs are period costs of Cellular Products. These period costs include, for example, salaries of salespersons, depreciation on computers and other equipment used in marketing, and the cost of leasing warehouse space for distribution. Operating income of Cellular Products is $32,000. **Operating income** is total revenues from operations minus cost of goods sold and operating costs (excluding interest expense and income taxes).

Newcomers to cost accounting frequently assume that indirect costs such as rent, telephone, and depreciation are always costs of the period in which they are incurred and are not associated with inventories. When these costs are incurred in marketing or in corporate headquarters, they are period costs. However, when these costs are incurred in manufacturing, they are manufacturing overhead costs and are inventoriable.

Recap of Inventoriable Costs and Period Costs

Exhibit 2-9 highlights the differences between inventoriable costs and period costs.

Panel A uses the manufacturing sector to illustrate these differences. The merchandising sector is shown in Panel B. First study Panel A. The manufacturing costs of finished goods include direct materials, other direct manufacturing costs such as direct manufacturing labor, and manufacturing overhead costs such as supervision, production control, and machine maintenance. All these costs are inventoriable: They are assigned to work-in-process inventory until the goods are completed and then to finished goods inventory until the goods are sold. All nonmanufacturing costs, such as R&D, design, and distribution costs, are period costs.

EXHIBIT 2-8	**General-Ledger T-Accounts for Cellular Products' Manufacturing Cost Flow**

Work-in-Process Inventory		Finished Goods Inventory		Cost of Goods Sold

Bal. Jan. 1, 2007	6,000	Cost of goods	Bal. Jan. 1, 2007	22,000	Cost of goods sold 108,000 ➔ 108,000
Direct materials used	76,000	manufactured 104,000 ———➤	104,000		
Direct manuf. labor	9,000				
Manuf. overhead costs	20,000		Bal. Dec. 31, 2007	18,000	
Bal. Dec. 31, 2007	7,000

EXHIBIT 2-9 **Relationships of Inventoriable Costs and Period Costs**

PANEL A: Manufacturing Company

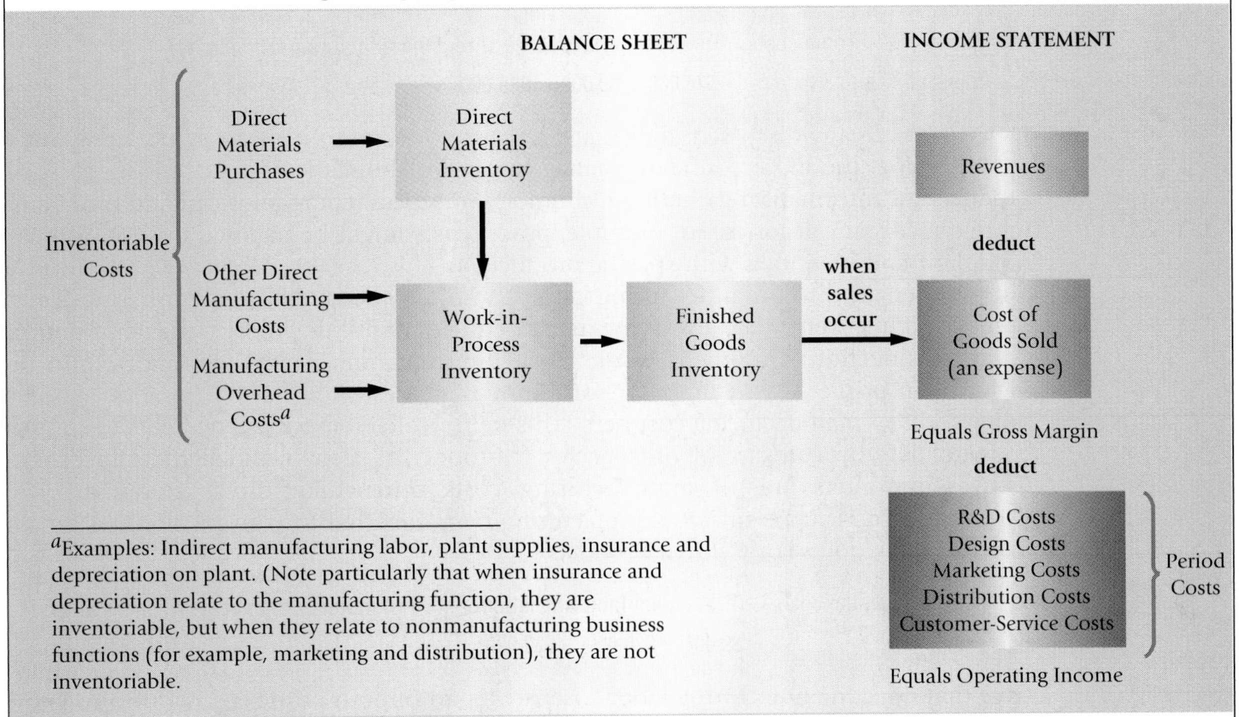

PANEL B: Merchandising Company (Retailer or Wholesaler)

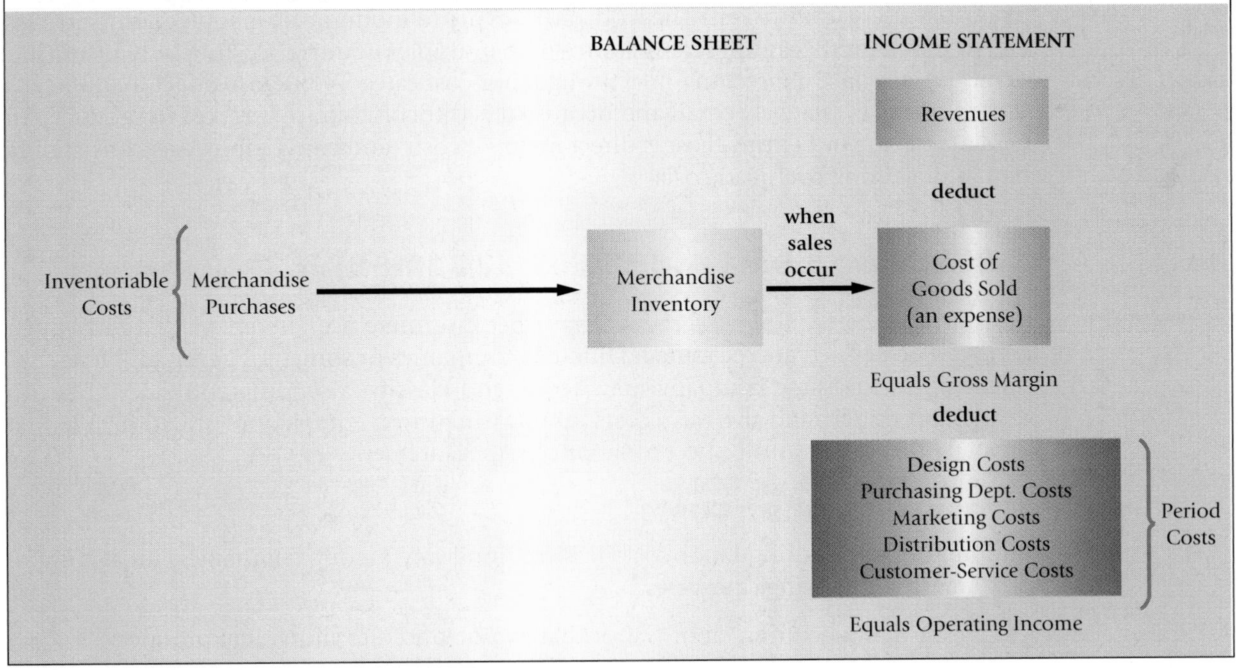

Now examine Panel B. A retailer or wholesaler buys goods for resale. The only inventoriable cost is the cost of merchandise. (This corresponds to the cost of finished goods manufactured for a manufacturing company.) Purchased goods are held as merchandise inventory, the cost of which is shown as an asset in the balance sheet. As the goods are sold, their costs are shown in the income statement as cost of goods sold. A retailer or wholesaler also has a variety of marketing, distribution, and customer-service costs, which are period costs. In the income statement, period costs are deducted from revenues without ever having been included as part of inventory.

Prime Costs and Conversion Costs

Two terms used to describe cost classifications in manufacturing costing systems are prime costs and conversion costs. **Prime costs** are all direct manufacturing costs. For Cellular Products,

$$\text{Prime costs} = \text{Direct material costs} + \text{Direct manufacturing labor costs}$$
$$= \$76{,}000 + \$9{,}000 = \$85{,}000$$

As we have already discussed, the greater the proportion of prime costs in a company's cost structure, the more confident managers can be about the accuracy of the costs of products. As information-gathering technology improves, companies can add more and more direct-cost categories. For example, power costs might be metered in specific areas of a plant and identified with specific products. In this case, prime costs would include direct materials, direct manufacturing labor, and direct metered power. Furthermore, if a production line were dedicated to the manufacture of a specific product, the depreciation on the production equipment would be a direct manufacturing cost and would be included in prime costs. Computer software companies often have a "purchased technology" direct manufacturing cost item. This item, which represents payments to suppliers who develop software algorithms for a product, is also included in prime costs. **Conversion costs** are all manufacturing costs other than direct material costs. Conversion costs represent all manufacturing costs incurred to convert direct materials into finished goods. For Cellular Products,

$$\text{Conversion costs} = \text{Direct manufacturing labor costs} + \text{Manufacturing overhead costs}$$
$$= \$9{,}000 + \$20{,}000 = \$29{,}000$$

Note that direct manufacturing labor costs are a part of both prime costs and conversion costs.

Question: Do prime costs + conversion costs = total manufacturing costs?

Answer: Only under the two-part classification: prime costs = direct material costs, and conversion costs = manufacturing overhead costs (which include direct manufacturing labor). Under the three-part classification, direct manufacturing labor is both a prime cost and a conversion cost, so the equation in the question would double-count direct manufacturing labor.

Some manufacturing operations such as computer-integrated manufacturing (CIM) plants have very few workers. The workers' roles are to monitor the manufacturing process and to maintain the equipment that produces multiple products. Costing systems in CIM plants do not have a direct manufacturing labor cost category because direct manufacturing labor cost is relatively small and because it is difficult to trace this cost to products. In CIM plants, the only prime cost is direct material costs, and conversion costs consist only of manufacturing overhead costs.

Measuring Costs Requires Judgment

Measuring costs requires judgment. That's because there are alternative ways in which costs can be defined and classified. Different companies or sometimes even different subunits within the same company may define and classify costs differently. Be careful to define and understand the ways costs are measured in a company or situation. We first illustrate this point with respect to labor cost measurement.

Measuring Labor Costs

Although manufacturing labor cost classifications vary among companies, most companies have the following categories:

- Direct manufacturing labor (labor that can be traced to individual products)
- Manufacturing overhead (examples of prominent labor components of manufacturing overhead follow):
  - Indirect labor (compensation)
    - Forklift truck operators (internal handling of materials)
    - Plant janitors
    - Plant guards
    - Rework labor (time spent by direct laborers redoing defective work)
    - Overtime premium paid to plant workers (explained next)
    - Idle time (explained next)

- Managers', department heads', and supervisors' salaries
- Payroll fringe costs, for example, health care premiums and pension costs (explained later)

All manufacturing labor compensation other than for direct manufacturing labor, managers' salaries, department heads' salaries, and supervisors' salaries is usually classified as *indirect labor costs,* a major component of manufacturing overhead. The indirect labor costs are commonly divided into many subclassifications to retain information on different categories of indirect labor. For example, the wages of forklift truck operators generally are not commingled with janitors' wages, although both are regarded as indirect labor costs.

Managers' salaries usually are not classified as indirect labor costs. Instead, the compensation of supervisors, department heads, and all others who are regarded as manufacturing management is placed in a separate classification of manufacturing overhead.

Overtime Premium and Idle Time

The purpose of classifying costs in detail is to associate an individual cost with a specific cause or reason for why it was incurred. Two classes of indirect labor—overtime premium and idle time—need special mention. **Overtime premium** is the wage rate paid to workers (for both direct labor and indirect labor) in *excess* of their straight-time wage rates. Overtime premium is usually considered to be a part of indirect costs or overhead. Consider an example from the service sector. George Flexner does home repairs for Sears Appliance Services. He is paid $20 per hour for straight-time and $30 per hour (time and a half) for overtime. His overtime premium is $10 per overtime hour. If he works 44 hours, including 4 overtime hours, in one week, his gross compensation would be classified as follows:

Direct service labor: 44 hours × $20 per hour	$880
Overtime premium: 4 hours × $10 per hour	40
Total compensation for 44 hours	$920

In this example, why is the overtime premium of direct labor usually considered an overhead cost rather than a direct cost? After all, it can be traced to specific repair jobs. Overtime premium is generally not considered a direct charge because the scheduling of repair jobs is usually either random or in accordance with minimizing overall travel time. For example, assume that jobs 1 through 5 are scheduled to be completed on a specific workday of 10 hours, including 2 overtime hours. Each job (service call) requires 2 hours. Should the job scheduled during hours 9 and 10 be assigned the overtime premium? Or should the premium be prorated over all five jobs? Prorating the overtime premium does not "penalize"—add to the cost of—a particular batch of work solely because it happened to be worked on during the overtime hours. *Instead, the overtime premium is considered to be attributable to the heavy overall volume of work. Its cost is regarded as part of service overhead, which is borne by all repair jobs.*

Sometimes overtime is not random. For example, a customer demanding a "rush job" may clearly be the sole source of overtime. In such instances, the overtime premium is regarded as a direct cost of that job.

Another subclassification of indirect labor is the idle time of both direct and indirect manufacturing or service labor. **Idle time** is wages paid for unproductive time caused by lack of orders, machine breakdowns, material shortages, poor scheduling, and the like. For example, if the Sears repair truck broke down for 3 hours, Flexner's earnings would be classified as follows:

Direct service labor: 41 hours × $20/hour	$820
Idle time (service overhead): 3 hours × $20/hour	60
Overtime premium (service overhead): 4 hours × $10/hour	40
Total earnings for 44 hours	$920

Clearly, the idle time is not related to a particular job, nor, as we have already discussed, is the overtime premium. Both overtime premium and idle time are considered overhead costs.

Benefits of Defining Accounting Terms

Managers, accountants, suppliers, and others will avoid many problems if they thoroughly understand and agree on the classifications and meanings of the cost terms introduced in this chapter and later in this book.

Consider the classification of manufacturing labor *payroll fringe costs* (for example, employer payments for employee benefits such as Social Security, life insurance, health insurance, and pensions). Some companies classify these costs as manufacturing overhead costs. In other companies, the fringe benefits related to direct manufacturing labor are treated as an additional direct manufacturing labor cost. Consider, for example, a direct laborer, such as a lathe operator, whose gross wages are computed on the basis of a stated wage rate of $20 an hour and fringe benefits totaling, say, $5 per hour. Some companies classify the $20 as direct manufacturing labor cost and the $5 as manufacturing overhead cost. Other companies classify the entire $25 as direct manufacturing labor cost. The latter approach is preferable because the stated wage and the fringe benefit costs together are a fundamental part of acquiring direct manufacturing labor services.

Caution: In every situation, pinpoint clearly what direct manufacturing labor includes and what direct manufacturing labor excludes. Achieving clarity may prevent disputes regarding cost-reimbursement contracts, income tax payments, and labor union matters. Consider that some countries such as Costa Rica and Mauritius offer substantial income tax savings to companies that locate plants within their borders. In some cases, to qualify for the tax benefits, the direct manufacturing labor costs of the plant must at least equal a specified percentage of the total manufacturing costs. Disputes have arisen regarding how to calculate the direct manufacturing labor percentage for qualifying for such tax benefits. For instance, are payroll fringe benefits on direct manufacturing labor part of direct manufacturing labor costs, or are they part of manufacturing overhead? Depending on how companies classify costs, you can see how they may show direct manufacturing labor as different percentages of total manufacturing costs. Consider a company with $5 million of payroll fringe costs (figures are assumed, in millions):

Classification A			**Classification B**		
	Costs	**Percentage**		**Costs**	**Percentage**
Direct materials	$ 40	40%	Direct materials	$ 40	40%
Direct manufacturing labor	20	20	Direct manufacturing labor	25	25
Manufacturing overhead	40	40	Manufacturing overhead	35	35
Total manufacturing costs	$100	100%	Total manufacturing costs	$100	100%

Classification A assumes payroll fringe costs are part of manufacturing overhead costs. In contrast, classification B assumes payroll fringe costs are part of direct manufacturing labor costs. If a country set the minimum percentage of direct labor costs at 25%, the company would receive a tax break using classification B, but no tax break using classification A. In addition to fringe benefits, other debated items are compensation for training time, idle time, vacations, sick leave, and overtime premium. To prevent disputes, contracts and laws should be as specific as possible regarding definitions and measurements.

8

Explain why product costs are computed in different ways for different purposes

. . . examples are pricing and product-mix decisions, government contracts, and financial statements

Different Meanings of Product Costs

Many cost terms found in practice have ambiguous meanings. Consider the term *product cost*. A **product cost** is the sum of the costs assigned to a product for a specific purpose. Different purposes can result in different measures of product cost, as the brackets on the value chain in Exhibit 2-10 illustrate:

- **Pricing and product-mix decisions.** For the purposes of making decisions about pricing and which products provide the most profits, the manager is interested in the overall (total) profitability of different products and, consequently, assigns costs incurred in all business functions of the value chain to the different products.

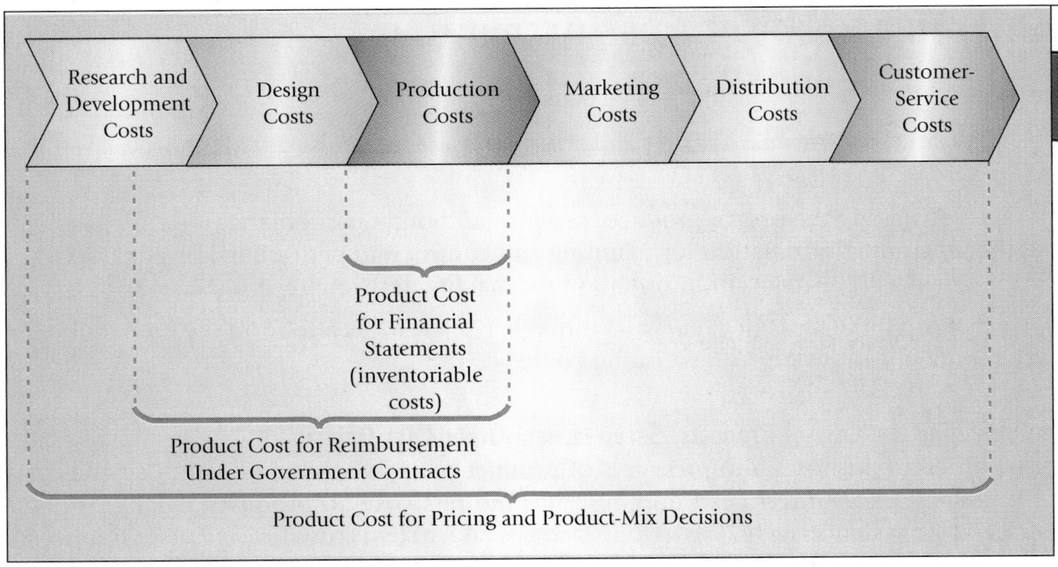

EXHIBIT 2-10

Different Product Costs for Different Purposes

- **Contracting with government agencies.** Government contracts often reimburse contractors on the basis of the "cost of a product" plus a prespecified margin of profit. Because of the cost-plus profit margin nature of the contract, government agencies provide detailed guidelines on the cost items they will allow and disallow when calculating the cost of a product. For example, some government agencies explicitly exclude marketing, distribution, and customer-service costs from the product costs that qualify for reimbursement, and they may only partially reimburse R&D costs. These agencies want to reimburse contractors for only those costs most closely related to delivering products under the contract. The second bracket in Exhibit 2-10 shows how the product-cost calculations for a specific contract may allow for all design and production costs but only part of R&D costs.
- **Preparing financial statements for external reporting under GAAP.** Under GAAP, only manufacturing costs can be assigned to inventories in the financial statements. For purposes of calculating inventory costs, product costs include only inventoriable (manufacturing) costs.

Generally, *inventoriable costs* are called *product costs* in financial accounting courses.

Exhibit 2-10 illustrates how product-cost measures range from a narrow set of costs for financial statements—a set that includes only inventoriable costs—to a broader set of costs for reimbursement under a government contract to a still broader set of costs for pricing and product-mix decisions.

This section focused on how different purposes result in the inclusion of different cost items of the value chain of business functions when product costs are calculated. The same caution about the need to be clear and precise about cost concepts and their measurement applies to each cost classification introduced in this chapter. Exhibit 2-11 summarizes the key cost classifications. The next section describes how the basic concepts introduced in this chapter lead to a framework for understanding cost accounting and cost management that can then be applied to the study of many topics, such as strategy evaluation, quality, and investment decisions.

Example: Numbers help illustrate the concepts in Exhibit 2-10. Using assumed numbers, the inventoriable cost of a testing device is $100 per unit, the device's cost for reimbursement under a government contract is $180, and the device's cost from throughout the value chain for a pricing decision is $300 per unit.

Study Tip: To review important terms and concepts in Chapters 1 and 2, work the crossword puzzle in the *Student Guide* (p. 18). The solution is on p. 22.

EXHIBIT 2-11

Alternative Classifications of Costs

1. Business function
   - a. Research and development
   - b. Design of products, services, or processes
   - c. Production
   - d. Marketing
   - e. Distribution
   - f. Customer service
2. Assignment to a cost object
   - a. Direct cost
   - b. Indirect cost
3. Cost behavior pattern in relation to changes in the level of activity or volume
   - a. Variable cost
   - b. Fixed cost
4. Aggregate or average
   - a. Total cost
   - b. Unit cost
5. Assets or expenses
   - a. Inventoriable cost
   - b Period cost

A Framework for Cost Accounting and Cost Management

9 **Describe a framework for cost accounting and cost management**
. . . three features that help managers make decisions

Three features of cost accounting and cost management across a wide range of applications are:

1. Calculating the cost of products, services, and other cost objects
2. Obtaining information for planning and control and performance evaluation
3. Analyzing the relevant information for making decisions

We develop these ideas in Chapters 3 through 12. The ideas also form the foundation for the study of various topics later in the book.

Calculating the Cost of Products, Services, and Other Cost Objects We have already seen the different purposes and measures of product costs. Whatever the purpose, the costing system traces direct costs and allocates indirect costs to products. Chapters 4 and 5 describe systems, such as activity-based costing systems, used to calculate total costs and unit costs of products and services. They also discuss how managers use this information to formulate strategy and make pricing, product mix, and cost-management decisions.

Obtaining Information for Planning and Control and Performance Evaluation Budgeting is the most commonly used tool for planning and control. A budget forces managers to look ahead, to translate strategy into plans, to coordinate and communicate within the organization, and to provide a benchmark for evaluating performance. Budgeting often plays a major role in affecting behavior and decisions because managers strive to meet budget targets. Chapter 6 describes budgeting systems.

At the end of a reporting period, managers compare actual results to planned performance. The manager's tasks are to understand why differences (called variances) between actual and planned performances arise and to use the information provided by these variances as feedback to promote learning and future improvement. Managers also use variances as well as nonfinancial measures, such as defect rates and customer satisfaction ratings, to control and evaluate the performance of various departments, divisions, and managers. Chapters 7 and 8 discuss variance analysis. Chapter 9 describes planning, control, and inventory-costing issues relating to capacity. Chapters 6, 7, 8, and 9 focus on the management accountant's role in implementing strategy.

Analyzing the Relevant Information for Making Decisions When making decisions about strategy design and strategy implementation, managers must understand which revenues and costs to consider and which ones to ignore. Management accountants help managers identify what information is relevant and what information is irrelevant. Consider a decision about whether to buy a product from an outside vendor or to make it in-house. The costing system indicates that it costs $25 per unit to make the product in-house. A vendor offers the product for $22 per unit. At first glance, it seems it will cost less for the company to buy the product rather than make it. However, suppose that, of the $25 to make the product in-house, $5 consists of plant lease costs that the company will have to pay whether the product is made or bought. Under this condition, it will cost less to make the product than to buy it. That's because making the product only costs an *additional* $20 per unit ($25 – $5), compared with an *additional* $22 per unit if it is bought. The $5 per unit of lease cost is irrelevant to the decision because it will be incurred whether the product is made or bought. Analyzing relevant information is a key aspect of making decisions.

When making strategic decisions about which products to produce, managers must know how revenues and costs vary with changes in output levels. For this purpose, managers need to distinguish fixed costs from variable costs. Chapter 3 analyzes how operating income changes with changes in output levels and how managers use this information to make decisions such as how much to spend on advertising. Chapter 10 describes methods to estimate the fixed and variable components of costs.

Chapter 11 applies the concept of relevance to making decisions in many different situations and describes methods managers use to maximize income given the resource constraints that they face. Chapter 12 describes how management accountants help managers determine prices and manage costs across the value chain and over a product's life cycle.

Later chapters in the book discuss topics such as strategy evaluation, customer profitability, quality, just-in-time systems, investment decisions, transfer pricing, and performance evaluation. Each of these topics invariably has product costing, planning and control, and decision-making perspectives. A command of the first 12 chapters is helpful to master these topics. For example, Chapter 13 on strategy describes the balanced scorecard, a set of financial and nonfinancial measures used to implement strategy that builds on the planning and control functions. The section on strategic analysis of operating income builds on ideas of product costing and variance analysis. The section on downsizing and managing capacity builds on ideas of relevant revenues and relevant costs.

PROBLEM FOR SELF-STUDY

Foxwood Company is a metal- and woodcutting manufacturer, selling products to the home construction market. Consider the following data for 2007:

Sandpaper	$ 2,000
Materials-handling costs	70,000
Lubricants and coolants	5,000
Miscellaneous indirect manufacturing labor	40,000
Direct manufacturing labor	300,000
Direct materials inventory, Jan. 1, 2007	40,000
Direct materials inventory, Dec. 31, 2007	50,000
Finished goods inventory, Jan. 1, 2007	100,000
Finished goods inventory, Dec. 31, 2007	150,000
Work in process inventory, Jan. 1, 2007	10,000
Work in process inventory, Dec. 31, 2007	14,000
Plant-leasing costs	54,000
Depreciation—plant equipment	36,000
Property taxes on plant equipment	4,000
Fire insurance on plant equipment	3,000
Direct materials purchased	460,000
Revenues	1,360,000
Marketing promotions	60,000
Marketing salaries	100,000
Distribution costs	70,000
Customer-service costs	100,000

Required

1. Prepare an income statement with a separate supporting schedule of cost of goods manufactured. For all manufacturing items, classify costs as direct costs or indirect costs and indicate by V or F whether each is basically a variable cost or a fixed cost (when the cost object is a product unit). If in doubt, decide on the basis of whether the total cost will change substantially over a wide range of units produced.
2. Suppose that both the direct material costs and the plant-leasing costs are for the production of 900,000 units. What is the direct material cost of each unit produced? What is the plant-leasing cost per unit? Assume the plant-leasing cost is a fixed cost.
3. Suppose Foxwood Company manufactures 1,000,000 units next year. Repeat the computation in requirement 2 for direct materials and plant-leasing costs. Assume the implied cost-behavior patterns persist.
4. As a management consultant, explain concisely to the company president why the unit cost for direct materials did not change in requirements 2 and 3 but the unit cost for plant-leasing costs did change.

SOLUTION

1.

Foxwood Company
Income Statement
For the Year Ended December 31, 2007

Revenues		$1,360,000
Cost of goods sold:		
Beginning finished goods, January 1, 2007	$ 100,000	
Cost of goods manufactured (see schedule below)	960,000	
Cost of goods available for sale	1,060,000	
Deduct ending finished goods, December 31, 2007	150,000	910,000
Gross margin (or gross profit)		450,000
Operating costs		
Marketing promotions	60,000	
Marketing salaries	100,000	
Distribution costs	70,000	
Customer-service costs	100,000	330,000
Operating income		$ 120,000

Foxwood Company
Schedule of Cost of Goods Manufactured
For the Year Ended December 31, 2007

Direct materials:		
Beginning inventory, January 1, 2007		$ 40,000
Purchases of direct materials		460,000
Cost of direct materials available for use		500,000
Ending inventory, December 31, 2007		50,000
Direct materials used		450,000 (V)
Direct manufacturing labor		300,000 (V)
Manufacturing overhead costs:		
Sandpaper	$ 2,000 (V)	
Materials-handling costs	70,000 (V)	
Lubricants and coolants	5,000 (V)	
Miscellaneous indirect manufacturing labor	40,000 (V)	
Plant-leasing costs	54,000 (F)	
Depreciation—plant equipment	36,000 (F)	
Property taxes on plant equipment	4,000 (F)	
Fire insurance on plant equipment	3,000 (F)	214,000
Manufacturing costs incurred during 2007		964,000
Beginning work in process, January 1, 2007		10,000
Total manufacturing costs to account for		974,000
Ending work in process, December 31, 2007		14,000
Cost of goods manufactured (to Income Statement)		$ 960,000

2.

Direct material unit cost = Direct materials used ÷ Units produced

= $450,000 ÷ 900,000 units = $0.50 per unit

Plant-leasing unit cost = Plant-leasing costs ÷ Units produced

= $54,000 ÷ 900,000 units = $0.06 per unit

3. The direct material costs are variable, so they would increase in total from $450,000 to $500,000 (1,000,000 units × $0.50 per unit). However, their unit cost would be unaffected: $500,000 ÷ 1,000,000 units = $0.50 per unit.

In contrast, the plant-leasing costs of $54,000 are fixed, so they would not increase in total. However, the plant-leasing cost per unit would decline from $0.060 to $0.054: $54,000 ÷ 1,000,000 units = $0.054 per unit.

4. The explanation would begin with the answer to requirement 3. As a consultant, you should stress that the unitizing (averaging) of costs that have different behavior patterns can be misleading. A common error is to assume that a total unit cost, which is often a sum of variable unit cost and fixed unit cost, is an indicator that total costs change in proportion to changes in production levels. The next chapter demonstrates the necessity for distinguishing between cost-behavior patterns. You must be wary, especially about average fixed cost per unit. Too often, unit fixed cost is erroneously regarded as being indistinguishable from unit variable cost.

DECISION POINTS

The following question-and-answer format summarizes the chapter's learning objectives. Each decision presents a key question related to a learning objective. The guidelines are the answer to that question.

Decision	Guidelines
1. How do managers choose a cost object?	A cost object is anything for which a separate measurement of cost is needed. Examples include a product, a service, a project, a customer, a brand category, an activity, and a department.
2. How do managers decide whether a cost is a direct or an indirect cost?	A direct cost is any cost that is related to a particular cost object and can be traced to that cost object in an economically feasible way. Indirect costs are related to the particular cost object but cannot be traced to it in an economically feasible way. The same cost can be direct for one cost object and indirect for other cost objects. This book uses *cost tracing* to describe the assignment of direct costs to a cost object and *cost allocation* to describe the assignment of indirect costs to a cost object.
3. How do managers decide whether a cost is a variable or a fixed cost?	A variable cost changes *in total* in proportion to changes in the related level of total activity or volume. A fixed cost remains unchanged *in total* for a given time period despite wide changes in the related level of total activity or volume.
4. How should costs be estimated?	In general, focus on total costs, not unit costs. When making total cost estimates, think of variable costs as an amount per unit and fixed costs as a total amount. The unit cost of a cost object should be interpreted cautiously when it includes a fixed-cost component.
5. How do you distinguish among manufacturing-, merchandising-, and service-sector companies?	Manufacturing-sector companies purchase materials and components and convert them into finished goods. Merchandising-sector companies purchase and then sell tangible products without changing their basic form. Service-sector companies provide services (intangible products) to their customers.
6. How do manufacturing companies categorize inventories?	The three categories of inventories found in many manufacturing companies depict stages in the conversion process: direct materials, work in process, and finished goods.
7. Which costs are initially treated as assets for external reporting, and which costs are expensed as they are incurred?	Inventoriable costs are all costs of a product that are regarded as an asset in the accounting period when they are incurred and then become cost of goods sold in the accounting period when the product is sold. Period costs are expensed in the accounting period in which they are incurred and are all of the costs in an income statement other than cost of goods sold.
8. How do managers assign costs to cost objects?	Managers can assign different costs to the same cost object depending on the purpose. For example, for the external reporting purpose in a manufacturing company, the inventoriable cost of a product includes only manufacturing costs. In contrast, costs from all business functions of the value chain often are assigned to a product for pricing and product-mix decisions.
9. What are the features of cost accounting and cost management?	Three features of cost accounting and cost management are (a) calculating the cost of products, services, and other cost objects; (b) obtaining information for planning and control and performance evaluation; and (c) analyzing the relevant information for making decisions.

TERMS TO LEARN

This chapter contains more basic terms than any other in this book. Do not proceed before you check your understanding of the following terms. Both the chapter and the Glossary at the end of the book contain definitions.

actual cost (p. 27)
average cost (p. 35)
budgeted cost (p. 27)
conversion costs (p. 42)
cost (p. 27)
cost accumulation (p. 27)
cost allocation (p. 27)
cost assignment (p. 27)
cost driver (p. 32)
cost object (p. 27)
cost of goods manufactured (p. 39)
cost tracing (p. 27)
direct costs of a cost object (p. 27)
direct manufacturing labor costs (p. 37)
direct material costs (p. 37)

direct materials inventory (p. 37)
factory overhead costs (p. 37)
finished-goods inventory (p. 37)
fixed cost (p. 30)
idle time (p. 43)
indirect costs of a cost object (p. 27)
indirect manufacturing costs (p. 37)
inventoriable costs (p. 37)
manufacturing overhead costs (p. 37)
manufacturing-sector companies (p. 36)
merchandising-sector companies (p. 36)
operating income (p. 40)
overtime premium (p. 43)
period costs (p. 38)
prime costs (p. 42)
product cost (p. 44)
relevant range (p. 33)
revenues (p. 38)
service-sector companies (p. 36)
unit cost (p. 35)
variable cost (p. 30)
work-in-process inventory (p. 37)
work in progress (p. 37)

PH Grade Assist

Prentice Hall Grade Assist (PHGA)

Your professor may ask you to complete selected exercises and problems in Prentice Hall Grade Assist (PHGA). PHGA is an online tool that can help you master the chapter's topics. It provides you with multiple variations of exercises and problems designated by the PHGA icon. You can rework these exercises and problems—each time with new data—as many times as you need. You also receive immediate feedback and grading.

ASSIGNMENT MATERIAL

Questions

2-1 Define cost object and give three examples.

2-2 Define direct costs and indirect costs.

2-3 Why do managers consider direct costs to be more accurate than indirect costs?

2-4 Name three factors that will affect the classification of a cost as direct or indirect.

2-5 Define variable cost and fixed cost. Give an example of each.

2-6 What is a cost driver? Give one example.

2-7 What is the relevant range? What role does the relevant-range concept play in explaining how costs behave?

2-8 Explain why unit costs must often be interpreted with caution.

2-9 Describe how manufacturing-, merchandising-, and service-sector companies differ from each other.

2-10 What are three different types of inventory that manufacturing companies hold?

2-11 Distinguish between inventoriable costs and period costs.

2-12 Do service-sector companies have inventoriable costs? Explain.

2-13 Define the following: direct material costs, direct manufacturing-labor costs, manufacturing overhead costs, prime costs, and conversion costs.

2-14 Describe the overtime-premium and idle-time categories of indirect labor.

2-15 Define product cost. Describe three different purposes for computing product costs.

Exercises

2-16 Computing and interpreting manufacturing unit costs. Minnesota Office Products (MOP) produces three different paper products at its Vaasa lumber plant: Supreme, Deluxe, and Regular. Each product has its own dedicated production line at the plant. It currently uses the following three-part classification for its manufacturing costs: direct materials, direct manufacturing labor, and manufacturing overhead costs. Total manufacturing overhead costs of the plant in July 2007 are $150 million ($20 million of which are fixed). This total amount is allocated to each product line on the basis of the direct manufacturing labor costs of each line. Summary data (in millions) for July 2007 are as follows:

	Supreme	Deluxe	Regular
Direct material costs	$84	$54	$62
Direct manufacturing labor costs	$14	$28	$ 8
Manufacturing overhead costs	$42	$84	$24
Units produced	80	120	100

Required

1. Compute the manufacturing cost per unit for each product produced in July 2007.
2. Suppose that in August 2007, production was 120 million units of Supreme, 160 million units of Deluxe, and 180 million units of Regular. Why might the July 2007 information on manufacturing cost per unit be misleading when predicting total manufacturing costs in August 2007?

2-17 Direct and indirect costs, effect of changing the classification of a cost item (continuation of 2-16). MOP hires Judy Shore, a cost consultant, who discovers that each production line has multiple energy meters, so it is economically feasible to trace $90 million of energy costs directly to the three product lines. The remaining $60 million of manufacturing overhead costs of the plant (including the $20 million of fixed costs) are allocated to each product on the basis of the direct manufacturing labor costs of each line. She reports the following revised numbers for July 2007:

Excel Lab
www.prenhall.com/horngren/cost12e

10	**Minnesota Office Products**		**(in millions)**		
11	**(after cost analysis by consultant)**	**Supreme**	**Deluxe**	**Regular**	**Total**
12	Direct material costs	$84	$54	$62	$200
13	Direct manufacturing labor costs	14	28	8	50
14	Direct energy costs	39.8	40.7	9.5	90
15	Other manufacturing overhead costs	16.8	33.6	9.6	60

If you want to use Excel to solve this exercise, go to the Excel Lab at **www.prenhall.com/horngren/cost12e** and download the template for Exercise 2-17.

Required

1. Why might MOP's managers prefer energy costs to be a direct cost rather than a manufacturing overhead cost?
2. Compute the manufacturing cost per unit for each product line after the cost analysis has been performed by Judy Shore.
3. Comment on the cost per unit for each product line before and after Shore's analysis.

2-18 Classification of costs, service sector. Consumer Focus is a marketing research firm that organizes focus groups for consumer-product companies. Each focus group has eight individuals who are paid $50 per session to provide comments on new products. These focus groups meet in hotels and are led by a trained, independent, marketing specialist hired by Consumer Focus. Each specialist is paid a fixed retainer to conduct a minimum number of sessions and a per session fee of $2,000. A Consumer Focus staff member attends each session to ensure that all the logistical aspects run smoothly.

Required

Classify each of the following cost items as:

a. Direct or indirect (D or I) costs with respect to each individual focus group.
b. Variable or fixed (V or F) costs with respect to how the total costs of Consumer Focus change as the number of focus groups conducted changes. (If in doubt, select on the basis of whether the total costs will change substantially if there is a large change in the number of groups conducted.)

You will have two answers (D or I; V or F) for each of the following items:

Cost Item	D or I	V or F
A. Payment to individuals in each focus group to provide comments on new products		
B. Annual subscription of Consumer Focus to *Consumer Reports* magazine		
C. Phone calls made by Consumer Focus staff member to confirm individuals will attend a focus group session (Records of individual calls are not kept.)		
D. Retainer paid to focus group leader to conduct 20 focus groups per year on new medical products		
E. Meals provided to participants in each focus group		
F. Lease payment by Consumer Focus for corporate office		
G. Cost of tapes used to record comments made by individuals in a focus group session (These tapes are sent to the company whose products are being tested.)		
H. Gasoline costs of Consumer Focus staff for company-owned vehicles (staff members submit monthly bills with no mileage breakdowns.)		

2-19 Classification of costs, merchandising sector. Home Entertainment Center (HEC) operates a large store in San Francisco. The store has both a video section and a music (compact disks and tapes) section. HEC reports revenues for the video section separately from the music section.

Required

Classify each of the following cost items as:

a. Direct or indirect (D or I) costs with respect to the total number of videos sold.

b. Variable or fixed (V or F) costs with respect to how the total costs of the video section change as the total number of videos sold changes. (If in doubt, select on the basis of whether the total costs will change substantially if there is a large change in the total number of videos sold.)

You will have two answers (D or I; V or F) for each of the following items:

Cost Item	D or I	V or F
A. Annual retainer paid to a video distributor		
B. Electricity costs of HEC store (single bill covers entire store)		
C. Costs of videos purchased for sale to customers		
D. Subscription to *Video Trends* magazine		
E. Leasing of computer software used for financial budgeting at HEC store		
F. Cost of popcorn provided free to all customers of HEC		
G. Earthquake insurance policy for HEC store		
H. Freight-in costs of videos purchased by HEC		

PH Grade Assist

2-20 Classification of costs, manufacturing sector. The Fremont, California, plant of New United Motor Manufacturing, Inc. (NUMMI), a joint venture of General Motors and Toyota, assembles two types of cars (Corollas and Geo Prisms). Separate assembly lines are used for each type of car.

Required

Classify each of the following cost items as:

a. Direct or indirect (D or I) costs with respect to the total number of cars of each type assembled (Corolla or Geo Prism).

b. Variable or fixed (V or F) costs with respect to how the total costs of the plant change as the total number of cars of each type assembled changes. (If in doubt, select on the basis of whether the total costs will change substantially if there is a large change in the total number of cars of each type assembled.)

You will have two answers (D or I; V or F) for each of the following items:

Cost Item	D or I	V or F
A. Cost of tires used on Geo Prisms		
B. Salary of public relations manager for NUMMI plant		
C. Annual awards dinner for Corolla suppliers		
D. Salary of engineer who monitors design changes on Geo Prism		
E. Freight costs of Corolla engines shipped from Toyota City, Japan, to Fremont, California		
F. Electricity costs for NUMMI plant (single bill covers entire plant)		
G. Wages paid to temporary assembly-line workers hired in periods of high production (paid on hourly basis)		
H. Annual fire-insurance policy cost for NUMMI plant		

2-21 Variable costs, fixed costs, total costs. Ana Compo is getting ready to open a small restaurant. She is on a tight budget and must choose between the following long-distance phone plans:

Plan A: Pay 10 cents per minute of long-distance calling.

Plan B: Pay a fixed monthly fee of $18 for up to 300 long-distance minutes, and 6 cents per minute thereafter (if she uses fewer than 300 minutes in any month, she still pays $18 for the month).

Plan C: Pay a fixed monthly fee of $24 for up to 480 long-distance minutes and 5 cents per minute thereafter (if she uses fewer than 480 minutes, she still pays $24 for the month).

Required

1. Draw a graph of the total monthly costs of the three plans for different levels of monthly long-distance calling.
2. Which plan should Compo choose if she expects to make 100 minutes of long-distance calls? 200 minutes? 500 minutes?

2-22 Variable costs and fixed costs. Consolidated Minerals (CM) owns the rights to extract minerals from beach sands on Fraser Island. CM has costs in three areas:

a. Payment to a mining subcontractor who charges $80 per ton of beach sand mined and returned to the beach (after being processed on the mainland to extract three minerals: ilmenite, rutile, and zircon).

b. Payment of a government mining and environmental tax of $50 per ton of beach sand mined.

c. Payment to a barge operator. This operator charges $150,000 per month to transport each batch of beach sand—up to 100 tons per batch per day—to the mainland and then return to Fraser Island (that is, 0 to 100 tons per day = $150,000 per month; 101 to 200 tons per day = $300,000 per month, and so on).

Each barge operates 25 days per month. The $150,000 monthly charge must be paid even if fewer than 100 tons are transported on any day and even if CM requires fewer than 25 days of barge transportation in that month.

CM is currently mining 180 tons of beach sands per day for 25 days per month.

Required

1. What is the variable cost per ton of beach sand mined? What is the fixed cost to CM per month?
2. Plot a graph of the variable costs and another graph of the fixed costs of CM. Your graphs should be similar to Exhibit 2-3, Panel A (p. 30), and Exhibit 2-4 (p. 34). Is the concept of relevant range applicable to your graphs? Explain.
3. What is the unit cost per ton of beach sand mined (a) if 180 tons are mined each day and (b) if 220 tons are mined each day? Explain the difference in the unit-cost figures.

2-23 Cost drivers and the value chain. A Johnson & Johnson analyst is preparing a presentation on cost drivers at one of its pharmaceutical drug subsidiaries. Unfortunately, both the list of its business functions and the accompanying list of representative cost drivers are accidentally randomized. The two lists now on the computer screen are:

Business Function	Representative Cost Driver
A. Production	1. Minutes of TV advertising time on *60 Minutes*
B. Research and development	2. Number of calls to toll-free customer telephone line
C. Marketing	3. Hours the Tylenol packaging line is in operation
D. Distribution	4. Number of packages shipped
E. Design of products/processes	5. Hours spent designing tamper-proof bottles
F. Customer service	6. Number of patents filed with U.S. Patent Office

Required

1. Match each business function with its representative cost driver.
2. Give a second example of a cost driver for each business function of Johnson & Johnson's pharmaceutical drug subsidiary.

2-24 Cost drivers and functions. The list of representative cost drivers in the right column of this table are randomized with respect to the list of functions in the left column. That is, they do not match.

Function	Representative Cost Driver
1. Accounting	A. Number of invoices sent
2. Personnel	B. Number of purchase orders
3. Data processing	C. Number of research scientists
4. Research and development	D. Hours of computer processing unit (CPU)
5. Purchasing	E. Number of new hires
6. Billing	F. Number of transactions processed

Required

1. Match each function with its representative cost driver.
2. Give a second example of a cost driver for each function.

2-25 Total costs and unit costs. A student association has hired a band and a caterer for a graduation party. The band will charge a fixed fee of $1,000 for an evening of music, and the caterer will charge a fixed fee of $500 for the party setup and an additional $10 per person who attends. Snacks and soft drinks will be provided by the caterer for the duration of the party. Students attending the party will pay $5 each at the door.

PH Grade Assist

Required

1. Draw a graph depicting the fixed cost, the variable cost, and the total cost to the student association for different attendance levels.
2. Suppose 100 people attend the party. What will be the total cost to the student association? What will be the cost per person?
3. Suppose 500 people attend the party. What will be the total cost to the student association and the cost per attendee?
4. Draw a graph depicting the cost per attendee for different attendance levels. As president of the student association, you want to request a grant to cover some of the party costs. Will you use the per attendee cost numbers to make your case? Why or why not?

2-26 Total costs and unit costs. Susan Wang is a well-known software engineer. Her specialty is writing software code used in maintaining the security of credit-card information. Wang is approached by the Electronic Commerce Group (ECG). They offer to pay her $100,000 for the right to use her code under license in their *e.procurement* software package. Wang rejects this offer because it provides her with no upside if the *e.procurement* package is a runaway success. Both parties eventually agree to a contract in which ECG pays Wang a flat fee of $100,000 for the right to use her code in up to 10,000 packages. If *e.procurement* sells more than 10,000 packages, Wang receives an additional $8 for each package sold beyond the 10,000 level.

Required

1. What is the unit cost to ECG of Wang's software code included in its *e.procurement* package if it sells (a) 2,000 packages, (b) 6,000 packages, (c) 10,000 packages, and (d) 20,000 packages? Comment on the results.
2. To predict ECG's total cost of using Wang's software code in *e.procurement*, which unit cost (if any) of (a) to (d) in requirement 1 would you recommend ECG use? Explain.

2-27 Inventoriable costs versus period costs. Each of the following cost items pertains to one of these companies: General Electric (a manufacturing-sector company), Safeway (a merchandising-sector company), and Google (a service-sector company):

- **a.** Perrier mineral water purchased by Safeway for sale to its customers
- **b.** Electricity used to provide lighting for assembly-line workers at a General Electric refrigerator-assembly plant
- **c.** Depreciation on Google's computer equipment used to update directories of Web sites
- **d.** Electricity used to provide lighting for Safeway's store aisles
- **e.** Depreciation on General Electric's computer equipment used for quality testing of refrigerator components during the assembly process
- **f.** Salaries of Safeway's marketing personnel planning local-newspaper advertising campaigns
- **g.** Perrier mineral water purchased by Google for consumption by its software engineers
- **h.** Salaries of Google's marketing personnel selling banner advertising

Required

1. Distinguish between manufacturing-sector, merchandising-sector, and service-sector companies.
2. Distinguish between inventoriable costs and period costs.
3. Classify each of the cost items (**a–h**) as an inventoriable cost or a period cost. Explain your answers.

Problems

2-28 Flow of Inventoriable Costs. Hofstra Plastics' selected data for August 2007 are presented here (in millions):

Direct materials inventory 8/1/2007	$ 90
Direct materials purchased	360
Direct materials used	375
Total manufacturing overhead	480
Variable manufacturing overhead	250
Total manufacturing costs	1,600
Work-in-process inventory 8/1/2007	200
Cost of goods manufactured	1,650
Finished goods inventory 8/1/2007	125
Cost of goods sold	1,700

Required

Calculate the following costs:

1. Direct materials inventory 8/31/2007
2. Fixed manufacturing overhead costs for August
3. Direct manufacturing labor costs for August
4. Work-in-process inventory 8/31/2007
5. Goods available for sale in August
6. Finished goods inventory 8/31/2007

PH Grade Assist

2-29 Computing cost of goods purchased and cost of goods sold. The following data are for Marvin Department Store. The account balances (in thousands) are for 2007.

Marketing, distribution, and customer-service costs	$ 37,000
Merchandise inventory, January 1, 2007	27,000
Utilities	17,000
General and administrative costs	43,000
Merchandise inventory, December 31, 2007	34,000
Purchases	155,000
Miscellaneous costs	4,000
Transportation-in	7,000
Purchase returns and allowances	4,000
Purchase discounts	6,000

Required

Compute (a) the cost of goods purchased and (b) the cost of goods sold.

2-30 Cost of goods manufactured. Consider the following account balances (in thousands) for the Canseco Company:

Excel Lab
www.prenhall.com/horngren/cost12e

	A	B	C
1	**Canseco Company**	**Beginning of 2007**	**End of 2007**
2			
3	Direct materials inventory	$22,000	$26,000
4	Work-in-process inventory	21,000	20,000
5	Finished goods inventory	18,000	23,000
6	Purchases of direct materials		75,000
7	Direct manufacturing labor		25,000
8	Indirect manufacturing labor		15,000
9	Plant Insurance		9,000
10	Depreciation -- plant, building, and equipment		11,000
11	Repairs and maintenance -- plant		4,000
12	Marketing, distribution, and customer-service costs		93,000
13	General and administrative costs		29,000

If you want to use Excel to solve this problem, go to the Excel Lab at **www.prenhall.com/horngren/cost12e** and download the template for Exhibit 2-7.

Required

1. Prepare a schedule for the cost of goods manufactured for 2007.
2. Revenues for 2007 were $300 million. Prepare the income statement for 2007.

2-31 Income statement and schedule of cost of goods manufactured. The Howell Corporation has the following account balances (in millions):

For Specific Date		For Year 2007	
Direct materials, Jan. 1, 2007	$15	Purchases of direct materials	$325
Work in process, Jan. 1, 2007	10	Direct manufacturing labor	100
Finished goods, Jan. 1, 2007	70	Depreciation—plant and equipment	80
Direct materials, Dec. 31, 2007	20	Plant supervisory salaries	5
Work in process, Dec. 31, 2007	5	Miscellaneous plant overhead	35
Finished goods, Dec. 31, 2007	55	Revenues	950
		Marketing, distribution, and customer-service costs	240
		Plant supplies used	10
		Plant utilities	30
		Indirect manufacturing labor	60

Required

Prepare an income statement and a supporting schedule of cost of goods manufactured for the year ended December 31, 2007. (For additional questions regarding these facts, see the next problem.)

2-32 Interpretation of statements (continuation of 2-31).

Required

1. How would the answer to Problem 2-31 be modified if you were asked for a schedule of cost of goods manufactured and sold instead of a schedule of cost of goods manufactured? Be specific.
2. Would the sales manager's salary (included in marketing, distribution, and customer-service costs) be accounted for any differently if the Howell Corporation were a merchandising-sector company instead of a manufacturing-sector company? Using the flow of manufacturing costs outlined in Exhibit 2-8 (p. 40), describe how the wages of an assembler in the plant would be accounted for in this manufacturing company.
3. Plant supervisory salaries are usually regarded as manufacturing overhead costs. When might some of these costs be regarded as direct manufacturing costs? Give an example.
4. Suppose that both the direct materials used and the plant and equipment depreciation are related to the manufacture of 1 million units of product. What is the unit cost for the direct materials assigned to those units? What is the unit cost for plant and equipment depreciation? Assume that yearly plant and equipment depreciation is computed on a straight-line basis.
5. Assume that the implied cost-behavior patterns in requirement 4 persist. That is, direct material costs behave as a variable cost, and plant and equipment depreciation behaves as a fixed cost. Repeat the computations in requirement 4, assuming that the costs are being predicted for the manufacture of 1.2 million units of product. How would the total costs be affected?
6. As a management accountant, explain concisely to the president why the unit costs differed in requirements 4 and 5.

2-33 Income statement and schedule of cost of goods manufactured. The following items (in millions) pertain to Chan Corporation:

For Specific Date		For Year 2007	
Work in process, Jan. 1, 2007	$10	Plant utilities	$ 5
Direct materials, Dec. 31, 2007	5	Indirect manufacturing labor	20
Finished goods, Dec. 31, 2007	12	Depreciation—plant	
Accounts payable, Dec. 31, 2007	20	and equipment	9
		Revenues	350
Accounts receivable, Jan. 1, 2007	50	Miscellaneous manufacturing	
Work in process, Dec. 31, 2007	2	overhead	10
Finished goods, Jan. 1, 2007	40	Marketing, distribution, and	
		customer-service costs	90
Accounts receivable, Dec. 31, 2007	30	Direct materials purchased	80
Accounts payable, Jan. 1, 2007	40	Direct manufacturing labor	40
Direct materials, Jan. 1, 2007	30	Plant supplies used	6
		Property taxes on plant	1

Chan's manufacturing costing system uses a three-part classification of direct materials, direct manufacturing labor, and manufacturing overhead costs.

Required

Prepare an income statement and a supporting schedule of cost of goods manufactured. (For additional questions regarding these facts, see the next problem.)

2-34 Terminology, interpretation of statements (continuation of 2-33).

Required

1. Calculate total prime costs and total conversion costs.
2. Compute total inventoriable costs and period costs.
3. Design costs and R&D costs are not considered product costs for financial statement purposes. When might some of these costs be regarded as product costs? Give an example.
4. Suppose that both the direct materials used and the depreciation on plant and equipment are related to the manufacture of 1 million units of product. Determine the unit cost for the direct materials assigned to those units and the unit cost for depreciation on plant and equipment. Assume that yearly depreciation is computed on a straight-line basis.
5. Assume that the implied cost-behavior patterns in requirement 4 persist. That is, direct material costs behave as a variable cost and depreciation on plant and equipment behaves as a fixed cost. Repeat the computations in requirement 4, assuming that the costs are being predicted for the manufacture of 1.5 million units of product. Determine the effect on total costs.
6. Assume that depreciation on the equipment (but not the plant) is computed based on the number of units produced because the equipment deteriorates with units produced. The depreciation rate on equipment is $4 per unit. Calculate the depreciation on equipment assuming (a) 1 million units of product are produced and (b) 1.5 million units of product are produced.

Excel Lab
www.prenhall.com/horngren/cost12e

2-35 Overtime premium. Ian Blacklaw and Gwen Benson are sales representatives for EMI, which installs and maintains music systems in office buildings, elevators, and other public areas. Sales representatives receive a base salary and a bonus of 10% of the actual gross margins on the orders they sell.

The direct manufacturing labor straight-time rate is $20 per hour, and the overtime rate is 50% higher. In costing each order, indirect manufacturing labor costs are assigned at a rate of 200% of direct manufacturing labor cost (excluding overtime premium). If overtime labor is used, whenever possible, it is charged to the rush order that caused the overtime. If overtime is caused by overall heavy production volume, not any particular rush order, it is allocated equally to all orders being worked on.

During January and February 2006, Blacklaw and Benson sold and delivered one system each to Westec and Pinnacle, respectively. Each order required 2,000 direct labor hours, for a total of 4,000 labor hours. Of these hours, 2,000 hours were overtime hours.

The following Excel spreadsheet summarizes the revenues and the costs other than overtime costs for each customer under different assumptions about which customer caused the rush order.

	A	B	C	D	E	F	G	H	I	J	K	L	M
9	**(in $000s)**	**Westec caused rush order**				**Pinnacle caused rush order**				**Neither caused rush order**			
10	**Customer**	**Westec**		**Pinnacle**		**Westec**		**Pinnacle**		**Westec**		**Pinnacle**	
11	**Sales Representative**	**I. Blacklaw**		**G. Benson**		**I. Blacklaw**		**G. Benson**		**I. Blacklaw**		**G. Benson**	
12	Revenues		$ 420,000		$ 460,000		$ 420,000		$ 460,000		$ 420,000		$ 460,000
13	Cost of goods sold:												
14	Direct Materials	$ 230,000		$ 260,000		$ 230,000		$ 260,000		$ 230,000		$ 260,000	
15	Direct manufacturing labor	40,000		40,000		40,000		40,000		40,000		40,000	
16	Indirect manufacturing labor	80,000		80,000		80,000		80,000		80,000		80,000	
17	Overtime costs	20,000											
18	Total cost of goods sold		370,000										
19	Gross Margin		50,000										
20	Bonus earned by salesperson		$ 5,000										

If you want to use Excel to solve this problem, go to the Excel Lab at **www.prenhall.com/horngren/cost12e** and download the template for Problem 2-35.

Required

1. Calculate the gross margin on each order if only Westec was a rush order.
2. Calculate the gross margin on each order if only Pinnacle was a rush order.
3. Calculate the gross margin on each order if neither of the two orders were rush orders.
4. Why do you think that Gary Shaw, EMI operations manager, is very particular about how overtime is tracked?

2-36 Fire loss, computing inventory costs. A distraught employee, Fang W. Arson, put a torch to a manufacturing plant on a blustery February 26. The resulting blaze destroyed the plant and its contents. Fortunately, certain accounting records were kept in another building. They reveal the following for the period from January 1, 2007, to February 26, 2007:

PH Grade Assist

Direct materials purchased	$160,000
Work in process, 1/1/2007	$34,000
Direct materials, 1/1/2007	$16,000
Finished goods, 1/1/2007	$30,000
Manufacturing overhead costs	40% of conversion costs
Revenues	$500,000
Direct manufacturing labor	$180,000
Prime costs	$294,000
Gross margin percentage based on revenues	20%
Cost of goods available for sale	$450,000

The loss is fully covered by insurance. The insurance company wants to know the historical cost of the inventories as a basis for negotiating a settlement, although the settlement is actually to be based on replacement cost, not historical cost.

Required

Calculate the cost of:

1. Finished goods inventory, 2/26/2007
2. Work-in-process inventory, 2/26/2007
3. Direct materials inventory, 2/26/2007

2-37 Comprehensive problem on unit costs, product costs. Tampa Office Equipment manufactures and sells metal shelving. It began operations on January 1, 2007. Costs incurred for 2007 are as follows (V stands for variable; F stands for fixed):

PH Grade Assist

Direct materials used	$140,000 V
Direct manufacturing-labor costs	30,000 V
Plant energy costs	5,000 V
Indirect manufacturing-labor costs	10,000 V
Indirect manufacturing-labor costs	16,000 F
Other indirect manufacturing costs	8,000 V
Other indirect manufacturing costs	24,000 F
Marketing, distribution, and customer-service costs	122,850 V
Marketing, distribution, and customer-service costs	40,000 F
Administrative costs	50,000 F

Variable manufacturing costs are variable with respect to units produced. Variable marketing, distribution, and customer-service costs are variable with respect to units sold.

Inventory data are:

	Beginning: January 1, 2007	**Ending: December 31, 2007**
Direct materials	0 lb.	2,000 lbs.
Work in process	0 units	0 units
Finished goods	0 units	? units

Production in 2007 was 100,000 units. Two pounds of direct materials are used to make one unit of finished product.

Revenues in 2007 were $436,800. The selling price per unit and the purchase price per pound of direct materials were stable throughout the year. The company's ending inventory of finished goods is carried at the average unit manufacturing costs for 2007. Finished-goods inventory at December 31, 2007, was $20,970.

Required

1. Calculate direct materials inventory, total cost, December 31, 2007.
2. Calculate finished-goods inventory, total units, December 31, 2007.
3. Calculate selling price in 2007.
4. Calculate operating income for 2007.

2-38 Cost analysis, litigation risk, ethics. Forever Young (FY) is a division of a large cosmetics company. It formulates and sells creams and lotions for toning and tightening facial skin. FY's scientists have developed Enhance, a drug that must be injected by a doctor and lasts for two to three months. Patients are not likely to be price-sensitive and therefore would be willing to pay the doctor $300 per treatment.

Sam Nash, Enhance's VP of marketing, has found a subcontractor who will produce Enhance to FY's exacting standards for $100 per treatment. FY plans to mark up each dose by 20% and sell it to physicians for $120. Amy Keely, the CEO, feels that Enhance is a thoroughly researched wonder drug and at these prices, it will be popular with doctors and their patients and will reverse the sagging division fortunes. Nash, who had previously been controller of FY, points out that the litigation risk from Enhance is greater than from FY's other products. He estimates that the potential litigation cost amounts to $110 per treatment. He suggests that they factor that cost into the upcoming presentation on Enhance to the board of directors, but Keely forbids it.

Required

1. Why might Amy Keely prevent Sam Nash from including the cost of potential litigation in the presentation of Enhance's economics and pricing?
2. If FY set prices by adding 20% to the total cost and the litigation cost were included, how much would FY charge doctors for a single shot of Enhance? How would that affect doctors' gross margins? How might this price affect the promotion of Enhance?
3. Nash discovers that FY may be able to purchase insurance to reduce its own litigation risk on Enhance. If FY wants doctors to enjoy a minimum gross margin of 40% and FY itself has a firm 20%-markup policy, what is the maximum per treatment litigation cost it would be willing to pay?
4. Keely tells Nash to stop worrying about a "mythical litigation issue" and get back to work on making Enhance a blockbuster treatment of choice. What should Nash do now?

Collaborative Learning Problem

2-39 Finding unknown amounts. An auditor for the Internal Revenue Service is trying to reconstruct some partially destroyed records of two taxpayers. For each of the cases in the accompanying list, find the unknowns designated by the letters A through D.

	Case 1 (in thousands)	Case 2 (in thousands)
Accounts receivable, 12/31	$ 6,000	$ 2,100
Cost of goods sold	A	20,000
Accounts payable, 1/1	3,000	1,700
Accounts payable, 12/31	1,800	1,500
Finished goods inventory, 12/31	B	5,300
Gross margin	11,300	C
Work in process inventory, 1/1	0	800
Work in process inventory, 12/31	0	3,000
Finished goods inventory, 1/1	4,000	4,000
Direct materials used	8,000	12,000
Direct manufacturing labor	3,000	5,000
Manufacturing overhead costs	7,000	D
Purchases of direct materials	9,000	7,000
Revenues	32,000	31,800
Accounts receivable, 1/1	2,000	1,400

Get Connected: Cost Accounting in the News

WWW

Go to www.prenhall.com/horngren/cost12e for additional online exercise(s) that explore issues affecting the accounting world today. These exercises offer you the opportunity to analyze and reflect on how cost accounting helps managers to make better decisions and handle the challenges of strategic planning and implementation.

CHAPTER 2 Video Case

THREE DOG BAKERY: Understanding Cost Terms

"Going to the dogs" has been good for Mark Beckloff and Dan Dye. Back in 1989, they founded the first bakery just for four-legged canine friends with little more than the desire to satisfy the finicky palate of their beloved 114-pound, deaf Great Dane, Gracie. The small venture has grown from a single store in downtown Kansas City to more than 40 locations worldwide, including Japan and Korea. Their dog treats are made from wholesome ingredients such as flour, eggs, carrots, spinach, peanut butter, and carob, and have clever names such as Rollovers, Pup Tarts, Scottie Biscottis, and Great Danish. Some treats are even frosted with honey-yogurt icings and decorated with colorful, edible flourishes. Special-occasion carrot or carob cakes can be personalized by an in-store pastry chef. The company regularly updates its 100+ product line to entice dog-lovers everywhere back to the stores again and again. Selling prices range from a few cents for a small biscuit to more than $20 for a special-order cake.

Three Dog Bakery has an 80,000-square-foot warehouse in Kansas City, containing manufacturing, distribution, and corporate offices, that prepares 70% of the goods sold. Except for slow summer months, the manufacturing operation runs 24 hours a day, 7 days a week, producing baked biscuits and carob-dipped items that can pack and ship well. There is one main assembly line with stations for mixing ingredients, mechanized cutting of shapes, extruding doughnut-shaped biscuits, placing biscuits on baking sheets, baking in ovens, cooling, carob-dipping (for selected biscuits), hand-packing into trays or containers, shrink-wrapping, and boxing. Most trays hold 12 specialty biscuits that are hand-packed. A conveyer belt is used for automated packing of small biscuits into 7-ounce tubs. Employees are cross-trained to perform multiple assembly-line functions and can work on every type of product produced at the plant.

For the remaining 30% of finished goods, each store has a specially outfitted kitchen used for preparing cakes, brownies, tarts, and other delicate or frosted items. Prepackaged mixes created back at the production facility are used to assure consistent quality across all stores. The retail outlets also sell nonfood products such as bowls, leashes, books, mugs, and T-shirts. Some stores even host "yappie hours" and in-store birthday parties for dog socialization. Customers don't have to visit a Three Dog Bakery to enjoy the treats, however. The company has a whimsical Web site at **www.threedog.com** that is home to the "dogalog" (well, it can't be called a "cat-alog," can it?). The site features all kinds of treats available for immediate shipping and accounts for 10% of the company's business now. In addition to its retail and e-commerce channels, Three Dog Bakery places heavy emphasis on its expanding wholesale business. The products were originally offered through national chains, such as PetsMart and Target, but are now finding success with high-end grocery stores that have lost much of their pet business to "big box" specialty pet stores and want a higher-end quality product to offer their shoppers. Even Wal-Mart can't ignore the appeal of Three Dog Bakery products. Dog lovers can find Lick 'n Crunch Cookies on the shelves there.

Annual revenues exceed $20 million for this privately held company. As for the pet market itself, there are more than 60 million pet dogs in the United States alone, with nearly every owner buying anywhere from one to five packages of treats per month. Two-thirds of pet owners give their pets gifts, more than half give Christmas presents, and 25% give birthday gifts. Pet owners spend in excess of $20 billion each year in an industry that includes animal products, food, and services. Owners who spend more than $300 per year on their dogs tend to be younger, more affluent, married, and have no children.

QUESTIONS

1. To what cost objects could Three Dog Bakery trace its costs?
2. Classify the following cost items as direct (D) or indirect (I), and fixed (F) or variable (V) with respect to the production department (you will have two answers for each item—D or I; F or V):

Cost Item	D or I	F or V
a. Salary of the production department manager who oversees manufacturing		
b. Salaries of founders Dan Dye and Mark Beckloff		
c. Cardboard trays used to package sets of 12 specialty biscuits		
d. Salary of the Web graphics designer who prepares the online dogalog illustrations and layout		
e. Annual maintenance service agreement for the conveyer belt		
f. Wages paid to assembly line workers who mix Scottie Biscotti ingredients in batches		
g. Utilities (water, electricity, waste) for the entire Kansas City warehouse		
h. Cost of flour, eggs, and honey-yogurt icing for the Pup Tarts		

3. What sectors—manufacturing, merchandising, or service—does Three Dog Bakery operate in? Why are they classified this way?
4. When Wal-Mart purchases Lick 'n Crunch Cookies for sale in its stores, is the purchase considered a period cost or an inventoriable cost? Why? What costs can Wal-Mart include as part of the purchase cost?

CHAPTER 3

COST-VOLUME-PROFIT ANALYSIS

LEARNING OBJECTIVES

1. **Understand the assumptions of cost-volume-profit (CVP) analysis**
2. **Explain the features of CVP analysis**
3. **Determine the breakeven point and output level needed to achieve a target operating income**
4. **Understand how income taxes affect CVP analysis**
5. **Explain CVP analysis in decision making and how sensitivity analysis helps managers cope with uncertainty**
6. **Use CVP analysis to plan variable and fixed costs**
7. **Apply CVP analysis to a company producing different products**
8. **Adapt CVP analysis to situations in which a product has more than one cost driver**
9. **Distinguish contribution margin from gross margin**

Becoming an entrepreneur and being your own boss is a dream for many people. Mary Frost is one of them. She discovered that selling Do-All Software, a home-office software package, at booths rented at software conventions was the perfect match for her skills and ambitions. There's a new computer convention coming up that she views as critical for exposure to new clients and growth. But the convention organizer has a complicated booth-rental plan, so Mary consults Joe Martinez, the management accountant, for help in deciding what to do.

Mary: Joe, this new convention in Chicago has thrown me for a loop. I'd like to rent a booth, but the conference organizers have offered us alternative ways to pay, and I'm not sure which option is best.

Joe: Okay, what are our choices?

Mary: Well, I was hoping to pay a fixed amount, but there are other options available. One of these options is to pay nothing up front and then pay a fixed percentage on whatever revenues we earn. The choices we make could significantly affect our profit or loss. I'd like to see an analysis of the options to help us make a decision. Can you help?

Joe: No problem. I'll put together a cost-volume-profit analysis to help evaluate the risks and rewards of the options. Will tomorrow work for you?

Mary: Yes, thanks. I also need to figure out whether to advertise. Because we're new to this convention, I don't know how well attended it will be or who else will be selling similar software. There's so much uncertainty.

Joe: Glad you told me. I'll work those issues into the analysis. At some point, Mary, we're going to have to examine whether additional spending is needed to upgrade our booth displays. We can start thinking about this expenditure, but in the meantime, let's get together tomorrow and see what needs to happen to make a profit or at least break even on the deal.

The scenario facing Mary and Joe is nothing new to organizations. Every day, managers at well-known companies such as Home Depot and Procter & Gamble use cost-volume-profit analysis to help answer questions such as those raised here. **Cost-volume-profit (CVP) analysis** examines the behavior of total revenues, total costs, and operating income as changes occur in the output level, the selling price, the variable cost per unit, or the fixed costs of a product. Home Depot, for example, might use CVP analysis to determine how many units of a new product must be sold to break even. Procter & Gamble might use it to better understand manufacturing costs for the Crest toothpaste product line or to help answer questions such as: How will total revenues and total costs be affected if the output level (the *volume* in CVP analysis) changes—for example, if we sell 1,000 more cases? If we expand our business into foreign markets, how will that affect costs, selling price, and output level? These questions have a common "what-if" theme. By examining the results of these what-if possibilities and alternatives, CVP analysis illustrates the profits from those possibilities and alternatives. In this way, CVP analysis guides managers' planning.

As you read this chapter, you will begin to understand the difficulties faced by capital-intensive companies that have high fixed costs. Many of these companies, such as US Airways and United Airlines in the airlines industry and Global Crossing and WorldCom in the telecommunications industry, are in bankruptcy. As sales declined at these companies during 2001 and 2002, high fixed costs led to substantial losses. CVP analysis helps management accountants alert managers to the risks and rewards of the decisions they make.

Cost-Volume-Profit Assumptions and Terminology

1

Understand the assumptions of cost-volume-profit (CVP) analysis

. . . for example, all costs are either variable or fixed with respect to output units

CVP analysis is based on several assumptions:

1. Changes in the levels of revenues and costs arise only because of changes in the number of product (or service) units produced and sold—for example, the number of television sets produced and sold by Sony Corporation or the number of packages delivered by Federal Express. The number of output units is the only revenue driver and the only cost driver. Just as a cost driver is any factor that affects costs, a **revenue driver** is a variable, such as volume, that causally affects revenues.
2. Total costs can be separated into two components: a fixed component that does not vary with output level and a variable component that changes with respect to output level. Furthermore, you know from Chapter 2 (Exhibit 2-5, p. 35) that variable costs include both direct variable costs and indirect variable costs of a product. Similarly, fixed costs include both direct fixed costs and indirect fixed costs of a product. (We discuss details of determining fixed and variable components of costs in Chapter 10.)
3. When represented graphically, the behaviors of total revenues and total costs are linear (meaning they can be represented as a straight line) in relation to output level within a relevant range (and time period).
4. Selling price, variable cost per unit, and total fixed costs (within a relevant range and time period) are known and constant. (This assumption is discussed later in the chapter and in the appendix to this chapter.)
5. The analysis either covers a single product or assumes that the proportion of different products when multiple products are sold will remain constant as the level of total units sold changes. (This assumption is discussed later in the chapter.)
6. All revenues and costs can be added, subtracted, and compared without taking into account the time value of money. (Chapter 21 considers the time value of money.)

Global surveys show that more than 50% of responding companies use some form of CVP analysis.

Study Tip: Go to **www.prenhall.com/harris** and print Chapter 3 from the *Student Guide.* Use the Highlights (pp. 23–26) to preview the chapter.

Assumption 3 holds if selling price and costs of production inputs are constant within the relevant range. Assumption 3 does not hold if reductions in selling price are necessary to spur sales at higher output levels or if variable cost per unit declines when output increases as employees learn to work more efficiently.

As the CVP assumptions make clear, an important feature of CVP analysis is distinguishing fixed from variable costs. Always keep in mind, however, that whether a cost is variable or fixed depends on the time period for a decision. The shorter the time horizon, the higher the percentage of total costs considered as fixed. Suppose an American Airlines plane will depart from its gate in the next hour and currently has 20 seats unsold. A potential passenger arrives with a transferable ticket from a competing airline. What are the variable costs to American of placing one more passenger in an otherwise empty seat? Variable costs (such as one more meal) would be negligible. Virtually all the costs in this decision situation (such as crew costs and baggage-handling costs) are fixed. Alternatively, suppose American must decide whether to include another city in its routes. This decision may have a one-year planning horizon. Many more costs, including crew costs, baggage-handling costs, and airport fees, would be regarded as variable; and fewer costs (for example, corporate-office costs) would be regarded as fixed in this decision. Always consider the relevant range, the length of the time horizon, and the specific decision situation when classifying costs as variable or fixed.

In the American Airlines example, be aware that a short-run decision can have long-run consequences. To illustrate, assume American accepts last-minute passengers at reduced fares because the contribution margin from these passengers is positive. This decision could have long-run consequences because future passengers might come to expect reduced fares at the last minute.

Many companies (and divisions and plants of companies) in industries such as airlines, automobiles, chemicals, plastics, and semiconductors have found that even the simplest possible CVP analysis can be helpful in making decisions about strategic and long-range planning, as well as decisions about product features and pricing. In some real-world settings, the six assumptions just described may not hold. For example, predicting total revenues and total costs may require multiple drivers of revenues and costs (such as number of output units, number of sales visits made to customers, and number of advertisements run). CVP analysis still may be useful in these situations, but the analysis becomes more complex. Always assess whether a simplified CVP analysis generates sufficiently accurate predictions of how total revenues and total costs behave. Use a more-complex approach with multiple revenue drivers, multiple cost drivers, and cost functions that are not linear only if doing so will significantly improve decisions.

Before explaining the basics of CVP analysis, we first clarify some terms.

$$\text{Operating income} = \text{Total revenues from operations} - \text{Cost of goods sold and operating costs (excluding income taxes)}$$

Net income is operating income plus nonoperating revenues (such as interest revenue) minus nonoperating costs (such as interest cost) minus income taxes. For simplicity, throughout this chapter we assume nonoperating revenues and nonoperating costs are zero. Thus, net income is computed as:

$$\text{Net income} = \text{Operating income} - \text{Income taxes}$$

Essentials of CVP Analysis

2
Explain the features of CVP analysis
. . . how operating income changes with changes in output level, selling price, variable costs, or fixed costs

In the Do-All Software example, the privilege of returning unsold packages means that cost of goods sold is variable with respect to the number of units sold.

Let's consider an example to see how CVP analysis works.

Example: As described in the conversation at the beginning of this chapter, Mary Frost is considering selling Do-All Software, a home-office software package, at a computer convention in Chicago. Mary can purchase this software from a computer software wholesaler at $120 per package, with the privilege of returning all unsold packages and receiving a full $120 refund per package. The packages would be sold for $200 each. She would pay $2,000 to Computer Conventions, Inc., for the booth rental for the convention. Assume there are no other costs. Mary is uncertain about how many packages she would be able to sell at the convention. To decide whether she should rent a booth, Mary wants to know what profits she would make for different quantities of packages that she might sell.

The booth-rental cost of $2,000 is a fixed cost because it will not change no matter how many packages Mary sells. The cost of the package itself is a variable cost because it increases in proportion to the number of packages sold. For each package that Mary sells, she will incur a cost of $120 to purchase it. Mary can use CVP analysis to examine changes in operating income as a result of selling different quantities of packages:

	Mary Sells 5 Packages		**Mary Sells 40 Packages**	
Revenues	$ 1,000	($200 per package × 5 packages)	$8,000	($200 per package × 40 packages)
Variable purchase costs	600	($120 per package × 5 packages)	4,800	($120 per package × 40 packages)
Fixed costs	2,000		2,000	
Operating income	$(1,600)		$1,200	

The only numbers that change from selling different quantities of packages are *total revenues* and *total variable costs*. The difference between total revenues and total variable costs is called **contribution margin**. Contribution margin indicates why operating income changes as the number of units sold changes. The contribution margin when Mary sells 5 packages is $400 ($1,000 in total revenues minus $600 in total variable costs); the contribution margin when Mary sells 40 packages is $3,200 ($8,000 in total revenues minus $4,800 in total variable costs). Be sure to subtract all variable costs when calculating the contribution margin. For example, if Mary had variable selling costs because she paid salespersons a commission on each package they sold at the convention, variable costs would include the cost of each package plus the sales commission.

Contribution margin per unit is a useful tool for calculating contribution margin and operating income. **Contribution margin per unit** is the difference between selling price and variable cost per unit. In the Do-All Software example, contribution margin per package, or per unit, is $200 – $120 = $80. Contribution margin can be calculated as:

$$\text{Contribution margin} = \text{Contribution margin per unit} \times \text{Number of units sold}$$

For example, when 40 packages are sold, contribution margin = $80 per unit × 40 units = $3,200.

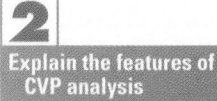

	A	B	C	D	E	F	G	H
1				Number of Packages Sold				
2				0	1	5	25	40
3	Revenues at	$ 200	per package	$ 0	$ 200	$ 1,000	$5,000	$8,000
4	Variable Costs at	$ 120	per package	0	120	600	3,000	4,800
5	Contribution Margin at	$ 80	per package	0	80	400	2,000	3,200
6	Fixed Costs	$2,000		2,000	2,000	2,000	2,000	2,000
7	Operating Income			$(2,000)	$(1,920)	$(1,600)	$ 0	$1,200

EXHIBIT 3-1

Contribution Income Statement for Different Quantities of Do-All Software Packages Sold

Contribution margin represents the amount of revenues minus variable costs that contributes to recovering fixed costs. Once fixed costs are fully recovered, the remaining contribution margin increases operating income. Exhibit 3-1 tabulates contribution margins for different quantities of packages sold and shows how contribution margin recovers fixed costs and generates operating income with increasing numbers of packages sold. The income statement in Exhibit 3-1 is called a **contribution income statement** because it groups costs into variable costs and fixed costs to highlight contribution margin. See how each additional package sold from 0 to 1 to 5 increases contribution margin by $80 per package, recovering more of the fixed costs and reducing the operating loss. If Mary sells 25 packages, contribution margin equals $2,000 ($80 per package × 25 packages), exactly recovering fixed costs and resulting in $0 operating income. If Mary sells 40 packages, contribution margin increases by another $1,200 ($3,200 – $2,000), all of which becomes operating income. As you look across Exhibit 3-1 from left to right, you see that the increase in contribution margin exactly equals the increase in operating income (or the decrease in operating loss).

Question: What is the basic difference between the income statement prepared under generally accepted accounting principles (IS/GAAP) and the contribution income statement (CIS)?

Answer: In the IS/GAAP, costs are separated into inventoriable costs and period costs. In the CIS, costs are separated according to how they behave (variable or fixed).

Instead of expressing contribution margin as a dollar amount per unit, we can express it as a percentage. **Contribution margin percentage** (also called **contribution margin ratio**) is contribution margin per unit divided by selling price.

In our example,

$$\text{Contribution margin percentage} = \frac{\$80}{\$200} = 0.40,\ \text{or } 40\%$$

Contribution margin percentage is contribution margin per dollar of revenues. In this example, it indicates that 40% of each dollar of revenues (equal to 40 cents) is contribution margin.

Mary can calculate total contribution margin for different output levels by multiplying the contribution margin percentage by the total revenues shown in Exhibit 3-1. For example, if Mary sells 40 packages, revenues will be $8,000 and contribution margin will equal 40% of $8,000, or 0.40 × $8,000 = $3,200. Mary earns operating income of $1,200 ($3,200 – $2,000) by selling 40 packages for $8,000.

Using data in Exhibit 3-1, contribution margin percentage (CM%) can also be calculated as contribution margin divided by total revenues. For example, if 40 packages are sold, CM% = $3,200 ÷ $8,000 = 40%.

The contribution income statement forms the basis of three alternative methods to express CVP relationships: the equation method, the contribution margin method, and the graph method. The equation method and the contribution margin method are most useful when managers are interested in determining operating income at a few specific levels of sales (for example 5, 15, 25, and 40 units sold). The graph method helps managers visualize the relationship between units sold and operating income over a wide range of quantities of units sold. As we shall see later in the chapter, we will use different methods for the different decisions that we analyze.

The complement of the contribution margin percentage (CM%) is the variable cost percentage (VC%). That is, CM% + VC% = 1. In the Do-All Software example, CM% = 40%, so VC% = 60%. Given variable cost of $120 per unit and VC% of 60%, selling price is $200 ($120 ÷ 0.60).

Equation Method

Think about the structure of the contribution income statement in Exhibit 3-1. Each column is expressed as an equation.

$$\text{Revenues} - \text{Variable costs} - \text{Fixed costs} = \text{Operating income}$$

How are revenues in each column calculated?

$$\text{Revenues} = \text{Selling price } (SP) \times \text{Quantity of output units sold } (Q)$$

Just remember the format of the contribution income statement and you can reconstruct this equation.

How are variable costs in each column calculated?

$$\text{Variable costs} = \text{Variable cost per unit } (VCU) \times \text{Quantity of output units sold } (Q)$$

So,

$$\left(\begin{array}{c}\text{Selling}\\ \text{price}\end{array} \times \begin{array}{c}\text{Quantity of output}\\ \text{units sold}\end{array}\right) - \left(\begin{array}{c}\text{Variable cost}\\ \text{per unit}\end{array} \times \begin{array}{c}\text{Quantity of output}\\ \text{units sold}\end{array}\right) - \begin{array}{c}\text{Fixed}\\ \text{costs}\end{array} = \begin{array}{c}\text{Operating}\\ \text{income}\end{array} \quad \textbf{(Eq. 1)}$$

We can use equation 1 to calculate operating income for different quantities of output units sold. For example, operating income when Mary sells 5 packages is:

$$(\$200 \times 5) - (\$120 \times 5) - \$2{,}000 = \$1{,}000 - \$600 - \$2{,}000 = -\$1{,}600$$

Contribution Margin Method

Equation 1 can be rearranged to emphasize contribution margin, which gives the contribution margin method its name.

Although common usage refers to three methods for CVP analysis, think of the methods not as distinct approaches but rather as variations of the equation for the contribution income statement.

$$\begin{array}{c}\text{Operating}\\ \text{income}\end{array} = \left[\left(\begin{array}{c}\text{Selling}\\ \text{price}\end{array} - \begin{array}{c}\text{Variable cost}\\ \text{per unit}\end{array}\right) \times \left(\begin{array}{c}\text{Quantity of output}\\ \text{units sold}\end{array}\right)\right] - \begin{array}{c}\text{Fixed}\\ \text{costs}\end{array}$$

$$\begin{array}{c}\text{Operating}\\ \text{income}\end{array} = \left(\begin{array}{c}\text{Contribution margin}\\ \text{per unit}\end{array} \times \begin{array}{c}\text{Quantity of output}\\ \text{units sold}\end{array}\right) - \begin{array}{c}\text{Fixed}\\ \text{costs}\end{array} \quad \textbf{(Eq. 2)}$$

In our Do-All Software example, contribution margin per unit is \$80 (\$200 – \$120), so when Mary sells 5 packages,

$$\text{Operating income} = (\$80 \times 5) - \$2{,}000 = -\$1{,}600$$

Graph Method

In the graph method, we represent total costs and total revenues graphically. Each is shown as a line on a graph. Exhibit 3-2 illustrates the graph method for Do-All Software. Because we have assumed that total costs and total revenues behave in a linear fashion, we need only two points to plot the line representing each of them.

EXHIBIT 3-2

Cost-Volume-Profit Graph for Do-All Software

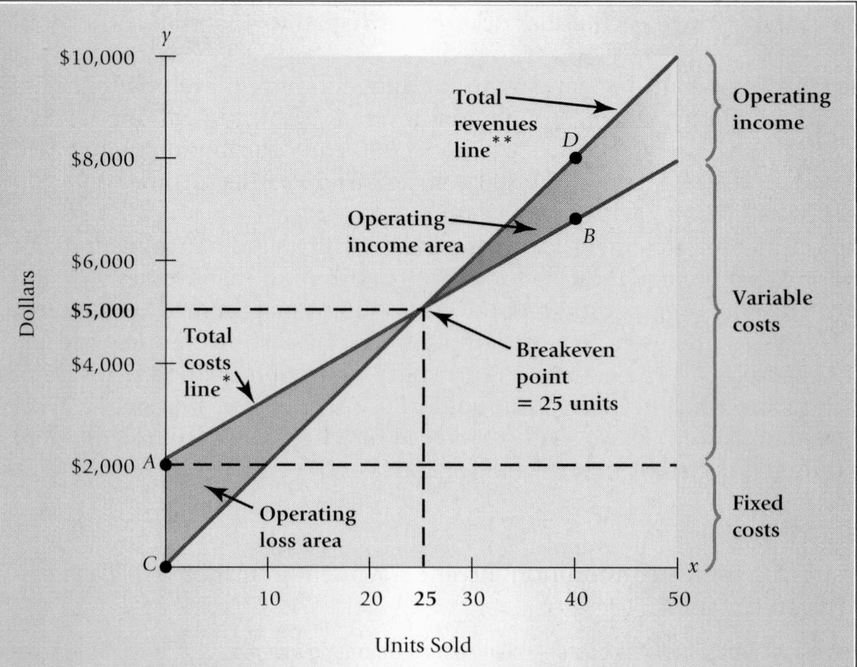

*Slope of the total costs line is the variable cost per unit = \$120

**Slope of the total revenues line is the selling price = \$200

Example: Even if total revenues and total costs are not linear throughout the range of 0 to 50 units as in Exhibit 3-2, a linear approximation may be acceptable within a relevant range, say, 15 to 40 units. If so, an alternative presentation follows:

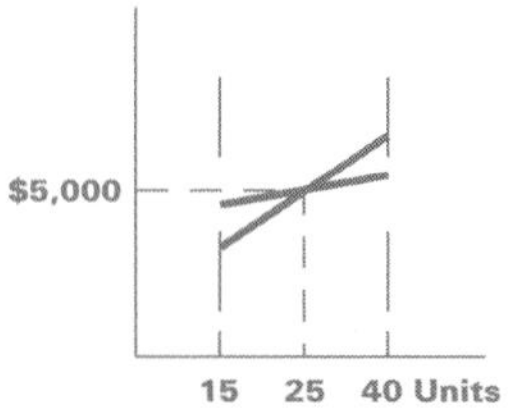

This graph illustrates that making inferences outside the range of 15 to 40 units is dangerous.

1. Total costs line The total costs line is the sum of fixed costs and variable costs. Fixed costs are \$2,000 at all output levels within the relevant range. To plot fixed costs, measure \$2,000 on the vertical axis (point *A*) and extend a line horizontally to the right from \$2,000 on the vertical axis. Variable costs are \$120 per unit. To plot the total costs line, use as one point the \$2,000 fixed costs at zero units sold (point *A*), because variable costs are \$0 when no units are sold. Select a second point by choosing any other convenient output level (say, 40 units sold) and determining the corresponding total costs. Total variable costs at this output level are \$4,800 (40 units × \$120 per unit). Because fixed costs are \$2,000 at all output levels within the relevant range, total costs at 40 units sold are \$6,800 (\$2,000 + \$4,800), which is point *B* in Exhibit 3-2. The total costs line is the straight line from point *A* through point *B*.

2. Total revenues line One convenient starting point is \$0 revenues at 0 units sold, which is point *C* in Exhibit 3-2. Select a second point by choosing any other convenient output level and determining the corresponding total revenues. At 40 units sold, total revenues are \$8,000 (\$200 per unit × 40 units), which is point *D* in Exhibit 3-2. The total revenues line is the straight line from point *C* through point *D*.

Profit or loss at any sales level can be determined by the vertical distance between the two lines at that level in Exhibit 3-2. For quantities fewer than 25 units sold, total costs exceed total revenues, and the mauve area indicates operating losses. For quantities greater than 25 units sold, total revenues exceed total costs, and the blue-green area indicates operating incomes. At 25 units sold, total revenues equal total costs. Mary will break even by selling 25 packages.

Breakeven Point and Target Income

3 Determine the breakeven point and output level needed to achieve a target operating income

. . . compare contribution margin and fixed costs

The **breakeven point (BEP)** is that quantity of output sold at which total revenues equal total costs—that is, the quantity of output sold at which the operating income is \$0. Managers are interested in the breakeven point because they want to avoid operating losses. The breakeven point tells them how much output they must sell to avoid a loss. We have already seen how to use the graph method to calculate the breakeven point. We now use the preceding data for Do-All Software to illustrate the breakeven point calculations using the equation method and the contribution margin method.

Recall the equation method (equation 1):

$$\left(\begin{matrix}\text{Selling}\\\text{price}\end{matrix}\times\begin{matrix}\text{Quantity of output}\\\text{units sold}\end{matrix}\right)-\left(\begin{matrix}\text{Variable cost}\\\text{per unit}\end{matrix}\times\begin{matrix}\text{Quantity of output}\\\text{units sold}\end{matrix}\right)-\begin{matrix}\text{Fixed}\\\text{costs}\end{matrix}=\begin{matrix}\text{Operating}\\\text{income}\end{matrix}$$

Using Do-All Software data, setting operating income equal to \$0 and denoting quantity of output units that must be sold by *Q*, we obtain:

$$\$200 \times Q - \$120 \times Q - \$2{,}000 = \$0$$
$$\$80 \times Q = \$2{,}000$$
$$Q = \$2{,}000 \div \$80 \text{ per unit} = 25 \text{ units}$$

If Mary sells fewer than 25 units, she will have a loss; if she sells 25 units, she will break even; and if she sells more than 25 units, she will make a profit. This breakeven point is expressed in units. It can also be expressed in terms of revenues: 25 units × \$200 selling price = \$5,000.

Recall the contribution margin method (equation 2):

$$\left(\begin{matrix}\text{Contribution}\\\text{margin per unit}\end{matrix}\times\begin{matrix}\text{Quantity of output}\\\text{units sold}\end{matrix}\right)-\text{Fixed costs}=\text{Operating income}$$

At the breakeven point, operating income is by definition \$0 and we obtain:

$$\text{Contribution margin per unit} \times \text{Breakeven number of units} = \text{Fixed cost} \qquad \text{(Eq. 3)}$$

Rearranging equation 3 and entering the data, we get:

$$\begin{matrix}\text{Breakeven}\\\text{number of units}\end{matrix}=\frac{\text{Fixed costs}}{\text{Contribution margin per unit}}=\frac{\$2{,}000}{\$80\text{ per unit}}=25\text{ units}$$

To calculate the breakeven point in terms of revenues, recall that in the Do-All Software example,

$$\frac{\text{Contribution margin}}{\text{percentage}} = \frac{\text{Contribution margin per unit}}{\text{Selling price}} = \frac{\$80}{\$200} = 0.40, \text{ or } 40\%.$$

That is, 40% of each dollar of revenue, or 40 cents, is contribution margin. To break even, contribution margin must equal fixed costs of $2,000. To earn $2,000 of contribution margin, revenues must equal $2,000 ÷ 0.40 = $5,000.

$$\frac{\text{Breakeven}}{\text{revenues}} = \frac{\text{Fixed costs}}{\text{Contribution margin \%}} = \frac{\$2{,}000}{0.40} = \$5{,}000$$

The breakeven point tells managers how much they must sell to avoid a loss. But managers are equally interested in how they will achieve the operating income targets underlying their strategies and plans.

Target Operating Income

We illustrate target operating income calculations by asking: How many units must Do-All Software sell to earn an operating income of $1,200? Using equation 1, we need to find Q where:

$$\$200 \times Q - \$120 \times Q - \$2{,}000 = \$1{,}200$$
$$\$80 \times Q = \$2{,}000 + \$1{,}200 = \$3{,}200$$
$$Q = \$3{,}200 \div \$80 \text{ per unit} = 40 \text{ units}$$

Alternatively, we could use the contribution margin method and equation 2,

The intuition for the formula is, "How many units must be sold to generate enough contribution margin to cover fixed costs and target operating income?"

$$\frac{\text{Quantity of output}}{\text{units required to be sold}} = \frac{\text{Fixed costs} + \text{Target operating income}}{\text{Contribution margin per unit}} \qquad \text{(Eq. 4)}$$

$$\frac{\text{Quantity of output}}{\text{units required to be sold}} = \frac{\$2{,}000 + \$1{,}200}{\$80 \text{ per unit}} = 40 \text{ units}$$

Proof:		
	Revenues, $200 per unit × 40 units	$8,000
	Variable costs, $120 per unit × 40 units	4,800
	Contribution margin, $80 per unit × 40 units	3,200
	Fixed costs	2,000
	Operating income	$1,200

The revenues needed to earn an operating income of $1,200 can also be calculated directly by recognizing (1) that $3,200 of contribution margin must be earned (fixed costs of $2,000 plus operating income of $1,200) and (2) that each dollar of revenue earns 40 cents of contribution margin. To earn $3,200 of contribution margin, revenues must equal $3,200 ÷ 0.40 = $8,000.

$$\text{Revenues needed to earn } \$1{,}200 = \frac{\$2{,}000 + \$1{,}200}{0.40} = \frac{\$3{,}200}{0.40} = \$8{,}000$$

The graph in Exhibit 3-2 is not helpful in answering the question of how many units Mary must sell to earn an operating income of $1,200. Why? Because it is not easy to determine in the graph the precise point at which the difference between the total revenues line and the total costs line is $1,200. However, recasting Exhibit 3-2 in the form of a profit-volume (PV) graph makes it possible to answer this question.

A **PV graph** shows how changes in the quantity of units sold affect operating income. Exhibit 3-3 is the PV graph for Do-All Software (fixed costs, $2,000; selling price, $200; and variable cost per unit, $120). The PV line can be drawn using two points. One

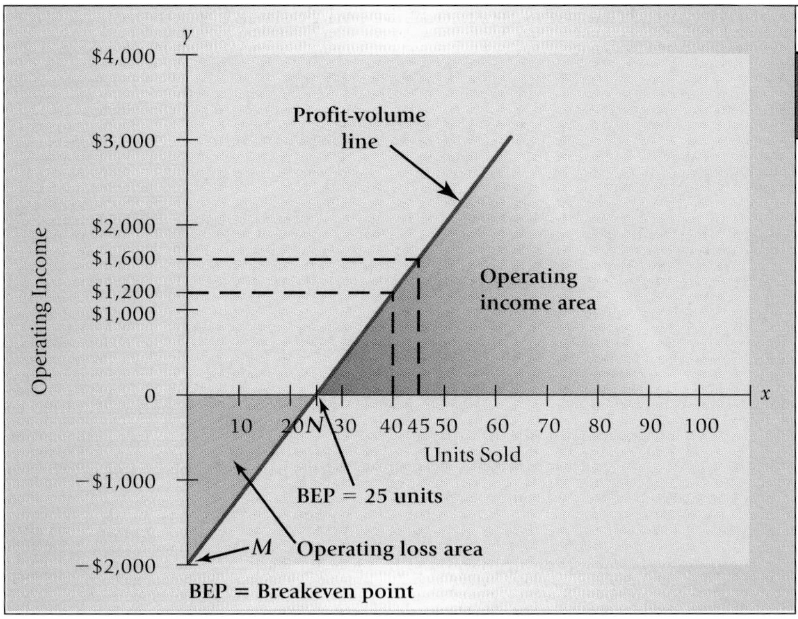

EXHIBIT 3-3

Profit-Volume Graph for Do-All Software

convenient point (*M*) is the operating loss at 0 units sold, which is equal to the fixed costs of $2,000, shown at –$2,000 on the vertical axis. A second convenient point (*N*) is the breakeven point, which is 25 units in our example (see p. 65). The PV line is the straight line from point *M* through point *N*. To find the number of units Mary must sell to earn an operating income of $1,200, draw a horizontal line corresponding to $1,200 on the vertical axis (that's the *y*-axis). At the point where this line intersects the PV line, draw a vertical line to the horizontal axis (that's the *x*-axis). The vertical line intersects the *x*-axis at 40 units, indicating that by selling 40 units Mary will earn an operating income of $1,200.

Target Net Income and Income Taxes

4 **Understand how income taxes affect CVP analysis**
. . . focus on net income

Thus far, we have ignored the effect of income taxes in our CVP analysis. In many companies, the income targets for managers in their strategic plans are expressed in terms of net income—operating income minus income taxes. That's because top management wants subordinate managers to take into account the effects their decisions have on operating income after income taxes are paid. Some decisions may not result in large operating incomes. But they may have favorable tax consequences and so may be attractive on a net income basis—the measure that drives shareholders' dividends and returns.

To make net income evaluations, CVP calculations for target income must be stated in terms of target net income instead of target operating income. For example, Mary may be interested in knowing the quantity of units she must sell to earn a net income of $960, assuming an income tax rate of 40%. Using the equation method,

$$\text{Revenues} - \text{Variable costs} - \text{Fixed costs} = \text{Target operating income}$$

And,

$$\text{Target net income} = (\text{Target operating income}) - (\text{Target operating income} \times \text{Tax rate})$$

$$\text{Target net income} = (\text{Target operating income})\ (1 - \text{Tax rate})$$

$$\text{Target operating income} = \frac{\text{Target net income}}{1 - \text{Tax rate}}$$

Substituting for target operating income:

$$\text{Revenues} - \text{Variable costs} - \text{Fixed costs} = \frac{\text{Target net income}}{1 - \text{Tax rate}}$$

Substituting numbers from our Do-All Software example:

$$\$200 \times Q - \$120 \times Q - \$2{,}000 = \frac{\$960}{1 - 0.40}$$

$$\$200 \times Q - \$120 \times Q - \$2{,}000 = \$1{,}600$$

$$\$80 \times Q = \$3{,}600$$

$$Q = \$3{,}600 \div \$80 \text{ per unit} = 45 \text{ units}$$

Example: Because no income taxes are paid at the breakeven point (BEP), income taxes do not affect the BEP. An increase in income tax rates, however, would increase the number of units that must be sold to generate a given net income (NI). In the Do-All Software example, when the income tax rate is 40%, sales of 45 units generate \$960 NI. If the income tax rate were 50%, sales of an extra 4 units (49 – 45) would be needed to generate \$960 NI:

Total operating income = \$960 ÷ (1 – 0.50) = \$1,920
Q = (\$2,000 + \$1,920) ÷ \$80/unit = 49 units

Study Tip: To check your understanding of CVP analysis, see the Featured Exercise, true–false statement 1, multiple-choice questions 5 and 6, and Review Exercise 1 (*Student Guide,* beginning p. 26). Fully explained solutions begin on p. 32. Note that these multiple-choice questions are from the CPA Exam and that Review Exercise 1 is from the CMA Exam. Studying CPA and CMA questions and answers is good preparation for both classroom exams and professional exams. Most *Student Guide* chapters contain at least five CPA/CMA questions and fully explained answers.

Alternatively, we can use the contribution margin method and equation 4 and substitute:

$$\text{Target operating income} = \frac{\text{Target net income}}{1 - \text{Tax rate}}$$

$$\begin{matrix}\text{Quantity of output} \\ \text{units required to be sold}\end{matrix} = \frac{\text{Fixed costs} + \dfrac{\text{Target net income}}{1 - \text{Tax rate}}}{\text{Contribution margin per unit}}$$

$$\begin{matrix}\text{Quantity of output} \\ \text{units required to be sold}\end{matrix} = \frac{\$2{,}000 + \dfrac{\$960}{1 - 0.40}}{\$80} = \frac{\$2{,}000 + \$1{,}600}{\$80 \text{ per unit}} = 45 \text{ units}$$

Proof:

Revenues, \$200 per unit × 45 units	\$9,000
Variable costs, \$120 per unit × 45 units	5,400
Contribution margin	3,600
Fixed costs	2,000
Operating income	1,600
Income taxes, \$1,600 × 0.40	640
Net income	\$ 960

Mary can also use the PV graph in Exhibit 3-3. For a target net income of \$960,

$$\text{Target operating income} = \frac{\text{Target net income}}{1 - \text{Tax rate}} = \frac{\$960}{1 - 0.40} = \$1{,}600$$

From Exhibit 3-3, to earn target operating income of \$1,600, Mary needs to sell 45 units.

Focusing the analysis on target net income instead of target operating income will not change the breakeven point. That's because, by definition, operating income at the breakeven point is \$0, and no income taxes are paid when there is no operating income.

Using CVP Analysis for Decision Making

5

Explain CVP analysis in decision making and how sensitivity analysis helps managers cope with uncertainty

. . . determine the effect on operating income of different assumptions

We have shown how CVP analysis is useful to determine breakeven quantities and to determine the quantities for achieving target operating income and target net income. Managers also use CVP analysis to guide other decisions, many of them strategic decisions. Consider a decision about choosing additional features for an existing product. Different choices can affect selling prices, variable cost per unit, fixed costs, units sold, and operating income. CVP analysis helps managers make product decisions by estimating the expected profitability of these choices. CVP analysis also helps managers make decisions such as how much to advertise, whether to expand into new markets, and how to price products.

Strategic decisions invariably entail risk. CVP analysis evaluates how operating income will be affected if the original predicted data are not achieved—say, if sales are 10% lower than estimated. Evaluating this risk affects other strategic decisions a company might make. For example, if the probability of a decline in sales seems high, a manager may take actions to shift the cost structure to have more variable costs and fewer fixed costs.

Decision to Advertise

Consider Do-All Software. Suppose Mary anticipates selling 40 units. Exhibit 3-3 indicates that Mary's operating income would be \$1,200. Mary is considering placing an advertisement describing the product and its features in the convention brochure. The advertisement will cost \$500. This cost is a fixed cost because it will not change regardless of the number of units Mary sells. She anticipates that advertising will increase sales by 10% to 44 packages. Should Mary advertise? The following table presents the CVP analysis.

	40 Packages Sold with No Advertising (1)	44 Packages Sold with Advertising (2)	Difference (3) = (2) – (1)
Revenues ($200 × 40; $200 × 44)	$8,000	$8,800	$ 800
Variable costs ($120 × 40; $120 × 44)	4,800	5,280	480
Contribution margin ($80 × 40; $80 × 44)	3,200	3,520	320
Fixed costs	2,000	2,500	500
Operating income	$1,200	$1,020	$(180)

Operating income decreases from $1,200 to $1,020, so Mary should not advertise. Note that Mary could focus only on the difference column and come to the same conclusion: If Mary advertises, contribution margin will increase by $320 (revenues, $800 – variable costs, $480), and fixed costs will increase by $500, resulting in a $180 decrease in operating income. As you become more familiar with CVP analysis, try evaluating decisions based on differences rather than mechanically working through the contribution income statement. Analyzing differences gets to the heart of CVP analysis and sharpens intuition by focusing only on the revenues and costs that will change by implementing new decisions.

Decision to Reduce Selling Price

Having decided not to advertise, Mary is contemplating whether to reduce the selling price to $175. At this price, she thinks she will sell 50 units. At this quantity, the software wholesaler who supplies Do-All Software will sell the packages to Mary for $115 per unit instead of $120. Should Mary reduce the selling price? No, as the following CVP analysis shows.

Contribution margin from lowering price to $175: ($175 – $115) per unit × 50 units	$3,000
Contribution margin from maintaining price at $200: ($200 – $120) per unit × 40 units	3,200
Change in contribution margin from lowering price	$ (200)

Decreasing the price will reduce contribution margin by $200 and, because the fixed costs of $2,000 will not change, it will also reduce operating income by $200.

Mary could also ask "At what price can I sell 50 units (purchased at $115 per unit) and continue to earn an operating income of $1,200?" The answer is $179, as the following calculations show.

Target operating income	$1,200
Add fixed costs	2,000
Target contribution margin	$3,200
Divided by number of units sold	÷ 50 units
Target contribution margin per unit	$ 64
Add variable cost per unit	115
Target selling price	$ 179

Mary should also examine the effects of other decisions, such as simultaneously increasing advertising costs and lowering prices. In each case, Mary will compare the changes in contribution margin (through the effects on selling prices, variable costs, and quantities of units sold) to the changes in fixed costs, and she will choose the alternative that gives the highest operating income.

Sensitivity Analysis and Uncertainty

Before choosing strategies and plans about how to implement strategies, managers frequently analyze the sensitivity of their decisions to changes in underlying assumptions. **Sensitivity analysis** is a "what-if" technique that managers use to examine how an outcome will change if the original predicted data are not achieved or if an underlying assumption changes. In the context of CVP analysis, sensitivity analysis answers such questions as, What will operating income be if the quantity of units sold decreases by 5% from the original prediction? And, What will operating income be if variable cost per unit increases by 10%? The sensitivity of operating income to various possible outcomes broadens managers' perspectives about what might actually occur *before* they commit costs.

When values of the CVP model's components are not known with certainty, they will need to be estimated, which requires judgment. Reasonable managers might disagree on their estimates of, say, variable cost per unit. Accountants perform sensitivity analysis to find out whether the different estimates of variable cost per unit significantly affect the results of CVP analysis and the decisions managers are considering.

Electronic spreadsheets, such as Excel, enable managers to conduct CVP-based sensitivity analyses in a systematic and efficient way. Using spreadsheets, managers can conduct sensitivity analysis to examine the effect and interaction of changes in selling price, variable cost per unit, fixed costs, and target operating income. Exhibit 3-4 displays a spreadsheet for the Do-All Software example. Mary can immediately see how many units need to be sold to achieve particular operating-income levels, given alternative levels of fixed costs and variable cost per unit that she may face. For example, 32 units are required to be sold to earn an operating income of \$1,200 if fixed costs are \$2,000 and variable cost per unit is \$100. Mary can also use Exhibit 3-4 to determine that she needs to sell 56 units to break even (earn operating income of \$0) if the booth rental at the Chicago convention is raised to \$2,800 (increasing fixed costs to \$2,800) and if the software supplier raises its price to \$150 (increasing variable cost to \$150 per unit). Mary can use information about costs and sensitivity analysis, together with realistic predictions about how much she can sell to decide if she should rent a booth at the convention.

Another aspect of sensitivity analysis is **margin of safety**, the amount by which budgeted (or actual) revenues exceed breakeven revenues. Expressed in units, *margin of safety* is the sales quantity minus the breakeven quantity. The margin of safety answers the "what-if" question: If budgeted revenues are above breakeven and drop, how far can they fall below budget before the breakeven point is reached? Such a fall could be due to a competitor introducing a better product, to poorly executed marketing programs, and so on. Assume that Mary has fixed costs of \$2,000, a selling price of \$200, and variable cost per unit of \$120. For 40 units sold, the budgeted revenues are \$8,000 and the budgeted operating income is \$1,200. The breakeven point for this set of assumptions is 25 units (\$2,000 ÷ \$80 per unit), or \$5,000 (\$200 per unit × 25 units). Mary can determine the margin of safety by using the following equation:

$$\text{Margin of safety} = \text{Budgeted revenues} - \text{Breakeven revenues} = \$8{,}000 - \$5{,}000 = \$3{,}000$$

$$\text{Margin of safety (in units)} = \text{Budgeted sales (units)} - \text{Breakeven sales (units)} = 40 - 25 = 15 \text{ units}$$

Sometimes margin of safety is expressed as a percentage:

$$\text{Margin of safety percentage} = \frac{\text{Margin of safety in dollars}}{\text{Budgeted (or actual) revenues}}$$

$$\text{In our example, margin of safety percentage} = \frac{\$3{,}000}{\$8{,}000} = 37.5\%$$

This means that revenues would have to decrease substantially, by 37.5%, to reach breakeven revenues. The high margin of safety gives Mary confidence that she is unlikely to suffer a loss.

EXHIBIT 3-4

Spreadsheet Analysis of CVP Relationships for Do-All Software

D5 =($A5+D$3)/(F1-$B5)

	A	B	C	D	E	F
1			Number of units required to be sold at $			200
2			Selling Price to Earn Target Operating Income of			
3		Variable Cost	\$0	\$1,200	\$1,600	\$2,000
4	Fixed Costs	per Unit	(Breakeven point)			
5	\$2,000	\$100	20	32[a]	36	40
6	\$2,000	\$120	25	40	45	50
7	\$2,000	\$150	40	64	72	80
8	\$2,400	\$100	24	36	40	44
9	\$2,400	\$120	30	45	50	55
10	\$2,400	\$150	48	72	80	88
11	\$2,800	\$100	28	40	44	48
12	\$2,800	\$120	35	50	55	60
13	\$2,800	\$150	56	80	88	96
14						

[a] $\frac{\text{Number of units}}{\text{required to be sold}} = \frac{\text{Fixed costs + Target operating income}}{\text{Contribution margin per unit}} = \frac{\$2{,}000 + \$1{,}200}{\$200 - \$100} = 32$

If, however, Mary expected to sell only 30 units, budgeted revenues would be \$6,000 (\$200 per unit × 30 units) and the margin of safety would equal:

$$\text{Budgeted revenues} - \text{Breakeven revenues} = \$6{,}000 - \$5{,}000 = \$1{,}000$$

$$\text{Margin of safety percentage} = \frac{\text{Margin of safety in dollars}}{\text{Budgeted (or actual) revenues}} = \frac{\$1{,}000}{\$6{,}000} = 16.67\%$$

This means that if revenues decrease by more than just 16.67%, Mary would suffer a loss. A low margin of safety increases the risk of a loss. If Mary does not have the tolerance for this level of risk, she will prefer not to rent a booth at the convention.

Sensitivity analysis is a simple approach to recognizing **uncertainty**, which is the possibility that an actual amount will deviate from an expected amount. Sensitivity analysis gives managers a good feel for the risks involved. A more-comprehensive approach to recognizing uncertainty is to compute expected values using probability distributions. This approach is illustrated in the appendix to this chapter.

Cost Planning and CVP

6

Use CVP analysis to plan variable and fixed costs

. . . compare risk of losses versus higher returns

Managers have the ability to choose the levels of fixed and variable costs in their cost structures. This is a strategic decision that managers make. In this section, we describe various factors that managers and management accountants consider as they make this decision.

Alternative Fixed-Cost/Variable-Cost Structures

CVP-based sensitivity analysis highlights the risks and returns as fixed costs are substituted for variable costs in a company's cost structure. In Exhibit 3-4, compare line 6 (fixed costs, \$2,000; variable cost per unit, \$120) and line 11 (fixed costs, \$2,800; variable cost per unit, \$100). See how the units required to be sold to break even are *higher* in line 11 (28 units, versus 25 units, in line 6) whereas the units required to be sold to earn \$2,000 of operating income are *lower* in line 11 (48 units, versus 50 units, in line 6). Line 11, with higher fixed costs, has more risk of loss (has a higher breakeven point) but offers a greater return (more operating income) as units sold increase. CVP analysis can help managers evaluate various fixed-cost/variable-cost structures. To consider these choices in more detail, let's return to Do-All Software. Mary is paying a \$2,000 booth-rental fee and incurring a variable cost per unit of \$120. Suppose Computer Conventions offers Mary three rental alternatives:

- **Option 1:** \$2,000 fixed fee
- **Option 2:** \$800 fixed fee plus 15% of convention revenues
- **Option 3:** 25% of convention revenues with no fixed fee

Mary is interested in how her choice of a rental agreement will affect the income she earns and the risks she faces. Exhibit 3-5 graphically depicts the profit-volume relationship for each option. The line representing the relationship between units sold and operating income for option 1 is the same as the line in the PV graph shown in Exhibit 3-3 (fixed costs of \$2,000 and contribution margin per unit of \$80). The line representing option 2 shows fixed costs of \$800 and a contribution margin per unit of \$50 [selling price, \$200, minus variable cost per unit, \$120, minus variable rental fees per unit, \$30, (0.15 × \$200)]. The line representing option 3 has fixed costs of \$0 and a contribution margin per unit of \$30 [\$200 − \$120 − \$50 (0.25 × \$200)].

If Mary sells 40 units, she should be indifferent across the three options. Each option results in operating income of \$1,200. The PV graph, however, highlights the different risks of loss and different returns associated with each option if sales differ from 40 units. The higher risk of a loss in option 1 is because of its higher fixed costs (\$2,000), which result in a higher breakeven point (25 units) and a lower margin of safety (40 − 25 = 15 units) relative to the other options. The line representing option 1 intersects the horizontal axis farther to the right than the lines representing options 2 and 3.

Consider operating income under each option if the number of units sold drops to 20. Exhibit 3-5 shows that option 1 leads to an operating loss, whereas options 2 and 3 continue to generate operating incomes. (A vertical line from X = 20 units sold cuts the

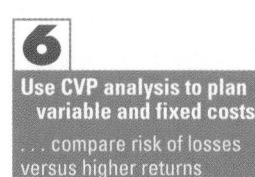

EXHIBIT 3-5

Profit-Volume Graph for Alternative Rental Options for Do-All Software

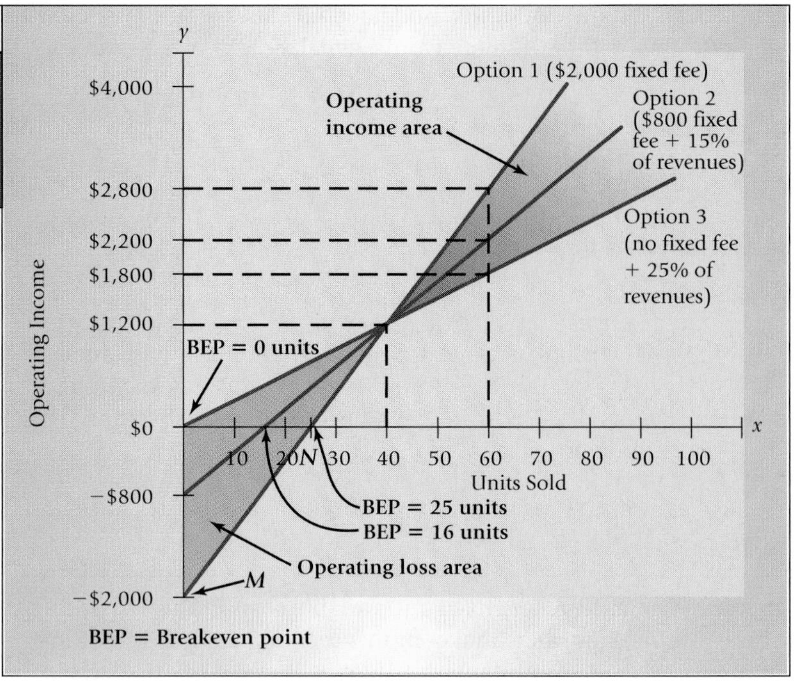

option 1 line below the horizontal axis in the mauve area and cuts the options 2 and 3 lines above the horizontal axis in the blue-green area.) The higher risk of loss in option 1, however, must be evaluated against its potential benefits. Option 1 has the highest contribution margin per unit because of its low variable costs. Once fixed costs are recovered at sales of 25 units, each additional unit sold adds $80 of contribution margin and, therefore, $80 of operating income per unit. For example, at sales of 60 units, option 1 shows an operating income of $2,800, greater than the operating incomes for sales of 60 units under options 2 and 3. By moving from option 1 toward option 3, Mary faces less risk of loss when demand is low, both because of lower fixed costs and because she loses less contribution margin per unit. She must, however, accept less operating income when demand is high because of the higher variable costs of option 3 compared with options 1 and 2.

The choice among options 1, 2, and 3 is a strategic decision that Mary faces. As in most strategic decisions, what she decides now will significantly affect her operating income (or loss), depending on the demand for Do-All Software. Faced with this uncertainty, Mary's choice will be influenced by her confidence in the level of demand for the software package and her willingness to risk losses if demand is low. For example, if Mary's tolerance for risk is high, she will choose option 1 with its high potential rewards. If, however, Mary is averse to taking risk, she will prefer option 3, where the rewards are smaller if sales are high but where she never suffers a loss if sales are low.

Operating Leverage

The risk-return trade-off across alternative cost structures can be measured as operating leverage. **Operating leverage** describes the effects that fixed costs have on changes in operating income as changes occur in units sold and, hence, in contribution margin. Organizations with a high proportion of fixed costs in their cost structures, as is the case under option 1, have high operating leverage. The line representing option 1 in Exhibit 3-5 is the steepest of the three lines. Small increases in sales lead to large increases in operating incomes. Small decreases in sales result in relatively large decreases in operating incomes, leading to a greater risk of operating losses. *At any given level of sales,*

$$\text{Degree of operating leverage} = \frac{\text{Contribution margin}}{\text{Operating income}}$$

The following table shows the **degree of operating leverage** at sales of 40 units for the three rental options.

	Option 1	Option 2	Option 3
1. Contribution margin per unit (p. 71)	\$ 80	\$ 50	\$ 30
2. Contribution margin (Row 1 × 40 units)	\$3,200	\$2,000	\$1,200
3. Operating income (from Exhibit 3-5)	\$1,200	\$1,200	\$1,200
4. Degree of operating leverage (Row 2 ÷ Row 3)	$\frac{\$3,200}{\$1,200} = 2.67$	$\frac{\$2,000}{\$1,200} = 1.67$	$\frac{\$1,200}{\$1,200} = 1.00$

These numbers indicate that, when sales are 40 units, a percentage change in sales and contribution margin will result in 2.67 times that percentage change in operating income for option 1, but the same percentage change (1.00) in operating income for option 3. Consider, for example, a sales increase of 50% from 40 to 60 units. Contribution margin will increase by 50% under each option. Operating income, however, will increase by 2.67 × 50% = 133% from \$1,200 to \$2,800 in option 1, but it will increase by only 1.00 × 50% = 50% from \$1,200 to \$1,800 in option 3 (see Exhibit 3-5). The degree of operating leverage at a given level of sales helps managers calculate the effect of fluctuations in sales on operating income.

Keep in mind that, in the presence of fixed costs, the degree of operating leverage is different at different levels of sales. For example, at sales of 60 units, the degree of operating leverage under each of the three options is as follows:

	Option 1	Option 2	Option 3
1. Contribution margin per unit (p. 71)	\$ 80	\$ 50	\$ 30
2. Contribution margin (Row 1 × 60 units)	\$4,800	\$3,000	\$1,800
3. Operating income (from Exhibit 3-5)	\$2,800	\$2,200	\$1,800
4. Degree of operating leverage (Row 2 ÷ Row 3)	$\frac{\$4,800}{\$2,800} = 1.71$	$\frac{\$3,000}{\$2,200} = 1.36$	$\frac{\$1,800}{\$1,800} = 1.00$

Example: Degree of operating leverage (DOL) is specific to a given level of sales as the starting point. If the starting point changes, the DOL changes. If the starting point were sales of 50 units, the DOL for option 1 would be:

$$\frac{CM}{CM - FC} = \frac{\$80 \times 50}{(\$80 \times 50) - \$2{,}000} = 2.00$$

The degree of operating leverage decreases from 2.67 (at sales of 40 units) to 1.71 (at sales of 60 units) under Option 1 and from 1.67 to 1.36 under Option 2. In general, whenever there are fixed costs, the degree of operating leverage decreases as the level of sales increases beyond the breakeven point. If fixed costs are \$0 as in Option 3, contribution margin equals operating income and the degree of operating leverage equals 1.00 at all sales levels.

But why must managers monitor operating leverage carefully? Consider companies such as US Airways, United Airlines, WorldCom, and Global Crossing. Their high operating leverage was a major reason for their financial problems. (See Focus on Values and Behaviors, p. 74.) Anticipating high demand for their products, these companies borrowed money to acquire assets, resulting in high fixed costs. As sales declined in 2001 and 2002, these companies suffered losses and could not generate sufficient cash to service their interest and debt, causing them to seek bankruptcy protection.

Could these problems have been avoided? Yes, if managers had not built up assets and fixed costs too quickly. They did so to take advantage of the opportunities they saw in the marketplace, but in so doing they significantly increased the risk of losses if demand for their products proved to be weak. Managers could also have reduced the magnitude of these problems by using equity rather than debt to finance the purchase of assets. Unlike debt, equity does not have a predetermined schedule of repayments. Equity financing would have given these companies more time to ride out the periods of weak demand for their services. So why didn't these companies use equity? Because relative to debt, equity financing is more costly. Managers and management accountants should always evaluate how the level of fixed costs and variable costs they choose will affect the risk-return trade-off. (See Concepts in Action, p. 75.)

To reduce their fixed costs, many companies are moving their manufacturing facilities from the United States to lower-cost countries such as Mexico and China. To substitute high fixed costs with lower variable costs, companies are purchasing products from lower-cost suppliers instead of manufacturing products themselves. These actions are reducing both costs and operating leverage. More recently, General Electric and Hewlett-Packard

F◎CUS ON VALUES AND BEHAVIORS

WORLDCOM: SIMPLY A MATTER OF POOR PLANNING?

A major benefit of CVP analysis is accurate planning. Conscientious planning requires management to make realistic assumptions about the future of the company by answering critical questions such as: How much will revenues be? What are the risks if revenues are lower than planned? What will costs be? Could costs be higher than expected? Realistic planning is particularly important in companies with large commitments of fixed costs, such as plant costs, loan and interest payments, and maintenance expenses, because lower-than-expected sales result in heavy losses. WorldCom, formerly the nation's second-largest telecommunications company, acquired companies and ramped up its investment in telecommunications infrastructure and equipment over a short period of time. When demand for its services fell, it began to face significant financial pressures. So what did the company do? It improperly booked billions of dollars of routine business costs as capital expenditures, overstating income by more than $11 billion by early 2002. The company also had loaned its then–chief executive officer, Bernard Ebbers, more than $400 million to cover personal stock trading losses.

Could WorldCom have avoided these problems if the assumptions underlying its financial projections had been realistic? Could CVP analysis have revealed to management that the company would face severe problems if its investment plans did not materialize? Yes, but reports in the financial press suggest that WorldCom's managers did not plan well. Even worse, they chose to manipulate financial statements to conceal the company's disastrous performance. The chief financial officer and finance executives failed in their responsibilities to be realistic, ask tough-minded, critical questions, and communicate results with integrity.

On June 25, 2002, WorldCom finally revealed its improper accounting practices. This led to a halt in the trading of its stock on the NASDAQ stock exchange and, just a few weeks later, Chapter 11 bankruptcy. On March 2, 2004, WorldCom's former chief financial officer, Scott Sullivan, finally admitted that, "as CFO at WorldCom, I participated with other members of WorldCom to conspire to paint a false and misleading picture of WorldCom's financial results." Bernard Ebbers, the former CEO, was indicted on charges of fraud, conspiracy, and making false statements in the $11 billion accounting scandal. He pleaded not guilty.

Sources: *"WorldCom Chief Turns Himself In to FBI," March 3, 2004,* Reuters.com *newswire; S. N. Mehta, "Is MCI Being Good Enough?"* Fortune, *October 27, 2003; B. Klayman, "MCI Reduces Earnings by $74.4 Billion," March 12, 2004,* Reuters.com.

began outsourcing service functions, such as post-sales customer service, by shifting their customer call centers to countries such as India, where costs are lower.

Effects of Sales Mix on Income

7 **Apply CVP analysis to a company producing different products**

. . . assume sales mix of products remains constant as total units sold changes

To help understand the sales-mix concept, imagine the software being sold only in bundles of five units: 3 Do-Alls and 2 Superwords. Such "bundling" is a good way to think of the sales-mix concept, even though the bundling need not be literally true.

Sales mix is the quantities of various products (or services) that constitute total unit sales of a company. Suppose Mary is now budgeting for a subsequent computer convention in Boston. She plans to sell two different software products—Do-All and Superword—and budgets the following:

	Do-All	Superword	Total
Units sold	60	40	100
Revenues, $200 and $100 per unit	$12,000	$4,000	$16,000
Variable costs, $120 and $70 per unit	7,200	2,800	10,000
Contribution margin, $80 and $30 per unit	$ 4,800	$1,200	6,000
Fixed costs			4,500
Operating income			$ 1,500

What is the breakeven point? In contrast to the single-product (or service) situation, the number of total units that must be sold to break even in a multiproduct company depends on the sales mix—the number of units of Do-All sold and the number of units of Superword sold. We assume that the budgeted sales mix (3 units of Do-All sold for every 2 units of Superword sold) will not change at different levels of total unit sales.

CONCEPTS IN ACTION

Influencing Cost Structures to Manage the Risk-Return Trade-Off at Amazon.com

Building up too much fixed costs can be hazardous to a company's health. Because fixed costs, unlike variable costs, do not automatically decrease as volume declines, companies with too much fixed costs can lose a considerable amount of money during lean times. Amazon.com, the Internet retailer, understood this concept well. Amazon began business using a "virtual" business model. When Amazon received a customer order for a book on its Web site, it immediately placed an order with a book wholesaler, which shipped the book directly to the customer. The "virtual" in Amazon's business model referred to the fact that Amazon was able to sell books from its Web site without having to invest in warehouses or inventory. Amazon incurred only the cost of acquiring books on an as-needed basis after it had received a confirmed order from a customer. Amazon essentially had a variable-cost structure: Costs were high when sales were strong, and costs were low when sales were weak. Without warehousing and inventory costs, Amazon avoided being stuck with fixed costs if business was slow. But this low-risk strategy came at a price: Purchasing books from wholesalers cost significantly more than purchasing books directly from publishers.

The competitive disadvantage from the higher cost of books became apparent in 1997, when Barnes & Noble, the largest "bricks and mortar"–based book retailer, opened an online store. Barnes & Noble already had a large distribution center to supply books to its "bricks and mortar" stores. It planned to use the same warehouse facility to fill the orders it received from online customers. Moreover, Barnes & Noble paid less for its books than Amazon because its distribution-center capacity enabled it to order books in the minimum-order quantities required by publishers. When it opened its online store, Barnes & Noble claimed it would offer "the lowest everyday prices of any online bookseller," as well as better service, because it controlled the product itself, rather than having to rely on a wholesaler to supply it. Barnes & Noble had higher fixed costs but lower variable costs than Amazon. At high volume levels, Barnes & Noble's costs would be lower than Amazon's costs.

In response to Barnes & Noble's threat, Amazon decided to build and acquire distribution centers of its own. Doing so increased Amazon's fixed costs, operating leverage, and risk but decreased its variable costs. Amazon was counting on a rapid expansion in sales, but in 2000 stock analysts estimated that Amazon's warehouse capacity was three to five times more than it needed. Even after acknowledging in 2001 that sales had fallen short of expectations and that two of its distribution facilities were closing, Amazon still needed to increase sales volume to enhance its chances of breaking even. As one analyst noted, "There are fixed costs associated with the technology and the distribution centers, so it helps to move more order volume through the technology infrastructure and distribution infrastructure." Finally, in 2002 when the company embarked on a strategy of broad discounting and free shipping, sales dramatically increased, decreasing the operating leverage and risk associated with Amazon's fixed costs while more fully utilizing its newly-developed distribution network.

Sources: Amazon.com financial statements, stock-analyst reports, and conversations with company management.

To compute the breakeven point, we calculate the *weighted-average contribution margin per unit* for the two products together at the budgeted sales mix.

$$\text{Weighted-average contribution margin per unit} = \frac{\left(\begin{array}{c}\text{Do-All's contribution}\\ \text{margin per unit}\end{array} \times \begin{array}{c}\text{Number of units}\\ \text{of Do-All sold}\end{array}\right) + \left(\begin{array}{c}\text{Superword's contribution}\\ \text{margin per unit}\end{array} \times \begin{array}{c}\text{Number of units}\\ \text{of Superword sold}\end{array}\right)}{\text{Number of units of Do-All sold} + \text{Number of units of Superword sold}}$$

$$= \frac{(\$80 \text{ per unit} \times 60 \text{ units}) + (\$30 \text{ per unit} \times 40 \text{ units})}{60 \text{ units} + 40 \text{ units}} = \frac{\$6{,}000}{100 \text{ units}} = \$60 \text{ per unit}$$

We then have

$$\text{Breakeven point} = \frac{\text{Fixed costs}}{\text{Weighted-average contribution margin per unit}} = \frac{\$4{,}500}{\$60 \text{ per unit}} = 75 \text{ units}$$

Because the ratio of Do-All sales to Superword sales is 60:40, or 3:2, the breakeven point is 45 (0.60 × 75) units of Do-All and 30 (0.40 × 75) units of Superword. At this mix, the contribution margin of $4,500 (Do-All $80 per unit × 45 units = $3,600 + Superword $30 per unit × 30 units = $900) equals the fixed costs of $4,500.

We can also calculate the breakeven point in revenues for the multiple-product situation using the weighted-average contribution margin percentage.

$$\begin{array}{c}\text{Weighted-average}\\ \text{contribution}\\ \text{margin percentage}\end{array} = \frac{\text{Total contribution margin}}{\text{Total revenues}} = \frac{\$6{,}000}{\$16{,}000} = 0.375, \text{ or } 37.5\%$$

$$\begin{array}{c}\text{Total revenues}\\ \text{required to}\\ \text{break even}\end{array} = \frac{\text{Fixed costs}}{\text{Weighted-average contribution margin percentage}} = \frac{\$4{,}500}{0.375} = \$12{,}000$$

The $16,000 of total revenues are in the ratio of 3:1 ($12,000:$4,000), or 75%:25% (p. 74). Hence the breakeven revenues of $12,000 should be split in the same ratio, 75%:25%. This amounts to breakeven revenues of $9,000 (75% × $12,000) of Do-All and $3,000 (25% × $12,000) of Superword. At a selling price of $200 for Do-All and $100 for Superword, breakeven equals 45 units ($9,000 ÷ $200) of Do-All and 30 units ($3,000 ÷ $100) of Superword.

An alternative approach to calculate the breakeven point is to recognize that if 5 total units are sold, 3 units will be Do-All and 2 units will be Superword. If 10 times as many total units are sold (5 × 10 = 50 units), 3 × 10 = 30 units will be Do-All and 2 × 10 = 20 units will be Superword. In general, if 5 × *S* (written as 5*S*) total units are sold, 3 × *S* (3*S*) units will be Do-All and 2 × *S* (2*S*) units will be Superword. To calculate the breakeven point:

$$\text{Revenues} - \text{Variable costs} - \text{Fixed costs} = \text{Operating income} = 0$$

Where,

$$\begin{aligned}\text{Revenues} &= \left(\begin{array}{c}\text{Selling price}\\ \text{of Do-All}\end{array} \times \begin{array}{c}\text{Number of units}\\ \text{of Do-All sold}\end{array}\right) + \left(\begin{array}{c}\text{Selling price}\\ \text{of Superword}\end{array} \times \begin{array}{c}\text{Number of units}\\ \text{of Superword sold}\end{array}\right)\\ &= \$200 \text{ per unit} \times 3S \text{ units} + \$100 \text{ per unit} \times 2S \text{ units}\\ &= \$600S + \$200S\\ &= \$800S\end{aligned}$$

$$\begin{aligned}\text{Variable costs} &= \left(\begin{array}{c}\text{Variable cost}\\ \text{per unit of Do-All}\end{array} \times \begin{array}{c}\text{Number of units}\\ \text{of Do-All sold}\end{array}\right) + \left(\begin{array}{c}\text{Variable cost}\\ \text{per unit of Superword}\end{array} \times \begin{array}{c}\text{Number of units}\\ \text{of Superword sold}\end{array}\right)\\ &= \$120 \text{ per unit} \times 3S \text{ units} + \$70 \text{ per unit} \times 2\text{S units}\\ &= \$360S + \$140S\\ &= \$500S\end{aligned}$$

To calculate the breakeven point,

$$\begin{aligned}\text{Revenues} - \text{Variable costs} - \text{Fixed costs} &= 0\\ \$800S - \$500S - \$4{,}500 &= 0\\ \$800S - \$500S &= \$4{,}500\\ \$300S &= \$4{,}500\\ S &= 15 \text{ units}\end{aligned}$$

$$\text{Number of units of Do-All to break even} = 3S = 3 \times 15 = 45 \text{ units}$$

$$\text{Number of units of Superword to break even} = 2S = 2 \times 15 = 30 \text{ units}$$

The breakeven point is 75 total units when the sales mix is 45 units of Do-All and 30 units of Superword. Note that the sales mix maintains the ratio of 3 units of Do-All to 2 units of Superword.

Alternative sales mixes (in units) that have a contribution margin of $4,500 and cause Mary to break even include (calculations not shown):

	Units									
Do-All	54	48	42	36	30	24	18	12	6	0
Superword	6	22	38	54	70	86	102	118	134	150
Total	60	70	80	90	100	110	120	130	140	150

Companies that sell multiple products adjust their mix to respond to demand changes. For example, as gasoline prices increase and customers want smaller cars, auto companies shift their production mix to produce additional smaller cars.

None of these sales mixes, however, describes the breakeven point in our example. Why? Because they do not match the budgeted sales mix of 3 units of Do-All for every 2 units of Superword. If the sales mix changes to 3 units of Do-All for every 7 units of Superword, you can see in the preceding table that the breakeven point increases from 75 units to 100 units, comprising 30 units of Do-All and 70 units of Superword. The breakeven quantity increases because the sales mix has shifted toward the lower-contribution-margin product, Superword, decreasing weighted-average contribution margin per unit.

In general, for any given total quantity of units sold, as the sales mix shifts toward units with higher contribution margins, operating income will be higher. If the mix shifts toward Do-All (say to 70% Do-All from 60% Do-All), which has a contribution margin of more than twice that of Superword, Mary's operating income will increase.

Multiple Cost Drivers

8

Adapt CVP analysis to situations in which a product has more than one cost driver

. . . basic concepts apply but simple formulas do not

Throughout the chapter we have assumed that the number of output units is the only revenue driver and the only cost driver. Now we describe how some aspects of CVP analysis can be adapted to the general case of multiple cost drivers.

Consider again the single-product Do-All Software example. Suppose Mary will incur a variable cost of $10 for preparing documents (including an invoice) for each customer who buys Do-All Software. That is, the cost driver of document-preparation costs is the number of customers who buy Do-All Software. Mary's operating income can then be expressed in terms of revenues and these costs:

$$\text{Operating income} = \text{Revenues} - \left(\begin{array}{c}\text{Cost of each}\\ \text{Do-All software}\\ \text{package}\end{array} \times \begin{array}{c}\text{Number of}\\ \text{packages}\end{array}\right) - \left(\begin{array}{c}\text{Cost of preparing}\\ \text{documents}\\ \text{for each customer}\end{array} \times \begin{array}{c}\text{Number of}\\ \text{customers}\end{array}\right) - \text{Fixed costs}$$

If Mary sells 40 packages to 15 customers, then

$$\begin{aligned}\text{Operating income} &= (\$200 \text{ per package} \times 40 \text{ packages}) - (\$120 \text{ per package} \times 40 \text{ packages})\\ &\quad - (\$10 \text{ per customer} \times 15 \text{ customers}) - \$2{,}000\\ &= \$8{,}000 - \$4{,}800 - \$150 - \$2{,}000 = \$1{,}050\end{aligned}$$

If instead Mary sells 40 packages to 40 customers, then

$$\begin{aligned}\text{Operating income} &= (\$200 \times 40) - (\$120 \times 40) - (\$10 \times 40) - \$2{,}000\\ &= \$8{,}000 - \$4{,}800 - \$400 - \$2{,}000 = \$800\end{aligned}$$

The number of packages sold is not the only determinant of Mary's operating income. For a given number of packages sold, Mary's operating income will be lower if she sells Do-All Software to more customers. Mary's costs depend on two cost drivers: the number of packages sold and the number of customers.

Just as in the case of multiple products, there is no unique breakeven point when there are multiple cost drivers. For example, Mary will break even if she sells 26 packages to 8 customers or 27 packages to 16 customers:

$$(\$200 \times 26) - (\$120 \times 26) - (\$10 \times 8) - \$2{,}000 = \$5{,}200 - \$3{,}120 - \$80 - \$2{,}000 = \$0$$

$$(\$200 \times 27) - (\$120 \times 27) - (\$10 \times 16) - \$2{,}000 = \$5{,}400 - \$3{,}240 - \$160 - \$2{,}000 = \$0$$

This example illustrates that CVP analysis can be adapted to multiple-cost-driver situations. However, in cases involving multiple cost drivers, the simple formulas described earlier in the chapter, for example, to calculate the breakeven point, cannot be used. That's because the same operating income can be achieved by various combinations of the cost drivers.

CVP Analysis in Service and Nonprofit Organizations

Thus far, our CVP analysis has focused on a merchandising company. CVP can also be applied to decisions by manufacturing, service, and nonprofit organizations. To apply CVP analysis in service and nonprofit organizations, we need to focus on measuring their output, which is different from the tangible units sold by manufacturing and merchandising companies. Examples of output measures in various service and nonprofit industries are:

Industry	Measure of Output
Airlines	Passenger miles
Hotels/motels	Room-nights occupied
Hospitals	Patient days
Universities	Student credit-hours

Consider an agency of the Massachusetts Department of Social Welfare with a \$900,000 budget appropriation (its revenues) for 2006. This nonprofit agency's purpose is to assist handicapped people seeking employment. On average, the agency supplements each person's income by \$5,000 annually. The agency's fixed costs, such as rent and administrative salaries, are \$270,000. It has no variable costs. The agency manager wants to know how many people could be assisted in 2006. We can use CVP analysis here by setting operating income to \$0. Let Q be the number of handicapped people to be assisted:

$$\text{Revenues} - \text{Variable costs} - \text{Fixed costs} = 0$$

$$\$900{,}000 - \$5{,}000Q - \$270{,}000 = 0$$

$$\$5{,}000Q = \$900{,}000 - \$270{,}000 = \$630{,}000$$

$$Q = \$630{,}000 \div \$5{,}000 \text{ per person} = 126 \text{ people}$$

Suppose the manager is concerned that the total budget appropriation for 2007 will be reduced by 15% to $\$900{,}000 \times (1 - 0.15) = \$765{,}000$. The manager wants to know how many handicapped people could be assisted with this reduced budget. Assume the same amount of monetary assistance per person:

$$\$765{,}000 - \$5{,}000Q - \$270{,}000 = 0$$

$$\$5{,}000Q = \$765{,}000 - \$270{,}000 = \$495{,}000$$

$$Q = \$495{,}000 \div \$5{,}000 \text{ per person} = 99 \text{ people}$$

Note the following two characteristics of the CVP relationships in this nonprofit situation:

1. The percentage drop in the number of people assisted, $(126 - 99) \div 126$, or 21.4%, is greater than the 15% reduction in the budget appropriation. That's because the \$270,000 in fixed costs still must be paid, leaving a proportionately lower budget to assist people. The percentage drop in service exceeds the percentage drop in budget appropriation.
2. Given the reduced budget appropriation (revenues) of \$765,000, the manager can adjust operations to stay within this appropriation in one or more of three basic ways: (a) reduce the number of people assisted from the current 126, (b) reduce the variable cost (the extent of assistance per person) from the current \$5,000 per person, or (c) reduce the total fixed costs from the current \$270,000.

Contribution Margin Versus Gross Margin

9

Distinguish contribution margin

. . . revenues minus variable costs

from gross margin

. . . revenues minus cost of goods sold

Let's contrast contribution margin, which provides information for CVP analysis, with gross margin discussed in Chapter 2.

$$\text{Gross margin} = \text{Revenues} - \text{Cost of goods sold}$$

$$\text{Contribution margin} = \text{Revenues} - \text{All variable costs}$$

Cost of goods sold in the merchandising sector is made up of goods purchased and then sold. Cost of goods sold in the manufacturing sector consists entirely of manufacturing costs (including fixed manufacturing costs). The phrase "all variable costs" refers to variable costs in all of the business functions of the value chain.

Service-sector companies can compute a contribution margin but not a gross margin. That's because service-sector companies do not have a cost of goods sold line item in their income statement.

This section distinguishes between contribution margin and gross margin in manufacturing and merchandising companies. This distinction does not apply to service companies because they have no cost of goods sold and therefore no gross margin.

Merchandising Sector

The most common difference between contribution margin and gross margin for companies in the merchandising sector is variable cost items that are not included in cost of goods sold. An example of such a variable cost item is commissions paid to salespersons as a percentage of revenues. Contribution margin is computed by deducting all variable costs from revenues, whereas gross margin is computed by deducting only cost of goods sold from revenues. The following example (figures assumed and in thousands) illustrates this difference:

Contribution Income Statement Emphasizing Contribution Margin			Financial Accounting Income Statement Emphasizing Gross Margin	
Revenues		$200	Revenues	$200
Variable cost of goods sold	$120		Cost of goods sold	120
Variable operating costs	43	163		
Contribution margin		37	Gross margin	80
Fixed operating costs		19	Operating costs ($43 + $19)	62
Operating income		$ 18	Operating income	$ 18

Variable operating costs of $43,000 are deducted from revenues when calculating contribution margin but are not deducted when calculating gross margin.

Manufacturing Sector

For companies in the manufacturing sector, contribution margin and gross margin differ in two respects: fixed manufacturing costs and variable nonmanufacturing costs. The following example (figures assumed and in thousands) illustrates this difference:

Contribution Income Statement Emphasizing Contribution Margin			Financial Accounting Income Statement Emphasizing Gross Margin	
Revenues		$1,000	Revenues	$1,000
Variable manufacturing costs	$250		Cost of goods sold ($250 + $160)	410
Variable nonmanufacturing costs	270	520		
Contribution margin		480	Gross margin	590
Fixed manufacturing costs	160		Nonmanufacturing costs	
Fixed nonmanufacturing costs	138	298	($270 + $138)	408
Operating income		$ 182	Operating income	$ 182

Fixed manufacturing costs of $160,000 are not deducted from revenues when computing contribution margin but are deducted when computing gross margin. Cost of goods sold in a manufacturing company includes all variable manufacturing costs and all fixed manufacturing costs ($250,000 + $160,000). Variable nonmanufacturing costs of $270,000 are deducted from revenues when computing contribution margin but are not deducted when computing gross margin.

Like contribution margin, gross margin can be expressed as a total, as an amount per unit, or as a percentage. For example, the **gross margin percentage** is the gross margin divided by revenues—59% ($590 ÷ $1,000) in our manufacturing-sector example.

PROBLEM FOR SELF-STUDY

Wembley Travel Agency specializes in flights between Los Angeles and London. It books passengers on United Airlines at $900 per round-trip ticket. Until last month, United paid Wembley a commission of 10% of the ticket price paid by each passenger. This commission was Wembley's only source of revenues. Wembley's fixed costs are $14,000 per month (for salaries, rent, and so on), and its variable costs are $20 per ticket purchased for a passenger. This $20 includes a $15 per ticket delivery fee paid to Federal Express. (To keep the analysis simple, we assume each round-trip ticket purchased is delivered in a separate package. Thus, the $15 delivery fee applies to each ticket.)

United Airlines has just announced a revised payment schedule for travel agents. It will now pay travel agents a 10% commission per ticket up to a maximum of $50. Any ticket costing more than $500 generates only a $50 commission, regardless of the ticket price.

Required

1. Under the old 10% commission structure, how many round-trip tickets must Wembley sell each month (a) to break even and (b) to earn an operating income of $7,000?
2. How does United's revised payment schedule affect your answers to (a) and (b) in requirement 1?

SOLUTION

1. Wembley receives a 10% commission on each ticket: 10% × $900 = $90. Thus,

Selling price	= $90 per ticket
Variable cost per unit	= $20 per ticket
Contribution margin per unit	= $90 − $20 = $70 per ticket
Fixed costs	= $14,000 per month

a. $$\text{Breakeven number of tickets} = \frac{\text{Fixed costs}}{\text{Contribution margin per unit}} = \frac{\$14{,}000}{\$70 \text{ per ticket}} = 200 \text{ tickets}$$

b. When target operating income = $7,000 per month:

$$\text{Quantity of tickets required to be sold} = \frac{\text{Fixed costs} + \text{Target operating income}}{\text{Contribution margin per unit}}$$

$$= \frac{\$14{,}000 + \$7{,}000}{\$70 \text{ per ticket}} = \frac{\$21{,}000}{\$70 \text{ per ticket}} = 300 \text{ tickets}$$

2. Under the new system, Wembley would receive only $50 on the $900 ticket. Thus,

Selling price	= $50 per ticket
Variable cost per unit	= $20 per ticket
Contribution margin per unit	= $50 − $20 = $30 per ticket
Fixed costs	= $14,000 per month

a. $$\text{Breakeven number of tickets} = \frac{\$14{,}000}{\$30 \text{ per ticket}} = 467 \text{ tickets (rounded up)}$$

b. $$\text{Quantity of tickets required to be sold} = \frac{\$21{,}000}{\$30 \text{ per ticket}} = 700 \text{ tickets}$$

The $50 cap on the commission paid per ticket causes the breakeven point to more than double (from 200 to 467 tickets) and the tickets required to be sold to earn $7,000 per month to also more than double (from 300 to 700 tickets). As would be expected, travel agents reacted very negatively to the United Airlines decision to change commission payments. Unfortunately for travel agents, other airlines also changed their commission structures in similar ways.

DECISION POINTS

The following question-and-answer format summarizes the chapter's learning objectives. Each decision presents a key question related to a learning objective. The guidelines are the answer to that question.

Decision	Guidelines
1. What assumptions must hold to apply CVP analysis?	CVP analysis requires simplifying assumptions, such as costs are either fixed or variable with respect to the number of output units (units produced and sold) and the relationship between total revenues and total costs is linear.

2. How can CVP analysis assist managers?	CVP analysis assists managers in understanding the behavior of a product's total costs, total revenues, and operating income as changes occur in the output level, selling price, variable costs, or fixed costs.
3. How do companies determine the breakeven point or the output needed to achieve a target operating income?	The breakeven point is the quantity of output at which total revenues equal total costs. The three methods for computing the breakeven point and the quantity of output to achieve target operating income are the equation method, the contribution margin method, and the graph method. Each method is merely a restatement of the others. Managers often select the method they find easiest to use in the specific decision situation.
4. How should companies incorporate income taxes into CVP analysis?	Income taxes can be incorporated into CVP analysis by using target net income rather than target operating income. The breakeven point is unaffected by income taxes because no income taxes are paid if there is no operating income.
5. How should companies cope with uncertainty or changes in underlying assumptions?	Sensitivity analysis, a "what-if" technique, examines how an outcome will change if the original predicted data are not achieved or if an underlying assumption changes. When making decisions, managers use CVP analysis to compare contribution margins and fixed costs under different assumptions.
6. How should companies choose between different variable-cost/fixed-cost structures?	Choosing the variable-cost/fixed-cost structure is a strategic decision for companies. CVP analysis highlights the risk of losses when revenues are low and the upside return when revenues are high for different proportions of variable and fixed costs in a company's cost structure.
7. Can CVP analysis be applied to a company producing multiple products?	CVP analysis can be applied to a company producing multiple products by assuming the sales mix of products sold remains constant as the total quantity of units sold changes.
8. Can CVP analysis be applied to a product that has multiple cost drivers?	The basic concepts of CVP analysis can be applied to multiple-cost-driver situations, but the simple formulas of the single-cost-driver case—for example, to calculate the breakeven point—cannot be used.
9. Can contribution margin and gross margin be used interchangeably?	These terms cannot be used interchangeably. Contribution margin is revenues minus all variable costs (throughout the value chain); gross margin is revenues minus cost of goods sold.

APPENDIX: DECISION MODELS AND UNCERTAINTY

This appendix explores the characteristics of uncertainty and describes an approach managers can use to make decisions in a world of uncertainty. We'll also illustrate the insights gained when uncertainty is recognized in CVP analysis.

Coping with Uncertainty[1]

Role of a Decision Model Uncertainty is the possibility that an actual amount will deviate from an expected amount. In the Do-All example, Mary might forecast sales at 40 units, but actual sales might turn out to be 30 units or 60 units. A decision model helps managers deal with such uncertainty. It is a formal method for making a choice, commonly involving both quantitative and qualitative analyses. The quantitative analysis usually includes the following steps:

Step 1: **Identify a choice criterion.** A **choice criterion** is an objective that can be quantified. This objective can take many forms. Most often the choice criterion is to maximize income or to minimize costs. The choice criterion provides a basis for choosing the best alternative action. Mary's choice criterion is to maximize expected operating income at the Chicago computer convention.

Step 2: **Identify the set of alternative actions to be considered.** We use the letter *a* with subscripts $_1$, $_2$, and $_3$ to distinguish each of Mary's three possible actions:

$$a_1 = \text{Pay \$2,000 fixed fee}$$

$$a_2 = \text{Pay \$800 fixed fee plus 15\% of convention revenues}$$

$$a_3 = \text{Pay 25\% of convention revenues with no fixed fee}$$

Step 3: **Identify the set of events that can occur.** An **event** is a possible relevant occurrence, such as the actual number of software packages Mary may sell at the convention. The set of events should be mutually exclusive and collectively exhaustive. Events are mutually exclusive if they cannot occur at the same time. Events are collectively exhaustive

[1]The presentation here draws (in part) from teaching notes prepared by R. Williamson.

> **Question:** What is the distinction between events and actions?
>
> **Answer:** *Events* are possible relevant occurrences that are uncontrollable states of nature. Managers assess the probabilities of various events occurring. *Actions* are choices made by managers. For a given decision, one action is selected and the other action(s) is rejected.

if, taken together, they make up the entire set of possible relevant occurrences (no other event can occur). Examples of mutually exclusive and collectively exhaustive events are growth, decline, or no change in industry demand, and increase, decrease, or no change in interest rates. Only one event out of the entire set of mutually exclusive and collectively exhaustive events will actually occur. Suppose Mary's only uncertainty is the number of units of Do-All Software that she can sell. For simplicity, suppose Mary estimates that sales will be either 30 or 60 units. We use the letter x with subscripts $_1$ and $_2$ to distinguish the set of mutually exclusive and collectively exhaustive events:

$$x_1 = 30 \text{ units}$$
$$x_2 = 60 \text{ units}$$

Step 4: Assign a probability to each event that can occur. A **probability** is the likelihood or chance that an event will occur. The decision model approach to coping with uncertainty assigns probabilities to events. A **probability distribution** describes the likelihood, or the probability, that each of the mutually exclusive and collectively exhaustive set of events will occur. In some cases, there will be much evidence to guide the assignment of probabilities. For example, the probability of obtaining heads in the toss of a coin is $1/2$ and that of drawing a particular playing card from a standard, well-shuffled deck is $1/52$. In business, the probability of having a specified percentage of defective units may be assigned with great confidence on the basis of production experience with thousands of units. In other cases, there will be little evidence supporting estimated probabilities—for example, expected sales of a new pharmaceutical product next year. Suppose that Mary, on the basis of past experience, assesses a 60% chance, or a $6/10$ probability, that she will sell 30 units and a 40% chance, or a $4/10$ probability, that she will sell 60 units. Using $P(x)$ as the notation for the probability of an event, the probabilities are:

$$P(x_1) = \frac{6}{10} = 0.60$$

$$P(x_2) = \frac{4}{10} = 0.40$$

The probabilities of these events add to 1.00 because they are mutually exclusive and collectively exhaustive.

Step 5: Identify the set of possible outcomes. Outcomes measure, in terms of the choice criterion, the predicted economic results of the various possible combinations of actions and events. The outcomes in the Do-All Software example take the form of six possible operating incomes that are displayed in a decision table in Exhibit 3-6. A **decision table** is a summary of the alternative actions, events, outcomes, and probabilities of events.

Distinguish actions from events. Actions are decision choices available to managers—for example, the particular rental alternatives that Mary can choose. Events are the set of all relevant occurrences that

EXHIBIT 3-6 Decision Table for Do-All Software

	A	B	C	D	E	F	G	H	I
1	Selling price =	$200		Operating Income					
2	Package cost =	$120		Under Each Possible Event					
3			Percentage						
4		Fixed	of Convention	Event x_1: Units Sold =		30	Event x_2: Units Sold =		60
5	Actions	Fee	Revenues	Probability(x_1) =		0.60	Probability(x_2) =		0.40
6	a_1: Pay $2,000 fixed fee	$2,000	0%	$400[l]			$2,800[m]		
7	a_2: Pay $800 fixed fee plus 15% of convention revenues	$ 800	15%	$700[n]			$2,200[p]		
8	a_3: Pay 25% of convention revenues with no fixed fee	$ 0	25%	$900[q]			$1,800[r]		
9									
10	[l]Operating Income = ($200 - $120)(30) - $2,000	=	$ 400						
11	[m]Operating Income = ($200 - $120)(60) - $2,000	=	$2,800						
12	[n]Operating Income = ($200 - $120 - 15% x $200)(30) - $800	=	$ 700						
13	[p]Operating Income = ($200 - $120 - 15% x $200)(60) - $800	=	$2,200						
14	[q]Operating Income = ($200 - $120 - 25% x $200)(30)	=	$ 900						
15	[r]Operating Income = ($200 - $120 - 25% x $200)(60)	=	$1,800						

EXHIBIT 3-7 **A Decision Model and Its Link to Performance Evaluation**

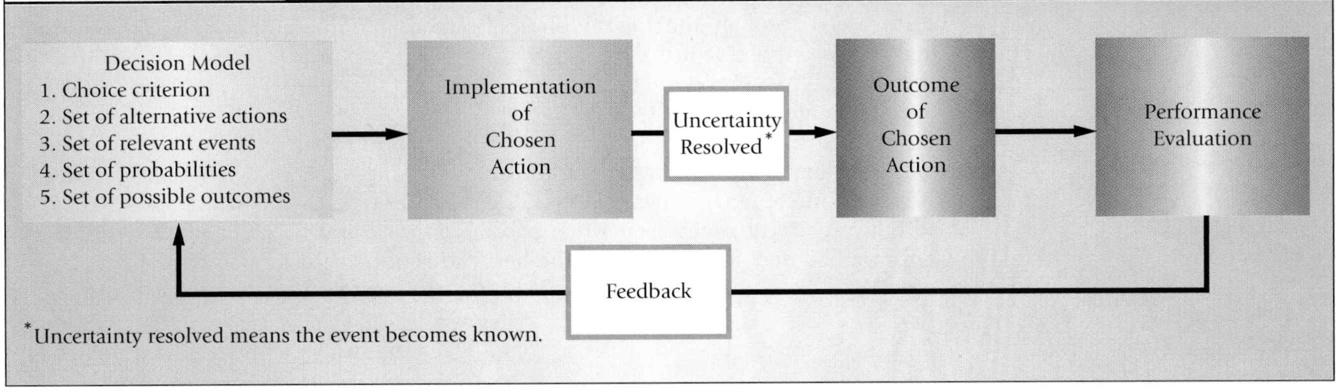

can happen—for example, the different quantities of software packages that may be sold at the convention. The outcome is operating income, which depends both on the action the manager selects (rental alternative chosen) and the event that occurs (the quantity of packages sold).

Exhibit 3-7 presents an overview of relationships among a decision model, the implementation of a chosen action, its outcome, and a subsequent performance evaluation. Thoughtful managers step back and evaluate what happened and learn from their experiences. This learning serves as feedback for adapting the decision model for future actions.

Expected Value An **expected value** is the weighted average of the outcomes, with the probability of each outcome serving as the weight. When the outcomes are measured in monetary terms, expected value is often called **expected monetary value**. Using information in Exhibit 3-6, the expected monetary value of each booth-rental alternative denoted by $E(a_1)$, $E(a_2)$, and $E(a_3)$ is:

Pay \$2,000 fixed fee:	$E(a_1) = 0.60(\$400) + 0.40(\$2,800) = \$1,360$
Pay \$800 fixed fee plus 15% of revenues:	$E(a_2) = 0.60(\$700) + 0.40(\$2,200) = \$1,300$
Pay 25% of revenues with no fixed fee:	$E(a_3) = 0.60(\$900) + 0.40(\$1,800) = \$1,260$

To maximize expected operating income, Mary should select action a_1—pay Computer Conventions a \$2,000 fixed fee.

To interpret the expected value of selecting action a_1, imagine that Mary attends many conventions, each with the probability distribution of operating incomes given in Exhibit 3-6. For a specific convention, Mary will earn operating income of either \$400, if she sells 30 units, or \$2,800, if she sells 60 units. But if Mary attends 100 conventions, she will expect to earn \$400 operating income 60% of the time (at 60 conventions), and \$2,800 operating income 40% of the time (at 40 conventions), for a total operating income of \$136,000 (\$400 × 60 + \$2,800 × 40). The expected value of \$1,360 is the operating income per convention that Mary will earn when averaged across all conventions (\$136,000 ÷ 100).

Consider the effect of uncertainty on the preferred action choice. If Mary were certain she would sell only 30 units (that is, $P(x_1) = 1$), she would prefer alternative a_3—pay 25% of convention revenues with no fixed fee. To follow this reasoning, examine Exhibit 3-6. When 30 units are sold, alternative a_3 yields the maximum operating income of \$900. Because fixed costs are \$0, booth-rental costs are lower, equal to \$1,500 (25% of revenues = 0.25 × \$200 per unit × 30 units) when sales are low.

However, if Mary were certain she would sell 60 software packages (that is, $P(x_2) = 1$), she would prefer alternative a_1—pay a \$2,000 fixed fee. Exhibit 3-6 indicates that when 60 units are sold, alternative $a_1$yields maximum operating income of \$2,800. Rental payments under a_2 and a_3 increase with units sold but are fixed under a_1.

Despite the high probability of selling only 30 units, Mary still prefers to take action a_1, that is, pay a fixed fee of \$2,000. That's because the high risk of low operating income (the 60% probability of selling only 30 units) is more than offset by the high return from selling 60 units, which has a 40% probability. If Mary were more averse to risk (measured in our example by the difference between operating incomes when 30 versus 60 units are sold), she might have preferred action a_2 or a_3. For example, action a_2 ensures an operating income of at least \$700, greater than the operating income of \$400 that she would earn under action a_1 if only 30 units were sold. Of course, choosing a_2 limits the upside potential to \$2,200 relative to \$2,800 under a_1, if 60 units are sold. If Mary is very concerned about downside risk, however, she may be willing to forgo some upside benefits to protect against a \$400 outcome by choosing a_2.[2]

[2]For more formal approaches, refer to J. Moore and L. Weatherford, *Decision Modeling with Microsoft Excel*, 6th ed. (Upper Saddle River, NJ: Prentice Hall, 2001).

Good Decisions and Good Outcomes Always distinguish between a good decision and a good outcome. One can exist without the other. Suppose you are offered a one-time-only gamble tossing a coin. You will win \$20 if the event is heads, but you will lose \$1 if the event is tails. As a decision maker, you proceed through the logical phases: gathering information, assessing outcomes, and making a choice. You accept the bet. Why? Because the expected value is \$9.50 [0.5(\$20) + 0.5(−\$1)]. The coin is tossed and the event is tails. You lose. From your viewpoint, this was a good decision but a bad outcome.

A decision can be made only on the basis of information that is available at the time of evaluating and making the decision. By definition, uncertainty rules out guaranteeing, after the fact, that the best outcome will always be obtained. As in our example, it is possible that bad luck will produce bad outcomes even when good decisions have been made. A bad outcome does not mean a bad decision was made. The best protection against a bad outcome is a good decision.

TERMS TO LEARN

This chapter and the Glossary at the end of the book contain definitions of the following important terms:

breakeven point (BEP) (p. 65)
choice criterion (p. 81)
contribution income statement (p. 63)
contribution margin (p. 62)
contribution margin per unit (p. 62)
contribution margin percentage (p. 63)
contribution margin ratio (p. 63)
cost-volume-profit (CVP) analysis (p. 60)
decision table (p. 82)
degree of operating leverage (p. 72)
event (p. 81)
expected monetary value (p. 83)
expected value (p. 83)
gross margin percentage (p. 79)
margin of safety (p. 70)
net income (p. 62)
operating leverage (p. 72)
outcomes (p. 82)
probability (p. 82)
probability distribution (p. 82)
PV graph (p. 66)
revenue driver (p. 61)
sales mix (p. 74)
sensitivity analysis (p. 69)
uncertainty (p. 71)

PH Grade Assist

Prentice Hall Grade Assist (PHGA)
Your professor may ask you to complete selected exercises and problems in Prentice Hall Grade Assist (PHGA). PHGA is an online tool that can help you master the chapter's topics. It provides you with multiple variations of exercises and problems designated by the PHGA icon. You can rework these exercises and problems—each time with new data—as many times as you need. You also receive immediate feedback and grading.

ASSIGNMENT MATERIAL

Note: To underscore the basic CVP relationships, the assignment material ignores income taxes unless stated otherwise.

Questions

3-1 Define cost-volume-profit analysis.

3-2 Describe the assumptions underlying CVP analysis.

3-3 Distinguish between operating income and net income.

3-4 Define contribution margin, contribution margin per unit, and contribution margin percentage.

3-5 Describe three methods that can be used to express CVP relationships.

3-6 Why is it more accurate to describe the subject matter of this chapter as CVP analysis rather than as breakeven analysis?

3-7 "CVP analysis is both simple and simplistic. If you want realistic analysis to underpin your decisions, look beyond CVP analysis." Do you agree? Explain.

3-8 How does an increase in the income tax rate affect the breakeven point?

3-9 Describe sensitivity analysis. How has the advent of the electronic spreadsheet affected the use of sensitivity analysis?

3-10 Give an example of how a manager can decrease variable costs while increasing fixed costs.

3-11 Give an example of how a manager can increase variable costs while decreasing fixed costs.

3-12 What is operating leverage? How is knowing the degree of operating leverage helpful to managers?

3-13 "There is no such thing as a fixed cost. All costs can be 'unfixed' given sufficient time." Do you agree? What is the implication of your answer for CVP analysis?

3-14 How can a company with multiple products compute its breakeven point?

3-15 "In CVP analysis, gross margin is a less-useful concept than contribution margin." Do you agree? Explain briefly.

Exercises

3-16 CVP computations. Fill in the blanks for each of the following independent cases.

Case	Revenues	Variable Costs	Fixed Costs	Total Costs	Operating Income	Contribution Margin Percentage
a.	—	$500	—	$ 800	$1,200	—
b.	$2,000	—	$300	—	$ 200	—
c.	$1,000	$700	—	$1,000	—	—
d.	$1,500	—	$300	—	—	40%

PH Grade Assist

3-17 CVP computations. Patel Manufacturing sold 180,000 units of its product for $25 per unit in 2005. Variable cost per unit is $20 and total fixed costs are $800,000.

Required

1. Calculate (a) contribution margin and (b) operating income.
2. Patel's current manufacturing process is labor intensive. Kate Schoenen, Patel's production manager, has proposed investing in state-of-the-art manufacturing equipment, which will increase the annual fixed costs to $2,500,000. The variable costs are expected to decrease to $10 per unit. Patel expects to maintain the same sales volume and selling price next year. How would acceptance of Schoenen's proposal affect your answers to (a) and (b) in requirement 1?
3. Should Patel accept Schoenen's proposal? Explain.

3-18 CVP analysis, changing revenues and costs. Sunshine Travel Agency specializes in flights between Toronto and Jamaica. It books passengers on Canadian Air. Sunshine's fixed costs are $22,000 per month. Canadian Air charges passengers $1,000 per round-trip ticket.

Required

Calculate the number of tickets Sunshine must sell each month to (a) break even and (b) make a target operating income of $10,000 per month in each of the following independent cases.

1. Sunshine's variable costs are $35 per ticket. Canadian Air pays Sunshine 8% commission on ticket price.
2. Sunshine's variable costs are $29 per ticket. Canadian Air pays Sunshine 8% commission on ticket price.
3. Sunshine's variable costs are $29 per ticket. Canadian Air pays $48 fixed commission per ticket to Sunshine. Comment on the results.
4. Sunshine's variable costs are $29 per ticket. It receives $48 commission per ticket from Canadian Air. It charges its customers a delivery fee of $5 per ticket. Comment on the results.

3-19 CVP exercises. The Super Donut owns and operates six doughnut outlets in and around Kansas City. You are given the following corporate budget data for next year:

Revenues	$10,000,000
Fixed costs	$ 1,700,000
Variable costs	$ 8,200,000

Variable costs change with respect to the number of doughnuts sold.

Required

Compute the budgeted operating income for each of the following deviations from the original budget data. (Consider each case independently.)

1. A 10% increase in contribution margin, holding revenues constant
2. A 10% decrease in contribution margin, holding revenues constant
3. A 5% increase in fixed costs
4. A 5% decrease in fixed costs
5. An 8% increase in units sold
6. An 8% decrease in units sold
7. A 10% increase in fixed costs and a 10% increase in units sold
8. A 5% increase in fixed costs and a 5% decrease in variable costs

PH Grade Assist

3-20 CVP exercises. The Doral Company manufactures and sells pens. Currently, 5,000,000 units are sold per year at $0.50 per unit. Fixed costs are $900,000 per year. Variable costs are $0.30 per unit.

Required

Consider each case separately:

1. **a.** What is the current annual operating income?
   b. What is the present breakeven point in revenues?

Compute the new operating income for each of the following changes:

2. A $0.04 per unit increase in variable costs
3. A 10% increase in fixed costs and a 10% increase in units sold
4. A 20% decrease in fixed costs, a 20% decrease in selling price, a 10% decrease in variable cost per unit, and a 40% increase in units sold

Compute the new breakeven point in units for each of the following changes:

5. A 10% increase in fixed costs
6. A 10% increase in selling price and a $20,000 increase in fixed costs

3-21 CVP analysis, income taxes. Diego Motors is a small car dealership. On average, it sells a car for $25,000, which it purchases from the manufacturer for $22,000. Each month, Diego Motors pays $50,000 in rent and utilities and $60,000 for salespeople's salaries. In addition to their salaries, salespeople are paid a commission of $500 for each car they sell. Diego Motors also spends $10,000 each month for local advertisements. Its tax rate is 40%.

Required

1. How many cars must Diego Motors sell each month to break even?
2. Diego Motors has a target monthly net income of $54,000. What is its target monthly operating income? How many cars must be sold each month to reach the target monthly net income of $54,000?

PH Grade Assist

3-22 CVP analysis, income taxes. The Rapid Meal has two restaurants that are open 24 hours a day. Fixed costs for the two restaurants together total $450,000 per year. Service varies from a cup of coffee to full meals. The average sales check per customer is $8.00. The average cost of food and other variable costs for each customer is $3.20. The income tax rate is 30%. Target net income is $105,000.

Required

1. Compute the revenues needed to earn the target net income.
2. How many customers are needed to break even? To earn net income of $105,000?
3. Compute net income if the number of customers is 150,000.

3-23 CVP analysis, sensitivity analysis. Hoot Washington is the newly elected leader of the Republican Party. Media Publishers is negotiating to publish *Hoot's Manifesto*, a new book that promises to be an instant best-seller. The fixed costs of producing and marketing the book will be $500,000. The variable costs of producing and marketing will be $4.00 per copy sold. These costs are before any payments to Hoot. Hoot negotiates an up-front payment of $3 million, plus a 15% royalty rate on the net sales price of each book. The net sales price is the listed bookstore price of $30, minus the margin paid to the bookstore to sell the book. The normal bookstore margin of 30% of the listed bookstore price is expected to apply.

Required

1. Prepare a PV graph for Media Publishers.
2. How many copies must Media Publishers sell to (a) break even and (b) earn a target operating income of $2 million?
3. Examine the sensitivity of the breakeven point to the following changes:
   a. Decreasing the normal bookstore margin to 20% of the listed bookstore price of $30.
   b. Increasing the listed bookstore price to $40 while keeping the bookstore margin at 30%.
   c. Comment on the results.

3-24 CVP analysis, margin of safety. Suppose Lattin Corp.'s breakeven point is revenues of $1,000,000. Fixed costs are $400,000.

Required

1. Compute the contribution margin percentage.
2. Compute the selling price if variable costs are $12 per unit.
3. Suppose 80,000 units are sold. Compute the margin of safety in units.

3-25 Operating leverage. Color Rugs is holding a two-week carpet sale at Jerry's Club, a local warehouse store. Color Rugs plans to sell carpets for $500 each. The company will purchase the carpets from a local distributor for $350 each, with the privilege of returning any unsold units for a full refund. Jerry's Club has offered Color Rugs two payment alternatives for the use of space.

- **Option 1:** A fixed payment of $5,000 for the sale period
- **Option 2:** 10% of total revenues earned during the sale period

Assume Color Rugs will incur no other costs.

Required

1. Calculate the breakeven point in units for (a) option 1 and (b) option 2.
2. At what level of revenues will Color Rugs earn the same operating income under either option?
3. **a.** For what range of unit sales will Color Rugs prefer option 1?
   b. For what range of unit sales will Color Rugs prefer option 2?
4. Calculate the degree of operating leverage at sales of 100 units for the two rental options.
5. Briefly explain and interpret your answer to requirement 4.

3-26 CVP analysis, international cost structure differences. Knitwear, Inc., is considering three countries for the sole manufacturing site of its new sweater: Singapore, Thailand, or the United States. All sweaters are to be sold to retail outlets in the United States at $32 per unit. These retail outlets add their own markup when selling to final customers. Fixed costs and variable cost per unit (sweater) differ in the three countries.

Excel Lab
www.prenhall.com/horngren/cost12e

	A	B	C	D
1		Annual	Variable	Variable
2		Fixed	Manufacturing	Marketing &
3		Costs	Cost	Distribution Cost
4	Country	(Millions)	per Sweater	per Sweater
5	Singapore	$ 6.5	$ 8.00	$11.00
6	Thailand	$ 4.5	$ 5.50	$11.50
7	United States	$12.0	$13.00	$ 9.00

If you want to use Excel to solve this exercise, go to the Excel Lab at **www.prenhall.com/horngren/cost12e** and download the template for Exercise 3-26.

Required

1. Compute the breakeven point for Knitwear, Inc., in each country in (a) units sold (b) revenues.
2. If Knitwear, Inc., plans to produce and sell 800,000 sweaters in 2005, what is the budgeted operating income for each of the three manufacturing locations? Comment on the results.

3-27 Sales mix, new and upgrade customers. Zapo 1-2-3 is a top-selling electronic spreadsheet product. Zapo is about to release version 5.0. It divides its customers into two groups: new customers and upgrade customers (those who previously purchased Zapo 1-2-3, 4.0 or earlier versions). Although the same physical product is provided to each customer group, sizable differences exist in selling prices and variable marketing costs:

	New Customers		Upgrade Customers	
Selling price		$210		$120
Variable costs				
Manufacturing	$25		$25	
Marketing	65	90	15	40
Contribution margin		$120		$ 80

The fixed costs of Zapo 1-2-3 5.0 are $14,000,000. The planned sales mix in units is 60% new customers and 40% upgrade customers.

Required

1. What is the Zapo 1-2-3 5.0 breakeven point in units, assuming that the planned 60%/40% sales mix is attained?
2. If the sales mix is attained, what is the operating income when 200,000 units are sold?
3. Show how the breakeven point in units changes with the following customer mixes:
   a. New 50%/Upgrade 50% **b.** New 90%/Upgrade 10% **c.** Comment on the results.

3-28 CVP analysis, multiple cost drivers. Susan Wong is a distributor of brass picture frames. For 2005, she plans to purchase frames for $30 each and sell them for $45 each. Susan's fixed costs are expected to be $240,000. Susan's only other costs will be variable costs of $60 per shipment for preparing the invoice and delivery documents, organizing the delivery, and following up for collecting accounts receivable. The $60 cost will be incurred each time Susan ships an order of picture frames, regardless of the number of frames in the order.

PH Grade Assist

Required

1. **a.** Suppose Susan sells 40,000 picture frames in 1,000 shipments in 2005. Calculate Susan's 2005 operating income.
   b. Suppose Susan sells 40,000 picture frames in 800 shipments in 2005. Calculate Susan's 2005 operating income.
2. Suppose Susan anticipates making 500 shipments in 2005. How many picture frames must Susan sell to break even in 2005?
3. Calculate another breakeven point for 2005, different from the one described in requirement 2. Explain briefly why Susan has multiple breakeven points.

3-29 Athletic scholarships, CVP analysis. Midwest University has an annual budget of $5,000,000 for athletic scholarships. Each athletic scholarship is for $20,000 per year. Fixed operating costs of the athletic scholarship program are $600,000, and variable operating costs are $2,000 per scholarship offered.

Required

1. Determine the number of athletic scholarships Midwest University can offer each year.
2. Suppose the total budget for next year is reduced by 22%. Fixed costs are to remain the same. Calculate the number of athletic scholarships that Midwest can offer next year.
3. As in requirement 2, assume a budget reduction of 22% and the same fixed costs. If Midwest wanted to offer the same number of athletic scholarships as it did in requirement 1, calculate the amount that will be paid to each student who receives a scholarship.

3-30 Contribution margin, decision making. Schmidt Men's Clothing's revenues and cost data for 2006 are:

Revenues		$ 500,000
Cost of goods sold (40% of sales)		200,000
Gross margin		300,000
Operating costs:		
Salaries fixed	$150,000	
Sales commissions (10% of sales)	50,000	
Depreciation of equipment and fixtures	12,000	
Store rent ($4,000 per month)	48,000	
Other operating costs	50,000	310,000
Operating income (loss)		$(10,000)

Mr. Schmidt, the owner of the store, is unhappy with the operating results. An analysis of other operating costs reveals that it includes $40,000 variable costs, which vary with sales volume, and $10,000 (fixed) costs.

Required

1. Compute the contribution margin of Schmidt Men's Clothing.
2. Compute the contribution margin percentage.
3. Mr. Schmidt estimates that he can increase revenues by 20% by incurring additional advertising costs of $10,000. Calculate the impact of the additional advertising costs on operating income.

Excel Lab
www.prenhall.com/horngren/cost12e

3-31 Contribution margin, gross margin, and margin of safety. Mirabella Cosmetics manufactures and sells a face cream to small ethnic stores in the greater New York area. It presents the monthly operating income statement shown here to George Lopez, a potential investor in the business. Help Mr. Lopez understand Mirabella's cost structure.

	A	B	C	D
1		**Mirabella Cosmetics**		
2		**Operating Income Statement, June 2005**		
3	Units Sold			10,000
4	Revenues			$100,000
5	Cost of Goods Sold			
6	Variable Manufacturing Costs		$55,000	
7	Fixed Manufacturing Costs		20,000	
8	Total			75,000
9	Gross Margin			25,000
10	Operating Costs			
11	Variable Marketing Costs		$ 5,000	
12	Fixed Marketing & Administration Costs		10,000	
13	Total Operating Costs			15,000
14	Operating Income			$ 10,000

If you want to use Excel to solve this exercise, go to the Excel Lab at **www.prenhall.com/horngren/cost12e** and download the template for Exercise 3-31.

Required

1. Recast the income statement to emphasize contribution margin.
2. Calculate the contribution margin percentage and breakeven point in units and revenues for June 2005.
3. What is the margin of safety (in units) for June 2005?
4. If sales in June were only 8,000 units and Mirabella's tax rate is 30%, calculate its net income.

3-32 Uncertainty, CVP analysis. (Chapter appendix) Angela Brady is considering promoting a world championship fight for boxer Mike Foreman. Brady will receive $16 for every cable-TV home that subscribes to the event. She will pay Foreman 25% of each $16 fee and a fixed fee of $2 million. In addition, she will incur fixed costs of $1 million and variable cost of $2 per cable-TV home that subscribes to this event. All ticket revenues from the fight go to the operator of the casino where the fight will take place.

Excel Lab www.prenhall.com/horngren/cost12e

The pay-per-view audience for such an event is uncertain, but Brady estimates the following probability distribution for it:

	A	B
1	Pay-per-view Audience (number of homes subscribing to the event)	Probability
2	100,000	0.05
3	200,000	0.10
4	300,000	0.30
5	400,000	0.35
6	500,000	0.15
7	1,000,000	0.05

If you want to use Excel to solve this exercise, go to the Excel Lab at **www.prenhall.com/horngren/cost12e** and download the template for Exercise 3-32.

Required

1. What is the expected payment Brady will make to Foreman?
2. If the only uncertainty is the size of the pay-per-view audience, what is the breakeven number of subscriber homes?
3. Based on the expected audience size, would you recommend Brady proceed with the plans for the fight?

Problems

3-33 CVP analysis, service firm. Wildlife Escapes generates average revenue of $4,000 per person on its five-day package tours to wildlife parks in Kenya. The variable costs per person are:

Airfare	$1,500
Hotel accommodations	1,000
Meals	300
Ground transportation	600
Park tickets and other costs	200
Total	$3,600

Annual fixed costs total $480,000.

Required

1. Calculate the number of package tours that must be sold to break even.
2. Calculate the revenue needed to earn a target operating income of $100,000.
3. If fixed costs increase by $24,000, what decrease in variable cost per person must be achieved to maintain the breakeven point calculated in requirement 1?

3-34 CVP, target operating income, service firm. Teddy Bear Daycare provides daycare for children Mondays through Fridays. Its monthly variable costs per child are:

Lunch and snacks	$100
Educational supplies	75
Other supplies (paper products, toiletries, etc.)	25
Total	$200

Monthly fixed costs consist of:

Rent	$2,000
Utilities	300
Insurance	300
Salaries	2,500
Miscellaneous	500
Total	$5,600

Teddy Bear charges each parent $600 per child.

Required

1. Calculate the breakeven point.
2. Teddy Bear's target operating income is $10,400 per month. Compute the number of children who must be enrolled to achieve the target operating income.
3. Teddy Bear lost its lease and had to move to another building. Monthly rent for the new building is $3,000. At the suggestion of parents, Teddy Bear plans to take children on field trips. Monthly costs of the field trips are $1,000. By how much should Teddy Bear increase fees per child to meet the target operating income of $10,400 per month, assuming the same number of children as in requirement 2?

3-35 CVP analysis. (CMA, adapted) Galaxy Disk's projected operating income for 2005 is $200,000, based on a sales volume of 200,000 units. Galaxy sells disks for $16 each. Variable costs consist of the $10 purchase price and a $2 shipping and handling cost. Galaxy's annual fixed costs are $600,000.

Required

1. Calculate Galaxy's breakeven point and margin of safety in units.
2. Calculate the company's operating income for 2005 if there is a 10% increase in projected unit sales.
3. For 2006, management expects that the unit purchase price of the disks will increase by 30%. Calculate the sales revenue Galaxy must generate for 2006 to maintain the current year's operating income if the selling price remains unchanged.

PH Grade Assist

3-36 CVP analysis, income taxes. (CMA, adapted) R. A. Ro and Company, a manufacturer of quality handmade walnut bowls, has had a steady growth in sales for the past five years. However, increased competition has led Mr. Ro, the president, to believe that an aggressive marketing campaign will be necessary next year to maintain the company's present growth. To prepare for next year's marketing campaign, the company's controller has prepared and presented Mr. Ro with the following data for the current year, 2005:

Variable cost (per bowl)	
Direct materials	$ 3.25
Direct manufacturing labor	8.00
Variable overhead (manufacturing, marketing, distribution, and customer service)	2.50
Total variable cost per bowl	$13.75
Fixed costs	
Manufacturing	$ 25,000
Marketing, distribution, and customer service	110,000
Total fixed costs	$135,000
Selling price	$25.00
Expected sales, 20,000 units	$500,000
Income tax rate	40%

Required

1. What is the projected net income for 2005?
2. What is the breakeven point in units for 2005?
3. Mr. Ro has set the revenue target for 2006 at a level of $550,000 (or 22,000 bowls). He believes an additional marketing cost of $11,250 for advertising in 2006, with all other costs remaining constant, will be necessary to attain the revenue target. What is the net income for 2006 if the additional $11,250 is spent and the revenue target is met?
4. What is the breakeven point in revenues for 2006 if the additional $11,250 is spent for advertising?
5. If the additional $11,250 is spent, what are the required 2006 revenues for 2006 net income to equal 2005 net income?
6. At a sales level of 22,000 units, what maximum amount can be spent on advertising if a 2006 net income of $60,000 is desired?

PH Grade Assist

3-37 CVP analysis, decision making. (M. Rajan, adapted) Tocchet Company manufactures CB1, a citizens band radio. The company's plant has an annual capacity of 50,000 units. Tocchet currently sells 40,000 units at a price of $105. It has the following cost structure:

Variable manufacturing cost per unit	$45
Fixed manufacturing costs	$800,000
Variable marketing and distribution cost per unit	$10
Fixed marketing and distribution costs	$600,000

Required

Consider each requirement independently.

1. The Marketing Department indicates that decreasing the selling price to $99 would increase sales to 50,000 units. This strategy will require Tocchet to increase its fixed marketing and distribution costs. Calculate the *maximum* increase in fixed marketing and distribution costs that will allow Tocchet to reduce the selling price to $99 and maintain its operating income.

2. The Manufacturing Department proposes changes in the manufacturing process to add new features to the CB1 product. These changes will increase fixed manufacturing costs by $100,000 and variable manufacturing cost per unit by $2. At its current sales quantity of 40,000 units, compute the *minimum* selling price that will allow Tocchet to add these new features and maintain its operating income.

3-38 CVP analysis, shoe stores. The WalkRite Shoe Company operates a chain of shoe stores that sell 10 different styles of inexpensive men's shoes with identical unit costs and selling prices. A unit is defined as a pair of shoes. Each store has a store manager who is paid a fixed salary. Individual salespeople receive a fixed salary and a sales commission. WalkRite is considering opening another store that is expected to have the revenue and cost relationships shown here:

Excel Lab www.prenhall.com/horngren/cost12e

	A	B	C	D	E
1	Unit Variable Data (per pair of shoes)			Annual Fixed Costs	
2	Selling Price	$30.00		Rent	$ 60,000
3	Cost of shoes	$19.50		Salaries	200,000
4	Sales commission	1.50		Advertising	80,000
5	Variable cost per unit	$21.00		Other fixed costs	20,000
6				Total fixed costs	$360,000

If you want to use Excel to solve this problem, go to the Excel Lab at **www.prenhall.com/horngren/cost12e** and download the template for Problem 3-38.

Required

Consider each question independently:

1. What is the annual breakeven point in (a) units sold and (b) revenues?
2. If 35,000 units are sold, what will be the store's operating income (loss)?
3. If sales commissions are discontinued and fixed salaries are raised by a total of $81,000, what would be the annual breakeven point in (a) units sold and (b) revenues?
4. Refer to the original data. If, in addition to his fixed salary, the store manager is paid a commission of $0.30 per unit sold, what would be the annual breakeven point in (a) units sold and (b) revenues?
5. Refer to the original data. If, in addition to his fixed salary, the store manager is paid a commission of $0.30 *per unit in excess of the breakeven point*, what would be the store's operating income if 50,000 units were sold?

3-39 CVP analysis, shoe stores (continuation of 3-38). Refer to requirement 3 of Problem 3-38. In this problem, assume the role of the owner of WalkRite.

If you want to use Excel to solve this problem, go to the Excel Lab at **www.prenhall.com/horngren/cost12e** and download the template for Problem 3-38.

Excel Lab www.prenhall.com/horngren/cost12e

Required

1. Calculate the number of units sold at which the owner of WalkRite would be indifferent between the original salary-plus-commissions plan for salespeople and the higher fixed-salaries-only plan.
2. As owner, which sales compensation plan would you choose if forecasted annual sales of the new store were at least 55,000 units? What do you think of the motivational aspect of your chosen compensation plan?
3. Suppose the target operating income is $168,000. How many units must be sold to reach the target operating income under (a) the original salary-plus-commissions plan and (b) the higher-fixed-salaries-only plan?
4. You open the new store on January 1, 2005, with the original salary-plus-commission compensation plan in place. Because you expect the cost of the shoes to rise due to inflation, you place a firm bulk order for 50,000 shoes and lock in the $19.50 price per unit. But, toward the end of the year, only 48,000 shoes are sold, and you authorize a markdown of the remaining inventory to $18 per unit. Finally, all units are sold. Salespeople, as usual, get paid a commission of 5% of revenues. What is the annual operating income for the store?

3-40 Alternative cost structures, sensitivity analysis. Refer to the data for the Do-All Software example on page 62. From a report drawn up by her marketing manager, Mary Frost knows that her customers are price-sensitive. The estimated demand at different prices is:

Excel Lab www.prenhall.com/horngren/cost12e

	A	B	C	D	E
1	Selling Price	$200	$230	$275	$300
2	Demand (number of packages)	42	30	20	15

If you want to use Excel to solve this problem, go to the Excel Lab at **www.prenhall.com/horngren/cost12e** and download the template for Problem 3-40.

Required

1. At what price should Mary sell Do-All at the convention to maximize operating income?
2. Repeat requirement 1 assuming that instead of paying a fixed fee of $2,000 for the booth rental, Mary pays a fee of $800 plus 15% of convention revenues.

3-41 Alternative fixed-cost/variable-cost structures. Cut-n-Sew is a small company that makes jackets for a ready-to-wear clothes designer at a selling price of $20. Cut-n-Sew is considering investing in a new plant. It can either invest in a more-manual plant or a more-automated plant. Both types of plants will have the same level of quality. The manual plant will have fixed costs of $20,000 per year, and a variable cost of $10 per jacket. The automated plant will have fixed costs of $30,000 per year, and a variable cost of $8 per jacket.

Required

1. What is the breakeven point in units for each type of plant?
2. Prepare a graph showing the profitability of the two types of plants at sales volumes of 2,000 to 7,000 units. At what anticipated sales volume will the two types of plants have the same operating income?
3. If Cut-n-Sew estimates sales of 4,000 jackets per year, which type of plant will it prefer to build?

3-42 CVP analysis, income taxes, sensitivity. (CMA, adapted) Almo Company manufactures and sells adjustable canopies that attach to motor homes and trailers. For its 2006 budget, Almo estimates the following:

Selling price	$400
Variable cost per canopy	$200
Annual fixed costs	$100,000
Net income	$240,000
Income tax rate	40%

The May income statement reported that sales were not meeting expectations. For the first five months of the year, only 350 units had been sold at the established price, with variable costs as planned, and it was clear that the net income projection for 2006 would not be reached unless some actions were taken. A management committee presented the following mutually exclusive alternatives to the president:

a. Reduce the selling price by $40. The sales organization forecasts that at this significantly reduced price, 2,700 units can be sold during the remainder of the year. Total fixed costs and variable cost per unit will stay as budgeted.
b. Lower variable cost per unit by $10 through the use of less-expensive direct materials and slightly modified manufacturing techniques. The selling price will also be reduced by $30, and sales of 2,200 units are expected for the remainder of the year.
c. Reduce fixed costs by $10,000 and lower the selling price by 5%. Variable cost per unit will be unchanged. Sales of 2,000 units are expected for the remainder of the year.

Required

1. If no changes are made to the selling price or cost structure, determine the number of units that Almo Company must sell (a) to break even and (b) to achieve its net income objective.
2. Determine which alternative Almo should select to achieve its net income objective. Show your calculations.

Excel Lab
www.prenhall.com/horngren/cost12e

3-43 Choosing between compensation plans, operating leverage. (CMA, adapted) Marston Corporation manufactures pharmaceutical products that are sold through a network of external sales agents. The agents are paid a commission of 18% of revenues. Marston is considering replacing the sales agents with its own salespeople, who would be paid a commission of 10% of revenues and total salaries of $2,080,000. The income statement for the year ending December 31, 2005, under the two scenarios is shown here.

	A	B	C	D	E
1			**Marston Corporation**		
2			**Income Statement**		
3			**For the Year Ended December 31, 2005**		
4		**Using Sales Agents**		**Using Own Sales Force**	
5	Revenues		$26,000,000		$26,000,000
6	Cost of goods sold				
7	Variable	$11,700,000		$11,700,000	
8	Fixed	2,870,000	14,570,000	2,870,000	14,570,000
9	Gross Margin		11,430,000		11,430,000
10	Marketing Costs				
11	Commissions	$ 4,680,000		$ 2,600,000	
12	Fixed Costs	3,420,000	8,100,000	5,500,000	8,100,000
13	Operating Income		$ 3,330,000		$ 3,330,000

If you want to use Excel to solve this problem, go to the Excel Lab at **www.prenhall.com/horngren/cost12e** and download the template for Problem 3-43.

Required

1. Calculate Marston's 2005 contribution margin percentage, breakeven revenues, and degree of operating leverage under the two scenarios.
2. Describe the advantages and disadvantages of each type of sales alternative.
3. In 2006, Marston uses its own salespeople, who demand a 15% commission. If all other cost behavior patterns are unchanged, how much revenue must the salespeople generate in order to earn the same operating income as in 2005?

3-44 Sales mix, three products. The Ronowski Company has three product lines of belts—A, B, and C—with contribution margins of $3, $2, and $1, respectively. The president foresees sales of 200,000 units in the coming period, consisting of 20,000 units of A, 100,000 units of B, and 80,000 units of C. The company's fixed costs for the period are $255,000.

PH Grade Assist

Required

1. What is the company's breakeven point in units, assuming that the given sales mix is maintained?
2. If the sales mix is maintained, what is the total contribution margin when 200,000 units are sold? What is the operating income?
3. What would operating income be if 20,000 units of A, 80,000 units of B, and 100,000 units of C were sold? What is the new breakeven point in units if these relationships persist in the next period?

3-45 Multiproduct breakeven, decision making. Evenkeel Corporation manufactures and sells one product—an infant car seat called Plumar—at a price of $50. Variable costs equal $20 per car seat. Fixed costs are $495,000. Evenkeel manufactures Plumar upon the receipt of orders from its customers. In 2005, it sold 30,000 units of Plumar. One of Evenkeel's customers, Glaston Corporation, has asked if in 2006 Evenkeel will manufacture a different style of car seat called Ridex. Glaston will pay $25 for each unit of Ridex. The variable cost for Ridex is estimated to be $15 per seat. Evenkeel has enough capacity to manufacture all the units of Plumar it can sell as well as the units of Ridex that Glaston wants without incurring any additional fixed costs. Evenkeel estimates that in 2006 it will sell 30,000 units of Plumar (assuming the same price and variable costs as in 2005) and 20,000 units of Ridex.

Andy Minton, the president of Evenkeel, checks the effect of accepting Glaston's offer on the breakeven revenues for 2006. Using the planned sales mix for 2006, he is surprised to find that the revenues required to break even appear to increase. He is not sure that his numbers are correct, but if they are, Andy feels inclined to reject Glaston's offer. He asks for your advice.

Required

1. Calculate the breakeven point in units and in revenues for 2005.
2. Calculate the breakeven point in units and in revenues for 2006 at the planned sales mix.
3. Explain why the breakeven point in revenues calculated in requirements 1 and 2 are different.
4. Should Andy accept Glaston's offer? Provide supporting calculations.

3-46 Sales mix, two products. The Goldman Company retails two products: a standard and a deluxe version of a luggage carrier. The budgeted income statement for next period is as follows:

	Standard Carrier	Deluxe Carrier	Total
Units sold	150,000	50,000	200,000
Revenues at $20 and $30 per unit	$3,000,000	$1,500,000	$4,500,000
Variable costs at $14 and $18 per unit	2,100,000	900,000	3,000,000
Contribution margins at $6 and $12 per unit	$ 900,000	$ 600,000	1,500,000
Fixed costs			1,200,000
Operating income			$ 300,000

Required

1. Compute the breakeven point in units, assuming that the planned sales mix is attained.
2. Compute the breakeven point in units (a) if only standard carriers are sold and (b) if only deluxe carriers are sold.
3. Suppose 200,000 units are sold but only 20,000 of them are deluxe. Compute the operating income. Compute the breakeven point in units. Compare your answer with the answer to requirement 1. What is the major lesson of this problem?

3-47 Gross margin and contribution margin. (R. Lambert, adapted) Foreman Fork, Inc.'s income statement for 2005 on production and sales of 200,000 units is as follows:

Revenues	$2,600,000
Cost of goods sold	1,600,000
Gross margin	1,000,000
Marketing and distribution costs	1,150,000
Operating income (loss)	$ (150,000)

Foreman's fixed manufacturing costs are $500,000 and variable marketing and distribution costs are $4 per unit.

Required

1. **a.** Calculate Foreman's variable manufacturing cost per unit for 2005.
   b. Calculate Foreman's fixed marketing and distribution costs for 2005.
2. Foreman's gross margin per unit is $5 ($1,000,000 ÷ 200,000 units). Sam Hogan, Foreman's president, believes that if production and sales had been 230,000 units, the company would have covered the $1,150,000 of marketing and distribution costs ($1,150,000 ÷ 5 = 230,000) and enabled Foreman to break even for the year. Calculate Foreman's operating income if production and sales equal 230,000 units. Explain briefly why Sam Hogan is wrong.
3. Calculate the breakeven point for 2005 in units and in revenues.

3-48 Ethics, CVP analysis. Allen Corporation produces a molded plastic casing, LX201, for desktop computers. Summary data from its 2005 income statement are as follows:

Revenues	$5,000,000
Variable costs	3,000,000
Fixed costs	2,160,000
Operating income	$ (160,000)

Jane Woodall, Allen's president, is very concerned about Allen Corporation's poor profitability. She asks Max Lemond, production manager, and Lester Bush, controller, to see if there are ways to reduce costs.

After two weeks, Max returns with a proposal to reduce variable costs to 52% of revenues by reducing the costs Allen currently incurs for safe disposal of wasted plastic. Lester is concerned that this would expose the company to potential environmental liabilities. He tells Max, "We would need to estimate some of these potential environmental costs and include them in our analysis." "You can't do that," Max replies. "We are not violating any laws. There is some possibility that we may have to incur environmental costs in the future, but if we bring it up now, this proposal will not go through because our senior management always assumes these costs to be larger than they turn out to be. The market is very tough, and we are in danger of shutting down the company. We don't want all our colleagues to lose their jobs. The only reason our competitors are making money is because they are doing exactly what I am proposing."

Required

1. Calculate Allen Corporation's breakeven revenues for 2005.
2. Calculate Allen Corporation's breakeven revenues if variable costs are 52% of revenues.
3. Calculate Allen Corporation's operating income for 2005 if variable costs had been 52% of revenues.
4. Given Max Lemond's comments, what should Lester Bush do?

Collaborative Learning Problem

Excel Lab
www.prenhall.com/horngren/cost12e

3-49 Deciding where to produce. (CMA, adapted) The Domestic Engines Co. produces the same power generators in two Illinois plants, a new plant in Peoria and an older plant in Moline. The following data are available for the two plants:

	A	B	C	D	E
1		Peoria		Moline	
2	Selling price		$150.00		$150.00
3	Variable manufacturing cost per unit	$72.00		$88.00	
4	Fixed manufacturing cost per unit	30.00		15.00	
5	Variable marketing and distribution cost per unit	14.00		14.00	
6	Fixed marketing and distribution cost per unit	19.00		14.50	
7	Total cost per unit		135.00		131.50
8	Operating income per unit		$ 15.00		$ 18.50
9	Production rate per day		400 units		320 units
10	Normal annual capacity usage		240 days		240 days
11	Maximum annual capacity		300 days		300 days

All fixed costs per unit are calculated based on a normal capacity usage consisting of 240 working days. When the number of working days exceeds 240, overtime charges raise the variable manufacturing costs of additional units by $3.00 per unit in Peoria and $8.00 per unit in Moline.

Domestic Engines Co. is expected to produce and sell 192,000 power generators during the coming year. Wanting to take advantage of the higher operating income per unit at Moline, the company's production manager has decided to manufacture 96,000 units at each plant, resulting in a plan in which Moline operates at capacity (320 units per day × 300 days) and Peoria operates at its normal volume (400 units per day × 240 days).

If you want to use Excel to solve this problem, go to the Excel Lab at **www.prenhall.com/horngren/cost12e** and download the template for Problem 3-49.

Required

1. Calculate the breakeven point in units for the Peoria plant and for the Moline plant.
2. Calculate the operating income that would result from the production manager's plan to produce 96,000 units at each plant.
3. Determine how the production of 192,000 units should be allocated between the Peoria and Moline plants to maximize operating income for Domestic Engines. Show your calculations.

Get Connected: Cost Accounting in the News

Go to www.prenhall.com/horngren/cost12e for additional online exercise(s) that explore issues affecting the accounting world today. These exercises offer you the opportunity to analyze and reflect on how cost accounting helps managers make better decisions and handle the challenges of strategic planning and implementation.

CHAPTER 3 Video Case

STORE 24: Cost-Volume-Profit Analysis

Modern convenience stores realize they have to offer more than late-night hours and a diverse product assortment to attract customers; they have to change with the times or face extinction. Over the years, convenience stores have stocked new products and services, such as gasoline, lottery tickets, and even Internet shopping and delivery services. A walk through any convenience store is likely to reveal in excess of 3,000 different products and services, often available 24 hours a day, seven days a week. There are close to 132,500 convenience stores scattered across the United States. The industry generated $337 billion in sales for 2003.

Store 24, based in Waltham, Massachusetts, operates 82 stores in its chain of convenience stores. Locations are primarily in the New England and Mid-Atlantic regions of the United States, where there are about 19,000 convenience stores—approximately 14% of the country's total. The average sale is $3.00, with a gross margin of 30%. As part of an accounting class assignment, Tanisha Jones made a visit to the Store 24 headquarters to learn more about the company. The class instructor directed students to find a local business that uses cost-volume-profit (CVP) analysis for decision making, and to identify a scenario where CVP analysis was used. Since Tanisha worked part time at the Store 24 in her neighborhood after school, she wanted to use her employer for the assignment.

Paul Doucette, Store 24's chief financial officer, agreed to meet Tanisha and help with her assignment. Paul assembled a set of reports and information Tanisha might find useful for the assignment. Paul told Tanisha that Store 24 uses CVP analysis in many situations. For example, company managers recently evaluated preparing in-store deli sandwiches for lunchtime customers versus prepackaged deli sandwiches provided by an outside vendor. The effect on income of the store's sales mix also had been reviewed, and sensitivity analysis had been performed to see the effect of changing the selling price of milk.

One recent use of CVP analysis that Paul thought would make a good illustration was the company's decision regarding the sale of money orders at its stores. Paul explained that this was a new product area for the company—a "financial service," much like what a bank would offer. By offering this new service, Store 24 hoped to boost its customer count. Previous studies had shown that customers were likely to buy more than just the items they originally intended to purchase. So, Store 24 wanted to boost sales revenue by giving customers another reason to come into the store—and buy more than intended.

Paul outlined for Tanisha the following information related to the analysis. The cost of renting the machine used in each store to prepare money orders is $30 per month. For each money order processed, Store 24 paid a processing fee of 6 cents. After conducting an informal survey of banks and other local businesses that offered money order services, Store 24 found most charging 99 cents for each money order transaction. Store 24 decided to price its money order fee at 79 cents to undercut the local competition. Paul estimated that a money order transaction would take one counter clerk 90 seconds to complete, versus only 30 seconds for ringing up a product sale. The average hourly wage for a store clerk is $9.00 per hour. Store 24 considered this labor cost as a variable cost.

QUESTIONS

1. What kinds of customers might be attracted to the money order service? Would you expect these customers to be typical of a convenience store such as Store 24?
2. What is the contribution margin per unit for money orders?
3. Using both the equation method and contribution margin method, how many money orders would each Store 24 location have to sell each month to break even on the service?
4. How many money orders would each Store 24 location need to sell to earn an operating income of $140 per month?
5. Studies have found that convenience store customers don't like to wait in line for service. What effect might the offering of money orders have if there's only one clerk staffed at the cash register each shift?

CHAPTER 4

JOB COSTING

LEARNING OBJECTIVES

1. **Describe the building-block concepts of costing systems**
2. **Distinguish job costing from process costing**
3. **Outline the seven-step approach to job costing**
4. **Distinguish actual costing from normal costing**
5. **Track the flow of costs in a job-costing system**
6. **Dispose of under- or overallocated manufacturing overhead costs at the end of the fiscal year using alternative methods**
7. **Apply variations from normal costing**

It's fair to say that no one likes to lose money. Whether a company is a new start-up venture providing marketing consulting services or an established manufacturer of custom-built motorcycles, knowledge of job cost—how much it costs to consult for a client job or to produce an individual motorcycle—is critical if profit is to be generated. But what costs need to be considered? Direct materials and labor only? Or something more? John Metz, owner and CEO of Robinson Company, realizes the importance of accurately determining job costs. His company manufactures and installs specialized machinery for the paper-making industry. John has called a meeting with Anita Patel, controller, to discuss the costs of a new job.

John: This new Western Pulp and Paper Company (WPP) job has me a bit worried. We've never made a machine quite like this one, and I'm wondering if our price quote of $15,000 for the job is adequate. We're also getting ready to bid on another similar job, so knowing how our costs are looking on the WPP job would help in preparing that bid.

Anita: We're only two months into the fiscal year, but our costing system shows that we should earn more than our usual profit margin on the WPP project.

John: When you say "profit margin," have you taken into account overhead costs as well as direct material and direct labor costs?

Anita: Yes—after all, we can't say we've made a profit unless our revenues exceed all our costs, not just the direct costs.

John: But Anita, how do you know what our overhead costs are for the WPP job this early in the year? Don't we have to wait until year-end to determine actual overhead?

Anita: Right again, John. Our accounting system does a good job of tracking job costs, but we won't know the final actual overhead costs until the end of December. However, we have a pretty good idea of our upcoming overhead costs, based on prior years' experience. Bottom line, I'd recommend pursuing more of these contracts.

John: That's great news. Thank you for your advice. I'll move forward right away on this new bid.

John Metz, like most business owners and managers, is right to be concerned about costs. DaimlerChrysler managers, for example, need to know how much it costs to manufacture the Mercedes S-Class. PriceWaterhouseCoopers needs to know what it costs to audit Novartis AG, the Swiss pharmaceutical company. When the costs and profitability of jobs are known, managers can confidently pursue their business strategies, develop pricing plans, and meet external reporting requirements. Costing systems are only one source of information for managers. When making decisions, managers combine cost information with noncost information, such as personal observations of operations, and nonfinancial performance measures, such as quality and customer satisfaction.

1

Describe the building-block concepts of costing systems

. . . the building blocks are cost object, direct costs, indirect costs, cost pools, and cost-allocation bases

Building-Block Concepts of Costing Systems

Let's review some terms discussed in Chapter 2 that we'll now use to introduce costing systems:

- **Cost object**—anything for which a measurement of costs is desired—for example, a product, such as an iMac computer, or a service, such as the cost of repairing an iMac computer.
- **Direct costs of a cost object**—costs related to a particular cost object that can be traced to that cost object in an economically feasible (cost-effective) way.
- **Indirect costs of a cost object**—costs related to a particular cost object that cannot be traced to that cost object in an economically feasible (cost-effective) way. Indirect costs are allocated to the cost object using a cost-allocation method.

Cost assignment is a general term for assigning costs, whether direct or indirect, to a cost object. *Cost tracing* is a specific term for assigning direct costs; *cost allocation* specifically refers to assigning indirect costs. The relationship among these three concepts can be graphically represented as

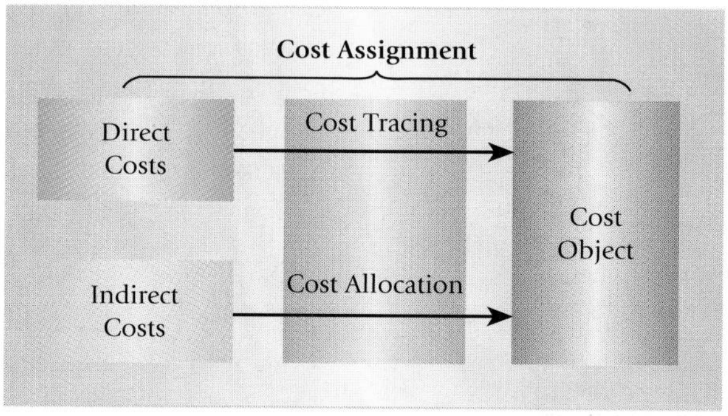

Throughout this chapter, the costs assigned to a cost object, for example, a product such as a Mini Cooper or a service such as an audit of MTV, include both variable and fixed costs. Managers use costs of products and services to guide long-run strategic decisions (for example, what mix of products and services to produce and sell and what prices to charge for them?) In making these decisions, managers include all costs for two reasons. First, in the long run more costs can be managed and fewer costs are regarded as fixed. Second, also in the long run, a business cannot survive unless the prices of the products and services it chooses to sell cover both variable and fixed costs.

We need to introduce and explain two more terms to discuss costing systems:

Study Tip: Student Guide Chapters 1 through 3 are available at **www.prenhall.com/harris**, and related study tips are in these Margin Notes. The print version of the *Student Guide* covers all 23 chapters of this book. To purchase the *Student Guide*, see the instructions at **www.prenhall.com/harris**.

1. **Cost pool.** A **cost pool** is a grouping of individual cost items. Cost pools can range from broad, such as all manufacturing-plant costs, to narrow, such as the costs of operating metal-cutting machines. Cost pools are often organized in conjunction with cost-allocation bases.

2. **Cost-allocation base.** How should a company allocate costs to operate metal-cutting machines—collected in a single cost pool—among different products? One way would be to allocate the costs on the basis of the number of machine-hours used to produce the different products. The **cost-allocation base** (in our example, the number of machine-hours) links in a systematic way an indirect cost or group of indirect costs (in our example, operating costs of all metal-cutting machines) to a cost object (in our example, different products). Companies often use the cost driver of indirect costs (number of machine-hours) as the cost-allocation base because of the cause-and-effect link between changes in the level of the cost driver and changes in indirect costs. A cost-allocation base can be either financial (such as direct labor costs) or nonfinancial (such as the number of machine-hours). When the cost object is a job, product, or customer, the cost-allocation base is also called a **cost-application base**.

The concepts represented by these five terms constitute the building blocks that we will use to design the costing systems described in this chapter.

Managers and management accountants choose cost objects to help them make decisions. As we described earlier, one major cost object of an accounting system is *products and services*. Another major cost object is *responsibility centers*, which are parts, segments, or subunits of an organization whose managers are accountable for specified activities. Examples of responsibility centers are departments or groups of departments (such as operations and sales at eBay), divisions (such as Cadillac and Buick at General Motors), and geographic territories (such as North America, Europe, and Asia Pacific at Nike).

The most common responsibility center is a department. Identifying department costs helps managers control the costs for which they are responsible. It also enables senior managers to evaluate the performance of their subordinates and the performance of subunits as economic investments. In manufacturing companies, the costs of the Manufacturing Department include all costs of materials, manufacturing labor, supervision, engineering, production, and quality control.

Be aware that supervision, engineering, and quality control costs, which are considered indirect or overhead costs when costing individual jobs or products, are considered direct costs of the Manufacturing Department. The reason is these costs are difficult to trace in an economically feasible way to individual jobs or products within the Manufacturing Department, but they are easily identified with and traced to the department itself.

These two cost objects—departments and products—represent two purposes of management accounting: providing information for (1) planning and control and (2) determining the cost of products. To illustrate, when manufacturing custom furniture, the cost of lumber and workers' wages are assigned to (1) the Production Department for control and performance evaluation (for example, did workers cut lumber and assemble furniture efficiently?) and (2) the finished pieces of furniture for inventory valuation. Estimating the cost of a piece of furniture *before* manufacturing occurs is often the basis of the pricing decision.

Job-Costing and Process-Costing Systems

2

Distinguish job costing

. . . job costing is used to cost a distinct product

from process costing

. . . process costing is used to cost masses of identical or similar units

Management accountants use two basic types of costing systems to assign costs to products or services:

1. **Job-costing system.** In this system, the cost object is a unit or multiple units of a distinct product or service called a **job**. Each job uses a different amount of resources. The product or service is often a single unit, such as a specialized machine made at Hitachi, a construction project managed by Bechtel Corporation, a repair job done at an Audi Service Center, or an advertising campaign produced by Saatchi and Saatchi. Each special machine made by Hitachi is unique and distinct. An advertising campaign for one client at Saatchi and Saatchi differs greatly from advertising campaigns for other clients. Job costing is also used to cost multiple units of a distinct product, such as the costs incurred by Raytheon Corporation to manufacture multiple units of the Patriot missile for the U.S. Department of Defense. Because the products and services are distinct, job-costing systems accumulate costs separately for each product or service.

2. **Process-costing system.** In this system, the cost object is masses of identical or similar units of a product or service. For example, Citibank provides the same service to all its customers when processing customer deposits. Intel provides the same product (say, a Pentium 4 chip) to each of its customers. Customers of Minute Maid all receive the same frozen orange juice product. In each period, process-costing systems divide the total costs of producing an identical or similar product or service by the total number of units produced to obtain a per-unit cost. This per-unit cost is the average unit cost that applies to each of the identical or similar units produced in that period.

Exhibit 4-1 presents examples of job costing and process costing in the service, merchandising, and manufacturing sectors.

These two types of costing systems are best considered as opposite ends of a continuum; in between, one type of system can blur into the other to some degree.

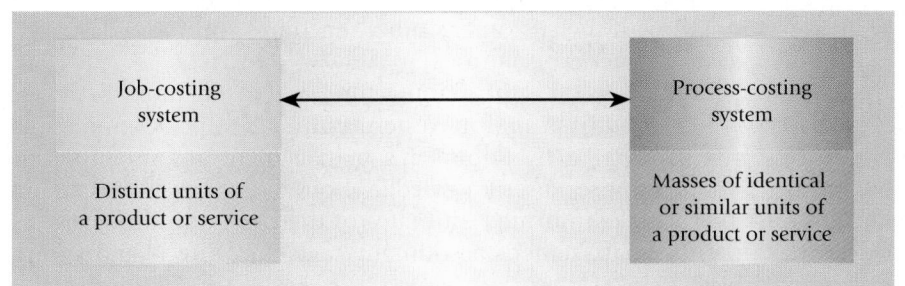

EXHIBIT 4-1

Examples of Job Costing and Process Costing in the Service, Merchandising, and Manufacturing Sectors

	Service Sector	Merchandising Sector	Manufacturing Sector
Job Costing Used	• Audit engagements done by Price WaterhouseCoopers • Consulting engagements done by McKinsey & Co. • Advertising-agency campaigns run by Ogilvy and Mather • Individual legal cases argued by Hale & Dorr • Computer-repair jobs done by CompUSA • Movies produced by Universal Studios	• L. L. Bean sending individual items by mail order • Special promotion of new products by Wal-Mart	• Assembly of individual aircrafts at Boeing • Construction of ships at Litton Industries
Process Costing Used	• Bank-check clearing at Bank of America • Postal delivery (standard items) by U.S. Postal Service	• Grain dealing by Arthur Daniel Midlands • Lumber dealing by Weyerhauser	• Oil refining by Shell Oil • Beverage production by PepsiCo

A company's costing system should be designed to supply managers with information for operating the business. The company's strategy and processes guide management accountants in designing the costing system. The costing system should never dictate the choice of strategy or processes.

Many companies have costing systems that are neither pure job costing nor pure process costing but have elements of both. Costing systems, therefore, need to be tailored to the underlying operations. For example, Kellogg Corporation uses job costing to calculate the total cost to manufacture each of its different and distinct types of products—such as Corn Flakes, Crispix, and Froot Loops—but process costing to calculate the per-unit cost of producing each identical box of Corn Flakes. In this chapter, we focus on job-costing systems. Chapters 17 and 18 discuss process-costing systems.

Actual Costing in Manufacturing

We illustrate job costing using the Robinson example from the vignette at the beginning of the chapter. Robinson uses actual-costing to determine the cost of individual jobs. **Actual costing** is a costing system that traces direct costs to a cost object by using the actual direct-cost rates times the actual quantities of the direct-cost inputs. It allocates indirect costs based on the actual indirect-cost rates times the actual quantities of the cost-allocation bases.

Robinson operates at capacity to manufacture and install specialized machinery for the paper-making industry at its Green Bay, Wisconsin, plant. In its job-costing system, Robinson accumulates costs incurred on a job in different parts of the value chain—for example, manufacturing, marketing, and customer service. To start, we focus on Robinson's manufacturing function (which also includes product installation). To make a machine, Robinson purchases some components from outside suppliers and makes others itself. Each of Robinson's jobs also has a service element: installing a machine at a customer's site, integrating it with the customer's other machines and processes, and ensuring the machine meets customer expectations.

The specific job we will focus on is the manufacture (and installation) of a small pulp machine, which converts wood to pulp, for Western Pulp and Paper Company in 2006. Based on cost estimates prepared by Robinson's management accountants, Robinson prices the job at $15,000. Robinson uses knowledge about its own costs to set a price that will make a profit and to make informed estimates of the costs of future jobs. The next section describes how the management accountant calculates direct- and indirect-cost rates and actual costs.

General Approach to Job Costing

3 **Outline the seven-step approach to job costing** . . . the seven-step approach is used to compute direct and indirect costs of a job

There are seven steps to assigning costs to an individual job—whether in the manufacturing, merchandising, or service sector.

Step 1: Identify the Job That Is the Chosen Cost Object. The cost object in the Robinson Company example is Job WPP 298, manufacturing a pulp machine for the Western Pulp and Paper Company in 2006. Robinson's managers and management accountants gather information to cost jobs through source documents. A **source document** is an original record (such as a labor time card on which an employee's work hours are recorded) that supports journal entries in an accounting system. The main source document for Job WPP 298 is a job-cost record. A **job-cost record**, also called a **job-cost sheet**, records and accumulates all the costs assigned to a specific job, starting when work begins. Exhibit 4-2 shows the job-cost record for the pulp machine ordered by Western Pulp and Paper Company. As we work our way through the various steps in costing Job WPP 298, follow the entries on the job-cost record in Exhibit 4-2.

Step 2: Identify the Direct Costs of the Job. Robinson identifies two direct-manufacturing cost categories: direct materials and direct manufacturing labor.

- **Direct materials:** On the basis of the engineering specifications and drawings provided by Western Pulp, a manufacturing engineer orders materials from the storeroom. The order is placed using a basic source document called a **materials-requisition record**, which contains information about the cost of direct materials used on a specific job and in a specific department. Exhibit 4-3,

EXHIBIT 4-2 **Source Documents at Robinson Company: Job-Cost Record**

JOB-COST RECORD

JOB NO: WPP 298 CUSTOMER: Western Pulp and Paper
Date Started: Feb. 3, 2006 Date Completed: Feb. 28, 2006

DIRECT MATERIALS

Date Received	Materials Requisition No.	Part No.	Quantity Used	Unit Cost	Total Costs
Feb. 3, 2006	2006: 198	MB 468-A	8	$14	$ 112
Feb. 3, 2006	2006: 199	TB 267-F	12	63	756
					•
					•
Total					$ 4,606

DIRECT MANUFACTURING LABOR

Period Covered	Labor-Time Record No.	Employee No.	Hours Used	Hourly Rate	Total Costs
Feb. 3–9, 2006	LT 232	551-87-3076	25	$18	$ 450
Feb. 3–9, 2006	LT 247	287-31-4671	5	19	95
					•
					•
Total					$ 1,579

MANUFACTURING OVERHEAD*

Date	Cost Pool Category	Allocation-Base	Allocation-Base Units Used	Allocation-Base Rate	Total Costs
Dec. 31, 2006	Manufacturing	Direct Manufacturing Labor-Hours	88 hours	$45	$ 3,960
Total					$ 3,960
TOTAL MANUFACTURING COST OF JOB					$10,145

*The Robinson Company uses a single manufacturing-overhead cost pool. The use of multiple overhead cost pools would mean multiple entries in the "Manufacturing Overhead" section of the job-cost record.

EXHIBIT 4-3 **Source Documents at Robinson Company: Materials-Requisition Record and Labor-Time Record**

PANEL A:

MATERIALS-REQUISITION RECORD

Materials-Requisition Record No.: 2006: 198

Job No.: WPP 298 Date: Feb. 3, 2006

Part No.	Part Description	Quantity	Unit Cost	Total Cost
MB 468-A	Metal Brackets	8	$14	$112

Issued By: B. Clyde Date: Feb. 3, 2006

Received By: L. Daley Date: Feb. 3, 2006

PANEL B:

LABOR-TIME RECORD

Labor-Time Record No.: LT 232

Employee Name: G. L. Cook Employee No.: 551-87-3076

Employee Classification Code: Grade 3 Machinist

Hourly Rate: $18

Week Start: Feb. 3, 2006 Week End: Feb. 9, 2006

Job No.	M	T	W	Th	F	S	Su	Total
WPP 298	4	8	3	6	4	0	0	25
JL 256	3	0	4	2	3	0	0	12
Maintenance	1	0	1	0	1	0	0	3
Total	8	8	8	8	8	0	0	40

Supervisor: R. Stuart Date: Feb. 10, 2006

Panel A, shows a materials-requisition record for the Robinson Company. See how the record specifies the job for which the material is requested (WPP 298), the description of the material (Part Number MB 468-A, metal brackets), the actual quantity (8), the actual unit cost ($14), and the actual total cost ($112). The $112 actual total cost also appears on the job-cost record in Exhibit 4-2. If we add the cost of all material requisitions, the total actual direct material cost is $4,606, which is shown on the job-cost record in Exhibit 4-2.

- **Direct manufacturing labor:** The accounting for direct manufacturing labor is similar to the accounting described for direct materials. The source document for direct manufacturing labor is a **labor-time record**, which contains information about the amount of labor time used for a specific job in a specific department. Exhibit 4-3, Panel B, shows a typical weekly labor-time record for a particular employee (G. L. Cook). Each day Cook records the time spent on individual jobs (in this case WPP 298 and JL 256), as well as the time spent on other tasks, such as maintenance of machines or cleaning, that are not related to a specific job.

The 25 hours that Cook spent on Job WPP 298 appears on the job-cost record in Exhibit 4-2 at a cost of $450 (25 hours × $18 per hour). Similarly, the job-cost record for Job JL 256 will carry a cost of $216 (12 hours × $18 per hour). The three hours of time spent on maintenance and cleaning at $18 per hour equals $54. This cost is part of indirect manufacturing costs because it is not traceable to any particular job. This indirect cost is included as part of the manufacturing-overhead cost pool allocated to jobs. The total direct manufacturing labor costs of $1,579 for the pulp machine that appear on the job-cost record in Exhibit 4-2 are the sum of all the direct manufacturing labor costs charged to this job by different employees.

All costs other than direct materials and direct manufacturing labor are classified as indirect costs.

Step 3: **Select the Cost-Allocation Bases to Use for Allocating Indirect Costs to the Job.** Indirect manufacturing costs are costs that are necessary to do a job but that cannot be traced to a specific job. It would be impossible to complete a job without incurring indirect costs such as supervision, manufacturing engineering, utilities, and repairs. Because these costs cannot be traced to a specific job, they must be allocated to all jobs in a systematic way. Different jobs require different quantities of indirect resources. The objective is to allocate the costs of indirect resources in a systematic way to their related jobs.

Companies often use multiple cost-allocation bases to allocate indirect costs (see Global Surveys of Company Practice, p. 103) because different indirect costs have different cost drivers. For example, some indirect costs such as depreciation and repairs of machines are more closely related to

GLOBAL SURVEYS OF COMPANY PRACTICE

Cost-Allocation Bases Used for Manufacturing Overhead

How do companies around the world allocate manufacturing overhead costs to products? The percentages in the following table indicate how frequently particular cost-allocation bases are used in costing systems in six countries. If the reported percentages for a country exceed 100%, that's because many companies surveyed use more than one cost-allocation base.

	United States[a]	Australia[b]	Ireland[c]	Japan[b]	New Zealand[d]	United Kingdom[d]
Direct labor	62%	73%	52%	68%	84%	78%
Machine-hours	12	17	22	27	53	60
Units of production	4	17	28	32	47	55
Direct material cost	5	14	7	36	44	40
Other	17	—	22	—	10	15

As the survey data identifies, a growing global trend is the use of multiple allocation bases for manufacturing overhead. Surveys also indicate that as companies begin to identify activity drivers of manufacturing overhead costs, such as setup hours and inspection hours, more of the manufacturing overhead costs are allocated to products using measures other than direct labor and machine-hours.[e]

[a] Cohen and Paquette, "Management Accounting Practices: Perceptions of Controllers."

[b] Wijewardena and De Zoysa, "A Comparative Analysis of Management Accounting Practices in Australia and Japan: An Empirical Investigation."

[c] Clarke, "Management Accounting Practices in Large Irish Manufacturing Firms."

[d] Lamminmaki and Drury, "A Comparison of New Zealand and British Product-Costing Practices."

[e] Groot, "Activity Based Costing in U.S. and Dutch Food Companies."

Full citations are in Appendix A at the end of the book.

machine-hours. Other indirect costs such as supervision and production support are more closely related to direct manufacturing labor-hours. Robinson, however, chooses direct manufacturing labor-hours as the sole allocation base for linking all indirect manufacturing costs to jobs. That's because, in its labor-intensive environment, Robinson believes that the number of direct manufacturing labor-hours is a good measure of how individual jobs use all the manufacturing overhead resources, such as salaries paid to supervisors, engineers, production support staff, and quality management staff. There is a strong cause-and-effect relationship between the direct manufacturing labor-hours required by an individual job—that's the cause—and the indirect manufacturing resources demanded by that job—that's the effect. In 2006, Robinson records 27,000 actual direct manufacturing labor-hours.

Step 4: Identify the Indirect Costs Associated with Each Cost-Allocation Base. Robinson believes that a single cost-allocation base—direct manufacturing labor-hours—can be used to allocate indirect manufacturing costs to jobs. Consequently, Robinson creates a single cost pool called manufacturing overhead costs. This pool represents all indirect costs of the Green Bay Manufacturing Department that are difficult to trace directly to individual jobs. In 2006, actual manufacturing overhead costs total $1,215,000.

As we saw in steps 3 and 4, managers first identify cost-allocation bases and then identify the costs related to each cost-allocation base, not the other way around. That's because managers must first understand the cost driver, the reasons why costs are being incurred (for example, for setting up machines, moving materials, or designing jobs), before they can determine the costs associated with each cost driver. The reason for not doing step 4 before step 3 is that there is nothing to guide the creation of the cost pools. As a result, the cost pools created may not have cost-allocation bases that are cost drivers of the costs in the cost pool.

Step 5: Compute the Rate per Unit of Each Cost-Allocation Base Used to Allocate Indirect Costs to the Job. For each cost pool, the actual **indirect-cost rate** is calculated by dividing total indirect costs in the pool (determined in step 4) by the total quantity of the cost-allocation base (determined in step 3). Robinson calculates the allocation rate for its single manufacturing overhead cost pool as follows:

$$\text{Actual manufacturing overhead rate} = \frac{\text{Actual manufacturing overhead costs}}{\text{Actual total quantity of cost-allocation base}}$$

$$= \frac{\$1{,}215{,}000}{27{,}000 \text{ direct manufacturing labor-hours}}$$

$$= \$45 \text{ per direct manufacturing labor-hour}$$

Step 6: Compute the Indirect Costs Allocated to the Job. The indirect costs of a job are computed by multiplying the actual quantity of each different allocation base (one allocation base for each cost pool) associated with the job by the indirect-cost rate of each allocation base (computed in step 5). To make the pulp machine, Robinson uses 88 direct manufacturing labor-hours, the cost-allocation base for its only manufacturing overhead cost pool (out of the 27,000 total direct manufacturing labor-hours for 2006). Manufacturing overhead costs allocated to the pulp machine job equal \$3,960 (\$45 per direct manufacturing labor-hour × 88 hours) and appear on the WPP 298 job-cost record in Exhibit 4-2.

Step 7: Compute the Total Cost of the Job by Adding All Direct and Indirect Costs Assigned to the Job. Exhibit 4-2 shows that the total manufacturing costs of the Western Pulp job are \$10,145.

Direct manufacturing costs		
Direct materials	\$4,606	
Direct manufacturing labor	1,579	\$ 6,185
Manufacturing overhead costs		
(\$45 per direct manuf. labor-hour × 88 hours)		3,960
Total manufacturing costs of job		\$10,145

Recall, Robinson was paid \$15,000 for the job. With that revenue, the actual-costing system shows a gross margin of \$4,855 (\$15,000 – \$10,145) and a gross-margin percentage of 32.4% (\$4,855 ÷ \$15,000 = 0.324).

Robinson's manufacturing managers and sales managers can use the gross-margin and gross-margin percentage calculations to compare the profitability of different jobs (see Concepts in Action on p. 106) to try to understand the reasons why some jobs show low profitability: Have direct materials been wasted? Was direct manufacturing labor too high? Were there ways to improve the efficiency of these jobs? Were these jobs simply underpriced? Job-cost analysis provides the information needed for judging the performance of manufacturing and sales managers and for making future improvements. (See Focus on Values and Behaviors, p. 107.)

Exhibit 4-4 is an overview of Robinson Company's job-costing system. This exhibit represents the concepts comprising the five building blocks—cost object, direct costs of a cost object, indirect costs of a cost object, indirect-cost pool, and cost-allocation base—of job-costing systems. Costing-system overviews such as Exhibit 4-4 are important learning tools. We urge you to sketch one when you need to understand a costing system in manufacturing, merchandising, or service companies. (The symbols in Exhibit 4-4 are used consistently in the costing-system overviews presented in this book. A triangle always identifies a direct cost; a rectangle, the indirect-cost pool; and an octagon, the cost-allocation base.) Note the parallel between the overview diagram and the cost of the pulp machine job described in step 7. Exhibit 4-4 shows two direct-cost categories (direct materials and direct manufacturing labor) and one indirect-cost category (manufacturing overhead) used to allocate indirect costs. The costs in step 7 also have three dollar amounts, each corresponding respectively to the two direct-cost and one indirect-cost categories.

Exhibit 4-4 presents concepts that appear throughout this book in a similar format. In the Robinson Company example, the cost object (a pulp machine for Western Pulp and Paper Company) has two direct costs (direct materials and direct manufacturing labor) and one indirect cost (manufacturing overhead) allocated on the basis of direct manufacturing labor-hours.

EXHIBIT 4-4

Job-Costing Overview for Determining Manufacturing Costs of Jobs at Robinson Company

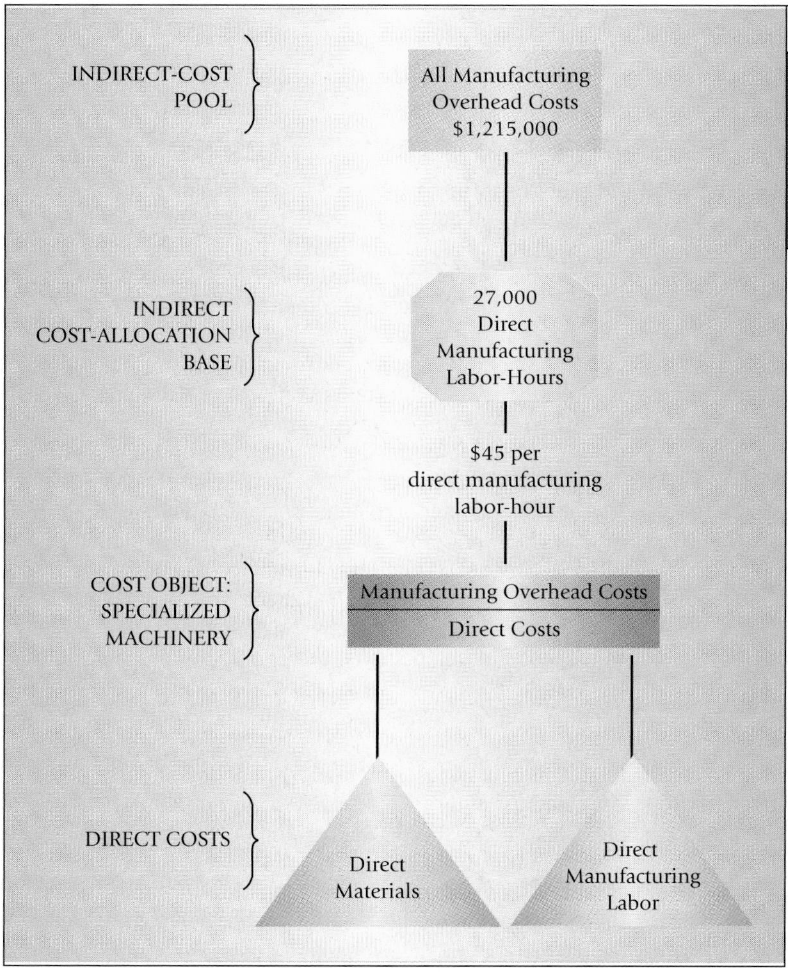

The Role of Technology

To improve the efficiency of their operations, managers use costing information about products and jobs to control materials, labor, and overhead costs. Modern information technology provides managers with quick and accurate product-cost information, making it easier to manage and control jobs. For example, in many costing systems, source documents exist only in the form of computer records. We next describe bar coding and other forms of online information recording that reduce human intervention and improve the accuracy of the records of materials and labor time for individual jobs.

Consider, for example, direct materials charged to jobs for product-costing purposes. Managers control these costs as materials are purchased and used. Using Electronic Data Interchange (EDI) technology, companies like Robinson order materials from their suppliers by clicking a few keys on a computer keyboard. EDI, an electronic computer link between a company and its suppliers, ensures that the order is transmitted quickly and accurately with minimum paperwork and costs. A bar code scanner records the receipt of incoming materials. The computer matches the receipt with the order, prints out a check to the supplier, and records the material received. When an operator on the production floor transmits a request for materials via a computer terminal, the computer prepares a materials-requisition record, instantly recording the issue of materials in the materials and job-cost records. Each day, the computer sums the materials-requisition records charged to a particular job or manufacturing department. A performance report is then prepared comparing budgeted costs and actual costs of direct materials. Direct material usage can be reported hourly—if the benefits exceed the cost of such frequent reporting.

Similarly, information about manufacturing labor is obtained as employees log into computer terminals and key in the job numbers, their employee numbers, and start and end times of their work on different jobs. The computer automatically prints the labor-time record and, using hourly rates stored for each employee, calculates the labor costs of

CONCEPTS IN ACTION

Job Costing on the Joint Strike Fighter Project

Northrop Grumman, Inc., is a leading provider of systems and technologies for the U.S. Department of Defense. Competitive bidding processes and increased public and congressional oversight make understanding costs critical in pricing decisions as well as in winning and retaining government contracts. Each job must be estimated individually because the unique end products demand different amounts of Northrop Grumman's resources.

In 2001, the team of Northrop Grumman, Lockheed Martin, and BAE Systems was awarded the System Design and Demonstration contract for the Joint Strike Fighter (JSF) project. This project, worth $200 billion over seven years, will create a family of supersonic, multi-role fighter airplanes designed for the U.S. Air Force, Navy, and Marine Corps, as well as the United Kingdom's Royal Air Force and Royal Navy. This project has five primary stages: (1) conceptualization, (2) design and review, (3) manufacturing, (4) assembly, and (5) testing and delivery. In the conceptualization phase, detailed plans for each aircraft model are created. Technologies for these plans are researched, developed, and approved during the design and review phase. Subsequently, thousands of components, created by the primary contractors and various subcontractors, are manufactured, assembled in multiple locations, and tested prior to delivery to the purchasing organizations. If they do not meet required specifications during testing, the fighter jets are reworked before delivery.

To ensure proper allocation and accounting of resources, JSF project managers use a job-costing system. The system first calculates the budgeted cost of direct materials and direct-labor hours for the project. It then allocates all overhead costs (supervisory salaries, rent, depreciation, materials handling, and so on) to jobs using budgeted direct material costs and direct-labor hours as allocation bases. Northrop Grumman's job-costing system allows managers to assign costs to processes and projects. Northrop Grumman continually estimates the profitability of these projects based on the percentage of work completed and the related revenue earned. Managers use the job-costing system to actively manage costs, while program representatives from the Department of Defense and members of Congress have access to clear, concise, and transparent costing data. Therefore, Northrop Grumman's job-costing system improves cost identification and management for all Department of Defense projects.

Source: Conversations with Stephen Bryant, Northrop Grumman, Inc., in October and November 2003.

individual jobs. Information technology also provides managers with instantaneous feedback to help control manufacturing overhead, jobs in process, jobs completed, and jobs shipped and installed at customer sites.

Time Period Used to Compute Indirect-Cost Rates

Robinson Company computes indirect-cost rates in step 5 of the job-costing system (p. 104) on an annual basis. Why does Robinson wait until the end of the fiscal year (annual accounting period) to calculate indirect-cost rates? Why doesn't Robinson calculate indirect-cost rates each week? or each month? Using weekly rates or monthly rates, Robinson would be able to calculate actual costs of jobs much earlier and not have to wait until the end of the fiscal year. There are two reasons for using longer periods, such as a year, to calculate indirect-cost rates. One reason is related to the dollar amount in the numerator. The other reason is related to the quantity in the denominator of the calculation.

1. **The numerator reason (indirect-cost pool).** The shorter the period, the greater the influence of seasonal patterns on the amount of costs. For example, if indirect-cost rates were calculated each month, costs of heating (included in the numerator) would be charged to production only during the winter months. But an annual period incorporates the effects of all four seasons into a single, annual indirect-cost rate.

FOCUS ON VALUES AND BEHAVIORS

ENRON'S CATASTROPHIC MISTAKES

Management accountants work as strategic business partners of managers. As members of cross-functional teams, management accountants design the job-costing systems underlying operations to help managers make strategic decisions and implement strategy. After all, job-costing systems help managers understand the profitability of different projects. Once the systems are in place, management accountants educate managers in how to use them.

Sometimes, however, there are catastrophic failures. Consider the high-profile bankruptcy of Enron, which, at the time it failed, was the seventh-largest corporation in the United States. Enron gave its managers powerful monetary incentives. To take advantage of these incentives, managers manipulated the numbers on which compensation was based. In its energy services division, executives inflated contract values that were derived from internal estimates. In overseas trading projects—for example, in India and Brazil—executives booked questionable profits. Yet it was the substantial off– balance sheet partnerships headed by CFO Andrew Fastow and propped up by an inflated stock price that ultimately caused the loss of thousands of jobs and billions of dollars in market value. The problems at Enron occurred because of faulty strategies, poor investments, and weak financial controls. To make matters worse, management at Enron attempted to conceal these problems with questionable accounting.

Enron's accounting and control system was poorly implemented. When questioned by the media about Enron's business model, operations, and financial results, senior executives refused to answer and claimed that anyone who asked questions didn't "get it." When Enron declared bankruptcy on December 2, 2001, senior officials responsible for its demise finally had to account for their actions. In fact, CFO Andrew Fastow has been sentenced to 10 years in prison, and Ken Lay, former chairman and CEO, has been indicted. Lay pleaded not guilty to all charges, which included lying to the public, investors, and Enron employees and making false statements. Unfortunately, for thousands of employees who lost their jobs and their savings, it was too late.

Sources: *Nelson D. Schwartz, "Enron Fallout: Wide But Not Deep,"* Fortune, *December 9, 2001; Bethany McLean, "Why Enron Went Bust,"* Fortune, *December 9, 2001. www.money.cnn.com/2004/07/08/news/newsmakers/lay; see article dated July 12, 2004 by Krysten Crawford.*

Levels of total indirect costs are also affected by nonseasonal erratic costs. Examples of nonseasonal erratic costs include costs incurred in a particular month that benefit operations during future months, costs of repairs and maintenance of equipment, and costs of vacation and holiday pay. If monthly indirect-cost rates were calculated, jobs done in a month with high, nonseasonal, erratic costs would be loaded with these costs. Pooling all indirect costs together over the course of a full year and calculating a single annual indirect-cost rate helps to smooth some of the erratic bumps in costs associated with shorter periods.

2. **The denominator reason (quantity of the allocation base).** Another reason for longer periods is the need to spread monthly fixed indirect costs over fluctuating levels of monthly output. Some indirect costs may be variable each month with respect to the cost-allocation base (for example, supplies), whereas other indirect costs are fixed each month (for example, property taxes and rent).

Suppose a company deliberately schedules its production to correspond with a highly seasonal sales pattern. Assume the following mix of variable indirect costs (such as supplies, repairs, and indirect manufacturing labor) and fixed indirect costs (plant depreciation and engineering support):

	Indirect Costs			Direct Manufacturing Labor-Hours	Allocation Rate per Direct Manufacturing Labor-Hour
	Variable (1)	Fixed (2)	Total (3)	(4)	(5) = (3) ÷ (4)
High-output month	$40,000	$60,000	$100,000	3,200	$31.25
Low-output month	10,000	60,000	70,000	800	87.50

In this example, the change in the indirect cost-allocation rate arises solely because of fixed costs. Variable cost per unit = $12.50 at both 3,200 and 800 hours. However, fixed cost per unit = $18.75 at 3,200 hours and = $75.00 at 800 hours. Fluctuations in the denominator affect only the fixed-cost portion of the cost rate.

You can see that variable indirect costs change in proportion to changes in direct manufacturing labor-hours. Therefore, the variable indirect-cost rate is the same in both the high-output months and the low-output months ($40,000 ÷ 3,200 labor-hours = $12.50 per labor-hour; $10,000 ÷ 800 labor-hours = $12.50 per labor-hour). If the variable indirect-cost rate is higher in high-output months (because of overtime payments or excessive machine maintenance caused by high output), variable indirect costs should be allocated at a higher rate to production in high-output months relative to production in low-output months. Consider now the fixed costs of $60,000. The fixed costs cause monthly total indirect-cost rates to vary considerably—from $31.25 per hour to $87.50 per hour. Few managers believe that identical jobs done in different months should be allocated indirect-cost charges per hour that differ so significantly ($87.50 ÷ $31.25 = 2.80, or 280%) because of fixed costs. In our example, management chooses a specific level of capacity based on a time horizon far beyond a mere month. An average, annualized rate based on the relationship of total annual indirect costs to the total annual level of output will smooth the effect of monthly variations in output levels.

The calculation of monthly indirect-cost rates is affected by the number of Monday-to-Friday workdays in a month. The number of workdays per month varies from 20 to 23 during a year. If separate rates are computed each month, jobs in February, having the fewest workdays in a month, would bear a greater share of indirect costs (such as depreciation and property taxes) than jobs in other months. Many managers believe such results to be an unrepresentative and unreasonable way to assign indirect costs to jobs. An annual period reduces the effect that the number of working days per month has on unit costs. In addition, setting annual overhead rates once a year saves management time that would be needed 12 times per year if overhead rates were set monthly.

Normal Costing

4

Distinguish actual costing

. . . actual costing uses actual indirect-cost rates

from normal costing

. . . normal costing uses budgeted indirect-cost rates

The difficulty of calculating actual indirect-cost rates on a weekly or monthly basis means managers cannot calculate the actual costs of jobs as they are completed. However, managers want a close approximation of the manufacturing costs of various jobs regularly during the year, not just at the end of the fiscal year. Managers want manufacturing costs (and other costs, such as marketing costs) for ongoing uses, including pricing jobs, monitoring and managing costs, and preparing interim financial statements. Because of the benefits of immediate access to job costs, few companies wait until the *actual* manufacturing overhead is finally known (at year-end) before allocating overhead costs to compute job costs. Instead, a *predetermined* or *budgeted* indirect-cost rate is calculated for each cost pool at the beginning of a fiscal year, and overhead costs are allocated to jobs as work progresses. For the numerator and denominator reasons already described, for each cost pool, the **budgeted indirect-cost rate** is computed as follows:

$$\text{Budgeted indirect-cost rate} = \frac{\text{Budgeted annual indirect costs}}{\text{Budgeted annual quantity of the cost-allocation base}}$$

Using budgeted indirect-cost rates gives rise to normal costing.

Normal costing is a costing system that traces direct costs to a cost object by using the actual direct-cost rates times the actual quantities of the direct-cost inputs and that allocates indirect costs based on the *budgeted* indirect-cost rates times the actual quantities of the cost-allocation bases. Both actual costing and normal costing trace direct costs to jobs in the same way. The actual quantities and actual rates of direct materials and direct manufacturing labor used on a job are known from the source documents as the work is done. The only difference between actual costing and normal costing is that actual costing uses *actual* indirect-cost rates, whereas normal costing uses *budgeted* indirect-cost rates to cost jobs. Exhibit 4-5 distinguishes between actual costing and normal costing.

We illustrate normal costing for the Robinson Company example using the seven-step procedure. The following budgeted data for 2006 are for its manufacturing operations:

	Budget
Total manufacturing overhead costs	$1,120,000
Total direct manufacturing labor-hours	28,000

Steps 1 and 2 are exactly as before: Step 1 identifies WPP 298 as the cost object; Step 2 calculates actual direct material costs of $4,606, and actual direct manufacturing labor costs of $1,579. Recall from Step 3 that Robinson uses a single cost-allocation base, direct

	Actual Costing	Normal Costing
Direct Costs	*Actual direct-cost rates* × actual quantities of direct-cost inputs	*Actual direct-cost rates* × actual quantities of direct-cost inputs
Indirect Costs	*Actual indirect-cost rates* × actual quantities of cost-allocation bases	*Budgeted indirect-cost rates* × actual quantities of cost-allocation bases

EXHIBIT 4-5

Actual Costing and Normal Costing Systems

manufacturing labor-hours, to allocate all manufacturing overhead costs to jobs. The budgeted quantity of direct manufacturing labor-hours for 2006 is 28,000 hours. In Step 4, Robinson groups all the indirect manufacturing costs into a single manufacturing overhead cost pool. In Step 5, the budgeted manufacturing overhead rate for 2006 is calculated as:

$$\text{Budgeted manufacturing overhead rate} = \frac{\text{Budgeted manufacturing overhead costs}}{\text{Budgeted total quantity of cost-allocation base}}$$

$$= \frac{\$1{,}120{,}000}{\text{28,000 direct manufacturing labor-hours}}$$

$$= \$40 \text{ per direct manufacturing labor-hour}$$

In Step 6, under a normal-costing system,

$$\begin{array}{c}\text{Manufacturing overhead costs}\\ \text{allocated to WPP 298}\end{array} = \begin{array}{c}\text{Budgeted manufacturing}\\ \text{overhead rate}\end{array} \times \begin{array}{c}\textit{Actual} \text{ quantity of direct}\\ \text{manufacturing labor-hours}\end{array}$$

$$= \begin{array}{c}\text{\$40 per direct manufacturing}\\ \text{labor-hour}\end{array} \times \begin{array}{c}\text{88 direct manufacturing}\\ \text{labor-hours}\end{array}$$

$$= \$3{,}520$$

In Step 7, the cost of the job under normal costing is $9,705, calculated as

Direct manufacturing costs		
Direct materials	$4,606	
Direct manufacturing labor	1,579	$6,185
Manufacturing overhead costs		
($40 × 88 actual direct manufacturing labor-hours)		3,520
Total manufacturing costs of job		$9,705

The manufacturing cost of the WPP 298 job is lower by $440 under normal costing ($9,705) than it is under actual costing ($10,145) because the budgeted indirect-cost rate is $40 per hour, whereas the actual indirect-cost rate is $45 per hour. That is, ($45 – $40) × 88 actual direct manufacturing labor-hours = $440.

As we discussed previously, manufacturing costs of a job are available much earlier under a normal-costing system. Consequently, Robinson's manufacturing and sales managers can evaluate the profitability of different jobs, the efficiency with which the jobs are done, and the pricing of different jobs as soon as the jobs are completed, while the experience is still fresh in everyone's mind. Another advantage of normal costing is that corrective actions can be implemented much sooner.

A Normal Job-Costing System in Manufacturing

5

Track the flow of costs in a job-costing system

. . . from purchase of materials to sale of finished goods

We now explain how a normal job-costing system operates in manufacturing. Continuing with the Robinson Company example, the following illustration considers events that occurred in February 2006.

General Ledger and Subsidiary Ledgers

You know by this point that a job-costing system has a separate job-cost record for each job. A summary of the job-cost record is typically found in a subsidiary ledger. The general ledger account Work-in-Process Control presents the total of these separate job-cost records pertaining to all unfinished jobs. The job-cost records and Work-in-Process Control account track job costs from when jobs are started until they are completed.

Think of subsidiary ledger accounts as "little" T-accounts that support the general ledger control T-account; for example, individual job-cost records are the support for Work-in-Process Control.

Exhibit 4-6 shows T-account relationships for Robinson Company's general ledger. The general ledger gives a "bird's-eye view" of the costing system. The amounts shown in Exhibit 4-6 are based on the transactions that follow. The explanation of transactions shows the subsidiary ledgers and the basic source documents that contain the underlying details—the "worm's-eye view." As you go through each of the following T-accounts, use Exhibit 4-6 as a road map to see how the various entries being made come together. General ledger accounts with "Control" in the titles (for example, Materials Control and Accounts Payable Control) have underlying subsidiary ledgers that contain additional details, such as each type of material in inventory and individual suppliers that Robinson must pay. The sum of all entries in underlying subsidiary ledgers equals the total amounts in the corresponding general ledger control accounts.

Software programs process the transactions in most accounting systems. Some programs make general ledger entries simultaneously with entries in the subsidiary ledger accounts. Other software programs make general ledger entries at, say, weekly or monthly intervals, with entries in the subsidiary ledger accounts made more frequently. The Robinson Company makes entries in its subsidiary ledger when transactions occur and then makes entries in its general ledger on a monthly basis.

A general ledger should be viewed as only one of many tools that assist management in planning and control. To control operations, managers use not only the source documents used to record amounts in the subsidiary ledgers, but also nonfinancial variables such as the percentage of jobs requiring rework.

EXHIBIT 4-6 **Manufacturing Job-Costing System Using Normal Costing: Diagram of General Ledger Relationships for February 2006**

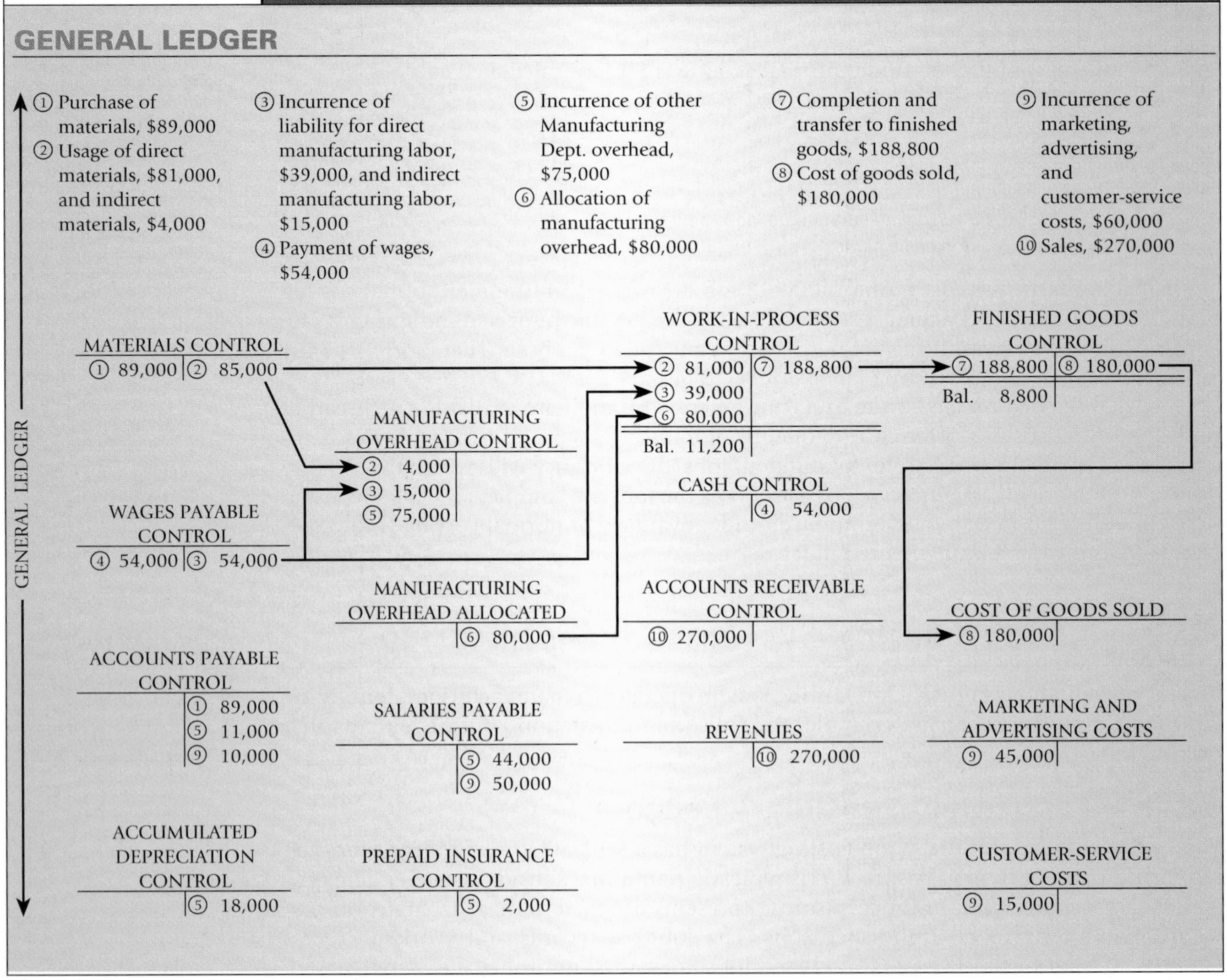

Explanations of Transactions

The following transaction-by-transaction analysis explains how a job-costing system serves the dual goals of product costing and department responsibility and control. These transactions track stages (a) through (d) from the purchase of materials and other manufacturing inputs, to conversion to work-in-process and finished goods, to the sale of finished goods:

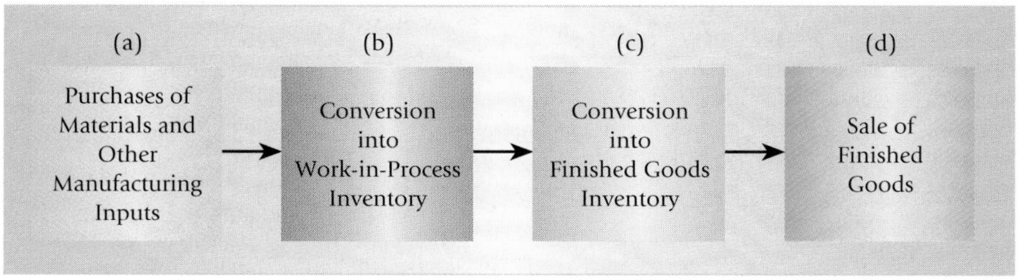

This graphic, which shows the *physical flow* of product through a manufacturing process, clarifies the economic transactions occurring. To more easily understand the first eight journal entries that follow, link the discussion of each entry to the graphic. For example, transaction 1 illustrates stage (a).

For each transaction, we discuss the accounts affected, the supporting records in the subsidiary ledger, the journal entry, and the posting to the general ledger.

1. *Transaction:* Purchases of materials (direct and indirect) on credit, $89,000.

   Account Analysis: The asset Materials Control is increased (debited) by $89,000, and the liability Accounts Payable Control is increased (credited) by $89,000.

   Subsidiary Records: The subsidiary ledger for materials at Robinson Company—called *Materials Records*—keeps a continuous record of quantity received, quantity issued to jobs, and inventory balances for each type of material. Panel A of Exhibit 4-7 shows the Materials Record for Metal Brackets (Part No. MB 468-A). In many companies, the source documents supporting the receipt and issue of materials are scanned into a computer. Software programs then automatically update the Materials Records and make all the necessary accounting entries in the subsidiary and general ledgers. The following journal entry accounts for all the $89,000 of February 2006 purchase transactions in the materials subsidiary ledger:

Journal Entry:	Materials Control	89,000	
	Accounts Payable Control		89,000

   Post to General Ledger (Exhibit 4-6):

   Materials Control

Debit	Credit
① 89,000	

   Accounts Payable Control

Debit	Credit
	① 89,000

   Materials Control includes all materials purchases, whether the items are classified as direct or indirect costs of products.

2. *Transaction:* Materials sent to the manufacturing floor: direct materials, $81,000, and indirect materials, $4,000.

   Account Analysis: The asset Work-in-Process Control account is increased (debited) by $81,000, and the Manufacturing Overhead Control account is increased (debited) by $4,000. The asset Materials Control is decreased (credited) by $85,000. The idea is that material costs "attach" to the work in process, thereby making the work in process a more valuable asset. Responsibility is fixed by using materials-requisition records as a basis for charging departments for the materials issued to them.

   Subsidiary Records: As direct materials are used, they are recorded as issued in the Materials Records (see Exhibit 4-7, Panel A, for a record of the Metal Brackets issued for the Western Pulp machine job). Direct materials are also charged to individual job records, which are the subsidiary ledger accounts for the Work-in-Process Control account in the general ledger. For example, the metal brackets used in the Western Pulp machine job appear as direct material costs of $112 in the subsidiary ledger under the job-cost record for WPP 298 (Exhibit 4-8, Panel A). The cost of direct materials used across all job-cost records for February 2006 is $81,000 (Exhibit 4-8, Panel A).

EXHIBIT 4-7 Subsidiary Ledger for Materials, Labor, and Manufacturing Department Overhead[1]

PANEL A: Materials Records by Type of Materials

Metal Brackets Part No. MB 468-A

Received	Issued					Balance
	Date	Req. No.	Qty.	Rate	Amt.	
①	2-3	2006: 198	8	$14	$112	
		②				

① ← Copies of invoices or receiving reports

② ← Copies of materials-requisition records

Total cost of all types of materials received in February, $89,000

Total cost of all types of materials issued in February, $85,000

PANEL B: Labor Records by Employee

G. L. Cook Empl. No. 551-87-3076

Week Endg.	Job No.	Hours Worked	Rate	Amt.
2-9	WPP 298	25	$18	$450
	JL 256	12	18	216
	Mntnce.	3	18	54
				$720
2-16		③		

③ ← Copies of labor-time record

Total cost of all direct and indirect manufacturing labor incurred in February, $54,000 ($39,000 + $15,000)

PANEL C: Manufacturing Department Overhead Records by Month

February 2006

Indir. Matr. Issued	Indir. Manuf. Labor	Supervn. & Eng.	Plant Utilities	Plant Deprn.	Plant Ins.
②	③	⑤	⑤	⑤	⑤
$4,000	$15,000	$44,000	$11,000	$18,000	$2,000

② ← Copies of materials requisitions

③ ← Manuf. labor-time record or payroll analysis

⑤ ← Payroll analysis invoices, special authorizations

Other manufacturing overhead costs incurred in February, $75,000

[1]The arrows show how the supporting documentation (for example, copies of materials requisition records) results in the journal entry number shown in circles (for example, journal entry number 2).

As indirect materials (for example, lubricants) are used, they are charged to the Manufacturing Department overhead records, which comprise the subsidiary ledger for Manufacturing Overhead Control (Exhibit 4-7, Panel C). The Manufacturing Department overhead records accumulate actual costs in individual overhead categories by each indirect-cost-pool account in the general ledger. Recall that Robinson has only one indirect-cost pool: Manufacturing Overhead. The cost of indirect materials used is not added directly to individual job records. Instead, the cost of these indirect materials is allocated to individual job records as a part of manufacturing overhead (transaction 6, which follows). The following journal entry accounts for all the February 2006 requisitions posted in the materials subsidiary ledger for direct materials ($81,000) and indirect materials ($4,000).

Journal Entry:			
	Work-in-Process Control	81,000	
	Manufacturing Overhead Control	4,000	
	Materials Control		85,000

Post to General Ledger (Exhibit 4-6):

Materials Control

①	89,000	②	85,000

Work-in-Process Control

②	81,000		

Manufacturing Overhead Control

②	4,000		

3. *Transaction:* Total manufacturing payroll incurred for February: direct, $39,000; indirect, $15,000.

EXHIBIT 4-8 **Subsidiary Ledger for Individual Jobs**[1]

PANEL A: Work-in-Process Inventory Records by Jobs

Job No. WPP 298

In-Process					Completed		Balance	
Date	Direct Materials	Direct Manuf. Labor	Allocated Manuf. Overhead	Total Cost	Date	Total Cost	Date	Total Cost
2-3	$ 112			$ 112				
2-9		$ 450		$ 450				
	•	•		•				
2-28	$4,606	$1,579	$3,520	$9,705	2-28	$9,705	2-28	$0
	(2)	(3)	(6)			(7)		

Sources: Copies of materials-requisition records (2); Copies of labor-time records (3); Budgeted rate × actual direct manuf. labor-hours (6); Completed job-cost record (7)

Total cost of direct materials issued to all jobs in Feb., $81,000

Total cost of direct manuf. labor used on all jobs in Feb., $39,000

Total manuf. overhead allocated to all jobs in Feb., $80,000

Total cost of all jobs completed and transferred to finished goods in Feb., $188,800

PANEL B: Finished Goods Inventory Records by Job

Job No. WPP 298

Received		Issued		Balance	
Date	Amt.	Date	Amt.	Date	Amt.
2-28	$9,705	2-28	$9,705	2-28	$0
	(7)		(8)		

Sources: Completed job-cost record (7); Costed sales invoice (8)

Total cost of all jobs transferred to finished goods in Feb., $188,800

Total cost of all jobs sold and invoiced in Feb., $180,000

[1]The arrows show how the supporting documentation (for example, copies of materials requisition records) results in the journal entry number shown in circles (for example, journal entry number 2).

Account Analysis: The asset Work-in-Process Control is increased (debited) by the direct manufacturing labor amount of $39,000, and Manufacturing Overhead Control is increased (debited) by the $15,000 of indirect manufacturing labor. The liability Wages Payable Control is increased (credited) by $54,000. Manufacturing labor costs increase Work-in-Process Control because these costs increase the cost of the work-in-process asset. Manufacturing labor helps to transform one asset—direct materials—into another asset—work in process—and then into another asset—finished goods.

Subsidiary Records: Labor-time records (see Exhibit 4-7, Panel B) are used to trace direct manufacturing labor to individual jobs and to accumulate the indirect manufacturing labor in Manufacturing Department overhead records (Exhibit 4-7, Panel C). The subsidiary ledger for employee labor records shows the $720 of wages owed to G. L. Cook, Employee No. 551-87-3076, for the week ending February 9. The sum of total wages owed to all employees for February 2006 is $54,000. The job-cost record for WPP 298 shows direct manufacturing labor costs of $450 for the time Cook spent on the Western Pulp machine job (Exhibit 4-8, Panel A). Total direct manufacturing labor costs recorded in all job-cost records (the subsidiary ledger for Work-in-Process Control) for February 2006 is $39,000. G. L. Cook's employee record shows $54 for maintenance, which is an indirect manufacturing labor cost. The total indirect manufacturing labor costs of $15,000 for February 2006 appear in the Manufacturing Department overhead records in the subsidiary ledger (Exhibit 4-7, Panel C). These costs, by definition, are not traced to an individual job. They are instead allocated to individual jobs as a part of manufacturing overhead (transaction 6, which follows). The journal entry for all the February 2006 manufacturing payroll for direct manufacturing labor ($39,000) and indirect manufacturing labor ($15,000) is

Journal Entry:	Work-in-Process Control	39,000	
	Manufacturing Overhead Control	15,000	
	Wages Payable Control		54,000

Post to General Ledger (Exhibit 4-6):

Wages Payable Control

		③	54,000

Work-in-Process Control

②	81,000		
③	39,000		

Manufacturing Overhead Control

②	4,000		
③	15,000		

4. *Transaction:* Payment of total manufacturing payroll for February, $54,000. (Because we are focusing on job-costing issues, payroll withholdings from employees, including taxes, are ignored in this example.) For convenience here, wages payable for the month are assumed to be completely paid at month's end.

   Account Analysis: The liability Wages Payable Control is decreased (debited) by $54,000, and the asset Cash Control is decreased (credited) by $54,000.

   Subsidiary Records: The subsidiary records for labor, overhead, and individual jobs are unaffected by this transaction.

Journal Entry:	Wages Payable Control	54,000	
	Cash Control		54,000

Post to General Ledger (Exhibit 4-6):

Wages Payable Control

④	54,000	③	54,000

Cash Control

		④	54,000

Utilities, depreciation, and insurance are debited to Manufacturing Overhead Control only if they are related to *producing the products*, and they are considered to be inventoriable costs (assets) until the products are sold. In contrast, utilities for a sales office, depreciation on executives' automobiles, and insurance on those automobiles are period costs and therefore are not part of manufacturing overhead.

5. *Transaction:* Additional manufacturing overhead costs incurred during February, $75,000. These costs consist of engineering and supervisory salaries, $44,000; plant utilities and repairs, $11,000; plant depreciation, $18,000; and plant insurance, $2,000.

   Account Analysis: The indirect-cost account, Manufacturing Overhead Control, is increased (debited) by $75,000. The liability, Salaries Payable Control, is increased (credited) by $44,000; the liability, Accounts Payable Control, is increased (credited) by $11,000; the asset Equipment Control is decreased (credited) by $18,000 by means of a contra (related) asset account, Accumulated Depreciation Control; and the asset Prepaid Insurance Control is decreased (credited) by $2,000.

   Subsidiary Records: The detail of each of these costs is entered in the appropriate columns of the individual Manufacturing Department overhead records that make up the subsidiary ledger for Manufacturing Overhead Control (see Exhibit 4-7, Panel C). The source documents for these entries include invoices (for example, a utility bill) and special schedules (for example, a depreciation schedule) from the responsible accounting officer. The following journal entry accounts for all $75,000 of February 2006 overhead transactions in the Manufacturing Department overhead records:

Journal Entry:	Manufacturing Overhead Control	75,000	
	Salaries Payable Control		44,000
	Accounts Payable Control		11,000
	Accumulated Depreciation Control		18,000
	Prepaid Insurance Control		2,000

Post to General Ledger (Exhibit 4-6):

Accounts Payable Control

	① 89,000
	⑤ 11,000

Manufacturing Overhead Control

② 4,000	
③ 15,000	
⑤ 75,000	

Accumulated Depreciation Control

	⑤ 18,000

Prepaid Insurance Control

	⑤ 2,000

Salaries Payable Control

	⑤ 44,000

6. *Transaction:* Allocation of manufacturing overhead to jobs, $80,000.

Account Analysis: The asset Work-in-Process Control is increased (debited) by $80,000. Manufacturing Overhead Control is, in effect, decreased (credited) by $80,000 via its contra (related) account, Manufacturing Overhead Allocated. **Manufacturing overhead allocated**—also called **manufacturing overhead applied**—is the amount of manufacturing overhead costs allocated to individual jobs based on the budgeted rate multiplied by actual quantity used of the allocation base. Manufacturing overhead allocated contains all manufacturing overhead costs. They are assigned to jobs using a cost-allocation base because these costs cannot be traced specifically to jobs in an economically feasible way. Under Robinson's normal-costing system, the budgeted manufacturing overhead rate for 2006 is $40 per direct manufacturing labor-hour.

Subsidiary Records: The job-cost record for each individual job in the subsidiary ledger will be debited for manufacturing overhead allocated for the actual direct manufacturing labor-hours used in that job. For example, the job-cost record for Job WPP 298 (Exhibit 4-8, Panel A) shows Manufacturing Overhead Allocated of $3,520 (budgeted rate of $40 per labor-hour × 88 actual direct manufacturing labor-hours used). We assume 2,000 actual direct manufacturing labor-hours were used for all jobs in February 2006, resulting in a total manufacturing overhead allocation of $40 per labor-hour × 2,000 direct manufacturing labor-hours = $80,000.

Journal Entry:		Debit	Credit
	Work-in-Process Control	80,000	
	Manufacturing Overhead Allocated		80,000

Post to General Ledger (Exhibit 4-6):

Manufacturing Overhead Allocated

	⑥ 80,000

Work-in-Process Control

② 81,000	
③ 39,000	
⑥ 80,000	

Keep in mind the distinct difference between transactions 5 and 6. In transaction 5, actual overhead costs incurred throughout the month are added (debited) to the Manufacturing Overhead Control account and the subsidiary manufacturing overhead records. These costs are not debited to Work-in-Process Control or the individual job-cost records. Manufacturing overhead costs are added (debited) to Work-in-Process Control and individual job-cost records *only when* manufacturing overhead costs are allocated in transaction 6. At the time those costs are allocated, Manufacturing Overhead Control is, *in effect,* decreased (credited) via its contra account, Manufacturing Overhead Allocated. Under the normal-costing system described in our illustration, the budgeted manufacturing overhead rate of $40 per direct manufacturing labor-hour is calculated at the beginning of the year on the basis of predictions of annual manufacturing overhead costs and the annual quantity of the cost-allocation base. Almost certainly, the actual amounts allocated will differ from the predictions. In a later section we discuss what to do with this difference.

Actual manufacturing overhead (MOH) is debited to MOH Control as incurred; the total actual MOH is not known until the end of the accounting period. Allocated MOH is the budgeted MOH rate (known at the *beginning* of the period) times the actual quantity of the MOH allocation base recorded upon completion of jobs (or the *end* of the period)—when usage of the allocation base is known.

7. *Transaction:* Completion and transfer to finished goods of individual jobs, $188,800.

Account Analysis: The asset Finished Goods Control is increased (debited) by $188,800, and the asset Work-in-Process Control is decreased (credited) by $188,800 to recognize the completion of jobs.

Subsidiary Records: Exhibit 4-8, Panel A, shows that Job WPP 298 was completed at a cost of $9,705. Job WPP 298 also simultaneously appears in the finished goods records of the subsidiary ledger. Given Robinson's use of normal costing, cost of goods completed consists of actual direct materials, actual direct manufacturing labor, and manufacturing overhead allocated to each job based on the budgeted manufacturing overhead rate times actual direct manufacturing labor-hours. The following journal entry accounts for the $188,800 total cost of all jobs completed in February 2006.

In transaction 7, the completed goods are moved out of the manufacturing area and into the finished-goods area. The $188,800 cost of completed goods is the "cost of goods manufactured." A *schedule* of cost of goods manufactured (for a different company) is presented in Exhibit 2-7, p. 39.

Journal Entry:			
	Finished Goods Control	188,800	
	Work-in-Process Control		188,800

Post to General Ledger (Exhibit 4-6):

Work-in-Process Control

②	81,000	⑦	188,800
③	39,000		
⑥	80,000		
Balance	11,200		

Finished Goods Control

⑦	188,800	

The debit balance of $11,200 in the Work-in-Process Control account represents the total costs of all jobs (per the job-cost records in the subsidiary ledger) that have not been completed as of the end of February 2006.

8. *Transaction:* Cost of Goods Sold, $180,000.

Account Analysis: The account Cost of Goods Sold is increased (debited) by $180,000. The asset Finished Goods Control is decreased (credited) by $180,000.

Subsidiary Records: Exhibit 4-8, Panel B, indicates that Job WPP 298 was sold and delivered to the customer in February 2006. The following journal entry accounts for the $180,000 total cost of all goods sold during February 2006.

Journal Entry:			
	Cost of Goods Sold	180,000	
	Finished Goods Control		180,000

Post to General Ledger (Exhibit 4-6):

Finished Goods Control

⑦	188,800	⑧	180,000
Balance	8,800		

Cost of Goods Sold

⑧	180,000	

The debit balance of $8,800 in the Finished Goods Control account represents the costs of all jobs that have been completed but not sold as of the end of February 2006.

9. *Transaction:* Marketing and customer-service payroll and advertising costs accrued for February:

Marketing Department salaries	$35,000
Advertising costs	10,000
Customer-Service Department salaries	15,000

Account Analysis: As described in Chapter 2, for financial accounting purposes, marketing and advertising costs of $45,000 ($35,000 + $10,000) and customer-service costs of $15,000 are *period costs* for February 2006 to be matched against February 2006's revenues. Unlike manufacturing costs, these costs are not added to Work-in-Process Control because these costs are not incurred to transform materials into a finished product.

Subsidiary Records: Just as in the case of the manufacturing payroll, Robinson maintains employee labor records in the subsidiary ledger for marketing and customer-service payroll as well as records for different types of advertising costs (print, television, and radio). The following journal entry accounts for all the February 2006 transactions in the Marketing, Advertising, and Customer-Service Department records.

Journal Entries:	Marketing and Advertising Costs	45,000	
	Customer-Service Costs	15,000	
	Salaries Payable Control		50,000
	Accounts Payable Control		10,000

Post to General Ledger (Exhibit 4-6):

Marketing and Advertising Costs

Debit	Credit
⑨ 45,000	

Salaries Payable Control

Debit	Credit
	⑤ 44,000
	⑨ 50,000

Customer-Service Costs

Debit	Credit
⑨ 15,000	

Accounts Payable Control

Debit	Credit
	① 89,000
	⑤ 11,000
	⑨ 10,000

10. *Transaction:* Sales revenues, all on credit, $270,000.

Account Analysis: The Revenues account is increased (credited) by $270,000. The asset Accounts Receivable Control is increased (debited) by $270,00. The $270,000 represents total amounts due from customers for sales made in February 2006.

Subsidiary Records: The February 2006 amounts due from each customer, including the $15,000 due from the sale of Job WPP 298, are recorded in the subsidiary ledger.

Journal Entry:	Accounts Receivable Control	270,000	
	Revenues		270,000

Post to General Ledger (Exhibit 4-6):

Accounts Receivable Control

Debit	Credit
⑩ 270,000	

Revenues

Debit	Credit
	⑩ 270,000

At this point, pause and review the 10 entries in this illustration. Exhibit 4-6 is a handy summary of all 10 general-ledger entries presented in T-account form. Be sure to trace each journal entry, step by step, to T-accounts in the general ledger in Exhibit 4-6.

Exhibit 4-9 presents Robinson's income statement for February 2006 using information from entries 8, 9, and 10. If desired, the cost of goods sold calculations can be further subdivided and presented in the format of Exhibit 2-7, p. 39.

EXHIBIT 4-9

Robinson Company Income Statement for the Month Ending February 28, 2006

Revenues		$270,000
Cost of goods sold ($180,000 + $14,000[1])		194,000
Gross margin		76,000
Operating costs		
Marketing and advertising costs	$45,000	
Customer-service costs	15,000	
Total operating costs		60,000
Operating income		$ 16,000

[1]Cost of goods sold has been increased by $14,000, the difference between the Manufacturing overhead control account ($94,000) and the Manufacturing overhead allocated ($80,000). In a later section of this chapter, we discuss this adjustment, which represents the amount by which actual manufacturing overhead cost exceeds the manufacturing overhead allocated to jobs during February 2006.

Nonmanufacturing Costs and Job Costing

Chapter 2 (pp. 44–45) pointed out that companies use product costs for different purposes. The product costs reported as inventoriable costs to shareholders may differ from product costs reported to tax authorities and may also differ from product costs reported to managers for guiding pricing and product-mix decisions. We emphasize that even though, as described previously, marketing and customer-service costs are expensed when incurred for financial accounting purposes, companies often trace or allocate these costs to individual jobs for pricing, product-mix, and cost-management decisions.

To identify marketing and customer-service costs of individual jobs, Robinson can use the same approach to job costing described earlier in this chapter in the context of manufacturing. Robinson can trace the direct marketing costs and customer-service costs to jobs. Robinson can then calculate a budgeted indirect-cost rate by dividing budgeted, indirect marketing costs plus indirect customer-service costs by the budgeted quantity of the cost-allocation base, say, revenues. Robinson can use this rate to allocate these indirect costs to jobs. For example, if this rate were 15% of revenues, Robinson would allocate \$2,250 to Job WPP 298 (0.15 × \$15,000, the revenue from the job). By assigning both manufacturing costs and nonmanufacturing costs to jobs, Robinson can compare all costs of the different jobs against the revenues they generate.

Budgeted Indirect Costs and End-of-Accounting-Year Adjustments

6

Dispose of under- or overallocated manufacturing overhead costs at the end of the fiscal year using alternative methods

. . . for example, writing off this amount to the Cost of Goods Sold account.

Using budgeted indirect-cost rates and normal costing instead of actual costing has the advantage that indirect costs can be assigned to individual jobs on an ongoing and timely basis, rather than only at the end of the fiscal year when actual costs are known. However, budgeted rates are unlikely to equal actual rates because they are based on estimates made up to 12 months before actual costs are incurred. We now consider adjustments that need to be made when, at the end of the fiscal year, indirect costs allocated differ from actual indirect costs incurred. Recall that for the numerator and denominator reasons discussed earlier (pp. 106–107), we do *not* expect actual overhead costs incurred each month to equal overhead costs allocated each month.

Underallocated indirect costs occur when the allocated amount of indirect costs in an accounting period is less than the actual (incurred) amount. **Overallocated indirect costs** occur when the allocated amount of indirect costs in an accounting period is greater than the actual (incurred) amount.

Underallocated (overallocated) indirect costs = Indirect costs incurred – Indirect costs allocated

Underallocated (overallocated) indirect costs are also called **underapplied (overapplied) indirect costs** and **underabsorbed (overabsorbed) indirect costs**.

Consider the manufacturing overhead indirect-cost pool at Robinson Company. There are two indirect-cost accounts in the general ledger that have to do with manufacturing overhead:

1. Manufacturing Overhead Control, the record of the actual costs in all the individual overhead categories (such as indirect materials, indirect manufacturing labor, supervision, engineering, power, and plant depreciation)
2. Manufacturing Overhead Allocated, the record of the manufacturing overhead allocated to individual jobs on the basis of the budgeted rate multiplied by actual direct manufacturing labor-hours

Assume the following annual data for the Robinson Company:

Manufacturing Overhead Control			Manufacturing Overhead Allocated	
Bal. Dec. 31, 2006	1,215,000		Bal. Dec. 31, 2006	1,080,000

The $1,080,000 credit balance in Manufacturing Overhead Allocated results from multiplying the 27,000 actual direct manufacturing labor-hours worked on all jobs in 2006 by the budgeted rate of $40 per direct manufacturing labor-hour.

The $135,000 difference (a net debit) is an underallocated amount because actual manufacturing overhead costs are greater than the allocated amount. This difference arises from two reasons related to the computation of the $40 budgeted hourly rate:

1. **Numerator reason (indirect-cost pool).** Actual manufacturing-overhead costs of $1,215,000 are greater than the budgeted amount of $1,120,000.
2. **Denominator reason (quantity of allocation base).** Actual direct manufacturing labor-hours of 27,000 are fewer than the budgeted 28,000 hours.

There are three main approaches to accounting for the $135,000 underallocated manufacturing overhead caused by Robinson underestimating manufacturing overhead costs and overestimating the quantity of the cost-allocation base: (1) adjusted allocation-rate approach, (2) proration approach, and (3) write-off to cost of goods sold approach.

Adjusted Allocation-Rate Approach

The **adjusted allocation-rate approach** restates all overhead entries in the general ledger and subsidiary ledgers using actual cost rates rather than budgeted cost rates. First, the actual manufacturing overhead rate is computed at the end of the fiscal year. Then, the manufacturing overhead costs allocated to every job during the year are recomputed using the actual manufacturing overhead rate (rather than the budgeted manufacturing overhead rate). Finally, end-of-year closing entries are made. The result is that at year-end, every job-cost record and finished goods record—as well as the ending Work-in-Process Control, Finished Goods Control, and Cost of Goods Sold accounts—accurately represent actual manufacturing overhead costs incurred.

The widespread adoption of computerized accounting systems has greatly reduced the cost of using the adjusted allocation-rate approach. Consider the Robinson example. The actual manufacturing overhead ($1,215,000) exceeds the manufacturing overhead allocated ($1,080,000) by 12.5% [($1,215,000 – $1,080,000) ÷ $1,080,000]. The actual 2006 manufacturing overhead rate is $45 per direct manufacturing labor-hour ($1,215,000 ÷ 27,000 hours) rather than the budgeted $40 per direct manufacturing labor-hour. At year-end, Robinson could increase the manufacturing overhead allocated to each job in 2006 by 12.5% using a single software command. The command would adjust both the subsidiary ledgers and the general ledger.

The adjusted allocation-rate approach "corrects" all MOH entries in the general and subsidiary ledgers to what they would have been if accountants had perfectly forecasted actual MOH costs *and* the actual quantity of the cost-allocation base used. Implementation of the adjusted allocation-rate approach becomes more feasible as technology improvements decrease information-processing costs.

Consider the Western Pulp machine job, WPP 298. Under normal costing, the manufacturing overhead allocated to the job is $3,520 (the budgeted rate of $40 per direct manufacturing labor-hour × 88 hours). Increasing the manufacturing overhead allocated by 12.5%, or $440 ($3,520 × 0.125), means the adjusted amount of manufacturing overhead allocated to Job WPP 298 equals $3,960 ($3,520 + $440). Note from page 104 that under actual costing, manufacturing overhead allocated to this job is also $3,960 (the actual rate of $45 per direct manufacturing labor-hour × 88 hours). Making this adjustment under normal costing for each job in the subsidiary ledgers ensures that all $1,215,000 of manufacturing overhead is allocated to jobs.

The adjusted allocation-rate approach yields the benefits of both the *timeliness and convenience of normal costing during the year and the accuracy of actual costing at year-end*. Each individual job-cost record and the end-of-year account balances for inventories and cost of goods sold are adjusted to actual costs. After-the-fact analysis of actual profitability of individual jobs provides managers with accurate and useful insights for future decisions about job pricing, which jobs to emphasize, and ways to manage job costs.

Proration Approach

Proration spreads underallocated overhead or overallocated overhead among ending work in process, finished goods, and cost of goods sold. Materials inventory is not included in this proration because no manufacturing overhead costs have been allocated to it. In our Robinson example, end-of-year proration is made to the ending balances in

Work-in-Process Control, Finished Goods Control, and Cost of Goods Sold. Assume the following actual results for Robinson Company in 2006:

	A	B	C
1	Account	Account Balance (Before Proration)	Allocated Manufacturing Overhead Included in Each Account Balance (Before Proration)
2	Work in Process Control	$ 50,000	$ 16,200
3	Finished Goods Control	75,000	31,320
4	Cost of Goods Sold	2,375,000	1,032,480
5		$2,500,000	$1,080,000

MOH Allocated is $135,000 less than MOH Control. That is, MOH Allocated is *underallocated.* Therefore, the amount of MOH Allocated that flowed into Work-in-Process Control and in turn into Finished Goods Control and Cost of Goods Sold is understated. Because all three of these accounts are understated, they would be increased under the proration approach.

How should Robinson prorate the underallocated $135,000 of manufacturing overhead at the end of 2006?

Robinson should prorate underallocated or overallocated amounts on the basis of the total amount of manufacturing overhead allocated (before proration) in the ending balances of Work-in-Process Control, Finished Goods Control, and Cost of Goods Sold. The $135,000 underallocated overhead is prorated over the three affected accounts in proportion to their total amount of manufacturing overhead allocated (before proration) in column 2 of the following table, resulting in the ending balances (after proration) in column 5 at actual costs.

	A	B	C	D	E	F	G
10		Account Balance (Before Proration)	Allocated Manufacturing Overhead Included in Each Account Balance (Before Proration)	Allocated Manufacturing Overhead Included in Each Account Balance as a Percent of Total	Proration of $135,000 of Underallocated Manufacturing Overhead		Account Balance (After Proration)
11	Account	(1)	(2)	(3) = (2) ÷ $1,080,000	(4) = (3) x $135,000		(5) = (1) + (4)
12	Work in Process Control	$ 50,000	$ 16,200	1.5%	0.015 x $135,000 =	$ 2,025	$ 52,025
13	Finished Goods Control	75,000	31,320	2.9%	0.029 x 135,000 =	3,915	78,915
14	Cost of Goods Sold	2,375,000	1,032,480	95.6%	0.956 x 135,000 =	129,060	2,504,060
15	Total	$2,500,000	$1,080,000	100.0%		$135,000	$2,635,000

Recall that the actual manufacturing overhead ($1,215,000) exceeds the manufacturing overhead allocated ($1,080,000) by 12.5%. The proration amounts in column 4 can also be derived by multiplying the balances in column 2 by 0.125. For example, the $3,915 proration to Finished Goods is 0.125 × $31,320. The journal entry to record this proration is:

Work-in-Process Control	2,025	
Finished Goods Control	3,915	
Cost of Goods Sold	129,060	
Manufacturing Overhead Allocated	1,080,000	
Manufacturing Overhead Control		1,215,000

If manufacturing overhead had been overallocated, the Work-in-Process Control, Finished Goods Control, and Cost of Goods Sold accounts would be decreased (credited) instead of increased (debited).

This journal entry restates the 2006 ending balances for Work-in-Process Control, Finished Goods Control, and Cost of Goods Sold to what they would have been if actual manufacturing overhead rates had been used rather than budgeted manufacturing overhead rates. This method reports the same 2006 ending balances in the general ledger as the adjusted allocation-rate approach.

Some companies use the proration approach but base it on the column 1 amounts of the preceding table—that is, the ending balances of Work-in-Process Control, Finished Goods Control, and Cost of Goods Sold before proration. It gives the same results as the previous proration *only if* the proportions of manufacturing overhead costs to total costs, and therefore direct costs, are the same in the Work-in-Process Control, Finished Goods Control, and Cost of Goods Sold accounts. In general, the proportion of direct costs to manufacturing overhead costs in the various accounts are not the same. That's because manufacturing overhead is usually allocated using a cost-allocation base such as direct manufacturing labor-hours rather than direct costs. The following table shows that prorations based on ending account balances will not be the same as the more-accurate prorations calculated earlier based on the amount of manufacturing overhead allocated to the accounts.

	A	B	C	D	E	F
1		**Account Balance (Before Proration)**	**Account Balance as a Percent of Total**	**Proration of $135,000 of Underallocated Manufacturing Overhead**		**Account Balance (After Proration)**
2	**Account**	**(1)**	**(2) = (1) ÷ $2,500,000**	**(3) = (2) x $135,000**		**(4) = (1) + (3)**
3	Work in Process Control	$ 50,000	2.0%	0.02 x $135,000 =	$ 2,700	$ 52,700
4	Finished Goods Control	75,000	3.0%	0.03 x 135,000 =	4,050	79,050
5	Cost of Goods Sold	2,375,000	95.0%	0.95 x 135,000 =	128,250	2,503,250
6	Total	$2,500,000	100.0%		$135,000	$2,635,000

However, proration based on ending balances is frequently justified as being an expedient way of approximating the more-accurate results from using indirect costs allocated.

Write-Off to Cost of Goods Sold Approach

Under this approach, the total under- or overallocated manufacturing overhead is included in this year's Cost of Goods Sold. For Robinson, the journal entry would be:

Cost of Goods Sold	135,000	
Manufacturing Overhead Allocated	1,080,000	
Manufacturing Overhead Control		1,215,000

Robinson's two Manufacturing Overhead accounts are closed with the difference between them included in cost of goods sold. The Cost of Goods Sold account after the write-off equals $2,510,000, the balance before the write-off of $2,375,000 *plus* the *underallocated* manufacturing overhead amount of $135,000.

Choice Among Approaches

Which of these three approaches is the best one to use? In making this decision, managers should be guided by the causes for underallocation or overallocation and how the information will be used. Many management accountants, industrial engineers, and managers argue that to the extent that the under- or overallocated overhead cost measures inefficiency during the period, it should be written off to Cost of Goods Sold instead of being prorated. This line of reasoning argues for applying a combination of the write-off and proration methods. For example, the portion of the underallocated overhead cost that is due to inefficiency (say, because of excessive spending) and that could have been avoided should be written off to Cost of Goods Sold, whereas the portion that is unavoidable should be prorated. Unlike full proration, this approach avoids carrying the costs of inefficiency as part of inventory assets.

Proration should be based on the manufacturing overhead allocated component in the ending balances of Work-in-Process Control, Finished Goods Control, and Cost of Goods Sold. This proration method results in the most accurate inventory and Cost of Goods Sold numbers being reported in the financial statements. Prorating to each individual job (as in the adjusted allocation-rate approach) is useful if the goal is to develop the most accurate record of individual job costs for profitability analysis purposes.

The write-off to Cost of Goods Sold is the simplest approach for dealing with under- or overallocated overhead. If the amount of under- or overallocated overhead is small—in comparison with total operating income or some other measure of materiality—the write-off to Cost of Goods Sold approach yields a good approximation to more-accurate, but more-complex, approaches. Companies are also becoming increasingly conscious of inventory control, and quantities of inventories are lower than they were in earlier years.

As a result, cost of goods sold tends to be higher in relation to the dollar amount of work-in-process and finished goods inventories. Also, the inventory balances of job-costing companies are usually small because goods are often made in response to customer orders. Consequently, as is true in our Robinson example, writing off, instead of prorating, under- or overallocated overhead is unlikely to cause significant distortions in financial statements. For all these reasons, the cost-benefit test favors the simplest approach—write-off to Cost of Goods Sold—because the more-complex attempts at accuracy represented by the other two approaches do not appear to provide sufficient additional useful information.

Study Tip: To check your understanding of job costing, see the Featured Exercise, true–false statement 5, multiple-choice questions 3 and 7, and Review Exercises 1 and 3 (*Student Guide*, beginning p. 39). Fully explained solutions begin on p. 40.

Note that regardless of which of the three approaches is used, the underallocated overhead is not carried in the overhead accounts beyond the end of the fiscal year. Why? Because the ending balances in Manufacturing Overhead Control and Manufacturing Overhead Allocated are closed to Work-in-Process Control, Finished Goods Control, and Cost of Goods Sold, and therefore become zero at the end of each year.

Multiple Overhead Cost Pools

The Robinson Company illustration assumed that a single manufacturing overhead cost pool with direct manufacturing labor-hours as the cost-allocation base was appropriate for allocating all manufacturing overhead costs to jobs. Robinson could have used multiple cost-allocation bases, say, direct manufacturing labor-hours and machine-hours, to allocate manufacturing overhead costs to jobs. But Robinson would use multiple cost-allocation bases only if its managers believed that the benefits of the information generated by adding one or more pools (more-accurate costing and pricing of jobs and better ability to manage costs) exceeded the additional costs of that costing system. (We discuss these issues in Chapter 5.)

To implement a normal-costing system with two overhead cost pools, Robinson would determine, say, the budgeted total direct manufacturing labor-hours and the budgeted total machine-hours for 2006, and identify the associated total budgeted overhead costs for each cost pool. It would then calculate two budgeted overhead rates, one based on direct manufacturing labor-hours and the other on machine-hours. Manufacturing overhead costs would be allocated to jobs using these two budgeted overhead rates and the actual direct manufacturing labor-hours and actual machine-hours used by various jobs. The general ledger would contain Manufacturing Overhead Control and Manufacturing Overhead Allocated amounts for each cost pool. End-of-year adjustments for under- or overallocated overhead costs would then be made separately for each cost pool.

Variations from Normal Costing: A Service-Sector Example

7

Apply variations from normal costing

. . . variations from normal costing use budgeted direct-cost rates

Job costing is also very useful in service industries such as accounting and consulting firms, advertising agencies, auto repair shops, and hospitals. In an accounting firm, each audit is a job. The costs of each audit are accumulated in a job-cost record, much like the document used by Robinson Company, based on the seven-step approach described earlier. On the basis of labor-time records, direct labor costs of the professional staff—audit partners, audit managers, and audit staff—are traced to individual jobs. Other direct costs such as travel, out-of-town meals and lodging, phone, fax, and copying are also traced to jobs. The costs of secretarial support, office staff, rent, and depreciation of furniture and equipment are indirect costs because these costs cannot be traced to jobs in an economically feasible way. Indirect costs are allocated to jobs, for example, using a cost-allocation base such as professional labor-hours.

In some service organizations, a variation from normal costing is helpful because actual direct-labor costs—the largest component of total costs—can be difficult to trace to jobs as they are completed. For example, in our audit illustration, the actual direct-labor costs may include bonuses that become known only at the end of the year (a numerator reason). Also, the hours worked each period might vary significantly depending on the number of working days each month and the demand from clients (a denominator reason). In situations like these, a company needing timely information during the progress of an audit (and not wanting to wait until the end of the fiscal year) will use budgeted rates for some direct costs and budgeted rates for indirect costs. All budgeted rates are calculated at the start of the fiscal year. In contrast, normal costing uses actual cost rates for all direct costs and budgeted cost rates only for indirect costs.

The mechanics of using budgeted rates for direct costs are similar to the methods employed when using budgeted rates for indirect costs in normal costing. We illustrate this for Lindsay and Associates, a public accounting firm. For 2006, Lindsay budgets total direct-labor costs of $14,400,000, total indirect costs of $12,960,000, and total direct (professional) labor-hours of 288,000. In this case,

$$\text{Budgeted direct-labor cost rate} = \frac{\text{Budgeted total direct-labor costs}}{\text{Budgeted total direct labor-hours}}$$

$$= \frac{\$14{,}400{,}000}{288{,}000 \text{ direct labor-hours}} = \$50 \text{ per direct labor-hour}$$

Assuming only one indirect-cost pool and total direct-labor costs as the cost- allocation base,

$$\begin{array}{c}\text{Budgeted}\\ \text{indirect-cost rate}\end{array} = \frac{\text{Budgeted total costs in indirect-cost pool}}{\text{Budgeted total quantity of cost-allocation base (direct-labor costs)}}$$

$$= \frac{\$12{,}960{,}000}{\$14{,}400{,}000} = 0.90, \text{ or } 90\% \text{ of direct-labor costs}$$

Suppose an audit of Tracy Transport, a client of Lindsay, completed in March 2006, uses 800 direct labor-hours. Lindsay calculates the direct-labor costs of the Tracy Transport audit by multiplying the budgeted direct-labor cost rate, $50 per direct labor-hour, by 800, the actual quantity of direct labor-hours. It allocates indirect costs to the Tracy Transport audit by multiplying the budgeted indirect-cost rate (90%) by the direct-labor costs assigned to the Tracy Transport job ($40,000). Assuming no other direct costs for travel and the like, the cost of the Tracy Transport audit is:

Direct-labor costs, $50 × 800	$40,000
Indirect costs allocated, 90% × $40,000	36,000
Total	$76,000

At the end of the fiscal year, the direct costs traced to jobs using budgeted rates will generally not equal the actual direct costs because the actual rate and the budgeted rate are developed at different times using different information. End-of-year adjustments for under- or overallocated direct costs would need to be made in the same way that adjustments are made for under- or overallocated indirect costs.

The Lindsay and Associates example illustrates that all costing systems do not exactly match either the actual-costing system or the normal-costing system described earlier in the chapter. As another example, engineering consulting firms often have some actual direct costs (cost of making blueprints or fees paid to outside experts), other direct costs (professional labor costs) traced to jobs using a budgeted rate, and indirect costs (engineering and office-support costs) allocated to jobs using a budgeted rate. Therefore, users of costing systems should be aware of the different systems that they may encounter.

Study Tip: To review important terms and concepts in Chapters 3 and 4, work the crossword puzzle (*Student Guide*, p. 45). The solution is on p. 48.

PROBLEM FOR SELF-STUDY

You are asked to bring the following incomplete accounts of Endeavor Printing, Inc., up to date through January 31, 2007. Consider the data that appear in the T-accounts as well as the following information in items (a) through (i).

Endeavor's normal-costing system has two direct-cost categories (direct material costs and direct manufacturing labor costs) and one indirect-cost pool (manufacturing overhead costs, which are allocated using direct manufacturing labor costs).

Materials Control	
12-31-2006 Bal. 15,000	

Wages Payable Control	
	1-31-2007 Bal 3,000

Work-in-Process Control	

Manufacturing Overhead Control	
1-31-2007 Bal. 57,000	

Finished Goods Control	
12-31-2006 Bal. 20,000	

Cost of Goods Sold	

Additional Information:

a. Manufacturing overhead is allocated using a budgeted rate that is set every December. Management forecasts next year's manufacturing overhead costs and next year's direct manufacturing labor costs. The budget for 2007 is $600,000 for manufacturing overhead costs and $400,000 for direct manufacturing labor costs.

b. The only job unfinished on January 31, 2007, is No. 419, on which direct manufacturing labor costs are $2,000 (125 direct manufacturing labor-hours) and direct material costs are $8,000.

c. Total direct materials issued to production during January are $90,000.

d. Cost of goods completed during January is $180,000.

e. Materials inventory as of January 31, 2007, is $20,000.

f. Finished goods inventory as of January 31, 2007, is $15,000.

g. All plant workers earn the same wage rate. Direct manufacturing labor-hours used for January total 2,500 hours. Other labor costs and supervision costs total $10,000.

h. The gross plant payroll paid in January equals $52,000. Ignore withholdings.

i. All "actual" manufacturing overhead incurred during January has already been posted.

j. All materials are direct materials.

Required

Calculate:

1. Materials purchased during January
2. Cost of Goods Sold during January
3. Direct manufacturing labor costs incurred during January
4. Manufacturing Overhead Allocated during January
5. Balance, Wages Payable Control, December 31, 2006
6. Balance, Work-in-Process Control, January 31, 2007
7. Balance, Work-in-Process Control, December 31, 2006
8. Manufacturing Overhead Underallocated or Overallocated for January 2007

SOLUTION

Amounts from the T-accounts are labeled "(T)"

1. From Materials Control T-account, Materials purchased: $90,000 (c) + $20,000 (e) – $15,000 (T) = $95,000
2. From Finished Goods Control T-account, Cost of Goods Sold: $20,000 (T) + $180,000 (d) – $15,000 (f) = $185,000
3. Direct manufacturing wage rate: $2,000 (b) ÷ 125 direct manufacturing labor-hours (b) = $16 per direct manufacturing labor-hour

   Direct manufacturing labor costs: 2,500 direct manufacturing labor-hours (g) × $16 per hour = $40,000
4. Manufacturing overhead rate: $600,000 (a) ÷ $400,000 (a) = 150%

   Manufacturing Overhead Allocated: 150% of $40,000 = 1.50 × $40,000 (see **3**) = $60,000
5. From Wages Payable Control T-account, Wages Payable Control, December 31, 2006: $52,000 (h) + $3,000 (T) – $40,000 (see **3**) – $10,000 (g) = $5,000
6. Work-in-Process Control, January 31, 2007: $8,000 (b) + $2,000 (b) + 150% of $2,000 (b) = $13,000 (This answer is used in item **7**.)

7. From Work-in-Process Control T-account, Work-in-Process Control, December 31, 2006: $180,000 (d) + $13,000 (see 6) – $90,000 (c) – $40,000 (see 3) – $60,000 (see 4) = $3,000

8. Manufacturing overhead overallocated: $60,000 (see 4) – $57,000 (T) = $3,000.

Entries in T-accounts are lettered in accordance with the preceding additional information and are numbered in accordance with the requirements above.

Materials Control

December 31, 2006	Bal. (given)	15,000			
	(1)	95,000*		(c)	90,000
January 31, 2007 Bal.	(e)	20,000			

Work-in-Process Control

December 31, 2006 Bal.	(7)	3,000		(d)	180,000
Direct materials	(c)	90,000			
Direct manufacturing labor	(b) (g) (3)	40,000			
Manufacturing overhead allocated	(g) (a) (4)	60,000			
January 31, 2007	Bal. (b) (6)	13,000			

Finished Goods Control

December 31, 2006 Bal.	(given)	20,000		(2)	185,000
	(d)	180,000			
January 31, 2007 Bal.	(f)	15,000			

Wages Payable Control

	(h)	52,000	December 31, 2006	(5)	5,000
				(g), (3)	40,000
				(g)	10,000
			January 31, 2007	(given)	3,000

Manufacturing Overhead Control

Total January charges (given)		57,000			

Manufacturing Overhead Allocated

				(g) (a) (4)	60,000

Cost of Goods Sold

	(f) (2)	185,000			

*Can be computed only after all other postings in the account have been found.

DECISION POINTS

The following question-and-answer format summarizes the chapter's learning objectives. Each decision presents a key question related to a learning objective. The guidelines are the answer to that question.

Decision	Guidelines
1. What are the building-block concepts of a costing system?	The building-block concepts of a costing system are cost object, direct costs of a cost object, indirect costs of a cost object, cost pool, and cost-allocation base. Costing-system overview diagrams represent these concepts in a systematic way. Costing systems aim to report cost numbers that reflect the way chosen cost objects (such as products or services) use the resources of an organization.

2. How do you distinguish job costing from process costing?

Job-costing systems assign costs to distinct units of a product or service. Process-costing systems assign costs to masses of identical or similar units and compute unit costs on an average basis. These two costing systems represent opposite ends of a continuum. The costing systems of many companies combine some elements of both job costing and process costing.

3. How do you implement a job-costing system?

A general approach to job costing requires identifying (a) the job, (b) the direct-cost categories, (c) the cost-allocation bases, (d) the indirect-cost categories, (e) the cost-allocation rates, (f) the allocated indirect costs of a job, and (g) the total direct and indirect costs of a job.

4. How do you distinguish actual costing from normal costing?

Actual costing and normal costing differ in the type of indirect-cost rates used:

	Actual Costing	Normal Costing
Direct-cost rates	Actual rates	Actual rates
Indirect-cost rates	Actual rates	Budgeted rates

Both systems use actual quantities of inputs for tracing direct costs and actual quantities of the allocation bases for allocating indirect costs.

5. What are the stages for recording transactions in a manufacturing job-costing system?

The transactions in a job-costing system in manufacturing track: (a) acquisition of materials and other manufacturing inputs; (b) their conversion into work in process; (c) their conversion into finished goods; and (d) the sale of finished goods. Each of the (a) to (d) stages in the manufacture/sale cycle are represented by journal entries in the costing system.

6. How should you dispose of under- or overallocated manufacturing overhead costs at the end of the fiscal year?

The two theoretically correct approaches to disposing of under- or overallocated manufacturing overhead costs at the end of the fiscal year are to adjust the allocation rate and to prorate on the basis of the total amount of the allocated manufacturing overhead cost in the ending balances of Work-in-Process Control, Finished Goods Control, and Cost of Goods Sold. Many companies, however, simply write off amounts of under- or overallocated manufacturing overhead to Cost of Goods Sold on the basis of practicality.

7. What variations from normal costing can be used?

In some variations from normal costing, organizations use budgeted rates to assign direct costs, as well as indirect costs, to jobs.

TERMS TO LEARN

This chapter and the Glossary at the end of this book contain definitions of:

actual costing (p. 100)
adjusted allocation-rate approach (p. 119)
budgeted indirect-cost rate (p. 108)
cost-allocation base (p. 98)
cost-application base (p. 98)
cost pool (p. 98)
indirect-cost rate (p. 104)
job (p. 99)
job-cost record (p. 101)
job-cost sheet (p. 101)
job-costing system (p. 99)
labor-time record (p. 102)
manufacturing overhead allocated (p. 115)
manufacturing overhead applied (p. 115)
materials-requisition record (p. 101)
normal costing (p. 108)
overabsorbed indirect costs (p. 118)
overallocated indirect costs (p. 118)
overapplied indirect costs (p. 118)
process-costing system (p. 99)
proration (p. 119)
source document (p. 101)
underabsorbed indirect costs (p. 118)
underallocated indirect costs (p. 118)
underapplied indirect costs (p. 118)

PH Grade Assist

Prentice Hall Grade Assist (PHGA)

Your professor may ask you to complete selected exercises and problems in Prentice Hall Grade Assist (PHGA). PHGA is an online tool that can help you master the chapter's topics. It provides you with multiple variations of exercises and problems designated by the PHGA icon. You can rework these exercises and problems—each time with new data—as many times as you need. You also receive immediate feedback and grading.

ASSIGNMENT MATERIAL

Questions

4-1 Define cost pool, cost tracing, cost allocation, and cost-allocation base.

4-2 How does a job-costing system differ from a process-costing system?

4-3 Why might an advertising agency use job costing for an advertising campaign by Pepsi, whereas a bank might use process costing to determine the cost of checking account deposits?

4-4 Describe the seven steps in job costing.

4-5 What are the two major cost objects that managers focus on in companies using job costing?

4-6 Describe three major source documents used in job-costing systems.

4-7 What is the main concern about source documents used to prepare job-cost records?

4-8 Give two reasons why most organizations use an annual period rather than a weekly or monthly period to compute budgeted indirect-cost rates.

4-9 Distinguish between actual costing and normal costing.

4-10 Describe two ways in which a house construction company may use job-cost information.

4-11 Comment on the following statement: "In a normal-costing system, the amounts in the Manufacturing Overhead Control account will always equal the amounts in the Manufacturing Overhead Allocated account."

4-12 Describe three different debit entries to the Work-in-Process Control T-account under normal costing.

4-13 Describe three alternative ways to dispose of under- or overallocated overhead costs.

4-14 When might a company use budgeted costs rather than actual costs to compute direct-labor rates?

4-15 Describe briefly why modern technology such as Electronic Data Interchange (EDI) is helpful to managers.

Exercises

4-16 Job costing, process costing. In each of the following situations, determine whether job costing or process costing would be more appropriate.

PH Grade Assist

- **a.** A CPA firm
- **b.** An oil refinery
- **c.** A custom furniture manufacturer
- **d.** A tire manufacturer
- **e.** A textbook publisher
- **f.** A pharmaceutical company
- **g.** An advertising agency
- **h.** An apparel manufacturing plant
- **i.** A flour mill
- **j.** A paint manufacturer
- **k.** A medical care facility
- **l.** A landscaping company
- **m.** A cola-drink-concentrate producer
- **n.** A movie studio
- **o.** A law firm
- **p.** A commercial aircraft manufacturer
- **q.** A management consulting firm
- **r.** A breakfast-cereal company
- **s.** A catering service
- **t.** A paper mill
- **u.** An auto repair shop

4-17 Actual costing, normal costing, accounting for manufacturing overhead. Destin Products uses a job-costing system with two direct-cost categories (direct materials and direct manufacturing labor) and one manufacturing overhead cost pool. Destin allocates manufacturing overhead costs using direct manufacturing labor costs. Destin provides the following information:

	Budget for 2007	Actual Results for 2007
Direct material costs	$1,500,000	$1,450,000
Direct manufacturing labor costs	1,000,000	980,000
Manufacturing overhead costs	1,750,000	1,862,000

Required

1. Compute the actual and budgeted manufacturing overhead rates for 2007.
2. During March, the job-cost record for Job 626 contained the following information:

Direct materials used	$40,000
Direct manufacturing labor costs	$30,000

   Compute the cost of Job 626 using (a) actual costing and (b) normal costing.
3. At the end of 2007, compute the under- or overallocated manufacturing overhead under normal costing. Why is there no under- or overallocated overhead under actual costing?

4-18 Job costing, normal and actual costing. Anderson Construction assembles residential houses. It uses a job-costing system with two direct-cost categories (direct materials and direct labor) and one indirect-cost pool (assembly support). Direct labor-hours is the allocation base for assembly support costs. In December 2006, Anderson budgets 2007 assembly-support costs to be $8,000,000 and 2007 direct labor-hours to be 160,000.

PH Grade Assist

At the end of 2007, Anderson is comparing the costs of several jobs that were started and completed in 2007.

	Laguna Model	Mission Model
Construction period	Feb–June 2007	May–Oct 2007
Direct materials	$106,450	$127,604
Direct labor	$36,276	$41,410
Direct labor-hours	900	1,010

Direct materials and direct labor are paid for on a contract basis. The costs of each are known when direct materials are used or when direct labor-hours are worked. The 2007 actual assembly-support costs were $6,888,000, and the actual direct labor-hours were 164,000.

Required

1. Compute the (a) budgeted indirect-cost rate and (b) actual indirect-cost rate. Why do they differ?
2. What are the job costs of the Laguna Model and the Mission Model using (a) normal costing and (b) actual costing?
3. Why might Anderson Construction prefer normal costing over actual costing?

4-19 Budgeted manufacturing overhead rate, allocated manufacturing overhead. Waheed Company uses normal costing. It allocates manufacturing overhead costs using a budgeted rate per machine-hour. The following data are available for 2006:

Budgeted manufacturing overhead costs	$2,850,000
Budgeted machine-hours	190,000
Actual manufacturing overhead costs	$2,910,000
Actual machine-hours	195,000

Required

1. Calculate the budgeted manufacturing overhead rate.
2. Calculate the manufacturing overhead allocated during 2006.
3. Calculate the amount of under- or overallocated manufacturing overhead.

4-20 Job costing, accounting for manufacturing overhead, budgeted rates. The Lynn Company uses a job-costing system at its Minneapolis plant. The plant has a Machining Department and an Assembly Department. Its job-costing system has two direct-cost categories (direct materials and direct manufacturing labor) and two manufacturing overhead cost pools (the Machining Department overhead, allocated to jobs based on actual machine-hours, and the Assembly Department overhead, allocated to jobs based on actual direct manufacturing labor costs). The 2007 budget for the plant is:

	Machining Department	Assembly Department
Manufacturing overhead	$1,800,000	$3,600,000
Direct manufacturing labor cost	$1,400,000	$2,000,000
Direct manufacturing labor-hours	100,000	200,000
Machine-hours	50,000	200,000

Required

1. Present an overview diagram of Lynn's job-costing system. Compute the budgeted manufacturing overhead rate for each department.
2. During February, the job-cost record for Job 494 contained the following:

	Machining Department	Assembly Department
Direct materials used	$45,000	$70,000
Direct manufacturing labor costs	$14,000	$15,000
Direct manufacturing labor-hours	1,000	1,500
Machine-hours	2,000	1,000

   Compute the total manufacturing overhead costs allocated to Job 494.
3. At the end of 2007, the actual manufacturing overhead costs were $2,100,000 in Machining and $3,700,000 in Assembly. Assume that 55,000 actual machine-hours were used in Machining and that actual direct manufacturing labor costs in Assembly were $2,200,000. Compute the over- or underallocated manufacturing overhead for each department.

PH Grade Assist

4-21 Job costing, consulting firm. Taylor & Associates, a consulting firm, has the following condensed budget for 2007:

Revenues		$20,000,000
Total costs:		
Direct costs		
Professional labor	$ 5,000,000	
Indirect costs		
Consulting support	13,000,000	18,000,000
Operating income		$ 2,000,000

Taylor has a single direct-cost category (professional labor) and a single indirect-cost pool (client support). Indirect costs are allocated to jobs on the basis of professional labor costs.

Required

1. Prepare an overview diagram of the job-costing system. Compute the 2007 budgeted indirect-cost rate for Taylor & Associates.

2. The markup rate for pricing jobs is intended to produce operating income equal to 10% of revenues. Compute the markup rate as a percentage of professional labor costs.
3. Taylor is bidding on a consulting job for Red Rooster, a fast-food chain specializing in poultry meats. The budgeted breakdown of professional labor on the job is as follows:

Professional Labor Category	Budgeted Rate per Hour	Budgeted Hours
Director	$200	3
Partner	100	16
Associate	50	40
Assistant	30	160

Compute the budgeted cost of the Red Rooster job. How much will Taylor bid for the job if it is to earn its target operating income of 10% of revenues?

4-22 Service industry, time period used to compute indirect cost rates. Printers, Inc., produces annual reports and marketing materials for large companies. There are three categories of costs in its normal job-costing system: direct materials, direct labor, and overhead (both variable and fixed), allocated on the basis of direct labor costs. Jill Liu, the controller, is concerned that an increasing number of clients are waiting until the last minute to send in their final orders, causing congestion and an increase in the variable manufacturing overhead rate because of higher overtime and facility and machine maintenance. This spike is during the "crazy" months of January, February, and March, when many companies are rushing to get out their annual reports and marketing materials. Liu obtains the following budgeted data for 2006:

Excel Lab
www.prenhall.com/horngren/cost12e

	A	B	C	D	E	F
1		Jan.-March	April-June	July-Sept.	Oct.-Dec.	Total
2	Direct materials	$900,000	$620,000	$595,000	$605,000	$2,720,000
3	Direct labor costs	$400,000	$280,000	$250,000	$270,000	$1,200,000
4	Variable overhead costs as a percentage of direct labor costs	90%	60%	60%	60%	
5	Fixed overhead costs	$300,000	$300,000	$300,000	$300,000	$1,200,000

If you want to use Excel to solve this exercise, go to the Excel Lab at **www.prenhall.com/horngren/cost12e** and download the template for Exercise 4-22.

Required

1. Consider Job 332, an order for 100,000 sales catalogs for the local mall. Actual direct material costs for this job are $10,000 and actual labor costs are $6,000. Calculate the cost of Job 332 (a) if it is completed in January–March 2006 and if the budgeted overhead rate for that quarter is used to allocate overhead costs, (b) if it is done in July–September 2006 and if the budgeted overhead rate for that quarter is used to allocate overhead costs, and (c) if the average budgeted overhead rate for the year 2006 is used to allocate overhead costs.
2. To cost each job, Printers, Inc., currently uses the budgeted variable overhead rate for the quarter in which the job is completed and a budgeted fixed overhead rate based on budgeted annual fixed overhead costs and budgeted annual direct labor costs. Calculate the cost of Job 332 using this method if it is done in (a) January–March 2006 and (b) July–September 2006.
3. Printers, Inc., prices each job at 125% of costs. Which method of costing jobs for pricing purposes would you recommend? Why? Explain briefly.

4-23 Accounting for manufacturing overhead. Consider the following selected cost data for the Pittsburgh Forging Company for 2006.

Budgeted manufacturing overhead	$7,000,000
Budgeted machine-hours	200,000
Actual manufacturing overhead	$6,800,000
Actual machine-hours	195,000

The company uses normal costing. Its job-costing system has a single manufacturing overhead cost pool. Costs are allocated to jobs using a budgeted machine-hour rate. Any amount of under- or overallocation is written off to Cost of Goods Sold.

Required

1. Compute the budgeted manufacturing overhead rate.
2. Prepare the journal entries to record the allocation of manufacturing overhead.
3. Compute the amount of under- or overallocation of manufacturing overhead. Is the amount material? Prepare a journal entry to dispose of this amount.

4-24 Job costing, journal entries. The University of Chicago Press is wholly owned by the university. It performs the bulk of its work for other university departments, which pay as though the press were an outside business enterprise. The press also publishes and maintains a stock of books for general sale. The Press uses normal costing to cost each job. Its job-costing system has two direct-cost categories (direct materials and direct manufacturing labor) and one indirect-cost pool (manufacturing overhead, allocated on the basis of direct manufacturing labor costs).

The following data (in thousands) pertain to 2007:

Direct materials and supplies purchased on credit	$ 800
Direct materials used	710
Indirect materials issued to various production departments	100
Direct manufacturing labor	1,300
Indirect manufacturing labor incurred by various production departments	900
Depreciation on building and manufacturing equipment	400
Miscellaneous manufacturing overhead* incurred by various production departments (ordinarily would be detailed as repairs, photocopying, utilities, etc.)	550
Manufacturing overhead allocated at 160% of direct manufacturing labor costs	?
Cost of goods manufactured	4,120
Revenues	8,000
Cost of goods sold	4,020
Inventories, December 31, 2006 (not 2007):	
Materials Control	100
Work-in-Process Control	60
Finished Goods Control	500

*The term manufacturing overhead is not used uniformly. Other terms that are often encountered in printing companies include *job overhead* and *shop overhead*.

Required

1. Prepare an overview diagram of the job-costing system at the University of Chicago Press.
2. Prepare journal entries to summarize the 2007 transactions. As your final entry, dispose of the year-end under- or overallocated manufacturing overhead as a write-off to Cost of Goods Sold. Number your entries. Explanations for each entry may be omitted.
3. Show posted T-accounts for all inventories, Cost of Goods Sold, Manufacturing Overhead Control, and Manufacturing Overhead Allocated.

4-25 Job costing, journal entries, and source documents (continuation of 4-24). For each journal entry in your answer to Exercise 4-24, (a) indicate the source document that would most likely authorize the entry, and (b) give a description of the entry in the subsidiary ledgers, if any entry needs to be made there.

4-26 Job costing, journal entries. Donnell Transport assembles prestige manufactured homes. Its job-costing system has two direct-cost categories (direct materials and direct manufacturing labor) and one indirect-cost pool (manufacturing overhead allocated at a budgeted $30 per machine-hour in 2007). The following data (in millions) pertain to operations for 2007:

Materials Control, beginning balance, January 1, 2007	$ 12
Work-in-Process Control, beginning balance, January 1, 2007	2
Finished Goods Control, beginning balance, January 1, 2007	6
Materials and supplies purchased on credit	150
Direct materials used	145
Indirect materials (supplies) issued to various production departments	10
Direct manufacturing labor	90
Indirect manufacturing labor incurred by various production departments	30
Depreciation on plant and manufacturing equipment	19
Miscellaneous manufacturing overhead incurred (ordinarily would be detailed as repairs, utilities, etc., with a corresponding credit to various liability accounts)	9
Manufacturing overhead allocated, 2,100,000 actual machine-hours	?
Cost of goods manufactured	294
Revenues	400
Cost of goods sold	292

Required

1. Prepare an overview diagram of Donnell Transport's job-costing system.
2. Prepare journal entries. Number your entries. Post to T-accounts. What is the ending balance of Work-in-Process Control?
3. Show the journal entry for disposing of under- or overallocated manufacturing overhead directly as a year-end write-off to Cost of Goods Sold. Post the entry to T-accounts.

4-27 Job costing, unit cost, ending work in process. Raymond Company produces pipes for concert-quality organs. Each job is unique. In April 2007, it completed all outstanding orders, and then, in May 2007, it worked on only two jobs, M1 and M2:

Excel Lab
www.prenhall.com/horngren/cost12e

	A	B	C
1	**Raymond Company, May 2007**	**Job M1**	**Job M2**
2	Direct materials	$ 75,000	$ 50,000
3	Direct manufacturing labor	275,000	200,000

Direct manufacturing labor is paid at the rate of $25 per hour. Manufacturing overhead costs are allocated at a budgeted rate of $20 per direct manufacturing labor-hour. Only Job M1 was completed in May.

If you want to use Excel to solve this exercise, go to the Excel Lab at **www.prenhall.com/horngren/cost12e** and download the template for Exercise 4-27.

Required

1. Compute the total cost for Job M1.
2. 1,500 pipes were produced for Job M1. Calculate the cost per pipe.
3. Prepare the journal entry transferring Job M1 to finished goods.
4. What is the ending balance in the Work-in-Process Control account?

4-28 Job costing; actual, normal, and variation from normal costing. Chirac & Partners, a Quebec-based public accounting partnership, specializes in audit services. Its job-costing system has a single direct-cost category (professional labor) and a single indirect-cost pool (audit support, which contains all costs of the Audit Support Department). Audit support costs are allocated to individual jobs using actual professional labor-hours. Chirac & Partners employs 10 professionals to perform audit services.

PH Grade Assist

Excel Lab
www.prenhall.com/horngren/cost12e

Budgeted and actual amounts for 2007 are as follows:

	A	B	C
1	**Chirac & Partners**		
2	**Budget for 2007**		
3	Professional labor compensation	$960,000	
4	Audit support department costs	$720,000	
5	Professional labor-hours billed to clients	16,000	hours
6			
7	**Actual results for 2007**		
8	Audit support department costs	$744,000	
9	Professional labor-hours billed to clients	15,500	hours
10	Actual professional labor cost rate	$58	per hour

If you want to use Excel to solve this exercise, go to the Excel Lab at **www.prenhall.com/horngren/cost12e** and download the template for Exercise 4-28.

Required

1. Compute the direct-cost rate and the indirect-cost rate per professional labor-hour for 2007 under (a) actual costing, (b) normal costing, and (c) the variation from normal costing that uses budgeted rates for direct costs.
2. Chirac's 2007 audit of Pierre & Co. was budgeted to take 110 hours of professional labor time. The actual professional labor time spent on the audit was 120 hours. Compute the cost of the Pierre & Co. audit using (a) actual costing, (b) normal costing, and (c) the variation from normal costing that uses budgeted rates for direct costs. Explain any differences in the job cost.

4-29 Research project costs, variation in overhead rates. Prentiss University is well-known for its groundbreaking academic research. Its professors regularly bid on and are awarded research projects funded by government and private agencies. Research teams use university resources such as laboratories, computers, office space, and libraries. For 2006, Prentiss' Dean of Research has collected the following budgeted costs of research projects in four academic departments:

Excel Lab
www.prenhall.com/horngren/cost12e

	A	B	C	D	E	F
1	**Cost Category**	**Department**				
2	**(000s)**	**Liberal Arts**	**Natural Sciences**	**Engineering**	**Business**	**Total**
3	Direct costs (travel, materials)	$1,200	$5,000	$5,500	$2,100	$13,800
4	Professors' salaries	1,000	1,600	1,500	2,000	6,100
5	Graduate students' stipends	700	1,500	2,500	500	5,200
6	Overhead costs such as office space, library, computers, and facilities	850	8,030	9,600	5,250	23,730

When a professor applies for a grant, Prentiss University requires him or her to submit a cost budget using the following cost categories: direct costs (say, for travel and project-specific materials), direct labor costs (for professors' and graduate students' time), and overhead costs (for use of university resources). Overhead costs are required to be calculated at an overhead rate of 210% of budgeted direct-labor costs of the project.

If you want to use Excel to solve this exercise, go to the Excel Lab at **www.prenhall.com/horngren/cost12e** and download the template for Exercise 4-29.

Required

1. Calculate a single common overhead rate across all departments based on budgeted total overhead costs and budgeted total direct labor costs.
2. Calculate the budgeted cost for research projects submitted to funding agencies by each academic department in 2006 using the method required by Prentiss University.
3. Calculate the budgeted cost of research projects in each academic department in 2006.
4. Professors in the Liberal Arts Department at Prentiss are beginning to lose many research projects to other small liberal arts colleges on the basis of cost. Why do you think this is happening?
5. If Liberal Arts professors are allowed to charge their own overhead rate of 50% of direct labor costs, what common overhead rate would Natural Sciences, Engineering, and Business have to apply based on budgeted overhead costs and budgeted direct labor costs of these departments?
6. What problems, if any, do you see arising from taking the approach proposed in requirement **5**?

Problems

4-30 Job costing, accounting for manufacturing overhead, budgeted rates. The Solomon Company uses a job-costing system at its Dover, Delaware, plant. The plant has a Machining Department and a Finishing Department. Solomon uses normal costing with two direct-cost categories (direct materials and direct manufacturing labor) and two manufacturing overhead cost pools (the Machining Department, with machine-hours as the allocation base, and the Finishing Department, with direct manufacturing labor costs as the allocation base). The 2006 budget for the plant is as follows:

	Machining Department	Finishing Department
Manufacturing overhead	$10,000,000	$8,000,000
Direct manufacturing labor costs	$ 900,000	$4,000,000
Direct manufacturing labor-hours	30,000	160,000
Machine-hours	200,000	33,000

Required

1. Prepare an overview diagram of Solomon's job-costing system.
2. What is the budgeted overhead rate in the Machining Department? In the Finishing Department?
3. During the month of January, the job-cost record for Job 431 shows the following:

	Machining Department	Finishing Department
Direct materials used	$14,000	$3,000
Direct manufacturing labor costs	$ 600	$1,250
Direct manufacturing labor-hours	30	50
Machine-hours	130	10

Compute the total manufacturing overhead allocated to Job 431.

4. Assuming that Job 431 consisted of 200 units of product, what is the cost per unit?
5. Amounts at the end of 2006 are as follows:

	Machining Department	Finishing Department
Manufacturing overhead incurred	$11,200,000	$7,900,000
Direct manufacturing labor costs	$ 950,000	$4,100,000
Machine-hours	220,000	32,000

Compute the under- or overallocated manufacturing overhead for each department and for the Dover plant as a whole.

6. Why might Solomon use two different manufacturing overhead cost pools in its job-costing system?

4-31 Service industry, job costing, law firm. Keating & Associates is a law firm specializing in labor relations and employee-related work. It employs 25 professionals (5 partners and 20 associates) who work directly with its clients. The average budgeted total compensation per professional for 2005 is $104,000. Each professional is budgeted to have 1,600 billable hours to clients in 2005. All professionals work for clients to their maximum 1,600 billable hours available. All professional labor costs are included in a single direct-cost category and are traced to jobs on a per-hour basis.

All costs of Keating & Associates other than professional labor costs are included in a single indirect-cost pool (legal support) and are allocated to jobs using professional labor-hours as the allocation base. The budgeted level of indirect costs in 2005 is $2,200,000.

Required

1. Prepare an overview diagram of Keating's job-costing system.
2. Compute the 2005 budgeted direct-cost rate per hour of professional labor.

3. Compute the 2005 budgeted indirect-cost rate per hour of professional labor.
4. Keating & Associates is considering bidding on two jobs:
   a. Litigation work for Richardson, Inc., which requires 100 budgeted hours of professional labor
   b. Labor contract work for Punch, Inc., which requires 150 budgeted hours of professional labor

   Prepare a cost estimate for each job.

4-32 Service industry, job costing, two direct- and two indirect-cost categories, law firm (continuation of 4-31). Keating has just completed a review of its job-costing system. This review included a detailed analysis of how past jobs used the firm's resources and interviews with personnel about what factors drive the level of indirect costs. Management concluded that a system with two direct-cost categories (professional partner labor and professional associate labor) and two indirect-cost categories (general support and secretarial support) would yield more-accurate job costs. Budgeted information for 2005 related to the two direct-cost categories is as follows:

	Professional Partner Labor	Professional Associate Labor
Number of professionals	5	20
Hours of billable time per professional	1,600 per year	1,600 per year
Total compensation (average per professional)	$200,000	$80,000

Budgeted information for 2005 relating to the two indirect-cost categories is

	General Support	Secretarial Support
Total costs	$1,800,000	$400,000
Cost-allocation base	Professional labor-hours	Partner labor-hours

Required

1. Compute the 2005 budgeted direct-cost rates for (a) professional partners and (b) professional associates.
2. Compute the 2005 budgeted indirect-cost rates for (a) general support and (b) secretarial support.
3. Compute the budgeted costs for the Richardson and Punch jobs, given the following information:

	Richardson, Inc.	Punch, Inc.
Professional partners	60 hours	30 hours
Professional associates	40 hours	120 hours

4. Comment on the results in requirement 3. Why are the job costs different from those computed in Problem 4-31?

4-33 Proration of overhead. (Z. Iqbal, adapted) The Zaf Radiator Company uses a normal-costing system with a single manufacturing overhead cost pool and machine-hours as the cost-allocation base. The following data are for 2007:

Budgeted manufacturing overhead	$4,800,000
Overhead allocation base	Machine-hours
Budgeted machine-hours	80,000
Manufacturing overhead incurred	$4,900,000
Actual machine-hours	75,000

Machine-hours data and the ending balances (before proration of under- or overallocated overhead) are as follows:

	Actual Machine-Hours	2007 End-of-Year Balance
Cost of Goods Sold	60,000	$8,000,000
Finished Goods Control	11,000	1,250,000
Work in Process Control	4,000	750,000

Required

1. Compute the budgeted manufacturing overhead rate for 2007.
2. Compute the under- or overallocated manufacturing overhead of Zaf Radiator in 2007. Dispose of this amount using
   a. Write-off to Cost of Goods Sold
   b. Proration based on ending balances (before proration) in Work-in-Process Control, Finished Goods Control, and Cost of Goods Sold
   c. Proration based on the allocated overhead amount (before proration) in the ending balances of Work-in-Process Control, Finished Goods Control, and Cost of Goods Sold
3. Which method do you prefer in requirement 2? Explain.

4-34 Normal costing, overhead allocation, working backward. (M. Rajan, adapted) Gibson Manufacturing uses normal costing for its job-costing system, which has two direct-cost categories (direct materials and direct manufacturing labor) and one indirect-cost category (manufacturing overhead). The following information is obtained for 2007:

- Total manufacturing costs, $8,000,000
- Manufacturing overhead allocated, $3,600,000 (allocated at a rate of 200% of direct manufacturing labor costs)
- Work-in-process inventory on January 1, 2007, $320,000
- Cost of finished goods manufactured, $7,920,000

Required

1. Use information in the first two bullet points to calculate (a) direct manufacturing labor costs in 2007 and (b) cost of direct materials used in 2007.
2. Calculate the ending work-in-process inventory on December 31, 2007.

PH Grade Assist

4-35 Proration of overhead, two indirect-cost pools. Glavine Corporation uses two manufacturing overhead cost pools: one for the overhead costs incurred in the Machining Department and another for overhead costs incurred in the Assembly Department. Glavine uses a normal-costing system. It allocates overhead costs to jobs from the Machining Department using a budgeted machine-hour overhead rate, and from the Assembly Department using a budgeted direct manufacturing labor-hour rate.

The following data are for 2006:

	Machining Department	Assembly Department
Budgeted manufacturing overhead rate	$60 per machine-hour	$40 per direct manuf. labor-hour
Actual manufacturing overhead costs	$6,200,000	$4,700,000

Machine-hours and direct manufacturing labor-hours data and ending balances are as follows:

	Actual Machine-Hours	Actual Direct Manufacturing Labor-Hours	Balance Before Proration, December 31, 2006
Cost of Goods Sold	67,500	90,000	$16,000,000
Finished Goods Control	4,500	4,800	750,000
Work-in-Process Control	18,000	25,200	3,250,000

Required

1. Compute the under- or overallocated overhead in *each* department in 2006. Dispose of the under- or overallocated amount in *each* department using:
   a. Write-off to Cost of Goods Sold.
   b. Proration based on ending balances (before proration) in Cost of Goods Sold, Finished Goods Control, and Work-in-Process Control.
   c. Proration based on the allocated overhead amount (before proration) in the ending balances of Cost of Goods Sold, Finished Goods Control, and Work-in-Process Control.
2. Explain which proration method you prefer in requirement 1.

4-36 General ledger relationships, under- and overallocation. (S. Sridhar, adapted) Needham Company uses normal costing in its job-costing system. Partially completed T-accounts and additional information for Needham for 2006 are as follows:

Direct Materials Control

1-1-2006	30,000	380,000
	400,000	

Work-in-Process Control

1-1-2006	20,000	
Dir. manuf. labor	360,000	

Finished Goods Control

1-1-2006	10,000	900,000
	940,000	

Manufacturing Overhead Control

540,000	

Manufacturing Overhead Allocated

Cost of Goods Sold

Additional Information:

a. Direct manufacturing labor wage rate was $15 per hour.
b. Manufacturing overhead was allocated at $20 per direct manufacturing labor-hour.
c. During the year, sales revenues were $1,090,000, and marketing and distribution costs were $140,000.

Required

1. What was the amount of direct materials issued to production during 2006?
2. What was the amount of manufacturing overhead allocated to jobs during 2006?
3. What was the total cost of jobs completed during 2006?
4. What was the balance of work-in-process inventory on December 31, 2006?
5. What was the cost of goods sold before proration of under- or overallocated overhead?
6. What was the under- or overallocated manufacturing overhead in 2006?
7. Dispose of the under- or overallocated manufacturing overhead using
   a. Write-off to Cost of Goods Sold
   b. Proration based on ending balances (before proration) in Work-in-Process Control, Finished Goods Control, and Cost of Goods Sold

8. Using each of the approaches in requirement 7, calculate Needham's operating income for 2006.
9. Which approach in requirement 7 do you recommend Needham use? Explain your answer briefly.

4-37 Overview of general ledger relationships. The Blakely Company is a small machine shop that uses normal costing in its job-costing system. The total debits and credits in certain accounts *one day before year-end* are as follows:

	December 30, 2005	
	Total Debits	**Total Credits**
Materials Control	$100,000	$ 70,000
Work-in-Process Control	320,000	305,000
Manufacturing Department Overhead Control	85,000	—
Finished Goods Control	325,000	300,000
Cost of Goods Sold	300,000	—
Manufacturing Overhead Allocated	—	90,000

All materials purchased are direct materials. Note that "total debits" in the inventory accounts would include beginning inventory balances on January 1, 2005, if any.

The total debits and total credits above *do not include* the following:

a. The manufacturing labor costs for the December 31 working day: direct manufacturing labor, $5,000, and indirect manufacturing labor, $1,000.
b. Miscellaneous manufacturing overhead incurred on December 31: $1,000.

Additional Information:

a. Manufacturing overhead has been allocated as a percentage of direct manufacturing labor costs through December 30.
b. Direct materials purchased during 2005 were $85,000.
c. No direct materials were returned to suppliers.
d. Direct manufacturing labor costs during 2005 totaled $150,000, not including the December 31 working day described previously.

Required

1. Use T-accounts to compute the January 1, 2005 beginning balances for the Materials Control, Work-in-Process Control, and Finished Goods Control accounts.
2. Prepare all adjusting and closing journal entries for the preceding accounts. Assume that all under- or overallocated manufacturing overhead is closed directly to Cost of Goods Sold.
3. Compute the ending inventory balances on December 31, 2005, after adjustments and closing, for Materials Control, Work-in-Process Control, and Finished Goods Control accounts.

4-38 General ledger relationships, under- and overallocation, service industry. Brody and Co., an engineering consulting firm, uses a variation from normal costing in its job-costing system. It charges jobs for fees paid to outside experts and costs of making blueprints at actual costs, professional direct-labor costs at a budgeted direct-labor rate, and engineering support overhead costs at a budgeted overhead rate.

PH Grade Assist

Brody maintains a "Jobs-in-Process Control" account in its general ledger that accumulates all costs of ongoing jobs. As a job is completed, Brody immediately bills the client and transfers the cost of the completed job to a "Cost of Jobs Billed" account.

The following data pertain to 2007:

1. Direct costs of fees and blueprints (all cash)	$ 150,000
2. Actual direct professional labor costs (all cash)	$1,500,000
3. Direct professional labor costs charged to jobs at a budgeted direct-labor rate of $50 per actual direct professional labor-hour	$1,450,000
4. Actual engineering support overhead costs (all cash)	$1,140,000
5. Engineering support overhead allocated at 80% of direct professional labor costs charged to jobs (80% × $1,450,000)	$1,160,000
6. Cost of jobs billed	$2,500,000
7. Revenues from jobs billed	$3,500,000

Required

1. Prepare summary journal entries for the above transactions using these accounts: Jobs-in-Process Control, Cost of Jobs Billed, Direct Professional Labor Control, Direct Professional Labor Costs Charged to Jobs, Engineering Support Overhead Control, Engineering Support Overhead Allocated, and Cash Control.
2. As your final entry, dispose of the year-end under- or overallocated account balances as direct write-offs to Cost of Jobs Billed.
3. Calculate Brody's gross margin percentage in 2007.

4-39 Allocation and proration of manufacturing overhead. (SMA, heavily adapted) Nicole Limited is a company that produces machinery to customer order. Its job-costing system (using normal costing) has two direct-cost categories (direct materials and direct manufacturing labor) and one indirect-cost pool (manufacturing overhead, allocated using a budgeted rate based on direct manufacturing labor costs). The budget for 2007 was:

Direct manufacturing labor	$420,000
Manufacturing overhead	$252,000

At the end of 2007, two jobs were incomplete: No. 1768B (total direct manufacturing labor costs were $11,000) and No. 1819C (total direct manufacturing labor costs were $39,000). Machine time totaled 287 hours for No. 1768B and 647 hours for No. 1819C. Direct materials issued to No. 1768B amounted to $22,000. Direct materials for No. 1819C were $42,000.

Total charges to the Manufacturing Overhead Control account for the year were $186,840. Direct manufacturing labor costs of all jobs were $400,000, representing 20,000 direct manufacturing labor-hours.

There were no beginning inventories. In addition to ending Work-in-Process Control, ending Finished Goods Control showed a balance of $156,000 (including direct manufacturing labor costs of $40,000). Revenues for 2007 totaled $2,700,680, cost of goods sold was $1,600,000, and marketing costs were $857,870. Nicole prices on a cost-plus basis. It currently uses a guideline of cost-plus 40% of cost.

Required

1. Prepare a detailed schedule showing the ending balances in the inventories accounts and Cost of Goods Sold (before considering any under- or overallocated manufacturing overhead). Show also the manufacturing overhead allocated included in these ending balances.
2. Calculate the under- or overallocated manufacturing overhead for 2007.
3. Prorate the amount computed in requirement 2 on the basis of
   a. The ending balances (before proration) of Work-in-Process Control, Finished Goods Control, and Cost of Goods Sold.
   b. The allocated overhead amount (before proration) in the ending balances of Work-in-Process Control, Finished Goods Control, and Cost of Goods Sold.
4. Assume that Nicole decides to write off to Cost of Goods Sold any under- or overallocated manufacturing overhead. Will operating income be higher or lower than the operating income that would have resulted from the proration in requirements 3a and 3b?
5. Calculate the cost of job No. 1819C if Nicole Limited had used the adjusted allocation-rate approach to dispose of under- or overallocated manufacturing overhead in 2007.

4-40 Job costing, contracting, ethics. Jack Halpern is the owner and CEO of Aerospace Comfort, a firm specializing in the manufacture of seats for airplanes. He has just received a copy of a letter written to the General Audit Section of the U.S. Navy. He believes it is from an ex-employee of Aerospace.

Dear Sir,

Aerospace Comfort manufactured 100 X7 seats for the Navy in 2007. You may be interested to know the following:

1. *Direct material costs billed for the 100 X7 seats were $25,000.*
2. *Direct manufacturing labor costs billed for 100 X7 seats were $6,000. These costs include 16 hours of setup labor at $25 per hour, an amount included in the manufacturing overhead cost pool as well. The $6,000 also includes 12 hours of design time at $50 an hour. Design time was explicitly identified as a cost the Navy would not reimburse.*
3. *Manufacturing overhead costs billed for 100 X7 seats were $9,000 (150% of direct manufacturing labor costs). This amount includes the 16 hours of setup labor at $25 per hour that is incorrectly included as part of direct manufacturing labor costs.*

You may also want to know that over 40% of the direct materials is purchased from Frontier Technology, a company that is 51% owned by Jack Halpern's brother. For obvious reasons, this letter will not be signed.

cc: The Wall Street Journal
Jack Halpern, CEO of Aerospace Comfort

Aerospace Comfort's contract states that the Navy reimburses Aerospace at 130% of total manufacturing costs. Assume that the facts in the letter are correct as you answer the following questions.

Required

1. What is the cost amount per X7 seat that Aerospace Comfort billed the Navy? Assume that the actual direct material costs were $25,000.
2. What is the amount per X7 seat that Aerospace Comfort should have billed the Navy? Assume that the actual direct material costs were $25,000.
3. What should the Navy do to tighten its procurement procedures to reduce the likelihood of such situations recurring in the future?

Collaborative Learning Problem

4-41 Service industry, job costing, accounting for overhead costs, budgeted rates. Jefferson Company, a commercial painting contractor, uses a normal-costing system to cost each job. Its job-costing system has two direct-cost categories (direct materials and direct labor) and one indirect-cost pool called overhead costs. To each job, Jefferson allocates overhead at a budgeted rate of 80% of direct labor costs.

Jefferson provides the following additional information for February 2007:

1. As of February 1, 2007, Job A21 was the only job in process, having incurred direct material costs of $30,000 and direct labor costs of $50,000.

2. Jobs A22, A23, and A24 were started during February.
3. Direct materials used during February were $150,000.
4. Direct labor costs for February were $120,000.
5. Actual overhead costs for February were $102,000.
6. On February 28, 2007, only job A24 was still in process, having incurred direct material costs of $20,000 and direct labor costs of $40,000.

Jefferson maintains a Jobs-in-Process Control account in its general ledger. As each job is completed, its cost is transferred to the Cost of Jobs Billed account. Each month, Jefferson closes any under- or overallocated overhead to Cost of Jobs Billed.

Required

1. Give one example of a direct cost and one example of an overhead cost for a job undertaken by Jefferson Company.
2. Calculate the overhead allocated to Job A21 as of February 1, 2007.
3. Calculate the overhead allocated to Job A24 as of February 28, 2007.
4. Calculate the under- or overallocated overhead for February 2007.
5. Calculate the Cost of Jobs Billed for February 2007.

Get Connected: Cost Accounting in the News

WWW

Go to www.prenhall.com/horngren/cost12e for additional online exercise(s) that explore issues affecting the accounting world today. These exercises offer you the opportunity to analyze and reflect on how cost accounting helps managers make better decisions and handle the challenges of strategic planning and implementation.

CHAPTER 4 Video Case

WHEELED COACH: Job Costing

What do you need in an emergency? If it's a medical emergency, Wheeled Coach has it covered. Based in Winter Park, Florida, Wheeled Coach (a subsidiary of Collins Industries) is the nation's largest manufacturer of custom-built ambulances that handle everything from routine hospital transports to full-scale trauma and disaster services. You might think that ambulances are pretty much all the same, but in fact, each Wheeled Coach ambulance is built from the ground up using 12 major platforms to meet the specific and unique requirements of every buyer. The custom nature of Wheeled Coach's business means that there are thousands of different configurations that plant personnel must be able to assemble efficiently. Because the vehicles are all distinct, Wheeled Coach uses a job-costing system to accumulate costs separately for each ambulance manufactured.

No vehicle begins production until all required materials are in inventory. Materials include Ford truck chassis, aluminum for framing, wood products for cabinets, and wiring for electrical systems. Wheeled Coach has close to 20,000 items, called stockkeeping units (SKUs), in its inventory, some of which arrive just-in-time for production. The goal of the company's six assembly lines is to roll a finished vehicle off the line each day. Close to 350 employees work four 10-hour days per week to achieve this goal. The main assembly lines are fed daily from subsidiary job shops near the main production floor. Some of the job shops include (1) carpentry for interior benches and cabinets, (2) upholstery for seating, (3) metal fabrication for the ambulance's shell, (4) paint shop for truck chassis prep, painting, and exterior detailing, (5) electrical for interior wiring, and (6) Plexiglas for interior cabinet window fabrication. All work is done to meet individual job specifications, so no finished goods inventory is made to stock. A detailed "bill of materials" is used to request and issue direct materials to the job shops and the main assembly floor.

To keep assembly moving each day, Wheeled Coach must balance its assembly-line work areas, called *cells*, so that just enough workers are assigned to work in the cell. Too many workers, and labor stands idle; too few workers, and the work tasks don't get finished by shift's end, backing up the line and triggering overtime. All work completed in each station moves into the next cell at day's end so that the workers are not kept waiting the following day.

QUESTIONS

1. Assume the following facts for Wheeled Coach: total direct labor for top-of-the-line ambulance Job 06-MX24D is 1,750 hours at a cost of $22,750. Direct materials for the job total $25,200. For 2006, Wheeled Coach recorded 700,000 actual direct manufacturing labor-hours, and actual indirect manufacturing costs totaled $21 million. Direct manufacturing labor-hours are used for allocating manufacturing overhead. Apply the seven steps in job costing to Wheeled Coach's operations.
2. Describe what types of source documents you would expect Wheeled Coach to use in their job-costing system.

CHAPTER 5

ACTIVITY-BASED COSTING AND ACTIVITY-BASED MANAGEMENT

LEARNING OBJECTIVES

1. **Explain how broad averaging undercosts and overcosts products or services**
2. **Present three guidelines for refining a costing system**
3. **Distinguish between simple and activity-based costing systems**
4. **Describe a four-part cost hierarchy**
5. **Cost products or services using activity-based costing**
6. **Explain how activity-based costing systems are used in activity-based management**
7. **Compare activity-based costing systems and department costing systems**
8. **Evaluate the costs and benefits of implementing activity-based costing systems**

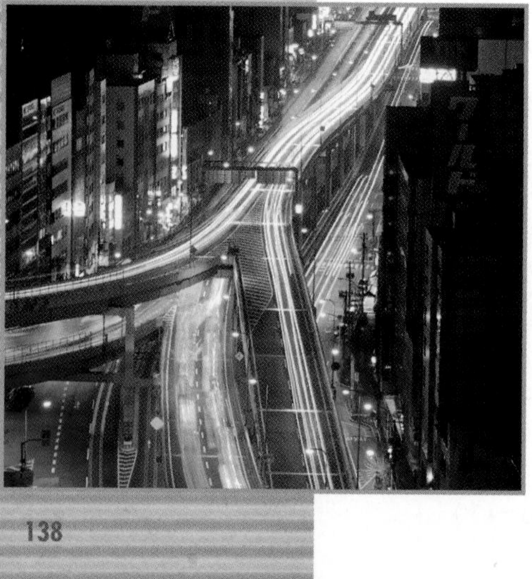

A good mystery never fails to capture the imagination. Money is stolen, property disappears, or someone meets with foul play. On the surface, what may appear unremarkable to the untrained eye may turn out to be quite a revelation when the facts and details are uncovered. Getting to the bottom of the case, understanding what happened and why, and taking action make the difference between a solved case and an unsolved one. The costing systems for some organizations are often mysteries, with unresolved questions. Are we pricing our products accurately? Why are we bleeding red ink?

At the beginning of this chapter, we're introduced to Plastim Corporation, a manufacturer of lenses for rear taillights in automobiles. There's a mystery in progress at the company, which appears to be buried in the company's costing system, because Plastim is facing a significant loss of business from a major customer. Cara Chu, the marketing manager for Plastim Corporation, has just received a disturbing letter from Giovanni Motors that requires investigation by Daniel Picard, manufacturing manager, and Walter McGraw, controller.

Cara: Well, this is certainly bad news. Giovanni Motors has notified us they plan to buy the simple S3 lenses from another vendor who is offering a much lower price. The loss of this business would be devastating, but we can't sell the lenses at a loss. Our pricing is based, in part, on what it costs to produce these lenses. Daniel, can we do anything to reduce our manufacturing costs?

Daniel: Walter will need to help me here, but our technology and manufacturing processes are pretty solid. I'm not saying there isn't room for improvement, but I'm not sure we can squeeze any more costs out of the production process for the S3 lenses.

Cara: Daniel, I know you have your hands full with producing both our complex CL5 lens and the simple S3 lens. I remember you once mentioned that it didn't seem quite right that the price of the CL5 lens was only twice that of the S3 lens when it was so much more difficult to make. At the time, I recall you questioned the adequacy of the costing system we use.

Daniel: Yes, but I just asked the question. The costing system may be part of the problem, but I am sure there are other explanations for why our costs for the simple lenses are more than our competitors'. Walter, what do you think?

Walter: Actually, I have just initiated a project to review our costing system but, given the urgency of this letter from Giovanni Motors, I will make it a top priority. In some cases, using a simple costing system like ours, with a single cost pool and a single indirect-cost rate to allocate indirect costs to jobs, products, or services, works just fine. This is true when those jobs, products, or services are alike in their consumption of indirect costs. If they're not alike, then inaccuracy can creep into the cost figures. A simple costing system just can't represent how different products use resources. Given Daniel's concerns, we probably need to refine our costing system. I'd like to dig a bit more and uncover additional facts before making any recommendations, however. Whatever we decide, we're going to need the buy-in of management at all levels.

Cara: Sounds good, Walter. I don't want our costing system plaguing us with more inaccurate information for crucial pricing decisions.

Like Plastim, most companies—such as Oracle, JP Morgan Chase, and Honda—offer more than one product (or service). To guide decision making, their costing systems must be able to recognize that different products may vary in their use of resources. For example, consider Dell Computer as it broadened its line of personal computers to include desktops, laptops, and servers. The three basic activities for manufacturing personal computers are (a) designing computers, (b) ordering component parts, and (c) configuring the assembly line so the manufacturing process is as efficient as possible. Finished machines are then packed and shipped to buyers. That sounds simple. And it is. But not simple enough so managers can assume that the cost to manufacture each type of computer is the same. If managers assumed that, they'd be making product decisions with flawed information. That's because different activities are needed to produce different computers in the different product lines. Recognizing this challenge, Dell refined its costing system to give managers the information they needed. John Jones, vice president and controller of Dell Americas Operations, noted that "Activity-based costing has really allowed Dell to go to the next level of understanding the profitability of each product it sells." The need for detailed costing information has never been so acute, given increased competitive pressures both foreign and domestic.

As competition intensifies, companies are increasingly producing a greater variety of products and services. Companies are finding, however, that producing different products and services places varying demands on their resources. Using broad averages to uniformly spread the cost of resources across different products results in inaccurate and misleading product costs. The need to measure more accurately how different products and services use resources has led companies such as American Express, Boeing, General Motors, and Exxon Mobil to refine their costing systems. One of the main ways companies around the world have refined their costing systems is through activity-based costing (ABC). We will describe how ABC systems help companies make better decisions about pricing and product mix. We also will show how ABC systems play a part in cost management decisions by improving product designs and efficiency. But before we focus on ABC systems, we take a look at simple costing systems that allocate costs broadly.

It's relatively easy to determine "accurate" costs of products (or services) when a company has only a few products. Companies turn to activity-based costing when they expand their product offerings and the products use different amounts of resources (such as supervision and quality control), which makes it more difficult to determine accurate costs.

Broad Averaging and Its Consequences

1

Explain how broad averaging undercosts and overcosts products or services

. . . this problem arises when reported costs of products do not equal their actual costs

Historically, companies (for example, television and automobile manufacturers) produced a limited variety of products. Indirect costs were a relatively small percentage of total costs. So, using simple costing systems to allocate costs broadly was easy, inexpensive, and reasonably accurate. However, as product diversity has increased, broad averaging has resulted in greater inaccuracy of product costs. For example, the use of a single, plantwide manufacturing overhead rate to allocate costs to products often produces unreliable cost data. The term *peanut-butter costing* (yes, that's what it's called) describes a particular costing approach that uses broad averages for assigning (or spreading, as in spreading peanut butter) the cost of resources uniformly to cost objects (such as products or services) when the individual products or services, in fact, use those resources in nonuniform ways.

Undercosting and Overcosting

The following example illustrates how averaging can provide inaccurate and misleading cost data. Consider the costing of a restaurant bill for four colleagues who meet monthly to discuss business developments. Each diner orders separate entrees, desserts, and drinks. The restaurant bill for the most recent meeting is:

	Entree	Dessert	Drinks	Total
Emma	$11	$ 0	$ 4	$ 15
James	20	8	14	42
Jessica	15	4	8	27
Matthew	14	4	6	24
Total	$60	$16	$32	$108
Average	$15	$ 4	$ 8	$ 27

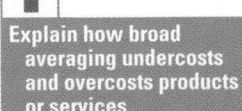

If the $108 total restaurant bill is divided evenly, $27 is the average cost per diner. This cost-averaging approach treats each diner the same. Emma would probably object to paying $27 because her actual cost is only $15; she ordered the lowest-cost entree, had no dessert, and had the lowest-cost drinks. When costs are averaged across all four diners, both Emma and Matthew are overcosted, James is undercosted, and Jessica is (by coincidence) accurately costed.

Broad averaging can lead to undercosting or overcosting of products or services:

- **Product undercosting**—a product consumes a high level of resources but is reported to have a low cost per unit (James's dinner).
- **Product overcosting**—a product consumes a low level of resources but is reported to have a high cost per unit (Emma's dinner).

Companies that undercost products may make sales that actually result in losses, although they may have the erroneous impression that these sales are profitable. That's because these sales may bring in less revenue than the cost of the resources they use. Companies that overcost products may overprice their products, losing market share to competitors producing similar products.

Product-Cost Cross-Subsidization

Product-cost cross-subsidization means that if a company undercosts one of its products, then it will overcost at least one of its other products. Similarly, if a company overcosts one of its products, it will undercost at least one of its other products. Product-cost cross-subsidization occurs when a cost is uniformly spread—meaning it is broadly averaged—across multiple products without a recognition of which products require what resources in what amounts.

In the restaurant-bill example, the amount of cost cross-subsidization of each diner can be readily computed *because all cost items can be traced as direct costs to each diner*. Calculating the amount of cost cross-subsidization is not as simple when there are indirect costs to be considered. Why? Because the resources represented by the indirect costs are used by two or more diners, so the amounts to be allocated to each diner are not so clear-cut—for example, how to allocate the cost of a bottle of wine shared by two or more diners.

To see the effects of broad averaging on direct and indirect costs, we consider Plastim Corporation's costing system.

Simple Costing System at Plastim Corporation

As mentioned earlier, Plastim Corporation manufactures lenses for the rear taillights of automobiles. A lens, made from black, red, orange, or white plastic, is the part of the lamp visible on the automobile's exterior. Lenses are made by injecting molten plastic into a mold to give the lamp its desired shape. The mold is cooled to allow the molten plastic to solidify, and the lens is removed.

Under its contract with Giovanni Motors, a major automobile manufacturer, Plastim makes two types of lenses: a complex lens, CL5, and a simple lens, S3. The complex lens is a large lens with special features, such as multicolor molding (when more than one color is injected into the mold) and complex shapes that wrap around the corner of the car. Manufacturing CL5 lenses is more complex because various parts in the mold must align and fit precisely. The S3 lens is simpler to make because it has a single color and few special features.

Design, Manufacturing, and Distribution Processes

The sequence of steps to design, produce, and distribute lenses, whether simple or complex, is:

- **Design products and processes.** Each year Giovanni Motors specifies some modifications to the simple and complex lenses. Plastim's Design Department designs the molds from which the lenses will be made and specifies the processes needed (that is, details of the manufacturing operations).
- **Manufacture lenses.** The lenses are molded, finished, cleaned, and inspected.
- **Ship and distribute lenses.** Finished lenses are packed and sent to Giovanni Motors.

Plastim is operating at capacity and incurs very low marketing costs. Because of its high-quality products, Plastim has minimal customer-service costs. Plastim's business environment is very competitive with respect to simple lenses. The letter from Giovanni's purchasing manager is of considerable concern because it indicates that a new supplier who makes only simple lenses is offering to supply the S3 lens to Giovanni at a price of $53, well below Plastim's $63 price. Unless Plastim can lower its selling price, it will lose the Giovanni business for the simple lens for the upcoming model year. Fortunately, the same competitive pressures do not exist for the complex lens, which Plastim currently sells to Giovanni at $137 per lens.

As the conversation at the beginning of the chapter suggests, Plastim's management has various options available. For example, Plastim can give up the Giovanni business in simple lenses if it is unprofitable. Or, Plastim can reduce the price of the simple lens and either accept a lower margin or aggressively seek to reduce costs. But to make these long-run strategic decisions, management needs to first understand the costs to make and sell the S3 and CL5 lenses. In determining these costs, Plastim assigns both variable and fixed costs to the S3 and CL5 lenses. Why? For two reasons. First because, in the long run, more costs can be managed and fewer costs are regarded as fixed. Second because, to survive and prosper in the long run, the prices charged for S3 and CL5 must exceed total costs (variable and fixed). Also, to guide their pricing and cost-management decisions, Plastim's managers assign all costs, both manufacturing and nonmanufacturing, to the S3 and CL5 lenses. Had the purpose been inventory costing to comply with generally accepted accounting principles, Plastim's management accountants would have assigned only manufacturing costs to the lenses.

Simple Costing System Using a Single Indirect-Cost Pool

Plastim has historically had a simple costing system that allocates indirect costs using a single indirect-cost rate, the type of system described in Chapter 4. We first describe Plastim's simple costing system and later contrast it with a different costing system: activity-based costing. (Note that instead of jobs, as in Chapter 4, we now have products as the cost objects.) Exhibit 5-1 shows an overview of Plastim's simple costing system. Use this exhibit as a guide as you study the following steps.

Step 1: **Identify the Products That Are the Chosen Cost Objects.** The cost objects are the 60,000 simple S3 lenses and the 15,000 complex CL5 lenses that Plastim produced in 2006. Plastim's goal is to calculate the total costs of designing, manufacturing, and distributing these lenses. Plastim determines the unit cost of each lens by dividing total costs of each type of lens by 60,000 units for S3 lenses and 15,000 units for CL5 lenses.

Step 2: **Identify the Direct Costs of the Products.** Plastim identifies the direct costs—direct materials and direct manufacturing labor—of the lenses as follows:

	60,000 Simple Lenses (S3)		15,000 Complex Lenses (CL5)		
	Total (1)	per Unit (2) = (1) ÷ 60,000	Total (3)	per Unit (4) = (3) ÷ 15,000	Total (5) = (1) + (3)
Direct materials	$1,125,000	$18.75	$675,000	$45.00	$1,800,000
Direct manufacturing labor	600,000	10.00	195,000	13.00	795,000
Total direct costs	$1,725,000	$28.75	$870,000	$58.00	$2,595,000

All other costs are classified as indirect costs.

Step 3: **Select the Cost-Allocation Bases to Use for Allocating Indirect Costs to the Products.** A majority of the indirect costs consist of salaries paid to supervisors, engineers, manufacturing support, and maintenance staff, all supporting direct manufacturing labor. Plastim uses direct manufacturing labor-hours as the only allocation base to allocate all indirect costs to S3 and CL5. In the current year, 2006, Plastim used 39,750 actual direct manufacturing labor-hours.

Step 4: **Identify the Indirect Costs Associated with Each Cost-Allocation Base.** Because Plastim uses only a single cost-allocation base, Plastim groups all indirect costs, totaling $2,385,000, into a single overhead cost pool.

EXHIBIT 5-1

Overview of Plastim's Simple Costing System

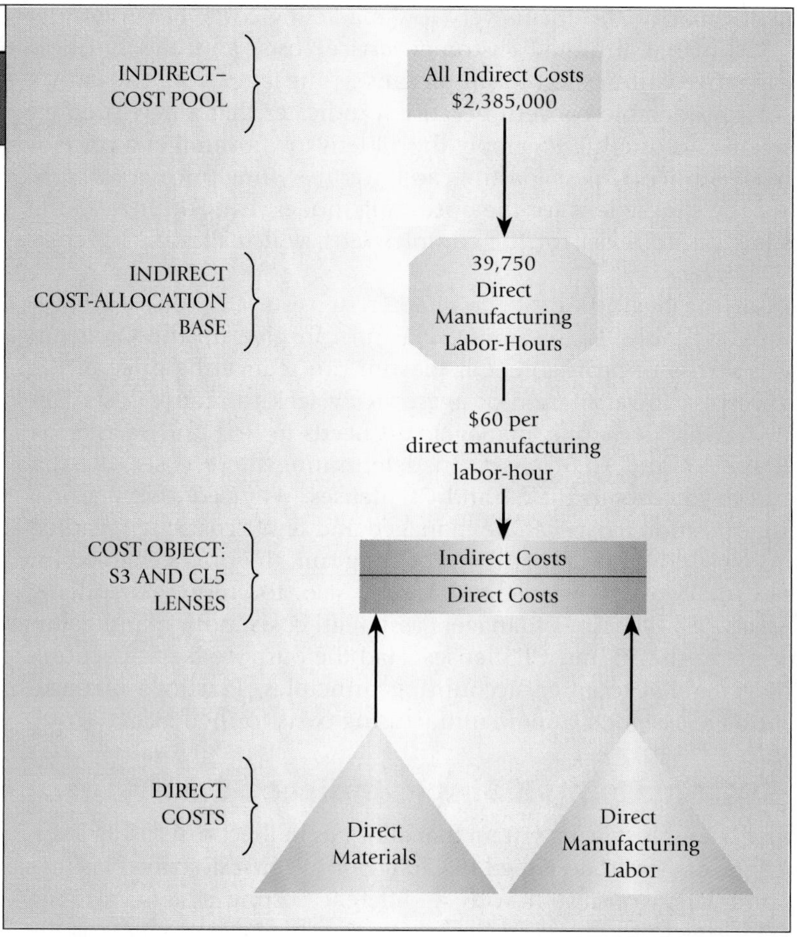

Step 5: Compute the Rate per Unit of Each Cost-Allocation Base Used to Allocate Indirect Costs to the Products.

$$\text{Actual indirect-cost rate} = \frac{\text{Actual total costs in indirect-cost pool}}{\text{Actual total quantity of cost-allocation base}}$$

$$= \frac{\$2{,}385{,}000}{39{,}750 \text{ direct manuf. labor-hours}}$$

$$= \$60 \text{ per direct manufacturing labor-hour}$$

Allocating indirect costs to both products at the $60 rate per direct manufacturing labor-hour is the peanut-butter costing approach.

Step 6: Compute the Indirect Costs Allocated to the Products. Plastim uses 30,000 total direct manufacturing labor-hours to make the S3 lenses and 9,750 total direct manufacturing labor-hours to make the CL5 lenses. Exhibit 5-2 shows indirect costs of $1,800,000 ($60 per direct manufacturing labor-hour × 30,000 direct manufacturing labor-hours) allocated to the simple lens and $585,000 ($60 per direct manufacturing labor-hour × 9,750 direct manufacturing labor-hours) allocated to the complex lens.

Step 7: Compute the Total Cost of the Products by Adding All Direct and Indirect Costs Assigned to the Products. Exhibit 5-2 presents the product costs for the simple and complex lenses. The direct costs are calculated in step 2 and the indirect costs in step 6. Be sure you see the parallel between the simple costing system overview diagram (Exhibit 5-1) and the costs calculated in step 7. Exhibit 5-1 shows two direct-cost categories and one indirect-cost category. Hence, the cost of each type of lens in step 7 (Exhibit 5-2) has three line items: two for direct costs and one for allocated indirect costs.

Plastim's management begins investigating why the unit cost of the S3 lens is $58.75, well above the $53 selling price quoted by Plastim's competitor. A possible explanation is that Plastim's technology and processes are inefficient in manufacturing and distributing the S3 lens. Further analysis of its operations indicates that such inefficiency is not the rea-

EXHIBIT 5-2 Plastim's Product Costs Using the Simple Costing System

	A	B	C	D	E	F	G
1		60,000			15,000		
2		Simple Lenses (S3)			Complex Lenses (CL5)		
3		Total	per Unit		Total	per Unit	Total
4		(1)	(2) = (1) ÷ 60,000		(3)	(4) = (3) ÷ 15,000	(5) = (1) + (3)
5	Direct materials	$1,125,000	$18.75		$ 675,000	$45.00	$1,800,000
6	Direct manufacturing labor	600,000	10.00		195,000	13.00	795,000
7	Total direct costs (Step 2)	1,725,000	28.75		870,000	58.00	2,595,000
8	Indirect costs allocated (Step 6)	1,800,000	30.00		585,000	39.00	2,385,000
9	Total costs (Step 7)	$3,525,000	$58.75		$1,455,000	$97.00	$4,980,000
10							

son. Plastim has years of experience in manufacturing and distributing lenses such as the S3. Because Plastim often makes process improvements, management is confident that their simple-lens technology and processes are not inferior to those of their competitors. However, management is less certain about Plastim's capabilities in manufacturing and distributing complex lenses because it has only recently started making this type of lens. Management is pleasantly surprised to learn that Giovanni Motors considers the price of the CL5 lens to be competitive. Although puzzling, even at these prices, Plastim earns a very large profit margin percentage (operating income ÷ revenues) on the CL5 lenses:

	60,000 Simple Lenses (S3)		15,000 Complex Lenses (CL5)		
	Total (1)	per Unit (2) = (1) ÷ 60,000	Total (3)	per Unit (4) = (3) ÷ 15,000	Total (5) = (1) + (3)
Revenues	$3,780,000	$63.00	$2,055,000	$137.00	$5,835,000
Costs	3,525,000	58.75	1,455,000	97.00	4,980,000
Operating income	$ 255,000	$ 4.25	$ 600,000	$ 40.00	$ 855,000
Profit margin percentage		6.75%		29.20%	

Plastim's management is surprised that this margin is low for the S3 lens, where the company has strong capabilities, but high on the newer, less-established CL5 lens. Because Plastim is not deliberately charging a low price for S3, management wonders whether the costing system is overcosting the simple S3 lens (assigning too much cost to it) and undercosting the complex CL5 lens (assigning too little cost to it).

Plastim's management is quite confident about the accuracy of the direct material costs and direct manufacturing labor costs of the lenses. They are confident because these costs can be traced to the lenses in an economically feasible way. However, management is less certain about the accuracy of the costing system in measuring the indirect resources used by each type of lens. The question facing management is, How might the system of allocating indirect costs to lenses be improved?

Accountants need to reevaluate the costing system if it yields numbers that don't agree with what operating and marketing managers intuitively expect or if costs/prices appear to be out of line with competitors' costs/prices.

Refining a Costing System

2 **Present three guidelines for refining a costing system**

. . . classify more costs as direct costs, expand the number of indirect-cost pools, and identify cost drivers

A **refined costing system** reduces the use of broad averages for assigning the cost of resources to cost objects (such as jobs, products, and services) and provides better measurement of the costs of indirect resources used by different cost objects—no matter how differently the different cost objects use indirect resources.

Many companies—such as John Deere, the American manufacturer of farm equipment; Kanthal, the Swedish manufacturer of heating elements; Owens and Minor, the American distributor of medical products; and The Cooperative Bank in the United Kingdom—have refined their costing systems. What has caused companies in such diverse industries, operating in different parts of the world, to do so? There are four principal reasons.

1. **Increase in product diversity.** Customers are demanding more customized products and, to differentiate themselves from competitors, companies are producing and selling many more products than in the past. Kanthal, for example, produces more than

10,000 different types of electrical heating wires and thermostats. Banks are offering many different types of accounts and services: special passbook accounts, ATM and credit cards, electronic payments, and investment and insurance services. These different products make different demands on the resources needed to produce them because of differences in volume, process, and complexity. The resources demanded by these different products cannot be measured by a simple costing system that allocates indirect costs on the basis of, say, direct manufacturing labor-hours. Using such a simple costing system will result in inaccurate and misleading product costs.

2. **Increase in indirect costs.** Advances in product and process technology have led to increases in indirect costs and decreases in direct costs, particularly direct manufacturing labor costs. For example, plant automation, such as computer-integrated manufacturing (CIM) and flexible manufacturing systems (FMS), has significantly reduced the direct manufacturing labor costs of products. Computers on the manufacturing floor give instructions to set up and run equipment quickly and automatically. The computers accurately measure hundreds of production parameters and directly control the manufacturing processes to achieve high-quality output. Managing more-complex technology and producing very diverse products requires committing an increasing amount of resources for various support functions, such as production scheduling and product and process design and engineering. Because direct manufacturing labor is not a cost driver of these costs, allocating indirect costs on the basis of direct manufacturing labor often does not accurately measure how resources are being used by different products.
3. **Advances in information technology.** Costing system refinements require more data gathering and more analysis and make the costing system more detailed. Improvements in information technology and the accompanying decline in the costs of tracking data make it more cost-effective to implement refinements in costing systems. It is more practical now to create systems that have multiple pools of indirect costs for allocating costs to products.
4. **Competition in product markets.** As markets have become more competitive, managers have felt the need to obtain more-accurate cost information to help them make important strategic decisions, such as how to price products and which products to sell. Making correct pricing and product mix decisions is critical in competitive markets because competitors quickly capitalize on a company's mistakes.

This chapter describes three guidelines for refining a costing system:

1. **Direct-cost tracing.** Classify as many of the total costs as direct costs of the cost object as is economically feasible. This guideline aims to reduce the amount of costs classified as indirect.
2. **Indirect-cost pools.** Expand the number of indirect-cost pools until each of these pools is more homogeneous. In a *homogeneous cost pool,* all of the costs have the same or a similar cause-and-effect (or benefits-received) relationship with the cost-allocation base. For example, a single indirect-cost pool containing both indirect machining costs and indirect distribution costs that are allocated to products using machine-hours is not homogeneous because machining costs and distribution costs do not have the same cause-and-effect relationship with machine-hours. Increases in machine-hours—the cause—have the effect of increasing machining costs but not distribution costs. Now suppose machining costs and distribution costs are subdivided into two separate indirect-cost pools using machine-hours as the cost-allocation base for the machining cost pool and the number of shipments as the cost-allocation base for the distribution cost pool. Each indirect-cost pool would now be homogeneous, which means that within each cost pool, all costs have the same cause-and-effect relationship with their respective cost-allocation base.
3. **Cost-allocation bases.** Use the cause-and-effect criterion, when possible, to identify the cost-allocation base (the cause) for each indirect-cost pool (the effect).

3

Distinguish between simple and activity-based costing systems

. . . unlike simple systems, ABC systems calculate costs of individual activities to cost products

Activity-Based Costing Systems

One of the best tools for refining a costing system is activity-based costing. **Activity-based costing (ABC)** refines a costing system by identifying individual activities as the fundamental cost objects. An **activity** is an event, task, or unit of work with a specified purpose—for example, designing products, setting up machines, operating machines, and distributing products. ABC systems calculate the costs of individual activities and assign costs to cost objects such as products and services on the basis of the activities needed to produce each product or service:[1]

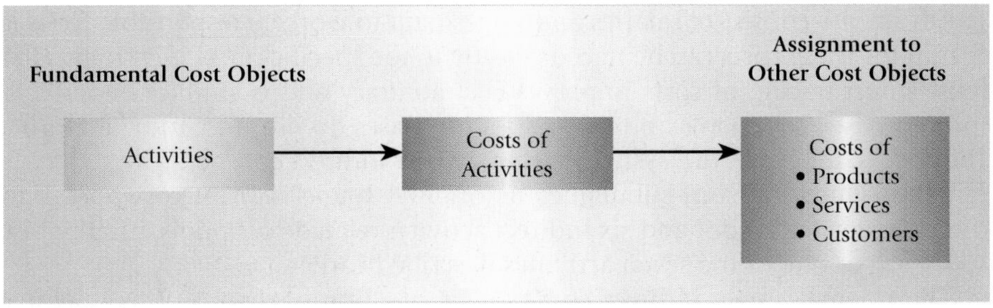

Activities consume resources (for example, workers are paid to pack and ship finished goods to customers). Then, products that consume the activities (packing and shipping) are allocated the costs of those activities.

Plastim's ABC System

After reviewing its simple costing system and the potential miscosting of product costs, Plastim decides to implement an ABC system. Direct costs can be traced to products easily, so the ABC system focuses on refining the assignment of indirect costs to departments, processes, products, and other cost objects. Plastim's ABC system identifies various activities that help explain why Plastim incurs the costs it currently classifies as indirect. To identify these activities, Plastim organizes a team comprised of managers from design, manufacturing, distribution, accounting, and administration.

Defining activities is not a simple matter. The team evaluates hundreds of tasks performed at Plastim before choosing the activities that form the basis of its ABC system. For example, it decides if maintenance of molding machines, operations of molding machines, process control, and product inspection should each be regarded as a separate activity or should be combined into a single activity. An activity-based costing system with many activities becomes complex and unwieldy to operate. An activity-based costing system with too few activities may not be rich enough to measure cause-and-effect relationships between cost drivers and various indirect costs. In choosing activities, Plastim's team identifies activities that account for a sizable fraction of indirect costs and combines other activities that have the same cost allocation base into a single activity. For example, the team decides to combine maintenance of molding machines, operations of molding machines, process control, and product inspection into a single activity—molding machine operations—because these activities have the same cost driver: molding machine-hours.

The team identifies the following seven activities by developing a flowchart of all the steps and processes needed to design, manufacture, and distribute S3 and CL5 lenses.

a. Design products and processes
b. Set up molding machines to ensure that the molds are properly held in place and parts are properly aligned before manufacturing starts
c. Operate molding machines to manufacture lenses
d. Clean and maintain the molds after lenses are manufactured
e. Prepare batches of finished lenses for shipment
f. Distribute lenses to customers
g. Administer and manage all processes at Plastim

These activity descriptions form the basis of the activity-based costing system—sometimes called an *activity list* or an *activity dictionary*. As we describe ABC systems,

[1]For more details on ABC systems, see R. Cooper and R. S. Kaplan, *The Design of Cost Management Systems* (Upper Saddle River, NJ: Prentice Hall, 1999), and G. Cokins, *Activity-Based Cost Management: An Executive's Guide* (Hoboken, NJ: John Wiley & Sons, 2001).

keep in mind the three guidelines for refining a costing system described on page 144.

1. **Direct-cost tracing.** ABC systems aim to reclassify some indirect costs as direct costs by evaluating if some of the costs currently classified as indirect can be traced to cost objects or products. In the Plastim example, the costs of the cleaning and maintenance activity consist of salaries and wages paid to workers responsible for cleaning the mold. These costs can be traced directly to the specific mold used to produce the lens. Direct tracing of costs improves cost accuracy and is simpler because, unlike indirect costs, cost pools and cost-allocation bases do not have to be identified.
2. **Indirect-cost pools.** ABC systems create smaller indirect cost pools linked to the different activities. Plastim subdivides its original single indirect cost pool into one direct-activity cost pool and six indirect activity–related cost pools, each pool corresponding to one of the seven activities described earlier.

   The original single indirect cost pool is not homogeneous. Why? Because the costs of some of the activities (for example, designing products and processes, setting up machines, and distributing lenses) that are lumped into the single cost pool have a weak cause-and-effect relationship with direct manufacturing labor-hours—for example, changes in direct manufacturing labor-hours have no effect on the costs of designing products and processes. Consequently, measuring the direct manufacturing labor-hours used by the S3 and CL5 lenses does not represent the costs of the indirect resources required by these two different lenses.

   Each of the new activity-related cost pools is homogeneous. Why? Because each activity cost pool includes only costs related to that activity (for example, the distribution cost pool includes only costs incurred for the distribution purpose). Among these distribution costs are the wages of truck drivers and the costs of moving cubic feet of packages.
3. **Cost-allocation bases.** For each activity cost pool, a measure of the activity performed serves as the cost-allocation base. For example, Plastim identifies setup-hours, the measure of setup activity (rather than direct manufacturing labor-hours), as the cost-allocation base for setup costs; and it identifies cubic feet of packages moved, the measure of distribution activity, as the cost-allocation base for distribution costs.

The logic of ABC systems is that more finely structured activity cost pools with activity-specific cost-allocation bases, which are cost drivers for the cost pool, lead to more-accurate costing of activities. Allocating costs to products by measuring the cost-allocation bases of different activities used by different products leads to more-accurate product costs. We illustrate this logic by focusing on the setup activity at Plastim.

Setting up molding machines frequently entails trial runs, fine-tuning, and adjustments. Improper setups cause quality problems such as scratches on the surface of the lens. The resources needed for each setup depend on the complexity of the manufacturing operation. Complex lenses require more setup resources per setup than simple lenses. Furthermore, complex lenses can be produced only in small batches because the molds for complex lenses need to be cleaned more often than molds for simple lenses. Relative to simple lenses, complex lenses not only use more resources per setup, but they also need more-frequent setups.

Setup data for the simple S3 lens and the complex CL5 lens are:

		Simple S3 Lens	Complex CL5 Lens	Total
1	Quantity of lenses produced	60,000	15,000	
2	Number of lenses produced per batch	240	50	
3 = (1) ÷ (2)	Number of batches	250	300	
4	Setup time per batch	2 hours	5 hours	
5 = (3) × (4)	Total setup-hours	500 hours	1,500 hours	2,000 hours

Of the $2,385,000 in the total indirect-cost pool, Plastim identifies the total costs of setups (consisting mainly of allocated costs of process engineers, quality engineers, supervisors, and setup equipment) to be $300,000. The following table illustrates the effect of using direct manufacturing labor-hours—the cost-allocation base for all indirect costs in Plastim's pre-ABC costing system—versus setup-hours—the cost-allocation base for setup costs in the ABC system—to allocate setup costs to the simple and complex lenses. Of the

$60 total rate per direct manufacturing labor-hour (p. 142), the setup cost per direct manufacturing labor-hour amounts to $7.54717 ($300,000 ÷ 39,750 total direct manufacturing labor-hours). The setup cost per setup-hour equals $150 ($300,000 ÷ 2,000 total setup-hours).

	Simple S3 Lens	Complex CL5 Lens	Total
Setup cost allocated using direct manufacturing labor-hours: $7.54717 × 30,000; $7.54717 × 9,750	$226,415	$ 73,585	$300,000
Setup cost allocated using setup-hours: $150 × 500; $150 × 1,500	$ 75,000	$225,000	$300,000

Which allocation base should Plastim use? Answer: Setup-hours, because following guidelines 2 and 3, there is a strong cause-and-effect relationship between setup-hours and setup-related overhead costs, but there is almost no relationship between direct manufacturing labor-hours and setup-related overhead costs. Setup costs depend on the number of batches and the complexity of the setups, so that's why setup-hours drive setup costs. Also, the CL5 lens uses more setup-hours than the S3 lens because the CL5 requires a greater number of setups and each setup is more complex. When direct manufacturing labor-hours rather than setup-hours are used to allocate setup costs, the simple S3 lens is overcosted. Why? Because the S3 lens uses a larger proportion of direct manufacturing labor-hours (30,000 ÷ 39,750 = 75.47%) compared to the proportion of setup-hours (500 ÷ 2,000 = 25%).

Note that setup-hours are related to batches (or groups) of lenses made, not individual lenses. Activity-based costing considers different levels of activities—for example, individual units of output versus batches of output—when identifying cause-and-effect relationships. As our discussion of setups illustrates, limiting cost drivers and cost-allocation bases to only units of output (such as direct manufacturing labor-hours) frequently will weaken the cause-and-effect relationship between the cost-allocation base and the costs in a cost pool. When the cost in a cost pool relates to batches of output (such as setup costs), the cost-allocation base must also relate to batches of output (for example, setup-hours).

Cost Hierarchies

4

Describe a four-part cost hierarchy

. . . a four-part cost hierarchy is used to categorize costs based on different types of cost drivers—for example, costs that vary with each unit of a product versus costs that vary with each batch of products.

A **cost hierarchy** categorizes indirect costs into different cost pools on the basis of the different types of cost drivers, or cost-allocation bases, or different degrees of difficulty in determining cause-and-effect (or benefits-received) relationships. ABC systems commonly use a cost hierarchy with four levels—output unit-level costs, batch-level costs, product-sustaining costs, and facility-sustaining costs—to identify cost-allocation bases that are, whenever possible, cost drivers of costs in activity cost pools.

Output unit-level costs are the costs of activities performed on each individual unit of a product or service. Molding machine operations costs (such as the costs of energy, machine depreciation, and repair) related to the activity of running the automated molding machines are output unit-level costs. They are output unit-level costs because, over time, the cost of this activity increases with additional units of output produced (or machine-hours used).

Suppose that in our Plastim example, each S3 lens requires 0.15 molding machine-hours. Then S3 lenses require a total of 9,000 molding machine-hours (0.15 molding machine-hours per lens × 60,000 lenses). Similarly, suppose each CL5 lens requires 0.25 molding machine-hours. Then the CL5 lenses require 3,750 molding machine-hours (0.25 molding machine-hours per lens × 15,000 lenses). The *total* molding machine operations costs allocated to S3 and CL5 depend on the quantity of each type of lens produced, regardless of the number of batches in which the lenses are made. Plastim's ABC system uses machine-hours—an output unit-level cost-allocation base—to allocate molding machine operations costs to products.

Batch-level costs are the costs of activities related to a group of units of products or services rather than to each individual unit of product or service. In the Plastim example, setup costs are batch-level costs. That's because, over time, the cost of this setup activity increases with setup-hours needed to produce batches of lenses. As described in the table on p. 146, the S3 lens requires 500 setup-hours (2 setup-hours per batch × 250 batches). The CL5 lens requires 1,500 setup-hours (5 setup-hours per batch × 300 batches). The total setup costs allocated to S3 and CL5 depend on the total setup-hours required by each type of lens, not on the number of units of S3 and CL5 produced. (Setup costs being a batch-level cost cannot be avoided by producing one less unit of S3 or CL5.) Plastim's ABC system uses setup-hours—a batch-level cost-allocation base—to allocate setup costs to products.

In companies that purchase many different types of direct materials (Plastim purchases mainly plastic pellets), procurement costs can be significant. Procurement costs include the costs of placing purchase orders, receiving materials, and paying suppliers. These costs are batch-level costs because they are related to the number of purchase orders placed rather than to the quantity or value of materials purchased. Other examples of batch-level costs are materials-handling and quality-inspection costs associated with batches of products produced.

Product-sustaining costs (or **service-sustaining costs**) are the costs of activities undertaken to support individual products or services regardless of the number of units or batches in which the units are produced. In the Plastim example, design costs are product-sustaining costs. Over time, design costs depend largely on the time spent by designers on designing and modifying the product, the mold, and the process. These design costs are a function of the complexity of the mold, measured by the number of parts in the mold multiplied by the area (in square feet) over which the molten plastic must flow (12 parts × 2.5 square feet, or 30 parts-square feet for the S3 lens, and 14 parts × 5 square feet, or 70 parts-square feet for the CL5 lens). In 2006, the total design costs allocated to S3 and CL5 depend on the complexity of the mold, regardless of the number of units or batches of production. Design costs cannot be avoided by producing fewer units or running fewer batches. Plastim's ABC system uses parts-square feet—a product-sustaining cost-allocation base—to allocate design costs to products. Other examples of product-sustaining costs are product research and development costs, costs of making engineering changes, and marketing costs to launch new products.

A major reason low-volume products are often undercosted is that low-volume products' *batch-level costs* and *product-sustaining costs* should be spread over the relatively few units of low-volume products rather than spread over all products using *output unit-level cost-allocation bases.*

Facility-sustaining costs are the costs of activities that cannot be traced to individual products or services but that support the organization as a whole. In the Plastim example, the general administration costs (including top management compensation, rent, and building security) are facility-sustaining costs. It is usually difficult to find a good cause-and-effect relationship between these costs and the cost-allocation base. This lack of a cause-and-effect relationship causes some companies to not allocate these costs to products and instead to deduct them separately from operating income. Other companies, such as Plastim, allocate facility-sustaining costs to products on some basis—for example, direct manufacturing labor-hours—because management believes all costs should be allocated to products. Allocating all costs to products or services becomes important when management wants to set selling prices on the basis of an amount of cost that includes all costs.

Implementing Activity-Based Costing at Plastim

5

Cost products or services using activity-based costing

. . . use cost rates for different activities to compute indirect costs of a product

Now that you know the basic concepts of ABC, let's use them to refine Plastim's simple costing system. We again follow the seven-step approach to costing and the three guidelines for refining costing systems (the guidelines are increasing direct-cost tracing, creating homogeneous indirect-cost pools, and identifying cost-allocation bases that have cause-and-effect relationships with costs in the cost pool). Exhibit 5-3 shows an overview of Plastim's ABC system. Use this exhibit as a guide as you study the following steps.

Step 1: **Identify the Products That Are the Chosen Cost Objects.** The cost objects are the S3 and CL5 lenses. Plastim's goal is to calculate, first, the total costs, and second, the per-unit costs of designing, manufacturing, and distributing these lenses.

Step 2: **Identify the Direct Costs of the Products.** Plastim identifies the following direct costs of the lenses: direct material costs, direct manufacturing labor costs, and mold cleaning and maintenance costs. Note that in the costing system it has been using, Plastim classified mold cleaning and maintenance costs as indirect costs and allocated them to products using direct manufacturing labor-hours. However, following guideline 1 for refining a costing system, mold cleaning and maintenance costs, consisting of workers' wages for cleaning molds after each batch of lenses is produced, can be traced directly as a batch-level cost because each type of lens can only be produced from a specific mold. Complex lenses incur more mold cleaning and maintenance costs than simple lenses because

Plastim produces more batches of complex lenses than simple lenses and because the molds of complex lenses are more difficult to clean. Direct manufacturing labor-hours is not a good cost driver of the demand that simple and complex lenses place on mold cleaning and maintenance resources.

Plastim's direct costs are:

		60,000 Simple Lenses (S3)		15,000 Complex Lenses (CL5)		
Description	**Cost Hierarchy Category**	**Total (1)**	**per Unit (2) = (1) ÷ 60,000**	**Total (3)**	**per Unit (4) = (3) ÷ 15,000**	**Total (5) = (1) + (3)**
Direct materials	Output unit-level	$1,125,000	$18.75	$ 675,000	$45.00	$1,800,000
Direct manuf. labor	Output unit-level	600,000	10.00	195,000	13.00	795,000
Mold cleaning & maintenance	Batch-level	120,000	2.00	150,000	10.00	270,000
Total direct costs		$1,845,000	$30.75	$1,020,000	$68.00	$2,865,000

All other costs are classified as indirect costs.

Step 3: Select the Cost-Allocation Bases to Use for Allocating Indirect Costs to the Products. Following guidelines 2 and 3 for refining a costing system, Plastim identifies six activities—design, set up molding machines, operate molding machines, set up batches for shipment, distribute lenses, and administer and manage processes—for allocating indirect costs to products. Exhibit 5-4, columns 2 and 4, show the cost hierarchy category, the cost-allocation base, and the quantity of the cost-allocation base for each activity described in column 1.

Identifying activities and cost drivers is not easy but necessary. Operating personnel have the best understanding of the company's production processes. In ABC, accountants often interview operating personnel to help identify activities and the related cost-allocation bases.

Identifying the cost-allocation bases defines the number of activity pools into which costs must be grouped in an ABC system. For example, rather than define the design activities of product design, process design, and prototyping as separate activities, Plastim defines these three activities together as a combined design activity and forms a homogeneous design cost pool. Why? Because the complexity of the mold is an appropriate cost driver for costs incurred in each of the three separate design activities.

A second consideration for choosing a cost-allocation base is the availability of reliable data and measures. Consider the problem of determining a cost-allocation base for the design activity. The driver of design cost, which is a product-sustaining cost, is the complexity of the mold; more-complex molds take more time to design. In its ABC system, Plastim measures complexity in terms of the number of parts in the mold and the surface area of the mold (parts-square feet). If these data are difficult to obtain or measure, Plastim may be forced to use some other measure of complexity, such as the amount of material flowing through the mold. A potential problem with this measure of complexity is that the quantity of material flow may not adequately represent the complexity of the design activity.

Step 4: Identify the Indirect Costs Associated with Each Cost-Allocation Base. In this step, overhead costs incurred by Plastim are assigned to activities (see Exhibit 5-4, column 3), to the extent possible, on the basis of a cause-and-effect relationship between the cost-allocation base for an activity and the costs of the activity. For example, all costs that have a cause-and-effect relationship to cubic feet of packages moved are assigned to the distribution cost pool. Of course, the strength of the cause-and-effect relationship between the cost-allocation base and the respective cost of the activity varies across cost pools. For example, the cause-and-effect relationship between direct manufacturing labor-hours and administration activity costs is not as strong as the relationship between setup-hours and setup activity costs.

Companies that have successfully implemented ABC usually limit the number of activities to 5 to 10 per department, at least in the initial implementation. More activities can be added if additional complexity is warranted. Identifying too many activities initially may bog the company down in too much detail, which might cause the ABC implementation to fail.

Some costs can be directly identified with a particular activity. For example, cost of materials used when designing products, salaries paid to design engineers, and depreciation of equipment used in the design department are directly identified with the design activity. Other costs need to be allocated across activities. For example, on the basis of interviews or time records,

EXHIBIT 5-3 Overview of Plastim's Activity-Based Costing System

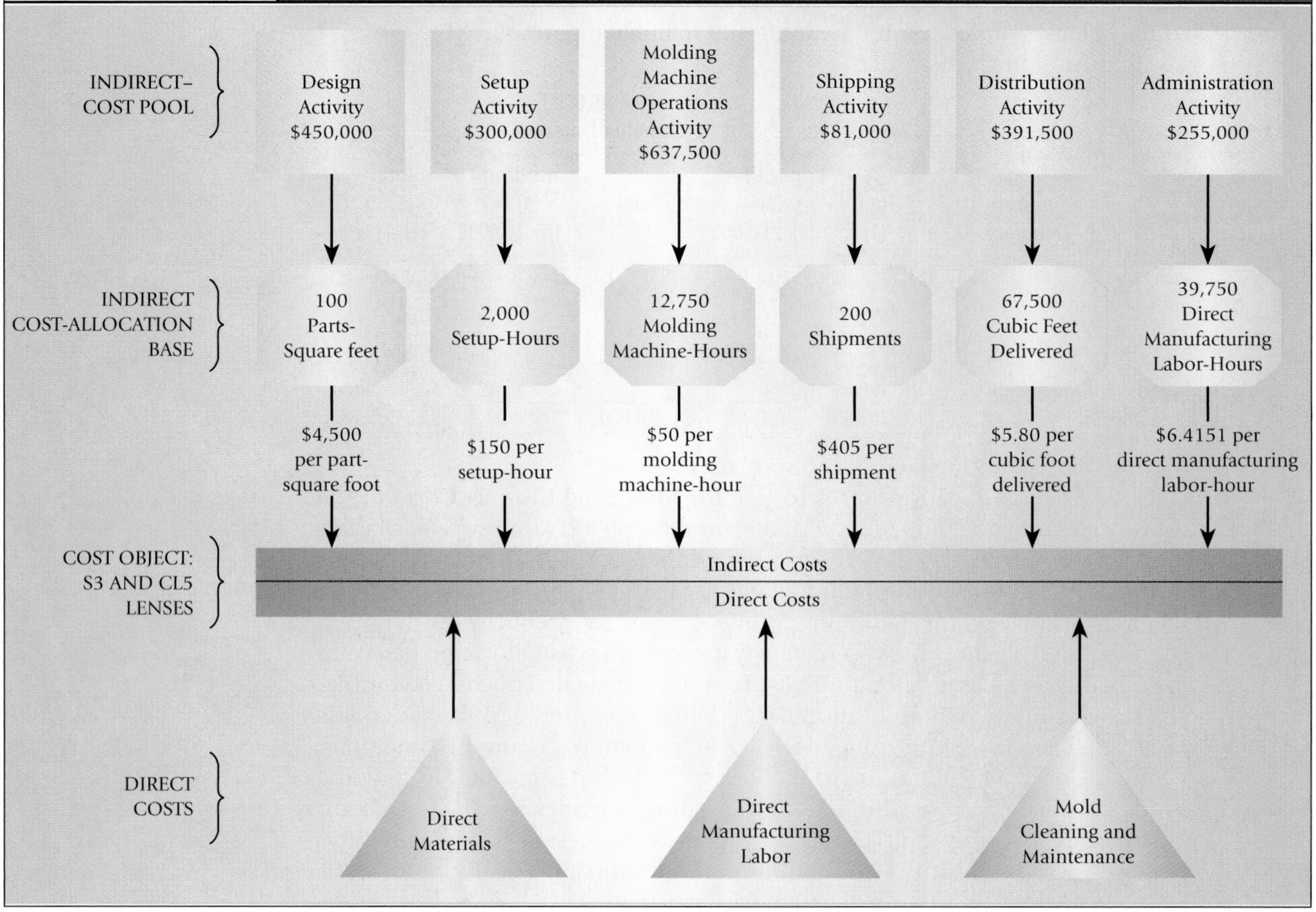

EXHIBIT 5-4 Activity-Cost Rates for Indirect-Cost Pools

	A	B	C	D	E	F	G	H
1			(Step 4)	(Step 3)		(Step 5)		
2	Activity	Cost Hierarchy Category	Total Indirect Costs	Cost-Allocation Base Quantity		Overhead Activity Cost-Allocation Rate		Cause-and-Effect Relationship Between Allocation Base and Activity Cost
3	(1)	(2)	(3)	(4)		(5) = (3) ÷ (4)		(6)
4	Design	Product-sustaining	$450,000	100	parts-square feet	$ 4,500	per part-square foot	Design Department indirect costs increase with more complex molds (more parts, larger surface area).
5	Setup of molding machines	Batch-level	$300,000	2,000	setup-hours	$ 150	per setup-hour	Indirect setup costs increase with setup-hours.
6	Molding machine operations	Output unit-level	$637,500	12,750	molding machine-hours	$ 50	per molding machine-hour	Indirect costs of operating molding machines increase with molding machine-hours.
7	Shipping	Batch-level	$ 81,000	200	shipments	$ 405	per shipment	Shipping costs incurred to prepare batches for shipment increase with the number of shipments.
8	Distribution	Output-unit-level	$391,500	67,500	cubic feet delivered	$ 5.80	per cubic foot delivered	Distribution costs increase with the cubic feet of packages delivered.
9	Administration	Facility sustaining	$255,000	39,750	direct manuf. labor-hours	$6.4151	per direct manuf. labor-hour	The demand for Administrative resources increases with direct manufacturing labor-hours.

EXHIBIT 5-5 Plastim's Product Costs Using Activity-Based Costing System

	A	B	C	D	E	F	G
1		60,000			15,000		
2		Simple Lenses (S3)			Complex Lenses (CL5)		
3		Total	per Unit		Total	per Unit	Total
4	**Cost Description**	(1)	(2) = (1) ÷ 60,000		(3)	(4) = (3) ÷ 15,000	(5) = (1) + (3)
5	Direct Costs						
6	Direct materials	$1,125,000	$18.75		$ 675,000	$ 45.00	$1,800,000
7	Direct manufacturing labor	600,000	10.00		195,000	13.00	795,000
8	Direct mold cleaning and maintenance costs	120,000	2.00		150,000	10.00	270,000
9	Total direct costs (Step 2)	1,845,000	30.75		1,020,000	68.00	2,865,000
10	Indirect Costs of Activities						
11	Design						
12	S3, 30 parts-sq.ft. x $4,500	135,000	2.25				450,000
13	CL5, 70 parts-sq.ft. x $4,500				315,000	21.00	
14	Setup of molding machines						
15	S3, 500 setup-hours x $150	75,000	1.25				300,000
16	CL5, 1,500 setup-hours x $150				225,000	15.00	
17	Molding machine operations						
18	S3, 9,000 molding machine-hours x $50	450,000	7.50				637,500
19	CL5, 3,750 molding machine-hours x $50				187,500	12.50	
20	Shipping						
21	S3, 100 shipments x $405	40,500	0.67				81,000
22	CL5, 100 shipments x $405				40,500	2.70	
23	Distribution						
24	S3, 45,000 cubic feet delivered x $5.80	261,000	4.35				391,500
25	CL5, 22,500 cubic feet delivered x $5.80				130,500	8.70	
26	Administration						
27	S3, 30,000 dir. manuf. labor-hours x $6.4151	192,453	3.21				255,000
28	CL5, 9,750 dir. manuf. labor-hours x $6.4151				62,547	4.17	
29	Total indirect costs allocated (Step 6)	1,153,953	19.23		961,047	64.07	2,115,000
30	Total Costs (Step 7)	$2,998,953	$49.98		$1,981,047	$132.07	$4,980,000
31							

manufacturing engineers and supervisors estimate the time spent on design, setting up of molding machines, and operating molding machines. The time spent on these activities serves as a basis for allocating each manufacturing engineer's and supervisor's salary costs to various activities. We illustrate these calculations for Gabriel Jackson, a manufacturing engineer at Plastim. The following table records the time Jackson spent on the different activities in 2006 and converts the time spent into dollar costs based on Jackson's salary.

Activity	Hours (1)	Rate per Hour (2)	Amount (3)
Design of products and processes	700	$25	$17,500
Setup of molding machines	400	25	10,000
Operation of molding machines	900	25	22,500
Total	2,000		$50,000

Other costs are similarly allocated to activity-cost pools using allocation bases that best describe the costs incurred to support the different activities. For example, rent costs are allocated on the basis of square-feet area used for different activities.

The point here is that all costs do not fit neatly into activity categories. Often, costs may first need to be allocated to activities before the costs of the activities can be allocated to products.

Step 5: Compute the Rate per Unit of Each Cost-Allocation Base Used to Allocate Indirect Costs to the Products. Exhibit 5-4, column 5, shows the calculation of the activity-cost rates using the quantity of the cost-allocation base selected in step 3 and the indirect costs of each activity calculated in step 4.

This chapter's activity-based cost calculations have been performed in Excel and illustrate how technology can aid in implementing ABC. The basic database is Exhibit 5-4, where activity cost rates are calculated for homogeneous indirect-cost pools. The Excel worksheet for Exhibit 5-5 draws on the Exhibit 5-4 database to calculate product costs. Companies use ABC software that has this same type of architecture that connects resources, activities, and cost objects.

Step 6: Compute the Indirect Costs Allocated to the Products. Exhibit 5-5 shows total indirect costs of $1,153,953 allocated to the simple lens and $961,047 allocated to the complex lens. To calculate total indirect costs of each lens, the total quantity of the cost-allocation base used for each activity by each type of lens (using data provided by Plastim's operations personnel) is multiplied by the cost-allocation rate calculated in step 5 (see Exhibit 5-4, column 5). For example, of the 2,000 total hours of the setup activity (Exhibit 5-4, column 4), the S3 lens uses 500 setup-hours and the CL5 lens uses 1,500 setup-hours. Therefore, total costs of setup activity allocated to the S3 lens are $75,000 (500 setup-hours × $150 per setup-hour) and to the CL5 lens are $225,000 (1,500 setup-hours × $150 per setup-hour). Setup cost per unit can then be calculated as $1.25 ($75,000 ÷ 60,000 units) for the S3 lens and $15 ($225,000 ÷ 15,000 units) for the CL5 lens.

Step 7: Compute the Total Cost of the Products by Adding All Direct and Indirect Costs Assigned to the Products. Exhibit 5-5 presents the product costs for the simple and complex lenses. The direct costs are calculated in step 2, and the indirect costs are calculated in step 6. The ABC system overview in Exhibit 5-3 shows three direct-cost categories and six indirect-cost categories. The cost of each lens type in Exhibit 5-5 has nine line items, three for direct costs and six for indirect costs. The differences between the ABC product costs of S3 and CL5 calculated in Exhibit 5-5 highlight how each of these products uses different amounts of direct and indirect costs in each activity area.

We emphasize two features of ABC systems. First, ABC systems focus on the long run and so identify all costs used by products, whether the costs are variable or fixed in the short run. As we saw in Chapter 3, if Plastim's managers were interested in short-run decisions, they would need to focus on only the variable costs of activities used by products and not all costs. Second, ABC systems recognize the hierarchy of costs to calculate total costs allocated to products. The per-unit costs can then be easily calculated by dividing total costs allocated to each product by the number of units of each product.

Comparing Alternative Costing Systems

Exhibit 5-6 compares the simple costing system using a single indirect-cost pool (Exhibit 5-1 and Exhibit 5-2) Plastim has been using and the ABC system (Exhibit 5-3 and Exhibit 5-5) that replaced it. We emphasize three points in Exhibit 5-6, consistent with the guidelines for refining a costing system: (1) ABC systems trace more costs as direct costs; (2) ABC systems create homogeneous cost pools linked to different activities; and (3) for each activity-cost pool, ABC systems seek a cost-allocation base that has a cause-and-effect relationship with costs in the cost pool.

The homogeneous cost pools and the choice of cost-allocation bases, tied to the cost hierarchy, give Plastim's managers greater confidence in the activity and product cost numbers from the ABC system. The bottom part of Exhibit 5-6 shows that allocating costs to lenses using only an output unit-level allocation base—direct manufacturing labor-hours, as in the single indirect-cost pool system used prior to ABC—overcosts the simple S3 lens by $8.77 per unit and undercosts the complex CL5 lens by $35.07 per unit. The CL5 lens uses a disproportionately larger amount of output unit-level, batch-level, and product-sustaining costs than is represented by the direct manufacturing labor-hour cost-allocation base. The S3 lens uses a disproportionately smaller amount of these costs.

The benefit of an ABC system is that it provides information to make better decisions. But the benefits of ABC must be weighed against its measurement and implementation costs. We will elaborate on these costs in a later section, when we discuss implementation of ABC systems.

6

Explain how activity-based costing systems are used in activity-based management

. . . such as pricing decisions, product-mix decisions, and cost reduction

Using ABC Systems for Improving Cost Management and Profitability

The emphasis of this chapter so far has been on the role of ABC systems in obtaining better product costs. **Activity-based management (ABM)** is a method of management decision-making that uses activity-based costing information to improve customer

EXHIBIT 5-6

Comparing Alternative Costing Systems

	Simple Costing System Using a Single Indirect-Cost Pool (1)	ABC System (2)	Difference (3) = (2) – (1)
Direct-cost categories	2 Direct materials Direct manufacturing labor	3 Direct materials Direct manufacturing labor Direct mold cleaning and maintenance labor	+1
Total direct costs	$2,595,000	$2,865,000	$270,000
Indirect-cost pools	1 Single indirect-cost pool allocated using direct manufacturing labor-hours	6 Design (parts-square feet)[1] Setup (setup-hours) Molding machine operations (molding machine-hours) Shipping (number of shipments) Distribution (cubic feet delivered) Administration (direct manufacturing labor-hours)	5
Total indirect costs	$2,385,000	$2,115,000	($270,000)
Total costs assigned to simple (S3) lens	$3,525,000	$2,998,953	($526,047)
Cost per unit of simple (S3) lens	$58.75	$49.98	($8.77)
Total costs assigned to complex (CL5) lens	$1,455,000	$1,981,047	$526,047
Cost per unit of complex (CL5) lens	$97.00	$132.07	$35.07

[1]Cost drivers for the various indirect-cost pools are shown in parentheses.

satisfaction and profitability. We define ABM broadly to include decisions about pricing and product mix, reduction of costs, improvement of processes, and product design.

Pricing and Product-Mix Decisions An ABC system gives managers cost information that helps in making and selling diverse products. With this information, managers can make pricing and product-mix decisions. For example, the ABC system indicates that Plastim can match its competitor's price of $53 for the S3 lens and still make a profit, because the ABC cost of S3 is $49.98 (see Exhibit 5-5). Without this information from the ABC system, Plastim managers might conclude erroneously that they would incur an operating loss on the S3 lens at a price of $53. This incorrect conclusion might cause Plastim to reduce its business in simple lenses and focus instead on complex lenses, where its single indirect-cost-pool system indicates it is very profitable.

Focusing on complex lenses would be a mistake. The ABC system indicates that the cost of making the complex lens is much higher—$132.07 versus $97 under the direct manufacturing labor-hour-based costing system Plastim had been using. As Plastim's operations staff had thought all along, Plastim has no competitive advantage in making CL5 lenses. At a price of $137 per lens for CL5, the profit margin is very small ($137.00 – $132.07 = $4.93). As Plastim reduces prices on simple lenses, it may need to negotiate a higher price on complex lenses.

Cost Reduction and Process Improvement Decisions Manufacturing and distribution personnel use ABC systems to focus on how and where to reduce costs. Managers set cost reduction targets in terms of reducing the cost per unit of the cost-allocation base in different activity areas. For example, the supervisor of the distribution activity area at Plastim could have a performance target of decreasing distribution cost per cubic foot of products deliv-

The core of the ABC approach is the analysis of activities. When Plastim analyzes its activity—setups of molding machines—the company may find ways to reduce setup time (the cost-management benefit of ABC) and better estimate setup cost per unit of product (the product-costing benefit of ABC). Remember, activities consume resources, and products consume activities.

ered from $5.80 to $5.40 by improving the efficiency of the distribution activity. Plastim seeks to reduce these costs without compromising customer service or the actual or perceived value (usefulness) customers obtain from the product or service. That is, Plastim will attempt to take out those costs that are *nonvalue added.*

Doing an analysis of the factors that cause costs to be incurred (cost drivers) reveals many opportunities for improving the way work is done. Management can evaluate whether particular nonvalue-added activities can be reduced or eliminated. Each of the cost-allocation bases in Plastim's ABC system is a nonfinancial variable (number of setup-hours, cubic feet delivered, and so on). Controlling physical items such as setup-hours or cubic feet delivered is often the most fundamental way that operating personnel manage costs. For example, Plastim can decrease distribution costs by packing the lenses in a way that reduces the bulkiness of the packages delivered.

The following table shows the reduction in distribution costs of the S3 and CL5 lenses as a result of actions that lower cost per cubic foot delivered (from $5.80 to $5.40) and total cubic feet of deliveries (from 45,000 to 40,000 for S3 and 22,500 to 20,000 for CL5).

	60,000 S3 Lenses		**15,000 CL5 Lenses**	
	Total (1)	**per Unit (2) = (1) ÷ 60,000**	**Total (3)**	**per Unit (4) = (3) ÷ 15,000**
Distribution costs (from Exhibit 5-5)				
S3, 45,000 cubic feet × $5.80/cubic foot	$261,000	$4.35		
CL5, 22,500 cubic feet × $5.80/cubic foot			$130,500	$8.70
Distribution costs as a result of process improvements				
S3, 40,000 cubic feet × $5.40/cubic foot	216,000	3.60		
CL5, 20,000 cubic feet × $5.40/cubic foot			108,000	7.20
Savings in distribution costs from process improvements	$ 45,000	$0.75	$ 22,500	$1.50

Taking the long-term strategic view of ABC systems, we assume in the preceding example that total distribution costs will decrease from $391,500 ($261,000 + $130,500) to $324,000 ($216,000 + $108,000) as Plastim reduces distribution cost per cubic foot and cubic feet of packages delivered. In the short run, however, distribution costs may be fixed and may not decrease. Suppose all $391,500 of distribution costs are fixed costs in the short run. In this case, how should costs be allocated to the S3 and CL5 lenses?

Many ABC systems distinguish *costs incurred* from *resources used* to design, manufacture, and deliver products and services. For the distribution activity, after process improvements,

Costs incurred = $391,500

Resources used = $216,000 (for S3 lens) + $108,000 (for CL5 lens) = $324,000

ABC systems focus on the resources used by each product and hence would allocate $216,000 to S3 and $108,000 to CL5 for a total of $324,000, which is less than the costs incurred of $391,500. The difference of $67,500 ($391,500 – $324,000) represents costs of unused but available distribution capacity—that is,

Costs incurred = Resources used + Costs of unused capacity

= $324,000 + $67,500 = $391,500

This unused capacity arises from efficiency improvements (using less distribution labor and space) that result in a decrease in the distribution cost per cubic foot from $5.80 to $5.40, as the following calculations show:

Number of cubic feet of lenses that Plastim can deliver as a result of efficiency improvements	= $391,500 / $5.40 per cubic foot	= 72,500 cubic feet
Number of cubic feet that Plastim needs to deliver (S3 lens, 40,000; CL5 lens, 20,000)	= 40,000 + 20,000	= 60,000 cubic feet
Unused distribution capacity		= 12,500 cubic feet

Costs of unused distribution capacity = 12,500 cubic feet × $5.40 per cubic foot = $67,500

An advantage of ABC systems is that they do not allocate the costs of unused capacity to products. Instead, these systems highlight the amount of unused capacity as a separate line item. Highlighting the unused capacity signals to managers an opportunity for reducing costs. Managers will seek to reduce unused capacity—for example, by redeploying labor to other uses or by laying off workers. At the same time, product costs for S3 and CL5 are not burdened by the cost of resources not supporting these products. Note that unused-capacity issues did not arise in our main Plastim Company example. That's because we assumed (for simplicity) that initially Plastim had no unused capacity. Chapter 9 discusses issues related to unused capacity in more detail.

Design Decisions Management can evaluate how its current product and process designs affect activities and costs as a way of identifying new designs to reduce costs. For example, design decisions that decrease complexity of the mold reduce costs of design, materials, labor, setups, molding machine operations, and mold cleaning and maintenance. Plastim's customers may be willing to give up some features of the lens in exchange for a lower price.

Had Plastim continued to use its direct manufacturing labor-hour-based system to choose among alternative designs, which design choices would Plastim have favored? Answer: Those designs that reduced direct manufacturing labor-hours the most. That's because the costing system would signal that reducing direct manufacturing labor-hours would reduce indirect costs. However, this would be a false signal. As our discussion of Plastim's ABC system reveals, the cause-and-effect relationship between direct manufacturing labor-hours and Plastim's indirect costs is weak, so reducing direct manufacturing labor-hours would have only a minimal effect on reducing indirect costs.

There are often more opportunities for cost reduction in the design stage than in the production stage.

Planning and Managing Activities As was the case with Plastim, most companies implementing ABC systems for the first time analyze actual costs to identify activity-cost pools and activity-cost rates. Many companies then use ABC systems for planning and managing activities. These companies specify budgeted costs for activities and use budgeted cost rates to cost products using normal costing. At year-end, budgeted costs and actual costs are compared to provide feedback on how well activities were managed. As activities and processes are changed, new activity-cost rates are calculated. At the end of the year, adjustments must also be made for underallocated or overallocated indirect costs for each activity area.

Our purpose in this chapter is to describe the basic building blocks of activity-based costing systems and to introduce activity-based management. We emphasize the effect ABC has on organizations and management, as cross-functional teams use ABC information to make decisions regarding pricing, design, cost reduction, and process improvement. Many of the cost drivers (for example, complexity of the mold) are nonfinancial variables, and ABC ties together financial and nonfinancial, or operational, factors. ABC also aids in performance management by identifying cost reduction targets for various activities.

Study Tip: To check your understanding of ABC, see the Featured Exercise, true–false statement 7, multiple-choice questions 5 and 6, and Review Exercises 3 and 4 (*Student Guide*, beginning p. 52). Fully explained solutions begin on p. 58

We will build on these ideas as we discuss various topics later in the book. Management decisions that use activity-based costing information are described in Chapter 6, where we discuss activity-based budgeting; Chapter 11, where we discuss outsourcing and adding or dropping business segments; in Chapter 12, where we evaluate alternative design choices to improve efficiency and reduce nonvalue-added costs; in Chapter 13, where we cover reengineering and downsizing; in Chapter 14, where we explore managing customer profitability; in Chapter 19, where we explain quality improvements; and in Chapter 20, where we describe how to evaluate suppliers.

Activity-Based Costing and Department Costing Systems

7

Compare activity-based costing systems and department costing systems

. . . both systems provide similar costs for products that use different activities within a department in a similar way

Companies often use costing systems that have features of ABC systems—such as multiple cost pools and multiple cost-allocation bases—but that do not emphasize individual activities. Many companies have evolved their costing systems from using a single indirect cost rate system to using separate indirect cost rates for each department (for example, design, manufacturing, distribution, and so on) or each subdepartment (for example, machining and assembly departments within manufacturing). Why do companies use department cost rates? Because the cost drivers of resources in each department or subdepartment differ from the single, companywide, cost-allocation base. ABC systems are a further refinement of department costing systems. In this section, we compare ABC systems and department costing systems.

Plastim uses the Design Department indirect cost rate to cost its design activity. Plastim calculates the design activity rate by dividing total Design Department costs by total parts-square feet, a measure of the complexity of the mold and the driver of Design Department costs. Plastim does not find it worthwhile to calculate separate activity rates within the Design Department for the different design activities, such as designing products, making temporary molds, and designing processes. Why? Because complexity of a mold is an appropriate cost-allocation base for costs incurred for all those design activities: The Design Department costs are homogeneous with respect to this cost-allocation base.

In contrast, using ABC, Plastim identifies in the Manufacturing Department, two activity cost pools—a setup cost pool and a molding machine operations cost pool—instead of using a single Manufacturing Department overhead cost pool. It identifies these activity cost pools for two reasons. First, each of these activities within manufacturing incurs significant costs and has a different cost driver. Second, the S3 and CL5 lenses do not use resources from these two activity areas in the same proportion. For example, CL5 uses 75% (1,500 ÷ 2,000) of the setup-hours but only 29.4% (3,750 ÷ 12,750) of the machine-hours. Using only machine-hours, say, to allocate all Manufacturing Department costs at Plastim would result in CL5 being undercosted because it would not be charged for the significant amounts of setup resources it actually uses.

Based on what we just explained, consider the following: Using department indirect cost rates to allocate costs to products results in the same product costs as activity cost rates if: (1) a single activity accounts for a sizable proportion of the department's costs; or (2) significant costs are incurred on different activities within a department but each activity has the same cost driver and hence cost-allocation base (as was the case in Plastim's Design Department); or (3) significant costs are incurred for different activities with different cost-allocation bases within a department but different products use resources from the different activity areas in the same proportions (for example, if CL5 had used 65%, say, of the setup-hours and 65% of the machine-hours).

When any one of these three conditions holds, department indirect cost rates and activity cost rates will give the same or similar cost information. In companies in which none of these conditions hold, department costing systems can be refined using ABC. Emphasizing activities leads to more-focused and homogeneous cost pools and aids in identifying cost-allocation bases for activities that have a better cause-and-effect relationship with the costs in activity cost pools. But the benefits of an ABC system must be balanced against its costs and limitations.

Implementing ABC Systems

8

Evaluate the costs and benefits of implementing activity-based costing systems

. . . measurement difficulties versus more accurate costs that aid in decision making

Managers choose the level of detail to use in a costing system by evaluating the expected costs of the costing system against the expected benefits that will come from using it to make better decisions. There are telltale signs that indicate when an ABC system is likely to provide the most benefits. Here are some of these signs:

- Significant amounts of indirect costs are allocated using only one or two cost pools.
- All or most indirect costs are identified as output unit-level costs (few indirect costs are described as batch-level costs, product-sustaining costs, or facility-sustaining costs).
- Products make diverse demands on resources because of differences in volume, process steps, batch size, or complexity.
- Products that a company is well suited to make and sell show small profits; whereas products that a company is less suited to produce and sell show large profits.
- Operations staff have significant disagreements with the accounting staff about the costs of manufacturing and marketing products and services.

When a company decides to implement ABC, it must make important choices about the level of detail to use. Should it choose many finely specified activities, cost drivers, and cost pools, or would a few suffice? For example, Plastim could identify a different rate per molding machine-hour for each different type of molding machine. In making such choices, managers weigh the benefits against the costs and limitations of implementing a more-detailed costing system.

The main costs and limitations of an ABC system are the operational complexities and measurements necessary to implement it. ABC systems require management to estimate costs of activity pools and to identify and measure cost drivers for these pools to serve as cost-allocation bases. Even basic ABC systems require many calculations to determine costs of products and services. Making the many measurements is costly. Activity cost rates also need to be updated regularly.

As ABC systems get very detailed and more cost pools are created, more allocations are necessary to calculate activity costs for each cost pool. This increases the chances of misidentifying the costs of different activity cost pools. For example, supervisors are likely to be more prone to incorrectly identify the time they spent on different activities if they have to allocate their time over five activities rather than only two activities.

At times, companies are also forced to use allocation bases for which data are readily available rather than allocation bases they would have liked to use. Consider materials-handling costs. A company might be forced to use the number of loads moved as the allocation base, instead of the complexity and distance of different loads moved, the preferred allocation base, simply because data on complexity and distance of moves are difficult to obtain. When measurement errors are large, activity-cost information can be misleading. For example, if the cost per load moved decreases, a company may conclude that it has become more efficient in its materials-handling operations. In fact, the lower cost per load moved may have resulted solely from moving many lighter loads over shorter distances.

Many companies such as Kanthal have found the strategic and operational benefits of a less-detailed ABC system to be good enough to not warrant incurring the costs and complexities of a more-detailed system. Other organizations, such as Hewlett-Packard, implement ABC in chosen divisions or functions. As improvements in information technology and accompanying declines in measurement costs continue, however, more-detailed ABC systems have become a practical alternative in many companies, such as The Cooperative Bank in the United Kingdom. As such trends continue, more-detailed ABC systems should be better able to pass the cost–benefit test.

Global Surveys of Company Practice (p. 158) suggest that ABC implementation varies among companies. Nevertheless, its framework and ideas provide a standard for judging whether any simple costing system is good enough for a particular management's purposes. Any contemplated changes in a simple costing system will inevitably be improved by ABC thinking. The Focus on Values and Behaviors feature (p. 159) describes some of the issues that management accountants must be sensitive to as they seek to immerse an organization with ABC thinking.

ABC in Service and Merchandising Companies

Although many of the early examples of ABC originated in manufacturing, ABC has many applications in service and merchandising companies. The Plastim example includes the application of ABC to a service activity—design—and to a merchandising activity—distribution. Companies such as The Cooperative Bank, Braintree Hospital, BCTel in the telecommunications industry, and Union Pacific in the railroad industry have implemented some form of ABC systems to identify profitable product mixes, improve efficiency, and satisfy customers. Similarly, many retail and wholesale companies—for example, Supervalu, a retailer and distributor of grocery store products and Owens and Minor, a medical supplies distributor—have used ABC systems.

The general approach to ABC in service and merchandising companies is similar to the ABC approach in manufacturing. Costs are divided into homogeneous cost pools and classified as output unit-level costs, batch-level costs, product-sustaining costs, service-sustaining costs, or facility-sustaining costs. The cost pools correspond to activities. Costs are allocated to products or customers using cost-allocation bases that have a cause-and-effect relationship with the costs in the cost pool. Service and merchandising companies must also confront the problems of measuring activity cost pools and identifying and measuring allocation bases.

GLOBAL SURVEYS OF COMPANY PRACTICE

Varying Interest in Activity-Based Costing

A number of companies around the world are investigating and implementing activity-based costing. However, ABC applications vary from organization to organization. Some companies use ABC as their basic, ongoing cost accounting system. Other organizations are more selective, so perhaps only a single business division uses ABC before it becomes a companywide initiative.

One study of 162 U.S.-based companies (including 29 service-sector companies) reported the following ranking of the primary applications for which ABC is used: (1) product/service costing, (2) cost reduction, and (3) process improvement.[a] Areas in which ABC-based information produced "significant" or "very significant" changes in decisions ranked as follows: (1) pricing strategy, (2) processes, and (3) product mix. Another recent survey of U.S. manufacturers reported that only 30 out of 145 respondents, or 20.6%, currently use ABC.[b] Unfortunately, the survey does not indicate why respondents are not using ABC. Some of these companies may already have information similar to the information developed by ABC systems. For other manufacturers, ABC may not be relevant or useful or the costs of implementing ABC may exceed the benefits.

Among United Kingdom companies, one survey indicates that 17.5% of businesses have implemented ABC and another 20.3% are considering using it.[c] For what applications are these firms using ABC?

Cost reduction	90.3%
Product/service pricing	68.9
Performance measurement/improvement	74.2
Cost modeling	64.5
Budgeting	54.8

A New Zealand survey found that 20.3% of respondents use ABC.[d] Other studies found that 20% of respondents from India and 11% of respondents from Singapore had implemented ABC systems.[e,f]

A survey of Irish manufacturing companies that have implemented ABC reported the following percentages for the benefits experienced: (1) more-accurate cost information for product costing and pricing (71%), (2) improved cost control and management (66%), (3) improved insight into cost drivers (58%), (4) better performance measures (46%), and (5) more-accurate customer profitability analysis (25%).[g] A survey of Irish service-sector companies reports similar percentages for the benefits experienced.[h]

The Irish survey also reported that the three most common implementation problems were assigning costs to activities, identifying and selecting cost drivers, and inadequate computer software. A survey of Dutch companies in the food and beverage industry cited problems of other priorities and lack of time, as well as the difficulty and cost of collecting data.[i]

---

[a] APQC/CAM-I, *Activity Based Management Consortium Study.*

[b] Sharman, "The Case for Management Accounting."

[c] Innes, "Activity-Based Costing in the U.K.'s Largest Companies."

[d] Cotton, "Note on a New Zealand Replication of the Innes et al. UK Activity-Based Costing Survey."

[e] Anderson and Lanen, "Economic Transition, Strategy, and the Evolution of Management Accounting Practices: The Case of India."

[f] Ghosh and Chan, "Management Accounting in Singapore—Well in Place?"

[g] Clarke, "Activity-Based Costing in Ireland: Barrier to, and Opportunities for, Change."

[h] Clarke and Mullins, "Activity-Based Costing in the Non-Manufacturing Sector in Ireland: A Preliminary Investigation."

[i] Groot, "Activity-Based Costing in U.S. and Dutch Food Companies."

Full citations are in Appendix A at the end of the book.

The Cooperative Bank followed the approach described in the preceding paragraph when it implemented ABC in its retail banking operations. It calculated the costs of various activities, such as performing ATM transactions, opening and closing accounts, administering mortgages, and processing Visa transactions. It then used the activity cost rates to calculate costs of various products, such as checking accounts, mortgages, and Visa cards. ABC information helped The Cooperative Bank to improve its processes and to identify profitable products and customer segments. The Concepts in Action feature (p. 160) describes ABC analysis in e-banking.

FOCUS ON VALUES AND BEHAVIORS

SUCCESSFULLY CHAMPIONING ABC

Successfully implementing ABC systems requires more than an understanding of the technical details. ABC implementation often represents a significant change in the costing system and, as the chapter indicates, it requires managers to make major choices with respect to the definition of activities and the level of detail. What then are some of the behavioral issues that the management accountant must be sensitive to?

1. **Gaining support of top management and creating a sense of urgency for the ABC effort.** This requires management accountants to lay out the vision for the ABC project and to clearly communicate its strategic benefits (for example, the resulting improvements in product and process design). It also requires selling the idea to end users, working with members of other departments and as business partners of the managers in the various areas affected by the ABC project. For example, at USAA Federal Savings Bank, project managers demonstrated how the information gained from ABC would provide insights into the efficiency of bank operations that was previously unavailable. Now the finance area communicates regularly with operations about new reports and proposed changes to the financial reporting package that managers receive.
2. **Creating a guiding coalition of managers throughout the value chain for the ABC effort.** ABC systems measure how the resources of an organization are used. Managers responsible for these resources have the best knowledge about activities and cost drivers. Getting managers to cooperate and take the initiative for implementing ABC is essential for gaining the required expertise, the proper credibility, and the necessary leadership. There are several other benefits to gaining wide participation among managers. First, implementing ABC requires a significant time commitment. If managers feel more involved in the process, they are more likely to be willing to commit their time to the ABC effort. Second, there inevitably will be some managers who may be, or may perceive themselves to be, negatively affected by the ABC information. In our Plastim example, the manager of the complex CL5 lens may feel that ABC disadvantages him because it assigns more costs to the CL5 lens. Involving managers who are skeptical of the ABC process and giving them an opportunity to express their concerns reduces the likelihood of these managers negatively affecting the process. Finally, engaging managers throughout the value chain creates greater opportunities for coordination and cooperation across the different functions. For example, an ABC analysis might reveal that a company is incurring high manufacturing costs because of quality problems in its plant. The best way to reduce costs may be to redesign the product. This requires that the design department and the manufacturing department work closely together.
3. **Educating and training employees in ABC as a basis for employee empowerment.** Disseminating information about ABC throughout all facets of an organization allows workers in all areas of a business to use their knowledge of ABC to make improvements. For example, WS Industries, an Indian manufacturer of insulators, not only shared ABC information with its workers but also established an incentive plan that gave employees a percentage of the cost savings. The results were dramatic because employees were empowered and motivated to implement numerous cost-saving projects.
4. **Seeking small short-run successes as proof that the ABC implementation is yielding results.** Too often, managers and management accountants seek big results and major changes far too quickly. In many situations, achieving a significant change overnight is difficult. However, showing how ABC information has helped improve a process and save costs, even if only in small ways, motivates the team to stay on course and build momentum. The credibility gained from small victories leads to additional and bigger improvements involving larger numbers of people and different parts of the organization. Eventually ABC and ABM will be rooted in the culture of the organization. Sharing short-run successes may also help motivate employees to be innovative. At USAA Federal Savings Bank, managers created a "process improvement" mailbox in Microsoft Outlook to facilitate the sharing of process improvement ideas.
5. **Recognizing that ABC information is not perfect because it balances the need for better information against the costs of creating a complex system that managers and employees may not understand.** The management accountant must help managers recognize both the value and the limitations of ABC and not oversell it. Open and honest communication about ABC ensures that managers use ABC thoughtfully to make good decisions. Critical judgments can then be made without being adversarial, and tough questions can be asked to help drive better decisions about the system.

CONCEPTS IN ACTION

Analyzing and Managing Multichannel Banking with Activity-Based Costing

Activity-based costing (ABC) can help banks, such as Wells Fargo and Bank of America, with strategic analysis, measurement, and management of their service delivery. This support is critical because banks offer consumers multiple service channels for transactions, including traditional branches, ATMs, and Internet banking. Because the costs for each channel are different, ABC can help answer questions such as, What costs are associated with branch transactions versus online transactions? Which channels help reduce overall costs? How much does it cost to get a new customer to use online banking? To answer these questions, ABC systems identify and measure the costs of activities aimed at servicing the customer.

Banking cost drivers are unique because the costs associated with each cost driver are different depending on whether customers use branch tellers, automated phone systems, or the Internet. Examples of these cost drivers include:

Activity	Cost Driver
1. Transaction processing—the costs associated with executing deposits, withdrawals, transfers, and other banking business	Number of transactions per channel
2. Product/service offerings—selecting service offerings, creating and developing new services, supporting existing offerings	Number of products/services per channel
3. Customer service—helping customers with problems and answering questions about service offerings	Number of inquiries per channel
4. Customer acquisition and retention—acquiring new customers and structuring programs to retain existing customers	Number of targeted customers per channel
5. Technology services—information technology support, including ATM maintenance, performance upgrades, and online banking service development	Number of support hours per channel

The activity costs are used to identify costs of different services within the different channels on the basis of the activities needed to support different service offerings. According to one recent report, ATM transactions are nine times cheaper and on-line banking fifteen times cheaper than traditional branch transactions. With such drastic cost differences, banks use ABC information to evaluate (1) the profits earned on customers that extensively use different transaction channels, (2) the profitability of placing new ATMs in high-traffic areas, and (3) the effectiveness of advertising that encourages existing customers to use online banking more.

Based on this cost information alone, it may appear that it is more profitable for banks to have all their customers rely exclusively on ATM and online banking. Not so fast! Research has shown that customers using online banking conduct many more transactions than other types of customers and use other channels of banking as well. The result: Conversion to online banking alone won't necessarily reduce banking costs, at least in the short run.

Sources: R. Brett, et al., "The Business Case for Right Channeling," *The TechStrategy Report* (June 2003); Conversations with Dr. Dennis Campbell, Harvard Business School (February 19, 2004 and February 26, 2004).

Activity-based costing raises some interesting issues when it is applied to a public service institution such as the U.S. Postal Service. The costs of delivering mail to remote locations are far greater than the costs of delivering mail within urban areas. However, the Postal Service simply cannot charge customers in remote areas higher prices. In this case, activity-based costing is valuable for understanding, managing, and reducing costs but often is not used for pricing decisions. The Problem for Self-Study describes an application of ABC in the merchandising sector.

PROBLEM FOR SELF-STUDY

Family Supermarkets (FS) has decided to increase the size of its Memphis store. It wants information about the profitability of individual product lines: soft drinks, fresh produce, and packaged food.

FS provides the following data for 2006 for each product line:

	Soft Drinks	Fresh Produce	Packaged Food
Revenues	$317,400	$840,240	$483,960
Cost of goods sold	$240,000	$600,000	$360,000
Cost of bottles returned	$ 4,800	$ 0	$ 0
Number of purchase orders placed	144	336	144
Number of deliveries received	120	876	264
Hours of shelf-stocking time	216	2,160	1,080
Items sold	50,400	441,600	122,400

FS also provides the following information for 2006:

Activity (1)	Description of Activity (2)	Total Costs (3)	Cost-Allocation Base (4)
1. Bottle returns	Returning of empty bottles to store	$ 4,800	Direct tracing to soft-drink line
2. Ordering	Placing of orders for purchases	$ 62,400	624 purchase orders
3. Delivery	Physical delivery and receipt of merchandise	$100,800	1,260 deliveries
4. Shelf-stocking	Stocking of merchandise on store shelves and ongoing restocking	$ 69,120	3,456 hours of shelf-stocking time
5. Customer support	Assistance provided to customers, including checkout and bagging	$122,880	614,400 items sold
Total		$360,000	

Required

1. Family Supermarkets currently allocates store support costs (all costs other than cost of goods sold) to product lines on the basis of cost of goods sold of each product line. Calculate the operating income and operating income as a percentage of revenues for each product line.
2. If Family Supermarkets allocates store support costs (all costs other than cost of goods sold) to product lines using an ABC system, calculate the operating income and operating income as a percentage of revenues for each product line.
3. Comment on your answers in requirements 1 and 2.

SOLUTION

1. The following table shows the operating income and operating income as a percentage of revenues for each product line. All store support costs (all costs other than cost of goods sold) are allocated to product lines using cost of goods sold of each product line as the cost-allocation base. Total store support costs equal $360,000 (cost of bottles returned, $4,800 + cost of purchase orders, $62,400 + cost of deliveries, $100,800 + cost of shelf-stocking, $69,120 + cost of customer support, $122,880). The allocation rate for store support costs = $360,000 ÷ $1,200,000 = 30% of cost of goods sold. To allocate support costs to each product line, FS multiplies the cost of goods sold of each product line by 0.30.

	Soft Drinks	Fresh Produce	Packaged Food	Total
Revenues	$317,400	$840,240	$483,960	$1,641,600
Cost of goods sold	240,000	600,000	360,000	1,200,000
Store support cost ($240,000; $600,000; $360,000) × 0.30	72,000	180,000	108,000	360,000
Total costs	312,000	780,000	468,000	1,560,000
Operating income	$ 5,400	$ 60,240	$ 15,960	$ 81,600
Operating income ÷ Revenues	1.70%	7.17%	3.30%	4.97%

2. Under an ABC system, FS identifies bottle-return costs as a direct cost because these costs can be traced to the soft drink product line. FS then calculates cost-allocation rates for each activity area (as in step 5 described in the chapter, p. 151). The activity rates are as follows:

Activity (1)	Cost Hierarchy (2)	Total Costs (3)	Quantity of Cost-Allocation Base (4)	Overhead Allocation Rate (5) = (3) ÷ (4)
Ordering	Batch-level	$ 62,400	624 purchase orders	$100 per purchase order
Delivery	Batch-level	$100,800	1,260 deliveries	$80 per delivery
Shelf-stocking	Output unit-level	$ 69,120	3,456 shelf-stocking-hours	$20 per stocking-hour
Customer support	Output unit-level	$122,880	614,400 items sold	$0.20 per item sold

Store support costs for each product line by activity are obtained by multiplying the total quantity of the cost-allocation base for each product line by the activity cost rate. Operating income and operating income as a percentage of revenues for each product line are as follows:

	Soft Drinks	Fresh Produce	Packaged Food	Total
Revenues	$317,400	$840,240	$483,960	$1,641,600
Cost of goods sold	240,000	600,000	360,000	1,200,000
Bottle-return costs	4,800	0	0	4,800
Ordering costs				
(144; 336; 144) purchase orders × $100	14,400	33,600	14,400	62,400
Delivery costs				
(120; 876; 264) deliveries × $80	9,600	70,080	21,120	100,800
Shelf-stocking costs				
(216; 2,160; 1,080) stocking-hours × $20	4,320	43,200	21,600	69,120
Customer-support costs				
(50,400; 441,600; 122,400) items sold × $0.20	10,080	88,320	24,480	122,880
Total costs	283,200	835,200	441,600	1,560,000
Operating income	$ 34,200	$ 5,040	$ 42,360	$ 81,600
Operating income ÷ Revenues	10.78%	0.60%	8.75%	4.97%

3. Managers believe the ABC system is more credible than the simple costing system. The ABC system distinguishes the different types of activities at FS more precisely. It also tracks more accurately how individual product lines use resources. Rankings of relative profitability—operating income as a percentage of revenues—of the three product lines under the simple costing system and under the ABC system are:

Simple Costing System		ABC System	
1. Fresh produce	7.17%	1. Soft drinks	10.78%
2. Packaged food	3.30%	2. Packaged food	8.75%
3. Soft drinks	1.70%	3. Fresh produce	0.60%

The percentage of revenues, cost of goods sold, and activity costs for each product line are as follows:

	Soft Drinks	Fresh Produce	Packaged Food
Revenues	19.34%	51.18%	29.48%
Cost of goods sold	20.00	50.00	30.00
Bottle returns	100.00	0	0
Activity areas:			
Ordering	23.08	53.84	23.08
Delivery	9.53	69.52	20.95
Shelf-stocking	6.25	62.50	31.25
Customer support	8.20	71.88	19.92

Soft drinks consume fewer resources than either fresh produce or packaged food. Soft drinks have fewer deliveries and require less shelf-stocking time than required for either fresh produce or packaged food. Most major soft-drink suppliers deliver merchandise to the store shelves and stock the shelves themselves. In contrast, the fresh produce area has the most deliveries and consumes a large percentage of shelf-stocking time. It also has the highest number of individual sales items. The simple costing system assumed that each product line used the resources in each activity area in the same ratio as their respective individual cost of goods sold to total cost of goods sold. Clearly, this assumption is incorrect. The simple costing system is an example of averaging that is too broad.

FS managers can use the ABC information to guide decisions such as how to allocate a planned increase in floor space. An increase in the percentage of space allocated to soft drinks is warranted. Note, however, that ABC information should be but one input into decisions about shelf-space allocation. FS may have minimum limits on the shelf space allocated to fresh produce because of shoppers' expectations that supermarkets will carry products from this product line. In many situations, companies cannot make product decisions in isolation but must consider the effect that deemphasizing a product might have on customer demand for other products.

Pricing decisions can also be made in a more-informed way with ABC information. For example, suppose a competitor announces a 5% reduction in soft-drink prices. Given the 10.77% margin FS currently earns on its soft-drink product line, it has flexibility to reduce prices and still make a profit on this product line. In contrast, the simple costing system erroneously reported that soft drinks only had a 1.70% margin, leaving little room to counter a competitor's pricing initiatives.

DECISION POINTS

The following question-and-answer format summarizes the chapter's learning objectives. Each decision presents a key question related to a learning objective. The guidelines are the answer to that question.

Decision	Guidelines
1. When does product undercosting or overcosting occur?	Product undercosting (overcosting) occurs when a product or service consumes a high (low) level of resources but is reported to have a low (high) cost. Broad averaging, or peanut-butter costing, a common cause of undercosting or overcosting, is the result of using broad averages that uniformly assign, or spread, the cost of resources to products when the individual products use those resources in a nonuniform way. Product-cost cross-subsidization exists when one undercosted (overcosted) product results in at least one other product being overcosted (undercosted).
2. How do managers refine a costing system?	Refining a costing system means making changes that result in cost numbers that better measure the way different cost objects, such as products, use different amounts of resources of the company. These changes can require additional direct-cost tracing, the choice of more-homogeneous indirect-cost pools, or the use of different cost-allocation bases.
3. What is the difference between the design of a simple costing system and an activity-based costing (ABC) system?	The ABC system differs from the simple system by its fundamental focus on activities. The ABC system typically has more-homogeneous indirect-cost pools than the simple system, and more cost drivers are used as cost-allocation bases.
4. What is a cost hierarchy?	A cost hierarchy categorizes costs into different cost pools on the basis of the different types of cost-allocation bases or different degrees of difficulty in determining cause-and-effect (or benefits-received) relationships. A four-part cost hierarchy consists of output unit-level costs, batch-level costs, product-sustaining or service-sustaining costs, and facility-sustaining costs.
5. How do managers cost products or services using ABC systems?	In ABC, costs of activities are used to assign costs to other cost objects such as products or services based on the activities the products or services consume.
6. How can ABC systems be used to manage better?	Activity-based management (ABM) is a management method of decision-making that uses ABC information to satisfy customers and improve profits. ABC systems are used for such management decisions as pricing, product-mix, cost reduction, process improvement, product and process redesign, and planning and managing activities.
7. When can department costing systems be used instead of ABC systems?	Cost information in department costing systems approximates cost information in ABC systems only when each department has a single activity, or a single cost-allocation base for different activities, or when different products use the different activities of the department in the same proportions.
8. When should managers use ABC systems?	ABC systems are likely to yield the most benefits when indirect costs are a high percentage of total costs or when products and services make diverse demands on indirect resources. The main costs of ABC systems are the complexity of the measurements necessary to implement and update the systems.

TERMS TO LEARN

This chapter and the Glossary at the end of this book contain definitions of:

activity (p. 144)
activity-based costing (ABC) (p. 144)
activity-based management (ABM) (p. 152)
batch-level costs (p. 147)
cost hierarchy (p. 147)
facility-sustaining costs (p. 148)
output unit-level costs (p. 147)
product-cost cross-subsidization (p. 140)
product overcosting (p. 140)
product-sustaining costs (p. 148)
product undercosting (p. 140)
refined costing system (p. 143)
service-sustaining costs (p. 148)

PH Grade Assist

Prentice Hall Grade Assist (PHGA)
Your professor may ask you to complete selected exercises and problems in Prentice Hall Grade Assist (PHGA). PHGA is an online tool that can help you master the chapter's topics. It provides you with multiple variations of exercises and problems designated by the PHGA icon. You can rework these exercises and problems—each time with new data—as many times as you need. You also receive immediate feedback and grading.

ASSIGNMENT MATERIAL

Questions

5-1 What is broad averaging and what consequences can it have on costs?

5-2 Why should managers worry about product overcosting or undercosting?

5-3 What is costing system refinement? Describe three guidelines for refinement.

5-4 What is an activity-based approach to designing a costing system?

5-5 Describe four levels of a cost hierarchy.

5-6 Why is it important to classify costs into a cost hierarchy?

5-7 What are the key reasons for product cost differences between simple costing systems and ABC systems?

5-8 Describe four decisions for which ABC information is useful.

5-9 "Department indirect-cost rates are never activity-cost rates." Do you agree? Explain.

5-10 Describe four signs that help indicate when ABC systems are likely to provide the most benefits.

5-11 What are the main costs and limitations of implementing ABC systems?

5-12 "ABC systems only apply to manufacturing companies." Do you agree? Explain.

5-13 "Activity-based costing is the wave of the present and the future. All companies should adopt it." Do you agree? Explain.

5-14 "Increasing the number of indirect-cost pools is guaranteed to sizably increase the accuracy of product or service costs." Do you agree? Why?

5-15 The controller of a retail company has just had a $50,000 request to implement an ABC system quickly turned down. A senior vice president, in rejecting the request, noted, "Given a choice, I will always prefer a $50,000 investment in improving things a customer sees or experiences, such as our shelves or our store layout. How does a customer benefit by our spending $50,000 on a supposedly better accounting system?" How should the controller respond?

Exercises

5-16 Cost hierarchy. Teledor, Inc., manufactures boom boxes (music systems with radio, cassette, and compact disc players) for several well-known companies. The boom boxes differ significantly in their complexity and their manufacturing batch sizes. The following costs were incurred in 2006.

- **a.** Indirect manufacturing labor costs such as supervision that supports direct manufacturing labor, $1,000,000
- **b.** Procurement costs of placing purchase orders, receiving materials, and paying suppliers related to the number of purchase orders placed, $500,000
- **c.** Cost of indirect materials, $250,000
- **d.** Costs incurred to set up machines each time a different product needs to be manufactured, $600,000
- **e.** Designing processes, drawing process charts, making engineering process changes for products, $800,000
- **f.** Machine-related overhead costs such as depreciation, maintenance, production engineering, $1,100,000 (These resources relate to the activity of running the machines.)
- **g.** Plant management, plant rent, and plant insurance, $900,000

Required

1. Classify each of the preceding costs as output unit-level, batch-level, product-sustaining, or facility-sustaining. Explain each answer.
2. Consider two types of boom boxes made by Teledor, Inc. One boom box is complex to make and is produced in many batches. The other boom box is simple to make and is produced in few batches. Suppose that Teledor needs the same number of machine-hours to make each type of boom box and that Teledor allocates all overhead costs using machine-hours as the only allocation base. How, if at all, would the boom boxes be miscosted? Briefly explain why.
3. How is the cost hierarchy helpful to Teledor in managing its business?

5-17 ABC, cost hierarchy, service. (CMA, adapted) Plymouth Test Laboratories does heat testing (HT) and stress testing (ST) on materials. Under its current simple costing system, Plymouth aggregates all operating costs of $1,200,000 into a single overhead cost pool. Plymouth calculates a rate per test-hour of $15 ($1,200,000 ÷ 80,000 total test-hours). HT uses 50,000 test-hours, and ST uses 30,000 test-hours. Gary Celeste, Plymouth's controller, believes that there is enough variation in test procedures and cost structures to establish separate costing and billing rates for HT and ST. The market for test services is becoming competitive. Without this information, any miscosting and mispricing of its services could cause Plymouth to lose business. Celeste divides Plymouth's costs into four activity-cost categories.

PH Grade Assist

a. Direct-labor costs, $240,000. These costs can be directly traced to HT, $180,000, and ST, $60,000.
b. Equipment-related costs (rent, maintenance, energy, and so on), $400,000. These costs are allocated to HT and ST on the basis of test-hours.
c. Setup costs, $350,000. These costs are allocated to HT and ST on the basis of the number of setup-hours required. HT requires 13,500 setup-hours, and ST requires 4,000 setup-hours.
d. Costs of designing tests, $210,000. These costs are allocated to HT and ST on the basis of the time required to design the tests. HT requires 2,800 hours, and ST requires 1,400 hours.

Required

1. Classify each activity cost as output unit-level, batch-level, product- or service-sustaining, or facility-sustaining. Explain each answer.
2. Calculate the cost per test-hour for HT and ST. Explain briefly the reasons why these numbers differ from the $15 per test-hour that Plymouth calculated using its simple costing system.
3. Explain the accuracy of the product costs calculated using the simple costing system and the ABC system. How might Plymouth's management use the cost hierarchy and ABC information to better manage its business?

5-18 Alternative allocation bases for a professional services firm. The Wolfson Group (WG) provides tax advice to multinational firms. WG charges clients for (a) direct professional time (at an hourly rate) and (b) support services (at 30% of the direct professional costs billed). The three professionals in WG and their rates per professional hour are:

PH Grade Assist

Professional	Billing Rate per Hour
Myron Wolfson	$500
Ann Brown	120
John Anderson	80

WG has just prepared the May 2005 bills for two clients. The hours of professional time spent on each client are as follows:

	Hours per Client	
Professional	**Seattle Dominion**	**Tokyo Enterprises**
Wolfson	15	2
Brown	3	8
Anderson	22	30
Total	40	40

Required

1. What amounts did WG bill to Seattle Dominion and Tokyo Enterprises for May 2005?
2. Suppose support services were billed at $50 per professional labor-hour (instead of 30% of professional labor costs). How would this change affect the amounts WG billed to the two clients for May 2005? Comment on the differences between the amounts billed in requirements 1 and 2.
3. How would you determine whether professional labor costs or professional labor-hours is the more appropriate allocation base for WG's support services?

5-19 Plantwide, department, and ABC indirect cost rates. Automotive Products (AP) designs and produces automotive parts. In 2007, actual variable manufacturing overhead is $308,600. AP's simple costing system allocates variable manufacturing overhead to its three customers based on machine-hours and prices its contracts based on full costs. One of its customers has regularly complained of being charged noncompetitive prices, so AP's controller Devon Smith realizes that it is time to examine the consumption of overhead resources more closely. He knows that there are three main departments that consume overhead

Excel Lab
www.prenhall.com/horngren/cost12e

resources: design, production, and engineering. Interviews with the department personnel and examination of time records yield the following detailed information:

	A	B	C	D	E	F
1			Variable	Usage of Cost Drivers by Customer Contract		
2	**Department**	**Cost Driver**	**Manufacturing Overhead in 2007**	**United Motors**	**Holden Motors**	**Leland Vehicle**
3	Design	CAD-design hours	$ 39,000	110	200	80
4	Engineering	Engineering hours	29,600	70	60	240
5	Production	Machine hours	240,000	120	2,800	1,080
6	Total		$308,600			
7						

If you want to use Excel to solve this exercise, go to the Excel Lab at **www.prenhall.com/horngren/cost12e** and download the template for Exercise 5-19.

Required

1. Compute the variable manufacturing overhead allocated to each customer in 2007 using the simple costing system that has machine-hours as the allocation base.
2. Compute the variable manufacturing overhead allocated to each customer in 2007 using department-based variable manufacturing overhead rates.
3. Comment on your answers in requirements 1 and 2. Which customer do you think was complaining about being overcharged in the simple system? If the new department-based rates are used to price contracts, which customer(s) will be unhappy? How would you respond to these concerns?
4. How else might AP use the information available from its department-by-department analysis of variable manufacturing overhead costs?
5. AP's managers are wondering if they should further refine the department-by-department costing system into an ABC system by identifying different activities within each department. Under what conditions would it not be worthwhile to further refine the department costing system into an ABC system?

PH Grade Assist

5-20 ABC, process costing. Parker Company produces mathematical and financial calculators. Data related to the two products are presented here.

	Mathematical	**Financial**
Annual production in units	50,000	100,000
Direct material costs	$150,000	$300,000
Direct manufacturing labor costs	$ 50,000	$100,000
Direct manufacturing labor-hours	2,500	5,000
Machine-hours	25,000	50,000
Number of production runs	50	50
Inspection hours	1,000	500

Total manufacturing overhead costs are:

	Total
Machining costs	$375,000
Setup costs	120,000
Inspection costs	105,000

Required

1. Compute the manufacturing overhead cost per unit for each product.
2. Compute the manufacturing cost per unit for each product.

Excel Lab
www.prenhall.com/horngren/cost12e

5-21 Activity-based costing, service company. Quikprint Corporation owns a small printing press that prints leaflets, brochures, and advertising materials. Quikprint classifies its various printing jobs as standard jobs or special jobs. Quikprint's simple job-costing system has two direct-cost categories (direct materials and direct labor) and a single indirect-cost pool. Quikprint allocates all indirect costs using printing machine-hours as the allocation base.

Quikprint is concerned about the accuracy of the costs assigned to standard and special jobs and therefore is planning to implement an activity-based costing system. Quickprint's ABC system would have the same direct-cost categories as its simple costing system. However, instead of a single indirect-cost pool there would now be six categories for assigning indirect costs: design, purchasing, setup, printing machine operations, marketing, and administration. To see how activity-based costing would affect the costs of standard and special jobs, Quikprint collects the following information for the fiscal year 2007 that just ended.

	A	B	C	D	E
1		**Standard Job**	**Special Job**	**Total**	**Cause-and-Effect Relationship between Allocation Base and Activity Cost**
2	Number of printing jobs	400	200		
3	Price per job	$1,200	$ 1,500		
4	Cost of supplies per job	$ 200	$ 250		
5	Direct manuf. labor cost per job	$ 180	$ 200		
6	Printing machine hours per job	10	10		
7	Cost of printing machine operations			$150,000	Indirect costs of operating printing machines increase with printing machine hours
8	Setup hours per job	4	7		
9	Setup costs			$ 90,000	Indirect setup costs increase with setup hours
10	Total number of purchase orders	400	500		
11	Purchase order costs			$ 36,000	Indirect purchase order costs increase with number of purchase orders
12	Total design costs	$8,000	$32,000	$ 40,000	Design costs are allocated to standard and special jobs based on a special study of the design department
13–14	Marketing costs	5% of sales price	5% of sales price	$ 39,000	
15	Administration costs			$ 47,000	Demand for administrative resources increases with direct manufacturing labor costs

If you want to use Excel to solve this exercise, go to the Excel Lab at **www.prenhall.com/horngren/cost12e** and download the template for Exercise 5-21.

Required

1. Calculate the cost of a standard job and a special job under the simple costing system.
2. Calculate the cost of a standard job and a special job under the activity-based costing system.
3. Compare the costs of a standard job and a special job in requirements 1 and 2. Why do the simple and activity-based costing systems differ in the cost of a standard job and a special job?
4. How might Quikprint use the new cost information from its activity-based costing system to better manage its business?

5-22 Allocation of costs to activities, unused capacity. Harmon Academy, a private school for boys, serves 500 students: 200 in the middle school (grades 6–8) and 300 in the high school (grades 9–12). Each school has its own assistant principal, and there is one principal, Brian Smith, for all of Harmon Academy. For any single student, almost all of Harmon's costs are indirect. Harmon currently has five indirect cost categories, which are listed in column A of the following table. Smith wants to develop an activity-based costing system for the school. He identifies four activities—academic instruction, administration, sports training, and community relationships—related to the educational enterprise, which are shown in columns B, C, D, and E of the following table.

Excel Lab
www.prenhall.com/horngren/cost12e

Smith and his team identify number of students as the cost driver of academic instruction and administration costs, and the number of team sports offered by the school as the cost driver of sports training costs. The cost of maintaining community relationships—dealing with the town board and participating in local activities—is a facility-sustaining cost that the school has to incur each year. This table shows the percentage of costs in each line item used by each activity.

	A	B	C	D	E	F
1		**Percentage of Costs Used by Each Activity**				
2	**Indirect Cost Categories**	**Academic Instruction**	**Administration**	**Sports Training**	**Community Relationships**	**2006 Expenditures**
3	Teachers' salaries and benefits	60%	20%	8%	12%	$4,000,000
4	Principals' salaries and benefits	10%	60%	5%	25%	400,000
5	Facilities cost	35%	15%	45%	5%	2,600,000
6	Office staff salaries and benefits	5%	60%	10%	25%	300,000
7	Sports program staff salaries and benefits	35%	10%	45%	10%	500,000
8						$7,800,000
9						

If you want to use Excel to solve this exercise, go to the Excel Lab at **www.prenhall.com/horngren/cost12e** and download the template for Exercise 5-22.

Required

1. What is the overall cost of educating each student? Of this cost, what percentage is the cost of academic instruction? Of administration?

2. Smith is dismayed at the high cost of sports training. Further examination reveals that $300,000 of those costs are for ice hockey, a sport pursued by a total of 40 students. What would the overall cost of educating each student be if the ice hockey program is eliminated and its cost saved?
3. For the 2007 school year, Harmon charges an annual fee of $1,000 for any student who wants to play ice hockey. As a result, 10 of the less-motivated students drop the sport. Assuming the costs of the school in 2007 are the same as in 2006, what is the overall cost of educating each student in 2007?
4. Consider the costs of the academic instruction activity and assume they are fixed in the short run. At these costs, Harmon could serve 600 students. What is the cost of the academic instruction resources used by Harmon's current 500 students? What is the cost of unused academic instruction capacity? What actions can Smith take to reduce the cost of academic instruction per student in the short run? In the long run?

PH Grade Assist

5-23 ABC, retail product-line profitability. Family Supermarkets (FS) decides to apply ABC analysis to three product lines: baked goods, milk and fruit juice, and frozen foods. It identifies four activities and their activity cost rates as:

Ordering	$100 per purchase order
Delivery and receipt of merchandise	$80 per delivery
Shelf-stocking	$20 per hour
Customer support and assistance	$0.20 per item sold

The revenues, cost of goods sold, store support costs, and activity-area usage of the three product lines are:

	Baked Goods	Milk and Fruit Juice	Frozen Products
Financial data			
Revenues	$57,000	$63,000	$52,000
Cost of goods sold	$38,000	$47,000	$35,000
Store support	$11,400	$14,100	$10,500
Activity-area usage (cost-allocation base)			
Ordering (purchase orders)	30	25	13
Delivery (deliveries)	98	36	28
Shelf-stocking (hours)	183	166	24
Customer support (items sold)	15,500	20,500	7,900

Under its simple costing system, FS allocated support costs to products at the rate of 30% of cost of goods sold.

Required

1. Use the simple costing system to prepare a product-line profitability report for FS.
2. Use the ABC system to prepare a product-line profitability report for FS.
3. What new insights does the ABC system in requirement 2 provide to FS managers?

PH Grade Assist

5-24 ABC, wholesale, customer profitability. Villeagas Wholesalers sells furniture items to four department-store chains (customers). Mr. Villeagas commented, "We apply ABC to determine product-line profitability. The same ideas apply to customer profitability, and we should find out our customer profitability as well." Villeagas Wholesalers sends catalogs to corporate purchasing departments on a monthly basis. The customers are entitled to return unsold merchandise within a six-month period from the purchase date and receive a full purchase price refund. The following data were collected from last year's operations:

	Chain			
	1	2	3	4
Gross sales	$50,000	$30,000	$100,000	$70,000
Sales returns:				
Number of items	100	26	60	40
Amount	$10,000	$ 5,000	$ 7,000	$ 6,000
Number of orders:				
Regular	40	150	50	70
Rush	10	50	10	30

Villeagas has calculated the following activity rates.

Activity	Cost-Driver Rate
Regular order processing	$20 per regular order
Rush order processing	$100 per rush order
Returned items processing	$10 per item
Catalogs and customer support	$1,000 per customer

Customers pay the transportation costs. The cost of goods sold averages 80% of sales.

Required

Determine the contribution to profit from each chain last year. Comment on your solution.

5-25 ABC, activity area cost-driver rates, product cross-subsidization. Idaho Potatoes (IP) processes potatoes into potato cuts at its highly automated Pocatello plant. It sells potatoes to the retail consumer market and to the institutional market, which includes hospitals, cafeterias, and university dormitories.

IP's simple costing system has a single direct-cost category (direct materials, which are the raw potatoes) and a single indirect-cost pool (production support). Support costs are allocated on the basis of pounds of potato cuts processed. Support costs include packaging materials. The 2006 total actual costs for producing 1,000,000 pounds of potato cuts (900,000 for the retail market and 100,000 for the institutional market) are:

Direct materials used	$150,000
Production support	$983,000

The simple costing system does not distinguish between potato cuts produced for the retail and the institutional markets.

At the end of 2006, IP unsuccessfully bid for a large institutional contract. Its bid was reported to be 30% above the winning bid. This feedback came as a shock because IP included only a minimum profit margin on its bid. Moreover, the Pocatello plant was acknowledged as the most efficient in the industry.

As a result of its review process of the lost contract bid, IP decided to explore ways to refine its costing system. First, it identified that $188,000 of the $983,000 pertaining to packaging materials could be traced to individual jobs ($180,000 for retail and $8,000 for institutional). These costs will now be classified as direct materials. The $150,000 of direct materials used were classified as $135,000 for retail and $15,000 for institutional. Second, it used ABC to examine how the two products (retail potato cuts and institutional potato cuts) used indirect support resources. The finding was that three activity areas could be distinguished.

- **Cleaning Activity Area**—IP uses 1,200,000 pounds of raw potatoes to yield 1,000,000 pounds of potato cuts. The cost-allocation base is pounds of raw potatoes cleaned. Costs in the cleaning activity area are $120,000.
- **Cutting Activity Area**—IP processes raw potatoes for the retail market independently of those processed for the institutional market. The production line produces (a) 250 pounds of retail potato cuts per cutting-hour and (b) 400 pounds of institutional potato cuts per cutting-hour. The cost-allocation base is cutting-hours on the production line. Costs in the cutting activity area are $231,000.
- **Packaging Activity Area**—IP packages potato cuts for the retail market independently of those packaged for the institutional market. The packaging line packages (a) 25 pounds of retail potato cuts per packaging-hour and (b) 100 pounds of institutional potato cuts per packaging-hour. The cost-allocation base is packaging-hours on the production line. Costs in the packaging activity area are $444,000.

Required

1. Using the simple costing system, what is the cost per pound of potato cuts produced by IP?
2. Calculate the cost rate per unit of the cost driver in the (a) cleaning, (b) cutting, and (c) packaging activity areas.
3. Suppose IP uses information from its activity cost rates to calculate costs incurred on retail potato cuts and institutional potato cuts. Using the ABC system, what is the cost per pound of (a) retail potato cuts and (b) institutional potato cuts?
4. Comment on the cost differences between the two costing systems in 1 and 3. How might IP use the information in 3 to make better decisions?

5-26 Activity-based costing, job-costing system. The Hewlett-Packard (HP) plant in Roseville, California, assembles and tests printed-circuit (PC) boards. The job-costing system at this plant has two direct-cost categories (direct materials and direct manufacturing labor) and seven indirect-cost pools. These indirect-cost pools represent the seven activity areas that operating personnel at the plant determined are sufficiently different (in terms of cost-behavior patterns or individual products being assembled) to warrant separate cost pools. The cost-allocation base chosen for each activity area is the cost driver at that activity area.

Debbie Berlant, a newly appointed marketing manager at HP, is attending a training session that describes how an activity-based costing approach was used to design the Roseville plant's job-costing system. Berlant is provided with the following incomplete information for a specific job (an order for a single PC board, No. A82):

Direct materials	$75.00	
Direct manufacturing labor	15.00	$90.00
Manufacturing overhead (see below)		?
Total manufacturing cost		$?

Manufacturing Overhead Cost Pool	Cost-Allocation Base	Cost-Allocation Rate	Units of Cost-Allocation Base Used on Job No. A82	Manufacturing Overhead Allocated to Job
1. Axial insertion	Axial insertions	0.08	45	?
2. Dip insertion	Dip insertions	0.25	?	6.00
3. Manual insertion	Manual insertions	?	11	5.50
4. Wave solder	Boards soldered	3.50	?	3.50
5. Backload	Backload insertions	?	6	4.20
6. Test	Budgeted time board is in test activity	90.00	0.25	?
7. Defect analysis	Budgeted time for defect analysis and repair	?	0.10	8.00

Required

1. Prepare an overview diagram of the activity-based job-costing system at the Roseville plant.
2. Fill in the blanks (noted by question marks) in the cost information provided to Berlant for Job No. A82.
3. Why might manufacturing managers and marketing managers favor this ABC job-costing system over the simple costing system, which had the same two direct-cost categories but only a single indirect-cost pool (manufacturing overhead allocated using direct manufacturing labor costs)?

5-27 ABC, product costing at banks, cross-subsidization. First International Bank (FIB) is examining the profitability of its Premier Account, a combined savings and checking account. Depositors receive a 7% annual interest rate on their average deposit. FIB earns an interest rate spread of 3% (the difference between the rate at which it lends money and the rate it pays depositors) by lending money for home loan purposes at 10%. Thus, FIB would gain $60 on the interest spread if a depositor had an average Premier Account balance of $2,000 in 2005 ($\$2,000 \times 3\% = \$60$).

The Premier Account allows depositors unlimited use of services such as deposits, withdrawals, checking accounts, and foreign currency drafts. Depositors with Premier Account balances of $1,000 or more receive unlimited free use of services. Depositors with minimum balances of less than $1,000 pay a $20-a-month service fee for their Premier Account.

FIB recently conducted an activity-based costing study of its services. It assessed the following costs for six individual services. The use of these services in 2005 by three customers is as follows:

	Activity-Based Cost per "Transaction"	Account Usage		
		Robinson	Skerrett	Farrel
Deposit/withdrawal with teller	$ 2.50	40	50	5
Deposit/withdrawal with automatic teller machine (ATM)	0.80	10	20	16
Deposit/withdrawal on prearranged monthly basis	0.50	0	12	60
Bank checks written	8.00	9	3	2
Foreign currency drafts	12.00	4	1	6
Inquiries about account balance	1.50	10	18	9
Average Premier Account balance for 2005		$1,100	$800	$25,000

Assume Robinson and Farrel always maintain a balance above $1,000, whereas Skerrett always has a balance below $1,000.

Required

1. Compute the 2005 profitability of the Robinson, Skerrett, and Farrel Premier Accounts at FIB.
2. What evidence is there of cross-subsidization among the three Premier Accounts? Why might FIB worry about this cross-subsidization if the Premier Account product offering is profitable as a whole?
3. What changes would you recommend for FIB's Premier Account?

Problems

5-28 Job costing with single direct-cost category, single indirect-cost pool, law firm. Wigan Associates is a recently formed law partnership. Ellery Hanley, the managing partner of Wigan Associates, has just finished a tense phone call with Martin Offiah, president of Widnes Coal. Offiah strongly complained about the price Wigan charged for some legal work done for Widnes Coal.

Hanley also received a phone call from its only other client (St. Helen's Glass), which was very pleased with both the quality of the work and the price charged on its most recent job.

Wigan Associates uses a cost-based approach to pricing (billing) each job. Currently it uses a simple costing system with a single direct-cost category (professional labor-hours) and a single indirect-cost pool (general support). Indirect costs are allocated to cases on the basis of professional labor-hours per case. The job files show the following:

	Widnes Coal	St. Helen's Glass
Professional labor	104 hours	96 hours

Professional labor costs at Wigan Associates are $70 an hour. Indirect costs are allocated to cases at $105 an hour. Total indirect costs in the most recent period were $21,000.

Required

1. Why is it important for Wigan Associates to understand the costs associated with individual jobs?
2. Compute the costs of the Widnes Coal and St. Helen's Glass jobs using Wigan's simple costing system.

5-29 Job costing with multiple direct-cost categories, single indirect-cost pool, law firm (continuation of 5-28). Hanley asks his assistant to collect details on those costs included in the $21,000 indirect-cost pool that can be traced to each individual job. After analysis, Wigan is able to reclassify $14,000 of the $21,000 as direct costs:

Other Direct Costs	Widnes Coal	St. Helen's Glass
Research support labor	$1,600	$ 3,400
Computer time	500	1,300
Travel and allowances	600	4,400
Telephones/faxes	200	1,000
Photocopying	250	750
Total	$3,150	$10,850

Hanley decides to calculate the costs of each job as if Wigan had used six direct cost-pools and a single indirect-cost pool. The single indirect-cost pool would have $7,000 of costs and would be allocated to each case using the professional labor-hours base.

Required

1. What is the revised indirect-cost allocation rate per professional labor-hour for Wigan Associates when total indirect costs are $7,000?
2. Compute the costs of the Widnes and St. Helen's jobs if Wigan Associates had used its refined costing system with multiple direct-cost categories and one indirect-cost pool.
3. Compare the costs of Widnes and St. Helen's jobs in requirement 2 with those in requirement 2 of Problem 5-28. Comment on the results.

5-30 Job costing with multiple direct-cost categories, multiple indirect-cost pools, law firm (continuation of 5-28 and 5-29). Wigan has two classifications of professional staff: partners and associates. Hanley asks his assistant to examine the relative use of partners and associates on the recent Widnes Coal and St. Helen's jobs. The Widnes job used 24 partner-hours and 80 associate-hours. The St. Helen's job used 56 partner-hours and 40 associate-hours. Therefore, totals of the two jobs together were 80 partner-hours and 120 associate-hours. Hanley decides to examine how using separate direct-cost rates for partners and associates and using separate indirect-cost pools for partners and associates would have affected the costs of the Widnes and St. Helen's jobs. Indirect costs in each indirect-cost pool would be allocated on the basis of total hours of that category of professional labor. From the total indirect cost-pool of $7,000, $4,600 is attributable to the activities of partners, and $2,400 is attributable to the activities of associates.

The rates per category of professional labor are as follows:

Category of Professional Labor	Direct Cost per Hour	Indirect Cost per Hour
Partner	$100.00	$4,600 ÷ 80 hours = $57.50
Associate	50.00	$2,400 ÷ 120 hours = $20.00

Required

1. Compute the costs of the Widnes and St. Helen's cases using Wigan's further refined system, with multiple direct-cost categories and multiple indirect-cost pools.
2. For what decisions might Wigan Associates find it more useful to use this job-costing approach rather than the approaches in Problem 5-28 or 5-29?

5-31 Plantwide, department, and activity-cost rates. (CGA, adapted) The Sayther Company manufactures and sells two products, A and B. The manufacturing activity is organized in two departments. Manufacturing overhead costs at its Portland plant are allocated to each product using a plantwide rate of $17 per direct manufacturing labor-hour. This rate is based on budgeted manufacturing overhead of $340,000 and 20,000 budgeted direct manufacturing labor-hours:

Manufacturing Department	Budgeted Manufacturing Overhead	Budgeted Direct Manufacturing Labor-Hours
1	$240,000	10,000
2	100,000	10,000
Total	$340,000	20,000

The number of direct manufacturing labor-hours required to manufacture each product is:

Manufacturing Department	Product A	Product B
1	4	1
2	1	4
Total	5	5

Per-unit costs for the two categories of direct manufacturing costs are:

Direct Manufacturing Costs	Product A	Product B
Direct material costs	$120	$150
Direct manufacturing labor costs	80	80

At the end of the year, there was no work in process. There were 200 finished units of product A and 600 finished units of product B on hand. Assume that the budgeted production level of the Portland plant was exactly attained.

Sayther sets the selling price of each product by adding 120% to its unit manufacturing costs; that is, if the unit manufacturing costs are $100, the selling price is $220 ($100 + $120). This 120% markup is designed to cover costs upstream to manufacturing (R&D and design) and costs downstream from manufacturing (marketing, distribution, and customer service), as well as to provide a profit.

Required

1. How much manufacturing overhead cost would be included in the inventory of products A and B if Sayther used (a) a plantwide overhead rate and (b) department overhead rates?
2. By how much would the selling prices of product A and product B differ if Sayther used a plantwide overhead rate instead of department overhead rates?
3. Should Sayther Company prefer plantwide or department overhead rates?
4. Under what conditions should Sayther Company further subdivide the department cost pools into activity cost pools?

5-32 Plantwide versus department overhead cost rates. (CMA, adapted) The MumsDay Corporation manufactures a complete line of fiberglass suitcases. MumsDay has three manufacturing departments (molding, component, and assembly) and two support departments (maintenance and power).

The sides of the cases are manufactured in the Molding Department. The frames, hinges, locks, and so forth are manufactured in the Component Department. The cases are completed in the Assembly Department. Varying amounts of materials, time, and effort are required for each of the various cases. The Maintenance Department and Power Department provide services to the three manufacturing departments.

MumsDay has always used a plantwide manufacturing overhead rate. Direct manufacturing labor-hours are used to allocate the overhead to each product. The budgeted rate is calculated by dividing the company's total budgeted manufacturing overhead cost by the total budgeted direct manufacturing labor-hours to be worked in the three manufacturing departments.

Whit Portlock, manager of Cost Accounting, has recommended that MumsDay use department overhead rates. Portlock has projected operating costs and production levels for the coming year. They are presented (in thousands) by department in the following table:

	Manufacturing Department		
	Molding	**Component**	**Assembly**
Manufacturing Department Operating Data			
Direct manufacturing labor-hours	500	2,000	1,500
Machine-hours	875	125	—
Manufacturing Department Costs			
Direct materials	$12,400	$30,000	$ 1,250
Direct manufacturing labor	3,500	20,000	12,000
Manufacturing department overhead	21,000	16,200	22,600
Total manufacturing departmental costs	$36,900	$66,200	$35,850
Use of Support Departments			
Estimated usage of maintenance resources in labor-hours for coming year	90	25	10
Estimated usage of power (in kilowatt-hours) for coming year	360	320	120

Estimated costs are $4,000 for the Maintenance Department and $18,400 for the Power Department and are in addition to the manufacturing department overhead costs shown in the table.

Required

1. Calculate the plantwide overhead rate for MumsDay Corporation for the coming year using the same method as used in the past.
2. Whit Portlock has been asked to develop department overhead rates for comparison with the plantwide rate. Follow these steps in developing the department rates:
   a. Allocate the Maintenance Department and Power Department costs to the three manufacturing departments.
   b. Calculate department overhead rates for the three manufacturing departments using a machine-hour allocation base for the Molding Department and a direct manufacturing labor-hour allocation base for the Component Department and Assembly Department.
3. Should the MumsDay Corporation use a plantwide rate or department rates to allocate overhead cost to its products? Explain your answer.
4. Under what conditions should MumsDay Corporation further subdivide the department cost pools into activity cost pools?

Excel Lab
www.prenhall.com/horngren/cost12e

5-33 Activity-based costing, unused capacity. Bronco Electric operates at capacity and manufactures and sells two types of motors: a special motor, Thermo, and a basic motor, Basca. Bronco's simple product costing system has two direct-cost categories (direct materials and direct manufacturing labor) and a single indirect-cost pool. Bronco allocates all indirect costs using direct manufacturing labor-hours as the allocation base.

Recently, a team of managers from product design, manufacturing, sales, and marketing decided to replace the single indirect-cost pool with seven indirect-cost pools: design, setups, materials handling, manufacturing operations, shipping, distribution, and administration. The two direct-cost categories were retained. The team felt that the simple costing system did not accurately represent the indirect resources demanded by each product. The team collected the following information for 2006, the year just ended.

	A	B	C	D	E	F	G
1				Basca	Thermo	Total	Cause-and-Effect Relationship Between Allocation Base and Activity Cost
2	Number of motors			30,000	15,000		
3	Selling price			$300	$400		
4	Direct material cost per motor			$100	$150		
5	Direct manufacturing labor-hours per motor at a direct manufacturing labor rate of	$20	per hour	2.0	2.5		
6	Total machine-hours			45,000	30,000		
7							
8	Manufacturing operations					$3,000,000	Indirect manufacturing operations costs increase with machine hours
9	Number of motors per batch			500	100		
10	Setup hours per batch			10	16		
11	Setup costs					$ 600,000	Indirect setup costs increase with setup hours
12	Number of different components per motor			55	75		
13	Materials-handling hours to move a load[1]			0.2	0.2		
14	Materials-handling costs					$ 582,000	Indirect materials-handling costs increase with materials-handling hours
15	Total number of components changed for each product			10	20		
16	Design costs					$ 900,000	Indirect design costs increase with number of components changed
17	Total number of shipments for each product			120	180		
18	Shipping costs					$ 90,000	Indirect costs incurred to prepare batches for shipment increase with number of shipments
19	Cubic feet per motor			1	1.5		
20	Distribution costs					$ 315,000	Indirect distribution costs increase with cubic feet of motors delivered
21							
22	Administration costs					$ 390,000	Demand for administrative resources increases with direct manufacturing labor-hours
23							
24	[1] Each load moves the quantity of a particular component required for the manufacturer of a batch of products. For example, because						
25	Basca has 55 different types of components, it takes 55 loads for all the components required to manufacture a batch of Basca to be						
26	transported from the store to the production area.						

If you want to use Excel to solve this problem, go to the Excel Lab at **www.prenhall.com/horngren/cost12e** and download the template for Problem 5-33.

Required

1. Calculate the cost per unit of Basca and Thermo under the simple costing system.
2. Calculate the cost per unit of Basca and Thermo under the activity-based costing system.
3. Compare the cost per unit for each product in requirements 1 and 2. Why do the simple and activity-based costing systems differ in the cost per unit for each product? Why might these differences be important for Bronco Electric?
4. Suppose distribution costs of $315,000 are fixed in the short run and that Bronco's distribution activity was operating at capacity in 2006. Bronco has found a way to reduce the bulkiness of the deliveries so that it now takes 0.9 cubic foot per motor for Basca and 1.2 cubic feet per motor for Thermo. What is the total cost of distribution resources used for Basca and Thermo? What is the cost of unused distribution capacity?
5. What actions can Bronco take to reduce distribution costs in the short run? In the long run?

5-34 Activity-based costing, merchandising. Pharmacare, Inc., a distributor of special pharmaceutical products, has three main market segments:

a. General supermarket chains
b. Drugstore chains
c. Mom-and-Pop single-store pharmacies

Excel Lab
www.prenhall.com/horngren/cost12e

Rick Flair, the new controller of Pharmacare, reported the following data for 2005:

	A	B	C	D	E
1	**Pharmacare, 2005**	**General**			
2		**Supermarket**	**Drugstore**	**Mom-and-Pop**	
3		**Chains**	**Chains**	**Single Stores**	**Pharmacare**
4	Revenues	$3,708,000	$3,150,000	$1,980,000	$8,838,000
5	Cost of goods sold	3,600,000	3,000,000	1,800,000	8,400,000
6	Gross Margin	$ 108,000	$ 150,000	$ 180,000	438,000
7	Other operating costs				301,080
8	Operating income				$ 136,920
9					

For many years, Pharmacare has used gross margin percentage [(Revenue − Cost of goods sold) ÷ Revenue] to evaluate the relative profitability of its market segments. But, Flair recently attended a seminar on activity-based costing and is considering using it at Pharmacare to analyze and allocate "other operating costs." He meets with all the key managers and several of his operations and sales staff and they agree that there are five key activities that drive other operating costs at Pharmacare:

Activity Area	Cost Driver
Order processing	Number of customer purchase orders
Line-item processing	Number of line items ordered by customers
Delivering to stores	Number of store deliveries
Cartons shipped to store	Number of cartons shipped
Stocking of customer store shelves	Hours of shelf-stocking

Each customer order consists of one or more line items. A line item represents a single product (such as Extra-Strength Tylenol Tablets). Each product line item is delivered in one or more separate cartons. Each store delivery entails the delivery of one or more cartons of products to a customer. Pharmacare's staff stacks cartons directly onto display shelves in customers' stores. Currently, there is no additional charge to the customer for shelf-stocking, and not all customers use Pharmacare for this activity. The level of each activity in the three market segments and the total cost incurred for each activity in 2005 is shown below:

	A	B	C	D	E
13	**Activity-based Cost Data**		**Activity Level**		
14	**Pharmacare, 2005**	**General**			**Total Cost**
15		**Supermarket**	**Drugstore**	**Mom-and-Pop**	**of Activity**
16	**Acitivity**	**Chains**	**Chains**	**Single Stores**	**in 2005**
17	Orders processed (number)	140	360	1,500	$ 80,000
18	Line items ordered (number)	1,960	4,320	15,000	63,840
19	Store deliveries made (number)	120	300	1,000	71,000
20	Cartons shipped to stores (number)	36,000	24,000	16,000	76,000
21	Shelf-stocking (hours)	360	180	100	10,240
22					$301,080
23					

If you want to use Excel to solve this problem, go to the Excel Lab at **www.prenhall.com/horngren/cost12e** and download the template for Problem 5-34.

Required

1. Compute the 2005 gross-margin percentage for each of Pharmacare's three market segments.
2. Compute the cost driver rates for each of the five activity areas.
3. Use the activity-based costing information to allocate the $301,080 of "other operating costs" to each of the market segments. Compute the operating income for each market segment.
4. Comment on the results. What new insights are available with the activity-based costing information?

5-35 Activity-based costing, product-cost cross-subsidization. Baker's Delight (BD) has been in the food-processing business three years. For its first two years (2005 and 2006), its sole product was raisin cake. All cakes were manufactured and packaged in one-pound boxes. BD used a normal costing system. The two direct-cost categories were direct materials and direct manufacturing labor. The sole indirect manufacturing cost category—manufacturing overhead—was allocated to products using pounds of production as the allocation base.

In its third year (2007), BD added a second product—layered carrot cake—which was also packaged in one-pound boxes. This product differs from raisin cake in several ways:

- More-expensive ingredients are used.
- More direct manufacturing labor time is required.
- More-complex manufacturing processing is required.

In 2007, BD continued to use its simple costing system, in which it allocated manufacturing overhead using total pounds (boxes) produced of raisin and layered carrot cakes.

Direct material cost in 2007 was $0.60 per pound of raisin cake and $0.90 per pound of layered carrot cake. Direct manufacturing labor cost in 2007 was $0.14 per pound of raisin cake and $0.20 per pound of layered carrot cake.

During 2007, BD sales staff reported greater-than-expected sales of layered carrot cake and less-than-expected sales of raisin cake. The budgeted and actual sales volume for 2007 is as follows:

	Budgeted	Actual
Raisin cake	160,000 pounds	120,000 pounds
Layered carrot cake	40,000 pounds	80,000 pounds

The budgeted manufacturing overhead for 2007 is $210,800.

At the end of 2007, Jonathan Davis, the controller of BD, decided to investigate how an activity-based costing system would have affected the product-cost numbers. After consultation with operating personnel, the single manufacturing overhead cost pool was subdivided into five activity areas. These activity areas, the cost-allocation base, the budgeted 2007 cost-allocation rate, and the quantity of the cost-allocation base used by the raisin and layered carrot cakes are as follows:

Activity	Cost-Allocation Base	Budgeted 2007 Cost per Unit of Cost-Allocation Base	Quantity of Cost-Allocation Base: Raisin Cake	Quantity of Cost-Allocation Base: Layered Carrot Cake
Mixing	Labor-hours	$0.04	600,000	640,000
Cooking	Oven-hours	$0.14	240,000	240,000
Cooling	Cool room-hours	$0.02	360,000	400,000
Creaming/Icing	Machine-hours	$0.25	0	240,000
Packaging	Machine-hours	$0.08	360,000	560,000

Required

1. Compute the 2007 product cost per pound of raisin cake and layered carrot cake produced using the simple costing system used in the 2005 to 2007 period.
2. Compute the 2007 product cost per pound of raisin cake and layered carrot cake produced using the activity-based costing system.
3. Explain the difference in product costs per pound computed in requirements 1 and 2.
4. Describe three uses Baker's Delight might make of the activity-based cost numbers.

5-36 ABC, health care. Uppervale Health Center runs three programs: (1) alcoholic rehabilitation, (2) drug addict rehabilitation, and (3) aftercare (counseling and support of patients after release from a mental hospital).

The center's budget for 2006 follows:

Professional salaries:		
4 physicians × $150,000	$ 600,000	
18 psychologists × $75,000	1,350,000	
20 nurses × $30,000	600,000	$2,550,000
Medical supplies		300,000
General overhead (administrative salaries, rent, utilities, etc.)		880,000
Total		$3,730,000

Muriel Clayton, the director of the center, is keen on determining the cost of each program. Clayton compiled the following data describing employee allocations to individual programs:

	Alcohol	Drug	Aftercare	Total Employees
Physicians		4		4
Psychologists	6	4	8	18
Nurses	4	6	10	20

Eighty patients are in residence in the alcohol program, each staying about six months. Thus, the clinic provides 40 patient-years of service in the alcohol program. Similarly, 100 patients are involved in the drug program for about six months each. Thus, the clinic provides 50 patient-years of service in the drug program.

Clayton has recently become aware of activity-based costing as a method to refine costing systems. She asks her accountant, Huey Deluth, how she should apply this technique. Deluth obtains the following information:

1. Consumption of medical supplies depends on the number of patient-years.
2. General overhead costs consists of:

Rent and clinic maintenance	$180,000
Administrative costs to manage patient charts, food, laundry	600,000
Laboratory services	100,000
Total	$880,000

3. Other information about individual departments are:

	Alcohol	Drug	Aftercare	Total
Square feet of space occupied by each program	9,000	9,000	12,000	30,000
Patient-years of service	40	50	60	150
Number of laboratory tests	400	1,400	700	2,500

Required

1. a. Selecting cost-allocation bases that you believe are the most appropriate for allocating indirect costs to programs, calculate the indirect cost rates for medical supplies; rent and clinic maintenance; administrative costs for patient charts, food, and laundry; and laboratory services.
   b. Using an activity-based costing approach to cost analysis, calculate the cost of each program and the cost per patient-year of the alcohol and drug programs.
   c. What benefits can Uppervale Health Center obtain by implementing the ABC system?
2. What factors, other than cost, do you think Uppervale Health Center should consider in allocating resources to its programs?

5-37 Activity-based job costing. Schramka Company manufactures a variety of prestige boardroom chairs. Its job-costing system uses an activity-based approach. There are two direct-cost categories (direct materials and direct manufacturing labor) and three indirect-cost pools. The cost pools represent three activity areas at the plant.

Manufacturing Activity Area	Budgeted Costs for 2007	Cost Driver Used as Allocation Base	Cost-Allocation Rate
Materials handling	$ 200,000	Parts	$ 0.25
Cutting	2,000,000	Parts	2.50
Assembly	2,000,000	Direct manufacturing labor-hours	25.00

Two styles of chairs were produced in March: the executive chair and the chairman chair. Their quantities, direct material costs, and other data for March 2007 are as follows:

	Units Produced	Direct Material Costs	Number of Parts	Direct Manufacturing Labor-Hours
Executive chair	5,000	$600,000	100,000	7,500
Chairman chair	100	25,000	3,500	500

The direct manufacturing labor rate is $20 per hour. Assume no beginning or ending inventory.

Required

1. Compute the March 2007 total manufacturing costs and unit costs of the executive chair and the chairman chair.
2. The upstream activities to manufacturing (R&D and design) and the downstream activities (marketing, distribution, and customer service) are analyzed, and the unit costs in 2007 are budgeted to be:

	Upstream Activities	Downstream Activities
Executive chair	$ 60	$110
Chairman chair	146	236

   Compute the full cost per unit of each chair. (Full cost of each chair is the sum of the costs of all business functions in the value chain.)
3. Compare the per-unit cost figures for the executive chair and the chairman chair computed in requirements 1 and 2. Why do the costs differ for each chair? Why might these differences be important to Schramka Company?

5-38 Activity-based job costing, unit-cost comparisons. The Tracy Corporation has a machining facility specializing in jobs for the aircraft-components market. Tracy's previous simple job-costing system had two direct-cost categories (direct materials and direct manufacturing labor) and a single indirect-cost pool (manufacturing overhead, allocated using direct manufacturing labor-hours). The indirect cost-allocation rate of the simple system for 2007 would have been $115 per direct manufacturing labor-hour.

Recently a team with members from product design, manufacturing, and accounting used an ABC approach to refine its job-costing system. The two direct-cost categories were retained. The team decided to replace the single indirect-cost pool with five indirect-cost pools. The cost pools represent five activity areas at the plant, each with its own supervisor and budget responsibility. Pertinent data are as follows:

Activity Area	Cost-Allocation Base	Cost-Allocation Rate
Materials handling	Parts	$ 0.40
Lathe work	Lathe turns	0.20
Milling	Machine-hours	20.00
Grinding	Parts	0.80
Testing	Units tested	15.00

Information-gathering technology has advanced to the point at which the data necessary for budgeting in these five activity areas are collected automatically.

Two representative jobs processed under the ABC system at the plant in the most recent period had the following characteristics:

	Job 410	Job 411
Direct material cost per job	$ 9,700	$59,900
Direct manufacturing labor cost per job	$750	$11,250
Number of direct manufacturing labor-hours per job	25	375
Parts per job	500	2,000
Lathe turns per job	20,000	60,000
Machine-hours per job	150	1,050
Units per job (all units are tested)	10	200

Required

1. Compute the manufacturing cost per unit for each job under the previous simple job-costing system.
2. Compute the manufacturing cost per unit for each job under the activity-based costing system.
3. Compare the per-unit cost figures for Jobs 410 and 411 computed in requirements 1 and 2. Why do the simple and the activity-based costing systems differ in the manufacturing cost per unit for each job? Why might these differences be important to Tracy Corporation?
4. How might Tracy Corporation use information from its ABC system to better manage its business?

5-39 ABC, implementation, ethics. (CMA, adapted) Applewood Electronics, a division of Elgin Corporation, manufactures two large-screen television models: the Monarch, which has been produced since 2001 and sells for $900, and the Regal, a newer model introduced in early 2004 that sells for $1,140. Based on the following income statement for the year ended November 30, 2005, senior management at Elgin have decided to concentrate Applewood's marketing resources on the Regal model and to begin to phase out the Monarch model.

Applewood Electronics
Income Statement
For the Fiscal Year Ended November 30, 2005

	Monarch	Regal	Total
Revenues	$19,800,000	$4,560,000	$24,360,000
Cost of goods sold	12,540,000	3,192,000	15,732,000
Gross margin	7,260,000	1,368,000	8,628,000
Selling and administrative expense	5,830,000	978,000	6,808,000
Operating income	$ 1,430,000	$ 390,000	$ 1,820,000
Units produced and sold	22,000	4,000	
Net income per unit sold	$65.00	$97.50	

Unit costs for Monarch and Regal are as follows:

	Monarch	Regal
Direct materials	$208	$584
Direct manufacturing labor		
Monarch (1.5 hours × $12)	18	
Regal (3.5 hours × $12)		42
Machine costs[a]		
Monarch (8 hours × $18)	144	
Regal (4 hours × $18)		72
Manufacturing overhead other than machine costs[b]	200	100
Total cost	$570	$798

[a]Machine costs include lease costs of the machine, repairs, and maintenance.

[b]Manufacturing overhead was allocated to products based on machine-hours at the rate of $25 per hour.

Applewood's controller, Susan Benzo, is advocating the use of activity-based costing and activity-based management and has gathered the following information about the company's manufacturing overhead costs for the year ended November 30, 2005.

Activity Center (Cost-Allocation Base)	Total Activity Costs	Units of the Cost-Allocation Base		
		Monarch	Regal	Total
Soldering (number of solder points)	$ 942,000	1,185,000	385,000	1,570,000
Shipments (number of shipments)	860,000	16,200	3,800	20,000
Quality control (number of inspections)	1,240,000	56,200	21,300	77,500
Purchase orders (number of orders)	950,400	80,100	109,980	190,080
Machine power (machine-hours)	57,600	176,000	16,000	192,000
Machine setups (number of setups)	750,000	16,000	14,000	30,000
Total manufacturing overhead	$4,800,000			

After completing her analysis, Benzo shows the results to Fred Duval, the Applewood division president. Duval does not like what he sees. "If you show headquarters this analysis, they are going to ask us to phase out the Regal line, which we have just introduced. This whole costing stuff has been a major problem for us. First Monarch was not profitable and now Regal."

"Looking at the ABC analysis, I see two problems. First, we do many more activities than the ones you have listed. If you had included all activities, maybe your conclusions would be different. Second, you used number of setups and number of inspections as allocation bases. The numbers would be different had you used setup-hours and inspection-hours instead. I know that measurement problems precluded you from using these other cost-allocation bases, but I believe you ought to make some adjustments to our current numbers to compensate for these issues. I know you can do better. We can't afford to phase out either product."

Benzo knows her numbers are fairly accurate. As a quick check, she calculates the profitability of Regal and Monarch using more and different allocation bases. The set of activities and activity rates she had used resulted in numbers that closely approximate those based on more-detailed analyses. She is confident that headquarters, knowing that Regal was introduced only recently, will not ask Applewood to phase it out. She is also aware that a sizable portion of Duval's bonus is based on division revenues. Phasing out either product would adversely affect his bonus. Still, she feels some pressure from Duval to do something.

Required

1. Using activity-based costing, calculate the profitability of the Regal and Monarch models.
2. Explain briefly why these numbers differ from the profitability of the Regal and Monarch models calculated using Applewood's existing simple costing system.
3. Comment on Duval's concerns about the accuracy and limitations of ABC.
4. How might Applewood find the ABC information helpful in managing its business?
5. What should Susan Benzo do?

Collaborative Learning Problem

5-40 Activity-based costing, cost hierarchy. (CMA, adapted) Coffee Bean, Inc. (CBI) buys coffee beans from around the world and roasts, blends, and packages them for resale. The major cost is direct materials; however, there is substantial manufacturing overhead in the predominantly automated roasting and packing process. The company uses relatively little direct labor.

Some of the coffees are very popular and sell in large volumes, whereas a few of the newer blends sell in very low volumes. CBI prices its coffee at budgeted cost, including allocated overhead, plus a markup on cost of 30%.

Data for the 2006 budget include manufacturing overhead of $3,000,000, which has been allocated on the basis of each product's budgeted direct-labor cost. The budgeted direct-labor cost for 2006 totals $600,000. Purchases and use of materials (mostly coffee beans) are budgeted to total $6,000,000.

The budgeted direct costs for one-pound bags of two of the company's products are:

	Mauna Loa	Malaysian
Direct materials	$4.20	$3.20
Direct labor	0.30	0.30

CBI's controller believes the existing simple costing system may be providing misleading cost information. She has developed an activity-based analysis of the 2006 budgeted manufacturing overhead costs, which is shown in the following table:

Activity	Cost Driver	Cost-Driver Rate
Purchasing	Purchase orders	$500
Materials handling	Loads moved	400
Quality control	Batches	240
Roasting	Roasting-hours	10
Blending	Blending-hours	10
Packaging	Packaging-hours	10

Budgeted data regarding the 2006 production of the Mauna Loa and Malaysian coffee follow. There will be no beginning or ending materials inventory for either of these coffees.

	Mauna Loa	Malaysian
Expected sales	100,000 pounds	2,000 pounds
Purchase orders	4	4
Batches	10	4
Loads moved	30	12
Roasting-hours	1,000	20
Blending-hours	500	10
Packaging-hours	100	2

Required

1. Using CBI's simple costing system:
   a. Determine the company's 2006 budgeted manufacturing overhead rate using direct-labor cost as the single allocation base.
   b. Determine the 2006 budgeted costs and selling prices of 1 pound of Mauna Loa coffee and 1 pound of Malaysian coffee.
2. Use the controller's activity-based approach to estimate the 2006 budgeted cost for 1 pound of
   a. Mauna Loa coffee
   b. Malaysian coffee

   Allocate all costs to the 100,000 pounds of Mauna Loa and the 2,000 pounds of Malaysian. Compare the results with those in requirement 1.
3. Examine the implications of your answers to requirement 2 for CBI's pricing and product-mix strategy.

WWW

Get Connected: Cost Accounting in the News

Go to www.prenhall.com/horngren/cost/2e for additional online exercise(s) that explore issues affecting the accounting world today. These exercises offer you the opportunity to analyze and reflect on how cost accounting helps managers to make better decisions and handle the challenges of strategic planning and implementation.

CHAPTER 5 Case

COLOMBO FROZEN YOGURT: Activity-Based Costing

As you've seen in this chapter, activity-based costing systems are useful in helping managers make better decisions about pricing, product mix, and cost management related to product design and efficiency. In fact, General Mills used ABC to identify and analyze the costs associated with the different channels used to market its Colombo frozen yogurt products.

Before performing ABC analysis, General Mills charged the same prices and provided the same promotions—$3 per case—to its customers, whether the customer was in the grocery (food purchased for later consumption or preparation at home) or the food-service (outside of home, immediate consumption) channel. Upon closer examination of the food-service channel, General Mills discovered segments within food service: destination yogurt shops or restaurants and impulse locations, located in business cafeterias and on college campuses and military bases. General Mills also noticed that sales dollars for frozen yogurt products were relatively constant, but profits were declining. The company sensed that destination yogurt shops may be more profitable than impulse locations, but it didn't have the information about profit differences to make changes. General Mills' logic was: Destination shops/restaurants focus on maximizing profit per square foot and managing the average sale per customer. However, impulse locations focus on cost per serving, and this segment of the business was growing at a much faster rate than the destination shop segment.

The sales data and income statements for last year by segment were:

Category	Impulse Locations	Yogurt Shops	Total
Sales in cases	1,200,000	300,000	1,500,000
Sales revenue	$23,880,000	$5,970,000	$29,850,000
Deduct: Promotions	3,600,000	900,000	4,500,000
Net sales	$20,280,000	$5,070,000	$25,350,000
Deduct: COGS	13,800,000	3,450,000	17,250,000
Gross margin	$ 6,480,000	$1,620,000	$ 8,100,000
Deduct: Merchandising	1,380,000	345,000	1,725,000
Deduct: SG&A*	948,000	237,000	1,185,000
Net income	$ 4,152,000	$1,038,000	$ 5,190,000

*Selling, general, and administrative expenses

Cost of goods sold includes $14,250,000 for ingredients, packaging, and storage, and $3,000,000 for pick, pack, and shipping. The product is the same across segments, so cost to produce is the same. However, pick, pack, and shipping costs vary if the order is for a full pallet. Full pallets cost $75 to pick and ship, whereas individual orders cost $2.25 per case. There are 75 cases in a pallet, with pallet and case usage by segment shown here:

	Impulse Segment	Yogurt Shops	Total
Cases in full pallets	60,000	240,000	300,000
Individual cases	1,140,000	60,000	1,200,000
Total cases	1,200,000	300,000	1,500,000

Merchandising costs consist mainly of kits at $500 each. A total of 3,450 kits were delivered last year, 90 of them to yogurt shops. For SG&A, costs were allocated to products based on gross sales dollars. When a random sample of the sales force was asked to keep diaries for 60 days, the resulting data revealed they spent much more time per sales dollar on yogurt sales than other General Mills products they represented. As a result, when SG&A costs were allocated based on time, the total allocation to yogurt jumped from $1,185,000 to $3,900,000. Of the total time spent on selling Colombo frozen yogurt, only 1% of that time was spent in shops.

QUESTIONS

1. How do the two segments identified by General Mills for Colombo frozen yogurt sales differ from each other?
2. Using ABC analysis, restate the income statements, above, to show new net income (*hint:* add a line item for shipping). What is net income per case?
3. Based on your analysis in question 2, what changes should General Mills make?

(IMA adapted; "Colombo Frozen Yogurt," John Guy and Jane Saly, *Cases from Management Accounting Practice*, Vol. 15, Institute of Management Accountants, 2000.) © IMA. Reprinted with permission from the Institute of Management Accountants, Montvale, N.J., **www.imanet.org**.

CHAPTER 6

MASTER BUDGET AND RESPONSIBILITY ACCOUNTING

LEARNING OBJECTIVES

1. Describe what the master budget is and explain its benefits
2. Describe the advantages of budgets
3. Prepare the operating budget and its supporting schedules
4. Use computer-based financial planning models in sensitivity analysis
5. Explain kaizen budgeting and how it is used for cost management
6. Prepare an activity-based budget
7. Describe responsibility centers and responsibility accounting
8. Explain how controllability relates to responsibility accounting

Budgets are a staple in the corporate world. Without budgets, it is difficult for managers and employees to know whether they're on target for growth and spending. Rex Jordan, the CEO of Stylistic Furniture, knows the critical role the budgeting process plays in his coffee table manufacturing business. As he prepares to address a group of senior managers regarding the 2007 budget process, he chooses his words carefully.

Rex: The year 2007 will be full of opportunity for us. The markets for our products are growing, so we need to plan for a significant increase in sales. Our sales force should continue to be in close touch with our customers and alert us to new opportunities. I know salespeople are sometimes tempted to underestimate budgeted revenues because it makes it easier for them to achieve their sales targets. But without accurate sales estimates, manufacturing, distribution, and customer service will find it difficult to deliver when sales growth occurs. All parts of the organization should know as early as possible what's expected of them so they can plan accordingly. As senior managers, you are responsible for performance, so I'm counting on your active participation and input into the budget process.

Abbie Suarez, Vice President Sales and Marketing: Rex, we're just as excited as you are about next year. My team is already working to identify not just new customers, but also ways to increase sales to our existing customer base.

Charlie Ballard, Executive Vice President: Rex, I think it's time we establish a cross-functional team to look at the effects our anticipated growth will have on manufacturing, distribution, and customer service. We can't afford to prepare budgets in departmental vacuums.

Rex: Sounds good. I'd like you to include Tina Larsen, our management accountant, on your team. She'll be able to challenge assumptions and make recommendations based on her knowledge of our financial position and current costs. With everyone's help, we'll have a clear picture of our plans and what we need to do to achieve them.

The meeting at Stylistic Furniture demonstrates how critical the budgeting process is to an organization. Southwest Airlines, for example, uses budgets to monitor and manage fuel costs. CostCo depends on its budget to maintain razor-thin margins due to strong competition from Wal-Mart. Managers at Ritz-Carlton prepare budgets for each hotel. Sales managers prepare revenue budgets, and then managers from every department, from housekeeping to the front desk, use the revenue budgets to prepare their own departmental budgets. Each budget is supported by anticipated occupancy, banquet hall use, and restaurant activity.

Budgeting is a common accounting tool companies use for implementing strategy. Budgeting aids in planning and controlling the actions companies must undertake to satisfy their customers and succeed in the marketplace. Budgets provide measures of the financial results a company expects from its planned activities. By planning, managers learn to anticipate potential problems and how to avoid them. Instead of facing unexpected problems, managers can focus their energies on exploiting opportunities. Remember that, "Few businesses plan to fail, but many of those that flop failed to plan."

Budgets and the Budgeting Cycle

A *budget* is (a) the quantitative expression of a proposed plan of action by management for a specified period and (b) an aid to coordinating what needs to be done to implement that plan. A budget generally includes both financial and nonfinancial aspects of the plan, and it serves as a blueprint for the company to follow in an upcoming period. A financial budget quantifies management's expectations regarding income, cash flows, and financial position. Just as financial statements are prepared for past periods, so can financial statements be prepared for future periods—for example, a budgeted income statement, a budgeted statement of cash flows, and a budgeted balance sheet. Underlying these financial budgets are nonfinancial budgets for, say, units manufactured or sold, number of employees, and number of new products being introduced to the marketplace.

Strategic Plans and Operating Plans

Budgeting is most useful when it is an integral part of a company's strategic analysis. *Strategy* specifies how an organization matches its own capabilities with the opportunities in the marketplace to accomplish its objectives. In developing successful strategies, managers consider questions such as:

- What are our objectives?
- Are the markets for our products local, regional, national, or global? What trends affect our markets? How are we affected by the economy, our industry, and our competitors?
- What organizational and financial structures serve us best?
- What are the risks and opportunities of alternative strategies, and what are our contingency plans if our preferred plan fails?

A company, such as Home Depot, can have a strategy of providing quality products or services at a low price. Pfizer or Porsche can have a strategy of providing a unique product or service that is priced higher than the products or services of competitors. Exhibit 6-1 shows that strategic plans are expressed through long-run budgets and operating plans via short-run budgets. But there is more to the story! The exhibit shows arrows pointing backward as well as forward. The backward arrows are a way of graphically indicating that budgets can lead to changes in plans and strategies. Budgets help managers assess strategic risks and opportunities by providing them with feedback about the likely effects of their strategies and plans. And sometimes the feedback signals to managers that they need to revise their plans and possibly their strategies.

Planning is setting goals and developing strategies to achieve those goals. Budgets show how resources will be deployed to implement strategy. The master budget helps managers implement their strategies.

DaimlerChrysler's decision about the pricing of its Dodge Durango illustrates how budgets helped its managers rework their operating plans. The Durango competes in the sport-utility vehicle (SUV) market with the lower-priced Subaru Forrester and Isuzu Rodeo, as well as the comparably priced Chevrolet Blazer. By reducing the Durango's price, DaimlerChrysler expected to increase demand for the Durango. The budget, however, indicated that, even with higher sales quantities, DaimlerChrysler would be unable to meet its financial targets for the Durango. For its strategy of reducing price to succeed, DaimlerChrysler also would need to reduce its manufacturing and marketing costs. This feedback led the Durango management team to develop new operating plans to use materials and labor more efficiently.

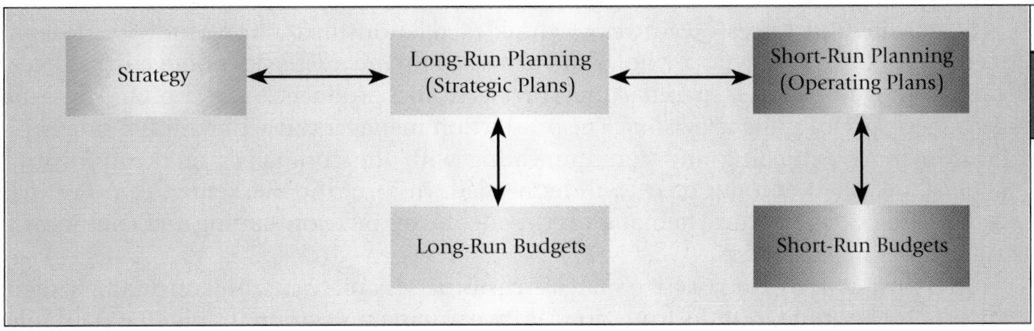

EXHIBIT 6-1
Strategy, Planning, and Budgets

Budgeting Cycle and Master Budget

Well-managed companies usually cycle through the following budgeting steps during the course of the fiscal year:

1. Working together, managers and management accountants plan the performance of the company as a whole and the performance of its subunits (such as departments or divisions). Taking into account past performance and anticipated changes in the future, managers at all levels agree on what is expected.
2. Senior managers give subordinate managers a frame of reference, a set of specific financial or nonfinancial expectations against which actual results will be compared.
3. Management accountants help managers investigate variations from plans, such as an unexpected decline in sales. If necessary, corrective action follows, such as a reduction in price to boost sales or cutting of costs to maintain profitability.
4. Managers and management accountants take into account market feedback, changed conditions, and their own experiences as they begin to make plans for the next period. For example, a decline in sales may cause managers to think about introducing a new product next period.

1

Describe what the master budget is

. . . the master budget is the initial budget prepared before the start of a period

and explain its benefits

. . . benefits include planning, coordination, and control

The preceding four steps describe the ongoing budget process. The working document at the core of this process is called the master budget. The **master budget** expresses management's operating and financial plans for a specified period (usually a fiscal year), and it includes a set of budgeted financial statements. The master budget is the initial plan of what the company intends to accomplish in the budget period. The master budget evolves from both operating and financing decisions made by managers.

- Operating decisions deal with how to best use the limited resources of an organization.
- Financing decisions deal with how to obtain the funds to acquire those resources.

The terminology used to describe budgets varies among companies. For example, budgeted financial statements are sometimes called **pro forma statements**. Some companies, such as Hewlett-Packard, refer to budgeting as *targeting*. And many companies, such as Nissan Motor and Owens Corning, refer to the budget as a *profit plan*.

The focus of this book is on how management accounting helps managers make operating decisions. That's why this chapter emphasizes operating budgets. Managers spend a significant part of their time preparing and analyzing budgets. The many advantages of budgeting make spending time on budgeting a worthwhile investment of managers' energies.

2

Describe the advantages of budgets

. . . advantages include helping to develop and implement strategic plans and motivate employees

Advantages of Budgets

Budgets are an integral part of management control systems. When administered thoughtfully by managers, budgets

- Promote coordination and communication among subunits within the company
- Provide a framework for judging performance
- Motivate managers and other employees

Coordination and Communication

Coordination is meshing and balancing all aspects of production or service and all departments in a company in the best way for the company to meet its goals. *Communication* is making sure those goals are understood and accepted by all employees.

The master budget helps coordinate the various business functions of the value chain, such as production, marketing, and customer service. Management accountants coordinate the budgeting process.

Coordination forces executives to think of relationships among individual departments and the company as a whole, and across companies. Consider budgeting at Pace, a United Kingdom-based manufacturer of electronic products. A key product is their decoder boxes for cable television. The production manager can achieve more-timely production by coordinating and communicating with the company's marketing team to understand when decoder boxes will be needed. In turn, the marketing team can make better predictions of future demand for decoder boxes by coordinating and communicating with Pace's customers.

Suppose BSKYB, one of Pace's largest customers, is planning to launch a new digital satellite service nine months from now. If Pace's marketing group is able to obtain information about the launch date for the satellite service, it can share this information with Pace's manufacturing group. The manufacturing group must then coordinate and communicate with Pace's materials-procurement group, and so on. The point to understand is that Pace is more likely to have satisfied customers (decoder boxes in the demanded quantities at the times demanded) if Pace coordinates and communicates both within its business functions and with its suppliers and customers during the budgeting process as well as the production process.

Framework for Judging Performance

Plans enable a company's managers to measure actual performance against budgets. Budgets can overcome two limitations of using past performance as a basis for judging actual results. One limitation is that past results often incorporate past miscues and substandard performance. Consider a cellular telephone company (Mobile Communications) examining the current-year (2007) performance of its sales force. Suppose the performance for 2006 incorporated the efforts of many salespeople who have since left Mobile because they did not have a good understanding of the marketplace. (The president of Mobile said, "They could not sell ice cream in a heat wave.") Using the sales record of those departed employees would set the performance bar for 2007 much too low.

The other limitation of using past performance is that future conditions can be expected to differ from the past. Consider again Mobile Communications. Suppose, in 2007, Mobile had a 20% revenue increase, compared with a 10% revenue increase in 2006. Does this increase indicate outstanding sales performance? Before you say yes, consider the following facts. In November 2006, an industry trade association forecast that the 2007 growth rate in industry revenues would be 40%, which also turned out to be the actual growth rate. As a result, Mobile's 20% actual revenue gain in 2007 takes on a negative connotation, even though it exceeded the 2006 actual growth rate of 10%. Using the 40% budgeted sales growth rate provides a better measure of the 2007 sales performance than using the 2006 actual growth rate of 10%.

However, it is important to remember that a company's budget should not be the only benchmark used to evaluate performance. Many companies also consider performance relative to peers as well as improvement over prior years. The problem with evaluating performance relative only to a budget is it creates an incentive for subordinates to set a target that is relatively easy to achieve.[1] Of course, managers at all levels recognize this incentive, and therefore they work to make the budget more challenging to achieve for the individuals who report to them. Negotiations occur among managers at each of these levels to understand what is possible and what is not. The budget is the end product of these negotiations.

Motivating Managers and Other Employees[2]

Research shows that challenging budgets improve employee performance. That's because falling short of budgeted numbers is viewed by employees as a failure. Most employees are motivated to work more intensely to avoid failure than to achieve success. As employees get closer to a goal, they work harder to achieve it. Therefore, many executives like to set demanding but achievable goals for their subordinate managers and employees. Creating a little anxiety improves performance, but overly ambitious and unachievable budgets increase anxiety without motivation—that's because employees see little chance of avoiding failure. General Electric's former CEO, Jack Welch, describes challenging budgets that subordinates buy into as energizing, motivating, and satisfying for managers and other employees, capable of unleashing out-of-the-box and creative thinking.

Challenges in Administering Budgets

Budgeting is a time-consuming process that involves all levels of management. Top managers want lower-level managers to participate in the budgeting process because lower-level managers have more specialized knowledge and first-hand experience with day-to-day

Managers often spend a lot of time working on budgets, which is costly. Studies of large companies report about 5% of staff positions are devoted to budgeting.

[1]See J. Hope and R. Fraser, *Beyond Budgeting* (Boston, MA: Harvard Business School Press, 2003) for several examples.

[2]For a more-detailed discussion, see R. Larnick, G. Wu, and C. Heath, "Raising the Bar on Goals," Graduate School of Business Publication, University of Chicago, Spring 1999.

aspects of running the business. Participation creates greater commitment and accountability toward the budget among lower-level managers. This is the bottom-up aspect of the budgeting process.

The widespread prevalence of budgets in companies ranging from major corporations with international presence to smaller local businesses indicates that the advantages of budgeting systems outweigh the costs. (See Global Surveys of Company Practice, p. 185.) To gain the benefits of budgeting, management at all levels of a company should understand and support the budget and all aspects of the management control system. Top management support is critical for obtaining lower-level management's participation in the formulation of budgets and for successful administration of budgets. Lower-level managers who feel that top management does not "believe" in a budget are unlikely to be active participants in a budget process.

Budgets should not be administered rigidly. Changing conditions usually call for changes in plans. A manager may commit to a budget, but a situation might develop in which some unplanned repairs or an unplanned advertising program would better serve the interests of the company. The manager should not defer the repairs or the advertising as a way of meeting the budget if doing so will hurt the company in the long run. Attaining the budget should not be an end in itself. In fact, critics of budgeting cite the temptation on the part of managers to administer budgets rigidly as one of the most negative aspects of budgeting.[3]

Time Coverage of Budgets

Budgets typically have a set period, such as a month, quarter, year, and so on. The set period can itself be broken into subperiods. For example, a 12-month cash budget may be broken into 12 monthly periods so that cash inflows and outflows can be better coordinated.

The motive for creating a budget should guide the period chosen for the budget. For example, consider budgeting for a new Harley-Davidson 500-cc motorcycle. If the purpose is to budget for the total profitability of this new model, a five-year period (or more) may be suitable and long enough to cover the product from design through to manufacture, sales, and after-sales support. In contrast, consider budgeting for a school play. If the purpose is to estimate all cash outlays, a six-month period from the planning stage to the final performance may be adequate.

The most frequently used budget period is one year, which is often subdivided into months and quarters. The budgeted data for a year are frequently revised as the year goes on. For example, at the end of the first quarter, the budget for the next three quarters can be changed in light of new information obtained during the first quarter.

Businesses are increasingly using rolling budgets. A **rolling budget**, also called a **continuous budget**, is a budget that is always available for a specified future period. It is created by continually adding a month, quarter, or year to the period that just ended. Consider Electrolux, the global appliance company, which has a three- to five-year strategic plan and a four-quarter rolling budget. A four-quarter rolling budget for the April 2007 to March 2008 period is superseded in the next quarter—that is in June 2007—by a four-quarter rolling budget for July 2007 to June 2008, and so on. There is always a 12-month budget (for the next year) in place. Rolling budgets constantly force Electrolux's management to think about the forthcoming 12 months, regardless of the quarter at hand.

3
Prepare the operating budget
. . . the budgeted income statement
and its supporting schedules
. . . such as cost of goods sold and nonmanufacturing costs

Steps in Developing an Operating Budget

The best way to explain how to prepare an operating budget is with an example. Consider Stylistic Furniture, the company we introduced at the start of the chapter. Its job-costing system for manufacturing costs has two direct-cost categories—direct materials and direct

[3] J. Hope and R. Fraser, *Beyond Budgeting* (Boston, MA: Harvard Business School Press, 2003), pp. 3–17.

GLOBAL SURVEYS OF COMPANY PRACTICE

Budget Practices Around the Globe

Surveys of financial officers of large companies throughout the United States, Europe, Asia, and Oceania indicate some interesting similarities and differences in budgeting practices. The use of master budgets is widespread; however, differences arise with respect to other dimensions of budgeting. U.S. controllers and managers, for example, favor participation by division managers and regard return on investment as the most important budget goal.[a] Similarly all of the Greek budget directors surveyed report that division managers participate in completing the master budget.[b] In contrast, fewer division managers in New Zealand and the United Kingdom participated in the budget committee process even though most executives in these countries place average to vital importance on adherence to budgets when evaluating managers.[c] Japanese companies have the smallest amount of participation by division managers in the budgeting process (relative to other countries surveyed) and regard sales revenue as the most important budget goal. A survey of Australian managers reported that budgeting is the management accounting practice that they benefit from the most.[d]

1. Percentage of companies that prepare a complete master budget:

United States	Australia	Finland[e]	Greece	India[f]	Japan[a]	New Zealand	Singapore[g]	Sweden[h]	U.K.
91%	100%	92%	93%	91%	93%	98%	97%	89%	95%

2. Percentage of companies reporting division-manager participation in budget committee discussions:

United States	Greece	India	Japan	New Zealand	U.K.
78%	93%	84%	67%	70%	71%

3. Ranking of the most important budget goals for division mangers (1 is most important):

	United States	Japan
Return on investment	1	4
Operating income	2	2
Sales revenue	3	1
Production costs	4	3

4. Percentage of executives who place importance on the budget when appraising management performance:

	New Zealand	United Kingdom
Not important	0%	1%
Below average importance	7	4
Average importance	22	14
Above average importance	45	39
Vital importance	26	28

What reduces the effectiveness of the planning and budgeting processes of companies? A survey of chief financial officers (CFOs) in the United States reported the following four factors in order of importance.[i]

1. Lack of a well-defined strategy
2. Lack of a clear linkage of strategy to operating plans
3. Lack of individual accountability for results
4. Lack of meaningful performance measures

Two planning methodologies viewed as "significant to extremely valuable" by more than 60% of CFOs surveyed were activity-based budgeting and rolling budget forecasts.

---

[a]Asada et al., "An Empirical Study."
[b]Ballas and Venieris, "A Survey of Management Accounting Practice."
[c]Guilding et al., "Budgeting and Standard Costing Practices."
[d]Crehnall and Smith, "Adoption and Benefits of Management Accounting."
[e]Ekholm and Wallin, "Is the Annual Budget Really Dead?"
[f]Joshi, "The International Diffusion of New Management Accounting."
[g]Ghosh and Chan, "Management Accounting in Singapore"
[h]Gladder et al., "Ekonomistyrning i Svenska Börsföretag."
[i]Lazere, "All Together Now."
Full citations are in Appendix A at the end of the book.

manufacturing labor—and one indirect-cost category—manufacturing overhead. Manufacturing overhead, both variable and fixed, is allocated to each coffee table using direct manufacturing labor-hours as the allocation base.

Exhibit 6-2 shows a diagram of the various parts of the master budget for Stylistic Furniture. The master budget comprises the financial projections of all the individual budgets for a company for a specified period, usually a fiscal year. The mauve boxes in Exhibit 6-2 represent the budgeted income statement and its supporting budget schedules—together called the **operating budget**. We show the revenues budget box in a light mauve color to indicate that it is often the starting point of the operating budget. The supporting schedules—shown in medium mauve—quantify the budgets for various business functions of the value chain, from research and development to administrative costs. These schedules build up to the budgeted income statement—the key summary statement in the operating budget—shown in dark mauve. The blue boxes in the exhibit are the **financial budget**, which is that part of the master budget made up of the capital expenditures budget, the cash budget, the budgeted balance sheet, and the budgeted statement of cash flows. A financial budget focuses on how operations and planned capital outlays affect cash—shown in light blue. The cash budget and the budgeted income statement can then be used to prepare two other summary financial statements—the budgeted balance sheet and the budgeted statement of cash flows—shown in medium blue. The master budget is finalized only after several rounds of discussions between top management and managers responsible for various business functions in the value chain.

To focus on how budgets help managers make accounting decisions, we now present the steps in preparing an operating budget for Stylistic Furniture for 2007. Use Exhibit 6-2 as a guide for the steps that follow. The appendix to this chapter presents Stylistic's cash budget, which is another key component of the master budget. We assume the following:

- The only source of revenues is sales of its single product, coffee tables. Nonsales-related revenues, such as interest income, is assumed to be zero. Units sold is the driver of revenues because selling prices are predicted to be unchanged throughout 2007.
- Work-in-process inventory is negligible and is ignored.
- Direct materials inventory and finished goods inventory are costed using the first-in, first-out (FIFO) method. Unit costs of direct materials purchased and finished goods sold remain unchanged throughout each budget year but can change from year to year.
- There are two types of direct materials: particle board (PB) and red oak (RO). Direct material costs are variable with respect to units of output—coffee tables.
- There are two types of direct manufacturing labor: laminating labor and machining labor. Direct manufacturing labor costs are variable with respect to direct manufacturing labor-hours. Direct manufacturing labor rates remain unchanged throughout each budget year but can change from year to year. Direct manufacturing labor workers are hired on an hourly basis; no overtime is worked.
- Manufacturing overhead has a variable component and a fixed component. The variable component is variable with respect to direct manufacturing labor-hours. For computing inventoriable costs, Stylistic allocates all manufacturing overhead costs, variable and fixed, using direct manufacturing labor-hours as the allocation base.
- Nonmanufacturing costs have a variable component and a fixed component. The variable component is variable with respect to the amount of revenues.[4]

Ending inventory is not just a "leftover"; it is a budgeted amount.

[4]To keep the Stylistic budget example straightforward, we assume all variable nonmanufacturing costs are variable with respect to amount of revenues. In practice, some of these costs may be variable with respect to non-revenue-based factors. For example, some distribution costs may be variable with respect to the weight of the item distributed or the distance moved to distribute the product. For case studies, see S. Player and D. Keys (ed.), *Activity-Based Management* (New York: MasterMedia, 1995).

EXHIBIT 6-2 Overview of the Master Budget for Stylistic Furniture

The budget for a merchandising company does not have a production budget, direct material costs budget, direct manufacturing labor costs budget, or a manufacturing overhead costs budget. In addition, a service company has neither a cost of goods sold budget nor an ending inventory budget. All the other budgets described in Exhibit 6-2 apply to merchandising and service companies.

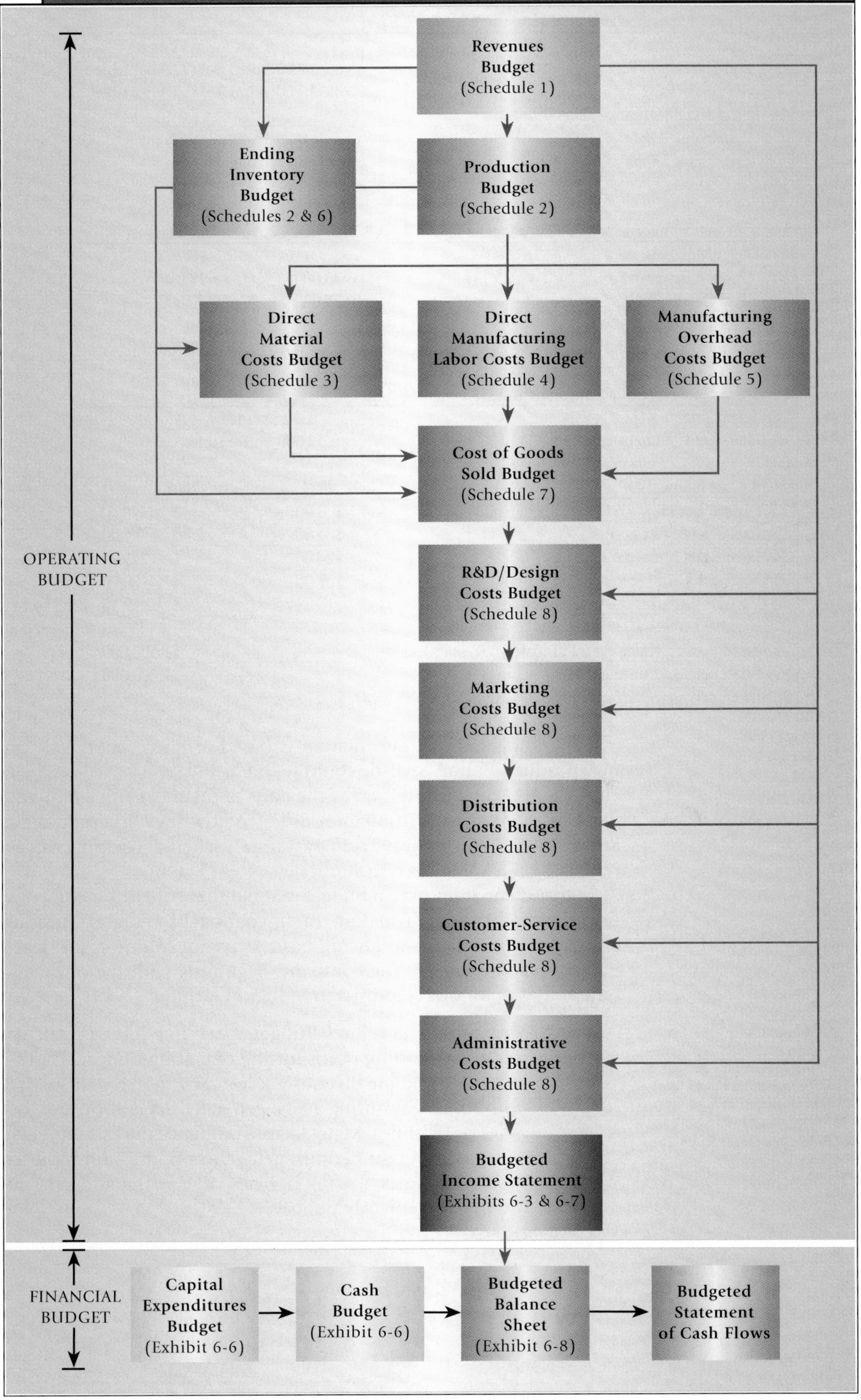

The following data are used in developing Stylistic's 2007 budget:

	A	B	C	D
1	a. Product specifications for each coffee table for 2007			
2	Direct Materials			
3	Particle Board (PB)	9.00	board feet (b.f.) per table	
4	Red Oak (RO)	10.00	board feet (b.f.) per table	
5	Direct Manufacturing Labor			
6	Laminating Labor	0.25	hours per table	
7	Machining Labor	3.75	hours per table	
8				
9		**Beginning**	**Target Ending**	
10	b. Inventory information in physical units for 2007	**Inventory**	**Inventory**	
11	Direct Materials			
12	Particle Board (b.f.)	20,000	18,000	
13	Red Oak (b.f.)	25,000	22,000	
14	Finished Goods			
15	Coffee tables (units)	5,000	3,000	
16				
17	c. Sales and revenue information for 2007			
18	Selling Price	$392	per table	
19	Units expected to be sold	52,000	coffee tables	
20				
21	d. Cost information	**2006**	**2007**	
22	Particle Board (per b.f.)	$ 3.90	$ 4.00	
23	Red Oak (per b.f.)	$ 5.80	$ 6.00	
24	Laminating labor (per hour)	$24.00	$ 25.00	
25	Machining labor (per hour)	$29.00	$ 30.00	
26	Variable manufacturing overhead costs		$ 9.50	per direct manufacturing labor-hour
27	Variable nonmanufacturing costs		13.5%	of revenues
28	Fixed manufacturing overhead costs		$1,600,000	
29	Fixed nonmanufacturing costs		$1,400,000	
30	Inventoriable (manufacturing) cost (per coffee table)	$ 275		

The budgeted cost information is based on the cost Stylistic expects to incur on its new production line. Stylistic could set budgeted costs based on the costs at the most efficient plant owned by Stylistic or the costs at the most efficient plant owned by any company in the industry. Companies differ in how they compute their budgeted amounts. Some companies rely heavily on past results when developing budgeted amounts; others rely on detailed engineering studies.

Most companies have a budget manual that contains a company's particular instructions and relevant information for preparing its budgets. Although the details differ among companies, the following basic steps are common for developing the operating budget for a manufacturing company. Beginning with the revenues budget, each of the other budgets follows step-by-step in logical fashion.

Because all of the budgets in Exhibit 6-2 flow from the revenues budget, accurate sales forecasts are needed. However, factors outside the company's control (such as competition and economic conditions) can make it difficult to accurately forecast sales.

Step 1: Prepare the Revenues Budget. A revenues budget, calculated in Schedule 1, is the usual starting point for the operating budget. That's because the production level and the inventory level—and therefore manufacturing costs—as well as nonmanufacturing costs, generally depend on the forecasted level of unit sales or revenues. Many factors influence the sales forecast, including the sales volume in recent periods, general economic and industry conditions, market research studies, pricing policies, advertising and sales promotions, competition, and regulatory policies.

	A	B	C	D
1	Schedule 1: Revenues Budget			
2	For the Year Ending December 31, 2007			
3				
4		**Selling Price**	**Units Sold**	**Total Revenues**
5	Coffee tables	$392	52,000	$20,384,000

The $20,384,000 is the amount of revenues in the budgeted income statement. The revenues budget is often the outcome of elaborate information gathering and discussions among sales managers and sales representatives who have a detailed understanding of customer needs, market potential, and competitors' products. Statistical approaches such as regression and trend analysis can also help in sales forecasting. These techniques use indicators of economic activity and past sales data to forecast future sales. Managers should use statistical analysis only as one input to forecast sales. In the final analysis, the sales forecast should represent the collective experience and judgment of managers.

The usual starting point for step 1 is to base revenues on expected demand. Occasionally, a factor other than demand limits budgeted revenues. For example, when demand is greater than available production capacity or a manufacturing input is in short supply, the revenues budget would be based on the maximum units that could be produced. Why? Because sales would be limited by the amount produced.

Regression and trend analysis are techniques that use sales data from recent periods to best represent how sales have changed over those periods. Extending this line into the future can help in predicting future sales.

Step 2: Prepare the Production Budget (in Units). After revenues are budgeted, the manufacturing manager prepares the production budget, which is calculated in Schedule 2. The total finished goods units to be produced depends on budgeted unit sales and expected changes in units of inventory levels:

$$\text{Budget production (units)} = \text{Budget sales (units)} + \text{Target ending finished goods inventory (units)} - \text{Beginning finished goods inventory (units)}$$

The nature of the product makes it difficult for some companies to synchronize production levels with expected sales. When inputs are available only seasonally, production occurs "in season." For example, a manufacturer of jellies makes the year's supply of strawberry jelly during strawberry harvest season.

	A	B
1	Schedule 2: Production Budget (in Units)	
2	For the Year Ending December 31, 2007	
3		
4		Coffee Tables
5	Budgeted unit sales (Schedule 1)	52,000
6	Add target ending finished goods inventory	3,000
7	Total required units	55,000
8	Deduct beginning finished goods inventory	5,000
9	Units of finished goods to be produced	50,000
10		

There is no need to memorize this schedule if you understand that the number of units to be produced is equal to the number of units needed (budgeted sales + ending FG inventory) minus the units already on hand (beginning FG inventory). The same idea applies to the purchases of each type of direct material. Keep all these computations in units and then multiply by the cost per unit at the end.

Step 3: Prepare the Direct Material Usage Budget and Direct Material Purchases Budget. The number of units to be produced, calculated in Schedule 2, is the

	A	B	C	D
1	Schedule 3A: Direct Material Usage Budget			
2	For the Year Ending December 31, 2007			
3				
4		Particle Board	Red Oak	
5		(PB)	(RO)	Total
6	Physical Units Budget			
7	PB required: 50,000 units × 9.00 b.f. per unit	450,000		
8	RO required: 50,000 units × 10.00 b.f. per unit		500,000	
9	To be used in production, b.f.	450,000	500,000	
10				
11	Cost Budget			
12	Available from beginning raw materials inventory:			
13	PB: $3.90 per b.f. × 20,000 b.f.	$ 78,000		
14	RO: $5.80 per b.f. × 25,000 b.f.		$ 145,000	
15	To be purchased this period:			
16	PB: $4.00 per b.f. × (450,000 - 20,000)b.f.	1,720,000		
17	RO: $6.00 per b.f. × (500,000 - 25,000) b.f.		2,850,000	
18	Direct materials to be used this period	$1,798,000	$2,995,000	$4,793,000
19				

key to computing the usage of direct materials in quantities and in dollars. The direct material quantities used depend on the efficiency with which materials are consumed to produce a table. Manufacturing managers are constantly seeking ways to make process improvements that increase quality and reduce waste, which reduces direct material usage and costs.

The purchasing manager prepares the budget for direct material purchases, calculated in Schedule 3B, based on the budgeted direct materials to be used, the beginning inventory of direct materials, and the target ending inventory of direct materials:

$$\text{Purchases of direct materials} = \text{Direct materials used in production} + \text{Target ending inventory of direct materials} - \text{Beginning inventory of direct materials}$$

Once we determine the number of units to be produced from the production budget (Schedule 2), we can budget for the manufacturing inputs—direct materials, direct labor, and overhead.

	A	B	C	D	E	F
1	Schedule 3B: Direct Material Purchases Budget					
2	For the Year Ending December 31, 2007					
3						
4		Particle Board		Red Oak		
5		(PB)		(RO)		Total
6	Physical Units Budget					
7	To be used in production (from Schedule 3A)	450,000	b.f.	500,000	b.f.	
8	Add target ending inventory	18,000	b.f.	22,000	b.f.	
9	Total requirements	468,000	b.f.	522,000	b.f.	
10	Deduct beginning inventory	20,000	b.f.	25,000	b.f.	
11	Purchases to be made	448,000	b.f.	497,000	b.f.	
12						
13	Cost Budget					
14	PB: 448,000 b.f. × $4.00 per b.f.	$1,792,000				
15	RO: 497,000 b.f. × $6.00 per b.f.			$2,982,000		
16	Purchases	$1,792,000		$2,982,000		$4,774,000
17						

Step 4: Prepare the Direct Manufacturing Labor Costs Budget. These costs depend on wage rates, production methods, and hiring plans. The manufacturing manager prepares the budget for direct manufacturing labor, calculated in Schedule 4:

	A	B	C	D	E	F	G
1	Schedule 4: Direct Manufacturing Labor Costs Budget						
2	For the Year Ending December 31, 2007						
3							
4		Laminating Labor		Machining Labor			
5		(LL)		(ML)		Total	
6	Labor-Hours Budget						
7	LL: 50,000 units × 0.25 hours/unit	12,500	hours				
8	ML: 50,000 units × 3.75 hours/unit			187,500	hours		
9		12,500	hours	187,500	hours	200,000	hours
10							
11	Cost Budget						
12	LL: $25.00 per hour × 12,500 hours	$312,500					
13	ML: $30.00 per hour × 187,500 hours			$5,625,000			
14		$312,500		$5,625,000		$5,937,500	
15							

Step 5: Prepare the Manufacturing Overhead Costs Budget. The total of these costs depends on how individual overhead costs vary with respect to the cost driver: direct manufacturing labor-hours. The calculations of budgeted manufacturing overhead costs appear in Schedule 5. The individual amounts for variable manufacturing overhead costs and fixed manufacturing overhead costs are based on input from Stylistic's operating personnel. The starting point for

these amounts is Stylistic's costs in the current and prior years. Based on efficiency improvements planned for 2007, the budgeted level of the cost driver (direct manufacturing labor-hours), and the cost of inputs, the manufacturing manager, aided by the management accountant, makes adjustments for cost changes expected in 2007.

In accordance with generally accepted accounting principles, Stylistic treats both variable and fixed manufacturing overhead as inventoriable costs. It inventories manufacturing overhead at the budgeted rate of $17.50 per direct manufacturing labor-hour (total budgeted manufacturing overhead, $3,500,000 ÷ 200,000 budgeted direct manufacturing labor-hours). Stylistic does not use a separate variable manufacturing overhead rate and a separate fixed manufacturing overhead rate. The budgeted manufacturing overhead cost per coffee table is $70 ($3,500,000 ÷ 50,000 coffee tables budgeted to be produced in 2007). The $70 budgeted manufacturing overhead cost per coffee table can also be calculated as $17.50 budgeted cost per direct manufacturing labor-hour × 4 budgeted direct manufacturing labor-hours per coffee table = $70.

	A	B	C
1	Schedule 5: Manufacturing Overhead Costs Budget		
2	For the Year Ending December 31, 2007		
3			
4		At Budgeted Level of 200,000	
5		Direct Manufacturing Labor-Hours	
6	Variable manufacturing overhead costs		
7	Supplies	$240,000	
8	Indirect manufacturing labor	620,000	
9	Power and energy	460,000	
10	Maintenance	300,000	
11	Miscellaneous	280,000	$1,900,000
12	Fixed manufacturing overhead costs		
13	Depreciation	$500,000	
14	Property taxes	350,000	
15	Property insurance	260,000	
16	Plant supervision	210,000	
17	Miscellaneous	280,000	$1,600,000
18	Total manufacturing overhead costs		$3,500,000
19			

Total variable overhead costs fluctuate in proportion to the quantity of the cost-allocation base (direct manufacturing labor-hours in the Stylistic example), whereas total fixed overhead costs remains constant over a relevant range of output.

Step 6: Prepare the Ending Inventories Budget. The management accountant prepares the ending inventories budget, calculated in Schedules 6A and 6B. Schedule 6A shows the computation of the unit cost of coffee tables started and completed in 2007. Under the FIFO method, this unit cost is used to calculate the cost of target ending inventories of finished goods in Schedule 6B.

	A	B	C	D	E	F	G
1	Schedule 6A: Unit Cost of Ending Finished Goods Inventory						
2	December 31, 2007						
3							
4		Cost per		Input per			
5		Unit of Input		Unit of Output		Total	
6	Direct Materials						
7	Particle board	$ 4.00	per b.f.	9.00	b.f.	$36.00	
8	Red oak	6.00	per b.f.	10.00	b.f.	60.00	$ 96.00
9	Direct Manufacturing Labor						
10	Laminating labor	$25.00	per hr.	0.25	hrs.	$ 6.25	
11	Machining labor	30.00	per hr.	3.75	hrs.	112.50	118.75
12	Manufacturing overhead costs	17.50	per hr.	4.00	hrs.		70.00
13	Total						$284.75
14							

This $284.75 unit cost for 2007 is more than the $275.00 unit cost for 2006 because of increases in direct material prices and direct manufacturing labor rates. As a result of this higher unit cost, Stylistic plans to increase the selling price of its coffee tables to $392, as shown in step 1.

	A	B	C	D	E	F	G
1	Schedule 6B: Ending Inventories Budget						
2	December 31, 2007						
3							
4		Cost per Unit		Units		Total	
5	Direct Materials						
6	Particle board	$ 4.00	per b.f.	18,000	b.f.	$ 72,000	
7	Red oak	6.00	per b.f.	22,000	b.f.	132,000	$204,000
8	Finished Goods						
9	Coffee tables	$284.75	per unit	3,000	units	$854,250	854,250
10	Total ending inventory						$1,058,250
11							

Step 7: Prepare the Cost of Goods Sold Budget. The manufacturing and purchase managers, together with the management accountant, use information from Schedules 3 through 6 to prepare Schedule 7.

The cost of goods manufactured portion of the cost of goods sold budget in Schedule 7 is a summarized form of the cost of goods manufactured schedule. For example, see Exhibit 2-7, Panel B, page 39. (Note, the Stylistic example assumes there is no beginning or ending work-in-process inventory.)

	A	B	C	D
1	Schedule 7: Cost of Goods Sold Budget			
2	For the Year Ending December 31, 2007			
3				
4	Beginning finished goods inventory,			
5	January 1, 2007, $275 × 5,000	Given		$ 1,375,000
6	Direct materials used	Schedule 3A	$4,793,000	
7	Direct manufacturing labor	Schedule 4	5,937,500	
8	Manufacturing overhead costs	Schedule 5	3,500,000	
9	Cost of goods manufactured			14,230,500
10	Cost of goods available for sale			15,605,500
11	Deduct ending finished goods inventory,			
12	December 31, 2007	Schedule 6B		854,250
13	Cost of goods sold			$14,751,250
14				

Step 8: Prepare the Nonmanufacturing Costs Budget. Schedules 2 through 7 cover budgeting for Stylistic's production function of the value chain. For brevity, other parts of the value chain are combined into a single schedule. Variable nonmanufacturing costs are variable with respect to the amount of revenues at the rate of 13.5% of revenues: $20,384,000 from Schedule 1 × 0.135 = $2,751,840. Variable product design costs represent royalty payments of 1.5%

	A	B	C	D
1	Schedule 8: Nonmanufacturing Costs Budget			
2	For the Year Ending December 31, 2007			
3				
4	Business Function	Variable Costs	Fixed Costs	Total Costs
5	R&D/Product design (Variable cost: $20,384,000 × 0.015)	$ 305,760	$ 250,000	$ 555,760
6	Marketing (Variable cost: $20,384,000 × 0.08)	1,630,720	290,000	1,920,720
7	Distribution (Variable cost: $20,384,000 × 0.025)	509,600	220,000	729,600
8	Customer service (Variable cost: $20,384,000 × 0.013)	264,992	240,000	504,992
9	Administrative (Variable cost: $20,384,000 × 0.002)	40,768	400,000	440,768
10		$2,751,840	$1,400,000	$4,151,840
11				

	A	B	C	D
1	Revenues	Schedule 1		$20,384,000
2	Cost of goods sold	Schedule 7		14,751,250
3	Gross margin			5,632,750
4	Operating costs			
5	R&D/Product design	Schedule 8	$ 555,760	
6	Marketing costs	Schedule 8	1,920,720	
7	Distribution costs	Schedule 8	729,600	
8	Customer-service costs	Schedule 8	504,992	
9	Administrative costs	Schedule 8	440,768	4,151,840
10	Operating income			$ 1,480,910
11				

EXHIBIT 6-3

Budgeted Income Statement for Stylistic Furniture for the Year Ending December 31, 2007

of revenues paid to the company that designed the table; variable marketing costs arise from the 8% sales commission on revenues paid to salespeople; variable distribution costs are 2.5% of revenues for insurance and freight; variable customer-service costs equal 1.3% of revenues paid to an outside party to service all warranty claims; and variable administrative costs equal 0.2% of revenues. Managers in the respective business functions of the value chain prepare the cost budgets presented in Schedule 8.

Step 9: **Prepare the Budgeted Income Statement.** The CEO and managers of various business functions, together with the management accountant, use information in Schedules 1, 7, and 8 to prepare the budgeted income statement, shown in Exhibit 6-3. The style used in Exhibit 6-3 is typical, but more details could be included in the income statement; the more details that are put in the income statement, the fewer supporting schedules that are needed for the income statement.

Budgeting is a cross-functional activity. Top management's strategies for achieving revenue and operating income goals influence the costs planned for the different business functions of the value chain. For example, a budgeted increase in sales based on spending more for marketing must be matched with higher production costs to ensure that there is an adequate supply of tables and with higher distribution costs to ensure timely delivery of tables to customers. As strategies change, the budgeted costs for different business functions of the value chain will also change. For example, a shift in strategy toward emphasizing product development and customer service will result in increased costs in these business functions of the operating budget.

Rex Jordan, the CEO of Stylistic Furniture, is very pleased with the 2007 budget. It calls for a substantial increase in operating income compared with 2006. As Rex studies the budget more carefully, however, he is struck by two comments appended to the budget: the first regarding the possibility of a 10% increase or decrease in the selling price of coffee tables and the second regarding the possibility of a 5% increase or decrease in the prices of direct materials (the particle board and the red oak). He asks Tina Larsen, the management accountant, to use Stylistic's financial planning model to evaluate how these outcomes will affect budgeted operating income.

Study Tip: To check your understanding of the operating budget, see multiple-choice question 3 and Review Exercise 1 (*Student Guide*, pp. 67–68). Fully explained answers are on pp. 71–72.

Computer-Based Financial Planning Models

4

Use computer-based financial planning models in sensitivity analysis

. . . for example, understand the effects of changes in selling prices and direct material prices on budgeted income

Many companies, including Stylistic, use Web-based budgeting tools (see Concepts in Action, p. 194) and software packages to reduce the computational burden and time required to prepare budgets. The software packages perform calculations for **financial planning models**, which are mathematical representations of the relationships among operating activities, financing activities, and other factors that affect the master budget. All software packages have a module on sensitivity analysis to assist managers in their planning and budgeting activities. *Sensitivity analysis* is a "what-if" technique that examines how a result will change if the original predicted data are not achieved or if an underlying assumption changes.

CONCEPTS IN ACTION

Web-Enabled Budgeting and Hendrick Motorsports

In recent years, many companies have implemented comprehensive software packages that manage budgeting and forecasting functions across the organization. One such option available is FRx® Software Corporation's Forecaster package. Forecaster is specifically designed for mid-market and corporate businesses wishing to gain control over their budgeting and forecasting process within a fully integrated, Web-based environment.

Among the many companies implementing Forecaster is Hendrick Motorsports. Featuring renowned drivers including Jeff Gordon, Hendrick is the premier NASCAR Nextel Cup stock car racing organization. Headquartered near Charlotte, North Carolina, Hendrick operates four full-time teams within the Nextel Cup series, which runs annually from early February through late November and features 36 races at 23 speedways across the United States. The Hendrick organization has over 400 employees, with tasks ranging from accounting and marketing to engine building and racecar driving. Such an environment features multiple functional areas and units, varied worksites, and ever-changing circumstances. Patrick Perkins, director of marketing, noted, "Racing is a fast business. It's just as fast off the track as it is on. With the work that we put into the development of our teams and technologies, and having to respond to change as well as anticipate change, I like to think of us in this business as change experts."

FRx Forecaster has allowed Hendrick's financial managers to seamlessly manage the planning and budgeting process. Authorized users from each functional area or team sign on to the application through the corporate intranet. Security on the system is tight: Access is limited to only the accounts that a manager is authorized to budget. Forecaster also allows users at the racetracks to access the application remotely, which allows managers to receive or update real time "actuals" from the system. This way, team managers know their allotted expenses for each race. Forecaster also provides users with additional features, including simplified functionality, human resource (labor) budgeting and planning data, seamless links with general ledger accounts, and the option to perform various what-if (sensitivity) analyses. Scott Lampe, chief financial officer, said, "Forecaster allows us to change our forecasts to respond to changes, either rules changes (such as changes in the Nextel Cup series' points system) or technology changes (such as the addition of restrictor plates), throughout the racing season."

FRx Forecaster and other similar packages are available from application service providers (ASPs)—described in the *Concepts in Action* box on page 33 in Chapter 2. With this setup, companies like Hendrick Motorsports can rent the application over the Internet rather than buy it, which can provide significant cost savings. Moreover, companies renting from an application service provider do not have to maintain or upgrade the software, because the ASP does all such work.

Web-enabled budgeting frees the finance department so it can focus on strategy, analysis, and decision making. It increases service levels to employees, reduces costs, accelerates the planning and budgeting cycles, and improves the value from budgeting. Patrick Perkins of Hendrick Motorsports agrees, "In racing, the team that wins is not only the team with the fastest car, but the team that is the most disciplined and prepared week in and week out. Forecaster allows us to respond to that changing landscape."

Sources: T. Powell, "Software Tends," *Journal of Cost Management* (January/February 1999), pp. 36–37; PR Newswire, "FRx Software Announces Availability of Forecaster 6.7," PR Newswire Web site **http://www.prnewswire.com** (July 31, 2003); FRx Software, "Hendrick Motorsports (Internet video)," FRx Software Web site **http://www.frxsoftware.com** (February 17, 2004); and Hendrick Motorsports, "About Hendrick Motorsports," Hendrick Motorsports Web site **http://www.hendrickmotorsports.com** (February 17, 2004).

To see how sensitivity analysis works, we consider the two parameters, selling price and direct material prices, identified as possibly affecting Stylistic Furniture's budget model for 2007. We consider nine combinations of different inputs for the two parameters:

1. Selling prices per table of $431.20 (10% increase), $392.00 (original budgeted price), and $352.80 (10% decrease)
2. Direct material purchase prices decreasing by 5% to $3.80 per board foot for particle board and $5.70 per board foot for red oak; remaining at the original budgeted price of $4.00 per board foot for particle board and $6.00 per board foot for red oak; and increasing by 5% to $4.20 per board foot for particle board and $6.30 per board foot for red oak

	A	B	C	D	E	F	G
1			Direct Material				
2			Purchase Prices		Budgeted Operating Income		
3		Selling	Particle	Red		Change from Master	
4	Scenario	Price	Board	Oak	Amount	Budget Base Case	
5	1	$431.20	$3.80	$5.70	$3,458,226	134%	Increase
6	2	431.20	4.00	6.00	3,244,126	119%	Increase
7	3	431.20	4.20	6.30	3,030,026	105%	Increase
8	4	392.00	3.80	5.70	1,695,010	14%	Increase
9	5[a]	392.00	4.00	6.00	1,480,910	0%	
10	6	392.00	4.20	6.30	1,266,810	14%	Decrease
11	7	352.80	3.80	5.70	(68,206)	105%	Decrease
12	8	352.80	4.00	6.00	(282,306)	119%	Decrease
13	9	352.80	4.20	6.30	(496,406)	134%	Decrease
14							
15	[a] Base case from Exhibit 6-3						

EXHIBIT 6-4

Effect of Changes in Budget Assumptions on Budgeted Operating Income for Stylistic Furniture

Exhibit 6-4 presents the budgeted operating income for the nine scenarios.

- Scenario 5 is the base case from Exhibit 6-3.
- Scenarios 2 and 8 illustrate the effects of changes in only the selling price.
- Scenarios 4 and 6 examine the effects of changes in only the direct material costs.
- Scenarios 1, 3, 7, and 9 pertain to simultaneous changes in both parameters.

Note that a change in Stylistic's selling price per table affects the variable nonmanufacturing costs, such as sales commissions, as well as revenues. Sensitivity analysis is especially useful in incorporating such interrelationships into budgeting decisions by managers.

Exhibit 6-4 shows wide variations in operating income ranging from $3,458,226 to $(496,406) as a result of changes in selling prices and direct material prices. The exhibit indicates that Stylistic will incur a loss if the selling price decreases by 10% to $352.80, regardless of what happens to direct material prices. The sensitivity analysis prompts Stylistic's managers to put in place contingency plans for cutting costs to reduce losses should selling prices decline during 2007. More generally, when the success or viability of a venture is highly dependent on attaining one or more targets, managers should frequently update their budgets as uncertainty is resolved. These updated budgets can help managers to adjust expenditure levels, change marketing strategies, and so on as circumstances change.

Instructors and students who, at this point, want to explore the cash budget and the budgeted balance sheet for the Stylistic Furniture example can skip ahead to the appendix on page 203.

Kaizen Budgeting

5

Explain kaizen budgeting

... budgeting for continuous improvement in labor-hours per unit

and how it is used for cost management

... to reduce costs

Chapter 1 noted the importance of continuous improvement, or *kaizen* in Japanese. **Kaizen budgeting** explicitly incorporates continuous improvement anticipated during the budget period into the budget numbers. Many companies that have cost reduction as a strategic focus, including General Motors in the United States and Citizens Watch and Toyota in Japan, use kaizen budgeting to continuously reduce costs.

Throughout our nine budgeting steps for Stylistic Furniture, we assumed 3.75 hours of machining labor time to manufacture each coffee table. A kaizen budgeting approach would incorporate continuous improvement, that is, reduction, in these direct manufacturing labor-hour requirements during 2007. For example:

	Budgeted Direct Machining Labor-Hours per Table
January–March 2007	3.75
April–June 2007	3.70
July–September 2007	3.65
October–December 2007	3.60

Much of the cost reduction associated with kaizen budgeting arises from many small improvements rather than "quantum leaps." A significant aspect of kaizen budgeting is the quantity and quality of employees' suggestions.

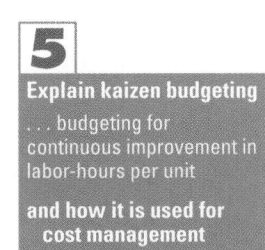

The implications of these direct manufacturing labor-hour reductions would also extend to reductions in variable manufacturing overhead costs, because direct manufacturing labor-hours is the driver of these costs. Unless Stylistic meets these continuous improvement goals, actual hours used will exceed budgeted hours in the latter quarters of the year. Should that happen, Stylistic's managers will explore reasons for the goals not being met and either adjust the targets or implement process changes that will accelerate continuous improvement.

Activity-Based Budgeting

6 **Prepare an activity-based budget**

. . . by budgeting the cost of activities needed to produce a product

Most budgeting models to date have used a small number of cost drivers that are predominantly output-based (units produced, units sold, or revenues). Due, in part, to the interest in activity-based costing (ABC), companies are now incorporating activity-based cost drivers in their budgets. A natural extension of activity-based costing is to use an activity-based approach to budgeting future costs. **Activity-based budgeting (ABB)** focuses on the budgeted cost of the activities necessary to produce and sell products and services. To illustrate ABB, we consider the setup activity at Stylistic. In Stylistic's operating budget outlined in steps 1 through 9 (pp. 188–193), the costs of the setup activity are embedded in the different line items (such as indirect manufacturing labor and plant supervision) that constitute the manufacturing overhead costs of $3,500,000 in Schedule 5. In ABB, the costs of this setup activity (as well as the costs of each of the other activities) would be separately estimated. Consider the following setup information for the laminating and machining areas in 2007:

	Laminating Setup	Machining Setup
1. Quantity of tables to be produced	50,000 tables	50,000 tables
2. Number of tables to be produced per batch	25 tables/batch	10 tables/batch
3. Number of batches (1) ÷ (2)	2,000 batches	5,000 batches
4. Setup time per batch	0.5 hour/batch	2.5 hours/batch
5. Total setup-hours (3) × (4)	1,000 hours	12,500 hours

At a rate of $25 per hour for laminating setup labor and $30 per hour for machining setup labor,

Laminating setup labor costs	
$25 per hour × 1,000 hours	$ 25,000
Machining setup labor costs	
$30 per hour × 12,500 hours	375,000
Total	$400,000

These variable setup costs of $400,000 are currently included as part of variable indirect manufacturing labor costs of $620,000 in step 5 of Stylistic's existing budget (see pp. 190–191).

The total costs of the setup activity for Stylistic also include the costs of supervisory time, calculated as follows.

1. Total setup-hours (1,000 hours for laminating + 12,500 hours for machining)	13,500 hours
2. Supervision time, 13,500 hours ÷ 10 (10 setup hours require 1 hour of supervisory labor time)	1,350
3. Supervision costs at $60 per hour, 1,350 hours × $60 per hour	$81,000

These fixed setup costs of $81,000 are currently included as part of fixed plant supervision costs of $210,000 in step 5 of Stylistic's budget (see pp. 190–191).

Total budgeted cost in Stylistic's setup activity is $481,000, consisting of $400,000 for setup labor-hours and $81,000 for supervision. As we discussed in Chapter 5, ABC analysis makes no distinction between short-run variable costs and short-run fixed costs. ABC analysis takes a long-run perspective in which all costs of an activity are treated as variable costs of that activity. The activity-cost buildup makes it easier for Stylistic to see how to reduce its budgeted setup costs for 2007. For example, Stylistic could:

- Increase the length of the production run per batch so that fewer batches (and therefore fewer setups) are needed for the budgeted production of 50,000 tables.
- Decrease the setup time per batch.
- Reduce the supervisory time needed per worker setup-hour, for instance by increasing the skill base of laminating or machining workers.

This illustration shows how ABB can provide more-detailed information that can improve decision making compared with budgeting based solely on output-based cost drivers. Should companies adopt ABC and ABB? As we discussed in Chapter 5, the answer for a specific company depends on management's evaluation of whether the expected benefits—for every department affected by the change—exceed the expected costs of installing and operating such systems.[5]

Finally, consider how the master budget, kaizen budgeting, and activity-based budgeting are related to one another. Think of kaizen budgeting and activity-based budgeting as building blocks for the master budget—kaizen budgeting, by incorporating continuous improvement standards in all steps of the master budget, and activity-based budgeting, by identifying activities and calculating budgeted indirect costs of activities in different business functions of the value chain (steps 5 and 8). Underlying master budgets are the thinking and ideas of kaizen budgeting and activity-based budgeting.

Budgeting and Responsibility Accounting

7

Describe responsibility centers

. . . a part of an organization that a manager is accountable for

and responsibility accounting

. . . measurement of plans and actual results that a manager is accountable for

To attain the goals described in the master budget, a company must coordinate the efforts of all its employees—from the top executive through all levels of management to every supervised worker. Coordinating the company's efforts means assigning responsibility to managers who are accountable for their actions in planning and controlling human and other resources. How each company structures its own organization significantly shapes how the company's efforts will be coordinated.

Organization Structure and Responsibility

Organization structure is an arrangement of lines of responsibility within the organization. A company such as British Petroleum may be organized primarily by business function: exploration, refining, and marketing, with each manager having decision-making authority over her function. Another company, such as Procter & Gamble, the household-products giant, may be organized by product line or brand. The managers of the individual divisions (toothpaste, soap, and so on) would each have decision-making authority concerning all the business functions (manufacturing, marketing, and so on) within that division.

Each manager, regardless of level, is in charge of a responsibility center. A **responsibility center** is a part, segment, or subunit of an organization whose manager is accountable for a specified set of activities. The higher the manager's level, the broader the responsibility center and, generally, the larger the number of his or her subordinates. **Responsibility accounting** is a system that measures the plans, budgets, actions, and actual results of each responsibility center. Four types of responsibility centers are:

Surveys show that companies generally establish budgetary reporting by responsibility center.

1. **Cost center**—the manager is accountable for costs only.
2. **Revenue center**—the manager is accountable for revenues only.
3. **Profit center**—the manager is accountable for revenues and costs.
4. **Investment center**—the manager is accountable for investments, revenues, and costs.

The Maintenance Department of a Marriott hotel is a cost center because the maintenance manager is responsible only for costs, so this budget emphasizes costs. The Sales Department is a revenue center because the sales manager is responsible primarily for revenues, so this budget emphasizes revenues. The hotel manager is in charge of a profit center because the manager is accountable for both revenues and costs, so this budget emphasizes revenues and costs. The regional manager responsible for investments in new hotel projects and for revenues and costs is in charge of an investment center, so this budget emphasizes revenues, costs, and the investment base.

A responsibility center can be structured to promote better alignment of individual and company goals. Until recently, OPD, an office products distributor, operated its Sales Department as a revenue center. Each salesperson received a commission of 3% of the revenues per order, regardless of its size, the cost of processing it, or the cost of delivering the office products. An analysis of customer profitability at OPD found that many customers were unprofitable. The main reason was the high ordering and delivery costs of small orders. OPD's managers decided to make the Sales Department a profit center, accountable

[5]For illustrative purposes, the ABB example uses the setup costs included in Stylistic's variable manufacturing overhead costs budget and fixed manufacturing overhead costs budget. ABB implementations in practice may include costs in many parts of the value chain. For an example, see S. Borjesson, "A Case Study on Activity-Based Budgeting," *Journal of Cost Management*, Vol. 10, No. 4, pp. 7–18.

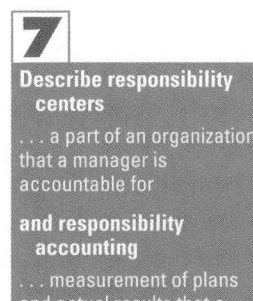

for revenues and costs, and to change the incentive system for salespeople to 15% of the monthly profitability per customer. The costs for each customer included the ordering and delivery costs. The effect of this change was immediate. The Sales Department began charging customers for ordering and delivery, and salespeople at OPD actively encouraged customers to consolidate their purchases into fewer orders. As a result, each order began producing larger revenues. Customer profitability increased because of a 40% reduction in ordering and delivery costs in one year.

Feedback

Budgets coupled with responsibility accounting provide feedback to top management about the performance relative to the budget of different responsibility center managers.

Differences between actual results and budgeted amounts—called *variances*—if properly used, can help managers implement and evaluate strategies in three ways:

1. ***Early warning.*** Variances alert managers early to events not easily nor immediately evident. Managers can then take corrective actions or exploit the available opportunities. For example, is a small decline in sales this period an indication of an even steeper decline to follow later in the year?
2. ***Performance evaluation.*** Variances inform managers about how well the company has performed in implementing its strategies. Were materials and labor used efficiently? Was R&D spending increased as planned? Did product warranty costs decrease as planned?
3. ***Evaluating strategy.*** Variances sometimes signal to managers that their strategies are ineffective. For example, a company seeking to compete by reducing costs and improving quality may find that it is achieving these goals but that it is having little effect on sales and profits. Top management may then want to reevaluate the strategy.

Responsibility and Controllability

8

Explain how controllability relates to responsibility accounting

. . . managers cannot control all of the costs that they are accountable for; responsibility accounting focuses on obtaining information, not fixing blame

Controllability is the degree of influence that a specific manager has over costs, revenues, or related items for which he is responsible. A **controllable cost** is any cost that is primarily subject to the influence of a given *responsibility center manager* for a given *period*. A responsibility accounting system could either exclude all uncontrollable costs from a manager's performance report or segregate such costs from the controllable costs. For example, a machining supervisor's performance report might be confined to direct materials, direct manufacturing labor, power, and machine maintenance costs and exclude costs such as rent and taxes paid on the plant.

In practice, controllability is difficult to pinpoint for at least two reasons:

If the purchasing manager forgets to order a direct-material item and must then place a rush order, the cost of the rush order is controllable by the purchasing manager. However, if suppliers increase their prices, that's something the purchasing manager cannot control. Nevertheless, the manager is still responsible in the sense that he is in the best position to explain the price increases, and he can influence prices and quality by bargaining and maintaining good supplier relations.

1. Few costs are clearly under the sole influence of one manager. For example, prices of direct materials may be influenced by a purchasing manager, but these prices also depend on market conditions beyond the manager's control. Quantities used may be influenced by a production manager, but quantities used also depend on the quality of materials purchased. Moreover, managers often work in teams. Think about how difficult it is to evaluate individual responsibility in a team situation.
2. With a long enough time span, all costs will come under somebody's control. However, most performance reports focus on periods of a year or less. A current manager may benefit from a predecessor's accomplishments or may inherit a predecessor's problems and inefficiencies. For example, present managers may have to work under undesirable contracts with suppliers or labor unions that were negotiated by their predecessors. How can we separate what the current manager actually controls from the results of decisions made by others? Exactly what is the current manager accountable for? Answers may not be clear-cut.

Executives differ in how they embrace the controllability notion when evaluating those reporting to them. Some CEOs regard the budget as a firm commitment that subordinates must meet. Failure to meet the budget is viewed unfavorably. Other CEOs believe a more risk-sharing approach with managers is preferable, in which noncontrollable factors and performance relative to competitors are taken into account when judging the performance of managers who fail to meet their budgets.

Managers should avoid overemphasizing controllability. Responsibility accounting is more far-reaching. It focuses on gaining *information and knowledge,* not only on control. *Responsibility accounting helps managers to first focus on whom they should ask to obtain information and not on whom they should blame.* For example, if actual revenues at a Marriott hotel are less than budgeted revenues, the managers of the hotel may be tempted to blame the sales manager for the poor performance. The fundamental purpose of responsibility accounting, however, is not to fix blame but to gather information to enable future improvement.

The question is, Who can tell us the most about the specific item in question, regardless of that person's ability to exert personal control over that item? For instance, purchasing managers may be held accountable for total purchase costs, not because of their ability to control market prices, but because of their ability to predict uncontrollable prices and to explain uncontrollable price changes. Similarly, managers at a Pizza Hut unit may be held responsible for operating income of their units, even though they (a) do not fully control selling prices nor the costs of many food items and (b) have minimal flexibility about what items to sell or the ingredients in the items they sell. They are, however, in the best position to explain differences between their actual operating incomes and their budgeted operating incomes.

Performance reports for responsibility centers are sometimes designed to change managers' behavior in the direction top management desires. For example, some companies have changed the accountability of a cost center to a profit center. That's because the manager will probably behave differently. A cost-center manager may emphasize production efficiency and deemphasize the pleas of sales personnel for faster service and rush orders. In a profit center, the manager is responsible for costs and revenues. Even though the manager still has no control over sales personnel, the manager can influence activities that affect sales and will more likely weigh the impact of decisions on costs and revenues rather than on costs alone.

Human Aspects of Budgeting

Why did we discuss the two major topics, the master budget and responsibility accounting, in the same chapter? Primarily to emphasize that human factors are crucial in budgeting. Too often, budgeting is thought of as a mechanical tool. The budgeting techniques themselves are free of emotion. However, the administration of budgeting requires education, persuasion, and intelligent interpretation.

To be effective, budgeting requires "honest" communication about the business from subordinates and lower-level managers to their bosses. But subordinates may try to build in *budgetary slack.* **Budgetary slack** describes the practice of underestimating budgeted revenues, or overestimating budgeted costs, to make budgeted targets more easily achievable. It frequently occurs when budget variances (the differences between actual results and budgeted amounts) are used to evaluate performance. Line managers are also unlikely to be "fully honest" in their budget communications if top management mechanically institutes across-the-board cost reductions (say, a 10% reduction in all areas) in the face of projected revenue reductions. Budgetary slack provides managers with a hedge against unexpected adverse circumstances. But budgetary slack also misleads top management about the true profit potential of the company, which leads to inefficient resource planning and allocation and poor coordination of activities across different parts of the company.

What can top management do to obtain accurate budget forecasts from lower-level managers? Several options exist.

To explain one approach, let's consider the plant manager of a beverage bottler who is suspected by top management of understating the productivity potential of the bottling lines in his forecasts for the coming year. His presumed motivation is to increase the likelihood of meeting next year's production bonus targets. Suppose top management could purchase a consulting firm's study that reports productivity levels—such as the number of bottles filled per hour—at a number of comparable plants owned by other bottling companies. This report shows that their own plant manager's productivity forecasts are well below actual productivity levels being achieved at other comparable plants.

Top management could share this independent information source with the plant manager and ask him to explain why his productivity differs from that at other comparable plants. They could also base part of the plant manager's compensation on his plant's productivity vis-a-vis other "benchmark" plants rather than on the forecasts he provided. Using external benchmark performance measures reduces a manager's ability to set budget levels that are easy to achieve.[6]

Another approach to reducing budgetary slack is for managers to involve themselves regularly in understanding what their subordinates are doing. Such involvement should not result in managers dictating the decisions and actions of subordinates. Rather, a manager's involvement should take the form of providing support, challenging in a motivational way the assumptions subordinates make, and enhancing mutual learning about the operations. Regular interaction with subordinates allows managers to become knowledgeable about the operations and diminishes the ability of subordinates to create slack in their budgets.

Part of top management's responsibility is to promote commitment among the employees to a set of core values and norms. These values and norms describe what constitutes acceptable and unacceptable behavior. For example, Johnson & Johnson (J&J) has a credo that describes its responsibilities to doctors, patients, employees, communities, and shareholders. Employees are trained in the credo to help them understand the behavior that is expected of them. Managers are often promoted from within and are therefore very familiar with the work of the employees reporting to them. Managers also have the responsibility to interact with and mentor their subordinates. These values and practices create a culture at J&J that discourages budgetary slack.

Some companies, such as IBM and Kodak, have designed innovative performance evaluation measures that reward managers based on the subsequent accuracy of the forecasts used in preparing budgets. For example, the *higher and more accurate* the budgeted profit forecasts of division managers, the higher their incentive bonuses.

Many of the best performing companies, such as General Electric, Microsoft, and Novartis, set "stretch" targets. Stretch targets are challenging but achievable levels of expected performance, intended to create a little discomfort and to motivate employees to exert extra effort and attain better performance.

Many managers regard budgets negatively. To them, the word budget is about as popular as, say, *downsizing*, *layoff*, or *strike*. Top managers must convince their subordinates that the budget is a tool designed to help them set and reach goals. But whatever the manager's perspective on budgets—pro or con—budgets are not remedies for weak management talent, faulty organization, or a poor accounting system.

The management style of executives is a factor in how budgets are perceived in companies. Some CEOs argue that "numbers always tell the story." An executive once noted that "you can miss your plan once, but you wouldn't want to miss it twice." Other CEOs believe "too much focus on making the numbers in a budget" can lead to poor decision making and unethical practices. (See the Focus on Values and Behaviors feature, p. 201.)

Budgeting in Multinational Companies

Multinational companies, such as Federal Express, Kraft, and Pfizer, have operations in many countries. An international presence carries with it positives—access to new markets and resources—and negatives—operating in less-familiar business environments and exposure to currency fluctuations. For example, multinational companies earn revenues and incur expenses in many different currencies, and they must translate their operating performance into a single currency (say, U.S. dollars) for reporting results to their

[6]For an excellent discussion of these issues, see Chapter 14 ("Formal Models in Budgeting and Incentive Contracts") of R. S. Kaplan and A. A. Atkinson, *Advanced Management Accounting*, 3rd ed. (Upper Saddle River, NJ: Prentice Hall, 1998).

FOCUS ON VALUES AND BEHAVIORS

MANAGEMENT ACCOUNTANTS: THE HEART OF THE BUDGETING PROCESS

An accurate budget is essential to a company's success. Billion-dollar companies—such as Intel, Amgen, and Microsoft—will spend as many as 25,000 person-days per year compiling and finalizing their budgets. Budgeting is a cross-functional activity that requires the knowledge and expertise of managers from all areas of an organization, including management accountants, who are central to the budgeting process. If a company is going to benefit from its budget, its management accountants must possess several skills. They need to be able to communicate well and to establish themselves as trusted partners of the management team. They must be able to simplify the budgeting process by adeptly sharing complex financial information with each business function without getting lost in technical details. Consider the following quote from a financial director at Boeing:

> *In wing manufacturing, [the staff focuses] on particular parts of the process in building the airplane. The demand for financial support is insatiable. [The staff] want to know and they need to know: What is the consequence of doing this? If we streamline this, how does it impact us financially? What does that do to us? Does it impact the value stream?*

Only management accountants can help the staff answer these critical questions.

Consider the Facilities & Operations Business Office of the Battelle Pacific Northwest National Laboratory. In 2000, budget managers worked with the company's management accountants to build a Web-based budget and planning system that streamlined the budget process. The system, which is still used throughout the company today, provides a single point of contact for overhead planning and budgeting and includes real-time data and standard analysis reporting. The results: higher quality and greater accuracy in the budgeting process, at a fraction of the time formerly spent on the process.

In addition to simplifying the budgeting process, management accountants work to ensure that managers' ideas and their resulting budgets are realistic. Management accountants must challenge faulty assumptions and incorrect logic ("let's assume a 10% increase in sales even though the overall market for the product is expected to decline") and probe for alternative approaches ("a 5% increase in sales is possible but this will require more resources to be devoted to marketing").

When it comes time to discuss the budget, some managers approach the negotiation process with an eye toward protecting their own interests. If managers make their budgets—or better, improve on them—financial rewards will come their way. So managers may intentionally ask for budget amounts that will help them achieve their targets but that will not maximize the company's overall profits. Addressing this issue of budgetary slack may be the most difficult role for management accountants because they must be able to deal with conflict and argue persuasively for more realistic targets.

Sources: *P. Smith, C. Goranson, and M. Astley, "Intranet Budgeting Does the Trick,"* Strategic Finance, *May 2003; L. Gray, "Why Budgeting Kills Your Company,"* Working Knowledge, *Harvard Business School, August 11, 2003; G. Siegal, J. Sorenson, and S. Richtermeyer, "Are You a Business Partner?"* Strategic Finance, *September 2003.*

shareholders each quarter. This translation is based on the average exchange rates that prevail during the quarter. That is, in addition to budgeting in different currencies, management accountants in multinational companies also need to budget for foreign exchange rates. This is difficult because management accountants need to anticipate potential changes that might take place during the year. Exchange rates are constantly fluctuating, so to reduce the possible negative impact on performance caused by unfavorable exchange rate movements, finance managers will frequently use sophisticated techniques such as forward, future, and option contracts to minimize exposure to foreign currency fluctuations. Besides currency issues, multinational companies need to understand the political, legal, and, in particular, economic environments of the different countries in which they operate. For example, in Turkey and some Latin American countries, annual inflation rates can be 100%, which leads to sharp declines in the value of the local currency.

Multinational companies find budgeting to be a valuable tool when operating in such uncertain environments. As circumstances and conditions change, companies revise their budgets. The purpose of budgeting is to help managers throughout the organization to learn and to adapt their plans to the changing conditions and to communicate and coordinate the actions that need to be taken throughout the company. When conditions are constantly changing, it is not meaningful to compare actual performance against the original budget to evaluate a manager's performance. Instead, performance evaluation is more subjective, based on how well the manager has managed in the uncertain environment.

PROBLEM FOR SELF-STUDY

Consider the Stylistic Furniture example described earlier. Suppose the selling price per table is $431.20, a 10% increase over the $392 selling price used in the chapter illustration. All other data are unchanged.

Required

Prepare a budgeted income statement, including all necessary detailed supporting budget schedules that are different from the schedules presented in the chapter. Indicate those schedules that will remain unchanged.

SOLUTION

Schedules 1 and 8 will change. Schedule 1 changes because a change in selling price affects revenues. Schedule 8 changes because revenues are a cost driver of variable nonmanufacturing costs. The remaining schedules will not change because a change in selling price has no effect on manufacturing costs. The revised schedules and the new budgeted income statement follow.

	A	B	C	D
1	Schedule 1: Revenues Budget			
2	For the Year Ending December 31, 2007			
3				
4		Selling Price	Units Sold	Total Revenues
5	Coffee tables	$431.20	52,000	$22,422,400

	A	B	C	D
1	Schedule 8: Nonmanufacturing Costs Budget			
2	For the Year Ending December 31, 2007			
3				
4	Business Function	Variable Costs	Fixed Costs (as in Schedule 8, p. 192)	Total Costs
5	R&D/Product design (Variable cost: $22,422,400 × 0.015)	$ 336,336	$ 250,000	$ 586,336
6	Marketing (Variable cost: $22,422,400 × 0.08)	1,793,792	290,000	2,083,792
7	Distribution (Variable cost: $22,422,400 × 0.025)	560,560	220,000	780,560
8	Customer service (Variable cost: $22,422,400 × 0.013)	291,491	240,000	531,491
9	Administrative (Variable cost: $22,422,400 × 0.002)	44,845	400,000	444,845
10		$3,027,024	$1,400,000	$4,427,024

	A	B	C	D
1	Stylistic Furniture Budgeted Income Statement			
2	For the Year Ending December 31, 2007			
3				
4	Revenues	Schedule 1		$22,422,400
5	Cost of goods sold	Schedule 7		14,751,250
6	Gross margin			7,671,150
7	Operating costs			
8	R&D/Product design	Schedule 8	$ 586,336	
9	Marketing costs	Schedule 8	2,083,792	
10	Distribution costs	Schedule 8	780,560	
11	Customer-service costs	Schedule 8	531,491	
12	Administrative costs	Schedule 8	444,845	4,427,024
13	Operating income			$ 3,244,126
14				

If we had also assumed that the price of the particle board had increased to $4.20 per board foot and the price of the red oak had increased to $6.30 per board foot (as in Scenario 3 in Exhibit 6-4, p. 193), Schedules 3A, 3B, 6A, 6B, and 7 would also have changed.

DECISION POINTS

The following question-and-answer format summarizes the chapter's learning objectives. Each decision presents a key question related to a learning objective. The guidelines are the answer to that question.

Decision	Guidelines
1. What is the master budget and why is it useful?	The master budget summarizes the financial projections of all the company's budgets. It expresses management's operating and financing plans—the formalized outline of the company's financial objectives and how they will be attained. Budgets are tools that, by themselves, are neither good nor bad. Budgets are useful when administered skillfully.
2. When should a company prepare budgets? What are the advantages of preparing budgets?	Budgets should be prepared when their expected benefits exceed their expected costs. The advantages of budgets include: (a) they compel strategic analysis and planning, (b) they promote coordination and communication among subunits of the company, (c) they provide a framework for judging performance, and (d) they motivate managers and other employees.
3. What is the operating budget and why is it useful?	The operating budget is the budgeted income statement and its supporting budget schedules. The starting point for the operating budget is generally the revenues budget. The following supporting schedules are derived from the revenues budget: production budget, direct material usage budget, direct material purchases budget, direct manufacturing labor budget, manufacturing overhead costs budget, ending inventories budget, cost of goods sold budget, R&D/product design budget, marketing budget, distribution budget, customer-service budget, and administrative budget.
4. How should managers consider what might happen if the assumptions underlying the budget change?	Managers should use computer-based financial planning models—mathematical statements of the relationships among operating activities, financing activities, and other factors that affect the budget. These models make it possible for management to conduct what-if (sensitivity) analysis of the effects on the master budget of changes in the original predicted data or changes in underlying assumptions and to develop plans to respond to changed conditions.
5. How can budgets include the effects of future improvements?	Kaizen budgeting is based on the idea that it is possible to continuously reduce costs over time. Costs in kaizen budgeting are based on improvements that are yet to be implemented rather than on current practices or methods.
6. How can a company prepare a budget based on costs of different activities?	Activity-based budgeting focuses on the budgeted costs of activities needed to produce and sell products and services. It is linked to activity-based costing but differs in its emphasis on future costs and future use of activity areas.
7. How do companies use responsibility centers and responsibility accounting?	A responsibility center is a part, segment, or subunit of an organization whose manager is accountable for a specified set of activities. Four types of responsibility centers are cost centers, revenue centers, profit centers, and investment centers. Responsibility accounting systems are useful because they measure the plans, budgets, actions, and actual results of each responsibility center.
8. Should performance reports of responsibility center managers only include costs the manager can control?	Controllable costs are costs primarily subject to the influence of a given responsibility center manager for a given time period. Performance reports of responsibility center managers often include costs, revenues, and investments that the managers cannot control. Responsibility accounting associates financial items with managers on the basis of which manager has the most knowledge and information about the specific items, regardless of the manager's ability to exercise full control.

APPENDIX: THE CASH BUDGET

The chapter illustrated the operating budget, which is one part of the master budget. The other part is the financial budget, which comprises the capital expenditures budget, the cash budget, the budgeted balance sheet, and the budgeted statement of cash flows. This appendix focuses on the cash budget and the budgeted balance sheet. Capital budgeting is discussed in Chapter 21. The budgeted statement of cash flows is beyond the scope of this book (and generally is covered in financial accounting and corporate finance courses).

If you have studied the statement of cash flows in a financial accounting course, be aware that the direct method of determining cash flows corresponds to the approach used in preparing the cash budget.

EXHIBIT 6-5

Balance Sheet for Stylistic Furniture, December 31, 2006

	A	B	C	D
1	**Assets**			
2	Current Assets			
3	Cash		$ 500,000	
4	Accounts receivable		1,881,600	
5	Direct materials inventory		223,000	
6	Finished goods inventory		1,375,000	$3,979,600
7	Property, plant and equipment			
8	Land		1,200,000	
9	Building and equipment	$2,300,000		
10	Accumulated depreciation	(800,000)	1,500,000	2,700,000
11	Total			$6,679,600
12				
13	**Liabilities and Stockholders' Equity**			
14	Current Liabilities			
15	Accounts payable		$ 384,000	
16	Income taxes payable		20,460	
17	Total current liabilities		404,460	
18	Long-term debt (interest at 10% per year)		2,400,000	
19	Total current and long-term liabilities			$2,804,460
20	Stockholders' equity			
21	Common stock, $0.01 par value, 300,000 shares outstanding		3,000	
22	Retained earnings		3,872,140	3,875,140
23	Total			$6,679,600
24				

Suppose Stylistic Furniture had the balance sheet for the year ended December 31, 2006, shown in Exhibit 6-5. The budgeted cash flows for 2007 are:

	A	B	C	D	E
1		**Quarters**			
2		**1**	**2**	**3**	**4**
3	Collections from customers	$5,331,200	$4,704,000	$4,704,000	$6,272,000
4	Disbursements				
5	Direct materials	960,000	1,152,000	1,152,000	1,536,000
6	Payroll	1,626,300	1,626,300	1,888,600	1,626,300
7	Other costs	1,580,460	1,580,460	1,580,460	1,580,460
8	Machinery purchase	0	0	1,800,000	0
9	Interest expense on long-term debt	60,000	60,000	60,000	60,000
10	Income taxes	100,000	120,460	100,000	100,000

The quarterly data are based on the budgeted cash effects of the operations formulated in Schedules 1 through 8 in the chapter, but the details of that formulation are not shown here to keep this illustration as brief and as focused as possible.

Long-term debt is $2.4 million at an annual interest rate of 10%, with $60,000 interest payable every quarter. The company wants to maintain a $100,000 minimum cash balance at the end of each quarter. The company can borrow or repay money at an interest rate of 12% per year. Management does not want to borrow any more short-term cash than is necessary. By special arrangement, interest is computed and paid when the principal is repaid. Assume, for simplicity, that borrowing takes place (in multiples of $1,000) at the beginning and repayment at the end of the quarter under consideration. Interest is computed to the nearest dollar.

Suppose the management accountant at Stylistic is given the preceding data and the other data contained in the budgets in the chapter (pp. 188–193). She is instructed as follows:

1. Prepare a cash budget for 2007 by quarter. That is, prepare a statement of cash receipts and disbursements by quarter, including details of borrowing, repayment, and interest.
2. Prepare a budgeted balance sheet on December 31, 2007.
3. Prepare a budgeted income statement for the year ended December 31, 2007. This statement should include interest expense and income taxes (at a rate of 36% of operating income). In April 2007, Stylistic will pay $120,640 of income taxes. This amount is the remaining payment due for the 2006 income tax year together with the $100,000 Stylistic pays each quarter of 2007 toward its 2007 income tax bill. Any remaining amount due is paid in April 2008.

	A	B	C	D	E	F
1		Quarters				Year as a
2		1	2	3	4	Whole
3	Cash balance, beginning	$ 500,000	$1,504,440	$1,669,220	$ 100,160	$ 500,000
4	Add receipts					
5	Collections from customers	5,331,200	4,704,000	4,704,000	6,272,000	21,011,200
6	Total cash available for needs (x)	5,831,200	6,208,440	6,373,220	6,372,160	21,511,200
7	Deduct disbursements					
8	Direct materials	960,000	1,152,000	1,152,000	1,536,000	4,800,000
9	Payroll	1,626,300	1,626,300	1,888,600	1,626,300	6,767,500
10	Other costs	1,580,460	1,580,460	1,580,460	1,580,460	6,321,840
11	Machinery purchase	0	0	1,800,000	0	1,800,000
12	Interest expense on long-term debt	60,000	60,000	60,000	60,000	240,000
13	Income taxes	100,000	120,460	100,000	100,000	420,460
14	Total disbursements (y)	4,326,760	4,539,220	6,581,060	4,902,760	20,349,800
15	Minimum cash balance desired	100,000	100,000	100,000	100,000	100,000
16	Total cash needed	4,426,760	4,639,220	6,681,060	5,002,760	20,449,800
17	Cash excess (deficiency)[a]	$1,404,440	$1,569,220	$ (307,840)	$1,369,400	$ 1,061,400
18	Financing					
19	Borrowing (at beginning)	$ 0	$ 0	$ 308,000	$ 0	$ 308,000
20	Repayment (at end)	0	0	0	(308,000)	(308,000)
21	Interest (at 12% per annum)[b]	0	0	0	(18,480)	(18,480)
22	Total effects of financing	$ 0	$ 0	$ 308,000	$ (326,480)	$ (18,480)
23	Cash balance, ending[c]	$1,504,440	$1,669,220	$ 100,160	$1,142,920	$ 1,142,920
24						
25	[a]Excess of total cash available over total cash needed before current financing.					
26	[b]Note that the short-term interest payments pertain only to the amount of principal being repaid at the end					
27	of a quarter: $308,000 x 0.12 x 0.5 = $18,480.					
28	[c]Ending cash balance = Total cash available for needs (x) - Total disbursements (y) + Total effects of financing.					

EXHIBIT 6-6

Cash Budget for Stylistic Furniture for the Year Ending December 31, 2007

Preparation of Budgets

1. The **cash budget** (Exhibit 6-6) is a schedule of expected cash receipts and disbursements. It predicts the effects on the cash position at the given level of operations. Exhibit 6-6 presents the cash budget by quarters to show the impact of cash flow timing on bank loans and their repayment. In practice, monthly—and sometimes weekly or even daily—cash budgets are critical for cash planning and control. Cash budgets help avoid unnecessary idle cash and unexpected cash deficiencies. They thus keep cash balances in line with needs. Ordinarily, the cash budget has these main sections:

a. The beginning cash balance plus cash receipts equals the total cash available before financing. Cash receipts depend on collections of accounts receivable, cash sales, and miscellaneous recurring sources, such as rental or royalty receipts. Information on the expected collectibility of accounts receivable is needed for accurate predictions. Key factors include bad-debt (uncollectible accounts) experience and average time lag between sales and collections.

b. Cash disbursements by Stylistic Furniture include:

i. *Direct material purchases*. Suppliers are paid in full three weeks after the goods are delivered.

ii. *Direct labor and other wage and salary outlays*. All payroll-related costs are paid in the month in which the labor effort occurs.

iii. *Other costs*. These depend on timing and credit terms. *Note, depreciation does not require a cash outlay.*

iv. *Other disbursements*. These include outlays for property, plant, equipment, and other long-term investments.

v. *Interest on long-term borrowing*.

vi. *Income tax payments*.

c. Short-term financing requirements depend on how the total cash available for needs [keyed as (x) in Exhibit 6-6] compares with the total cash disbursements [keyed as (y)], plus the minimum ending cash balance desired. The financing plans will depend on the relationship between total cash available for needs and total cash needed. If there is a deficiency of cash, loans will be obtained. If there is excess cash, any outstanding loans will be repaid.

d. The ending cash balance.

There's no need to memorize the format of the cash budget if you remember that it's similar to the way your bank statement works: beginning balance + deposits (receipts) – disbursements = ending balance (before financing). This ending balance reveals how much must be borrowed or can be repaid/invested.

Keep in mind three points about cash budgets: (1) The ending balance (EB) of cash in one quarter is the beginning balance (BB) of cash in the next quarter. (2) In the "Year as a Whole" column, receipts and disbursements are totaled for the four quarters. However, the BB in that column is the BB for quarter 1, and the EB is the EB for quarter 4. (3) Depreciation is not a cash disbursement.

EXHIBIT 6-7

Budgeted Income Statement for Stylistic Furniture for the Year Ending December 31, 2007

	A	B	C	D
1	Revenues	Schedule 1		$20,384,000
2	Cost of goods sold	Schedule 7		14,751,250
3	Gross margin			5,632,750
4	Operating costs			
5	R&D/Product design	Schedule 8	$ 555,760	
6	Marketing costs	Schedule 8	1,920,720	
7	Distribution costs	Schedule 8	729,600	
8	Customer-service costs	Schedule 8	504,992	
9	Administrative costs	Schedule 8	440,768	4,151,840
10	Operating income			1,480,910
11	Interest expense			258,480
12	Income before income taxes			1,222,430
13	Income taxes			440,075
14	Net Income			$ 782,355
15				

The cash budget in Exhibit 6-6 shows the pattern of short-term "self-liquidating" cash loans. In quarter 3, Stylistic budgets a $307,840 cash deficiency. Hence, it undertakes short-term borrowing of $308,000 for six months. Seasonal peaks of production or sales often result in heavy cash disbursements for purchases, payroll, and other operating outlays as the products are produced and sold. Cash receipts from customers typically lag behind sales. The loan is *self-liquidating* in the sense that the borrowed money is used to acquire resources that are used to produce and sell finished goods, and the proceeds from sales are used to repay the loan. This self-liquidating cycle is the movement from cash to inventories to receivables and back to cash.

2. The budgeted income statement is presented in Exhibit 6-7. It is merely the budgeted operating income statement in Exhibit 6-3 (p. 193) expanded to include interest expense and income taxes.
3. The budgeted balance sheet is presented in Exhibit 6-8. Each item is projected in light of the details of the business plan as expressed in all the previous budget schedules. For example, the ending balance of accounts receivable of $1,254,400 is computed by adding the budgeted revenues of $20,384,000 (from Schedule 1) to the beginning balance of accounts receivable of $1,881,600 (from Exhibit 6-5) and subtracting cash receipts of $21,011,200 (from Exhibit 6-6).

For simplicity, the cash receipts and disbursements were given explicitly in this illustration. Usually, the receipts and disbursements are calculated based on the lags between the items reported on the accrual basis of accounting in an income statement and balance sheet and their related cash receipts and disbursements. Consider accounts receivable. In the first three quarters, Stylistic esti-

EXHIBIT 6-8

Budgeted Balance Sheet for Stylistic Furniture, December 31, 2007

	A	B	C	D
1	**Assets**			
2	Current Assets			
3	Cash		$1,142,920	
4	Accounts receivable		1,254,400	
5	Direct materials inventory		204,000	
6	Finished goods inventory		854,250	$3,455,570
7	Property, plant and equipment			
8	Land		1,200,000	
9	Building and equipment	$4,100,000		
10	Accumulated depreciation	(1,300,000)	2,800,000	4,000,000
11	Total			$7,455,570
12				
13	**Liabilities and Stockholders' Equity**			
14	Current Liabilities			
15	Accounts payable		$ 358,000	
16	Income taxes payable		40,075	
17	Total current liabilities		398,075	
18	Long-term debt (interest at 10% per year)		2,400,000	
19	Total current and long-term liabilities			$2,798,075
20	Stockholders' equity			
21	Common stock, $0.01 par value, 300,000 shares outstanding		3,000	
22	Retained earnings		4,654,495	4,657,495
23	Total			$7,455,570
24				

mates that 70% of all sales made in a quarter are collected in the same quarter and 30% are collected in the following quarter. In the fourth quarter, Stylistic anticipates, based on its prior history, that it will collect slightly less than 80% of sales (79.445%). Estimated collections from customers each quarter are calculated in the following table (assuming sales by quarter of $4,928,000, $4,608,000, $4,745,143, and $6,102,857 that equal 2007 budgeted sales of $20,384,000).

Schedule of Cash Collections

	Quarters			
	1	2	3	4
Accounts receivable balance on 1-1-2007 (p. 204) (Fourth quarter sales from prior year collected in first quarter of 2007)	$1,881,600			
From first-quarter 2007 sales ($4,928,000 × 0.70; $4,928,000 × 0.30)	3,449,600	$1,478,400		
From second-quarter 2007 sales ($4,608,000 × 0.70; $4,608,000 × 0.30)		3,225,600	$1,382,400	
From third-quarter 2007 sales ($4,745,143 × 0.70; $4,745,143 × 0.30)			3,321,600	$1,423,543
From fourth-quarter 2007 sales (estimated collections from sales of $6,102,857)				4,848,457
Total collections	$5,331,200	$4,704,000	$4,704,000	$6,272,000

Note that the quarterly cash collections from customers calculated in this schedule equal the cash collections by quarter shown on page 204. Furthermore, the difference between fourth-quarter sales and the cash collected from fourth-quarter sales, $6,102,857 − $4,848,457 = $1,254,400 appears as accounts receivable in the budgeted balance sheet as of December 31, 2007 (see Exhibit 6-8).

Study Tip: To check your understanding of cash budgeting, see Featured Exercise 2, multiple-choice question 8, and Review Exercise 3 (*Student Guide*, beginning p. 65). Fully explained answers begin on page 71.

Sensitivity Analysis and Cash Flows

Exhibit 6-4 (p. 195) shows how differing assumptions about selling prices of coffee tables and direct material prices led to differing amounts for budgeted operating income for Stylistic Furniture. A key use of sensitivity analysis is to budget cash flow. Exhibit 6-9 outlines the short-term borrowing implications of the nine combinations examined in Exhibit 6-4. Scenarios 7 to 9, with the lower selling price per table ($352.80), require large amounts of short-term borrowing in quarters 3 and 4. Scenario 9, with the combination of a 10% lower selling price and 5% higher direct material costs, requires the largest amount of borrowing by Stylistic Furniture. Sensitivity analysis helps managers anticipate such outcomes and take steps to minimize the effects of expected reductions in cash flows from operations.

EXHIBIT 6-9

Sensitivity Analysis: Effects of Key Budget Assumptions in Exhibit 6-4 on 2007 Short-Term Borrowing for Stylistic Furniture

	A	B	C	D	E	F	G	H	I
1			Direct Material						
2			Purchase Costs		Budgeted	Short-Term Borrowing by Quarter			
3		Selling	Particle	Red	Operating			Quarters	
4	Scenario	Price	Board	Oak	Income	1	2	3	4
5	1	$431.20	$3.80	$5.70	$3,458,226	$0	$0	$ 0	$ 0
6	2	431.20	4.00	6.00	3,244,126	0	0	0	0
7	3	431.20	4.20	6.30	3,030,026	0	0	0	0
8	4	392.00	3.80	5.70	1,695,010	0	0	145,000	0
9	5	392.00	4.00	6.00	1,480,910	0	0	308,000	0
10	6	392.00	4.20	6.30	1,266,810	0	0	472,000	0
11	7	352.80	3.80	5.70	(68,206)	0	0	1,413,000	717,000
12	8	352.80	4.00	6.00	(282,306)	0	0	1,576,000	997,000
13	9	352.80	4.20	6.30	(496,406)	0	0	1,739,000	1,276,000

TERMS TO LEARN

The chapter and the Glossary at the end of the book contain definitions of:

activity-based budgeting (ABB) (p. 196)
budgetary slack (p. 199)
cash budget (p. 205)
continuous budget (p. 184)
controllability (p. 198)
controllable cost (p. 198)
cost center (p. 197)
financial budget (p. 186)
financial planning models (p. 193)
investment center (p. 197)
kaizen budgeting (p. 195)
master budget (p. 182)
operating budget (p. 186)
organization structure (p. 197)
pro forma statements (p. 182)
profit center (p. 197)
responsibility accounting (p. 197)
responsibility center (p. 197)
revenue center (p. 197)
rolling budget (p. 184)

PH Grade Assist

Prentice Hall Grade Assist (PHGA)
Your professor may ask you to complete selected exercises and problems in Prentice Hall Grade Assist (PHGA). PHGA is an online tool that can help you master the chapter's topics. It provides you with multiple variations of exercises and problems designated by the PHGA icon. You can rework these exercises and problems—each time with new data—as many times as you need. You also receive immediate feedback and grading.

ASSIGNMENT MATERIAL

Questions

6-1 What are the four elements of the budgeting cycle?

6-2 Define master budget.

6-3 "Strategy, plans, and budgets are unrelated to one another." Do you agree? Explain.

6-4 "Budgeted performance is a better criterion than past performance for judging managers." Do you agree? Explain.

6-5 "Production managers and marketing managers are like oil and water. They just don't mix." How can a budget assist in reducing battles between these two areas?

6-6 "Budgets meet the cost-benefit test. They force managers to act differently." Do you agree? Explain.

6-7 Define rolling budget. Give an example.

6-8 Outline the steps in preparing an operating budget.

6-9 "The sales forecast is the cornerstone for budgeting." Why?

6-10 How can sensitivity analysis be used to increase the benefits of budgeting?

6-11 Define kaizen budgeting.

6-12 Describe how nonoutput-based cost drivers can be incorporated into budgeting.

6-13 Explain how the choice of the type of responsibility center (cost, revenue, profit, or investment) affects behavior.

6-14 What are some additional considerations that arise when budgeting in multinational companies?

6-15 "Cash budgets must be prepared before the operating income budget." Do you agree? Explain.

Exercises

6-16 **Sales budget, service setting.** In 2006, McGrath & Sons, a small environmental-testing firm, performed 11,000 radon tests for $250 each and 15,200 lead tests for $200 each. Because newer homes are being built with lead-free pipes, lead-testing volume is expected to decrease by 10% next year. However, awareness of radon-related health hazards is expected to result in a 5% increase in radon-test volume each year in the near future. Jim McGrath feels that if he lowers his price for lead testing to $190 per test, he will have to face only a 5% decline in lead-test sales in 2007.

Required

1. Prepare a 2007 sales budget for McGrath & Sons assuming that they hold prices at 2006 levels.
2. Prepare a 2007 sales budget for McGrath & Sons assuming that they lower the price of a lead test to $190. Should McGrath lower the price of a lead test in 2007 if its goal is to maximize sales revenue?

6-17 **Sales and production budget.** The Mendez Company expects sales in 2007 of 100,000 units of serving trays. Mendez's beginning inventory for 2007 is 7,000 trays; target ending inventory, 11,000 trays. Compute the number of trays budgeted for production in 2007.

6-18 **Direct material budget.** Inglenook Co. produces wine. The company expects to produce 1,500,000 two-liter bottles of Chablis in 2007. Inglenook purchases empty glass bottles from an outside vendor. Its target ending inventory of such bottles is 50,000; its beginning inventory is 20,000. For simplicity, ignore breakage. Compute the number of bottles to be purchased in 2007.

6-19 **Budgeting material purchases.** The Mahoney Company has prepared a sales budget of 42,000 finished units for a three-month period. The company has an inventory of 22,000 units of finished goods on hand at December 31 and has a target finished goods inventory of 24,000 units at the end of the succeeding quarter.

It takes three gallons of direct materials to make one unit of finished product. The company has an inventory of 90,000 gallons of direct materials at December 31 and has a target ending inventory of 110,000 gallons at the end of the succeeding quarter. How many gallons of direct materials should be purchased during the three months ending March 31?

6-20 Revenues and production budget. Purity, Inc., bottles and distributes mineral water from the company's natural springs in northern Oregon. Purity markets two products: twelve-ounce disposable plastic bottles and four-gallon reusable plastic containers.

PH Grade Assist

Required

1. For 2007, Purity marketing managers project monthly sales of 400,000 twelve-ounce bottles and 100,000 four-gallon containers. Average selling prices are estimated at $0.25 per twelve-ounce bottle and $1.50 per four-gallon container. Prepare a revenues budget for Purity, Inc., for the year ending December 31, 2007.
2. Purity begins 2007 with 900,000 twelve-ounce bottles in inventory. The vice president of operations requests that twelve-ounce ending inventory on December 31, 2007, be no less than 600,000 bottles. Based on sales projections as budgeted above, what is the minimum number of twelve-ounce bottles Purity must produce during 2007?
3. The VP of operations requests that ending inventory of four-gallon containers on December 31, 2007, be 200,000 units. If the production budget calls for Purity to produce 1,300,000 four-gallon containers during 2007, what is the beginning inventory of four-gallon containers on January 1, 2007?

6-21 Direct material usage, unit costs, and gross margins (continuation of 6-20). Purity, Inc., bottles and distributes mineral water from the company's natural springs in northern Oregon. Purity markets two products: 12-ounce disposable plastic bottles and 4-gallon reusable plastic containers. The 12-ounce bottles are purchased from Plastico, a plastics manufacturer, at a cost of 6 cents per bottle. The 4-gallon containers are sterilized and put back into service at a cost of 30 cents per container. Spring water is extracted at a direct labor cost of 1 cent per 8 ounces (there are 128 ounces in a gallon). Manufacturing overhead is allocated at the rate of 15 cents per unit. (Note: A unit can be a 12-ounce bottle *or* a 4-gallon container). In 2007, the production budget calls for the production of 4,500,000 12-ounce bottles and 1,300,000 4-gallon containers.

Required

1. Assume 4-gallon containers are fully depreciated, so the only cost incurred is that of sterilization. Beginning and ending inventories for 4-gallon containers are zero. There are 500,000 empty 12-ounce bottles in beginning inventory on January 1, 2007. The vice president of operations would like to end 2007 with 300,000 empty 12-ounce bottles in inventory. Accounting for sterilization as the only cost of the 4-gallon containers, prepare a direct material usage budget (relating to both bottles and containers) in both units and dollars.
2. The cost of direct manufacturing labor is captured through the extraction cost as detailed above. Based on the data given, prepare a direct manufacturing labor budget for 2007.
3. Calculate the manufacturing cost per unit for each product.
4. Assuming average selling prices as in Exercise 6-20, what is the expected average gross margin per unit for each product?
5. Consider Purity's choice of the cost-allocation base for manufacturing overhead. Can you suggest alternative cost-allocation bases?

6-22 Revenues, production, and purchases budgets. The Suzuki Co. in Japan has a division that manufactures two-wheel motorcycles. Its budgeted sales for Model G in 2007 is 800,000 units. Suzuki's target ending inventory is 100,000 units, and its beginning inventory is 120,000 units. The company's budgeted selling price to its distributors and dealers is 400,000 yen (¥) per motorcycle.

Suzuki buys all its wheels from an outside supplier. No defective wheels are accepted. (Suzuki's needs for extra wheels for replacement parts are ordered by a separate division of the company.) The company's target ending inventory is 30,000 wheels, and its beginning inventory is 20,000 wheels. The budgeted purchase price is 16,000 yen (¥) per wheel.

Required

1. Compute the budgeted revenues in yen.
2. Compute the number of motorcycles to be produced.
3. Compute the budgeted purchases of wheels in units and in yen.

6-23 Budgets for production and direct manufacturing labor. (CMA, adapted) Roletter Company makes and sells artistic frames for pictures of weddings, graduations, and other special events. Bob Anderson, the controller, is responsible for preparing Roletter's master budget and has accumulated the following information for 2007:

	2007				
	January	**February**	**March**	**April**	**May**
Estimated sales in units	10,000	12,000	8,000	9,000	9,000
Selling price	$54.00	$51.50	$51.50	$51.50	$51.50
Direct manufacturing labor-hours per unit	2.0	2.0	1.5	1.5	1.5
Wage per direct manufacturing labor-hour	$10.00	$10.00	$10.00	$11.00	$11.00

Besides wages, direct manufacturing labor-related costs include pension contributions of $0.50 per hour, worker's compensation insurance of $0.15 per hour, employee medical insurance of $0.40 per hour, and social security taxes. Assume that as of January 1, 2007, the social security tax rates are 7.5% for employers and 7.5% for employees. The cost of employee benefits paid by Roletter on its employees is treated as a direct manufacturing labor cost.

Roletter has a labor contract that calls for a wage increase to $11 per hour on April 1, 2007. New labor-saving machinery has been installed and will be fully operational by March 1, 2007. Roletter expects to have 16,000 frames on hand at December 31, 2006, and it has a policy of carrying an end-of-month inventory of 100% of the following month's sales plus 50% of the second following month's sales.

Required

Prepare a production budget and a direct manufacturing labor budget for Roletter Company by month and for the first quarter of 2007. Both budgets may be combined in one schedule. The direct manufacturing labor budget should include labor-hours, and show the details for each labor cost category.

Excel Lab www.prenhall.com/horngren/cost12e

PH Grade Assist

6-24 Activity-based budgeting. The Chelsea store of Family Supermarket (FS), a chain of small neighborhood grocery stores, is preparing its activity-based budget for January 2008. FS has three product categories: soft drinks, fresh produce, and packaged food. The following table shows the four activities that consume indirect resources at the Chelsea store, the cost drivers and their rates, and the cost-driver amount budgeted to be consumed by each activity in January 2008.

	A	B	C	D	E	F
1			January 2008	January 2008 Budgeted		
2			Budgeted	Amount of Cost Driver Used		
3	Activity	Cost Driver	Cost-Driver Rate	Soft Drinks	Fresh Produce	Packaged Food
4	Ordering	Number of purchase orders	$ 90	14	24	14
5	Delivery	Number of deliveries	$ 82	12	62	19
6	Shelf-stocking	Hours of stocking time	$ 21	16	172	94
7	Customer support	Number of items sold	$0.18	4,600	34,200	10,750

If you want to use Excel to solve this exercise, go to the Excel Lab at **www.prenhall.com/horngren/cost12e** and download the template for Exercise 6-24.

Required

1. What is the total budgeted indirect cost at the Chelsea store in January 2008? What is the total budgeted cost of each activity at the Chelsea store for January 2008? What is the budgeted indirect cost of each product category for January 2008?
2. Which product category has the largest fraction of total budgeted indirect costs?
3. Given your answer in requirement 2, what advantage does FS gain by using an activity-based approach to budgeting over, say, allocating indirect costs to products based on cost of goods sold?

Excel Lab www.prenhall.com/horngren/cost12e

PH Grade Assist

6-25 Kaizen approach to activity-based budgeting (continuation of 6-24). Family Supermarkets (FS) has a kaizen (continuous improvement) approach to budgeting monthly activity costs for each month of 2008. Each successive month, the budgeted cost-driver rate decreases by 0.2% relative to the preceding month (so, for example, February's budgeted cost-driver rate is 0.998 times January's budgeted cost-driver rate, and March's budgeted cost-driver rate is 0.998 times the budgeted February 2008 rate). FS assumes that the budgeted amount of cost-driver usage remains the same each month.

If you want to use Excel to solve this exercise, go to the Excel Lab at **www.prenhall.com/horngren/cost12e** and download the template for Exercise 6-24.

Required

1. What is the total budgeted cost for each activity and the total budgeted indirect cost for March 2008?
2. What are the benefits of using a kaizen approach to budgeting? What are the limitations of this approach, and how might FS management overcome them?

PH Grade Assist

6-26 Responsibility and controllability. Consider each of the following independent situations:

1. A very successful salesman at Amcorp Computers regularly ignores the published sales catalog and offers lowered prices to his customers in order to close sales. The VP of sales notices that revenues are substantially lower than budgeted.
2. Every "special deal" offered to a customer by any salesperson at Amcorp Computers has to be cleared by the VP of sales. Revenues for the second quarter have been lower than budgeted.
3. The shipping department of Amcorp has limited capacity, and sales orders are being cancelled by customers because of delays in delivery. Revenues for the past month have been lower than budgeted.
4. At Planetel Corp., a manufacturer of telecommunications equipment, the production supervisor notices that a significantly larger number of direct manufacturing labor-hours were used than had been budgeted. Investigation revealed that it was due to a decline in educational standards required by the HR department when they interviewed applicants for hourly production jobs six months earlier.
5. At Planetel Corp., a relatively new production supervisor finds that more direct manufacturing labor-hours were used than had been budgeted. Interviews revealed that workers were unhappy with his management style and were intentionally working slowly and inefficiently.
6. At Planetel Corp., the production supervisor traces the excessive consumption of direct materials (relative to the budget) to the fact that waste was high on machines that had not been properly maintained.

Required

For each situation described, determine where (that is, with whom) (a) responsibility and (b) controllability lie. Suggest what might be done to solve the problem or to improve the situation.

6-27 Cash flow analysis, chapter appendix. (CMA, adapted) TabComp, Inc., is a retail distributor for MZB-33 computer hardware and related software and support services. TabComp prepares annual sales forecasts of which the first six months for 2006 are presented here.

Cash sales account for 25% of TabComp's total sales, 30% of the total sales are paid by bank credit card, and the remaining 45% are on open account (TabComp's own charge accounts). The cash sales and cash from bank credit-card sales are received in the month of the sale. Bank credit-card sales are subject to a 4% discount deducted at the time of the daily deposit. The cash receipts for sales on open account are 70% in the month following the sale and 28% in the second month after the sale. The remaining accounts receivable are estimated to be uncollectible.

TabComp's month-end inventory requirements for computer hardware units are 30% of the next month's sales. A one-month lead time is required for delivery from the manufacturer. Thus, orders for computer hardware units are placed on the 25th of each month to assure that they will be in the store by the first day of the month needed. The computer hardware units are purchased under terms of n/45 (payment in full within 45 days of invoice), measured from the time the units are delivered to TabComp. TabComp's purchase price for the computer units is 60% of the selling price.

TabComp Inc.
Sales Forecast First Six Months of 2006

	Hardware Sales		Software	Total
	Units	**Dollars**	**Sales and Support**	**Revenues**
January	130	$ 390,000	$160,000	$ 550,000
February	120	360,000	140,000	500,000
March	110	330,000	150,000	480,000
April	90	270,000	130,000	400,000
May	100	300,000	125,000	425,000
June	125	375,000	225,000	600,000
Total	675	$2,025,000	$930,000	$2,955,000

Required

1. Calculate the cash that TabComp, Inc., can expect to collect during April 2006. Be sure to show all of your calculations.
2. TabComp, Inc., is determining how many MZB-33 computer hardware units to order on January 25, 2006.
   a. Determine the projected number of computer hardware units that will be ordered.
   b. Calculate the dollar amount of the order that TabComp will place for these computer hardware units.
3. As part of the annual budget process, TabComp prepares a cash budget by month for the entire year. Explain why a company such as TabComp prepares a cash budget by month for the entire year.

Problems

6-28 Budget schedules for a manufacturer. Sierra Furniture is an elite desk manufacturer. It makes two products:

- Executive desks—3′ × 5′ oak desks
- Chairman desks—6′ × 4′ red oak desks

The budgeted direct-cost inputs for each product in 2006 are:

	Executive Line	Chairman Line
Oak top	16 square feet	0
Red oak top	0	25 square feet
Oak legs	4	0
Red oak legs	0	4
Direct manufacturing labor	3 hours	5 hours

Unit data pertaining to the direct materials for March 2006 are:

Actual Beginning Direct Materials Inventory (3/1/2006)

	Executive Line	Chairman Line
Oak top (square feet)	320	0
Red oak top (square feet)	0	150
Oak legs	100	0
Red oak legs	0	40

Target Ending Direct Materials Inventory (3/31/2006)

	Executive Line	Chairman Line
Oak top (square feet)	192	0
Red oak top (square feet)	0	200
Oak legs	80	0
Red oak legs	0	44

Unit cost data for direct-cost inputs pertaining to February 2006 and March 2006 are:

	February 2006 (actual)	March 2006 (budgeted)
Oak top (per square foot)	$18	$20
Red oak top (per square foot)	23	25
Oak legs (per leg)	11	12
Red oak legs (per leg)	17	18
Manufacturing labor cost per hour	30	30

Manufacturing overhead (both variable and fixed) is allocated to each desk on the basis of budgeted direct manufacturing labor-hours per desk. The budgeted variable manufacturing overhead rate for March 2006 is $35 per direct manufacturing labor-hour. The budgeted fixed manufacturing overhead for March 2006 is $42,500. Both variable and fixed manufacturing overhead costs are allocated to each unit of finished goods.

Data relating to finished goods inventory for March 2006 are:

	Executive	Chairman Line
Beginning inventory in units	20	5
Beginning inventory in dollars (cost)	$10,480	$4,850
Target ending inventory in units	30	15

Budgeted sales for March 2006 are 740 units of the executive line and 390 units of the chairman line. The budgeted selling prices per unit in March 2006 are $1,020 for the executive-line desk and $1,600 for the chairman-line desk. Assume the following in your answer:

- Work-in-process inventories are negligible and ignored.
- Direct materials inventory and finished goods inventory are costed using the FIFO method.
- Unit costs of direct materials purchased and finished goods are constant in March 2006.

Required

1. Prepare the following budgets for March 2006:
   a. Revenues budget
   b. Production budget in units
   c. Direct material usage budget and direct material purchases budget
   d. Direct manufacturing labor budget
   e. Manufacturing overhead budget
   f. Ending inventory budget (direct materials and finished goods)
   g. Cost of goods sold budget
2. Suppose Sierra Furniture decides to incorporate continuous improvement into its budgeting process. Describe two areas where Sierra could incorporate continuous improvement into the budget schedules in requirement 1.

PH Grade Assist

6-29 Sensitivity analysis, changing budget assumptions, kaizen approach. Choco Chips produces two brands of chocolate chip cookies: Chippo and Chokko. The cookies are produced from only two ingredients: chocolate chips and cookie dough. Chippo is 50% chips by weight and 50% dough, whereas Chokko is 25% chips by weight and 75% dough; there is negligible loss while baking the cookies.

Packages of either brand weigh 1 pound. Choco Chips's master budget projects sales of 500,000 packages of each brand in 2007, at $3 per package. Forecasted 2007 ingredients' costs are $2 per pound of chocolate chips and $1 per pound of cookie dough. A total of 5,000 direct manufacturing labor-hours—40% for Chippo and 60% for Chokko—are budgeted, at $20 per hour. Manufacturing overhead costs are expected to be $160,000, allocated between the two products on the basis of packages produced. There is no beginning or ending inventory.

Required

1. Calculate budgeted gross margins for each product and for Choco Chips in 2007.
2. By working with its current suppliers, Choco Chips estimates it could reduce the cost of ingredients by 3%. Calculate Choco Chips's revised budgeted gross margin in 2007.
3. An analysis of all activities by a cross-functional team responsible for continuous improvement shows that if the company purchases better-quality ingredients from a different supplier costing 5% more than the original ingredients, there will be fewer quality-related production line stoppages, which will reduce manufacturing overhead costs and direct manufacturing labor-hours by 2%. Calculate Choco Chips's revised 2007 budgeted gross margin under this scenario.
4. Based on budgeted gross margin alone, which of the three scenarios here do you think Choco Chips's management would prefer? What other factors would you consider before choosing between (2) and (3) above?

6-30 Revenue and production budgets. (CPA, adapted) The Scarborough Corporation manufactures and sells two products: Thingone and Thingtwo. In July 2006, Scarborough's budget department gathered the following data to prepare budgets for 2007:

2007 Projected Sales

Product	Units	Price
Thingone	60,000	$165
Thingtwo	40,000	$250

2007 Inventories in Units

Product	Expected Target January 1, 2007	December 31, 2007
Thingone	20,000	25,000
Thingtwo	8,000	9,000

The following direct materials are used in the two products:

Direct Material	Unit	Amount Used per Unit Thingone	Thingtwo
A	pound	4	5
B	pound	2	3
C	each	0	1

Projected data for 2007 with respect to direct materials are as follows:

Direct Material	Anticipated Purchase Price	Expected Inventories January 1, 2007	Target Inventories December 31, 2007
A	$12	32,000 lb.	36,000 lb.
B	5	29,000 lb.	32,000 lb.
C	3	6,000 units	7,000 units

Projected direct manufacturing labor requirements and rates for 2007 are as follows:

Product	Hours per Unit	Rate per Hour
Thingone	2	$12
Thingtwo	3	16

Manufacturing overhead is allocated at the rate of $20 per direct manufacturing labor-hour.

Required

Based on the preceding projections and budget requirements for Thingone and Thingtwo, prepare the following budgets for 2007:

1. Revenues budget (in dollars)
2. Production budget (in units)
3. Direct material purchases budget (in quantities)
4. Direct material purchases budget (in dollars)
5. Direct manufacturing labor budget (in dollars)
6. Budgeted finished goods inventory at December 31, 2007 (in dollars)

6-31 Budgeted income statement. (CMA, adapted) Easecom Company is a manufacturer of video-conferencing products. Regular units are manufactured to meet marketing projections, and specialized units are made after an order is received. Maintaining the video-conferencing equipment is an important area of customer satisfaction. With the recent downturn in the computer industry, the video-conferencing equipment segment has suffered, leading to a decline in Easecom's financial performance. The following income statement shows results for 2007.

Easecom Company
Income Statement
For the Year Ended December 31, 2007 (in thousands)

Revenues:		
Equipment	$6,000	
Maintenance contracts	1,800	
Total revenues		$7,800
Cost of goods sold		4,600
Gross margin		3,200
Operating costs		
Marketing	600	
Distribution	150	
Customer maintenance	1,000	
Administration	900	
Total operating costs		2,650
Operating income		$ 550

Easecom's management team is in the process of preparing the 2008 budget and is studying the following information:

1. Selling prices of equipment are expected to increase by 10% as the economic recovery begins. The selling price of each maintenance contract is expected to remain unchanged from 2007.
2. Equipment sales in units are expected to increase by 6%, with a corresponding 6% growth in units of maintenance contracts.
3. Cost of each unit sold is expected to increase by 3% to pay for the necessary technology and quality improvements.

4. Marketing costs are expected to increase by $250,000, but administration costs are expected to remain at 2007 levels.
5. Distribution costs vary in proportion to the number of units of equipment sold.
6. Two maintenance technicians are to be hired at a total cost of $130,000, which covers wages and related travel costs. The objective is to improve customer service and shorten response time.
7. There is no beginning or ending inventory of equipment.

Required Prepare a budgeted income statement for the year ending December 31, 2008.

6-32 Responsibility of purchasing agent. (Adapted from a description by R. Villers) Mark Richards is the purchasing agent for the Hart Manufacturing Company. Kent Sampson is head of the Production Planning and Control Department. Every six months, Sampson gives Richards a general purchasing program. Richards gets specifications from the Engineering Department. He then selects suppliers and negotiates prices. When he took this job, Richards was informed very clearly that he bore responsibility for meeting the general purchasing program once he accepted it from Sampson.

During week 24, Richards is advised that Part No. 1234—a critical part—would be needed for assembly on Tuesday morning of week 32. He found that the regular supplier could not deliver. He called everywhere and finally found a supplier in the Midwest who accepted the commitment.

He followed up by e-mail. Yes, the supplier assured him, the part would be ready. The matter was so important that on Thursday of week 31, Richards checked by phone. Yes, the shipment had left in time. Richards was reassured and did not check further. But on Tuesday of week 32, the part had not arrived. Inquiry revealed that the shipment had been misdirected by the railroad and was still in Chicago.

Required What department should bear the costs of time lost in the plant due to the delayed shipment? Why? As purchasing agent, do you think it is fair that such costs be charged to your department?

6-33 Activity-based budgeting. Anderson Manufacturing, Inc., manufactures two types of valves, 300,000 simple valves (SV2) and 100,000 complex valves (CL9). Anderson uses activity-based costing and activity-based budgeting. The following table contains cost-driver and budgeted indirect-cost information for 2007 for the different activities.

Activity	Cost Driver	Items in Cost Pool (fixed cost + cost per unit of cost driver)
Machining	Machine hours	Indirect materials $0 + $10 per machine-hour
		Indirect labor $20,000 + $15 per machine-hour
		Utilities $0 + $5 per machine-hour
Setups and quality assurance	Production runs	Indirect materials $0 + $1,000 per prod. run
		Indirect labor $0 + $1,200 per prod. run
		Inspection $80,000 + $2,000 per prod. run
Procurement	Purchase orders	Indirect materials $0 + $4 per purch. order
		Indirect labor $45,000 + $0 per purch. order
Design	Engineering hours	Engineering $75,000 + $50 per engg.-hour
Materials handling	Square feet of materials handled	Indirect materials $0 + $2 per sq ft
		Indirect labor $30,000 + $0 per sq ft

Additional budget data for 2007, describing the amount of activity resources used by the two types of valves follows:

	Quantity of Cost Driver Used By		
Activity	**SV2**	**CL9**	**Total Budgeted Volume of Cost Driver**
a. Machining	6,500	3,500	10,000 machine-hours
b. Setups and quality assurance	20	20	40 production runs
c. Procurement	8,000	7,000	15,000 purchase orders
d. Design	25	75	100 engineering-hours
e. Materials handling	60,000	40,000	100,000 square feet

Required

1. Calculate the total budgeted cost for each activity in 2007 and the cost-driver rate for each activity.
2. Use the cost-driver rates calculated in requirement 1 to calculate budgeted indirect costs allocated to each product in total and per unit.
3. What advantages might Anderson gain by using an activity-based budgeting approach over, say, an approach that allocates the cost of these activities to products as a percentage of the cost of goods sold.

6-34 Comprehensive operating budget, budgeted balance sheet. Slopes, Inc., manufactures and sells snowboards. Slopes manufactures a single model, the Pipex. In the summer of 2006, Slopes's management accountant gathered the following data to prepare budgets for 2007:

Materials and labor requirements

Direct materials	
Wood	5 board feet (b.f.) per snowboard
Fiberglass	6 yards per snowboard
Direct manufacturing labor	5 hours per snowboard

Slopes's CEO expects to sell 1,000 snowboards during 2007 at an estimated retail price of $450 per board. Further, he expects 2007 beginning inventory of 100 boards and would like to end 2007 with 200 snowboards in stock.

Direct materials inventories

	Beginning Inventory 1/1/2007	Ending Inventory 12/31/2007
Wood	2,000	1,500
Fiberglass	1,000	2,000

Variable manufacturing overhead is $7 per direct manufacturing labor-hour. There are also $66,000 in fixed manufacturing overhead costs budgeted for 2007. Slopes combines both variable and fixed manufacturing overhead into a single rate based on direct manufacturing labor-hours. Variable marketing costs are allocated at the rate of $250 per sales visit. The marketing plan calls for 30 sales visits during 2007. Finally, there are $30,000 in fixed nonmanufacturing costs budgeted for 2007.

Other data includes:

	2006 Unit Price	2007 Unit Price
Wood	$28.00 per b.f.	$30.00 per b.f.
Fiberglass	$ 4.80 per yard	$ 5.00 per yard
Direct manufacturing labor	$24.00 per hour	$25.00 per hour

The inventoriable unit cost for ending finished goods inventory on December 31, 2006, is $374.80. Assume Slopes uses a FIFO inventory method for both direct materials and finished goods. Ignore work in process in your calculations.

Budgeted balances at December 31, 2007, in the selected accounts are:

Cash	$ 10,000
Property, plant, and equipment (net)	850,000
Current liabilities	17,000
Long-term liabilities	178,000
Stockholders' equity	800,000

Required

1. Prepare the 2007 revenues budget (in dollars).
2. Prepare the 2007 production budget (in units).
3. Prepare the direct material usage and purchases budgets.
4. Prepare a direct manufacturing labor budget.
5. Prepare a manufacturing overhead budget.
6. What is the budgeted manufacturing overhead rate?
7. What is the budgeted manufacturing overhead cost per output unit?
8. Calculate the cost of a snowboard manufactured in 2007.
9. Prepare an ending inventory budget for both direct materials and finished goods.
10. Prepare a cost of goods sold budget.
11. Prepare the budgeted income statement for Slopes, Inc., for the year ending December 31, 2007.
12. Prepare the budgeted balance sheet for Slopes, Inc., as of December 31, 2007.

6-35 Cash budgeting, chapter appendix. Retail outlets purchase snowboards from Slopes, Inc., throughout the year. However, in anticipation of late summer and early fall purchases, outlets ramp up inventories from May through August. Outlets are billed when boards are ordered. Invoices are payable within 60 days. From past experience, Slopes's accountant projects 20% of invoices are paid in the month invoiced, 50% are paid in the following month, and 30% of invoices are paid two months after the month of invoice. The average selling price per snowboard is $450.

To meet demand, Slopes increases production from April through July, because the snowboards are produced a month prior to their projected sale. Direct materials are purchased in the month of production and are paid for during the following month (terms are payment in full within 30 days of the invoice date). During this period there is no production for inventory, and no materials are purchased for inventory.

Direct manufacturing labor and manufacturing overhead are paid monthly. Variable manufacturing overhead is incurred at the rate of $7 per direct manufacturing labor-hour. Variable marketing costs are driven by the number of sales visits. However, there are no sales visits during the months studied. Slopes, Inc., also incurs fixed manufacturing overhead costs of $5,500 per month and fixed nonmanufacturing overhead costs of $2,500 per month.

Projected Sales

May	80 units	August	100 units
June	120 units	September	60 units
July	200 units	October	40 units

Direct Materials and Direct Manufacturing Labor Utilization and Cost

	Units per Board	Price per Unit	Unit
Wood	5	$30	Board feet
Fiberglass	6	5	Yard
Direct manufacturing labor	5	25	Hour

The beginning cash balance for July 1, 2007, is $10,000. On October 1, 2006, Slopes had a cash crunch and borrowed $30,000 on a 6% one-year note with interest payable monthly. The note is due October 1, 2007. Using the information provided, you will need to determine whether Slopes will be in a position to pay off this short-term debt on October 1, 2007.

Required

1. Prepare a cash budget for the months of July through September 2007. Show supporting schedules for the calculation of receivables and payables.
2. Will Slopes be in a position to pay off the $30,000 one-year note that is due on October 1, 2007? If not, what actions would you recommend to Slopes's management?
3. Suppose Slopes is interested in maintaining a minimum cash balance of $10,000. Will the company be able to maintain such a balance during all three months analyzed? If not, suggest a suitable cash management strategy.

Excel Lab
www.prenhall.com/horngren/cost12e

6-36 Cash budget, fill in the blanks, chapter appendix. Starport, Inc., assembles and launches commercial satellites. Along with the numbers provided in Problem Exhibit 6-36 below, you are provided with the following budgeting information:

- Starport's CEO insists that Starport maintain a minimum quarterly cash balance of $15 million. Cash in excess of this minimum balance is not invested outside; it is held in the company's cash account.
- In the event of a cash deficiency, Starport will borrow only as much as is needed to maintain the minimum cash balance. Short-term loans carry an interest rate of 12% per year, calculated from the beginning of the quarter in which the loan is initiated through the end of the quarter in which the loan is repaid.
- In the second quarter, Starport plans to buy and pay for new launch-pad machinery costing $85 million.
- On January 1, 2005, Starport raised $100 million through the issue of a five-year 12% bond. Interest on this long-term debt is payable quarterly.

If you want to use Excel to solve this problem, go to the Excel Lab at **www.prenhall.com/horngren/cost12e** and download the template for Problem 6-36.

Required

Use the available information to complete Starport's cash budget. If you are unable to calculate any of the missing numbers, make an assumption and continue.

	A	B	C	D	E	F
1	**Starport, Inc.**					
2	**Cash Budget for the Year Ending December 31, 2007 (in thousands)**					
3						
4		**Quarters**				**Year as a**
5		**1**	**2**	**3**	**4**	**Whole**
6	Cash balance, beginning	$ 15,000	?	?	?	?
7	Add receipts					
8	Collections from customers	385,000	?	?	$365,000	$1,360,000
9	Total cash available for needs	?	$347,000	$310,000	?	?
10	Deduct disbursements					
11	Direct materials	175,000	125,000	?	155,000	?
12	Payroll	?	110,000	95,000	118,000	448,000
13	Other costs	50,000	45,000	40,000	49,000	?
14	Machinery purchase	0	?	0	0	85,000
15	Interest costs (bond)	?	?	?	?	?
16	Income taxes	15,000	14,000	12,000	?	61,000
17	Total disbursements	368,000	?	260,000	345,000	?
18	Minimum cash balance desired	?	?	?	?	15,000
19	Total cash needed	?	?	?	?	1,370,000
20	Cash excess (deficiency)	?	$ (50,000)	?	?	$ 5,000
21	Financing					
22	Borrowing (at beginning)	$ 0	?	$ 0	$ 0	?
23	Repayment (at end)	0	$ 0	0	(50,000)	$ (50,000)
24	Interest (at 12% per annum)	0	0	0	(4,500)	(4,500)
25	Total effects of financing	$ 0	?	$ 0	$ (54,500)	$ (4,500)
26	Cash balance, ending	$ 32,000	?	?	$ 15,500	?
27						

6-37 Cash budgeting, chapter appendix. On December 1, 2007, the Itami Wholesale Co. is attempting to project cash receipts and disbursements through January 31, 2008. On this latter date, a note will be payable in the amount of $100,000. This amount was borrowed in September to carry the company through the seasonal peak in November and December.

Selected general ledger balances on December 1 are:

Cash	$ 10,000	
Accounts receivable	280,000	
Allowance for bad debts		$15,800
Inventory	87,500	
Accounts payable		92,000

Sales terms call for a 2% discount if payment is made within the first 10 days of the month after sale, with the balance due by the end of the month after sale. Experience has shown that 70% of the billings will be collected within the discount period, 20% by the end of the month after purchase, and 8% in the following month. The remaining 2% will be uncollectable. There are no cash sales.

The average selling price of the company's products is $100 per unit. Actual and projected sales are:

October actual	$ 180,000
November actual	250,000
December estimated	300,000
January estimated	150,000
February estimated	120,000
Total estimated for year ending June 30, 2008	$1,500,000

All purchases are payable within 15 days. Thus, approximately 50% of the purchases in a month are due and payable in the next month. The average unit purchase cost is $70. Target ending inventories are 500 units plus 25% of the next month's unit sales.

Total budgeted marketing, distribution, and customer-service costs for the year are $400,000. Of this amount, $150,000 are considered fixed (and include depreciation of $30,000). The remainder vary with sales. Both fixed and variable marketing, distribution, and customer-service costs are paid as incurred.

Required

Prepare a cash budget for December 2007 and January 2008. Supply supporting schedules for collections of receivables; payments for merchandise; and marketing, distribution, and customer-service costs.

6-38 Comprehensive budget, fill in schedules. The manager of Newport Stationery Store is working on the final quarter's budget for 2007. She has the following information:

PH Grade Assist

Excel Lab www.prenhall.com/horngren/cost12e

1.

	A	B
1	**Newport Stationery Store**	
2	**Balance Sheet as of September 30, 2007**	
3	Current Assets	
4	Cash	$ 12,000
5	Accounts Receivable	10,000
6	Inventory	63,600
7	Equipment -- net	100,000
8	Liabilities as of September 30	None

2.

D	E	F	G	H
Recent and anticipated sales:				
September	**October**	**November**	**December**	**January**
$40,000	$48,000	$60,000	$80,000	$36,000

3. Credit sales: Sales are 75% cash, 25% on credit. Credit accounts are all collected within 30 days of sale. The accounts receivable on September 30 are the result of September's credit sales (25% of $40,000).
4. Gross margin averages 30% of revenues. Newport treats cash discounts on purchases as "other income" in the income statement.
5. Monthly operating costs: Salaries and wages average 15% of revenues; rent 5%; other operating costs, excluding depreciation, 4%. These costs are paid in cash each month. Depreciation is $1,000 per month.
6. Inventory purchases: Newport always keeps a basic minimum inventory of $30,000. Each month it purchases just enough inventory to cover the following month's sales. The inventory on September 30 is the $30,000 minimum inventory plus cost of sales equal to 70% (100% – gross margin of 30%) of October's anticipated sales of $48,000 [$30,000 + (0.7 × $48,000) = $63,600]. Terms on inventory purchases are 2/10, n/30. (Payments on purchases are to be made in 30 days; a 2% discount is available if full payment is made within 10 days of purchase.) Newport takes all available discounts by paying in the month of the purchase.
7. Equipment purchases: In October, Newport will spend $600 on light fixtures, and in November, $400; these amounts will be capitalized.
8. A minimum cash balance of $8,000 must be maintained. All borrowing—in multiples of $1,000—occurs at the beginning of the month; all repayments are made at month-end. Loans are repaid when sufficient cash is available, and interest is paid only at the time of repaying the principal. The interest rate is 18%

per year. Management does not want to borrow any more cash than is necessary and wants to repay as soon as cash is available.

If you want to use Excel to solve this problem, go to the Excel Lab at **www.prenhall.com/horngren/cost12e** and download the template for Problem 6-38.

Required

1. Complete the following schedules A through F.
2. What do you think is the most logical type of loan for Newport to take when it needs cash? Explain your reasoning.
3. Prepare a budgeted income statement for the fourth quarter and a budgeted balance sheet as of December 31, 2007. Ignore income taxes.
4. Some simplifications have been made in the design of this problem. What complicating factors may arise in compiling cash and financing budgets in a business such as Newport Stationery Store?

	A	B	C	D	E
1	**Schedule A**				
2	**Budgeted Monthly Cash Receipts**				
3	**Item**	**September**	**October**	**November**	**December**
4	Total sales	$40,000	$48,000	$60,000	$80,000
5	Credit sales	10,000	12,000		
6	Cash sales				
7	Receipts:				
8	Cash sales		$36,000		
9	Collections on accounts receivable		10,000		
10	Total		$46,000		
11	**Schedule B**				
12	**Budgeted Monthly Cash Disbursements for Purchases**				
13	**Item**	**October**	**November**	**December**	**4th Quarter**
14	Purchases (70% of next month's sales)	$42,000			
15	Deduct 2% cash discount	840			
16	Total disbursements	$41,160			
17	**Schedule C**				
18	**Budgeted Monthly Cash Disbursements for Operations**				
19	**Item**	**October**	**November**	**December**	**4th Quarter**
20	Salaries and wages	$ 7,200			
21	Rent	2,400			
22	Other cash operating costs	1,920			
23	Total disbursements	$11,520			
24	**Schedule D**				
25	**Budgeted Total Monthly Cash Disbursements**				
26	**Item**	**October**	**November**	**December**	**4th Quarter**
27	Purchases	$41,160			
28	Cash operating costs	11,520			
29	Light fixtures	600			
30	Total disbursements	$53,280			
31	**Schedule E**				
32	**Budgeted Cash Receipts and Disbursements**				
33	**Item**	**October**	**November**	**December**	**4th Quarter**
34	Total receipts	$46,000			
35	Total disbursements	53,280			
36	Net cash increase (decrease)	$ (7,280)			
37	**Schedule F**				
38	**Financing Required**				
39	**Item**	**October**	**November**	**December**	**4th Quarter**
40	Beginning cash balance	$12,000			
41	Net cash increase (decrease)	(7,280)			
42	Cash position before borrowing	4,720			
43	Minimum cash balance required	8,000			
44	Cash excess (deficiency)	(3,280)			
45	Borrowing required	4,000			
46	Interest payments				
47	Borrowing repaid				
48	Ending cash balance	$ 8,720			

6-39 Budgetary slack and ethics. (CMA) It is fall 2006 and Marge Atkins, the new management accountant at Norton Company, a manufacturer of baby furniture, is working on the 2007 budget. Scott Ford, the northeast sales manager, whose sales team will easily meet its $2,000,000 sales budget this year, has projected sales of $2,200,000 in 2007. But, in conversations with individual salespeople, Atkins learns that each salesperson is expecting to make sales of at least 20% more in 2007 than in the current year. When Atkins asks Ford about this, he says, "Well, not meeting projections is so bad for the morale of the sales team...and you know how the top brass froths at the mouth when we miss our target by even a little bit... so, we give ourselves a little breathing room." Intrigued, Atkins investigates further and finds that Pete Granger, the production manager, makes similar adjustments, padding estimated costs by about 10% to come up with the budgeted costs.

Required

1. As a management accountant, should Marge Atkins take the position that the behavior described by Scott Ford and Pete Granger is unethical? Refer to the Standards of Ethical Conduct for Management Accountants described in Chapter 1 (p. 16).
2. How would you suggest Marge Atkins handle this situation?

Collaborative Learning Problem

6-40 Comprehensive Review of Budgeting, Cash Budgeting, Chapter Appendix. Wilson Beverages bottles two soft drinks under license to Cadbury Schweppes at its Manchester plant. All inventory is in direct materials and finished goods at the end of each working day. There is no work-in-process inventory.

The two soft drinks bottled by Wilson Beverages are lemonade and diet lemonade. The syrup for both soft drinks is purchased from Cadbury Schweppes.

Wilson Beverages uses a lot size of 1,000 cases as the unit of analysis in its budgeting. (Each case contains 24 bottles.) Direct materials are expressed in terms of lots, in which one lot of direct materials is the input necessary to yield one lot (1,000 cases) of beverage. The following purchase prices are forecast for direct materials in 2005:

	Lemonade	Diet Lemonade
Syrup	$1,200 per lot	$1,100 per lot
Containers (bottles, caps, etc.)	$1,000 per lot	$1,000 per lot
Packaging	$ 800 per lot	$ 800 per lot

All direct material purchases are on account.

The two soft drinks are bottled using the same equipment. The only difference in the bottling process for the two soft drinks is the syrup.

Summary data used in developing budgets for 2005 are

1. Sales
   - Lemonade, 1,080 lots at $9,000 selling price per lot
   - Diet lemonade, 540 lots at $8,500 selling price per lot

   All sales are on account.
2. Beginning (January 1, 2005) inventory of direct materials
   - Syrup for lemonade, 80 lots at $1,100 purchase price per lot
   - Syrup for diet lemonade, 70 lots at $1,000 purchase price per lot
   - Containers, 200 lots at $950 purchase price per lot
   - Packaging, 400 lots at $900 purchase price per lot
3. Beginning (January 1, 2005) inventory of finished goods
   - Lemonade, 100 lots at $5,300 per lot
   - Diet lemonade, 50 lots at $5,200 per lot
4. Target ending (December 31, 2005) inventory of direct materials
   - Syrup for lemonade, 30 lots
   - Syrup for diet lemonade, 20 lots
   - Containers, 100 lots
   - Packaging, 200 lots
5. Target ending (December 31, 2005) inventory of finished goods
   - Lemonade, 20 lots
   - Diet lemonade, 10 lots
6. Each lot requires 20 direct manufacturing labor-hours at the 2005 budgeted rate of $25 per hour. Direct manufacturing labor costs are paid at the end of each month.
7. Variable manufacturing overhead is forecast to be $600 per hour of bottling time; bottling time is the time the filling equipment is in operation. It takes two hours to bottle one lot of lemonade and two hours to bottle one lot of diet lemonade. Assume all variable manufacturing overhead costs are paid during the same month when incurred.

   Fixed manufacturing overhead is forecast to be $1,200,000 for 2005. Included in the fixed manufacturing overhead forecast is $400,000 for depreciation. All manufacturing overhead costs are paid as incurred.
8. Hours of budgeted bottling time is the sole cost-allocation base for all fixed manufacturing overhead.
9. Administration costs are forecast to be 10% of the cost of goods manufactured for 2005. Marketing costs are forecast to be 12% of revenues for 2005. Distribution costs are forecast to be 8% of revenues for 2005. All these costs are paid during the month when incurred. Assume there are no depreciation or amortization expenses.
10. Budgeted beginning balances on January 1, 2005:

Accounts receivable (from sales)	$550,000
Accounts payable (for direct materials)	300,000
Cash	100,000

11. Budgeted ending balances on December 31, 2005:

Accounts receivable (from sales)	$600,000
Accounts payable (for direct materials)	400,000

12. Budgeted equipment purchase in May $1,350,000
13. Estimated income tax expense for 2005 $ 625,000

Required Assume Wilson Beverages uses the first-in, first-out method for costing all inventories. On the basis of the preceding data, prepare the following budgets for 2005:

- **a.** Revenues budget (in dollars)
- **b.** Production budget (in units)
- **c.** Direct materials usage budget (in units and dollars)
- **d.** Direct materials purchases budget
- **k.** Administration costs budget (in units and dollars)
- **e.** Direct manufacturing labor budget
- **f.** Manufacturing overhead costs budget
- **g.** Ending finished goods inventory budget
- **h.** Cost of goods sold budget
- **i.** Marketing costs budget
- **j.** Distribution costs budget
- **l.** Budgeted income statement
- **m.** Cash budget

Get Connected: Cost Accounting in the News

Go to www.prenhall.com/horngren/cost12e for additional online exercise(s) that explore issues affecting the accounting world today. These exercises offer you the opportunity to analyze and reflect on how cost accounting helps managers to make better decisions and handle the challenges of strategic planning and implementation.

CHAPTER 6 Video Case

RITZ-CARLTON HOTELS: Budgets and Responsibility Accounting

"Ladies and gentlemen serving ladies and gentlemen." That's the motto of the Ritz-Carlton. With locations ranging from the United States to Bahrain to China, the grand 58-hotel chain is known for its indulgent luxury and sumptuous surroundings. This aura of old-world elegance stands in stark contrast to its rather heavy emphasis, behind the scenes of course, on cost control and budgets. Yet it is this very approach that makes it possible for the Ritz-Carlton to offer the legendary grandeur all guests expect during their stay.

A hotel's performance is the responsibility of the general manager and controller at each location worldwide. Local forecasts and budgets are prepared annually and are the basis of subsequent performance evaluations. Preparation of the annual budget begins with the sales budget, prepared by the hotel's sales director. Budgeted sources of revenue include hotel rooms; convention, wedding, and meeting facilities; merchandise; and food and beverage. The controller then seeks input from all employees—from maintenance staff to kitchen workers—about anticipated payroll changes, operating costs, and planned events or promotions that might affect costs. Standard costs, based on cost per occupied room, are used to build the budget for guest room stays. Other standards are used for meeting rooms and food and beverages. The completed sales budget and annual operating budget are sent to corporate headquarters. From there, actual monthly performance against plan is monitored.

On the 25th of each month, budgets for the next three months are reviewed to be sure goals are still accurate. Accuracy can be critical for a business whose occupancy can fluctuate significantly from day to day, depending on group or company bookings, special events, or changes in local competition. Any changes are communicated to corporate headquarters, with explanations of revisions provided as needed. Managers of each hotel meet daily to review performance to date, and have the ability to adjust prices in the reservation system if they so choose. Adjusting prices can be particularly important if a large group cancels at the last minute or if other unforeseen events cause occupancy to drop suddenly, as happened after the World Trade Center terrorist attacks in 2001.

Meeting the monthly budgeted goals is primarily the responsibility of each hotel's controller. The controller of each hotel receives a monthly report from corporate headquarters that shows how the hotel performed against budget, as well as against the actual performance of other Ritz-Carlton hotels. Ideas for boosting revenues and reducing costs are regularly shared among hotel controllers, who recognize the value of contributing to the entire organization's success, not just the success of their own hotel properties.

QUESTIONS

1. The Ritz-Carlton gives all employees at each of its hotels the chance to meet with their hotel's controller to review budgets and reports on actual performance, as a form of participatory budgeting. What advantages or disadvantages do you see with this approach?
2. What factors might affect the Ritz-Carlton's annual sales forecast for room occupancy, restaurants, and use of meetings rooms and conference facilities?
3. How is uncertainty handled in Ritz-Carlton's budgeting process?
4. The Ritz-Carlton uses responsibility accounting for its worldwide hotel and resort operations. What levels of responsibility reports would you expect to see throughout the company?

CHAPTER 7

FLEXIBLE BUDGETS, DIRECT-COST VARIANCES, AND MANAGEMENT CONTROL

LEARNING OBJECTIVES

1. **Distinguish a static budget from a flexible budget**
2. **Develop flexible budgets and compute flexible-budget variances and sales-volume variances**
3. **Explain why standard costs are often used in variance analysis**
4. **Compute price variances and efficiency variances for direct-cost categories**
5. **Understand how managers use variances**
6. **Perform variance analysis in activity-based costing systems**
7. **Describe benchmarking and how it is used in cost management**

Do you remember the anxiety you felt in school on report card day? You had planned to make straight A's, but your report card contained a B in one subject and a C in another. What happened? You probably evaluated reasons for the difference—study habits, absences, or extra-curricular activities—and made changes so that your grade expectations for the next report card stood a greater chance of being met. Businesses also have report cards in the form of performance reports. Managers prepare budgets describing the expected performance for a period. At the end of the period, actual performance is compared against the budgets, and any variance is explained. Then, corrective action is taken. Larry Farrell, the CEO of Webb Company—a jacket manufacturer—is very disappointed by his company's April 2006 monthly performance report. Rosie Guerrero, controller, has been asked to shed some light on what happened.

Larry: Rosie, is our April performance report correct? I can't believe we budgeted operating income of $108,000 but earned only $14,900. Where did we go wrong?

Rosie: You can see from the variance report I prepared that one reason for this difference is that our unit sales were 2,000 jackets fewer than what we'd planned. We did achieve a higher selling price than budgeted, but our direct materials, direct labor, and manufacturing overhead costs were much higher than they should have been.

Larry: How did we lose control so quickly? We really need to learn from this and come up with a solution—fast. Any ideas?

Rosie: To be honest, we don't seem to have the edge in the market that we used to enjoy, but we also had some production problems that negatively affected our costs. Although it's a bit early to tell, we are looking at the quality of the materials, jacket design, worker skill, and machine maintenance as potential reasons. I'm leaving no stone unturned in getting to the bottom of this problem.

Larry: Thanks, Rosie. You know I'm not trying to fix the blame. I just want to know what went wrong and take action so that we don't experience this again. If you can give me your final analysis next week, the management team can begin work on correcting the problems and devising plans to prevent them from occurring in the future.

Like the Webb Company, many companies regularly track actual and budgeted performance. When variances occur, managers seek to find reasons for the differences and then work to make improvements. McDonald's, the well-known fast-food chain, has an extensive budgeting system in place, starting at the individual restaurant level. Store managers budget for sales, food costs, and labor expenses. Throughout each day, managers check budgeted performance against actual activity and make any necessary adjustments. For example, if business is slower than expected, employees may be released early from their shifts. Through each store's point-of-sale terminal system, store results are reported to regional managers and eventually to corporate headquarters, where a higher-level investigation of variances is performed. The results of this investigation may lead to more employee training or different advertising campaigns to attract more customers.

In Chapter 6, you saw how budgets help managers with their planning function. We now turn to how budgets—specifically flexible budgets—are used to evaluate variances, which assist managers in their control function. Variances enable managers to compare actual results with planned performance. Flexible budgets and variances help managers gain insights into why actual results differ from planned performance. That "why" is what this chapter and the next are about.

The Use of Variances

Each **variance** we compute is the difference between an amount based on an actual result and the corresponding budgeted amount. The budgeted amount is a point of reference for making comparisons.

Variances are where the planning and control functions come together to assist managers in implementing their strategies. **Management by exception** is the practice of concentrating on areas not operating as expected (such as a large shortfall in sales of a product) and giving less attention to areas operating as expected. In other words, managers usually pay more attention to areas with large variances. Consider actual scrap and rework costs at a Maytag appliances plant. Suppose its actual costs are much higher than budgeted costs. The variances will guide managers to seek explanations and to take early corrective action, ensuring that future operations result in less scrap and rework. Sometimes a large positive variance may occur, such as a significant decrease in manufacturing costs of a product. Managers will try to understand the reasons for this decrease—for example, better operator training or changes in manufacturing methods—so these practices can be appropriately continued.

Master the material in this chapter before moving on to the next chapter. Chapter 8 builds on concepts introduced here.

Variances are also used in performance evaluation and to motivate managers. Production-line managers at Maytag may have quarterly efficiency incentives linked to achieving a budgeted amount of operating costs.

Sometimes variances suggest a change in strategy. Excessive defect rates for a new product may suggest a flawed product design. Managers may then want to reevaluate their product strategies.

Static Budgets and Static-Budget Variances

1

Distinguish a static budget

... the master budget based on output planned at start of period

from a flexible budget

... the budget that is adjusted (flexed) to recognize the actual output level

Let's take a closer look at variances by examining Webb Company's accounting system. Note as you study the exhibits in this chapter that "level" followed by a number denotes the amount of detail shown by a variance analysis. Level 0 reports the least detail, level 1 offers more information, and so on.

Consider the following facts about Webb Company—an example we use in this chapter. As mentioned earlier, Webb manufactures and sells jackets. The jackets require tailoring and many hand operations. Webb sells exclusively to distributors, who in turn sell to independent clothing stores and retail chains. For simplicity, we assume that Webb's only costs are manufacturing costs; it incurs no costs in other value-chain functions, such as marketing and distribution. We also assume that all units manufactured in April 2006 are sold in April 2006. Therefore, all direct materials are purchased and used in the same budget period, and there is no direct materials inventory at either the beginning or the end of the period. There are also no work-in-process or finished goods inventories at either the beginning or the end of the period. The Problem for Self-Study (pp. 242–243) relaxes some of these assumptions. Webb has three variable-cost categories. The budgeted variable cost per jacket for each category is:

Cost Category	Variable Cost per Jacket
Direct material costs	$60
Direct manufacturing labor costs	16
Variable manufacturing overhead costs	12
Total variable costs	$88

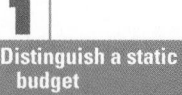

The *number of units manufactured* is the cost driver for direct materials, direct manufacturing labor, and variable manufacturing overhead. The relevant range for the cost driver is from 0 to 12,000 jackets. Budgeted and actual data for April 2006 follow:

Budgeted fixed manufacturing costs for production between 0 and 12,000 jackets	$276,000
Budgeted selling price	$120 per jacket
Budgeted sales	12,000 jackets
Actual sales	10,000 jackets

The **static budget**, or master budget, is based on the level of output planned at the start of the budget period. The master budget is called a static budget because the budget for the period is developed around a single (static) planned output level. Exhibit 7-1, column 3, presents the static budget for Webb Company for April 2006 that was prepared at the end of 2005. For each line item in the income statement, Exhibit 7-1, column 1, displays data for the actual April results. For example, actual revenues are $1,250,000, and the actual selling price is $1,250,000 ÷ 10,000 jackets = $125 per jacket—compared with the budgeted selling price of $120 per jacket. Similarly, actual direct material costs are $621,600, and the direct material cost per jacket is $621,600 ÷ 10,000 = $62.16 per jacket—compared with the budgeted direct material cost per jacket of $60. We describe potential reasons and explanations for these differences as we discuss different variances throughout the chapter.

The **static-budget variance** (see Exhibit 7-1, column 2) is the difference between the actual result and the corresponding budgeted amount in the static budget.

A **favorable variance**—denoted F in this book—has the effect of increasing operating income relative to the budgeted amount. For revenue items, F means actual revenues exceed budgeted revenues. For cost items, F means actual costs are less than budgeted costs. An **unfavorable variance**—denoted U in this book—has the effect of decreasing operating income relative to the budgeted amount. Unfavorable variances are also called *adverse variances* in some countries, for example, the United Kingdom.

EXHIBIT 7-1

Static-Budget-Based Variance Analysis for Webb Company for April 2006[a]

Level 0 Analysis

Actual operating income	$ 14,900
Static-budget operating income	108,000
Static-budget variance for operating income	$ 93,100 U

Level 1 Analysis

	Actual Results (1)	Static-Budget Variances (2) = (1) – (3)	Static Budget (3)
Units sold	10,000	2,000 U	12,000
Revenues	$1,250,000	$190,000 U	$1,440,000
Variable costs			
Direct materials	621,600	98,400 F	720,000
Direct manufacturing labor	198,000	6,000 U	192,000
Variable manufacturing overhead	130,500	13,500 F	144,000
Total variable costs	950,100	105,900 F	1,056,000
Contribution margin	299,900[b]	84,100 U	384,000[c]
Fixed costs	285,000	9,000 U	276,000
Operating income	$ 14,900	$ 93,100 U	$ 108,000

$93,100 U
Static-budget variance

[a]F = favorable effect on operating income; U = unfavorable effect on operating income.
[b]Contribution margin percentage = $299,900 ÷ $1,250,000 = 24.0%.
[c]Contribution margin percentage = $384,000 ÷ $1,440,000 = 26.7%.

The unfavorable variance of $93,100 in Exhibit 7-1 for level 0 is simply calculated by subtracting static-budget operating income of $108,000 from actual operating income of $14,900:

$$\text{Static-budget variance for operating income} = \text{Actual result} - \text{Static-budget amount}$$
$$= \$14{,}900 - \$108{,}000$$
$$= \$93{,}100\ \text{U}$$

Level 1 analysis in Exhibit 7-1 provides managers with more detailed information on the static-budget variance for operating income of $93,100 U. The level 1 analysis indicates how the line items that make up operating income—revenues, individual variable costs, and fixed costs—add up to the static-budget variance of $93,100. The budgeted contribution margin percentage of 26.7% decreases to 24.0% for the actual results.

Remember, Webb only produced and sold 10,000 jackets, although managers anticipated an output of 12,000 jackets in the static budget. *Managers want to know how much of the static-budget variance is because of inaccurate forecasting of output units sold and how much is because of Webb's performance in manufacturing and selling 10,000 jackets.* Managers, therefore, create a flexible budget, which makes it possible for them to gain a more in-depth understanding of deviations from the static budget.

Flexible Budgets

2

Develop flexible budgets

... proportionately increase variable costs; keep fixed costs the same

and compute flexible-budget variances

... each flexible-budget variance is the difference between an actual result and a flexible-budget amount

and sales-volume variances

... each sales-volume variance is the difference between a flexible-budget amount and a static-budget amount

A **flexible budget** calculates budgeted revenues and budgeted costs based on *the actual output in the budget period.* The flexible budget is prepared at the end of the period (April 2006), after the actual output of 10,000 jackets is known. The flexible budget is the budget that Webb would have prepared at the start of the budget period if it had correctly forecast the actual output of 10,000 jackets. In preparing the flexible budget:

- The budgeted selling price is the same $120 per jacket used in preparing the static budget.
- The budgeted variable costs are the same $88 per jacket used in the static budget.
- The budgeted fixed costs are the same static-budget amount of $276,000 because the 10,000 jackets produced falls within the relevant range of 0 to 12,000 jackets for which fixed costs are $276,000.

The *only* difference between the static budget and the flexible budget is that the static budget is prepared for the planned output of 12,000 jackets, whereas the flexible budget is based on the actual output of 10,000 jackets. The static budget is being "flexed," or adjusted, from 12,000 jackets to 10,000 jackets. In preparing the flexible budget for 10,000 jackets, all costs are assumed to be either variable or fixed with respect to the number of jackets produced.

Webb develops its flexible budget in three steps.

Step 1: **Identify the Actual Quantity of Output.** In April 2006, Webb produced and sold 10,000 jackets.

Step 2: **Calculate the Flexible Budget for Revenues Based on Budgeted Selling Price and Actual Quantity of Output.**

$$\text{Flexible-budget revenues} = \$120 \text{ per jacket} \times 10{,}000 \text{ jackets}$$
$$= \$1{,}200{,}000$$

Step 3: **Calculate the Flexible Budget for Costs Based on Budgeted Variable Cost per Output Unit, Actual Quantity of Output, and Budgeted Fixed Costs.**

Flexible-budget variable costs	
Direct materials, $60 per jacket × 10,000 jackets	$ 600,000
Direct manufacturing labor, $16 per jacket × 10,000 jackets	160,000
Variable manufacturing overhead, $12 per jacket × 10,000 jackets	120,000
Total flexible-budget variable costs	880,000
Flexible-budget fixed costs	276,000
Flexible-budget total costs	$1,156,000

Question: If the flexible budget (FB) is based on *actual output,* which isn't known until the end of the period, how can it be a *budget*?

Answer: The FB shows the costs that should have been incurred (the budgeted costs) to achieve the actual output level. The FB is the budget managers would have prepared at the beginning of the period if they had perfectly predicted the actual output level.

EXHIBIT 7-2 **Level 2 Flexible-Budget-Based Variance Analysis for Webb Company for April 2006[a]**

Level 2 Analysis

	Actual Results (1)	**Flexible-Budget Variances (2) = (1) – (3)**	**Flexible Budget (3)**	**Sales-Volume Variances (4) = (3) – (5)**	**Static Budget (5)**
Units sold	10,000	0	10,000	2,000 U	12,000
Revenues	$1,250,000	$50,000 F	$1,200,000	$240,000 U	$1,440,000
Variable costs					
Direct materials	621,600	21,600 U	600,000	120,000 F	720,000
Direct manufacturing labor	198,000	38,000 U	160,000	32,000 F	192,000
Variable manufacturing overhead	130,500	10,500 U	120,000	24,000 F	144,000
Total variable costs	950,100	70,100 U	880,000	176,000 F	1,056,000
Contribution margin	299,900	20,100 U	320,000	64,000 U	384,000
Fixed manufacturing costs	285,000	9,000 U	276,000	0	276,000
Operating income	$ 14,900	$29,100 U	$ 44,000	$ 64,000 U	$ 108,000

Level 2 — $29,100 U Flexible-budget variance; $64,000 U Sales-volume variance

Level 1 — $93,100 U Static-budget variance

[a]F = favorable effect on operating income; U = unfavorable effect on operating income.

These three steps enable Webb to prepare a flexible budget, as shown in Exhibit 7-2, column 3. Webb uses the flexible budget to move to a level 2 variance analysis that further subdivides the $93,100 unfavorable static-budget variance for operating income.

Flexible-Budget Variances and Sales-Volume Variances

Exhibit 7-2 shows the level 2 flexible-budget-based variance analysis for Webb, which subdivides the level 1 $93,100 unfavorable static-budget variance for operating income into two parts: a flexible-budget variance of $29,100 U and a sales-volume variance of $64,000 U. The **sales-volume variance** is the difference between a flexible-budget amount and the corresponding static-budget amount. The **flexible-budget variance** is the difference between an actual result and the corresponding flexible-budget amount based on the actual output level in the budget period.

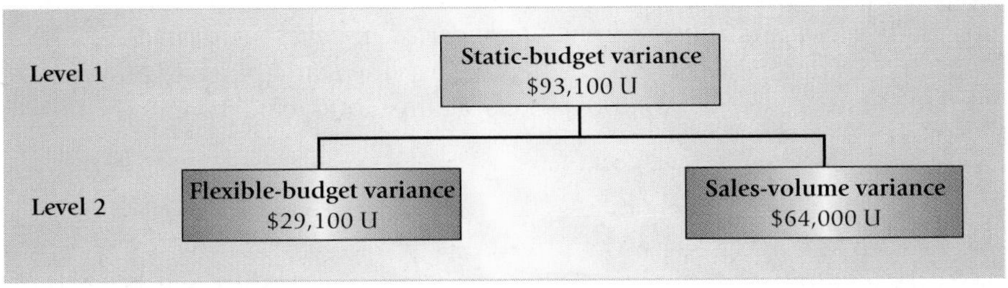

The levels of variance analysis can be likened to peeling an onion. With each deeper level of analysis, the manager peels away another layer, gaining further insight.

Sales-Volume Variances

Keep in mind that the flexible-budget amounts in column 3 of Exhibit 7-2 and the static-budget amounts in column 5 are both computed using budgeted selling prices, budgeted variable cost per jacket, and budgeted fixed costs. The difference between the static-budget and the flexible-budget amounts is called the sales-volume variance because it represents the difference caused *solely* by the difference in the 10,000 actual quantity

Sales-volume variances arise solely from the differences between the budgeted output level used to develop the static budget and the actual output level used to develop the flexible budget.

(or volume) of jackets sold and the 12,000 quantity of jackets expected to be sold in the static budget.

$$\text{Sales-volume variance for operating income} = \text{Flexible-budget amount} - \text{Static-budget amount}$$
$$= \$44{,}000 - \$108{,}000$$
$$= \$64{,}000\ \text{U}$$

The sales-volume variance in operating income for Webb measures the change in budgeted contribution margin because Webb sold only 10,000 jackets rather than the budgeted 12,000.

$$\text{Sales-volume variance for operating income} = \left(\text{Budgeted contribution margin per unit}\right) \times \left(\text{Actual units sold} - \text{Static-budget units sold}\right)$$
$$= \left(\text{Budgeted selling price} - \text{Budgeted variable cost per unit}\right) \times \left(\text{Actual units sold} - \text{Static-budget units sold}\right)$$
$$= (\$120 \text{ per jacket} - \$88 \text{ per jacket}) \times (10{,}000 \text{ jackets} - 12{,}000 \text{ jackets})$$
$$= \$32 \text{ per jacket} \times (-2{,}000 \text{ jackets})$$
$$= \$64{,}000\ \text{U}$$

Webb's managers determine that the unfavorable sales-volume variance could be because of one or more of the following reasons:

1. The overall demand for jackets is not growing at the rate that was anticipated.
2. Competitors are taking away market share from Webb.
3. Webb did not adapt quickly to changes in customer preferences and tastes.
4. Budgeted sales targets were set without careful analysis of market conditions.
5. Quality problems developed that led to customer dissatisfaction with Webb's jackets.

How Webb responds to the unfavorable sales-volume variance will be influenced by what management believes to be the cause of the variance. For example, if Webb's managers believe the unfavorable sales-volume variance was caused by market-related reasons (reasons 1, 2, 3, or 4), the sales manager would be in the best position to explain what happened and to suggest corrective actions, such as sales promotions, that may be needed. If, however, managers believe the unfavorable sales-volume variance was caused by quality problems (reason 5), the manufacturing manager would be in the best position to analyze the causes and to suggest strategies for improvement, such as changes in the manufacturing process or investments in new machines.

Exhibit 7-2, column 4, shows a sales-volume variance for each of the line items in the income statement. Separating the effects of inaccurate forecasting of output units sold—the sales-volume variance—from the static-budget variance enables managers to compare actual revenues earned and costs incurred for April 2006 against the revenues and costs Webb would have budgeted for the 10,000 jackets actually produced and sold—the flexible budget. *These flexible-budget variances are a better measure of operating performance because they compare actual revenues to budgeted revenues and actual costs to budgeted costs for the same 10,000 jackets of output.* In contrast, the static-budget variances compare actual revenues and costs for 10,000 jackets against budgeted revenues and costs for 12,000 jackets.

Flexible-Budget Variances

The first three columns of Exhibit 7-2 compare actual results with flexible-budget amounts. Flexible-budget variances are in column 2 for each line item in the income statement:

$$\text{Flexible-budget variance} = \text{Actual result} - \text{Flexible-budget amount}$$

The operating income line in Exhibit 7-2 shows the flexible-budget variance is \$29,100 U (\$14,900 − \$44,000). The \$29,100 U arises because actual selling price, actual variable cost per unit, and actual fixed costs differ from their budgeted amounts. The actual results and budgeted amounts for the selling price and variable cost per unit are:

	Actual Result	Budgeted Amount
Selling price	\$125.00 (\$1,250,000 ÷ 10,000 jackets)	\$120.00 (\$1,200,000 ÷ 10,000 jackets)
Variable cost per jacket	\$ 95.01 (\$ 950,100 ÷ 10,000 jackets)	\$ 88.00 (\$ 880,000 ÷ 10,000 jackets)

The flexible-budget variance for revenues is called the **selling-price variance** because it arises solely from the difference between the actual selling price and the budgeted selling price:

$$\text{Selling-price variance} = \left(\text{Actual selling price} - \text{Budgeted selling price}\right) \times \text{Actual units sold}$$

$$= (\$125 \text{ per jacket} - \$120 \text{ per jacket}) \times 10{,}000 \text{ jackets}$$

$$= \$50{,}000 \text{ F}$$

Webb has a favorable selling-price variance because the \$125 actual selling price exceeds the \$120 budgeted amount, which increases operating income. Marketing managers are generally in the best position to understand and explain the reason for this selling price difference. For example, was it because of better quality? Or was it because of an overall increase in market prices? Webb's managers concluded it was because of a general increase in prices.

The flexible-budget variance for total variable costs is unfavorable (\$70,100 U) for the actual output of 10,000 jackets. It's unfavorable because of one or both of the following:

- Webb used greater quantities of inputs (such as direct manufacturing labor-hours) relative to the budgeted quantities of inputs.
- Webb incurred higher prices per unit for the inputs (such as the wage rate per direct manufacturing labor-hour) relative to the budgeted prices per unit of the inputs.

Higher input quantities relative to the budget and/or higher input prices relative to the budget could be the result of Webb deciding to produce a better product than what was planned in the budget or the result of inefficiencies in Webb's manufacturing and purchasing, or both. *You should always think of variance analysis as providing suggestions for further investigation rather than as establishing conclusive evidence of good or bad performance.*

The actual fixed costs of \$285,000 are \$9,000 more than the budgeted amount of \$276,000. This higher cost decreases operating income, making this flexible-budget variance unfavorable.

In the rest of this chapter, we will focus on variable direct-cost input variances. Chapter 8 emphasizes indirect (overhead) cost variances.

Price Variances and Efficiency Variances for Direct-Cost Inputs

To gain further insight, almost all companies subdivide the level 2 flexible-budget variance for direct-cost inputs into two more-detailed variances, which are level 3 variances:

1. A price variance that reflects the difference between an actual input price and a budgeted input price
2. An efficiency variance that reflects the difference between an actual input quantity and a budgeted input quantity

Managers generally have more control over efficiency variances than price variances. That's because the quantity of inputs used is primarily affected by factors inside the company, but price changes are primarily due to market forces outside the company.

The information available from these level 3 variances helps managers to better understand past performance and take corrective actions to implement superior strategies in the future.

Obtaining Budgeted Input Prices and Budgeted Input Quantities

To calculate price and efficiency variances, Webb needs to obtain budgeted input prices and budgeted input quantities. Webb's three main sources for this information are:

1. **Actual input data from past periods.** Most companies have past data on actual input prices and actual input quantities. These past prices and quantities could be used as the budgeted prices and quantities in a flexible budget. The advantage of past data is that they represent quantities and prices that are "real" rather than hypothetical and can serve

as benchmarks for continuous improvement. Another advantage is that past data are typically available at low cost. However, there are limitations to using past data. Past data can include inefficiencies such as wastage of direct materials. Past data also do not incorporate any changes expected for the budget period.

2. **Data from other companies that have similar processes.** The benefit of using this data is that the budget numbers represent competitive benchmarks from other companies. The main difficulty of using this source is that comparable input-price and input-quantity data from other companies may not be available.

3

Explain why standard costs are often used in variance analysis

. . . standard costs exclude past inefficiencies and take into account future changes

3. **Standards developed by Webb.** A **standard** is a carefully determined price, cost, or quantity. A standard is usually expressed on a per-unit basis. Consider how Webb determines its direct labor standards. Webb conducts engineering studies to obtain a detailed breakdown of the steps required to make a jacket. Each step is assigned a standard time based on work performed by a *skilled* worker using equipment operating in an *efficient* manner. There are two advantages of using standard times: (i) they aim to exclude past inefficiencies and (ii) they aim to take into account changes expected to occur in the budget period. An example of (ii) is the decision by Webb, for strategic reasons, to lease new sewing machines that operate at a faster speed and enable output to be produced with lower defect rates. Similarly, Webb determines the standard quantity of square yards of cloth required by a skilled operator to make each jacket.

When developing standards for indirect costs, using detailed engineering studies to determine the standard times spent by support staff on different products is quite difficult. Instead, management accountants develop standard times based on interviews that identify the time spent by support staff on various activities (such as setups, supervision, and quality control) and the amount of time of each activity required by different products.

The term "standard" refers to many different things. Always clarify its meaning and how it is being used. A **standard input** is a carefully determined quantity of input—such as square yards of cloth or direct manufacturing labor-hours—required for one unit of output, such as a jacket. A **standard price** is a carefully determined price that a company expects to pay for a unit of input. In the Webb example, the standard wage rate that Webb expects to pay its operators is an example of a standard price of a direct manufacturing labor-hour. A **standard cost** is a carefully determined cost of a unit of output—for example, the standard direct manufacturing labor cost of a jacket at Webb.

$$\frac{\text{Standard cost per output unit for}}{\text{each variable direct-cost input}}\!$$

Standard cost per output unit for each variable direct-cost input = Standard input allowed for one output unit × Standard price per input unit

Standard direct material cost per jacket: 2 square yards of cloth input allowed per output unit (jacket) manufactured, at \$30 standard price per square yard

Standard direct material cost per jacket = 2 square yards × \$30 per square yard = \$60

Standard direct manufacturing labor cost per jacket: 0.8 manufacturing labor-hour of input allowed per output unit manufactured, at \$20 standard price per hour

Standard direct manufacturing labor cost per jacket = 0.8 labor-hour × \$20 per labor-hour = \$16

How are the words "budget" and "standard" related? Budget is the broader term. To clarify: Budgeted input prices, budgeted input quantities, and budgeted costs need *not* be based on standards. However, when standards *are* used to obtain budgeted input quantities and budgeted input prices, the terms "standard" and "budget" are used interchangeably. The standard quantity of each input per unit of output and the standard price of each input determine the standard, or budgeted, cost of each input per unit of output. See how the standard-cost computations for direct materials and direct manufacturing labor equal the budgeted direct material cost per jacket of \$60 and the budgeted direct manufacturing labor cost of \$16 referred to earlier (p. 222).

In its standard costing system, Webb uses standards that are attainable through efficient operations but that allow for normal disruptions. An alternative is to set more-challenging standards that are more difficult to attain. As we discussed in Chapter 6, setting challenging standards can increase motivation and performance. If, however, standards are regarded by workers as essentially unachievable, it can increase frustration and hurt performance. The Global Surveys of Company Practice feature describes the widespread use of standard costs.

GLOBAL SURVEYS OF COMPANY PRACTICE

The Widespread Use of Standard Costs

Surveys from around the world report widespread use of standard costs by manufacturers. The following data are representative of surveys conducted in nine countries:

	Percentage of Respondents Using Standard Costs in Their Accounting System
United States[a]	76%
Ireland[b]	87%
China[c]	87%
United Kingdom[d]	76%
New Zealand[d]	73%
India[e]	68%
Singapore[f]	56%
Australia[g]	92%
Japan[g]	90%

What explains the popularity of standard costs? A survey of Australian and Japanese companies reports the following purposes for using standard costs (1, most important; 7, least important):[g]

	Australia	Japan
Product costing	1	4
Budgeting	2	1
Inventory valuation	3	6
Management control	4	3
Cost control	5	2
Cost reduction	6	5
Simplification of bookkeeping	7	7

[a]Ernst & Young, "2003 Survey of Management Accounting."
[b]Clarke, "Management Accounting Practices."
[c]Firth, "The Diffusion of Managerial Accounting."
[d]Lamminmaki & Drury, "A Comparison of New Zealand and British Product-Costing Practices."
[e]Anderson & Lanen, "Economic Transition."
[f]Ghosh & Chan, "Management Accounting in Singapore."
[g]Wijewardena & De Zoysa, "A Comparative Analysis of Management Accounting Practices in Australia and Japan."
Full citations are in Appendix A at the end of the book.

Data for Calculating Webb's Price Variances and Efficiency Variances

4

Compute price variances
. . . each price variance is the difference between an actual input price and a budgeted input price

and efficiency variances
. . . each efficiency variance is the difference between an actual input quantity and a budgeted input quantity for actual output

for direct-cost categories

Consider Webb's two direct-cost categories. The actual cost for each of these categories for the 10,000 jackets manufactured and sold in April 2006 is:

Direct materials purchased and used	
1. Square yards of cloth input purchased and used	22,200
2. Actual price incurred per square yard	$28
3. Direct material costs (22,200 × $28) [shown in Exhibit 7-2, column 1]	$621,600
Direct manufacturing labor	
1. Direct manufacturing labor-hours	9,000
2. Actual price incurred per direct manufacturing labor-hour	$22
3. Direct manufacturing labor costs (9,000 × $22) [shown in Exhibit 7-2, column 1]	$198,000

For simplicity, we assume the quantity of direct materials used equals the quantity of direct materials purchased. Let's use this Webb Company data to illustrate the price variance and the efficiency variance for direct-cost inputs.

A **price variance** is the difference between actual price and budgeted price multiplied by actual input quantity, such as direct materials purchased or used. A price variance is sometimes called an **input-price variance** or **rate variance**, especially when referring to a price variance for direct labor. An **efficiency variance** is the difference between actual input quantity used—such as square yards of cloth of direct materials—and budgeted input quantity allowed for actual output, multiplied by budgeted price. An efficiency variance is sometimes called a **usage variance**.

We use a *columnar solution format* as a helpful and intuitive approach to compute variances—for example, see Exhibits 7-2 and 7-3.

Exhibit 7-3 shows how the price variance and the efficiency variance subdivide the flexible-budget variance. Consider direct materials. The direct materials flexible-budget variance of \$21,600 U is the difference between actual costs incurred (actual input quantity × actual price) of \$621,600 shown in column 1 and the flexible budget (budgeted input quantity allowed for actual output × budgeted price) of \$600,000 shown in column 3. Column 2 (actual input quantity × budgeted price) is inserted between column 1 and column 3. The difference between columns 1 and 2 is the price variance of \$44,400 F. This price variance occurs because the same actual input quantity (22,200 sq. yds.) is multiplied by *actual price* (\$28) in column 1 and *budgeted price* (\$30) in column 2. The difference between columns 2 and 3 is the efficiency variance of \$66,000 U, because the same budgeted price (\$30) is multiplied by *actual input quantity* (22,200 sq. yds) in column 2 and *budgeted input quantity allowed for actual output* (20,000 sq. yds.) in column 3. See how the direct materials price variance, \$44,400 F, plus the direct materials efficiency variance, \$66,000 U, equals the direct materials flexible-budget variance, \$21,600 U. Let's explore price variances and efficiency variances in greater detail so we can see how managers use these variances to improve their future performance.

Price Variances

The formula for computing the price variance is:

$$\text{Price variance} = \left(\text{Actual price of input} - \text{Budgeted price of input}\right) \times \text{Actual quantity of input}$$

EXHIBIT 7-3 **Columnar Presentation of Variance Analysis: Direct Costs for Webb Company for April 2006[a]**

Level 3 Analysis

	Actual Costs Incurred (Actual Input Quantity × Actual Price) (1)		**Actual Input Quantity × Budgeted Price (2)**		**Flexible Budget (Budgeted Input Quantity Allowed for Actual Output × Budgeted Price) (3)**
Direct Materials	(22,200 sq. yds. × \$28/sq. yd.) \$621,600		(22,200 sq. yds. × \$30/sq. yd.) \$666,000		(10,000 units × 2 sq. yds./unit × \$30/sq. yd.) \$600,000
Level 3		\$44,400 F Price variance		\$66,000 U Efficiency variance	
Level 2			\$21,600 U Flexible-budget variance		
Direct Manufacturing Labor	9,000 hours × \$22/hr. \$198,000		9,000 hours × \$20/hr. \$180,000		10,000 units × 0.8 hrs./unit × \$20/hr. \$160,000
Level 3		\$18,000 U Price variance		\$20,000 U Efficiency variance	
Level 2			\$38,000 U Flexible-budget variance		

[a]F = favorable effect on operating income; U = unfavorable effect on operating income.

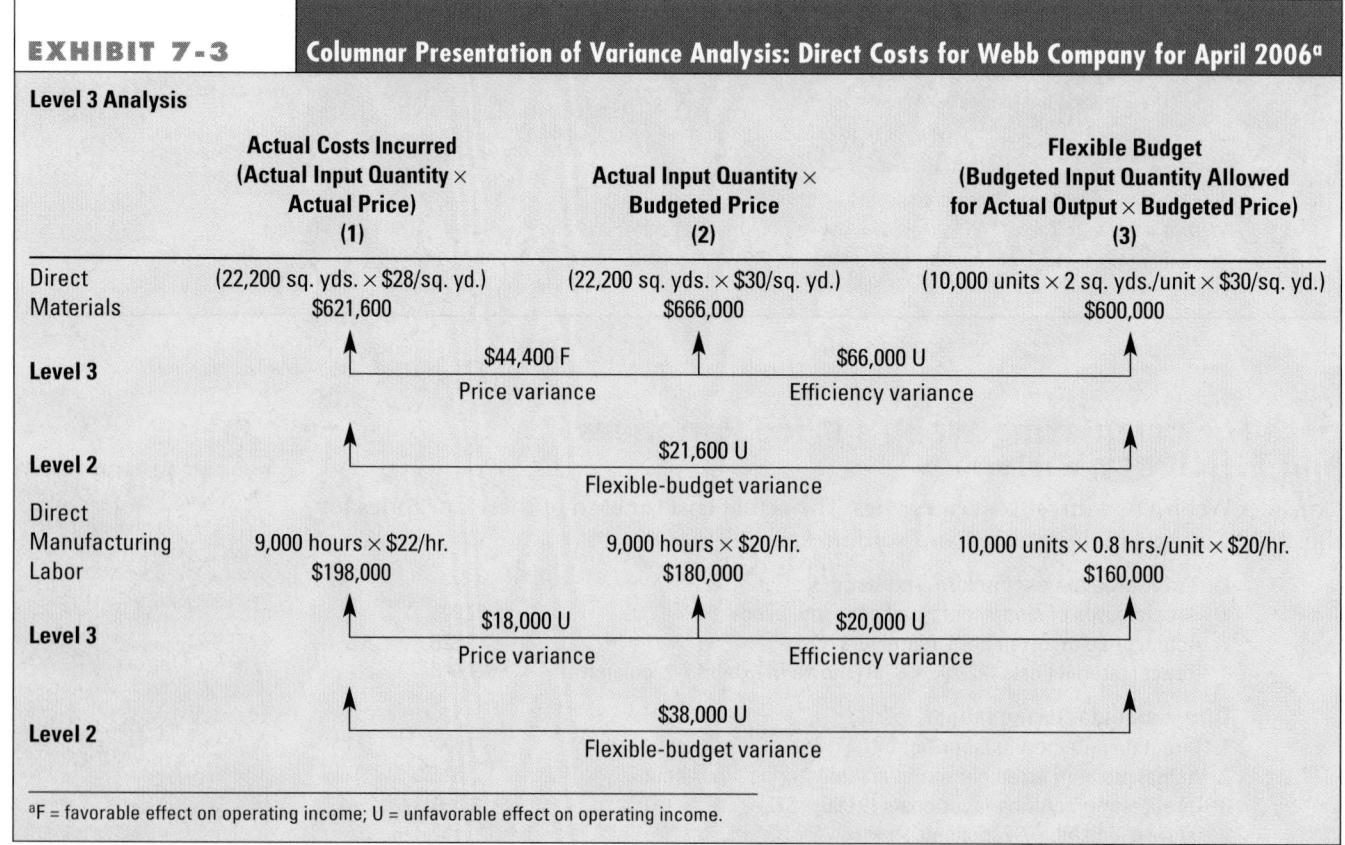

Price variances for Webb's two direct-cost categories are:

Direct-Cost Category	(Actual price of input − Budgeted price of input)	×	Actual quantity of input	=	Price Variance
Direct materials	($28 per sq. yard − $30 per sq. yard)	×	22,200 square yards	=	$44,400 F
Direct manufacturing labor	($22 per hour − $20 per hour)	×	9,000 hours	=	18,000 U

The direct materials price variance is favorable because actual price of cloth is less than budgeted price, resulting in an increase in operating income. The direct manufacturing labor price variance is unfavorable because actual wage rate paid to labor is more than the budgeted rate, resulting in a decrease in operating income.

Always consider a broad range of possible causes for a price variance. For example, Webb's favorable direct materials price variance could be because of one or more of the following:

- Webb's purchasing manager negotiated the direct materials prices more skillfully than was planned for in the budget.
- The purchasing manager changed to a lower-price supplier.
- Webb's purchasing manager ordered larger quantities than the quantities budgeted, thereby obtaining quantity discounts.
- Direct material prices decreased unexpectedly because of, say, industry oversupply.
- Budgeted purchase prices of direct materials were set too high without careful analysis of market conditions.
- The purchasing manager received favorable prices because he was willing to accept unfavorable terms on factors other than prices (such as lower-quality material).

Webb's response to a direct materials price variance depends on what is believed to be the cause of the variance. Assume Webb's managers attribute the favorable price variance to the purchasing manager ordering in larger quantities than budgeted, thereby receiving quantity discounts. Webb could examine if purchasing in these larger quantities resulted in higher storage costs. If the increase in storage and inventory holding costs exceeds the quantity discounts, purchasing in larger quantities is not beneficial. Some companies have reduced their materials storage areas to prevent their purchasing managers from ordering in larger quantities.

Efficiency Variance

For any actual level of output, the efficiency variance is the difference between actual quantity of input used and budgeted quantity of input allowed to produce actual output, multiplied by budgeted price:

$$\text{Efficiency Variance} = \left(\begin{array}{c}\text{Actual}\\ \text{quantity of}\\ \text{input used}\end{array} - \begin{array}{c}\text{Budgeted quantity}\\ \text{of input allowed}\\ \text{for actual output}\end{array}\right) \times \begin{array}{c}\text{Budgeted price}\\ \text{of input}\end{array}$$

The idea here is that a company is inefficient if it uses a larger quantity of input than the budgeted quantity for actual output units produced; the company is efficient if it uses a smaller quantity of inputs than budgeted for actual output units produced.

The efficiency variances for each of Webb's direct-cost categories are:

Direct-Cost Category	(Actual quantity of input used − Budgeted quantity of input allowed for actual output)	×	Budgeted price of input	=	Efficiency Variance
Direct materials	[22,200 sq. yds. − (10,000 units × 2 sq. yds./unit)]	×	$30 per sq. yard		
	= (22,200 sq. yds. − 20,000 sq. yds.)	×	$30 per sq. yard	=	$66,000 U
Direct manuf. labor	[9,000 hours − (10,000 units × 0.8 hour/unit)]	×	$20 per hour		
	= (9,000 hours − 8,000 hours)	×	$20 per hour	=	20,000 U

The two manufacturing efficiency variances—direct materials efficiency variance and direct manufacturing labor efficiency variance—are each unfavorable because more input was used than was budgeted, resulting in a decrease in operating income.

The flexible budget for inputs is based on the *budgeted quantity of inputs allowed for the actual output level (BQIA).* To understand BQIA in the Webb example, distinguish *inputs* (square yards of cloth, direct manufacturing labor-hours) from *output* (jackets). BQIA is computed by multiplying the actual quantity of output produced times how much of each input should have been used per output unit.

CONCEPTS IN ACTION

Weapons Against Waste: Variance Analysis at Sandoz

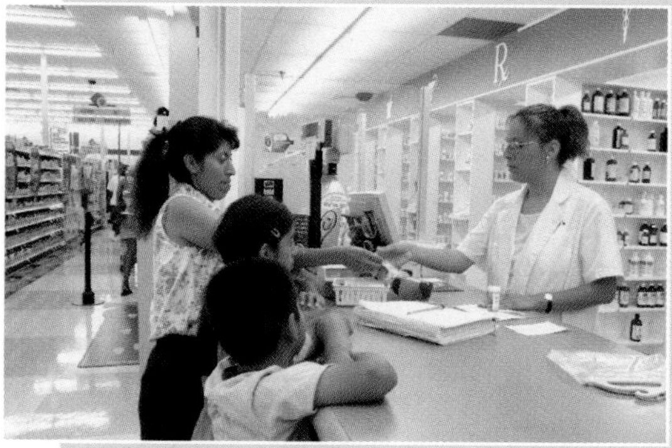

Sandoz US, a subsidiary of Swiss-based Novartis AG, develops generic pharmaceutical substitutes for market-leading therapeutic drugs. To ensure success, Sandoz must develop and deliver its products to wholesalers and retailers at the lowest possible cost. Because the generic drug industry is so competitive, an intricate understanding of product costs is critical. Variance analysis helps managers assess and maintain product profitability.

At its Broomfield, Colorado, manufacturing facility, Sandoz uses standard costs, based on the recipes for each product, to predict the costs associated with producing batches of each generic drug. To monitor and control costs, the plant controller regularly reviews detailed costing information received from the managers on the production floor. The plant controller then uses variance analysis to improve operations. Variance analysis helps support improvements in the manufacturing process, forecast financial results, and set manufacturing standards. Most importantly, it also helps managers find the root cause of process deficiencies. Let's take a closer look at how Sandoz's managers use variance analysis.

Materials cost variances are reviewed on a weekly basis and are analyzed in terms of yield loss. Yield loss is a measure of direct materials efficiency—that is, the difference between the actual quantity of materials used and the expected quantity of materials that should have been used.

Each week, management accountants at Sandoz analyze which products have the top dollar value and the highest volume of yield losses. They forward their findings to production for review, and year-to-date trends are examined by engineers and scientists to determine if changes in processes, materials, and equipment are necessary or if the standards that have been set require modification. Maintaining accurate standards is important because managers use standards to plan direct materials purchases. Inaccuracies about direct material requirements could lead to direct material stockouts, cycle time increases, and customer back orders.

But direct material costs are not the only costs getting attention. Consider direct manufacturing labor costs. Management accountants calculate a standard direct manufacturing labor rate for each manufacturing area (for example, mixing, blending, tableting, and packaging). Managers then review direct manufacturing labor efficiency variances, and management accountants report and track products and work centers with consistently high unfavorable variances. Teams of workers analyze root causes and recommend process and equipment enhancements to improve direct manufacturing labor efficiency and to make standard labor-time adjustments. Accurate labor-time standards are critical because they drive direct manufacturing labor staffing levels.

How has variance analysis and standard costing helped Sandoz? Over the years, the plant has decreased yield and destruction losses, enhancing the company's ability to deliver products that meet customers' expectations and contributing significantly to overall profitability.

Source: Conversations with and documents prepared by Eric Evans and Erich Erchr on March 20, 2004, and May 28, 2004.

As with price variances, there is a broad range of possible causes for these efficiency variances (see also the Concepts in Action feature above). For example, Webb's unfavorable efficiency variance for direct manufacturing labor could be because of one or more of the following:

- Webb's personnel manager hired underskilled workers.
- Webb's production scheduler inefficiently scheduled work, resulting in more manufacturing labor time than budgeted being used per jacket.
- Webb's maintenance department did not properly maintain machines, resulting in more manufacturing labor time than budgeted being used per jacket.
- Budgeted time standards were set too tight without careful analysis of the operating conditions and the employees' skills.

Suppose Webb's managers determine that the unfavorable variance is because of poor machine maintenance. Webb may then establish a team consisting of plant engineers and machine operators to develop a maintenance schedule that will reduce future breakdowns and thereby prevent adverse effects on labor time and product quality.

Summary of Variances

Exhibit 7-4 provides a summary of the level 1, 2, and 3 variances. Note how the variances in level 3 aggregate to the variances in level 2 and how the variances in level 2 aggregate to the variances in level 1.

The following computations show why actual operating income is $14,900 when the static budget operating income is $108,000. The numbers in the computations can be found in Exhibits 7-2 and 7-3.

Static budget operating income			$108,000
Unfavorable sales-volume variance for operating income			(64,000)
Flexible-budget operating income			44,000
Flexible-budget variances for operating income:			
Favorable selling-price variance		$ 50,000	
Direct materials variances:			
Favorable direct materials price variance	$ 44,400		
Unfavorable direct materials efficiency variance	(66,000)		
Unfavorable direct materials variance		(21,600)	
Direct manufacturing labor variances:			
Unfavorable direct manufacturing labor price variance	(18,000)		
Unfavorable direct manufacturing labor efficiency variance	(20,000)		
Unfavorable direct manufacturing labor variance		(38,000)	
Unfavorable variable manufacturing overhead variance		(10,500)	
Unfavorable fixed manufacturing overhead variance		(9,000)	
Unfavorable flexible-budget variance for operating income			(29,100)
Actual operating income			$ 14,900

The summary of variances highlights three main effects.

1. Webb sold 2,000 fewer units than budgeted, resulting in an unfavorable sales-volume variance of $64,000. Sales declined because of quality problems and new styles of jackets introduced by Webb's competitors.
2. Webb sold units at a higher price than budgeted, resulting in a favorable selling-price variance of $50,000. Webb's prices, however, were lower than the prices charged by Webb's competitors.
3. Manufacturing costs for the actual output produced were higher than budgeted—direct materials by $21,600; direct manufacturing labor by $38,000; variable manufacturing overhead by $10,500; and fixed manufacturing overhead by $9,000—because of poor quality of cloth, poor maintenance of machines, and underskilled workers.

We now present Webb's journal entries under its standard costing system.

EXHIBIT 7-4 **Summary of Levels 1, 2, and 3 Variance Analysis**

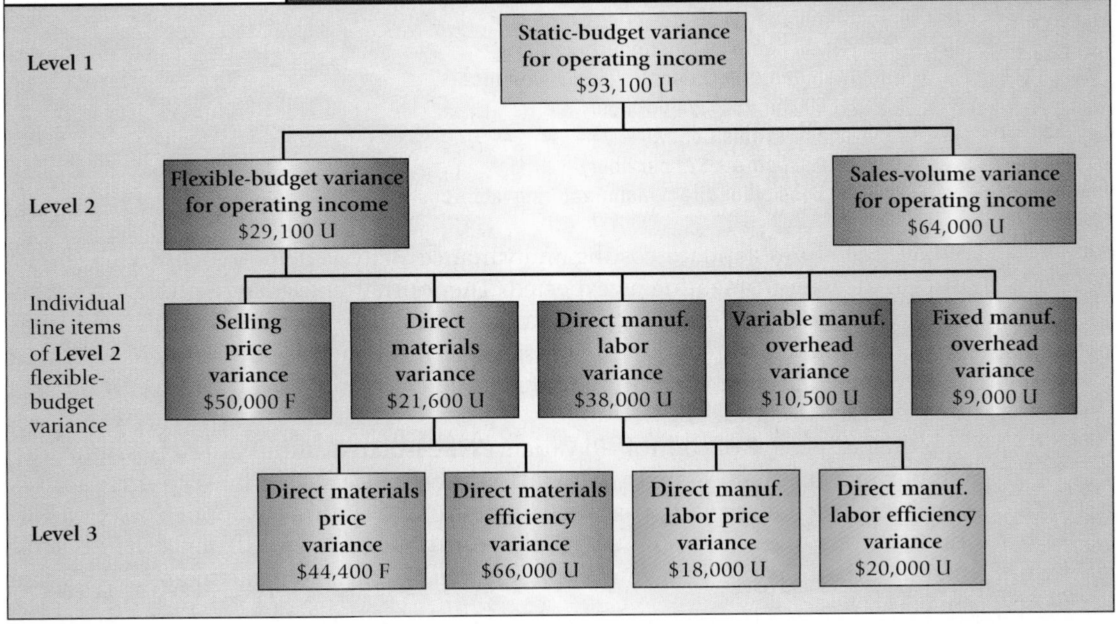

Journal Entries Using Standard Costs

Chapter 4 illustrated journal entries when normal costing is used. We will now illustrate journal entries for Webb Company using standard costs. Our focus is on direct materials and direct manufacturing labor. All the numbers included in the following journal entries are found in Exhibit 7-3.

Note: In each of the following entries, unfavorable variances are always debits (they decrease operating income), and favorable variances are always credits (they increase operating income).

JOURNAL ENTRY 1A: Isolate the direct materials price variance at the time of purchase by increasing (debiting) Direct Materials Control at standard prices. This is the earliest time possible to isolate this variance.

Unfavorable variances reduce operating income, so they're recorded as debits, like expenses. Favorable variances increase operating income, so they're recorded as credits, like revenues (or contra expenses).

1a. Direct Materials Control		
(22,200 square yards × \$30 per square yard)	666,000	
Direct Materials Price Variance		
(22,200 square yards × \$2 per square yard)		44,400
Accounts Payable Control		
(22,200 square yards × \$28 per square yard)		621,600
To record direct materials purchased.		

JOURNAL ENTRY 1B: Isolate the direct materials efficiency variance at the time the direct materials are used by increasing (debiting) Work-in-Process Control at standard quantities allowed for actual output units manufactured times standard prices.

1b. Work-in-Process Control		
(10,000 jackets × 2 yards per jacket × \$30 per square yard)	600,000	
Direct Materials Efficiency Variance		
(2,200 square yards × \$30 per square yard)	66,000	
Direct Materials Control		
(22,200 square yards × \$30 per square yard)		666,000
To record direct materials used.		

JOURNAL ENTRY 2: Isolate the direct manufacturing labor price variance and efficiency variance at the time this labor is used by increasing (debiting) Work-in-Process Control at standard quantities allowed for actual output units manufactured at standard prices. Note that Wages Payable Control measures the actual amounts payable to workers based on actual hours worked and actual wage rates.

Unlike materials, labor cannot be stored for future use, so there is only one journal entry for both the purchase and use of direct manufacturing labor.

2. Work-in-Process Control		
(10,000 jackets × 0.80 hour per jacket × \$20 per hour)	160,000	
Direct Manufacturing Labor Price Variance		
(9,000 hours × \$2 per hour)	18,000	
Direct Manufacturing Labor Efficiency Variance		
(1,000 hours × \$20 per hour)	20,000	
Wages Payable Control		
(9,000 hours × \$22 per hour)		198,000
To record liability for direct manufacturing labor costs.		

Recall from Chapter 4 that under both actual costing and normal costing, direct materials and direct manufacturing labor are calculated at actual costs.

We have seen how standard costing and variance analysis help to focus management attention on areas not operating as expected. The journal entries here point to another advantage of standard costing systems—that is, standard costs simplify product costing. As each unit is manufactured, costs are assigned to it using the standard cost of direct materials, the standard cost of direct manufacturing labor and, as you will see in Chapter 8, standard overhead cost.

From the perspective of control, all variances are isolated at the earliest possible time. For example, by isolating the direct materials price variance at the time of purchase, corrective actions—such as seeking cost reductions from the current supplier or obtaining price quotes from other potential suppliers—can be taken immediately when a large unfavorable variance is first known rather than waiting until after the materials are used in production.

At the end of the fiscal year, the variance accounts are written off to cost of goods sold if they are immaterial in amount. For simplicity, we assume that the balances in the different direct cost variance accounts as of April 2006 are also the balances at the end of 2006 and therefore immaterial in total. Webb would record the following journal entry to write off the direct cost variance accounts to Cost of Goods Sold.

Cost of goods sold	59,600	
Direct Materials Price Variance	44,400	
Direct Materials Efficiency Variance		66,000
Direct Manufacturing Labor Price Variance		18,000
Direct Manufacturing Labor Efficiency Variance		20,000

Alternatively, assuming Webb has inventories at the end of the fiscal year, the variance accounts are prorated between cost of goods sold and various inventory accounts using the methods described in Chapter 4 (pp. 119–121). For example, Direct Materials Price Variance is prorated among Materials Control, Work-in-Process Control, Finished Goods Control and Cost of Goods Sold on the basis of the standard costs of direct materials in each account's ending balance. Direct Materials Efficiency Variance is prorated among Work-in-Process Control, Finished Goods Control and Cost of Goods Sold on the basis of the direct material costs in each account's ending balance (after proration of the direct materials price variance).

Many accountants, industrial engineers, and managers maintain that to the extent that variances measure inefficiency or abnormal efficiency during the year, they should be written off instead of being prorated among inventories and cost of goods sold. This reasoning argues for applying a combination of the write-off and proration methods for each individual variance. Consider the efficiency variance. The portion of the efficiency variance that is due to inefficiency and could have been avoided should be written off to cost of goods sold while the portion that is unavoidable should be prorated. If another variance, such as the direct materials price variance, is considered unavoidable because it is entirely caused by general market conditions, it should be prorated. Unlike full proration, this approach avoids carrying the costs of inefficiency as part of inventoriable costs.

Study Tip: To check your understanding of direct-cost variances, see the Featured Exercises 1 and 2, true–false statements 1 and 6, multiple-choice questions 1 and 7, and Review Exercise 1 (*Student Guide*, beginning on p. 77.) Fully explained answers begin on page 84.

Implementing Standard Costing

Standard costing provides valuable information for the management and control of materials, labor, and other activities related to production.

Standard Costing and Information Technology

Modern information technology promotes the increased use of standard costing systems for product costing and control. Companies such as Dell and Sandoz (the manufacturer of generic pharmaceuticals) store standard prices and standard quantities in their computer systems. A bar code scanner records the receipt of materials, immediately costing each material using its stored standard price. The receipt of materials is then matched with the purchase order to record accounts payable and to isolate the direct materials price variance.

The direct materials efficiency variance is calculated as output is completed by comparing the standard quantity of direct materials that should have been used with the computerized request for direct materials submitted by an operator on the production floor. Labor variances are calculated as employees log into production-floor terminals and punch in their employee numbers, start and end times, and the quantity of product they helped produce. Managers use this instantaneous feedback from variances to initiate immediate corrective action, as needed.

Wide Applicability of Standard Costing

Companies that have implemented total quality management and computer-integrated manufacturing (CIM) systems, as well as companies in the service sector, find standard costing to be a useful tool. Companies implementing total quality management programs use standard costing to control materials costs. Service-sector companies such as

Total quality management, and CIM systems are described in Chapter 1 (p. 6 and p. 4, respectively).

McDonald's are labor intensive and use standard costs to control labor costs. Companies that have implemented CIM, such as Toyota, use flexible budgeting and standard costing to manage activities such as materials handling and setups.

Management Uses of Variances

Managers and management accountants use variances to evaluate performance, to trigger organization learning, and to make continuous improvements. But in doing so, managers must recognize that variances can have multiple causes.

Multiple Causes of Variances

Managers must not interpret variances in isolation of each other. The causes of variances in one part of the value chain can be the result of decisions made in another part of the value chain. Consider an unfavorable direct materials efficiency variance on Webb's production line. Possible operational causes of this variance across the value chain of the company are:

1. Poor design of products or processes
2. Poor work on the production line because of underskilled workers or faulty machines
3. Inappropriate assignment of labor or machines to specific jobs
4. Congestion due to scheduling a large number of rush orders from Webb's sales representatives
5. Webb's suppliers not manufacturing cloth materials of uniformly high quality

Item 5 offers an even broader reason for the cause of the unfavorable direct materials efficiency variance by considering inefficiencies in the supply chain of companies—in this case, by the cloth suppliers for Webb's jackets. Whenever possible, managers must attempt to understand the root causes of the variances.

When to Investigate Variances

Investigating variances entails activities ranging from phone calls and e-mails to engineering analyses of the production processes, which can be expensive. Detailed investigation is warranted only when the expected benefits (for example, reduced costs or better decisions because of more-accurate data) exceed the expected costs of the investigation.

Managers realize that a standard is not a single measure but rather a range of possible acceptable input quantities, costs, output quantities, or prices. Consequently, they expect small variances to arise. A variance within an acceptable range is considered to be an "in-control occurrence" and calls for no investigation or action by managers. So when would managers need to investigate variances?

Frequently, managers investigate variances based on subjective judgments or rules of thumb. For critical items, such as product defects, even a small variance may prompt investigations and actions. For other items, such as direct material costs, labor costs, and repair costs, companies generally have rules such as "investigate all variances exceeding $5,000 or 25% of budgeted cost, whichever is lower." The idea is that a 4% variance in direct material costs of $1 million—a $40,000 variance—deserves more attention than a 20% variance in repair costs of $10,000—a $2,000 variance. Variance analysis is subject to the same cost-benefit test as all other phases of a management control system.

5

Understand how managers use variances

. . . managers use variances to improve future performance

Performance Measurement Using Variances

Managers often use variance analysis when evaluating the performance of their subordinates. Two attributes of performance are commonly evaluated:

1. **Effectiveness:** the degree to which a predetermined objective or target is met—for example, sales, customer satisfaction, and quality of Motorola's new line of cell phones.
2. **Efficiency:** the relative amount of inputs used to achieve a given output level—the smaller the quantity of inputs used to make a given number of cell phones or the greater the number of cell phones made from a given quantity of input, the greater the efficiency.

Killing a fly with a sledge hammer is effective but not efficient. Killing a fly with a fly swatter is both effective and efficient.

As we discussed earlier, managers must be sure they understand the causes of a variance before using it for performance evaluation. Suppose a Webb purchasing manager has just negotiated a deal that results in a favorable price variance for direct materials. The deal could have achieved a favorable variance for any or all of the following reasons:

1. The purchasing manager bargained effectively with suppliers.
2. The purchasing manager secured a discount for buying in bulk with fewer purchase orders. However, buying larger quantities than necessary for the short run resulted in excessive inventory.

3. The purchasing manager accepted a bid from the lowest-priced supplier after only minimal effort to check quality amid concerns about the supplier's materials.

If the purchasing manager's performance is evaluated solely on price variances, then the evaluation will be positive. Reason 1 would support this favorable conclusion: The purchasing manager bargained effectively. Reasons 2 and 3 have short-run gains, buying in bulk or making only minimal effort to check the supplier's quality-monitoring procedures. However, these short-run gains could be offset by higher inventory storage costs or higher inspection costs and defect rates on Webb's production line, leading to unfavorable direct manufacturing labor and direct materials efficiency variances. Webb may ultimately lose more money because of reasons 2 and 3 than it gains from the favorable price variance. *Bottom line: Managers should not automatically interpret a favorable variance as "good news."*

Managers benefit from variance analysis because it highlights individual aspects of performance. However, if any single performance measure (for example, a labor efficiency variance or a consumer rating report) receives excessive emphasis, managers will tend to make decisions that will cause the particular performance measure to look good. These actions may conflict with the company's overall goals, inhibiting the goals from being achieved. This faulty perspective on performance usually arises when top management designs a performance evaluation and reward system that does not emphasize total company objectives.

Organization Learning

The goal of variance analysis is for managers to understand why variances arise, to learn, and to improve future performance. For instance, to reduce the unfavorable direct materials efficiency variance, Webb's managers may seek improvements in product design, in the commitment of workers to do the job right the first time, and in the quality of supplied materials, among other improvements. Sometimes an unfavorable direct materials efficiency variance may signal a need to change product strategy, perhaps because the product cannot be made at a low enough cost. Variance analysis should not be a tool to "play the blame game" (that is, seeking a person to blame for every unfavorable variance). Rather, it should help the company learn about what happened and how to perform better in the future.

Managers need to strike a delicate balance between the two uses of variances we have discussed: performance evaluation and organization learning. Variance analysis is helpful for performance evaluation, but an overemphasis on performance evaluation and meeting individual variance targets can undermine learning and continuous improvement. Why? Because achieving the standard becomes an end in and of itself. As a result, managers will seek targets that are easy to attain rather than targets that are challenging and that require creativity and resourcefulness. For example, if performance evaluation is overemphasized, Webb's manufacturing manager will prefer an easy standard that allows workers ample time to manufacture a jacket; he will then have little incentive to improve processes and methods to reduce manufacturing time and cost.

An overemphasis on performance evaluation may also cause managers to take actions to achieve the budget and avoid an unfavorable variance, even if such actions could hurt the company in the long run. For example, the manufacturing manager may push workers to produce jackets within the time allowed, even if this action could lead to poorer quality jackets being produced, which could later hurt revenues. Such negative impacts are less likely to occur if variance analysis is seen as a way of promoting organization learning. (See the Focus on Values and Behaviors feature, p. 238.)

Continuous Improvement

Managers can also use variance analysis to create a virtuous cycle of continuous improvement. How? By repeatedly identifying causes of variances, initiating corrective actions, and evaluating results of actions. Improvement opportunities are often easier to identify when products are first produced. Once the easy opportunities have been identified ("the low-hanging fruit picked"), much more ingenuity may be required to identify successive improvement opportunities. Some companies use kaizen budgeting (Chapter 6, p. 195) to specifically target reductions in budgeted costs over successive periods. The advantage of kaizen budgeting is that it makes continuous improvement goals explicit.

There is a trade-off between pushing for too much continuous improvement and the motivational problems associated with judging performance against a goal that workers perceive to be unattainable. Management must recognize that the rate of improvement will likely decrease over time, after the "easy" improvements are achieved first.

FOCUS ON VALUES AND BEHAVIORS

STARBUCKS, McDONALD'S, AND JOHNSON & JOHNSON: MAKING GOOD USE OF VARIANCES

There aren't many accounting processes that generate as much interest and anxiety among managers as analyzing reports comparing actual performance with budgeted performance. That's because managers are accountable for achieving their negotiated budgets and don't want to be perceived as a failure among their colleagues. But the main goal of variance analysis is not to fix blame but to learn, and it's ultimately the responsibility of top managers and management accountants to set the right tone so improvements can be made. Managers at Starbucks, for example, are responsible for making sure that each new store's sales meet or exceed expectations. This is not a small task. In March 2004, projected corporate sales growth was 12%, contributing to an overall monthly revenue increase of $494 million. Starbucks currently has 8,000 stores globally and plans to grow to around 25,000 locations worldwide, approaching McDonald's in its number of retail outlets. Management accountants at the company are intimately involved in establishing budgeted performance and monitoring actual performance for each of the company's stores.

Whether it's Starbucks, McDonald's, or any other major corporation, management accountants must be able to provide managers with clear and precise explanations for variances. They must do so in a thoughtful, constructive, and helpful way. Instead of simply pointing out problems, they need to understand the reasons for the variances and help develop solutions and action plans for tackling the issues. Rather than focusing only on negative performance, management accountants should also discuss the positive outcomes. Ideally, variances should be addressed by teams so that there is shared responsibility and accumulation of ideas from all areas of the organization. McDonald's, for example, established a systemwide response to upgrading its coffee offerings due to increased competition from Starbucks.

Another organization in which management accountants take a learning approach to variance analysis is Johnson & Johnson, the giant pharmaceutical and consumer products company. Johnson & Johnson conducts business via hundreds of subsidiary companies within a highly decentralized structure. Management accountants in these subsidiary companies use variances to help managers discover and correct problems. This is often done in meetings that bring together the entire senior management team of the subsidiary company. A Johnson & Johnson executive remarked that "managers are forced to review their businesses in depth for costs, trends, manufacturing efficiency, marketing plans, and their competitive situation. Program and action plans result. . . . These meetings force us to think about how we should respond and to look at both the upside and downside of changes in the business. They really get our creative juices flowing."

Variance analyses are critical to an organization's success. Management accountants must never waver from accurately presenting the numbers and from persuading managers to be realistic about performance. Learning from past mistakes and implementing corrective action plans quickly can happen only when management accountants are successful in their roles as motivators, communicators, and team players.

Sources: *Allison Linn, "Starbucks Lays Out Aggressive Growth Plans,"* Seattle Post-Intelligence, *March 30, 2004; "Schaeffer's Market Observation Features Starbucks: SBUX," Businesswire.com, April 1, 2004; Andy Serwer, "Starbucks to Go,"* Fortune, *January 26, 2004; R. Simons,* Codman and Shurtleff Inc.: Planning and Control System, *Harvard Business School case number 9-187-081.*

To control the process, the supervisor cannot wait for an accounting report with variances reported in dollars. Instead he uses personal observation and timely nonfinancial performance measures. For example, a Nissan plant compiles data such as defect rates and production-schedule attainment and broadcasts them in ticker-tape fashion on screens throughout the plant.

Even though lower-level control depends primarily on nonfinancial performance measures, there are two reasons why these results need to be reported in dollars: (1) to compare different variances for performance evaluation and strategic planning and (2) to decide which variance to investigate.

Financial and Nonfinancial Performance Measures

Almost all companies use a combination of financial and nonfinancial performance measures for planning and control rather than relying exclusively on either type of measure. In Webb's cutting room, cloth is laid out and cut into pieces, which are then matched and assembled. Managers exercise control in the cutting room by observing workers and by focusing on *nonfinancial measures,* such as number of square yards of cloth used to produce 1,000 jackets or percentage of jackets started and completed without requiring any rework. Production workers at Webb find these nonfinancial measures easy to understand. At the same time, production managers at Webb will likely also use *financial measures* to evaluate the overall cost efficiency with which operations are being run and to help guide decisions about, say, changing the mix of inputs used in manufacturing jackets. Financial measures are often critical in a company because they indicate the economic impact of diverse physical activities in a way that allows managers to make trade-offs—increase the costs of one physical activity (say, cutting) to reduce the costs of another physical measure (say, defects).

We next describe how the management insights gained from standard costing and variance analysis are helpful to companies that use activity-based costing systems.

Variance Analysis and Activity-Based Costing

Activity-based costing (ABC) systems focus on individual activities as the fundamental cost objects. ABC systems classify the costs of various activities into a cost hierarchy—output unit-level costs, batch-level costs, product-sustaining costs, and facility-sustaining costs (see pp. 147–148). In this section, we show how a company that has an ABC system and batch-level direct costs can benefit from variance analysis. Batch-level costs are the costs of activities related to a group of units of products or services rather than to each individual unit of product or service.

6 **Perform variance analysis in activity-based costing systems**
... by comparing budgeted costs and actual costs of activities

Relating Batch Costs to Product Output

Consider Lyco Brass Works, which manufactures many different types of faucets and brass fittings. Because of the wide range of products it produces, Lyco uses an activity-based costing system. In contrast, Webb uses a simple costing system because it makes only one type of jacket. One of Lyco's products is Elegance, a decorative brass faucet for home spas. Lyco produces Elegance in batches. For each product Lyco makes, it uses dedicated materials-handling labor to bring materials to the production floor, transport work in process from one work center to the next, and take the finished goods to the shipping area. Therefore, materials-handling labor costs for Elegance are direct costs of Elegance. Because the materials for a batch are moved together, materials-handling labor costs vary with number of batches rather than with number of units in a batch. Materials-handling labor costs are variable direct batch-level costs.

Information regarding Elegance for 2007 follows:

	Static-Budget Amount	Actual Result
1. Units of Elegance produced and sold	180,000	151,200
2. Batch size (units per batch)	150	140
3. Number of batches (Line 1 ÷ Line 2)	1,200	1,080
4. Materials-handling labor-hours per batch	5	5.25
5. Total materials-handling labor-hours (Line 3 × Line 4)	6,000	5,670
6. Cost per materials-handling labor-hour	$14	$14.50
7. Total materials-handling labor costs (Line 5 × Line 6)	$84,000	$ 82,215

To prepare the flexible budget for materials-handling labor costs, Lyco starts with the actual units of output produced, 151,200 units, and proceeds with the following steps.

Step 1: Using Budgeted Batch Size, Calculate the Number of Batches That Should Have Been Used to Produce Actual Output. At the budgeted batch size of 150 units per batch, Lyco should have produced the 151,200 units of output in 1,008 batches (151,200 units ÷ 150 units per batch).

Step 2: Using Budgeted Materials-Handling Labor-Hours per Batch, Calculate the Number of Materials-Handling Labor-Hours That Should Have Been Used. At the budgeted quantity of 5 hours per batch, 1,008 batches should have required 5,040 materials-handling labor-hours (1,008 batches × 5 hours per batch).

Step 3: Using Budgeted Cost per Materials-Handling Labor-Hour, Calculate the Flexible-Budget Amount for Materials-Handling Labor-Hours. The flexible-budget amount is 5,040 materials-handling labor-hours × $14 budgeted cost per materials-handling labor-hour = $70,560.

Note how the flexible-budget calculations for materials-handling labor costs focus on batch-level quantities (materials-handling labor-hours per batch rather than per unit). The flexible-budget variance for materials-handling labor costs can then be calculated as:

$$\text{Flexible-budget variance} = \text{Actual costs} - \text{Flexible-budget costs}$$

$$= (5{,}670 \text{ hours} \times \$14.50 \text{ per hour}) - (5{,}040 \text{ hours} \times \$14 \text{ per hour})$$

$$= \$82{,}215 - \$70{,}560$$

$$= \$11{,}655 \text{ U}$$

The unfavorable variance indicates that materials-handling labor costs were $11,655 higher than the flexible-budget target.

Price and Efficiency Variances

We can get some insight into the possible reasons for this $11,655 unfavorable variance by examining the price and efficiency components of the flexible-budget variance.

$$\text{Price variance} = \left(\begin{matrix}\text{Actual price} \\ \text{of input}\end{matrix} - \begin{matrix}\text{Budgeted price} \\ \text{of input}\end{matrix}\right) \times \begin{matrix}\text{Actual quantity} \\ \text{of input}\end{matrix}$$
$$= (\$14.50 \text{ per hour} - \$14 \text{ per hour}) \times 5{,}670 \text{ hours}$$
$$= \$0.50 \text{ per hour} \times 5{,}670 \text{ hours}$$
$$= \$2{,}835 \text{ U}$$

The unfavorable price variance for materials-handling labor indicates that the $14.50 actual cost per materials-handling labor-hour exceeds the $14.00 budgeted cost per materials-handling labor-hour. This variance could be the result of Lyco's human resources manager negotiating wage rates less skillfully or of wage rates increasing unexpectedly due to scarcity of labor.

$$\text{Efficiency variance} = \left(\begin{matrix}\text{Actual} \\ \text{quantity of} \\ \text{input used}\end{matrix} - \begin{matrix}\text{Budgeted quantity} \\ \text{of input allowed} \\ \text{for actual output}\end{matrix}\right) \times \begin{matrix}\text{Budgeted} \\ \text{price} \\ \text{of input}\end{matrix}$$
$$= (5{,}670 \text{ hours} - 5{,}040 \text{ hours}) \times \$14 \text{ per hour}$$
$$= 630 \text{ hours} \times \$14 \text{ per hour}$$
$$= \$8{,}820 \text{ U}$$

The unfavorable efficiency variance indicates that the 5,670 actual materials-handling labor-hours exceeded the 5,040 budgeted materials-handling labor-hours for actual output. Possible reasons for the unfavorable efficiency variance are:

- Smaller actual batch sizes of 140 units, instead of the budgeted batch sizes of 150 units, resulting in Lyco producing the 151,200 units in 1,080 batches instead of 1,008 (151,200 ÷ 150) batches
- Higher actual materials-handling labor-hours per batch of 5.25 hours instead of budgeted materials-handling labor-hours of 5 hours

Reasons for smaller-than-budgeted batch sizes could include quality problems when batch sizes exceed 140 faucets and high costs of carrying inventory.

Possible reasons for larger actual materials-handling labor-hours per batch are:

- Inefficient layout of the Elegance production line
- Materials-handling labor having to wait at work centers before picking up or delivering materials
- Unmotivated, inexperienced, and underskilled employees
- Very tight standards for materials-handling time

Identifying the reasons for the efficiency variance helps Lyco's managers develop a plan for improving materials-handling labor efficiency.

Focus on Hierarchy

Flexible-budget quantity computations focus at the appropriate level of the cost hierarchy. For example, because materials handling is a batch-level cost, the flexible-budget quantity calculations are made at the batch level—the quantity of materials-handling labor-hours that Lyco should have used based on the number of batches it should have used to produce the actual quantity of 151,200 units. If a cost had been a product-sustaining cost—such as product design cost—the flexible-budget quantity computations would focus at the product-sustaining level, for example, by evaluating the actual complexity of product design relative to the budget.

Benchmarking and Variance Analysis

7 **Describe benchmarking and how it is used in cost management**

. . . benchmarking compares actual performance against the best levels of performance

The budgeted amounts in the Webb Company and Lyco Brass Works illustrations are based on analysis of operations within their own respective companies. We now turn to the situation in which companies develop standards based on an analysis of operations at other companies. **Benchmarking** is the continuous process of comparing the levels of performance in producing products and services and executing activities against the best levels of performance in competing companies or in companies having similar processes. When benchmarks are used as standards, managers and management accountants know that the company will be competitive in the marketplace if it can attain the standards.

Companies develop benchmarks and calculate variances on items that are the most important to their businesses. For example, McDonald's calculates average waiting-to-order time, order-delivery time, and window time for their drive-through lines.

Consider the cost per available seat mile (ASM) for United Airlines; ASMs equal the total seats in a plane multiplied by the distance travelled. Assume United uses data from each of nine competing U.S. airlines in its benchmark cost comparisons. Summary data are in Exhibit 7-5. The benchmark companies are ranked from lowest to highest cost per ASM in column 1. Also reported in Exhibit 7-5 are revenue per ASM, gross margin per ASM, labor cost per ASM, fuel cost per ASM, and total available seat miles (a measure of airline size).

How well did United manage its costs? The answer depends on which specific benchmark is being used for comparison. United's actual cost of $0.1104 per ASM is above the average cost of $0.0992 per ASM of the nine other airlines. However, United's cost per ASM is 82% higher than JetBlue Airways, the lowest-cost competitor at $0.0608 per ASM [($0.1104 − $0.0608) ÷ $0.0608 = 82%)]. So why is United's cost per ASM so high? Column 4 suggests that labor cost is one reason ($0.0385 for United compared with $0.0196 for JetBlue). These benchmarking data alert management at United that they need to cut labor costs to become more cost competitive with their lower-cost competitors.

Finding appropriate benchmarks is a major issue in implementing benchmarking. Many companies purchase benchmark data from consulting firms.

Using benchmarks such as those in Exhibit 7-5 is not without problems. For example, one problem is ensuring the benchmark numbers are comparable. In other words, there needs to be an "apples to apples" comparison. Differences can exist across companies in their strategies, inventory costing methods, depreciation methods, and so on. For example, JetBlue serves fewer cities and has mostly long-haul flights compared with United, which serves almost all major U.S. cities and several international cities and has both long-haul and short-haul flights. Southwest Airlines differs from United because it specializes in short-haul direct flights and offers fewer services on board its planes. Because United's strategy is different from the strategies of JetBlue and Southwest, one might expect its cost per ASM to be different too. United's strategy is more comparable to the strategies of American, Continental, Delta, Northwest, and U.S. Airways. Note that its costs per ASM are more competitive with these airlines. But United competes head-to-head

EXHIBIT 7-5 **Available Seat Mile (ASM) Benchmark Comparison of United Airlines with Nine Other Airlines**

Airline	Cost per ASM (1)	Revenue per ASM (2)	Gross Margin per ASM (3) = (2) – (1)	Labor Cost per ASM (4)	Fuel Cost per ASM (5)	Total ASMs (Millions) (6)
United Airlines	$0.1104	$0.1006	–$0.0098	$0.0385	$0.0152	136,630
Airlines used as benchmarks:						
JetBlue Airways	$0.0608	$0.0732	$0.0124	$0.0196	$0.0108	13,639
Southwest Airlines	$0.0760	$0.0827	$0.0067	$0.0310	$0.0116	71,790
America West Airlines	$0.0794	$0.0786	–$0.0008	$0.0234	$0.0131	27,888
Delta Airlines	$0.1048	$0.0970	–$0.0078	$0.0472	$0.0144	134,383
Northwest Airlines	$0.1103	$0.1073	–$0.0030	$0.0441	$0.0175	88,593
Continental Airlines	$0.1106	$0.1132	$0.0026	$0.0390	$0.0160	78,385
American Airlines	$0.1107	$0.1056	–$0.0051	$0.0440	$0.0168	165,209
Alaska Airlines	$0.1184	$0.1175	–$0.0009	$0.0451	$0.0088	17,341
U.S. Airways	$0.1220	$0.1178	–$0.0042	$0.0459	$0.0143	58,017
Average of airlines used as benchmarks	$0.0992	$0.0992	$0.0000	$0.0377	$0.0137	72,805

Source: Individual companies' 10-K reports. All data are for the year ending December 31, 2003.

with JetBlue and Southwest in several cities and markets, so it still needs to benchmark against these carriers as well.

United's management accountants can use benchmarking data to address several questions. How do plane size and type, duration of flights, and so on affect the cost per ASM? Do airlines differ in their fixed cost/variable cost structures? Can performance be improved by rerouting flights, using different types of aircraft on different routes, or changing the frequency or timing of specific flights? What explains revenue differences per ASM across airlines? Is it differences in perceived quality of service or differences in competitive power at specific airports? Management accountants are more valuable to managers when they use benchmarking data to provide insight into *why* costs or revenues differ across companies, or within plants of the same company, as distinguished from simply reporting the magnitude of such differences.

PROBLEM FOR SELF-STUDY

O'Shea Company manufactures ceramic vases. It uses its standard costing system when developing its flexible-budget amounts. In April 2007, 2,000 finished units were produced. The following information is related to its two direct manufacturing cost categories: direct materials and direct manufacturing labor.

Direct materials used were 4,400 kilograms (kg). The standard direct materials input allowed for one output unit is 2 kilograms at $15 per kilogram. O'Shea purchased 5,000 kilograms of materials at $16.50 per kilogram, a total of $82,500. (This Problem for Self-Study illustrates how to calculate direct materials variances when the quantity of materials *purchased* in a period differs from the quantity of materials *used* in that period.)

Actual direct manufacturing labor-hours were 3,250, at a total cost of $66,300. Standard manufacturing labor time allowed is 1.5 hours per output unit, and the standard direct manufacturing labor cost is $20 per hour.

Required

1. Calculate the direct materials price variance and efficiency variance, and the direct manufacturing labor price variance and efficiency variance. Base the direct materials price variance on a flexible budget for *actual quantity purchased*, but base the direct materials efficiency variance on a flexible budget for *actual quantity used*.
2. Prepare journal entries for a standard costing system that isolates variances at the earliest possible time.

SOLUTION

1. Exhibit 7-6 shows how the columnar presentation of variances introduced in Exhibit 7-3 can be adjusted for the difference in timing between purchase and use of materials. Note, in particular, the two sets of computations in column 2 for direct materials—the $75,000 for direct materials purchased and the $66,000 for direct materials used. The direct materials price variance is calculated on purchases so that managers responsible for the purchase can immediately identify and isolate reasons for the variance and initiate any desired corrective action. The efficiency variance is the responsibility of the production manager, so this variance is identified only at the time materials are used.

2\.

Materials Control (5,000 kg × $15 per kg)	75,000	
Direct Materials Price Variance (5,000 kg × $1.50 per kg)	7,500	
Accounts Payable Control (5,000 kg × $16.50 per kg)		82,500
Work in Process Control (2,000 units × 2 kg per unit × $15 per kg)	60,000	
Direct Materials Efficiency Variance (400 kg × $15 per kg)	6,000	
Materials Control (4,400 kg × $15 per kg)		66,000
Work in Process Control (2,000 units × 1.5 hours per unit × $20 per hour)	60,000	
Direct Manufacturing Labor Price Variance (3,250 hours × $0.40 per hour)	1,300	
Direct Manufacturing Labor Efficiency Variance (250 hours × $20 per hour)	5,000	
Wages Payable Control (3,250 hours × $20.40 per hour)		66,300

Note: All the variances are debits because they are unfavorable and therefore reduce operating income.

EXHIBIT 7-6 Columnar Presentation of Variance Analysis for O'Shea Company: Direct Materials and Direct Manufacturing Labor for April 2007[a]

Level 3 Analysis

	Actual Costs Incurred (Actual Input Quantity × Actual Price) (1)		Actual Input Quantity × Budgeted Price (2)		Flexible Budget (Budgeted Input Quantity Allowed for Actual Output × Budgeted Price) (3)
Direct Materials	(5,000 kg × $16.50/kg) $82,500	$7,500 U Price variance	(5,000 kg × $15.00/kg) $75,000 (4,400 kg × $15.00/kg) $66,000	$6,000 U Efficiency variance	(2,000 units × 2 kg/unit × $15.00/kg) $60,000
Direct Manufacturing Labor	(3,250 hrs. × $20.40/hr.) $66,300	$1,300 U Price variance	(3,250 hrs. × $20.00/hr.) $65,000	$5,000 U Efficiency variance	(2,000 units × 1.50 hrs./unit × $20.00/hr.) $60,000

[a]F = favorable effect on operating income; U = unfavorable effect on operating income.

DECISION POINTS

The following question-and-answer format summarizes the chapter's learning objectives. Each decision presents a key question related to a learning objective. The guidelines are the answer to that question.

Decision	Guidelines
1. How does a flexible budget differ from a static budget, and why should companies use flexible budgets?	A static budget is based on the level of output planned at the start of the budget period. A flexible budget is adjusted (flexed) to recognize the actual output level of the budget period. Flexible budgets help managers gain more insight into the causes of variances than is available from static budgets.
2. How can managers develop a flexible budget and compute the flexible-budget variance and the sales-volume variance?	Managers use a three-step procedure to develop a flexible budget. When all costs are either variable with respect to output units or fixed, these three steps require only information about budgeted selling price, budgeted variable cost per output unit, budgeted fixed costs, and actual quantity of output units. The static-budget variance can be subdivided into a flexible-budget variance (the difference between an actual result and the corresponding flexible-budget amount) and a sales-volume variance (the difference between the flexible-budget amount and the corresponding static-budget amount).
3. What is a standard cost, and what are its purposes?	A standard cost is a carefully determined cost based on efficient operations. The purposes of a standard cost are to exclude past inefficiencies and to take into account changes expected to occur in the budget period.
4. Why should a company calculate price and efficiency variances?	The computation of price and efficiency variances helps managers gain insight into two different—but not independent—aspects of performance. The price variance focuses on the difference between actual input price and budgeted input price. The efficiency variance focuses on the difference between actual quantity of input and budgeted quantity of input allowed for actual output.
5. How do managers use variances?	Managers use variances for performance evaluation, organization learning, and continuous improvement. When using variances for these purposes, managers consider several variances together rather than focusing only on an individual variance.

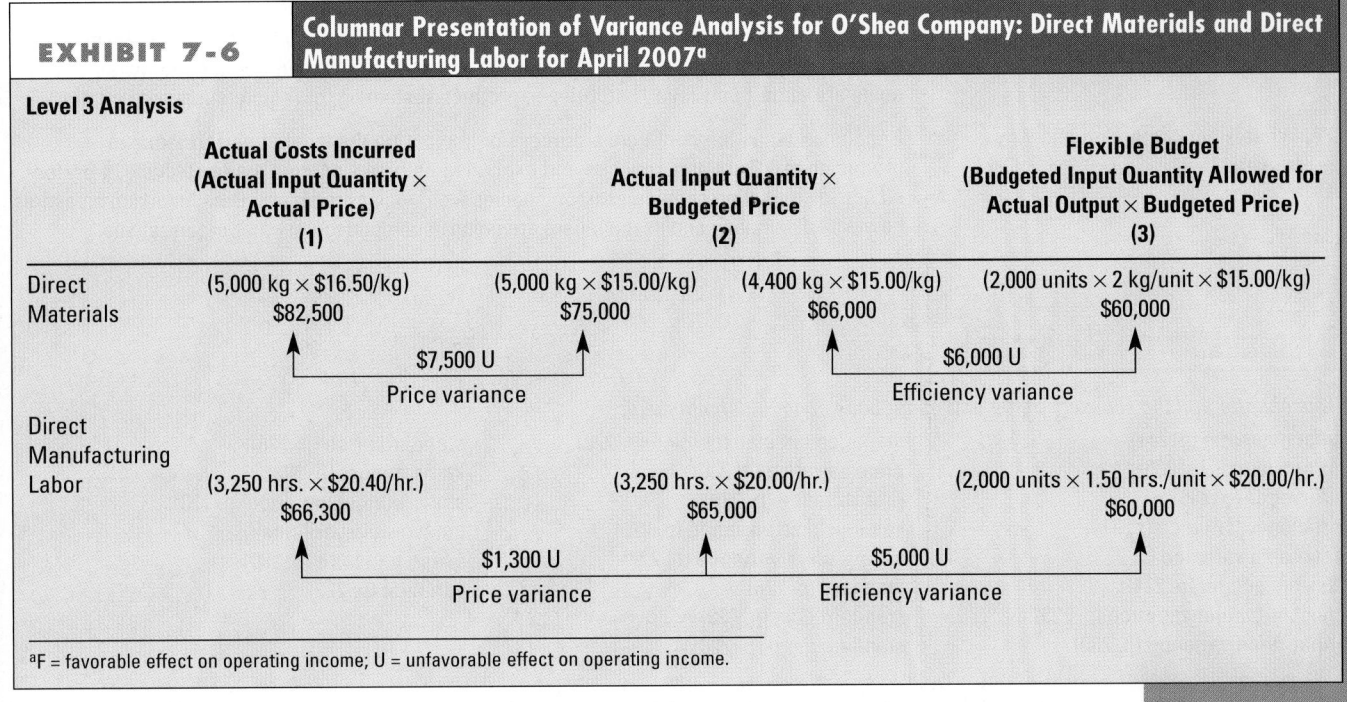

6. Can variance analysis be used with an activity-based costing system?

Variance analysis can be applied to activity costs (such as setup costs) to gain insight into why actual activity costs differ from activity costs in the static budget or in the flexible budget. Interpreting cost variances for different activities requires understanding whether the costs are output unit-level, batch-level, product-sustaining, or facility-sustaining costs.

7. What is benchmarking and why is it useful?

Benchmarking is the continuous process of comparing the level of performance in producing products and services and executing activities against the best levels of performance in competing companies or companies with similar processes. Benchmarking measures how well a company and its managers are doing in comparison to other organizations.

TERMS TO LEARN

This chapter and the Glossary at the end of the book contain definitions of:

benchmarking (p. 241)
effectiveness (p. 236)
efficiency (p. 236)
efficiency variance (p. 230)
favorable variance (p. 223)
flexible budget (p. 224)
flexible-budget variance (p. 225)
input-price variance (p. 230)
management by exception (p. 222)
price variance (p. 230)
rate variance (p. 230)
sales-volume variance (p. 225)
selling-price variance (p. 227)
standard (p. 228)
standard cost (p. 228)
standard input (p. 228)
standard price (p. 228)
static budget (p. 223)
static-budget variance (p. 223)
unfavorable variance (p. 223)
usage variance (p. 230)
variance (p. 222)

PH Grade Assist

Prentice Hall Grade Assist (PHGA)
Your professor may ask you to complete selected exercises and problems in Prentice Hall Grade Assist (PHGA). PHGA is an online tool that can help you master the chapter's topics. It provides you with multiple variations of exercises and problems designated by the PHGA icon. You can rework these exercises and problems—each time with new data—as many times as you need. You also receive immediate feedback and grading.

ASSIGNMENT MATERIAL

Questions

7-1 What is the relationship between management by exception and variance analysis?

7-2 What are two possible sources of information a company might use to compute the budgeted amount in variance analysis?

7-3 Distinguish between a favorable variance and an unfavorable variance.

7-4 What is the key difference between a static budget and a flexible budget?

7-5 Why might managers find a level 2 flexible-budget analysis more informative than a level 1 static-budget analysis?

7-6 Describe the steps in developing a flexible budget.

7-7 List four reasons for using standard costs.

7-8 How might a manager gain insight into the causes of a flexible-budget variance for direct materials?

7-9 List three causes of a favorable direct materials price variance.

7-10 Describe three reasons for an unfavorable direct manufacturing labor efficiency variance.

7-11 How does variance analysis help in continuous improvement?

7-12 Why might an analyst examining variances in the production area look beyond that business function for explanations of those variances?

7-13 Comment on the following statement made by a plant manager: "Meetings with my plant accountant are frustrating. All he wants to do is pin the blame on someone for the many variances he reports."

7-14 How can variances be used to analyze costs in individual activity areas?

7-15 "Benchmarking against other companies enables a company to identify the lowest-cost producer. This amount should become the performance measure for next year." Do you agree?

Exercises

7-16 Flexible budget. Brabham Enterprises manufactures tires for the Formula I motor racing circuit. For August 2006, it budgeted to manufacture and sell 3,000 tires at a variable cost of $74 per tire and total fixed costs of $54,000. The budgeted selling price was $110 per tire. Actual results in August 2006 were 2,800 tires manufactured and sold at a selling price of $112 per tire. The actual total variable costs were $229,600, and the actual total fixed costs were $50,000.

Required

1. Prepare a performance report (akin to Exhibit 7-2, p. 225) that uses a flexible budget and a static budget.
2. Comment on the results in requirement 1.

7-17 Flexible budget. Connor Company's budgeted prices for direct materials, direct manufacturing labor, and direct marketing (distribution) labor per attaché case are $40, $8, and $12, respectively. The president is pleased with the following performance report:

	Actual Costs	Static Budget	Variance
Direct materials	$364,000	$400,000	$36,000 F
Direct manufacturing labor	78,000	80,000	2,000 F
Direct marketing (distribution) labor	110,000	120,000	10,000 F

Actual output was 8,800 attaché cases. Assume all three direct-cost items above are variable costs.

Required

Is the president's pleasure justified? Prepare a revised performance report that uses a flexible budget and a static budget.

7-18 Flexible-budget preparation and analysis. Bank Management Printers, Inc., produces luxury checkbooks with three checks and stubs per page. Each checkbook is designed for an individual customer and is ordered through the customer's bank. The company's operating budget for September 2007 included these data:

Number of checkbooks	15,000
Selling price per book	$20
Variable cost per book	$8
Fixed costs for the month	$145,000

The actual results for September 2007 were:

Number of checkbooks produced and sold	12,000
Average selling price per book	$21
Variable cost per book	$7
Fixed costs for the month	$150,000

The executive vice president of the company observed that the operating income for September was much less than anticipated, despite a higher-than-budgeted selling price and a lower-than-budgeted variable cost per unit. As the company's management accountant, you have been asked to provide explanations for the disappointing September results.

Bank Management develops its flexible budget on the basis of budgeted per-output-unit revenue and per-output-unit variable costs without detailed analysis of budgeted inputs.

Required

1. Prepare a level 1 analysis of the September performance.
2. Prepare a level 2 analysis of the September performance.
3. Why might Bank Management find the level 2 analysis more informative than the level 1 analysis? Explain your answer.

7-19 Flexible budget, working backward. The Spencer Company designs and manufactures ball bearings for extreme-performance machinery. The following table is a partially complete level 2 variance analysis for Spencer Company for the year ended December 31, 2007.

Excel Lab
www.prenhall.com/horngren/cost12e

	A	B	C	D	E	F
1		**Performance Report, Year Ended December 31, 2007**				
2		**Actual Results**	**Flexible-Budget Variances**	**Flexible Budget**	**Sales-Volume Variances**	**Static Budget**
3		**(1)**	**(2) = (1) - (3)**	**(3)**	**(4) = (3) - (5)**	**(5)**
4	Units sold	650,000	______	______	______	600,000
5	Revenues (sales)	$3,575,000				$2,100,000
6	Variable costs	2,575,000	______	______	______	1,200,000
7	Contribution margin	1,000,000				900,000
8	Fixed costs	700,000	______	______	______	600,000
9	Operating income	$ 300,000	______	______	______	$ 300,000
10						
11		↑		↑		↑
12	Level 2		Flexible-budget variance		Sales-volume variance	
13		↑				↑
14	Level 1			Static-budget variance		

If you want to use Excel to solve this exercise, go to the Excel Lab at **www.prenhall.com/horngren/cost12e** and download the template for Exercise 7-19.

Required

1. Complete the analysis in the preceding table. Calculate all the required variances. (If your work is accurate, you will find that the total static-budget variance is $0.)
2. What are the actual and budgeted selling prices? What are the actual and budgeted variable costs per unit?
3. Jack Spence, CEO, was delighted with the lack of a static-budget variance. Is his reaction appropriate? Review the variances you have calculated and discuss possible causes and potential problems.
4. What is the most important lesson of this exercise?

Excel Lab
www.prenhall.com/horngren/cost12e

7-20 Flexible-budget and sales volume variances. Marron, Inc., produces the basic fillings used in many popular frozen desserts and treats—vanilla and chocolate ice creams, puddings, meringues, and fudge. Marron uses standard costing and carries over no inventory from one month to the next. The ice cream product group's results for June 2007 were:

	A	B	C
1	**Performance Report, June 2007**		
2		**Actual Results**	**Static Budget**
3	Units (pounds)	525,000	500,000
4	Revenues	$3,360,000	$3,250,000
5	Variable manufacturing costs	1,890,000	1,750,000
6	Contribution margin	$1,470,000	$1,500,000
7			

Ted Levine, the business manager for ice cream products, is pleased that more pounds of ice cream were sold than budgeted and that revenues were up. Unfortunately, variable manufacturing costs went up too. The bottom line is that contribution margin declined by $30,000, which is less than 1% of the budgeted revenues of $3,250,000. Overall, Levine feels that the business is running fine.

If you want to use Excel to solve this exercise, go to the Excel Lab at **www.prenhall.com/horngren/cost12e** and download the template for Exercise 7-20.

Required

1. Calculate the static-budget variance in units, revenues, variable manufacturing costs, and contribution margin? What percentage is each static-budget variance relative to its static-budget amount?
2. Break down each static-budget variance into a flexible-budget variance and a sales-volume variance (level 2 analysis).
3. Calculate the selling-price variance?
4. Assume the role of management accountant at Marron. How would you present the results to Ted Levine? Should he be more concerned? If so, why?

7-21 Price and efficiency variances. Peterson Foods manufactures pumpkin scones. For January 2007, it budgeted to purchase and use 15,000 pounds of pumpkin at $0.89 a pound. Actual purchases and usage for January 2007 were 16,000 pounds at $0.82 a pound. It budgets for 60,000 pumpkin scones. Actual output was 60,800 pumpkin scones.

Required

1. Compute the flexible-budget variance.
2. Compute the price and efficiency variances.
3. Comment on the results in requirements 1 and 2.

7-22 Materials and manufacturing labor variances. Consider the following data collected for Great Homes, Inc.:

	Direct Materials	Direct Manufacturing Labor
Cost incurred: actual inputs × actual prices	$200,000	$90,000
Actual inputs × standard prices	214,000	86,000
Standard inputs allowed for actual output × standard prices	225,000	80,000

Required

Compute the price, efficiency, and flexible-budget variances for direct materials and direct manufacturing labor.

PH Grade Assist

7-23 Price and efficiency variances. CellOne is a cellular phone service reseller. CellOne contracts with major cellular operators for airtime in bulk and then resells service to retail customers. CellOne budgeted to sell 7,800,000 minutes in the month ended March 31, 2007. Actual minutes sold totaled only 7,500,000. Due to fluctuations in hourly usage, CellOne "overbuys" airtime from cellular operators. CellOne plans to buy 10% more airtime than it plans to sell. For example, CellOne's budget called for the purchase of 8,580,000 minutes, based on the plan to sell 7,800,000 minutes. In what follows, think of purchased airtime as direct materials.

CellOne budgets purchased airtime to cost 4.5 cents per minute. Actual purchased airtime in 2007 averaged 5.0 cents per minute. CellOne incurs direct labor costs due to the employment of technicians. One hour of technical support is required for every 5,000 minutes of airtime sold. In practice, only 1,600 hours of technical support were used. Technical support was planned at $60 per hour. Actual technical support costs averaged $62 per hour.

Required

1. Calculate the flexible-budget variance for direct materials and direct labor costs. [Use the 8,250,000 (7,500,000 × 1.10) minutes in the flexible budget.]
2. Calculate the price and efficiency variances for direct materials and labor costs.

7-24 Direct materials and direct manufacturing labor variances. GloriaDee, Inc., designs and manufactures T-shirts. It sells its T-shirts to brand-name clothes retailers in lots of one dozen. GloriaDee's June 2007 static budget and actual results for direct inputs are:

Static Budget

Number of T-shirt lots (1 lot = 1 dozen)	500
Per lot of T-shirts:	
Direct materials	12 meters at $1.50 per meter = $18.00
Direct manufacturing labor	2 hours at $8.00 per hour = $16.00

Actual Results

Number of T-shirt lots sold	550
Total direct inputs:	
Direct materials	7,260 meters at $1.75 per meter = $12,705
Direct manufacturing labor	1,045 hours at $8.10 per hour = $8,464.50

GloriaDee has a policy of analyzing all input variances when they add up to more than 10% of the total cost of materials and labor in the flexible budget, and this is true in June 2007. The production manager discusses the sources of the variances: "A new type of material was purchased in June. This led to faster cutting and sewing, but the workers used more material than usual as they learned to work with it. For now, the standards are fine."

Required

1. Calculate the direct materials and direct manufacturing labor price and efficiency variances in June 2007. What is the total flexible-budget variance for both inputs (direct materials and direct manufacturing labor) combined? What percentage is this variance of the total cost of direct materials and direct manufacturing labor in the flexible budget?
2. Gloria Denham, the CEO, is concerned about the input variances. But, she likes the quality and feel of the new material and agrees to use it for one more year. In June 2008, GloriaDee again produces 550 lots of T-shirts. Relative to June 2007, 2% less direct material is used, direct material price is down 5%, and 2% less direct manufacturing labor is used. Labor price has remained the same as in June 2007. Calculate the direct materials and direct manufacturing labor price and efficiency variances in June 2008. What is the total flexible-budget variance for both inputs (direct materials and direct manufacturing labor) combined? What percentage is this variance of the total cost of direct materials and direct manufacturing labor in the flexible budget?
3. Comment on the June 2008 results. Would you continue the "experiment" of using the new material?

7-25 Price and efficiency variances, journal entries. Chemical, Inc., has set up the following standards per finished unit for direct materials and direct manufacturing labor:

Direct materials: 10 lbs. at $3 per lb.	$30.00
Direct manufacturing labor: 0.5 hours at $20 per hour	10.00

The number of finished units budgeted for March 2007 was 10,000; 9,810 units were actually produced.

Actual results in March 2007 were:

Direct materials: 98,073 lbs. used	
Direct manufacturing labor: 4,900 hours	$102,900

Assume that there was no beginning inventory of either direct materials or finished units.

During the month, materials purchases amounted to 100,000 lbs., at a total cost of $310,000. Input-price variances are isolated upon purchase. Input-efficiency variances are isolated at the time of usage.

Required

1. Compute the March 2007 price and efficiency variances of direct materials and direct manufacturing labor.
2. Prepare journal entries to record the variances in requirement 1.
3. Comment on the March 2007 price and efficiency variances of Chemical, Inc.
4. Why might Chemical, Inc., calculate direct materials price variances and direct materials efficiency variances with reference to different points in time?

7-26 Continuous improvement (continuation of 7-25). Chemical, Inc., adopts a continuous-improvement approach to setting monthly standard costs. Assume the standard direct material cost of $30 per unit and the standard direct manufacturing labor cost of $10 per unit pertain to January 2007. The standard quantities for February 2007 are 0.997 of the standard quantities for January. The standard quantities for March 2007 are 0.997 of the standard quantities for February 2007. Assume the same information for March 2007 as in Exercise 7-25, except for these revised standard quantities.

Required

1. Compute the March 2007 standard quantities for direct materials and direct manufacturing labor.
2. Compute the March 2007 price and efficiency variances for direct materials and direct manufacturing labor.

7-27 Materials and manufacturing labor variances, standard costs. Consider the following selected data regarding the manufacture of a line of upholstered chairs:

	Standards per Chair
Direct materials	2 square yards of input at $10 per square yard
Direct manufacturing labor	0.5 hour of input at $20 per hour

The following data were compiled regarding *actual performance:* actual output units (chairs) produced, 20,000; square yards of input purchased and used, 37,000; price per square yard, $10.20; direct manufacturing labor costs, $176,400; actual hours of input, 9,000; labor price per hour, $19.60.

Required

1. Show computations of price and efficiency variances for direct materials and direct manufacturing labor. Give a plausible explanation of why each variance occurred.
2. Suppose 60,000 square yards of materials were purchased (at $10.20 per square yard), even though only 37,000 square yards were used. Suppose further that variances are identified at their most timely control point; accordingly, direct materials price variances are isolated and traced at the time of purchase to the Purchasing Department rather than to the Production Department. Compute the price and efficiency variances under this approach.

7-28 Journal entries and T-accounts (continuation of 7-27). Prepare journal entries and post them to T-accounts for all transactions in Exercise 7-27, including requirement 2. Summarize in three sentences how these journal entries differ from the normal-costing entries described in Chapter 4, pages 111–117.

7-29 Flexible budget. (Refer to data in Exercise 7-27). Suppose the static budget was for 24,000 units of output. The general manager is thrilled about the following report:

	Actual Results	Static Budget	Variance
Direct materials	$377,400	$480,000	$102,600 F
Direct manufacturing labor	$176,400	$240,000	$63,600 F

Required

Is the manager's glee warranted? Prepare a report that provides a more-detailed explanation of why the static budget was not achieved. Actual output was 20,000 units.

PH Grade Assist

7-30 Activity-based costing, flexible-budget variances for finance-function activities. Josh Sanchez is the chief financial officer of Bouquets.com, an Internet company that enables customers to order deliveries of flowers by accessing its Web site. Sanchez is concerned with the efficiency and effectiveness of the finance function. He collects the following information for three finance activities in 2007:

			Rate per Unit of Cost Driver	
Activity	**Activity Level**	**Cost Driver**	**Static Budget**	**Actual**
Receivables	Output unit	Remittances	$0.639	$0.75
Payables	Batch	Invoices	2.900	2.80
Travel expenses	Batch	Travel claims	7.600	7.40

The output measure is the number of deliveries, which is the same as the number of remittances. The following is additional information.

	Static-Budget Amounts	Actual Amounts
Number of deliveries	1,000,000	948,000
Batch size in terms of deliveries:		
Payables	5	4.468
Travel expenses	500	501.587

Required

1. Calculate the flexible-budget variance for each activity in 2007.
2. Calculate the price and efficiency variances for each activity in 2007.

7-31 Price and efficiency variances, benchmarking. Garden Art Co. produces molded plastic garden pots and other plastic containers. In June 2007, Garden Art produces 1,000 lots (each lot is 12 dozen pots) of its most popular line of pots, the 14-inch "Grecian urns," at each of its two plants, which are located in Mineola and Bayside. The production manager, Joyce Montel, asks her assistant, Kevin Cheriton, to find out the precise per-unit budgeted variable costs at the two plants and the variable costs of a competitor, Miraclo, who offers similar-quality urns at cheaper prices. Cheriton pulls together the following information for each lot:

Per lot	Mineola Plant	Bayside Plant	Miraclo
Direct materials	13.50 lbs. @ $9.20 per lb.	14.00 lbs. @ $9.00 per lb.	13.00 lbs. @ $8.80 per lb.
Direct labor	3 hrs. @ $10.15 per hr.	2.7 hrs. @ $10.20 per hr.	2.5 hrs. @ $10.00 per hr.
Variable overhead	$12 per lot	$11 per lot	$11 per lot

Required

1. What is the budgeted variable cost per lot at the Mineola Plant, the Bayside Plant, and at Miraclo?
2. Using the Miraclo data as the standards, calculate the direct materials and direct manufacturing labor price and efficiency variances for the Mineola and Bayside plants.
3. What advantage does Garden Art get by using Miraclo's benchmark data as standards in calculating its variances? Identify two issues that Montel should keep in mind in using the Miraclo benchmark data as the standards.

Problems

7-32 Flexible budget, direct materials and direct manufacturing labor variances. Tuscany Statuary manufactures bust statues of famous historical figures. All statues are the same size. Each unit requires the same amount of resources. The following information is from the static budget for 2007:

PH Grade Assist

Expected production and sales	5,000 units
Direct materials	50,000 pounds
Direct manufacturing labor	20,000 hours
Total fixed costs	$1,000,000

Standard quantities, standard prices, and standard unit costs follow for direct materials and direct manufacturing labor.

	Standard Quantity	Standard Price	Standard Unit Cost
Direct materials	10 pounds	$10 per pound	$100
Direct manufacturing labor	4 hours	$40 per hour	$160

During 2007, actual number of units produced and sold was 6,000. Actual cost of direct materials used was $594,000, based on 54,000 pounds purchased at $11 per pound. Direct manufacturing labor-hours actually used were 25,000, at the rate of $38 per hour. This resulted in actual direct manufacturing labor costs of $950,000. Actual fixed costs were $1,005,000. There were no beginning or ending inventories.

Required

1. Calculate sales-volume variance and flexible-budget variance for operating income.
2. Compute price and efficiency variances for direct materials and direct manufacturing labor.

7-33 Static budget, flexible budget, service sector, professional labor efficiency, and effectiveness. Meridian Financial Services (MFS) is a mortgage broker. It helps prospective homeowners find low-cost mortgage loans and helps existing homeowners refinance their current loans. MFS charges clients a fee equal to 0.5% of the loan amount. MFS's static budget and its actual results for November 2007 are:

Excel Lab
www.prenhall.com/horngren/cost12e

	A	B	C	D	E	F	G	H	I	J	K
1		Static Budget					Actual Results				
2	Number of loans	90					120				
3	Average loan amount	$200,000					$224,000				
4	Commission	0.50%	of loan amount				0.50%	of loan amount			
5	Variable costs per loan application										
6	Professional labor	6.00	hrs.	at	$40	per hr.	7.2	hrs.	at	$42	per hr.
7	Loan filing fees	$ 100					$ 100				
8	Credit checks	$ 120					$ 125				
9	Courier mailings	$ 50					$ 54				
10	Office support (fixed costs)	$ 31,000					$ 33,500				

If you want to use Excel to solve this problem, go to the Excel Lab at **www.prenhall.com/horngren/cost12e** and download the template for Problem 7-33.

Required

1. Prepare a static budget for November 2007.
2. Prepare a level 2 variance analysis for November 2007; identify sales-volume and flexible-budget variances for operating income.
3. Compute professional-labor price and efficiency variances for November 2007 (labor price is computed on a per-hour basis).
4. What factors would you consider in evaluating the effectiveness of professional labor in November 2007?

7-34 Comprehensive variance analysis, responsibility issues. (CMA, adapted) Horizons Unlimited manufactures a full line of well-known sunglasses frames and lenses. Horizons uses a standard costing system to set attainable standards for direct materials, labor, and overhead costs. Standards have been reviewed and revised annually, as necessary. Department managers, whose evaluations and bonuses are affected by their department's performance, have been held responsible to explain variances in their department performance reports.

Recently, the manufacturing variances in the Visionaire prestige line of sunglasses have caused some concern. For no apparent reason, unfavorable materials and labor variances have occurred. At the monthly staff meeting, Jim Denton, manager of the Visionaire line, will be expected to explain his variances and suggest ways of improving performance. Denton will be asked to explain the following performance report for 2007:

	Actual Results	Static-Budget Amounts
Units sold	4,850	5,000
Revenues	$397,700	$400,000
Variable manufacturing costs	234,643	216,000
Fixed manufacturing costs	72,265	75,000
Gross margin	90,792	109,000

Denton collected the following information:

a. Three items comprised the standard variable manufacturing costs in 2007:
- Direct materials: Frames. Static budget cost of $33,000. The standard input for 2007 is 3.00 ounces per unit.
- Direct materials: Lenses. Static budget costs of $93,000. The standard input for 2007 is 6.00 ounces per unit.
- Direct manufacturing labor: Static budget costs of $90,000. The standard input for 2007 is 1.20 hours per unit.

Assume there are no variable manufacturing overhead costs.

b. The actual variable manufacturing costs in 2007 were:
- Direct materials: Frames. Actual costs of $37,248. Actual ounces used were 3.20 ounces per unit.
- Direct materials: Lenses. Actual costs of $100,492. Actual ounces used were 7.00 ounces per unit.
- Direct manufacturing labor: Actual costs of $96,903. The actual labor rate was $14.80 per hour.

Required

1. Prepare a report that includes:
   a. Selling-price variance
   b. Sales-volume variance and flexible-budget variance for operating income in the format of the level 2 analysis in Exhibit 7-2
   c. Price and efficiency variances for:
   - Direct materials: frames
   - Direct materials: lenses
   - Direct manufacturing labor
2. Give three possible explanations for each of the three price and efficiency variances at Horizons in requirement 1c.

7-35 Service sector, solve for unknowns. Hideki Repair Shop specializes in replacing car mufflers. Hideki uses a standard costing system based on a standard wage rate and standard labor hours to replace each muffler. Some labor records for the month of August were lost, but the following information was available. Actual hours of input were 1,000. The direct labor flexible-budget variance was $3,500 favorable. The standard labor price was $30.00 per hour. The labor price variance for August was $1,000 unfavorable.

Required

1. Calculate actual labor price per hour.
2. Calculate standard labor hours for actual total output achieved in August.

Excel Lab www.prenhall.com/horngren/cost12e

PH Grade Assist

7-36 Level 2 variance analysis, solve for unknowns. Homerun Headgear manufactures and distributes baseball caps to ballparks and other sports venues. Homerun's plan for 2006 forecast sales of 600,000 caps. However, only 500,000 caps were sold. Based on the following data, calculate the missing numbers and complete the analysis.

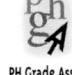

	A	B	C	D	E	F	G	H
1	**Homerun Headgear Performance Report, Year Ended December 31, 2006**							
2		**Actual Results**	**Flexible-Budget Variances**		**Flexible Budget**	**Sales-Volume Variances**		**Static Budget**
3		**(1)**	**(2) = (1) - (3)**		**(3)**	**(4) = (3) - (5)**		**(5)**
4	Units sold	500,000						600,000
5	Revenues (sales)	$5,000,000						$4,800,000
6	Variable costs	1,400,000						1,800,000
7	Contribution margin		$1,100,000	F		$500,000	U	
8	Fixed costs	1,150,000			$1,000,000			1,000,000
9	Operating income							
10								
11								
12	Level 2		Flexible-budget variance			Sales-volume variance		
13								
14	Level 1				Static-budget variance			

If you want to use Excel to solve this problem, go to the Excel Lab at **www.prenhall.com/horngren/cost12e** and download the template for Problem 7-36.

Required

1. Calculate the budgeted and actual selling prices.
2. Assuming that the driver for variable costs is units sold, what are the budgeted and actual variable costs per unit?
3. Calculate the flexible-budget operating income.
4. Calculate the flexible-budget variance for operating income.
5. Calculate the sales-volume variance for operating income.
6. Calculate the static-budget variance for operating income.

7-37 Direct labor and direct materials variances, missing data. (CMA, heavily adapted). Morro Bay Surfboards manufactures fiberglass surfboards. The standard cost of direct materials and direct manufacturing labor is $100 per board. This includes 20 pounds of direct materials, at the budgeted price of $2 per pound, and five hours of direct manufacturing labor, at the budgeted rate of $12 per hour. Following are the data for the month of July:

PH Grade Assist

Units completed	6,000 units
Direct material purchases	150,000 pounds
Cost of direct material purchases	$292,500
Actual direct manufacturing labor-hours	32,000 hours
Actual direct-labor cost	$368,000
Direct materials efficiency variance	$ 12,500 U

There were no beginning inventories.

Required

1. Compute direct manufacturing labor variances for July.
2. Compute the actual pounds of direct materials used in production in July.
3. Calculate the actual price per pound of direct materials purchased.
4. Calculate the direct materials price variance.

7-38 Direct materials and manufacturing labor variances, solving unknowns. (CPA, adapted) On May 1, 2007, Bovar Company began the manufacture of a new paging machine known as Dandy. The company installed a standard costing system to account for manufacturing costs. The standard costs for a unit of Dandy follow:

Direct materials (3 lbs. at $5 per lb.)	$15.00
Direct manufacturing labor (1/2 hour at $20 per hour)	10.00
Manufacturing overhead (75% of direct manufacturing labor costs)	7.50
	$32.50

The following data were obtained from Bovar's records for the month of May:

	Debit	**Credit**
Revenues		$125,000
Accounts payable control (for May's purchases of direct materials)		68,250
Direct materials price variance	$3,250	
Direct materials efficiency variance	2,500	
Direct manufacturing labor price variance	1,900	
Direct manufacturing labor efficiency variance		2,000

Actual production in May was 4,000 units of Dandy, and actual sales in May were 2,500 units.

The amount shown earlier for direct materials price variance applies to materials purchased during May. There was no beginning inventory of materials on May 1, 2007.

Required

Compute each of the following items for Bovar for the month of May. Show your computations.

1. Standard direct manufacturing labor-hours allowed for actual output produced
2. Actual direct manufacturing labor-hours worked
3. Actual direct manufacturing labor wage rate
4. Standard quantity of direct materials allowed (in pounds)
5. Actual quantity of direct materials used (in pounds)
6. Actual quantity of direct materials purchased (in pounds)
7. Actual direct materials price per pound

7-39 Responsibility for variances. The Quincy Company uses standard costing. Direct materials are purchased by Maria Suarez, the purchasing manager. Andy Blake is responsible for production. There are no beginning or ending inventories for May 2007.

The standard price of the chemical used as the principal direct material was $2 per pound. The standard quantity was 6 pounds per case of finished product.

The standard price for direct manufacturing labor was $14 per hour. The standard quantity of labor was 0.5 hour per case of finished product.

During the past month, Quincy produced 10,000 cases of finished product. Actual labor costs were $78,000 for 6,500 actual hours. During May, 71,000 pounds of chemicals were acquired and consumed at a price of $1.80 per pound.

Required

1. Calculate the direct materials price variance, the direct materials efficiency variance, the direct manufacturing labor price variance, and the direct manufacturing labor efficiency variance.
2. As the supervisor of the purchasing manager and the production manager, how would you assign responsibility for each of the variances calculated in requirement 1 to each manager under the following two scenarios:
   a. The direct materials variances are attributable to the purchase of poor-quality materials.
   b. The quality of direct materials is fine but the production manager used cheaper, less-skilled workers in May.

7-40 Comprehensive variance analysis review. FlexMem, Inc., manufactures diskettes. The CFO has provided you with the following budgeted standards for the month of February 2007:

Average selling price per diskette	$4.00
Total direct material cost per diskette	$0.85
Direct manufacturing labor	
Direct manufacturing labor cost per hour	$15.00
Average labor productivity rate (diskettes per hour)	300
Direct marketing cost per unit	$0.30
Fixed overhead	$900,000

Sales of 1,500,000 units are budgeted for February. Actual February results are:

- Unit sales and production totaled 80% of plan.
- Actual average selling price declined to $3.70.
- Productivity dropped to 250 diskettes per hour.
- Actual direct manufacturing labor cost is $15 per hour.
- Actual total direct material cost per unit dropped to $0.80.
- Actual direct marketing costs were $0.30 per unit.
- Fixed overhead costs were $30,000 below plan.

Required

Calculate the following:

1. Static-budget and actual operating income
2. Static-budget variance for operating income
3. Flexible-budget operating income
4. Flexible-budget variance for operating income
5. Sales-volume variance for operating income
6. Price and efficiency variances for direct manufacturing labor
7. Flexible-budget variance for direct manufacturing labor

Excel Lab
www.prenhall.com/horngren/cost12e

7-41 Comprehensive variance analysis. Electronic System Solutions (ESS) is a subcontractor for a large auto parts supplier. Given design specifications, it manufactures an electronic weight-sensing unit for the front passenger seats of cars. ESS uses a standard costing system. The standards are set at the beginning of each year.

Early in the second quarter of 2007, ESS faced two production-related crises: it had to change its direct materials supplier and had to negotiate and sign a new short-term labor agreement with its highly-skilled and somewhat combative workers' union. Sari Noonan, a management accountant at ESS, described the changes at a management meeting: "Well, let's get the bad news out of the way—the new materials are more expensive per pound than our standards for 2007 and the new labor contract also raises the cost of direct labor relative to our 2007 standards. But, there's good news . . . the new materials are of better quality so there will be less waste and less rework, and we suspect that the per-unit direct manufacturing labor cost will come down as a result. Now we just have to wait and see how things pan out."

At the end of the second quarter, Noonan and her boss, Jim Shaw, reviewed the following results with the management team:

	A	B	C	D	E	F	G	H	I	J	K	L	M	N	O	P	Q	R	S
1		**Variable Costs Per Unit**																	
2	**Per Unit Variable Costs**	**Standard**						**First-Quarter 2007 Actual Results**						**Second-Quarter 2007 Actual Results**					
3	Direct materials	2.2	lbs	at	$5.70	per lb	$12.54	2.3	lbs	at	$5.80	per lb	$13.34	2.0	lbs	at	$6.00	per lb	$12.00
4	Direct manufacturing labor	0.5	hrs	at	$12	per hr	$6.00	0.52	hrs	at	$ 12	per hr	$6.24	0.45	hrs	at	$ 14	per hr	$ 6.30
5	Other variable costs						$10.00						$10.00						$ 9.85
6							$28.54						$29.58						$28.15
7																			

	U	V	W	X
1				
2		**Static Budget for Each Quarter Based on 2007 Standards**	**First-Quarter 2007 Results**	**Second-Quarter 2007 Results**
3	Units	10,000	11,000	12,000
4	Selling price	$70	$ 72	$ 71.50
5	Sales	$700,000	$792,000	$858,000
6	Variable costs			
7	Direct materials	125,400	146,740	144,000
8	Direct manufacturing labor	60,000	68,640	75,600
9	Other variable costs	100,000	110,000	118,200
10	Total variable costs	285,400	325,380	337,800
11	Contribution margin	414,600	466,620	520,200
12	Fixed costs	170,000	165,000	171,000
13	Operating income	$244,600	$301,620	$349,200

Noonan and Shaw were both relieved and concerned about the results. The anticipated savings in material waste and rework seemed to have materialized, but, as Jim Shaw put it, "I know exactly what the union is going to harp on—that even at $14-per-hour labor, actual unit costs are below standard unit costs, and operating income just continues to climb, etcetera, etcetera. I think we'd better brace for more pressure to raise wages."

If you want to use Excel to solve this problem, go to the Excel Lab at **www.prenhall.com/horngren/cost12e** and download the template for Problem 7-41.

Required

1. Prepare a detailed variance analysis of the second-quarter results relative to the static budget. Show how much of the improvement in operating income arose due to changes in sales volume and how much arose for other reasons. Calculate variances that isolate the effects of price and usage changes in direct materials and direct manufacturing labor.
2. Use the results of requirement 1 to prepare a rebuttal to the union's anticipated demands in light of the second-quarter results.
3. Jim Shaw thinks that "we can negotiate better if we change the standards." Without performing any calculations, discuss the pros and cons of immediately changing the standards.

7-42 Comprehensive variance analysis. (CMA) Aunt Molly's Old Fashioned Cookies bakes cookies for retail stores. The company's best-selling cookie is Chocolate Nut Supreme, a gourmet cookie that sells for $8 per pound. The standard monthly production level is 400,000 pounds, and the standard inputs and costs per pound are:

Excel Lab
www.prenhall.com/horngren/cost12e

	A	B	C	D	E
1		**Quantity per**		**Standard**	
2	**Cost Item**	**Pound of Cookies**		**Unit Costs**	
3	Direct materials				
4	Cookie mix	10	oz.	$0.02	/oz.
5	Milk chocolate	5	oz.	0.15	/oz.
6	Almonds	1	oz.	0.50	/oz.
7					
8	Direct manufacturing labor[a]				
9	Mixing	1	min.	14.40	/hr.
10	Baking	2	min.	18.00	/hr.
11					
12	Variable overhead[b]	3	min.	32.40	/hr.
13	[a]Direct manufacturing labor rates include employee benefits.				
14	[b]Allocated on the basis of direct manufacturing labor-hours.				

Karen Blair, the company's management accountant, prepares monthly budget reports based on these standard costs. Molly Cates, the company president, is disappointed with the April results shown here:

	Performance Report, April 2007				
18		Actual	Budget	Variance	
19	Units (pounds)	450,000	400,000	50,000	F
20	Revenues	$3,555,000	$3,200,000	$355,000	F
21	Direct materials	865,000	580,000	285,000	U
22	Direct manufacturing labor	348,000	336,000	12,000	U

Cates notes that despite a sizable increase in the pounds of cookies sold in April, Chocolate Nut Supreme's contribution to the company's overall profitability has been lower than expected. Blair gathers the following information to help analyze the situation:

25	Usage Report, April 2007			
26	Cost Item	Quantity		Actual Cost
27	Direct Materials			
28	Cookie mix	4,650,000	oz.	$ 93,000
29	Milk chocolate	2,660,000	oz.	532,000
30	Almonds	480,000	oz.	240,000
31				
32	Direct manufacturing labor			
33	Mixing	450,000	min.	108,000
34	Baking	800,000	min.	240,000

If you want to use Excel to solve this problem, go to the Excel Lab at **www.prenhall.com/horngren/cost12e** and download the template for Problem 7-42.

Required Compute the following variances. Comment on the variances, with particular attention to the variances that may be related to each other and the controllability of each variance:

1. Selling-price variance
2. Direct materials price variance
3. Direct materials efficiency variance
4. Direct manufacturing labor efficiency variance

7-43 Flexible budgeting, activity-based costing, variance analysis. Toymaster, Inc., produces a toy car, TGC, in batches. After each batch of TGC is run, the molds are cleaned. The labor costs of cleaning the molds can be traced to TGC because TGC can only be produced from a specific mold. The following information pertains to June 2007:

	Static-Budget Amounts	Actual Amounts
Units of TGC produced and sold	30,000	22,500
Batch size (units per batch)	250	225
Cleaning labor-hours per batch	3	3.5
Cleaning labor cost per hour	$14	$12.50

Required

1. Calculate the flexible-budget variance for total cleaning labor costs in June 2007.
2. Calculate the price and efficiency variances for total cleaning labor costs in June 2007. Comment on the results.

Collaborative Learning Exercise

7-44 Price and efficiency variances, problems in standard-setting, benchmarking. Savannah Fashions manufactures shirts for retail chains. Jorge Andersen, the controller, is becoming increasingly disenchanted with Savannah's standard costing system. The budgeted and actual amounts for direct materials and direct manufacturing labor for July 2007 were:

	Budgeted Amounts	Actual Amounts
Shirts manufactured	4,000	4,488
Direct material costs	$20,000	$20,196
Direct material units (rolls of cloth)	400	408
Direct manufacturing labor costs	$18,000	$18,462
Direct manufacturing labor-hours	1,000	1,020

There were no beginning or ending inventories of materials.

Standard costs are based on a study of the operations conducted by an independent consultant six months earlier. Andersen observes that since that study he has rarely seen an unfavorable variance of any magnitude. He notes that even at their current output levels, the workers seem to have a lot of time for sitting around and gossiping. Andersen is concerned that the production manager, Charlie Fenton, is aware of this but does not want to tighten up the standards because the lax standards make his performance look good.

Required

1. Compute the price and efficiency variances of Savannah Fashions for direct materials and direct manufacturing labor in July 2007.
2. Describe the types of actions the employees at Savannah Fashions may have taken to reduce the accuracy of the standards set by the independent consultant. Why would employees take those actions? Is this behavior ethical?
3. If Andersen does nothing about the standard costs, will his behavior violate any of the Standards of Ethical Conduct for Management Accountants described in Exhibit 1-7 on p. 16?
4. What actions should Andersen take?
5. Andersen can obtain benchmarking information about the estimated costs of Savannah's major competitors from Benchmarking Clearing House. Discuss the pros and cons of using the Benchmarking Clearing House information to compute the variances in requirement 1.

Get Connected: Cost Accounting in the News

Go to www.prenhall.com/horngren/cost12e for additional online exercise(s) that explore issues affecting the accounting world today. These exercises offer you the opportunity to analyze and reflect on how cost accounting helps managers to make better decisions and handle the challenges of strategic planning and implementation.

CHAPTER 7 Case

MANAGEMENT CONTROL AT STARBUCKS

Quick—where's the nearest Starbucks coffee shop? Down the block, at the airport, in your office building? Seems like they're everywhere, doesn't it? With more than 8,000 locations worldwide and long-run plans to grow to 25,000, new stores open at a rate of about 3.5 stores per day. This explosive growth means Starbucks, which doesn't franchise, must carefully train its personnel in each location on the fine points of serving a product that demanding customers expect to be consistent all day, every day. Their secret? Not just fine coffee; it's close attention to fundamental cost accounting principles.

The store manager in your local Starbucks probably doesn't look like an accountant. Yet behind the coffee bar, she receives and reviews a number of key reports that focus her attention on the standards set by corporate headquarters in Seattle. Even when a new Starbucks store opens down the street and cannibalizes 30% of the existing stores' sales, the manager knows that, in the broader picture, it means lower delivery costs, shorter customer lines, and increased foot traffic for all stores in the area.

The typical Starbucks menu offers bulk coffees in the bold, smooth, and mild categories; classic drinks such as frappuccinos, and coffees and espresso drinks with prices ranging from $1.40 for a tall freshly brewed coffee to $4.45 for a high-end iced venti white chocolate mocha. Depending on store location, a single barista (the person making the drinks) may serve about 20 drinks per hour, generating somewhere in the neighborhood of $60 to $80 an hour in revenue. The costs behind those revenues are primarily barista labor, starting at $7.75 an hour (increasing to more than $8.00 after a year); and materials, or ingredients such as coffee, milk, and flavorings. Overhead for store leases, utilities, insurance, water, and other costs are reported to the store manager, but they're only held accountable for variations in the labor costs and ingredient costs.

Chances are good you are one of the millions of people who queue up 18 times a month for your pricey coffee fix. Maybe you even linger to read the paper, hold a meeting, or use the in-store wireless network. Starbucks wants you to come back repeatedly, not only for its product offerings, but because they deliver solid customer service and consistency as a result of strict adherence to their stated standards, morning to night, around the globe.

QUESTIONS

1. Assume each Starbucks store tracks direct labor and direct material costs for each of its drinks, with the standard costs for a single grande cappuccino as follows:

Labor	$0.40
Coffee	0.70
Dairy products	0.35
Cup and lid	0.07
Stirrers, napkins	0.03

   Suppose actual output for one week is 1,000 grande cappuccino drinks. The actual total cost of coffee used to make these drinks was $730. The manager of the store has no control over the price paid for the coffee provided by Starbucks—this is a predetermined price. What is the total direct materials variance for coffee for this drink? Is this a price or an efficiency variance? Is it favorable or unfavorable? Why?
2. Nonfinancial measures are important to the operations of each Starbucks. For example, cleanliness of public areas is one such measure. Another measure covers achieving the company's "third place" concept (in which home and work are the first two places in a person's life, Starbucks is third). What other nonfinancial measures do you think the company might use? Why do nonfinancial measures matter in cost accounting?

CHAPTER 8

FLEXIBLE BUDGETS, OVERHEAD COST VARIANCES, AND MANAGEMENT CONTROL

LEARNING OBJECTIVES

1. **Explain the similarities and differences in planning variable overhead costs and fixed overhead costs**
2. **Identify the features of standard costing**
3. **Compute the variable overhead efficiency variance and the variable overhead spending variance**
4. **Explain how the variable overhead efficiency variance differs from the efficiency variance for a direct cost**
5. **Compute a budgeted fixed overhead cost rate**
6. **Explain two concerns when interpreting the production-volume variance as a measure of the economic cost of unused capacity**
7. **Show how the 4-variance analysis approach reconciles the actual overhead incurred with the overhead amounts allocated during the period**
8. **Calculate overhead variances in activity-based costing**

What do this week's weather forecast, courtroom witness testimony, and organization performance have in common? Most of the time, reality doesn't match expectations. It doesn't rain when forecast, the witness swears the defendant was at the scene of the crime even though a solid alibi exists, and organizations discover at month-end their skyrocketing costs have significantly reduced profits. Differences, or variances, are all around us.

For organizations, variances are often complex and can have serious and unpleasant consequences. Getting to the root of their causes is critical if performance is to be improved. That's why Larry Farrell, CEO of Webb Company, has called a meeting of his sales, manufacturing, purchasing, and finance managers. The performance report for April 2006 is not even close to expectations, and he wants to know why.

Larry: I'm very concerned about the unfavorable manufacturing overhead variances in this April report: $10,500 for variable manufacturing overhead and $55,000 for fixed manufacturing overhead. The manufacturing overhead efficiency and total spending variances also are unfavorable. Can someone help me understand what happened?

Ben Shuman, vice president, sales: Larry, the market for our jackets has definitely softened. We're trying to determine whether it's a change in customer preferences or a response to the new styles our competitors have brought to the market.

Rosie Guerrero, controller: We do know we produced and sold 2,000 fewer jackets than we budgeted. As a result of lower production, we spent a lot of money on fixed costs for manufacturing capacity that we didn't use. We also spent more on fixed costs than planned. I already have a team working to suggest ways to address these problems. We're also taking a look at the reasons for the unfavorable variable overhead efficiency variance we incurred. Inadequate machine maintenance and lower worker skill levels may be the culprits.

Larry: All right. Obviously we all know this is not good news, but let's learn from this problem and focus on finding solutions.

Webb is not the only company that must deal with the challenges of managing overhead costs. Chemical, paper, and steel companies such as Du Pont, International Paper, and U.S. Steel incur large costs to construct and maintain their manufacturing plants and equipment. These costs are part of overhead. Internet companies such as Amazon.com and Yahoo! invest large amounts in software that enables them to provide a broad range of services to their customers in a timely and reliable way. These costs are part of their overhead.

In this chapter we will examine how flexible budgets and variance analysis can help managers plan and control overhead costs. Chapter 7 emphasized the direct-cost categories of direct materials and direct manufacturing labor. In this chapter, we focus on the indirect-cost categories of variable manufacturing overhead and fixed manufacturing overhead. Finally, we explain why managers should be careful when interpreting variances based on overhead-cost concepts developed primarily for financial reporting purposes.

It is not unusual for more than 50% of a company's total product costs throughout the value chain to be classified as overhead. Increased automation, more-complex production and distribution processes, and product proliferation increase overhead costs.

Planning of Variable and Fixed Overhead Costs

1

Explain the similarities and differences in planning variable overhead costs and fixed overhead costs

. . . for both, plan only essential activities and be efficient; fixed overhead costs are usually determined well before the budget period begins

We'll use the Webb Company example again to illustrate planning and control of variable and fixed overhead costs. Recall, Webb manufactures jackets that are sold to distributors, who in turn sell to independent clothing stores and retail chains. For simplicity, we assume Webb's only costs are *manufacturing* costs. Variable manufacturing overhead costs for Webb include energy, machine maintenance, engineering support, indirect materials, and indirect manufacturing labor. Fixed manufacturing overhead costs include plant-leasing costs, some administrative costs (such as the plant manager's salary), and depreciation on plant equipment.

Planning Variable Overhead Costs

To effectively plan variable overhead costs for a product or service, managers must eliminate the activities that do not add value to the product or service. By doing this, managers are able to focus their attention solely on the activities that will create a superior product or service for their customers. Webb's managers examine how each of the variable overhead costs they incur relates to delivering a superior product or service to customers. For example, customers expect Webb's jackets to last. So managers at Webb consider sewing to be an essential activity. Therefore, maintenance activities for sewing machines—included in Webb's variable overhead costs—are also essential activities for which management must plan. In addition, such maintenance should be done in a cost-effective way. This means, for example, scheduling equipment maintenance in a systematic way rather than waiting for sewing machines to break down.

The two ways of managing variable overhead costs are (1) eliminate nonvalue-added costs (for example, consume less electricity by using more energy-efficient equipment) and (2) reduce consumption of the cost-allocation bases (for example, redesign products to require fewer machine-hours of processing time).

Planning Fixed Overhead Costs

Effective planning of fixed overhead costs is similar to effective planning for variable overhead costs—planning to undertake only essential activities and then planning to be efficient in that undertaking. But in planning fixed overhead costs, there is one more strategic issue that managers must take into consideration: choosing the appropriate level of capacity or investment that will benefit the company in the long run. Consider Webb's leasing of sewing machines, each having a fixed cost per year. Leasing insufficient machine capacity—say, because Webb underestimates demand or because of limited space in the plant—will result in an inability to meet demand and lost sales of jackets. Leasing more machines than necessary—if Webb overestimates demand—will result in additional fixed leasing costs on machines not fully used during the year.

The two ways of managing fixed overhead costs are (1) eliminate nonvalue-added costs (for example, arrange to have vendors deliver direct materials to the production floor just when needed, which enables a warehouse lease to be terminated) and (2) plan for appropriate capacity levels.

The planning of fixed overhead costs differs from the planning of variable overhead costs in one important respect: timing. At the start of a budget period, management will have made most of the decisions that determine the level of fixed overhead costs to be incurred. But, it's the day-to-day, ongoing operating decisions that mainly determine the level of variable overhead costs incurred in that period.

Standard Costing at Webb Company

2

Identify the features of standard costing

. . . uses standard prices and standard quantities of inputs to cost products

Webb uses standard costing. The development of standards for Webb's direct manufacturing costs was described in Chapter 7. This chapter discusses the development of standards for Webb's manufacturing overhead costs. **Standard costing** is a costing system that (a) traces direct costs to output produced by multiplying the standard prices or rates by the standard quantities of inputs allowed for actual outputs produced and (b) allocates overhead costs on the basis of the standard overhead-cost rates times the standard quantities of the allocation bases allowed for the actual outputs produced.

The standard cost of Webb's jackets can be computed at the start of the budget period. This feature of standard costing simplifies record keeping. That's because no record need be kept of the actual overhead costs or of the actual quantities of the cost-allocation bases used for making the jackets. What is needed are the standard overhead cost rates for variable and fixed overhead. Webb's management accountants calculate these cost rates based on the planned amounts of variable and fixed overhead and the standard quantities of the allocation bases. We describe these computations in the following sections. Note that once standards have been set, the costs of using standard costing are low relative to the costs of using actual costing or normal costing.

Developing Budgeted Variable Overhead Cost Rates

Budgeted variable overhead cost-allocation rates can be developed in four steps. We use the Webb example to illustrate these steps. Throughout the chapter, we use the broader term "budgeted rate" rather than "standard rate" to be consistent with the term used in describing normal costing in earlier chapters. In standard costing, the budgeted rates are standard rates.

Step 1: **Choose the Period to Be Used for the Budget.** Webb uses a 12-month budget period to help smooth out seasonal effects.

Step 2: **Select the Cost-Allocation Bases to Use in Allocating Variable Overhead Costs to Output Produced.** Webb's operating managers select machine-hours as the cost-allocation base because they believe, on the basis of the planning process, that machine-hours is the only cost driver of variable manufacturing overhead. On the basis of an engineering study, Webb estimates it will take 0.40 of a machine-hour per actual output unit. For its budgeted output of 144,000 jackets in 2006, Webb budgets 57,600 (0.40 × 144,000) machine-hours

Step 3: **Identify the Variable Overhead Costs Associated with Each Cost-Allocation Base.** Webb groups in a single cost pool all of its variable manufacturing overhead costs, including costs of energy, machine maintenance, engineering support, indirect materials, and indirect manufacturing labor. Webb's total budgeted variable manufacturing overhead costs for 2006 are $1,728,000.

Step 4: **Compute the Rate per Unit of Each Cost-Allocation Base Used to Allocate Variable Overhead Costs to Output Produced.** Dividing the amount in step 3 ($1,728,000) by the amount in step 2 (57,600 machine-hours), Webb estimates a rate of $30 per standard machine-hour for allocating its variable manufacturing overhead costs.

The budgeted variable manufacturing overhead (BVMOH) cost rate differs from the budgeted price of direct materials (DM) or direct manufacturing labor (DML). The BVMOH cost rate encompasses costs of *many diverse VMOH items per unit of the cost-allocation base.* In the Webb example, the BVMOH cost rate is $30 per machine-hour—that is, Webb expects to spend $30 on a "market basket" of VMOH items. The market-basket aspect of the BVMOH cost rate makes VMOH variances more difficult to interpret than DM and DML variances.

In standard costing, the variable overhead rate per unit of the cost-allocation base ($30 per machine-hour for Webb) is generally expressed as a standard rate per output unit. Webb calculates the budgeted variable overhead cost rate per output unit as:

$$\begin{aligned}\text{Budgeted variable overhead cost rate per output unit} &= \text{Budgeted input allowed per output unit} \times \text{Budgeted variable overhead cost rate per input unit}\\ &= 0.40 \text{ hours per jacket} \times \$30 \text{ per hour}\\ &= \$12 \text{ per jacket}\end{aligned}$$

Webb uses $12 per jacket as the budgeted variable overhead cost rate in both its static budget for 2006 and in the monthly performance reports it prepares during 2006.

Exhibit 8-1 shows how Webb's variable manufacturing overhead costs are expected to change with respect to output units (jackets) for the planning and control (budgeting) purpose and also for the inventory costing purpose. As the number of jackets manufactured increases, budgeted variable manufacturing overhead costs (for the planning and control purpose of cost accounting) and variable manufacturing overhead costs allocated to output units (for the inventory costing purpose) increase at the rate of $12 per jacket. The graphs for the two purposes are identical.

Exhibit 8-1 presents an overall picture of how total variable manufacturing overhead would behave. Of course, variable manufacturing overhead costs consist of many items,

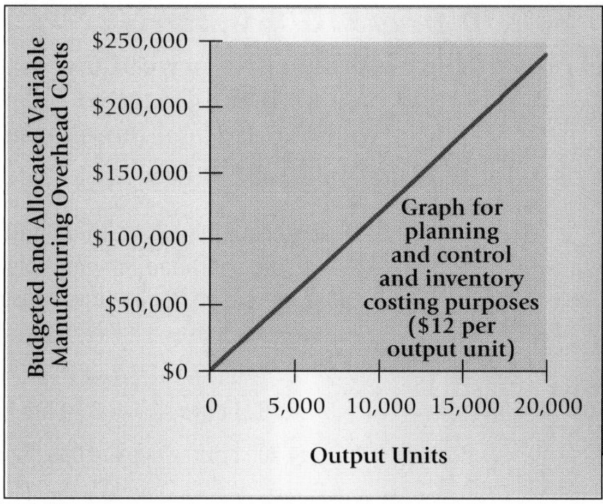

EXHIBIT 8-1

Behavior of Variable Manufacturing Overhead Costs: Budgeted for Planning and Control Purposes and Allocated for Inventory Costing Purposes for Webb Company for April 2006

including energy, repairs, indirect manufacturing labor, and so on. Managers help control variable manufacturing overhead costs by budgeting each line item and then investigating possible causes for any significant variances.

Variable Overhead Cost Variances

We now illustrate how the budgeted variable manufacturing overhead rate is used in computing Webb's variable manufacturing overhead cost variances. The following data are for April 2006, when Webb produced and sold 10,000 jackets:

	Actual Result	Flexible-Budget Amount
1. Output units (jackets)	10,000	10,000
2. Machine-hours per output unit	0.45	0.40
3. Machine-hours (1 × 2)	4,500	4,000
4. Variable manufacturing overhead costs	$130,500	$120,000
5. Variable manufacturing overhead costs per machine-hour (4 ÷ 3)	$29.00	$30.00
6. Variable manufacturing overhead costs per output unit (4 ÷ 1)	$13.05	$12.00

In the Webb example, be sure to distinguish budgeted VMOH cost per unit of output ($12 per jacket) from budgeted VMOH cost per unit of the input cost-allocation base ($30 per machine-hour). Either cost rate can be used to compute VMOH allocated: 10,000 × (0.40 × $30) = $120,000, or 10,000 × $12 = $120,000.

As we saw in Chapter 7, the flexible budget enables Webb to highlight the differences between actual costs and actual quantities versus budgeted costs and budgeted quantities for the actual output level of 10,000 jackets.

Flexible-Budget Analysis

The **variable overhead flexible-budget variance** measures the difference between actual variable overhead costs incurred and flexible-budget variable overhead amounts.

In this chapter, we again use a columnar solution format as a helpful and intuitive approach to compute variances. Examples include Exhibits 8-2, 8-3, and 8-5.

$$\text{Variable overhead flexible-budget variance} = \text{Actual costs incurred} - \text{Flexible-budget amount}$$
$$= \$130{,}500 - \$120{,}000$$
$$= \$10{,}500\text{ U}$$

This $10,500 unfavorable flexible-budget variance means Webb's actual variable manufacturing overhead exceeded the flexible-budget amount by $10,500 for the 10,000 jackets actually produced and sold. Webb's managers would want to know the reasons why actual costs exceeded the flexible-budget amount. Did Webb use more machine-hours than planned to produce the 10,000 jackets? If so, was it because workers were less skilled than expected in using machines? Or did Webb spend more on variable overhead costs, such as maintenance?

Just as we illustrated in Chapter 7 with the flexible-budget variance for direct-cost items, Webb's managers can get further insight into the reason for the $10,500 unfavorable variance (a level 2 variance) by subdividing it into the level 3 efficiency variance and spending variance.

Variable Overhead Efficiency Variance

3 **Compute the variable overhead efficiency variance**
... difference between actual quantity of cost-allocation base and budgeted quantity of cost-allocation base

and the variable overhead spending variance
... difference between actual variable overhead cost rate and budgeted variable overhead cost rate

The **variable overhead efficiency variance** is the difference between actual quantity of the cost-allocation base used and budgeted quantity of the cost-allocation base that should have been used to produce actual output, multiplied by budgeted variable overhead cost per unit of the cost-allocation base.

$$\text{Variable overhead efficiency variance} = \left(\begin{array}{c}\text{Actual quantity of}\\ \text{variable overhead}\\ \text{cost-allocation base}\\ \text{used for actual}\\ \text{output}\end{array} - \begin{array}{c}\text{Budgeted quantity of}\\ \text{variable overhead}\\ \text{cost-allocation base}\\ \text{allowed for}\\ \text{actual output}\end{array}\right) \times \begin{array}{c}\text{Budgeted variable}\\ \text{overhead cost per unit}\\ \text{of cost-allocation base}\end{array}$$

$$= (4{,}500 \text{ hours} - 0.40 \text{ hrs./unit} \times 10{,}000 \text{ units}) \times \$30 \text{ per hour}$$

$$= (4{,}500 \text{ hours} - 4{,}000 \text{ hours}) \times \$30 \text{ per hour}$$

$$= \$15{,}000 \text{ U}$$

4 **Explain how the variable overhead efficiency variance**
... focuses on quantity of cost-allocation base used

differs from the efficiency variance for a direct cost
... focuses on quantity of materials or labor-hours used

The unfavorable VMOH efficiency variance does not mean workers wasted VMOH items and used more VMOH per machine-hour. This variance arose because Webb used too much of the cost-allocation base, machine-hours. Because the machines ran an extra 500 hours, they used extra VMOH items, such as electricity, maintenance, and supplies.

Columns 2 and 3 of Exhibit 8-2 depict the variable overhead efficiency variance. Note the variance arises solely because of the difference between actual quantity (4,500 hours) and budgeted quantity (4,000 hours) of the cost-allocation base. The variable overhead efficiency variance is computed the same way as the efficiency variance for direct-cost items (Chapter 7, p. 231). But the interpretation of the variable overhead efficiency variance differs from the interpretation of direct-cost efficiency variances. In Chapter 7, efficiency variances for direct-cost items are based on differences between actual inputs used and budgeted inputs allowed for actual output produced. For example, an efficiency variance for direct manufacturing labor for Webb will indicate whether more or fewer direct manufacturing labor-hours are used per jacket than were budgeted for actual output produced. In contrast, the efficiency variance for variable overhead cost is based on *the efficiency with which the cost-allocation base is used.* Webb's unfavorable variable overhead efficiency variance of $15,000 means that the actual machine-hours (the cost-allocation base) of 4,500 hours turned out to be higher than the budgeted machine-hours of 4,000 hours allowed to manufacture 10,000 jackets.

The following table shows possible causes for Webb's actual machine-hours exceeding budgeted machine-hours and management's potential responses to each of these causes.

Possible Causes for Exceeding Budget	Potential Management Responses
1. Workers were less skilled than expected in using machines.	**1.** Encourage the human resources department to implement better employee-hiring practices and training procedures.
2. Production scheduler inefficiently scheduled jobs, resulting in more machine-hours used than budgeted.	**2.** Improve plant operations by installing production scheduling software.
3. Machines were not maintained in good operating condition.	**3.** Ensure preventive maintenance is done on all machines.
4. Webb's sales staff promised a distributor a rush delivery, which resulted in more machine-hours used than budgeted.	**4.** Coordinate production schedules with sales staff and distributors and share information with them.
5. Budgeted machine time standards were set too tight.	**5.** Commit more resources to develop appropriate standards.

Management's response to this $15,000 U variance would be guided by which cause(s) best describes the April 2006 results. Note how, depending on the cause(s) of the variance, corrective actions may need to be taken not just in manufacturing but also in other business functions of the value chain, such as sales and distribution.

Webb's managers discovered that one reason the machines operated below budgeted efficiency levels in April 2006 was because of insufficient maintenance performed in the prior two months. A former plant manager delayed maintenance in a presumed attempt to meet monthly budget cost targets. As we discussed in Chapter 6, managers should not be focused on meeting short-run budget targets if it is likely to result in harmful long-run consequences. Webb is now strengthening its internal maintenance procedures so that

EXHIBIT 8-2 **Columnar Presentation of Variable Manufacturing Overhead Variance Analysis: Webb Company for April 2006[a]**

	Actual Costs Incurred: Actual Input Quantity × Actual Rate (1)		Actual Input Quantity × Budgeted Rate (2)		Flexible Budget: Budgeted Input Quantity Allowed for Actual Output × Budgeted Rate (3)
	(4,500 hrs. × $29/hr.) = $130,500		(4,500 hrs. × $30/hr.) = $135,000		(0.40 hrs./unit × 10,000 units × $30/hr.) 4,000 hrs. × $30/hr. $120,000
Level 3		$4,500 F Spending variance		$15,000 U Efficiency variance	
Level 2			$10,500 U Flexible-budget variance		

[a]F = favorable effect on operating income; U = unfavorable effect on operating income.

failure to do monthly maintenance as completely as needed will raise a "red flag" that must be immediately explained to management. Underskilled workers was another reason for actual machine-hours exceeding budgeted machine-hours. As a result, Webb is initiating steps to improve hiring and training practices.

Variable Overhead Spending Variance

The **variable overhead spending variance** is the difference between actual variable overhead cost per unit of the cost-allocation base and budgeted variable overhead cost per unit of the cost-allocation base, multiplied by actual quantity of variable overhead cost-allocation base used for actual output.

$$\begin{aligned}\text{Variable overhead spending variance} &= \left(\begin{array}{c}\text{Actual variable}\\ \text{overhead cost per}\\ \text{unit of cost-allocation base}\end{array} - \begin{array}{c}\text{Budgeted variable}\\ \text{overhead cost per}\\ \text{unit of cost-allocation base}\end{array}\right) \times \begin{array}{c}\text{Actual quantity of}\\ \text{variable overhead}\\ \text{cost-allocation base}\\ \text{used for actual output}\end{array}\\ &= (\$29 \text{ per machine-hour} - \$30 \text{ per machine-hour}) \times 4{,}500 \text{ machine-hours}\\ &= (-\$1 \text{ per machine-hour}) \times 4{,}500 \text{ machine-hours}\\ &= \$4{,}500 \text{ F}\end{aligned}$$

Webb operated in April 2006 with a lower-than-budgeted variable overhead cost per machine-hour. Hence, there is a favorable variable overhead spending variance. Columns 1 and 2 in Exhibit 8-2 depict this variance.

To understand the favorable variable overhead spending variance and its implications, Webb's managers need to recognize why *actual* variable overhead cost per unit of the cost-allocation base ($29 per machine-hour) is *lower* than *budgeted* variable overhead cost per unit of the cost-allocation base ($30 per machine-hour). The 4,500 actual machine-hours are 12.5% greater than the flexible-budget amount of 4,000 machine-hours [(4,500 − 4,000) ÷ 4,000 = 0.125, or 12.5%]. Actual variable overhead costs of $130,500 are only 8.75% greater than the flexible-budget amount of $120,000 [($130,500 − $120,000) ÷ $120,000 = 0.0875, or 8.75%]. Relative to the flexible budget, the percentage increase in actual variable overhead costs is *less* than the percentage increase in machine-hours. Consequently, actual variable overhead cost per machine-hour is lower than the budgeted amount.

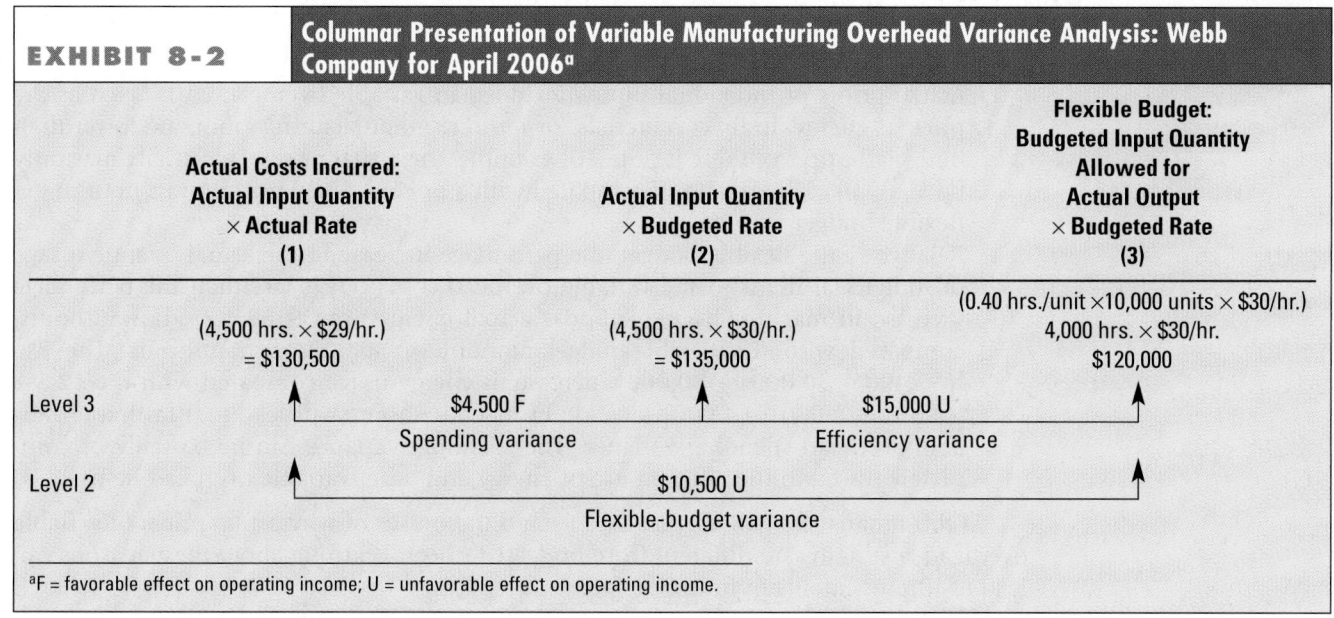

Recall, variable manufacturing overhead costs include costs of energy, machine maintenance, indirect materials, and indirect manufacturing labor. Two reasons why the percentage increase in actual variable manufacturing overhead costs is less than the percentage increase in machine-hours are:

1. Actual prices of individual inputs included in variable overhead costs, such as the price of energy, indirect materials, or indirect manufacturing labor, are lower than budgeted prices of these inputs. For example, the actual price of electricity may only be $0.09 per kilowatt-hour, compared with a price of $0.10 per kilowatt-hour in the flexible budget.
2. Relative to the flexible budget, the percentage increase in the actual quantity usage of individual items in the variable overhead-cost pool is less than the percentage increase in machine-hours. Suppose actual energy used is 32,400 kilowatt-hours, compared with the flexible-budget amount of 30,000 kilowatt-hours. The 8% [(32,400 − 30,000) ÷ 30,000] increase in energy usage compared with the 12.5% [(4,500 − 4,000) ÷ 4,000] increase in machine-hours will lead to a favorable variable overhead spending variance. The spending variance can be partially or completely traced to the efficient use of energy and other variable overhead items.

Webb's managers will need to understand the causes of why actual prices of variable overhead cost items are different from budgeted prices. Learning about these reasons can lead to improvements in future periods.

The price effects could be the result of skillful negotiation on the part of the purchasing manager, oversupply in the market, or lower quality of inputs such as indirect materials. Webb's response would depend on what is believed to be the cause of the variance. For example, if the concerns are about quality, Webb would want to put in place new quality management systems.

Similarly, Webb's managers would need to understand the possible causes for the efficiency with which variable overhead costs are used. These causes include skill levels of workers, maintenance of machines and the efficiency of the manufacturing process. Webb's managers discovered that Webb used fewer supervision resources per machine-hour because of manufacturing process improvements. As a result, they began organizing cross-functional teams to see if more process improvements could be achieved.

Is a favorable variable overhead spending variance always desirable? No. For example, the variable overhead spending variance would be favorable if Webb's managers purchased lower-priced poor-quality indirect materials, hired less-talented supervisors, or performed less machine maintenance. These decisions, however, are likely to hurt product quality and harm the long-run prospects of the business.

To clarify the concepts of variable overhead efficiency variance and variable overhead spending variance, consider the following example, assuming that (a) energy is the only item of variable overhead cost and machine-hours is the cost-allocation base, (b) actual machine-hours used to produce actual output equals budgeted machine-hours, and (c) actual price of energy equals budgeted price. Under those assumptions, there would be no efficiency variance, but there could be a spending variance. The company has been efficient with respect to the number of machine-hours used to produce the actual output. But it could be using too much energy—not because of excessive machine-hours but because of wastage (using more energy per machine-hour). The cost of this higher energy usage would be measured by the spending variance. Managers would try to find ways to reduce energy consumption per machine-hour via better machine maintenance or by making modifications to the manufacturing process.

The variable manufacturing overhead variances computed in this section can be summarized as follows:

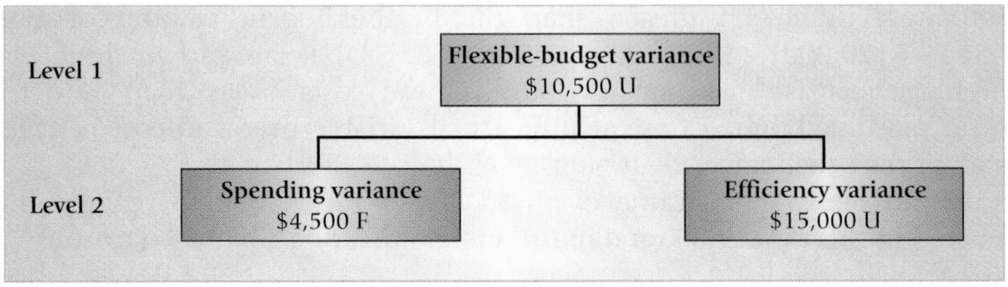

Journal Entries for Variable Manufacturing Overhead Costs and Variances

We now prepare journal entries for Variable Manufacturing Overhead Control and the contra account Variable Manufacturing Overhead Allocated.

Entries for variable manufacturing overhead for April 2006 (data from Exhibit 8-2) are:

1.	Variable Manufacturing Overhead Control	130,500	
	Accounts Payable Control and various other accounts		130,500
	To record actual variable manufacturing overhead costs incurred.		
2.	Work-in-Process Control	120,000	
	Variable Manufacturing Overhead Allocated		120,000
	To record variable manufacturing overhead cost allocated, (0.40 machine-hour/unit × 10,000 units × $30/machine-hour). (The costs accumulated in Work-in-Process Control are transferred to Finished Goods Control when production is completed and to Cost of Goods Sold when the products are sold.)		
3.	Variable Manufacturing Overhead Allocated	120,000	
	Variable Manufacturing Overhead Efficiency Variance	15,000	
	Variable Manufacturing Overhead Control		130,500
	Variable Manufacturing Overhead Spending Variance		4,500
	To record variances for the accounting period.		

These variances are the underallocated or overallocated variable overhead costs. At the end of the fiscal year, the variance accounts are written off to cost of goods sold if immaterial in amount. If the variances are material in amount, they are prorated among Work-in-Process Control, Finished Goods Control, and Cost of Goods Sold on the basis of the variable manufacturing overhead allocated to these accounts, as described in Chapter 4, pp. 119–121. As we discussed in Chapter 7, only unavoidable costs are prorated. Any part of the variances attributable to avoidable inefficiency are written off in the period. Assume that the balances in the variable overhead variance accounts as of April 2006 are also the balances at the end of the 2006 fiscal year and are immaterial in amount. The following journal entry records the write-off to cost of goods sold.

Cost of Goods Sold	10,500	
Variable Manufacturing Overhead Spending Variance	4,500	
Variable Manufacturing Overhead Efficiency Variance		15,000

We next consider fixed overhead costs.

Developing Budgeted Fixed Overhead Rates

5
Compute a budgeted fixed overhead cost rate
. . . budgeted fixed costs divided by level of cost-allocation base

Fixed manufacturing overhead costs are, by definition, a lump sum of costs that remains unchanged in total for a given period despite wide changes in the level of total activity or volume related to those overhead costs. Fixed costs are usually included in flexible budgets, but they remain the same total amount within the relevant range of activity regardless of the output level chosen to "flex" the variable costs and revenues. Recall from Exhibit 7-2, p. 225, and the steps in developing a flexible budget that the fixed-cost amount is the same $276,000 in the static budget and in the flexible budget. Do not assume, however, that fixed manufacturing overhead costs can never be changed. Managers can reduce fixed costs by selling equipment or by laying off employees. But they are fixed in the sense that, unlike variable costs such as direct material costs, fixed costs do not *automatically* increase or decrease with the level of activity within the relevant range. The steps in developing the budgeted fixed overhead rate are:

Step 1: **Choose the Period to Use for the Budget.** As with variable overhead costs, the budget period for fixed costs is typically 12 months. Chapter 4 (pp. 106–108) provides two reasons for using annual overhead rates rather than, say, monthly rates: the numerator reason—such as reducing the influence of seasonality—and the denominator reason—such as reducing the effect of varying output and number of days in a month. In addition, setting annual overhead rates once a year saves management the time they would need 12 times during the year if budget rates had to be set monthly.

Step 2: **Select the Cost-Allocation Base to Use in Allocating Fixed Overhead Costs to Output Produced.** Webb uses machine-hours as the only cost-allocation base for fixed manufacturing overhead costs. Why? Because Webb's managers believe that, in the long run, fixed manufacturing overhead costs will increase or decrease to the levels needed to support the amount of machine-hours. Therefore, in the long run, the amount of machine-hours used is the only cost driver of fixed manufacturing overhead costs. The amount of machine-hours is the denominator in the budgeted fixed overhead rate computation and is called the **denominator level**. In manufacturing settings, the denominator level is called, more specifically, the **production-denominator level**. For simplicity, we assume Webb expects to operate at capacity in fiscal year 2006—with a budgeted amount of 57,600 machine-hours for a budgeted output of 144,000 jackets.[1]

Step 3: **Identify the Fixed Overhead Costs Associated with Each Cost-Allocation Base.** Because Webb identifies only a single cost-allocation base—machine-hours—to allocate fixed manufacturing overhead costs, it groups all its fixed manufacturing overhead costs in a single cost pool. Costs in this pool include depreciation on plant and equipment, plant and equipment leasing costs, and some administrative costs (such as the plant manager's salary). Webb's fixed manufacturing overhead budget for 2006 is $3,312,000.

Step 4: **Compute the Rate per Unit of Each Cost-Allocation Base Used to Allocate Fixed Overhead Costs to Output Produced.** Dividing the $3,312,000 from step 3 by the 57,600 machine-hours from step 2, Webb estimates a fixed manufacturing overhead cost rate of $57.50 per machine-hour:

$$\begin{array}{c}\text{Budgeted fixed}\\ \text{overhead cost per}\\ \text{unit of cost-allocation}\\ \text{base}\end{array} = \frac{\begin{array}{c}\text{Budgeted total costs}\\ \text{in fixed overhead cost pool}\end{array}}{\begin{array}{c}\text{Budgeted total quantity of}\\ \text{cost-allocation base}\end{array}} = \frac{\$3{,}312{,}000}{57{,}600} = \$57.50 \text{ per machine-hour}$$

In standard costing, the $57.50 fixed overhead cost per machine-hour is usually expressed as a standard cost per output unit. Recall that Webb's engineering study estimates that it will take 0.40 machine-hour per output unit. Webb can now calculate the budgeted fixed overhead cost per output unit as:

$$\begin{array}{c}\text{Budgeted fixed}\\ \text{overhead cost per}\\ \text{output unit}\end{array} = \begin{array}{c}\text{Budgeted quantity of}\\ \text{cost-allocation}\\ \text{base allowed per}\\ \text{output unit}\end{array} \times \begin{array}{c}\text{Budgeted fixed}\\ \text{overhead cost}\\ \text{per unit of}\\ \text{cost-allocation base}\end{array}$$

$$= 0.40 \text{ of a machine-hour per jacket} \times \$57.50 \text{ per machine-hour}$$

$$= \$23.00 \text{ per jacket}$$

When preparing monthly budgets for 2006, Webb divides the $3,312,000 annual total fixed costs into 12 equal monthly amounts of $276,000.

Fixed Overhead Cost Variances

The flexible-budget amount for a fixed-cost item is also the amount included in the static budget prepared at the start of the period. No adjustment is required for differences between actual output and budgeted output for fixed costs. That's because fixed costs are

[1]Because Webb plans its capacity over multiple periods, anticipated demand in 2006 could be such that budgeted output for 2006 is less than capacity. Companies vary in the denominator levels they choose; some may choose budgeted ouptut and others may choose capacity. In either case, the basic approach and analysis presented in this chapter is unchanged. Chapter 9 discusses choosing a denominator level and its implications in more detail.

EXHIBIT 8-3

Columnar Presentation of Fixed Manufacturing Overhead Variance Analysis: Webb Company for April 2006[a]

	Actual Costs Incurred (1)	Flexible Budget: Same Budgeted Lump Sum (as in Static Budget) Regardless of Output Level (2)	Allocated: Budgeted Input Quantity Allowed for Actual Output × Budgeted Rate (3)
			(0.40 hrs./unit × 10,000 units × $57.50/hr.)
			(4,000 hrs. × $57.50/hr.)
	$285,000	$276,000	$230,000
Level 3	9,000 U — Spending variance		$46,000 U — Production-volume variance
Level 2	$9,000 U — Flexible-budget variance		

[a]F = favorable effect on operating income; U = unfavorable effect on operating income.

unaffected by changes in the output level within the relevant range. At the start of 2006, Webb budgeted fixed manufacturing overhead costs to be $276,000 per month. The actual amount for April 2006 turned out to be $285,000. The **fixed overhead flexible-budget variance** is the difference between actual fixed overhead costs and fixed overhead costs in the flexible budget:

$$\text{Fixed overhead flexible-budget variance} = \text{Actual costs incurred} - \text{Flexible-budget amount}$$
$$= \$285,000 - \$276,000$$
$$= \$9,000\text{ U}$$

The variance is unfavorable because $285,000 actual fixed manufacturing overhead costs exceed the $276,000 budgeted for April 2006, which decreases that month's operating income by $9,000.

The flexible-budget variance for fixed manufacturing overhead (FMOH) is not subdivided into separate price and efficiency variances. The $9,000 unfavorable flexible-budget variance for FMOH arose because Webb incurred more FMOH costs than the lump-sum amount budgeted. That's why it's called a spending variance.

The variable overhead flexible-budget variance described earlier in this chapter was subdivided into a spending variance and an efficiency variance. There is not an efficiency variance for fixed costs. That's because a given lump sum of fixed costs will be unaffected by how efficiently machine-hours are used to produce output in a given budget period. As we will see later on, this does not mean that a company cannot be efficient or inefficient in its use of fixed-cost resources. As Exhibit 8-3 shows, because there is no efficiency variance, the **fixed overhead spending variance,** a level 3 variance, is the same amount as the level 2 fixed overhead flexible-budget variance:

$$\text{Fixed overhead spending variance} = \text{Actual costs incurred} - \text{Flexible-budget amount}$$
$$= \$285,000 - \$276,000$$
$$= \$9,000\text{ U}$$

Reasons for the unfavorable spending variance could be higher plant-leasing costs, higher depreciation on plant and equipment, and higher administrative costs such as a higher-than-budgeted salary paid to the plant manager. Webb investigated this variance and found that there was a $9,000 per month unexpected increase in its equipment-leasing costs. However, management concluded that the new lease rates were competitive with lease rates available elsewhere. If this were not the case, management would look to lease equipment from other suppliers.

Production-Volume Variance

We now consider a variance—the production-volume variance—that only arises for fixed costs.

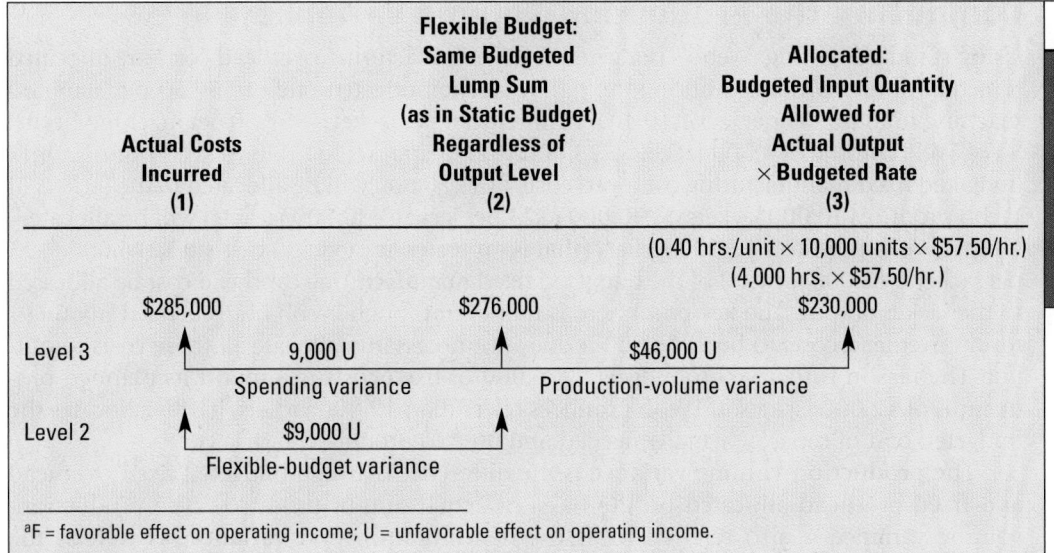

6

Explain two concerns when interpreting the production-volume variance as a measure of the economic cost of unused capacity

. . . extra capacity may be needed to satisfy uncertain demand surges; does not take into account the effect of price decreases that may be needed to fill capacity

Computing the Production-Volume Variance

Using standard costing, Webb's budgeted fixed manufacturing overhead costs are allocated to actual output produced during the period at the budgeted rate of \$57.50 per standard machine-hour or \$23 per jacket (0.40 machine-hour per jacket × \$57.50 per machine-hour). So, if Webb produces 1,000 jackets, \$23,000 (\$23 per jacket × 1,000 jackets) out of April's budgeted fixed manufacturing overhead costs of \$276,000 will be allocated to the jackets. If Webb produces 10,000 jackets, \$230,000 (\$23 per jacket × 10,000 jackets) will be allocated. Only if Webb produces 12,000 jackets (that is, operates at capacity), will all \$276,000 (\$23 per jacket × 12,000 jackets) of the budgeted fixed manufacturing overhead cost be allocated to the jacket output. The key point here is that even though Webb budgets fixed manufacturing overhead costs to be \$276,000 it does not necessarily allocate all these costs to output. The reason is that Webb budgets \$276,000 of fixed costs to support its planned production of 12,000 jackets. If Webb produces fewer than 12,000 jackets, it only allocates the budgeted cost of capacity actually needed and used to produce the jackets.

The **production-volume variance** is the difference between budgeted fixed overhead and fixed overhead allocated on the basis of actual output produced. The production-volume variance is also referred to as the **denominator-level variance**, as well as the **output-level overhead variance**.

The formula for calculating the production-volume variance, expressed in terms of allocation-base units (machine-hours for Webb), is:

Question: When the production-volume variance is unfavorable, what is the relationship between FMOH allocated and budgeted FMOH?

Answer: FMOH allocated is *less than* budgeted FMOH, as in the Webb example.

$$\text{Production-volume variance} = \begin{matrix}\text{Budgeted}\\\text{fixed}\\\text{overhead}\end{matrix} - \begin{matrix}\text{Fixed overhead allocated using}\\\text{budgeted input allowed for}\\\text{actual output units produced}\end{matrix}$$

$$= \$276{,}000 - (0.40 \text{ hours per unit} \times 10{,}000 \text{ units} \times \$57.50 \text{ per hour})$$

$$= \$276{,}000 - \$230{,}000$$

$$= \$46{,}000 \text{ U}$$

The computations based on the allocation-base units can also be expressed in terms of the budgeted fixed cost per output unit:

$$\text{Production-volume variance} = \begin{matrix}\text{Budgeted}\\\text{fixed}\\\text{overhead}\end{matrix} - \begin{matrix}\text{Fixed overhead allocated using}\\\text{budgeted cost per output unit}\\\text{allowed for actual output produced}\end{matrix}$$

$$= \$276{,}000 - (\$23 \text{ per jacket} \times 10{,}000 \text{ jackets})$$

$$= \$276{,}000 - \$230{,}000$$

$$= \$46{,}000 \text{ U}$$

As shown in Exhibit 8-3, the budgeted fixed overhead (\$276,000) will be the lump sum shown in the static budget and also in any flexible budget within the relevant range. Fixed overhead allocated (\$230,000) is the amount of fixed overhead costs allocated to each unit of output (\$23) multiplied by the number of output units produced during the budget period (10,000 units). The \$46,000 U production-volume variance can also be thought of as \$23 per jacket × 2,000 jackets that were *not* produced (12,000 jackets planned − 10,000 jackets produced). We will explore possible causes for the unfavorable production-volume variance and its management implications in the following section.

Exhibit 8-4 is a graphic presentation of the production-volume variance. Exhibit 8-4 shows that for planning and control purposes, fixed manufacturing overhead costs do not change in the 0- to 12,000-unit relevant range. Contrast this behavior of fixed costs with how these costs are depicted for the inventory costing purpose in Exhibit 8-4. Under generally accepted accounting principles, fixed manufacturing overhead costs are allocated as an inventoriable cost to the output units produced. Every output unit that Webb manufactures will increase the fixed manufacturing overhead allocated to products by \$23. That is, for purposes of allocating fixed manufacturing overhead costs to jackets, these costs are viewed *as if* they had a variable-cost behavior pattern. As the graph in Exhibit 8-4 shows, the difference between the fixed manufacturing overhead costs budgeted of \$276,000 and the \$230,000 of costs allocated is the \$46,000 unfavorable production-volume variance.

When allocating FMOH for the inventory-costing purpose, we "unitize" FMOH (we treat FMOH *as if* it were a variable cost). In contrast, budgeted FMOH is fixed over a wide range of output levels. The production-volume variance is zero only if FMOH allocated *equals* budgeted FMOH. If so, the actual output level (expressed in terms of the FMOH cost-allocation base) is equal to the denominator level used to compute the budgeted FMOH cost rate.

Inventoriable costs are all costs of a product that are regarded as assets and expensed as cost of goods sold when the product is sold.

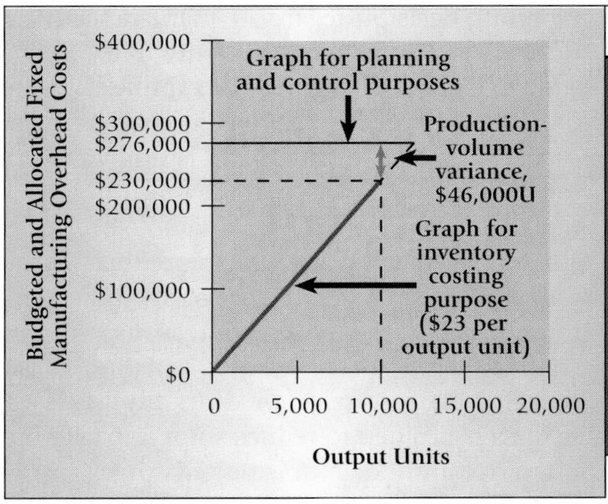

EXHIBIT 8-4

Behavior of Fixed Manufacturing Overhead Costs: Budgeted for Planning and Control Purposes and Allocated for Inventory Costing Purposes for Webb Company for April 2006

Managers should always be careful to distinguish the behavior of fixed costs from how fixed costs are allocated to products. In particular, managers should not use the unitization of fixed manufacturing overhead costs for planning and control decisions that are based on how fixed costs behave. When forecasting fixed costs, managers should concentrate on total lump-sum costs.

Interpreting the Production-Volume Variance

Lump-sum fixed costs represent costs of acquiring capacity, such as plant and equipment leases, that do not decrease automatically if the resources needed turn out to be less than the resources acquired. Sometimes, costs are fixed for contractual reasons such as a lease contract; at other times, costs are fixed because of lumpiness in acquiring and disposing of capacity—for example, Webb may only be able to add capacity to produce jackets in increments of say 1,000 jackets. If this is the case, Webb may choose capacity levels of 10,000, 11,000, or 12,000 jackets but nothing in between.

Webb's management would want to analyze why this overcapacity occurred. Is demand weak? Should Webb reevaluate its product and marketing strategies? Is there a quality problem? Or did Webb make a strategic mistake by acquiring too much capacity? The causes of the $46,000 unfavorable production-volume variance will drive the actions Webb's managers will take in response to this variance.

In contrast, a favorable production-volume variance indicates an overallocation of fixed overhead costs. That is, the standard overhead costs allocated to the actual output produced exceed the budgeted fixed overhead costs of $276,000. The favorable production-volume variance corrects for the fixed costs recorded in excess of $276,000.

Be careful when drawing conclusions regarding a company's decisions about capacity planning and how that capacity was used from the type (that is, favorable, F, or unfavorable, U) or the magnitude associated with a production-volume variance. To interpret the $46,000 unfavorable variance, Webb should consider why it sold only 10,000 jackets in April. Suppose a new competitor had gained market share by pricing below Webb's selling price. To sell the budgeted 12,000 jackets, Webb might have had to reduce its own selling price on all 12,000 jackets. Suppose it decided that selling 10,000 jackets at a higher price yielded higher operating income than selling 12,000 jackets at a lower price. The problem is the production-volume variance does not take into account such information. That's why Webb should not interpret the $46,000 U amount as the total economic cost of selling 2,000 jackets fewer than the 12,000 jackets budgeted. If, however, Webb's managers anticipate they will not need capacity beyond 10,000 jackets, they may reduce the excess capacity, say, by cancelling the lease on some of the machines.

Companies plan their plant capacity strategically on the basis of market information about how much capacity will be needed over some future time horizon. For 2006, Webb's budgeted quantity of output is equal to the maximum capacity of the plant for that budget period. Actual demand (and quantity produced) turned out to be below the budgeted quantity of output, so Webb reports an unfavorable production-volume variance for April 2006. However, it would be incorrect to conclude that Webb's management made a poor planning decision regarding plant capacity. Demand for Webb's jackets might be highly uncertain. Given this uncertainty and the cost of not having sufficient capacity to meet sudden demand surges (for example, lost contribution margins and reduced follow-on business), Webb's management may have made a wise choice in planning 2006 plant capacity. Of course, if demand is unlikely to pick up again, Webb's managers may look to cancel the lease on some of the machines or to sublease the machines to other parties with the goal of reducing the unfavorable production-volume variance.

Managers must always explore the why of a variance before concluding that the label unfavorable or favorable necessarily indicates, respectively, poor or good management performance. Understanding the reasons for a variance also helps managers decide on future courses of action (see the Concepts in Action feature, p. 269). Should they try to reduce capacity, increase sales, or do nothing? Based on their analysis of the situation, Webb's managers decided to reduce some capacity but continued to maintain some excess capacity to accommodate unexpected surges in demand. Chapter 9 and Chapter 13 examine these issues in more detail.

Next, we describe the journal entries Webb would make to record fixed overhead costs using standard costing.

Journal Entries for Fixed Manufacturing Overhead Costs and Variances

We illustrate journal entries for fixed manufacturing overhead costs for April 2006 using Fixed Manufacturing Overhead Control and the contra account Fixed Manufacturing Overhead Allocated (data from Exhibit 8-3).

1.	Fixed Manufacturing Overhead Control	285,000	
	Salaries Payable, Accumulated Depreciation, and various other accounts		285,000
	To record actual fixed overhead costs incurred.		
2.	Work-in-Process Control	230,000	
	Fixed Manufacturing Overhead Allocated		230,000
	To record fixed manufacturing overhead costs allocated, (0.40 machine-hour/unit × 10,000 units × $57.50/machine-hour). (The costs accumulated in Work-in-Process Control are transferred to Finished Goods Control when production is completed and to Cost of Goods Sold when the products are sold.)		
3.	Fixed Manufacturing Overhead Allocated	230,000	
	Fixed Manufacturing Overhead Spending Variance	9,000	
	Fixed Manufacturing Overhead Production-Volume Variance	46,000	
	Fixed Manufacturing Overhead Control		285,000
	To record variances for the accounting period.		

Note how the fixed manufacturing overhead spending variance and the fixed manufacturing overhead production-volume variance record the $55,000 ($285,000 – $230,000) of fixed manufacturing overhead costs that have been incurred but not allocated to jackets. These variances are the underallocated fixed overhead costs that we introduced in normal costing in Chapter 4.

At the end of the fiscal year, the fixed manufacturing overhead spending variance is written off to cost of goods sold if it is immaterial in amount, or prorated among Work-in-Process Control, Finished Goods Control, Cost of Goods Sold, and the Production-Volume Variance on the basis of fixed manufacturing overhead allocated to these accounts as described in Chapter 4, pages 119–121. Some companies combine the write-off and proration methods—that is, they write off the portion of the variance that is due to inefficiency and could have been avoided and prorate the portion of the variance that is unavoidable. Assume that the balance in the Fixed Overhead Spending Variance account as of April 2006 is also the balance at the end of 2006 and is immaterial in amount. The following journal entry records the write-off to Cost of Goods Sold.

Cost of Goods Sold	9,000	
Fixed Manufacturing Overhead Spending Variance		9,000

CONCEPTS IN ACTION

Variance Analysis and Standard Costing: Helping Sandoz Manage Overhead Costs

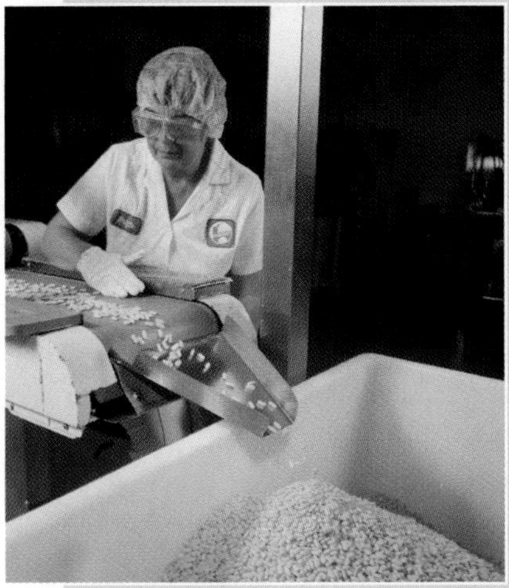

How does a major manufacturing company, such as Sandoz US, maintain its competitive advantage? In addition to its intricate analysis of direct cost variances, Sandoz must also tackle the challenge of accounting for overhead cost variances. Let's examine how Sandoz uses variance analysis and standard costing to manage its overhead costs.

Each year, Sandoz prepares an overhead budget based on a detailed production plan, planned overhead spending, and other factors, including inflation, efficiency initiatives, and anticipated capital expenditures and depreciation. Sandoz then uses activity-based costing techniques to assign budgeted overhead costs to different work centers (for example, mixing, blending, tableting, testing, and packaging). Finally, overhead costs are assigned to products based on the activity levels required by each product at each work center. The resulting standard product cost is used in product profitability analysis and as a basis for making pricing decisions. The two main focal points in Sandoz's performance analyses are overhead absorption analysis and manufacturing overhead variance analysis.

Each month, absorption analysis compares actual production and actual costs to the standard costs of processed inventory. The monthly analysis evaluates two key trends: 1. Are costs in line with the budget? If not, the reasons are examined and the accountable managers notified. 2. Are production volume and product mix conforming to plan? If not, machine capacities are reviewed and adjusted if the absorption trend is deemed to be permanent. Absorption analysis acts as a compass for plant management to determine if they are on budget and have an appropriate capacity level to efficiently satisfy the needs of their customers.

Manufacturing overhead variances are examined at the work center level. These variances help determine when equipment is not running as expected, which leads to repair or replacement. Variances also help in identifying inefficiencies in processing and setup and cleaning times, which leads to more efficient ways to use equipment. Sometimes, manufacturing overhead variance analysis leads to the review and improvement of the standards themselves—a critical element in planning the level of plant capacity. Management reviews current and future capacity utilization on a monthly basis, using standard hours entered into the plant's Enterprise Resource Planning system. The standards are a useful tool in identifying capacity constraints and future capital needs.

As the plant controller remarked, "Standard costing at Sandoz produces costs that are not only understood by management accountants and industrial engineers, but by decision makers in marketing and on the production floor. Management accountants at Sandoz achieve this by having a high degree of process understanding and involvement. The result is better pricing and product mix decisions, lower waste, process improvements, and efficient capacity choices—all contributing to overall profitability."

Source: Conversations with and documents prepared by Eric Evans and Erich Erchr on March 20, 2004, and May 28, 2004.

We now address the production-volume variance. Assume that the balance in Fixed Manufacturing Overhead Production-Volume Variance as of April 2006 is also the balance at the end of 2006. Also assume that some of the jackets manufactured during 2006 are in work in process and finished goods inventory at the end of the year. A strong argument is often made by many management accountants for writing off to Cost of Goods Sold and not prorating an unfavorable production-volume variance. Proponents of this argument contend that the unfavorable production-volume variance of \$46,000 measures the cost of resources expended for 2,000 jackets that were not produced (\$23 per jacket × 2,000 jackets = \$46,000). Prorating these costs would inappropriately result in allocating fixed costs incurred for the 2,000 jackets that were not produced to the jackets that were produced. The jackets produced already bear their representative share of fixed costs of \$23 per jacket. Therefore, this argument favors charging the unfavorable production-volume variance against the year's revenues so that fixed costs of unused capacity are not carried in work in process and finished goods inventory.

There is, however, an alternative view. This view regards the denominator level chosen as a 'soft' rather than a 'hard' measure of the fixed resources required and needed to

FOCUS ON VALUES AND BEHAVIORS

THE CHALLENGES OF OVERHEAD VARIANCES

Management accountants are constantly monitoring all aspects of a company's financial activities, which gives them a unique perspective into overhead variance analysis. Because overhead variances are challenging for managers to understand, management accountants must acquire a deep understanding of operations and processes so they can provide an in-depth examination of the company's performance. Armed with this knowledge, management accountants can explain to managers the reasons for the variances and help them develop action plans to improve performance and promote learning.

When it comes to selecting the quantity of the cost-allocation base for allocating variable and fixed overhead costs to output produced, managers may be tempted to choose a lower capacity level (denominator) to avoid unfavorable variances and the resulting negative effects on operating income. For exampe, if Webb's management team had used 48,000 budgeted machine-hours (that is, 120,000 jackets per year or 10,000 jackets per month) instead of 57,600 machine-hours as the denominator, Webb would not have experienced an unfavorable production-volume variance. But Webb's management accountants should ask if this is the right choice. For example, is 48,000 machine-hours too conservative a figure? Wouldn't the effect of increasing the budgeted fixed overhead cost per output unit be to increase inventory values and inflate operating income? Wouldn't it mislead managers about available capacity? Management accountants must always act to ensure the accuracy of reported numbers even if it means reporting lower profits.

produce each jacket. Suppose for example that, either because of the design of the jacket or the functioning of the machines, it took more machine-hours than previously thought to manufacture each jacket. Consequently, Webb could make only 10,000 jackets rather than the planned 12,000 in April. In this case, the $276,000 of budgeted fixed manufacturing overhead costs support the production of the 10,000 jackets manufactured. Under this reasoning, prorating the fixed overhead production-volume variance would appropriately spread fixed manufacturing overhead costs among Work-in-Process Control, Finished Goods Control, and Cost of Goods Sold.

What about a favorable production-volume variance? Suppose Webb manufactured 13,800 jackets in April 2006.

$$\text{Production-Volume Variance} = \begin{array}{c}\text{Budgeted}\\ \text{fixed}\\ \text{overhead}\end{array} - \begin{array}{c}\text{Fixed overhead allocated using}\\ \text{budgeted cost per output unit}\\ \text{allowed for actual output produced}\end{array}$$

$$= \$276{,}000 - (\$23 \text{ per jacket} \times 13{,}800 \text{ jackets})$$

$$= \$276{,}000 - \$317{,}400 = \$41{,}400 \text{ F}$$

Because actual production exceeded the planned capacity level, clearly the fixed manufacturing overhead costs of $276,000 supported production of, and so should be allocated to, all 13,800 jackets. Prorating the favorable production-volume variance achieves this outcome and reduces the amounts in Work-in-Process Control, Finished Goods Control, and Cost of Goods Sold. Proration is also the more conservative approach in the sense that it results in a lower operating income than if all of the favorable production-volume variance were credited to Cost of Goods Sold.

One more point is relevant to the discussion of whether to prorate the production-volume variance or to write it off to cost of goods sold. If variances are always written off to cost of goods sold, a company could set its standards to either increase (for financial reporting purposes) or decrease (for tax purposes) operating income. For example, Webb could generate a favorable (unfavorable) production-volume variance by setting the denominator level used to allocate fixed overhead costs low (high) and thereby increase (decrease) operating income. (See also the Focus on Values and Behaviors feature above.) The proration method has the effect of approximating the allocation of fixed costs based on actual costs and actual output so it is not susceptible to the manipulation of operating income via the choice of the denominator level.

There is no clear-cut or preferred approach for closing out the production-volume variance. The appropriate accounting procedure is a matter of judgment and depends on the circumstances of each case. Variations of the proration method may be desirable. For example, a company may choose to write off a portion of the production-volume variance and prorate the rest. The goal is to write off that part of the production-volume variance that represents the cost of capacity not used to support the production of output during the period. The rest of the production-volume variance is prorated to Work-in-Process Control, Finished Goods Control, and Cost of Goods Sold.

If Webb were to write off the production-volume variance to cost of goods sold, it would make the following journal entry.

Cost of Goods Sold	46,000	
Fixed Manufacturing Overhead Production-Volume Variance		46,000

Integrated Analysis of Overhead Cost Variances

7 **Show how the 4- variance analysis approach reconciles the actual overhead incurred with the overhead amounts allocated during the period**

. . . the 4-variance analysis approach identifies spending and efficiency variances for variable overhead costs and spending and production-volume variances for fixed overhead costs

As our discussion indicates, the variance calculations for variable manufacturing overhead and fixed manufacturing overhead differ.

- Variable manufacturing overhead has no production-volume variance.
- Fixed manufacturing overhead has no efficiency variance.

Exhibit 8-5 presents an integrated summary of the variable overhead variances and the fixed overhead variances computed using standard costs for April 2006. Exhibit 8-5 indicates the columns for which no variances are calculated. Panel A shows the variances for variable manufacturing overhead; Panel B shows the variances for fixed manufacturing overhead. As you study Exhibit 8-5, note how the columns in Panels A and B are aligned to measure the different variances. In both Panels A and B,

- The difference between columns 1 and 2 measures the spending variance.
- The difference between columns 2 and 3 measures the efficiency variance (if applicable).
- The difference between columns 3 and 4 measures the production-volume variance (if applicable).

Panel A has an efficiency variance; Panel B has no efficiency variance. A lump-sum amount of fixed costs will be unaffected by the degree of operating efficiency in a given budget period.

Panel A does not have a production-volume variance. That's because the amount of variable overhead allocated is always the same as the flexible-budget amount. Variable costs never have any unused capacity. When production and sales decline from 12,000 jackets to 10,000 jackets, budgeted variable overhead costs proportionately decline. Fixed costs are different. Panel B has a production-volume variance (see Exhibit 8-4) because Webb had to acquire the fixed manufacturing overhead resources it had committed to when it planned production of 12,000 jackets, even though it produced only 10,000 jackets and did not use some of its capacity.

4-, 3-, 2-, and 1-Variance Analysis

When all four overhead variances in Exhibit 8-5 are presented together—spending variance and efficiency variance for variable manufacturing overhead and spending variance and production-volume variance for fixed manufacturing overhead—it is called a 4-variance analysis:

4-Variance Analysis

	Spending Variance	Efficiency Variance	Production-Volume Variance
Variable manufacturing overhead	$4,500 F	$15,000 U	Never a variance
Fixed manufacturing overhead	$9,000 U	Never a variance	$46,000 U

Some companies do not distinguish variable manufacturing overhead incurred from fixed manufacturing overhead incurred in their costing systems and instead combine them into total manufacturing overhead incurred. Companies do this to simplify their accounting systems because making the distinction between variable and fixed costs is often not clear-cut. As we saw in Chapter 2 and will see in Chapter 10, many costs such as supervision, quality control, and materials handling have both variable- and fixed-cost components

EXHIBIT 8-5 Columnar Presentation of Integrated Variance Analysis: Webb Company for April 2006[a]

PANEL A: Variable Manufacturing Overhead

Actual Costs Incurred: Actual Input Quantity × Actual Rate (1)	Actual Input Quantity × Budgeted Rate (2)	Flexible Budget: Budgeted Input Quantity Allowed for Actual Output × Budgeted Rate (3)	Allocated: Budgeted Input Quantity Allowed for Actual Output × Budgeted Rate (4)
		(0.40 hrs./unit × 10,000 units × $30/hr.)	(0.40 hrs./unit × 10,000 units × $30/hr.)
(4,500 hrs. × $29/hr.)	(4,500 hrs. × $30/hr.)	(4,000 hrs. × $30/hr.)	(4,000 hrs. × $30/hr.)
$130,500	$135,000	$120,000	$120,000

- (1)–(2): $4,500 F — Spending variance
- (2)–(3): $15,000 U — Efficiency variance
- (3)–(4): Never a variance
- (1)–(3): $10,500 U — Flexible-budget variance
- (3)–(4): Never a variance
- (1)–(4): $10,500 U — Underallocated variable overhead (Total variable overhead variance)

PANEL B: Fixed Manufacturing Overhead

Actual Costs Incurred (1)	Same Budgeted Lump Sum (as in Static Budget) Regardless of Output Level (2)	Flexible Budget: Same Budgeted Lump Sum (as in Static Budget) Regardless of Output Level (3)	Allocated: Budgeted Input Quantity Allowed for Actual Output × Budgeted Rate (4)
			(0.40 hrs./unit × 10,000 units × $57.50/hr)
			(4,000 hrs. × $57.50/hr)
$285,000	$276,000	$276,000	$230,000

- (1)–(2): $9,000 U — Spending variance
- (2)–(3): Never a variance
- (3)–(4): $46,000 U — Production-volume variance
- (1)–(3): $9,000 U — Flexible-budget variance
- (3)–(4): $46,000 U — Production-volume variance
- (1)–(4): $55,000 U — Underallocated fixed overhead (Total fixed overhead variance)

[a]F = favorable effect on operating income; U = unfavorable effect on operating income.

that may not be easy to separate. Managers can then use a 3-variance analysis that combines the two spending variances.

3-Variance Analysis

	Spending Variance	Efficiency Variance	Production-Volume Variance
Total manufacturing overhead	$4,500 U	$15,000 U	$46,000 U

The accounting for 3-variance analysis is simpler than for 4-variance analysis, but some information is lost. For this reason, managers prefer using 4-variance analysis if they can identify the variable and fixed components of manufacturing overhead. Because 3-variance analysis combines variable and fixed overhead spending variances when reporting overhead cost variances, it is sometimes called *combined variance analysis.*

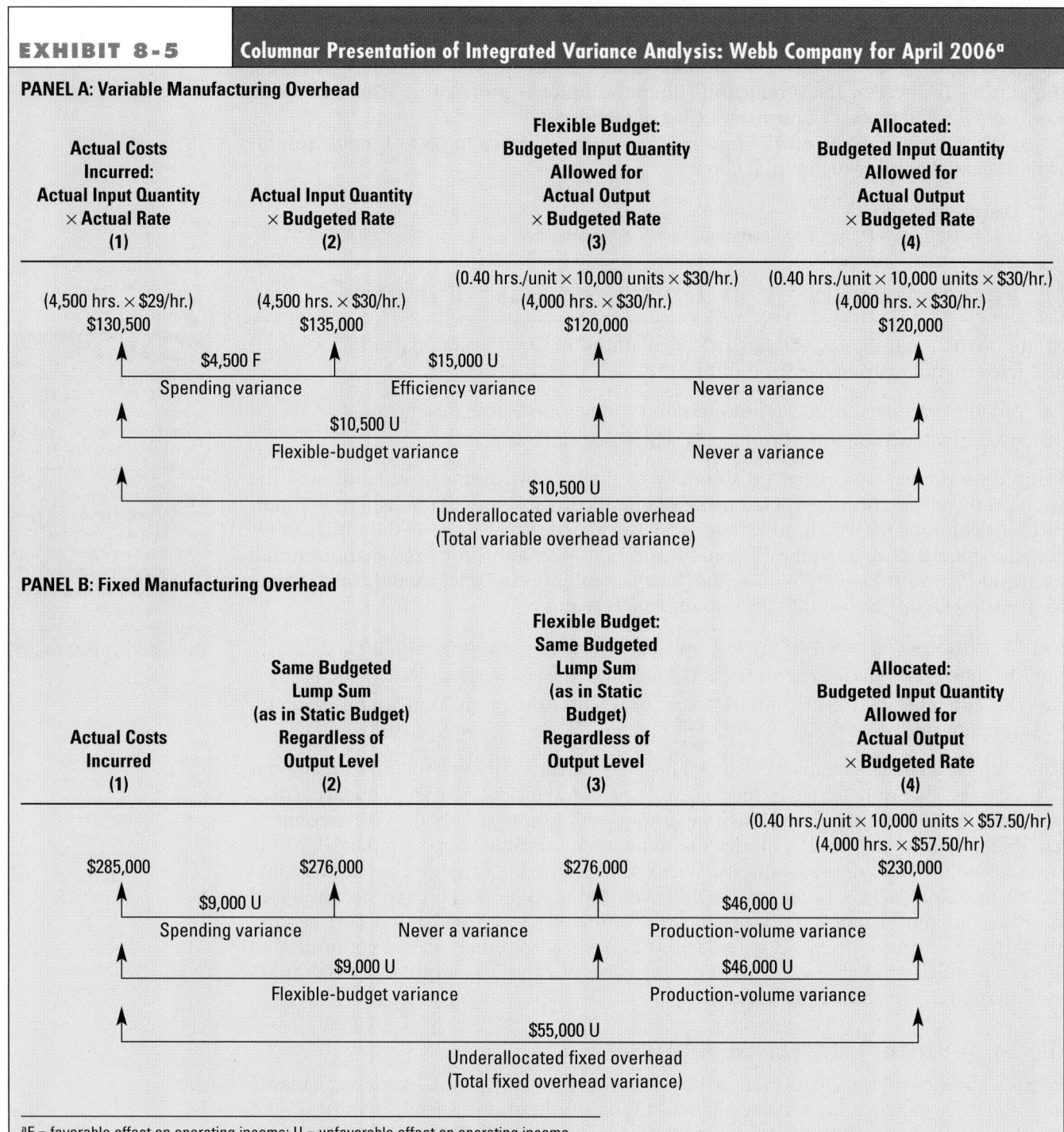

A 2-variance analysis aggregates the spending and efficiency variances from the 3-variance analysis.

2-Variance Analysis

	Flexible-Budget Variance	Production-Volume Variance
Total manufacturing overhead	$19,500 U	$46,000 U

The 2-variance analysis compares actual costs to the flexible budget to compute the flexible-budget variance and the budgeted and allocated fixed costs to compute the production-volume variance. Unlike 3-variance analysis, 2-variance analysis does not use information about the actual inputs (machine-hours) used in April (the information required in Exhibit 8-5, Panel A, column 2, to subdivide the variable manufacturing overhead flexible-budget variance into the spending variance and the efficiency variance).

A 1-variance analysis combines the flexible-budget variance and the production-volume variance from 2-variance analysis:

1-Variance Analysis

	Total Overhead Variance
Total manufacturing overhead	$65,500 U

The single variance of $65,500 U in 1-variance analysis is called **total-overhead variance.** Using figures from Exhibit 8-5, the $65,500 U total-overhead variance is the difference between (a) the total actual manufacturing overhead incurred ($130,500 + $285,000 = $415,500) and (b) the manufacturing overhead allocated ($120,000 + $230,000 = $350,000) to the actual output produced. This variance equals the underallocated (or underapplied) overhead costs that we first discussed in Chapter 4's normal costing, page 118.

Study Tip: To check your understanding of overhead variance analysis, see the Featured Exercise, true–false statement 4, multiple-choice questions 2 and 4, and Review Exercises 1 and 3 (*Student Guide*, beginning p. 92. Fully explained answers begin on p. 100.)

Detailed 4-variance analyses are more common in large, complex businesses. That's because it is impossible for managers at a company such as General Electric to keep track of all that is happening within their areas of responsibility. The detailed 4-variance analyses help managers identify and focus attention on the areas not operating as expected. Managers of small businesses understand their operations better based on personal observations and nonfinancial measures. They find less value in doing the additional measurements (such as distinguishing variable from fixed manufacturing overhead) required for 4-variance analyses. Regardless of the level of detail, the Global Surveys of Company Practice, p. 274, indicate widespread use of variance analysis in organizations.

As you have seen in the case of other variances, the variances in Webb's 4-variance analysis are not necessarily independent of each other. For example, Webb may purchase lower-quality machine fluids (leading to a favorable variable overhead spending variance), which results in the machines taking longer to operate than budgeted (causing an unfavorable variable overhead efficiency variance), and producing less than budgeted output (causing an unfavorable production-volume variance).

Production-Volume Variance and Sales-Volume Variance

As we complete our study of variance analysis for Webb Company, it is helpful to step back to see the "big picture." Exhibit 7-2, page 225, subdivided the static-budget variance of $93,100 U into a flexible-budget variance of $29,100 U and a sales-volume variance of $64,000 U. In Chapters 7 and 8, we presented level 3 variances that subdivided, whenever possible, individual flexible-budget variances for selling price, direct materials, direct manufacturing labor, variable overhead, and fixed overhead. Here is a summary:

Selling price	$50,000 F
Direct materials (Price, $44,400 F + Efficiency, $66,000 U)	21,600 U
Direct manufacturing labor (Price, $18,000 U + Efficiency, $20,000 U)	38,000 U
Variable overhead (Spending, $4,500 F + Efficiency, $15,000 U)	10,500 U
Fixed overhead (Spending, $9,000 U)	9,000 U
Total flexible budget variance	$29,100 U

GLOBAL SURVEYS OF COMPANY PRACTICE

Variance Analysis and Control Decisions

There is widespread usage of the variances discussed in Chapters 7 and 8. A survey of United Kingdom companies reported the following percentages[a]:

Variance	Percentage of Companies Computing Variance	Percentage of Companies Viewing the Variance as "Above Average Importance" or "Vitally Important" in Control Decisions
Sales volume	77%	70%
Selling price	75	69
Materials price	94	69
Materials efficiency	80	66
Labor price	63	36
Labor efficiency	73	65
Overhead spending	89	69
Production volume	41	28

In addition, a recent survey of 270 Danish chief management accountants found that 74% consider variance analysis "important" or "very important."[b] Another survey of U.K. and New Zealand manufacturers found that after adopting modern management techniques, including just-in-time and advanced manufacturing technologies, 87% of U.K. and 84% of New Zealand respondents experienced either no change or an increased importance in the role of variance analysis in their control systems.[c]

[a]Drury et al., *A Survey of Management Accounting. . . .*

[b]Mouritsen, "Five Aspects of Accounting Departments. . . ."

[c]Guilding et al., "Budgeting and Standard Costing Practices. . . ."

Full citations are in Appendix A at the end of the book.

But we also calculated one other variance in Chapter 8, the production-volume variance, which is not part of the flexible-budget variance. The question that remains is where does the production-volume variance fit into the "big picture"? As we shall see, the production-volume variance is a level 3 variance that subdivides the sales-volume variance.

Under our assumption of actual production and sales of 10,000 jackets, Webb's costing system debits to Work-in-Process Control the standard costs of the 10,000 jackets produced, which are then transferred to Finished Goods and finally to Cost of Goods Sold:

Direct materials (Chapter 7, p. 234, Entry 1b)	
($60 per jacket × 10,000 jackets)	$ 600,000
Direct manufacturing labor (Chapter 7, p. 234, Entry 2)	
($16 per jacket × 10,000 jackets)	160,000
Variable manufacturing overhead (Chapter 8, p. 263, Entry 2)	
($12 per jacket × 10,000 jackets)	120,000
Fixed manufacturing overhead (Chapter 8, p. 268, Entry 2)	
($23 per jacket × 10,000 jackets)	230,000
Cost of goods sold at standard cost	
($111 per jacket × 10,000 jackets)	$1,110,000

Webb's costing system also records the revenues from the 10,000 jackets sold at the budgeted selling price of $120 per jacket. The net effect of these entries on Webb's budgeted operating income is as follows:

Revenues at budgeted selling price	
($120 per jacket × 10,000 jackets)	$1,200,000
Cost of goods sold at standard cost	
($111 per jacket × 10,000 jackets)	1,110,000
Operating income based on budgeted profit per jacket	
($9 per jacket × 10,000 jackets)	$ 90,000

The crucial point to keep in mind is that in standard costing, fixed manufacturing overhead cost is treated as if it is a variable cost. That is, in determining the budgeted operating income of \$90,000, only \$230,000 (\$23 per jacket × 10,000 jackets) of fixed manufacturing overhead is considered, whereas the budgeted fixed manufacturing overhead costs are \$276,000. Webb's accountants then record the \$46,000 unfavorable production-volume variance (the difference between budgeted fixed manufacturing overhead costs, \$276,000, and allocated fixed manufacturing overhead costs, \$230,000, p. 268, Entry 3) and the various flexible-budget variances (including the fixed manufacturing overhead spending variance) that total \$29,100 unfavorable (see Exhibit 7-2, p. 225). This results in actual operating income of \$14,900 as follows:

Operating income based on budgeted profit per jacket ($9 per jacket × 10,000 jackets)	$90,000
Unfavorable production-volume variance	(46,000)
Flexible-budget operating income (Exhibit 7-2)	44,000
Unfavorable flexible-budget variance for operating income (Exhibit 7-2)	(29,100)
Actual operating income (Exhibit 7-2)	$14,900

Nowhere in Webb's costing system is any entry made for the static-budget operating income of \$108,000 (p. 223). The reason is that standard costing records only budgeted revenues, standard costs, and variances for the 10,000 jackets actually produced and sold, not for the 12,000 jackets that were *planned* to be produced and sold. Therefore, the sales-volume variance of 64,000 U, the difference between static-budget operating income, \$108,000, and flexible-budget operating income, \$44,000 (Exhibit 7-2, p. 225), is never actually recorded in standard costing. Nevertheless, the sales-volume variance is useful because it helps managers understand the lost contribution margin from selling 2,000 fewer jackets (the sales-volume variance assumes fixed costs remain at the budgeted level of \$276,000).

Similarly, the difference between static-budget operating income of \$108,000 for 12,000 jackets and budgeted operating income for 10,000 jackets of \$90,000 is also not recorded in Webb's costing system. This *operating-income volume variance* of \$18,000 U (\$108,000 − \$90,000) is smaller than the sales-volume variance of \$64,000 U. That's because Webb's costing system assumes fixed costs behave in a variable manner and so assumes fixed costs are only the allocated fixed costs of \$230,000 rather than the budgeted fixed costs of \$276,000 assumed in the sales-volume variance calculations. Of course, the difference between the allocated and budgeted fixed costs is precisely the production-volume variance of \$46,000 U. Therefore,

Operating-income volume variance	$18,000 U
Production-volume variance	46,000 U
Equals sales-volume variance	$64,000 U

That is, the level 2 sales-volume variance can be subdivided into level 3 production-volume and operating-income volume variances

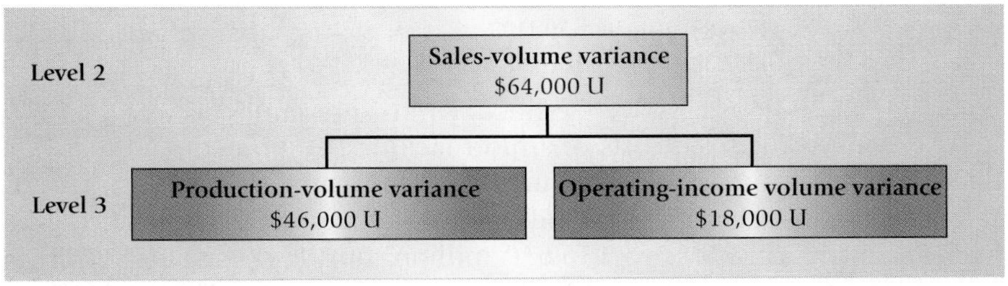

Financial and Nonfinancial Performance Measures

MOH cost items can be controlled on the production floor through personal observation and timely nonfinancial measures of individual items (for example, overtime authorization, idle time, and defect rates). The accounting system transforms these nonfinancial measures into financial measures that inform managers of the materiality (significance) of the variances.

The overhead variances discussed in this chapter are examples of financial performance measures. Managers also find that nonfinancial measures provide useful information. Nonfinancial measures that Webb likely would find helpful in planning and controlling its overhead costs are:

1. Quantity of actual indirect materials used per machine-hour, relative to quantity of budgeted indirect materials used per machine-hour

There is debate over the relative weights to be given to financial and nonfinancial measures. For example, some experts maintain that nonfinancial measures, such as product quality and customer satisfaction, should be given more emphasis than financial measures. Chapter 13 considers this issue in detail.

2. Actual energy used per machine-hour, relative to budgeted energy used per machine-hour
3. Actual machine-hours per jacket, relative to budgeted machine-hours per jacket

These performance measures, like the financial variances discussed in this chapter and Chapter 7, are best considered as signals to direct managers' attention to problems. These nonfinancial performance measures probably would be reported daily or hourly on the production floor. The manufacturing overhead variances we discussed in this chapter capture the financial effects of items such as 1, 2, and 3, which in many cases first appear as nonfinancial performance measures.

Both financial and nonfinancial performance measures are used to evaluate the performance of managers. Exclusive reliance on either is always too simplistic because each gives a different perspective on performance. Nonfinancial measures (such as those described above) provide feedback on individual aspects of a manager's performance, whereas financial measures evaluate the overall effect of and the tradeoffs among different nonfinancial performance measures.

Overhead Cost Variances in Nonmanufacturing and Service Settings

Our Webb Company example examines variable manufacturing overhead costs and fixed manufacturing overhead costs. Should the overhead costs of the nonmanufacturing areas of the company be examined using the variance analysis framework discussed in this chapter? Variable-cost information pertaining to nonmanufacturing, as well as manufacturing, costs is often used in pricing decisions and decisions about which products to emphasize. Variance analysis of all variable overhead costs is considered when making such decisions and when managing costs. For example, managers in industries in which distribution costs are high, such as automobiles, consumer durables, cement and steel, may use standard costing to give reliable and timely information on variable distribution overhead spending variances and efficiency variances.

Consider service-sector companies such as airlines, hospitals, hotels, and railroads. The measures of output commonly used in these companies are passenger-miles flown, patient-days provided, room-days occupied, and ton-miles of freight hauled, respectively. Few costs can be traced to these outputs in a cost-effective way. The majority of costs are fixed overhead costs (for example, costs of equipment, buildings, and staff). Using capacity effectively is the key to profitability, and fixed overhead variances can help managers in this task.

Consider the following data for United Airlines for 2000 and 2003. Available seat miles (ASMs) are the actual seats in an airplane multiplied by the distance traveled.

Year	Total ASMs (Millions) (1)	Revenue per ASM (2)	Cost per ASM (3)	Gross Margin per ASM (4) = (2) – (3)
2000	175,485	$0.1103	$0.1066	$0.0037
2003	136,630	$0.1006	$0.1104	–$0.0098

Retail businesses, such as Kmart, also have high capacity-related fixed costs (lease and occupancy costs). Sales declines result in unused capacity and unfavorable fixed-cost variances. Kmart reduced fixed costs by closing some of its stores, but it also had to file for Chapter 11 bankruptcy.

After September 11, 2001, as air travel declined, United's revenues decreased but a majority of its costs comprising fixed costs of airport facilities, equipment, and personnel did not. United had a large unfavorable production-volume variance as its capacity remained underutilized. As column 1 of the table indicates, United responded by reducing its capacity from 175,485 million ASMs to 136,630 million, but it was unable to fill even the planes it had left, so revenue per ASM declined (column 2) and cost per ASM increased (column 3). United filed for Chapter 11 bankruptcy and began seeking government guarantees to obtain the loans it needed to bring it out of bankruptcy.

8

Calculate overhead variances in activity-based costing

. . . compare budgeted and actual overhead costs of activities

Activity-Based Costing and Variance Analysis

ABC systems classify costs of various activities into a cost hierarchy: output unit-level, batch-level, product-sustaining, and facility-sustaining (see pp. 147–148). The basic principles and concepts for variable manufacturing overhead costs and fixed manufacturing overhead costs presented earlier in the chapter can be applied to ABC systems. In this section, we illustrate variance analysis for variable batch-level setup overhead costs and fixed batch-level setup overhead costs. Batch-level costs are costs of activities that are related to a group of units of products or services rather than to each individual unit.

We continue the Chapter 7 example of Lyco Brass Works, which manufactures Elegance, a line of decorative brass faucets for home spas. Lyco produces Elegance in batches. To manufacture a batch of Elegance, Lyco must set up the machines and molds. Setups are a highly skilled activity. Hence, a separate Setup Department is responsible for setting up machines and molds for different batches of products. Setup costs are overhead costs of products.

Setup costs consist of some costs that are variable and some that are fixed with respect to the number of setup-hours. Variable setup costs consist of wages paid to direct setup labor and indirect support labor, costs of maintenance of setup equipment, and costs of indirect materials and energy used during setups. Fixed setup costs consist of salaries paid to engineers and supervisors and costs of leasing setup equipment.

Information regarding Elegance for 2007 follows:

	Static-Budget Amount	Actual Amount
1. Units of Elegance produced and sold	180,000	151,200
2. Batch size (units per batch)	150	140
3. Number of batches (Line 1 ÷ Line 2)	1,200	1,080
4. Setup-hours per batch	6	6.25
5. Total setup-hours (Line 3 × Line 4)	7,200	6,750
6. Variable overhead cost per setup-hour	\$20	\$21
7. Variable setup overhead costs (Line 5 × Line 6)	\$144,000	\$141,750
8. Total fixed setup overhead costs	\$216,000	\$220,000

Flexible Budget and Variance Analysis for Variable Setup Overhead Costs

To prepare the flexible budget for variable setup overhead costs, Lyco starts with the actual units of output produced, 151,200 units, and proceeds in the following steps.

Step 1: Using Budgeted Batch Size, Calculate the Number of Batches That Should Have Been Used to Produce Actual Output. Lyco should have manufactured the 151,200 units of output in 1,008 batches (151,200 units ÷ 150 units per batch).

Step 2: Using Budgeted Setup-Hours per Batch, Calculate the Number of Setup-Hours That Should Have Been Used. At the budgeted quantity of 6 setup-hours per batch, 1,008 batches should have required 6,048 setup-hours (1,008 batches × 6 setup-hours per batch).

Step 3: Using Budgeted Variable Cost per Setup-Hour, Calculate the Flexible Budget for Variable Setup Overhead Costs. The flexible-budget amount is 6,048 setup-hours × \$20 per setup-hour = \$120,960.

Flexible-budget variance for variable setup overhead costs = Actual costs incurred − Flexible-budget costs

= (6,750 hours × \$21 per hour) − (6,048 hours × \$20 per hour)

= \$141,750 − \$120,960

= \$20,790 U

Exhibit 8-6 presents the variances for variable setup overhead costs in columnar form.

EXHIBIT 8-6

Columnar Presentation of Variable Setup Overhead Variance Analysis for Lyco Brass Works for 2007[a]

	Actual Costs Incurred: Actual Input Quantity × Actual Rate (1)		Actual Input Quantity × Budgeted Rate (2)		Flexible Budget: Budgeted Input Quantity Allowed for Actual Output × Budgeted Rate (3)
	(6,750 hours × \$21 per hour)		(6,750 hours × \$20 per hour)		(6,048 hours × \$20 per hour)
	\$141,750		\$135,000		\$120,960
Level 3		\$6,750 U Spending variance		\$14,040 U Efficiency variance	
Level 2			\$20,790 U Flexible-budget variance		

[a]F = favorable effect on operating income; U = unfavorable effect on operating income.

The flexible-budget variance for variable setup overhead costs can be subdivided into efficiency and spending variances.

Because setup costs are at the batch level, the budgeted quantity of input allowed for actual output is calculated at the batch level. The quantity of setup-hours allowed is based on the number of batches it should have taken to produce the actual quantity of output. Although both ABC systems and traditional costing systems allocate MOH costs to output units produced, ABC has the advantage that there are better cause-and-effect relationships between the cost-allocation bases chosen and the related cost pools.

$$\begin{aligned}\text{Variable setup overhead efficiency variance} &= \left(\begin{array}{c}\text{Actual quantity of variable overhead}\\ \text{cost-allocation base used for}\\ \text{actual output}\end{array} - \begin{array}{c}\text{Budgeted quantity of variable overhead}\\ \text{cost-allocation base allowed for}\\ \text{actual output}\end{array}\right) \times \begin{array}{c}\text{Budgeted variable overhead cost per}\\ \text{unit of cost-allocation base}\end{array}\\ &= (6{,}750 \text{ hours} - 6{,}048 \text{ hours}) \times \$20 \text{ per hour}\\ &= 702 \text{ hours} \times \$20 \text{ per hour}\\ &= \$14{,}040\ \text{U}\end{aligned}$$

The unfavorable variable setup overhead efficiency variance of \$14,040 arises because the 6,750 actual setup-hours exceed the 6,048 setup-hours Lyco should have used for the number of units it produced. Two reasons for the unfavorable efficiency variance are (1) smaller actual batch sizes of 140 units per batch, instead of budgeted batch sizes of 150 units, which resulted in Lyco producing the 151,200 units in 1,080 batches instead of 1,008 batches; and (2) higher actual setup-hours per batch of 6.25 hours instead of the budgeted 6 hours.

Explanations for smaller-than-budgeted batch sizes could include (1) quality problems if batch sizes exceed 140 units (faucets) and (2) high costs of carrying inventory. Explanations for higher actual setup-hours per batch include (1) problems with equipment; (2) undermotivated, inexperienced, or underskilled employees; and (3) inappropriate setup-time standards.

Lyco's variable setup overhead spending variance is calculated as follows:

$$\begin{aligned}\text{Variable setup overhead spending variance} &= \left(\begin{array}{c}\text{Actual variable overhead cost per}\\ \text{unit of cost-allocation base}\end{array} - \begin{array}{c}\text{Budgeted variable overhead cost per}\\ \text{unit of cost-allocation base}\end{array}\right) \times \begin{array}{c}\text{Actual quantity of variable overhead}\\ \text{cost-allocation base}\\ \text{used for actual output}\end{array}\\ &= (\$21 \text{ per hour} - \$20 \text{ per hour}) \times 6{,}750 \text{ hours}\\ &= \$1 \text{ per hour} \times 6{,}750 \text{ hours}\\ &= \$6{,}750\ \text{U}\end{aligned}$$

The unfavorable spending variance indicates that Lyco operated in 2007 with a higher-than-budgeted variable overhead cost per setup-hour. Two main reasons that could account for the unfavorable spending variance are (1) actual prices of individual items included in variable overhead, such as setup labor, indirect support labor, or energy, are higher than budgeted prices; and (2) actual quantity usage of individual items, such as indirect support labor and energy, increased more than the increase in setup-hours, due perhaps to setups becoming more complex because of equipment problems. Thus, equipment problems could lead to an unfavorable efficiency variance because setup-hours increase, but they could also lead to an unfavorable spending variance, because each setup-hour requires more resources from the setup cost pool than was budgeted.

Identifying the reasons for these variances is important because it helps managers take corrective action that will be incorporated in future budgets. We now consider fixed setup overhead costs.

Flexible Budget and Variance Analysis for Fixed Setup Overhead Costs

Lyco's fixed setup overhead flexible-budget variance is calculated as follows:

$$\begin{aligned}\text{Fixed-setup overhead flexible-budget variance} &= \text{Actual costs incurred} - \text{Flexible-budget costs}\\ &= \$220{,}000 - \$216{,}000\\ &= \$4{,}000\text{ U}\end{aligned}$$

Note that the flexible-budget amount for fixed setup overhead costs equals the static-budget amount of $216,000. That's because there is no "flexing" of fixed costs.

The fixed setup overhead spending variance is the same amount as the fixed overhead flexible-budget variance (because fixed overhead costs have no efficiency variance).

$$\begin{aligned}\text{Fixed-setup overhead spending variance} &= \text{Actual costs incurred} - \text{Flexible-budget costs}\\ &= \$220{,}000 - \$216{,}000\\ &= \$4{,}000\text{ U}\end{aligned}$$

The unfavorable fixed setup overhead spending variance could be because of higher leasing costs of new setup equipment or higher salaries paid to engineers and supervisors. Lyco may have incurred these costs to alleviate some of the difficulties it was having in setting up machines.

To calculate the production-volume variance, Lyco first computes the budgeted cost-allocation rate for fixed setup overhead costs using the same four-step approach described on pages 263–264.

Step 1: Choose the Period to Use for the Budget. Lyco uses a period of 12 months (the year 2007).

Step 2: Select the Cost-Allocation Base to Use in Allocating Fixed Overhead Costs to Output Produced. Lyco uses budgeted setup-hours as the cost-allocation base for fixed setup overhead costs. Budgeted setup-hours in the static budget for 2007 are 7,200 hours.

Step 3: Identify the Fixed Overhead Costs Associated with the Cost-Allocation Base. Lyco's fixed setup overhead cost budget for 2007 is $216,000.

Step 4: Compute the Rate per Unit of the Cost-Allocation Base Used to Allocate Fixed Overhead Costs to Output Produced. Dividing the $216,000 from step 3 by the 7,200 setup-hours from step 2, Lyco estimates a fixed setup overhead cost rate of $30 per setup-hour:

$$\begin{aligned}\text{Budgeted fixed setup overhead cost per unit of cost-allocation base} &= \frac{\text{Budgeted total costs in fixed overhead cost pool}}{\text{Budgeted total quantity of cost-allocation base}} = \frac{\$216{,}000}{7{,}200\text{ setup-hours}}\\ &= \$30\text{ per setup-hour}\end{aligned}$$

$$\begin{aligned}\text{Production-volume variance for fixed setup overhead costs} &= \text{Budgeted fixed setup overhead costs} - \text{Fixed setup overhead allocated using budgeted input allowed for actual output units produced}\\ &= \$216{,}000 - (1{,}008\text{ batches} \times 6\text{ hours/batch}) \times \$30/\text{hour}\\ &= \$216{,}000 - (6{,}048\text{ hours} \times \$30/\text{hour})\\ &= \$216{,}000 - \$181{,}440\\ &= \$34{,}560\text{ U}\end{aligned}$$

Exhibit 8-7 presents the variances for fixed setup overhead costs in columnar form.

EXHIBIT 8-7

Columnar Presentation of Fixed Setup Overhead Variance Analysis: Lyco Brass Works for 2007[a]

	Actual Costs Incurred (1)		Flexible Budget: Same Budgeted Lump Sum (as in Static Budget) Regardless of Output Level (2)		Allocated: Budgeted Input Quantity Allowed for Actual Output × Budgeted Rate (3)
					(1,008[b] batches × 6 hours/batch × $30/hour) (6,048 hours × $30/hour)
	$220,000		$216,000		$181,440
Level 3		$4,000 U Spending variance		$34,560 U Production-volume variance	
Level 2		$4,000 U Flexible-budget variance			

[a]F = favorable effect on operating income; U = unfavorable effect on operating income.
[b]1,008 batches = 151,200 units ÷ 150 units per batch.

Study Tip: To review important terms and concepts in Chapters 7 and 8, work the crossword puzzle (*Student Guide*, p. 99). The solution is on p. 104.

During 2007, Lyco planned to produce 180,000 units of Elegance but actually produced 151,200 units. The unfavorable production-volume variance measures the amount of extra fixed setup costs that Lyco incurred for setup capacity it had but did not use. One interpretation is that the unfavorable $34,560 production-volume variance represents inefficient use of setup capacity. However, Lyco may have earned higher operating income by selling 151,200 units at a higher price than 180,000 units at a lower price. As a result, the production-volume variance should be interpreted cautiously because it does not consider effects on selling prices and operating income.

PROBLEM FOR SELF-STUDY

Maria Lopez is the newly appointed president of Laser Products. She is examining the May 2007 results for the Aerospace Products Division. This division manufactures wing parts for satellites. Lopez's current concern is with manufacturing overhead costs at the Aerospace Products Division. Both variable and fixed manufacturing overhead costs are allocated to the wing parts on the basis of laser-cutting-hours. The following budget information is available:

Budgeted variable manufacturing overhead rate	$200 per hour
Budgeted fixed manufacturing overhead rate	$240 per hour
Budgeted laser-cutting time per wing part	1.5 hours
Budgeted production and sales for May 2007	5,000 wing parts
Budgeted fixed manufacturing overhead costs for May 2007	$1,800,000

Actual results for May 2007 are:

Wing parts produced and sold	4,800 units
Laser-cutting-hours used	8,400 hours
Variable manufacturing overhead costs	$1,478,400
Fixed manufacturing overhead costs	$1,832,200

Required

1. Compute the spending variance and the efficiency variance for variable manufacturing overhead.
2. Compute the spending variance and the production-volume variance for fixed manufacturing overhead.
3. Give two explanations for each of the variances calculated in requirements 1 and 2.

SOLUTION

1. and 2. See Exhibit 8-8.

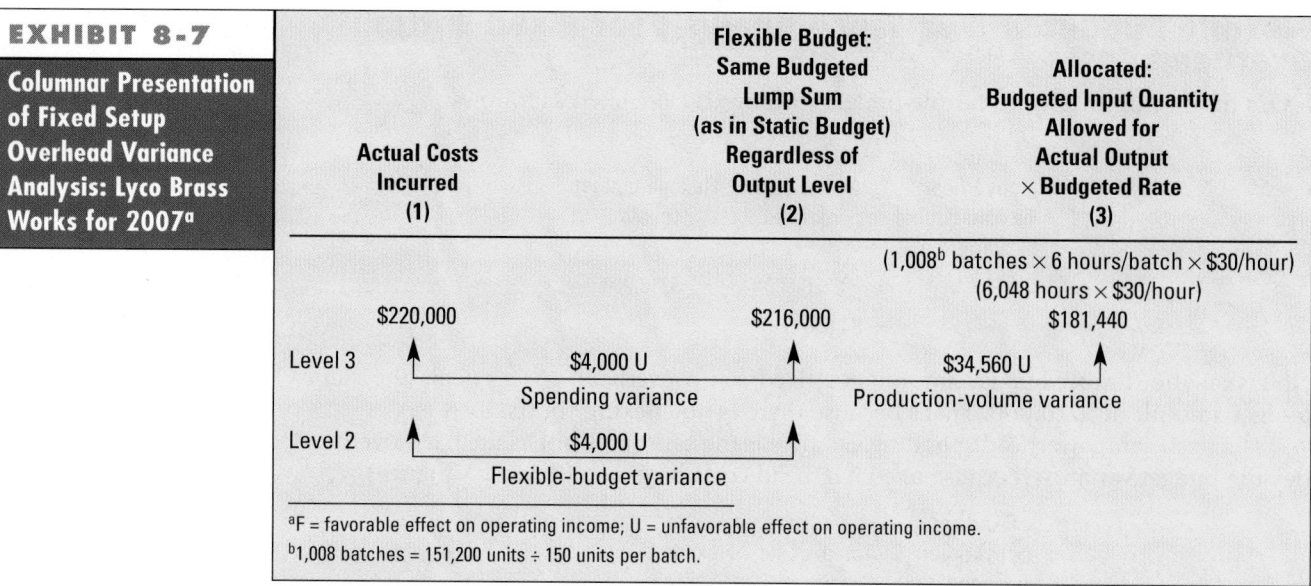

EXHIBIT 8-8 **Columnar Presentation of Integrated Variance Analysis: Laser Products for May 2007[a]**

PANEL A: Variable Manufacturing Overhead

Actual Costs Incurred: Actual Input Quantity × Actual Rate (1)	Actual Input Quantity × Budgeted Rate (2)	Flexible Budget: Budgeted Input Quantity Allowed for Actual Output × Budgeted Rate (3)	Allocated: Budgeted Input Quantity Allowed for Actual Output × Budgeted Rate (4)
		(1.5 hrs./unit × 4,800 units × $200/hr.)	(1.5 hrs./unit × 4,800 units × $200/hr.)
(8,400 hrs. × $176/hr.)	(8,400 hrs. × $200/hr.)	(7,200 hrs. × $200/hr.)	(7,200 hrs. × $200/hr.)
$1,478,400	$1,680,000	$1,440,000	$1,440,000

(1)–(2): $201,600 F, Spending variance; (2)–(3): $240,000 U, Efficiency variance; (3)–(4): Never a variance

(1)–(3): $38,400 U, Flexible-budget variance; (3)–(4): Never a variance

(1)–(4): $38,400 U, Underallocated variable overhead (Total variable overhead variance)

PANEL B: Fixed Manufacturing Overhead

Actual Costs Incurred (1)	Same Budgeted Lump Sum (as in Static Budget) Regardless of Output Level (2)	Flexible Budget: Same Budgeted Lump Sum (as in Static Budget) Regardless of Output Level (3)	Allocated: Budgeted Input Quantity Allowed for Actual Output × Budgeted Rate (4)
			(1.5 hrs./unit × 4,800 units × $240/hr.)
			(7,200 hrs. × $240/hr.)
$1,832,200	$1,800,000	$1,800,000	$1,728,000

(1)–(2): $32,200 U, Spending variance; (2)–(3): Never a variance; (3)–(4): $72,000 U, Production-volume variance

(1)–(3): $32,200 U, Flexible-budget variance; (3)–(4): $72,000 U, Production-volume variance

(1)–(4): $104,200 U, Underallocated fixed overhead (Total fixed overhead variance)

[a]F = favorable effect on operating income; U = unfavorable effect on operating income.

Source: From "The Case for Management Accounting" by Paul Sherman. Used with permission from STRATEGIC FINANCE, October 2003, published by the Institute of Management Accountants, Montvale, NJ, www.imanet.org.

3. *a.* Variable manufacturing overhead spending variance, $201,600 F. One possible reason for this variance is that actual prices of individual items included in variable overhead (such as cutting fluids) are lower than budgeted prices. A second possible reason is that the percentage increase in the actual quantity usage of individual items in the variable overhead cost pool is less than the percentage increase in laser-cutting-hours compared to the flexible budget.

b. Variable manufacturing overhead efficiency variance, $240,000 U. One possible reason for this variance is inadequate maintenance of laser machines, causing them to take more laser-cutting time per wing part. A second possible reason is use of undermotivated, inexperienced, or underskilled workers with the laser-cutting machines, resulting in more laser-cutting time per wing part.

c. Fixed manufacturing overhead spending variance, $32,200 U. One possible reason for this variance is that the actual prices of individual items in the fixed-cost pool unexpectedly increased from the prices budgeted (such as an unexpected increase in machine leasing costs). A second possible reason is misclassification of items as fixed that are in fact variable.

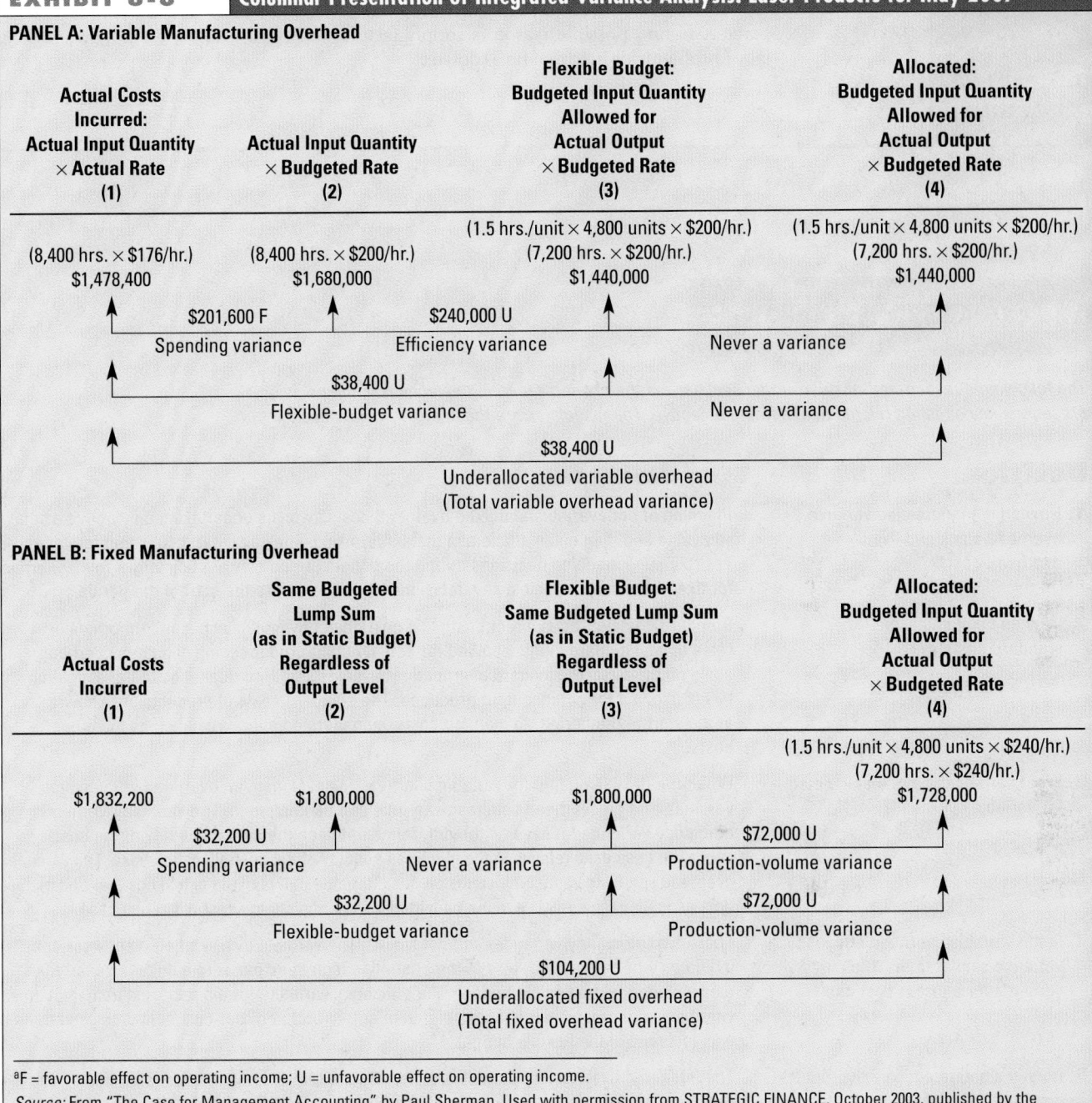

d. Production-volume variance, $72,000 U. Actual production of wing parts is 4,800 units, compared with 5,000 units budgeted. One possible reason for this variance is demand factors, such as a decline in an aerospace program that led to a decline in demand for aircraft parts. A second possible reason is supply factors, such as a production stoppage due to labor problems or machine breakdowns.

DECISION POINTS

The following question-and-answer format summarizes the chapter's learning objectives. Each decision presents a key question related to a learning objective. The guidelines are the answer to that question.

Decision	Guidelines
1. How do managers plan variable overhead costs and fixed overhead costs?	Planning of both variable and fixed overhead costs involves undertaking only activities that add value and then being efficient in that undertaking. The key difference is that for variable-cost planning, ongoing decisions during the budget period play a much larger role; whereas for fixed-cost planning, most key decisions are made before the start of the period.
2. Why do companies use standard costing?	Standard costing traces direct costs to a cost object by multiplying standard prices or rates times standard inputs allowed for actual output produced and allocates overhead costs on the basis of standard overhead rates times standard quantities of the allocation bases allowed for actual output produced. The standard costs of products are known at the start of the period. To manage costs, managers compare actual costs to standard costs.
3. What variances can be calculated for variable overhead?	When the flexible budget for variable overhead is developed, an overhead efficiency variance and an overhead spending variance can be computed. The variable overhead efficiency variance focuses on the difference between the actual quantity of the cost-allocation base used relative to the budgeted quantity of the cost-allocation base. The variable overhead spending variance focuses on the difference between the actual cost per unit of the cost-allocation base relative to the budgeted cost per unit of the cost-allocation base.
4. Is the variable overhead efficiency variance similar to the efficiency variance for a direct-cost item?	These two efficiency variances are not similar. The variable overhead efficiency variance indicates whether more or less of the cost-allocation base per output unit was used than was included in the flexible budget. The efficiency variance for a direct-cost item indicates whether more or less of the input per unit of output of that direct-cost item was used than was included in the flexible budget.
5. How is a budgeted fixed overhead cost rate calculated?	The budgeted fixed overhead cost rate is calculated by dividing the budgeted fixed overhead costs by the denominator level of the cost-allocation base.
6. How should managers interpret the production-volume variance?	Managers should interpret cautiously the production-volume variance as a measure of the economic cost of unused capacity. One caution: management may have maintained some extra capacity to meet uncertain demand surges that are important to satisfy. Another caution: the production-volume variance focuses only on fixed overhead costs. The production-volume variance does not take into account any decreases in the selling price of output necessary to spur extra demand that would, in turn, make use of any idle capacity.
7. What is the most detailed way for a company to reconcile actual overhead incurred with the amount allocated during a period?	A 4-variance analysis presents spending and efficiency variances for variable overhead costs and spending and production-volume variances for fixed overhead costs. By analyzing these four variances together, managers can reconcile the actual overhead costs with the amount of overhead allocated to output produced during a period.
8. Can the flexible-budget variance approach for analyzing overhead costs be used in activity-based costing?	Yes, flexible budgets in ABC systems give insight into why actual overhead activity costs differ from budgeted overhead activity costs. Using output and input measures for an activity, a 4-variance analysis can be conducted.

TERMS TO LEARN

The chapter and the Glossary at the end of the book contain definitions of:

denominator level (p. 264)
denominator-level variance (p. 266)
fixed overhead flexible-budget variance (p. 265)
fixed overhead spending variance (p. 265)
output-level overhead variance (p. 266)
production-denominator level (p. 264)
production-volume variance (p. 266)
standard costing (p. 257)
total-overhead variance (p. 273)
variable overhead efficiency variance (p. 260)
variable overhead flexible-budget variance (p. 259)
variable overhead spending variance (p. 261)

PH Grade Assist

Prentice Hall Grade Assist (PHGA)
Your professor may ask you to complete selected exercises and problems in Prentice Hall Grade Assist (PHGA). PHGA is an online tool that can help you master the chapter's topics. It provides you with multiple variations of exercises and problems designated by the PHGA icon. You can rework these exercises and problems—each time with new data—as many times as you need. You also receive immediate feedback and grading.

ASSIGNMENT MATERIAL

Questions

8-1 How do managers plan for variable overhead costs?

8-2 How does the planning of fixed overhead costs differ from the planning of variable overhead costs?

8-3 How does standard costing differ from actual costing?

8-4 What are the steps in developing a budgeted variable overhead cost-allocation rate?

8-5 The spending variance for variable manufacturing overhead is affected by several factors. Explain.

8-6 Assume variable manufacturing overhead is allocated using machine-hours. Give three possible reasons for a favorable variable overhead efficiency variance.

8-7 Describe the difference between a direct materials efficiency variance and a variable manufacturing overhead efficiency variance.

8-8 What are the steps in developing a budgeted fixed overhead rate?

8-9 Why is the flexible-budget variance the same amount as the spending variance for fixed manufacturing overhead?

8-10 Explain how the analysis of fixed manufacturing overhead costs differs for (a) planning and control on the one hand and (b) inventory costing for financial reporting on the other hand.

8-11 Provide one caveat that will affect whether a production-volume variance is a good measure of the economic cost of unused capacity.

8-12 "The production-volume variance should always be written off to Cost of Goods Sold." Do you agree? Explain.

8-13 What are the variances in a 4-variance analysis?

8-14 "Overhead variances should be viewed as interdependent rather than independent." Give an example.

8-15 Describe how flexible-budget variance analysis can be used in the control of costs of activity areas.

Exercises

8-16 Variable manufacturing overhead, variance analysis. Esquire Clothing is a manufacturer of designer suits. The cost of each suit is the sum of three variable costs (direct material costs, direct manufacturing labor costs, and manufacturing overhead costs) and one fixed-cost category (manufacturing overhead costs). Variable manufacturing overhead cost is allocated to each suit on the basis of budgeted direct manufacturing labor-hours per suit. For June 2007, each suit is budgeted to take four labor-hours. Budgeted variable manufacturing overhead cost per labor-hour is $12. The budgeted number of suits to be manufactured in June 2007 is 1,040.

PH Grade Assist

Actual variable manufacturing costs in June 2007 were $52,164 for 1,080 suits started and completed. There were no beginning or ending inventories of suits. Actual direct manufacturing labor-hours for June were 4,536.

Required

1. Compute the flexible-budget variance, the spending variance, and the efficiency variance for variable manufacturing overhead.
2. Comment on the results.

8-17 Fixed manufacturing overhead, variance analysis (continuation of 8-16). Esquire Clothing allocates fixed manufacturing overhead to each suit using budgeted direct manufacturing labor-hours per suit. Data pertaining to fixed manufacturing overhead costs for June 2007 are budgeted, $62,400, and actual, $63,916.

Required

1. Compute the spending variance for fixed manufacturing overhead. Comment on the results.
2. Compute the production-volume variance for June 2007. What inferences can Esquire Clothing draw from this variance?

8-18 Variable manufacturing overhead variance analysis. The French Bread Company bakes baguettes for distribution to upscale grocery stores. The company has two direct-cost categories: direct materials and direct manufacturing labor. Variable manufacturing overhead is allocated to products on the basis of standard direct manufacturing labor-hours. Following is some budget data for the French Bread Company:

Direct manufacturing labor use	0.02 hours per baguette
Variable manufacturing overhead	$10.00 per direct manufacturing labor-hour

The French Bread Company provides the following additional data for the year ended December 31, 2007:

Planned (budgeted) output	3,200,000 baguettes
Actual production	2,800,000 baguettes
Direct manufacturing labor	50,400 hours
Actual variable manufacturing overhead	$680,400

Required

1. What is the denominator level used for allocating variable manufacturing overhead? (That is, for how many direct manufacturing labor-hours is French Bread budgeting?)
2. Prepare a variance analysis of variable manufacturing overhead. Use Exhibit 8-5 (p. 272) for reference.
3. Discuss the variances you have calculated and give possible explanations for them.

8-19 Fixed manufacturing overhead variance analysis. The French Bread Company bakes baguettes for distribution to upscale grocery stores. The company has two direct-cost categories: direct materials and direct manufacturing labor. Fixed manufacturing overhead is allocated to products on the basis of standard direct manufacturing labor-hours. Following is some budget data for the French Bread Company:

Direct manufacturing labor use	0.02 hours per baguette
Fixed manufacturing overhead	$4.00 per direct labor-hour

The French Bread Company provides the following additional data for the year ended December 31, 2007:

Planned (budgeted) output	3,200,000 baguettes
Actual production	2,800,000 baguettes
Actual direct manufacturing labor	50,400 hours
Actual fixed manufacturing overhead	$272,000

Required

1. Prepare a variance analysis of fixed manufacturing overhead cost. Use Exhibit 8-5 (p. 272) as a guide.
2. Is fixed overhead underallocated or overallocated? By what amount?
3. Comment on your results. Discuss the variances and explain what may be driving them.

Excel Lab
www.prenhall.com/horngren/cost12e

PH Grade Assist

8-20 Manufacturing overhead, variance analysis. Zircon, Inc., assembles its CardioX product at its Scottsdale plant. Fixed and variable manufacturing overheads are allocated to each CardioX unit using budgeted assembly-hours. Budgeted assembly time is two hours per unit. The following table shows the budgeted amounts and actual results related to overhead for March 2007.

	A	B	C
1	**Zircon (March 2007)**	**Actual Results**	**Static Budget**
2	Units of CardioX assembled and sold	5,400	5,000
3	Hours of assembly time	10,280	
4	Variable manufacturing overhead cost per hour of assembly time		$ 30.00
5	Variable manufacturing overhead costs	$310,500	
6	Fixed manufacturing overhead costs	$514,000	$480,000

If you want to use Excel to solve this exercise, go to the Excel Lab at **www.prenhall.com/horngren/cost12e** and download the template for Exercise 8-20.

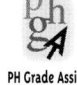

1. Prepare an analysis of all variable manufacturing overhead and fixed manufacturing overhead variances using the columnar approach in Exhibit 8-5 (p. 272).
2. Prepare journal entries for Zircon's March 2007 variable and fixed manufacturing overhead costs and variances; write off these variances to cost of goods sold for the quarter ending March 2007.
3. How does the planning and control of variable manufacturing overhead costs differ from the planning and control of fixed manufacturing overhead costs?

Required

8-21 4-variance analysis, fill in the blanks. Use the following manufacturing overhead data to fill in the following blanks:

PH Grade Assist

	Variable	Fixed
Actual costs incurred	$11,900	$6,000
Costs allocated to products	9,000	4,500
Flexible budget: Budgeted input allowed for actual output produced × budgeted rate	9,000	5,000
Actual input × budgeted rate	10,000	5,000

Use F for favorable and U for unfavorable:

	Variable	Fixed
(1) Spending variance	$____	$____
(2) Efficiency variance	____	____
(3) Production-volume variance	____	____
(4) Flexible-budget variance	____	____
(5) Underallocated (overallocated) manufacturing overhead	____	____

8-22 Straightforward 4-variance overhead analysis. The Lopez Company uses standard costing in its manufacturing plant for auto parts. The standard cost of a particular auto part, based on a denominator level of 4,000 output units per year, included 6 machine-hours of variable manufacturing overhead at $8 per hour and 6 machine-hours of fixed manufacturing overhead at $15 per hour. Actual output produced was 4,400 units. Variable manufacturing overhead incurred was $245,000. Fixed manufacturing overhead incurred was $373,000. Actual machine-hours were 28,400.

PH Grade Assist

Required

1. Prepare an analysis of all variable manufacturing overhead and fixed manufacturing overhead variances, using the 4-variance analysis in Exhibit 8-5 (p. 272).
2. Prepare journal entries using the 4-variance analysis.
3. Describe how individual variable manufacturing overhead items are controlled from day to day. Also, describe how individual fixed manufacturing overhead items are controlled.

8-23 Straightforward coverage of manufacturing overhead, standard-costing system. The Singapore division of a Canadian telecommunications company uses standard costing for its machine-paced production of telephone equipment. Data regarding production during June are as follows:

Variable manufacturing overhead costs incurred	$155,100
Variable manufacturing overhead cost rate	$12 per standard machine-hour
Fixed manufacturing overhead costs incurred	$401,000
Fixed manufacturing overhead budgeted	$390,000
Denominator level in machine-hours	13,000
Standard machine-hour allowed per unit of output	0.30
Units of output	41,000
Actual machine-hours used	13,300
Ending work-in-process inventory	0

Required

1. Prepare an analysis of all manufacturing overhead variances. Use the 4-variance analysis framework illustrated in Exhibit 8-5 (p. 272).
2. Prepare journal entries for manufacturing overheads and their variances.
3. Describe how individual variable manufacturing overhead items are controlled from day to day. Also, describe how individual fixed manufacturing overhead items are controlled.

8-24 Overhead variances, service sector. Meals on Wheels (MOW) operates a meal home-delivery service. It has agreements with 20 restaurants to pick up and deliver meals to customers who phone or fax orders to MOW. MOW allocates variable and fixed overhead costs on the basis of delivery time. MOW's owner, Josh Carter, obtains the following information for May 2007 overhead costs:

Excel Lab
www.prenhall.com/horngren/cost12e

	A	B	C
1	**Meals on Wheels (May 2007)**	**Actual Results**	**Static Budget**
2	Output units (number of deliveries)	8,800	10,000
3	Hours per delivery		0.70
4	Hours of delivery time	5,720	
5	Variable overhead cost per hour of delivery time		$ 1.50
6	Variable overhead costs	$10,296	
7	Fixed overhead costs	$38,600	$35,000

If you want to use Excel to solve this exercise, go to the Excel Lab at **www.prenhall.com/horngren/cost12e** and download the template for Exercise 8-24.

Required

1. Compute spending and efficiency variances for MOW's variable overhead in May 2007.
2. Compute the spending variance and production-volume variance for MOW's fixed overhead in May 2007.
3. Comment on MOW's overhead variances and suggest how Josh Carter might manage MOW's variable overhead differently from its fixed overhead costs.

8-25 Total overhead, 3-variance analysis. Wright-Patterson Air Force Base has an extensive repair facility for jet engines. It developed standard costing and flexible budgets to account for this activity. Budgeted variable overhead at a level of 8,000 standard monthly direct labor-hours was $64,000; budgeted total overhead at 10,000 standard direct labor-hours was $197,600. The standard cost allocated to repair output included a total overhead rate of 120% of standard direct labor costs. Total overhead incurred for October was $249,000. Direct labor costs incurred were $202,440. The direct labor price variance was $9,640 unfavorable. The direct labor flexible-budget variance was $14,440 unfavorable. The standard labor price was $16 per hour. The production-volume variance was $14,000, favorable.

Required

1. Compute the direct labor efficiency variance and the spending, efficiency, and production-volume variances for overhead. Also, compute the denominator level.
2. Describe how individual variable manufacturing overhead items are controlled from day to day. Also, describe how individual fixed manufacturing overhead items are controlled.

PH Grade Assist

8-26 Overhead variances, missing information. Blakely Printing budgets 12,000 machine-hours for June 2007. The budgeted variable overhead rate is $6 per machine-hour. At the end of June, its managers reported a $250 favorable spending variance for variable overhead and a $1,050 unfavorable spending variance for fixed overhead. For the pages actually printed, they should have used 9,900 machine-hours, but they actually used 10,000 machine-hours. Total overhead costs were $80,000.

Required

1. In the columnar presentation below for June 2007's variable manufacturing overhead variance analysis, calculate (a) through (e). Will variable overhead be over- or underallocated? By how much?

	Actual Costs Incurred: Actual Input Quantity × Actual Rate (1)	Actual Input Quantity × Budgeted Rate (2)	Flexible Budget: Budgeted Input Quantity Allowed for Actual Output × Budgeted Rate (3)
	(b)	(a)	(c)
Level 3	← $250 F Spending variance →	← (d) Efficiency variance →	
Level 2	← (e) Flexible-budget variance →		

2. In the columnar presentation below for June 2007's fixed manufacturing overhead variance analysis, calculate (a) through (e). Will fixed manufacturing overhead be over- or underallocated? By how much?

	Actual Costs Incurred: (1)	Flexible Budget: Same Budgeted Lump Sum (as in Static Budget) Regardless of Output Level (2)	Allocated: Budgeted Input Quantity Allowed for Actual Output × Budgeted Rate (3)
	(a)	(b)	9,900 hours × (c)
Level 3	← $1,050 U Spending variance →	← (d) Production volume variance →	
Level 2	← (e) Flexible-budget variance →		

PH Grade Assist

8-27 Identifying favorable and unfavorable variances. Consider a company that uses standard costing and allocates variable and fixed manufacturing overhead based on machine-hours. For each independent scenario given, indicate whether each of the variances will be favorable or unfavorable or, in case of insufficient information, indicate "cannot be determined."

Scenario	Variable Overhead Spending Variance	Variable Overhead Efficiency Variance	Fixed Overhead Spending Variance	Fixed Overhead Production-Volume Variance
Actual machine hours are 10% greater than flexible-budget machine-hours				
Production output is 20% less than budgeted				
Production output is 10% more than budgeted; actual machine-hours are 5% less than budgeted				
Production output is 15% more than budgeted, and actual fixed overhead is 6% more than budgeted				
Relative to the flexible budget, actual machine-hours are 10% greater, and actual variable overhead costs are 8% greater				

8-28 Flexible-budget variances, review of Chapters 7 and 8. The *Monthly Herald* uses standard costing and reports the following results in August 2008 for its monthly newspaper:

Excel Lab
www.prenhall.com/horngren/cost12e

	A	B	C
1		**Actual Results**	**Static Budget**
2	Number of copies	320,000	300,000
3	Number of pages of newsprint	17,280,000	15,000,000
4	Cost of newsprint (direct materials)	\$ 224,640	\$ 180,000
5	Variable overhead costs	\$ 63,936	\$ 60,000
6	Fixed overhead costs	\$ 97,000	\$ 90,000

Newsprint—the special paper on which the newspaper is printed—is the only direct-cost category. Variable and fixed overhead costs are allocated using budgeted rates on the basis of newsprint pages. Each copy of the *Monthly Herald* has only 50 newsprint pages, but in August 2008, the printing machines jammed frequently during printing runs and damaged a lot of newsprint pages.

If you want to use Excel to solve this exercise, go to the Excel Lab at **www.prenhall.com/horngren/cost12e** and download the template for Exercise 8-28.

Required

1. Prepare a comprehensive set of flexible-budget variances at the *Monthly Herald* in August 2008 for direct materials, variable overhead, and fixed overhead.
2. Comment on the results in requirement 1.

Problems

8-29 Comprehensive variance analysis. FlatScreen manufactures flat-panel LCD displays. The displays are sold to major PC manufacturers. Following is some manufacturing overhead data for FlatScreen for the year ended December 31, 2006:

PH Grade Assist

Manufacturing Overhead	Actual Results	Flexible Budget	Allocated Amount
Variable	\$1,532,160	\$1,536,000	\$1,536,000
Fixed	7,004,160	6,961,920	7,526,400

FlatScreen's budget was based on the assumption that 17,760 units (panels) would be manufactured during 2006. The planned allocation rate was 2 machine-hours per unit. Actual number of machine-hours used during 2006 was 36,480. The static-budget variable manufacturing overhead costs equal \$1,420,800.

Required

Compute the following quantities (you should be able to do so in the prescribed order):

a. Budgeted number of machine-hours planned
b. Budgeted fixed manufacturing overhead costs per machine-hour
c. Budgeted variable manufacturing overhead costs per machine-hour
d. Budgeted number of machine-hours allowed for actual output produced
e. Actual number of output units
f. Actual number of machine-hours used per panel

8-30 Journal entries (continuation of 8-29).

Required

PH Grade Assist

1. Prepare journal entries for variable and fixed manufacturing overhead (you will need to calculate the various variances to accomplish this).
2. Overhead variances are written off to the Cost of Goods Sold (COGS) account at the end of the fiscal year. Show how COGS is adjusted through journal entries.

8-31 Graphs and overhead variances. The Carvelli Company is a manufacturer of housewares and uses standard costing. Manufacturing overhead (both variable and fixed) is allocated to products on the basis of budgeted machine-hours. The budget for 2007 included:

Variable manufacturing overhead	$9 per machine-hour
Fixed manufacturing overhead	$72,000,000
Denominator level	4,000,000 machine-hours

Required

1. Prepare two graphs, one for variable manufacturing overhead and one for fixed manufacturing overhead. Each graph should display how Carvelli's total manufacturing overhead costs will be depicted for the purposes of (a) planning and control and (b) inventory costing.
2. Suppose that 3,500,000 machine-hours were allowed for actual output produced in 2007, but 3,800,000 actual machine-hours were used. Actual manufacturing overhead was $36,100,000, variable, and $72,200,000, fixed. Compute (a) the variable manufacturing overhead spending and efficiency variances and (b) the fixed manufacturing overhead spending and production-volume variances. Use the columnar presentation illustrated in Exhibit 8-5 (p. 272).
3. What is the amount of the under- or overallocated variable manufacturing overhead and the under- or overallocated fixed manufacturing overhead? Why are the flexible-budget variance and the under- or overallocated overhead amount always the same for variable manufacturing overhead but rarely the same for fixed manufacturing overhead?
4. Suppose the denominator level was 3,000,000 rather than 4,000,000 machine-hours. What variances in requirement 2 would be affected? Recompute them.

8-32 4-variance analysis, find the unknowns. Consider each of the following situations—cases A, B, and C—independently. Data refer to operations for April 2007. For each situation, assume standard costing. Also assume the use of a flexible budget for control of variable and fixed manufacturing overhead based on machine-hours.

	Cases		
	A	**B**	**C**
(1) Fixed manufacturing overhead incurred	$10,600	—	$12,000
(2) Variable manufacturing overhead incurred	$ 7,000	—	—
(3) Denominator level in machine-hours	500	—	1,100
(4) Standard machine-hours allowed for actual output achieved	—	650	—
(5) Fixed manufacturing overhead (per standard machine-hour)	—	—	—
Flexible-budget data:			
(6) Variable manufacturing overhead (per standard machine-hour)	—	$8.50	$5.00
(7) Budgeted fixed manufacturing overhead	$10,000	—	$11,000
(8) Budgeted variable manufacturing overhead[a]	—	—	—
(9) Total budgeted manufacturing overhead[a]	—	$12,525	—
Additional data:			
(10) Standard variable manufacturing overhead allocated	$ 7,500	—	—
(11) Standard fixed manufacturing overhead allocated	$10,000	—	—
(12) Production-volume variance	—	$500 U	$500 F
(13) Variable manufacturing overhead spending variance	$ 950 F	$0	$350 U
(14) Variable manufacturing overhead efficiency variance	—	$0	$100 U
(15) Fixed manufacturing overhead spending variance	—	$300 F	—
(16) Actual machine-hours used	—	—	—

[a]For standard machine-hours allowed for actual output produced.

Required

Fill in the blanks under each case. [*Hint:* Prepare a worksheet similar to that in Exhibit 8-5 (p. 272). Fill in the knowns and then solve for the unknowns.]

PH Grade Assist

8-33 Flexible budgets, 4-variance analysis. (CMA, adapted) Nolton Products uses standard costing. It allocates manufacturing overhead (both variable and fixed) to products on the basis of standard direct manufacturing labor-hours (DLH). Nolton develops its manufacturing overhead rate from the current annual budget. The manufacturing overhead budget for 2007 is based on budgeted output of 720,000 units, requiring 3,600,000 DLH. The company is able to schedule production uniformly throughout the year.

A total of 66,000 output units requiring 315,000 DLH was produced during May 2007. Manufacturing overhead (MOH) costs incurred for May amounted to $375,000. The actual costs, compared with the annual budget and $\frac{1}{12}$ of the annual budget, are as follows:

Annual Manufacturing Overhead Budget 2007

	Total Amount	Per Output Unit	Per DLH Input Unit	Monthly MOH Budget May 2007	Actual MOH Costs for May 2007
Variable MOH					
Indirect manufacturing labor	$ 900,000	$1.25	$0.25	$ 75,000	$ 75,000
Supplies	1,224,000	1.70	0.34	102,000	111,000
Fixed MOH					
Supervision	648,000	0.90	0.18	54,000	51,000
Utilities	540,000	0.75	0.15	45,000	54,000
Depreciation	1,008,000	1.40	0.28	84,000	84,000
Total	$4,320,000	$6.00	$1.20	$360,000	$375,000

Calculate the following amounts for Nolton Products for May 2007: **Required**

1. Total manufacturing overhead costs allocated
2. Variable manufacturing overhead spending variance
3. Fixed manufacturing overhead spending variance
4. Variable manufacturing overhead efficiency variance
5. Production-volume variance

Be sure to identify each variance as favorable (F) or unfavorable (U).

8-34 Overhead analysis, sensitivity to denominator volume. Armstrong Corporation produces thermostats and has no inventories. Armstrong uses standard costing and allocates all overhead on the basis of machine-hours. It budgets 0.30 of a machine-hour to manufacture each unit. The following information is for 2007:

Excel Lab
www.prenhall.com/horngren/cost12e

	A	B	C
1		**Actual Results**	**Static Budget**
2	Production and sales in units	110,000	120,000
3	Machine-hours	30,000	36,000
4	Fixed manufacturing overhead	$440,000	$450,000
5	Variable manufacturing overhead	$960,000	
6	Variable manuf. overhead rate per machine-hour		$ 30

If you want to use Excel to solve this problem, go to the Excel Lab at **www.prenhall.com/horngren/cost12e** and download the template for Problem 8-34.

Required

1. Calculate the variable manufacturing overhead spending and efficiency variances.
2. Calculate the fixed manufacturing overhead spending and production-volume variances.
3. Suppose Armstrong had budgeted for 150,000 units instead of 120,000 units and 45,000 (150,000 × 0.30) machine-hours instead of 36,000 machine-hours. All other information in the table remains the same. Recalculate the variable manufacturing overhead variances and the fixed manufacturing overhead variances in requirements 1 and 2.
4. Armstrong writes off all variances to cost of goods sold. How would Armstrong's operating income change if it budgeted for 150,000 units of production and sales rather than 120,000 units?

8-35 Sales-volume variance, production-volume variance. Morano Company budgeted production and sales at its maximum capacity of 20,000 units for 2006. However, Morano was able to produce and sell only 18,000 units for the year. There are no beginning or ending inventories. Other data for 2006 follow:

Budgeted fixed overhead costs	$500,000
Budgeted selling price	$100
Budgeted variable cost per unit	$40

Required

1. Calculate the static-budget operating income, the flexible-budget operating income, and the operating income based on the budgeted profit per unit.
2. Compute sales-volume variance, production-volume variance, and operating income volume variance. What do each of these variances measure?

8-36 Activity-based costing, variance analysis. Toymaster, Inc., produces a plastic toy car, TGC, in batches. To manufacture a batch of TGCs, Toymaster must set up the machines. Setup costs are batch-level costs. A separate Setup Department is responsible for setting up machines for TGC.

PH Grade Assist

Setup overhead costs consist of some costs that are variable and some that are fixed with respect to the number of setup-hours. The following information pertains to 2007.

	Static-Budget Amounts	Actual Results
Units of TGC produced and sold	30,000	22,500
Batch size (number of units per batch)	250	225
Setup-hours per batch	5	5.25
Variable overhead cost per setup-hour	$25	$24
Total fixed setup overhead costs	$18,000	$17,535

Required

1. For variable setup overhead costs, compute the efficiency and spending variances. Comment on the results.
2. For fixed setup overhead costs, compute the spending and the production-volume variances. Comment on the results.

8-37 Activity-based costing, variance analysis. Asma Surgical Instruments, Inc., makes a special line of forceps, SFA, in batches. Asma randomly selects forceps from each SFA batch for quality-testing purposes. Quality testing costs are batch-level costs. A separate quality-testing section is responsible for SFA quality testing.

Quality-testing costs consist of some variable and some fixed costs in relation to quality-testing hours. The following information is for 2007:

	Static-Budget Amounts	Actual Results
Units of SFA produced and sold	21,000	22,000
Batch size (number of units per batch)	500	550
Testing-hours per batch	5.5	5.4
Variable overhead cost per testing-hour	$40	$42
Total fixed testing overhead costs	$28,875	$27,216

Required

1. For variable testing overhead costs, compute the efficiency and spending variances. Comment on the results.
2. For fixed testing overhead costs, compute the spending and the production-volume variances. Comment on the results.

Excel Lab
www.prenhall.com/horngren/cost12e

8-38 Comprehensive overhead variance analyses. Happy Valley is a large wine-producing region in southern Oregon. The Brando Brothers Wine Company, which has a huge following among wine connoisseurs, buys select wines in bulk from the area's wineries and blends and bottles the wine for sale under its own label. Its variable overhead costs (power, cleaning supplies, and the like) and fixed overhead costs (salaries of skilled vintners involved in quality-control and building-related costs) are allocated on the basis of bottling machine-hours. For the quarter ending September 30, 2008, the Brando operation reports the following:

	A	B	C
1		Actual Results	Static Budget
2	Production volume (bottles)	450,000	420,000
3	Bottling machine-hours	3,000	2,800
4	Variable overhead	$153,000	$140,000
5	Fixed overhead	$960,000	$980,000

If you want to use Excel to solve this problem, go to the Excel Lab at **www.prenhall.com/horngren/cost12e** and download the template for Problem 8-38.

Required

1. Compute the variable overhead spending and efficiency variances. Prepare journal entries to record these variances for the quarter.
2. Compute the fixed overhead spending and production-volume variances. Prepare journal entries to record these variances for the quarter.
3. End-of-quarter balances in Work-in-Process Control and Finished Goods Control are $900,000 and $1,500,000, respectively, and Cost of Goods Sold for the quarter is $2,400,000. Prepare journal entries to close out the variable overhead variances and the fixed overhead spending variance to Cost of Goods Sold. Prepare a journal entry to close out the production-volume variance by allocating it among Work in Process Control, Finished Goods Control, and Cost of Goods Sold using end-of-quarter balances in these accounts.
4. The plant manager is given a bonus based on how well she controls cost of goods sold each quarter. She is an advocate for writing off the production-volume variance to cost of goods sold. Discuss the possible implications of such an arrangement.

8-39 Comprehensive review of Chapters 7 and 8, working backward from given variances. The Mancusco Company uses a flexible budget and standard costs to aid planning and control of its machining manufacturing operations. Its costing system for manufacturing has two direct-cost categories (direct materials and direct manufacturing labor—both variable) and two overhead-cost categories (variable manufacturing overhead and fixed manufacturing overhead, both allocated using direct manufacturing labor-hours).

At the 40,000 budgeted direct manufacturing labor-hour level for August, budgeted direct manufacturing labor is $800,000, budgeted variable manufacturing overhead is $480,000, and budgeted fixed manufacturing overhead is $640,000.

The following actual results are for August:

Direct materials price variance (based on purchases)	$176,000 F
Direct materials efficiency variance	69,000 U
Direct manufacturing labor costs incurred	522,750
Variable manufacturing overhead flexible-budget variance	10,350 U
Variable manufacturing overhead efficiency variance	18,000 U
Fixed manufacturing overhead incurred	597,460
Fixed manufacturing overhead spending variance	42,540 F

The standard cost per pound of direct materials is $11.50. The standard allowance is three pounds of direct materials for each unit of product. During August, 30,000 units of product were produced. There was no beginning inventory of direct materials. There was no beginning or ending work in process. In August, the direct materials price variance was $1.10 per pound.

In July, labor unrest caused a major slowdown in the pace of production, resulting in an unfavorable direct manufacturing labor efficiency variance of $45,000. There was no direct manufacturing labor price variance. Labor unrest persisted into August. Some workers quit. Their replacements had to be hired at higher wage rates, which had to be extended to all workers. The actual average wage rate in August exceeded the standard average wage rate by $0.50 per hour.

Required

1. Compute the following for August:
   a. Total pounds of direct materials purchased
   b. Total number of pounds of excess direct materials used
   c. Variable manufacturing overhead spending variance
   d. Total number of actual direct manufacturing labor-hours used
   e. Total number of standard direct manufacturing labor-hours allowed for the units produced
   f. Production-volume variance
2. Describe how Mancusco's control of variable manufacturing overhead items differs from its control of fixed manufacturing overhead items.

8-40 Review of Chapters 7 and 8, 3-variance analysis. (CPA, adapted) The Beal Manufacturing Company's costing system has two direct-cost categories: direct materials and direct manufacturing labor. Manufacturing overhead (both variable and fixed) is allocated to products on the basis of standard direct manufacturing labor-hours (DLH). At the beginning of 2007, Beal adopted the following standards for its manufacturing costs:

	Input	Cost per Output Unit
Direct materials	3 lbs. at $5 per lb.	$ 15.00
Direct manufacturing labor	5 hrs. at $15 per hr.	75.00
Manufacturing overhead:		
Variable	$6 per DLH	30.00
Fixed	$8 per DLH	40.00
Standard manufacturing cost per output unit		$160.00

The denominator level for total manufacturing overhead per month in 2007 is 40,000 direct manufacturing labor-hours. Beal's flexible budget for January 2007 was based on this denominator level. The records for January indicated the following:

Direct materials purchased	25,000 lbs. at $5.20 per lb.
Direct materials used	23,100 lbs.
Direct manufacturing labor	40,100 hrs. at $14.60 per hr.
Total actual manufacturing overhead (variable and fixed)	$600,000
Actual production	7,800 output units

Required

1. Prepare a schedule of total standard manufacturing costs for the 7,800 output units in January 2007.
2. For the month of January 2007, compute the following variances, indicating whether each is favorable (F) or unfavorable (U):
   a. Direct materials price variance, based on purchases
   b. Direct materials efficiency variance
   c. Direct manufacturing labor price variance
   d. Direct manufacturing labor efficiency variance
   e. Total manufacturing overhead spending variance
   f. Variable manufacturing overhead efficiency variance
   g. Production-volume variance

Collaborative Learning Problem

8-41 Overhead variances, ethics. New Mexico Company uses standard costing. The company prepared its static budget for 2007 at 1,000,000 machine-hours for the year. Total budgeted overhead cost is $12,500,000. The variable overhead rate is $10 per machine-hour ($20 per unit). Actual results for 2007 follow:

Machine-hours	960,000 hours
Output	498,000 units
Variable overhead	$10,080,000
Fixed overhead spending variance	$600,000 U

Required

1. Compute for the fixed overhead
   - **a.** Budgeted amount
   - **b.** Budgeted cost per machine-hour
   - **c.** Actual cost
   - **d.** Production-volume variance
2. Compute the variable overhead spending variance and the variable overhead efficiency variance.
3. Jerry Remich, the controller, prepares the variance analysis. It is common knowledge in the company that he and Ron Monroe, the production manager, are not on the best of terms. In a recent executive committee meeting, Monroe had complained about the lack of usefulness of the accounting reports he receives. To get back at him, Remich manipulated the actual fixed overhead amount by assigning a greater-than-normal share of allocated costs to the production area. And, he decided to depreciate all of the newly acquired production equipment using the double-declining-balance method rather than the straight-line method, contrary to the company practice. As a result, there was a sizable unfavorable fixed overhead spending variance. He boasted to one of his confidants, "I am just returning the favor." Discuss Remich's actions and their ramifications.

Get Connected: Cost Accounting in the News

Go to www.prenhall.com/horngren/cost12e for additional online exercise(s) that explore issues affecting the accounting world today. These exercises offer you the opportunity to analyze and reflect on how cost accounting helps managers to make better decisions and handle the challenges of strategic planning and implementation.

CHAPTER 8 Case

TEVA SPORT SANDALS: Variable Overhead Variances

Teva Sport Sandals was founded in the 1980s by a seasoned river guide, Mark Thatcher, who was tired of losing his flip-flop sandals every time he took a raft ride down the Colorado River. Thatcher knew firsthand how thong-style rubber sandals abandoned his feet when he was slogging through mud and water. He figured a thong-style sandal with a heel strap on the back would be the answer to keeping sandals on. His new sandal creation was called the "Teva" (which means "nature" in Hebrew), and it was an immediate hit with water sports enthusiasts on the river and with others nowhere near a river.

Today Teva sandals are manufactured under license by Deckers Outdoor Corporation of Goleta, California. More than 60 styles for men, women, and children are available through retail sports stores, catalogs, and department stores around the world. The entire line of sandals also is sold direct to consumers through Teva's Web site at **www.teva.com**. Sandal styles are updated by designers at Deckers annually for each new selling season. Those new sandal specifications are converted into sandal prototypes by the in-house Fabrication Department.

Upon approval of the prototype designs, detailed sandal specifications are given to Pat Devaney, Deckers' vice president of production, development, and sourcing. Pat has responsibility for negotiating the best possible prices for finished sandals with the plant in China that manufactures the sandals. The specifications are critical to the negotiations. Some of the direct materials are sourced within China to help reduce the costs and prices of finished goods. Other direct materials must be imported. Either way, Deckers and the manufacturing plant in China work together to arrive at the best price. Once the specification and price negotiations are finished, the plant begins production according to the schedule set during negotiations.

The managers at the manufacturing plant in China have responsibility for controlling production costs. For illustration purposes, let's assume the following data apply to a recent month of sandal manufacturing for the plant (all amounts in U.S. dollars). Overhead is allocated based on machine-hours.

	Actual Results	Flexible-Budget Amount
Output units (pairs of sandals)	150,000	150,000
Machine-hours	67,500	60,000
Machine-hours per output unit	0.45	0.40
Variable manufacturing overhead costs	$1,950,000	$1,800,000
Variable manufacturing overhead cost per machine-hour	$28.89	$30.00
Variable manufacturing overhead cost per output unit	$13.00	$12.00

The plant manager's performance bonus is tied, in part, to his or her control of manufacturing overhead costs. There is an unfavorable variable overhead flexible-budget variance of $150,075 for this month's production of 150,000 pairs of sandals. The manager is interested in finding out what happened and why.

QUESTIONS

1. Compute the spending variance and the efficiency variance for variable manufacturing overhead.
2. What do the spending and efficiency variances mean? What are possible causes?
3. What explanation(s) should the plant manager give for the unfavorable variable overhead flexible-budget variance this month?

CHAPTER 9

INVENTORY COSTING AND CAPACITY ANALYSIS

LEARNING OBJECTIVES

1. Identify what distinguishes variable costing from absorption costing
2. Prepare income statements under absorption costing and variable costing
3. Explain differences in operating income under absorption costing and variable costing
4. Understand how absorption costing can provide undesirable incentives for managers to build up finished goods inventory
5. Differentiate throughput costing from variable costing and absorption costing
6. Describe the various capacity concepts that can be used in absorption costing
7. Understand the major factors management considers in choosing a capacity level to compute the budgeted fixed manufacturing cost rate
8. Describe how attempts to recover fixed costs of capacity may lead to price increases and lower demand
9. Explain how the capacity level chosen to calculate the budgeted fixed overhead cost rate affects the production-volume variance

There's nothing like a good incentive to influence actions. Organizations, for example, offer managers financial rewards and bonuses when key goals are met. The more desirable the prize, the greater the likelihood it will be pursued. Yet on the path to achieving the goals, dysfunctional activity may occur.

Claudia Jackson, president of Stassen Company, an optical consumer-products manufacturer, has just returned from a visit to the warehouse, which is stocked to the ceiling with finished telescopes. She is not happy, and for good reason. The most recent market feedback points to a decline in demand for Stassen's telescopes. As she contemplates the effect of the inventory buildup on the company's financial reports, Gary Dobbs, CFO, stops by her office.

Gary: Claudia, do you have a minute? I want to talk with you about our inventory situation.

Claudia: Yes, absolutely. I just returned from the warehouse, and it's overflowing with telescopes. This buildup can't be good.

Gary: You're right. We need to think about how we're valuing our inventory and the effects our incentives have on plant managers. We can value inventory based only on variable manufacturing costs or on both variable and fixed manufacturing costs. The income we report is directly affected by our choice.

Claudia: You bring up a good point about incentives. I know we paid some big bonuses last quarter, and I can't help but wonder if the full warehouse isn't somehow related to that.

Gary: Here's what I'll do. My team will put together a memo describing our options, complete with alternative income statement scenarios for the next three years. You'll see that one method will report a higher income figure in one period but a lower figure in another. The reason relates to how costs flow into and out of inventory at the end of the year, compared with the beginning of the year.

Claudia: Just what I need. Let's get together to review our options next week and get this problem fixed, quick.

Just like at Stassen, few numbers capture the attention of managers in the way that reported operating income does. Capital-intensive companies such as Aluminum Company of America (Alcoa), AT&T, Cessna, Delta Airlines, and Harley-Davidson have high fixed costs. Because of the negative effects fixed costs can have on operating income, how to manage the capacity decisions that generate these fixed costs, such as the number of planes Delta Airlines should have in its fleet, is among the most important strategic decisions these companies make. In their early histories, companies such as AT&T and Delta Airlines experienced demand for their products that exceeded their capacity to supply. Later, as they added capacity and demand declined, these companies had to drastically cut capacity by closing plants, selling planes, and laying off thousands of workers. Unlike variable costs, fixed costs do not automatically go away as output declines. Because fixed costs are harder to reduce, managers must plan them carefully.

Besides managing capacity levels, managers in companies and industries with high fixed costs care about decisions that affect their operating income numbers. Consider the following:

- Planning decisions of managers, such as a decision to introduce a new line of Harley-Davidson motorcycles, typically include analyses of how such decisions would affect future operating income.
- Top management uses operating income numbers to evaluate the performance of managers. Operating income also affects a company's stock price. Therefore, any stock-based compensation—such as stock options that managers receive—would also be affected.

This chapter examines two types of cost accounting choices for inventories that affect the operating income of manufacturing companies:

1. *The inventory-costing choice* determines which manufacturing costs are treated as inventoriable costs. Recall from Chapter 2 (pp. 37–38), *inventoriable costs* are all costs of a product that are regarded as assets when they are incurred and expensed as cost of goods sold when the product is sold. There are three types of inventory costing: absorption costing, variable costing, and throughput costing. We discuss each in Part One of this chapter.
2. *The denominator-level capacity choice* relates to the preselected level of the cost-allocation base used to set budgeted fixed manufacturing cost rates. There are four choices of capacity levels: theoretical capacity, practical capacity, normal capacity utilization, and master-budget capacity utilization. We discuss each in Part Two of this chapter.

Choosing between absorption costing (AC) and variable costing (VC) is only one of several issues pertaining to inventory costing in manufacturing companies. For example, managers also must choose a cost flow assumption such as FIFO, LIFO, or weighted average. (The abbreviations AC and VC are used throughout the Margin Notes in this chapter.)

PART ONE: INVENTORY COSTING FOR MANUFACTURING COMPANIES

The two common methods of costing inventories in manufacturing companies are variable costing and absorption costing. We discuss them first and then explain throughput costing, a more recent and less common method.

Variable Costing and Absorption Costing

The easiest way to understand the difference between variable costing and absorption costing is with an example. We present data for Stassen Company, which we introduced at the beginning of the chapter.

Data for Stassen Company for 2006

Stassen uses standard costing:

- Direct costs are traced to products using standard prices and standard inputs allowed for actual outputs produced.
- Indirect (overhead) manufacturing costs are allocated using standard indirect rates times standard inputs allowed for actual outputs produced.

To evaluate the performance of the telescope product line, Stassen's management wants to prepare an income statement for 2006 (the fiscal year just ended). The operating information for the year is:

	A	B
1		**Units**
2	Beginning inventory	0
3	Production	800
4	Sales	600
5	Ending inventory	200

Actual price and cost data for 2006 are:

	A	B
10	Selling Price	$ 100
11	Variable manufacturing cost per unit	
12	Direct material cost per unit	$ 11
13	Direct manufacturing labor cost per unit	4
14	Manufacturing overhead cost per unit	5
15	Total variable manufacturing cost per unit	$ 20
16	Variable marketing cost per unit sold (all indirect)	$ 19
17	Fixed manufacturing costs (all indirect)	$12,000
18	Fixed marketing costs (all indirect)	$10,800

For simplicity and to focus on the main ideas, we assume the following about Stassen:

Be aware that variable manufacturing costs often vary with the output level produced, whereas variable nonmanufacturing costs (for example, sales commissions) often vary with the amount of revenues.

- Stassen incurs manufacturing and marketing costs only. The cost driver for all variable manufacturing costs is units produced; the cost driver for variable marketing costs is units sold. There are no batch-level costs and no product-sustaining costs.
- Work-in-process inventory is zero.
- The budgeted level of production for 2006 is 800 units, which is used to calculate the budgeted fixed manufacturing cost per unit. The actual production for 2006 is 800 units.
- Stassen budgeted sales of 600 units for 2006, which is the same as the actual sales for 2006.
- There are no price variances, no efficiency variances, and no spending variances. Therefore, the *budgeted* (standard) price and cost data for 2006 are the same as the *actual* price and cost data. Our first example, based on data for 2006, has no production-volume variance for manufacturing costs. Later examples, based on data for 2007 and 2008, have production-volume variances. The Stassen Company's income statements show no variances other than the production-volume variance, where applicable.
- All variances are written off to cost of goods sold in the period (year) in which they occur.

1

Identify what distinguishes variable costing

. . . fixed manufacturing costs excluded from inventoriable costs

from absorption costing

. . . fixed manufacturing costs included in inventoriable costs

Variable costing is a method of inventory costing in which all variable manufacturing costs are included as inventoriable costs. All fixed manufacturing costs are excluded from inventoriable costs and are instead treated as costs of the period in which they are incurred.

Absorption costing is a method of inventory costing in which all variable manufacturing costs and all fixed manufacturing costs are included as inventoriable costs. That is, inventory "absorbs" all manufacturing costs.

Under both variable costing and absorption costing, all variable manufacturing costs are inventoriable costs and all nonmanufacturing costs in the value chain (such as research and development and marketing), whether variable or fixed, are period costs and are recorded as expenses when incurred.

To summarize: How fixed manufacturing costs are accounted for is the main difference between variable costing and absorption costing.

- Under variable costing, fixed manufacturing costs are treated as an expense of the period.
- Under absorption costing, fixed manufacturing costs are inventoriable costs. In our example, the standard fixed manufacturing cost is $15 per unit ($12,000 ÷ 800 units) produced.

For Stassen, inventoriable costs per unit produced in 2006 under the two methods are:

	Variable Costing		Absorption Costing	
Variable manufacturing cost per unit produced				
Direct materials	$11.00		$11.00	
Direct manufacturing labor	4.00		4.00	
Manufacturing overhead	5.00	$20.00	5.00	$20.00
Fixed manufacturing cost per unit produced		—		15.00
Total inventoriable cost per unit produced		$20.00		$35.00

Comparing Income Statements for One Year

What will Stassen's operating income be if it uses variable costing or absorption costing? The differences in these methods are apparent in Exhibit 9-1. Panel A shows the variable-costing income statement and Panel B the absorption-costing income statement for Stassen's telescope product line for 2006. The variable-costing income statement uses the contribution-margin format introduced in Chapter 3. The absorption-costing income statement uses the gross-margin format introduced in Chapter 2. Why these differences in format? The distinction between variable costs and fixed costs is central to variable costing, and it is highlighted by the contribution-margin format. Similarly, the distinction between manufacturing and nonmanufacturing costs is central to absorption costing, and it is highlighted by the gross-margin format.

Absorption-costing income statements need not differentiate between variable and fixed costs. However, we will make this distinction between variable and fixed costs in the Stassen example to show how individual line items are classified differently under variable costing and absorption costing. See in Exhibit 9-1, Panel B, that under absorption costing, inventoriable cost is \$35 per unit because fixed manufacturing costs allocated at the rate of \$15 per unit and variable manufacturing costs of \$20 per unit are assigned to each unit of product.

See how the fixed manufacturing costs of \$12,000 are accounted for under variable costing and absorption costing in Exhibit 9-1. The income statement under variable costing deducts the \$12,000 lump sum as an expense for 2006. In contrast, the income statement under absorption costing regards each finished unit as absorbing \$15 of fixed manufacturing cost. Under absorption costing, the \$12,000 (\$15 per unit × 800 units) is initially treated as an inventoriable cost in 2006. Of this, \$9,000 (\$15 per unit × 600 units sold) subsequently becomes a part of cost of goods sold in 2006, and \$3,000 (\$15 per unit × 200 units) remains an asset—part of ending finished goods inventory on December 31, 2006. Operating income is \$3,000 higher under absorption costing compared with variable costing, because only \$9,000 of fixed manufacturing costs are expensed under absorption costing, whereas all \$12,000 of fixed manufacturing costs are expensed under variable costing. Note that the variable manufacturing cost of \$20 per unit is accounted for the same way in both income statements in Exhibit 9-1.

2

Prepare income statements under absorption costing

. . . using the gross-margin format

and variable costing

. . . using the contribution-margin format

The VC income statement uses the contribution-margin format that distinguishes variable costs from fixed costs. This format highlights the lump-sum fixed manufacturing overhead (FMOH) costs that are expensed in the period incurred. The AC income statement uses the gross-margin format that distinguishes manufacturing costs from nonmanufacturing costs.

Two items distinguish gross margin (GM) from contribution margin (CM): (1) FMOH costs and (2) variable nonmanufacturing (VNM) costs. AC expenses FMOH costs related to units sold (as part of cost of goods sold) in calculating GM. In contrast, VC expenses total FMOH costs after calculating CM. Also, in AC, all nonmanufacturing costs are subtracted from GM, but in VC, VNM costs are subtracted in calculating CM.

EXHIBIT 9-1 Comparison of Variable Costing and Absorption Costing for Stassen Company: Telescope Product-Line Income Statements for 2006

	A	B	C	D	E	F	G
1	**Panel A: VARIABLE COSTING**				**Panel B: ABSORPTION COSTING**		
2	Revenues: \$100 x 600 units		\$60,000		Revenues: \$100 x 600 units		\$60,000
3	Variable cost of goods sold				Cost of goods sold		
4	Beginning Inventory	\$ 0			Beginning Inventory	\$ 0	
5	Variable manufacturing costs: \$20 x 800 units	16,000			Variable manufacturing costs: \$20 x 800 units	16,000	
6					Allocated fixed manufacturing costs: \$15 x 800 units	12,000	
7	Cost of goods available for sale	16,000			Cost of goods available for sale	28,000	
8	Deduct ending inventory: \$20 x 200 units	(4,000)			Deduct ending inventory: \$35 x 200 units	(7,000)	
9	Variable cost of goods sold		12,000		Cost of goods sold		21,000
10	Variable marketing costs: \$19 x 600 units sold		11,400				
11	Contribution margin		36,600		Gross Margin		39,000
12	Fixed manufacturing costs		12,000		Variable marketing costs: \$19 x 600 units sold		11,400
13	Fixed marketing costs		10,800		Fixed marketing costs		10,800
14	Operating income		\$13,800		Operating Income		\$16,800
15							
16	Manufacturing costs expensed in Panel A:				Manufacturing costs expensed in Panel B:		
17	Variable cost of goods sold		\$12,000				
18	Fixed manufacturing costs		12,000				
19	Total		\$24,000		Cost of goods sold		\$21,000
20							

These points can be summarized as follows:

	Variable Costing	Absorption Costing
Variable manufacturing costs: $20 per telescope produced	Inventoriable	Inventoriable
Fixed manufacturing costs: $12,000 per year	Deducted as an expense of the period	Inventoriable at $15 per telescope produced using budgeted denominator level of 800 units produced per year ($12,000 ÷ 800 units = $15 per unit)

The difference between VC and AC operating incomes is a *matter of timing.* Under VC, FMOH costs are expensed in the period incurred. Under AC, FMOH costs are allocated to output produced and are not expensed until those units are sold.

The basis of the difference between variable costing and absorption costing is how fixed manufacturing costs are accounted for. If inventory levels change, operating income will differ between the two methods because of the difference in accounting for fixed manufacturing costs. To see this, let's compare telescope sales of 600, 700, and 800 units by Stassen in 2006, when 800 units were produced. Of the $12,000 total fixed manufacturing costs, the amount expensed in the 2006 income statement would be:

	A	B	C	D	E	F	G
1			Variable Costing			Absorption Costing	
2						Fixed Manufacturing Costs	
3	Units	Ending	Fixed Manufacturing Costs			Included in Inventory	Amount Expensed
4	Sold	Inventory	Included in Inventory	Amount Expensed		= $15 x Ending Inventory	= $15 x Units Sold
5	600	200	$0	$12,000		$3,000	$ 9,000
6	700	100	$0	$12,000		$1,500	$10,500
7	800	0	$0	$12,000		$ 0	$12,000

This chapter's appendix describes how the choice of variable costing or absorption costing affects the breakeven quantity of sales.

Sometimes the term **direct costing** is used to describe the inventory-costing method we call *variable costing*. However, direct costing is not an accurate description for two reasons:

1. Variable costing does not include all direct costs as inventoriable costs. Only direct variable manufacturing costs are included. Any direct fixed manufacturing costs and any direct nonmanufacturing costs are excluded from inventoriable costs.
2. Variable costing includes as inventoriable costs not only direct manufacturing costs but also variable manufacturing overhead costs.

Note also that *variable costing* is a less-than-perfect term to describe this inventory-costing method because not all variable costs are inventoriable costs. Only variable manufacturing costs are inventoriable.

Explaining Differences in Operating Income

3

Explain differences in operating income under absorption costing

. . . affected by unit level of production and unit level of sales

and variable costing

. . . affected only by unit level of sales

To get a more-comprehensive view of the effects of variable costing and absorption costing, Stassen's management accountants prepare income statements for three years of operations.

Data for Stassen Company for 2006, 2007, and 2008

In both 2007 and 2008, Stassen has a production-volume variance because actual telescope production differs from the budgeted level of production of 800 units per year used to calculate budgeted fixed manufacturing cost per unit. The actual quantities sold for 2007 and 2008 are the same as the sales quantities budgeted for these respective years, which are given in units in the following table:

Chapter 8 (pp. 266–268) discusses the computation and interpretation of the production-volume variance (PVV).

	E	F	G	H
1		2006	2007	2008
2	Beginning inventory	0	200	50
3	Production	800	500	1,000
4	Sales	600	650	750
5	Ending inventory	200	50	300

All other 2006 data given earlier for Stassen also apply for 2007 and 2008.

Comparing Income Statements for Three Years

Exhibit 9-2 presents the income statement under variable costing in Panel A and the income statement under absorption costing in Panel B for 2006, 2007, and 2008. As you study Exhibit 9-2, note that the 2006 columns in both Panels A and B show the same figures as Exhibit 9-1. The 2007 and 2008 columns are similar to 2006 *except for the production-volume variance line item under absorption costing in Panel B.* Keep in mind the following points about absorption costing as you study Panel B of Exhibit 9-2:

1. The $15 fixed manufacturing cost rate is based on the budgeted denominator level of 800 units in 2006, 2007, and 2008 ($12,000 ÷ 800 units = $15 per unit). Whenever production—that's the quantity produced, not the quantity sold—deviates from the denominator level, there will be a production-volume variance. The amount of Stassen's

EXHIBIT 9-2 **Comparison of Variable Costing and Absorption Costing for Stassen Company: Telescope Product-Line Income Statements for 2006, 2007, and 2008**

	A	B	C	D	E	F	G
1	**Panel A: VARIABLE COSTING**						
2		**2006**		**2007**		**2008**	
3	Revenues: $100 x 600; 650; 750 units		$60,000		$65,000		$75,000
4	Variable cost of goods sold						
5	Beginning Inventory: $20 x 0; 200; 50 units	$ 0		$ 4,000		$ 1,000	
6	Variable manufacturing costs: $20 x 800; 500; 1,000 units	16,000		10,000		20,000	
7	Cost of goods available for sale	16,000		14,000		21,000	
8	Deduct ending inventory: $20 x 200; 50; 300 units	(4,000)		(1,000)		(6,000)	
9	Variable cost of goods sold		12,000		13,000		15,000
10	Variable marketing costs: $19 x 600; 650; 750 units		11,400		12,350		14,250
11	Contribution margin		36,600		39,650		45,750
12	Fixed manufacturing costs		12,000		12,000		12,000
13	Fixed marketing costs		10,800		10,800		10,800
14	Operating income		$13,800		$16,850		$22,950
15							
16	**Panel B: ABSORPTION COSTING**						
17		**2006**		**2007**		**2008**	
18	Revenues: $100 x 600; 650; 750 units		$60,000		$65,000		$75,000
19	Cost of goods sold						
20	Beginning Inventory: $35 x 0; 200; 50 units	$ 0		$ 7,000		$ 1,750	
21	Variable manufacturing costs: $20 x 800; 500; 1,000 units	16,000		10,000		20,000	
22	Allocated fixed manufacturing costs: $15 x 800; 500; 1,000 units	12,000		7,500		15,000	
23	Cost of goods available for sale	28,000		24,500		36,750	
24	Deduct ending inventory: $35 x 200; 50; 300 units	(7,000)		(1,750)		(10,500)	
25	Adjustment for production-volume variance[a]	0		4,500 U		(3,000) F	
26	Cost of goods sold		21,000		27,250		23,250
27	Gross Margin		39,000		37,750		51,750
28	Variable marketing costs: $19 x 600; 650; 750 units		11,400		12,350		14,250
29	Fixed marketing costs		10,800		10,800		10,800
30	Operating Income		$16,800		$14,600		$26,700
31							
32	[a] Production-volume variance = Budgeted fixed manufacturing costs − Fixed manufacturing overhead allocated using budgeted cost per output unit allowed for actual output produced (Panel B, line 22)						
33	2006: $12,000 - ($15 x 800) = $12,000 - $12,000 = $0						
34	2007: $12,000 - ($15 x 500) = $12,000 - $7,500 = $4,500 U						
35	2008: $12,000 - ($15 x 1,000) = $12,000 - $15,000 = 3,000 F						
36							
37	Production-volume variance can also be calculated as						
38	Fixed manufacturing cost per unit x (Denominator level - Actual output units produced)						
39	2006: $15 x (800 - 800) units = $15 x 0 = $0						
40	2007: $15 x (800 - 500) units = $15 x 300 = $4,500 U						
41	2008: $15 x (800 - 1,000) units = $15 x (200) = $(3,000) F						

production-volume variance is determined by multiplying $15 per unit by the difference between the actual level of production and the denominator level.

In 2007, production was 500 units, 300 lower than the denominator level of 800 units. The result is an unfavorable production-volume variance of $4,500 ($15 per unit × 300 units). The year 2008 has a favorable production-volume variance of $3,000 ($15 per unit × 200 units), due to production of 1,000 units, which exceeds the denominator level of 800 units.

Recall how standard costing works under absorption costing. Each time a unit is manufactured, $15 of fixed manufacturing costs is included in the cost of goods manufactured and available for sale. In 2007, when 500 units are manufactured, $7,500 ($15 per unit × 500 units) of fixed manufacturing costs are included in the cost of goods available for sale (see Exhibit 9-2, Panel B, line 22). Total fixed manufacturing costs for 2007 are $12,000. The production-volume variance of $4,500 U equals the difference between $12,000 and $7,500. In Panel B, note how, for each year, the fixed manufacturing costs included in the cost of goods available for sale plus the production-volume variance always equals $12,000.

The PVV is the difference between the lump-sum budgeted FMOH and FMOH allocated to output produced. Because FMOH costs aren't allocated to output produced under VC (FMOH costs are expensed in the period incurred), there is no PVV under VC.

2. The production-volume variance, which relates only to fixed manufacturing overhead, exists under absorption costing but not under variable costing. That's because under variable costing, fixed manufacturing costs of $12,000 are always treated as an expense of the period, regardless of the level of production (and sales).

Here's a summary (using information from Exhibit 9-2) of the operating-income differences for Stassen Company during the 2006 to 2008 period:

	2006	2007	2008
1. Absorption-costing operating income	$16,800	$14,600	$26,700
2. Variable-costing operating income	13,800	16,850	22,950
3. Difference: (1) – (2)	3,000	(2,250)	3,750
4. Difference as a % of absorption-costing operating income	17.9%	(15.4%)	14.0%

The percentage differences in the preceding table illustrate why managers whose performance is measured by reported income are concerned about the choice between variable costing and absorption costing.

Why do variable costing and absorption costing usually report different operating income numbers? In general, if inventory increases during an accounting period, less operating income will be reported under variable costing than absorption costing. Conversely, if inventory decreases, more operating income will be reported under variable costing than absorption costing. The difference in reported operating income is due solely to (a) moving fixed manufacturing costs into inventories as inventories increase and (b) moving fixed manufacturing costs out of inventories as inventories decrease.

The difference between operating income under absorption costing and variable costing can be computed by formula 1, which focuses on fixed manufacturing costs in beginning inventory and ending inventory:

	A	B	C	D	E	F	G	H
1	**Formula 1**							
2						**Fixed manufacturing**		**Fixed manufacturing**
3		**Absorption-costing**	-	**Variable-costing**	=	**costs in ending inventory**	-	**costs in beginning inventory**
4		**operating income**		**operating income**		**under absorption costing**		**under absorption costing**
5	**2006**	$16,800	-	$13,800	=	($15 per unit x 200 units)	-	($15 per unit x 0 units)
6				$ 3,000	=	$3,000		
7								
8	**2007**	$14,600	-	$16,850	=	($15 per unit x 50 units)	-	($15 per unit x 200 units)
9				($ 2,250)	=	($2,250)		
10								
11	**2008**	$26,700	-	$22,950	=	($15 per unit x 300 units)	-	($15 per unit x 50 units)
12				$ 3,750	=	$3,750		

Fixed manufacturing costs in ending inventory are deferred to a future period under absorption costing. For example, $3,000 of fixed manufacturing overhead is deferred to 2007 at December 31, 2006. Under variable costing, all $12,000 of fixed manufacturing costs are treated as an expense of 2006.

Recall that,

$$\text{Beginning inventory} + \text{Cost of goods manufactured} = \text{Cost of goods sold} + \text{Ending inventory}$$

Therefore, instead of focusing on fixed manufacturing costs in ending and beginning inventory, we could alternatively focus on fixed manufacturing costs in units produced and units sold. This approach highlights how fixed manufacturing costs move between units produced and units sold during the fiscal year.

16	**Formula 2**							
17						**Fixed manufacturing costs**		**Fixed manufacturing costs**
18		**Absorption-costing**	-	**Variable-costing**	=	**inventoried in units produced**	-	**in cost of goods sold**
19		**operating income**		**operating income**		**under absorption costing**		**under absorption costing**
20	**2006**	$16,800	-	$13,800	=	($15 per unit x 800 units)	-	($15 per unit x 600 units)
21				$ 3,000	=	$3,000		
22								
23	**2007**	$14,600	-	$16,850	=	($15 per unit x 500 units)	-	($15 per unit x 650 units)
24				($ 2,250)	=	($2,250)		
25								
26	**2008**	$26,700	-	$22,950	=	($15 per unit x 1,000 units)	-	($15 per unit x 750 units)
27				$ 3,750	=	$3,750		

There is increasing pressure on managers to reduce inventory levels. Some companies are achieving steep reductions in inventory levels using policies such as just-in-time production—a production system under which products are manufactured only when needed. Formula 1 illustrates that, as Stassen reduces its inventory levels, operating income differences between absorption costing and variable costing become immaterial. Consider, for example, the formula for 2006. If instead of 200 units in ending inventory, Stassen had only 2 units in ending inventory, the difference between absorption-costing operating income and variable-costing operating income would drop from $3,000 to $30 [($15 per unit × 2) − ($15 per unit × 0)].

Effect of Sales and Production on Operating Income

Given a constant contribution margin per unit and constant fixed costs, the period-to-period change in operating income under variable costing is *driven solely by changes in the quantity of units actually sold*. Consider the variable-costing operating income of Stassen in (a) 2007 versus 2006 and (b) 2008 versus 2007.

Recall that,

$$\begin{aligned}\text{Contribution margin per unit} &= \text{Selling price} - \text{Variable manufacturing cost per unit} - \text{Variable marketing cost per unit}\\ &= \$100 \text{ per unit} - \$20 \text{ per unit} - \$19 \text{ per unit}\\ &= \$61 \text{ per unit}\end{aligned}$$

$$\text{Change in variable-costing operating income} = \text{Contribution margin per unit} \times \text{Change in quantity of units sold}$$

(a) 2007 vs. 2006: $16,850 − $13,800 = $61 per unit × (650 units − 600 units)

$3,050 = $3,050

(b) 2008 vs. 2007: $22,950 − $16,850 = $61 per unit × (750 units − 650 units)

$6,100 = $6,100

Under variable costing, Stassen managers cannot increase operating income by "producing for inventory." Why not? Because, as you can see from the preceding computations, only the quantity of units sold drives operating income. We'll explain later in this chapter that absorption costing enables managers to increase operating income by increasing the unit level of sales, as well as by producing more units. Before you proceed to the next section, make sure you examine Exhibit 9-3 for a detailed comparison of the differences between variable costing and absorption costing.

Study Tip: To check your understanding of variable costing and absorption costing, see the Featured Exercise, true–false statement 4, multiple-choice questions 5 and 7, and Review Exercise 1 (*Student Guide*, beginning p. 108). Fully explained answers begin on p. 116.

EXHIBIT 9-3 **Comparative Income Effects of Variable Costing and Absorption Costing**

Question	Variable Costing	Absorption Costing	Comment
Are fixed manufacturing costs inventoried?	No	Yes	Basic theoretical question of when these costs should be expensed
Is there a production-volume variance?	No	Yes	Choice of denominator level affects measurement of operating income under absorption costing only
Are classifications between variable and fixed costs routinely made?	Yes	Infrequently	Absorption costing can be easily modified to obtain subclassifications for variable and fixed costs, if desired (for example, see Exhibit 9-1, Panel B)
How do changes in unit inventory levels affect operating income?[a]			Differences are attributable to the timing of when fixed manufacturing costs are expensed
Production = sales	Equal	Equal	
Production > sales	Lower[b]	Higher[c]	
Production < sales	Higher	Lower	
What are the effects on cost-volume-profit relationship (for a given level of fixed costs and a given contribution margin per unit)?	Driven by unit level of sales	Driven by (a) unit level of sales, (b) unit level of production, and (c) chosen denominator level	Management control benefit: Effects of changes in production level on operating income are easier to understand under variable costing

[a]Assuming that all manufacturing variances are written off as period costs, that no change occurs in work-in-process inventory, and no change occurs in the budgeted fixed manufacturing cost rate between accounting periods.

[b]That is, lower operating income than under absorption costing.

[c]That is, higher operating income than under variable costing.

Performance Measures and Absorption Costing

Absorption costing is the required inventory method for external reporting in most countries. A majority of companies use absorption costing for internal accounting as well. Why? Because it is cost-effective and less confusing to managers to use one common method of inventory costing for both external and internal reporting and performance evaluation. A common method of inventory costing can also help prevent managers from taking actions that make their performance measure look good but hurt the income they report to shareholders. Another advantage of absorption costing is that it measures the cost of all manufacturing resources, whether variable or fixed, necessary to produce inventory. Many companies use inventory costing information for long-run decisions such as pricing and choosing a product mix. For these long-run decisions, inventory costs should include both variable *and* fixed costs.

One problem with absorption costing is that it enables a manager to increase operating income in a specific period by increasing production—even if there is no customer demand for the additional production! (See the Focus on Values and Behaviors feature, p. 303.) Stassen's managers may be tempted to do this to get higher bonuses based on absorption-costing operating income. Generally, higher operating income also has a positive effect on stock price, which increases managers' stock-based compensation.

To reduce the undesirable incentives to build up inventories that absorption costing can create, many companies also use variable costing for internal reporting. Variable costing focuses attention on distinguishing variable manufacturing costs from fixed manufacturing costs. This distinction is important for short-run decision making (as in cost-volume-profit analysis in Chapter 3 and in planning and control in Chapters 6, 7, and 8).

The different advantages of variable costing and absorption costing benefits companies that use both methods for internal reporting—variable costing for short-run decisions and performance evaluation and absorption costing for long-run decisions (see the Global Surveys of Company Practice feature, p. 305). In the next section, we explore in more detail the challenges that arise from absorption costing.

FOCUS ON VALUES AND BEHAVIORS

BRISTOL-MYERS/SQUIBB'S QUESTIONABLE INVENTORY STRATEGY

How many units should be produced? What denominator level should be used to calculate the budgeted fixed manufacturing overhead rate? How should the production-volume variance be disposed of at the end of the fiscal year? The choices that managers and management accountants make affect performance evaluations, compensation, and reported operating income. The challenge facing companies is that the answers to these questions are far from clear-cut, which requires managers and management accountants to exercise considerable judgment.

Management accountants may face pressure from managers to make choices that increase (or sometimes decrease) operating income. Consider the case of Bristol-Myers/Squibb (BMS), the New York–based pharmaceutical company. Between 1999 and 2001, the company produced much more product than it sold to consumers. This action increased operating income under absorption costing. But BMS went much further, by offering incentives to wholesalers to build their inventories and then recording deliveries to wholesalers as revenues. This step allowed BMS to meet its quarterly revenue forecasts. Following an investigation, the U.S. Department of Justice and the Securities and Exchange Commission concluded that the loading of inventories onto wholesalers could not be recognized as revenues. BMS was charged with overstating revenues by $2.5 billion from 1999 through 2001. In a 2004 interview, Chief Financial Officer Andrew Bonfield stated that the company is working to "improve the transparency and quality of its financial disclosures."

The problems at Bristol-Myers/Squibb illustrate why management accountants must possess a strong sense of integrity to guide their decisions. They must help managers run their businesses as effectively as possible, not overproducing solely to make numbers look better or to push finished goods onto wholesalers and distributors to meet sales targets. They must also prepare reports that accurately represent what happened, allocating only the appropriate fixed costs to inventory. Commitment to these goals is what companies demand from their management accountants.

Source: *Barbara Martinez, "Bristol-Myers Again Restates Results,"* The Wall Street Journal, *March 16, 2004.*

Undesirable Buildup of Inventories

4

Understand how absorption costing can provide undesirable incentives for managers to build up finished goods inventory

. . . producing more units for inventory absorbs fixed manufacturing costs and increases operating income

Recall that one motivation for an undesirable buildup of inventories could be because a manager's bonus is based on reported absorption-costing operating income. Assume that Stassen's managers have such a bonus plan. Exhibit 9-4 shows how Stassen's absorption-costing operating income for 2007 changes as the production level changes. This exhibit assumes that the production-volume variance is written off to cost of goods sold at the end of each year. Beginning inventory of 200 units and sales of 650 units for 2007 are unchanged from the case shown in Exhibit 9-2. *As you review Exhibit 9-4, keep in mind that the computations are basically the same as those in Exhibit 9-2.*

Exhibit 9-4 shows that production of only 450 units meets the 2007 sales budget of 650 units (200 units from beginning inventory + 450 units produced). Operating income at this production level is $13,850. By producing more than 450 units, commonly referred to as *producing for inventory,* Stassen increases absorption-costing operating income. Each additional unit in 2007 ending inventory will increase operating income by $15. For example, if 800 units are produced, ending inventory will be 350 units and operating income will be $19,100. This amount is $5,250 more than the operating income with zero ending inventory ($19,100 – $13,850, or 350 units × $15 per unit = $5,250). Under absorption costing, the company, by producing 350 units for inventory, includes $5,250 of fixed manufacturing costs in finished goods inventory, so they are not expensed in 2007.

Can't top management implement checks and balances that limit managers from producing for inventory under absorption costing? The answer is yes, as we will see in the next section, but producing for inventory cannot be completely prevented. There are many subtle ways a manager can produce for inventory that, if done to a limited extent, may not be easy to detect. For example,

- A plant manager may switch to manufacturing products that absorb the highest amount of fixed manufacturing costs, regardless of the customer demand for these products (called "cherry picking" the production line). Production of items that absorb the least or lower fixed manufacturing costs may be delayed, resulting in failure to meet promised customer delivery dates (which, over time, can result in unhappy customers).

EXHIBIT 9-4 **Effect on Absorption-Costing Operating Income of Different Production Levels for Stassen Company: Telescope Product-Line Income Statement for 2007 at Sales of 650 Units**

	A	B	C	D	E	F	G	H	I	J	K
1	**Unit Data**										
2	Beginning inventory	200		200		200		200		200	
3	Production	450		500		650		800		900	
4	Goods available for sale	650		700		850		1,000		1,100	
5	Sales	650		650		650		650		650	
6	Ending inventory	0		50		200		350		450	
7											
8	**Income Statement**										
9	Revenues	$65,000		$65,000		$65,000		$65,000		$65,000	
10	Cost of goods sold										
11	Beginning inventory ($35 x 200 units)	7,000		7,000		7,000		7,000		7,000	
12	Variable manufacturing costs ($20 x production)	9,000		10,000		13,000		16,000		18,000	
13	Allocated fixed manufacturing costs ($15 x production)	6,750		7,500		9,750		12,000		13,500	
14	Cost of goods available for sale	22,750		24,500		29,750		35,000		38,500	
15	Deduct ending inventory ($35 x ending inventory)	0		(1,750)		(7,000)		(12,250)		(15,750)	
16	Adjustment for production-volume variance[a]	5,250	U	4,500	U	2,250	U	0		(1,500)	F
17	Cost of goods sold	28,000		27,250		25,000		22,750		21,250	
18	Gross margin	37,000		37,750		40,000		42,250		43,750	
19	Marketing costs ($10,800 + $19 per unit x 650 units sold)	23,150		23,150		23,150		23,150		23,150	
20	Operating income	$13,850		$14,600		$16,850		$19,100		$20,600	
21											
22	[a] Production-volume variance = Budgeted fixed manufacturing costs - Allocated fixed manufacturing costs (Income Statement, line 13)										
23	At production of 450 units: $12,000 - $6,750 = $5,250 U										
24	At production of 500 units: $12,000 - $7,500 = $4,500 U										
25	At production of 650 units: $12,000 - $9,750 = $2,250 U										
26	At production of 800 units: $12,000 - $12,000 = $0										
27	At production of 900 units: $12,000 - $13,500 = $1,500 F										

- A plant manager may accept a particular order to increase production, even though another plant in the same company is better suited to handle that order.
- To increase production, a manager may defer maintenance beyond the current period. Although operating income in this period may increase as a result, future operating income could decrease by a larger amount if repair costs increase and equipment becomes less efficient .

The example in Exhibit 9-4 focuses on only one year (2007). A Stassen manager who built up ending inventories of telescopes to 450 units in 2007 would have to further increase ending inventories in 2008 to increase that year's operating income by producing for inventory. There are limits to how much inventory levels can be increased over time (because of physical constraints on storage space and management supervision and controls). Such limits reduce the likelihood of incurring some of absorption costing's undesirable effects.

Proposals for Revising Performance Evaluation

Top management, with help from the controller and management accountants, can take several steps to reduce the undesirable effects of absorption costing.

- Focus on careful budgeting and inventory planning to reduce management's freedom to build up excess inventory. For example, the budgeted monthly balance sheets have estimates of the dollar amount of inventories. If actual inventories exceed these dollar amounts, top management can investigate the inventory buildups.
- Incorporate a carrying charge for inventory in the internal accounting system. For example, the company could assess an inventory carrying charge of 1% per month on the investment tied up in inventory and for spoilage and obsolescence when it eval-

GLOBAL SURVEYS OF COMPANY PRACTICE

Usage of Variable Costing and Absorption Costing by Companies

Surveys of company practice in the United States, Scandinavia, and Asia report that approximately 20% to 55% of companies use variable costing in their internal accounting system. In addition, up to 30% of companies use both variable costing and absorption costing:

	United States[a]	China[b]	Estonia[c]	Finland[d]	India[e]	Malaysia[f]	Norway[g]
Variable costing used	24%	32%	39%	42%	50%	23%	55%
Absorption costing used	76	68	55	31	48	46	29
Both systems used	—	6	28	2	31	16	—

Surveys to date have not extensively examined the usage of throughput costing.

Many companies using variable costing for internal reporting, short run decisions, and performance evaluation, also use absorption costing for external reporting or tax reporting. Companies that use variable costing for internal accounting make an adjustment at the end of the quarter (for quarterly reporting) or at the end of the fiscal year (for annual reporting) to prorate fixed manufacturing overhead to inventory and cost of goods sold to prepare absorption-costing statements for external reporting. The most common problem reported by companies using variable costing is the difficulty of classifying costs into fixed or variable categories.

[a] Ernst & Young, "2003 Survey of Management Accounting."
[b] Firth, M., "The Diffusion of Managerial Accounting."
[c] Haldma, T., and K. Lääts, "Contingencies Influencing."
[d] Lukka, K., and M. Granlund, "Cost Accounting in Finland."
[e] Joshi, P., "The International Diffusion."
[f] Chun, L., et al, "Are Management Accounting Systems."
[g] Bjornenak, T., "Conventional Wisdom and Costing Practices."
Full citations are in Appendix A at the end of the book.

uates a manager's performance. An increasing number of companies are beginning to adopt this inventory carrying charge.

- Change the period used to evaluate performance. Critics of absorption costing give examples in which managers take actions that maximize quarterly or annual income at the potential expense of long-run income. When their performance is evaluated over a three- to five-year period, managers will be less tempted to produce for inventory.
- Include nonfinancial as well as financial variables in the measures used to evaluate performance (see the Concepts in Action feature, p. 306). Examples of nonfinancial measures that can be used to monitor the performance of Stassen's managers in 2008 (see data on the bottom of p. 298) are:

$$\textbf{(a)}\ \frac{\text{Ending inventory in units in 2008}}{\text{Beginning inventory in units in 2008}} = \frac{300}{50} = 6$$

$$\textbf{(b)}\ \frac{\text{Units produced in 2008}}{\text{Units sold in 2008}} = \frac{1{,}000}{750} = 1.3$$

Top management would want to see production equal to sales and relatively stable levels of inventory. Companies that manufacture or sell several products could report these two measures for each of the products they manufacture and sell.

5
Differentiate throughput costing
. . . direct material costs inventoried
from variable costing
. . . variable manufacturing costs inventoried
and absorption costing
. . . variable and fixed manufacturing costs inventoried

Throughput Costing

Some managers maintain that even variable costing promotes an excessive amount of costs being inventoried. They argue that only direct materials are "truly variable." **Throughput costing**, which also is called **super-variable costing** because it is an extreme form of vari-

CONCEPTS IN ACTION

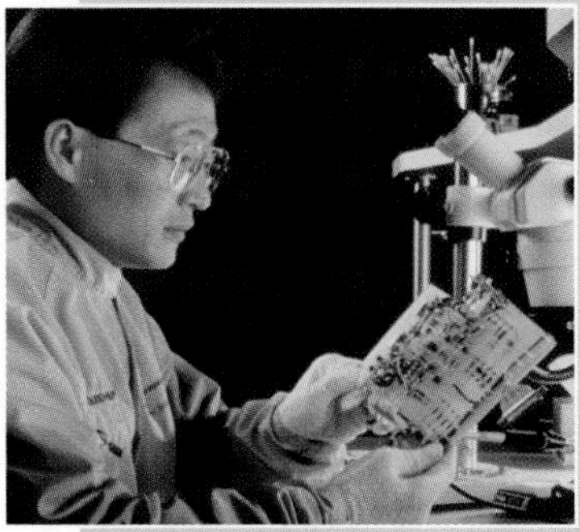

Yield Improvements and the Production-Volume Variance at Analog Devices

Analog Devices, Inc. (ADI) produces integrated circuits and systems used in computers, broadband modems, medical instruments, and consumer electronics. Improving yield—the quantity of good die produced on a silicon wafer divided by the total number of die that could be printed and produced on the wafer—is critical to delivering high-quality products at low cost.

For internal-reporting purposes, ADI uses variable costing. Fixed costs—comprising fixed overhead costs—are allocated to products only for the purposes of external reporting. The denominator level used to allocate standard fixed overhead costs to products is machine capacity assuming efficient operations—for example, machines working six hours per day. However, suppose running the machines only four hours a day is adequate to meet actual demand. The result is an unfavorable production-volume variance because budgeted fixed overhead costs exceed the overhead costs allocated to production.

How do improvements in yield affect ADI's production-volume variance? As yields improve, machines need to be run for even fewer hours to produce the actual output. That's because fewer silicon wafers need to be started to get the desired quantity of good product. Consequently, even fewer of the budgeted fixed overhead costs get allocated to production, the costs in inventory decline, and the unfavorable production-volume variance gets bigger. As the production-volume variance is written off to cost of goods sold at year-end, profit margins decline. Thus, quality improvements can have negative operating-income effects!

The performance evaluation of production planners at ADI was weighted more toward satisfying customer orders than reducing inventory levels. Thus, even as yields improved, planners were reluctant to reduce the number of wafer starts until they were sure that the higher yields would continue. They did not want to be in a position in which ADI lacked inventory to meet customer requests. Building up inventory also improved short-run operating income.

Commenting on the tensions and trade-offs, ADI's chairman and president warned, "Unless quality improvement and other more-fundamental performance measures are elevated to the same level of importance as financial measures, when conflicts arise, financial considerations win out." However, believing in the long-run benefits of higher quality, ADI continued to improve yield, and it developed performance measures that gave incentives to production planners and operations managers to not produce more product simply to absorb more fixed overhead costs into inventory. This strategy has proven very successful. ADI is a leading semiconductor company with 2003 revenues of over $2 billion and 60,000 customers worldwide.

Source: Analog Devices: The Half-Life System, Harvard Business School case number 9-190-061, Analog Devices 2003 Annual Report, and discussions with company management.

able costing, is a method of inventory costing in which only direct material costs are included as inventoriable costs. All other costs are costs of the period in which they are incurred. In particular, variable direct manufacturing labor costs and variable manufacturing overhead costs are regarded as period costs and are deducted as expenses of the period.

Advocates of throughput costing maintain that, in the short run, manufacturing costs other than direct materials are relatively fixed. They view costs relating to workers, equipment, occupancy, and so on as relatively fixed with respect to providing productive capacity during the period.

Exhibit 9-5 is the throughput-costing income statement for Stassen Company for 2006, 2007, and 2008. *Throughput contribution* equals revenues minus all direct material cost of the goods sold. Compare the operating income amounts reported in Exhibit 9-5 with those for absorption costing and variable costing:

	2006	2007	2008
Absorption-costing operating income	$16,800	$14,600	$26,700
Variable-costing operating income	13,800	16,850	22,950
Throughput-costing operating income	12,000	18,200	20,700

Only the $11 direct material cost per unit is inventoriable under throughput costing, compared with $35 per unit for absorption costing and $20 per unit for variable costing. When the production quantity exceeds sales, as in 2006 and 2008, throughput costing results in the largest amount of expenses in the current period's income statement. Advocates of throughput costing say it provides less incentive to produce for inventory than either variable costing or, especially, absorption costing. Throughput costing is a

	A	B	C	D	E
1		**2006**	**2007**	**2008**	
2	Revenues: $100 x 600; 650; 750 units	$60,000	$65,000	$75,000	
3	Direct material cost of goods sold				
4	Beginning Inventory: $11 x 0; 200; 50 units	0	2,200	550	
5	Direct materials: $11 x 800; 500; 1,000 units	8,800	5,500	11,000	
6	Cost of goods available for sale	8,800	7,700	11,550	
7	Deduct ending inventory: $11 x 200; 50; 300 units	(2,200)	(550)	(3,300)	
8	Direct material cost of goods sold	6,600	7,150	8,250	
9	Throughput contribution[a]	53,400	57,850	66,750	
10	Manufacturing costs (other than direct materials)[b]	19,200	16,500	21,000	
11	Marketing costs[c]	22,200	23,150	25,050	
12	Operating income	$12,000	$18,200	$20,700	
13					
14	[a]Throughput contribution equals revenues minus all direct material costs of goods sold.				
15	[b]Fixed manuf. costs + [(variable manuf. labor + variable manuf. overhead) × units produced];				
16	$12,000 + [($4 + $5) × 800; 500; 1,000 units]				
17	[c]Fixed marketing costs + (variable marketing cost per unit × units sold);				
18	$10,800 + ($19 × 600; 650; 750 units)				

EXHIBIT 9-5

Throughput Costing for Stassen Company: Telescope Product-Line Income Statements for 2006, 2007, and 2008

more recent phenomenon in comparison with variable costing and absorption costing and has avid supporters, but so far it has not been widely adopted.[1]

Comparison of Alternative Inventory-Costing Methods

Variable costing and absorption costing (as well as throughput costing) may be combined with actual, normal, or standard costing. Exhibit 9-6 compares product costing under six alternative inventory-costing systems.

Variable Costing	Absorption Costing
Actual costing	Actual costing
Normal costing	Normal costing
Standard costing	Standard costing

For example, a company might use AC based on standard costing for external financial reporting and VC based on standard costing for internal reporting.

Variable costing has been controversial among accountants—not because of disagreement about the need to delineate between variable and fixed costs for internal planning and control, but as it pertains to *external reporting*. Accountants who favor variable costing for external reporting maintain that the fixed portion of manufacturing costs is more closely related to the capacity to produce than to the actual production of specific units. Hence, fixed costs should be expensed, not inventoried.

Accountants who support absorption costing for *external reporting* maintain that inventories should carry a fixed-manufacturing-cost component. Why? Because both variable manufacturing costs and fixed manufacturing costs are necessary to produce goods. Therefore, both types of costs should be inventoried in order to match all manufacturing costs to revenues, regardless of their different behavior patterns.

For external reporting to shareholders, companies around the globe tend to follow the generally accepted accounting principle that all manufacturing costs are inventoriable. For tax reporting in the United States, all manufacturing costs plus some product design and administrative costs (such as legal costs) must be included as inventoriable costs.[2] Administrative costs must be allocated between those costs related to manufacturing activities (inventoriable costs) and those not related to manufacturing.

Accountants who favor VC argue that FMOH costs are incurred to create the capacity to produce units. Once the capacity is created, FMOH costs should be expensed in the period incurred, regardless of how much of that capacity is actually used.

VC isn't acceptable for external financial reporting or tax reporting. If a company uses VC, it must be in addition to AC. These companies have decided that the benefits of VC outweigh its costs.

[1]See E. Goldratt, *The Theory of Constraints* (New York: North River Press, 1990); E. Noreen, D. Smith, and J. Mackey, *The Theory of Constraints and Its Implications for Management Accounting* (New York: North River Press, 1995).

[2]Section 1.471-11 of the U.S. Internal Revenue Code (Inventories of Manufacturers) states that "both direct and indirect production costs must be taken into account in the computation of inventoriable costs in accordance with the 'full absorption' method of inventory costing . . . Costs are considered to be production costs to the extent that they are incident to and necessary for production or manufacturing operations or processes. Production costs include direct production costs and fixed and variable indirect production costs." Case law is useful to examine when determining the precise boundaries between inventoriable and noninventoriable costs.

EXHIBIT 9-6 **Comparison of Alternative Inventory-Costing Systems**

			Actual Costing	Normal Costing	Standard Costing
Absorption Costing	Variable Costing	Variable Direct Manufacturing Cost	Actual prices × Actual quantity of inputs used	Actual prices × Actual quantity of inputs used	Standard prices × Standard quantity of inputs allowed for actual output achieved
		Variable Manufacturing Overhead Costs	Actual variable overhead rates × Actual quantity of cost-allocation bases used	Budgeted variable overhead rates × Actual quantity of cost-allocation bases used	Standard variable overhead rates × Standard quantity of cost-allocation bases allowed for actual output achieved
		Fixed Direct Manufacturing Costs	Actual prices × Actual quantity of inputs used	Actual prices × Actual quantity of inputs used	Standard prices × Standard quantity of inputs allowed for actual output achieved
		Fixed Manufacturing Overhead Costs	Actual fixed overhead rates × Actual quantity of cost-allocation bases used	Budgeted fixed overhead rates × Actual quantity of cost-allocation bases used	Standard fixed overhead rates × Standard quantity of cost-allocation bases allowed for actual output achieved

A key issue in absorption costing is the choice of the capacity level used to compute fixed manufacturing cost per unit produced. Part Two of this chapter discusses this issue.

PROBLEM FOR SELF-STUDY

Assume Stassen Company on January 1, 2006, decides to contract with another company to preassemble a large percentage of the components of its telescopes. The revised manufacturing cost structure during the 2006-to-2008 period is:

Variable manufacturing cost per unit produced	
Direct materials	$30.50
Direct manufacturing labor	2.00
Manufacturing overhead	1.00
Total variable manufacturing cost per unit produced	$33.50
Fixed manufacturing costs	$1,200

Under the revised cost structure, a larger percentage of Stassen's manufacturing costs are variable with respect to units produced. The denominator level of production used to calculate budgeted fixed manufacturing cost per unit in 2006, 2007, and 2008 is 800 units. Assume no other change from the data underlying Exhibits 9-1 and 9-2. Summary information pertaining to absorption-costing operating income and variable-costing operating income with this revised cost structure is:

	2006	2007	2008
Absorption-costing operating income	$16,800	$18,650	$24,000
Variable-costing operating income	16,500	18,875	23,625
Difference	$ 300	$ (225)	$ 375

Required

1. Compute the budgeted fixed manufacturing cost per unit in 2006, 2007, and 2008.
2. Explain the difference between absorption-costing operating income and variable-costing operating income in 2006, 2007, and 2008, focusing on fixed manufacturing costs in beginning and ending inventory.
3. Why are these differences smaller than the differences in Exhibit 9-2?

SOLUTION

1.
$$\text{Budgeted fixed manufacturing cost per unit} = \frac{\text{Budgeted fixed manufacturing costs}}{\text{Budgeted production units}}$$
$$= \frac{\$1{,}200}{800 \text{ units}}$$
$$= \$1.50 \text{ per unit}$$

2.
$$\begin{pmatrix}\text{Absorption-costing} & & \text{Variable-costing}\\ \text{operating} & - & \text{operating}\\ \text{income} & & \text{income}\end{pmatrix} = \begin{pmatrix}\text{Fixed manufacturing} & & \text{Fixed manufacturing costs}\\ \text{costs in ending inventory} & - & \text{in beginning inventory}\\ \text{under absorption costing} & & \text{under absorption costing}\end{pmatrix}$$

2006: $\$16{,}800 - \$16{,}500 = (\$1.50 \text{ per unit} \times 200 \text{ units}) - (\$1.50 \text{ per unit} \times 0 \text{ units})$

$\$300 = \$300$

2007: $\$18{,}650 - \$18{,}875 = (\$1.50 \text{ per unit} \times 50 \text{ units}) - (\$1.50 \text{ per unit} \times 200 \text{ units})$

$-\$225 = -\$225$

2008: $\$24{,}000 - \$23{,}625 = (\$1.50 \text{ per unit} \times 300 \text{ units}) - (\$1.50 \text{ per unit} \times 50 \text{ units})$

$\$375 = \$375$

3. Subcontracting a large part of manufacturing has greatly reduced the magnitude of fixed manufacturing costs. This reduction, in turn, means differences between absorption costing and variable costing are much smaller than in Exhibit 9-2.

PART TWO: DENOMINATOR-LEVEL CAPACITY CONCEPTS AND FIXED-COST CAPACITY ANALYSIS

Determining the "right" level of capacity is one of the most strategic and most difficult decisions managers face. Having too much capacity to produce relative to capacity needed to meet demand means incurring some costs of unused capacity. Having too little capacity to produce means that demand from some customers may be unfilled. These customers may go to other sources of supply and never return. We now consider issues that arise with capacity costs.

Alternative Denominator-Level Capacity Concepts for Absorption Costing

6

Describe the various capacity concepts that can be used in absorption costing

. . . theoretical capacity, practical capacity, normal capacity utilization, and master-budget capacity utilization

Earlier chapters, especially Chapters 4, 5, and 8, have highlighted how normal costing and standard costing report costs in an ongoing timely manner throughout a fiscal year. The choice of the capacity level used to allocate budgeted fixed manufacturing costs to products can greatly affect the operating income reported under normal costing or standard costing and the product-cost information available to managers.

Consider Bushells Company, which produces 12-ounce bottles of iced tea at its Sydney bottling plant. The annual fixed manufacturing costs of the bottling plant are $5,400,000. Bushells currently uses absorption costing with standard costs for external reporting purposes, and it calculates its budgeted fixed manufacturing rate on a per-case basis (one case is twenty-four 12-ounce bottles of iced tea). We will now examine four different capacity levels used as the denominator to compute the budgeted fixed manufacturing cost rate: theoretical capacity, practical capacity, normal capacity utilization, and master-budget capacity utilization.

Theoretical Capacity and Practical Capacity

In business and accounting, *capacity* ordinarily means a "constraint," an "upper limit." **Theoretical capacity** is the level of capacity based on producing at full efficiency all the time. Bushells can produce 10,000 cases of iced tea per shift when the bottling lines are operating at maximum speed. If we assume 360 days per year, the theoretical annual capacity for three 8-hour shifts per day is:

$$10{,}000 \text{ cases per shift} \times 3 \text{ shifts per day} \times 360 \text{ days} = 10{,}800{,}000 \text{ cases}$$

Theoretical capacity is theoretical in the sense that it does not allow for any plant maintenance, interruptions because of bottle breakage on the filling lines, or any other factor. Theoretical capacity represents an ideal goal of capacity utilization. Theoretical capacity levels are unattainable in the real world, but they provide a benchmark for a company to aspire to.

Practical capacity is the level of capacity that reduces theoretical capacity by considering unavoidable operating interruptions, such as scheduled maintenance time, shutdowns for holidays, and so on. Assume that practical capacity is the practical production rate of 8,000 cases per shift (as opposed to 10,000 cases per shift under theoretical capacity) for three shifts per day for 300 days a year (as distinguished from 360 days a year under theoretical capacity). The practical annual capacity is:

$$8{,}000 \text{ cases per shift} \times 3 \text{ shifts per day} \times 300 \text{ days} = 7{,}200{,}000 \text{ cases}$$

Engineering and human resource factors are both important when estimating theoretical or practical capacity. Engineers at the Bushells plant can provide input on the technical capabilities of machines for filling bottles. Human-safety factors, such as increased injury risk when the line operates at faster speeds, are also necessary considerations in estimating practical capacity.

Normal Capacity Utilization and Master-Budget Capacity Utilization

Both theoretical capacity and practical capacity measure capacity levels in terms of what a plant can *supply*—available capacity. In contrast, normal capacity utilization and master-budget capacity utilization measure capacity levels in terms of *demand* for the output of the plant—the amount of the available capacity that the plant expects to use based on the demand for its products. In many cases, budgeted demand is well below production capacity available.

Normal capacity utilization is the level of capacity utilization that satisfies average customer demand over a period (say, two to three years) that includes seasonal, cyclical, and trend factors. **Master-budget capacity utilization** is the level of capacity utilization that managers expect for the current budget period, which is typically one year. These two capacity-utilization levels can differ—for example, when an industry, such as automobiles or semiconductors, has cyclical periods of high and low demand or when management believes that budgeted production for the coming period is not representative of long-run demand.

Consider Bushells' master budget for 2007, based on demand for and production of 4,000,000 cases of tea per year.[3] Despite using this master-budget capacity-utilization level of 4,000,000 cases for 2007, top management believes that over the next three years the normal (average) annual production level will be 5,000,000 cases. They view 2007's budgeted production level of 4,000,000 cases to be "abnormally" low. That's because a major competitor (Tea-Mania) has been sharply reducing its selling price and spending large amounts on advertising. Bushells expects that the competitor's lower price and advertising blitz will not be a long-run phenomenon and that, in 2008, Bushells' production and sales will be higher.

Effect on Budgeted Fixed Manufacturing Cost Rate

Choosing a denominator level arises only under AC. Both VC and throughput costing expense the lump-sum FMOH costs in the period incurred.

We now illustrate how each of these four denominator levels affects the budgeted fixed manufacturing cost rate. Bushells has budgeted (standard) fixed manufacturing costs (all of which are overhead costs) of $5,400,000 for 2007. This lump-sum amount is incurred to provide the capacity to bottle iced tea. This lump sum includes, among other costs, leasing costs for bottling equipment and the compensation of the plant manager. The

[3]Management plans to run one shift for 300 days in 2007 at a speed of 8,000 cases per shift. A second shift will run for 200 days (in the warmer months) at the same speed of 8,000 cases per shift. Thus, budgeted production for 2007 is (300 days × 8,000 cases/day) + (200 days × 8,000 cases/day) = 4,000,000 cases.

budgeted fixed manufacturing cost rates for 2007 for each of the four capacity-level concepts are:

	A	B	C	D
1		Budgeted Fixed	Budgeted	Budgeted Fixed
2	Denominator-Level	Manufacturing	Capacity Level	Manufacturing
3	Capacity Concept	Costs per Year	(in Cases)	Cost per Case
4	(1)	(2)	(3)	(4) = (2) ÷ (3)
5	Theoretical capacity	$5,400,000	10,800,000	$0.50
6	Practical capacity	$5,400,000	7,200,000	$0.75
7	Normal capacity utilization	$5,400,000	5,000,000	$1.08
8	Master-budget capacity utilization	$5,400,000	4,000,000	$1.35

The significant difference in cost rates (from $0.50 to $1.35) arises because of large differences in budgeted capacity levels under the different capacity concepts.

Budgeted (standard) variable manufacturing cost is $5.20 per case. The total budgeted (standard) manufacturing cost per case for alternative capacity-level concepts is:

11		Budgeted Variable	Budgeted Fixed	Budgeted Total
12	Denominator-Level	Manufacturing	Manufacturing	Manufacturing
13	Capacity Concept	Cost per Case	Cost per Case	Cost per Case
14	(1)	(2)	(3)	(4) = (2) + (3)
15	Theoretical capacity	$5.20	$0.50	$5.70
16	Practical capacity	$5.20	$0.75	$5.95
17	Normal capacity utilization	$5.20	$1.08	$6.28
18	Master-budget capacity utilization	$5.20	$1.35	$6.55

Because different denominator-level capacity concepts yield different budgeted fixed manufacturing costs per case, Bushells must decide which capacity level to use. There is no requirement that Bushells use the same capacity-level concept, say, for management planning and control, external reporting to shareholders, and income tax purposes.

Choosing a Capacity Level

7

Understand the major factors management considers in choosing a capacity level to compute the budgeted fixed manufacturing cost rate

. . . managers must consider the effect a capacity level has on product costing, capacity management, pricing decisions, and financial statements

As we just saw, at the start of each fiscal year, managers determine different denominator levels for the different capacity concepts and calculate different budgeted fixed manufacturing costs per unit. We now discuss the problems with and effects of different denominator-level choices for different purposes, including (a) product costing and capacity management, (b) pricing, (c) performance evaluation, (d) external reporting, and (e) regulatory requirements. We also describe the difficulties managers face in forecasting chosen denominator-level capacity concepts.

Product Costing and Capacity Management

Data from normal costing or standard costing are often used in pricing or product-mix decisions. As the Bushells example illustrates, use of theoretical capacity results in an unrealistically small fixed manufacturing cost per case because it is based on an idealistic and unattainable level of capacity. Theoretical capacity is rarely used to calculate budgeted fixed manufacturing cost per unit because it departs significantly from the real capacity available to a company.

Many companies favor practical capacity as the denominator to calculate budgeted fixed manufacturing cost per unit. Practical capacity in the Bushells example represents the maximum number of cases (7,200,000) that Bushells intends to produce per year for the $5,400,000 it will spend on capacity each year. If Bushells had consistently planned to produce fewer cases of iced tea, say 4,000,000 cases each year, it would have built a smaller plant and incurred lower costs.

Bushells budgets $0.75 in fixed manufacturing cost per case based on the $5,400,000 it costs to acquire the capacity to produce 7,200,000 cases. This level of plant capacity is an important strategic decision that managers make well before Bushells uses the capacity and even before Bushells knows how much of the capacity it will actually use. That is, budgeted fixed manufacturing cost of $0.75 per case measures the *cost per case of supplying the capacity*.

Demand for Bushells' iced tea in 2007 is expected to be 4,000,000 cases, which is 3,200,000 cases lower than the practical capacity of 7,200,000 cases. However, the cost of *supplying* the capacity needed to make 4,000,000 cases is still $0.75 per case. That's because it costs Bushells $5,400,000 per year to acquire the capacity to make 7,200,000 cases. The capacity and its cost are fixed *in the short run*; unlike variable costs, the capacity supplied does not automatically reduce to match the capacity needed in 2007. As a result, not all of the capacity supplied at $0.75 per case will be needed or used in 2007. Using practical capacity as the denominator level, managers can subdivide the cost of resources supplied into used and unused components. At the supply cost of $0.75 per case, manufacturing resources that Bushells will use equal $3,000,000 ($0.75 per case × 4,000,000 cases). Manufacturing resources that Bushells will not use are $2,400,000 [$0.75 per case × (7,200,000 - 4,000,000) cases].

Using practical capacity as the denominator level fixes the cost of capacity at the cost of supplying the capacity, regardless of the demand for the capacity. Highlighting the cost of capacity acquired but not used directs managers' attention to taking actions to manage unused capacity, perhaps by designing new products to fill unused capacity, leasing out unused capacity to others, or by eliminating unused capacity. In contrast, using either of the capacity levels based on the demand for Bushells' iced tea—master-budget capacity utilization or normal capacity utilization—hides the amount of unused capacity. If Bushells had used master-budget capacity utilization as the capacity level, it would have calculated budgeted fixed manufacturing cost per case as $1.35 ($5,400,000 ÷ 4,000,000 cases). This calculation does not use data about practical capacity, so it does not separately identify the cost of unused capacity. Note, however, that the cost of $1.35 per case includes a charge for unused capacity: the $0.75 fixed manufacturing resource that would be used to produce each case at practical capacity plus the cost of unused capacity allocated to each case, $0.60 per case ($2,400,000 ÷ 4,000,000 cases).

From the perspective of long-run product costing, which cost of capacity should Bushells use for pricing purposes or for benchmarking its product cost structure against competitors: $0.75 per case based on practical capacity? or $1.35 per case based on master-budget capacity utilization? Probably, the $0.75 per case based on practical capacity. Why? Because $0.75 per case represents budgeted cost per case of only the capacity used to produce the product, and it explicitly excludes the cost of any unused capacity. Bushells' customers will be willing to pay a price that covers the cost of the capacity actually used but will not want to pay for capacity that is not used to produce the product and provides no other benefits to them. Customers expect Bushells to manage its unused capacity or to bear the cost of unused capacity, not pass it along to them. Moreover, if Bushells' competitors manage unused capacity more effectively, the cost of capacity in the competitors' cost structures (which guides competitors' pricing decisions) is likely to approach $0.75 per case. In the next section we show how the use of normal capacity utilization or master-budget capacity utilization can result in setting selling prices that are not competitive.

Pricing Decisions and the Downward Demand Spiral

8

Describe how attempts to recover fixed costs of capacity may lead to price increases and lower demand

. . . this situation is the downward demand spiral, which explains why customers are unwilling to pay for a company's unused capacity

The **downward demand spiral** for a company is the continuing reduction in the demand for its products that occurs when prices of competitors' products are not met and (as demand drops further) higher and higher unit costs result in more and more reluctance to meet competitors' prices.

The easiest way to understand the downward demand spiral is via an example. Assume Bushells uses master-budget capacity utilization of 4,000,000 cases for product costing in 2007. The resulting manufacturing cost is $6.55 per case ($5.20 variable manufacturing cost per case + $1.35 fixed manufacturing cost per case). Assume a competitor (Lipton Iced Tea) in December 2006 offers to supply a major customer of Bushells (a customer who was expected to purchase 1,000,000 cases in 2007) iced tea at $6.25 per case. The Bushells manager, not wanting to show a loss on the account and wanting to recoup all costs in the long run, declines to match the competitor's price and the account is lost. The lost account means budgeted fixed manufacturing costs of $5,400,000 will be spread over the remaining master-budget volume of 3,000,000 cases at a rate of $1.80 per case ($5,400,000 ÷ 3,000,000 cases).

Suppose yet another Bushells customer—who also accounts for 1,000,000 cases of budgeted volume—receives a bid from a competitor at a price of $6.60 per case. The Bushells manager compares this bid with his revised unit cost of $7.00 ($5.20 + $1.80), declines to match the competition, and the account is lost. Planned output would shrink further to 2,000,000 units. Budgeted fixed manufacturing cost per case for the remaining 2,000,000 cases now would be $2.70 ($5,400,000 ÷ 2,000,000 cases). The following table shows the effect of spreading fixed manufacturing costs over a shrinking amount of master-budget capacity utilization:

Master-Budget Capacity Utilization Denominator Level (Cases) (1)	Budgeted Variable Manufacturing Cost per Case (2)	Budgeted Fixed Manufacturing Cost per Case [$5,400,000 ÷ (1)] (3)	Budgeted Total Manufacturing Cost per Case (4) = (2) + (3)
4,000,000	$5.20	$1.35	$ 6.55
3,000,000	5.20	1.80	7.00
2,000,000	5.20	2.70	7.90
1,000,000	5.20	5.40	10.60

The use of practical capacity as the denominator to calculate budgeted fixed manufacturing cost per case would avoid the recalculation of unit costs when expected demand levels change. That's because the fixed cost rate would be calculated based on *capacity available* rather than *capacity used to meet demand.* Managers who use reported unit costs in a mechanical way to set prices are less likely to promote a downward demand spiral when they use practical capacity than when they use normal capacity utilization or master-budget capacity utilization.

Using practical capacity as the denominator level also gives the manager a more-accurate idea of the resources needed and used to produce a case by excluding the cost of unused capacity. As discussed earlier, the cost of manufacturing resources supplied to produce a case is $5.95 ($5.20 variable manufacturing cost per case plus $0.75 fixed manufacturing cost per case). This cost is lower than the prices offered by Bushells' competitors and would have correctly led the manager to match the prices and retain the accounts (assuming for purposes of this discussion that Bushells has no other costs). If, however, the prices offered by competitors were lower than $5.95 per case, the Bushells manager would not recover the cost of resources used to supply cases. This would signal to the manager that Bushells was noncompetitive even if it had no unused capacity. The only way then for Bushells to be profitable and retain customers in the long run would be to reduce its manufacturing cost per case.

Performance Evaluation

Consider how the choice between normal capacity utilization, master-budget capacity utilization, and practical capacity affects how a marketing manager is evaluated. Normal capacity utilization is often used as a basis for long-run plans. Normal capacity utilization depends on the time span selected and the forecasts made for each year. *However, normal capacity utilization is an average that provides no meaningful feedback to the marketing manager for a particular year.* Using normal capacity utilization as a reference for judging current performance of a marketing manager is an example of misusing a long-run measure for a short-run purpose. Master-budget capacity utilization, rather than normal capacity utilization or practical capacity, is what should be used for evaluating a marketing manager's performance in the current year. That's because the master budget is the principal short-run planning and control tool. Managers feel more obligated to reach the levels specified in the master budget, which should have been carefully set in relation to the maximum opportunities for sales in the current year.

When large differences exist between practical capacity and master-budget capacity utilization, several companies (such as Texas Instruments, Polysar, and Sandoz) classify the difference as *planned unused capacity*. One reason for this approach is performance evaluation. Consider our Bushells iced-tea example. The managers in charge of capacity planning usually do not make pricing decisions. Top management decided to build an iced-tea plant with 7,200,000 cases of practical capacity, focusing on demand over the next five years. But Bushells' marketing managers, who are mid-level managers, make the pricing decisions. These marketing managers believe they should be held accountable only for the manufacturing overhead costs related to their potential customer base in 2007. The master-budget capacity utilization suggests a customer base in 2007 of 4,000,000 cases ($\frac{5}{9}$ of the 7,200,000 practical capacity). Using responsibility accounting

Similar issues arise for manufacturing managers who are evaluated on the basis of master-budget capacity utilization and are held accountable for manufacturing overhead costs.

principles (see Chapter 6, pp. 196–199), only $\frac{5}{9}$ of the budgeted total fixed manufacturing costs ($\$5{,}400{,}000 \times \frac{5}{9} = \$3{,}000{,}000$) would be attributed to the fixed capacity costs of meeting 2007 demand. The remaining $\frac{4}{9}$ of the numerator ($\$5{,}400{,}000 \times \frac{4}{9} = \$2{,}400{,}000$) would be separately shown as the capacity cost of meeting increases in long-run demand expected to occur beyond 2007.[4]

9

Explain how the capacity level chosen to calculate the budgeted fixed overhead cost rate affects the production-volume variance

. . . if the capacity level is greater (less) than actual production, there is an unfavorable (favorable) production-volume variance

External Reporting

The magnitude of the favorable/unfavorable production-volume variance under absorption costing will be affected by the choice of the denominator level used to calculate budgeted fixed manufacturing cost per case. Assume the following actual operating information for Bushells in 2007:

20	Beginning inventory	0	
21	Production	4,400,000	cases
22	Sales	4,000,000	cases
23	Ending inventory	400,000	cases
24	Selling price	$8	per case
25	Variable manufacturing cost	$5.20	per case
26	Fixed manufacturing costs	$5,400,000	
27	Operating (nonmanufacturing) costs	$2,810,000	

There is no beginning inventory for 2007 and no price, spending, or efficiency variances in manufacturing costs.

Recall from Chapter 8 the equation used to calculate the production-volume variance:

$$\text{Production-volume variance} = \begin{pmatrix}\text{Budgeted}\\ \text{fixed}\\ \text{manufacturing}\\ \text{overhead}\end{pmatrix} - \begin{pmatrix}\text{Fixed manufacturing overhead allocated using}\\ \text{budgeted cost per output unit}\\ \text{allowed for actual output produced}\end{pmatrix}$$

The higher the denominator level, (1) the lower the budgeted FMOH cost rate, (2) the lower the amount of FMOH allocated to output produced (because the budgeted FMOH cost rate is lower), and (3) the higher the unfavorable PVV (because the higher the denominator level, the more likely actual output will fall short of that level).

The four different capacity-level concepts result in four different budgeted fixed manufacturing overhead cost rates per unit. The different rates will result in different amounts of fixed manufacturing overhead costs allocated to the 4,400,000 cases actually produced and different amounts of production-volume variance. Using the budgeted fixed manufacturing costs of $5,400,000 (equal to actual fixed manufacturing costs) and the rates calculated on page 311 for different denominator levels, the production-volume variance computations are as follows:

Production-volume variance (theoretical capacity) = \$5,400,000 − (4,400,000 cases × \$0.50 per case)
= \$5,400,000 − \$2,200,000
= \$3,200,000 U

Production-volume variance (practical capacity) = \$5,400,000 − (4,400,000 cases × \$0.75 per case)
= \$5,400,000 − \$3,300,000
= \$2,100,000 U

Production-volume variance (normal capacity utilization) = \$5,400,000 − (4,400,000 cases × \$1.08 per case)
= \$5,400,000 − \$4,752,000
= \$648,000 U

Production-volume variance (master-budget capacity utilization) = \$5,400,000 − (4,400,000 cases × \$1.35 per case)
= \$5,400,000 − \$5, 940,000
= \$540,000 F

[4]For further discussion, see T. Klammer, *Capacity Measurement and Improvement* (Chicago: Irwin, 1996). This research was facilitated by CAM-I, an organization promoting innovative cost management practices. CAM-I's research on capacity costs explores ways in which companies can identify types of capacity costs that can be reduced (or eliminated) without affecting the required output to meet customer demand. An example is improving processes to successfully eliminate the costs of capacity held in anticipation of handling difficulties due to imperfect coordination with suppliers and customers.

How Bushells disposes of its production-volume variance at the end of the fiscal year will determine the effect this variance will have on the company's operating income. We now discuss the three alternative approaches Bushells can use to dispose of the production-volume variance. These approaches were first discussed in Chapter 4 (pp. 119–122).

1. **Adjusted allocation-rate approach.** This approach restates all amounts in the general and subsidiary ledgers by using actual rather than budgeted cost rates. Given that actual fixed manufacturing costs are $5,400,000 and actual production is 4,400,000 cases, the recalculated fixed manufacturing cost is $1.23 per case ($5,400,000 ÷ 4,400,000 cases, rounded up to the nearest cent). The adjusted allocation-rate approach results in the choice of the capacity level used to calculate the budgeted fixed manufacturing cost per case having no effect on year-end financial statements. In effect, actual costing is adopted at the end of the fiscal year.
2. **Proration approach.** The underallocated or overallocated overhead is spread among ending balances in Work-in-Process Control, Finished Goods Control, and Cost of Goods Sold. The proration restates the ending balances in these accounts to what they would have been if actual cost rates had been used rather than budgeted cost rates. The proration approach also results in the choice of the capacity level used to calculate the budgeted fixed manufacturing cost per case having no effect on year-end financial statements.
3. **Write-off variances to cost of goods sold approach.** Exhibit 9-7 shows how use of this approach affects Bushells' operating income for 2007. Recall that Bushells had no beginning inventory, production of 4,400,000 cases, and sales of 4,000,000 cases. Therefore, the ending inventory on December 31, 2007, is 400,000 cases. Using master-budget capacity utilization as the denominator level results in assigning the highest amount of fixed manufacturing cost per case to the 400,000 cases in ending inventory (see the line item "deduct ending inventory" in Exhibit 9-7). Accordingly, operating income is highest using master-budget capacity utilization. The differences in operating

EXHIBIT 9-7 **Income-Statement Effects of Using Alternative Capacity-Level Concepts: Bushells Company for 2007**

	A	B	C	D	E	F	G	H	I
1		Theoretical Capacity		Practical Capacity		Normal Capacity Utilization		Master-Budget Capacity Utilization	
2	Denominator level in cases	10,800,000		7,200,000		5,000,000		4,000,000	
3	Revenues[a]	$32,000,000		$32,000,000		$32,000,000		$32,000,000	
4	Cost of goods sold								
5	Beginning inventory	0		0		0		0	
6	Variable manufacturing costs[b]	22,880,000		22,880,000		22,880,000		22,880,000	
7	Fixed manufacturing costs[c]	2,200,000		3,300,000		4,752,000		5,940,000	
8	Cost of goods available for sale	25,080,000		26,180,000		27,632,000		28,820,000	
9	Deduct ending inventory[d]	(2,280,000)		(2,380,000)		(2,512,000)		(2,620,000)	
10	Total COGS (at standard costs)	22,800,000		23,800,000		25,120,000		26,200,000	
11	Adjustment for production-volume variance	3,200,000	U	2,100,000	U	648,000	U	(540,000)	F
12	Total cost of goods sold	26,000,000		25,900,000		25,768,000		25,660,000	
13	Gross margin	6,000,000		6,100,000		6,232,000		6,340,000	
14	Operating costs	2,810,000		2,810,000		2,810,000		2,810,000	
15	Operating income	$ 3,190,000		$ 3,290,000		$ 3,422,000		$ 3,530,000	
16									
17	[a]$8.00 × 4,000,000 units = $32,000,000			[d]Ending inventory costs:					
18	[b]$5.20 × 4,400,000 units = $22,880,000			($5.20 + $0.50) × 400,000 units = $2,280,000					
19	[c]Fixed manufacturing overhead costs:			($5.20 + $0.75) × 400,000 units = $2,380,000					
20	$0.50 × 4,400,000 units = $2,200,000			($5.20 + $1.08) × 400,000 units = $2,512,000					
21	$0.75 × 4,400,000 units = $3,300,000			($5.20 + $1.35) × 400,000 units = $2,620,000					
22	$1.08 × 4,400,000 units = $4,752,000								
23	$1.35 × 4,400,000 units = $5,940,000								

income for the four denominator-level concepts in Exhibit 9-7 are due to different amounts of fixed manufacturing overhead being inventoried at the end of 2007:

	Fixed Manufacturing Overhead in Dec. 31, 2007, Inventory
Theoretical capacity	400,000 cases × $0.50 per case = $200,000
Practical capacity	400,000 cases × 0.75 per case = 300,000
Normal capacity utilization	400,000 cases × 1.08 per case = 432,000
Master-budget capacity utilization	400,000 cases × 1.35 per case = 540,000

In Exhibit 9-7, for example, the $108,000 difference ($3,530,000 – $3,422,000) in operating income between master-budget capacity utilization and normal capacity utilization is due to the difference in fixed manufacturing overhead inventoried ($540,000 – $432,000).

Study Tip: To check your understanding of the denominator-level capacity concepts for absorption costing, see true–false statement 8, multiple-choice questions 8 and 9, and Review Exercise 2 (*Student Guide*, beginning p. 111). Fully explained answers begin on p. 116.

What is the common reason and explanation for the increasing operating-income numbers in Exhibit 9-4 (p. 304) and Exhibit 9-7? It is the amount of fixed manufacturing costs incurred in 2007 that is included in ending inventory at the end of the year. As this amount increases, so does operating income. The amount of fixed manufacturing costs inventoried depends on two factors: the number of units in ending inventory and the rate at which fixed manufacturing costs are allocated to each unit. Exhibit 9-4 shows the effect on operating income of increasing the number of units in ending inventory (by increasing production). Exhibit 9-7 shows the effect on operating income of increasing the fixed manufacturing cost allocated per unit (by decreasing the denominator level used to calculate the rate).

Chapter 8 (pp. 269–271) discusses the various issues managers and management accountants must consider when deciding whether to prorate the production-volume variance among inventories and cost of goods sold or to simply write off the variance to cost of goods sold. The basic objective is to write off the portion of the production-volume variance that represents the cost of capacity not used to support the production of output during the period. Determining this amount is almost always a matter of judgment.

Regulatory Requirements

For tax reporting purposes in the United States, the Internal Revenue Service (IRS) requires companies to use practical capacity to calculate budgeted fixed manufacturing cost per unit. At year-end, proration of any variances between inventories and cost of goods sold is required (unless the variance is immaterial in amount) to calculate the company's operating income.[5]

Difficulties in Forecasting Chosen Denominator-Level Concept

Note: Practical capacity need not be constant over time. For example, improvements in plant layout and increases in worker efficiency both can result in significant increases in practical capacity for the same plant over time.

Practical capacity measures the available supply of capacity. Managers can usually use engineering studies and human-resource considerations (such as worker safety) to obtain a reliable estimate of this denominator level for the budget period. However, it is more difficult to estimate normal capacity utilization reliably. For example, many U.S. steel companies in the 1980s believed they were in the downturn of a demand cycle that would have an upturn within two or three years. After all, steel had been a cyclical business in which upturns followed downturns, making the notion of normal capacity utilization appear reasonable. Unfortunately, the steel cycle in the 1980s did not turn up; some companies and numerous plants closed. Some marketing managers are prone to overestimate their ability to regain lost sales and market share. Their estimate of "normal" demand for their product may be based on an overly optimistic outlook. Master-budget capacity utilization typically focuses only on the expected capacity utilization for the next year.

[5]U.S. tax reporting requires the use of either the adjusted allocation-rate approach or the proration approach. Section 1.471-11 of the U.S. Internal Revenue Code states: "The proper use of the standard cost method requires that a taxpayer must reallocate to the goods in ending inventory a pro rata portion of any net negative or net positive overhead variances."

Therefore, master-budget capacity utilization can be more reliably estimated than normal capacity utilization.

Capacity Costs and Denominator-Level Issues

We now present more factors that affect the planning and control of capacity costs.

1. Costing systems, such as normal costing or standard costing, do not recognize uncertainty the way managers recognize it. Managers use a *single* amount rather than a range of possible amounts as the denominator level when calculating budgeted fixed manufacturing cost per unit in absorption costing. Yet, managers face uncertainty about demand: they even face uncertainty about their capability to supply. Bushells' plant has an estimated practical capacity of 7,200,000 cases. The estimated master-budget capacity utilization for 2007 is 4,000,000 cases. These estimates are uncertain. Managers recognize uncertainty in their capacity-planning decisions. Bushells built its current plant with a 7,200,000-case practical capacity in part to provide the capability to meet possible demand surges. Even if these demand surges do not occur in a given period, it would be wrong to conclude all capacity not used in a given period is wasted resources. *The gains from meeting sudden demand surges may well require having unused capacity in some periods.*
2. The fixed manufacturing cost rate is based on a numerator—budgeted fixed manufacturing costs—and a denominator—some measure of capacity or capacity utilization. Our discussion so far has emphasized issues concerning the choice of the denominator. Challenging issues also arise in measuring the numerator. For example, deregulation of the U.S. electric utility industry has resulted in many electric utilities becoming unprofitable. This situation has led to write-downs in the values of the utilities' plants and equipment. The write-downs reduce the numerator because there is less depreciation expense included in the calculation of fixed capacity cost per kilowatt-hour of electricity produced. The difficulty managers face in this situation is that the amount of write-downs is not clear-cut but rather a matter of judgment.
3. Capacity costs arise in nonmanufacturing parts of the value chain, as well as with the manufacturing function emphasized in this chapter. Bushells may acquire a fleet of vehicles capable of distributing the practical capacity of its iced-tea plant. When actual production is below practical capacity, there will be unused-capacity cost issues with the distribution function, as well as with the manufacturing function.

   As you saw in Chapter 8, capacity cost issues are prominent in many service-sector companies, such as airlines, hospitals, and railroads, even though these companies carry no inventory and so have no inventory costing issues. For example, in calculating the fixed overhead cost per patient-day in its obstetrics and gynecology department, a hospital must decide what denominator level to use: practical capacity, normal capacity utilization, or master-budget capacity utilization. Its decision may have implications for capacity management, as well as pricing and performance evaluation.
4. For simplicity and to focus on the main ideas about choosing a denominator to calculate a budgeted fixed manufacturing cost rate, our Bushells example assumed that all fixed manufacturing costs had a single cost driver: cases of iced tea produced. As you saw in Chapter 5, activity-based costing systems have multiple overhead cost pools at the output-unit, batch, product-sustaining, and facility-sustaining levels, each with its own cost driver. In calculating activity cost rates (for fixed costs of setups and material handling, say), management must choose a capacity level for the quantity of the cost driver (setup-hours or loads moved). Should it use practical capacity, normal capacity utilization, or master-budget capacity utilization? For all the reasons described in this chapter (such as pricing and capacity management), most proponents of activity-based costing argue that practical capacity should be used as the denominator level to calculate activity cost rates.

PROBLEM FOR SELF-STUDY

Suppose Bushells Company is computing its operating income for 2009. That year's results are identical to the results for 2007, shown in Exhibit 9-7, except that master-budget capacity utilization for 2009 is 6,000,000 cases instead of 4,000,000 cases. Production in 2009 is 4,400,000 cases. There is no beginning inventory on January 1, 2009, and there are no variances other than the production-volume variance. Bushells writes off this variance to cost of goods sold. Sales in 2009 are 4,000,000 cases.

Required

How would the results for Bushells Company in Exhibit 9-7 differ if the year were 2009 rather than 2007? Show your computations.

SOLUTION

The only change in Exhibit 9-7 results would be for the master-budget capacity utilization level. The budgeted fixed manufacturing cost rate for 2009 is:

$$\frac{\$5,400,000}{6,000,000 \text{ cases}} = \$0.90 \text{ per case}$$

The manufacturing cost per case is \$6.10 (\$5.20 + \$0.90). So, the production-volume variance for 2009 is:

$$(6,000,000 \text{ cases} - 4,400,000 \text{ cases}) \times \$0.90 \text{ per case} = \$1,440,000, \text{ or } \$1,440,000 \text{ U}$$

The income statement for 2009 shows:

Revenues: \$8.00 per case × 4,000,000 cases	\$32,000,000
Cost of goods sold	
Beginning inventory	0
Variable manufacturing costs: \$5.20 per case × 4,400,000 cases	22,880,000
Fixed manufacturing costs: \$0.90 per case × 4,400,000 cases	3,960,000
Cost of goods available for sale	26,840,000
Deduct ending inventory: \$6.10 per case × 400,000 cases	(2,440,000)
Cost of goods sold (at standard costs)	24,400,000
Adjustment for variances	1,440,000 U
Cost of goods sold	25,840,000
Gross margin	6,160,000
Operating costs	2,810,000
Operating income	\$ 3,350,000

The higher denominator level used to calculate budgeted fixed manufacturing cost per case in the 2009 master budget means that fewer fixed manufacturing costs are inventoried in 2009 (\$0.90 per case × 400,000 cases = \$360,000) than in 2007 (\$1.35 per case × 400,000 cases = \$540,000), given identical sales and production levels and assuming the production-volume variance is written off to cost of goods sold. This difference of \$180,000 (\$540,000 − \$360,000) results in operating income being lower by \$180,000 in 2009 relative to 2007 (\$3,530,000 − \$3,350,000).

DECISION POINTS

The following question-and-answer format summarizes the chapter's learning objectives. Each decision presents a key question related to a learning objective. The guidelines are the answer to that question.

Decision	Guidelines
1. How does variable costing differ from absorption costing?	Variable costing and absorption costing differ in only one respect: how to account for fixed manufacturing costs. Under variable costing, fixed manufacturing costs are excluded from inventoriable costs and are a cost of the period in which they are incurred. Under absorption costing, fixed manufacturing costs are inventoriable and become a part of cost of goods sold in the period when sales occur.
2. What formats do companies use when preparing income statements under variable costing and absorption costing?	The variable-costing income statement is based on the contribution-margin format. The absorption-costing income statement is based on the gross-margin format.

3. How do the level of sales and the level of production affect operating income under variable costing and absorption costing?	Under variable costing, operating income is driven by the unit level of sales. Under absorption costing, operating income is driven by the unit level of production, the unit level of sales, and the denominator level.
4. Why might managers build up finished goods inventory if they use absorption costing?	When absorption costing is used, managers can increase current operating income by producing more units for inventory. Producing for inventory absorbs more fixed manufacturing costs into inventory and reduces costs expensed in the period. Critics of absorption costing label this manipulation of income as the major negative consequence of treating fixed manufacturing costs as inventoriable costs.
5. How does throughput costing differ from variable costing and absorption costing?	Throughput costing treats all costs except direct materials as costs of the period in which they are incurred. Throughput costing results in a lower amount of manufacturing costs being inventoried than either variable or absorption costing.
6. What are the various capacity levels a company can use to compute the budgeted fixed manufacturing cost rate?	Capacity levels can be measured in terms of capacity supplied—theoretical capacity or practical capacity. Capacity can also be measured in terms of output demanded—normal capacity utilization or master-budget capacity utilization.
7. What are the major factors managers consider in choosing the capacity level to compute the budgeted fixed manufacturing cost rate?	The major factors managers consider in choosing the capacity level to compute the budgeted fixed manufacturing cost rate are (a) effect on product costing and capacity management, (b) effect on pricing decisions, (c) effect on performance evaluation, (d) effect on financial statements, (e) regulatory requirements, and (f) difficulties in forecasting chosen capacity-level concepts.
8. Should a company with high fixed costs and unused capacity raise selling prices to try to fully recoup its costs?	No, companies with high fixed costs and unused capacity may encounter ongoing and increasingly greater reductions in demand if they continue to raise selling prices to try to fully recoup variable and fixed costs from a declining sales base. This phenomenon is called the downward demand spiral.
9. How does the capacity level chosen to compute the budgeted fixed overhead cost rate affect the production-volume variance?	When the chosen capacity level exceeds the actual production level, there will be an unfavorable production-volume variance; when the chosen capacity level is less than the actual production level, there will be a favorable production-volume variance.

APPENDIX: BREAKEVEN POINTS IN VARIABLE COSTING AND ABSORPTION COSTING

Chapter 3 introduced cost-volume-profit analysis. If variable costing is used, the breakeven point (that's where operating income is \$0) is computed in the usual manner. There is only one breakeven point in this case, and it depends on (1) fixed (manufacturing and operating) costs and (2) contribution margin per unit.

The formula for computing breakeven point under variable costing is a special case of the more-general target operating income formula from Chapter 3 (p. 66):

$$\text{Let } Q = \text{Number of units sold to earn the target operating income}$$

$$\text{Then } Q = \frac{\text{Total fixed costs} + \text{Target operating income}}{\text{Contribution margin per unit}}$$

Breakeven occurs when the target operating income is \$0. In our Stassen illustration for 2007 (see Exhibit 9-2, p. 299):

$$Q = \frac{(\$12{,}000 + \$10{,}800) + \$0}{\$100 - (\$20 + \$19)} = \frac{\$22{,}800}{\$61}$$

$$= 374 \text{ units (rounded up to the nearest unit)}$$

Proof of breakeven point:

Revenues, \$100 × 374 units	\$37,400
Variable costs, \$39 × 374 units	14,586
Contribution margin, \$61 × 374 units	22,814
Fixed costs	22,800
Operating income	\$ 14

Operating income is not \$0 because the breakeven number of units is rounded up to 374 from 373.77.

If absorption costing is used, the required number of units to be sold to earn a specific target operating income is not unique because of the number of variables involved. The following formula shows the factors that will affect the target operating income under absorption costing:

Remember, "Total fixed costs" in this formula includes *all* fixed costs (not just FMOH costs).

$$Q = \frac{\text{Total fixed costs} + \text{Target operating income} + \left[\text{Fixed manufacturing cost rate} \times \left(\text{Breakeven sales in units} - \text{Units produced}\right)\right]}{\text{Contribution margin per unit}}$$

This formula shows that under AC, there's a unique breakeven point for each different quantity of units produced. Also, there's an inverse relationship between the quantity of units produced and the quantity of units needed to be sold to break even. The more units produced, the more FMOH costs allocated to those units, and the fewer the units needed to be sold to break even.

In this formula, the numerator is the sum of three terms (from the perspective of the two "+" signs), compared with two terms in the numerator of the variable-costing formula stated earlier. The additional term in the numerator under absorption costing is:

$$\left[\text{Fixed manufacturing cost rate} \times \left(\text{Breakeven sales in units} - \text{Units produced}\right)\right]$$

This term reduces the fixed costs that need to be recovered when units produced exceed the breakeven sales quantity. When production exceeds the breakeven sales quantity, some of the fixed manufacturing costs that are expensed under variable costing are not expensed under absorption costing; they are instead included in finished goods inventory.

For Stassen Company in 2007, one breakeven point, Q, under absorption costing for production of 500 units is:

$$Q = \frac{(\$12{,}000 + \$10{,}800) + \$0 + [\$15(Q - 500)]}{\$100 - (\$20 + \$19)}$$

$$= \frac{\$22{,}800 + \$15Q - \$7{,}500}{\$61}$$

$$\$61Q = \$15{,}300 + \$15Q$$

$$\$46Q = \$15{,}300$$

$$Q = 333 \text{ (rounded up to the nearest unit)}$$

Proof of breakeven point:

Revenues, $100 × 333 units		$33,300
Cost of goods sold		
Cost of goods sold at standard cost, $35 × 333 units	$11,655	
Production-volume variance, $15 × (800 – 500) units	4,500 U	16,155
Gross margin		17,145
Operating costs		
Variable operating costs, $19 × 333 units	6,327	
Fixed operating costs	10,800	17,127
Operating income		$ 18

Operating income is not $0 because the breakeven number of units is rounded up to 333 from 332.61.

The breakeven point under absorption costing depends on (1) fixed manufacturing costs, (2) fixed operating costs, (3) contribution margin per unit, (4) unit level of production, and (5) the capacity level chosen as the denominator to set the fixed manufacturing cost rate. For Stassen in 2007, a combination of 333 units sold, fixed manufacturing costs of $12,000, fixed operating costs of $10,800, contribution margin per unit of $61, 500 units produced, and an 800-unit denominator level would result in an operating income of $0. *Note, however, that there are many combinations of these five factors that would give an operating income of $0.* For example, a combination of 284 units sold, 650 units produced, fixed manufacturing costs of $12,000, fixed operating costs of $10,800, and an 800-unit denominator level also results in an operating income of $0 under absorption costing.

Proof of breakeven point:

Revenues, $100 × 284 units		$28,400
Cost of goods sold		
Cost of goods sold at standard cost, $35 × 284 units	$ 9,940	
Production-volume variance, $15 × (800 – 650) units	2,250 U	12,190
Gross margin		16,210
Operating costs		
Variable operating costs, $19 × 284 units	5,396	
Fixed operating costs	10,800	16,196
Operating income		$ 14

Operating income is not $0 because the breakeven number of units is rounded up to 284 from 283.70.

Suppose actual production in 2007 were equal to the denominator level, 800 units, and there were no units sold and no fixed operating costs. All the units produced would be placed in inventory, so all the fixed manufacturing costs would be included in inventory. There would be no production-volume variance. Under these conditions, the company could break even with no sales whatsoever! In contrast, under variable costing, the operating loss would be equal to the fixed manufacturing costs of $12,000.

TERMS TO LEARN

This chapter and the Glossary at the end of the book contain definitions of:

absorption costing (p. 296)
direct costing (p. 298)
downward demand spiral (p. 312)
master-budget capacity utilization (p. 310)
normal capacity utilization (p. 310)
practical capacity (p. 310)
super-variable costing (p. 305)
theoretical capacity (p. 309)
throughput costing (p. 305)
variable costing (p. 296)

PH Grade Assist

Prentice Hall Grade Assist (PHGA)
Your professor may ask you to complete selected exercises and problems in Prentice Hall Grade Assist (PHGA). PHGA is an online tool that can help you master the chapter's topics. It provides you with multiple variations of exercises and problems designated by the PHGA icon. You can rework these exercises and problems—each time with new data—as many times as you need. You also receive immediate feedback and grading.

ASSIGNMENT MATERIAL

Questions

9-1 Differences in operating income between variable costing and absorption costing are due solely to accounting for fixed costs. Do you agree? Explain.

9-2 Why is the term *direct costing* a misnomer?

9-3 Do companies in either the service sector or the merchandising sector make choices about absorption costing versus variable costing?

9-4 Explain the main conceptual issue under variable costing and absorption costing regarding the timing for the release of fixed manufacturing overhead as expense.

9-5 "Companies that make no variable-cost/fixed-cost distinctions must use absorption costing, and those that do make variable-cost/fixed-cost distinctions must use variable costing." Do you agree? Explain.

9-6 The main trouble with variable costing is that it ignores the increasing importance of fixed costs in manufacturing companies. Do you agree? Why?

9-7 Give an example of how, under absorption costing, operating income could fall even though the unit sales level rises.

9-8 What are the factors that affect the breakeven point under (a) variable costing and (b) absorption costing?

9-9 Critics of absorption costing have increasingly emphasized its potential for leading to undesirable incentives for managers. Give an example.

9-10 What are two ways of reducing the negative aspects associated with using absorption costing to evaluate the performance of a plant manager?

9-11 What denominator-level capacity concepts emphasize the output a plant can supply? What denominator-level capacity concepts emphasize the output customers demand for products produced by a plant?

9-12 Describe the downward demand spiral and its implications for pricing decisions.

9-13 Will the financial statements of a company always differ when different choices at the start of the accounting period are made regarding the denominator-level capacity concept?

9-14 What is the IRS's requirement for tax reporting regarding the choice of a denominator-level capacity concept?

9-15 "The difference between practical capacity and master-budget capacity utilization is the best measure of management's ability to balance the costs of having too much capacity and having too little capacity." Do you agree? Explain.

Exercises

Excel Lab www.prenhall.com/horngren/cost12e

PH Grade Assist

9-16 Variable and absorption costing, explaining operating-income differences. Nascar Motors assembles and sells motor vehicles and uses standard costing. Actual data relating to April and May 2006 are:

	A	B	C
1		**April**	**May**
2	Unit data		
3	Beginning inventory	0	150
4	Production	500	400
5	Sales	350	520
6	Variable costs		
7	Manufacturing cost per unit produced	$ 10,000	$ 10,000
8	Operating cost per unit sold	3,000	3,000
9	Fixed costs		
10	Manufacturing costs	$2,000,000	$2,000,000
11	Operating costs	600,000	600,000

The selling price per vehicle is $24,000. The budgeted level of production used to calculate the budgeted fixed manufacturing cost per unit is 500 units. There are no price, efficiency, or spending variances. Any production-volume variance is written off to cost of goods sold in the month in which it occurs.

If you want to use Excel to solve this exercise, go to the Excel Lab at **www.prenhall.com/horngren/cost12e** and download the template for Exercise 9-16.

Required

1. Prepare April and May 2006 income statements for Nascar Motors under (a) variable costing and (b) absorption costing.
2. Prepare a numerical reconciliation and explanation of the difference between operating income for each month under variable costing and absorption costing.

Excel Lab www.prenhall.com/horngren/cost12e

9-17 Throughput costing (continuation of 9-16). The variable manufacturing costs per unit of Nascar Motors are:

	A	B	D
1		**April**	**May**
7	Direct material cost per unit	$6,700	$6,700
8	Direct manufacturing labor cost per unit	1,500	1,500
9	Manufacturing overhead cost per unit	1,800	1,800

If you want to use Excel to solve this exercise, go to the Excel Lab at **www.prenhall.com/horngren/cost12e** and download the template for Exercise 9-16.

Required

1. Prepare income statements for Nascar Motors in April and May of 2006 under throughput costing.
2. Contrast the results in requirement 1 with those in requirement 1 of Exercise 9-16.
3. Give one motivation for Nascar Motors to adopt throughput costing.

9-18 Variable and absorption costing, explaining operating-income differences. BigScreen Corporation manufactures and sells 50-inch television sets and uses standard costing. Actual data relating to January, February, and March of 2007 are:

	January	**February**	**March**
Unit data			
Beginning inventory	0	300	300
Production	1,000	800	1,250
Sales	700	800	1,500
Variable costs			
Manufacturing cost per unit produced	$900	$900	$900
Operating cost per unit sold	$600	$600	$600
Fixed costs			
Manufacturing costs	$400,000	$400,000	$400,000
Operating costs	$140,000	$140,000	$140,000

The selling price per unit is $2,500. The budgeted level of production used to calculate the budgeted fixed manufacturing cost per unit is 1,000 units. There are no price, efficiency, or spending variances. Any production-volume variance is written off to cost of goods sold in the month in which it occurs.

Required

1. Prepare income statements for BigScreen in January, February, and March of 2007 under (a) variable costing and (b) absorption costing.
2. Explain the difference in operating income for January, February, and March under variable costing and absorption costing.

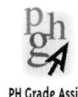

9-19 Throughput costing (continuation of 9-18). The variable manufacturing costs per unit of BigScreen Corporation are:

PH Grade Assist

	January	February	March
Direct material cost per unit	$500	$500	$500
Direct manufacturing labor cost per unit	100	100	100
Manufacturing overhead cost per unit	300	300	300
	$900	$900	$900

Required

1. Prepare income statements for BigScreen in January, February, and March of 2007 under throughput costing.
2. Contrast the results in requirement 1 with those in requirement 1 of Exercise 9-18.
3. Give one motivation for BigScreen to adopt throughput costing.

9-20 Variable versus absorption costing. The Zwatch Company manufactures trendy, high-quality moderately priced watches. As Zwatch's senior financial analyst, you are asked to recommend a method of inventory costing. The CFO will use your recommendation to prepare Zwatch's 2007 income statement. The following data are for the year ended December 31, 2007:

Beginning inventory, January 1, 2007	85,000 units
Ending inventory, December 31, 2007	34,500 units
2007 sales	345,400 units
Selling price (to distributor)	$22.00 per unit
Variable manufacturing cost per unit, including direct materials	$5.10 per unit
Variable operating cost per unit sold	$1.10 per unit sold
Fixed manufacturing costs	$1,440,000
Denominator-level machine-hours	6,000
Standard production rate	50 units per machine-hour
Fixed operating costs	$1,080,000

Assume standard costs per unit are the same for units in beginning inventory and units produced during the year. Also, assume no price, spending, or efficiency variances. Any production-volume variance is written off to cost of goods sold in the month in which it occurs.

Required

1. Prepare income statements under variable and absorption costing for the year ended December 31, 2007.
2. What is Zwatch's operating income as percentage of revenues under each costing method?
3. Explain the difference in operating income between the two methods.
4. Which costing method would you recommend to the CFO? Why?

9-21 Absorption and variable costing. (CMA) Osawa, Inc., planned and actually manufactured 200,000 units of its single product in 2007, its first year of operation. Variable manufacturing cost was $20 per unit produced. Variable operating cost was $10 per unit sold. Planned and actual fixed manufacturing costs were $600,000. Planned and actual fixed operating costs totaled $400,000. Osawa sold 120,000 units of product at $40 per unit.

Required

1. Osawa's 2007 operating income using absorption costing is (a) $440,000, (b) $200,000, (c) $600,000, (d) $840,000, or (e) none of these. Show supporting calculations.
2. Osawa's 2007 operating income using variable costing is (a) $800,000, (b) $440,000, (c) $200,000, (d) $600,000, or (e) none of these. Show supporting calculations.

9-22 Absorption versus variable costing. Sonnenheim, a pharmaceutical company, has a new division that will produce and market Mimic for treatment of hair loss. Each patient who has been prescribed Mimic purchases a year's worth of treatment at a time, which is sold in a single package. For 2007, its first year of producing and selling Mimic, Sonnenheim estimates sales of 50,000 packages and so produces 50,000 packages. Actual 2007 sales are 44,800 packages. The average wholesale selling price is $1,200 per package. Sonnenheim's actual 2007 costs are:

Excel Lab
www.prenhall.com/horngren/cost12e

	A	B
1	Variable cost per unit	
2	Manufacturing cost per package produced	
3	Direct materials	$ 55
4	Direct manufacturing labor	45
5	Manufacturing overhead	120
6	Marketing cost per package sold	75
7	Fixed costs	
8	Manufacturing costs	$ 7,358,400
9	R&D	4,905,600
10	Marketing	15,622,400

If you want to use Excel to solve this exercise, go to the Excel Lab at **www.prenhall.com/horngren/cost12e** and download the template for Exercise 9-22.

Required

1. Calculate the operating income under variable costing.
2. Each package of Mimic produced is allocated $165 in fixed manufacturing costs. If the production-volume variance is written off to cost of goods sold, and there are no price, spending, or efficiency variances, calculate the operating income under absorption costing.
3. Explain the differences in operating incomes obtained in requirement 1 and requirement 2.
4. Sonnenheim's management is considering implementing a bonus for the Mimic plant manager based on gross margin under absorption costing. What incentives will this create for the plant manager? Do you think this new bonus plan is a good idea? Explain briefly.

9-23 Comparison of actual-costing methods. The Rehe Company sells its razors at $3 per unit. The company uses a first-in, first-out actual costing system. A fixed manufacturing cost rate is computed at the end of each year by dividing the actual fixed manufacturing costs by the actual production units. The following data are related to its first two years of operation:

	2006	2007
Sales	1,000 units	1,200 units
Production	1,400 units	1,000 units
Costs:		
Variable manufacturing	$ 700	$ 500
Fixed manufacturing	700	700
Variable operating	1,000	1,200
Fixed operating	400	400

Required

1. Prepare income statements based on variable costing for each of the two years.
2. Prepare income statements based on absorption costing for each of the two years.
3. Prepare a numerical reconciliation and explanation of the difference between operating income for each year under absorption costing and variable costing.
4. Critics have claimed that a widely used accounting system has led to undesirable buildups of inventory levels. (a) Is variable costing or absorption costing more likely to lead to such buildups? Why? (b) What can be done to counteract undesirable inventory buildups?

Excel Lab
www.prenhall.com/horngren/cost12e

9-24 Variable and absorption costing, sales, and operating-income changes. Headsmart, a three-year-old company, has been producing and selling a single type of bicycle helmet. Headsmart uses standard costing. After reviewing the income statements for the first three years, Stuart Weil, president of Headsmart, commented: "I was told by our accountants—and in fact, I have memorized—that our breakeven volume is 50,000 units. I was happy that we reached that sales goal in each of our first two years. But, here's the strange thing: in our first year, we sold 50,000 units and indeed we broke even. Then, in our second year we sold the same volume and had a positive operating income. I didn't complain, of course . . . but here's the bad part. In our third year, we *sold 20% more* helmets, but our *operating income fell by more than 80%* relative to the second year! We didn't change our selling price or cost structure over the past three years and have no price, efficiency, or spending variances . . . so what's going on?!"

	A	B	C	D
1	**Absorption Costing**			
2		**2006**	**2007**	**2008**
3	Sales (units)	50,000	50,000	60,000
4	Revenues	$2,100,000	$2,100,000	$2,520,000
5	Cost of goods sold			
6	Beginning inventory	0	0	380,000
7	Production	1,900,000	2,280,000	1,900,000
8	Available for sale	1,900,000	2,280,000	2,280,000
9	Deduct ending inventory	0	(380,000)	0
10	Adjustment for production-volume variance	0	(240,000)	0
11	Cost of goods sold	1,900,000	1,660,000	2,280,000
12	Gross margin	200,000	440,000	240,000
13	Selling and administrative expenses (all fixed)	200,000	200,000	200,000
14	Operating income	$ 0	$ 240,000	$ 40,000
15				
16	Beginning inventory	0	0	10,000
17	Production (units)	50,000	60,000	50,000
18	Sales (units)	50,000	50,000	60,000
19	Ending inventory	0	10,000	0
20	Variable manufacturing cost per unit	$ 14	$ 14	$ 14
21	Fixed manufacturing overhead costs	$1,200,000	$1,200,000	$1,200,000
22	Fixed manuf. costs allocated per unit produced	$ 24	$ 24	$ 24

If you want to use Excel to solve this exercise, go to the Excel Lab at **www.prenhall.com/horngren/cost12e** and download the template for Exercise 9-24.

Required

1. What denominator level is Headsmart using to allocate fixed manufacturing costs to the bicycle helmets? How is Headsmart disposing of any favorable or unfavorable production-volume variance at the end of the year? Explain your answer briefly.
2. How did Headsmart's accountants arrive at the breakeven volume of 50,000 units?
3. Prepare a variable costing–based income statement for each year. Explain the variation in variable-costing operating income for each year based on contribution margin per unit and sales volume.
4. Reconcile the operating incomes under variable costing and absorption costing for each year, and use this information to explain to Stuart Weil the positive operating income in 2007 and the drop in operating income in 2008.

9-25 Capacity management, denominator-level capacity concepts. Each of the following items is identified by a number:

PH Grade Assist

1. Should be used for performance evaluation
2. Measures the denominator level in terms of demand for the output of the plant
3. Represents the expected level of capacity utilization for the next budget period
4. Is based on producing at full efficiency all the time
5. Takes into account seasonal, cyclical, and trend factors
6. Measures the denominator level in terms of what a plant can supply
7. Represents an ideal benchmark
8. Highlights the cost of capacity acquired but not used
9. Hides the cost of capacity acquired but not used
10. Should be used for long-term pricing purposes
11. If used as the denominator-level concept, would avoid the restatement of unit costs when expected demand levels change

Required

Match each of the items with one or more of the following denominator-level capacity concepts by putting the appropriate letter(s) by each number:

a. Theoretical capacity
b. Practical capacity
c. Normal capacity utilization
d. Master-budget capacity utilization

9-26 Denominator-level problem. The Spalding Sails company produces the Spalding 26, a very popular 26-foot recreational sail boat. Spalding Sails takes pride in the high quality it builds into its affordable boats. The company has been in business for 35 years. Management has recently adopted absorption costing and is debating which denominator-level concept to use. The Spalding 26 sells for an average price of $15,000. Budgeted fixed manufacturing overhead costs for 2007 are estimated at $3,800,000. Spalding uses subassembly operators that provide component parts. The following are the denominator-level options that management has been considering:

a. Theoretical capacity—based on two shifts, completion of four boats per shift, and a 360-day year—$2 \times 4 \times 360 = 2{,}880$.
b. Practical capacity—theoretical capacity adjusted for unavoidable interruptions, breakdowns, and so forth—$2 \times 3 \times 300 = 1{,}800$.
c. Normal capacity utilization—estimated at 1,000 units.
d. Master-budget capacity utilization—the strengthening stock market and a record number of baby boomers retiring over the coming year has prompted the Marketing Department to issue an estimate for 2007 of 1,200 units.

Required

1. Calculate the budgeted fixed manufacturing overhead cost rates under the four denominator-level concepts.
2. What are the benefits to Spalding Sails of using either theoretical capacity or practical capacity?
3. Under a cost-based pricing system, what are the negative aspects of a master-budget denominator level? What are the positive aspects?

9-27 Capacity usage of activities, alternative denominator-level capacities. Harris Corporation, which produces two types of doll houses—Beachcomber and Hilltop—has collected the following 2007 data for the budgeted fixed costs of its three manufacturing overhead activities and its two products:

PH Grade Assist

Excel Lab www.prenhall.com/horngren/cost12e

	A	B	C	D	E	F	G	H	I
1				Denominator-level capacity			Activity consumption by product		
2	Activity	Cost	Cost Driver	Theoretical	Practical		Beachcomber	Hilltop	
3	Machine setup	$500,000	No. of setup hours	5,000	4,500	setup hours	3,200	1,400	setup hours
4	Material handling	$200,000	Material pounds	100,000	95,000	material pounds	44,000	41,000	material pounds
5	Quality Inspection	$300,000	No. of inspections	20,000	18,000	inspections	8,500	10,000	inspections

Harris Corporation uses standard costing, has no price, efficiency, or spending variances and writes off any production-volume variances to cost of goods sold.

If you want to use Excel to solve this exercise, go to the Excel Lab at **www.prenhall.com/horngren/cost12e** and download the template for Exercise 9-27.

Required

1. If theoretical capacity is used as the denominator level, calculate (a) the costs allocated to each product for each activity and (b) the production-volume variance for each activity.
2. If practical capacity is used as the denominator level, calculate (a) the costs allocated to each product for each activity and (b) the production-volume variance for each activity.
3. Consider the different purposes cost information is used for, such as, product costing and capacity management, pricing, performance evaluation, external reporting, and regulatory requirements. For each of these different purposes, comment on the pros and cons of using theoretical capacity and practical capacity as the denominator levels.

9-28 Capacity usage, cost behavior, service firm. A division of Finn & Sawyer processes delinquent bill collections for a number of companies in the Atlanta area. Its 5 employees are budgeted to earn a total of $200,000 each year, a fixed cost. They have the capacity to process 100,000 bills during the year. Variable bill-processing costs are budgeted at $75,000 per year. Finn & Sawyer's biggest customer, A&S Security Services, accounts for about 40% of the bills processed each year, and it pays $3 per bill processed. During 2007, 80,000 bills were actually processed. There were no price, efficiency, or spending variances.

Required

1. Calculate Finn & Sawyer's budgeted full cost (variable and fixed) to process one bill, using practical capacity of 100,000 bills as the denominator level.
2. What was the cost of unused capacity in 2007? Is any of the cost of unused capacity attributable to variable costs? Explain.
3. Based on data from the past five years, Finn & Sawyer's controller suggests using 80,000 bills per year as the denominator level. What is the budgeted full cost to process one bill using 80,000 bills per year as the denominator level?
4. Is A&S Security an attractive customer considering the new budgeted cost calculated in requirement 3? What should Finn & Sawyer do with regard to this customer?

PH Grade Assist

9-29 Variable and absorption costing and breakeven points (chapter appendix). Shasta Hills, a winery in northern California, manufactures a premium cabernet and sells primarily to distributors. Wine is sold in cases of one dozen bottles. In the year ended December 31, 2007, Shasta Hills sold 242,400 cases at an average selling price of $94 per case. The following additional data are for Shasta Hills for the same year (assume constant unit costs and no price, spending, efficiency, or production-volume variances):

Beginning inventory, January 1, 2007	32,600 cases
Ending inventory, December 31, 2007	24,800 cases
Fixed manufacturing costs	$3,753,600
Fixed operating costs	$6,568,800
Variable costs	
Direct materials	
Grapes	$16 per case
Bottles, corks, and crates	$10 per case
Direct labor	
Bottling	$6 per case
Winemaking	$14 per case
Aging	$2 per case

Required

1. Calculate the number of cases Shasta Hills produced in 2007.
2. Find the breakeven point (number of cases) in 2007
   a. under variable costing
   b. under absorption costing
3. Grape costs are expected to increase 25% in 2008. Assuming all other data are the same, calculate the minimum number of cases Shasta Hills must sell in 2008 to break even
   a. under variable costing
   b. under absorption costing

Problems

9-30 Variable costing versus absorption costing. The Mavis Company uses an absorption-costing system based on standard costs. Total variable manufacturing cost, including direct material cost, is $3 per unit; the standard production rate is 10 units per machine-hour. Total budgeted and actual fixed manufacturing overhead costs are $420,000. Fixed manufacturing overhead is allocated at $7 per machine-hour ($420,000 ÷ 60,000 machine-hours of denominator level). Selling price is $5 per unit. Variable operating cost, which is driven by units sold, is $1 per unit. Fixed operating costs are $120,000. Beginning inventory in 2007 is 30,000 units; ending inventory is 40,000 units. Sales in 2007 are 540,000 units. The same standard unit costs persisted throughout 2006 and 2007. For simplicity, assume that there are no price, spending, or efficiency variances.

Required

1. Prepare an income statement for 2007 assuming that the production-volume variance is written off at year-end as an adjustment to cost of goods sold.
2. The president has heard about variable costing. She asks you to recast the 2007 statement as it would appear under variable costing.
3. Explain the difference in operating income as calculated in requirements 1 and 2.
4. Graph how fixed manufacturing overhead is accounted for under absorption costing. That is, there will be two lines: one for the budgeted fixed manufacturing overhead (which is equal to the actual

fixed manufacturing overhead in this case) and one for the fixed manufacturing overhead allocated. Show how the production-volume variance might be indicated in the graph.

5. Critics have claimed that a widely used accounting system has led to undesirable buildups of inventory levels. (a) Is variable costing or absorption costing more likely to lead to such buildups? Why? (b) What can be done to counteract undesirable inventory buildups?

9-31 Breakeven under absorption costing (chapter appendix). Refer to Problem 9-30.

Required

1. Compute the breakeven point (in units) under variable costing.
2. Compute the breakeven point (in units) under absorption costing.
3. Suppose that production is exactly equal to the denominator level, but no units are sold. Fixed manufacturing costs are unaffected. Assume, however, that all operating costs are avoided. Compute operating income under (a) variable costing and (b) absorption costing. Explain the difference between your answers.

9-32 Variable costing and absorption costing, All-Fixed Company. (R. Marple, adapted) It is the end of 2007. The All-Fixed Company began operations in January 2006. The company is so named because it has no variable costs. All its costs are fixed; they do not vary with output.

PH Grade Assist

The All-Fixed Company is located on the bank of a river and has its own hydroelectric plant to supply power, light, and heat. The company manufactures a synthetic fertilizer from air and river water and sells its product at a price that is not expected to change. It has a small staff of employees, all paid fixed annual salaries. The output of the plant can be increased or decreased by adjusting a few dials on a control panel.

The following budgeted and actual data are for the operations of the All-Fixed Company. All-Fixed uses budgeted production as the denominator level and writes off any production-volume variance to cost of goods sold.

	2006	2007[a]
Sales	10,000 tons	10,000 tons
Production	20,000 tons	0 tons
Selling price	$30 per ton	$30 per ton
Costs (all fixed):		
Manufacturing	$280,000	$280,000
Operating	$ 40,000	$ 40,000

[a]Management adopted the policy, effective January 1, 2007, of producing only as much product as needed to fill sales orders. During 2007, sales were the same as for 2006 and were filled entirely from inventory at the start of 2007.

Required

1. Prepare income statements with one column for 2006, one column for 2007, and one column for the two years together, using (a) variable costing and (b) absorption costing.
2. What is the breakeven point under (a) variable costing and (b) absorption costing?
3. What inventory costs would be carried in the balance sheet on December 31, 2006 and 2007, under each method?
4. Assume that the performance of the top manager of the company is evaluated and rewarded largely on the basis of reported operating income. Which costing method would the manager prefer? Why?

9-33 Comparison of variable costing and absorption costing. Hinkle Company uses standard costing. Tim Bartina, the new president of Hinkle Company, is presented with the following data for 2006:

Excel Lab
www.prenhall.com/horngren/cost12e

	A	B	C
1	Hinkle Company		
2	Income Statements for the Year Ended December 31, 2006		
3		Variable	Absorption
4		Costing	Costing
5	Revenues	$9,000,000	$9,000,000
6	Cost of goods sold (at standard costs)	4,680,000	5,860,000
7	Fixed manufacturing overhead (budgeted)	1,200,000	-
8	Fixed manufacturing overhead variances (all unfavorable):		
9	Spending	100,000	100,000
10	Production volume	-	400,000
11	Total marketing and administrative costs (all fixed)	1,500,000	1,500,000
12	Total costs	7,480,000	7,860,000
13	Operating income	$1,520,000	$1,140,000
14			
15	Inventories (at standard costs)		
16	December 31, 2005	$1,200,000	$1,720,000
17	December 31, 2006	66,000	206,000

If you want to use Excel to solve this problem, go to the Excel Lab at **www.prenhall.com/horngren/cost12e** and download the template for Problem 9-33.

Required

1. At what percentage of denominator level was the plant operating during 2006?
2. How much fixed manufacturing overhead was included in the 2005 and the 2006 ending inventory under absorption costing?
3. Reconcile and explain the difference in 2006 operating incomes under variable and absorption costing.
4. Tim Bartina is concerned: He notes that despite an increase in sales over 2005, 2006 operating income has actually declined under absorption costing. Explain how this occurred.

Excel Lab
www.prenhall.com/horngren/cost12e

9-34 Alternative denominator-level capacity concepts, effect on operating income. Lucky Lager has just purchased the Austin Brewery. The brewery is two years old and uses absorption costing. It will "sell" its product to Lucky Lager at $68 per barrel. Paul Brandon, Lucky Lager's controller, obtains the following information about Austin Brewery's capacity and budgeted fixed costs for 2006:

	A	B	C	D	E
1		**Budgeted Fixed**	**Days of**	**Hours of**	
2	**Denominator-Level**	**Manufacturing**	**Production**	**Production**	**Barrels**
3	**Capacity Concept**	**Overhead per Period**	**per Period**	**per Day**	**per Hour**
4	Theoretical capacity	$42,000,000	365	24	600
5	Practical capacity	$42,000,000	350	20	500
6	Normal capacity utilization	$42,000,000	350	20	400
7	Master-budget capacity utilization for each half year				
8	(a) January-June 2006	$21,000,000	175	20	320
9	(b) July-December 2006	$21,000,000	175	20	480

If you want to use Excel to solve this problem, go to the Excel Lab at **www.prenhall.com/horngren/cost12e** and download the template for Problem 9-34.

Required

1. Compute the budgeted fixed manufacturing overhead rate per barrel for each of the denominator-level capacity concepts. Explain why they are different.
2. In 2006, the Austin Brewery reported these production results:

12	Beginning inventory in barrels, 1-1-2006	0
13	Production in barrels	2,600,000
14	Ending inventory in barrels, 12-31-2006	200,000
15	Actual variable manufacturing costs	$120,380,000
16	Actual fixed manufacturing overhead costs	$ 40,632,000

There are no variable cost variables. Fixed manufacturing overhead cost variances are written off to cost of goods sold in the period in which they occur. Compute the Austin Brewery's operating income when the denominator-level capacity is (a) theoretical capacity, (b) practical capacity, and (c) normal capacity utilization.

Excel Lab
www.prenhall.com/horngren/cost12e

9-35 Motivational considerations in denominator-level capacity selection (continuation of 9-34). If you want to use Excel to solve this problem, go to the Excel Lab at **www.prenhall.com/horngren/cost12e** and download the template for Problem 9-34.

Required

1. If the plant manager of the Austin Brewery gets a bonus based on operating income, which denominator-level capacity concept would he prefer to use? Explain.
2. What denominator-level capacity concept would Lucky Lager prefer to use for U.S. income-tax reporting? Explain.
3. How might the IRS limit the flexibility of an absorption-costing company like Lucky Lager in attempting to minimize its taxable income?

Excel Lab
www.prenhall.com/horngren/cost12e

9-36 Denominator-level choices, changes in inventory levels, effect on operating income. Accel Partners uses absorption costing based on standard costs and reports the following data for 2007:

	A	B	C
1	Theoretical capacity	360,000	units
2	Practical capacity	300,000	units
3	Normal capacity utilization	240,000	units
4	Selling price	$30	per unit
5	Beginning inventory	25,000	units
6	Production	260,000	units
7	Sales volume	280,000	units
8	Variable budgeted manufacturing cost	$3	per unit
9	Total budgeted fixed manufacturing costs	$3,600,000	
10	Total budgeted operating costs (all fixed)	$1,000,000	

There are no price, spending, or efficiency variances. The production-volume variance is written off to cost of goods sold. For each choice of denominator level, the budgeted production cost per unit is also the cost per unit of beginning inventory.

If you want to use Excel to solve this problem, go to the Excel Lab at **www.prenhall.com/horngren/cost12e** and download the template for Problem 9-36.

Required

1. What is the production-volume variance in 2007 when the denominator level is (a) theoretical capacity, (b) practical capacity, and (c) normal capacity utilization?
2. Prepare absorption costing–based income statements for Accel Partners using theoretical capacity, practical capacity, and normal capacity utilization as the denominator levels.
3. Why is the operating income under normal capacity utilization lower than the other two scenarios?
4. Reconcile the difference in operating income based on theoretical capacity and practical capacity with the difference in fixed manufacturing overhead included in inventory.

9-37 Effects of denominator-level choice. The Wong Company installed standard costs and a flexible budget on January 1, 2006. The president has been pondering how fixed manufacturing overhead should be allocated to products. Machine-hours has been chosen as the allocation base. Her remaining uncertainty is the denominator level for machine-hours. She decides to wait for the first month's results before making a final choice of what denominator level should be used from that day forward.

PH Grade Assist

In January 2006, the actual units of output had a standard of 70,000 machine-hours allowed. If the company used practical capacity as the denominator level, the fixed manufacturing overhead spending variance would be $10,000, unfavorable, and the production-volume variance would be $36,000, unfavorable. If the company used normal capacity utilization as the denominator level, the production-volume variance would be $20,000, favorable. Budgeted fixed manufacturing overhead was $120,000 for the month.

Required

1. Compute the denominator level, assuming that the normal-capacity-utilization concept is chosen.
2. Compute the denominator level, assuming that the practical-capacity concept is chosen.
3. Suppose you are the executive vice president. You want to maximize your 2006 bonus, which depends on 2006 operating income. Assume that the production-volume variance is written off to cost of goods sold at year-end. Which denominator level would you favor? Why?

9-38 Downward demand spiral. MetaTech Company manufactures and sells one type of large optical storage system. Its practical annual capacity is 5,000 units, and, for the past few years, its budgeted and actual sales and production volume have been 5,000 units per year. MetaTech's budgeted and actual variable manufacturing costs are $100 per unit, and budgeted and actual total fixed manufacturing costs are $1,500,000 per year. MetaTech calculates full manufacturing cost per unit as the sum of the variable manufacturing cost per unit and the fixed manufacturing costs allocated to the budgeted units produced. Selling price is set at a 100% markup to full manufacturing cost per unit.

Required

1. Compute MetaTech's selling price.
2. Recent competition from abroad has caused a drop in budgeted production and sales volume to 4,000 units per year, and analysts are predicting further declines. If MetaTech continues to use budgeted production as the denominator level, calculate its new selling price.
3. Comment on the effect changes in budgeted production have on selling price. Suggest another denominator level that MetaTech might use for its pricing decision. Justify your choice.
4. MetaTech has received an offer to buy identical storage units for $400 each instead of manufacturing the units in-house. Shutting down the manufacturing plant would reduce fixed costs to $300,000 per year. Should MetaTech accept this offer? Why or why not?

9-39 Denominator level, production-volume variance, working backward. National Electronics, Inc. acquired plant assets based on long-range demand forecasts for its products. National uses standard costing. Its budgeted fixed manufacturing overhead costs for 2007 were $10,400,000. For each of the denominator-level capacity alternatives (measured in machine-hours), its 2007 production-volume variance was:

PH Grade Assist

Excel Lab www.prenhall.com/horngren/cost12e

	A	B	C
1	**Denominator-Level**	**Production-Volume**	
2	**Capacity Concept**	**Variance**	
3	Theoretical capacity	$5,200,000	U
4	Practical capacity	2,600,000	U
5	Normal capacity utilization	2,080,000	U
6	Master-budget capacity utilization	1,600,000	F

If you want to use Excel to solve this problem, go to the Excel Lab at **www.prenhall.com/horngren/cost12e** and download the template for Problem 9-39.

Required

1. How much fixed manufacturing overhead was allocated for each denominator-level capacity?
2. For 2007 actual output, 1,200,000 budgeted machine-hours were allowed. What was the budgeted fixed manufacturing overhead rate per machine-hour for each denominator-level capacity?
3. Using your answer to requirement 2, what was the capacity in machine-hours for each denominator-level capacity?

9-40 Cost allocation, downward demand spiral. Mission One operates a chain of 10 hospitals in the Los Angeles area. Its central food-catering facility, MedChef, prepares and delivers meals to the hospitals. It has the capacity to deliver up to 3,650,000 meals a year. In 2007, based on estimates from each hospital controller, MedChef budgeted for 2,555,000 meals a year. Budgeted fixed costs in 2007 were $3,832,500. Each hospital was charged $5.30 per meal—$3.80 variable costs plus $1.50 allocated budgeted fixed cost.

Recently, the hospitals have been complaining about the quality of MedChef's meals and their rising costs. In mid-2007, Mission One's president announces that all Mission One hospitals and support facilities will be run as profit centers. Hospitals will be free to purchase quality-certified services from outside the system. Roy Jenkins, MedChef's controller, is preparing the 2008 budget. He hears that three hospitals have decided to use outside suppliers for their meals; this will reduce the 2008 estimated demand to 2,190,000 meals. No change in variable cost per meal or total fixed costs is expected in 2008.

Required

1. How did Jenkins calculate the budgeted fixed cost per meal of $1.50 in 2007?
2. Using the same approach to calculating budgeted fixed cost per meal and pricing as in 2007, how much would hospitals be charged for each MedChef meal in 2008? What would their reaction be?
3. Suggest an alternative cost-based price per meal that Jenkins might propose and that might be more acceptable to the hospitals. What would MedChef and Jenkins have to do to make this price profitable in the long run?

9-41 Cost allocation, responsibility accounting, ethics (continuation of 9-40). In 2008, only 2,017,100 MedChef meals were produced and sold to the hospitals. Jenkins suspects that hospital controllers had systematically inflated their 2008 meal estimates.

Required

1. Recall that MedChef uses the master-budget capacity utilization to allocate fixed costs and to price meals. What was the effect of production-volume variance on MedChef's operating income in 2008?
2. Why might hospital controllers deliberately overestimate their future meal counts?
3. What other evidence should Mission One's controller seek in order to investigate Jenkins' concerns?
4. Suggest two specific steps that Mission One's controller might take to reduce hospital controllers' incentives to inflate their estimated meal counts.

Collaborative Learning Problem

9-42 Absorption, variable, and throughput costing. The Waterloo, Ontario, plant of Maple Leaf Motors assembles the Icarus motor vehicle. The standard unit manufacturing cost per vehicle in 2006 is:

Direct materials	$6,000
Direct manufacturing labor	1,800
Variable manufacturing overhead	2,000
Fixed manufacturing overhead	?

The Waterloo plant is highly automated. Practical capacity per month is 4,000 vehicles. Variable manufacturing overhead is allocated to vehicles on the basis of assembly time. The standard assembly time per vehicle is 20 hours. Fixed manufacturing overhead in 2006 is allocated on the basis of the standard assembly time for the budgeted normal capacity utilization of the plant. In 2006, the budgeted normal capacity utilization is 3,000 vehicles per month. The budgeted monthly fixed manufacturing overhead is $7,500,000.

On January 1, 2006, there is zero beginning inventory of Icarus vehicles. The actual unit production and sales figures for the first three months of 2006 are:

	January	February	March
Production	3,200	2,400	3,800
Sales	2,000	2,900	3,200

Assume no direct materials variances, no direct manufacturing labor variances, and no manufacturing overhead spending or efficiency variances in the first three months of 2006.

Bret Hart, a vice president of Maple Leaf Motors, is the manager of the Waterloo plant. His compensation includes a bonus that is 0.5% of quarterly operating income. Operating income is calculated using absorption costing. Maple Leaf Motors prepares absorption-costing income statements monthly, which includes an adjustment to cost of goods sold for the production-volume variance occurring in that month.

The Waterloo plant "sells" each Icarus to Maple Leaf's marketing subsidiary at $16,000 per vehicle. No marketing costs are incurred by the Waterloo plant.

Required

1. Compute (a) the fixed manufacturing overhead cost per unit and (b) the total manufacturing cost per unit.
2. Compute the monthly operating income for January, February, and March under absorption costing. What amount of bonus is paid each month to Bret Hart?
3. How much would use of variable costing change Hart's bonus each month if the same 0.5% figure were applied to variable-costing operating income?
4. Explain the differences in Hart's bonuses in requirements 2 and 3.

5. How much would use of throughput costing change Hart's bonus if the same 0.5% figure were applied to throughput-costing operating income?
6. Outline different approaches Maple Leaf Motors could use to reduce possible undesirable behavior associated with the use of absorption costing at its Waterloo plant.

Get Connected: Cost Accounting in the News

Go to www.prenhall.com/horngren/cost12e for additional online exercise(s) that explore issues affecting the accounting world today. These exercises offer you the opportunity to analyze and reflect on how cost accounting helps managers to make better decisions and handle the challenges of strategic planning and implementation.

CHAPTER 9 Video Case

CAVCO INDUSTRIES Capacity Analysis

Forget what you think you know about manufactured homes—the floral vinyl walls, squeaky floors, and decidedly "cookie-cutter" look. From "tape and texture" walls to stucco-and-tile exterior finishes, Cavco Industries of Phoenix, Arizona, produces manufactured housing for the twenty-first century that rivals the construction and design elements found in traditional site-built homes. In business for over 40 years, Cavco sells manufactured homes, camping cabins, "Park Model" homes under 400 square feet in size, and commercial buildings. The company has several hundred floor plans to choose from, or it can customize floor plans to fit the design specifications of the buyer. Sales have risen about 7% annually over the past three years.

Cavco relies on lean manufacturing and just-in-time inventory management techniques at its three manufacturing facilities. With thousands of stockkeeping units (SKUs), direct materials inventory turns over every week. The most expensive inventory items consist of wood and wood products, steel, drywall, and petroleum-based products. There are about 50 different stations in the main assembly lines on Cavco's production floor. They are fed daily by subsidiary job shops close by, such as the in-house cabinetmaking shop and flooring shop. Nothing is ever made to stock, so the bills of materials coming from independent-dealer orders drive the release of direct materials onto the floor at each station in assembly.

At each plant, the manager schedules production so tightly that there is rarely downtime at any station in an assembly line. Efficiency is so consistent that budgeted direct materials and direct manufacturing labor usually match the actual costs incurred at month-end. Instead of computing a budgeted overhead allocation rate at the beginning of the year and adjusting at year-end, the company applies actual plant overhead (consisting of utilities, engineering, purchasing, and plant manager salaries) each month so managers can see how they did and make adjustments before the next month's production activities get too far along. Once each home section (called a "floor") is completed, it is driven out of the plant by independent shippers, title passes to the dealer, sales revenue is booked, and the home is taken to its destination. With no unsold finished goods in stock at month-end, the only materials to account for each month are those not yet released into production and those in work-in-process inventory.

QUESTIONS

1. Assume Cavco has dedicated one of its manufacturing plants to building camping cabins. Budgeted annual fixed manufacturing costs for this facility are $2,000,000 and include the items listed in the case. The amount will remain the same, even though shifts per day and days worked per week may fluctuate. The master budget for 2006 is based on one-shift production of 2 camping cabins per day over a four-day workweek. The plant is closed on Mondays for building and equipment maintenance. The company also shuts down production for one week in July and one week at the end of December. Normal capacity utilization is based on one-shift production of two cabins per day, five days a week, with maintenance performed in the evenings. Practical capacity is two cabins a day, five days a week for three shifts. Theoretical capacity is three shifts a day, seven days a week, throughout the year. If every camping cabin built in this plant takes the same amount of time to complete, what is the 2006 budgeted fixed manufacturing overhead cost rate per cabin under theoretical capacity, practical capacity, normal capacity utilization, and master-budget capacity utilization?
2. Assume the standard variable manufacturing cost for a camping cabin is $10,000. Compute the total standard manufacturing cost per cabin under theoretical capacity, practical capacity, normal capacity utilization, and master-budget capacity utilization.
3. Cavco does not have any finished goods inventory at month-end. What kinds of undesirable behaviors on the part of plant managers are they avoiding?

CHAPTER 10

DETERMINING HOW COSTS BEHAVE

LEARNING OBJECTIVES

1. **Explain the two assumptions frequently used in cost-behavior estimation**
2. **Describe linear cost functions and three common ways in which they behave**
3. **Understand various methods of cost estimation**
4. **Outline six steps in estimating a cost function using quantitative analysis**
5. **Describe three criteria used to evaluate and choose cost drivers**
6. **Explain and give examples of nonlinear cost functions**
7. **Distinguish the cumulative average-time learning model from the incremental unit-time learning model**
8. **Be aware of data problems encountered in estimating cost functions**

What is the value of looking at the past? Perhaps it is to recall fond memories or to extend your knowledge of historical events. Maybe your return to the past is done to better understand and predict the future. When an organization looks at the past, it's typically done to analyze the results of decisions made so that, in the future, the best outcomes are repeated and the mistakes avoided. When Elegant Rugs' general manager, Wendy Stevens, called her management accountant, Julio Colon, into her office, she had both the past and the future on her mind.

Wendy: Julio, I've been thinking about our manufacturing operations and some of our recent successes. The new contemporary designs have been a huge success for the company. Yet I know that we can't expect to repeat our success without an understanding of how we got there. I'd like to see how we can use actual costs to predict costs in the future. Can you help me with this?

Julio: Sure. We have a number of techniques at our disposal, all of which require that we separate fixed costs from variable costs. Some of them are pretty simple to use, such as the industrial engineering method, the conference method, and the account analysis method. But they're not as accurate as some other approaches. I know how you like precision, so I'd recommend we use a more sophisticated method—regression analysis.

Wendy: Ah yes! I recall using this technique in business school, although I'll admit it's been a while since I've used regression analysis. Can you give me a quick refresher?

Julio: All right. Predicting costs, such as direct materials and direct labor, is fairly easy. The challenge is in determining manufacturing overhead costs for our different carpet types. To do this, we first need to identify the cost drivers of different overhead costs. We then use regression analysis and past data to estimate the relationship between the amount of the cost driver and overhead cost. This helps us predict the cost per unit of the cost driver and overhead costs for the different styles of carpets.

Wendy: I can see the benefits of predicting costs. With our upcoming introduction of new styles of carpet, we'll be able to determine which ones will likely be the most profitable. We should also be able to predict how our costs will decrease as we learn through experience how to make the new styles more efficiently. Thanks, Julio. Let's meet again next week to review your regression results.

Managers must understand how costs behave to make strategic decisions and operating decisions. For example, managers at Sony must determine which alternative product design for the new line of Plasma televisions is most profitable. Managers at GE might consider whether a component part for its new line of dishwashers should be made or bought. At Bank of America, managers might want to explore the effect a 5% increase in customers is expected to have on operating income. The management team at Gap, Inc., would want to learn why the variable overhead efficiency variance is so large. Managers at Owens and Minor would want to know which cost drivers to choose in its activity-based costing system.

Knowledge of cost behavior is needed to answer these questions. This chapter will focus on how managers determine cost-behavior patterns—that is, how they understand how costs change in relation to changes in activity levels, in the quantity of products produced, and so on.

General Issues in Estimating Cost Functions

Managers are able to understand cost behavior through cost functions. A **cost function** is a mathematical description of how a cost changes with changes in the level of an activity relating to that cost. Examples of activities are preparing setups for production runs and operating machines. Cost functions can be plotted on a graph by measuring the level of an activity, such as number of batches produced or number of machine-hours used, on the horizontal axis (called the *x*-axis) and the amount of total costs corresponding to—or preferably, dependent on—the levels of that activity on the vertical axis (called the *y*-axis).

Basic Assumptions and Examples of Cost Functions

1

Explain the two assumptions frequently used in cost-behavior estimation

... cost functions are linear and have a single cost driver

Managers often estimate cost functions based on two assumptions:

1. Variations in the level of a single activity (the cost driver) explain the variations in the related total costs.
2. Cost behavior is approximated by a linear cost function within the relevant range. Recall that a relevant range is the range of the activity in which there is a relationship between total cost and the level of activity. For a **linear cost function** represented graphically, total cost versus the level of a single activity related to that cost is a straight line within the relevant range.

2

Describe linear cost functions

... graph of cost function is a straight line

and three common ways in which they behave

... variable, fixed, and mixed

We use these two assumptions throughout most, but not all, of this chapter. Not all cost functions are linear and can be explained by a single activity. Later sections will discuss cost functions that do not rely on these assumptions.

To see the role of cost functions in business decisions, consider the negotiations between Cannon Services and World Wide Communications (WWC) for exclusive use of a telephone line between New York and Paris. WWC offers Cannon the choice of any one of three alternative cost structures. These cost structures were introduced in Chapter 2.

- **Alternative 1:** $5 per phone-minute used. Total cost to Cannon varies with the number of phone-minutes used. That is, the number of phone-minutes used is the only factor whose change causes a change in total cost.

Panel A in Exhibit 10-1 presents this *variable cost* for Cannon Services. Total cost (measured vertically on the *y*-axis) changes in proportion to the number of phone-minutes used (measured horizontally on the *x*-axis) within the relevant range. Under alternative 1, there is no fixed cost. Total cost simply increases by $5 for every additional phone-minute used. Panel A illustrates the $5 **slope coefficient**, the amount by which total cost changes when a one-unit change occurs in the level of activity (one phone-minute in the Cannon example).

We write the cost function in Panel A of Exhibit 10-1 as

$$y = \$5X$$

where X measures the actual number of phone-minutes used (on the *x*-axis), and y measures the total cost of the phone-minutes used (on the *y*-axis) calculated using the cost function. *Throughout the chapter, uppercase letters, such as X, refer to the actual observations, and lowercase letters, such as y, represent estimates or calculations made using a cost function.*

- **Alternative 2:** $10,000 per month. Total cost will be $10,000 per month, regardless of the number of phone-minutes used. (We use the same activity measure, number of phone-minutes used, to compare cost-behavior patterns under the three alternatives.) With this alternative, the cost is fixed, not variable.

Panel B in Exhibit 10-1 presents this *fixed cost* for Cannon Services. The fixed cost of $10,000 is called a **constant**; it is the component of total cost that does not vary with changes in the level of the activity. Under alternative 2, the constant accounts for all the

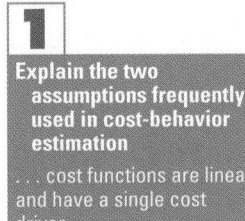

EXHIBIT 10-1 Examples of Linear Cost Functions

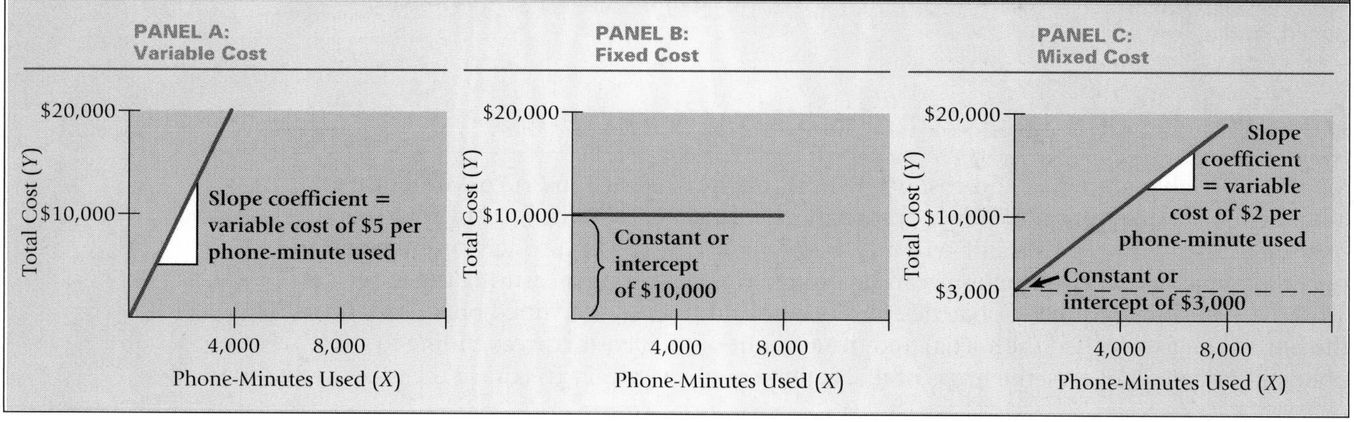

cost because there is no variable cost. Graphically, the slope coefficient of the cost function is zero; this cost function intersects the *y*-axis at the constant value, and therefore the *constant* is also called the **intercept**.

We write the cost function in Panel B as

$$y = \$10{,}000$$

- **Alternative 3:** \$3,000 per month plus \$2 per phone-minute used. This is an example of a mixed cost. A **mixed cost**—also called a **semivariable cost**—is a cost that has both fixed and variable elements. Under this alternative, the cost has one component that is fixed regardless of the number of phone-minutes used—a fixed cost of \$3,000 per month—and another component that is variable with respect to the number of phone-minutes used—a variable cost of \$2 per phone-minute used.

Panel C in Exhibit 10-1 presents this mixed cost for Cannon Services. Unlike the graphs for alternatives 1 and 2, Panel C has both a constant, or intercept, value of \$3,000 and a slope coefficient of \$2.

We write the cost function in Panel C of Exhibit 10-1 as

$$y = \$3{,}000 + \$2X$$

In the case of a mixed cost, total cost in the relevant range increases as the number of phone-minutes used increases. Note, total cost does not vary strictly in proportion to the number of phone-minutes used within the relevant range. For example, when 4,000 phone-minutes are used, the total cost equals \$11,000 [\$3,000 + (\$2 per phone-minute × 4,000 phone-minutes)], but when 8,000 phone-minutes are used, total cost equals \$19,000 [\$3,000 + (\$2 per phone-minute × 8,000 phone-minutes)]. Although the number of phone-minutes used has doubled, total cost has increased by only about 73% [(\$19,000 − \$11,000) ÷ \$11,000].

Cannon's managers must understand the cost-behavior patterns in the three alternatives to choose the best deal with WWC. Suppose Cannon expects to use at least 4,000 phone-minutes per month. Its cost for 4,000 phone-minutes under the three alternatives would be as follows:

- **Alternative 1** \$20,000 (\$5 per phone-minute × 4,000 phone-minutes)
- **Alternative 2** \$10,000
- **Alternative 3** \$11,000 [\$3,000 + (\$2 per phone-minute × 4,000 phone-minutes)]

Alternative 2 is the least costly. Moreover, if Cannon were to use more than 4,000 phone-minutes, as is likely to be the case, alternatives 1 and 3 would be even more costly. Cannon's managers, therefore, should choose alternative 2.

Note that the graphs in Exhibit 10-1 are linear. That is, they appear as straight lines. We simply need to know the constant, or intercept, amount (commonly designated *a*) and the slope coefficient (commonly designated *b*). For any linear cost function based on a single activity (recall our two assumptions discussed at the start of the chapter), knowing *a* and *b* is sufficient to describe and graphically plot all the values within the relevant range of number of phone-minutes used. We write a general form of this linear cost function as

$$y = a + bX$$

Under alternative 1, a = \$0 and b = \$5 per phone-minute used; under alternative 2, a = \$10,000 and b = \$0 per phone-minute used; and under alternative 3, a = \$3,000 and b = \$2 per phone-minute used. To plot the mixed-cost function in Panel C, we draw a line starting from the point marked \$3,000 on the y-axis and increasing at a rate of \$2 per phone-minute used, so that at 1,000 phone-minutes, total costs increase by \$2,000 (\$2 per phone-minute × 1,000 phone-minutes) to \$5,000 (\$3,000 + \$2,000) and at 2,000 phone-minutes, total costs increase by \$4,000 (\$2 per phone-minute × 2,000 phone-minutes) to \$7,000 (\$3,000 + \$4,000) and so on.

Brief Review of Cost Classification

Let's review briefly Chapter 2's three criteria for classifying a cost into its variable and fixed components.

Choice of Cost Object A particular cost item could be variable with respect to one cost object and fixed with respect to another cost object. Consider Super Shuttle, an airport transportation company. If the fleet of vans it owns is the cost object, then the annual van registration and license costs would be variable costs with respect to the number of vans owned. But if a particular van is the cost object, then the registration and license costs for that van are fixed costs with respect to the miles driven during a year.

Time Horizon Whether a cost is variable or fixed with respect to a particular activity depends on the time horizon being considered in the decision situation. The longer the time horizon, other things being equal, the more likely that the cost will be variable. For example, inspection costs at Boeing Company are typically fixed in the short run with respect to inspection-hours used because inspectors earn a fixed salary in a given year regardless of the number of inspection-hours of work done. But in the long run, Boeing's total inspection costs will vary with the inspection-hours required: More inspectors will be hired if more inspection-hours are needed, and some inspectors will be reassigned to other tasks or laid off if fewer inspection-hours are needed.

Relevant Range Managers should never forget that variable and fixed cost-behavior patterns are valid for linear cost functions only within the given relevant range. Outside the relevant range, variable and fixed cost-behavior patterns change, causing costs to become nonlinear (nonlinear means the plot of the relationship on a graph is not a straight line). For example, Exhibit 10-2 plots the relationship (over several years) between total direct manufacturing labor costs and the number of snowboards produced each year by Ski Authority at its Vermont plant. In this case, the nonlinearities outside the relevant range occur because of labor and other inefficiencies (first because workers are learning to produce snowboards and later because capacity limits are being stretched). Knowing the proper relevant range is essential to properly classify costs.

If you've taken a microeconomics course, the cost function in Exhibit 10-2 should look familiar. Below the relevant range, total costs increase at a decreasing rate due to economies of scale. Above the relevant range, diminishing marginal returns cause total costs to increase at an increasing rate.

EXHIBIT 10-2

Linearity Within Relevant Range for Ski Authority, Inc.

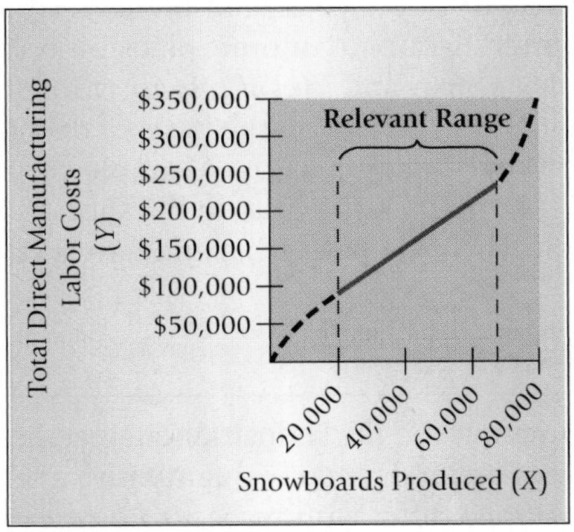

Cost estimation underlies many topics in cost accounting. Examples include CVP analysis (Chapter 3), flexible budgets and variances (Chapters 7 and 8), and variable costing (Chapter 9).

Cost Estimation

The Cannon Services/WWC example illustrates variable-, fixed-, and mixed-cost functions using information about *future* cost structures proposed to Cannon by WWC. Often, however, cost functions are estimated from *past* cost data. Managers use **cost estimation** to measure a relationship based on data from past costs and the related level of an activity. For example, marketing managers at Volkswagen could use cost estimation to understand what causes their marketing costs to change from year to year (for example, the number of cars sold or the number of new car models introduced) and the fixed and variable components of these costs (see Global Surveys of Company Practice, p. 337). Managers are interested in estimating past cost-behavior functions primarily because these estimates can help them make more-accurate **cost predictions**, or forecasts, about future costs. Better cost predictions help managers make more-informed planning and control decisions, such as preparing next year's marketing budget. But better management decisions, cost predictions, and estimation of cost functions can be achieved only if managers correctly identify the factors that affect costs.

The Cause-and-Effect Criterion in Choosing Cost Drivers

The most important issue in estimating a cost function is determining whether a cause-and-effect relationship exists between the level of an activity and the costs related to that level of activity. Without a cause-and-effect relationship, managers will be unable to estimate or predict costs and, therefore, will have difficulty managing those costs. The cause-and-effect relationship might arise as a result of:

- **A physical relationship between the level of activity and costs.** An example is when units of production is used as the activity that affects direct material costs. Producing more units requires more direct materials, which results in higher total direct material costs.
- **A contractual arrangement.** In alternative 1 of the Cannon Services example described earlier, number of phone-minutes used is specified in the contract as the level of activity that affects the telephone line costs.
- **Knowledge of operations.** An example is when number of parts is used as the activity measure of ordering costs. A product with many parts will incur higher ordering costs than a product with few parts.

For many years, church attendance and alcohol consumption were positively correlated. This did not occur because attending church increased people's alcohol consumption or because drinking alcohol promoted piety. Rather, it occurred because of the *increasing population* and its independent effects on both church attendance and alcohol consumption. The lesson: high correlation between two variables does not necessarily mean that a cause-and-effect relationship exists.

Managers must be careful not to interpret a high correlation, or connection, in the relationship between two variables to mean that either variable causes the other. For example, higher production generally results in higher material costs and higher labor costs. Material costs and labor costs are highly correlated, but neither causes the other.

Only a cause-and-effect relationship—not merely correlation—establishes an economically plausible relationship between the level of an activity and its costs. Economic plausibility is critical because it gives analysts and managers confidence that the estimated relationship will appear again and again in other sets of data from the same situation.

Recall from Chapter 2 that when a cause-and-effect relationship exists between a change in the level of an activity and a change in the level of total costs, we refer to the activity measure as a *cost driver*. Because economic plausibility is essential for cost estimation, we use the terms *level of activity* and *level of cost driver* interchangeably when estimating cost functions. To identify cost drivers on the basis of data gathered over time, always use a long time horizon. Why? Because, as our example of inspection costs at Boeing Company illustrates (p. 335), costs may be fixed in the short run (during which time they have no cost driver), but they are usually variable and have a cost driver in the long run.

3

Understand various methods of cost estimation

. . . for example, the regression analysis method determines the line that best fits past data

Cost Estimation Methods

Four methods of cost estimation are the industrial engineering method, the conference method, the account analysis method, and the quantitative analysis method (which takes different forms). These methods differ with respect to how expensive they are to imple-

GLOBAL SURVEYS OF COMPANY PRACTICE

International Comparison of Cost Classification by Companies

Organizations differ in classifying individual costs. A variable-cost item in one organization can be a fixed-cost item in another organization. Consider labor costs. Home construction companies often classify labor cost as a variable cost. These companies rapidly adjust their labor force in response to changes in the demand for housing construction. In contrast, oil-refining companies often classify labor cost as a fixed cost. The labor force is stable even when sizable changes occur in the volume or type of oil products refined.

Surveys indicate significant differences in the percentage of companies in various countries that classify individual cost categories as variable, fixed, or mixed. A lower percentage of U.S. and Australian companies treat labor costs as a fixed cost compared with Japanese companies.

	U.S. Companies			Japanese Companies			Australian Companies		
Cost Category	Variable	Mixed	Fixed	Variable	Mixed	Fixed	Variable	Mixed	Fixed
Production labor	86%	6%	8%	52%	5%	43%	70%	20%	10%
Setup labor	60	25	15	44	6	50	45	33	22
Materials-handling labor	48	34	18	23	16	61	40	30	30
Quality-control labor	34	36	30	13	12	75	21	27	52
Tooling	32	35	33	31	26	43	25	28	47
Energy	26	45	29	42	31	27	—	—	—
Building occupancy	1	6	93	0	0	100	—	—	—
Depreciation	1	7	92	0	0	100	—	—	—

Source: Adapted from the NAA Tokyo Affiliate, "Management Accounting in the Advanced Manufacturing," and Joye and Blayney, "Cost and Management Accounting."
Full citations are in Appendix A at the end of the book.

ment, the assumptions they make, and the information they provide about the accuracy of the estimated cost function. They are not mutually exclusive and many organizations use a combination of these methods.

Industrial Engineering Method

The **industrial engineering method**, also called the **work-measurement method**, estimates cost functions by analyzing the relationship between inputs and outputs in physical terms. Consider Elegant Rugs, a carpet manufacturer that uses inputs of cotton, wool, dyes, direct manufacturing labor, machine time, and power. Production output is square yards of carpet. Time-and-motion studies analyze the time required to perform the various operations to produce the carpet. For example, a time-and-motion study may conclude that to produce 10 square yards of carpet requires one hour of direct manufacturing labor. Standards and budgets transform these physical input measures into costs. The result is an estimated cost function relating direct manufacturing labor costs to the cost driver, square yards of carpet produced.

The industrial engineering method is rooted in studies performed and techniques developed by scientific management pioneers Frank and Lillian Gilbreth in the early twentieth century.

The industrial engineering method is a very thorough and detailed way to estimate a cost function when there is a physical relationship between inputs and outputs, but it can be very time-consuming. Some government contracts mandate its use. Many organizations, such as Bose and Nokia, use it to estimate manufacturing costs but find it too costly or impractical for analyzing their entire cost structure. For example, physical relationships between inputs and outputs are difficult to specify for some individual cost items, such as R&D and advertising.

Conference Method

The **conference method** estimates cost functions on the basis of analysis and opinions about costs and their drivers gathered from various departments of a company (purchasing, process engineering, manufacturing, employee relations, and so on). The Cooperative

Bank in the United Kingdom has a Cost-Estimating Department that develops cost functions for its retail banking products (checking accounts, VISA cards, mortgages, and so on) based on the consensus of estimates from personnel of the particular departments.

The conference method encourages interdepartmental cooperation. The pooling of expert knowledge from each business function of the value chain gives the conference method credibility. Because the conference method does not require detailed analysis of data, cost functions and cost estimates can be developed quickly. However, the emphasis on opinions rather than systematic estimation means that the accuracy of the cost estimates depends largely on the care and skill of the people providing the inputs.[1]

Account Analysis Method

The **account analysis method** estimates cost functions by classifying various cost accounts as variable, fixed, or mixed with respect to the identified level of activity. Typically, managers use qualitative rather than quantitative analysis when making these cost-classification decisions. The account analysis approach is widely used because it is reasonably accurate, cost-effective, and easy to use.

Consider indirect manufacturing labor costs for a small production area (or cell) at Elegant Rugs, which uses state-of-the-art automated weaving machines to produce carpets for homes and offices. Indirect manufacturing labor costs include wages paid for supervision, maintenance, quality control, and setups. During the most recent 12-week period, Elegant Rugs ran the machines in the cell for a total of 862 hours and incurred total indirect manufacturing labor costs of \$12,501. Using qualitative analysis, the manager and the cost analyst determine that indirect manufacturing labor costs are mixed costs. As machine-hours vary, one component of the cost (such as supervision cost) is fixed, whereas another component (such as maintenance cost) is variable. The goal is to use account analysis to estimate a linear cost function for indirect manufacturing labor costs with number of machine-hours as the cost driver. The cost analyst uses experience and judgment to separate total indirect manufacturing labor costs (\$12,501) into costs that are fixed (\$2,157) and costs that are variable (\$10,344) with respect to the number of machine-hours used. Variable cost per machine-hour is \$10,344 ÷ 862 machine-hours = \$12 per machine-hour. The linear cost equation, $y = a + bX$, in this example is:

Indirect manufacturing labor costs = \$2,157 + (\$12 per machine-hour × Number of machine-hours)

The indirect manufacturing labor cost per machine-hour is \$12,501 ÷ 862 machine-hours = \$14.50 per machine-hour. Management at Elegant Rugs can use the cost function to estimate the indirect manufacturing labor costs of using, say, 950 machine-hours to produce carpet in the next 12-week period. Estimated costs equal \$2,157 + (950 machine-hours × \$12 per machine-hour) = \$13,557. The indirect manufacturing labor cost per machine-hour decreases to \$13,557 ÷ 950 machine-hours = \$14.27 per machine-hour, as fixed costs of \$2,157 are spread over a greater number of machine-hours.

To obtain reliable estimates of the fixed and variable components of cost, organizations such as Target take care to ensure that individuals thoroughly knowledgeable about the operations make the cost-classification decisions. Supplementing the account analysis method with the conference method improves credibility.

Quantitative Analysis Method

The industrial engineering, conference, and account analysis methods require less historical data than most quantitative analyses. Consequently, cost estimation for a new product will usually begin with one or more of these three methods. Quantitative analysis may be used for this product later on, after the company collects the necessary historical data.

Quantitative analysis uses a formal mathematical method to fit cost functions to past data observations. Excel is a useful tool for performing quantitative analysis. Columns B and C of Exhibit 10-3 show the breakdown of Elegant Rugs's total machine-hours (862) and total indirect manufacturing labor costs (\$12,501) into weekly data for the most recent 12-week period. Note that the data are paired—for each week there is data for the number of machine-hours and corresponding indirect manufacturing labor costs. For example, week 12 shows 48 machine-hours and indirect manufacturing labor costs of \$963. The next section uses the data in Exhibit 10-3 to illustrate how to estimate a cost function using quantitative analysis.

---

[1]The conference method is further described in W. Winchell, *Realistic Cost Estimating for Manufacturing,* 2nd ed. (Dearborn, MI: Society for Manufacturing Engineers, 1989).

	A	B	C
1	Week	Cost Driver: Machine-Hours	Indirect Manufacturing Labor Costs
2		(X)	(Y)
3	1	68	$1,190
4	2	88	1,211
5	3	62	1,004
6	4	72	917
7	5	60	770
8	6	96	1,456
9	7	78	1,180
10	8	46	710
11	9	82	1,316
12	10	94	1,032
13	11	68	752
14	12	48	963
15	Total	862	$12,501
16			

EXHIBIT 10-3

Weekly Indirect Manufacturing Labor Costs and Machine-Hours for Elegant Rugs

Steps in Estimating a Cost Function Using Quantitative Analysis

There are six steps in estimating a cost function using a quantitative analysis of a past cost relationship.

4

Outline six steps in estimating a cost function using quantitative analysis

. . . the end result (step 6) is to evaluate the cost driver of the estimated cost function

Step 1: Choose the dependent variable
Step 2: Identify the independent variable, or cost driver
Step 3: Collect data on the dependent variable and the cost driver
Step 4: Plot the data
Step 5: Estimate the cost function
Step 6: Evaluate the cost driver of the estimated cost function

Let's take a closer look at quantitative analysis using the Elegant Rugs example.

Step 1: **Choose the dependent variable.** Choice of the **dependent variable** (the cost to be predicted) will depend on the cost function being estimated. In the Elegant Rugs example, the dependent variable is indirect manufacturing labor costs.

Step 2: **Identify the independent variable, or cost driver.** The **independent variable** (level of activity or cost driver) is the factor used to predict the dependent variable (costs). When the cost is an indirect cost, as with Elegant Rugs, the independent variable is also called a cost-allocation base. Although these terms are sometimes used interchangeably, we use the term *cost driver* to describe the independent variable. Frequently, the cost analyst, working with the management team, will cycle through the six steps several times, trying alternative economically plausible cost drivers to identify a cost driver that best fits the data.

A cost driver should have an *economically plausible* relationship with the dependent variable and be measurable. Economic plausibility means that the relationship (describing how changes in the cost driver lead to changes in the costs being considered) is based on a physical relationship, a contract, or knowledge of operations and makes economic sense to the operating manager and the management accountant. All the individual items of costs included in the dependent variable should have the same cost driver. When all items of costs in the dependent variable do not have the same cost driver, the cost analyst should investigate the possibility of estimating more than one cost function, one for each cost item/cost driver pair.

The chapter focuses on a single independent variable or cost driver. The appendix to this chapter (pp. 361–363) describes how multiple cost drivers can be used to predict a cost.

As an example, consider several types of fringe benefits paid to employees and the cost drivers of the benefits:

Fringe Benefit	Cost Driver
Health benefits	Number of employees
Cafeteria meals	Number of employees
Pension benefits	Salaries of employees
Life insurance	Salaries of employees

The costs of health benefits and cafeteria meals can be combined into one cost pool because they both have the same cost driver—the number of employees. Pension benefits and life insurance costs have a different cost driver—the salaries of employees—and, therefore, should not be combined with health benefits and cafeteria meals. Instead, pension benefits and life insurance should be combined into a separate cost pool. Using that cost pool, pension benefits and life insurance costs can be estimated using salaries of employees receiving these benefits as the cost driver.

Step 3: Collect data on the dependent variable and the cost driver. This is usually the most difficult step in cost analysis. Cost analysts obtain data from company documents, from interviews with managers, and through special studies. These data may be time-series data or cross-sectional data.

Time-series data pertain to the same entity (organization, plant, activity, and so on) over successive past periods. Weekly observations of indirect manufacturing labor costs and number of machine-hours at Elegant Rugs are examples of time-series data. The ideal time-series database would contain numerous observations for a company whose operations have not been affected by economic or technological change. A stable economy and technology ensure that data collected during the estimation period represent the same underlying relationship between the cost driver and the dependent variable. Moreover, the periods (for example, daily, weekly, or monthly) used to measure the dependent variable and the cost driver should be consistent throughout the observations.

Cross-sectional data pertain to different entities during the same period. For example, studies of loans processed and the related personnel costs at 50 individual, yet similar branches of a bank during March 2006 would produce cross-sectional data for that month. Later on in the chapter, we describe the problems that arise in data collection.

Step 4: Plot the data. The general relationship between the cost driver and the costs can be readily observed in a graphical representation of the data, which is commonly called a plot of the data. Moreover, the plot highlights extreme observations (observations outside the general pattern) that analysts should check. Was there an error in recording the data or an unusual event, such as a work stoppage, that makes these observations unrepresentative of the normal relationship between the cost driver and the costs? Plotting the data also provides insight into whether the relationship is approximately linear and what the relevant range of the cost function is.

If there were extreme observations, the manager would need to find out if these observations were correct or the result of an error. If correct, managers would include the observations if they were representative and discard them if they were unusual.

Exhibit 10-4 is a plot of the weekly data from columns B and C of the Excel spreadsheet in Exhibit 10-3. This graph provides strong visual evidence of a positive linear relationship between number of machine-hours and indirect manufacturing labor costs (that is, when machine-hours go up, so do indirect manufacturing labor costs). There do not appear to be any extreme observations in Exhibit 10-4. The relevant range is from 46 to 96 machine-hours per week (weeks 8 and 6, respectively).

Step 5: Estimate the cost function. We will show two ways to estimate the cost function for our Elegant Rugs data. One uses the high-low method, and the other uses regression analysis, the two most frequently described forms of quantitative analysis. We show these after Step 6.

Step 6: Evaluate the cost driver of the estimated cost function. In this step, we describe criteria for evaluating the cost driver of the estimated cost function. We do this after illustrating the high-low method and regression analysis.

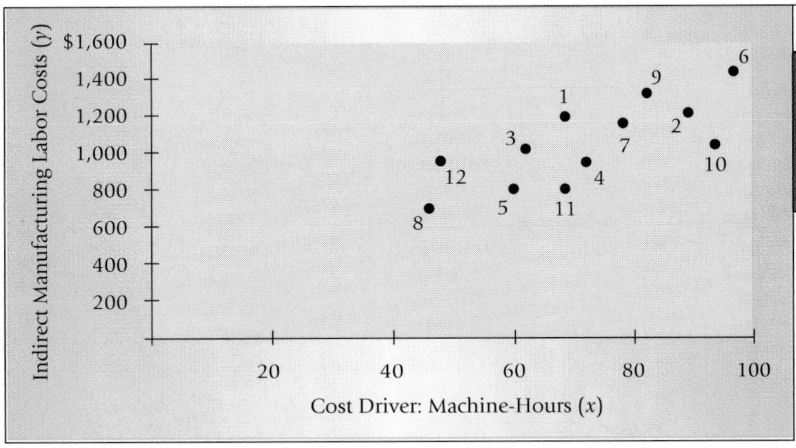

EXHIBIT 10-4

Plot of Weekly Indirect Manufacturing Labor Costs and Machine-Hours for Elegant Rugs

High-Low Method

The simplest form of quantitative analysis is the **high-low method**. It uses only the highest and lowest observed values of the cost driver within the relevant range and their respective costs. The cost function is estimated by using these two points to calculate the slope coefficient and the constant or intercept. We illustrate the high-low method using data from Exhibit 10-3.

	Cost Driver: Machine-Hours (X)	Indirect Manufacturing Labor Costs (Y)
Highest observation of cost driver (week 6)	96	$1,456
Lowest observation of cost driver (week 8)	46	710
Difference	50	$ 746

The slope coefficient, b, is calculated as:

$$\text{Slope coefficient} = \frac{\text{Difference between costs associated with highest and lowest observations of the cost driver}}{\text{Difference between highest and lowest observations of the cost driver}}$$

$$= \$746 \div 50 \text{ machine-hours} = \$14.92 \text{ per machine-hour}$$

To compute the constant, we can use either the highest or the lowest observation of the cost driver. Both calculations yield the same answer because the solution technique solves two linear equations with two unknowns, the slope coefficient and the constant. Because

$$y = a + bX$$
$$a = y - bX$$

therefore, at the highest observation of the cost driver, the constant, a, is calculated as:

$$\text{Constant} = \$1{,}456 - (\$14.92 \text{ per machine-hour} \times 96 \text{ machine-hours}) = \$23.68$$

And at the lowest observation of the cost driver,

$$\text{Constant} = \$710 - (\$14.92 \text{ per machine-hour} \times 46 \text{ machine-hours}) = \$23.68$$

Thus, the high-low estimate of the cost function is:

$$y = a + bX$$
$$y = \$23.68 + (\$14.92 \text{ per machine-hour} \times \text{Number of machine-hours})$$

The maroon line in Exhibit 10-5 shows the estimated cost function using the high-low method (based on the data in Exhibit 10-3). The estimated cost function is a straight line

EXHIBIT 10-5

High-Low Method for Weekly Indirect Manufacturing Labor Costs and Machine-Hours for Elegant Rugs

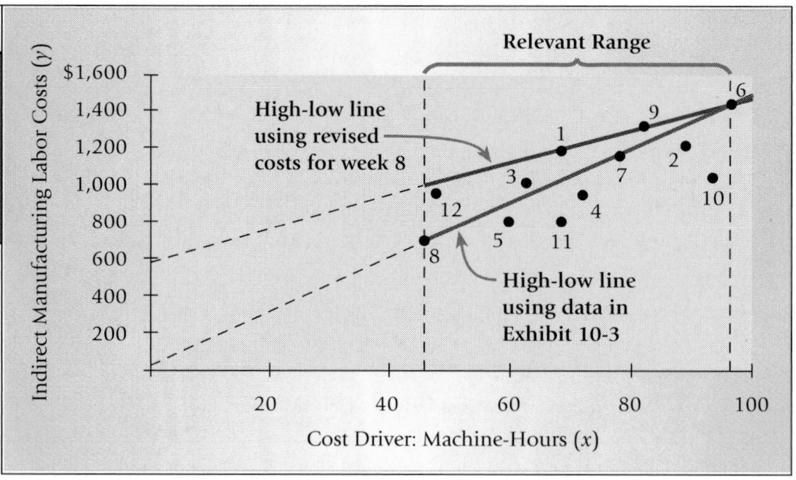

joining the observations with the highest and lowest values of the cost driver (machine-hours). The intercept (a = \$23.68), the point where the dashed extension of the maroon line meets the y-axis, is the constant component of the equation that provides the best linear approximation of how a cost behaves *within the relevant range* of 46 to 96 machine-hours. The intercept should *not* be interpreted as an estimate of the fixed costs of Elegant Rugs if no machines were run. That's because running no machines and shutting down the plant—that is, using zero machine-hours—is *outside the relevant range*.

Suppose indirect manufacturing labor costs in week 6 were $1,280, instead of $1,456, while 96 machine-hours were used. In this case, the highest observation of the cost driver (96 machine-hours in week 6) will not coincide with the newer highest observation of the costs ($1,316 in week 9). How would this change affect our high-low calculation? Given that the cause-and-effect relationship runs *from* the cost driver *to* the costs in a cost function, we choose the highest and lowest observations of the cost driver (the factor that causes the costs to change). The high-low method would still estimate the new cost function using data from weeks 6 (high) and 8 (low).

There is a danger of relying on only two observations to estimate a cost function. Suppose that because a labor contract guarantees certain minimum payments in week 8, indirect manufacturing labor costs in week 8 were $1,000, instead of $710, when only 46 machine-hours were used. The blue-green line in Exhibit 10-5 shows the cost function that would be estimated by the high-low method using this revised cost. Other than the two points used to draw the line, all other data lie on or below the line! In this case, choosing the highest and lowest observations for machine-hours would result in an estimated cost function that poorly describes the underlying linear cost relationship between number of machine-hours and indirect manufacturing labor costs.

Sometimes the high-low method is modified so that the two observations chosen are a *representative high* and a *representative low*. Managers use this modification to avoid having extreme observations, which arise from abnormal events and affect the cost function. The modification allows managers to estimate a cost function that is representative of the relationship between the cost driver and costs and therefore is more useful for making decisions (such as pricing and performance evaluation) based on the estimated cost function. The advantage of the high-low method is that it is simple to compute and easy to understand; the disadvantage is that it ignores information from all but two observations when estimating the cost function.

Regression Analysis Method

If you've taken a statistics course, you might not think there is much connection between regression analysis and accounting. But this section shows an important accounting application for regression analysis.

The regression analysis method of quantitative analysis uses all available data to estimate the cost function. **Regression analysis** is a statistical method that measures the average amount of change in the dependent variable associated with a unit change in one or more independent variables. In the Elegant Rugs example, the dependent variable is total indirect manufacturing labor costs. The independent variable, or cost driver, is number of machine-hours. **Simple regression** analysis estimates the relationship between the dependent variable and *one* independent variable. **Multiple regression** analysis estimates the relationship between the dependent variable and *two or more* independent variables.

Multiple regression analysis for Elegant Rugs might use as the independent variables, or cost drivers, number of machine-hours and number of batches. The appendix to this chapter will explore simple regression and multiple regression in more detail.

In later sections, we will illustrate how Excel performs the calculations associated with regression analysis. The following discussion emphasizes how managers interpret and use the output from Excel to make critical strategic decisions. Exhibit 10-6 shows the line developed using regression analysis that best fits the data in columns B and C of Exhibit 10-3. Excel estimates the cost function to be

$$y = \$300.98 + \$10.31X$$

The regression line in Exhibit 10-6 is derived using the least-squares technique (explained in more detail in the appendix). The least-squares technique determines the regression line by minimizing the sum of the squared vertical differences from the data points (the various points in the graph) to the regression line. The vertical difference, called **residual term**, measures the distance between actual cost and estimated cost for each observation. Exhibit 10-6 shows the residual term for the week 1 data. The line from the observation to the regression line is drawn perpendicular to the horizontal axis, or *x*-axis. The smaller the residual terms, the better the fit between actual cost observations and estimated costs. *Goodness of fit* indicates the strength of the relationship between the cost driver and costs. The regression line in Exhibit 10-6 rises from left to right. The positive slope of this line and small residual terms indicate that, on average, indirect manufacturing labor costs increase as the number of machine-hours increases. The vertical dashed lines in Exhibit 10-6 indicate the relevant range, the range within which the cost function applies.

The regression line is fitted through a set of observations so that it best represents the underlying relationship or pattern in the observations.

The estimate of the slope coefficient, *b*, indicates that indirect manufacturing labor costs vary at the average amount of $10.31 for every machine-hour used within the relevant range. Management can use the regression equation when budgeting for future indirect manufacturing labor costs. For instance, if 90 machine-hours are budgeted for the upcoming week, the predicted indirect manufacturing labor costs would be

$$y = \$300.98 + (\$10.31 \text{ per machine-hour} \times 90 \text{ machine-hours}) = \$1{,}228.88$$

The regression method is more accurate than the high-low method because the regression equation estimates costs using information from all observations, whereas the high-low equation uses information from only two observations. The inaccuracies of the high-low method can mislead managers. Consider the high-low equation in the preceding section, y = $23.68 + $14.92 per machine-hour. For 90 machine-hours, the predicted weekly cost based on the high-low equation is $23.68 + ($14.92 per machine-hour × 90 machine-hours) = $1,366.48. Suppose that for 7 weeks over the next 12-week period, Elegant Rugs runs its machines for 90 hours each week. Assume average indirect manufacturing labor costs for those 7 weeks are $1,300. Based on the high-low prediction of $1,366.48, Elegant Rugs would conclude it has performed well because actual costs are less than predicted costs. But comparing the $1,300 performance with the more-accurate $1,228.88 prediction of the regression model tells a

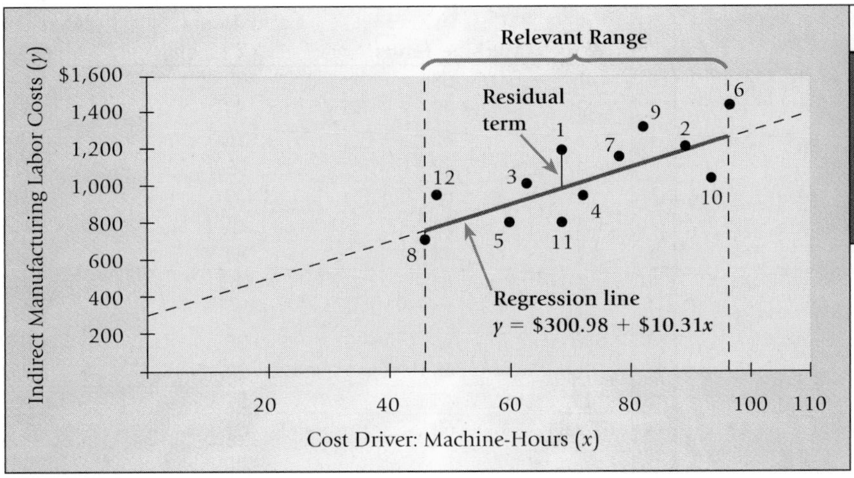

EXHIBIT 10-6

Regression Model for Weekly Indirect Manufacturing Labor Costs and Machine-Hours for Elegant Rugs

much different story and would probably prompt Elegant Rugs to search for ways to improve its cost performance.

Accurate cost estimation helps managers predict future costs and evaluate the success of cost-reduction initiatives. Suppose the manager at Elegant Rugs is interested in evaluating whether recent strategic decisions that led to changes in the production process and resulted in the data in Exhibit 10-3 have reduced indirect manufacturing labor costs, such as supervision, maintenance, and quality control. Using data on number of machine-hours used and indirect manufacturing labor costs of the previous process, the manager estimates the regression equation,

$$y = \$545.26 + (\$15.86 \text{ per machine-hour} \times \text{number of machine-hours})$$

The constant ($300.98 versus $545.26) and the slope coefficient ($10.31 versus $15.86) are both smaller than before. It appears that the new process has decreased indirect manufacturing labor costs.

Evaluating Cost Drivers of the Estimated Cost Function

How does a company determine the best cost driver when estimating a cost function? In many cases, the choice of a cost driver is aided substantially by understanding both operations and cost accounting.

To see why understanding operations is needed, consider the costs to maintain and repair metal-cutting machines at Helix Corporation, a manufacturer of treadmills. Helix schedules repairs and maintenance at a time when production is at a low level to avoid having to take machines out of service when they are needed most. An analysis of the monthly data will then show high repair costs in months of low production and low repair costs in months of high production. Someone unfamiliar with operations might conclude that there is an inverse relationship between production and repair costs. The engineering link between units produced and repair costs, however, is usually clear-cut. Over time, there is a cause-and-effect relationship: the higher the level of production, the higher the repair costs. To estimate the relationship correctly, operating managers and analysts will recognize that repair costs will tend to lag behind periods of high production, and hence, they will use production of the prior period as the cost driver.

In other cases, choosing a cost driver is more subtle and difficult. Consider again indirect manufacturing labor costs at Elegant Rugs. Management believes that both the number of machine-hours and the number of direct manufacturing labor-hours are plausible cost drivers of indirect manufacturing labor costs. However, management is not sure which is the better cost driver. (See the Focus on Values and Behaviors feature on p. 346.) Exhibit 10-7 presents weekly data (in Excel) on indirect manufacturing labor costs and number of

EXHIBIT 10-7

Weekly Indirect Manufacturing Labor Costs, Machine-Hours, and Direct Manufacturing Labor-Hours for Elegant Rugs

	A	B	C	D
1	Week	Original Cost Driver: Machine-Hours	Alternative Cost Driver: Direct Manufacturing Labor-Hours (X)	Indirect Manufacturing Labor Costs (Y)
2	1	68	30	$ 1,190
3	2	88	35	1,211
4	3	62	36	1,004
5	4	72	20	917
6	5	60	47	770
7	6	96	45	1,456
8	7	78	44	1,180
9	8	46	38	710
10	9	82	70	1,316
11	10	94	30	1,032
12	11	68	29	752
13	12	48	38	963
14	Total	862	462	$12,501
15				

machine-hours for the most recent 12-week period from Exhibit 10-3, together with data on the number of direct manufacturing labor-hours for the same period.

What guidance do the different cost-estimation methods provide for choosing among cost drivers? The industrial engineering method relies on analyzing physical relationships between cost drivers and costs, relationships that are difficult to specify in this case. The conference method and the account analysis method use subjective assessments to choose a cost driver and to estimate the fixed and variable components of the cost function. In these cases, managers must rely on their best judgment. Managers cannot use these methods to test and try alternative cost drivers. The major advantages of quantitative methods are that they are objective—a given data set and estimation method result in a unique estimated cost function—and managers can use them to evaluate different cost drivers. We use the regression analysis approach to illustrate how to evaluate different cost drivers.

First, the cost analyst at Elegant Rugs enters data in columns C and D of Exhibit 10-7 in Excel and estimates the following regression equation of indirect manufacturing labor costs based on number of direct manufacturing labor-hours:

$$y = \$744.67 + \$7.72X$$

Exhibit 10-8 shows the plots of the data points for number of direct manufacturing labor-hours and indirect manufacturing labor costs, and the regression line that best fits the data. Exhibit 10-6 shows the corresponding graph when number of machine-hours is the cost driver. To decide which of the two cost drivers Elegant Rugs should choose, the analyst compares the machine-hour regression equation and the direct manufacturing labor-hour regression equation. There are three criteria used to make this evaluation.

1. **Economic plausibility.** Both cost drivers are economically plausible. However, in the state-of-the-art, highly automated production environment at Elegant Rugs, managers familiar with the operations believe that costs such as machine maintenance are likely to be more closely related to number of machine-hours used than to number of direct manufacturing labor-hours used.
2. **Goodness of fit.** Compare Exhibits 10-6 and 10-8. The vertical differences between actual costs and predicted costs are much smaller for the machine-hours regression than for the direct manufacturing labor-hours regression. Number of machine-hours used, therefore, has a stronger relationship—or goodness of fit—with indirect manufacturing labor costs.
3. **Significance of independent variable.** Again compare Exhibits 10-6 and 10-8 (both of which have been drawn to the same scale). The machine-hours regression line has a steep slope relative to the slope of the direct manufacturing labor-hours regression line. *For the same (or more) scatter of observations about the line (goodness of fit)*, a flat, or slightly sloped regression line indicates a weak relationship between the cost driver and costs. In our example, changes in direct manufacturing labor-hours appear to have a small influence or effect on indirect manufacturing labor costs.

As in most applications, the cost function in the Elegant Rugs example is not valid at shutdown ($x = 0$) because that point is outside the relevant range (see Exhibit 10-8). That is, the y-intercept, \$744.67, is not the fixed costs at 0 direct manufacturing labor-hours because at shutdown many costs can be avoided (for example, laying off salaried personnel). In this example, the \$744.67 is simply the constant component of the regression equation that provides the best linear fit of the data.

5

Describe three criteria used to evaluate and choose cost drivers

. . . economically plausible relationships, goodness of fit, and significant effect of the cost driver on costs

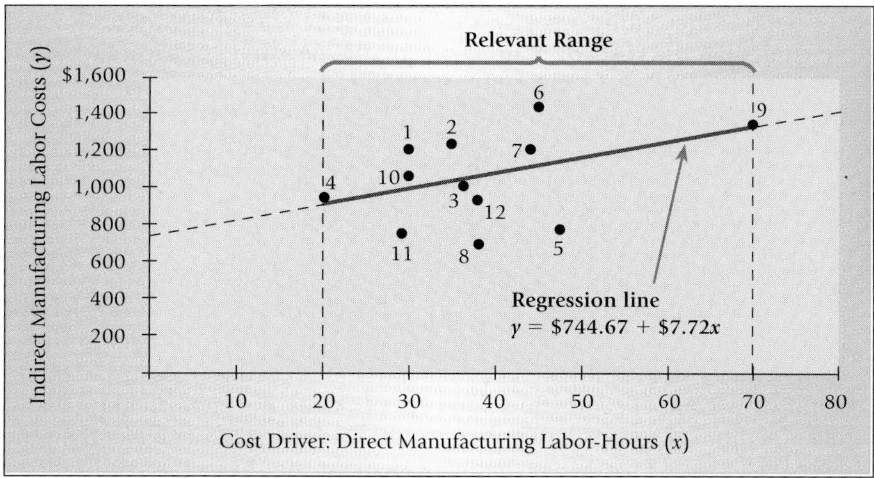

EXHIBIT 10-8

Regression Model for Weekly Indirect Manufacturing Labor Costs and Direct Manufacturing Labor-Hours for Elegant Rugs

FOCUS ON VALUES AND BEHAVIORS

BOEING'S MANAGEMENT ACCOUNTANTS: EMBRACING OPPORTUNITIES AND TACKLING CHALLENGES

Understanding how costs behave is a valuable technical skill. Managers look to management accountants to help them identify cost drivers, estimate cost relationships, and determine the fixed and variable components of costs. To be effective, management accountants must have a clear understanding of the business operations and must be seen as vital members of the management team. They must also be able to convey their findings so that managers who are unfamiliar with the technical details can understand the issues in a way that is helpful when making decisions.

Let's consider an example. Chicago-based Boeing landed the role of lead systems integrator (LSI) for a multiyear, $14.8-billion defense missile-shield contract with the U.S. government. This deal could lead to 20 years and $100 billion worth of work on military combat systems. The contract shifts Boeing toward more software-based programs and more management roles instead of pure military hardware manufacturing. This is a great opportunity for Boeing, but these new opportunities also create many challenges. As LSI, Boeing must hire contractors and collect fees for overseeing projects, which means examining unfamiliar categories of costs. For Boeing's management accountants, helping to determine the underlying cost drivers involved in this strategic shift—from manufacturer to contractor—is critical, as is the ability to help managers estimate new cost relationships and fixed and variable costs.

Determining cost drivers is not simply an analytical skill but one that requires good judgment. A manager may exert pressure on management accountants to favor one cost driver over another—perhaps because it reduces the costs assigned to the manager's pet project or because it makes the manager's performance look better. If management accountants want to ensure that their analysis is sound and that the decisions based on their analysis are value-enhancing, they should never be persuaded by unethical pressures from management.

Source: *Julie Creswell, "Boeing's Defense,"* Fortune, *April 19, 2004.*

In the Elegant Rugs example, machine-hours dominated direct manufacturing labor-hours on all three criteria. But what if this were not the case? Then, economic plausibility would be the most important criterion. Statistical techniques can be used to evaluate tradeoffs between the other two criteria: goodness of fit and significance of independent variable.

Based on this evaluation, managers at Elegant Rugs select number of machine-hours as the cost driver and use the cost function y = \$300.98 + (\$10.31 per machine-hour × number of machine-hours) to predict future indirect manufacturing labor costs.

Why is choosing the correct cost driver to estimate indirect manufacturing labor costs important? Consider the following strategic decision that management at Elegant Rugs must make. The company is thinking of introducing a new style of carpet that, from a manufacturing standpoint, is similar to the carpets it has manufactured in the past. Sales of 650 square yards of this carpet are expected each week. Management estimates 72 machine-hours and 21 direct manufacturing labor-hours would be required per week to produce the 650 square yards of carpet needed. Using the machine-hour regression equation, Elegant Rugs would predict indirect manufacturing labor costs of y = \$300.98 + (\$10.31 per machine-hour × 72 machine-hours) = \$1,043.30. If it used direct manufacturing labor-hours as the cost driver, it would incorrectly predict costs of \$744.67 + (\$7.72 per labor-hour × 21 labor-hours) = \$906.79. If Elegant Rugs chose similarly incorrect cost drivers for other indirect costs as well and systematically underestimated costs, it would conclude that the costs of manufacturing the new style of carpet would be low and basically fixed (fixed because the regression line is nearly flat). But the actual costs driven by number of machine-hours used and other correct cost drivers would be higher. By failing to identify the proper cost drivers, management would be misled into believing the new style of carpet would be more profitable than it actually is. It might decide to introduce the new style of carpet, whereas if Elegant identifies the correct cost driver it might decide not to introduce the new carpet.

Incorrectly estimating the cost function would also have repercussions for cost management and cost control. Suppose number of direct manufacturing labor-hours were used as the cost driver, and actual indirect manufacturing labor costs for the new carpet were \$970. Actual costs would then be higher than the predicted costs of \$906.79. Management would feel compelled to find ways to cut costs. In fact, on the basis of the preferred machine-hour cost driver, the plant would have actual costs lower than the \$1,043.30 predicted costs—a performance that management should seek to replicate, not change!

Cost Drivers and Activity-Based Costing

Activity-based costing (ABC) systems focus on individual activities—such as product design, machine setup, materials handling, distribution, and customer service—as the fundamental cost objects. To implement ABC systems, managers must identify a cost driver for each activity. For example, using methods described in this chapter, the manager must decide whether the number of loads moved or the weight of loads moved is the cost driver of materials-handling costs.

To choose the cost driver and use it to estimate the cost function in our materials-handling example, the manager collects data on materials-handling costs and the quantities of the two competing cost drivers over a reasonably long period. Why a long period? Because in the short run, materials-handling costs may be fixed and, therefore, will not vary with changes in the level of the cost driver. In the long run, however, there is a clear cause-and-effect relationship between materials-handling costs and the cost driver. Suppose number of loads moved is the cost driver of materials-handling costs. Increases in the number of loads moved will require more materials-handling labor and equipment; decreases will result in equipment being sold and labor being reassigned to other tasks.

ABC systems have a great number and variety of cost drivers and cost pools. That means ABC systems require many cost relationships to be estimated. In estimating the cost function for each cost pool, the manager must pay careful attention to the cost hierarchy. For example, if a cost is a batch-level cost such as setup cost, the manager must only consider batch-level cost drivers like number of setup-hours. In some cases, the costs in a cost pool may have more than one cost driver. In the Elegant Rugs example, the cost drivers for indirect manufacturing labor costs could be machine-hours and number of production batches of carpet manufactured. Furthermore, it may be difficult to subdivide the indirect manufacturing labor costs into two cost pools and to measure the costs associated with each cost driver. In these cases, companies use multiple regression to estimate costs based on more than one independent variable. The appendix to this chaper discusses multiple regression in more detail.

A cost hierarchy categorizes costs into different cost pools on the basis of the different types of cost drivers. A common four part cost hierarchy is output unit-level costs, batch-level costs, product-sustaining costs, and facility-sustaining costs (see pp. 147–148).

As the Concepts in Action feature (p. 348) indicates, managers implementing ABC systems use a variety of methods—industrial engineering, conference, and regression analysis—to estimate slope coefficients. In making these choices, managers trade off level of detail, accuracy, feasibility, and costs of estimating cost functions.

Nonlinearity and Cost Functions

6

Explain and give examples of nonlinear cost functions

. . . graph of cost function is not a straight line, for example, because of quantity discounts or costs changing in steps

In practice, cost functions are not always linear. A **nonlinear cost function** is a cost function for which the graph of total costs (based on the level of a single activity) is not a straight line within the relevant range. To see what a nonlinear cost function looks like, return to Exhibit 10-2 (p. 335), but now let's expand the relevant range from 0 to 80,000 snowboards produced from the original relevant range of 20,000 to 65,000. You can see that the cost function over this expanded range is graphically represented by a line that is not a straight line.

Consider another example. Economies of scale in advertising may enable an advertising agency to double the number of advertisements generated for less than double the costs. Even direct material costs are not always linear variable costs because of quantity discounts on direct material purchases. As shown in Exhibit 10-9 (p. 349), Panel A, total direct material costs rise as the units of direct materials purchased increase. But, because of quantity discounts, these costs rise more slowly (as indicated by the slope coefficient) as the units of direct materials purchased increase. This cost function has b = \$25 per unit for 1 to 1,000 units purchased, b = \$15 per unit for 1,001 to 2,000 units purchased, and b = \$10 per unit for 2,001 to 3,000 units purchased. The direct material cost per unit falls at each price break—that is, the cost per unit decreases with larger purchase orders. If managers are interested in understanding cost behavior over the relevant range from 1 to 3,000 units, the cost function is nonlinear—not a straight line. If, however, managers are only interested in understanding cost behavior over a more narrow relevant range (for example, from 1 to 1,000 units), the cost function is linear.

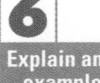

CONCEPTS IN ACTION

Activity-Based Costing: Identifying Cost and Revenue Drivers

Many cost estimation methods presented in this chapter are essential to service- and retail-sector implementations of activity-based costing. To determine the cost of an activity in the banking industry, ABC systems often rely on expert analyses and opinions gathered from operating personnel (the conference method). For example, the Loan Department staff at the Cooperative Bank in the United Kingdom subjectively estimate the costs of the loan processing activity and the quantity of the related cost driver—the number of loans processed, a batch-level cost driver, as distinguished from the amount of the loans, an output unit-level cost driver—to derive the cost of processing a loan.

ABC systems in government agencies, in contrast, frequently use input-output relationships (the industrial engineering method) to identify cost drivers and the cost of an activity. The City of Indianapolis Department of Transportation uses work-measurement methods to determine the direct and indirect costs associated with its 35 primary activities. At the federal government level, similar processes have helped the U.S. Postal Service determine the cost of each post office transaction and the Patent and Trademark Office identify the costs of each patent examination.

Regression analysis is another helpful tool for determining the cost drivers of activities. Consider how fuel service retailers (that is, gas stations with convenience stores) identify the principal cost driver for labor within their operations. Two possible cost drivers are gasoline sales and convenience store sales. Gasoline sales are batch-level activities because payment transactions occur only once for each gasoline purchase, regardless of the volume of gasoline purchased; whereas convenience store sales are output unit-level activities that vary based on the amount of food, drink, and other products sold. Fuel service retailers generally use convenience store sales as the basis for assigning labor costs because multiple regression analyses confirm that convenience store sales, not gasoline sales, are the major cost driver of labor.

Can these cost estimation methods also be used to identify drivers of revenue? For example, how should banks structure their certificate of deposit (CD) offerings? At First Tennessee Banking Corporation, the cost of processing a CD is fixed regardless of the amount of the certificate, but the revenue is a function of the dollar amount of the certificate. Therefore, a 90-day $500 CD that is reopened four times a year generates only $5 a year on a 1% interest spread, which is considerably less revenue than the cost of processing the transactions. By applying ABC concepts and using the conference method, First Tennessee found that 30% of its CD offerings were providing 88% of CD profits, while another 30% of CDs were serviced at a loss of 7%. As a result of these findings, management worked to enhance revenues through a combination of higher minimum balances, new products, and process redesign.

Source: Based on "The Cooperative Bank," Harvard Business School Case No. N9-195-196; City of Indianapolis: "Activity-Based Costing of City Services (A)," Harvard Business School Case No. N9-196-115; Barton, T., and J. MacArthur, "Activity-Based Costing and Predatory Pricing: The Case of the Petroleum Retail Industry," *Management Accounting Quarterly* (Spring 2003); Carter, T., A. Sedaghat, and T. Williams, "How ABC Changed the Post Office," *Management Accounting* (February 1998); Peckenpaugh, J., "Teaching the ABCs," *Government Executive* (April 2002); and Sweeney, R., and J. Mays, "ABM," *Management Accounting* (March 1997).

Step cost functions are also examples of nonlinear cost functions. A **step cost function** is a cost function in which the cost remains the same over various ranges of the level of activity, but the cost increases by discrete amounts—that is, increases in steps—as the level of activity increases from one range to the next. Panel B in Exhibit 10-9 shows a *step variable-cost function,* a step cost function in which cost remains the same over *narrow* ranges of the level of activity in each relevant range. Panel B presents the relationship between units of production and setup costs. The pattern is a step cost function because, as we described in Chapter 5 on activity-based costing, setup costs are related to each production batch started. If the relevant range is considered to be from 0 to 6,000 production units, the cost function is nonlinear. However, as shown by the blue-green line in Panel B, managers often approximate step variable costs with a continuously-variable cost function. This type of step cost pattern also occurs when production inputs such as materials-handling labor, supervision, and process engineering labor are acquired in discrete quantities but used in fractional quantities.

EXHIBIT 10-9 Examples of Nonlinear Cost Functions

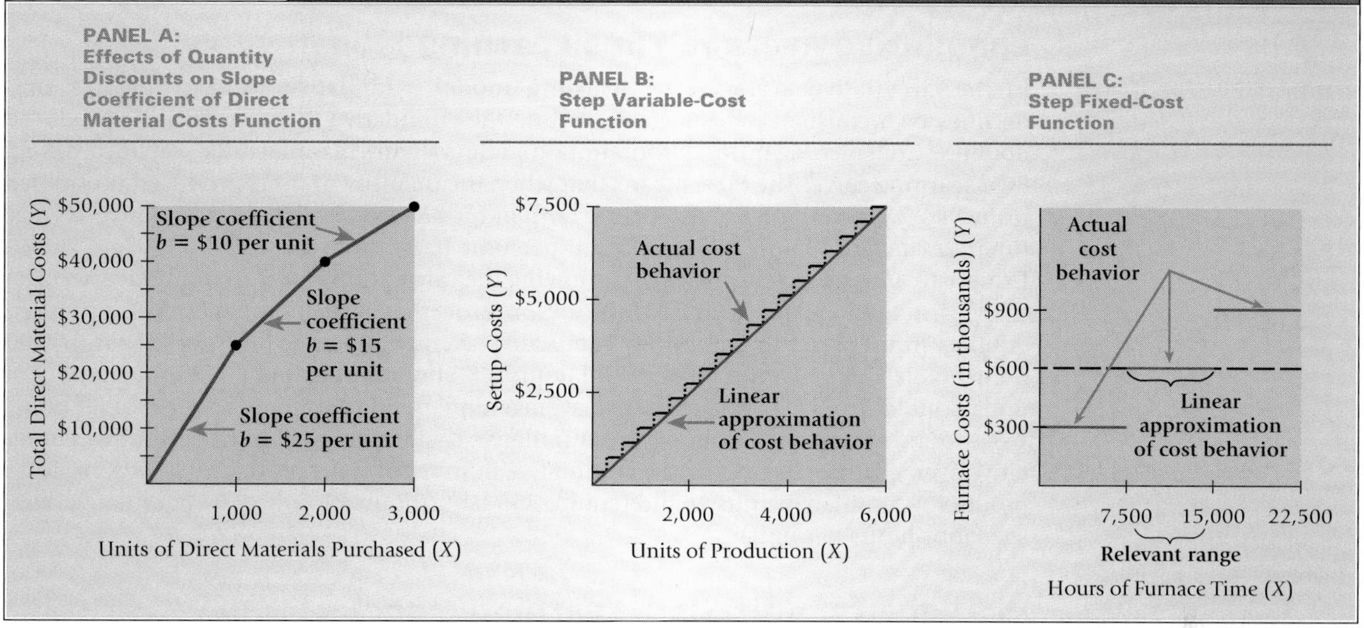

Panel C in Exhibit 10-9 shows a *step fixed-cost function* for Crofton Steel, a company that operates large heat-treatment furnaces to harden steel parts. Looking at Panel C and Panel B, you can see that the main difference between a step variable-cost function and a step fixed-cost function is that the cost in a step fixed-cost function remains the same over *wide* ranges of the activity in each relevant range. The ranges indicate the number of furnaces being used (each furnace costs $300,000). The cost increases from one range to the next higher range when the hours of furnace time needed require the use of another furnace. The relevant range of 7,500 to 15,000 hours of furnace time indicates that the company expects to operate with two furnaces at a cost of $600,000. Management considers the cost of operating furnaces as a fixed cost within this relevant range of operation. However, if the relevant range is considered to be from 0 to 22,500 hours, the cost function is nonlinear: The graph in Panel C is not a single straight line; it is three broken lines.

Effective cost management utilizes a particular level of step fixed costs as fully as possible (that is, on a particular step, operate as far to the right side as feasible). For example, in Panel C of Exhibit 10-9, needing 15,000 hours of furnace time will fully utilize two furnaces.

Learning Curves and Nonlinear Cost Functions

Nonlinear cost functions also result from learning curves. A **learning curve** is a function that measures how labor-hours per unit decline as units of production increase because workers are learning and becoming better at their jobs. Managers use learning curves to predict how labor-hours, or labor costs, will increase as more units are produced.

The aircraft-assembly industry first documented the effect that learning has on efficiency. In general, as workers become more familiar with their tasks, their efficiency improves. Managers learn how to improve the scheduling of work shifts. Managers learn how to operate the plant better. As a result of improved efficiency, unit costs decrease as productivity increases, and the unit-cost function behaves nonlinearly. These nonlinearities must be considered when estimating and predicting unit costs.

Managers have extended the learning-curve notion to other business functions in the value chain, such as marketing, distribution, and customer service, and to costs other than labor costs. The term *experience curve* describes this broader application of the learning curve. An **experience curve** is a function that measures the decline in cost per unit in various business functions of the value chain—marketing, distribution, and so on—as the amount of these activities increases. For companies such as Dell Computer, Wal-Mart, and McDonald's, learning curves and experience curves are key elements of their strategies. These companies use learning curves and experience curves to reduce costs and increase customer satisfaction, market share, and profitability.

We now describe two learning-curve models: the cumulative average-time learning model and the incremental unit-time learning model.

7

Distinguish the cumulative average-time learning model

. . . average time per unit declines by constant percentage, as units produced double

from the incremental unit-time learning model

. . . incremental time to produce last unit declines by constant percentage, as units produced double

Cumulative Average-Time Learning Model

In the **cumulative average-time learning model**, cumulative average time per unit declines by a constant percentage each time the cumulative quantity of units produced doubles. Consider Rayburn Corporation, a radar systems manufacturer. Rayburn has an 80% learning curve. The 80% means that when the quantity of units produced is doubled from X to $2X$, cumulative average time *per unit* for $2X$ units is 80% of cumulative average time *per unit* for X units. Average time per unit has dropped by 20% (100% – 80%). Exhibit 10-10 is an Excel spreadsheet showing the calculations for the cumulative average-time learning model for Rayburn Corporation. Note that as the number of units produced doubles from 1 to 2 in column 1, cumulative average time per unit declines from 100 hours to 80% of 100 hours (0.80 × 100 hours = 80 hours) in column 2. As the number of units doubles from 2 to 4, cumulative average time per unit declines to 80% of 80 hours = 64 hours, and so on. To obtain the cumulative total time in column 3, multiply cumulative average time per unit by the cumulative number of units produced. For example, to produce 4 cumulative units would require 256 labor-hours (4 units × 64 cumulative average labor-hours per unit).

Question: Does a higher learning percentage (say, 90% rather than 80%) indicate a faster rate of learning?

Answer: No, a higher learning percentage actually indicates a *slower* rate of learning. For example, consider in Exhibit 10-10 the row for two cumulative units. Under this 80% learning curve, the cumulative average time per unit is 80 labor-hours. If the rate of learning had been 90%, the cumulative average time per unit would have been 90 labor-hours (100 × 0.90).

Incremental Unit-Time Learning Model

In the **incremental unit-time learning model**, incremental time needed to produce the last unit declines by a constant percentage each time the cumulative quantity of units produced doubles. Again, consider Rayburn Corporation and an 80% learning curve. The 80% here means that when the quantity of units produced is doubled from X to $2X$, the time needed to produce the last unit when $2X$ total units are produced is 80% of the time needed to produce the last unit when X total units are produced. Exhibit 10-11 is an Excel spreadsheet showing the calculations for the incremental unit-time learning model for Rayburn Corporation based on an 80% learning curve. Note how when units produced double from 2 to 4 in column 1, the time to produce unit 4 (the last unit when 4 units are produced) is 64 hours in column 2, which is 80% of the 80 hours needed to produce

EXHIBIT 10-10 Cumulative Average-Time Learning Model for Rayburn Corporation

	A	B	C	D	E
1		80% Learning Curve			
2					
3	Cumulative	Cumulative		Cumulative	Individual Unit
4	Number	Average Time		Total Time:	Time for Xth
5	of Units (X)	per Unit (y)*: Labor Hours		Labor-Hours	Unit: Labor Hours
6	(1)	(2)		(3) = (1) × (2)	(4)
7	1	100.00		100.00	100.00
8	2	80.00	= (100 × 0.8)	160.00	60.00
9	3	70.21		210.63	50.63
10	4	64.00	= (80 × 0.8)	256.00	45.37
11	5	59.56		297.80	41.80
12	6	56.17		337.02	39.22
13	7	53.45		374.15	37.13
14	8	51.20	= (64 × 0.8)	409.60	35.45
15	9	49.29		443.61	34.01
16	10	47.65		476.50	32.89
17	11	46.21		508.31	31.81
18	12	44.93		539.16	30.85
19	13	43.79		569.27	30.11
20	14	42.76		598.64	29.37
21	15	41.82		627.30	28.66
22	16	40.96	= (51.2 × 0.8)	655.36	28.06
23					
24					
25					

E9 = D9 - D8 = 210.63 - 160.00

*The mathematical relationship underlying the cumulative average-time learning model is:

$$y = aX^b$$

where y = Cumulative average time (labor-hours) per unit
X = Cumulative number of units produced
a = Time (labor-hours) required to produce the first unit
b = Factor used to calculate cumulative average time to produce units

The value of b is calculated as

$$\frac{\ln(\text{learning-curve \% in decimal form})}{\ln 2}$$

For an 80% learning curve, $b = \ln 0.8/\ln 2 = -0.2231/0.6931 = -0.3219$.
When X=3, a=100, b=-0.3219,
$y = 100 \times 3^{-0.3219} = 70.21$ labor hours
The cumulative total time when X=3 is 70.21 × 3 = 210.63 labor-hours

The individual unit times in column 4 are calculated using the data in column 3. For example, the individual unit time for the third unit is 50.63 labor-hours (210.63 - 160.00). Numbers in the table may not be exact because of rounding.

EXHIBIT 10-11 Incremental Unit-Time Learning Model for Rayburn Corporation

	A	B	C	D	E
1		80% Learning Curve			
2					
3	Cumulative Number of Units (X)	Individual Unit Time for Xth Unit (y)*: Labor Hours		Cumulative Total Time: Labor-Hours	Cumulative Average Time per Unit: Labor-Hours
4	(1)	(2)		(3)	(4) = (3) ÷ (1)
5	1	100.00		100.00	100.00
6	2	80.00	= (100 × 0.8)	180.00	90.00
7	3	70.21		250.21	83.40
8	4	64.00	= (80 × 0.8)	314.21	78.55
9	5	59.56		373.77	74.75
10	6	56.17		429.94	71.66
11	7	53.45		483.39	69.06
12	8	51.20	= (64 × 0.8)	534.59	66.82
13	9	49.29		583.88	64.88
14	10	47.65		631.53	63.15
15	11	46.21		677.74	61.61
16	12	44.93		722.67	60.22
17	13	43.79		766.46	58.96
18	14	42.76		809.22	57.80
19	15	41.82		851.04	56.74
20	16	40.96	= (51.2 × 0.8)	892.00	55.75

D7 = D6 + B7 = 180.00 + 70.21

*The mathematical relationship underlying the incremental unit-time learning model is:

$$y = aX^b$$

where y = Time (labor-hours) taken to produce the last single unit
X = Cumulative number of units produced
a = Time (labor-hours) required to produce the first unit
b = Factor used to calculate incremental unit time to produce units

$$= \frac{\ln(\text{learning-curve \% in decimal form})}{\ln 2}$$

For an 80% learning curve, $b = \ln 0.8 \div \ln 2 = -0.2231 \div 0.6931 = -0.3219$
When X=3, a=100, b=-0.3219,
$y = 100 \times 3^{-0.3219} = 70.21$ labor hours
The cumulative total time when X=3 is 100 + 80 + 70.21 = 250.21 labor-hours.
Numbers in the table may not be exact because of rounding.

unit 2 (the last unit when 2 units are produced). We obtain the cumulative total time in column 3 by summing individual unit times in column 2. For example, to produce 4 cumulative units would require 314.21 labor-hours (100.00 + 80.00 + 70.21 + 64.00).

Exhibit 10-12 presents graphs using Excel for the cumulative average-time learning model (using data from Exhibit 10-10) and the incremental unit-time learning model (using data from Exhibit 10-11). Panel A graphically illustrates cumulative average time per unit as a function of cumulative units produced for each model. The curve for the cumulative average-time learning model is plotted using the data from Exhibit 10-10, column 2, versus column 1. The curve for the incremental unit-time learning model is plotted using the data from Exhibit 10-11, column 4, versus column 1. Panel B graphically illustrates cumulative total labor-hours as a function of cumulative units produced for each model. The curve for the cumulative average-time learning model is plotted using the data from Exhibit 10-10, column 3, versus column 1. The curve for the incremental unit-time learning model is plotted using the data from Exhibit 10-11, column 3, versus column 1.

EXHIBIT 10-12 Plots for Cumulative Average-Time Learning Model and Incremental Unit-Time Learning Model for Rayburn Corporation

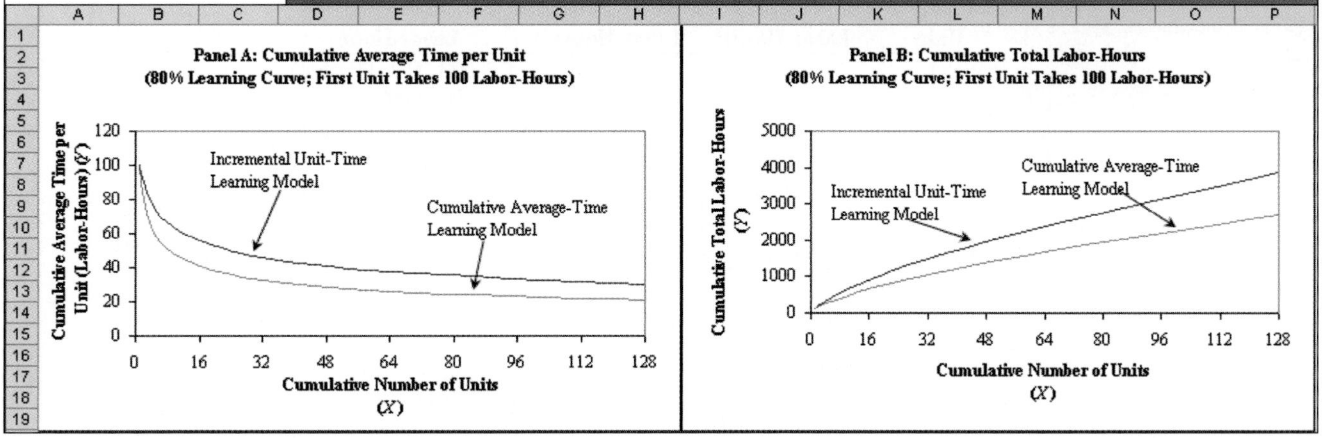

The incremental unit-time model predicts a higher cumulative total time to produce two or more units than the cumulative average-time model, assuming the same learning rate for both models. That is, in Exhibit 10-12, Panel B, the graph for the 80% incremental unit-time model lies above the graph for the 80% cumulative average-time model. If we compare the results in Exhibit 10-10 (column 3) with the results in Exhibit 10-11 (column 3), to produce 4 cumulative units, the 80% incremental unit-time learning model predicts 314.21 labor-hours versus 256.00 labor-hours predicted by the 80% cumulative average-time learning model. That's because under the cumulative average-time learning model *average labor-hours needed to produce all 4 units* is 64 hours; the labor-hour amount needed to produce unit 4 is much less than 64 hours—it is 45.37 hours (see Exhibit 10-10). Under the incremental unit-time learning model, the labor-hour amount needed to produce unit 4 is 64 hours, and the labor-hours needed to produce the first three units are more than 64 hours, so average time needed to produce all 4 units is more than 64 hours.

Study Tip: To check your understanding of the material in the body of this chapter, see the Featured Exercise (parts a through d); true–false statements 2 and 6; multiple-choice questions 4, 6, and 7; and Review Exercises 1 and 2 (*Student Guide*, beginning p. 127). Fully explained answers begin on p. 132.

How do managers choose which of these models to use? They make their choices on a case-by-case basis. For example, if the behavior of manufacturing labor-hour usage as production levels increase follows a pattern like the one predicted by the cumulative average-time learning model, then the cumulative average-time learning model should be used. Engineers, plant managers, and workers are good sources of information on the amount and type of learning actually occurring as production increases. Plotting this information is helpful in selecting the appropriate model.[2]

Setting Prices, Budgets, and Standards

How do companies use learning curves? Consider the data in Exhibit 10-10 for the cumulative average-time learning model at Rayburn Corporation. Suppose variable costs subject to learning effects consist of direct manufacturing labor, at $20 per hour, and related overhead, at $30 per direct manufacturing labor-hour. Managers should predict the costs shown in Exhibit 10-13.

These data show that the effects of the learning curve could have a major influence on decisions. For example, managers at Rayburn Corporation might set an extremely low selling price on its radar systems to generate high demand. As its production increases to meet this growing demand, cost per unit drops. Rayburn "rides the product down the learning curve" as it establishes a larger market share. Although it may have earned little operating income on its first unit sold—it may actually have lost money on that unit—Rayburn earns more operating income per unit as output increases.

U.S. laws prohibit price discrimination—charging different customers different prices for the same product or service—if the intent is to lessen or prevent competition.

Alternatively, subject to legal and other considerations, Rayburn's managers might set a low price on just the final 8 units. After all, the total labor and related overhead costs per unit for these final 8 units are predicted to be only $12,288 ($32,768 – $20,480). On these final 8 units, the $1,536 cost per unit ($12,288 ÷ 8 units) is much lower than the $5,000 cost per unit of the first unit produced.

EXHIBIT 10-13

Predicting Costs Using Learning Curves at Rayburn Corporation

	A	B	C	D	E	F
1		**Cumulative**				
2	**Cumulative**	**Average Time**	**Cumulative**	**Cumulative Costs**		**Additions to**
3	**Number of**	**per Unit:**	**Total Time:**	**at $50 per**		**Cumulative**
4	**Units**	**Labor-Hours[a]**	**Labor-Hours[a]**	**Labor-Hour**		**Costs**
5	1	100.00	100.00	$ 5,000	(100.00 x $50)	$ 5,000
6	2	80.00	160.00	8,000	(160.00 x $50)	3,000
7	4	64.00	256.00	12,800	(256.00 x $50)	4,800
8	8	51.20	409.60	20,480	(409.60 x $50)	7,680
9	16	40.96	655.36	32,768	(655.36 x $50)	12,288
10						
11	[a] Based on the cumulative average-time learning model. See Exhibit 10-10 for the computation					
12	of these amounts.					

[2]For details, see C. Bailey, "Learning Curve Estimation of Production Costs and Labor-Hours Using a Free Excel Add-In," *Management Accounting Quarterly*, Summer 2000. Free software for estimating learning curves is available at Dr. Bailey's Web site (**www.profbailey.com**).

Many companies, such as Pizza Hut and Home Depot, incorporate learning-curve effects when evaluating performance. The Nissan Motor Company expects its workers to learn and improve on the job and evaluates performance accordingly. It sets assembly-labor efficiency standards for new models of cars after taking into account the learning that will occur as more units are produced.

The learning-curve models examined in Exhibits 10-10 to 10-13 assume that learning is driven by a single variable (production output). Other models of learning have been developed (by companies such as Analog Devices and Yokogowa Hewlett-Packard) that focus on how quality—rather than manufacturing labor-hours—will change over time, regardless of whether more units are produced. Studies indicate that factors other than production output, such as job rotation and organizing workers into teams, contribute to learning that improves quality.

Data Collection and Adjustment Issues

8

Be aware of data problems encountered in estimating cost functions

. . . for example, unreliable data and poor recordkeeping, extreme observations, treating fixed costs as if they are variable, and a changing relationship between a cost driver and cost

The ideal database for estimating cost functions quantitatively has two characteristics:

1. **The database should contain numerous reliably measured observations of the cost driver (the independent variable) and the related costs (the dependent variable).** Errors in measuring the costs and the cost driver are serious. They result in inaccurate estimates of the effect of the cost driver on costs.
2. **The database should consider for the cost driver many values spanning a wide range.** Using only a few values of the cost driver that are grouped closely considers too small a segment of the relevant range and reduces the confidence in the estimates obtained.

Unfortunately, cost analysts typically do not have the advantage of working with a database having both characteristics. This section outlines some frequently encountered data problems and steps the cost analyst can take to overcome these problems.

1. The time period for measuring the dependent variable (for example, machine-lubricant costs) does not properly match the period for measuring the cost driver. This problem often arises when accounting records are not kept on the accrual basis. Consider a cost function with machine-lubricant costs as the dependent variable and number of machine-hours as the cost driver. Assume that the lubricant is purchased sporadically and stored for later use. Records maintained on the cash basis will indicate little lubricant consumption in many months and large lubricant consumption in other months. These records present an obviously inaccurate picture of what is actually taking place. The analyst should use accrual accounting to measure consumption of machine lubricants to better match costs with the cost driver in this example.
2. Fixed costs are allocated as if they are variable. For example, costs such as depreciation, insurance, or rent may be allocated to products to calculate cost per unit of output. *The danger is to regard these costs as variable rather than as fixed. They seem to be variable because of the allocation methods used.* To avoid this problem, the analyst should distinguish carefully fixed costs from variable costs and not treat allocated fixed cost per unit as a variable cost.
3. Data are either not available for all observations or are not uniformly reliable. Missing cost observations often arise from a failure to record a cost or from classifying a cost incorrectly. For example, marketing costs may be understated because costs of sales visits to customers may be incorrectly recorded as customer-service costs. Recording data manually rather than electronically tends to result in a higher percentage of missing observations and erroneously entered observations. Errors also arise when data on cost drivers originate outside the internal accounting system. For example, the Accounting Department may obtain data on testing-hours for medical instruments from the company's Manufacturing Department and data on number of items shipped to customers from the Distribution Department. One or both of these departments might not keep accurate records. To minimize these problems, the cost analyst should design data collection reports that regularly and routinely obtain the required data and should follow up immediately whenever data are missing.
4. Extreme values of observations occur from errors in recording costs (for example, a misplaced decimal point), from nonrepresentative periods (for example, from a period in which a major machine breakdown occurred or from a period in which

a delay in delivery of materials from an international supplier curtailed production), or from observations outside the relevant range. Analysts should adjust or eliminate unusual observations before estimating a cost relationship.

5. There is no homogeneous relationship between the cost driver and the individual cost items in the dependent variable-cost pool. A homogeneous relationship exists when each activity whose costs are included in the dependent variable has the same cost driver. In this case, a single cost function can be estimated. As discussed in step 2 for estimating a cost function using quantitative analysis (p. 339), when the cost driver for each activity is different, separate cost functions, each with its own cost driver, should be estimated for each activity. Alternatively, as discussed on pp. 361–363, the cost function should be estimated with more than one independent variable using multiple regression.
6. The relationship between the cost driver and the cost is not stationary. That is, the underlying process that generated the observations has not remained stable over time. For example, the relationship between number of machine-hours and manufacturing overhead costs is unlikely to be stationary when the data cover a period in which new technology was introduced. One way to see if the relationship is stationary is to split the sample into two parts and estimate separate cost relationships—one for the period before the technology was introduced and one for the period after the technology was introduced. Then, if the estimated coefficients for the two periods are similar, the analyst can pool the data to estimate a single cost relationship. When feasible, pooling data provides a larger data set for the estimation, which increases confidence in the cost predictions being made.
7. Inflation has affected costs, the cost driver, or both. For example, inflation may cause costs to change even when there is no change in the level of the cost driver. To study the underlying cause-and-effect relationship between the level of the cost driver and costs, the analyst should remove purely inflationary price effects from the data by dividing each cost by the price index on the date the cost was incurred.

In many cases, a cost analyst must expend considerable effort to reduce the effect of these problems before estimating a cost function on the basis of past data.

PROBLEM FOR SELF-STUDY

The Helicopter Division of Aerospatiale is examining helicopter assembly costs at its plant in Marseilles, France. It has received an initial order for eight of its new land-surveying helicopters. Aerospatiale can adopt one of two methods of assembling the helicopters:

	A	B	C	D	E
1		**Labor-Intensive Assembly Method**		**Machine-Intensive Assembly Method**	
2	Direct material cost per helicopter	$40,000		$36,000	
3	Direct assembly labor time for first helicopter	2,000	labor-hours	800	labor-hours
4	Learning curve for assembly labor time per helicopter	85%	cumulative average time[a]	90%	incremental unit time[b]
5	Direct assembly labor cost	$ 30	per hour	$ 30	per hour
6	Equipment-related indirect manufacturing cost	$ 12	per direct-assemby labor-hour	$ 45	per direct-assemby labor-hour
7	Materials-handling-related indirect manufacturing cost	50%	of direct material cost	50%	of direct material cost
8					
9		ln 0.85	-0.162519		
10	[a]Using the formula (p. 350), for an 85% learning curve, b =		= = -0.234465		
11		ln 2	0.693147		
12		ln 0.90	-0.105361		
13	[b]Using the formula (p. 351), for a 90% learning curve, b =		= = -0.152004		
14		ln 2	0.693147		

Required

1. How many direct-assembly labor-hours are required to assemble the first eight helicopters under (a) the labor-intensive method and (b) the machine-intensive method?
2. What is the total cost of assembling the first eight helicopters under (a) the labor-intensive method and (b) the machine-intensive method?

SOLUTION

1. *a.* The following calculations show the labor-intensive assembly method based on an 85% cumulative average-time learning model (using Excel):

	G	H	I	J	K
1					
2		**Cumulative**			**Incremental**
3	**Cumulative**	**Average Time**		**Cumulative**	**Time for**
4	**Number**	**per Unit (y):**		**Total Time:**	**Xth unit:**
5	**of Units**	**Labor-Hours**		**Labor-Hours**	**Labor-Hours**
6	**(1)**	**(2)**		**(3) = (1) x (2)**	**(4)**
7	1	2,000		2,000	2,000
8	2	1,700	(2,000 x 0.85)	3,400	1,400
9	3	1,546		4,638	1,238
10	4	1,445	(1,700 x 0.85)	5,780	1,142
11	5	1,371		6,855	1,075
12	6	1,314		7,884	1,029
13	7	1,267		8,869	985
14	8	1,228.25	(1,445 x 0.85)	9,826	957

Cumulative average-time per unit for the *X*th unit in column 2 is calculated as $y = aX^b$; see Exhibit 10-10 (p. 350). For example, when $X = 3$, $y = 2{,}000 \times 3^{-0.234465} = 1{,}546$ labor-hours.

b. The following calculations show the machine-intensive assembly method based on a 90% incremental unit-time learning model:

	G	H	I	J	K
16		**Incremental**			**Cumulative**
17	**Cumulative**	**Unit Time**		**Cumulative**	**Average Time**
18	**Number**	**for Xth Unit (y):**		**Total Time:**	**per Unit:**
19	**of Units**	**Labor-Hours**		**Labor-Hours**	**Labor-Hours**
20	**(1)**	**(2)**		**(3)**	**(4) = (3) ÷ (1)**
21	1	800		800	800
22	2	720	(800 x 0.9)	1,520	760
23	3	677		2,197	732
24	4	648	(720 x 0.9)	2,845	711
25	5	626		3,471	694
26	6	609		4,080	680
27	7	595		4,675	668
28	8	583	(648 x 0.9)	5,258	657

Individual unit time for the *X*th unit in column 2 is calculated as $y = aX^b$; see Exhibit 10-11 (p. 351). For example, when $X = 3$, $y = 800 \times 3^{-0.152004} = 677$ labor-hours.

2. Total costs of assembling the first eight helicopters are:

	O	P	Q
1		**Labor-Intensive**	**Machine-Intensive**
2		**Assembly Method**	**Assembly Method**
3		**(using data from part 1a)**	**(using data from part 1b)**
4	Direct materials:		
5	8 helicopters x $40,000; $36,000 per helicopter	$320,000	$288,000
6	Direct assembly labor:		
7	9,826 hours; 5,258 hours x $30/hour	294,780	157,740
8	Indirect manufacturing costs		
9	Equipment related		
10	9,826 hours x $12/hour; 5,258 hours x $45/hour	117,912	236,610
11	Materials-handling related		
12	0.50 x $320,000; $288,000	160,000	144,000
13	Total assembly costs	$892,692	$826,350
14			

The machine-intensive method's assembly costs are $66,342 lower than the labor-intensive method ($892,692 – $826,350).

DECISION POINTS

The following question-and-answer format summarizes the chapter's learning objectives. Each decision presents a key question related to a learning objective. The guidelines are the answer to that question.

Decision	Guidelines
1. What assumptions are usually made when estimating a cost function?	The two assumptions frequently made in cost-behavior estimation are (a) changes in the level of a single activity explain changes in total costs and (b) cost behavior can adequately be approximated by a linear function of the activity level within the relevant range.
2. What is a linear cost function and what types of cost behavior can it represent?	A linear cost function is a cost function in which, within the relevant range, the graph of total costs based on the level of a single activity is a straight line. Linear cost functions can be described by a constant, *a*, which represents the estimate of the total cost component that, within the relevant range, does not vary with changes in the level of the activity; and a slope coefficient, *b,* which represents the estimate of the amount by which total costs change for each unit change in the level of the activity within the relevant range. Three types of linear cost functions are variable, fixed, and mixed (or semivariable).
3. What are the different methods that can be used to estimate a cost function?	Four methods for estimating cost functions are the industrial engineering method, the conference method, the account analysis method, and the quantitative analysis method (which includes the high-low method and the regression analysis method). If possible, the cost analyst should apply more than one method. Each method is a check on the others.
4. What are the steps to estimate a cost function using quantitative analysis?	There are six steps to estimate a cost function using quantitative analysis: (a) Choose the dependent variable; (b) identify the cost driver; (c) collect data on the dependent variable and the cost driver; (d) plot the data; (e) estimate the cost function; and (f) evaluate the cost driver of the estimated cost function. In most situations, working closely with operations managers, the cost analyst will cycle through these steps several times before identifying an acceptable cost function.
5. How should a company evaluate and choose cost drivers?	Three criteria for evaluating and choosing cost drivers are (a) economic plausibility, (b) goodness of fit, and (c) significance of independent variable.
6. What is a nonlinear cost function and how does it arise?	A nonlinear cost function is a cost function in which the graph of total costs based on the level of a single activity is not a straight line within the relevant range. Nonlinear costs can arise because of quantity discounts, step cost functions, and learning-curve effects.
7. What are two types of learning curve models that a company can use?	The learning curve is an example of a nonlinear cost function. Labor-hours per unit decline as units of production increase. In the cumulative average-time learning model, cumulative average-time per unit declines by a constant percentage each time the cumulative quantity of units produced doubles. In the incremental unit-time learning model, incremental unit time (the time needed to produce the last unit) declines by a constant percentage each time the cumulative quantity of units produced doubles. A company should use the model that better fits its observed labor-hour usage.
8. What are the common data problems a company must watch for when estimating costs?	The most difficult task in cost estimation is collecting high-quality, reliably measured data on the costs and the cost driver. Common problems include missing data, extreme values of observations, changes in technology, and distortions resulting from inflation.

APPENDIX: REGRESSION ANALYSIS

	A	B	C
1	Week	Cost Driver: Machine-Hours	Indirect Manufacturing Labor Costs
2		(X)	(Y)
3	1	68	$1,190
4	2	88	1,211
5	3	62	1,004
6	4	72	917
7	5	60	770
8	6	96	1,456
9	7	78	1,180
10	8	46	710
11	9	82	1,316
12	10	94	1,032
13	11	68	752
14	12	48	963
15	Total	862	$12,501
16			

This appendix describes estimation of the regression equation, several commonly used regression statistics, and how to choose among cost functions that have been estimated by regression analysis. We use the data for Elegant Rugs presented in Exhibit 10-3 (p. 339) and displayed here again for easy reference.

Estimating the Regression Line

The least-squares technique for estimating the regression line minimizes the sum of the squares of the vertical deviations from the data points to the estimated regression line (also called *residual term* in Exhibit 10-6, p. 343). The objective is to find the values of a and b in the linear cost function $y = a + bX$, where y is the *predicted* cost value as distinguished from the *observed* cost value, which we denote by Y. We wish to find the numerical values of a and b that minimize $\Sigma(Y - y)^2$, the sum of the squares of the vertical deviations between Y and y. Generally, these computations are done using software packages such as Excel. For the data in our example,[3] a = \$300.98 and b = \$10.31, so that the equation of the regression line is y = \$300.98 + \$10.31X.

Goodness of Fit

Goodness of fit measures how well the predicted values, y, based on the cost driver, X, match actual cost observations, Y. The regression analysis method computes a measure of goodness of fit, called the coefficient of determination. The **coefficient of determination, r^2**, measures the percentage of variation in Y explained by X (the independent variable). That is, the coefficient of determination indicates the proportion of the variance of Y that is explained by the independent variable X (where $\bar{Y} = \Sigma Y \div n$). It is more convenient to express the coefficient of determination as 1 minus the proportion of total variance that is *not* explained by the independent variable—that is, 1 minus the ratio of unexplained variation to total variation. The unexplained variance arises because of differences between the actual values, Y, and the predicted values, y, which in the Elegant Rugs example is given by[4]

$$r^2 = 1 - \frac{\text{Unexplained variation}}{\text{Total variation}} = 1 - \frac{\Sigma(Y - y)^2}{\Sigma(Y - \bar{Y})^2} = 1 - \frac{290{,}824}{607{,}699} = 0.52$$

The calculations indicate that r^2 increases as the predicted values, y, more closely approximate the actual observations, Y. The range of r^2 is from 0 (implying no explanatory power) to 1 (implying perfect explanatory power). Generally, an r^2 of 0.30 or higher passes the goodness-of-fit test. However, do not rely exclusively on goodness of fit. It can lead to the indiscriminate inclusion of independent variables that increase r^2 but have no economic plausibility as cost drivers. *Goodness of fit has meaning only if the relationship between the cost drivers and costs is economically plausible.*

Significance of Independent Variables

Do changes in the economically plausible independent variable result in significant changes in the dependent variable? Or alternatively stated, is the slope coefficient, b, of the regression line statistically significant (that is, different from \$0)? Recall, for example, that in the regression of number of machine-hours and indirect manufacturing labor costs in the Elegant Rugs illustration, b is estimated from a sample of 12 weekly observations. The estimate b is subject to random factors, as are all sample statistics. That is, a different sample of 12 data points would undoubtedly give a different estimate of b. The **standard error of the estimated coefficient** indicates how much the estimated value b is

To obtain reliable cost functions, managers find it helpful to consult with a technical expert on regression analysis.

[3]The formulae for a and b are:

$$a = \frac{(\Sigma Y)(\Sigma X^2) - (\Sigma X)(\Sigma XY)}{n(\Sigma X^2) - (\Sigma X)(\Sigma X)} \text{ and } b = \frac{n(\Sigma XY) - (\Sigma X)(\Sigma Y)}{n(\Sigma X^2) - (\Sigma X)(\Sigma X)}$$

where for the Elegant Rugs data in Exhibit 10-3,

n = number of data points = 12
ΣX = sum of the given X values = 68 + 88 + ⋯ + 48 = 862
ΣX^2 = sum of squares of the X values = $(68)^2 + (88)^2 + \cdots + (48)^2$ = 4,624 + 7,744 + ⋯ + 2,304 = 64,900
ΣY = sum of given Y values = 1,190 + 1,211 + ⋯ + 963 = 12,501
ΣXY = sum of the amounts obtained by multiplying each of the given X values by the associated observed Y value = (68)(1,190) + (88)(1,211) + ⋯ + (48)(963)
= 80,920 + 106,568 + ⋯ + 46,224 = 928,716

$$a = \frac{(12{,}501)(64{,}900) - (862)(928{,}716)}{12(64{,}900) - (862)(862)} = \$300.98$$

$$b = \frac{12(928{,}716) - (862)(12{,}501)}{12(64{,}900) - (862)(862)} = \$10.31$$

[4]From footnote 3, ΣY = 12,501 and $\bar{Y}$ = 12,501 ÷ 12 = 1,041.75

$$\Sigma(Y - \bar{Y})^2 = (1{,}190 - 1{,}041.75)^2 + (1{,}211 - 1{,}041.75)^2 + \cdots + (963 - 1{,}041.75)^2 = 607{,}699$$

Each value of X generates a predicted value of y. For example, in week 1, y = \$300.98 + (\$10.31 × 68) = \$1002.06; in week 2, y = \$300.98 + (\$10.31 × 88) = \$1,208.26; and in week 12, y = \$300.98 + (\$10.31 × 48) = \$795.86.

$$\Sigma(Y - y)^2 = (1{,}190 - 1{,}002.06)^2 + (1{,}211 - 1{,}208.26)^2 + \cdots + (963 - 795.86)^2 = 290{,}824$$

likely to be affected by random factors. The *t*-value of the *b* coefficient measures how large the value of the estimated coefficient is relative to its standard error. With 12 observations and two parameters *a* and *b* to be estimated, a cutoff *t*-value with an absolute value greater than 2.228 suggests that the *b* coefficient is significantly different from \$0.[5] In other words, a relationship exists between the independent variable and the dependent variable that cannot be attributed to random chance alone.

Exhibit 10-14 shows a convenient format (in Excel) for summarizing the regression results for number of machine-hours and indirect manufacturing labor costs. The *t*-value (called *t* Stat in the Excel output) for the slope coefficient *b* is \$10.31 ÷ \$3.12 = 3.30, which exceeds the cutoff *t*-value of 2.228. Therefore, the coefficient of the machine-hours variable is significantly different from \$0—that is, the probability is low (less than 5%) that random factors could have caused the coefficient *b* to be positive. Alternatively, we can restate our conclusion in terms of a *confidence interval*: There is less than a 5% chance that the true value of the machine-hours coefficient lies outside the range \$10.31 ± (2.228 × \$3.12), or \$10.31 ± \$6.95, or from \$3.36 to \$17.26. Therefore, we can conclude that changes in the number of machine-hours do affect indirect manufacturing labor costs. Similarly, using data from Exhibit 10-14, the *t*-value for the constant term *a* is \$300.98 ÷ \$229.75 = 1.31, which is less than 2.228. This *t*-value indicates that, within the relevant range, the constant term is *not* significantly different from zero. The Durbin-Watson statistic in Exhibit 10-14 will be discussed in the following section.

Specification Analysis of Estimation Assumptions

Specification analysis is the testing of the assumptions of regression analysis. If the assumptions of (1) linearity within the relevant range, (2) constant variance of residuals, (3) independence of residuals, and (4) normality of residuals all hold, then the simple regression procedures give reliable estimates of coefficient values. This section provides a brief overview of specification analysis. When these assumptions are not satisfied, more-complex regression procedures are necessary to obtain the best estimates.[6]

1. **Linearity within the relevant range.** A common assumption—and one that appears to be reasonable in many business applications—is that a linear relationship exists between the independent variable *X* and the dependent variable *Y* within the relevant range. If a linear regression model is used to estimate a nonlinear relationship, however, the coefficient estimates obtained will be inaccurate.

   When there is only one independent variable, the easiest way to check for linearity is to study the data plotted in a scatter diagram, a step that often is unwisely skipped. Exhibit 10-6 (p. 343) presents a scatter diagram for the indirect manufacturing labor costs and machine-hours variables of Elegant Rugs shown in Exhibit 10-3 (p. 339). The scatter diagram reveals that linearity appears to be a reasonable assumption for these data.

EXHIBIT 10-14 **Simple Regression Results with Indirect Manufacturing Labor Costs as Dependent Variable and Machine-Hours as Independent Variable (Cost Driver) for Elegant Rugs**

	A	B	C	D	E	F
1		**Coefficients**	**Standard Error**	**t Stat**		= Coefficient/Standard Error
2		**(1)**	**(2)**	**(3) = (1) ÷ (2)**		= B3/C3
3	Intercept	\$300.98	\$229.75	1.31 ⟶		=300.98/229.75
4	Independent Variable: Machine-Hours (*X*)	\$ 10.31	\$ 3.12	3.30		
5						
6	**Regression Statistics**					
7	R Square	0.52				
8	Durbin-Watson Statistic	2.05				

[5]The cutoff *t*-value for inferring that a *b* coefficient is significantly different from 0 is a function of the number of degrees of freedom in regression analysis. The number of degrees of freedom is calculated as the sample size minus the number of parameters (in this example, two, *a* and *b*) estimated in the regression. The cutoff *t*-value of 2.00 assumes 60 degrees of freedom. The smaller the sample size, the greater is the cutoff *t*-value. For 10 degrees of freedom, the cutoff *t*-value is 2.228.

[6]For details see, for example, W. H. Greene, *Econometric Analysis*, 4th ed. (Upper Saddle River, NJ: Prentice Hall, 2000).

The learning-curve models discussed in this chapter (pp. 349–353) are examples of nonlinear cost functions. Costs increase when the level of production increases, but by lesser amounts than would occur with a linear cost function. In this case, the analyst should estimate a nonlinear cost function that incorporates learning effects.

2. **Constant variance of residuals.** The vertical deviation of the observed value Y from the regression line estimate y is called the *residual term, disturbance term,* or *error term,* $u = Y - y$. The assumption of constant variance implies that the residual terms are unaffected by the level of the cost driver. The assumption also implies that there is a uniform scatter, or dispersion, of the data points about the regression line as in Exhibit 10-15, Panel A. This assumption is likely to be violated, for example, in cross-sectional estimation of costs in operations of different sizes. For example, suppose Elegant Rugs has production areas of varying sizes. The company collects data from these different production areas to estimate the relationship between machine-hours and indirect manufacturing labor costs. It is very possible that the residual terms in this regression will be larger for the larger production areas that have higher machine-hours and higher indirect manufacturing labor costs. There would not be a uniform scatter of data points about the regression line (see Exhibit 10-15, Panel B). Constant variance is also known as *homoscedasticity.* Violation of this assumption is called *heteroscedasticity*.

   Heteroscedasticity does not affect the accuracy of the regression estimates a and b. It does, however, reduce the reliability of the estimates of the standard errors and thus affects the precision with which inferences about the population parameters can be drawn from the regression estimates.

3. **Independence of residuals.** The assumption of independence of residuals is that the residual term for any one observation is not related to the residual term for any other observation. The problem of *serial correlation* (also called *autocorrelation*) in the residuals arises when there is a systematic pattern in the sequence of residuals such that the residual in observation n conveys information about the residuals in observations $n + 1$, $n + 2$, and so on. The scatter diagram helps in identifying autocorrelation. Autocorrelation does not exist in Panel A, but it does in Panel B of Exhibit 10-16. Observe the systematic pattern of the residuals in Panel B—positive residuals for extreme (high and low) quantities of direct materials used and negative residuals for moderate quantities of direct materials used. One reason for this observed pattern at low values of the cost driver is the "stickiness" of costs. As direct materials used decrease below 400 tons, materials-handling costs do not decline. No such pattern exists in Panel A.

   Like nonconstant variance of residuals, serial correlation does not affect the accuracy of the regression estimates a and b. It does, however, affect the standard errors of the coefficients, which in turn affect the precision with which inferences about the population parameters can be drawn from the regression estimates.

   The Durbin-Watson statistic is one measure of serial correlation in the estimated residuals. For samples of 10 to 20 observations, a Durbin-Watson statistic in the 1.10-to-2.90 range indicates that the residuals are independent. The Durbin-Watson statistic for the regression results of Elegant Rugs in Exhibit 10-14 is 2.05. Therefore, an assumption of independence in the estimated residuals is reasonable for this regression model.

EXHIBIT 10-15 Constant Variance of Residuals Assumption

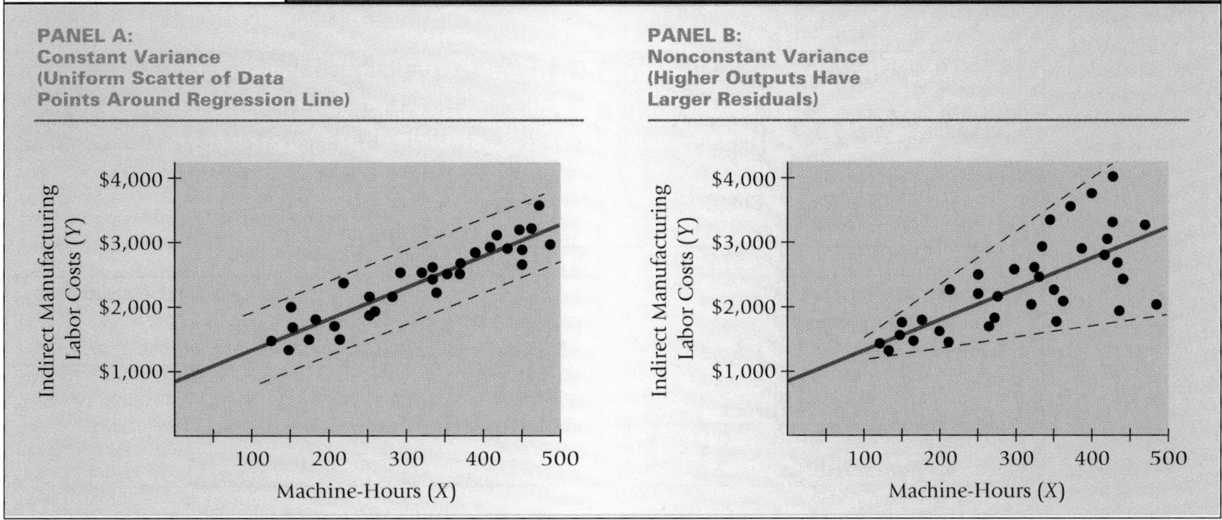

EXHIBIT 10-16 Independence of Residuals Assumption

PANEL A:
Independence of Residuals
(No Pattern in Residuals)

PANEL B:
Serial Correlation in Residuals
(A Pattern of Positive Residuals for Extreme Direct Materials Used; Negative Residuals for Moderate Direct Materials Used)

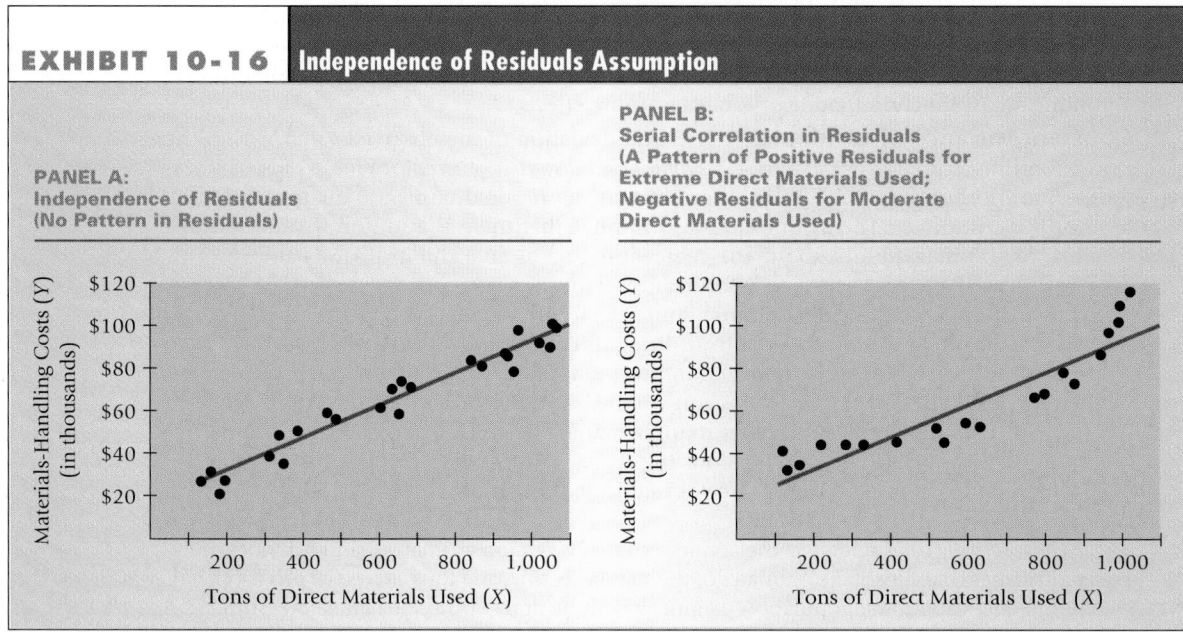

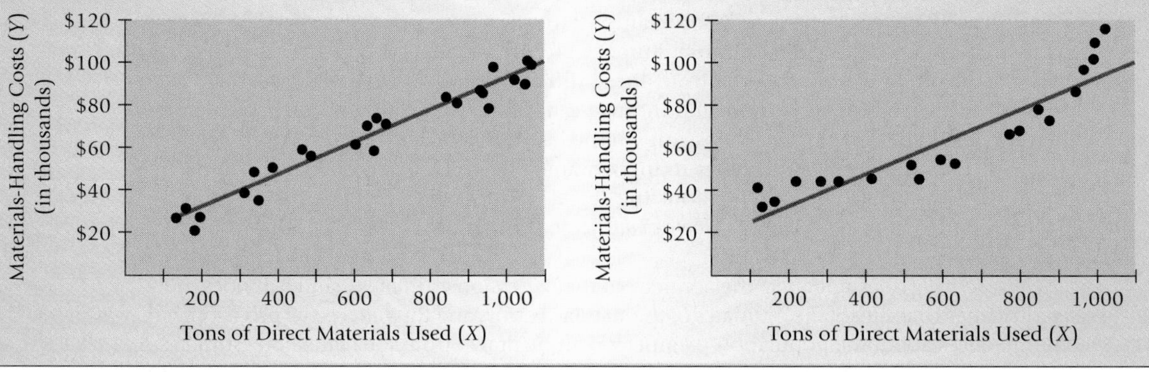

4. **Normality of residuals.** The normality of residuals assumption means that the residuals are distributed normally around the regression line. This assumption is necessary for making inferences about *y*, *a*, and *b*.

Using Regression Output to Choose Cost Drivers of Cost Functions

Consider the two choices of cost drivers we described earlier in this chapter for indirect manufacturing labor costs (y):

$$y = a + (b \times \text{Number of machine-hours})$$

$$y = a + (b \times \text{Number of direct manufacturing labor-hours})$$

Exhibits 10-6 and 10-8 show plots of the data for the two regressions. Exhibit 10-14 reports regression results for the cost function using number of machine-hours as the independent variable. Exhibit 10-17 presents comparable regression results (in Excel) for the cost function using number of direct manufacturing labor-hours as the independent variable.

On the basis of the material presented in this appendix, which regression is better? Exhibit 10-18 compares these two cost functions in a systematic way. For several criteria, the cost function based on machine-hours is preferable to the cost function based on direct manufacturing labor-hours. The economic plausibility criterion is especially important.

EXHIBIT 10-17 Simple Regression Results with Indirect Manufacturing Labor Costs as Dependent Variable and Direct Manufacturing Labor-Hours as Independent Variable (Cost Driver) for Elegant Rugs

	A	B	C	D	E	F	G	H
1		**Coefficients**	**Standard Error**	**t Stat**				
2		**(1)**	**(2)**	**(3) = (1) ÷ (2)**				
3	Intercept	$744.67	$217.61	3.42				
4	Independent Variable: Direct Manufacturing Labor-Hours (X)	$ 7.72	$ 5.40	1.43 →		= Coefficient/Standard Error = B4/C4 = 7.72/5.40		
5								
6	**Regression Statistics**							
7	R Square	0.17						
8	Durbin-Watson Statistic	2.26						

EXHIBIT 10-18

Comparison of Alternative Cost Functions for Indirect Manufacturing Labor Costs Estimated with Simple Regression for Elegant Rugs

Criterion	Cost Function 1: Machine-Hours as Independent Variable	Cost Function 2: Direct Manufacturing Labor-Hours as Independent Variable
Economic plausibility	A positive relationship between indirect manufacturing labor costs (technical support labor) and machine-hours is economically plausible in Elegant Rugs' highly automated plant.	A positive relationship between indirect manufacturing labor costs and direct manufacturing labor-hours is economically plausible, but less so than machine-hours in Elegant Rugs' highly automated plant on a week-to-week basis.
Goodness of fit[a]	$r^2 = 0.52$ Excellent goodness of fit.	$r^2 = 0.17$ Poor goodness of fit.
Significance of independent variable(s)	The *t*-value of 3.30 is significant.	The *t*-value of 1.43 is not significant.
Specification analysis of estimation assumptions	Plot of the data indicates that assumptions of linearity, constant variance, independence of residuals, (Durbin-Watson statistic = 2.05), and normality of residuals hold, but inferences drawn from only 12 observations are not reliable.	Plot of the data indicates that assumptions of linearity, constant variance, independence of residuals (Durbin-Watson statistic = 2.26) and normality of residuals hold, but inferences drawn from only 12 observations are not reliable.

[a]If the number of observations available to estimate the machine-hours regression differs from the number of observations available to estimate the direct manufacturing labor-hours regression, an *adjusted* r^2 can be calculated to take this difference (in degrees of freedom) into account. Programs such as Excel calculate and present *adjusted* r^2.

Do not always assume that any one cost function will perfectly satisfy all the criteria in Exhibit 10-18. A cost analyst must often make a choice among "imperfect" cost functions, in the sense that the data of any particular cost function will not perfectly meet one or more of the assumptions underlying regression analysis. For example, both of the cost functions in Exhibit 10-18 are imperfect because, as stated in the section on specification analysis of estimation assumptions, inferences drawn from only 12 observations are not reliable.

Multiple Regression and Cost Hierarchies

In some cases, a satisfactory estimation of a cost function may be based on only one independent variable, such as number of machine-hours. In many cases, however, basing the estimation on more than one independent variable (that is, *multiple regression*) is more economically plausible and improves accuracy. The most widely used equations to express relationships between two or more independent variables and a dependent variable are linear in the form

$$Y = a + b_1X_1 + b_2X_2 + \cdots + u$$

where

Y = Cost to be predicted

$X_1, X_2, \ldots$ = Independent variables on which the prediction is to be based

$a, b_1, b_2, \ldots$ = Estimated coefficients of the regression model

u = Residual term that includes the net effect of other factors not in the model as well as measurement errors in the dependent and independent variables

Multiple regression analysis is useful for estimating total costs when different levels of the cost hierarchy are involved. This example uses number of machine-hours (an output unit-level cost driver) and number of production batches (a batch-level cost driver).

Example Consider the Elegant Rugs data in Exhibit 10-19. The company's ABC analysis indicates that indirect manufacturing labor costs include large amounts incurred for setup and changeover costs when a new batch of carpets is started. Management believes that in addition to number of

EXHIBIT 10-19

Weekly Indirect Manufacturing Labor Costs, Machine-Hours, Direct Manufacturing Labor-Hours, and Number of Production Batches for Elegant Rugs

	A	B	C	D	E
1	Week	Machine-Hours (X_1)	Number of Production Batches (X_2)	Direct Manufacturing Labor-Hours	Indirect Manufacturing Labor Costs (Y)
2	1	68	12	30	$ 1,190
3	2	88	15	35	1,211
4	3	62	13	36	1,004
5	4	72	11	20	917
6	5	60	10	47	770
7	6	96	12	45	1,456
8	7	78	17	44	1,180
9	8	46	7	38	710
10	9	82	14	70	1,316
11	10	94	12	30	1,032
12	11	68	7	29	752
13	12	48	14	38	963
14	Total	862	144	462	$12,501
15					

machine-hours (an output unit-level cost driver), indirect manufacturing labor costs are also affected by the number of batches of carpet produced during each week (a batch-level driver). Elegant Rugs estimates the relationship between two independent variables, number of machine-hours and number of production batches of carpet manufactured during the week, and indirect manufacturing labor costs.

Exhibit 10-20 presents results (in Excel) for the following multiple regression model, using data in columns B, C, and E of Exhibit 10-19:

$$y = \$42.58 + \$7.60X_1 + \$37.77X_2$$

where X_1 is the number of machine-hours and X_2 is the number of production batches. It is economically plausible that both number of machine-hours and number of production batches would help explain variations in indirect manufacturing labor costs at Elegant Rugs. The r^2 of 0.52 for the simple regression using number of machine-hours (Exhibit 10-14) increases to 0.72 with the multiple regression in Exhibit 10-20. The *t*-values suggest that the independent variable coefficients of both number of machine-hours ($7.60) and number of production batches ($37.77) are significantly different from zero (t = 2.74 is the *t*-value for number of machine-hours, and t = 2.48 is the *t*-value for number of production batches). The multiple regression model in Exhibit 10-20 satisfies both economic plausibility and statistical criteria, and it explains much greater variation (that is, r^2

EXHIBIT 10-20

Multiple Regression Results with Indirect Manufacturing Labor Costs and Two Independent Variables or Cost Drivers (Machine-Hours and Production Batches) for Elegant Rugs

	A	B	C	D	E	F	G
1		Coefficients	Standard Error	t Stat			
2		(1)	(2)	(3) = (1) ÷ (2)			
3	Intercept	$42.58	$213.91	0.20			
4	Independent variable 1: Machine-hours (*X1*)	$ 7.60	$ 2.77	2.74 →	= Coefficient/Standard Error = B4/C4 = 7.60/2.77		
5	Independent variable 2: Number of production batches (*X2*)	$37.77	$ 15.25	2.48			
6							
7	**Regression Statistics**						
8	R Square	0.72					
9	Durbin-Watson Statistic	2.49					

of 0.72 versus r^2 of 0.52) in indirect manufacturing labor costs than the simple regression model using only number of machine-hours as the independent variable. Number of machine-hours and number of production batches are both important cost drivers of indirect manufacturing labor costs at Elegant Rugs.

In Exhibit 10-20, the slope coefficients—$7.60 for number of machine-hours and $37.77 for number of production batches—measure the change in indirect manufacturing labor costs associated with a unit change in an independent variable (assuming that the other independent variable is held constant). For example, indirect manufacturing labor costs increase by $37.77 when one more production batch is added, assuming that the number of machine-hours is held constant.

An alternative approach would create two separate cost pools for indirect manufacturing labor costs: one for costs related to number of machine-hours and another for costs related to number of production batches. Elegant Rugs would then estimate the relationship between the cost driver and the costs in each cost pool. The difficult task under this approach is to properly subdivide the indirect manufacturing labor costs into the two cost pools.

Multicollinearity

A major concern that arises with multiple regression is multicollinearity. **Multicollinearity** exists when two or more independent variables are highly correlated with each other. Generally, users of regression analysis believe that a *coefficient of correlation* between independent variables greater than 0.70 indicates multicollinearity. Multicollinearity increases the standard errors of the coefficients of the individual variables. That is, variables that are economically and statistically significant will appear not to be significantly different from zero.

The coefficients of correlation between the potential independent variables for Elegant Rugs in Exhibit 10-19 are:

Combinations of Pairs of Independent Variables	Coefficient of Correlation
Machine-hours and direct manufacturing labor-hours	0.12
Machine-hours and production batches	0.40
Direct manufacturing labor-hours and production batches	0.31

These results indicate that multiple regressions using any pair of the independent variables in Exhibit 10-19 are not likely to encounter multicollinearity problems.

When multicollinearity exists, try to obtain new data that do not suffer from multicollinearity problems. Do not drop an independent variable (cost driver) that should be included in a model because it is correlated with another independent variable. Omitting such a variable will cause the estimated coefficient of the independent variable included in the model to be biased away from its true value.

Study Tip: To check your understanding of the material in the appendix, see the Featured Exercise (parts e through h), true–false statements 10 and 12, and Review Exercise 3 (*Student Guide,* beginning p. 127). Fully explained answers begin on p. 132.

TERMS TO LEARN

This chapter and the Glossary at the end of this book contain definitions of:

account analysis method (p. 338)
coefficient of determination (r^2) (p. 357)
conference method (p. 337)
constant (p. 333)
cost estimation (p. 336)
cost function (p. 333)
cost predictions (p. 336)
cumulative average-time learning model (p. 350)
dependent variable (p. 339)
experience curve (p. 349)
high-low method (p. 341)
incremental unit-time learning model (p. 350)
independent variable (p. 339)
industrial engineering method (p. 337)
intercept (p. 334)
learning curve (p. 349)
linear cost function (p. 333)
mixed cost (p. 334)
multicollinearity (p. 363)
multiple regression (p. 342)
nonlinear cost function (p. 347)
regression analysis (p. 342)
residual term (p. 343)
semivariable cost (p. 334)
simple regression (p. 342)
slope coefficient (p. 333)
specification analysis (p. 358)
standard error of the estimated coefficient (p. 357)
step cost function (p. 348)
work-measurement method (p. 337)

PH Grade Assist

Prentice Hall Grade Assist (PHGA)
Your professor may ask you to complete selected exercises and problems in Prentice Hall Grade Assist (PHGA). PHGA is an online tool that can help you master the chapter's topics. It provides you with multiple variations of exercises and problems designated by the PHGA icon. You can rework these exercises and problems—each time with new data—as many times as you need. You also receive immediate feedback and grading.

ASSIGNMENT MATERIAL

Questions

10-1 What two assumptions are frequently made when estimating a cost function?

10-2 Describe three alternative linear cost functions.

10-3 What is the difference between a linear and a nonlinear cost function? Give an example of each type of cost function.

10-4 "High correlation between two variables means that one is the cause and the other is the effect." Do you agree? Explain.

10-5 Name four approaches to estimating a cost function.

10-6 Describe the conference method for estimating a cost function. What are two advantages of this method?

10-7 Describe the account analysis method for estimating a cost function.

10-8 List the six steps in estimating a cost function on the basis of an analysis of a past cost relationship. Which step is typically the most difficult for the cost analyst?

10-9 When using the high-low method, should you base the high and low observations on the dependent variable or on the cost driver?

10-10 Describe three criteria for evaluating cost functions and choosing cost drivers.

10-11 Define learning curve. Outline two models that can be used when incorporating learning into the estimation of cost functions.

10-12 Discuss four frequently encountered problems when collecting cost data on variables included in a cost function.

10-13 What are the four key assumptions examined in specification analysis in the case of simple regression?

10-14 "All the independent variables in a cost function estimated with regression analysis are cost drivers." Do you agree? Explain.

10-15 "Multicollinearity exists when the dependent variable and the independent variable are highly correlated." Do you agree? Explain.

Exercises

10-16 Estimating a cost function. The controller of the Ijiri Company wants you to estimate a cost function from the following two observations in a general ledger account called Maintenance:

Month	Machine-Hours	Maintenance Costs Incurred
January	4,000	$3,000
February	7,000	3,900

Required

1. Estimate the cost function for maintenance.
2. Can the constant in the cost function be used as an estimate of fixed maintenance cost per month? Explain.

PH Grade Assist

10-17 Identifying variable-, fixed-, and mixed-cost functions. The Pacific Corporation operates car rental agencies at more than 20 airports. Customers can choose from one of three contracts for car rentals of one day or less:

- Contract 1: $50 for the day
- Contract 2: $30 for the day plus $0.20 per mile traveled
- Contract 3: $1 per mile traveled

1. Plot separate graphs for each of the three contracts, with costs on the vertical axis and miles traveled on the horizontal axis.
2. Express each contract as a linear cost function of the form $y = a + bX$.
3. Identify each contract as a variable-, fixed-, or mixed-cost function.

Required

10-18 Various cost-behavior patterns. (CPA, adapted) Select the graph that matches the numbered manufacturing cost data. Indicate by letter which graph best fits the situation or item described.

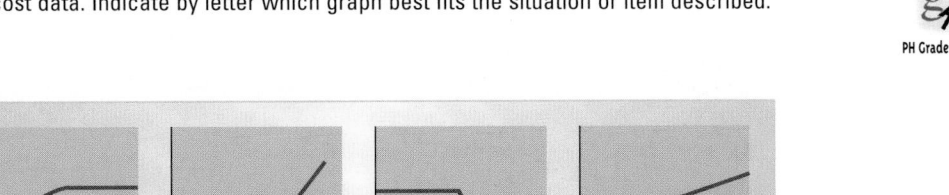

PH Grade Assist

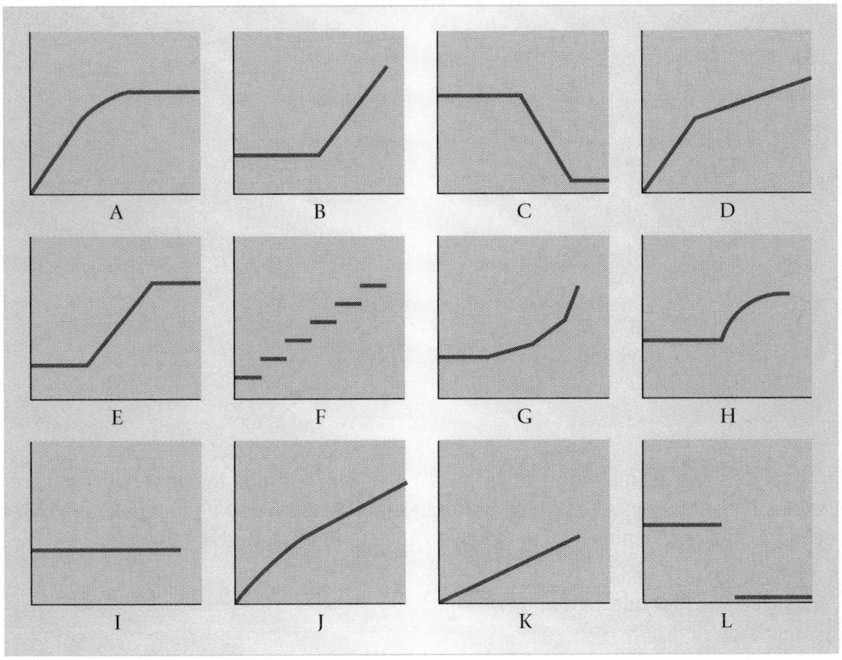

The vertical axes of the graphs represent total cost, and the horizontal axes represent units produced during a calendar year. In each case, the zero point of dollars and production is at the intersection of the two axes. The graphs may be used more than once.

Required

1. Annual depreciation of equipment, where the amount of depreciation charged is computed by the machine-hours method.
2. Electricity bill—a flat fixed charge, plus a variable cost after a certain number of kilowatt-hours are used, in which the quantity of kilowatt-hours used varies proportionately with quantity of units produced.
3. City water bill, which is computed as follows:

First 1,000,000 gallons or less	\$1,000 flat fee
Next 10,000 gallons	\$0.003 per gallon used
Next 10,000 gallons	\$0.006 per gallon used
Next 10,000 gallons	\$0.009 per gallon used
and so on	and so on

   The gallons of water used vary proportionately with the quantity of production output.
4. Cost of direct materials, where direct material cost per unit produced decreases with each pound of material used (for example, if 1 pound is used, the cost is \$10; if 2 pounds are used, the cost is \$19.98; if 3 pounds are used, the cost is \$29.94), with a minimum cost per unit of \$9.20.
5. Annual depreciation of equipment, where the amount is computed by the straight-line method. When the depreciation schedule was prepared, it was anticipated that the obsolescence factor would be greater than the wear-and-tear factor.
6. Rent on a manufacturing plant donated by the city, where the agreement calls for a fixed-fee payment unless 200,000 labor-hours are worked, in which case no rent is paid.
7. Salaries of repair personnel, where one person is needed for every 1,000 machine-hours or less (that is, 0 to 1,000 hours requires one person, 1,001 to 2,000 hours requires two people, and so on).
8. Cost of direct materials used (assume no quantity discounts).
9. Rent on a manufacturing plant donated by the county, where the agreement calls for rent of \$100,000 to be reduced by \$1 for each direct manufacturing labor-hour worked in excess of 200,000 hours, but a minimum rental fee of \$20,000 must be paid.

10-19 Matching graphs with descriptions of cost and revenue behavior. (D. Green, adapted) Given here are a number of graphs.

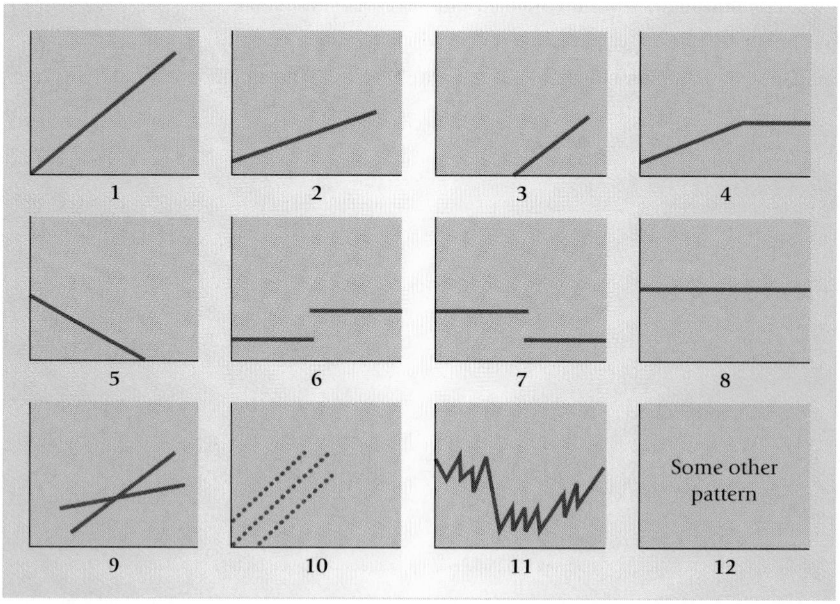

The horizontal axis represents the units produced over the year and the vertical axis represents total cost or revenues. Indicate by number which graph best fits the situation or item described. Some graphs may be used more than once; some may not apply to any of the situations.

a. Direct material costs
b. Supervisors' salaries for one shift and two shifts
c. A cost-volume-profit graph
d. Mixed costs—for example, car rental fixed charge plus a rate per mile driven
e. Depreciation of plant, computed on a straight-line basis
f. Data supporting the use of a variable-cost rate, such as manufacturing labor cost of $14 per unit produced
g. Incentive bonus plan that pays managers $0.10 for every unit produced above some level of production
h. Interest expense on $2 million borrowed at a fixed rate of interest

PH Grade Assist

10-20 Account analysis method. Lorenzo operates a car wash. Incoming cars are put on an automatic conveyor belt. Cars are washed as the conveyor belt carries the car from the start station to the finish station. After the car moves off the conveyor belt, the car is dried manually. Workers then clean and vacuum the inside of the car. Lorenzo serviced 80,000 cars in 2006. Lorenzo reports the following costs for 2006.

Account Description	Costs
Car wash labor	$240,000
Soap, cloth, and supplies	32,000
Water	28,000
Electric power to move conveyor belt	72,000
Depreciation	64,000
Salaries	46,000

Required

1. Classify each account as variable or fixed with respect to the number of cars washed. Explain.
2. Lorenzo expects to wash 90,000 cars in 2007. Use the cost classification you developed in requirement 1 to estimate Lorenzo's total costs in 2007. Depreciation is computed on a straight-line basis.

10-21 Account analysis method. Gower, Inc., a manufacturer of plastic products, reports the following manufacturing costs and account analysis classification for the year ended December 31, 2006.

Account	Classification	Amount
Direct materials	All variable	$300,000
Direct manufacturing labor	All variable	225,000
Power	All variable	37,500
Supervision labor	20% variable	56,250
Materials-handling labor	50% variable	60,000
Maintenance labor	40% variable	75,000
Depreciation	0% variable	95,000
Rent, property taxes, and administration	0% variable	100,000

Gower, Inc., produced 75,000 units of product in 2006. Gower's management is estimating costs for 2007 on the basis of 2006 numbers. The following additional information is available for 2007.

a. Direct materials prices in 2007 are expected to increase by 5% compared with 2006.
b. Under the terms of the labor contract, direct manufacturing labor wage rates are expected to increase by 10% in 2007 compared with 2006.
c. Power rates and wage rates for supervision, materials handling, and maintenance are not expected to change from 2006 to 2007.
d. Depreciation costs are expected to increase by 5%, and rent, property taxes, and administration costs are expected to increase by 7%.
e. Gower, Inc., expects to manufacture and sell 80,000 units in 2007.

Required

1. Prepare a schedule of variable, fixed, and total manufacturing costs for each account category in 2007. Estimate total manufacturing costs for 2007.
2. Calculate Gower's total manufacturing cost per unit in 2006, and estimate total manufacturing cost per unit in 2007.
3. How can you obtain better estimates of fixed and variable costs? Why would these better estimates be useful to Gower?

10-22 Estimating a cost function, high-low method. Reisen Travel offers helicopter service from suburban towns to John F. Kennedy International Airport in New York City. Each of its 10 helicopters makes between 1,000 and 2,000 round-trips per year. The records indicate that a helicopter that has made 1,000 round-trips in the year incurs an average operating cost of $300 per round-trip, and one that has made 2,000 round-trips in the year incurs an average operating cost of $250 per round-trip.

Required

1. Using the high-low method, estimate the linear relationship $y = a + bX$, where y is the total annual operating cost of a helicopter and X is the number of round-trips it makes to JFK airport during the year.
2. Give examples of costs that would be included in a and in b.
3. If Reisen Travel expects each helicopter to make, on average, 1,200 round-trips in the coming year, what should its estimated operating budget for the helicopter fleet be?

10-23 Estimating a cost function, high-low method. Laurie Daley is examining customer-service costs in the southern region of Capitol Products. Capitol Products has more than 200 separate electrical products that are sold with a 6-month guarantee of full repair or replacement with a new product. When a product is returned by a customer, a service report is prepared. This service report includes details of the problem and the time and cost of resolving the problem. Weekly data for the most recent 10-week period are:

Week	Customer-Service Department Costs	Number of Service Reports
1	$13,845	201
2	20,624	276
3	12,941	122
4	18,452	386
5	14,843	274
6	21,890	436
7	16,831	321
8	21,429	328
9	18,267	243
10	16,832	161

Required

1. Plot the relationship between customer-service costs and number of service reports. Is the relationship economically plausible?
2. Use the high-low method to compute the cost function, relating customer-service costs to the number of service reports.
3. What variables, in addition to number of service reports, might be cost drivers of monthly customer-service costs of Capitol Products?

10-24 Linear cost approximation. Terry Lawler, managing director of the Memphis Consulting Group, is examining how overhead costs behave with changes in monthly professional labor-hours billed to clients. Assume the following historical data:

Total Overhead Costs	Professional Labor-Hours Billed to Clients
$340,000	3,000
400,000	4,000
435,000	5,000
477,000	6,000
529,000	7,000
587,000	8,000

Required

1. Compute the linear cost function, relating total overhead cost to professional labor-hours, using the representative observations of 4,000 and 7,000 hours. Plot the linear cost function. Does the constant component of the cost function represent the fixed overhead costs of the Memphis Consulting Group? Why?
2. What would be the predicted total overhead costs for (a) 5,000 hours and (b) 8,000 hours using the cost function estimated in requirement 1? Plot the predicted costs and actual costs for 5,000 and 8,000 hours.
3. Lawler had a chance to accept a special job that would have boosted professional labor-hours from 4,000 to 5,000 hours. Suppose Lawler, guided by the linear cost function, rejected this job because it would have brought a total increase in contribution margin of $38,000, before deducting the predicted increase in total overhead cost, $43,000. What is the total contribution margin actually forgone?

10-25 Cost-volume-profit and regression analysis. Garvin Corporation manufactures a children's bicycle, model CT8. Garvin currently manufactures the bicycle frame. During 2005, Garvin made 30,000 frames at a total cost of $900,000. Ryan Corporation has offered to supply as many frames as Garvin wants at a cost of $28.50 per frame. Garvin anticipates needing 36,000 frames each year for the next few years.

Required

1. **a.** What is the average cost of manufacturing a bicycle frame in 2005? How does it compare to Ryan's offer?
   b. Can Garvin use the answer in requirement 1a to determine the cost of manufacturing 36,000 bicycle frames? Explain.
2. Garvin's cost analyst uses annual data from past years to estimate the following regression equation with total manufacturing costs of the bicycle frame as the dependent variable and bicycle frames produced as the independent variable:

$$y = \$432{,}000 + \$15X$$

   During the years used to estimate the regression equation, the production of bicycle frames varied from 28,000 to 36,000. Using this equation, estimate how much it would cost Garvin to manufacture 36,000 bicycle frames. How much more or less costly is it to manufacture the frames rather than to acquire them from Ryan?
3. What other information would you need in order to be confident that the equation in requirement 2 accurately predicts the cost of manufacturing bicycle frames?

10-26 Regression analysis, service company. (CMA, adapted) Bob Jones owns a catering company that prepares food and beverages for banquets and parties. For a standard party the cost on a per-person basis is:

Food and beverages	$15
Labor (0.5 hour × $10 per hour)	5
Overhead (0.5 hour × $14 per hour)	7
Total cost per person	$27

Jones is quite certain about his estimates of the food, beverages, and labor costs but is not as comfortable with the overhead estimate. The overhead estimate was based on the actual data for the past 12 months, which are presented here. These data indicate that overhead costs vary with the direct labor-hours used. The $14 estimate was determined by dividing total overhead costs for the 12 months by total labor-hours.

Month	Labor-Hours	Overhead Costs
January	2,500	$ 55,000
February	2,700	59,000
March	3,000	60,000
April	4,200	64,000
May	7,500	77,000
June	5,500	71,000
July	6,500	74,000
August	4,500	67,000
September	7,000	75,000
October	4,500	68,000
November	3,100	62,000
December	6,500	73,000
Total	57,500	$805,000

Jones has recently become aware of regression analysis. He estimated the following regression equation with overhead costs as the dependent variable and labor-hours as the independent variable:

$$y = \$48{,}271 + \$3.93X$$

Required

1. Plot the relationship between overhead costs and labor-hours. Draw the regression line and evaluate it using the criteria of economic plausibility, goodness of fit, and slope of the regression line.
2. Using data from the regression analysis, what is the variable cost per person for a standard party?
3. Bob Jones has been asked to prepare a bid for a 200-person standard party to be given next month. Determine the minimum bid price that Jones would be willing to submit to recoup variable costs.

10-27 High-low method, regression analysis, distribution costs. Kara Jones, manager of distribution at Angel Foods, has the following data about monthly distribution costs and the number of packages shipped each month during the past year. To quickly assess the variable cost of a shipment of packages, she has been using the rule-of-thumb that it costs $0.50 to ship one package. Now she wants to better analyze the cost-and-cost-driver relationship, and in particular, she wants to assess whether she needs a new rule-of-thumb to estimate distribution costs.

Excel Lab www.prenhall.com/horngren/cost12e

	A	B	C
1	**Month**	**Distribution Costs**	**Number of Packages Shipped**
2	January	$ 28,000	51,000
3	February	20,000	43,000
4	March	17,000	28,000
5	April	32,000	67,000
6	May	40,000	73,000
7	June	24,000	54,000
8	July	22,000	37,000
9	August	35,000	72,000
10	September	42,000	71,000
11	October	23,000	56,000
12	November	33,000	52,000
13	December	22,000	45,000
14	Total	$338,000	649,000

If you want to use Excel to solve this exercise, go to the Excel Lab at **www.prenhall.com/horngren/cost12e** and download the template for Exercise 10-27.

Required

1. Plot the relationship between distribution costs and number of packages shipped.
2. Express Kara Jones's rule-of-thumb as a cost equation in the form:

$$\text{Distribution cost} = b_1 \times \text{Number of packages shipped}$$

   Plot this line on the same graph as requirement 1.
3. Estimate the relationship,

$$\text{Distribution cost} = a_2 + (b_2 \times \text{Number of packages shipped})$$

   by the high-low method. Plot this line on the same graph by connecting the high and low points.
4. Jones's staff analyst estimates the following regression equation:

$$\text{Distribution cost} = \$1{,}349 + (\$0.496 \times \text{Number of packages shipped})$$

   Plot this regression line on the same graph.
5. Jones anticipates shipping 40,000 packages in the next month. What is the predicted distribution cost using (a) Jones's rule-of-thumb, (b) the relationship estimated by the high-low method, and (c) the estimated regression equation. Which predicted cost should Jones use, and why?

10-28 Learning curve, cumulative average-time learning model. Global Defense manufactures radar systems. It has just completed the manufacture of its first newly designed system, RS-32. Manufacturing data for the RS-32 follows:

PH Grade Assist

Excel Lab www.prenhall.com/horngren/cost12e

	A	B	C
1	Direct material cost	$80,000	per unit of RS-32
2	Direct manufacturing labor time for first unit	3,000	direct manufacturing labor-hours
3	Learning curve for manufacturing labor time per radar system	90%	cumulative average time[a]
4	Direct manufacturing labor cost	$ 25	per direct manufacturing labor-hour
5	Variable manufacturing overhead cost	$ 15	per direct manufacturing labor-hour
6			
7	[a]Using the formula (p. 350), for a 90% learning curve, $b = \frac{\ln 0.90}{\ln 2}$	$= \frac{-0.105361}{0.693147} = -0.152004$	
8			

If you want to use Excel to solve this exercise, go to the Excel Lab at **www.prenhall.com/horngren/cost12e** and download the template for Exercise 10-28.

Required

Calculate the total variable costs of producing 2, 4, and 8 units.

Excel Lab www.prenhall.com/horngren/cost12e PH Grade Assist

10-29 Learning curve, incremental unit-time learning model. Assume the same information for Global Defense as in Exercise 10-28, except that Global Defense uses a 90% incremental unit-time learning model as a basis for predicting direct manufacturing labor-hours. (A 90% learning curve means $b = -0.152004$.)

If you want to use Excel to solve this exercise, go to the Excel Lab at **www.prenhall.com/horngren/cost12e** and download the template for Exercise 10-28.

Required

1. Calculate the total variable costs of producing 2, 3, and 4 units.
2. If you solved Exercise 10-28, compare your cost predictions in the two exercises for 2 and 4 units. Why are the predictions different?

Problems

10-30 High-low method. Ken Howard, financial analyst at JVR Corporation, is examining the behavior of quarterly maintenance costs for budgeting purposes. Howard collects the following data on machine-hours worked and maintenance costs for the past 12 quarters:

Quarter	Machine-Hours	Maintenance Costs
1	90,000	$185,000
2	110,000	220,000
3	100,000	200,000
4	120,000	240,000
5	85,000	170,000
6	105,000	215,000
7	95,000	195,000
8	115,000	235,000
9	95,000	190,000
10	115,000	225,000
11	105,000	180,000
12	125,000	250,000

Required

1. Estimate the cost function for the quarterly data using the high-low method.
2. Plot and comment on the estimated cost function.
3. Howard anticipates that JVR will operate machines for 90,000 hours in quarter 13. Calculate the predicted maintenance costs in quarter 13 using the cost function estimated in requirement 1.

Excel Lab www.prenhall.com/horngren/cost12e

10-31 High-low and regression methods, small business. Rudolph & Sons is a small mail-order distribution company that faces high seasonal demand, and in the peak months, ramps up its hiring considerably. As a small business owner, Mr. Rudolph is concerned about the cost of health insurance for his employees. He has the following insurance cost data for the past 15 months of operations:

	A	B	C
1	Month	Number of Employees	Insurance Costs
2	November	119	$ 44,930
3	December	131	48,326
4	January	148	54,260
5	February	50	33,110
6	March	54	32,880
7	April	56	33,200
8	May	53	33,130
9	June	64	32,100
10	July	76	36,400
11	August	80	33,120
12	September	84	34,340
13	October	93	37,600
14	November	106	39,900
15	December	118	44,670
16	January	140	51,107
17	15-month total	1,372	$589,073

Jake Rudolph, the owner's son, has just earned a business degree. He estimates the following relationship using regression analysis:

$$\text{Monthly insurance costs} = \$19,740 + (\$214 \text{ per worker} \times \text{Number of employees})$$

The fit of the regression is excellent ($r^2 = 0.92$) so Jake Rudolph has a high degree of confidence in the estimated relationship. When he explains his findings, his father searches for his insurance contract, which reveals that Mr. Rudolph actually pays $32,000 per month for up to 80 employees and $300 per month for each additional employee. Actual monthly costs are higher because of claims filed by employees.

If you want to use Excel to solve this problem, go to the Excel Lab at **www.prenhall.com/horngren/cost12e** and download the template for Problem 10-31.

Required

1. Plot the data for insurance costs (y-axis) and number of employees (x-axis) on a graph.
2. Plot the relationship between number of employees and insurance costs as described in the insurance contract.
3. Estimate the relationship between number of employees and insurance costs using the high-low method, and plot it on the same graph. Using the high-low estimation, what is the predicted monthly insurance cost for 75 employees? For 130 employees?
4. Plot the regression line. What is the monthly insurance cost predicted by the regression line for 75 employees? For 130 employees?
5. Suppose the Rudolphs do not know the terms of the actual insurance contract, but they have a vague recollection that it is flat and fixed up to a certain number of employees and increasing linearly after that level. Which of the two estimated lines—using the high-low method or using regression—would you suggest they use to predict monthly insurance costs, and why?

10-32 High-low method; regression analysis. (CIMA, adapted) Anna Martinez, the financial manager at the Casa Real restaurant, is checking to see if there is any relationship between newspaper advertising and sales revenues at the restaurant. She obtains the following data for the past 10 months:

PH Grade Assist

Month	Revenues	Advertising Costs
March	$50,000	$2,000
April	70,000	3,000
May	55,000	1,500
June	65,000	3,500
July	55,000	1,000
August	65,000	2,000
September	45,000	1,500
October	80,000	4,000
November	55,000	2,500
December	60,000	2,500

She estimates the following regression equation:

$$\text{Monthly revenues} = \$39{,}502 + (8.723 \times \text{Advertising costs})$$

Required

1. Plot the relationship between advertising costs and revenues.
2. Draw the regression line and evaluate it using the criteria of economic plausibility, goodness of fit, and slope of the regression line.
3. Use the high-low method to compute the cost function, relating advertising costs and revenues.
4. Using (a) the regression equation and (b) the high-low equation, what is the increase in revenues for each $1,000 spent on advertising within the relevant range? Which method should Martinez use to predict the effect of advertising costs on revenues? Explain briefly.

10-33 Regression analysis, activity-based costing, choosing cost drivers. Larry Chu, the plant controller at Rohan Plastics, wants to identify cost drivers for support overhead costs. Indirect support consists of skilled staff responsible for the efficient functioning of all aspects (setup, production, maintenance, and quality control) of the plastic injection molding facility. In talking to the support staff, Chu has the impression that the staff spends a sizable portion of their time ensuring that the equipment is set up correctly and checking that the first units of production in each batch are of good quality.

PH Grade Assist

Chu has collected the following data for the past 12 months:

Month	Support Overhead Costs	Machine-Hours	Number of Batches
January	$ 84,000	2,250	309
February	41,000	2,400	128
March	63,000	2,850	249
April	44,000	2,100	159
May	44,000	2,700	216
June	48,000	2,250	174
July	66,000	3,800	264
August	46,000	3,600	162
September	33,000	1,850	147
October	66,000	3,300	219
November	81,000	3,750	303
December	57,000	2,000	106
Total	$673,000	32,850	2,436

Chu estimates the following two regression equations:

$$y = \$28{,}089 + (\$10.23 \times \text{Machine-hours})$$

$$y = \$16{,}031 + (\$197.30 \times \text{Number of batches})$$

where y is the monthly support overhead costs.

Required

1. Plot the monthly data and the regression lines for each of the following cost functions:
   a. Support overhead costs = $a + (b \times \text{Machine-hours})$
   b. Support overhead costs = $a + (b \times \text{Number of batches})$
   Which cost driver for support overhead costs would you choose? Explain.
2. Chu anticipates 2,600 machine-hours and 300 batches for next month. Using the cost driver you chose in requirement 1, what amount of support overhead costs should Chu budget?
3. Assume facts in Requirement 2. Chu adds 20% to costs to determine target revenues (and hence prices). Costs other than support overhead are expected to equal $125,000 next month. Compare the target revenue numbers obtained if the cost driver is (i) machine-hours or (ii) number of batches. What would happen if Chu chose the cost driver you did not choose in requirement 1 to set target revenues and prices? Describe any other implications of choosing the "other" cost driver and cost function.

10-34 Interpreting regression results, matching time periods. Brickman Apparel produces equipment for the extreme-sports market. It has four peak periods, each lasting two months, for manufacturing the merchandise suited for spring, summer, fall, and winter. In the off-peak periods, Brickman schedules equipment maintenance and runs advertising to generate demand for its upcoming seasonal merchandise. Brickman's controller, Sascha Green, wants to understand the drivers of equipment maintenance costs and the effect of advertising expenditures on sales. A regression analysis of two years of monthly data yields the following relationships:

$$\text{Maintenance costs} = \$21{,}000 - (\$2.20 \text{ per machine-hour} \times \text{Number of machine-hours})$$

$$\text{Sales revenue} = \$310{,}000 - (\$1.80 \times \text{advertising expenditure})$$

Upon examining the results, Green comments, "So, all I have to do to reduce maintenance costs is run my machines longer?! And, clearly our advertising function is broken: the more we spend on advertising, the lower our sales revenue."

Required

1. Explain why Green made this comment.
2. Suggest a more economically plausible relationship between monthly maintenance costs and monthly machine-hours. Justify your choice.
3. Suggest a more economically plausible relationship between monthly sales and advertising expenditures. Justify your choice.

Excel Lab
www.prenhall.com/horngren/cost12e

10-35 Cost estimation, cumulative average-time learning curve. The Nautilus Company, which is under contract to the U.S. Navy, assembles troop deployment boats. As part of its research program, it completes the assembly of the first of a new model (PT109) of deployment boats. The Navy is impressed with the PT109. It requests that Nautilus submit a proposal on the cost of producing another seven PT109s.

Nautilus reports the following cost information for the first PT109 assembled and uses an 85% cumulative average-time learning model as a basis for forecasting direct manufacturing labor-hours for the next seven PT109s. (An 85% learning curve means $b = -0.234465$.):

	A	B	C
1	Direct materials	$100,000	
2	Direct manufacturing labor time for first boat	10,000	labor-hours
3	Direct manufacturing labor rate	$ 30	per direct manufacturing labor-hour
4	Variable manufacturing overhead cost	$ 20	per direct manufacturing labor-hour
5	Other manufacturing overhead	25%	of direct manufacturing labor costs
6	Tooling costs[a]	$ 50,000	
7	Learning curve for manufacturing labor time per boat	85%	cumulative average time[b]
8			
9	[a] Tooling can be reused at no extra cost because all of its cost has been assigned to the first deployment boat.		
10			
11	[b] Using the formula (p. 350), for an 85% learning curve, $b = \frac{\ln 0.85}{\ln 2} = \frac{-0.162519}{0.693147} = -0.234465$		
12			

If you want to use Excel to solve this problem, go to the Excel Lab at **www.prenhall.com/horngren/cost12e** and download the template for Problem 10-35.

Required

1. Calculate predicted total costs of producing the seven PT109s for the Navy. (Nautilus will keep the first deployment boat assembled, costed at $725,000, as a demonstration model for potential customers.)
2. What is the dollar amount of the difference between (a) the predicted total costs for producing the seven PT109s in requirement 1, and (b) the predicted total costs for producing the seven PT109s, assuming that there is no learning curve for direct manufacturing labor? That is, for (b) assume a linear function for units produced and direct manufacturing labor-hours.

10-36 Cost estimation, incremental unit-time learning model. Assume the same information for the Nautilus Company as in Problem 10-35 with one exception. This exception is that Nautilus uses an 85% incremental unit-time learning model as a basis for predicting direct manufacturing labor-hours on its assembling operations. (An 85% learning curve means $b = -0.234465$.)

Excel Lab
www.prenhall.com/horngren/cost12e

If you want to use Excel to solve this problem, go to the Excel Lab at **www.prenhall.com/horngren/cost12e** and download the template for Problem 10-35.

Required

1. Prepare a prediction of the total costs for producing the seven PT109s for the Navy.
2. If you solved requirement 1 of Problem 10-35, compare your cost prediction there with the one you made here. Why are the predictions different?

10-37 Evaluating different simple regression models, nonprofit (chapter appendix). Kevin Schonberg manages the Fallen Leaf Summer Camp. He has been camp manager for two years and has been asked to help rein in the costs of running the camp. With that in mind, he would like to cut back the number of week-long educational and recreational minicourses offered to the campers, but his marketing manager points out that the minicourses are a big draw. So, at the very least, Kevin wants to understand how course overhead costs are related to the number of minicourses offered and the number of campers who attend the camp. A few moments at the financial manager's computer yields the following data:

Excel Lab
www.prenhall.com/horngren/cost12e

	A	B	C	D
1	Year	Course Overhead Costs	Number of Minicourses Offered	Number of Campers
2	1	$24,500	15	1,700
3	2	34,100	18	2,500
4	3	30,100	25	1,300
5	4	35,700	27	2,350
6	5	34,700	27	1,950
7	6	40,800	29	2,450
8	7	41,800	44	2,850
9	8	35,700	36	1,950
10	9	40,300	42	1,750
11	10	52,000	37	1,850
12	11	54,500	51	2,800
13	12	66,300	52	3,800

Jill Day, a camp counselor and business student, is hired for a few hours each evening to run some simple analyses as necessary. She reports the following regression relationships:

Regression 1: Course overhead costs = $a + (b \times$ Number of minicourses offered)

	F	G	H	I
15		Coefficients	Standard Error	t Stat
16	Constant	$13,462.67	$5,649.30	2.38
17	Independent variable 1: Number of minicourses	$ 816.25	$ 159.03	5.13
18	$r^2 =$	0.72		
19	Durbin-Watson statistic =	1.87		

Regression 2: Course overhead costs = $a + (b \times$ Number of campers)

	F	G	H	I
22		Coefficients	Standard Error	t Stat
23	Constant	$11,746.66	$8,613.47	1.36
24	Independent variable 1: Number of campers	$ 12.83	$ 3.65	3.51
25	$r^2 =$	0.55		
26	Durbin-Watson statistic =	0.88		

If you want to use Excel to solve this problem, go to the Excel Lab at **www.prenhall.com/horngren/cost12e** and download the template for Problem 10-37.

Required

1. On two separate graphs, plot the course overhead costs against the number of minicourses and against the number of campers. On each graph, superimpose the corresponding plot of the relationship estimated by regression 1 or 2.
2. Evaluate the two estimated regression models. Use the format in Exhibit 10-18 (p. 361).
3. What insights do the analyses provide about controlling overhead costs at the summer camp?

Excel Lab
www.prenhall.com/horngren/cost12e

10-38 Evaluating multiple regression models, nonprofit (continuation of 10-37) (chapter appendix). If you want to use Excel to solve this problem, go to the Excel Lab at **www.prenhall.com/horngren/cost12e** and download the template for Problem 10-37.

Required

1. Given the findings in Problem 10-37, should Schonberg and his financial manager ask Jill Day to come in and run a multiple regression model to better understand the drivers of overhead costs? Why? Be specific.
2. Schonberg opts for the multiple regression analysis, and Day reports the following results:

	F	G	H	I
29		**Coefficients**	**Standard Error**	**t Stat**
30	Constant	$6,055.38	$6,087.81	0.99
31	Independent variable 1: Number of minicourses	$ 607.07	$ 171.56	3.54
32	Independent variable 2: Number of campers	$ 6.36	$ 3.09	2.06
33	r^2 =	0.81		
34	Durbin-Watson statistic =	1.91		

   The coefficient of correlation between number of minicourses and number of campers is 0.59. Use the format in Exhibit 10-18 (p. 361) to evaluate the multiple regression model. (Assume linearity, constant variance of residuals, and normality of residuals.) Should Schonberg use the multiple regression model to predict course overhead costs instead of the two simple regression models of Problem 10-37?
3. How might Schonberg use these regression results to manage overhead costs?

10-39 Purchasing Department cost drivers, activity-based costing, simple regression analysis (chapter appendix). Fashion Flair operates a chain of 10 retail department stores. Each department store makes its own purchasing decisions. Barry Lee, assistant to the president of Fashion Flair, is interested in better understanding the drivers of Purchasing Department costs. For many years, Fashion Flair has allocated Purchasing Department costs to products on the basis of the dollar value of merchandise purchased. A $100 item is allocated 10 times as many overhead costs associated with the Purchasing Department as a $10 item.

Lee recently attended a seminar titled "Cost Drivers in the Retail Industry." In a presentation at the seminar, Couture Fabrics, a leading competitor that has implemented activity-based costing, reported number of purchase orders and number of suppliers to be the two most important cost drivers of Purchasing Department costs. The dollar value of merchandise purchased in each purchase order was not found to be a significant cost driver. Lee interviewed several members of the Purchasing Department at the Fashion Flair store in Miami. They believed that Couture Fabrics' conclusions also applied to their Purchasing Department.

Lee collects the following data for the most recent year for Fashion Flair's 10 retail department stores:

Department Store	Purchasing Department Costs (PDC)	Dollar Value of Merchandise Purchased (MP$)	Number of Purchase Orders (No. of PO's)	Number of Suppliers (No. of S's)
Baltimore	$1,523,000	$ 68,315,000	4,357	132
Chicago	1,100,000	33,456,000	2,550	222
Los Angeles	547,000	121,160,000	1,433	11
Miami	2,049,000	119,566,000	5,944	190
New York	1,056,000	33,505,000	2,793	23
Phoenix	529,000	29,854,000	1,327	33
Seattle	1,538,000	102,875,000	7,586	104
St. Louis	1,754,000	38,674,000	3,617	119
Toronto	1,612,000	139,312,000	1,707	208
Vancouver	1,257,000	130,944,000	4,731	201

Lee decides to use simple regression analysis to examine whether one or more of three variables (the last three columns in the table) are cost drivers of Purchasing Department costs. Summary results for these regressions are as follows:

Regression 1: PDC = $a + (b \times$ MP\$)

Variable	Coefficient	Standard Error	*t*-Value
Constant	\$1,039,061	\$343,439	3.03
Independent variable 1: MP\$	0.0031	0.0037	0.84

$r^2 = 0.08$; Durbin-Watson statistic = 2.41

Regression 2: PDC = $a + (b \times$ No. of PO's)

Variable	Coefficient	Standard Error	*t*-Value
Constant	\$730,716	\$265,419	2.75
Independent variable 1: No. of PO's	\$156.97	\$64.69	2.43

$r^2 = 0.42$; Durbin-Watson statistic = 1.98

Regression 3: PDC = a + ($b \times$ No. of S's)

Variable	Coefficient	Standard Error	*t*-Value
Constant	\$814,862	\$247,821	3.29
Independent variable 1: No. of S's	\$3,875	\$1,697	2.28

$r^2 = 0.39$; Durbin-Watson statistic = 1.97

Required

1. Compare and evaluate the three simple regression models estimated by Lee. Graph each one. Also, use the format employed in Exhibit 10-18 (p. 361) to evaluate the information.
2. Do the regression results support the Couture Fabrics' presentation about the Purchasing Department's cost drivers? Which of these cost drivers would you recommend in designing an ABC system?
3. How might Lee gain additional evidence on drivers of Purchasing Department costs at each of Fashion Flair's stores?

10-40 Purchasing Department cost drivers, multiple regression analysis (continuation of 10-39) (chapter appendix). Barry Lee decides that the simple regression analysis used in Problem 10-39 could be extended to a multiple regression analysis. He finds the following results for two multiple regression analyses:

Regression 4: PDC = $a + (b_1 \times$ No. of PO's) + ($b_2 \times$ No. of S's)

Variable	Coefficient	Standard Error	*t*-Value
Constant	\$485,384	\$257,477	1.89
Independent variable 1: No. of PO's	\$123.22	\$57.69	2.14
Independent variable 2: No. of S's	\$2,952	\$1,476	2.00

$r^2 = 0.63$; Durbin-Watson statistic = 1.90

Regression 5: PDC = $a + (b_1 \times$ No. of PO's) + ($b_2 \times$ No. of S's) + ($b_3 \times$ MP\$)

Variable	Coefficient	Standard Error	*t*-Value
Constant	\$494,684	\$310,205	1.59
Independent variable 1: No. of PO's	\$124.05	\$63.49	1.95
Independent variable 2: No. of S's	\$2,984	\$1,622	1.84
Independent variable 3: MP\$	–0.0002	0.0030	–0.07

$r^2 = 0.63$; Durbin-Watson statistic = 1.90

The coefficients of correlation between combinations of pairs of the variables are:

	PDC	MP\$	No. of PO's
MP\$	0.29		
No. of PO's	0.65	0.27	
No. of S's	0.63	0.34	0.29

Required

1. Evaluate regression 4 using the criteria of economic plausibility, goodness of fit, significance of independent variables and specification analysis. Compare regression 4 with regressions 2 and 3 in Problem 10-39. Which one of these models would you recommend that Lee use? Why?
2. Compare regression 5 with regression 4. Which one of these models would you recommend that Lee use? Why?
3. Lee estimates the following data for the Baltimore store for next year: dollar value of merchandise purchased, \$75,000,000; number of purchase orders, 3,900; number of suppliers, 110. How much should Lee budget for Purchasing Department costs for the Baltimore store for next year?
4. What difficulties do not arise in simple regression analysis that may arise in multiple regression analysis? Is there evidence of such difficulties in either of the multiple regressions presented in this problem? Explain.
5. Give two examples of decisions in which the regression results reported here (and in Problem 10-39) could be informative.

Collaborative Learning Problem

10-41 High-low method, alternative regression functions, accrual accounting adjustments, ethics. Trevor Kennedy, the cost analyst at a can manufacturing plant of United Packaging, is examining the relationship between total engineering support costs reported in the plant records and machine-hours. These costs have two components: (1) labor, which is paid monthly, and (2) materials and parts, which are purchased from an outside vendor every three months. After further discussion with the operating manager, Kennedy discovers that the materials and parts numbers reported in the monthly records are on an "as purchased," or cash accounting basis and not on an "as used," or accrual accounting basis. By examining materials and parts usage records, Kennedy is able to restate the materials and parts costs to an "as used" basis. (No restatement of the labor costs was necessary.) The reported and restated costs are as follows:

Month	Labor: Reported Costs (1)	Materials and Parts: Reported Costs (2)	Materials and Parts: Restated Costs (3)	Total Engineering Support: Reported Costs (4) = (1) + (2)	Total Engineering Support: Restated Costs (5) = (1) + (3)	Machine-Hours (6)
March	$347	$847	$182	$1,194	$529	30
April	521	0	411	521	932	63
May	398	0	268	398	666	49
June	355	961	228	1,316	583	38
July	473	0	348	473	821	57
August	617	0	349	617	966	73
September	245	821	125	1,066	370	19
October	487	0	364	487	851	53
November	431	0	290	431	721	42

The regression results for total engineering support reported costs as the dependent variable, are:

Regression 1: Engineering support reported costs = $a + (b \times$ Machine-hours)

Variable	Coefficient	Standard Error	*t*-Value
Constant	$1,393.20	$305.68	4.56
Independent variable 1: Machine-hours	–$14.23	$6.15	–2.31

$r^2 = 0.43$; Durbin-Watson statistic = 2.26

The regression results for total engineering support restated costs as the dependent variable, are:

Regression 2: Engineering support restated costs = $a + (b \times$ Machine-hours)

Variable	Coefficient	Standard Error	*t*-Value
Constant	$176.38	$53.99	3.27
Independent variable 1: Machine-hours	$11.44	$1.08	10.59

$r^2 = 0.94$; Durbin-Watson statistic = 1.31

Required

1. Plot the cost functions relating (i) the *reported costs* for total engineering support to machine-hours and (ii) the *restated costs* for total engineering support to machine-hours. Comment on the plots.
2. Use the high-low method to compute estimates of the cost functions $y = a + bX$ for (a) reported engineering support costs and machine-hours and (b) restated engineering support costs and machine-hours.
3. Contrast and evaluate the cost function estimated with regression analysis using restated data for materials and parts with the cost function estimated with regression analysis using the data reported in the plant records. Use the comparison format employed in Exhibit 10-18 (p. 361).
4. Of all the cost functions estimated in requirements 2 and 3, which one would you choose to best represent the relationship between engineering support costs and machine-hours? Explain briefly.
5. What problems might Kennedy encounter when restating the materials and parts costs recorded to an "as used," or accrual accounting basis?
6. Why is it important for Kennedy to choose the correct cost function? That is, illustrate two potential problems Kennedy could encounter by choosing a cost function other than the one you chose in requirement 4.
7. John Mason, the plant manager, is not pleased when he sees the restated numbers. He tells Kennedy, "I think the restated engineering support costs are too high. Please recheck your numbers. They ought to be lower." Kennedy is aware that lower costs will result in a higher bonus for Mason. He is also certain that his numbers are correct. What should Kennedy do?

Get Connected: Cost Accounting in the News

Go to www.prenhall.com/horngren/cost12e for additional online exercise(s) that explore issues affecting the accounting world today. These exercises offer you the opportunity to analyze and reflect on how cost accounting helps managers to make better decisions and handle the challenges of strategic planning and implementation.

CHAPTER 10 Case

U.S. BREWING INDUSTRY: Cost Estimation

Hobie Leland, Jr., has been assigned to a project to estimate the cost-volume relationship of Ace Brewing Company. Leland first analyzes Ace's internal records and discovers that since 1986, Ace has been a single-line-of-business company. Prior to 1986, it also owned a soft-drink company (Hoff Beverage Company), and the accounting records did not separately report the costs associated with the brewing and soft-drink operations. Leland decides to base his analysis on the 1986 to 2004 period and collects the data in Exhibit 10-21.

QUESTIONS

1. Estimate the following linear relationship between cost of sales (C_t) and barrels of beer sold (V_t) from 1986 to 2004 using (a) the high-low method and (b) regression analysis.

$$C_t = a + b\,V_t$$

Evaluate the results.

2. One problem in using time series data to estimate cost-volume relationships arises from inflation. One technique proposed to deal with this problem is to deflate the dependent variable by a price index (P_t). The "Wholesale Price Index of Beer" from 1986 to 2004 is presented in Exhibit 10-21. Estimate the following linear relationship using regression analysis:

$$\frac{C_t}{P_t} = a + b \cdot V_t$$

Evaluate the results.

3. Leland remembered a warning from his college days: Serial correlation in the residuals is frequently encountered in regressions using time series data. A common approach to serial correlation of the residuals is to estimate the model in the first differences of the variables as follows:

$$\left(\frac{C_t}{P_t} - \frac{C_{t-1}}{P_{t-1}}\right) = a + b(V_t - V_{t-1})$$

Estimate this relationship for Ace using regression analysis. Is serial correlation in the residuals less of a problem than with the model estimated in 2 above? Explain.

4. Which regression equation would you choose to estimate the cost-volume relationship of Ace? Explain.

EXHIBIT 10-21
Ace Brewing Company: 1986 to 2004

Year	Cost of Goods Sold (in millions)	Barrels Sold (in millions)	Wholesale Price Index of Beer
1986	$166.943	5.844	0.533
1987	184.981	6.672	0.533
1988	206.666	7.444	0.535
1989	229.200	8.219	0.536
1990	252.122	9.047	0.540
1991	285.380	10.123	0.552
1992	313.070	10.910	0.557
1993	305.044	10.225	0.570
1994	324.391	10.517	0.596
1995	367.779	11.797	0.611
1996	395.559	12.600	0.612
1997	431.398	13.128	0.623
1998	530.769	14.297	0.719
1999	630.160	15.669	0.759
2000	696.039	17.037	0.769
2001	688.045	16.003	0.794
2002	720.258	15.367	0.848
2003	765.303	15.115	0.933
2004	832.018	15.091	1.000

CHAPTER 11

DECISION MAKING AND RELEVANT INFORMATION

LEARNING OBJECTIVES

1. Use the five-step decision process to make decisions
2. Distinguish relevant from irrelevant costs and revenues in decision situations
3. Understand the difference between quantitative and qualitative factors in decision making
4. Beware of two potential problems in relevant-cost analysis
5. Explain the opportunity-cost concept and why it is used in decision making
6. Know how to choose which products to produce when there are capacity constraints
7. Discuss factors managers must consider when adding or dropping customers or segments
8. Explain why book value of equipment is irrelevant in equipment-replacement decisions
9. Explain how conflicts can arise between the decision model used by a manager and the performance-evaluation model used to evaluate the manager

How many decisions have you made today? Maybe you made a big one, such as accepting a job offer or finally deciding to buy a new car. Or maybe your decisions were as simple as settling on your plans for the weekend or where to eat out for dinner. Whether decisions are significant or routine, most people follow a simple, logical decision making process. This process involves gathering information, making predictions, making a choice, acting on the choice, and evaluating results. And it works for organizations as well as individuals.

Barbara Bailey is CEO of Soho Company. Her company manufactures three-in-one stereos consisting of a compact disc (CD) player, cassette deck, and digital radio. Over the past few weeks she has faced several major decisions. One of them involved whether to make or buy the CD player. Yesterday, she and her management team decided to add a new product line.

As Barbara looked over the volumes of financial information she'd used to make her decisions while preparing for the next week's board meeting, she observed something she hadn't noticed before. She called Alex Gilbert, the CFO, into her office.

Barbara: Alex, I was just reviewing all the financial reports you have been giving me over the past few weeks. It seems there is a lot of variation in the numbers, which I didn't notice until now. For example, certain fixed costs were included for some of the decision scenarios but excluded for others. Sometimes the costs recorded in the accounting system were totally ignored, and sometimes costs not recorded in the system were included in the analysis. I want to be sure that I understand these numbers before the board meeting.

Alex: The key concept is relevance. Remember when you asked me to analyze the different alternatives? You asked me what revenues and costs would change if we chose one alternative over another. The analysis I prepared for each decision contained only the relevant revenues and costs for the decision. For different decisions and different alternatives, the relevant revenues and costs were not the same.

Barbara: Terrific, but I think I still need more detail on how you arrived at the numbers.

Alex: Let's meet tomorrow morning to review the numbers. I also will highlight the strategic and qualitative aspects of each decision.

Barbara: Yes, that sounds great. Thanks, Alex.

Corporations around the world use a decision process similar to the one at Soho company. Citibank gathers information about financial markets, consumer preferences, and economic trends before determining whether to offer new services to customers. Macy's examines the relevant information related to domestic and international clothing manufacturing before choosing its vendors. And Porsche gathers cost information to decide whether it should manufacture a component part or purchase it from a supplier. The decision process may not always be an easy one, but as Napoleon Bonaparte said, "Nothing is more difficult, and therefore more precious, than to be able to decide."

Information and the Decision Process

Shareholders want managers to make decisions that are in the shareholders' best interest.

Managers usually follow a *decision model* for choosing among different courses of action. A **decision model** is a formal method of making a choice, and it often involves both quantitative and qualitative analyses. Management accountants work with managers by analyzing and presenting relevant data to guide decisions.

Consider a strategic decision facing management at Precision Sporting Goods, a manufacturer of golf clubs: Should it reorganize its manufacturing operations to reduce manufacturing labor costs? Assume that there are only two alternatives: do not reorganize or reorganize.

1

Use the five-step decision process to make decisions

. . . the five steps are obtain information, make predictions, choose an alternative, implement the decision, and evaluate performance

The reorganization will eliminate all manual handling of materials. The current manufacturing line uses 20 workers—15 workers operate machines, and 5 workers handle materials. The 5 materials-handling workers have been hired on contracts that permit layoffs without additional payments. Each worker puts in 2,000 hours annually. The cost of reorganization (consisting mostly of new equipment leases) is predicted to be $90,000 each year. The predicted production output of 25,000 units will be unaffected by the decision. Also unaffected will be the predicted selling price of $250, the direct material cost per unit of $50, manufacturing overhead of $750,000, and marketing costs of $2,000,000.

Managers typically use the five-step decision process described in Exhibit 11-1 to make decisions such as do not reorganize or reorganize. In this exhibit, study the sequence of the

EXHIBIT 11-1

Five-Step Decision Process for Precision Sporting Goods

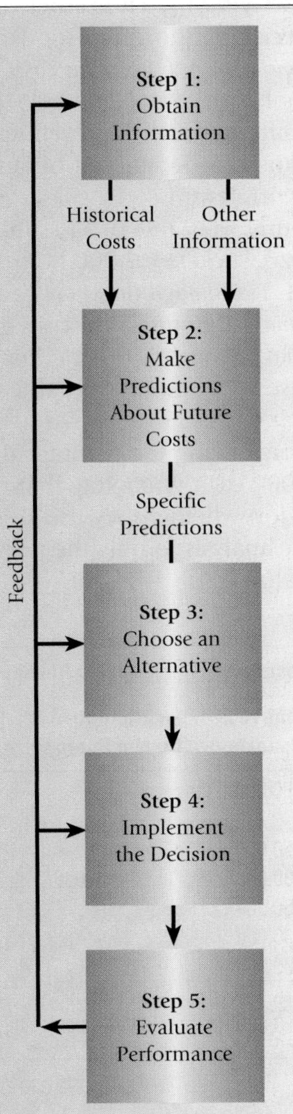

Historical hourly wage rates are $14 per hour. However, a recently negotiated increase in employee benefits of $2 per hour will increase wages to $16 per hour in the future. The reorganization of manufacturing operations is expected to reduce the number of workers from 20 to 15 by eliminating all 5 workers who handle materials. The reorganization is likely to have negative effects on employee morale.

Managers use information from step 1 together with an assessment of probability as a basis for predicting future manufacturing labor costs. Under the existing do-not-reorganize alternative, costs are predicted to be $640,000 (20 workers × 2,000 hours per worker per year × $16 per hour). Under the reorganize alternative, costs are predicted to be $480,000 (15 workers × 2,000 hours per worker per year ×$16 per hour). Recall, the reorganization is predicted to cost $90,000 per year.

Managers compare the predicted benefits of the different alternatives in step 2 ($640,000 – $480,000 = $160,000—that is, savings from eliminating materials-handling labor costs, 5 workers × 2,000 hours per worker per year × $16 per hour= $160,000) and compare the savings to the cost of the reorganization ($90,000) along with other considerations (such as likely negative effects on employee morale). Management chooses the reorganize alternative.

The manager implements the decision reached in step 3 by reorganizing manufacturing operations.

Evaluating performance after the decision is implemented in step 4 provides critical feedback for managers, and the five-step sequence is then repeated in whole or in part. Managers learn from actual results that the new manufacturing labor costs are $540,000, rather than the predicted $480,000, because of lower-than-expected manufacturing labor productivity. This (now) historical information can help managers make better subsequent predictions that allow for more learning time. Alternatively, managers may improve implementation via employee training and better supervision.

steps and note how step 5 evaluates performance to provide feedback about actions taken in the previous steps. This feedback might affect future predictions, the prediction methods used, the way choices are made, or the implementation of the decision.

2

Distinguish relevant from irrelevant costs and revenues in decision situations

... only costs and revenues that are expected to occur in the future and differ among alternative courses of action are relevant

The Concept of Relevance

Much of this chapter focuses on step 3 in Exhibit 11-1 and on the concepts of relevant costs and relevant revenues when choosing among alternatives.

Relevant Costs and Relevant Revenues

Relevant costs are *expected future costs* and **relevant revenues** are *expected future revenues* that differ among the alternative courses of action being considered. Be sure you understand that to be relevant costs and relevant revenues they *must*

- **Occur in the future**—every decision deals with selecting a course of action based on its expected future results—and
- **Differ among the alternative courses of action**—costs and revenues that do not differ will not matter and, hence, will have no bearing on the decision being made.

It's essential to understand the concept of relevance; it is used extensively in this chapter and in many chapters that follow.

The question is always, What difference will an action make?

Exhibit 11-2 presents the financial data underlying the choice between the do-not-reorganize and reorganize alternatives for Precision Sporting Goods. The first two columns present *all data*. The last two columns present *only relevant costs*—the $640,000 and $480,000 expected future manufacturing labor costs and the $90,000 expected future reorganization costs that differ between the two alternatives. The revenues, direct materials, manufacturing overhead, and marketing items can be ignored because they do not differ between the alternatives and, therefore, are irrelevant.

Note, the past (historical) manufacturing hourly wage rate of $14 and total past (historical) manufacturing labor costs of $560,000 (20 workers × 2,000 hours per worker per year × $14 per hour) do not appear in Exhibit 11-2. *Although they may be a useful basis for making informed predictions of the expected future manufacturing labor costs of $640,000 and $480,000, historical costs themselves are past costs that, therefore, are irrelevant to decision making.* Past costs are also called **sunk costs** because they are unavoidable and cannot be changed no matter what action is taken.

Some managers may prefer to focus only on relevant revenues and relevant costs (for example, the right-most two columns in Exhibit 11-2). Why? Because managers reduce their information load by excluding irrelevant data. Research has shown that when inundated with data, managers tend to make poorer decisions, take longer to decide, and have more confidence in their decisions.

The analysis in Exhibit 11-2 indicates that reorganizing the manufacturing operations will increase predicted operating income by $70,000 each year. Note that the managers at Precision Sporting Goods reach the same conclusion whether they use all data or include only relevant data in the analysis. By confining the analysis to only the relevant data, man-

EXHIBIT 11-2

Determining Relevant Revenues and Relevant Costs for Precision Sporting Goods

	All Revenues and Costs		Relevant Revenues and Costs	
	Alternative 1: Do Not Reorganize	**Alternative 2: Reorganize**	**Alternative 1: Do Not Reorganize**	**Alternative 2: Reorganize**
Revenues[a]	$6,250,000	$6,250,000	—	—
Costs:				
Direct materials[b]	1,250,000	1,250,000	—	—
Manufacturing labor	640,000[c]	480,000[d]	$ 640,000[c]	$ 480,000[d]
Manufacturing overhead	750,000	750,000	—	—
Marketing	2,000,000	2,000,000	—	—
Reorganization costs	—	90,000	—	90,000
Total costs	4,640,000	4,570,000	640,000	570,000
Operating income	$1,610,000	$1,680,000	$(640,000)	$(570,000)
	$70,000 Difference		$70,000 Difference	

[a]25,000 units × $250 per unit = $6,250,000
[b]25,000 units × $50 per unit = $1,250,000
[c]20 workers × 2,000 hours per worker × $16 per hour = $640,000
[d]15 workers × 2,000 hours per worker × $16 per hour = $480,000

EXHIBIT 11-3

Key Features of Relevant Information

- Past (historical) costs may be helpful as a basis for making *predictions*. However, past costs themselves are always irrelevant when making *decisions*.
- Different alternatives can be compared by examining differences in expected total future revenues and costs.
- Not all expected future revenues and costs are relevant. Expected future revenues and costs that do not differ among alternatives are irrelevant and, hence, can be eliminated from the analysis. The key question is always, What difference will an action make?
- Appropriate weight must be given to qualitative factors and quantitative nonfinancial factors.

agers can clear away the clutter of potentially confusing irrelevant data. Focusing on the relevant data is especially helpful when all the information needed to prepare a detailed income statement is unavailable. Understanding which costs are relevant and which are irrelevant helps the decision maker concentrate on obtaining only the pertinent data and saves time.

Qualitative and Quantitative Relevant Information

3

Understand the difference between quantitative
. . . outcomes that are measured in numerical terms

and qualitative factors in decision making
. . . outcomes that are difficult to measure accurately in numerical terms

Managers divide the outcomes of alternatives into two broad categories: *quantitative* and *qualitative*. **Quantitative factors** are outcomes that are measured in numerical terms. Some quantitative factors are financial; they can be expressed in monetary terms. Examples include the costs of direct materials, direct manufacturing labor, and marketing. Other quantitative factors are nonfinancial; they can be measured numerically, but they are not expressed in monetary terms. Reduction in new product-development time for a manufacturing company and the percentage of on-time flight arrivals for an airline company are examples of quantitative nonfinancial factors. **Qualitative factors** are outcomes that are difficult to measure accurately in numerical terms. Employee morale is an example.

Relevant-cost analysis generally emphasizes quantitative factors that can be expressed in financial terms. *But just because qualitative factors and quantitative nonfinancial factors cannot be measured easily in financial terms does not make them unimportant.* In fact, managers must at times give more weight to these factors. For example, managers at Precision Sporting Goods carefully considered the negative effect on employee morale of laying off materials-handling workers, a qualitative factor, before choosing the reorganize alternative. Trading off nonfinancial and financial considerations is seldom easy.

Exhibit 11-3 summarizes the key features of relevant information.

An Illustration of Relevance: Choosing Output Levels

The concept of relevance applies to all decision situations. In this and the following several sections, we present some of these decision situations. We start by considering decisions that affect output levels. For example, managers must choose whether to introduce a new product or to try to sell more units of an existing product. Managers are interested in the effects that changes in output levels will have on the company and on operating income.

One-Time-Only Special Orders

One type of decision that affects output levels is accepting or rejecting special orders when there is idle production capacity and the special orders have no long-run implications. We use the term **one-time-only special order** to describe these conditions.

Example 1: Surf Gear manufactures quality beach towels at its highly automated Burlington, North Carolina, plant. The plant has a production capacity of 48,000 towels each month. Current monthly production is 30,000 towels. Retail department stores account for all existing sales. Expected results for the coming month (August) are shown in Exhibit 11-4. (These amounts are predictions based on past costs.) We assume all costs can be classified as either fixed or variable with respect to a single cost driver (units of output).

EXHIBIT 11-4

Budgeted Income Statement for August, Absorption-Costing Format for Surf Gear[a]

	A	B	C	D
1		**Total**	**Per Unit**	
2	Units sold	30,000		
3				
4	Revenues	$600,000	$20.00	
5	Cost of goods sold (manufacturing costs)			
6	Variable manufacturing costs	225,000	7.50[b]	
7	Fixed manufacturing costs	135,000	4.50[c]	
8	Total cost of goods sold	360,000	12.00	
9	Marketing costs			
10	Variable marketing costs	150,000	5.00	
11	Fixed marketing costs	60,000	2.00	
12	Total marketing costs	210,000	7.00	
13	Full costs of the product	570,000	19.00	
14	Operating income	$ 30,000	$ 1.00	
15				
16	[a] Surf Gear incurs no R&D, product-design, distribution or customer-service costs			
17	[b] Variable maufacturing cost per unit = Direct material cost per unit + Direct maufacturing labor cost per unit + Variable maufacturing overhead per unit			
18				
19	= $6.00 + $0.50 + $1.00 = $7.50			
20	[c] Fixed maufacturing cost per unit = Fixed direct maufacturing labor cost per unit + Fixed maufacturing overhead per unit			
21				
22	= $1.50 + $3.00 = $4.50			

As a result of a strike at its existing towel supplier, a luxury hotel chain has offered to buy 5,000 towels from Surf Gear in August at $11 per towel. No subsequent sales to this hotel chain are anticipated. Fixed manufacturing costs are tied to the 48,000-towel production capacity. That is, fixed manufacturing costs relate to the production capacity available, regardless of the capacity used. If Surf Gear accepts the special order, it will use existing idle capacity to produce the 5,000 towels, and fixed manufacturing costs will not change. No marketing costs will be necessary for the 5,000-unit one-time-only special order. Accepting this special order is not expected to affect the selling price or the quantity of towels sold to regular customers. Should Surf Gear accept the hotel chain's offer?

Exhibit 11-4 presents data for this example on an absorption-costing basis (that is, both variable and fixed manufacturing costs are included in inventoriable costs and cost of goods sold). In this exhibit, the manufacturing cost of $12 per unit and the marketing cost of $7 per unit include both variable and fixed costs. The sum of all costs (variable and fixed) in a particular business function of the value chain, such as manufacturing costs or marketing costs, are called **business function costs**. **Full costs of the product**, in this case $19 per unit, are the sum of all variable and fixed costs in all business functions of the value chain (R&D, design, production, marketing, distribution, and customer service). For Surf Gear, full costs of the product consist of costs in manufacturing and marketing because these are the only business functions. No marketing costs are necessary for the special order, so the manager of Surf Gear will focus only on manufacturing costs. Based on the manufacturing cost per unit of $12—which is greater than the $11-per-unit price offered by the hotel chain—the manager might decide to reject the offer.

Exhibit 11-5 separates manufacturing and marketing costs into their variable- and fixed-cost components and presents data in the format of a contribution income statement. The relevant revenues and costs are the expected future revenues and costs that differ as a result of accepting the special offer—revenues of $55,000 ($11 per unit × 5,000 units) and variable manufacturing costs of $37,500 ($7.50 per unit × 5,000 units). The fixed manufacturing costs and all marketing costs (*including variable marketing costs*) are irrelevant in this case. That's because these costs will not change in total whether the special order is accepted or rejected. Surf Gear would gain an additional $17,500 (relevant revenues, $55,000 – relevant costs, $37,500) in operating income by accepting the special order. In this example, comparing total amounts for 30,000 units versus 35,000 units or focusing only on the relevant amounts in the difference column in Exhibit 11-5 avoids a misleading implication—the implication that would result from comparing the $11-per-

Question: Could the special order affect Surf Gear's regular business?

Answer: Yes, unless Surf Gear has effectively segmented its market so that the special order to the hotel chain does not affect the regular business to the retail department stores.

	A	B	D	F	H
1		Without the Special Order		With the Special Order	Difference: Relevant Amounts
2		30,000		35,000	for the
3		Units to be Sold		Units to be Sold	5,000
4		Per Unit	Total	Total	Units Special Order
5		(1)	(2) = (1) x 30,000	(3)	(4) = (3) - (2)
6	Revenues	$20.00	$600,000	$655,000	$55,000[a]
7	Variable costs:				
8	Manufacturing	7.50	225,000	262,500	37,500[b]
9	Marketing	5.00	150,000	150,000	0[c]
10	Total variable costs	12.50	375,000	412,500	37,500
11	Contribution margin	7.50	225,000	242,500	17,500
12	Fixed costs:				
13	Manufacturing	4.50	135,000	135,000	0[d]
14	Marketing	2.00	60,000	60,000	0[d]
15	Total fixed costs	6.50	195,000	195,000	0
16	Operating income	$ 1.00	$ 30,000	$ 47,500	$17,500
17					
18	[a] 5,000 units × $11.00 per unit = $55,000.				
19	[b] 5,000 units × $7.50 per unit = $37,500.				
20	[c] No variable marketing costs would be incurred for the 5,000-unit one-time-only special order.				
21	[d] Fixed manufacturing costs and fixed marketing costs would be unaffected by the special order.				

EXHIBIT 11-5

One-Time-Only Special-Order Decision for Surf Gear: Comparative Contribution Income Statements

Exhibit 11-5 illustrates two keys to analyzing relevant costs and relevant revenues for decisions: (1) distinguish relevant costs and revenues from irrelevant ones and (2) use the contribution income statement to focus on whether each variable cost and each fixed cost is affected by the alternatives under consideration.

unit selling price against the manufacturing cost per unit of $12 (Exhibit 11-4), which includes both variable and fixed manufacturing costs.

The assumption of no long-run or strategic implications is crucial to management's analysis of the one-time-only special-order decision. Suppose Surf Gear concludes that the retail department stores (its regular customers) will demand a lower price if it sells towels at $11 apiece to the luxury hotel chain. In this case, revenues from regular customers will be relevant. Why? Because the future revenues from regular customers will differ depending on whether the special order is accepted or rejected. The relevant-revenue and relevant-cost analysis of the hotel-chain order would have to be modified to consider both the short-run benefits from accepting the order and the long-run consequences on profitability if prices were lowered to all regular customers.

Potential Problems in Relevant-Cost Analysis

4

Beware of two potential problems in relevant-cost analysis

... (1) making incorrect general assumptions, such as all variable costs are relevant and all fixed costs are irrelevant and (2) focusing only on unit costs, not on total costs

Managers should avoid two potential problems in relevant-cost analysis. First, they must watch out for incorrect general assumptions, such as all variable costs are relevant and all fixed costs are irrelevant. In the Surf Gear example, the variable marketing cost of $5 per unit is irrelevant because Surf Gear will incur no extra marketing costs by accepting the special order. But fixed manufacturing costs could be relevant. The extra production of 5,000 towels per month does not affect fixed manufacturing costs because we assumed that the relevant range is from 30,000 to 48,000 towels per month. In some cases, however, producing the extra 5,000 towels might increase fixed manufacturing costs. Suppose Surf Gear would need to run three shifts of 16,000 towels per shift to achieve full capacity of 48,000 towels per month. Increasing the monthly production from 30,000 to 35,000 would require a partial third shift because two shifts could produce only 32,000 towels. The extra shift would increase fixed manufacturing costs, thereby making these additional fixed manufacturing costs relevant for this decision.

Second, unit-cost data can potentially mislead decision makers in two ways:

1. **When irrelevant costs are included.** Consider the $4.50 of fixed manufacturing cost per unit (direct manufacturing labor, $1.50 per unit, plus manufacturing overhead, $3.00 per unit) included in the $12-per-unit manufacturing cost in the one-time-only special-order decision (see Exhibits 11-4 and 11-5). This $4.50-per-unit cost is irrelevant, given the assumptions in our example, so it should be excluded.

2. **When the same unit costs are used at different output levels.** Generally, managers use total costs rather than unit costs because total costs are easier to work with and reduce the chance for erroneous conclusions. Then, if desired, the total costs can be unitized. In the Surf Gear example, total fixed manufacturing costs remain at $135,000 even if Surf Gear accepts the special order and produces 35,000 towels. Including the fixed manufacturing cost per unit of $4.50 as a cost of the special order would lead to the erroneous conclusion that total fixed manufacturing costs would increase to $157,500 ($4.50 per towel × 35,000 towels).

The best way for managers to avoid these two potential problems is to keep focusing on (1) total revenues and total costs (rather than unit revenue and unit cost) and (2) the relevance concept. Managers should always require all items included in an analysis to be expected total future revenues and expected total future costs that differ among the alternatives.

Insourcing-versus-Outsourcing and Make-versus-Buy Decisions

We now apply the concept of relevance to another strategic decision: whether a company should make a component part or buy it from a supplier. We again assume idle capacity.

Outsourcing and Idle Facilities

Outsourcing is purchasing goods and services from outside vendors rather than **insourcing**, which is producing the same goods or providing the same services within the organization. For example, Kodak prefers to manufacture its own film (insourcing), but it has IBM do its data processing (outsourcing). Toyota relies on outside vendors to supply some component parts but chooses to manufacture other parts internally.

Decisions about whether a producer of goods or services will insource or outsource are also called **make-or-buy decisions**. Sometimes qualitative factors dominate management's make-or-buy decision. For example, Dell Computer buys the Pentium chip for its personal computers from Intel because Dell does not have the know-how and technology to make the chip itself. To maintain the secrecy of its formula, Coca-Cola does not outsource the manufacture of its concentrate. Surveys of companies indicate they consider the most important factors in the make-or-buy decision to be quality, dependability of suppliers, and cost.

Example 2: The Soho Company, mentioned earlier, manufactures a three-in-one stereo consisting of a CD player, a cassette deck, and a digital radio. Columns 1 and 2 of the following table show the current costs for manufacturing the CD-player unit of the stereo system based on an analysis of various manufacturing activities:

	Total Current Costs of Producing 1,000,000 Units in 2,500 Batches (1)	Current Cost per Unit (2) = (1) ÷ 1,000,000	Expected Total Costs of Producing 1,000,000 Units in 5,000 Batches Next Year (3)	Expected Cost per Unit (4) = (3) ÷ 1,000,000
Direct materials	$ 9,000,000	$ 9.00	$ 9,000,000	$ 9.00
Direct manufacturing labor	2,400,000	2.40	2,400,000	2.40
Variable manufacturing overhead costs of power and utilities	1,600,000	1.60	1,600,000	1.60
Mixed (variable and fixed) manufacturing overhead costs of materials handling and setup	1,750,000	1.75	2,000,000	2.00
Fixed manufacturing overhead costs of plant lease, insurance, and administration	3,000,000	3.00	3,000,000	3.00
Total manufacturing costs	$17,750,000	$17.75	$18,000,000	$18.00

Currently, materials-handling and setup activities occur each time a batch of CD players is made. Soho produces 1,000,000 CD players in 2,500 batches, with 400 units in each batch. The number of batches is the cost driver for these costs. Total materials-handling costs and setup costs equal fixed costs of $500,000 plus variable costs of $500 per batch [$500,000 + (2,500 batches × $500 per batch) = $1,750,000]. Soho is considering whether to produce CD players in smaller batch sizes. Soho anticipates producing the 1,000,000 CD players next year in 5,000 batches of 200 units per batch. Through continuous improvement, the company expects to reduce variable costs for materials handling and setup to $300 per batch. No other changes in variable cost per unit or fixed costs are anticipated.

Another manufacturer offers to sell Soho 1,000,000 CD players next year for $16 per unit on whatever delivery schedule Soho wants. Assume that financial factors will be the basis of this make-or-buy decision. Should Soho make or buy the CD player?

Columns 3 and 4 of the preceding table indicate the expected total costs and expected cost per unit of producing 1,000,000 CD players next year. Direct material costs, direct manufacturing labor costs, and variable manufacturing overhead costs that vary with units produced are not expected to change because Soho plans to continue to produce 1,000,000 units next year at the same variable cost per unit as this year. Materials-handling and setup costs are expected to increase, even with no change in total production quantity. That's because these costs will vary with the number of batches, not the number of units produced. Soho's managers expect total materials-handling costs and setup costs to be $2,000,000 [$500,000 + (5,000 batches × the cost per batch of $300)]. Soho expects fixed manufacturing overhead costs to remain the same. The expected manufacturing cost per unit for next year is $18. At first glance, it appears that the company should buy CD players because the expected $18-per-unit cost of making the CD player is more than the $16 per unit to buy it. But a make-or-buy decision is often not obvious. To make a decision, management needs to answer the question: What is the difference in relevant costs between the alternatives?

For the moment, suppose (a) the capacity now used to make the CD players will become idle next year if the CD players are purchased and (b) the $3,000,000 of fixed manufacturing overhead will continue to be incurred next year, regardless of the decision made. Assume the $500,000 in fixed salaries to support materials handling and setup will not be incurred if the manufacture of CD players is completely shut down.

Exhibit 11-6 presents the relevant-cost computations. Note that Soho will *save* $1,000,000 by making CD players rather than buying them from the outside supplier. Making CD players is the preferred alternative.

Note how the key concepts of relevance presented in Exhibit 11-3 apply here:

- Current-cost data in Example 2, columns 1 and 2 (p. 384), play no role in the analysis in Exhibit 11-6 because for next year's make-or-buy decision these costs are past costs and, hence, irrelevant. They only help in predicting future costs.

EXHIBIT 11-6

Relevant (Incremental) Items for Make-or-Buy Decision for CD Players at Soho Company

	Total Relevant Costs		Relevant Cost Per Unit	
Relevant Items	**Make**	**Buy**	**Make**	**Buy**
Outside purchase of parts		$16,000,000		$16.00
Direct materials	$ 9,000,000		$ 9.00	
Direct manufacturing labor	2,400,000		2.40	
Variable manufacturing overhead	1,600,000		1.60	
Mixed (variable and fixed) materials-handling and setup overhead	2,000,000		2.00	
Total relevant costs[a]	$15,000,000	$16,000,000	$15.00	$16.00
Difference in favor of making CD players	$ 1,000,000		$ 1.00	

[a]The $3,000,000 of plant-lease, plant-insurance, and plant-administration costs could be included under both alternatives. Conceptually, they do not belong in a listing of relevant costs because these costs are irrelevant to the decision. Practically, some managers may want to include them in order to list all costs that will be incurred under each alternative.

- Exhibit 11-6 shows $2,000,000 of future materials-handling and setup costs under the make alternative but not under the buy alternative. Why? Because buying CD players and not manufacturing them will save $2,000,000 in future variable costs per batch and avoidable fixed costs. The $2,000,000 represents future costs that differ between the alternatives and so is relevant to the make-or-buy decision.
- Exhibit 11-6 excludes the $3,000,000 of plant-lease, insurance, and administration costs under both alternatives. Why? Because these future costs will not differ between the alternatives, so they are irrelevant.

A common term in decision making is *incremental cost*. An **incremental cost** is the additional total cost incurred for an activity. In Exhibit 11-6, the incremental cost of making CD players is the additional total cost of $15,000,000 that Soho will incur if it decides to make CD players. The $3,000,000 of fixed manufacturing overhead is not an incremental cost because Soho will incur these costs whether or not it makes CD players. Similarly, the incremental cost of buying CD players from an outside supplier is the additional total cost of $16,000,000 that Soho will incur if it decides to buy CD players. A **differential cost** is the difference in total cost between two alternatives. In Exhibit 11-6, the differential cost between the make-CD-players and buy-CD-players alternatives is $1,000,000 ($16,000,000 – $15,000,000). Note that *incremental cost* and *differential cost* are sometimes used interchangeably in practice. When faced with these terms, always be sure what they mean.

We define *incremental revenue* and *differential revenue* similarly to incremental cost and differential cost. **Incremental revenue** is the additional total revenue from an activity. **Differential revenue** is the difference in total revenue between two alternatives.

Strategic and Qualitative Factors

Strategic and qualitative factors affect outsourcing decisions. For example, Soho may prefer to manufacture CD players in-house to retain control over the design, quality, reliability, and delivery schedules of the CD players it uses in its stereos. Conversely, despite the cost advantages documented in Exhibit 11-6, Soho may prefer to outsource, become a smaller and leaner organization, and focus on areas of its core competencies—the manufacture and sale of stereos. As an example of focus, advertising companies, such as J. Walter Thompson, only do the creative and planning aspects of advertising (their core competencies), and they outsource production activities, such as film, photographs, and illustrations.

Outsourcing is not without risks. As a company's dependence on its suppliers increases, suppliers could increase prices and let quality and delivery performance slip. To minimize these risks, companies generally enter into long-run contracts specifying costs, quality, and delivery schedules with their suppliers. Intelligent managers build close partnerships or alliances with a few key suppliers. Toyota goes so far as to send its own engineers to improve suppliers' processes. Suppliers of companies such as Ford, Hyundai, Panasonic, and Sony have researched and developed innovative products, met demands for increased quantities, maintained quality and on-time delivery, and lowered costs—actions that the companies themselves would not have had the competencies to achieve. The Concepts in Action feature (p. 387) describes how companies are outsourcing services to lower-cost countries, which is also called *offshoring*.

Outsourcing decisions invariably have a long-run horizon in which the financial costs and benefits of outsourcing become more uncertain. Almost always, strategic and qualitative factors such as those described here become important determinants of the outsourcing decision. Weighing all these factors requires the exercise of considerable management judgment and care.

5

Explain the opportunity-cost concept and why it is used in decision making

. . . in all decisions, it is important to consider the contribution to income forgone by choosing a particular alternative and rejecting others

Opportunity Costs and Outsourcing

For purposes of the introductory example, the calculations in Exhibit 11-6 assumed that the capacity currently used to make CD players will remain idle if Soho purchases the parts from the outside manufacturer. However, the released capacity can be used for other, more-profitable purposes. The choice Soho's managers are faced with then is not whether to make or buy but how best to use available production capacity.

CONCEPTS IN ACTION

The Benefits and Costs of "Offshoring"

Recently, companies and public policy experts have engaged in a significant debate about "offshoring," which is the outsourcing of jobs to other countries. This increasingly prevalent practice involves replacing domestic employees with professionals in other countries at substantially lower labor costs. Typically, companies headquartered in the United States have outsourced jobs to India, China, Russia, Israel, and Ireland.

Offshoring is popular with companies because it yields significant cost savings. Within the high-tech sector, for example, a software developer for IBM in the United States costs $56 an hour, whereas one in China costs only $12.50 an hour, including salary and benefits. Similar opportunities for cost savings are found in the customer-service, technical-support, manufacturing, and supply-chain functions. Savings resulting from offshoring increase profits or are passed on to consumers via lower prices. McKinsey & Company, a consulting firm, estimates that in the long run outsourcing could result in as much as a 50% increase in profits for some American businesses.

However, offshoring does not come without costs, and these costs can be significant. A recent study by Hewitt Associates found that many companies fail to account for many of the costs associated with offshoring. Hewitt found, for example, that fewer than half of the companies had considered the effect of higher taxes in the countries where they were offshoring jobs, about 75% had not considered the impact of offshoring on costs in the rest of the supply chain, and only 34% had considered the costs of shutting down domestic facilities.

The economic impact of offshoring has so far been small. For example, even though American spending on offshore IT software and services rose from $2.5 billion to $10 billion during the 1998 to 2003 period, offshoring was responsible for fewer than 10% of the overall domestic job losses experienced within that sector. Furthermore, the U.S. Bureau of Labor Statistics predicts that there will be more than one million additional jobs for computer specialists in America before 2012. Nevertheless, outsourcing raises questions about how workers can be retrained and prepared for new high-skilled jobs.

Sources: M. Baily, *Exploding the Myths About Offshoring* (April 2004). Available from McKinsey & Company. **http://www.mckinsey.com/knowledge/mgi/reports/Offshoring/exploding_myths.asp**; W. Bulkeley, "IBM Documents Give Rare Look at Sensitive Plans on 'Offshoring'," *The Wall Street Journal*, January 19, 2004; D. Legard, "Gartner: Backlash Against Offshoring to Vanish by 2006," Infoword.com, June 15, 2004. **http://www.infoworld.com/article/04/06/15/HNoffshorebacklash_1.html**; *Offshoring: Is it a Win–Win Game?* (May 2004). Available from McKinsey & Company. **http://www.mckinsey.com/knowledge/mgi/reports/offshore.asp**; A. Reynolds, "Offshoring Which Jobs?" *Washington Times*, June 6, 2004. **http://www.cato.org/dailys/06-13-04.html**; "Study Notes Offshoring Downside," CNN/*Money*, March 5, 2004. **http://money.cnn.com/2004/03/04/news/economy/outsourcing_costs/**; *The Comprehensive Impact of Offshore IT Software and Services Outsourcing on the U.S. Economy and the IT Industry* (March 2004). Available from Global Insight. **http://www.globalinsight.com/publicDownload/genericContent/03-30-04_execsum.pdf**; "The Great Hollowing-Out Myth," *The Economist*, February 19, 2004. **http://www.economist.com/agenda/PrinterFriendly.cfm?Story_ID=2454530**

Example 3: Suppose that if Soho decides to buy CD players for its stereos from the outside supplier, then Soho's best use of the capacity that becomes available is to produce 500,000 Discmans, a portable, stand-alone CD player. From a manufacturing standpoint, Discmans are similar to stereo CD players. With help from operating managers, John Marquez, Soho's management accountant, estimates the following future revenues and costs if Soho decides to manufacture and sell Discmans:

Incremental future revenues		$8,000,000
Incremental future costs		
Direct materials	$3,400,000	
Direct manufacturing labor	1,000,000	
Variable overhead (such as power, utilities)	600,000	
Materials-handling and setup overheads	500,000	
Total incremental future costs		5,500,000
Incremental future operating income		$2,500,000

Because of capacity constraints, Soho can make either CD players for its stereo unit or Discmans, but not both. Which of the following three alternatives should Soho choose?

1. Make stereo CD players and do not make Discmans
2. Buy stereo CD players and do not make Discmans
3. Buy stereo CD players and make Discmans

You probably will find the total-alternatives approach easier to understand. To use it, merely analyze the cash flows into and out of the company. We suggest you use the total-alternatives approach until you are sufficiently comfortable with the concept of opportunity cost to use the opportunity-cost approach.

Exhibit 11-7, Panel A, summarizes the "total-alternatives" approach—the future costs and revenues for *all* alternatives. Alternative 3, buying stereo CD players and using the available capacity to make and sell Discmans, is the preferred alternative. The future incremental costs of buying stereo CD players from an outside supplier ($16,000,000) are more than the future incremental costs of making stereo CD players in-house ($15,000,000). But Soho can use the capacity freed up by buying stereo CD players to gain $2,500,000 in operating income (incremental future revenues of $8,000,000 minus total incremental future costs of $5,500,000) by making and selling Discmans. The *net relevant* costs of buying stereo CD players and making and selling Discmans are $16,000,000 – $2,500,000 = $13,500,000.

The Opportunity-Cost Approach

Deciding to use a resource in a particular way causes a manager to give up the opportunity to use the resource in alternative ways. This lost opportunity is a cost that the manager must take into consideration when making a decision. **Opportunity cost** is the contribution to operating income that is forgone or rejected by not using a limited resource in its next-best alternative use. For example, the (relevant) cost of going to school for an MBA degree is not only the cost of tuition, books, lodging, and food, but also the income forgone (opportunity cost) by studying rather than working. Presumably the estimated future benefits of obtaining an MBA (for example, a higher-paying career) will exceed these costs. (See the Concepts in Action feature on p. 390 for a discussion on opportunity costs at Delta Airlines.)

Exhibit 11-7, Panel B, displays the opportunity-cost approach for analyzing the alternatives faced by Soho. *When using the opportunity-cost approach, Soho's managers should focus on the costs of making or buying stereo CD players.*

EXHIBIT 11-7

Total-Alternatives Approach and Opportunity-Cost Approach to Make-or-Buy Decisions for Soho Company

	Alternatives for Soho		
Relevant Items	**1. Make Stereo CD Players and Do Not Make Discmans**	**2. Buy Stereo CD Players and Do Not Make Discmans**	**3. Buy Stereo CD Players and Make Discmans**
PANEL A Total-Alternatives Approach to Make-or-Buy Decisions			
Total incremental future costs of making/buying stereo CD players (from Exhibit 11-6)	$15,000,000	$16,000,000	$16,000,000
Deduct excess of future revenues over future costs from Discmans	0	0	(2,500,000)
Total relevant costs under total-alternatives approach	$15,000,000	$16,000,000	$13,500,000
Panel B Opportunity-Cost Approach to Make-or-Buy Decisions			
Total incremental future costs of making/buying stereo CD players (from Exhibit 11-6)	$15,000,000	$16,000,000	$16,000,000
Opportunity cost: Profit contribution forgone because capacity will not be used to make Discmans, the next-best alternative	2,500,000	2,500,000	0
Total relevant costs under opportunity-cost approach	$17,500,000	$18,500,000	$16,000,000

Note that the differences in costs across the columns in Panels A and B are the same: The cost of alternative 3 is $1,500,000 less than the cost of alternative 1, and $2,500,000 less than the cost of alternative 2.

Consider alternative 1, make stereo CD players and do not make Discmans, and ask, What are all the costs of making stereo CD players under this alternative? Certainly, Soho will incur $15,000,000 of incremental costs to make stereo CD players. But is this the entire cost? No, because by deciding to use limited manufacturing resources to make stereo CD players, Soho will give up the opportunity to earn $2,500,000 by not using these resources to make Discmans. Therefore, the relevant costs of making stereo CD players are the incremental costs of $15,000,000 plus the opportunity cost of $2,500,000.

Next consider alternative 2, buy stereo CD players and do not make Discmans. The incremental cost of buying stereo CD players will be $16,000,000. Similar to alternative 1, there is also an opportunity cost of $2,500,000 as a result of deciding not to make Discmans.

Finally, consider alternative 3, buy stereo CD players and make Discmans. The incremental cost of buying stereo CD players will be $16,000,000. The opportunity cost is zero. Why? Because by choosing this alternative, Soho will not forgo the profit it can earn from making and selling Discmans.

Panel B leads management to the same conclusion as Panel A: buying stereo CD players and making Discmans is the preferred alternative.

Panels A and B of Exhibit 11-7 describe two consistent approaches to decision making with capacity constraints. The total-alternatives approach in Panel A includes all future incremental costs and revenues. For example, under alternative 3, the additional future operating income from *using capacity to make and sell Discmans* ($2,500,000) is subtracted from the future incremental cost of buying stereo CD players ($16,000,000). The opportunity-cost analysis in Panel B takes the opposite approach. It focuses on stereo CD players. *Whenever capacity is not going to be used to make and sell Discmans,* the future forgone operating income is added as an opportunity cost of making or buying stereo CD players, as in alternatives 1 and 2. (Note that when Discmans are made, as in alternative 3, there is no "opportunity cost of not making Discmans.") Therefore, whereas Panel A *subtracts* $2,500,000 under alternative 3, Panel B *adds* $2,500,000 under alternative 1 and also under alternative 2. Panel B highlights the idea that when capacity is constrained, the relevant revenues and costs of any alternative equal the incremental future revenues and costs *plus* the opportunity cost. However, when more than two alternatives are being considered simultaneously, it is generally easier to use the total-alternatives approach.

Opportunity costs are not incorporated into formal financial accounting records. Why? Because historical record keeping is limited to transactions involving alternatives that were *actually selected,* rather than alternatives that were rejected. Rejected alternatives do not produce transactions and so they are not recorded. If Soho makes stereo CD players, it will not make Discmans, and it will not record any accounting entries for Discmans. Yet the opportunity cost of making stereo CD players, which equals the operating income that Soho forgoes by not making Discmans, is a crucial input into the make-or-buy decision. Consider again Exhibit 11-7, Panel B. On the basis of only the incremental costs systematically recorded in the accounting system, it is less costly for Soho to make rather than buy stereo CD players. Recognizing the opportunity cost of $2,500,000 leads to the different conclusion that it is preferable to buy stereo CD players.

Suppose Soho has sufficient capacity to make Discmans even if it makes stereo CD players. In this case, Soho has a fourth alternative: make stereo CD players and make Discmans. For this alternative, the opportunity cost of making stereo CD players is $0 because Soho does not give up the $2,500,000 operating income from making Discmans even if it chooses to make stereo CD players. The relevant costs are $15,000,000 (incremental costs of $15,000,000 plus opportunity cost of $0). Under these conditions, Soho would prefer to make stereo CD players, rather than buy them, and also make Discmans.

Besides quantitative considerations, the make-or-buy decision should consider strategic and qualitative factors as well. If Soho decides to buy stereo CD players from an outside supplier, it should consider factors such as the supplier's reputation for quality and timely delivery. Soho would also want to consider the strategic consequences of selling Discmans. For example, will selling Discmans take Soho's focus away from its stereo business?

CONCEPTS IN ACTION

Delta Airlines, the Internet, and Opportunity Costs

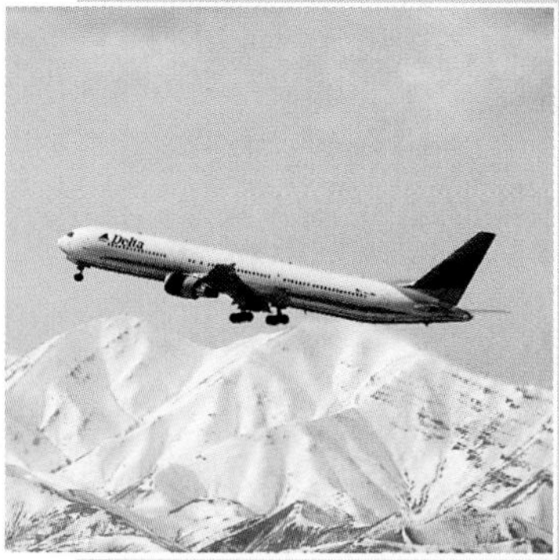

What are the relevant costs for Delta Airlines to fly a customer on a round-trip flight from Orlando to San Francisco, leaving on Saturday, June 12, 2004, and returning on Tuesday, June 15, 2004? The incremental costs are very small—mainly food costs of, say, $20—because the other costs are fixed—the plane, pilots, ticket agents, fuel, airport landing fees, and baggage handlers. The question is, What are the opportunity costs? To determine the opportunity costs, Delta Airlines must assess what profit it has forgone by selling a seat to a particular customer. The profit forgone depends on whether the flight is full—meaning the plane is operating at capacity. Delta would normally charge $440 for this round-trip ticket. If seats are available, the opportunity cost is zero. If the flight is full, the opportunity cost is $420 ($440 – $20), or the profit Delta would make selling the same seat to another customer. The relevant cost is $440—the incremental cost of $20 plus the opportunity cost of $420.

If a customer calls or uses the Internet to purchase the ticket in early May 2004, Delta computes the relevant costs to be $440 because it expects that flight will be full. But what if on Wednesday, June 9, 2004, Delta finds that the plane will not be full? The relevant cost for each remaining seat on the flight will be only the $20 incremental cost, and Delta can lower its prices well below $440—to, say, $150—and still make an incremental profit on each additional seat sold. Waiting until the last minute and recognizing that opportunity costs are zero enables Delta to lower its prices drastically in hopes of attracting more customers while still earning a profit on each additional passenger.

The Internet makes it possible for Delta to tell potential customers cheaply and quickly about lowered fares. Using what is called "push" technology, Delta broadcasts information about all flights on which seats are available to subscribers who have registered free of charge on Delta Airlines' Web page at **www.delta.com**. Each Wednesday, an e-mail is sent to every subscriber indicating departure and arrival cities for which cheap fares, often from $80 to $200, are available. The requirement? Travel must start that Saturday and end the following Monday or Tuesday. By waiting until midweek to announce the fares, Delta can be certain that unfilled seats are available and that the opportunity costs for the fares it offers are therefore zero. In addition, Delta offers seats to various Web sites specializing in last-minute travel packages, including Site 59 (**www.site59.com**), LastMinuteTravel (**www.lastminutetravel.com**), and Priceline (**www.priceline.com**). Delta Airlines' low-fare subscription service and offerings through last-minute travel Web sites are good examples of how a company that has a good understanding of relevant costs can take advantage of its low variable-cost structure using the Internet.

Carrying Costs of Inventory

To see another example of an opportunity cost, consider the following data for Soho:

Annual estimated stereo CD player requirements for next year	1,000,000 units
Cost per unit when each purchase is equal to 10,000 units	$16.00
Cost per unit when each purchase is equal to or greater than 500,000 units; $16 minus 1% discount	$15.84
Cost of a purchase order	$500
Alternatives under consideration:	
A. Make 100 purchases of 10,000 units each during next year	
B. Make 2 purchases of 500,000 units during the year	
Average investment in inventory:	
A. (10,000 units × $16.00 per unit) ÷ 2[a]	$80,000
B. (500,000 units × $15.84 per unit) ÷ 2[a]	$3,960,000
Annual rate of return if cash is invested elsewhere (for example, bonds or stocks) at the same level of risk as investment in inventory	9%

[a]The example assumes that stereo-CD-player purchases will be used up uniformly throughout the year. The average investment in inventory during the year is the cost of the inventory when a purchase is received plus the cost of inventory just before the next purchase is delivered (in our example, zero) divided by 2.

Soho will pay cash for the stereo CD players it buys. Which purchasing alternative is more economical for Soho? The following table presents the two alternatives.

	Alternative A: Make 100 Purchases of 10,000 Units Each During the Year (1)	Alternative B: Make 2 Purchases of 500,000 Units Each During the Year (2)	Difference (3) = (1) – (2)
Annual purchase-order costs (100 purch. orders × $500/purch. order; 2 purch. orders × $500/purch. order)	$ 50,000	$ 1,000	$ 49,000
Annual purchase costs (1,000,000 units × $16.00/unit; 1,000,000 units × $15.84/unit)	16,000,000	15,840,000	160,000
Annual rate of return that could be earned if investment in inventory were invested elsewhere at the same level of risk (opportunity cost) (0.09 × $80,000; 0.09 × $3,960,000)	7,200	356,400	(349,200)
Relevant costs	$16,057,200	$16,197,400	$(140,200)

The opportunity cost of holding inventory is the income forgone by tying up money in inventory and not investing it elsewhere. The opportunity cost would not be recorded in the accounting system because, once the alternative of investing money elsewhere is rejected, there are no transactions related to this alternative to record. On the basis of the costs recorded in the accounting system (purchase-order costs and purchase costs), Soho would erroneously conclude that making two purchases of 500,000 units each is the less costly alternative. Column 3, however, indicates that, consistent with the trends toward holding smaller inventories, purchasing smaller quantities of 10,000 units 100 times a year is preferred to purchasing 500,000 units twice during the year. Why? Because the lower opportunity cost of holding smaller inventory exceeds the higher purchase and ordering costs. If the opportunity cost of money tied up in inventory were greater than 9% per year, or if other incremental benefits of holding lower inventory were considered—such as lower insurance, materials-handling, storage, obsolescence, and breakage costs—making 100 purchases would be even more economical.

Product-Mix Decisions Under Capacity Constraints

6

Know how to choose which products to produce when there are capacity constraints

. . . select the product with the highest contribution margin per unit of the limiting resource

We now examine how the concept of relevance applies to **product-mix decisions**—the decisions made by a company about which products to sell and in what quantities. These decisions usually have only a short-run focus because the level of capacity can be expanded in the long run. For example, BMW, the German car manufacturer, must continually adapt the mix of its different models of cars (for example, 325i, 525i, and 740i) to short-run fluctuations in selling prices and demand. To determine product mix, a company maximizes operating income, given constraints such as capacity and demand. Throughout this section, we assume that as short-run changes in product mix occur, the only costs that change are costs that are variable with respect to the number of units produced (and sold). Under this assumption, the analysis of individual product contribution margins provides insight into the product mix that maximizes operating income.

Example 4: Power Recreation assembles two engines—a snowmobile engine and a boat engine—at its Lexington, Kentucky, plant.

	Snowmobile Engine	Boat Engine
Selling price	$800	$1,000
Variable cost per unit	560	625
Contribution margin per unit	$240	$ 375
Contribution margin percentage ($240 ÷ $800; $375 ÷ $1,000)	30%	37.5%

Assume that only 600 machine-hours are available daily for assembling engines. Additional capacity cannot be obtained in the short run. Power Recreation can sell as many engines as it produces. The constraining resource, then, is machine-hours. It takes two machine-hours to produce one snowmobile engine and five machine-hours to produce one boat engine. What product mix should Power Recreation's managers choose to maximize its operating income?

In terms of contribution margin per unit and contribution margin percentage, boat engines are more profitable than snowmobile engines. The product that Power Recreation should produce and sell, however, is not necessarily the product with the higher individual contribution margin per unit or contribution margin percentage. Managers should choose the product with *the highest contribution margin per unit of the constraining resource (factor)*. That's the resource that restricts or limits the production or sale of products.

	Snowmobile Engine	Boat Engine
Contribution margin per unit	$240	$375
Machine-hours required to produce one unit	2 machine-hours	5 machine-hours
Contribution margin per machine-hour		
$240 per unit ÷ 2 machine-hours/unit	$120/machine-hour	
$375 per unit ÷ 5 machine-hours/unit		$75/machine-hour
Total contribution margin for 600 machine-hours		
$120/machine-hour × 600 machine-hours	$72,000	
$75/machine-hour × 600 machine-hours		$45,000

Producing snowmobile engines earns more contribution margin per machine-hour, which is the constraining resource in this example. Therefore, choosing to produce and sell snowmobile engines maximizes *total* contribution margin and operating income. Other constraints in manufacturing settings can be the availability of direct materials, components, or skilled labor, as well as financial and sales factors. In a retail department store, the constraining resource may be linear feet of display space. Regardless of the specific constraining resource, managers should always focus on maximizing *total* contribution margin by choosing products that give the highest contribution margin per unit of the constraining resource.

In many cases a manufacturer or retailer has the challenge of trying to maximize total operating income for a variety of products, each with more than one constraining resource. Some constraints may require a manufacturer or retailer to stock minimum quantities of products even if these products are not very profitable. For example, supermarkets must stock less-profitable products because customers will be willing to shop at a supermarket only if it carries a wide range of products that customers desire. To determine the most profitable production schedules and the most profitable product mix, you need to determine what is the maximum total contribution margin in the face of many constraints. Optimization techniques, such as the linear programming technique discussed in the appendix to this chapter, help solve these more-complex problems.

Finally, there is the question of managing the bottleneck constraint to increase output and, therefore, contribution margin. Can the available machine-hours for assembling engines be increased beyond 600, for example, by reducing idle time? Can the time needed to assemble each snowmobile engine (two machine-hours) and each boat engine (five machine-hours) be reduced, for example, by reducing setup time and processing time of assembly? Can quality be improved so that constrained capacity is used to produce only good units rather than some good and some defective units? Can some of the assembly operations be outsourced to allow more engines to be built? Implementing any of these options will likely require Power Recreation to incur incremental costs. Power Recreation will implement only those options whose benefits of higher contribution margins exceed the costs. *Instructors and students who, at this point, want to explore these issues in more detail can go to the section in Chapter 19, pages 675–677, titled "Theory of Constraints and Throughput Contribution Analysis" and then return to this chapter without any loss of continuity.*

Customer Profitability, Activity-Based Costing, and Relevant Costs

Not only must companies make choices regarding which products and how much of each product to produce, they must often make decisions about adding or dropping a product line or a business segment. Similarly, if the cost object is a customer, companies must make decisions about adding or dropping customers (analogous to a product line) or a branch office (analogous to a business segment). We illustrate relevant-revenue and relevant-cost analysis for these kinds of decisions using customers rather than products as the cost object.

7

Discuss factors managers must consider when adding or dropping customers or segments

. . . managers should focus on how total costs differ among alternatives and ignore allocated overhead costs

Example 5: Allied West, the West Coast sales office of Allied Furniture, a wholesaler of specialized furniture, supplies furniture to three local retailers: Vogel, Brenner, and Wisk. Exhibit 11-8 presents expected revenues and costs of Allied West by customer for the upcoming year using its activity-based costing system. Allied West assigns costs to customers based on the activities needed to support each customer. Information on Allied West's costs for different activities at various levels of the cost hierarchy follows:

- Furniture-handling labor costs vary with the number of units of furniture shipped to customers.
- Allied West reserves different areas of the warehouse to stock furniture for different customers. For simplicity, assume that furniture-handling equipment in an area and depreciation costs on the equipment are identified with individual customers (customer-level costs). Any equipment not used remains idle. The equipment has a one-year useful life and zero disposal value.
- Allied West allocates rent to each customer on the basis of the amount of warehouse space reserved for that customer.
- Marketing costs vary with the number of sales visits made to customers.
- Sales-order costs are batch-level costs that vary with the number of sales orders received from customers; delivery-processing costs are batch-level costs that vary with the number of shipments made.
- Allied West allocates fixed general-administration costs (facility-level costs) to customers on the basis of customer revenues.
- Allied Furniture allocates its fixed corporate-office costs to sales offices on the basis of the square feet area of each sales office. Allied West allocates these costs to customers on the basis of customer revenues.

The Allied West example illustrates a keep-or-discontinue decision, but the object of the decision is a *customer* rather than a *product*. The example uses Chapter 5's activity-based costing concepts.

In the following sections, we consider these decisions that Allied West's managers face: Should Allied West drop the Wisk account? Should it add a fourth customer, Loral? Should Allied Furniture close down Allied West? Should it open another sales office, Allied South, whose revenues and costs are identical to those of Allied West?

EXHIBIT 11-8

Customer Profitability Analysis for Allied West

	Customer			
	Vogel	Brenner	Wisk	Total
Revenues	$500,000	$300,000	$400,000	$1,200,000
Cost of goods sold	370,000	220,000	330,000	920,000
Furniture-handling labor	41,000	18,000	33,000	92,000
Furniture-handling equipment cost written off as depreciation	12,000	4,000	9,000	25,000
Rent	14,000	8,000	14,000	36,000
Marketing support	11,000	9,000	10,000	30,000
Sales-order and delivery processing	13,000	7,000	12,000	32,000
General administration	20,000	12,000	16,000	48,000
Allocated corporate-office costs	10,000	6,000	8,000	24,000
Total costs	491,000	284,000	432,000	1,207,000
Operating income	$ 9,000	$ 16,000	$(32,000)	$ (7,000)

Relevant-Revenue and Relevant-Cost Analysis of Dropping a Customer

Exhibit 11-8 indicates a loss of $32,000 on the Wisk account. Allied West's managers believe the reason for the loss is that Wisk places many low-margin orders with Allied, resulting in high sales-order, delivery-processing, furniture-handling, and marketing costs. Allied West is considering several possible actions with respect to the Wisk account: reducing its own costs of supporting Wisk by becoming more efficient, cutting back on some of the services it offers Wisk, asking Wisk to place fewer orders that are larger than the present ones, charging Wisk higher prices, or dropping the Wisk account. The following analysis focuses on the operating-income effect of dropping the Wisk account.

To determine what to do, Allied West's managers must answer the question, What are the relevant revenues and relevant costs? Information about the effect of dropping the Wisk account follows.

- Dropping the Wisk account will save cost of goods sold, furniture-handling labor, marketing support, sales-order, and delivery-processing costs incurred on the account.
- Dropping the Wisk account will leave idle the warehouse space and furniture-handling equipment currently used to supply products to Wisk.
- Dropping the Wisk account will have no effect on fixed general-administration costs or corporate-office costs.

Exhibit 11-9, column 1, presents the relevant-revenue and relevant-cost analysis using data from the Wisk column in Exhibit 11-8. Allied West's operating income will be $15,000 lower if it drops the Wisk account—the cost savings from dropping the Wisk account, $385,000, will not be enough to offset the loss of $400,000 in revenues—so Allied West's managers decide to keep the account. Note that there is no opportunity cost of using warehouse space for Wisk because without Wisk, the space and equipment will remain idle.

Depreciation is a past cost, therefore it is irrelevant; rent, general-administration, and corporate-office costs are irrelevant because they are future costs that will not change if Allied West drops the Wisk account. For purposes of this decision, Allied West's managers should be particularly mindful of allocated overhead costs such as corporate-office costs. They should ignore amounts allocated to the sales office and individual customers. The question Allied West's managers must ask when deciding whether corporate-office costs are relevant is, Will expected total corporate-office costs decrease as a result of dropping the Wisk account? In our example, they will not, so these costs are irrelevant. *If expected total corporate-office costs* decreased by dropping the Wisk account, those savings would be relevant even if *the amount allocated to Allied West did not change.*

Now suppose that if Allied West drops the Wisk account, it could lease the extra warehouse space to Sanchez Corporation for $20,000 per year. Then $20,000 would be

EXHIBIT 11-9

Relevant-Revenue and Relevant-Cost Analysis for Dropping the Wisk Account and Adding the Loral Account

	(Loss in Revenues) and Savings in Costs from Dropping Wisk Account (1)	Incremental Revenues and (Incremental Costs) from Adding Loral Account (2)
Revenues	$(400,000)	$400,000
Cost of goods sold	330,000	(330,000)
Furniture-handling labor	33,000	(33,000)
Furniture-handling equipment cost written off as depreciation	0	(9,000)
Rent	0	0
Marketing support	10,000	(10,000)
Sales-order and delivery processing	12,000	(12,000)
General administration	0	0
Corporate-office costs	0	0
Total costs	385,000	(394,000)
Effect on operating income (loss)	$ (15,000)	$ 6,000

In making the decision to keep or drop the Wisk account, depreciation expense is *not* relevant because it is a sunk cost. Likewise, total costs that don't change are irrelevant—*regardless of how they might be allocated.*

Allied's opportunity cost of continuing to use the warehouse to service Wisk. Allied West would gain $5,000 by dropping the Wisk account ($20,000 from lease revenue minus lost operating income of $15,000). Before reaching a decision, Allied West's managers must examine whether Wisk can be made more profitable so that supplying products to Wisk earns more than the $20,000 from leasing to Sanchez. The managers must also consider strategic factors such as the effect of the decision on Allied West's reputation for developing stable, long-run business relationships with its customers.

Relevant-Revenue and Relevant-Cost Analysis of Adding a Customer

Suppose that in addition to Vogel, Brenner, and Wisk, Allied West's managers are evaluating the profitability of adding a customer, Loral. Allied West is already incurring annual costs of $36,000 for warehouse rent and $48,000 for general-administration costs. These costs together with *actual total* corporate-office costs will not change if Loral is added as a customer. Loral has a customer profile much like Wisk's. Suppose Allied West's managers predict revenues and costs of doing business with Loral to be the same as the revenues and costs described under the Wisk column of Exhibit 11-8. In particular, Allied West would have to acquire furniture-handling equipment for the Loral account costing $9,000, with a one-year useful life and zero disposal value. Should Allied West add Loral as a customer?

Exhibit 11-9, column 2, shows incremental revenues exceed incremental costs by $6,000. On the basis of this analysis, Allied West's managers would recommend adding Loral as a customer. Rent, general-administration, and corporate-office costs are irrelevant because these costs will not change if Loral is added as a customer. However, the cost of new equipment to support the Loral order (written off as depreciation of $9,000 in Exhibit 11-9, column 2) is relevant. That's because this cost can be avoided if Allied West decides not to add Loral as a customer. Note the critical distinction here: *Depreciation cost is irrelevant in deciding whether to drop Wisk as a customer because depreciation is a past cost, but the cost of purchasing new equipment that will then be written off as depreciation in the future is relevant in deciding whether to add Loral as a customer.*

Relevant-Revenue and Relevant-Cost Analysis of Closing or Adding Branch Offices or Segments

Companies periodically confront decisions about closing or adding branch offices or business segments. For example, given Allied West's expected loss of $7,000 (see Exhibit 11-8), should it be closed? Assume that closing Allied West will have no effect on total corporate-office costs.

Exhibit 11-10, column 1, presents the relevant-revenue and relevant-cost analysis using data from the Total column in Exhibit 11-8. The revenue losses of $1,200,000 will exceed

EXHIBIT 11-10

Relevant-Revenue and Relevant-Cost Analysis for Closing Allied West and Opening Allied South

	(Loss in Revenues) and Savings in Costs from Closing Allied West (1)	Incremental Revenues and (Incremental Costs) from Opening Allied South (2)
Revenues	$(1,200,000)	$1,200,000
Cost of goods sold	920,000	(920,000)
Furniture-handling labor	92,000	(92,000)
Furniture-handling equipment cost written off as depreciation	0	(25,000)
Rent	36,000	(36,000)
Marketing support	30,000	(30,000)
Sales-order and delivery processing	32,000	(32,000)
General administration	48,000	(48,000)
Corporate-office costs	0	0
Total costs	1,158,000	(1,183,000)
Effect on operating income (loss)	$ (42,000)	$ 17,000

the cost savings of $1,158,000, leading to a decrease in operating income of $42,000. Allied West should not be closed. The key reasons are that closing Allied West will not save depreciation cost of $25,000, which is a past or sunk cost, or actual total corporate-office costs. Corporate-office costs allocated to various sales offices will change *but the total amount of these costs will not decline*. The $24,000 no longer allocated to Allied West will be allocated to other sales offices. Therefore, the $24,000 of allocated corporate-office costs should not be included as expected cost savings from closing Allied West.

Now suppose Allied Furniture has the opportunity to open another sales office, Allied South, whose revenues and costs would be identical to Allied West's costs, including a cost of $25,000 to acquire furniture-handling equipment with a one-year useful life and zero disposal value. Opening this office will have no effect on total corporate-office costs. Should Allied Furniture open Allied South? Exhibit 11-10, column 2, indicates that it should do so because opening Allied South will increase operating income by $17,000. As before, the cost of new equipment (written off as depreciation) is relevant. But the point here is to ignore *allocated* corporate-office costs and focus on *total* corporate-office costs. Total corporate-office costs will not change if Allied South is opened, therefore these costs are irrelevant.

Irrelevance of Past Costs and Equipment-Replacement Decisions

8

Explain why book value of equipment is irrelevant in equipment-replacement decisions

. . . it is a past cost

At several points in this chapter, when discussing the concept of relevance, we reasoned that past (historical or sunk) costs are irrelevant to decision making. That's because a decision cannot change something that has already happened. We now apply this concept to decisions about replacing equipment. We stress the idea that **book value**—original cost minus accumulated depreciation—of existing equipment is a past cost that is irrelevant.

Example 6: Toledo Company is considering replacing a metal-cutting machine with a newer model. The new machine is more efficient than the old machine, but it has a shorter life. Revenues from aircraft parts ($1.1 million per year) will be unaffected by the replacement decision. Here's the data the management accountant prepares for the existing (old) machine and the replacement (new) machine:

	Old Machine	New Machine
Original cost	$1,000,000	$600,000
Useful life	5 years	2 years
Current age	3 years	0 years
Remaining useful life	2 years	2 years
Accumulated depreciation	$600,000	Not acquired yet
Book value	$400,000	Not acquired yet
Current disposal value (in cash)	$40,000	Not acquired yet
Terminal disposal value (in cash 2 years from now)	$0	$0
Annual operating costs (maintenance, energy, repairs, coolants, and so on)	$800,000	$460,000

Toledo Corporation uses straight-line depreciation. To focus on relevance, we ignore the time value of money and income taxes.[1] Should Toledo replace its old machine?

Exhibit 11-11 presents a cost comparison of the two machines. Consider why each of the four items in Toledo's equipment-replacement decision is relevant or irrelevant:

1. **Book value of old machine, $400,000.** Irrelevant, because it is a past cost. All past costs are "down the drain." Nothing can change what has already been spent or what has already happened.
2. **Current disposal value of old machine, $40,000.** Relevant, because it is an expected future benefit that will only occur if the machine is replaced.

Although the book value of old equipment is irrelevant in a keep-or-replace decision, managers may still be concerned about book value for two reasons: (1) If the equipment is replaced, the entire "Loss on Disposal" will appear in the current period's income statement, and (2) it's undesirable to admit to a loss.

[1]See Chapter 21 for a discussion of time-value-of-money and income-tax considerations in capital investment decisions.

EXHIBIT 11-11

Operating Income Comparison: Replacement of Machine, Relevant and Irrelevant Items for Toledo Company

	Two Years Together		
	Keep (1)	Replace (2)	Difference (3) = (1) – (2)
Revenues	$2,200,000	$2,200,000	—
Operating costs			
Cash operating costs ($800,000/yr. × 2 years; $460,000/yr. × 2 years)	1,600,000	920,000	$ 680,000
Book value of old machine			
Periodic write-off as depreciation or	400,000	—	—
Lump-sum write-off	—	400,000[a]	
Current disposal value of old machine	—	(40,000)[a]	40,000
New machine cost, written off periodically as depreciation	—	600,000	(600,000)
Total operating costs	2,000,000	1,880,000	120,000
Operating income	$ 200,000	$ 320,000	$(120,000)

[a]In a formal income statement, these two items would be combined as "loss on disposal of machine" of $360,000.

3. **Loss on disposal, $360,000.** This is the difference between amounts in items 1 and 2. It is a meaningless combination blurring the distinction between the irrelevant book value and the relevant disposal value. Each should be considered separately, as was done in items 1 and 2.
4. **Cost of new machine, $600,000.** Relevant, because it is an expected future cost that will only occur if the machine is purchased.

Exhibit 11-11 should clarify these four assertions. Column 3 in Exhibit 11-11 shows that the book value of the old machine does not differ between the alternatives and could be ignored for decision-making purposes. No matter what the timing of the write-off—whether a lump-sum charge in the current year or depreciation charges over the next two years—the total amount is still $400,000 because it is a past (historical) cost. In contrast, the $600,000 cost of the new machine is relevant because it would not be incurred by deciding not to replace. Note that the operating income from replacing is $120,000 higher for the two years together.

To provide focus, Exhibit 11-12 concentrates only on relevant items. Note that the same answer—higher operating income as a result of lower costs of $120,000 by replacing the machine—is obtained even though the book value is omitted from the calculations. The only relevant items are the cash operating costs, the disposal value of the old machine, and the cost of the new machine, which is represented as depreciation in Exhibit 11-12.[2]

EXHIBIT 11-12

Cost Comparison: Replacement of Machine, Relevant Items Only, for Toledo Company

	Two Years Together		
	Keep (1)	Replace (2)	Difference (3) = (1) – (2)
Cash operating costs	$1,600,000	$ 920,000	$680,000
Current disposal value of old machine	—	(40,000)	40,000
New machine, written off periodically as depreciation	—	600,000	(600,000)
Total relevant costs	$1,600,000	$1,480,000	$120,000

[2]Other applications of relevant revenues and relevant costs appear in Chapter 12, for pricing decisions; Chapter 16, for sell-or-process-further decisions; Chapter 19, for quality management, costs of time, and the theory of constraints; Chapter 20, for just-in-time purchasing and production, and supplier evaluation; Chapter 21, for capital budgeting; and Chapter 22, for transfer pricing.

Decisions and Performance Evaluation

Consider our equipment-replacement example in light of the five-step sequence in Exhibit 11-1 (p. 379).

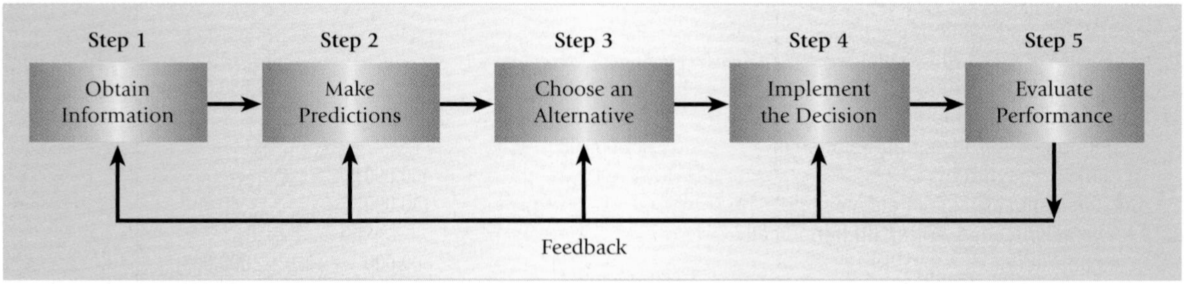

9

Explain how conflicts can arise between the decision model used by a manager and the performance-evaluation model used to evaluate the manager

. . . tell managers to take a multiple-year view in decision making but judge their performance only on the basis of the current year's operating income

The decision model analysis (step 3), which is presented in Exhibits 11-11 and 11-12, dictates replacing the machine rather than keeping it. In the real world, however, would the manager replace? An important factor in replacement decisions is the manager's perception of whether the decision model is consistent with how the manager's performance is judged (the performance-evaluation model in step 5).

From the perspective of their own careers, it's no surprise that managers tend to favor the alternative that makes their performance look better. If the performance-evaluation model conflicts with the decision model, the performance-evaluation model often prevails in influencing managers' decisions. For example, if the promotion or bonus of the manager at Toledo hinges on his or her first year's operating income performance under accrual accounting, the manager's temptation *not* to replace will be overwhelming. Why? Because the accrual accounting model for measuring performance will show a higher first-year operating income if the old machine is kept rather than replaced (as the following table shows):

First-Year Results: Accrual Accounting

	Keep		Replace	
Revenues		$1,100,000		$1,100,000
Operating costs				
Cash-operating costs	$800,000		$460,000	
Depreciation	200,000		300,000	
Loss on disposal	—		360,000	
Total operating costs		1,000,000		1,120,000
Operating income (loss)		$ 100,000		$ (20,000)

Even though top management's goals encompass the two-year period (consistent with the decision model), the manager will focus on first-year results if his or her evaluation is based on short-run measures such as the first-year's operating income.

Resolving the conflict between the decision model and the performance-evaluation model is frequently a baffling problem in practice. In theory, resolving the difficulty seems obvious: Design models that are consistent. Consider our replacement example. Year-by-year effects on operating income of replacement can be budgeted for the two-year planning horizon. The manager then would be evaluated on the expectation that the first year would be poor and the next year would be much better.

The practical difficulty is that accounting systems rarely track each decision separately. Performance evaluation focuses on responsibility centers for a specific period, not on projects or individual items of equipment over their useful lives. Thus, the impacts of many different decisions are combined in a single performance report. Top management, through the reporting system, is rarely aware of particular desirable alternatives that were *not* chosen by lower-level managers.

Consider another conflict between the decision model and the performance-evaluation model. Suppose a manager buys a particular machine only to discover shortly thereafter that a better machine could have been purchased instead. The decision model may suggest replacing the machine that was just bought with the better machine, but will the manager do so? Probably not. Why? Because replacing the machine so soon after its purchase may

Study Tip: To check your understanding of the material in this chapter, see Featured Exercises 1 and 2, true–false statements 1 and 8, multiple-choice questions 1 and 2, and Review Exercises 2 and 3 (*Student Guide*, beginning p. 140). Fully explained answers begin on p. 147.

FOCUS ON VALUES AND BEHAVIORS

BEYOND THE WALLS OF THE ACCOUNTING DEPARTMENT

It is not unusual to find management accountants on the manufacturing floor, at the warehouse, in the offices of marketing and sales managers, and in customer-service centers. Why do management accountants spend so much time "in the field"? To properly apply relevant-revenue and relevant-cost concepts to decisions, management accountants must have a good understanding of the business context of decisions. Such an understanding often will lead management accountants to ask questions not considered by others: Is this really a one-time-only special order? What else, if anything, could we do with freed up capacity if we outsourced a component part? Which resource is constrained and what is the contribution margin per unit of the constrained resource? How would *total* costs change if we dropped a customer or product line? Managers expect management accountants to articulate clearly why these questions are important. Therefore, management accountants need to build the skill to communicate concepts of relevance and opportunity cost in the simplest possible terms. Management accountants also have the responsibility to make managers aware of qualitative and nonfinancial factors such as the negative effect on employee morale of laying off workers.

Management accountants also need to be alert and informed about conflicts that can arise between models of decision making and performance evaluation. When such conflicts occur, management accountants have the responsibility to explain to managers why the decisions being made are not in the best long-run interests of the company and propose changes in the performance-evaluation model that will minimize these conflicts.

Many companies—such as Cisco Systems, General Electric, and Novartis—design systems that seek to align decision-making models and performance-evaluation models. For example, these companies evaluate the performance of their business-unit managers on the basis of division operating income reduced by an imputed interest cost representing the holding cost of assets, such as inventory and accounts receivable. In this way, the opportunity costs of holding assets that managers include in their decision models are also considered when evaluating the managers' performance, even though these opportunity costs are not recorded in the financial accounting system. As a result, managers in these companies constantly seek ways to increase operating income while reducing investments in assets.

reflect badly on the manager's capabilities and performance. If the manager's bosses have no knowledge of the better machine, the manager may prefer to keep the recently purchased machine rather than alert them to the better machine. (See the Focus on Values and Behaviors feature above.)

PROBLEM FOR SELF-STUDY

Wally Lewis is manager of the engineering development division of Goldcoast Products. Lewis has just received a proposal signed by all 10 of his engineers to replace the workstations with networked personal computers (networked PCs). Lewis is not enthusiastic about the proposal.

Data on workstations and networked PCs are:

	Workstations	Networked PCs
Original cost	$300,000	$135,000
Useful life	5 years	3 years
Current age	2 years	0 years
Remaining useful life	3 years	3 years
Accumulated depreciation	$120,000	Not acquired yet
Current book value	$180,000	Not acquired yet
Current disposal value (in cash)	$95,000	Not acquired yet
Terminal disposal value (in cash 3 years from now)	$0	$0
Annual computer-related cash operating costs	$40,000	$10,000
Annual revenues	$1,000,000	$1,000,000
Annual noncomputer-related operating costs	$880,000	$880,000

Lewis's annual bonus includes a component based on division operating income. He has a promotion possibility next year that would make him a group vice president of Goldcoast Products.

Required

1. Compare the costs of workstations and networked PCs. Consider the cumulative results for the three years together, ignoring the time value of money and income taxes.
2. Why might Lewis be reluctant to purchase the networked PCs?

SOLUTION

1. The following table considers all cost items when comparing future costs of workstations and networked PCs:

All Items	Three Years Together Workstations (1)	Networked PCs (2)	Difference (3) = (1) – (2)
Revenues	$3,000,000	$3,000,000	—
Operating costs			
Noncomputer-related operating costs	2,640,000	2,640,000	—
Computer-related cash operating costs	120,000	30,000	$ 90,000
Workstations' book value			
Periodic write-off as depreciation or	180,000	—	—
Lump-sum write-off	—	180,000	
Current disposal value of workstations	—	(95,000)	95,000
Networked PCs, written off periodically as depreciation	—	135,000	(135,000)
Total operating costs	2,940,000	2,890,000	50,000
Operating income	$ 60,000	$ 110,000	$(50,000)

Alternatively, the analysis could focus on only those items in the preceding table that differ between the alternatives.

Relevant Items	Three Years Together Workstations	Networked PCs	Difference
Computer-related cash operating costs	$120,000	$ 30,000	$ 90,000
Current disposal value of workstations	—	(95,000)	95,000
Networked PCs, written off periodically as depreciation	—	135,000	(135,000)
Total relevant costs	$120,000	$ 70,000	$ 50,000

The analysis suggests that it is cost-effective to replace the workstations with the networked PCs.

2. The accrual-accounting operating incomes *for the first year* under the keep-workstations versus the buy-networked-PCs alternatives are:

	Keep Workstations		Buy Networked PCs	
Revenues		$1,000,000		$1,000,000
Operating costs				
Noncomputer-related operating costs	$880,000		$880,000	
Computer-related cash operating costs	40,000		10,000	
Depreciation	60,000		45,000	
Loss on disposal of workstations	—		85,000[a]	
Total operating costs		980,000		1,020,000
Operating income (loss)		$ 20,000		$ (20,000)

[a]$85,000 = Book value of workstations, $180,000 – Current disposal value, $95,000.

Lewis would be less happy with the expected operating loss of $20,000 if the networked PCs are purchased than he would be with the expected operating income of $20,000 if the workstations are kept. Buying the networked PCs would eliminate the component of his bonus based on operating income. He might also perceive the $20,000 operating loss as reducing his chances of being promoted to a group vice president.

DECISION POINTS

The following question-and-answer format summarizes the chapter's learning objectives. Each decision presents a key question related to a learning objective. The guidelines are the answer to that question.

Decision	**Guidelines**
1. What is the five-step process that can be used to make decisions?	The five-step decision process is (a) obtain information, (b) make predictions, (c) choose an alternative, (d) implement the decision, and (e) evaluate performance to provide feedback.
2. When is a revenue or cost item relevant for a particular decision?	To be relevant for a particular decision, a revenue or cost item must meet two criteria: (a) it must be an expected future revenue or expected future cost, and (b) it must differ among alternative courses of action.
3. Should both quantitative and qualitative factors be considered in making decisions?	Yes, because the outcomes of alternative actions can be quantitative and qualitative. Quantitative outcomes are measured in numerical terms. Some quantitative outcomes can be expressed in financial terms, others cannot. Qualitative factors, such as employee morale, are difficult to measure accurately in numerical terms. Consideration must be given to both quantitative and qualitative factors in making decisions.
4. What potential problems should be avoided in relevant-cost analysis?	Two potential problems to avoid in relevant-cost analysis are (a) making incorrect general assumptions—such as all variable costs are relevant and all fixed costs are irrelevant—and (b) losing sight of total amounts, focusing instead on unit amounts.
5. What is an opportunity cost and why should it be included when making decisions?	Opportunity cost is the contribution to income that is forgone or rejected by not using a limited resource in its next-best alternative use. Opportunity cost is included in decision making because it represents the best alternative way in which an organization may have used its resources had it not made the decision it did.
6. When resources are constrained, how should managers choose which of multiple products to produce and sell?	Under these conditions, managers should select the product that yields the highest contribution margin per unit of the constraining or limiting resource (factor).
7. In deciding to add or drop customers or to add or discontinue branch offices or segments, how should managers take into account allocated overhead costs?	Managers should focus on whether total overhead costs will change when making decisions about adding or dropping customers or adding or discontinuing branch offices and segments. Managers should ignore allocated overhead costs.
8. Is book value of existing equipment relevant in equipment-replacement decisions?	Book value of existing equipment is a past (historical or sunk) cost and, therefore, is irrelevant in equipment-replacement decisions.
9. How can conflicts arise between the decision model used by a manager and the performance-evaluation model used to evaluate that manager?	Top management faces a persistent challenge: making sure that the performance-evaluation model of lower-level managers is consistent with the decision model. A common inconsistency is to tell these managers to take a multiple-year view in their decision making but then to judge their performance only on the basis of the current year's operating income.

APPENDIX: LINEAR PROGRAMMING

In this chapter's Power Recreation example (pp. 391–392), suppose both the snowmobile and boat engines must be tested on a very expensive machine before they are shipped to customers. The available machine-hours for testing are limited. Production data are:

Department	Available Daily Capacity in Hours	Use of Capacity in Hours per Unit of Product: Snowmobile Engine	Use of Capacity in Hours per Unit of Product: Boat Engine	Daily Maximum Production in Units: Snowmobile Engine	Daily Maximum Production in Units: Boat Engine
Assembly	600 machine-hours	2.0 machine-hours	5.0 machine-hours	300[a] snow engines	120 boat engines
Testing	120 testing-hours	1.0 machine-hour	0.5 machine-hour	120 snow engines	240 boat engines

[a]For example, 600 machine-hours ÷ 2.0 machine-hours per snowmobile engine = 300, the maximum number of snowmobile engines that the Assembly Department can make if it works exclusively on snowmobile engines.

EXHIBIT 11-13

Operating Data for Power Recreation

	Department Capacity (per Day) In Product Units				
	Assembly	**Testing**	**Selling Price**	**Variable Cost per Unit**	**Contribution Margin per Unit**
Only snowmobile engines	300	120	\$ 800	\$560	\$240
Only boat engines	120	240	\$1,000	\$625	\$375

Exhibit 11-13 summarizes these and other relevant data. In addition, as a result of material shortages for boat engines, Power Recreation cannot produce more than 110 boat engines per day. How many engines of each type should Power Recreation produce and sell daily to maximize operating income?

Because there are multiple constraints, a technique called *linear programming* or *LP* can be used to determine the number of each type of engine Power Recreation should produce. LP models typically assume that all costs are either variable or fixed with respect to a single cost driver (units of output). As we shall see, LP models also require certain other linear assumptions to hold. When these assumptions fail, other decision models should be considered.[3]

The Power Recreation example is an accounting application of linear programming, a technique taught in courses such as operations management, management science, or quantitative analysis for business decisions.

Steps in Solving an LP Problem

We use the data in Exhibit 11-13 to illustrate the three steps in solving an LP problem. Throughout this discussion, S equals the number of units of snowmobile engines produced and sold, and B equals the number of units of boat engines produced and sold.

S and B in the objective function and in the constraints always appear in linear form—for example, they never appear as S^2 or B^2 or $\sqrt{S}$ or $\sqrt{B}$, etc. As you see in Exhibit 11-14, the plots of the objective function and the constraints are linear—they appear as straight lines.

Step 1: **Determine the objective function.** The **objective function** of a linear program expresses the objective or goal to be maximized (say, operating income) or minimized (say, operating costs). In our example, the objective is to find the combination of snowmobile engines and boat engines that maximizes total contribution margin. Fixed costs remain the same regardless of the product-mix decision and are irrelevant. The linear function expressing the objective for the total contribution margin (*TCM*) is:

$$TCM = \$240S + \$375B$$

Step 2: **Specify the constraints.** A **constraint** is a mathematical inequality or equality that must be satisfied by the variables in a mathematical model. The following linear inequalities express the relationships in our example:

Assembly Department constraint	$2S + 5B \leq 600$
Testing Department constraint	$1S + 0.5B \leq 120$
Materials-shortage constraint for boat engines	$B \leq 110$
Negative production is impossible	$S \geq 0$ and $B \geq 0$

The three solid lines on the graph in Exhibit 11-14 show the existing constraints for Assembly and Testing and the materials-shortage constraint.[4] The feasible or technically possible alternatives are those combinations of quantities of snowmobile engines and boat engines that satisfy all the constraining resources or factors. The shaded "area of feasible solutions" in Exhibit 11-14 shows the boundaries of those product combinations that are feasible.

Step 3: **Compute the optimal solution.** **Linear programming (LP)** is an optimization technique used to maximize the *objective function* when there are multiple *constraints*. We present two approaches for finding the optimal solution using LP: trial-and-error approach and graphic approach. These approaches are easy to use in our example because there are only two variables in the objective function and a small number of constraints. Understanding these approaches provides insight into LP. In most real-world LP applications, managers use computer software packages to calculate the optimal solution.[5]

---

[3]Other decision models are described in J. Moore and L. Weatherford, *Decision Modeling with Microsoft Excel*, 6th ed. (Upper Saddle River, NJ: Prentice Hall, 2001); and S. Nahmias, *Production and Operations Analysis*, 4th ed. (New York: McGraw-Hill/Irwin, 2001).

[4]As an example of how the lines are plotted in Exhibit 11-14, use equal signs instead of inequality signs and assume for the Assembly Department that $B = 0$; then $S = 300$ (600 machine-hours ÷ 2 machine-hours per snowmobile engine). Assume that $S = 0$; then $B = 120$ (600 machine-hours ÷ 5 machine-hours per boat engine). Connect those two points with a straight line.

[5]Although the trial-and-error and graphic approaches can be useful for two variables, they are impractical when more variables exist. Standard computer software packages rely on the simplex method. The *simplex method* is an iterative step-by-step procedure for determining the optimal solution to an LP problem. It starts with a specific feasible solution and then tests it by substitution to see whether the result can be improved. These substitutions continue until no further improvement is possible and the optimal solution is obtained.

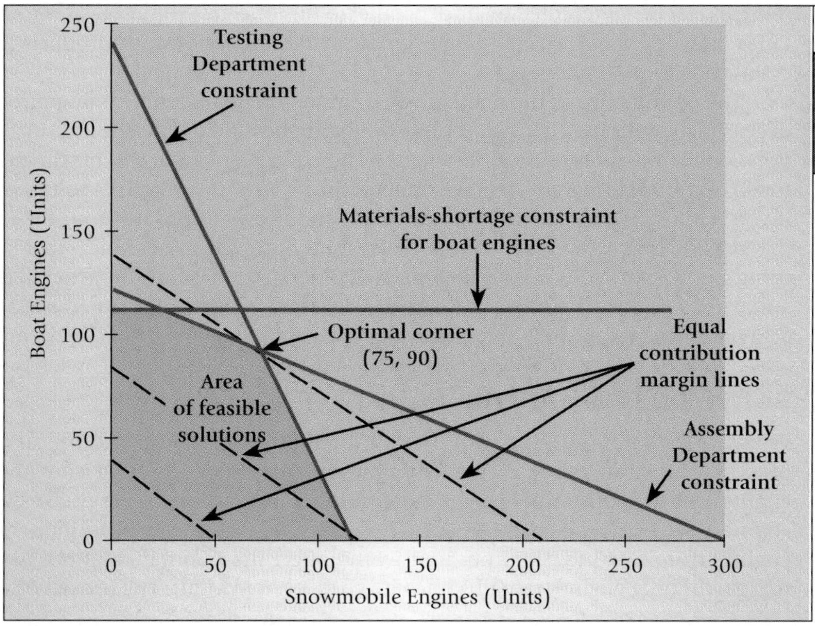

EXHIBIT 11-14

Linear Programming: Graphic Solution for Power Recreation

Trial-and-error approach The optimal solution can be found by trial and error, by working with coordinates of the corners of the area of feasible solutions.

First, select any set of corner points and compute the total contribution margin. Five corner points appear in Exhibit 11-14. It is helpful to use simultaneous equations to obtain the exact coordinates in the graph. To illustrate, the corner point (*S* = 75, *B* = 90) can be derived by solving the two pertinent constraint inequalities as simultaneous equations:

	$2S + 5B = 600$	(1)
	$1S + 0.5B = 120$	(2)
Multiplying (2) by 2:	$2S + 1B = 240$	(3)
Subtracting (3) from (1):	$4B = 360$	
Therefore,	$B = 360 \div 4 = 90$	
Substituting for *B* in (2):	$1S + 0.5(90) = 120$	
	$S = 120 - 45 = 75$	

Given *S* = 75 snowmobile engines and *B* = 90 boat engines, *TCM* = ($240 per snowmobile engine × 75 snowmobile engines) + ($375 per boat engine × 90 boat engines) = $51,750.

Second, move from corner point to corner point and compute the total contribution margin at each corner point.

Trial	Corner Point (*S*, *B*)	Snowmobile Engines (*S*)	Boat Engines (*B*)	Total Contribution Margin
1	(0, 0)	0	0	$240(0) + $375(0) = $0
2	(0, 110)	0	110	$240(0) + $375(110) = $41,250
3	(25, 110)	25	110	$240(25) + $375(110) = $47,250
4	(75, 90)	75	90	$240(75) + $375(90) = $51,750[a]
5	(120, 0)	120	0	$240(120) + $375(0) = $28,800

[a]The optimal solution.

The optimal product mix is the mix that yields the highest total contribution: 75 snowmobile engines and 90 boat engines. To understand the solution, consider what happens when moving from the point (25, 110) to (75, 90). Power Recreation gives up $7,500 [$375 × (110 – 90)] in contribution margin from boat engines while gaining $12,000 [$240 × (75 – 25)] in contribution margin from snowmobile engines. This results in a net increase in contribution margin of $4,500 ($12,000 – $7,500), from $47,250 to $51,750.

Graphic approach Consider all possible combinations that will produce the same total contribution margin of, say, $12,000. That is,

$$\$240S + \$375B = \$12{,}000$$

This set of $12,000 contribution margins is a straight dashed line through [*S* = 50 ($12,000 ÷ $240); *B* = 0)] and [*S* = 0, *B* = 32 ($12,000 ÷ $375)] in Exhibit 11-14. Other equal total contribution margins can be represented by lines parallel to this one. In Exhibit 11-14, we show three dashed lines. Lines drawn farther from the origin represent more sales of both products and higher amounts of equal contribution margins.

The optimal line is the one farthest from the origin but still passing through a point in the area of feasible solutions. This line represents the highest total contribution margin. The optimal solution—the number of snowmobile engines and boat engines that will maximize the objective function, total contribution margin—is the corner point ($S = 75$, $B = 90$). This solution will become apparent if you put a straight-edge ruler on the graph and move it outward from the origin and parallel with the $12,000 line. Move the ruler as far away from the origin as possible—that is, increase the total contribution margin—without leaving the area of feasible solutions. In general, the optimal solution in a maximization problem lies at the corner where the dashed line intersects an extreme point of the area of feasible solutions. Moving the ruler out any farther puts it outside the area of feasible solutions.

Sensitivity Analysis

As the Power Recreation example illustrates, large changes in contribution margin per unit of products may not affect the optimal product mix if there are no other nearby corner points.

What are the implications of uncertainty about the accounting or technical coefficients used in the objective function (such as the contribution margin per unit of snowmobile engines or boat engines) or the constraints (such as the number of machine-hours it takes to make a snowmobile engine or a boat engine)? Consider how a change in the contribution margin of snowmobile engines from $240 to $300 per unit would affect the optimal solution. Assume the contribution margin for boat engines remains unchanged at $375 per unit. The revised objective function will be:

$$TCM = \$300S + \$375B$$

Using the trial-and-error approach to calculate the total contribution margin for each of the five corner points described in the previous table, the optimal solution is still ($S = 75$, $B = 90$). What if the contribution margin of snowmobile engines falls to $160 per unit? The optimal solution remains the same ($S = 75$, $B = 90$). Thus, big changes in the contribution margin per unit of snowmobile engines have no effect on the optimal solution in this case. That's because, although the slopes of the equal contribution margin lines in Exhibit 11-14 change as the contribution margin of snowmobile engines changes from $240 to $300 to $160 per unit, the farthest point at which the equal contribution margin lines intersect the area of feasible solutions is still ($S = 75$, $B = 90$).

TERMS TO LEARN

This chapter and the Glossary at the end of the book contain definitions of:

book value (p. 396)
business function costs (p. 382)
constraint (p. 402)
decision model (p. 379)
differential cost (p. 386)
differential revenue (p. 386)
full costs of the product (p. 382)
incremental cost (p. 386)
incremental revenue (p. 386)
insourcing (p. 384)
linear programming (LP) (p. 402)
make-or-buy decisions (p. 384)
objective function (p. 402)
one-time-only special order (p. 381)
opportunity cost (p. 388)
outsourcing (p. 384)
product-mix decisions (p. 391)
qualitative factors (p. 381)
quantitative factors (p. 381)
relevant costs (p. 380)
relevant revenues (p. 380)
sunk costs (p. 380)

PH Grade Assist

Prentice Hall Grade Assist (PHGA)
Your professor may ask you to complete selected exercises and problems in Prentice Hall Grade Assist (PHGA). PHGA is an online tool that can help you master the chapter's topics. It provides you with multiple variations of exercises and problems designated by the PHGA icon. You can rework these exercises and problems—each time with new data—as many times as you need. You also receive immediate feedback and grading.

ASSIGNMENT MATERIAL

Questions

11-1 Outline the five-step sequence in a decision process.

11-2 Define relevant costs. Why are historical costs irrelevant?

11-3 "All future costs are relevant." Do you agree? Why?

11-4 Distinguish between quantitative and qualitative factors in decision making.

11-5 Describe two potential problems that should be avoided in relevant-cost analysis.

11-6 "Variable costs are always relevant, and fixed costs are always irrelevant." Do you agree? Why?

11-7 "A component part should be purchased whenever the purchase price is less than its total manufacturing cost per unit." Do you agree? Why?

11-8 Define opportunity cost.

11-9 "Managers should always buy inventory in quantities that result in the lowest purchase cost per unit." Do you agree? Why?

11-10 "Management should always maximize sales of the product with the highest contribution margin per unit." Do you agree? Why?

11-11 "A branch office or business segment that shows negative operating income should be shut down." Do you agree? Explain briefly.

11-12 "Cost written off as depreciation on equipment already purchased is always irrelevant." Do you agree? Why?

11-13 "Managers will always choose the alternative that maximizes operating income or minimizes costs in the decision model." Do you agree? Why?

11-14 Describe the three steps in solving a linear programming problem.

11-15 How might the optimal solution of a linear programming problem be determined?

Exercises

11-16 Disposal of assets. Answer the following questions.

PH Grade Assist

1. A company has an inventory of 1,000 assorted parts for a line of missiles that has been discontinued. The inventory cost is $80,000. The parts can be either (a) remachined at total additional costs of $30,000 and then sold for $35,000 or (b) sold as scrap for $2,000. Which action is more profitable? Show your calculations.
2. A truck, costing $100,000 and uninsured, is wrecked its first day in use. It can be either (a) disposed of for $10,000 cash and replaced with a similar truck costing $102,000 or (b) rebuilt for $85,000, and thus be brand-new as far as operating characteristics and looks are concerned. Which action is less costly? Show your calculations.

11-17 The careening personal computer. (W. A. Paton) An employee in the Accounting Department of a company was moving a personal computer from one room to another. As he came alongside an open stairway, he slipped and the computer got away from him. It careened down the stairs with a great racket and wound up at the bottom, completely destroyed. Hearing the crash, the office manager came rushing out and turned rather pale when he saw what had happened. "Someone tell me quickly," the manager yelled, "if that is one of our fully depreciated items." A check of the accounting records showed that the smashed computer was, indeed, one of those items that had been written off. "Thank God!" exclaimed the manager.

Required

Explain and comment on the point of this anecdote.

11-18 Multiple choice. (CPA) Choose the best answer.

PH Grade Assist

1. The Woody Company manufactures slippers and sells them at $10 a pair. Variable manufacturing cost is $4.50 a pair, and allocated fixed manufacturing cost is $1.50 a pair. It has enough idle capacity available to accept a one-time-only special order of 20,000 pairs of slippers at $6 a pair. Woody will not incur any marketing costs as a result of the special order. What would the effect on operating income be if the special order could be accepted without affecting normal sales? (a) $0, (b) $30,000 increase, (c) $90,000 increase, or (d) $120,000 increase. Show your calculations.
2. The Reno Company manufactures Part No. 498 for use in its production line. The manufacturing cost per unit for 20,000 units of Part No. 498 is as follows:

Direct materials	$ 6
Direct manufacturing labor	30
Variable manufacturing overhead	12
Fixed manufacturing overhead allocated	16
Total manufacturing cost per unit	$64

The Tray Company has offered to sell 20,000 units of Part No. 498 to Reno for $60 per unit. Reno will make the decision to buy the part from Tray if there is an overall savings of at least $25,000 for Reno. If Reno accepts Tray's offer, $9 per unit of the fixed overhead allocated would be eliminated. Furthermore, Reno has determined that the released facilities could be used to save relevant costs in the manufacture of Part No. 575. For Reno to achieve an overall savings of $25,000, the amount of relevant costs that would have to be saved by using the released facilities in the manufacture of Part No. 575 would be (a) $80,000, (b) $85,000, (c) $125,000, or (d) $140,000. Show your calculations.

11-19 Special order, activity-based costing. (CMA, adapted) The Award Plus Company manufactures medals for winners of athletic events and other contests. Its manufacturing plant has the capacity to produce 10,000 medals each month. Current production and sales are 7,500 medals per month. The company normally charges $150 per medal. Cost information for the current activity level is as follows:

Variable costs that vary with number of units produced	
Direct materials	$ 262,500
Direct manufacturing labor	300,000
Variable costs (for setups, materials handling, quality control, and so on) that vary with number of batches, 150 batches × $500 per batch	75,000
Fixed manufacturing costs	275,000
Fixed marketing costs	175,000
Total costs	$1,087,500

Award Plus has just received a special one-time-only order for 2,500 medals at $100 per medal. Accepting the special order would not affect the company's regular business. Award Plus makes medals for its existing customers in batch sizes of 50 medals (150 batches × 50 medals per batch = 7,500 medals). The special order requires Award Plus to make the medals in 25 batches of 100 each.

Required

1. Should Award Plus accept this special order? Show your calculations.
2. Suppose plant capacity were only 9,000 medals instead of 10,000 medals each month. The special order must either be taken in full or rejected completely. Should Award Plus accept the special order? Show your calculations.
3. As in requirement 1, assume that monthly capacity is 10,000 medals. Award Plus is concerned that if it accepts the special order, its existing customers will immediately demand a price discount of $10 in the month in which the special order is being filled. They would argue that Award Plus's capacity costs are now being spread over more units and that existing customers should get the benefit of these lower costs. Should Award Plus accept the special order under these conditions? Show your calculations.

11-20 Make versus buy, activity-based costing. The Svenson Corporation manufactures cellular modems. It manufactures its own cellular modem circuit boards (CMCB), an important part of the cellular modem. It reports the following cost information about the costs of making CMCBs in 2006 and the expected costs in 2007:

	Current Costs in 2006	Expected Costs in 2007
Variable manufacturing costs		
Direct material cost per CMCB	$ 180	$ 170
Direct manufacturing labor cost per CMCB	50	45
Variable manufacturing cost per batch for setups, materials handling, and quality control	1,600	1,500
Fixed manufacturing cost		
Fixed manufacturing overhead costs that can be avoided if CMCBs are not made	320,000	320,000
Fixed manufacturing overhead costs of plant depreciation, insurance, and administration that cannot be avoided even if CMCBs are not made	800,000	800,000

Svenson manufactured 8,000 CMCBs in 2006 in 40 batches of 200 each. In 2007, Svenson anticipates needing 10,000 CMCBs. The CMCBs would be produced in 80 batches of 125 each.

The Minton Corporation has approached Svenson about supplying CMCBs to Svenson in 2007 at $300 per CMCB on whatever delivery schedule Svenson wants.

Required

1. Calculate the total expected manufacturing cost per unit of making CMCBs in 2007.
2. Suppose the capacity currently used to make CMCBs will become idle if Svenson purchases CMCBs from Minton. On the basis of financial considerations alone, should Svenson make CMCBs or buy them from Minton? Show your calculations.
3. Now suppose that if Svenson purchases CMCBs from Minton, its best alternative use of the capacity currently used for CMCBs is to make and sell special circuit boards (CB3s) to the Essex Corporation. Svenson estimates the following incremental revenues and costs from CB3s:

Total expected incremental future revenues	$2,000,000
Total expected incremental future costs	$2,150,000

On the basis of financial considerations alone, should Svenson make CMCBs or buy them from Minton? Show your calculations.

11-21 Inventory decision, opportunity costs. Lawnox, a manufacturer of lawn mowers, predicts that it will purchase 240,000 spark plugs next year. Lawnox estimates that 20,000 spark plugs will be required each month. A supplier quotes a price of $8 per spark plug. The supplier also offers a special discount option: If all 240,000 spark plugs are purchased at the start of the year, a discount of 5% off the $8 price will be given. Lawnox can invest its cash at 8% per year. It costs Lawnox $200 to place each purchase order.

Required

1. What is the opportunity cost of interest forgone from purchasing all 240,000 units at the start of the year instead of in 12 monthly purchases of 20,000 units per order?
2. Would this opportunity cost be recorded in the accounting system? Why?

3. Should Lawnox purchase 240,000 units at the start of the year or 20,000 units each month? Show your calculations.

11-22 Relevant costs, contribution margin, product emphasis. The Beach Comber is a take-out food store at a popular beach resort. Susan Sexton, owner of the Beach Comber, is deciding how much refrigerator space to devote to four different drinks. Pertinent data on these four drinks are as follows:

	Cola	Lemonade	Punch	Natural Orange Juice
Selling price per case	$18.00	$19.20	$26.40	$38.40
Variable cost per case	$13.50	$15.20	$20.10	$30.20
Cases sold per foot of shelf space per day	25	24	4	5

Sexton has a maximum front shelf space of 12 feet to devote to the four drinks. She wants a minimum of 1 foot and a maximum of 6 feet of front shelf space for each drink.

Required

1. Compute the contribution margin per case of each type of drink.
2. A co-worker of Sexton's recommends that she maximize the shelf space devoted to those drinks with the highest contribution margin per case. Evaluate this recommendation.
3. What shelf-space allocation for the four drinks would you recommend for the Beach Comber? Show your calculations.

11-23 Selection of most profitable product. Body-Builders, Inc., produces two basic types of weight-lifting equipment, Model 9 and Model 14. Pertinent data are as follows:

Excel Lab
www.prenhall.com/horngren/cost12e

	A	B	C
1		**Per Unit**	
2		**Model 9**	**Model 14**
3	Selling price	$100.00	$70.00
4	Costs		
5	Direct material	28.00	13.00
6	Direct manufacturing labor	15.00	25.00
7	Variable manufacturing overhead*	25.00	12.50
8	Fixed manufacturing overhead*	10.00	5.00
9	Marketing (all variable)	14.00	10.00
10	Total cost	92.00	65.50
11	Operating income	$ 8.00	$ 4.50
12			
13	*Allocated on the basis of machine-hours.		

The weight-lifting craze is such that enough of either Model 9 or Model 14 can be sold to keep the plant operating at full capacity. Both products are processed through the same production departments.

If you want to use Excel to solve this exercise, go to the Excel Lab at **www.prenhall.com/horngren/cost12e** and download the template for Exercise 11-23.

Required

Which products should be produced? Briefly explain your answer.

11-24 Which base to close, relevant-cost analysis, opportunity costs. The U.S. Defense Department has the difficult decision of deciding which military bases to shut down. Military and political factors obviously matter, but cost savings are also an important factor. Consider two naval bases located on the West Coast—one in Alameda, California, and the other in Everett, Washington. The Navy has decided that it needs only one of those two bases permanently, so one must be shut down. The decision regarding which base to shut down will be made on cost considerations alone. The following information is available:

a. The Alameda base was built at a cost of $100 million. The operating costs of the base are $400 million per year. The base is built on land owned by the Navy, so the Navy pays nothing for the use of the property. If the base is closed, the land will be sold to developers for $500 million.
b. The Everett base was built at a cost of $150 million on land leased by the Navy from private citizens. The Navy can choose to lease the land permanently for a lease payment of $3 million per year. If it decides to keep the Everett base open, the Navy plans to invest $60 million in a fixed income note, which at 5% interest will earn the $3 million the government needs for the lease payments. The land and buildings will immediately revert back to the owner if the base is closed. The operating costs of the base, excluding lease payments, are $300 million per year.
c. If the Alameda base is shut down, the Navy will have to transfer some personnel to the Everett facility. As a result, the yearly operating costs at Everett will increase by $100 million per year. If the Everett facility is closed down, no extra costs will be incurred to operate the Alameda facility.

Required The California delegation in Congress argues that it is cheaper to shut down the Everett base for two reasons: (1) It would save $100 million per year in additional costs required to operate the Everett base, and (2) it would save the lease payment of $3 million per year. (Recall that the Alameda base requires no cash payments for use of the land because the land is owned by the Navy.) Do you agree with the California delegation's arguments and conclusions? In your answer, identify and explain all costs that you consider relevant and all costs that you consider irrelevant for the base-closing decision.

PH Grade Assist

11-25 Closing and opening stores. Sanchez Corporation runs two convenience stores, one in Connecticut and one in Rhode Island. Operating income for each store in 2007 is as follows:

	Connecticut Store	Rhode Island Store
Revenues	$1,070,000	$860,000
Operating costs		
Cost of goods sold	750,000	660,000
Lease rent (renewable each year)	90,000	75,000
Labor costs (paid on an hourly basis)	42,000	42,000
Depreciation of equipment	25,000	22,000
Utilities (electricity, heating)	43,000	46,000
Allocated corporate overhead	50,000	40,000
Total operating costs	1,000,000	885,000
Operating income (loss)	$ 70,000	$(25,000)

The equipment has a zero disposal value. In a senior management meeting, Maria Lopez, the management accountant at Sanchez Corporation, makes the following comment, "Sanchez can increase its profitability by closing down the Rhode Island store or by adding another store like it."

Required

1. By closing down the Rhode Island store, Sanchez can reduce overall corporate overhead costs by $44,000. Calculate Sanchez's operating income if it closes the Rhode Island store. Is Maria Lopez's statement about the effect of closing the Rhode Island store correct? Explain.
2. Calculate Sanchez's operating income if it keeps the Rhode Island store open and opens another store with revenues and costs identical to the Rhode Island store (including a cost of $22,000 to acquire equipment with a one-year useful life and zero disposal value). Opening this store will increase corporate overhead costs by $4,000. Is Maria Lopez's statement about the effect of adding another store like the Rhode Island store correct? Explain.

11-26 Choosing customers. Broadway Printers operates a printing press with a monthly capacity of 2,000 machine-hours. Broadway has two main customers: Taylor Corporation and Kelly Corporation. Data on each customer for January follows:

	Taylor Corporation	Kelly Corporation	Total
Revenues	$120,000	$80,000	$200,000
Variable costs	42,000	48,000	90,000
Contribution margin	78,000	32,000	110,000
Fixed costs (allocated)	60,000	40,000	100,000
Operating income	$ 18,000	$(8,000)	$ 10,000
Machine-hours required	1,500 hours	500 hours	2,000 hours

Kelly Corporation indicates that it wants Broadway to do an *additional* $80,000 worth of printing jobs during February. These jobs are identical to the existing business Broadway did for Kelly in January in terms of variable costs and machine-hours required. Broadway anticipates that the business from Taylor Corporation in February will be the same as that in January. Broadway can choose to accept as much of the Taylor and Kelly business for February as its capacity allows. Assume that total machine-hours and fixed costs for February will be the same as in January.

Required What action should Broadway take to maximize its operating income? Show your calculations.

11-27 Relevance of equipment costs. The Auto Wash Company has just today paid for and installed a special machine for polishing cars at one of its several outlets. It is the first day of the company's fiscal year. The machine costs $20,000. Its annual cash operating costs total $15,000. The machine will have a four-year useful life and a zero terminal disposal value.

After the machine has been used for only one day, a salesperson offers a different machine that promises to do the same job at annual cash operating costs of $9,000. The new machine will cost $24,000 cash, installed. The "old" machine is unique and can be sold outright for only $10,000, minus $2,000 removal cost. The new machine, like the old one, will have a four-year useful life and zero terminal disposal value.

Revenues, all in cash, will be $150,000 annually, and other cash costs will be $110,000 annually, regardless of this decision.

For simplicity, ignore income taxes and the time value of money.

Required

1. **a.** Prepare a statement of cash receipts and disbursements for each of the four years under each alternative. What is the cumulative difference in cash flow for the four years taken together?
   b. Prepare income statements for each of the four years under each alternative. Assume straight-line depreciation. What is the cumulative difference in operating income for the four years taken together?
   c. What are the irrelevant items in your presentations in requirements a and b? Why are they irrelevant?
2. Suppose the cost of the "old" machine was $1 million rather than $20,000. Nevertheless, the old machine can be sold outright for only $10,000, minus $2,000 removal cost. Would the net differences in requirements 1a and 1b change? Explain.
3. Is there any conflict between the decision model and the incentives of the manager who has just purchased the "old" machine and is considering replacing it a day later?

11-28 Equipment upgrade versus replacement. (A. Spero, adapted) The TechMech Company produces and sells 6,000 modular computer desks per year at a selling price of $500 each. Its current production equipment, purchased for $1,500,000 and with a five-year useful life, is only two years old. It has a terminal disposal value of $0 and is depreciated on a straight-line basis. The equipment has a current disposal price of $600,000. However, the emergence of a new molding technology has led TechMech to consider either upgrading or replacing the production equipment. The following table presents data for the two alternatives:

Excel Lab
www.prenhall.com/horngren/cost12e

	A	B	C
1		**Upgrade**	**Replace**
2	One-time equipment costs	$2,700,000	$4,200,000
3	Variable manufacturing cost per desk	$140	$80
4	Remaining useful life of equipment (years)	3	3
5	Terminal disposal value of equipment	$0	$0

All equipment costs will continue to be depreciated on a straight-line basis. For simplicity, ignore income taxes and the time value of money.

If you want to use Excel to solve this exercise, go to the Excel Lab at **www.prenhall.com/horngren/cost12e** and download the template for Exercise 11-28.

Required

1. Should TechMech upgrade its production line or replace it? Show your calculations.
2. Now suppose the one-time equipment cost to replace the production equipment is somewhat negotiable. All other data are as given previously. What is the maximum one-time equipment cost that TechMech would be willing to pay to replace the old equipment rather than upgrade it?
3. Assume that the capital expenditures to replace and upgrade the production equipment are as given in the original exercise, but that the production and sales quantity is not known. For what production and sales quantity would TechMech (i) upgrade the equipment or (ii) replace the equipment?
4. Assume that all data are as given in the original exercise. Dan Doria is TechMech's manager, and his bonus is based on operating income. Because he is likely to relocate after about a year, his current bonus is his primary concern. Which alternative would Doria choose? Explain.

Problems

11-29 Special order. Autodeck Company produces sound systems for cars and sells them to automotive manufacturers for $100 each. Full capacity is 20,000 systems per month, but it is currently producing 18,000 systems per month for its regular customers. The company reports the following monthly results:

Excel Lab
www.prenhall.com/horngren/cost12e

	A	B	C
1		**Per Unit**	**Total**
2	Revenue	$100	$1,800,000
3	Direct materials	25	450,000
4	Direct manufacturing labor	10	180,000
5	Variable manufacturing overhead	22	396,000
6	Fixed manufacturing overhead	3	54,000
7	Variable selling expenses	19	342,000
8	Fixed selling expenses	2	36,000
9	Total costs	81	1,458,000
10	Operating income	$ 19	$ 342,000
11			

Autodeck's manager, Gus Bronson, receives a call regarding a one-time special order: Telluride Automotive needs 2,000 systems and will pay $65 per system. Autodeck will incur no selling costs for the special order.

If you want to use Excel to solve this problem, go to the Excel Lab at **www.prenhall.com/horngren/cost12e** and download the template for Problem 11-29.

Required

1. Should Bronson accept this one-time special order? What would monthly operating income be if Autodeck did accept Telluride's order?
2. Telluride's manager calls again: They've run some new calculations, and they really need 2,500 systems at the same $65 price. It will have to be an all-or-nothing deal. Bronson thinks, "Now they're pushing it . . . Telluride's order will displace some of the volume I sell to my regular customers who are a lot more profitable for us." Assuming that Autodeck's regular customer relationships will not suffer due to a small one-time volume reduction, and based on financial considerations alone, what should Bronson do? Provide specific calculations and explain your reasoning.
3. Assuming that Autodeck's regular customer relationships will not suffer due to a small one-time volume reduction, up to what volume is Autodeck better off supplying to Telluride at a selling price of $65?

11-30 Contribution approach, relevant costs. Air Frisco has leased a single jet aircraft that it operates between San Francisco and the Fijian Islands. Only tourist-class seats are available on its planes. An analyst has collected the following information:

Seating capacity per plane	360 passengers
Average number of passengers per flight	200 passengers
Average one-way fare	$500
Variable fuel costs	$14,000 per flight
Food and beverage service costs (no charge to passenger)	$20 per passenger
Commission to travel agents paid by Air Frisco (all tickets are booked by travel agents)	8% of fare
Fixed annual lease costs allocated to each flight	$53,000 per flight
Fixed ground-services (maintenance, check in, baggage handling) costs allocated to each flight	$7,000 per flight
Fixed flight-crew salaries allocated to each flight	$4,000 per flight

Assume that fuel costs are unaffected by the actual number of passengers on a flight.

Required

1. Calculate the total contribution margin from passengers that Air Frisco earns on each one-way flight between San Francisco and Fiji.
2. The Market Research Department of Air Frisco indicates that lowering the average one-way fare to $480 will increase the average number of passengers per flight to 212. On the basis of financial considerations alone, should Air Frisco lower its fare? Show your calculations.
3. Travel International, a tour operator, approaches Air Frisco with the possibility of chartering its aircraft. The terms of charter are as follows: (a) For each one-way flight, Travel International will pay Air Frisco $74,500 to charter the plane and to use its flight crew and ground-service staff; (b) Travel International will pay for fuel costs; and (c) Travel International will pay for all food costs. On the basis of financial considerations alone, should Air Frisco accept Travel International's offer? Show your calculations. What other factors should Air Frisco consider in deciding whether to charter its plane to Travel International?

11-31 Relevant costs, opportunity costs. Larry Miller, the general manager of Basil Software, must decide when to release the new version of Basil's spreadsheet package, Easyspread 2.0. Development of Easyspread 2.0 is complete; however, the diskettes, compact discs, and user manuals have not yet been produced. The product can be shipped starting July 1, 2006.

The major problem is that Basil has overstocked the previous version of its spreadsheet package, Easyspread 1.0. Miller knows that once Easyspread 2.0 is introduced, Basil will not be able to sell any more units of Easyspread 1.0. Rather than just throwing away the inventory of Easyspread 1.0, Miller is wondering if it might be better to continue to sell Easyspread 1.0 for the next three months and introduce Easyspread 2.0 on October 1, 2006, when the inventory of Easyspread 1.0 will be sold out.

The following information is available:

	Easyspread 1.0	Easyspread 2.0
Selling price	$150	$185
Variable cost per unit of diskettes, compact discs, user manuals	20	25
Development cost per unit	65	95
Marketing and administrative cost per unit	35	40
Total cost per unit	120	160
Operating income per unit	$ 30	$ 25

Development cost per unit for each product equals the total costs of developing the software product divided by the anticipated unit sales over the life of the product. Marketing and administrative costs are fixed costs in 2006, incurred to support all marketing and administrative activities of Basil Software. Marketing and administrative costs are allocated to products on the basis of the budgeted revenues of each product. The preceding unit costs assume Easyspread 2.0 will be introduced on October 1, 2006.

Required

1. On the basis of financial considerations alone, should Miller introduce Easyspread 2.0 on July 1, 2006, or wait until October 1, 2006? Show your calculations, clearly identifying relevant and irrelevant revenues and costs.
2. What other factors might Larry Miller consider in making a decision?

11-32 Opportunity costs. (H. Schaefer) The Wolverine Corporation is working at full production capacity producing 10,000 units of a unique product, Rosebo. Manufacturing cost per unit for Rosebo is as follows:

Direct materials	$ 2
Direct manufacturing labor	3
Manufacturing overhead	5
Total manufacturing cost	$10

Manufacturing overhead cost per unit is based on variable cost per unit of $2 and fixed costs of $30,000 (at full capacity of 10,000 units). Marketing cost per unit, all variable, is $4, and the selling price is $20.

A customer, the Miami Company, has asked Wolverine to produce 2,000 units of Orangebo, a modification of Rosebo. Orangebo would require the same manufacturing processes as Rosebo. Miami has offered to pay Wolverine $15 for a unit of Orangebo plus half of the marketing cost per unit.

Required

1. What is the opportunity cost to Wolverine of producing the 2,000 units of Orangebo? (Assume that no overtime is worked.)
2. The Buckeye Corporation has offered to produce 2,000 units of Rosebo for Wolverine so that Wolverine may accept the Miami offer. That is, if Wolverine accepts the Buckeye offer, Wolverine would manufacture 8,000 units of Rosebo and 2,000 units of Orangebo and purchase 2,000 units of Rosebo from Buckeye. Buckeye would charge Wolverine $14 per unit to manufacture Rosebo. On the basis of financial considerations alone, should Wolverine accept the Buckeye offer? Show your calculations.
3. Suppose Wolverine had been working at less than full capacity, producing 8,000 units of Rosebo at the time the Miami offer was made. Calculate the minimum price Wolverine should accept for Orangebo under these conditions. (Ignore the previous $15 selling price.)

11-33 Product mix, special order. (N. Melumad, adapted) Pendleton Engineering makes cutting tools for metalworking operations. It makes two types of tools: R3, a regular cutting tool, and HP6, a high-precision cutting tool. R3 is manufactured on a regular machine, but HP6 must be manufactured on both the regular machine and a high-precision machine. The following information is available.

	R3	**HP6**
Selling price	$100	$150
Variable manufacturing cost per unit	$ 60	$100
Variable marketing cost per unit	$ 15	$ 35
Budgeted total fixed overhead costs	$350,000	$550,000
Hours required to produce 1 unit on the regular machine	1.0	0.5

Additional information includes:

a. Pendleton faces a capacity constraint on the regular machine of 50,000 hours per year.
b. The capacity of the high-precision machine is not a constraint.
c. Of the $550,000 budgeted fixed overhead costs of HP6, $300,000 are lease payments for the high-precision machine. This cost is charged entirely to HP6 because Pendleton uses the machine exclusively to produce HP6. The lease agreement for the high-precision machine can be canceled at any time without penalties.
d. All other overhead costs are fixed and cannot be changed.

Required

1. What product mix—that is, how many units of R3 and HP6—will maximize Pendleton's operating income? Show your calculations.
2. Suppose Pendleton can increase the annual capacity of its regular machines by 15,000 machine-hours at a cost of $150,000. Should Pendleton increase the capacity of the regular machines by 15,000 machine-hours? By how much will Pendleton's operating income increase? Show your calculations.
3. Suppose that the capacity of the regular machines has been increased to 65,000 hours. Pendleton has been approached by Carter Corporation to supply 20,000 units of another cutting tool, S3, for $120 per unit. Pendleton must either accept the order for all 20,000 units or reject it totally. S3 is exactly like R3 except that its variable manufacturing cost is $70 per unit. (It takes one hour to produce one unit of S3 on the regular machine, and variable marketing cost equals $15 per unit.) What product mix should Pendleton choose to maximize operating income? Show your calculations.

11-34 Dropping a product line, selling more units. The Northern Division of Grossman Corporation makes and sells tables and beds. The following estimated revenue and cost information from the division's activity-based costing system is available for 2005.

	4,000 Tables	5,000 Beds	Total
Revenues ($125 × 4,000; $200 × 5,000)	$500,000	$1,000,000	$1,500,000
Variable direct materials and direct manufacturing labor costs ($75 × 4,000; $105 × 5,000)	300,000	525,000	825,000
Depreciation on equipment used exclusively by each product line	42,000	58,000	100,000
Marketing and distribution costs			
$40,000 (fixed) + ($750 per shipment × 40 shipments)	70,000		205,000
$60,000 (fixed) + ($750 per shipment × 100 shipments)		135,000	
Fixed general-administration costs of the division allocated to product lines on the basis of revenues	110,000	220,000	330,000
Corporate-office costs allocated to product lines on the basis of revenues	50,000	100,000	150,000
Total costs	572,000	1,038,000	1,610,000
Operating income (loss)	$(72,000)	$ (38,000)	$ (110,000)

Additional information includes:

a. On January 1, 2005, the equipment has a book value of $100,000 and zero disposal value. Any equipment not used will remain idle.

b. Fixed marketing and distribution costs of a product line can be avoided if the line is discontinued.

c. Fixed general-administration costs of the division and corporate-office costs will not change if sales of individual product lines are increased or decreased or if product lines are added or dropped.

Required

1. On the basis of financial considerations alone, should the Northern Division discontinue the tables product line, assuming the released facilities remain idle? Show your calculations.
2. What would be the effect on Northern Division's operating income if it were to sell 4,000 more tables? Assume that to do so the division would have to acquire additional equipment costing $42,000 with a one-year useful life and zero terminal disposal value. Assume further that the fixed marketing and distribution costs would not change but that the number of shipments would double. Show your calculations.
3. Given the Northern Division's expected operating loss of $110,000, should Grossman Corporation shut it down? Assume that shutting down the Northern Division will have no effect on corporate-office costs but will lead to savings of all general-administration costs of the division. Show your calculations.
4. Suppose Grossman Corporation has the opportunity to open another division, the Southern Division, whose revenues and costs are expected to be identical to the Northern Division's revenues and costs (including a cost of $100,000 to acquire equipment with a one-year useful life and zero terminal disposal value). Opening the new division will have no effect on corporate-office costs. Should Grossman open the Southern Division? Show your calculations.

11-35 Make or buy, unknown level of volume. (A. Atkinson) Oxford Engineering manufactures small engines. The engines are sold to manufacturers who install them in such products as lawn mowers. The company currently manufactures all the parts used in these engines but is considering a proposal from an external supplier who wishes to supply the starter assemblies used in these engines.

The starter assemblies are currently manufactured in Division 3 of Oxford Engineering. The costs relating to the starter assemblies for the past 12 months were as follows:

Direct materials	$200,000
Direct manufacturing labor	150,000
Manufacturing overhead	400,000
Total	$750,000

Over the past year, Division 3 manufactured 150,000 starter assemblies. The average cost for each starter assembly is $5 ($750,000 ÷ 150,000).

Further analysis of manufacturing overhead revealed the following information. Of the total manufacturing overhead, only 25% is considered variable. Of the fixed portion, $150,000 is an allocation of general overhead that will remain unchanged for the company as a whole if production of the starter assemblies is discontinued. A further $100,000 of the fixed overhead is avoidable if production of the starter assemblies is discontinued. The balance of the current fixed overhead, $50,000, is the division manager's salary. If production of the starter assemblies is discontinued, the manager of Division 3 will be transferred to Division 2 at the same salary. This move will allow the company to save the $40,000 salary that would otherwise be paid to attract an outsider to this position.

Required

1. Tidnish Electronics, a reliable supplier, has offered to supply starter-assembly units at $4 per unit. Because this price is less than the current average cost of $5 per unit, the vice president of manufacturing is eager to accept this offer. On the basis of financial considerations alone, should the outside

offer be accepted? Show your calculations. (*Hint:* Production output in the coming year may be different from production output in the past year.)

2. How, if at all, would your response to requirement 1 change if the company could use the vacated plant space for storage and, in so doing, avoid $50,000 of outside storage charges currently incurred? Why is this information relevant or irrelevant?

11-36 Make versus buy, activity-based costing, opportunity costs. (N. Melumad and S. Reichelstein, adapted) The Ace Company produces bicycles. This year's expected production is 10,000 units. Currently, Ace makes the chains for its bicycles. Ace's management accountant reports the following costs for making the 10,000 bicycle chains:

	Cost per Unit	Costs for 10,000 Units
Direct materials	$4.00	$ 40,000
Direct manufacturing labor	2.00	20,000
Variable manufacturing overhead (power and utilities)	1.50	15,000
Inspection, setup, materials handling		2,000
Machine rent		3,000
Allocated fixed costs of plant administration, taxes, and insurance		30,000
Total costs		$110,000

Ace has received an offer from an outside vendor to supply any number of chains Ace requires at $8.20 per chain. The following additional information is available:

a. Inspection, setup, and materials-handling costs vary with the number of batches in which the chains are produced. Ace produces chains in batch sizes of 1,000 units. Ace will produce the 10,000 units in 10 batches.

b. Ace rents the machine used to make the chains. If Ace buys all of its chains from the outside vendor, it does not need to pay rent on this machine.

Required

1. Assume that if Ace purchases the chains from the outside supplier, the facility where the chains are currently made will remain idle. On the basis of financial considerations alone, should Ace accept the outside supplier's offer at the anticipated production (and sales) volume of 10,000 units? Show your calculations.
2. For this question, assume that if the chains are purchased outside, the facilities where the chains are currently made will be used to upgrade the bicycles by adding mud flaps and reflectors. As a consequence, the selling price of bicycles will be raised by $20. The variable cost per unit of the upgrade would be $18, and additional tooling costs of $16,000 would be incurred. On the basis of financial considerations alone, should Ace make or buy the chains, assuming that 10,000 units are produced (and sold)? Show your calculations.
3. The sales manager at Ace is concerned that the estimate of 10,000 units may be high and believes that only 6,200 units will be sold. Production will be cut back, freeing up work space. This space can be used to add the mud flaps and reflectors whether Ace buys the chains or makes them in-house. At this lower output, Ace will produce the chains in eight batches of 775 units each. On the basis of financial considerations alone, should Ace purchase the chains from the outside vendor? Show your calculations.

11-37 Multiple choice, comprehensive problem on relevant costs. The following are the Class Company's unit costs of manufacturing and marketing a high-style pen at an output level of 20,000 units per month:

Manufacturing cost	
Direct materials	$1.00
Direct manufacturing labor	1.20
Variable manufacturing overhead cost	0.80
Fixed manufacturing overhead cost	0.50
Marketing cost	
Variable	1.50
Fixed	0.90

Required

The following situations refer only to the preceding data; there is *no connection* between the situations. Unless stated otherwise, assume a regular selling price of $6 per unit. Choose the best answer to each question. Show your calculations.

1. For an inventory of 10,000 units of the high-style pen presented in the balance sheet, the appropriate unit cost to use is (a) $3.00, (b) $3.50, (c) $5.00, (d) $2.20, or (e) $5.90.
2. The pen is usually produced and sold at the rate of 240,000 units per year (an average of 20,000 per month). The selling price is $6 per unit, which yields total annual revenues of $1,440,000. Total costs are $1,416,000, and operating income is $24,000, or $0.10 per unit. Market research estimates that unit sales

could be increased by 10% if prices were cut to $5.80. Assuming the implied cost-behavior patterns continue, this action, if taken, would

a. Decrease operating income by $7,200

b. Decrease operating income by $0.20 per unit ($48,000) but increase operating income by 10% of revenues ($144,000), for a net increase of $96,000

c. Decrease fixed cost per unit by 10%, or $0.14, per unit, and thus decrease operating income by $0.06 ($0.20 – $0.14) per unit

d. Increase unit sales to 264,000 units, which at the $5.80 price would give total revenues of $1,531,200 and lead to costs of $5.90 per unit for 264,000 units, which would equal $1,557,600, and result in an operating loss of $26,400

e. None of these

3. A contract with the government for 5,000 units of the pens calls for the reimbursement of all manufacturing costs plus a fixed fee of $1,000. No variable marketing costs are incurred on the government contract. You are asked to compare the following two alternatives:

Sales Each Month to	Alternative A	Alternative B
Regular customers	15,000 units	15,000 units
Government	0 units	5,000 units

Operating income under alternative B is greater than that under alternative A by (a) $1,000, (b) $2,500, (c) $3,500, (d) $300, or (e) none of these.

4. Assume the same data with respect to the government contract as in requirement 3 except that the two alternatives to be compared are:

Sales Each Month to	Alternative A	Alternative B
Regular customers	20,000 units	15,000 units
Government	0 units	5,000 units

Operating income under alternative B relative to that under alternative A is (a) $4,000 less, (b) $3,000 greater, (c) $6,500 less, (d) $500 greater, or (e) none of these.

5. The company wants to enter a foreign market in which price competition is keen. The company seeks a one-time-only special order for 10,000 units on a minimum-unit-price basis. It expects that shipping costs for this order will amount to only $0.75 per unit, but the fixed costs of obtaining the contract will be $4,000. The company incurs no variable marketing costs other than shipping costs. Domestic business will be unaffected. The selling price to break even is (a) $3.50, (b) $4.15, (c) $4.25, (d) $3.00, or (e) $5.00.

6. The company has an inventory of 1,000 units of pens that must be sold immediately at reduced prices. Otherwise, the inventory will become worthless. The unit cost that is relevant for establishing the minimum selling price is (a) $4.50, (b) $4.00, (c) $3.00, (d) $5.90, or (e) $1.50.

7. A proposal is received from an outside supplier who will make and ship the high-style pens directly to the Class Company's customers as sales orders are forwarded from Class's sales staff. Class's fixed marketing costs will be unaffected, but its variable marketing costs will be slashed by 20%. Class's plant will be idle, but its fixed manufacturing overhead will continue at 50% of present levels. How much per unit would the company be able to pay the supplier without decreasing operating income? (a) $4.75, (b) $3.95, (c) $2.95, (d) $5.35, or (e) none of these.

11-38 Make or buy (continuation of 11-37). Assume that, as in requirement 7 of Problem 11-37, a proposal is received from an outside supplier who will make and ship high-style pens directly to the Class Company's customers as sales orders are forwarded from Class's sales staff. If the supplier's offer is accepted, the present plant facilities will be used to make a new pen whose unit costs will be:

Variable manufacturing cost	$5.00
Fixed manufacturing cost	1.00
Variable marketing cost	2.00
Fixed marketing cost	0.50

Total fixed manufacturing overhead will be unchanged from the original level given at the beginning of Problem 11-37. Fixed marketing costs for the new pens are over and above the fixed marketing costs incurred for marketing the high-style pens at the beginning of Problem 11-37. The new pen will sell for $9. The minimum desired operating income on the two pens taken together is $50,000 per year.

Required

What is the maximum purchase cost per unit that the Class Company would be willing to pay for subcontracting the production of the high-style pens?

Excel Lab
www.prenhall.com/horngren/cost12e

11-39 Product mix, constrained resource. Taylor Boat Yard produces and sells a line of small boats for recreational use. Production is a machine-intensive process, with the parts for each boat being manufactured on a series of machines run by highly skilled operators. Taylor's variable costs are direct material costs, variable machining costs, variable manufacturing overhead costs, and sales commissions. Marion Taylor, the owner, is planning production for the coming year and collects the following data:

	A	B	C	D	E
1		Estimated		Direct	Variable
2		Demand	Selling	Material	Machining
3		(units)	Price	Cost Per Unit	Cost Per Unit
4	Cruiser-LX	1,800	$3,000	$750	$600
5	Cruiser-EX	2,400	2,400	650	500
6	Boater-LX	4,500	2,100	500	500
7	Boater-EX	4,200	2,000	500	400
8	Canoe Star	39,000	800	100	200

- Salespeople are paid a 5% commission on each Cruiser or Boater sold, and a 10% commission on each Canoe Star sold. All other marketing and administrative costs are fixed and, along with the fixed manufacturing costs, total $8,750,000.
- Annual capacity is 60,000 machine-hours, which is limited by the availability of machines. Machining costs are $200 per hour, and variable manufacturing overhead equals $50 per machine-hour.
- Taylor Boat Yard holds negligible inventories to minimize the business risk of changing fads in recreational boating.

If you want to use Excel to solve this problem, go to the Excel Lab at **www.prenhall.com/horngren/cost12e** and download the template for Problem 11-39.

Required

1. Calculate the machine-hours required to satisfy the estimated demand for each type of boat.
2. What is the contribution margin per unit earned from each type of boat?
3. Advise Marion Taylor about the most profitable production levels of the five products.
4. Suppose Taylor Boat Yard can lease additional machining capacity on an as-needed basis. What is the maximum amount that Marion Taylor would be willing to pay for each hour of additional machining capacity in the coming year?

11-40 Optimal product mix. (CMA adapted, chapter appendix) Della Simpson, Inc., sells two popular brands of cookies: Della's Delight and Bonny's Bourbon. Della's Delight goes through the Mixing and Baking departments, and Bonny's Bourbon, a filled cookie, goes through the Mixing, Filling, and Baking departments.

Excel Lab
www.prenhall.com/horngren/cost12e

Michael Shirra, vice president for sales, believes that at the current price, Della Simpson can sell all of its daily production of Della's Delight and Bonny's Bourbon. Both cookies are made in batches of 3,000. In each department, the time required per batch and the total time available each day are as follows:

	A	B	C	D
1		Department Minutes		
2		Mixing	Filling	Baking
3	Della's Delight	30	0	10
4	Bonny's Bourbon	15	15	15
5	Total available per day	660	270	300

Revenue and cost data for each type of cookie are:

	A	B	C
7		Della's	Bonny's
8		Delight	Bourbon
9	Revenue per batch	$ 475	$ 375
10	Variable cost per batch	175	125
11	Contribution margin per batch	$ 300	$ 250
12	Monthly fixed costs		
13	(allocated to each product)	$18,650	$22,350

If you want to use Excel to solve this problem, go to the Excel Lab at **www.prenhall.com/horngren/cost12e** and download the template for Problem 11-40.

Required

1. Using *D* to represent the batches of Della's Delight and *B* to represent the batches of Bonny's Bourbon made and sold each day, formulate Shirra's decision as an LP model.
2. Compute the optimal number of batches of each type of cookie that Della Simpson, Inc., should make and sell each day to maximize operating income.

Excel Lab www.prenhall.com/horngren/cost12e

11-41 Make versus buy, ethics. (CMA, adapted) Lynn Hart is a management accountant at Paibec Corporation. Paibec is under intense cost competition. Hart has been asked to evaluate whether Paibec should continue to manufacture MTR-2000 or purchase it from Marley Company. Marley has submitted a bid to supply the 32,000 MTR-2000 units that Paibec will need for 2006 at a price of $17.30 each. Paibec has capacity available to produce 32,000 units.

From plant records and interviews with John Porter, the plant manager, Hart gathered the following information regarding Paibec's costs to manufacture 30,000 units of MTR-2000 in 2005:

	A	B
1		**Costs for**
2		**30,000**
3		**units in 2005**
4	Direct materials	$195,000
5	Direct manufacturing labor	120,000
6	Plant space rental	84,000
7	Equiment leasing	36,000
8	Other manufacturing overhead	225,000
9	Total manufacturing costs	$660,000
10		

Additionally, Porter tells her that:

- Plant rental and equipment lease are annual contracts that are going to be expensive to wiggle out of. Porter estimates it will cost $10,000 to terminate the plant rental contract and $5,000 to terminate the equipment-lease contract.
- 40% of the other manufacturing overhead is variable, proportionate to the direct manufacturing labor costs. The fixed component of other manufacturing overhead is expected to remain the same whether MTR-2000 is manufactured by Paibec or outsourced to Marley.
- Paibec's just-in-time policy means that inventory is negligible.

Hart is aware that cost studies can be threatening to current employees because the findings may lead to reorganizations and layoffs. She knows that Porter is concerned that outsourcing MTR-2000 will result in some of his close friends being laid off. Therefore, she performs her own independent analysis of competitive and other economic data, which reveals that:

- Prices of direct materials are likely to be higher by 8% in 2006 compared to 2005.
- Direct manufacturing labor rates are likely to be higher by 5% in 2006 compared to 2005.
- The plant-rental contract can, in fact, be terminated by paying $10,000. Paibec will not have any need for this space if MTR-2000 is outsourced.
- The equipment lease can be terminated by paying $3,000.

John Porter argues that Hart is ignoring the amazing continuous improvement that is occurring at the plant and that increases in direct material prices and direct manufacturing labor rates assumed by Hart will not occur. But Hart is very confident about the accuracy of the information she has collected.

If you want to use Excel to solve this problem, go to the Excel Lab at **www.prenhall.com/horngren/cost12e** and download the template for Problem 11-41.

Required

1. On the basis of the material and labor cost estimates originally compiled with Porter's help, should Hart recommend that MTR-2000 be produced at Paibec or purchased from Marley? Show your calculations.
2. On the basis of Hart's own independent estimates, should she recommend that MTR-2000 be produced or purchased? Show your calculations.
3. What other factors should Hart examine before recommending whether Paibec should manufacture or buy MTR-2000?
4. What should Hart do in response to Porter's inputs and comments?

Collaborative Learning Problem

Excel Lab www.prenhall.com/horngren/cost12e

11-42 Optimal product mix. (CMA, adapted) Omnisport manufactures and sells sports equipment. It currently produces and sells 5,000 pairs (units) of in-line skates each year, operating at maximum machine capacity. Omnisport's market research has revealed that it could sell 8,000 pairs of in-line skates annually. Calcott Inc., a nearby supplier, has offered to supply up to 6,000 pairs of in-line skates at a price of $75 per pair. However, Jack Petrone, Omnisport's product manager, has noticed the current snowboarding craze and believes that Omnisport could sell up to 12,000 pairs (units) of snowboard bindings annually. Omnisport's management accountant summarizes the available data:

	A	B	C	D
1		Manufactured	Snowboard	Purchased
2		Inline Skates	Bindings	Inline Skates
3		(pair)	(pair)	(pair)
4	Selling Price	$98	$60	$98
5	Cost per unit			
6	Purchase cost	-	-	75
7	Direct material	20	20	-
8	Variable machine operating cost ($16 per machine hour)	24	8	-
9	Variable and fixed manufacturing overhead (allocation base: machine hours)	18	6	-
10	Variable marketing and administrative cost	9	8	4

- Fixed manufacturing overhead costs of $30,000 are not affected by the product-mix decision.
- Fixed manufacturing overhead costs are allocated to products based on a machine-hour rate, which is calculated by dividing total fixed manufacturing overhead costs of $30,000 by machine-hour capacity.
- Fixed marketing and administrative costs of $60,000 are not affected by the product-mix decision.

If you want to use Excel to solve this problem, go to the Excel Lab at **www.prenhall.com/horngren/cost12e** and download the template for Problem 11-42.

Required

1. How many machine-hours does each pair of manufactured in-line skates need? Each pair of snowboard bindings? If Omnisport produces only 12,000 pairs of snowboard bindings, what would be the cost of unused manufacturing capacity?
2. Calculate the variable manufacturing overhead rate per machine-hour.
3. Calculate the contribution margin per unit for manufactured in-line skates, snowboard bindings, and purchased in-line skates. Calculate the contribution margin per machine-hour for the two manufactured products.
4. Calculate the quantity of each product that Omnisport should manufacture and sell or purchase and sell to maximize operating income. What is the maximum operating income Omnisport can earn?

Get Connected: Cost Accounting in the News

Go to www.prenhall.com/horngren/cost12e for additional online exercise(s) that explore issues affecting the accounting world today. These exercises offer you the opportunity to analyze and reflect on how cost accounting helps managers to make better decisions and handle the challenges of strategic planning and implementation.

CHAPTER 11 Video Case

STORE 24: Decision Making and Relevant Information

As suppliers of primarily commodity convenience products, the convenience store industry faces lots of competitive pressure. Gas stations are encroaching on convenience store territory with new minimart stores. And neighborhood drugstores are expanding their turf by charging less for products that used to be the exclusive domain of the convenience store—products such as cigarettes, food service, packaged beverages, candy, snacks, and milk products. Convenience stores are battling back by offering a deeper selection of products. Because drugstore chains, in particular, must maintain a certain amount of square footage for pharmacy and nonfood items, they can't always carry the latest, coolest items.

Store 24, based in Waltham, Massachusetts, is all too familiar with these industry trends. The company has responded by offering speedy service—in and out in under 30 seconds—redesigned layouts to put the best-selling items within easy reach, and updated product offerings. The company's 82 stores operate throughout the northeastern United States, in both urban and suburban locations.

One recent day, President and CEO Bob Gordon met with CFO Paul Doucette to discuss a proposal from a new vendor to stock its line of fruit-flavored waters in Store 24's refrigerated cases. The water comes in 16-ounce, single-serve clear plastic bottles. There are three flavors available: Mandarin-Tangerine,

Very Cherry Berry, and Citrus-Melon. Although product-inventory ordering decisions are generally left to individual store managers, this decision is being considered by headquarters staff because it's a new vendor who must pass approval before Store 24 puts the company on its approved-vendor list. If the vendor is approved, the flavored waters will displace another company's product in the refrigerated beverage case in each store because there is a fixed amount of space in those cases.

Although layouts vary among Store 24 locations, each store has nine refrigerated beverage cases, with eight shelves per case. The current cold-beverage product mix is:

Dairy (milk and related beverages)	1 case
Gatorade and sports drinks	1 case
Juice products	1 case
Beer	2 cases
Soda	3 cases
Water (plain and sparkling)	1 case

As it turns out, the only place Store 24 could stock the new flavored waters is in the case that currently holds plain and sparkling water products. All other cases are dedicated to the products they carry through contractual arrangements with those vendors. The water case holds four shelves of 24-ounce, single-serve bottles of plain water and four shelves of 24-ounce, single-serve bottles of sparkling water. Each shelf is 36 inches wide and 12 inches deep. The fixed costs of operating each refrigerated case are $2,000 annually for depreciation and $600 annually for utilities and maintenance.

As for the products, a 24-ounce, round plastic bottle occupies 3 inches of shelf space; a 16-ounce, round plastic bottle occupies 2 inches of shelf space. Products can't be stacked. The selling price of a single 24-ounce bottle of plain water is $1.25, with a variable cost per bottle of $0.813. The selling price of a single 24-ounce bottle of sparkling water is $1.75, with a variable cost per bottle of $1.225. The suggested selling price of the 16-ounce bottle of flavored water is $1.50, with a variable cost per bottle of $1.125.

QUESTIONS

1. Using Exhibit 11-1 (p. 379), describe Store 24's five-step decision process for deciding whether to carry the new fruit-flavored water.
2. What is the contribution margin per bottle of each product? What is the contribution margin ratio for each product? What is the contribution margin per square foot of shelf space for each product (16-ounce flavored water, 24-ounce plain water, 24-ounce sparkling water)?
3. What is the constraining resource?
4. On the basis of financial considerations alone, should Store 24 stock the new flavored waters in place of some of the plain and sparkling water products? Explain briefly.
5. What factors should Store 24 consider in deciding how much shelf space it should devote to each of the three water products: plain, sparkling, and flavored?

Industry data source: Extracted from **Convenience Store News**, May 28, 2001.

CHAPTER 12

PRICING DECISIONS AND COST MANAGEMENT

LEARNING OBJECTIVES

1. **Discuss the three major influences on pricing decisions**
2. **Distinguish short-run from long-run pricing decisions**
3. **Price products using the target-costing approach**
4. **Apply the concepts of cost incurrence and locked-in costs**
5. **Price products using the cost-plus approach**
6. **Use life-cycle budgeting and costing when making pricing decisions**
7. **Describe two pricing practices in which noncost factors are important when setting prices**
8. **Explain the effects of antitrust laws on pricing**

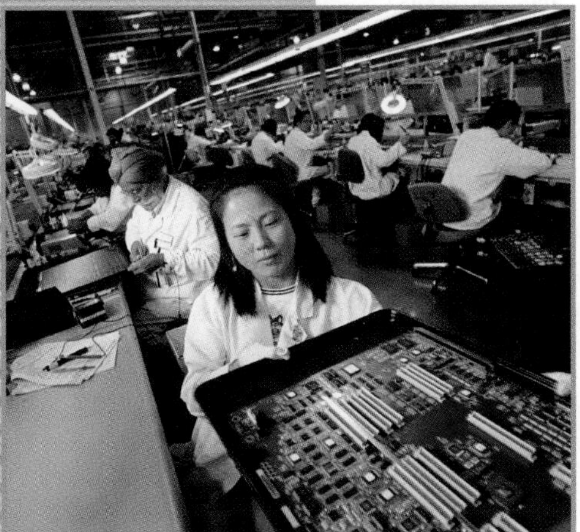

When was the last time you filled a shopping basket with merchandise and then told the sales clerk at the checkout how much you were willing to pay? If you tried this, you'd likely get some funny looks. Yet one Internet-based company allows you to do just that. At Priceline.com, the company doesn't set selling prices for airline tickets, hotel rooms, and rental cars; its customers do. When a match between the customer's named price and Priceline's travel partners is found, both parties get the deal they want.

Most companies, however, don't operate this way. Instead, tremendous effort is devoted to analyzing costs and prices. If the price is too high, the sale will be lost. Too low, and earnings targets won't be hit. Astel Computers understands this concept well. Astel manufactures two brands of personal computers (PCs)—Deskpoint, Astel's top-of-the-line product, and Provalue, a less-powerful Pentium chip–based machine. Recently, Edward Crane, CEO, couldn't believe the numbers he was seeing. The report showed that Astel would close 2007 with a profit of $100 per unit on Provalue. The report also indicated that, to be competitive in 2008, Astel would need to reduce the price of the Provalue computer to $800, a 20% reduction. Edward's contemplation was interrupted by Denise Sullivan, management accountant, and Hector Jackson, manufacturing vice president.

Edward: Just who I needed to see—come in. Is this report right, Denise? It looks like our only hope of making a good profit next year will be to significantly cut costs on Provalue *and* sell more units at the same time. How are we going to do this?

Denise: Based on our research, we know our target price for Provalue next year is $800. Two years ago we implemented an activity-based costing system that identifies the cost drivers for different costs. We now have a basis for finding ways to reduce costs either by eliminating activities or reducing the costs of those activities.

Hector: Let me jump in here. We've already started to do value engineering—an evaluation of all business functions with the objective of reducing costs while still meeting customer needs. With Provalue, we're looking at a new design that should drive down costs for direct materials, testing, distribution, and customer service over the entire life cycle of the new model.

Edward: Great! We really have no choice but to innovate and improve. Let's meet again next week for an update on your findings. We're getting ready to renegotiate some of our key supplier contracts next month, so the sooner we know what we need to do, the better.

The situation facing Astel is not at all uncommon. Companies such as Harrods Department Stores, Nokia, and the Grand Canyon Railway are constantly making product and service pricing decisions. These are strategic decisions that affect the quantity produced and sold, and therefore, costs and revenues. To make these decisions, managers need to understand cost behavior patterns and cost drivers. They can then evaluate demand at different prices and manage costs across the value chain and over a product's life cycle to achieve profitability.

1 **Discuss the three major influences on pricing decisions**
. . . customers, competitors, and costs

This framework of customers, competitors, and costs is consistent with economics courses.

Major Influences on Pricing Decisions

Consider for a moment how managers at Adidas might price their newest line of sneakers, or how decision makers at Microsoft would determine how much to charge for a monthly subscription of MSN Internet service. How companies price a product or a service ultimately depends on the demand and supply for it. Three influences on demand and supply are customers, competitors, and costs.

Customers, Competitors, and Costs

Customers Customers influence price through their effect on the demand for a product or service, based on factors such as the features of a product and its quality. Companies must always examine pricing decisions through the eyes of their customers. Too high a price relative to the value customers place on a product may cause customers to choose a competing or substitute product.

Competitors No business operates in a vacuum. Companies must always be aware of the actions of their competitors. At one extreme, alternative or substitute products of competitors can affect demand and force a company to lower its prices. At the other extreme, a company without a competitor can set higher prices. When there are competitors, knowledge of rivals' technology, plant capacity, and operating policies enables a company to estimate its competitors' costs—valuable information in setting its own prices.

Suppose the yen weakens from \$1 = 110 yen in 2005 to \$1 = 120 yen in 2006. A product that costs 1,320 yen can then be purchased for \$12 (1,320 yen ÷ 110 yen per \$1) in 2005 and for \$11 (1,320 yen ÷ 120 yen per \$1) in 2006.

Because competition spans international borders, costs and pricing decisions are also affected by fluctuations in the exchange rates between different countries' currencies. For example, if the yen weakens against the U.S. dollar, Japanese products become cheaper for American consumers and, consequently, more competitive in U.S. markets.

Costs Costs influence prices because they affect supply. As companies supply more product, the cost of producing each additional unit initially declines but then eventually increases. Companies supply products so long as the additional revenue from selling one more unit exceeds the additional cost of producing it. The lower the cost of producing a product, the greater the quantity of product the company is willing to supply. Managers who understand the cost of producing their companies' products set prices that make the products attractive to customers while maximizing their companies' operating incomes. In computing the relevant costs for a pricing decision, the manager must consider relevant costs in all business functions of the value chain, from R&D to customer service.

If each company in an industry is selling a somewhat-different product, a company can charge a price for its product that is different from other companies' prices.

Surveys of how managers make pricing decisions reveal that companies weigh customers, competitors, and costs differently. At one extreme, companies operating in a perfectly competitive market sell very similar commodity-type products, such as wheat, rice, steel, and aluminum. These companies have no control over setting prices and must accept the price determined by a market consisting of many participants. Cost information helps a company decide only on the output level that maximizes its operating income. In less-competitive markets, such as those for cameras, televisions, and cellular phones, products are differentiated and all three factors affect prices: The value customers place on a product and the prices charged for competing products affect demand, and the costs of producing and delivering the product influence supply. As competition lessens even more, the key factor affecting pricing decisions is the customer's willingness to pay, not costs or competitors. At the other extreme, there are monopolies. A monopolist has no competitors and has much more leeway to set high prices. Nevertheless, there are limits. The higher the price a monopolist sets, the lower the demand for the monopolist's product. Monopolist companies must choose the price–quantity combination that maximizes operating income.

2 **Distinguish short-run**
. . . less-than-one-year time horizon with mostly incremental costs being relevant
from long-run pricing decisions
. . . more-than-one-year time horizon with all product costs being relevant

Time Horizon of Pricing Decisions

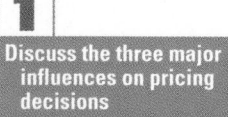

Short-run pricing decisions typically have a time horizon of less than a year and include decisions such as (a) pricing a *one-time-only special order* with no long-run implications and (b) adjusting product mix and output volume in a competitive market. Long-run pricing decisions have a time horizon of a year or longer and include pricing a product in a major market in which there is some leeway in setting price. Two key differences affect pricing for the long run versus the short run.

1. Costs that are often irrelevant for short-run pricing decisions, such as fixed costs that cannot be changed, are generally relevant in the long run because costs can be altered in the long run.
2. Profit margins in long-run pricing decisions are often set to earn a reasonable return on investment. Short-run pricing is more opportunistic: Prices are decreased when demand is weak and increased when demand is strong.

Costing and Pricing for the Short Run

Consider a short-run pricing decision facing the management team at Astel Computers. Datatech Corporation has asked Astel to bid on supplying 5,000 Provalue computers over the next three months. After this three-month period, Datatech is unlikely to place any future sales orders with Astel. Datatech will sell Provalue computers under its own brand name in regions and markets where Astel does not sell Provalue. Whether Astel accepts or rejects this order will not affect Astel's revenues—neither the units sold nor the selling price—from exisiting sales channels.

Relevant Costs for Short-Run Pricing Decisions

Before Astel can bid on Datatech's offer, Astel's managers must first estimate how much it will cost to supply the 5,000 computers. Similar to the Surf Gear example in Chapter 11, the relevant costs Astel's managers must focus on include all direct and indirect costs throughout the value chain that will change in total by accepting the one-time-only special order from Datatech. Astel's managers outline the relevant costs in the following table:

Direct materials ($460 per computer × 5,000 computers)	$2,300,000
Direct manufacturing labor ($64 per computer × 5,000 computers)	320,000
Fixed costs of additional capacity to manufacture Provalue	250,000
Total costs	$2,870,000*

*No additional costs will be required for R&D, design, marketing, distribution, or customer service.

For some decisions, it's erroneous to assume that variable costs are relevant and fixed costs are irrelevant. For example, in the Astel-Datatech special-order decision, the fixed costs of additional capacity to manufacture Provalue are relevant.

The relevant cost per computer is $574 ($2,870,000 ÷ 5,000). Therefore, any selling price above $574 will improve Astel's profitability in the short run. Astel's managers also know that one of its competitors with a highly efficient plant has significant idle capacity and is eager to win the Datatech contract. Armed with all this information, what price should Astel's managers bid for the 5,000-computer order?

Strategic and Other Factors in Short-Run Pricing

In choosing how much to bid, Astel's managers must be strategic. If, based on its market intelligence, Astel believes its competitor will bid between $596 and $610 per computer, Astel could bid $595 per computer and still increase operating income by $105,000 (relevant revenues, $595 × 5,000 = $2,975,000 minus relevant costs, $2,870,000). Management's strategy is to bid as high above $574 as possible while remaining lower than competitors' bids.

Astel's managers must also consider other effects of its pricing decision, such as whether Datatech will undercut Astel's selling price in Astel's current markets. If Astel's managers believe this is a significant risk, the relevant costs of the bidding decision should include the contribution margin lost on sales to existing customers. If Astel's managers view the threat to its existing business from accepting the Datatech order to be serious enough, they may decide not to bid for the Datatech business, or they may quote Datatech a price close to the price Astel charges its other customers. After carefully evaluating the situation, Astel's managers conclude that Datatech will not undercut prices to Astel's customers, so Astel makes a bid to supply Provalue computers at a price of $595 each.

Astel's short-run pricing decision focused on identifying a sufficiently low price at which Astel would still make a profit. That's because we assumed (a) Astel has access to extra capacity and (b) a competitor with an efficient plant and idle capacity was likely to make a low bid. However, short-run pricing does not always work this way. Companies may experience strong demand for their products in the short run, but they may have limited capacity. In these cases, companies strategically increase prices in the short run to as much as the market will bear. We observe high short-run prices in the case of new products or new models of older products, such as microprocessors, computer chips, cellular telephones, and software.

Costing and Pricing for the Long Run

Just think how frustrated consumers get when, over the course of a year, the prices of items such as gasoline and airline tickets bounce around a lot.

Short-run pricing decisions are responses to short-run demand and supply conditions, and the relevant costs are only those costs that will change in the short run. Long-run pricing is a strategic decision designed to build long-run relationships with customers based on stable and predictable prices. Buyers—whether a person buying a box of Wheaties, Bechtel Corporation buying a fleet of tractors, or General Foods Corporation buying audit services—typically prefer stable and predictable prices over a long time horizon. A stable price reduces the need for continuous monitoring of suppliers' prices, improves planning, and builds long-run buyer–seller relationships. But to charge a stable price and earn the target long-run return, a company must, over the long run, know and manage its costs of supplying product to customers. As we will see, relevant costs for long-run pricing decisions include *all* future fixed and variable costs.

Calculating Product Costs for Long-Run Pricing Decisions

Let's return to the Astel example. However, this time we will consider the long-run pricing decision for Provalue.

Astel has no beginning or ending inventory of Provalue in 2007 and manufactures and sells 150,000 units during the year. The manufacturing cost of Provalue is calculated using activity-based costing (ABC). Astel has three direct manufacturing costs—direct materials, direct manufacturing labor, and direct machining costs—and three manufacturing overhead cost pools—ordering and receiving components, testing and inspection of final product, and rework (correcting and fixing errors and defects)—in its accounting system. Astel treats machining costs as a direct cost of Provalue because it is manufactured on machines that are dedicated to the production of Provalue only.[1]

Astel uses a long-run time horizon to price Provalue. Over this horizon, Astel's management observes the following:

- Direct material costs vary with number of units of Provalue produced.
- Direct manufacturing labor costs vary with number of direct manufacturing labor-hours used.
- Direct machining costs, such as rental charges, do not vary with number of machine-hours used over this time horizon, so they are fixed in the long run based on Astel's capacity of 300,000 machine-hours. Each unit of Provalue requires 2 machine-hours. Therefore, the entire machining capacity is used to manufacture Provalue (2 machine-hours per unit × 150,000 units = 300,000 machine-hours).
- Ordering and receiving, testing and inspection, and rework costs vary with the quantity of their respective cost driver. For example, ordering and receiving costs vary with the number of orders. Staff members responsible for placing orders can be reassigned or laid off in the long run if fewer orders need to be placed, or the number of staff members can be increased in the long run to process more orders.

The following Excel spreadsheet summarizes direct costs, manufacturing overhead cost pools, the cost driver for each activity, details leading up to the total quantity of the cost driver needed to produce 150,000 units, and the cost per unit of each cost driver.

[1]Recall that Astel makes two types of PCs: Deskpoint and Provalue. If Deskpoint and Provalue had shared the same machines, Astel would have allocated machining costs on the basis of the budgeted machine-hours used to manufacture the two products and would have treated these costs as fixed overhead costs. The basic analysis of Provalue would be exactly as described in the chapter except that machining costs would appear as overhead rather than direct fixed costs.

	A	B	C	D	E	F	G	H
1					PROVALUE			
2					150,000	output units		
3	**Cost Category**	**Cost Driver**	**Details of Cost Driver Quantities**				**Total Quantity of Cost Driver**	**Cost per Unit of Cost Driver**
4	**(1)**	**(2)**	**(3)**		**(4)**		**(5) = (3) x (4)**	**(6)**
5	**Direct Manufacturing Costs**							
6	Direct materials	No. of kits	1	kit per output unit	150,000	output units	150,000	$460
7	Direct manufacturing labor (DML)	DML hours	3.2	DML hours per output unit	150,000	output units	480,000	$ 20
8	Direct machining (fixed)	Machine-hours					300,000	$ 38
9	**Manufacturing Overhead Costs**							
10	Ordering and receiving	No. of orders	50	orders per component	450	components	22,500	$ 80
11	Testing and inspection	Testing-hours	30	testing-hours per output unit	150,000	output units	4,500,000	$ 2
12	Rework				8%	defect rate		
13		Rework-hours	2.5	rework-hours per defective unit	12,000[a]	defective units	30,000	$ 40
14								
15	[a] 8% defect rate × 150,000 output units = 12,000 defective units							

Exhibit 12-1 indicates that the total cost of manufacturing Provalue is $102 million, and the manufacturing cost per unit is $680. Manufacturing, however, is just one business function in the value chain. To set long-run prices, Astel's managers must calculate the *full cost* of producing and selling Provalue.

EXHIBIT 12-1

Manufacturing Costs of Provalue for 2007 Using Activity-Based Costing

	A	B	C
1		**Total Manufacturing**	
2		**Costs for**	**Manufacturing**
3		**150,000 Units**	**Cost per Unit**
4		**(1)**	**(2) = (1) ÷ 150,000**
5	Direct manufacturing costs		
6	Direct material costs		
7	(150,000 units x $460 per unit)	$ 69,000,000	$460
8	Direct manufacturing labor costs		
9	(480,000 hours x $20 per hour)	9,600,000	64
10	Direct machining costs		
11	(300,000 machine-hours x $38 per machine-hour)	11,400,000	76
12	Direct manufacturing costs	90,000,000	600
13			
14	Manufacturing overhead costs		
15	Ordering and receiving costs		
16	(22,500 orders x $80 per order)	1,800,000	12
17	Testing and inspection costs		
18	(4,500,000 hours x $2 per hour)	9,000,000	60
19	Rework costs		
20	(30,000 rework hours x $40 per hour)	1,200,000	8
21	Manufacturing overhead costs	12,000,000	80
22	Total manufacturing costs	$102,000,000	$680
23			

EXHIBIT 12-2

Product Profitability of Provalue for 2007 Using Value-Chain Activity-Based Costing

	A	B	C
1		Total Amounts	
2		for 150,000 Units	Per Unit
3		(1)	(2) = (1) ÷ 150,000
4	Revenues	$150,000,000	$1,000
5	Cost of goods sold[a] (from Exhibit 12-1)	102,000,000	680
6	Operating costs[b]		
7	R&D costs	5,400,000	36
8	Design costs of product and process	6,000,000	40
9	Marketing costs	15,000,000	100
10	Distribuiton costs	3,600,000	24
11	Customer-service costs	3,000,000	20
12	Operating costs	33,000,000	220
13	Full cost of the product	135,000,000	900
14	Operating income	$ 15,000,000	$ 100
15			
16	[a]Cost of goods sold = Total manufacturing costs because there is no beginning or		
17	ending inventory of Provalue in 2007		
18	[b]Numbers for operating cost line-items are assumed without supporting calculations		

For its nonmanufacturing business functions in the value chain, Astel's managers identify direct costs and choose cost drivers and cost pools for indirect costs that measure cause-and-effect relationships. Astel's managers allocate costs to Provalue based on the quantity of cost-driver units that Provalue uses. Exhibit 12-2 summarizes the operating income for Provalue for 2007 based on an activity-based analysis of costs in all business functions. (For brevity, supporting calculations for nonmanufacturing business functions are not given.) Astel earns $15 million from Provalue, or $100 per unit sold in 2007.

Alternative Long-Run Pricing Approaches

How do companies use product cost information to make long-run pricing decisions? Two different approaches for pricing decisions are:

1. Market-based
2. Cost-based, which is also called cost-plus

The market-based approach to pricing starts by management asking, Given what our customers want and how our competitors will react to what we do, what price should we charge? The cost-based approach to pricing starts by management asking, Given what it costs us to make this product, what price should we charge that will recoup our costs and achieve a target return on investment?

Companies operating in *competitive* markets (for example, commodities such as steel, oil, and natural gas) use the market-based approach. The items produced or services provided by one company are very similar to items produced or services provided by others. Companies in these markets must accept the prices set by the market.

Companies operating in *less competitive* markets offering products or services that differ from each other (for example, automobiles, computers, management consulting, and legal services), can use either the market-based or cost-based approach as the starting point for pricing decisions. Some companies first look at costs and then consider customers or competitors—the cost-based approach. Others start by considering customers and competitors and then look at costs—the market-based approach. Both approaches consider customers, competitors, and costs. Only their starting points differ. Management must always keep in mind market forces, regardless of which pricing approach is used. For instance, a price set via cost-plus thinking may simply be unacceptable to customers, perhaps because a competitor has introduced a new, lower-priced product. So the "plus" in cost-plus is reduced to a price acceptable to the market.

Companies operating in markets that are *not competitive* favor cost-based approaches. That's because these companies do not need to respond or react to competitors' prices.

We consider first the market-based approach.

Target Costing for Target Pricing

Market-based pricing starts with a target price. A **target price** is the estimated price for a product or service that potential customers will pay. This estimate is based on an understanding of customers' perceived value for a product or service and how competitors will price competing products or services. Having this understanding of customers and competitors has become important for three reasons:

1. Competition from lower-cost producers has meant that prices cannot be increased.
2. Products are on the market for shorter periods of time, leaving less time and opportunity to recover from pricing mistakes.
3. Customers have become more knowledgeable and demand quality products at reasonable prices.

3

Price products using the target-costing approach

. . . target costing identifies an estimated price customers are willing to pay and then computes a target cost to earn the desired profit

Understanding Customers' Perceived Value

A company's sales and marketing organization, through close contact and interaction with customers, is usually in the best position to identify customers' needs and their perceived value for a product or service. Companies also conduct market research studies about product features that customers want and the prices they are willing to pay for those features.

Doing Competitor Analysis

To gauge how competitors might react to a prospective price, a company needs to understand competitors' technologies, products or services, costs, and financial conditions. For example, knowing competitors' technologies and products helps a company (a) to evaluate how distinctive its own products or services will be in the market and (b) to determine the prices it might be able to charge as a result of being distinctive. Where does a company obtain information about its competitors? Usually from customers, suppliers, and employees of competitors. Another source of information is *reverse engineering*—that's disassembling and analyzing competitors' products to determine product designs and materials and to become acquainted with the technologies competitors use. Many companies, including Ford, General Motors, and PPG Industries, have departments whose sole purpose is to analyze competitors with respect to these considerations.

Implementing Target Pricing and Target Costing

There are five steps in developing target prices and target costs. We illustrate these steps using our Provalue example.

Step 1: **Develop a product that satisfies the needs of potential customers.** Based on an understanding of customer requirements and an analysis of competitors' products, Astel plans the product features and design modifications for Provalue. Astel's market research indicates that customers do not value Provalue's extra features, such as special audio features and designs that accommodate upgrades that can make the PC run faster. They want Astel to redesign Provalue into a no-frills but reliable PC and to sell it at a much lower price.

Step 2: **Choose a target price.** Based on Astel's research of its competitors' products and technologies, Astel expects its competitors to lower the prices of PCs that compete with Provalue by 15%. Astel's management wants to respond aggressively by reducing Provalue's price by 20%, from \$1,000 to \$800 per unit. At this lower price, Astel's marketing manager forecasts an increase in annual sales from 150,000 to 200,000 units.

Step 3: **Derive a target cost per unit by subtracting target operating income per unit from the target price.** The target price is the basis for calculating target cost. *Target cost per unit* is the target price minus *target operating income per unit.* **Target operating income per unit** is the operating income that a company aims to earn per unit of a product or service sold. **Target cost per unit** is the estimated long-run cost per unit of a product or service that enables the company to achieve its target operating income per unit when selling at the target

Target pricing and target costing are used in different industries and companies around the world—Ford, General Motors, Toyota, and Daihatsu in the automobile industry; Matsushita, Panasonic, and Sharp in the electronics industry; and Compaq and Toshiba in the personal-computer industry.

price.[2] Target cost per unit is often lower than the existing *full cost per unit of the product.* Target cost per unit is really just that—a target—something the company must commit to achieve.

To earn the target return on the capital invested in the business, Astel's management needs a 10% target operating income on target revenues.

Total target revenues	= \$800 per unit × 200,000 units = \$160,000,000
Total target operating income	= 10% × \$160,000,000 = \$16,000,000
Target operating income per unit	= \$16,000,000 ÷ 200,000 units = \$80 per unit
Target cost per unit	= Target price − Target operating income per unit
	= \$800 per unit − \$80 per unit = \$720 per unit
Total current full costs of Provalue	= \$135,000,000 (from Exhibit 12-2)
Current full cost per unit of Provalue	= \$135,000,000 ÷ 150,000 units = \$900 per unit (from Exhibit 12-2)

Provalue's \$720 target cost per unit is well below its existing \$900 unit cost. Astel must reduce its unit cost by \$180 to reach its goal. Cost-reduction efforts need to extend to all parts of the value chain—from R&D to customer service—including seeking lower prices from suppliers for materials and components.

What costs do Astel's managers include in the target-cost calculations? The relevant costs are *all* future costs, both variable and fixed, because in the long run, a company's prices and revenues must recover all its costs. If all these costs cannot be recovered, the company's best alternative is to shut down—an action that results in forgoing all future revenues and saving all future costs, whether fixed or variable. Contrast relevant costs for long-run pricing decisions (all variable and fixed costs) with relevant costs for short-run pricing decisions (costs that change in the short run, mostly but not exclusively variable costs).

Step 4: **Perform cost analysis.** This step analyzes which aspects of a product or service to target for cost reduction. For Provalue, Astel's managers consider the following:

- The function performed by different component parts such as the motherboard, disc drives, and the graphics and video cards.
- The current costs of the different component parts.
- The importance that customers place on different product features. For example, Astel's targeted customers place greater emphasis on the reliability of the computer than on video quality.
- How different features relate to the functions performed by different component parts. For example, the reliability of the computer can be enhanced by using a simpler motherboard. However, the newly designed computer may not be able to support the top-of-the-line video card, but this is of little concern to Astel because video quality is not as important to Astel's targeted customers.

Step 5: **Perform value engineering to achieve target cost. Value engineering** is a systematic evaluation of all aspects of the value chain, with the objective of reducing costs while improving quality and satisfying customer needs. As we describe next, value engineering encompasses improvements in product designs, changes in materials specifications, and modifications in process methods. (See the Concepts in Action feature on p. 427 to learn about IKEA's approach to target pricing and target costing.)

Value Engineering, Cost Incurrence, and Locked-In Costs

Traditional cost accounting systems don't classify costs as value-added or nonvalue-added. To obtain this information, management accountants must work closely with production and marketing personnel.

To implement value engineering, managers distinguish value-added activities and costs from nonvalue-added activities and costs in producing a product or service. A **value-added cost** is a cost that, if eliminated, would reduce the actual or perceived value or utility (usefulness) customers obtain from using the product or service. Examples are costs of specific product features and attributes desired by customers. For Provalue, these features and attributes are adequate memory, desired preloaded software, clear images on the monitor, and prompt customer service. A **nonvalue-added cost** is a cost that, if eliminated, would not reduce the actual or perceived value or utility (usefulness) customers obtain from

[2]For a more-detailed discussion of target costing, see S. Ansari, J. Bell, and The CAM-I Target Cost Core Group, *Target Costing: The Next Frontier in Strategic Cost Management* (Homewood, IL: Irwin McGraw-Hill, 1997).

CONCEPTS IN ACTION

Extreme Target Pricing and Cost Management at IKEA

For millions of loyal customers throughout the world, Swedish furniture giant IKEA has achieved an almost cult-like status. Known for products with unpronounceable names, flat packaging, and do-it-yourself instructions, IKEA has grown from humble beginnings to become the world's largest furniture retailer with 186 stores in 31 countries. How did this happen? Through aggressive target pricing, coupled with relentless cost management. IKEA's prices typically run 30% to 50% below their competitors' prices.

To achieve such low prices, the process of driving down costs begins with product conceptualization. First, product developers identify gaps in IKEA's current product portfolio. For example, product developers might identify the need to create a new low-price, modern-style couch designed for smaller apartments. Second, product developers and their team survey competitors to determine how much they charge for similar items, then select a target price that is 30% to 50% less than the competitor's price. With a product concept and price established, product developers then determine what materials will be used and what manufacturer will do the assembly work—all before the new item is even designed. A brief describing the new couch's target cost and basic specifications is submitted for bidding among IKEA's 1,800 suppliers in 55 countries. Suppliers vie to offer the most attractive bid. Subsequently, internal and freelance designers compete to determine the product's final design based on price, function, and materials to be used. This value-engineering process promotes volume-based cost efficiencies throughout the design and production process.

But aggressive cost management does not stop there! All IKEA products are designed to be shipped unassembled in flat packages. The company estimates that shipping costs would be six times greater if all products were shipped assembled. In addition, IKEA stores *do not* offer many of the amenities their competitors offer, including salespeople, conspicuous price reductions, and product delivery. Although this perhaps is inconvenient to some potential customers, the relentless focus on lean design, efficiency, and low prices remains a hallmark at IKEA. As founder Ingvar Kamprad once noted, "Waste of resources is a mortal sin at IKEA. Expensive solutions are often a sign of mediocrity, and an idea without a price tag is never acceptable."

Sources: L. Margonelli, "How IKEA Designs Its Sexy Price Tags," *Business 2.0* (October 2002); R. Cooper and W. Chew, "Control Tomorrow's Costs Through Today's Designs," *Harvard Business Review* (January-February 1996); *Ingvar Kamprad and IKEA*, Harvard Business School case number 9-390-132; O. Burkeman, "The Miracle of Älmhult," *The Guardian* (June 17, 2004).

using the product or service. It is a cost that the customer is unwilling to pay for. Examples of nonvalue-added costs are costs of producing defective products and machine breakdowns. Successful companies keep nonvalue-added costs to a minimum.

Activities and their costs do not always fall neatly into value-added or nonvalue-added categories. Some costs, such as supervision and production control, fall in a gray area because they include mostly value-added but also some nonvalue-added aspects. Despite these troublesome gray areas, attempts to distinguish value-added from nonvalue-added costs provide a useful overall framework for value engineering.

Some materials-handling and inspection costs are necessary to move the product through the manufacturing process and to ensure its quality. Companies implementing TQM practices seek to improve product design and the manufacturing process while reducing materials-handling and inspection costs.

In the Provalue example, direct materials, direct manufacturing labor, and direct machining costs are value-added costs. Ordering, receiving, testing, and inspection costs fall in the gray area. Customers perceive some portion, but not all, of these costs as necessary for adding value. Rework costs, including costs of delivering reworked products, are nonvalue-added costs because these costs could have been avoided if a defective product had not been produced in the first place.

Astel's goal in value engineering is to reduce, and possibly eliminate, nonvalue-added costs such as rework costs by reducing defect rates. Astel's value-engineering effort also seeks to increase efficiency by reducing value-added costs such as direct manufacturing labor costs by reducing direct manufacturing labor-hours or cost per direct manufacturing labor-hour to make each unit of Provalue.

4
Apply the concepts of cost incurrence
. . . when resources are consumed
and locked-in costs
. . . when resources are committed to be incurred in the future

To do value engineering, Astel's managers must distinguish when costs are incurred from when costs are locked in. **Cost incurrence** describes when a resource is consumed (or benefit forgone) to meet a specific objective. Costing systems emphasize cost incurrence. For

EXHIBIT 12-3

Pattern of Cost Incurrence and Locked-In Costs for Provalue

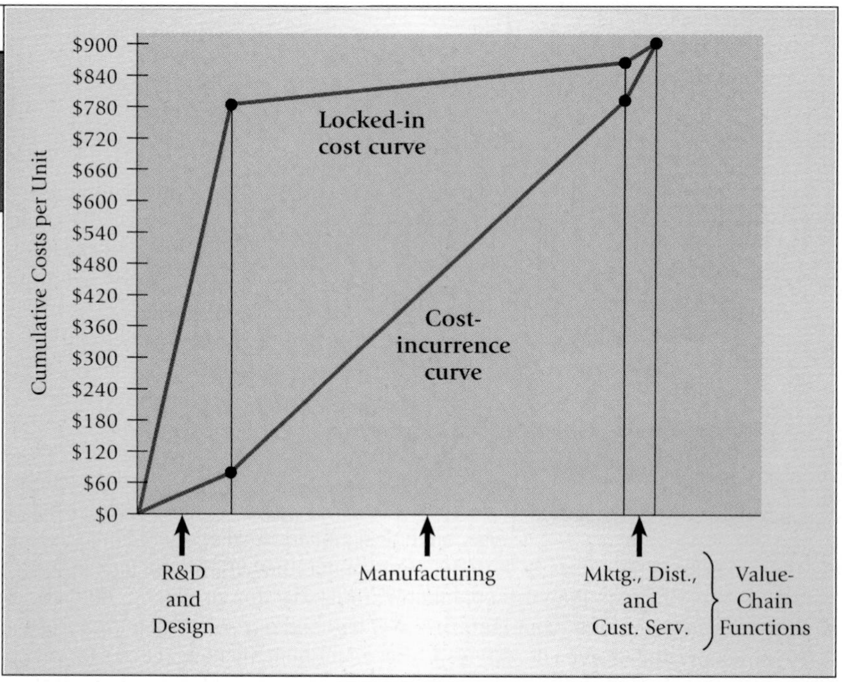

example, Astel's costing system recognizes direct material costs of Provalue as each unit of Provalue is assembled and sold. But Provalue's direct material cost per unit is *locked in*, or *designed in*, much earlier, when product designers choose the components that will go into Provalue. **Locked-in costs—designed-in costs**—are costs that have not yet been incurred but, based on decisions that have already been made, will be incurred in the future.

To manage costs well, a company must identify how design choices lock in costs, *before* the costs are incurred. Consider quality costs. If Astel experiences quality problems during manufacturing, its ability to improve quality and reduce scrap is limited by Provalue's design. Scrap and rework costs are incurred during manufacturing, but they are often locked in much earlier in the value chain by faulty design. Similarly, in the software industry, costs of developing software are often locked in at the design-and-analysis stage. Costly and difficult-to-fix errors that appear during coding and testing are frequently locked in by bad software designs.

Exhibit 12-3 illustrates how the locked-in cost curve and the cost-incurrence curve might appear in the case of Provalue. The bottom curve, graphically representing cost incurrence, uses information from Exhibit 12-2 to plot the cumulative cost per unit incurred in different business functions of the value chain. The top curve plots how cumulative costs are locked in. (The specific numbers underlying this curve are not presented.) Total cumulative cost per unit for both curves is $900. *However, the graph emphasizes the wide divergence between the time when costs are locked in and when they are incurred.* For example, once the product is designed and the operations to manufacture, market, distribute, and support the product are determined, more than 86% ($780 ÷ $900) of the unit cost of Provalue is locked in. Costs such as direct materials, direct manufacturing labor, and many other manufacturing, marketing, distribution, and customer-service costs are all locked in at the end of the design stage, when only about 8% ($76 ÷ $900) of the unit cost is actually incurred!

Value-Chain Analysis and Cross-Functional Teams

Companies are always wanting to make improvements and cut costs. For example, because direct material costs are often significant, many manufacturers work closely with their suppliers to achieve the target direct material costs.

To help reduce costs, Astel's managers must focus on the design stage. The company organizes a cross-functional value-engineering team consisting of marketing managers, product designers, manufacturing engineers, purchasing managers, suppliers, dealers, and management accountants. The team evaluates the impact of design innovations and modifications on all business functions of the value chain. They choose modifications that have the greatest value to their customers relative to the costs required to provide those features. Here are some of the team's ideas:

- Use a simpler, more-reliable motherboard without complex features.
- Design Provalue so that various parts snap-fit together, rather than solder together, to decrease direct manufacturing labor-hours and the related costs.

FOCUS ON VALUES AND BEHAVIORS

PRICING DECISIONS ARE NOT ARBITRARY

Before decision makers at Toyota, IKEA, PALM, and Apple can determine the price of their products, they have a lot to consider. What do our customers want, and what prices are they willing to pay? What are our competitors doing? How can we manage costs to achieve profitability? At each of these companies, management accountants play an important role in helping to answer these questions.

To successfully influence pricing decisions, manage costs, answer the needs of customers, and outdo competitors, management accountants must understand the intricacies of each part of the value chain. At the same time, their colleagues in R&D, manufacturing, and marketing must consider management accountants as integral members of their teams. But why is it important to create a culture of cross-functionality? Consider Toyota Corporation. Toyota's management accountants created "cost sheets" based on their understanding of various processes. These cost sheets helped Toyota's line managers evaluate costs of alternative designs, which contributed to continuous reduction in costs, sales growth, and profitability.

Management accountants must always create a culture of information sharing. They must be able to bring to the attention of manufacturing and marketing managers the cost and profitability of different design alternatives. They need to be comfortable presenting cost information even when design data are incomplete and ambiguous, and they must be ready to refine cost estimates as design details become clearer. If management accountants are unable to perform these tasks, pricing problems will ensue which could benefit competitors and alienate customers.

As we have seen many times before, the role of the management accountant also includes potential ethical obstacles. As it relates to pricing decisions, management accountants must always be careful that their pricing proposals are ethical and legal—no matter how profitable such actions might be in the short run. Consider newspaper reports alleging Medicare fraud. Companies apparently have been charging Medicare, the U.S. government's medical program for senior citizens, higher prices than allowable and for services that were never delivered. In such a situation, it is the management accountant's responsibility to protest illegal or unethical pricing actions. Failure to do so can result in multimillion-dollar fines and significant damage to a company's reputation.

- Simplify the Provalue design and use fewer components to decrease ordering and receiving costs and also decrease testing and inspection costs.
- Design Provalue to be lighter and smaller to reduce distribution and packaging costs.
- Design Provalue to reduce repair costs at customer sites to lower customer-service costs.

Management accountants use their understanding of the technical and business aspects of the entire value chain to quickly estimate cost savings and to explain the cost implications of alternative design choices to the team. (See also the Focus on Values and Behaviors feature above.) These cost estimates are based on the parts and processes required by the new design.

> Many Japanese companies use cost tables to make cost estimates. Cost tables are databases of cost information for different materials, component parts, and processes.

After going through the cost analysis, Astel's management team feels it has two alternatives: respond less aggressively to its competitors or replace Provalue with a newly designed computer that has fewer complex features and therefore is less costly to make. Astel decides to go with the second alternative.

Do not assume that costs are always locked in at the design stage. In some industries (such as bulk chemical manufacturing, legal, and consulting) costs are locked in and incurred at about the same time. If costs are not locked in early, cost reduction can be achieved right up to the time when costs are incurred. In these cases, costs are lowered through improved operating efficiency and productivity (for example, reducing the time it takes to do a task), rather than better design. Many companies combine value engineering with *kaizen*, or *continuous improvement* methods that seek to improve productivity and eliminate waste during production and delivery of products.

In summary, the target-pricing, target-costing, and value-engineering process has five key aspects:

1. Understanding customer requirements and competitor actions
2. Selecting a target price and determining a target cost
3. Anticipating how costs are locked in before they are incurred
4. Improving product and process designs to achieve target costs and better quality
5. Using cross-functional teams to coordinate actions that need to be taken throughout the value chain

Achieving the Target Cost per Unit for Provalue

As we saw in the preceding section, value engineering often has strategic implications. At Astel, value engineering leads management to discontinue Provalue and introduce Provalue II, a high-quality, highly reliable, no-frills computer that has fewer features and meets customers' price expectations. Provalue II has a simplified motherboard and fewer component parts, requires fewer machine-hours to manufacture, is easier to test, and has lower defect rates. Exhibit 12-4 uses an activity-based approach to compare cost-driver quantities and rates for the 150,000 units of Provalue and the 200,000 units of Provalue II in 2008.

Note how value engineering reduces both value-added costs (by designing Provalue II to use less-costly direct materials and fewer direct manufacturing labor-hours) and nonvalue-added costs (by simplifying Provalue II's design to reduce the percentage of units that require rework). For simplicity, we assume that value engineering will not reduce the \$20 cost per direct manufacturing labor-hour, the \$80 cost per order, the \$2 cost per testing-hour, or the \$40 cost per rework-hour. By making these activities more efficient, value engineering can also reduce costs by reducing these cost-driver rates (see the Problem for Self-Study, p. 441).

The only costs that value engineering cannot reduce are the total fixed machining costs. Regardless of whether Astel uses all 300,000 machine-hours of capacity available to it for manufacturing Provalue II, Astel will incur machining costs of \$11,400,000 (300,000 machine-hours × \$38 per machine-hour). But Astel uses value engineering to reduce the

EXHIBIT 12-4 Cost-Driver Quantities and Rates for Provalue and Provalue II for 2008 Using Activity-Based Costing

	A	B	C	D	E	F	G	H	I	J	K	L	M	N
1			PROVALUE						PROVALUE II					
2					150,000	output units					200,000	output units		
3	Cost Category	Cost Driver	Details of Cost Driver Quantities				Total Quantity of Cost Driver	Cost per Unit of Cost Driver	Details of Cost Driver Quantities				Total Quantity of Cost Driver	Cost per Unit of Cost Driver
4	(1)	(2)	(3)		(4)		(5)=(3)×(4)	(6)	(7)		(8)		(9)=(7)×(8)	(10)
5	**Direct Manufacturing Costs**													
6	Direct materials	No. of kits	1	kit per output unit	150,000	output units	150,000	\$460	1	kit per output unit	200,000	output units	200,000	\$385
7	Direct manuf. labor (DML)	DML hours	3.2	DML hours per output unit	150,000	output units	480,000	\$ 20	2.65	DML hours per output unit	200,000	output units	530,000	\$ 20
8	Direct machining (fixed)	Machine-hours					300,000	\$ 38					300,000	\$ 38
9	**Manufacturing Overhead Costs**													
10	Ordering and receiving	No. of orders	50	orders per component	450	components	22,500	\$ 80	50	orders per component	425	components	21,250	\$ 80
11	Testing and inspection	Testing-hours	30	testing-hours per output unit	150,000	output units	4,500,000	\$ 2	15	testing-hours per output unit	200,000	output units	3,000,000	\$ 2
12	Rework				8%	defect rate					6.5%	defect rate		
13		Rework-hours	2.5	rework-hours per defective unit	12,000[a]	defective units	30,000	\$ 40	2.5	rework-hours per defective unit	13,000[b]	defective units	32,500	\$ 40
14														
15	[a] 8% defect rate × 150,000 output units = 12,000 defective units													
16	[b] 6.5% defect rate × 200,000 output units = 13,000 defective units													

EXHIBIT 12-5 Target Manufacturing Costs of Provalue II for 2008

	A	B	C	D	E	F
1		PROVALUE II				PROVALUE
2		Estimated		Estimated		Manufacturing
3		Manufacturing Costs		Manufacturing		Cost Per Unit
4		for 200,000 Units		Cost per Unit		(Exhibit 12-1)
5		(1)		(2) = (1) ÷ 200,000		(3)
6	Direct manufacturing costs					
7	Direct material costs					
8	(200,000 units x $385 per unit)	$ 77,000,000		$385.00		$460.00
9	Direct manufacturing labor costs					
10	(530,000 hours x $20 per hour)	10,600,000		53.00		64.00
11	Direct machining costs					
12	(300,000 machine-hours x $38 per machine-hour)	11,400,000		57.00		76.00
13	Direct manufacturing costs	99,000,000		495.00		600.00
14	Manufacturing overhead costs					
15	Ordering and receiving costs					
16	(21,250 orders x $80 per order)	1,700,000		8.50		12.00
17	Testing and inspection costs					
18	(3,000,000 hours x $2 per hour)	6,000,000		30.00		60.00
19	Rework costs					
20	(32,500 rework hours x $40 per hour)	1,300,000		6.50		8.00
21	Manufacturing overhead costs	9,000,000		45.00		80.00
22	Total manufacturing costs	$108,000,000		$540.00		$680.00

machine-hours required to make Provalue II to 1.5 hours per unit. This reduction allows Astel to use the available machine capacity to make and sell more units of Provalue II (200,000 units versus 150,000 units for Provalue), thereby reducing the machining cost per unit.

Exhibit 12-5 presents the target manufacturing costs of Provalue II, using data for the quantity of the cost driver and the cost-driver rate from the Provalue II columns in Exhibit 12-4. For comparison, Exhibit 12-5 also shows the manufacturing cost per unit of Provalue from Exhibit 12-1. The new design is expected to reduce the total manufacturing cost per unit by $140 (from $680 to $540) at the expected sales quantity of 200,000 units. Using an analysis similar to the one used in manufacturing, Astel's managers estimate the expected effect of the new design on costs in other business functions of the value chain. Exhibit 12-6 shows that the estimated full unit cost of the product equals $720—the target cost per unit for Provalue II. Astel's goals are to sell Provalue II at the target price, achieve target cost, and earn the target operating income.[3] At the end of 2008, Astel's managers will compare actual costs and target costs to gain insight about improvements that can be made in subsequent target-costing efforts.

In summary, for target pricing and target costing to be effective, Astel's management accountants need to

- Determine costs of different activities and distinguish value-added from non-value-added costs
- Identify costs throughout the value chain and summarize the effects that design changes will have on those costs
- Estimate costs of different features, functions, and component parts

Unless managed properly, value engineering and target costing can have undesirable effects:

- Employees may feel frustrated if they fail to attain targets.
- The cross-functional team may add too many features just to accommodate the different wishes of team members.
- A product may be in development for a long time as alternative designs are evaluated repeatedly.

[3]For more details, see R. Cooper and R. Slagmulder, *Target Costing and Value Engineering* (Portland, OR: Productivity Press, 1997).

EXHIBIT 12-6

Target Product Profitability of Provalue II for 2008

	A	B	C	D
1		**Estimated**		**Estimated**
2		**Total Amounts**		**Total Amount**
3		**for 200,000 Units**		**Per Unit**
4		**(1)**		**(2) = (1) ÷ 200,000**
5	Revenues	$160,000,000		$800
6	Cost of goods sold[a] (from Exhibit 12-5)	108,000,000		540
7	Operating costs[b]			
8	R&D costs	4,000,000		20
9	Design costs of product and process	6,000,000		30
10	Marketing costs	18,000,000		90
11	Distribuiton costs	4,400,000		22
12	Customer-service costs	3,600,000		18
13	Total operating costs	36,000,000		180
14	Full cost of the product	144,000,000		720
15	Operating income	$ 16,000,000		$ 80
16				
17	[a]Cost of goods sold = Total manufacturing costs because there is no beginning or			
18	ending inventory for Provalue II in 2008.			
19	[b]Numbers for operating-cost line items are assumed without supporting calculations			

- Organizational conflicts may develop as the burden of cutting costs falls unequally on different business functions in the company's value chain, for example, more on manufacturing than on marketing.

To avoid these pitfalls, target-costing efforts should always (a) encourage employee participation and celebrate small improvements toward achieving the target, (b) focus on the customer, (c) pay attention to schedules, and (d) set cost-cutting targets for all value-chain functions to build a culture of teamwork and cooperation.

5

Price products using the cost-plus approach

. . . cost-plus pricing is based on some measure of cost plus a markup

Cost-Based (Cost-Plus) Pricing

Instead of using the market-based approach for their long-run pricing decisions, managers sometimes use a cost-based approach. The general formula for setting a cost-based price adds a markup component to the cost base to determine a prospective selling price. Because a markup is added, cost-based pricing is often called cost-plus pricing, with the plus referring to the markup component. Managers use the cost-plus pricing formula only as a starting point for pricing decisions. Therefore, the markup component is rarely a rigid number. Instead, it is flexible, depending on the behavior of customers and competitors. The markup component is ultimately determined by the market.[4]

Cost-Plus Target Rate of Return on Investment

We illustrate a cost-plus pricing formula for our Astel example. Assume Astel's engineers have redesigned Provalue into Provalue II and that Astel uses a 12% markup on the full unit cost of the product in developing the prospective selling price.

Cost base (full unit cost of Provalue II, Exhibit 12-6)	$720.00
Markup component of 12% (0.12 × $720)	86.40
Prospective selling price	$806.40

How is the markup percentage of 12% determined? One way is to choose a markup to earn a *target rate of return on investment*. The **target rate of return on investment** is the target annual operating income that an organization aims to achieve divided by invested capital. Invested capital can be defined in many ways. In this chapter, we define invested capital as total assets—that is, long-term assets plus current assets. Suppose Astel's (pre-

[4]Exceptions are pricing of electricity and natural gas in many countries, where prices are set by the government on the basis of costs plus a return on invested capital. Chapter 15 discusses the use of costs to set prices in the defense-contracting industry. In these situations where products are not subject to competitive forces, cost accounting techniques substitute for markets as the basis for setting prices.

tax) target rate of return on investment is 18% and Provalue II's capital investment is $96 million. The target annual operating income for Provalue II is:

Invested capital	$96,000,000
Target rate of return on investment	18%
Target annual operating income (0.18 × $96,000,000)	$17,280,000
Target operating income per unit of Provalue II ($17,280,000 ÷ 200,000 units)	$86.40

This calculation indicates that Astel needs to earn a target operating income of $86.40 on each unit of Provalue II. The markup of $86.40 expressed as a percentage of the full product cost per unit of $720 equals 12% ($86.40 ÷ $720).

Do not confuse the 18% target rate of return on investment with the 12% markup percentage.

- The 18% target rate of return on investment expresses Astel's expected annual operating income as a percentage of investment.
- The 12% markup expresses operating income per unit as a percentage of the full product cost per unit.

Astel first calculates target rate of return on investment and then determines markup percentage.

Alternative Cost-Plus Methods

Companies sometimes find it difficult to determine the specific amount of capital they invested to support a specific product. That's because computing the specific amount of invested capital requires knowing, for example, the allocations of investments in equipment and buildings to produce individual products—a difficult and somewhat arbitrary task. Some companies prefer to use alternative cost bases and markup percentages that still earn a return on invested capital but do not require explicit calculations of invested capital to set price.

We illustrate these alternatives using the Astel example. Exhibit 12-7 separates the cost per unit for each business function of the value chain into its variable- and fixed-cost components (without providing details of the calculations). The following table illustrates some alternative cost bases for Provalue II using assumed markup percentages.

Cost Base	Estimated Cost per Unit (1)	Markup Percentage (2)	Markup Component (3) = (1) × (2)	Prospective Selling Price (4) = (1) + (3)
Variable manufacturing cost	$483.00	65%	$313.95	$796.95
Variable cost of the product	547.00	45	246.15	793.15
Manufacturing cost	540.00	50	270.00	810.00
Full cost of the product	720.00	12	86.40	806.40

EXHIBIT 12-7

Estimated Cost Structure of Provalue II for 2008

Business Function	Estimated Variable Cost per Unit	Estimated Fixed Cost per Unit[a]	Business-Function Cost per Unit
R&D	$ 8	$ 12	$ 20
Design of product/process	10	20	30
Manufacturing	483	57	540
Marketing	25	65	90
Distribution	13	9	22
Customer service	8	10	18
Total	$547	$173	$720
	↑ Per-unit variable cost of the product	↑ Per-unit fixed cost of the product	↑ Per-unit full cost of the product

[a]Based on budgeted annual capacity of 200,000 units.

The different cost bases and markup percentages give four prospective selling prices that are close to each other. In practice, a company will choose a cost base that it regards as reliable and a markup percentage that is based on its experience in pricing products to recover its costs and earn a target return on investment. For example, a company may choose the full cost of the product as a base if it is unsure about distinguishing variable costs from fixed costs.

The markup percentages in the preceding table vary a great deal, from a high of 65% on variable manufacturing cost to a low of 12% on full cost of the product. Why the wide variation? Because cost bases that include fewer costs have a higher markup percentage to compensate for the costs excluded from the base. The markup percentage also depends on the extent of competition in the marketplace. Markups and profit margins tend to be lower in more-competitive markets.

Surveys indicate that most managers use the full cost of the product for their cost-based pricing decisions (see Global Surveys of Company Practice on p. 435)—that is, they include both fixed and variable costs when calculating the cost per unit. Managers cite the following advantages for including fixed cost per unit in the cost base for pricing decisions:

Suppose the full cost of a product based on sales of 1,000 units is:

Variable cost per unit	$30
Fixed cost per unit (avoidable if product is discontinued)	20
Full cost per unit	$50

A manager may be tempted to cut price to, say, $35 because the product still gives a positive contribution margin. However, if sales are only 1,000 units, the $5,000 of contribution margin would not recover the $20,000 ($20 per unit × 1,000 units) of fixed costs, and the product would not be profitable. Using full cost per unit measures the costs that must be recovered over the long run if the product is to be profitable.

1. **Full recovery of all costs of the product.** For long-run pricing decisions, full cost of the product informs managers of the minimum cost they need to recover to continue in business. Using just the variable cost as a base does not give managers this information. There is then a temptation, as has happened in the airline industry, to engage in excessive long-run price cutting as long as prices provide a positive contribution margin. Long-run price cutting, however, will result in losses if long-run revenues are less than the long-run full cost of the product.
2. **Price stability.** Managers believe that basing prices on the full cost of the product promotes price stability, because it limits the ability and temptations of salespersons to cut prices. Managers prefer price stability because it facilitates more-accurate forecasting and planning.
3. **Simplicity.** A full-cost formula for pricing does not require a detailed analysis of cost-behavior patterns to separate costs into fixed and variable components for each product. Many costs—for example, testing, inspection, and setups—have both variable- and fixed-cost components. Determining the variable cost of each activity and product is not straightforward.

Including fixed cost per unit in the cost base for pricing is not without problems. Allocating fixed costs to products can be arbitrary. Also, calculating fixed cost per unit requires a denominator level that is likely only an estimate of capacity or expected units of future sales. Errors in these estimates will cause actual full cost per unit of the product to differ from the estimated amount.

Cost-Plus Pricing and Target Pricing

The selling prices computed under cost-plus pricing are *prospective* prices. Suppose Astel's initial product design results in a $750 cost for Provalue II. Assuming a 12% markup, Astel sets a prospective price of $840 [$750 + (0.12 × $750)]. In the competitive personal computer market, customer and competitor reactions to this price may force Astel to reduce the markup percentage and lower the price to, say, $800. Astel may then want to redesign Provalue II to reduce the cost to $720 per unit, as in our example, and achieve a markup close to 12% while keeping the price at $800. The eventual design and cost-plus price chosen must balance the trade-offs among costs, markup, and customer reactions.

The target-pricing approach reduces the need to go back and forth among prospective cost-plus prices, customer reactions, and design modifications. Relative to cost-plus pricing, target pricing first determines product characteristics and target price on the basis of customer preferences and expected competitor responses. Market considerations and target price focus and motivate managers to perform value engineering and to design products to achieve target cost.

To attract new clients, public accounting firms often deliberately bid less than their expected full cost on first-time audits, a practice called *low-balling*, in anticipation that profits from future audits will more than make up for the initial shortfall.

Suppliers who provide unique products and services—accountants and management consultants, for example—usually use cost-plus pricing. Professional service firms set prices based on hourly cost-plus billing rates of partners, managers, and associates. These prices are, however, reduced in competitive situations. Professional service firms also take a multiple-year client perspective when deciding prices. Certified public accountants, for example, sometimes charge a client a low price initially and a higher price later.

GLOBAL SURVEYS OF COMPANY PRACTICE

Differences in Pricing Practices and Cost-Management Methods in Various Countries

Surveys of financial managers of the largest industrial companies in several countries indicate similarities and differences in pricing practices around the world. The use of cost-based pricing appears to be more prevalent in the United States and Hong Kong than in Canada, Denmark, and Ireland.

Ranking of pricing method used as a starting point to price products (1 is most important):

	United States[a]	Canada[b]	Denmark[c]	Hong Kong	Ireland[d]
Market-based	2	1	1	2	1
Cost-based	1	2	2	1	2

Hong Kong and Canadian survey data indicate that when managers are determining the most appropriate pricing method, they consider the following factors: buyer demand, supply and cost of goods and services, the degree of competition, and desired profit.

Among firms using market-based pricing methods, companies in the United States use target costing less frequently than companies in Australia and India.

Use of target costing among firms:

	United States[e]	Australia[f]	India[g]
Percentage of firms using target costing	26%	38%	35%

When, subject to market considerations, costs are used for pricing decisions, the pattern is consistent—overwhelmingly, companies around the globe prefer to use full costs of the product rather than variable costs.

Ranking of cost methods used in pricing decisions (1 is most important):

	United States	China[h]	Ireland	New Zealand[i]	United Kingdom
Based on full costs of the product	1	1	1	1	1
Based on variable costs of the product	2	2	2	2	2

[a]Grant Thornton, *Survey.*
[b]Ogunmokun, Chan, and Li, "An Exploratory Study."
[c]Israelsen, Andersen, Rohde, and Sorensen, "Management Accounting."
[d]Clarke, "Management Accounting Practices."
[e]Ernst & Young, "2003 Survey."
[f]Crehnall and Smith, "Adoption."
[g]Joshi, "The International Diffusion."
[h]Firth, "The Diffusion."
[i]Lamminmaki and Drury, "A Comparison."
Full citations are in Appendix A at the end of the book.

Service companies such as home repairs, automobile repairs, and architectural firms use a cost-plus pricing method called the *time-and-materials method.* Individual jobs are priced based on materials and labor time. The price charged for materials equals the cost of materials plus a markup. The price charged for labor represents the cost of labor, allocated overhead, and a markup. Therefore, the price charged for each cost item includes its own markup.

6

Use life-cycle budgeting and costing when making pricing decisions

. . . accumulate all costs of a product from initial R&D to final customer service for each year of its life

Life-cycle costing can be implemented by coding revenues and costs by product as well as by functional account (for example, R&D, advertising, etc.) in journal entries. Data can then be compiled for each product.

For example, continuous advances in technology shorten product life cycles, making it more desirable to use life-cycle budgeting and life-cycle costing.

At the beginning of a product's life cycle, it's difficult to determine how successful the product will be. Therefore, the earlier costs are locked in, the riskier the product.

Life-Cycle Product Budgeting and Costing

Companies sometimes need to consider target prices and target costs for a product over a multiple-year product life cycle. The **product life cycle** spans the time from initial R&D on a product to when customer service and support is no longer offered for that product. For automobile companies such as DaimlerChrysler, Ford, and Nissan, the product life cycle for different car models ranges from 12 to 15 years. For pharmaceutical products, the life cycle at companies such as Pfizer, Merck, and Glaxo Smith Kline may be 15 to 20 years. And for banks such as Wachovia and BankOne, a product such as a newly designed savings account with specific privileges can have a life cycle of 10 to 20 years. The sales part of the product life cycle has four stages: when a product is introduced to the market, when sales grow, when sales stabilize as the product matures, and when sales decline as the product loses market acceptance.

In **life-cycle budgeting**, managers estimate the revenues and business function costs of the value chain attributable to each product from its initial R&D to its final customer service and support. **Life-cycle costing** tracks and accumulates business function costs of the value chain attributable to each product from initial R&D to final customer service and support. Life-cycle budgeting and life-cycle costing span several financial reporting years.

Life-Cycle Budgeting and Pricing Decisions

Budgeted life-cycle costs can provide information needed for strategically evaluating pricing decisions. Consider Insight, Inc., a computer software company, which is developing a new accounting package, "General Ledger." Assume the following budgeted amounts for General Ledger over a six-year product life cycle:

Years 1 and 2		
R&D costs		$240,000
Design costs		160,000
Years 3 to 6		
	Total Fixed Costs	**Variable Cost per Package**
Production costs	$100,000	$25
Marketing costs	70,000	24
Distribution costs	50,000	16
Customer-service costs	80,000	30

To be profitable, Insight must generate enough revenues to recover the costs in all six business functions of the value chain and, in particular, its high fixed nonproduction costs, which total $600,000. Exhibit 12-8 presents the life-cycle budget for General Ledger for three alternative selling-price/sales-quantity combinations.

Several features make life-cycle budgeting particularly important:

1. **Nonproduction costs are large.** Production costs are commonly visible on a product-by-product basis in most accounting systems. However, costs associated with R&D, design, marketing, distribution, and customer service are less visible on a product-by-product basis. When nonproduction costs are significant, as in the General Ledger example, identifying these costs by product is essential for target pricing, target costing, value engineering, and cost management.
2. **The development period for R&D and design is long and costly.** In the General Ledger example, R&D and design span two years and constitute more than 30% of total costs for each of the three combinations of selling price and predicted sales quantity. When a high percentage of total life-cycle costs are incurred before any production begins and before any revenues are received, the company especially needs accurate revenue and cost predictions for the product. It uses this information to decide whether to begin the costly R&D and design activities.
3. **Many costs are locked in at R&D and design stages—even if R&D and design costs themselves are small.** In our General Ledger example, a poorly designed accounting software package that is difficult to install and use would result in higher marketing,

EXHIBIT 12-8

Budgeted Life-Cycle Revenues and Costs for "General Ledger" Software Package of Insight, Inc.[a]

	Alternative Selling-Price/ Sales-Quantity Combinations		
	A	B	C
Selling price per package	$400	$480	$600
Sales quantity in units	5,000	4,000	2,500
Life-cycle revenues ($400 × 5,000; $480 × 4,000; $600 × 2,500)	$2,000,000	$1,920,000	$1,500,000
Life-cycle costs			
R&D costs	240,000	240,000	240,000
Design costs of product/process	160,000	160,000	160,000
Production costs $100,000 + ($25 × 5,000); $100,000 + ($25 × 4,000); $100,000 + ($25 × 2,500)	225,000	200,000	162,500
Marketing costs $70,000 + ($24 × 5,000); $70,000 + ($24 × 4,000); $70,000 + ($24 × 2,500)	190,000	166,000	130,000
Distribution costs $50,000 + ($16 × 5,000); $50,000 + ($16 × 4,000); $50,000 + ($16 × 2,500)	130,000	114,000	90,000
Customer-service costs $80,000 + ($30 × 5,000); $80,000 + ($30 × 4,000); $80,000 + ($30 × 2,500)	230,000	200,000	155,000
Total life-cycle costs	1,175,000	1,080,000	937,500
Life-cycle operating income	$ 825,000	$ 840,000	$ 562,500

[a]This exhibit does not take into consideration the time value of money when computing life-cycle revenues or life-cycle costs. Chapter 21 outlines how this important factor can be incorporated into such calculations.

distribution, and customer-service costs over several subsequent periods. These costs would be even higher if the product failed to meet promised quality-performance levels. A life-cycle revenue-and-cost budget prevents these relationships among business-function costs from being overlooked in decision making. Life-cycle budgeting highlights costs throughout the product's life cycle and so facilitates target pricing, target costing, and value engineering at the design stage before costs are locked in. The amounts presented in Exhibit 12-8 are the outcome of value engineering.

Insight decides to sell the General Ledger package for $480 per package because this price maximizes life-cycle operating income. Insight's managers will eventually compare actual costs incurred to life-cycle budgets to obtain feedback and learn about how to estimate costs for subsequent products. Exhibit 12-8 assumes that the selling price per package is the same over the entire life cycle. For strategic reasons, however, Insight may decide to skim the market—charging higher prices to customers eager to try General Ledger when it is first introduced and lowering prices later as the product matures. In these later stages, Insight may even add new features to differentiate the product to maintain prices and sales. The life-cycle budget will then incorporate this strategy.

Management of environmental costs provides another example of life-cycle costing and value engineering. Environmental laws—for example, the U.S. Clean Air Act and the U.S. Superfund Amendment and Reauthorization Act—have introduced tougher environmental standards, imposed stringent cleanup requirements, and introduced severe penalties for polluting the air and contaminating subsurface soil and groundwater. Environmental costs are often locked in at the product- and process-design stage. To avoid environmental liabilities, companies in industries such as oil refining and chemical processing do value engineering and design products and processes to manufacture the products to prevent and reduce pollution over the product's life cycle. Laptop computer manufacturers—for example, Hewlett Packard and Apple—have introduced costly recycling programs to ensure that nickel-cadmium batteries that can leak hazardous chemicals into the soil are disposed of in an environmentally safe way at the end of the batteries' life.

Hewlett-Packard (HP) has a substantial share of the computer printer market. To maintain market share, HP "cuts short" a printer's product life by bringing a newer version to market while the "old" version still has substantial market share. Why does HP "cannibalize" its own products? Because being first to market helps gain market share.

Study Tip: To check your understanding of the material in this chapter, see the Featured Exercise, multiple-choice questions 3 and 7, and Review Exercises 1 and 2 (*Student Guide*, beginning p. 155). Fully explained answers begin on p. 161.

Customer Life-Cycle Costing

A different notion of life-cycle costs is *customer life-cycle costs.* **Customer life-cycle costs** focus on the total costs incurred by a customer to acquire, use, maintain, and dispose of a product or service. Customer life-cycle costs for a car include the cost of the car itself plus the costs of operating and maintaining the car minus the disposal value of the car. Customer life-cycle costs can be an important consideration in the pricing decision.

Boeing Corporation paid special attention to customer life-cycle costs when it designed the Boeing 777. The plane's design allows mechanics easier access to different parts of the plane for routine maintenance. The goal: to reduce the time and cost of plane maintenance and thereby decrease a large component of the life-cycle cost of owning a plane.

For example, Ford's goal is to design cars that require minimal maintenance for 100,000 miles. Ford expects to charge a higher price and/or to gain greater market share by selling cars designed to meet this goal. Similarly, Maytag, the home-appliance manufacturer, charges higher prices for models that save electricity and have low maintenance costs.

Considerations Other than Costs in Pricing Decisions

7

Describe two pricing practices in which noncost factors are important when setting prices

. . . price discrimination—charging different customers different prices for the same product; and peak-load pricing—charging higher prices when demand approaches capacity

In some cases, cost is *not* a major factor in setting prices. Consider the prices airlines charge for a round-trip flight from San Francisco to Cleveland. A coach-class ticket for a flight with 21-day advance purchase is $350 if the passenger stays in Cleveland over a Saturday night. It is $1,600 if the passenger returns without staying over a Saturday night. Can this price difference be explained by the difference in the cost to the airline of these round-trip flights? No; it costs airlines the same amount to transport the passenger from San Francisco to Cleveland and back, whether or not the passenger stays in Cleveland over a Saturday night. To explain this difference in price, we must recognize the potential for *price discrimination*.

Price discrimination is the practice of charging different customers different prices for the same product or service. How does price discrimination work in our airline example? The demand for airline tickets comes from two main sources: business travelers and pleasure travelers. Some travelers must travel to conduct business for their organizations, so their demand for air travel is relatively insensitive to price. Insensitivity of demand to price changes is called *demand inelasticity*. Airlines can earn higher operating income by charging business travelers higher prices, because higher prices have little effect on their demand for air travel. Also, business travelers generally go to their destinations, complete their work, and return home without staying over a Saturday night. Pleasure travelers, however, usually don't need to return home during the week, and they prefer to spend weekends at their destinations. Because they pay for their tickets themselves, pleasure travelers' demand is more price-elastic—that is, they are much more sensitive to price than business travelers. Therefore, it is profitable for the airlines to charge low fares to stimulate demand among pleasure travelers.

How can airlines keep fares high for business travelers while, at the same time, keeping fares low for pleasure travelers? Requiring a Saturday night stay discriminates between the two customer segments. The airlines price-discriminate to take advantage of different sensitivities to prices exhibited by business travelers and pleasure travelers. Price differences exist even though there is no cost difference in serving the two segments of customers.

What if economic conditions weaken such that business travelers become more sensitive to price? The airlines may then need to lower the prices charged to business travelers. Following the events of Septemebr 11, 2001, airlines started offering discounted fares on certain routes without requiring a Saturday night stay to stimulate business travel. Business travel picked up and airlines started filling more seats than they otherwise would have. Unfortunately, travel did not pick up enough, and the airline industry as a whole suffered severe losses over the next three years.

For the 2004 Summer Olympics in Athens, hotels charged very high rates and required multiple-night stays. Airlines also charged high fares for flights into and out of many cities in the region for roughly a month around the time of the Games. Given that demand was expected to far exceed capacity, the hospitality industry and airlines employed peak-load pricing to increase their profits.

In addition to price discrimination, pricing decisions also consider other noncost factors such as capacity constraints. **Peak-load pricing** is the practice of charging a higher price for the same product or service when the demand for it approaches the physical limit of the capacity to produce that product or service. Prices charged during periods when demand on the production capacity is high represent what customers are willing to pay for the product or service. These prices are greater than the prices charged when slack or excess capacity is available. Peak-load pricing occurs in the telephone, telecommunications, hotel, car rental, and electric-utility industries. Consider the daily rental rates charged by Avis Corporation in January 2004 for mid-sized cars rented at Boston's Logan Airport:

Monday through Thursday	$80 per day
Friday through Sunday	$21 per day

Avis's actual daily costs of renting a car are the same whether the car is rented on a weekday or on a weekend. Why the difference in prices? One explanation is that there is a greater demand for cars on weekdays because of business activity. Faced with capacity limits, Avis charges peak-load prices at levels the market will bear.

A second explanation is that the rental rates are a form of price discrimination. On weekdays, demand for cars comes largely from business travelers, who need to rent cars and who are insensitive to prices. Higher rental rates on weekdays are profitable because they have little effect on demand. Weekend rental demand comes from pleasure travelers, who are price-sensitive. Lower rates stimulate demand from these individuals and increase Avis's operating income. Under either explanation, the pricing decision is not primarily driven by cost considerations.

The Concepts in Action feature in Chapter 11 (p. 390) discusses Delta Airlines' Internet pricing of seats on flights with excess capacity (flights with unsold seats)—an example of price discrimination and nonpeak-load pricing.

Another example of considerations other than costs affecting prices occurs when the same product is sold in different countries. Consider software, books, and medicines produced in one country and sold globally. The prices charged in each country vary much more than the costs of delivering the product to each country. These price differences arise because of differences in the purchasing power of consumers in different countries (a form of price discrimination) and government restrictions that may limit the prices that can be charged.

Effects of Antitrust Laws on Pricing

8

Explain the effects of antitrust laws on pricing

. . . antitrust laws attempt to counteract pricing below costs to drive out competitors or fixing prices artificially high to harm consumers

Legal considerations affect pricing decisions. Companies are not always free to charge whatever price they like. For example, under the U.S. Robinson-Patman Act, a manufacturer cannot price-discriminate between two customers if the intent is to lessen or prevent competition for customers. Two key features of price-discrimination laws are:

1. Price discrimination is permissible if differences in prices can be justified by differences in costs.
2. Price discrimination is illegal only if the intent is to lessen or prevent competition.

The price discrimination by airlines and car rental companies described earlier is legal because their practices do not hinder competition.

To comply with U.S. antitrust laws, such as the Sherman Act, the Clayton Act, the Federal Trade Commission Act, and the Robinson-Patman Act, pricing must not be predatory.[5] A company engages in **predatory pricing** when it deliberately prices below its costs in an effort to drive competitors out of the market and restrict supply, and then raises prices rather than enlarge demand.[6]

The U.S. Supreme Court established the following conditions to prove that predatory pricing has occurred:

- The predator company charges a price below an appropriate measure of its costs, and
- The predator company has a reasonable prospect of recovering in the future, through larger market share or higher prices, the money it lost by pricing below cost.

The Supreme Court has not specified the "appropriate measure of costs."[7]

[5]Discussion of the Sherman Act and the Clayton Act is in A. Barkman and J. Jolley, "Cost Defenses for Antitrust Cases," *Management Accounting* 67 (no. 10): 37–40.

[6]For more details, see W. Viscusi, J. Vernon, and J. Harrington, *Economics of Regulation and Antitrust*, 3rd ed. (Cambridge, MA: MIT Press, 2000); and J. L. Goldstein, "Single Firm Predatory Pricing in Antitrust Law: The Rose Acre Recoupment Test and the Search for an Appropriate Judicial Standard," *Columbia Law Review* 91 (1991): 1557–1592.

[7]*Brooke Group v. Brown & Williamson Tobacco,* 113 S. Ct. (1993); T. J. Trujillo, "Predatory Pricing Standards Under Recent Supreme Court Decisions and Their Failure to Recognize Strategic Behavior as a Barrier to Entry," *Iowa Journal of Corporation Law* (Summer 1994): 809–831.

Most courts in the United States have defined the "appropriate measure of costs" as the short-run marginal or average variable costs.[8] In *Adjustor's Replace-a-Car v. Agency Rent-a-Car*, Adjustor's (the plaintiff) claimed that it was forced to withdraw from the Austin and San Antonio, Texas, markets because Agency had engaged in predatory pricing.[9] To prove predatory pricing, Adjuster pointed to "the net loss from operations" in Agency's income statement, calculated after allocating Agency's headquarters overhead. The judge, however, ruled that Agency had not engaged in predatory pricing because the price it charged for a rental car never dropped below its average variable costs.

It would be wise for companies that have concerns about their conformance with antitrust laws to have accounting systems that incorporate the following procedures:

- Collect data and keep detailed records of variable costs for all business functions of the value chain.
- Review all proposed prices below variable costs in advance, with a presumption that claims of predatory intent will occur.

The Supreme Court decision in *Brooke Group v. Brown & Williamson Tobacco* (*BWT*) increased the difficulty of proving predatory pricing. The Court ruled that pricing below average variable costs is not predatory if the company does not have a reasonable chance of later increasing prices or market share to recover its losses.[10] The defendant, BWT, a cigarette manufacturer, sold brand-name cigarettes and had 12% of the cigarette market. The introduction of generic cigarettes threatened BWT's market share. BWT responded by introducing its own version of generics priced below average variable cost, thereby making it difficult for generic manufacturers to continue in business. The Supreme Court ruled that BWT's action was a competitive response and not predatory pricing. That's because, given BWT's small 12% market share and the existing competition within the industry, it would be unable to later charge a monopoly price to recoup its losses.

Closely related to predatory pricing is dumping. Under U.S. laws, **dumping** occurs when a non-U.S. company sells a product in the United States at a price below the market value in the country where it is produced, and this lower price materially injures or threatens to materially injure an industry in the United States. If dumping is proven, an antidumping duty can be imposed under U.S. tariff laws equal to the amount by which the foreign price exceeds the U.S. price. Cases related to dumping have occurred in the cement, computer, lumber, steel, semiconductor, and sweater industries. In late 2001, the U.S. International Trade Commission ruled that the dumping of certain steel products from 23 nations, including China and Japan, harmed domestic producers. In March 2002, President George W. Bush, acting on the International Trade Commission's recommendation, levied three-year tariffs on all producers from these nations.

Eight of the countries affected by the U.S. steel tariffs appealed President Bush's decision to the dispute settlement panel of the World Trade Organization (WTO). The WTO is an international institution created with the goal of promoting and regulating trade practices among countries by lowering import duties and tariffs. In July 2003, the dispute settlement panel ruled that no dumping had occurred and that the tariffs were inconsistent with WTO rules. After losing an appeal to the full WTO appellate body and under mounting international pressure and threats to impose retaliatory tariffs on U.S. products, the United States complied with the WTO ruling and rescinded the steel tariffs in December 2003.

Another violation of antitrust laws is collusive pricing. **Collusive pricing** occurs when companies in an industry conspire in their pricing and production decisions to achieve a price above the competitive price and so restrain trade. For example, in 2002, video-games manufacturer Nintendo was fined €149 million by the European Commission for colluding with seven distributors to prevent the export of products to EU countries where video game prices were low. In 2004, the U.S. Department of Justice fined Bayer AG $66 million for colluding with various companies to artificially regulate prices in the rubber chemicals market.

---

[8]An exception is *McGahee v. Northern Propane Gas Co.* [858 F, 2d 1487 (1988)], in which the Eleventh Circuit Court held that prices below average total cost constitute evidence of predatory intent. For more discussion, see P. Areeda and D. Turner, "Predatory Pricing and Related Practices under Section 2 of Sherman Act," *Harvard Law Review* 88 (1975): 697–733. For an overview of case law, see W. Viscusi, J. Vernon, and J. Harrington, *Economics of Regulation and Antitrust*, 3rd ed. (Cambridge, MA: MIT Press, 2000). See also the "Legal Developments" section of the *Journal of Marketing* for summaries of court cases.

[9]*Adjustor's Replace-a-Car, Inc. v. Agency Rent-a-Car*, 735 2d 884 (1984).

[10]*Brooke Group v. Brown & Williamson Tobacco*, 113 S. Ct. (1993).

PROBLEM FOR SELF-STUDY

Reconsider the Astel Computer example (pp. 430–432). Astel's marketing manager realizes that a further reduction in price is necessary to sell 200,000 units of Provalue II. To maintain a target profitability of $16 million, or $80 per unit (the same amounts shown in Exhibit 12-6), Astel will need to reduce costs of Provalue II by $6 million, or $30 per unit. Astel targets a reduction of $4 million, or $20 per unit, in manufacturing costs, and $2 million, or $10 per unit, in marketing, distribution, and customer-service costs. The cross-functional team assigned to this task proposes the following changes to manufacture a different version of Provalue, called Provalue III:

1. Reduce direct materials and ordering costs by purchasing subassembled components rather than individual components.
2. Reengineer ordering and receiving to reduce ordering and receiving costs per order.
3. Reduce testing time and the labor and power required per hour of testing.
4. Develop new rework procedures to reduce rework costs per hour.

No changes are proposed in direct manufacturing labor costs per unit and in total machining costs.

The following table summarizes the cost-driver quantities and the cost per unit of each cost driver for Provalue III compared with Provalue II.

	A	B	C	D	E	F	G	H	I	J	K	L	M	N
1			PROVALUE II						PROVALUE III					
2					200,000 output units						200,000 output units			
3	Cost Category	Cost Driver	Details of Cost Driver Quantities				Total Quantity of Cost Driver	Cost per Unit of Cost Driver	Details of Cost Driver Quantities				Total Quantity of Cost Driver	Cost per Unit of Cost Driver
4	(1)	(2)	(3)		(4)		(5)=(3)×(4)	(6)	(7)		(8)		(9)=(7)×(8)	(10)
5	**Direct Manufacturing Costs**													
6	Direct materials	No. of kits	1	kit per output unit	200,000	output units	200,000	$385	1	kit per output unit	200,000	output units	200,000	$ 375
7	Direct manuf. labor (DML)	DML hours	2.65	DML hours per output unit	200,000	output units	530,000	$ 20	2.65	DML hours per output unit	200,000	output units	530,000	$ 20
8	Direct machining (fixed)	Machine-hours					300,000	$ 38					300,000	$ 38
9	**Manufacturing Overhead Costs**													
10	Ordering and receiving	No. of orders	50	orders per compo-nent	425	compo-nents	21,250	$ 80	50	orders per compo-nent	400	compo-nents	20,000	$ 60
11	Testing and inspection	Testing-hours	15	testing-hours per output unit	200,000	output units	3,000,000	$ 2	14	testing-hours per output unit	200,000	output units	2,800,000	$1.70
12	Rework				6.5%	defect rate					6.5%	defect rate		
13		Rework-hours	2.5	rework-hours per defective unit	13,000[a]	defec-tive units	32,500	$ 40	2.5	rework-hours per defective unit	13,000[a]	defec-tive units	32,500	$ 32
14														
15	[a] 6.5% defect rate x 200,000 output units = 13,000 defective units													

Required

Will the proposed changes achieve Astel's targeted reduction of $4 million, or $20 per unit, in manufacturing costs for Provalue III? Show your computations.

SOLUTION

Exhibit 12-9 presents the manufacturing costs for Provalue III based on the proposed changes. Manufacturing costs will decline from $108 million, or $540 per unit (Exhibit 12-5), to $104 million, or $520 per unit (Exhibit 12-9), and will achieve the target reduction of $4 million, or $20 per unit.

EXHIBIT 12-9 Target Manufacturing Costs of Provalue III for 2008 Based on Proposed Changes

	A	B	C	D
1		Estimated		Estimated
2		Manufacturing Costs		Manufacturing
3		for 200,000 Units		Cost per Unit
4		(1)		(2) = (1) ÷ 200,000
5	Direct manufacturing costs			
6	Direct material costs			
7	(200,000 units x $375 per unit)	$75,000,000		$375.00
8	Direct manufacturing labor costs			
9	(530,000 hours x $20 per hour)	10,600,000		53.00
10	Direct machining costs			
11	(300,000 machine-hours x $38 per machine-hour)	11,400,000		57.00
12	Direct manufacturing costs	97,000,000		485.00
13				
14	Manufacturing overhead costs			
15	Ordering and receiving costs			
16	(20,000 orders x $60 per order)	1,200,000		6.00
17	Testing and inspection costs			
18	(2,800,000 hours x $1.70 per hour)	4,760,000		23.80
19	Rework costs			
20	(32,500 rework hours x $32 per hour)	1,040,000		5.20
21	Manufacturing overhead costs	7,000,000		35.00
22	Total manufacturing costs	$104,000,000		$520.00
23				

DECISION POINTS

The following question-and-answer format summarizes the chapter's learning objectives. Each decision presents a key question related to a learning objective. The guidelines are the answers to that question.

Decision	Guidelines
1. What are the three major influences on pricing decisions?	Customers, competitors, and costs influence prices through their effects on demand and supply; customers and competitors affect demand, and costs affect supply.
2. How do short-run pricing decisions differ from long-run pricing decisions?	Short-run pricing decisions focus on a time horizon of less than a year and have no long-run implications. Long-run pricing decisions focus on a time horizon of a year or longer. The time horizon appropriate to a decision on pricing dictates which costs are relevant, how costs are managed, and the profit that must be earned.
3. How do companies price products using target costing?	One approach to long-run pricing is to use a target price. Target price is the estimated price that potential customers are willing to pay for a product or service. Target operating income per unit is subtracted from the target price to determine target cost per unit. Target cost per unit is the estimated long-run cost of a product or service that when sold enables the company to achieve target operating income per unit. The challenge for the company is to make the cost improvements necessary through value-engineering methods to achieve the target cost.
4. Why is it important to distinguish cost incurrence from locked-in costs?	Cost incurrence describes when a resource is sacrificed. Locked-in costs are costs not yet incurred but which, based on decisions that have already been made, will be incurred in the future. To reduce costs, techniques such as value engineering are most effective *before* costs are locked in.
5. How do companies price products using the cost-plus approach?	The cost-plus approach to pricing adds a markup component to a cost base as the starting point for pricing decisions. Many different costs, such as full cost of the product or manufacturing cost, can serve as the cost base in applying the cost-plus formula. Prices are then modified on the basis of customers' reactions and competitors' responses. Therefore, the size of the "plus" is determined by the marketplace.

6. What are life-cycle budgeting and life-cycle costing, and when should companies use these techniques?

Life-cycle budgeting estimates and life-cycle costing tracks and accumulates the costs (and revenues) attributable to a product from its initial R&D to its final customer service and support. These life-cycle techniques are particularly important when (a) nonproduction costs are large, (b) a high percentage of total life-cycle costs are incurred before production begins and before any revenues are earned, and (c) a high fraction of the life-cycle costs are locked in at the R&D and design stages.

7. What are price discrimination and peak-load pricing?

Price discrimination is charging some customers a higher price for a given product or service than other customers. Peak-load pricing is charging a higher price for the same product or service when demand approaches physical-capacity limits. Under price discrimination and peak-load pricing, prices differ among market segments even though the cost of providing the product or service is approximately the same.

8. How do antitrust laws affect pricing?

To comply with antitrust laws, a company must not engage in predatory pricing, dumping, or collusive pricing, which lessen competition; put another company at a competitive disadvantage; or harm consumers.

TERMS TO LEARN

The chapter and the Glossary at the end of the book contain definitions of:

collusive pricing (p. 440)
cost incurrence (p. 427)
customer life-cycle costs (p. 438)
designed-in costs (p. 428)
dumping (p. 440)
life-cycle budgeting (p. 436)
life-cycle costing (p. 436)
locked-in costs (p. 428)
nonvalue-added cost (p. 426)
peak-load pricing (p. 438)
predatory pricing (p. 439)
price discrimination (p. 438)
product life cycle (p. 436)
target cost per unit (p. 425)
target operating income per unit (p. 425)
target price (p. 425)
target rate of return on investment (p. 432)
value-added cost (p. 426)
value engineering (p. 426)

PH Grade Assist

Prentice Hall Grade Assist (PHGA)

Your professor may ask you to complete selected exercises and problems in Prentice Hall Grade Assist (PHGA). PHGA is an online tool that can help you master the chapter's topics. It provides you with multiple variations of exercises and problems designated by the PHGA icon. You can rework these exercises and problems—each time with new data—as many times as needed. You also receive immediate feedback and grading.

ASSIGNMENT MATERIAL

Questions

12-1 What are the three major influences on pricing decisions?

12-2 "Relevant costs for pricing decisions are full costs of the product." Do you agree? Explain.

12-3 Give two examples of pricing decisions with a short-run focus.

12-4 How is activity-based costing useful for pricing decisions?

12-5 Describe two alternative approaches to long-run pricing decisions.

12-6 What is a target cost per unit?

12-7 Describe value engineering and its role in target costing.

12-8 Give two examples of a value-added cost and two examples of a nonvalue-added cost.

12-9 "It is not important for a company to distinguish between cost incurrence and locked-in costs." Do you agree? Explain.

12-10 What is cost-plus pricing?

12-11 Describe three alternative cost-plus pricing methods.

12-12 Give two examples in which the difference in the costs of two products or services is much smaller than the difference in their prices.

12-13 What is life-cycle budgeting?

12-14 What are three benefits of using a product life-cycle reporting format?

12-15 Define predatory pricing, dumping, and collusive pricing.

Exercises

12-16 Relevant-cost approach to pricing decisions, special order. The following financial data apply to the videotape production plant of the Dill Company for October 2006:

	Budgeted Manufacturing Cost per Videotape
Direct materials	$1.50
Direct manufacturing labor	0.80
Variable manufacturing overhead	0.70
Fixed manufacturing overhead	1.00
Total manufacturing cost	$4.00

Variable manufacturing overhead varies with the number of units produced. Fixed manufacturing overhead of $1 per tape is based on budgeted fixed manufacturing overhead of $150,000 per month and budgeted production of 150,000 tapes per month. The Dill Company sells each tape for $5.

Marketing costs have two components:

- Variable marketing costs (sales commissions) of 5% of revenues
- Fixed monthly costs of $65,000

During October 2006, Lyn Randell, a Dill Company salesperson, asked the president for permission to sell 1,000 tapes at $3.80 per tape to a customer not in Dill's normal marketing channels. The president refused this special order because the selling price was below the total budgeted manufacturing cost.

Required

1. What would have been the effect on monthly operating income of accepting the special order?
2. Comment on the president's "below manufacturing costs" reasoning for rejecting the special order.
3. What other factors should the president consider before accepting or rejecting the special order?

12-17 Relevant-cost approach to short-run pricing decisions. The San Carlos Company is an electronics business with eight product lines. Income data for one of the products (XT-107) for June 2007 are:

Revenues, 200,000 units at average price of $100 each		$20,000,000
Variable costs		
Direct materials at $35 per unit	$ 7,000,000	
Direct manufacturing labor at $10 per unit	2,000,000	
Variable manufacturing overhead at $5 per unit	1,000,000	
Sales commissions at 15% of revenues	3,000,000	
Other variable costs at $5 per unit	1,000,000	
Total variable costs		14,000,000
Contribution margin		6,000,000
Fixed costs		5,000,000
Operating income		$ 1,000,000

Abrams, Inc., an instruments company, has a problem with its preferred supplier of XT-107 components. This supplier has had a three-week labor strike. Abrams approaches the San Carlos sales representative, Sarah Holtz, about providing 3,000 units of XT-107 at a price of $80 per unit. Holtz informs the XT-107 product manager, Jim McMahon, that she would accept a flat commission of $6,000 rather than the usual 15% of revenues if this special order were accepted. San Carlos has the capacity to produce 300,000 units of XT-107 each month, but demand has not exceeded 200,000 units in any month in the past year.

Required

1. If the 3,000-unit order from Abrams is accepted, how much will operating income increase or decrease? (Assume the same cost structure as in June 2007.)
2. McMahon ponders whether to accept the 3,000-unit special order. He is afraid of the precedent that might be set by cutting the price. He says, "The price is below our full cost of $95 per unit. I think we should quote a full price, or Abrams will expect favored treatment again and again if we continue to do business with them." Do you agree with McMahon? Explain.

PH Grade Assist

12-18 Short-run pricing, capacity constraints. Vermont Hills Dairy, maker of specialty cheeses, produces a soft cheese from the milk of Holstein cows raised on a special corn-based diet. One kilogram of soft cheese, which has a contribution margin of $8, requires 4 liters of milk. A well-known gourmet restaurant has asked Vermont Hills to produce 2,000 kilograms of a hard cheese from the same milk of Holstein cows. Knowing that the dairy has sufficient unused capacity, Elise Princiotti, owner of Vermont Hills, calculates the costs of making one kilogram of the desired hard cheese:

Milk (10 liters × $1.50 per liter)	$15
Variable direct manufacturing labor	5
Variable manufacturing overhead	3
Fixed manufacturing cost allocated	6
Total manufacturing cost	$29

1. Suppose Vermont Hills can acquire all the Holstein milk that it needs. What is the minimum price per kilogram it should charge for the hard cheese?
2. Now suppose that the Holstein milk is in short supply. Every kilogram of hard cheese produced by Vermont Hills will reduce the quantity of soft cheese that it can make and sell. What is the minimum price per kilogram it should charge to produce the hard cheese?

Required

12-19 Value-added, nonvalue-added costs. The Marino Repair Shop repairs and services machine tools. A summary of its costs (by activity) for 2007 is as follows:

PH Grade Assist

a. Materials and labor for servicing machine tools	$800,000
b. Rework costs	75,000
c. Expediting costs caused by work delays	60,000
d. Materials-handling costs	50,000
e. Materials-procurement and inspection costs	35,000
f. Preventive maintenance of equipment	15,000
g. Breakdown maintenance of equipment	55,000

Required

1. Classify each cost as value-added, nonvalue-added, or in the gray area in between.
2. For any cost classified in the gray area, assume 65% is value-added and 35% is nonvalue-added. How much of the total of all seven costs is value-added and how much is nonvalue-added?
3. Marino is considering the following changes: (a) introducing quality-improvement programs whose net effect will be to reduce rework and expediting costs by 75% and materials and labor costs for servicing machine tools by 5%; (b) working with suppliers to reduce materials-procurement and inspection costs by 20% and materials-handling costs by 25%; and (c) increasing preventive-maintenance costs by 50% to reduce breakdown-maintenance costs by 40%. Calculate the effect of programs (a), (b), and (c) on value-added costs, nonvalue-added costs, and total costs. Comment briefly.

12-20 Target operating income, value-added costs, service company. Carasco Associates prepares architectural drawings to conform to local structural-safety codes. Its income statement for 2007 is:

Revenues	$680,000
Salaries of professional staff (8,000 hours × $50 per hour)	400,000
Travel	18,000
Administrative and support costs	160,000
Total costs	578,000
Operating income	$102,000

Following is the percentage of time spent by professional staff on various activities:

Making calculations and preparing drawings for clients	75%
Checking calculations and drawings	4
Correcting errors found in drawings (not billed to clients)	7
Making changes in response to client requests (billed to clients)	6
Correcting own errors regarding building codes (not billed to clients)	8
Total	100%

Assume administrative and support costs vary with professional-labor costs.

Consider each requirement independently.

Required

1. How much of the total costs in 2007 are value-added, nonvalue-added, or in the gray area in between? Explain your answers briefly. What actions can Carasco take to reduce its costs?
2. Suppose Carasco could eliminate all errors so that it did not need to spend any time making corrections and, as a result, could proportionately reduce professional-labor costs. Calculate Carasco's operating income.
3. Now suppose Carasco could take on as much business as it could complete, but it could not add more professional staff. Assume Carasco could eliminate all errors so that it does not need to spend any time correcting errors. Assume Carasco could use the time saved to increase revenues proportionately. Assume travel costs will remain at $18,000. Calculate Carasco's operating income.

12-21 Target prices, target costs, activity-based costing. Snappy Tiles is a small distributor of marble tiles. Snappy identifies its three major activities and cost pools as ordering, receiving and storage, and shipping, and it reports the following details for 2006:

PH Grade Assist

Activity	Cost Driver	Quantity of Cost Driver	Cost per Unit of Cost Driver
1. Placing and paying for orders of marble tiles	Number of orders	500	$50 per order
2. Receiving and storage	Loads moved	4,000	$30 per load
3. Shipping of marble tiles to retailers	Number of shipments	1,500	$40 per shipment

For 2006, Snappy buys 250,000 marble tiles at an average cost of $3 per tile and sells them to retailers at an average price of $4 per tile. Assume Snappy has no fixed costs and no inventories.

Required

1. Calculate Snappy's operating income for 2006.
2. For 2007, retailers are demanding a 5% discount off the 2006 price. Snappy's suppliers are only willing to give a 4% discount. Snappy expects to sell the same quantity of marble tiles in 2007 as in 2006. If all other costs and cost-driver information remain the same, calculate Snappy's operating income for 2007.
3. Suppose further that Snappy decides to make changes in its ordering and receiving-and-storing practices. By placing long-run orders with its key suppliers, Snappy expects to reduce the number of orders to 200 and the cost per order to $25 per order. By redesigning the layout of the warehouse and reconfiguring the crates in which the marble tiles are moved, Snappy expects to reduce the number of loads moved to 3,125 and the cost per load moved to $28. Will Snappy achieve its target operating income of $0.30 per tile in 2007? Show your calculations.

PH Grade Assist

12-22 Target costs, effect of product-design changes on product costs. Medical Instruments uses a manufacturing costing system with one direct-cost category (direct materials) and three indirect-cost categories:

a. Setup, production order, and materials-handling costs that vary with the number of batches
b. Manufacturing-operations costs that vary with machine-hours
c. Costs of engineering changes that vary with the number of engineering changes made

In response to competitive pressures at the end of 2006, Medical Instruments used value-engineering techniques to reduce manufacturing costs. Actual information for 2006 and 2007 is:

	2006	2007
Setup, production-order, and materials-handling costs per batch	$ 8,000	$ 7,500
Total manufacturing-operations cost per machine-hour	$55	$50
Cost per engineering change	$12,000	$10,000

The management of Medical Instruments wants to evaluate whether value engineering has succeeded in reducing the target manufacturing cost per unit of one of its products, HJ6, by 10%.

Actual results for 2006 and 2007 for HJ6 are:

	Actual Results for 2006	Actual Results for 2007
Units of HJ6 produced	3,500	4,000
Direct material cost per unit of HJ6	$1,200	$1,100
Total number of batches required to produce HJ6	70	80
Total machine-hours required to produce HJ6	21,000	22,000
Number of engineering changes made	14	10

Required

1. Calculate the manufacturing cost per unit of HJ6 in 2006.
2. Calculate the manufacturing cost per unit of HJ6 in 2007.
3. Did Medical Instruments achieve the target manufacturing cost per unit for HJ6 in 2007? Explain.
4. Explain how Medical Instruments reduced the manufacturing cost per unit of HJ6 in 2007.

12-23 Cost-plus target return on investment pricing. John Beck is the managing partner of a business that has just finished building a 60-room motel. Beck anticipates that he will rent these rooms for 16,000 nights next year (or 16,000 room-nights). All rooms are similar and will rent for the same price. Beck estimates the following operating costs for next year:

Variable operating costs	$3 per room-night
Fixed costs	
Salaries and wages	$175,000
Maintenance of building and pool	37,000
Other operating and administration costs	140,000
Total fixed costs	$352,000

The capital invested in the motel is $960,000. The partnership's target return on investment is 25%. Beck expects demand for rooms to be uniform throughout the year. He plans to price the rooms at full cost plus a markup on full cost to earn the target return on investment.

Required

1. What price should Beck charge for a room-night? What is the markup as a percentage of the full cost of a room-night?
2. Beck's market research indicates that if the price of a room-night determined in requirement 1 is reduced by 10%, the expected number of room-nights Beck could rent would increase by 10%. Should Beck reduce prices by 10%? Show your calculations.

Excel Lab
www.prenhall.com/horngren/cost12e

12-24 Cost-plus, target pricing, working backward. (S. Sridhar, adapted) Waterbury, Inc., manufactures and sells RF17, a specialty raft used for whitewater rafting. In 2007, it reported the following:

	A	B
1		**2007**
2	Units produced and sold	20,000
3	Investment	$2,400,000
4	Full cost per unit	$ 300
5	Rate of return on investment	20%
6	Markup percentage on variable cost	50%

If you want to use Excel to solve this exercise, go to the Excel Lab at **www.prenhall.com/horngren/cost12e** and download the template for Exercise 12-24.

Required

1. What was the selling price in 2007? What was the percentage markup on full cost? What was the variable cost per unit?
2. Waterbury is considering raising its selling price to $348. However, at this price, its sales volume is predicted to fall by 10%. If Waterbury's cost structure (variable cost per unit and total fixed costs) remains unchanged and if its demand forecast is accurate, should it raise the selling price to $348?
3. In 2008, due to increased competition, Waterbury must reduce its selling price to $315 in order to sell 20,000 units. The manager of the rafts division reduces annual investment to $2,100,000 but still demands a 20% target rate of return on investment. If fixed costs cannot be changed in this time frame, what is the target variable cost per unit?

12-25 Life-cycle product costing, activity-based costing. Destin Products makes digital watches. Destin is preparing a product-life-cycle budget for a new watch, MX3. Development on the new watch is to start shortly. Estimates for MX3 are as follows:

Life-cycle units manufactured and sold	400,000
Selling price per watch	$40
Life-cycle costs	
R&D and design costs	$1,000,000
Manufacturing	
Variable cost per watch	$15
Variable cost per batch	$600
Watches per batch	500
Fixed costs	$1,800,000
Marketing	
Variable cost per watch	$3.20
Fixed costs	$1,000,000
Distribution	
Variable cost per batch	$280
Watches per batch	160
Fixed costs	$720,000
Customer-service cost per watch	$1.50

Ignore the time value of money.

Required

1. Calculate the budgeted life-cycle operating income for the new watch.
2. What percentage of the budgeted total product life-cycle costs will be *incurred* by the end of the R&D and design stages?
3. An analysis reveals that 80% of the budgeted total product life-cycle costs of the new watch will be *locked in* at the R&D and design stages. What are the implications for managing MX3's costs?
4. Destin's Market Research Department estimates that reducing MX3's price by $3 will increase life-cycle unit sales by 10%. If unit sales increase by 10%, Destin plans to increase manufacturing and distribution batch sizes by 10% as well. Assume that all variable costs per watch, variable costs per batch, and fixed costs will remain the same. Should Destin reduce MX3's price by $3? Show your calculations.

12-26 Considerations other than cost in pricing. In an advertisement in a San Francisco newspaper, three hotel chains published their weekend and weekday daily room rates for various cities in California.

		Daily Rate	
Hotel	**City**	**Weekend**	**Weekday**
Westin	Palo Alto	$149	$319
Westin	Santa Clara	89	239
Sheraton	San Francisco (airport)	109	219
Sheraton	Sunnyvale	89	209
Four Points	Pleasanton	75	169
Four Points	Sunnyvale	89	209

Weekend rates required Friday and/or Saturday night stay.

Required

1. Are there differences in incremental costs to hotels for weekend stays compared with weekday stays?
2. Explain the reason(s) why hotels charge lower rates for weekend stays compared with weekday stays.

3. In the same advertisement, two hotels published their room rates for Anaheim (where Disneyland is located), and one hotel published its room rate for Fisherman's Wharf in San Francisco (a popular tourist attraction). Interestingly, the weekend rates in each of these three cases were the same as weekday rates. Explain how this situation differs from the one in requirement 2.

Problems

12-27 Relevant-cost approach to pricing decisions. Stardom, Inc., cans peaches for sale to food distributors. All costs are classified as either manufacturing or marketing. Stardom prepares monthly budgets. The March 2007 budgeted absorption-costing income statement is as follows:

Revenues (1,000 crates × $100 a crate)	$100,000
Cost of goods sold	60,000
Gross margin	40,000
Marketing costs	30,000
Operating income	$ 10,000
Normal markup percentage:	
$40,000 ÷ $60,000 = 66.7% of absorption cost	

Monthly costs are classified as fixed or variable (with respect to the number of crates produced for manufacturing costs and with respect to the number of crates sold for marketing costs):

	Fixed	Variable
Manufacturing	$20,000	$40,000
Marketing	16,000	14,000

Stardom has the capacity to can 1,500 crates per month. The relevant range in which monthly fixed manufacturing costs will be "fixed" is from 500 to 1,500 crates per month.

Required

1. Calculate the markup percentage based on total variable costs.
2. Assume that a new customer approaches Stardom to buy 200 crates at $55 per crate for cash. The customer does not require any marketing effort. Additional manufacturing costs of $2,000 (for special packaging) will be required. Stardom believes that this is a one-time-only special order because the customer is discontinuing business in six weeks' time. Stardom is reluctant to accept this 200-crate special order because the $55-per-crate price is below the $60-per-crate absorption cost. Do you agree with this reasoning? Explain.
3. Assume that the new customer decides to remain in business. How would this longevity affect your willingness to accept the $55-per-crate offer? Explain.

PH Grade Assist

12-28 Target rate of return on investment, activity-based costing. Electronic Arts (EA) distributes video games to retail stores and video-game parlors. It has a simple business model: Order the video games, catalog the games on EA's Web site, deliver and provide on-site support, and bill and collect from the customers. EA reported the following costs in April 2006:

Activity	Cost Driver	Quantity	Cost per Unit of Cost Driver
Ordering	Number of game vendors	40	$250 per vendor
Cataloging	Number of new titles	20	$100 per title
Delivery and support	Number of deliveries	400	$15 per delivery
Billing and collection	Number of customers	300	$50 per customer

In April 2006, EA purchased 12,000 video-game disks at an average cost of $15 per disk, and it sold them at an average price of $22 per disk. The catalog on the Web site and the customer interactions that occur during delivery are EA's main marketing inputs. EA incurs no other costs.

Required

1. Calculate EA's operating income for April 2006. If the monthly investment in EA is $300,000, what rate of return on investment does the business earn?
2. The current crop of game systems is maturing, and prices for games are beginning to decline. EA anticipates that from May onward, it will be able to sell 12,000 game disks each month for an average of $18 per disk, and it will have to pay vendors an average of $12 per disk. Assuming other costs are the same as in April, will EA be able to earn its 15% target rate of return on investment?
3. EA's small workforce gathers as a team and considers process improvements. They recommend "firing" the marginal vendors—those who need a lot of "hand holding" but whose titles are not very popular. They agree that they should shift some of their resources from vendor relationships and cataloging to delivery and customer relationships. In May 2006, EA reports the following support costs:

Activity	Cost Driver	Quantity	Cost per Unit of Cost Driver
Ordering	Number of game vendors	30	$200 per vendor
Cataloging	Number of new titles	15	$100 per title
Delivery and support	Number of deliveries	450	$20 per delivery
Billing and collection	Number of customers	300	$50 per customer

At a selling price of $18 and a cost of $12 per disk, how many game disks must EA sell in May 2006 to earn its 15% target rate of return on investment?

12-29 Product costs, target costing, activity-based costing. Executive Power (EP) manufactures and sells computers and computer peripherals to several nationwide retail chains. John Farnham is the manager of the printer division whose best-selling printers are P-81 and P-63.

Excel Lab www.prenhall.com/horngren/cost12e

The manufacturing cost of each printer is calculated using activity-based costing. EP has one direct-manufacturing cost category (direct materials) and five manufacturing overhead cost pools. The current quantities of cost drivers per output unit are shown in columns E and F. Competitors are now experimenting with outsourcing and have introduced lower-priced comparable models of printers. Farnham gathers the P-series design-and-manufacturing team. They agree to a target cost of $675 per unit for P-81 and $435 per unit for P-63. The team brainstorms on alternatives to the current design-and-manufacturing system. Their revised designs (P-81 REV and P-63 REV) will have the quantities of cost drivers per output unit shown in columns G and H:

	A	B	C	D	E	F	G	H	I
1	**Indirect Manufacturing**		**Cost per Unit of**		**Quantity of Cost Driver Per Output Unit**				
2	**Cost Pool**	**Cost Driver**	**Cost Driver**		**P-81**	**P-63**	**P-81 REV**	**P-63 REV**	
3	Materials handling	Number of parts	$ 0.80		90	50	75	42	parts
4	Assembly management	Hours of assembly time	$48.00		2.8	1.8	2.0	1.5	assembly-hours
5	Machine insertion of parts	No. of machine inserted parts	$ 0.75		49	31	59	29	parts
6	Manual insertion of parts	No. of manually inserted parts	$ 1.90		41	19	16	13	parts
7	Quality testing	Testing hours	$35.00		1.2	1.0	1.2	0.9	testing-hours
8									
9	Direct material cost per unit				$400.50	$286.50	$385.00	$260.00	

If you want to use Excel to solve this problem, go to the Excel Lab at **www.prenhall.com/horngren/cost12e** and download the template for Problem 12-29.

Required

1. What is the current manufacturing cost per unit of P-81 and P-63?
2. Does the planned product-and-process redesign achieve the target unit cost for P-81 REV and P-63 REV?
3. Farnham makes one more push for the P-series to remain competitive: He finds that he can reduce the supervisory staff so that the assembly-management activity will now cost only $40 per hour. However, this would mean more-vigilant testing: 1.6 testing-hours per unit of P-81 REV and 0.95 testing-hours per unit of P-63 REV. Should Farnham reduce the supervisory staff? Will this change help EP achieve the target costs for P-81 REV and P-63 REV?

12-30 Target prices, target costs, value engineering, cost incurrence, locked-in costs, activity-based costing. Cutler Electronics makes a radio-cassette player, CE100, which has 80 components. Cutler sells 7,000 units each month for $70 each. The costs of manufacturing CE100 are $45 per unit, or $315,000 per month. Monthly manufacturing costs incurred are:

Direct material costs	$182,000
Direct manufacturing labor costs	28,000
Machining costs (fixed)	31,500
Testing costs	35,000
Rework costs	14,000
Ordering costs	3,360
Engineering costs (fixed)	21,140
Total manufacturing costs	$315,000

Cutler's management identifies the activity cost pools, the cost drivers for each activity, and the cost per unit of the cost driver for each overhead cost pool as follows:

Manufacturing Activity	Description of Activity	Cost Driver	Cost per Unit of Cost Driver
1. Machining costs	Machining components	Machine-hour capacity	$4.50 per machine-hour
2. Testing costs	Testing components and final product (Each unit of CE100 is tested individually.)	Testing-hours	$2 per testing-hour
3. Rework costs	Correcting and fixing errors and defects	Units of CE100 reworked	$20 per unit
4. Ordering costs	Ordering of components	Number of orders	$21 per order
5. Engineering costs	Designing and managing of products and processes	Engineering-hour capacity	$35 per engineering-hour

Cutler's management views direct material costs and direct manufacturing labor costs as variable with respect to the units of CE100 manufactured. Over a long-run horizon, each of the overhead costs described in the preceding table varies, as described, with the chosen cost drivers.

The following additional information describes the existing design:

a. Testing and inspection time per unit is 2.5 hours.
b. 10% of the CE100s manufactured are reworked.
c. Cutler places two orders with each component supplier each month. Each component is supplied by a different supplier.
d. It currently takes 1 hour to manufacture each unit of CE100.

In response to competitive pressures, Cutler must reduce its price to $62 per unit and its costs by $8 per unit. No additional sales are anticipated at this lower price. However, Cutler stands to lose significant sales if it does not reduce its price. Manufacturing has been asked to reduce its costs by $6 per unit. Improvements in manufacturing efficiency are expected to yield a net savings of $1.50 per radio-cassette player, but that is not enough. The chief engineer has proposed a new modular design that reduces the number of components to 50 and also simplifies testing. The newly designed radio-cassette player, called "New CE100" will replace CE100.

The expected effects of the new design are as follows:

a. Direct material cost for the New CE100 is expected to be lower by $2.20 per unit.
b. Direct manufacturing labor cost for the New CE100 is expected to be lower by $0.50 per unit.
c. Machining time required to manufacture the New CE100 is expected to be 20% less, but machine-hour capacity will not be reduced.
d. Time required for testing the New CE100 is expected to be lower by 20%.
e. Rework is expected to decline to 4% of New CE100s manufactured.
f. Engineering-hours capacity will remain the same.

Assume that the cost per unit of each cost driver for CE100 continues to apply to New CE100.

Required

1. Calculate Cutler's manufacturing cost per unit of New CE100.
2. Will the new design achieve the per-unit cost-reduction targets that have been set for the manufacturing costs of New CE100? Show your calculations.
3. The problem describes two strategies to reduce costs: (a) improving manufacturing efficiency and (b) modifying product design. Which strategy has more impact on Cutler's costs? Why? Explain briefly.

Excel Lab
www.prenhall.com/horngren/cost12e

12-31 Cost-plus pricing. Bryant Company specializes in assembling and tuning mass-produced musical instruments used by children learning music at the elementary-school level. Galliano's, a large distributor, has asked Bryant to bid on the assembly of 5,000 violins. Galliano's will supply all the necessary materials (violin parts and support materials). Don Bryant, owner of Bryant Company, assembles the following information:

	A	B	C
1	Assembly rate	4	violins per direct manufacturing labor hour
2	Variable direct manufacturing labor cost	$ 60	per direct manufacturing labor hour
3	Variable overhead cost	$ 20	per direct manufacturing labor hour
4	Fixed overhead cost	$ 50	per direct manufacturing labor hour
5	Incremental administrative costs	$10,000	

If you want to use Excel to solve this problem, go to the Excel Lab at **www.prenhall.com/horngren/cost12e** and download the template for Problem 12-31.

Required

1. Calculate the minimum price per violin that Bryant should bid for Galliano's order.
2. Galliano offers to pay full cost plus a maximum markup of 20%. Galliano's defines full cost as all variable costs plus fixed overhead plus incremental administrative costs. Calculate Bryant's bid price per violin using full cost plus the maximum markup allowed by Galliano's.
3. Further discussion with Galliano's reveals that the highest bid they will entertain is $33 per violin. What factors should Bryant consider in making a decision about whether to put in a bid at that price?

Excel Lab
www.prenhall.com/horngren/cost12e

12-32 Cost-plus, time and materials. Mazzoli Brothers is an auto repair shop. Mazzoli's cost accounting system tracks two cost categories: direct labor (working on the cars) and direct materials (parts). Mazzoli uses a time-and-materials pricing system, with direct labor marked up 100% and direct materials marked up 50% to recover indirect costs of support staff, support materials, and shared machines and tools, and to earn a profit.

Johanna White brings her car to the shop. The head mechanic, Luke Bariess, concludes her car's problem is with the clutch plate. He considers two options: replace the clutch plate or repair it. The cost information available to Bariess follows:

	A	B	C	D
1		Labor		Materials
2	Repair option	3.5	hours	$ 40
3	Replace option	1.5	hours	$200
4	Markup	100%		50%
5				
6	Labor rate	$30	per labor-hour	

If you want to use Excel to solve this problem, go to the Excel Lab at **www.prenhall.com/horngren/cost12e** and download the template for Problem 12-32.

Required

1. Why might Mazzoli use different markup rates for direct materials and for direct labor?
2. If Bariess presents White with the replace or repair options, what price would he quote for each?
3. If the two options were equally safe and effective for the three years that White intends to use the car before junking it, which option would she choose?
4. If Bariess's objective is to maximize profits, which option would Bariess recommend to White? Is this the option chosen by White in requirement 3? Comment on your answers in requirements 3 and 4.

12-33 Cost-plus and market-based pricing. California Temps, a large labor contractor, supplies contract labor to building-construction companies. For 2007, California Temps has budgeted to supply 80,000 hours of contract labor. Its variable costs are $12 per hour, and its fixed costs are $240,000. Roger Mason, the general manager, has proposed a cost-plus approach for pricing labor at full cost plus 20%.

PH Grade Assist

Required

1. Calculate the price per hour that California Temps should charge based on Mason's proposal.
2. The marketing manager supplies the following information on demand levels at different prices:

Price per Hour	Demand (Hours)
$16	120,000
17	100,000
18	80,000
19	70,000
20	60,000

   California Temps can meet any of these demand levels. Fixed costs will remain unchanged for all the demand levels. On the basis of this additional information, calculate the price per hour that California Temps should charge to maximize operating income.
3. Comment on your answers to requirements 1 and 2. Why are they the same or different?

12-34 Cost-plus and market-based pricing. (CMA, adapted) Best Test Laboratories evaluates the reaction of materials to extreme increases in temperature. Much of the company's early growth was attributable to government contracts. Recent growth has come from diversification and expansion into commercial markets. Environmental testing at Best Test now includes:

Heat testing	(HTT)	Arctic-condition testing	(ACT)
Air-turbulence testing	(ATT)	Aquatic testing	(AQT)
Stress testing	(SST)		

Currently, all of the budgeted operating costs are collected in a single overhead pool. All of the estimated testing-hours are also collected in a single pool. One rate per test-hour is used for all five types of testing. This hourly rate is marked up by 45% to recover administrative costs and taxes, and to earn a profit.

Rick Shaw, Best Test's controller, believes that there is enough variation in the test procedures and cost structure to establish separate costing rates and billing rates at a 45% mark up. He also believes that the inflexible rate structure currently being used is inadequate in today's competitive environment. After analyzing the following data, he has recommended new rates for Best Test's upcoming fiscal year.

The budgeted total test-laboratory costs for the coming year are:

Test pool labor (10 employees)	$ 420,000
Supervision	72,000
Equipment depreciation	178,460
Heat	170,000
Electricity	124,000
Water	74,000
Setup	58,000
Indirect materials	104,000
Operating supplies	62,000
Total test-lab costs	$1,262,460
Total estimated test-hours	106,000

Shaw has determined the resource usage by test type in the following table:

	HTT	ATT	SST	ACT	AQT
Test pool labor employees	3	2	2	1	2
Supervision	40%	15%	15%	15%	15%
Depreciation	$48,230	$22,000	$39,230	$32,000	$37,000
Heat	50%	5%	5%	30%	10%
Electricity	30%	10%	10%	40%	10%
Water	—	—	20%	20%	60%
Setup	20%	15%	30%	15%	20%
Indirect materials	15%	15%	30%	20%	20%
Operating supplies	10%	10%	25%	20%	35%
Test-hours	29,680	12,720	27,560	22,260	13,780
Competitors' hourly billing rates	$17.50	$19.00	$15.50	$16.00	$20.00

Required

1. Compute the single pool hourly cost and hourly billing rate for Best Test Laboratories.
2. Compute the five separate hourly billing rates for Best Test Laboratories.
3. Discuss what effect the new cost-plus method will have on the pricing structure for each of the five test types. Given the competitors' hourly billing rates, how might Best Test modify its pricing?
4. In general, identify at least three other internal or external factors that influence pricing structure.

Excel Lab
www.prenhall.com/horngren/cost12e

12-35 Life-cycle costing. Consider Insight, Inc.'s development of the "General Ledger" package described in this chapter. Suppose Insight had the choice to develop either GL1 or GL2, both general-ledger packages that have the same functionality. GL1 is designed for a broad range of applications and is robustly implemented. GL2's design and implementation is "rough and ready," meaning the basic functionality is made available quickly and extra resources are spent in marketing and customizing the product for specialized customer segments. The budgeted amounts for GL1 and GL2 over a six-year product life cycle are:

	A	B	C	D	E
1		GL1		GL2	
2	**Years 1 & 2**				
3	R&D Costs	$240,000		$150,000	
4	Design Costs	160,000		75,000	
5					
6	**Years 3 to 6**	**Total**	**Variable Cost**	**Total**	**Variable Cost**
7		**Fixed Costs**	**Per Package**	**Fixed Costs**	**Per Package**
8	Production costs	$100,000	$25	$100,000	$25
9	Marketing costs	70,000	24	90,000	40
10	Distribution costs	50,000	16	80,000	25
11	Customer service costs	80,000	30	100,000	50

If you want to use Excel to solve this problem, go to the Excel Lab at **www.prenhall.com/horngren/cost12e** and download the template for Problem 12-35.

Required

1. Suppose that at a selling price of $480, Insight's marketing team forecasts total life-cycle sales of 4,000 units for either GL1 or GL2. Ignoring the time value of money, what would the predicted total life-cycle costs and life-cycle operating incomes be for GL1 and GL2? Which product should Insight choose? Explain.
2. How do GL1 and GL2 differ in their cost structures (the percentage of total costs in each cost category)? Which product would Insight view as more risky? Explain.
3. Jori Yellin is division manager for financial and accounting products at Insight. The General Ledger is one of her division's products. If Yellin's performance evaluation and bonus are linked to division operating income and she is unlikely to be at Insight beyond years 1 and 2, which product (GL1 or GL2) is she likely to endorse?

12-36 Airline pricing, considerations other than cost in pricing. Air Americo is about to introduce a daily round-trip flight from New York to Los Angeles and is determining how it should price its round-trip tickets.

The market research group at Air Americo segments the market into business and pleasure travelers. It provides the following information on the effects of two different prices on the number of seats expected to be sold and the variable cost per ticket, including the commission paid to travel agents:

		Number of Seats Expected to Be Sold	
Price Charged	**Variable Cost per Ticket**	**Business**	**Pleasure**
$ 500	$ 80	200	100
2,000	180	190	20

Pleasure travelers start their travel during one week, spend at least one weekend at their destination, and return the following week or thereafter. Business travelers usually start and complete their travel within the same work week. They do not stay over weekends.

Assume that round-trip fuel costs are fixed costs of $24,000 and that fixed costs allocated to the round-trip flight for airplane-lease costs, ground services, and flight-crew salaries total $188,000.

Required

1. If you could charge different prices to business travelers and pleasure travelers, would you? Show your computations.
2. Explain the key factor (or factors) for your answer in requirement 1.
3. How might Air Americo implement price discrimination? That is, what plan could the airline formulate so that business travelers and pleasure travelers each pay the price desired by the airline?

12-37 Ethics and pricing. Baker, Inc., is preparing to submit a bid for a ball-bearings order. Greg Lazarus, controller of the Bearings Division of Baker, has asked John Decker, the cost analyst, to prepare the bid. To determine the amount of the bid, Baker's policy is to mark up the full costs of the order by 10%. Lazarus tells Decker that he is keen on winning the bid and that the bid amount he calculates should be competitive.

Decker prepares the following costs for the bid:

Direct materials		$40,000
Direct manufacturing labor		10,000
Overhead costs		
Design and parts administration	$4,000	
Production order	5,000	
Setup	5,500	
Materials handling	6,500	
General and administration	9,000	
Total overhead costs		30,000
Full product costs		$80,000

All direct costs and 30% of overhead costs are incremental costs of the order.

Lazarus reviews the numbers and says, "Your costs are way too high. You have allocated too many overhead costs to this order. You know our fixed overhead is not going to change if we win this order and manufacture the bearings. Rework your numbers. You have got to make the costs lower."

Decker verifies that his numbers are correct. He knows that Lazarus wants this order because the additional revenues from the order would lead to a big bonus for Lazarus and the senior division managers. Decker knows that if he does not come up with a lower bid, Lazarus will be very upset.

Required

1. Using Baker's pricing policy and based on Decker's estimates, calculate the total amount Baker should bid for the ball-bearings order.
2. Calculate the incremental costs of the ball-bearing order. Why do you think Baker uses full costs of the order rather than incremental costs in its bidding decisions?
3. Evaluate whether Lazarus' suggestion to Decker to use lower cost numbers is unethical. Would it be unethical for Decker to change his analysis so that a lower cost can be calculated? What steps should Decker take to resolve this situation?

Collaborative Learning Problem

12-38 Target prices, target costs, value engineering. Avery, Inc., manufactures component parts. One product, TX-40-1, has annual sales of 50,000 units. Avery sells TX-40-1 for $40.60 per unit. Avery has three direct-cost categories (direct materials, direct manufacturing labor, and direct machining) and three activity-based indirect-cost categories (setup, testing, and engineering). All R&D and design costs are included in the engineering cost category. There are no marketing, distribution, or customer-service costs. Over the long run, management views indirect costs as variable with respect to each of their cost drivers. Details of costs and cost drivers for TX-40-1 are shown in columns (3) to (6) in the table on page 454.

Excel Lab
www.prenhall.com/horngren/cost12e

Facing competitive pressures, Avery wants to reduce the price of TX-40-1 to $34.80 to maintain its current unit sales level. Avery's engineers, given the task of reducing the cost of TX-40-1, have proposed a modified product and process design. The new version of the original product is called TX-40-2. Details of costs and cost drivers for TX-40-2 are shown in columns (7) to (10) in the table on page 454.

If you want to use Excel to solve this problem, go to the Excel Lab at **www.prenhall.com/horngren/cost12e** and download the template for Problem 12-38.

Required

1. Fill in the gray cells in the Excel spreadsheet, and then calculate the full cost per unit for TX-40-1 using activity-based costing.
2. What is the markup percentage on the full cost per unit for TX-40-1?
3. What is the target cost per unit for TX-40-2 if Avery wants to maintain the same markup percentage on the full cost per unit as for TX-40-1?
4. Will the design of TX-40-2 achieve the target cost calculated in requirement 3? Explain.
5. What price will Avery charge for TX-40-2 if it uses the same markup percentage on the full cost per unit for TX-40-2 as it did for TX-40-1?

	A	B	C	D	E	F	G	H	I	J	K	L	M	N
1			TX-40-1						TX-40-2					
2					50,000	output units					50,000	output units		
3	**Cost Category**	**Cost Driver**	**Details of Cost Driver Quantities**				**Total Quantity of Cost Driver**	**Cost per Unit of Cost Driver**	**Details of Cost Driver Quantities**				**Total Quantity of Cost Driver**	**Cost per Unit of Cost Driver**
4	**(1)**	**(2)**	**(3)**		**(4)**		**(5)**	**(6)**	**(7)**		**(8)**		**(9)**	**(10)**
5	Direct materials	No. of kits	1	kit per output unit	50,000	output units		$ 17	1	kit per output unit	50,000	output units		$ 14
6	Direct manuf. labor (DML)	DML hours	0.25	DML hours per output unit	50,000	output units		$ 24	0.25	DML hours per output unit	50,000	output units		$ 21
7	Direct machining (fixed)	Machine-hours					50,000	$ 3					50,000	$ 3
8	Setup	Setup-hours	12	setup-hours per batch	100	batches		$ 25	6	setup-hours per batch	100	batches		$ 25
9	Testing	Testing-hours	2.5	testing-hours per output unit	50,000	output units		$ 2	2	testing-hours per output unit	50,000	output units		$ 2
10	Engineering	Engg. hours					1,700	$100					1,700	$100

Get Connected: Cost Accounting in the News

WWW

Go to www.prenhall.com/horngren/cost12e for additional online exercise(s) that explore issues affecting the accounting world today. These exercises offer you the opportunity to analyze and reflect on how cost accounting helps managers to make better decisions and handle the challenges of strategic planning and implementation.

CHAPTER 12 Video Case

GRAND CANYON RAILWAY: Pricing

Riders of the Grand Canyon Railway have a choice of three classes of service: Coach class, the Club Car, which includes bar service; and the Chief Car, which offers first-class service. Because capacity in each railcar is fixed, managers rely on a wide range of information to determine the best mix of prices to charge in filling seats. Peak-load pricing is practiced during the summer season when demand for travel approaches capacity.

The railway's cost structure is heavily weighted toward fixed costs, such as depreciation on railroad tracks, engines, physical facilities, and administrative salaries. Pricing must cover variable costs to make a contribution toward recouping these fixed costs. Costs are driven by a number of factors. Passenger-driven unit costs include food and beverages; trip-driven unit costs include fuel, engineers, and entertainment; and facility-sustaining costs include advertising and railroad-track costs.

Managers use monthly reports of future bookings and past travel patterns to estimate future operating income. They analyze data on pricing promotions to determine which ones are most profitable. Based on this information, managers recently reduced the discounts given to travelers. Although the number of passengers decreased by 12% in a recent year, profitability increased 67%.

QUESTIONS

1. What are the implications of the Grand Canyon Railway's cost structure?
2. Should managers try to fill empty seats in the Club and Chief cars on the day of departure? Explain briefly.
3. Explain why profitability increased even though the number of passengers decreased.

CHAPTER 13

STRATEGY, BALANCED SCORECARD, AND STRATEGIC PROFITABILITY ANALYSIS

LEARNING OBJECTIVES

1. **Recognize which of two generic strategies a company is using**
2. **Understand what comprises reengineering**
3. **Describe the four perspectives of the balanced scorecard**
4. **Analyze changes in operating income to evaluate strategy**
5. **Distinguish engineered costs from discretionary costs**
6. **Identify unused capacity and how to manage it**

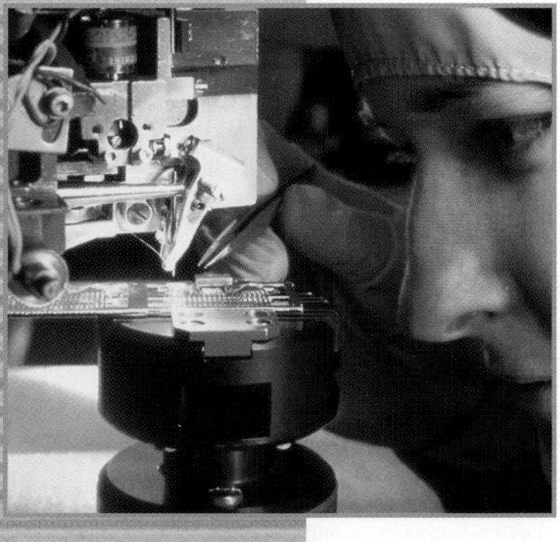

Olive Garden wants to know. So do Barnes and Noble, Pepsi, and L. L. Bean. Even the local car dealer and your transit authority have taken an interest. They all want to know how they are doing and how they score against customer-service measures they work hard to meet. As a consumer of their products and services, you're in the perfect position to provide feedback to help them improve future performance. Chipset, Inc., maker of linear integrated circuit devices (LICDs) used in modems and communication networks, wants to know how it scores as well. The company has recently implemented a balanced scorecard that includes measurements of customer experiences. Yet CEO Jim Brady realizes there is more work to be done and has assembled his senior staff to address the situation at the start of 2007.

Jim: Thank you all for coming today. We've just completed a very successful year, in large part due to the commitment and hard work that you and your staff put in. We'll review last year's performance at our annual retreat at month's end. The goal today is to plan for that meeting. I've asked Sharon to take the lead in pulling together the data we may need.

Sharon Wilson (Chief Financial Officer): Thanks, Jim. You all know we embarked on two major strategic initiatives last year: quality improvement and reengineering our order-delivery process. Both these initiatives were intended to improve responsiveness to customers. We also implemented a balanced scorecard to see how well we are doing on the financial side, in our customers' opinions, in manufacturing, and in developing our people. I will distribute the latest scorecard before the retreat.

Stuart Nixon (VP, Manufacturing): I'm wondering if you plan to include all the performance targets our departments put together. I'd like to see how our actual performance compares with what we expected.

Sharon: Not only that, but with your help, I plan to include explanations of any differences.

Rosa Diaz (VP, Marketing): As part of our strategy of being a low-cost manufacturer, we reduced product prices and grew market share. Will the scorecard include an analysis of the data related to this strategy as well?

Sharon: Yes. In fact, we're testing some new software that performs an analysis of operating income from a strategic standpoint. We plan to plug in performance data from 2005 and 2006 to see how much of our income growth can be traced to our new strategy. I'll include a copy of the results in everybody's packets for the retreat.

Jim: Great. If there are more suggestions, let Sharon know by the end of the week. I want our annual retreat to be productive in addition to the usual fun, so let's be thinking about what improvements we need to make this year.

This chapter focuses on how management-accounting information helps Chipset and companies such as Subway, Pitney-Bowes, JetBlue, and Futura Industries to implement and evaluate their strategies. Strategy drives the operations of a company and guides managers' short-run and

In today's fast-changing business environment, the management accountant must have a clear understanding of where a company is headed and how all business functions of the value chain work together.

long-run decisions. We describe the balanced scorecard approach to implementing strategy and how to analyze operating income to evaluate strategy. We also show how management accounting information helps strategic initiatives, such as productivity improvement, reengineering, and downsizing.

What Is Strategy?

Strategy specifies how an organization matches its own capabilities with the opportunities in the marketplace to accomplish its objectives. In formulating its strategy, an organization must thoroughly understand its industry. Industry analysis focuses on five forces: (1) competitors, (2) potential entrants into the market, (3) equivalent products, (4) bargaining power of customers, and (5) bargaining power of input suppliers.[1] The collective effect of these forces shapes an organization's profit potential. In general, profit potential decreases with greater competition, stronger potential entrants, products that are similar, and more-demanding customers and suppliers. We illustrate these five forces for Chipset, Inc. Chipset produces a single specialized product, CX1. This standard, high-performance microchip can be used in multiple applications. Chipset designed CX1 with extensive input from customers.

1. **Competitors.** Chipset has many growth opportunities. Its CX1 model enjoys a reputation for superior features relative to competing products. However, severe competition exists with respect to price, timely delivery, and quality. Companies in the industry have high fixed costs, and therefore pressures persist to use capacity fully and to cut selling prices. Price reductions spur growth because LICDs can then be used in DSL lines for major corporations such as Earthlink and Verizon. Quality is essential because LICD failure disrupts the communication network.
2. **Potential entrants into the market.** The integrated-circuits industry does not attract potential new entrants because competition keeps profit margins small and new manufacturing facilities require a lot of capital. Companies that have been making LICDs are further down the learning curve, so they know how to lower costs. Existing companies, such as Chipset, also have the advantage of close relationships with customers and suppliers that have been built up over the years.
3. **Equivalent products.** Chipset employs a technology that allows its customers to use CX1 to best meet their needs. CX1 has a flexible design that is easily integrated into the end products, such as DSL networks, of Chipset's customers. This reduces the risk of equivalent products or new technologies replacing CX1 during the next few years. Such a risk decreases even more if Chipset continuously improves CX1's design and processes to reduce production costs and lower CX1's prices.
4. **Bargaining power of customers.** Customers such as Earthlink and Verizon have bargaining power because each buys large quantities of CX1. Customers can also obtain microchips from other suppliers. Therefore, signing contracts to deliver microchips is important to Chipset. Customers recognize these circumstances, so they negotiate hard with Chipset to keep prices down.
5. **Bargaining power of input suppliers.** To deliver a superior product, Chipset purchases high-quality materials, such as silicon wafers, pins for connectivity, and plastic or ceramic packaging from its suppliers and employs skilled engineers, technicians, and manufacturing labor. Materials suppliers and employees have some bargaining power to demand higher prices and wages.

1
Recognize which of two generic strategies a company is using
. . . product differentiation or cost leadership

In summary, strong competition and the bargaining powers of customers and suppliers put significant pressure on Chipset's selling prices. To respond to these challenges, Chipset must choose one of two basic strategies: *differentiating its product* or *achieving cost leadership*.

[1]M. Porter, *Competitive Strategy* (New York: Free Press, 1980); M. Porter, *Competitive Advantage* (New York: Free Press, 1985); and M. Porter, "What Is Strategy?" *Harvard Business Review* (November–December 1996): 61–78.

Product differentiation is an organization's ability to offer products or services perceived by its customers to be superior and unique relative to the products or services of its competitors. Hewlett-Packard has successfully differentiated its products in the electronics industry, as have Pfizer in the pharmaceutical industry and Coca-Cola in the soft drink industry. These companies have achieved differentiation through innovative product R&D, careful development and promotion of their brands, and the rapid push of products to market. Differentiation increases brand loyalty and the willingness of customers to pay higher prices.

Cost leadership is an organization's ability to achieve lower costs relative to competitors through productivity and efficiency improvements, elimination of waste, and tight cost control. Cost leaders in their respective industries include Home Depot and Lowe's (building products), Texas Instruments (consumer electronics), and Emerson Electric (electric motors). These companies all provide products and services that are similar to—not differentiated from—those of their competitors, but they are provided at a lower cost to the customer. Lower selling prices, rather than unique products or services, provide a competitive advantage for these cost leaders.

When the only computers were mainframes, IBM was able to differentiate its product through superior service. When the PC was introduced, selling price to the end user (and therefore, cost leadership) became much more important as the product changed to one with many more potential customers (both businesses and individuals).

What strategy should Chipset follow? CX1 is already somewhat differentiated from competing products. Differentiating CX1 further will be costly, but Chipset may be able to charge a higher price. Conversely, reducing the cost of CX1 will allow the company to reduce price and spur growth. The CX1 technology allows Chipset's customers to achieve different performance levels by simply altering the number of CX1 units in their products. The existing technology and design provide a more cost-effective solution than designing new customized microchips for different applications. Customers want Chipset to keep the current design of CX1 but lower its price. Chipset's current engineering staff is more skilled at making product and process improvements than at creatively designing brand-new products and technologies. Chipset concludes that it should follow a cost-leadership strategy. Successful cost leadership also is expected to increase Chipset's market share and help the company grow. Chipset's challenge is to effectively implement its cost-leadership strategy.

Strategy Implementation and the Balanced Scorecard

Management accountants design reports to help managers track progress in implementing strategy. Many organizations, such as Allstate Insurance, Bank of Montreal, BP, and Dow Chemical, have introduced a *balanced scorecard* approach to manage the implementation of their strategies.

The Balanced Scorecard

The **balanced scorecard** translates an organization's mission and strategy into a set of performance measures that provides the framework for implementing its strategy.[2] The balanced scorecard does not focus solely on achieving financial objectives. It also highlights the nonfinancial objectives that an organization must achieve to meet its financial objectives. The scorecard measures an organization's performance from four perspectives: (1) financial, (2) customer, (3) internal business processes, and (4) learning and growth. A company's strategy influences the measures it uses to track performance in each of these perspectives.

Why is this tool called a balanced scorecard? Because it balances the use of financial and nonfinancial performance measures to evaluate short-run and long-run performance in a single report. The balanced scorecard reduces managers' emphasis on short-run financial performance, such as quarterly earnings. That's because the key strategic nonfinancial and operational indicators, such as product quality and customer satisfaction, measure changes that a company is making for the long run. The financial benefits of these long-run changes may not appear immediately in short-run earnings; however, given the company's strategy, strong improvement in nonfinancial measures usually indicates the creation of future eco-

Performance measures in the balanced scorecard must be closely linked with the company's strategy. When the measures are linked (assuming a sound strategy), the company is able to focus on what it needs to do to be successful.

[2]See R. S. Kaplan and D. P. Norton, *The Balanced Scorecard* (Boston: Harvard Business School Press, 1996); R. S. Kaplan and D. P. Norton, *The Strategy-Focused Organization: How Balanced Scorecard Companies Thrive in the New Business Environment* (Boston: Harvard Business School Press, 2001); and R. S. Kaplan and D. P. Norton, *Strategy Maps: Converting Intangible Assets into Tangible Outcomes* (Boston: Harvard Business School Press, 2004).

nomic value. For example, an increase in customer satisfaction, as measured by customer surveys and repeat purchases, signals a strong likelihood of higher sales and income in the future. By balancing the mix of financial and nonfinancial measures, the balanced scorecard broadens management's attention to short-run *and* long-run performance. Never lose sight of the key point. In for-profit companies, the goal of the balanced scorecard is to improve a company's overall financial performance. Nonfinancial measures simply serve as leading indicators for the hard-to-measure long-run financial goals.

We illustrate the four perspectives of the balanced scorecard using the Chipset example. The measures Chipset's managers choose for each perspective relate to the action plans for furthering Chipset's cost leadership strategy: *improve quality* and *reengineer processes*. As a result of these actions, Chipset expects to reduce costs and downsize, eliminating excess capacity. However, Chipset's management team does not want to cut personnel to the extent that it would adversely affect employee morale and hinder future growth.

2

Understand what comprises reengineering

. . . redesigning business processes to improve performance by reducing cost and improving quality

Quality Improvement and Reengineering at Chipset

To improve product quality—that is, reduce defect rates and improve yields in its manufacturing process—Chipset must maintain process parameters within tight ranges. To achieve this goal, Chipset needs real-time data about manufacturing-process parameters, such as temperature and pressure, and more-effective process-control methods. Chipset must also train its workers in quality-management techniques to help them identify the causes of defects and ways to prevent them. Following this training, Chipset needs to empower its workers to use their own initiative to make decisions and take actions that will improve quality.

Real-time data means instantaneous and continuous data about process parameters.

A second element of Chipset's strategy is reengineering its order-delivery process. Some of Chipset's customers have complained about the length of time that elapses between ordering products and their delivery. **Reengineering** is the fundamental rethinking and redesign of business processes to achieve improvements in critical measures of performance, such as cost, quality, service, speed, and customer satisfaction.[3] To illustrate reengineering, consider the order-delivery system at Chipset in 2005. When Chipset received an order from a customer, a copy was sent to manufacturing, where a production scheduler began planning the manufacturing of the ordered products. Frequently, a considerable amount of time passed before production began on the ordered product. After manufacturing was complete, CX1 chips moved to the Shipping Department, which matched the quantities of CX1 to be shipped against customer orders. Often, completed CX1 chips stayed in inventory until a truck became available for shipment. If the quantity to be shipped was less than the number of chips requested by the customer, a special shipment was made for the balance of the chips. Shipping documents moved to the Billing Department for issuing invoices. Special staff in the Accounting Department followed up with customers for payments.

Reengineering is closely related to value engineering (Chapter 12, p. 426). Reengineering focuses on redesigning business processes to improve performance and satisfy customers. Value engineering relies on product design modifications, changes in material specifications, and the like to improve performance and satisfy customers.

The many transfers of CX1 chips and/or information about them across departments (sales, manufacturing, shipping, billing, and accounting) to satisfy a customer order slowed down the process and created delays. Furthermore, no single individual was responsible for fulfilling each customer order. A cross-functional team from the various departments has reengineered the order-delivery process for 2006. The goals were to make the entire organization more customer-focused and to reduce delays by eliminating the number of interdepartment transfers. Under the new system, a customer-relationship manager is responsible for each customer and negotiates long-term contracts specifying quantities and prices. The customer-relationship manager works closely with the customer and with manufacturing to specify delivery schedules for CX1 one month in advance of shipment. The schedule of customer orders is sent electronically to manufacturing. Completed chips are shipped directly from the manufacturing plant to customer sites. Each shipment automatically triggers an invoice that is sent electronically to the customer. Customers transfer funds electronically to Chipset's bank.

Successful reengineering projects involve entire functional areas within the company. The gains arise from integration of effort and elimination of unnecessary steps and waiting time.

The experiences of many companies, such as AT&T, Banca di America e di Italia, Cigna Insurance, Cisco, Pepsi, and Siemens Nixdorf, indicate that the benefits from reengineer-

[3]See M. Hammer and J. Champy, *Reengineering the Corporation: A Manifesto for Business Revolution* (New York: Harper, 1993); E. Ruhli, C. Treichler, and S. Schmidt, "From Business Reengineering to Management Reengineering—A European Study," *Management International Review* (1995): 361–371; and K. Sandberg, "Reengineering Tries a Comeback—This Time for Growth, Not Just for Cost Savings," *Harvard Management Update* (November 2001).

ing are most significant when it cuts across functional lines to focus on an entire business process (as in the Chipset example). Reengineering only the shipping or invoicing activity at Chipset rather than the entire order-delivery process would not be particularly beneficial. Successful reengineering efforts involve changing roles and responsibilities, eliminating unnecessary activities and tasks, using information technology, and developing employee skills. Chipset's balanced scorecard for 2006 tracks Chipset's progress in reengineering its order-delivery process from both the nonfinancial and financial perspectives.

Four Perspectives of the Balanced Scorecard

3 **Describe the four perspectives of the balanced scorecard**
... financial, customer, internal business process, learning and growth

Exhibit 13-1 presents Chipset's balanced scorecard. It highlights the four perspectives of performance: financial, customer, internal business process, and learning and growth. At the beginning of 2006, the company's managers specify the objectives, measures, initiatives (necessary actions to achieve the objectives) and target performance (the first four columns of Exhibit 13-1).

Competitor benchmarks provide the basis for target performance levels for financial and nonfinancial measures. These benchmarks indicate the performance levels necessary to meet customer needs, compete effectively, and achieve financial goals. Chipset wants to use the balanced scorecard targets to drive the organization to higher levels of performance. Managers therefore set targets to achieve a level of performance distinctly better than competitors. Chipset's managers complete the fifth column, reporting actual performance at the end of 2006. This column shows how well Chipset performed relative to target performance.

In setting the target performance in a balanced scorecard, the company shouldn't just aim to be better than it has been in the past. It must strive to be among the "best in class" among its competitors.

1. **Financial perspective.** This perspective evaluates the profitability of the strategy. Because cost reduction relative to competitors' costs and sales growth are Chipset's key strategic initiatives, the financial perspective focuses on how much of operating income results from reducing costs and selling more units of CX1.
2. **Customer perspective.** This perspective identifies targeted customer and market segments and measures the company's success in these segments. To monitor its growth objectives, Chipset uses measures such as market share in the communication-networks segment, number of new customers, and customer-satisfaction ratings.
3. **Internal-business-process perspective.** This perspective focuses on internal operations that create value for customers that, in turn, furthers the financial perspective by increasing shareholder value. Chipset determines internal-business-process improvement targets after benchmarking against its main competitors. We discussed in Chapter 12 that there are different sources of competitor cost analysis: published financial statements, prevailing prices, customers, suppliers, former employees, industry experts, and financial analysts. Chipset also physically disassembles competitors' products to compare them with its own products and designs. This activity helps Chipset estimate competitors' costs. The internal-business-process perspective comprises three subprocesses:

- **Innovation process:** Creating products, services, and processes that will meet the needs of customers. Chipset aims to lower costs and promote growth by improving the technology of its manufacturing process.
- **Operations process:** Producing and delivering existing products and services that will meet the needs of customers. Chipset's strategic initiatives are (a) improving manufacturing quality, (b) reducing delivery time to customers, and (c) meeting specified delivery dates.
- **Postsales-service process:** Providing service and support to the customer after the sale of a product or service. Chipset monitors how quickly and accurately it is responding to customer-service requests.

4. **Learning-and-growth perspective.** This perspective identifies the capabilities the organization must excel at to achieve superior internal processes that create value for customers and shareholders. Chipset's learning and growth perspective emphasizes three capabilities: (1) employee capabilities, measured by the percentage of employees trained in process and quality management; (2) information-system capabilities, measured by the percentage of manufacturing processes with real-time feedback; and (3) motivation, measured by employee satisfaction and the percentage of manufacturing and sales employees (line employees) empowered to manage processes.

EXHIBIT 13-1 **The Balanced Scorecard for Chipset, Inc., for 2006**

Objectives	Measures	Initiatives	Target Performance	Actual Performance
Financial Perspective				
Increase shareholder value	Operating income from productivity gain	Manage costs and unused capacity	$2,000,000	$2,012,500
	Operating income from growth	Build strong customer relationships	$3,000,000	$3,420,000
	Revenue growth		6%	6.48%[a]
Customer Perspective				
Increase market share	Market share in communication-networks segment	Identify future needs of customers	6%	7%
Increase customer satisfaction	Number of new customers	Identify new target-customer segments	1	1[b]
	Customer-satisfaction ratings	Increase customer focus of sales organization	90% of customers give top two ratings	87% of customers give top two ratings
Internal-Business-Process Perspective				
Improve manufacturing quality and productivity	Yield	Identify root causes of problems and improve quality	78%	79.3%
Reduce delivery time to customers	Order-delivery time	Reengineer order-delivery process	30 days	30 days
Meet specified delivery dates	On-time delivery	Reengineer order-delivery process	92%	90%
Improve postsales service	Service response time	Improve customer-service process	Within 4 hours	Within 3 hours
Improve processes	Number of major improvements in manufacturing and business processes	Organize teams from manufacturing and sales to modify processes	5	5
Improve manufacturing capability	Percentage of processes with advanced controls	Organize R&D/manufacturing teams to implement advanced controls	75%	75%
Learning-and-Growth Perspective				
Align employee and organization goals	Employee-satisfaction ratings	Employee participation and suggestions program to build teamwork	80% of employees give top two ratings	88% of employees give top two ratings
Develop process skill	Percentage of employees trained in process and quality management	Employee training programs	90%	92%
Empower workforce	Percentage of line workers empowered to manage processes	Have supervisors act as coaches rather than decision makers	85%	90%
Enhance information-system capabilities	Percentage of manufacturing processes with real-time feedback	Improve online and offline data gathering	80%	80%

[a](Revenues in 2006 – Revenues in 2005) ÷ Revenues in 2005 = ($28,750,000 – $27,000,000) ÷ $27,000,000 = 6.48%.

[b]Number of customers increased from seven to eight in 2006.

The arrows in Exhibit 13-1 indicate the cause-and-effect linkages—how gains in the learning-and-growth perspective lead to improvements in internal business processes, which in turn lead to higher customer satisfaction and market share, and finally lead to superior financial performance. Note how the scorecard describes elements of Chipset's strategy implementation. Worker empowerment, training, and information systems improve employee satisfaction and lead to manufacturing and business-process improvements that in turn improve quality and reduce delivery time. The result is increased customer satisfaction and higher market share. These initiatives have been successful from a financial perspective. Chipset has earned significant operating income from its cost leadership strategy, and that strategy has also led to growth.

In Exhibit 13-1, note how each of the four perspectives focuses management on different elements of the business, with different measures, initiatives, and target performance. All four perspectives are linked to the company's strategy and are expected to positively affect financial performance over time.

Implementing a Balanced Scorecard

To successfully implement a balanced scorecard requires commitment and leadership from top management. At Chipset, the team building the balanced scorecard (headed by the vice president of strategic planning) conducted interviews with senior managers, probed executives about customers, competitors, and technological developments, and sought proposals for balanced scorecard objectives across the four perspectives. The team then met to discuss the responses and to build a prioritized list of objectives.

In a meeting with all senior managers, the team sought to achieve consensus on the scorecard objectives and to establish a cause-and-effect linkage across the chosen objectives. Senior management was then divided into four groups, with each group responsible for one of the perspectives. In addition, each group broadened the base of inputs by including representatives from the next-lower levels of management and key functional managers. The groups identified measures for each objective and the sources of information for each measure. The groups then met to finalize scorecard objectives, measures, targets, and the initiatives to achieve the targets.

The final balanced scorecard was communicated to all employees and will be used by top management to evaluate the performance of managers throughout the company. Too often, scorecards are seen by only a select group of managers. By limiting the scorecard's exposure, an organization loses the opportunity for widespread organization engagement and alignment. (See also the Focus on Values and Behaviors feature on p. 462.)

Employees quickly learn that the aspects of their performance that are measured are what's important. That is, the act of collecting and reporting various numbers that employees are responsible for can be a powerful motivator. The company needs to choose these performance measures with care and consider how they may affect employee behavior.

Aligning the Balanced Scorecard to Strategy

Different strategies call for different scorecards. Suppose Visilog, another company in the microchip industry, follows a product-differentiation strategy in designing custom chips for modems and communication networks. Visilog designs its balanced scorecard to fit its strategy. For example, in the financial perspective, Visilog evaluates how much of its operating income comes from charging premium prices for its products. In the customer perspective, Visilog measures the percentage of its revenues from new products and new customers. In the internal-business-process perspective, Visilog measures new product development time. In the learning-and-growth perspective, Visilog measures the development of advanced manufacturing capabilities to produce custom chips. Visilog does use some of the measures described in Chipset's balanced scorecard in Exhibit 13-1. For example, revenue growth, customer satisfaction ratings, order-delivery time, on-time delivery, percentage of frontline workers empowered to manage processes, and employee-satisfaction ratings are also important measures under the product-differentiation strategy. The point is to align the balanced scorecard with company strategy.[4] Exhibit 13-2 presents some common measures found on company scorecards in the service, retail, and manufacturing sectors.

[4]For simplicity, we have presented the balanced scorecard in the context of companies that have followed either a cost-leadership or a product-differentiation strategy. Of course, a company may have some products for which cost leadership is critical and other products for which product differentiation is important. The company will then develop separate scorecards to implement the different product strategies. In still other contexts, product differentiation may be of primary importance, but some cost leadership must also be achieved. The balanced scorecard measures would then be linked in a cause-and-effect way to this strategy.

FOCUS ON VALUES AND BEHAVIORS

THE NEW WAVE OF ACCOUNTING: CONTRIBUTING TO STRATEGY

As competition intensifies, organizations increasingly want management accountants involved in the design and implementation of strategy. To be effective members of the strategy team, management accountants must understand the economic environment of their industry as well as their organization's customers and competitors. In response to the changing business landscape, management accountants have begun to develop this understanding.

When implementing strategic measurement systems such as the balanced scorecard, it is important for management accountants to have a broad view. Management accountants are more likely to gain support from managers throughout the value chain if they are able to demonstrate a solid understanding of the external business environment as well as internal business issues such as human resources, operations, and distribution. Without this range of knowledge, it would be difficult for management accountants to work with managers to assemble a scorecard that represents the realities of the business.

By communicating the benefits of strategic measurement systems, management accountants gain credibility and support among managers and other employees whose performance will be held accountable against the metrics in the scorecard. Management accountants need to explain, openly and honestly, any costs and limitations of these measures. At no point should they oversell the measures. Rather, management accountants should educate and train managers and employees in how to use these strategic measurement systems to run their businesses better.

Strategic decisions also entail tough choices—shutting down a division, reallocating resources, or downsizing capacity. Many companies such as AT&T, Boeing, Kodak, General Motors, and Lucent Technologies have faced these complicated situations. Management accountants are responsible for presenting the data for these difficult decisions, which makes it crucial that they always present the correct financial details despite pressures they may face to slant the facts one way or another.

Features of a Good Balanced Scorecard

A well-designed balanced scorecard has several features:

1. It tells the story of a company's strategy, articulating a sequence of cause-and-effect relationships—the links among the various perspectives that describe how strategy will be implemented. Each measure in the scorecard is part of a cause-and-effect chain, from strategy formulation to financial outcomes.
2. The balanced scorecard helps to communicate the strategy to all members of the organization by translating the strategy into a coherent and linked set of understandable and measurable operational targets. Guided by the scorecard, managers and employees take actions and make decisions to achieve the company's strategy. To focus these actions, some companies, such as Cigna Property and Casualty Insurance, Johnson & Johnson, and Wells Fargo, have developed scorecards at the division and department levels.

EXHIBIT 13-2

Frequently Cited Balanced Scorecard Measures

Financial Perspective
Operating income, revenue growth, revenues from new products, gross margin percentage, cost reductions in key areas, economic value added[a] (EVA®), return on investment[a]

Customer Perspective
Market share, customer satisfaction, customer-retention percentage, time taken to fulfill customers' requests, number of customer complaints

Internal-Business-Process Perspective
Innovation Process: Operating capabilities, number of new products or services, new-product development times, and number of new patents
Operations Process: Yield, defect rates, time taken to deliver product to customers, percentage of on-time deliveries, average time taken to respond to orders, setup time, manufacturing downtime
Postsales Service Process: Time taken to replace or repair defective products, hours of customer training for using the product

Learning-and-Growth Perspective
Employee education and skill levels, employee-satisfaction ratings, employee turnover rates, information system availability, percentage of processes with advanced controls, percentage of employee suggestions implemented, percentage of compensation based on individual and team incentives

[a]These measures are described in Chapter 23.

3. In for-profit companies, the balanced scorecard must motivate managers to take actions that eventually result in improvements in financial performance. Managers sometimes tend to focus too much on innovation, quality, and customer satisfaction as ends in themselves. For example, Xerox spent heavily to increase customer satisfaction without a resulting financial payoff. The company later discovered that a measure of customer loyalty, not general customer satisfaction, was a leading indicator of future financial performance. A balanced scorecard emphasizes nonfinancial measures as part of a program to achieve future financial performance. When financial and nonfinancial performance measures are properly linked, most, if not all, of the nonfinancial measures serve as leading indicators of lagging future financial performance. In the Chipset example, improvements in nonfinancial factors have, in fact, already led to improvements in financial factors.

In contrast to for-profit companies, nonprofit organizations have primary objectives such as number of people served and other service goals.

4. The balanced scorecard limits the number of measures, identifying only the most critical ones. The purpose is to focus managers' attention on measures that most affect the implementation of strategy.

5. The balanced scorecard highlights less-than-optimal trade-offs that managers may make when they fail to consider operational and financial measures together. For example, a company whose strategy is innovation and product differentiation could achieve superior short-run financial performance by reducing spending on R&D. A good balanced scorecard would signal that the short-run financial performance might have been achieved by taking actions that hurt future financial performance because a leading indicator of that performance, R&D spending and R&D output, has declined.

Are you surprised by the limited number of performance measures in a balanced scorecard? Well, individuals' limits on processing information and perceiving tradeoffs among various measures translate into the idea that "fewer is better." That is, management needs to specify only the critical measures so that employees focus their efforts on improving items that will make a difference in achieving the company's strategic goals.

Pitfalls in Implementing a Balanced Scorecard

Pitfalls to avoid in implementing a balanced scorecard include the following:

1. Managers should not assume the cause-and-effect linkages are precise. They are merely hypotheses. Over time, a company must gather evidence of the strength and timing of the linkages among the nonfinancial and financial measures. With experience, organizations should alter their scorecards to include those nonfinancial objectives and measures that are the best leading indicators of financial performance (a lagging indicator). Understanding that the scorecard evolves over time helps managers to avoid unproductively trying to design the "perfect" scorecard at the outset.

Managers should expect a company's balanced scorecard to evolve over time as better measures are found and the linkages between processes and profits are better understood. As the business environment and strategy change over time, the items in the scorecard also will need to change.

2. Managers should not seek improvements across all of the measures all of the time. Trade-offs may need to be made across various strategic goals. For example, strive for quality and on-time performance but not beyond a point at which further improvement in these objectives may be inconsistent with long-run profit maximization.

For more discussion on how companies use the balanced scorecard to compete based on quality and time, see Chapter 19.

3. Managers should not use only objective measures in the balanced scorecard. Chipset's balanced scorecard includes both objective measures (such as operating income from cost leadership, market share, and manufacturing yield) and subjective measures (such as customer- and employee-satisfaction ratings). When using subjective measures, though, management must be careful that the benefits of this potentially rich information are not lost by using measures that are inaccurate or that can be easily manipulated.

4. Managers should not fail to consider both costs and benefits of initiatives such as spending on information technology and R&D before including these objectives in the balanced scorecard. Otherwise, managers may focus on measures that will not result in overall long-run financial benefits.

5. Managers should not ignore nonfinancial measures when evaluating managers and other employees. Managers tend to focus on what their performance is measured by. Excluding nonfinancial measures when evaluating performance will reduce the significance and importance that managers give to nonfinancial measures. The Global Surveys of Company Practice feature (see p. 464) indicates that companies implementing the balanced scorecard assign weights to nonfinancial performance measures when evaluating management performance. However, they still assign more than 50% weight to financial results.

GLOBAL SURVEYS OF COMPANY PRACTICE

Widening the Performance-Measurement Lens Using the Balanced Scorecard

A recent survey of 100 large U.S. companies indicates that 60% use some variation of the balanced scorecard.[a] Frequently, scorecards are used by segments of an organization rather than the entire organization. Moreover, many companies use modifications of the full balanced scorecards, which are more accurately described as partial balanced scorecards. Of these adopters, more than 80% are either using or planning to use the scorecard or variations of it for incentive compensation purposes.

As the following table shows, companies using the scorecard cite the broadening of the performance measures as the most important reason for adopting it.

Reason	Percentage Citing as Highly Important
Combines operational and financial measures	88%
Minimizes reliance on a single measure	67%
Shows if improvement in one area adversely affects another area	35%

Surveys also indicate that the balanced scorecard helps in designing performance measures that communicate strategy and in identifying drivers of key financial performance measures.[b] Despite the broadening of performance measures, companies continue to assign more weight to financial results in performance evaluation.

Performance-Measure Category	Average Relative Weight
Financial perspective	55%
Customer perspective	19%
Internal-business-process perspective	12%
Learning-and-growth perspective	14%

The balanced scorecard concept continues to spread across the globe, but, to date, scorecards have not been implemented widely outside the United States. A survey of leading German, Swiss, and Austrian companies found only 26% of companies had adopted balanced scorecards, while another 13% were just beginning implementation.[c] Respondents implementing comprehensive balanced scorecards identified primarily strategic, not financial, benefits to adoption (ranked by response frequency):

- Improving alignment of strategic objectives with actions
- Clarifying and communicating strategy
- Developing a consistent system of objectives in the company
- Giving stronger consideration to nonfinancial drivers of performance

Despite the wide range of scorecard-related benefits, surveys also indicate some problems in implementing the balanced scorecard. Among American companies, strategic challenges include (1) difficulty in evaluating the relative importance of different measures, (2) problems in measuring and quantifying important qualitative data, (3) lack of clarity resulting from a large number of measures, and (4) time and expense necessary for designing and maintaining the scorecard. Additionally, some companies in Hong Kong noted that implementation was expensive and time-intensive.[d] These companies also noted that they faced resistance from staff and middle management, and that existing operations and IT systems were not equipped for implementation.

Despite these challenges, surveys indicate that executives continue to find the balanced scorecard effective and useful. In fact, an increasing number of companies in Scandinavia,[e] Finland,[f] Portugal,[g] and Singapore,[h] are implementing the balanced scorecard.

[a] Towers Perrin, "CompScan Report."
[b] M. Frigo, "2001 CMG Survey"
[c] S. Speckbacher, J. Bischof, and T. Pfeiffer, "A Descriptive Analysis."
[d] "Hong Kong."
[e] C. Ax, and T. Bjornenak, "The Building and Diffusion."
[f] T. Malmi, "Balanced Scorecard in."
[g] L. Rodrigues, and G. Sousa, "The Use of the Balanced Scorecard."
[h] A. Chia, and H. Hoon, "Adoption and Creating."
Full citations are in Appendix A at the end of the book.

Evaluating the Success of Strategy and Implementation

To evaluate how successful Chipset's strategy and its implementation have been, its management compares the target- and actual-performance columns in the balanced scorecard (Exhibit 13-1). Chipset met most targets set on the basis of competitor benchmarks. Chipset will continue to seek improvements on the targets it did not achieve, but meeting most targets suggests that the strategic initiatives that Chipset identified and measured for learning and growth resulted in improvements in internal business processes, customer measures, and financial performance.

How would Chipset know if it had problems in implementation? If it did not meet its targets on the two perspectives that are more internally focused: learning and growth and internal business processes.

What if Chipset performed well on learning and growth and internal business processes, but customer measures and financial performance in this year and in the next few years did not improve? Chipset's managers would then conclude that Chipset did a good job of implementation (the various internal nonfinancial measures it targeted improved) but that its strategy was faulty (there was no effect on customers or on long-run financial performance and value creation). Management failed to identify the correct causal links. It implemented the wrong strategy well! Management would then reevaluate the strategy and the factors that drive it.

Now what if Chipset performed well on its various nonfinancial measures and operating income over this year and the next few years also increased? Chipset's managers might be tempted to declare the success of these strategies from the increase in operating income. Unfortunately, management still would be unable to conclude with any confidence that Chipset did a good job of formulating and implementing its strategy. Why? Because operating income can increase simply because entire markets are expanding, not because a company's strategy has been successful. Also, changes in operating income might occur because of factors outside the strategy. For example, a company such as Chipset that has chosen a cost-leadership strategy may find that its operating-income increase instead resulted incidentally from, say, some degree of product differentiation. *Managers and management accountants need to evaluate the success of a strategy by linking the sources of operating-income increases to the strategy.*

For Chipset to conclude that it was successful in implementing its strategy, it must demonstrate that improvements in its financial performance and operating income over time resulted from achieving targeted cost savings and growth in market share. Fortunately, the top two rows of Chipset's balanced scorecard in Exhibit 13-1 show that operating-income gains from productivity ($2,012,500) and growth ($3,420,000) exceeded the targets. The next section of this chapter describes how these numbers were calculated. To be sure that the strategy has been successful, Chipset's management would like to see similar gains in subsequent years.

Chipset's management accountants subdivide changes in operating income into components that can be identified with product differentiation, cost leadership, and growth. Why growth? Because successful cost leadership or product differentiation generally increases market share and helps a company to grow. Subdividing the change in operating income to evaluate the success of a strategy is conceptually similar to the variance analysis discussed in Chapters 7 and 8. One difference, however, is that management accountants compare actual operating performance over two different periods, not actual to budgeted numbers in the same time period as in variance analysis.

Strategic Analysis of Operating Income

4 **Analyze changes in operating income to evaluate strategy**
. . . growth, price recovery, and productivity

The following illustration explains how to subdivide the change in operating income from one period to *any* future period. The individual components describe company performance with regard to cost leadership, product differentiation, and growth.[5] We illus-

[5]For other details, see R. Banker, S. Datar, and R. Kaplan, "Productivity Measurement and Management Accounting," *Journal of Accounting, Auditing and Finance* (1989): 528–554; and A. Hayzen and J. Reeve, "Examining the Relationships in Productivity Accounting," *Management Accounting Quarterly* (2000).

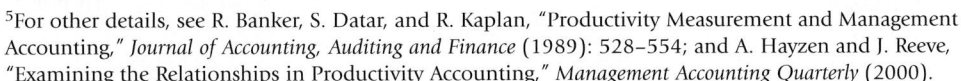

This section is difficult but important. This strategic analysis is an example of how the management accountant can add significant insight and value for the management team in assessing the effectiveness of implementing their strategy.

trate the analysis using data from 2005 and 2006 because Chipset implemented key elements of its strategy in late 2005 and expects the financial consequences of these strategies to begin to appear in 2006. Suppose the financial consequences of these strategies had been expected to affect operating income in, say, 2007 only. Then we could just as easily have compared 2005 to 2007. If necessary, we could also have compared 2005 to 2006 and 2007 taken together.

Chipset's data for 2005 and 2006 follow.

	2005	2006
1. Units of CX1 produced and sold	1,000,000	1,150,000
2. Selling price	$27	$25
3. Direct materials (square centimeters of silicon wafers)	3,000,000	2,900,000
4. Direct material cost per square centimeter	$1.40	$1.50
5. Manufacturing processing capacity (in square centimeters of silicon wafer)	3,750,000	3,500,000
6. Conversion costs (all manufacturing costs other than direct material costs)	$16,050,000	$15,225,000
7. Conversion cost per unit of capacity (Row 6 ÷ Row 5)	$4.28	$4.35
8. R&D employees	40	39
9. R&D costs	$4,000,000	$3,900,000
10. R&D cost per employee (Row 9 ÷ Row 8)	$100,000	$100,000

Chipset provides the following additional information.

1. Conversion costs for each year depend on production capacity defined in terms of the quantity of square centimeters of silicon wafers that can be processed. Such costs do not vary with the actual quantity of silicon wafers processed. (Because direct manufacturing labor costs are small and are tied to capacity, Chipset includes these costs with manufacturing overhead costs as part of conversion costs rather than as a separate cost category.) To reduce conversion costs, management would have to reduce capacity by selling some of the manufacturing equipment and by reassigning manufacturing personnel to other tasks or laying them off.

2. At the start of each year, management uses its discretion to determine the amount of R&D work to be done. This work is independent of the actual quantity of CX1 produced and sold or silicon wafers processed.

3. Chipset's marketing and sales costs are small relative to the other costs. Chipset has fewer than 10 customers, each purchasing roughly the same quantities of CX1. Because of the highly technical nature of the product, Chipset uses a cross-functional team for its marketing and sales activities. Engineers from R&D work closely with customers to understand their needs regarding upgrades of CX1 and to market CX1 to them. Once a contract to supply chips is signed, the customer-relationship manager located in the manufacturing area is responsible for ensuring that quality products are delivered at the time agreed on. This cross-functional approach ensures that, although marketing and sales costs are small, the entire Chipset organization remains focused on increasing customer satisfaction and market share. (The Problem for Self-Study at the end of this chapter describes a situation in which marketing, sales, and customer-service costs are significant.)

4. Chipset's asset structure is very similar in 2005 and 2006. Operating income for each year is as follows.

	2005	2006
Revenues ($27 per unit × 1,000,000 units; $25 per unit × 1,150,000 units)	$27,000,000	$28,750,000
Costs		
Direct material costs ($1.40/sq. cm. × 3,000,000 sq. cm.; $1.50/sq. cm. × 2,900,000 sq. cm.)	4,200,000	4,350,000
Conversion costs ($4.28/sq. cm. × 3,750,000 sq. cm.; $4.35/sq. cm. × 3,500,000 sq. cm.)	16,050,000	15,225,000
R&D costs ($100,000 × 40 employees; $100,000 × 39 employees)	4,000,000	3,900,000
Total costs	24,250,000	23,475,000
Operating income	$ 2,750,000	$ 5,275,000
Change in operating income	$2,525,000 F	

The goal of Chipset's managers is to evaluate how much of the $2,525,000 increase in operating income was caused by the successful implementation of the company's cost-leadership strategy. To do this, management accountants analyze three main factors: growth, price recovery, and productivity.

The **growth component** measures the change in operating income attributable solely to the change in the quantity of output sold between 2005 and 2006.

The **price-recovery component** measures the change in operating income attributable solely to changes in Chipset's prices of inputs and outputs between 2005 and 2006. The price-recovery component measures the change in output price compared with the changes in input prices. A company that has successfully pursued a strategy of product differentiation will be able to increase its output price faster than the increase in its input prices, boosting profit margins and operating income: It will show a large positive price-recovery component.

The **productivity component** measures the change in costs attributable to a change in the quantity of inputs used in 2006 relative to the quantity of inputs that would have been used in 2005 to produce the 2006 output. The productivity component measures the amount by which operating income increases by using inputs productively to lower costs. A company that has successfully pursued a strategy of cost leadership will be able to produce a given quantity of output with a smaller quantity of inputs: It will show a large positive productivity component. Given Chipset's strategy of cost leadership, we expect the increase in operating income to be attributable to the productivity and growth components, not to price recovery. We now examine these three components in detail.

The calculations here resemble those in Chapters 7 and 8. The growth component calculations resemble the sales-volume variance; the price-recovery component calculations resemble the price and spending variances; and the productivity component calculations resemble the efficiency variances.

Growth Component of Change in Operating Income

The growth component of the change in operating income measures the increase in revenues minus the increase in costs from selling more units of CX1 in 2006 (1,150,000 units) than in 2005 (1,000,000 units), *assuming nothing else has changed*. That is, the growth-component calculations use 2005 output prices, input prices, efficiencies, and capacity relationships.

Revenue effect of growth

$$\text{Revenue effect of growth} = \left(\begin{array}{c}\text{Actual units of}\\ \text{output sold}\\ \text{in 2006}\end{array} - \begin{array}{c}\text{Actual units of}\\ \text{output sold}\\ \text{in 2005}\end{array}\right) \times \begin{array}{c}\text{Selling}\\ \text{price}\\ \text{in 2005}\end{array}$$

$$= (1{,}150{,}000 \text{ units} - 1{,}000{,}000 \text{ units}) \times \$27 \text{ per unit}$$

$$= \$4{,}050{,}000 \text{ F}$$

This component is favorable (F) because the increase in output sold in 2006 increases operating income. Components that decrease operating income are unfavorable (U).

Note that Chipset uses the 2005 price of CX1 here and focuses only on the increase in units sold between 2005 and 2006. That's because the objective of the revenue effect of the growth component is to isolate the increase in revenues between 2005 and 2006 due solely to the change in the units sold, *assuming* the 2005 selling price continues into 2006.

Cost effect of growth The cost effect of growth measures how much costs would have changed in 2005 if Chipset had produced 1,150,000 units of CX1 instead of 1,000,000 units. To measure the cost effect of growth, Chipset's managers distinguish variable costs such as direct material costs from fixed costs such as conversion costs and R&D costs. That's because as units produced (and sold) increase, variable costs increase proportionately but fixed costs, generally, do not change.

$$\begin{array}{c}\text{Cost effect of}\\ \text{growth for}\\ \text{variable costs}\end{array} = \left(\begin{array}{c}\text{Units of input}\\ \text{required to}\\ \text{produce 2006}\\ \text{output in 2005}\end{array} - \begin{array}{c}\text{Actual units of}\\ \text{input used}\\ \text{to produce}\\ \text{2005 output}\end{array}\right) \times \begin{array}{c}\text{Input}\\ \text{price}\\ \text{in 2005}\end{array}$$

$$\begin{array}{c}\text{Cost effect of}\\ \text{growth for}\\ \text{direct materials}\end{array} = \left(3{,}000{,}000 \text{ sq. cm.} \times \frac{1{,}150{,}000 \text{ units}}{1{,}000{,}000 \text{ units}} - 3{,}000{,}000 \text{ sq. cm.}\right) \times \$1.40 \text{ per sq. cm.}$$

$$= (3{,}450{,}000 \text{ sq. cm.} - 3{,}000{,}000 \text{ sq. cm.}) \times \$1.40 \text{ per sq. cm.} = \$630{,}000 \text{ U}$$

$$\text{Cost effect of growth for fixed costs} = \left(\begin{array}{c}\text{Actual units of capacity in}\\ \text{2005 if adquate to produce}\\ \text{2006 output in 2005}\\ \text{OR}\\ \text{If 2005 capacity inadequate}\\ \text{to produce 2006 output in 2005,}\\ \text{units of capacity required}\\ \text{to produce 2006 output in 2005}\end{array} - \begin{array}{c}\text{Actual units}\\ \text{of capacity}\\ \text{in 2005}\end{array}\right) \times \begin{array}{c}\text{Price per}\\ \text{unit of}\\ \text{capacity}\\ \text{in 2005}\end{array}$$

$$\text{Cost effect of growth for conversion costs} = (3{,}750{,}000 \text{ sq. cm.} - 3{,}750{,}000 \text{ sq. cm.}) \times \$4.28 \text{ per sq. cm.} = \$0$$

Conversion costs are fixed costs at a given level of capacity. Chipset has manufacturing capacity to process 3,750,000 square centimeters of silicon wafers in 2005 at a cost of $16,050,000, or $4.28 per square centimeter (rows 5, 6, and 7 of data on p. 466). To produce 1,150,000 units of output in 2005, Chipset would have needed to process 3,450,000 square centimeters of direct materials. Chipset has adequate capacity to produce 1,150,000 units, so conversion costs would not change.

$$\text{Cost effect of growth for R \& D costs} = (40 \text{ employees} - 40 \text{ employees}) \times \$100{,}000 \text{ per employee} = \$0$$

R&D costs are fixed discretionary costs that would not have changed in 2005 if Chipset had produced and sold more units of CX1.

In summary, the net increase in operating income attributable to growth equals:

Revenue effect of growth		$4,050,000 F
Cost effect of growth		
Direct material costs	$630,000 U	
Conversion costs	0	
R&D costs	0	630,000 U
Change in operating income due to growth		$3,420,000 F

Price-Recovery Component of Change in Operating Income

Assuming that the 2005 relationship between inputs and outputs continued in 2006, the price-recovery component of the change in operating income measures solely the effect of price changes on revenues and costs to produce and sell the 1,150,000 units of CX1 in 2006.

Revenue effect of price recovery

$$\text{Revenue effect of price recovery} = \left(\begin{array}{c}\text{Selling price}\\ \text{in 2006}\end{array} - \begin{array}{c}\text{Selling price}\\ \text{in 2005}\end{array}\right) \times \begin{array}{c}\text{Actual units}\\ \text{of output}\\ \text{sold in 2006}\end{array}$$

$$= (\$25 \text{ per unit} - \$27 \text{ per unit}) \times 1{,}150{,}000 \text{ units}$$

$$= \$2{,}300{,}000 \text{ U}$$

Note that the calculation focuses on revenue changes caused by changes in the selling price of CX1 between 2005 and 2006.

Cost effect of price recovery Chipset's management accountants calculate the cost effects of price recovery separately for variable costs and for fixed costs, just as they did when calculating the cost effect of growth.

$$\text{Cost effect of price recovery for variable costs} = \left(\begin{array}{c}\text{Input price}\\ \text{in 2006}\end{array} - \begin{array}{c}\text{Input price}\\ \text{in 2005}\end{array}\right) \times \begin{array}{c}\text{Units of input}\\ \text{required to}\\ \text{produce 2006}\\ \text{output in 2005}\end{array}$$

$$\text{Cost effect of price recovery for direct materials} = (\$1.50 \text{ per sq. cm.} - \$1.40 \text{ per sq. cm.}) \times 3{,}450{,}000 \text{ sq. cm.} = \$345{,}000 \text{ U}$$

Recall that the direct materials of 3,450,000 square centimeters required to produce 2006 output in 2005 had already been calculated when computing the cost effect of growth (p. 467).

$$\text{Cost effect of price recovery for fixed costs} = \left(\begin{array}{c}\text{Price per}\\ \text{unit of}\\ \text{capacity}\\ \text{in 2006}\end{array} - \begin{array}{c}\text{Price per}\\ \text{unit of}\\ \text{capacity}\\ \text{in 2005}\end{array}\right) \times \begin{array}{c}\text{Actual units of capacity in}\\ \text{2005, if adequate to produce}\\ \text{2006 output in 2005}\\ \text{OR}\\ \text{If 2005 capacity inadequate to}\\ \text{produce 2006 output in 2005,}\\ \text{units of capacity required to}\\ \text{produce 2006 output in 2005}\end{array}$$

Cost effects of price recovery for fixed costs are:

Conversion costs: ($4.35 per sq. cm. – $4.28 per sq. cm.) × 3,750,000 sq. cm. = $262,500 U

R&D costs: ($100,000 per employee – $100,000 per employee) × 40 employees = $0

Recall that the units of capacity in these calculations equal the 2005 capacity because adequate capacity is available in 2005 to produce 2006 output—3,750,000 sq. cm. of conversion capacity and 40 employees of R&D capacity. The detailed analyses of capacities were presented when computing the cost effect of growth (p. 468).

In summary, the net decrease in operating income attributable to price recovery equals:

Revenue effect of price recovery		$2,300,000 U
Cost effect of price recovery		
Direct material costs	$345,000 U	
Conversion costs	262,500 U	
R&D costs	0	607,500 U
Change in operating income due to price recovery		$2,907,500 U

The price-recovery analysis indicates that, even as the prices of its inputs increased, the selling prices of CX1 decreased and Chipset could not pass on input-price increases to its customers.

Productivity Component of Change in Operating Income

The productivity component of the change in operating income uses 2006 input prices to measure how costs have decreased as a result of using fewer inputs, a better mix of inputs, and/or less capacity to produce 2006 output, compared with the inputs and capacity that would have been used in 2005.

The productivity-component calculations use 2006 prices and output. That's because the productivity component isolates the change in costs between 2005 and 2006 caused solely by the change in the quantities, mix, and/or capacities of inputs.[6]

$$\text{Cost effect of productivity for variable costs} = \left(\begin{array}{c}\text{Actual units of}\\ \text{input used}\\ \text{to produce}\\ \text{2006 output}\end{array} - \begin{array}{c}\text{Units of input}\\ \text{required to}\\ \text{produce 2006}\\ \text{output in 2005}\end{array}\right) \times \begin{array}{c}\text{Input}\\ \text{price}\\ \text{in 2006}\end{array}$$

[6]Note that the productivity-component calculation uses actual 2006 input prices, whereas its counterpart, the efficiency variance in Chapters 7 and 8, uses budgeted prices. (In effect, the budgeted prices correspond to 2005 prices). Year 2006 prices are used in the productivity calculation because Chipset wants its managers to choose input quantities to minimize costs in 2006 based on currently prevailing prices. If 2005 prices had been used in the productivity calculation, managers would choose input quantities based on irrelevant input prices that prevailed a year ago! Using budgeted prices in Chapters 7 and 8 does not pose a similar problem. That's because, unlike 2005 prices that describe what happened a year ago, budgeted prices represent prices that are expected to prevail in the current period. Moreover, budgeted prices can be changed, if necessary, to bring them in line with actual current-period prices.

Using the 2006 data given on page 466 and the calculation of units of input required to produce 2006 output in 2005 when discussing the cost effects of growth (p. 467),

$$\text{Cost effect of productivity for direct materials} = (2{,}900{,}000 \text{ sq. cm.} - 3{,}450{,}000 \text{ sq. cm.}) \times \$1.50 \text{ per sq. cm}$$

$$= 550{,}000 \text{ sq. cm.} \times \$1.50 \text{ per sq. cm.} = \$825{,}000 \text{ F}$$

Chipset's quality and yield improvements reduced the quantity of direct materials needed to produce output in 2006 relative to 2005.

$$\begin{array}{c}\text{Cost effect of}\\ \text{productivity for}\\ \text{fixed costs}\end{array} = \left(\begin{array}{c}\text{Actual units of}\\ \text{capacity}\\ \text{in 2006}\end{array} - \begin{array}{c}\text{Actual units of capacity in}\\ \text{2005, if adequate to produce}\\ \text{2006 output in 2005}\\ \text{OR}\\ \text{If 2005 capacity inadequate}\\ \text{to produce 2006 output in 2005,}\\ \text{units of capacity required to}\\ \text{produce 2006 output in 2005}\end{array}\right) \times \begin{array}{c}\text{Price per}\\ \text{unit of}\\ \text{capacity}\\ \text{in 2006}\end{array}$$

Using the 2006 data given on page 466, and the analyses of capacity required to produce 2006 output in 2005 when discussing the cost effect of growth (p. 468),

Cost effects of productivity for fixed costs are

Conversion costs: (3,500,000 sq. cm. – 3,750,000 sq. cm.) × \$4.35 per sq. cm. = \$1,087,500 F

R&D costs: (39 employees – 40 employees) × \$100,000 per employee = \$100,000 F

Note that productivity improvements do not occur automatically for fixed costs. When the company needs less capacity, the only way to save some of these costs is for management to reduce capacity (for example, in equipment/facilities and/or personnel).

Chipset's managers decreased manufacturing capacity in 2006 to 3,500,000 square centimeters. They did so by selling off old equipment and laying off workers. R&D capacity decreased because Chipset's managers did not replace an engineer who quit.

In summary, the net increase in operating income attributable to productivity equals

Cost effect of productivity	
Direct material costs	\$ 825,000 F
Conversion costs	1,087,500 F
R&D costs	100,000 F
Change in operating income due to productivity	\$2,012,500 F

The productivity component indicates that Chipset was able to increase operating income by improving quality and productivity, eliminating capacity, and reducing costs. The appendix to this chapter examines partial and total factor productivity changes between 2005 and 2006 and describes how the management accountant can obtain a deeper understanding of Chipset's cost-leadership strategy. Note that the productivity component focuses exclusively on costs, so there is no revenue effect for this component.

Exhibit 13-3 summarizes the growth, price-recovery, and productivity components of the changes in operating income. Exhibit 13-4 graphically presents the causes of the changes in operating income between 2005 and 2006. Generally, companies that have been successful at cost leadership will show favorable productivity and growth components. Companies that have successfully differentiated their products will show favorable price-recovery and growth components. In Chipset's case, consistent with its strategy and its implementation, productivity contributed \$2,012,500 to the increase in operating income, and growth contributed \$3,420,000. Operating income suffered because, even as input prices increased, the selling price of CX1 decreased. Had Chipset been able to differentiate its product and charge a higher price, the price-recovery effects might have been less unfavorable or perhaps even favorable. As a result, Chipset's managers plan to evaluate some modest changes in product features that might help differentiate CX1 somewhat from competing products.

EXHIBIT 13-3 **Strategic Analysis of Profitability**

	Income Statement Amounts in 2005 (1)	Revenue and Cost Effects of Growth Component in 2006 (2)	Revenue and Cost Effects of Price-Recovery Component in 2006 (3)	Cost Effect of Productivity Component in 2006 (4)	Income Statement Amounts in 2006 (5) = (1) + (2) + (3) + (4)
Revenues	$27,000,000	$4,050,000 F	$2,300,000 U	—	$28,750,000
Costs	24,250,000	630,000 U	607,500 U	$2,012,500 F	23,475,000
Operating income	$ 2,750,000	$3,420,000 F	$2,907,500 U	$2,012,500 F	$ 5,275,000
			$2,525,000 F		
			Change in operating income		

Further Analysis of Growth, Price-Recovery, and Productivity Components

As in all variance and profit analysis, Chipset's managers want to more closely analyze the change in operating income. In the Chipset example, growth might have been helped by an increase in industry market size. Therefore, at least part of the increase in operating income may be attributable to favorable economic conditions in the industry rather than to any successful implementation of strategy. Some of the growth might also have come as a result of a management decision at Chipset to take advantage of its productivity gains by decreasing selling price. In this case, the increase in operating income from cost leadership must include the productivity gain, any increase in operating income from productivity-related growth in market share, and any decrease in operating income from lowering prices.

The analysis described in this section gives management more information to evaluate the success of the organization's strategy and its implementation. For example, by analyzing the effect of the market growth rate in the industry, Chipset's managers can isolate the effect of what they have accomplished (with either cost leadership or product differentiation) versus what resulted from changes in the marketplace.

To illustrate these ideas, consider again the Chipset example and the following additional information.

- The market growth rate in the industry is 10% in 2006. Of the 150,000 (1,150,000 – 1,000,000) units of increased sales of CX1 between 2005 and 2006, 100,000 (0.10 × 1,000,000) units are due to an increase in industry market size (which Chipset should have benefited from regardless of its productivity gains), and the remaining 50,000 units are due to an increase in market share.
- During 2006, Chipset experienced a $1.35, or 5%, decline in the price of CX1 (0.05 × $27 = $1.35). Taking advantage of productivity gains, management reduced the price of CX1 by an additional $0.65, which led to the 50,000-unit increase in market share. [Recall that the total decrease in the price of CX1 is from $27 to $25, or $2 ($1.35 + $0.65).]

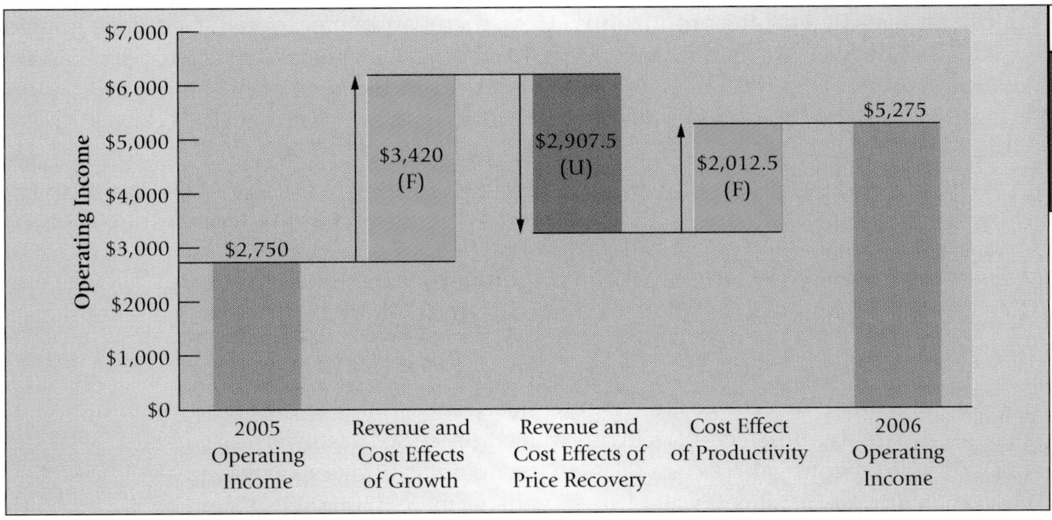

EXHIBIT 13-4 **Graphical Presentation of Strategic Analysis of Profitability (in thousands)**

The effect of the industry-market-size factor on operating income (rather than any specific strategic actions) is:

Change in operating income due to growth in industry market size

$$\$3{,}420{,}000 \text{ (Exhibit 13-3, column 2)} \times \frac{100{,}000 \text{ units}}{150{,}000 \text{ units}} \qquad \$2{,}280{,}000 \text{ F}$$

Lacking a differentiated product, Chipset experiences a $1.35 decline in output prices even while the prices of its inputs increase.

The effect of product differentiation on operating income is:

Change in operating income due to a decline in the selling price of CX1 (other than the strategic reduction in price included as part of the cost-leadership component) $1.35/unit × 1,150,000 units	$1,552,500 U
Change in prices of inputs (cost effect of price recovery)	607,500 U
Change in operating income due to product differentiation	$2,160,000 U

The effect of cost leadership on operating income is:

Productivity component	$2,012,500 F
Effect of strategic decision to reduce price ($0.65/unit × 1,150,000 units)	747,500 U
Growth in market share due to productivity improvement and strategic decision to reduce prices	
$\$3{,}420{,}000 \text{ (Exhibit 13-3, column 2)} \times \frac{50{,}000 \text{ units}}{150{,}000 \text{ units}}$	1,140,000 F
Change in operating income due to cost leadership	$2,405,000 F

A summary of the change in operating income between 2005 and 2006 follows.

Change due to industry market size	$2,280,000 F
Change due to product differentiation	2,160,000 U
Change due to cost leadership	2,405,000 F
Change in operating income	$2,525,000 F

Under different assumptions of how the change in selling price affects the quantity of CX1 sold, the analysis will attribute different amounts to the different strategies. The point to understand here is that, consistent with its cost-leadership strategy, the productivity gains of $2,012,500 Chipset made in 2006 were a big part of the increase in operating income in 2006. The Problem for Self-Study on page 476 describes the analysis of the growth, price-recovery, and productivity components for a company following a product-differentiation strategy. The Concepts in Action feature (p. 473) describes the problems of dot-com companies that emphasized growth and did not achieve cost leadership or product differentiation.

Downsizing and the Management of Capacity

As we saw in our discussion of the productivity component, fixed costs are tied to capacity. Unlike variable costs, fixed costs do not change automatically with changes in activity level (for example, fixed conversion costs do not change with changes in the quantity of silicon wafers started into production). How then can managers reduce capacity-based fixed costs? By measuring and managing unused capacity. **Unused capacity** is the amount of productive capacity available over and above the productive capacity employed to meet consumer demand in the current period. To understand unused capacity, it is necessary to distinguish *engineered costs* from *discretionary costs*.

5

Distinguish engineered costs

. . . a cause-and-effect relationship exists between output produced and costs incurred

from discretionary costs

no cause-and-effect relationship exists between output produced and costs incurred

Engineered costs result from a cause-and-effect relationship between the cost driver—output—and the (direct or indirect) resources used to produce that output. In the Chipset example, direct material costs are *direct engineered costs*. Conversion costs are an example of *indirect engineered costs*. Consider 2006. The output of 1,150,000 units of CX1 and the efficiency with which inputs are converted into outputs result in 2,900,000 square centimeters of silicon wafers being started into production. Manufacturing-conversion-cost resources used to produce 1,150,000 units of CX1 equal $12,615,000 ($4.35 per sq. cm. × 2,900,000 sq. cm.), assuming that the cost of resources used increases proportionately with the number of square centimeters of silicon wafers processed. Conversion costs are higher ($15,225,000) because these costs relate to the manufacturing capacity to process 3,500,000 square centimeters of silicon wafer ($4.35 per sq. cm. × 3,500,000 sq. cm. = $15,225,000).

CONCEPTS IN ACTION

Growth-versus-Profitability Choices of Dot-Com Companies

Competitive advantage comes from product differentiation or cost leadership. Successful implementation of these strategies helps a company be profitable and grow. During the dot-com boom in the late 1990s, many dot-com companies pursued a strategy of short-run growth to gain brand recognition and market share, with the goal of later translating such growth into higher prices (via product differentiation) or lower costs (via cost leadership). The most spectacular failures of dot-com companies occurred in companies that followed the "get big fast" model but then failed to differentiate their products or reduce their costs.

One such example is Webvan. At Webvan, customers ordered groceries online. Webvan then delivered these groceries to customers' homes. The benefit to customers was that they avoided the hassle of driving, parking, and standing in line at the supermarket. Webvan's model was to get big fast. *The New York Times* noted that "long before it began to get the bugs out of its initial 100,000-square-foot distribution center in Oakland, California, Webvan began a three-year program to replicate the facility in 26 cities nationwide, at a cost of $35 million each." Webvan also spent large amounts of money on marketing to establish its brand. The operational challenges of an online grocery business are immense. Webvan never generated anywhere near the sales volume it was expecting. The low margins of the retail grocery business, perishable inventory, and large amounts of unused capacity led to heavy losses. In July 2001, Webvan filed for bankruptcy, having spent almost all of the $1.2 billion of its invested capital.

Webvan did not become profitable because its cost structure was higher than the bricks-and-mortar grocery stores it competed against. Lower costs due to productivity increases or economies of scale did not materialize. Despite brand recognition, Webvan did not have a favorable price-recovery component of operating income because customers were unwilling to pay premium prices for the convenience of online grocery shopping. Without a cost leadership or product differentiation advantage, the growth component of operating income was unfavorable because costs exceeded revenues. The more Webvan sold, the more money it lost, leading to its eventual bankruptcy. Long-run success depends on gaining cost leadership or product differentiation, which Webvan never achieved.

Since Webvan's bankruptcy, new entrants have cautiously entered the online grocery-shopping market. These firms, including Ahold's Peapod and Safeway.com, began operations by minimizing initial investment and costs. Peapod, for example, shares warehousing facilities and operations with local Ahold-owned supermarkets including Giant, Bi-Lo, and Stop and Shop. Like other online grocers, Peapod follows a product-differentiation strategy, charging premium prices for the convenience of online shopping. Additionally, and unlike Webvan, online grocers now have minimum orders, typically $50. These leaner operations and higher prices have proven successful for these second-generation entrants. Peapod alone had revenues of $150 million in 2003, and Safeway.com was responsible for increasing profitability of its parent company.

Source: J. Moran, "Online Grocery Services Are on the Rebound," *Hartford Courant* (July 8, 2004); S. Hansel, "An Ambitious Internet Grocer Is Out of Both Cash and Ideas," *The New York Times* (July 10, 2001); S. Kapner, "Early Winner in Online Food; Local and Simple Ways Work for British Grocer," *The New York Times* (July 20, 2001); "Business and Finance," *The Wall Street Journal* (August 9, 1999); and Webvan's 2001 10K filings.

Although these costs are fixed in the short run, over the long run there is a cause-and-effect relationship between output and manufacturing capacity required (and conversion costs needed). Engineered costs can be variable or fixed in the short run.

Discretionary costs have two important features: (1) They arise from periodic (usually annual) decisions regarding the maximum amount to be incurred; and (2) they have no measurable cause-and-effect relationship between output and resources used. There is often a delay between when a resource is acquired and when it is used. Examples of discretionary costs include advertising, executive training, R&D, and corporate-staff department costs such as legal, human resources, and public relations. Unlike engineered costs, a noteworthy aspect of discretionary costs is that managers are seldom confident that the "correct" amounts are being spent. The founder of Lever Brothers, an international consumer-products company, once noted, "Half the money I spend on advertising is

EXHIBIT 13-5

Differences Between Engineered Costs and Discretionary Costs

	Engineered Costs (Examples: Manufacturing, Distribution)	Discretionary Costs (Examples: R&D, Advertising, Public Relations)
Type of process or activity	**a.** Detailed and physically observable **b.** Repetitive	**a.** Black box (knowledge of process is sketchy or unavailable) **b.** Nonrepetitive or nonroutine
Level of uncertainty (the possibility that actual costs will deviate from expected costs)	Moderate or small	Large

Source: This exhibit is a modification of one suggested by H. Itami.

wasted; the trouble is, I don't know which half!" In the Chipset example, R&D costs are discretionary costs because there is no measurable cause-and-effect relationship between output of 1,150,000 units produced and the R&D resources needed or used.[7]

Exhibit 13-5 summarizes two key distinctions between engineered and discretionary costs: the type of process and the level of uncertainty represented in a cost.

6

Identify unused capacity

. . . capacity available minus capacity used

and how to manage it

. . . downsize to reduce capacity

Identifying Unused Capacity for Engineered and Discretionary Overhead Costs

How does the distinction between engineered and discretionary costs help a manager understand and manage unused capacity? Actually, each of these costs has a very different relationship to capacity. Consider engineered conversion costs. As shown in Exhibit 13-6, Chipset management indicates that manufacturing capacity can be added or reduced in increments to process 250,000 square centimeters of silicon wafers. At each level, conversion costs are fixed. For example, conversion costs are fixed at $13,050,000 if Chipset wants enough capacity to process between 2,750,001 and 3,000,000 square centimeters of silicon wafers. If Chipset wants to process say, 3,100,000 square centimeters, it would need to increase its capacity to 3,250,000 square centimeters, an increase of 250,000 square centimeters of capacity at a cost of $1,087,500.

At the start of 2006, Chipset had capacity to process 3,750,000 square centimeters of silicon wafers. Quality and productivity improvements made during 2006 enabled Chipset to produce 1,150,000 units of CX1 by processing 2,900,000 square centimeters of silicon wafers. Chipset calculates its unused manufacturing capacity as 850,000 (3,750,000 − 2,900,000) square centimeters of silicon-wafer processing capacity at the beginning of 2006. At the 2006 conversion cost of $4.35 per square centimeter,

$$\begin{aligned}\begin{matrix}\text{Cost of}\\\text{unused capacity}\end{matrix} &= \begin{matrix}\text{Cost of capacity}\\\text{at the beginning}\\\text{of the year}\end{matrix} - \begin{matrix}\text{Manufacturing resources}\\\text{used during the year}\end{matrix}\\&= (3{,}750{,}000 \text{ sq. cm.} \times \$4.35 \text{ per sq. cm.}) - (2{,}900{,}000 \text{ sq. cm.} \times \$4.35 \text{ per sq. cm.})\\&= \$16{,}312{,}500 - \$12{,}615{,}000 = \$3{,}697{,}500\end{aligned}$$

The absence of a cause-and-effect relationship makes identifying unused capacity for discretionary costs difficult. Management cannot determine the R&D resources used for the actual output produced to compare to R&D capacity. And without a measure of capacity used, it is not possible to compute unused capacity.

[7]Managers also describe some costs as infrastructure costs—costs that arise from having property, plant, and equipment and a functioning organization. Examples are depreciation, long-run lease rental, and the acquisition of long-run technical capabilities. These costs are generally fixed costs because they are committed to and acquired before they are used. Infrastructure costs can be engineered or discretionary. For instance, manufacturing-overhead cost incurred at Chipset to acquire manufacturing capacity is an infrastructure cost that is an example of an engineered cost. In the long run, there is a cause-and-effect relationship between output and manufacturing-overhead costs needed to produce that output. R&D cost incurred to acquire technical capability is an infrastructure cost that is an example of a discretionary cost. There is no measurable cause-and-effect relationship between output and R&D cost incurred.

EXHIBIT 13-6 **Engineered Costs and Unused Capacity at Chipset, Inc., in 2006**

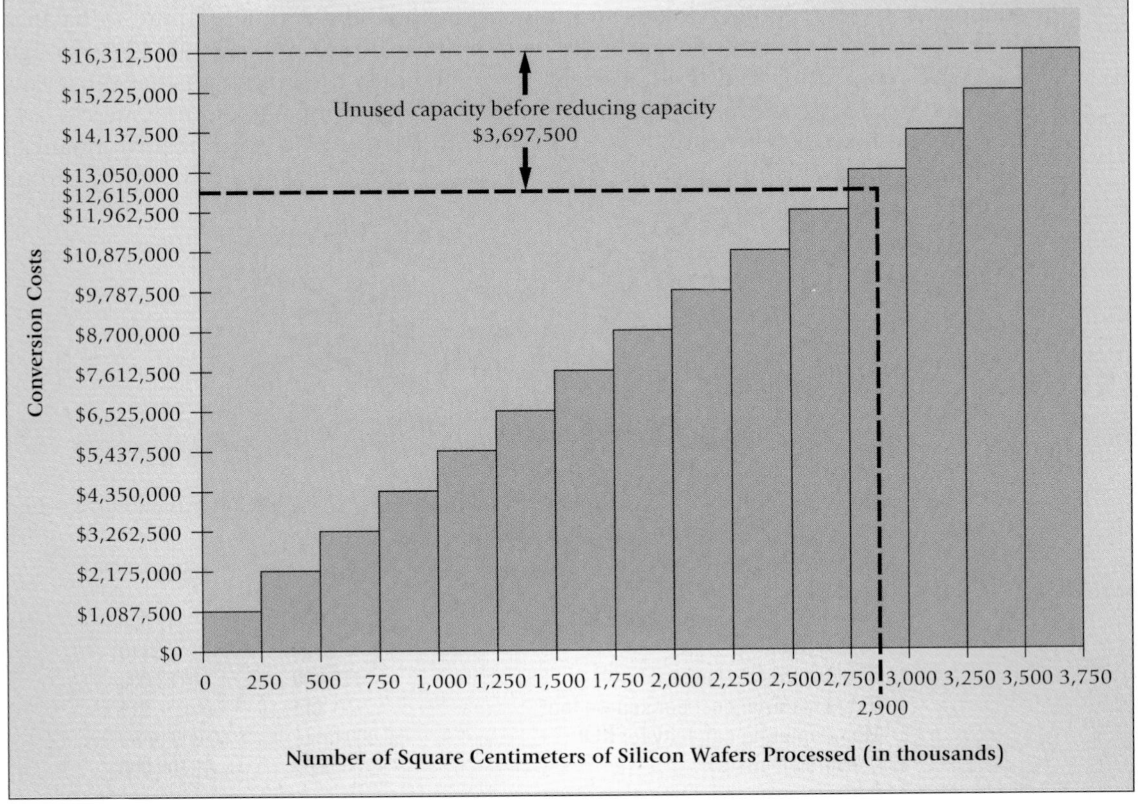

Managing Unused Capacity

What actions can Chipset management take when it identifies unused capacity? In general, it has two alternatives: Chipset can attempt to eliminate the unused capacity, or it can attempt to grow output to utilize the unused capacity.

In recent years, many companies have *downsized* in an attempt to eliminate their unused capacity. **Downsizing** (also called **rightsizing**) is an integrated approach of configuring processes, products, and people to match costs to the activities that need to be performed to operate effectively and efficiently in the present and future. Companies such as AT&T, Delta Airlines, General Motors, IBM, and Scott Paper have downsized to focus on their core businesses and have instituted organization changes to increase efficiency, reduce costs, and improve quality. However, downsizing often means eliminating jobs, which can have an adverse effect on employee morale and the culture of a company. Downsizing is best done in the context of a company's overall strategy and by retaining individuals who have strong management, leadership, and technical skills and experience.

Consider Chipset's alternatives with respect to its unused manufacturing capacity. Because it needed to process 2,900,000 square centimeters of silicon wafers in 2006, it could have reduced capacity to 3,000,000 square centimeters (recall, manufacturing capacity can be added or reduced only in increments of 250,000 sq. cm.), resulting in cost savings of $3,262,500 [(3,750,000 sq. cm. – 3,000,000 sq. cm.) × $4.35 per sq. cm.]. Chipset's strategy, however, was not only to reduce costs but also to grow its business. So early in 2006, Chipset reduced its manufacturing capacity by only 250,000 square centimeters—from 3,750,000 square centimeters to 3,500,000 square centimeters—saving $1,087,500 ($4.35 per sq. cm. × 250,000 sq. cm.). It retained some unused capacity for future growth. By avoiding greater reductions in capacity, it also maintained the morale of its skilled and capable workforce. The success of this strategy will depend on Chipset achieving the future growth it has projected.

Because identifying unused capacity for discretionary costs is difficult, downsizing or otherwise, managing this unused capacity is also difficult. Chipset's management uses judgment and discretion to reduce R&D costs by $100,000 in 2006. Its goal is to reduce

Study Tip: To check your understanding of the material in this chapter, see the Featured Exercise, true–false statements 5 and 9, multiple-choice questions 3 and 5, and Review Exercise 1 (*Student Guide*, beginning p. 170). Fully explained answers begin on p. 178.

R&D costs without significantly affecting the output of the R&D activity. Greater reductions in R&D costs could harm the business by slowing down needed product and process improvements. Chipset must meet its need for cost reductions without compromising quality, continuous improvement, and future growth. Delta Airlines' failure to balance these factors led its board of directors to replace the airline's CEO in 1997. Even though aggressive cost cutting had restored Delta to profitability, the board felt that those cuts had compromised customer satisfaction, a key to the company's future success and growth. The new CEO refocused the company on its customers with positive financial results, but the events of September 11, 2001, hurt Delta just as it did the entire airline industry.

PROBLEM FOR SELF-STUDY

Following a strategy of product differentiation, Westwood Corporation makes a high-end kitchen range hood, KE8. Westwood's data for 2005 and 2006 follow:

	2005	2006
1. Units of KE8 produced and sold	40,000	42,000
2. Selling price	$100	$110
3. Direct materials (square feet)	120,000	123,000
4. Direct material cost per square foot	$10	$11
5. Manufacturing capacity for KE8	50,000 units	50,000 units
6. Conversion costs	$1,000,000	$1,100,000
7. Conversion cost per unit of capacity (Row 6 ÷ Row 5)	$20	$22
8. Selling and customer-service capacity	30 customers	29 customers
9. Selling and customer-service costs	$720,000	$725,000
10. Cost per customer of selling and customer-service capacity (Row 9 ÷ Row 8)	$24,000	$25,000

Westwood produced no defective units and reduced direct material usage per unit of KE8 in 2006. Conversion costs in each year are tied to manufacturing capacity. Selling and customer-service costs are related to the number of customers that the selling and service functions are designed to support. Westwood has 23 customers (wholesalers) in 2005 and 25 customers in 2006.

Required

1. Describe briefly the elements you would include in Westwood's balanced scorecard.
2. Calculate the growth, price-recovery, and productivity components that explain the change in operating income from 2005 to 2006.
3. Suppose during 2006, the market size for high-end kitchen range hoods grew 3% in terms of number of units and all increases in market share (that is, increases in the number of units sold greater than 3%) are due to Westwood's product-differentiation strategy. Calculate how much of the change in operating income from 2005 to 2006 is due to the industry-market-size factor, cost leadership, and product differentiation.
4. How successful has Westwood been in implementing its strategy? Explain.

SOLUTION

1. The balanced scorecard should describe Westwood's product-differentiation strategy. Elements that should be included in its balanced scorecard are:
   - **Financial perspective** Increase in operating income from higher margins on KE8 and from growth
   - **Customer perspective** Market share in the high-end market and customer satisfaction
   - **Internal business process perspective** Manufacturing quality, order-delivery time, on-time delivery, and new product features added, development time for new products and improvements in manufacturing processes
   - **Learning-and-growth perspective** Percentage of employees trained in process and quality management and employee satisfaction ratings

2. Operating income for each year is:

	2005	2006
Revenues		
($100 per unit × 40,000 units; $110 per unit × 42,000 units)	$4,000,000	$4,620,000
Costs		
Direct material costs		
($10 per sq. ft. × 120,000 sq. ft.; $11 per sq. ft. × 123,000 sq. ft.)	1,200,000	1,353,000
Conversion costs		
($20 per unit × 50,000 units; $22 per unit × 50,000 units)	1,000,000	1,100,000
Selling and customer-service costs		
($24,000 per customer × 30 customers; $25,000 per customer × 29 customers)	720,000	725,000
Total costs	2,920,000	3,178,000
Operating income	$1,080,000	$1,442,000
Change in operating income	$362,000 F	

Growth Component of Operating Income Change

$$\text{Revenue effect of growth} = \left(\begin{matrix}\text{Actual units of}\\ \text{output sold}\\ \text{in 2006}\end{matrix} - \begin{matrix}\text{Actual units of}\\ \text{output sold}\\ \text{in 2005}\end{matrix}\right) \times \begin{matrix}\text{Selling}\\ \text{price}\\ \text{in 2005}\end{matrix}$$

$$= (42{,}000 \text{ units} - 40{,}000 \text{ units}) \times \$100 \text{ per unit} = \$200{,}000 \text{ F}$$

$$\begin{matrix}\text{Cost effect}\\ \text{of growth for}\\ \text{variable costs}\end{matrix} = \left(\begin{matrix}\text{Units of input}\\ \text{required to produce}\\ \text{2006 output in 2005}\end{matrix} - \begin{matrix}\text{Actual units of input}\\ \text{used to produce}\\ \text{2005 output}\end{matrix}\right) \times \begin{matrix}\text{Input}\\ \text{price}\\ \text{in 2005}\end{matrix}$$

$$\begin{matrix}\text{Cost effect}\\ \text{of growth for}\\ \text{direct materials}\end{matrix} = \left(120{,}000 \text{ sq. ft} \times \frac{42{,}000 \text{ units}}{40{,}000 \text{ units}} - 120{,}000 \text{ sq. ft.}\right) \times \$10 \text{ per sq. ft.}$$

$$= (126{,}000 \text{ sq. ft.} - 120{,}000 \text{ sq. ft.}) \times \$10 \text{ per sq. ft.} = \$60{,}000 \text{ U}$$

$$\begin{matrix}\text{Cost effect}\\ \text{of growth for}\\ \text{fixed costs}\end{matrix} = \left(\begin{matrix}\text{Actual units of capacity in}\\ \text{2005, because adequate capacity}\\ \text{exists to produce 2006 output in 2005}\end{matrix} - \begin{matrix}\text{Actual units}\\ \text{of capacity}\\ \text{in 2005}\end{matrix}\right) \times \begin{matrix}\text{Price per}\\ \text{unit of}\\ \text{capacity}\\ \text{in 2005}\end{matrix}$$

Cost effects of growth for fixed costs are:

Conversion costs: (50,000 units – 50,000 units) × $20 per unit = $0

Selling and customer-service costs: (30 customers – 30 customers) × $24,000 per customer = $0

In summary, the net increase in operating income attributable to growth equals:

Revenue effect of growth		$200,000 F
Cost effect of growth		
Direct material costs	$60,000 U	
Conversion costs	0	
Selling and customer-service costs	0	60,000 U
Change in operating income due to growth		$140,000 F

Price-Recovery Component of Operating-Income Change

$$\begin{matrix}\text{Revenue effect of}\\ \text{price recovery}\end{matrix} = \left(\begin{matrix}\text{Selling price}\\ \text{in 2006}\end{matrix} - \begin{matrix}\text{Selling price}\\ \text{in 2005}\end{matrix}\right) \times \begin{matrix}\text{Actual units}\\ \text{of output}\\ \text{sold in 2006}\end{matrix}$$

$$= (\$110 \text{ per unit} - \$100 \text{ per unit}) \times 42{,}000 \text{ units} = \$420{,}000 \text{ F}$$

$$\begin{matrix}\text{Cost effect of}\\ \text{price recovery}\\ \text{for variable costs}\end{matrix} = \left(\begin{matrix}\text{Input}\\ \text{price}\\ \text{in 2006}\end{matrix} - \begin{matrix}\text{Input}\\ \text{price}\\ \text{in 2005}\end{matrix}\right) \times \begin{matrix}\text{Units of input}\\ \text{required to produce}\\ \text{2006 output in 2005}\end{matrix}$$

Direct material costs: ($11 per sq. ft. – $10 per sq. ft.) × 126,000 sq. ft. = $126,000 U

$$\text{Cost effect of price recovery for fixed costs} = \left(\begin{matrix}\text{Price per unit of capacity in 2006}\end{matrix} - \begin{matrix}\text{Price per unit of capacity in 2005}\end{matrix}\right) \times \begin{matrix}\text{Actual units of capacity in 2005, because adequate capacity exists to produce 2006 output in 2005}\end{matrix}$$

Cost effects of price recovery for fixed costs are:

Conversion costs: ($22 per unit – 20 per unit) × 50,000 units = $100,000 U
Selling and cust.-service costs: ($25,000 per cust. – $24,000 per cust.) × 30 customers = $30,000 U

In summary, the net increase in operating income attributable to price recovery equals:

Revenue effect of price recovery		$420,000 F
Cost effect of price recovery		
Direct material costs	$126,000 U	
Conversion costs	100,000 U	
Selling and customer-service costs	30,000 U	256,000 U
Change in operating income due to price recovery		$164,000 F

Productivity Component of Operating-Income Change

$$\text{Cost effect of productivity for variable costs} = \left(\begin{matrix}\text{Actual units of input used to produce 2006 output}\end{matrix} - \begin{matrix}\text{Units of input required to produce 2006 output in 2005}\end{matrix}\right) \times \begin{matrix}\text{Input price in 2006}\end{matrix}$$

$$\text{Cost effect of productivity for direct materials} = (123{,}000 \text{ sq. ft.} - 126{,}000 \text{ sq. ft.}) \times \$11 \text{ per sq. ft.} = \$33{,}000 \text{ F}$$

$$\text{Cost effect of productivity for fixed costs} = \left(\begin{matrix}\text{Actual units of capacity in 2006}\end{matrix} - \begin{matrix}\text{Actual units of capacity in 2005, because adequate capacity exists to produce 2006 output in 2005}\end{matrix}\right) \times \begin{matrix}\text{Price per unit of capacity in 2006}\end{matrix}$$

Cost effects of productivity for fixed costs are:

Conversion costs: (50,000 units – 50,000 units) × $20 per unit = $0
Selling and customer-service costs: (29 customers – 30 customers) × $25,000/customer = $25,000 F

In summary, the net increase in operating income attributable to productivity equals:

Cost effect of productivity:	
Direct material costs	$33,000 F
Conversion costs	0
Selling and customer-service costs	25,000 F
Change in operating income due to productivity	$58,000 F

A summary of the change in operating income between 2005 and 2006 follows:

	Income Statement Amounts in 2005 (1)	Revenue and Cost Effects of Growth Component in 2006 (2)	Revenue and Cost Effects of Price-Recovery Component in 2006 (3)	Cost Effect of Productivity Component in 2006 (4)	Income Statement Amounts in 2006 (5) = (1) + (2) + (3) + (4)
Revenue	$4,000,000	$200,000 F	$420,000 F	—	$4,620,000
Costs	2,920,000	60,000 U	256,000 U	$58,000 F	3,178,000
Operating income	$1,080,000	$140,000 F	$164,000 F	$58,000 F	$1,442,000

$362,000 F

Change in operating income

3. *Effect of the industry-market-size factor on operating income*
Of the increase in sales from 40,000 to 42,000 units, 3%, or 1,200 units (0.03 × 40,000), is due to growth in market size, and 800 units (2,000 – 1,200) are due to an increase in market share. The change in Westwood's operating income from the industry-market-size factor rather than specific strategic actions is:

$$\$140{,}000 \text{ (column 2 of preceding table)} \times \frac{1{,}200 \text{ units}}{2{,}000 \text{ units}} \qquad \underline{\$\ 84{,}000} \text{ F}$$

Effect of product differentiation on operating income

Increase in the selling price of KE8 (revenue effect of the price-recovery component)	$420,000 F
Increase in prices of inputs (cost effect of the price-recovery component)	256,000 U
Growth in market share due to product differentiation	
$\$140{,}000 \text{ (column 2 of preceding table)} \times \frac{800 \text{ units}}{2{,}000 \text{ units}}$	56,000 F
Change in operating income due to product differentiation	$220,000 F

Effect of cost leadership on operating income

Productivity component	$ 58,000 F

A summary of the net increase in operating income from 2005 to 2006 follows:

Change due to the industry-market-size factor	$ 84,000 F
Change due to product differentiation	220,000 F
Change due to cost leadership	58,000 F
Change in operating income	$362,000 F

4. The analysis of operating income indicates that a significant amount of the increase in operating income resulted from Westwood's successful implementation of its product-differentiation strategy. The company was able to continue to charge a premium price for KE8 while increasing market share. Westwood was also able to earn additional operating income from improving its productivity.

DECISION POINTS

The following question-and-answer format summarizes the chapter's learning objectives. Each decision presents a key question related to a learning objective. The guidelines are the answer to that question.

Decision	**Guidelines**
1. What are two generic strategies a company can use?	Two generic strategies are product differentiation and cost leadership. Product differentiation is offering products and services that are perceived by customers as being superior and unique. Cost leadership is achieving low costs relative to competitors.
2. What is reengineering?	Reengineering is the rethinking of business processes, such as the order-delivery process, to improve critical performance measures such as cost, quality, and customer satisfaction.
3. How can an organization translate its strategy into a set of performance measures?	An organization can develop a balanced scorecard that provides the framework for a strategic measurement and management system. The balanced scorecard measures performance from four perspectives: (1) financial, (2) customer, (3) internal business processes, and (4) learning and growth.
4. How can a company analyze changes in operating income to evaluate the success of its strategy?	To evaluate the success of its strategy, a company can subdivide the change in operating income into growth, price-recovery, and productivity components. The growth component measures the change in revenues and costs from selling more or less units, assuming no changes in prices of outputs and inputs or efficiencies. The price-recovery component measures changes in revenues and costs as a result solely of changes in the prices of outputs and inputs. The productivity component measures the decrease in costs from using fewer inputs, a better mix of inputs, and reducing capacity. A company is considered successful in implementing its strategy when changes in operating income align closely with its strategy.
5. How can a company distinguish engineered costs from discretionary costs?	Engineered costs result from a cause-and-effect relationship between output and the resources needed to produce that output. Discretionary costs arise from periodic (usually annual) management decisions regarding the amount to be incurred. Discretionary costs are not tied to a cause-and-effect relationship between inputs and outputs.
6. How can a company identify unused capacity, and if it is present, how can unused capacity be managed?	Identifying unused capacity is easier for engineered costs than for discretionary costs. Downsizing is an approach to managing unused capacity that matches costs to the activities that need to be performed to operate effectively.

APPENDIX: PRODUCTIVITY MEASUREMENT

Productivity measures the relationship between actual inputs used (both quantities and costs) and actual outputs produced. The lower the inputs for a given quantity of outputs or the higher the outputs for a given quantity of inputs, the higher the productivity. Measuring productivity improvements over time highlights the specific input-output relationships that contribute to cost leadership.

Partial Productivity Measures

Partial-productivity (PP) measures are partial in the sense that they measure the amount of output produced per unit of an individual input. PP measures are based on physical inputs and outputs; they do not use input prices.

Partial productivity, the most frequently used productivity measure, compares the quantity of output produced with the quantity of an individual input used. In its most common form, partial productivity is expressed as a ratio:

$$\text{Partial productivity} = \frac{\text{Quantity of output produced}}{\text{Quantity of input used}}$$

The higher the ratio, the greater the productivity.
Consider direct materials productivity at Chipset in 2006.

$$\begin{aligned}\text{Direct materials partial productivity} &= \frac{\text{Quantity of CX1 units produced during 2006}}{\text{Quantity of direct materials used to produce CX1 in 2006}}\\ &= \frac{\text{1,150,000 units of CX1}}{\text{2,900,000 sq. cm. of direct materials}}\\ &= \text{0.397 units of CX1 per sq. cm. of direct materials}\end{aligned}$$

Note direct materials partial productivity ignores Chipset's other inputs, manufacturing conversion capacity, and R&D. Partial-productivity measures become more meaningful when comparisons are made that examine productivity changes over time, either across different facilities or relative to a benchmark. Exhibit 13-7 presents partial-productivity measures for Chipset's inputs for 2006 and the comparable 2005 inputs that would have been used to produce 2006 output, using information from the productivity-component calculations on pages 469–470. These measures compare actual inputs used in 2006 to produce 1,150,000 units of CX1 with inputs that would have been used in 2006 had the input–output relationship from 2005 continued in 2006.

Evaluating Changes in Partial Productivities

Note how the partial-productivity measures differ for variable-cost and fixed-cost components. For variable-cost elements, such as direct materials, productivity improvements measure the reduction in input resources used to produce output (3,450,000 square centimeters of silicon wafers to 2,900,000 square centimeters). For fixed-cost elements such as manufacturing conversion capacity, partial productivity measures the reduction in overall capacity from 2005 to 2006 (3,750,000 square centimeters of silicon wafers to 3,500,000 square centimeters) regardless of the amount of capacity actually used in each period.

An advantage of partial-productivity measures is that they focus on a single input. As a result, they are simple to calculate and easily understood by operations personnel. Managers and operators examine these numbers to understand the reasons underlying productivity changes—better training of workers, lower labor turnover, better incentives, improved methods, or substitution of materials for labor. Isolating the relevant factors helps Chipset implement and sustain these practices in the future.

EXHIBIT 13-7

Comparing Chipset's Partial Productivities in 2005 and 2006

Input (1)	Partial Productivity in 2006 (2)	Comparable Partial Productivity Based on 2005 Input–Output Relationships (3)	Percentage Change from 2005 to 2006 (4)
Direct materials	$\frac{1,150,000}{2,900,000} = 0.397$	$\frac{1,150,000}{3,450,000} = 0.333$	$\frac{0.397 - 0.333}{0.333} = 19.2\%$
Manufacturing conversion capacity	$\frac{1,150,000}{3,500,000} = 0.329$	$\frac{1,150,000}{3,750,000} = 0.307$	$\frac{0.329 - 0.307}{0.307} = 7.2\%$
R&D	$\frac{1,150,000}{39} = 29,487$	$\frac{1,150,000}{40} = 28,750$	$\frac{29,487 - 28,750}{28,750} = 2.6\%$

For all their advantages, partial-productivity measures also have serious drawbacks. Because partial productivity focuses on only one input at a time rather than on all inputs simultaneously, managers cannot evaluate the effect on overall productivity, if (say) manufacturing-conversion-capacity partial productivity increases while direct materials partial productivity decreases. Total factor productivity (TFP), or total productivity, is a measure of productivity that considers all inputs simultaneously.

Total Factor Productivity

Total factor productivity (TFP) is the ratio of the quantity of output produced to the costs of all inputs used based on current-period prices.

$$\text{Total factor productivity} = \frac{\text{Quantity of output produced}}{\text{Costs of all inputs used}}$$

TFP considers all inputs simultaneously and the trade-offs across inputs based on current input prices. Do not think of all productivity measures as physical measures lacking financial content—how many units of output are produced per unit of input. TFP is intricately tied to minimizing total cost—a financial objective.

Calculating and Comparing Total Factor Productivity

We first calculate Chipset's TFP in 2006, using 2006 prices and 1,150,000 units of output produced (based on information from the first part of the productivity-component calculations on pp. 469–470).

$$\begin{aligned}\text{Total factor productivity for 2006 using 2006 prices} &= \frac{\text{Quantity of output produced in 2006}}{\text{Costs of inputs used in 2006 based on 2006 prices}}\\ &= \frac{1{,}150{,}000}{(2{,}900{,}000 \times \$1.50) + (3{,}500{,}000 \times \$4.35) + (39 \times \$100{,}000)}\\ &= \frac{1{,}150{,}000}{\$23{,}475{,}000}\\ &= 0.048988 \text{ units of output per dollar of input cost}\end{aligned}$$

By itself, the 2006 TFP of 0.048988 units of CX1 per dollar of input costs is not particularly helpful. We need something to compare the 2006 TFP against. One alternative is to compare TFPs of other similar companies in 2006. However, finding similar companies and obtaining accurate comparable data are often difficult. Companies, therefore, usually compare their own TFPs over time. In the Chipset example, we use as a benchmark TFP calculated using the inputs that Chipset would have used in 2005 to produce 1,150,000 units of CX1 at 2006 prices (that is, we use the costs calculated from the second part of the productivity-component calculations on pp. 469–470). Why do we use 2006 prices? Because using the current year's prices in both calculations controls for input-price differences and focuses the analysis on adjustments the manager made in quantities of inputs in response to changes in prices.

$$\begin{aligned}\text{Benchmark TFP} &= \frac{\text{Quantity of output produced in 2006}}{\text{Costs of inputs that would have been used in 2005 to produce 2006 output}}\\ &= \frac{1{,}150{,}000}{(3{,}450{,}000 \times \$1.50) + (3{,}750{,}000 \times \$4.35) + (40 \times \$100{,}000)}\\ &= \frac{1{,}150{,}000}{\$25{,}487{,}500}\\ &= 0.045120 \text{ units of output per dollar of input cost}\end{aligned}$$

Using 2006 prices, TFP increased 8.6% [(0.048988 – 0.045120) ÷ 0.045120 = 0.086, or 8.6%] from 2005 to 2006. Note that the 8.6% increase in TFP also equals the $2,012,500 gain (Exhibit 13-3, column 4) divided by the $23,475,000 of actual costs incurred in 2006 (Exhibit 13-3, column 5). Total factor productivity increased because Chipset produced more output per dollar of input cost in 2006 relative to 2005, measured in both years using 2006 prices. The gain in TFP occurs because Chipset increases the partial productivities of individual inputs and, consistent with its strategy, seeks the least-expensive combination of inputs to produce CX1. Note that increases in TFP cannot be due to differences in input prices because we used 2006 prices to evaluate both the inputs that Chipset would have used in 2005 to produce 1,150,000 units of CX1 and the inputs actually used in 2006.

Be aware of the intuition underlying the benchmark TFP calculation. We want to assess whether employees, in producing this period's outputs, used a combination of inputs that is more cost-effective than simply continuing last period's combination. Our objective is to see if the current period combination of inputs (at current-period prices) is more cost-effective than simply continuing (at current-period prices) the input combination used in the prior period.

Using Partial and Total Factor Productivity Measures

A major advantage of TFP is that it measures the combined productivity of all inputs used to produce output and explicitly considers gains from using fewer physical inputs as well as substitution among inputs. Managers can analyze these numbers to understand the reasons for changes in TFP—for example, better human resource management practices, higher quality of materials, or improved manufacturing methods.

Although TFP measures are comprehensive, operations personnel find financial TFP measures more difficult to understand and less useful than physical partial-productivity measures. For example, companies that are more labor intensive than Chipset use manufacturing-labor partial-productivity measures. However, if productivity-based bonuses depend on gains in manufacturing-labor partial productivity alone, workers have incentives to substitute materials (and capital) for labor. This substitution improves their own productivity measure, while possibly decreasing the overall productivity of the company as measured by TFP. To overcome these incentive problems, some companies—for example, TRW, Eaton, and Whirlpool—explicitly adjust bonuses based on manufacturing-labor partial productivity for the effects of other factors such as investments in new equipment and higher levels of scrap. That is, they combine partial productivity with TFP-like measures.

Many companies such as Behlen Manufacturing, a steel fabricator, and Motorola, a microchip manufacturer, use both partial productivity and total factor productivity to evaluate performance. *Partial productivity and TFP measures work best together because the strengths of one offset the weaknesses of the other.*

TERMS TO LEARN

This chapter and the Glossary at the end of the book contain definitions of:

balanced scorecard (p. 457)
cost leadership (p. 457)
discretionary costs (p. 473)
downsizing (p. 475)
engineered costs (p. 472)
growth component (p. 467)
partial productivity (p. 480)
price-recovery component (p. 467)
product differentiation (p. 457)
productivity (p. 480)
productivity component (p. 467)
reengineering (p. 458)
rightsizing (p. 475)
total factor productivity (TFP) (p. 481)
unused capacity (p. 472)

PH Grade Assist

Prentice Hall Grade Assist (PHGA)

Your professor may ask you to complete selected exercises and problems in Prentice Hall Grade Assist (PHGA). PHGA is an online tool that can help you master the chapter's topics. It provides you with multiple variations of exercises and problems designated by the PHGA icon. You can rework these exercises and problems—each time with new data—as many times as you need. You also receive immediate feedback and grading.

ASSIGNMENT MATERIAL

Questions

13-1 Define strategy.

13-2 Describe the five key forces to consider when analyzing an industry.

13-3 Describe two generic strategies.

13-4 What are four key perspectives in the balanced scorecard?

13-5 What is reengineering?

13-6 Describe three features of a good balanced scorecard.

13-7 What are three important pitfalls to avoid when implementing a balanced scorecard?

13-8 Describe three key components in doing a strategic analysis of operating income.

13-9 Why might an analyst incorporate the industry-market-size factor and the interrelationships among the growth, price-recovery, and productivity components into a strategic analysis of operating income?

13-10 How does an engineered cost differ from a discretionary cost?

13-11 "The distinction between engineered and discretionary costs is irrelevant when identifying unused capacity." Do you agree? Comment briefly.

13-12 What is downsizing?

13-13 What is a partial-productivity measure?

13-14 What is total factor productivity?

13-15 "We are already measuring total factor productivity. Measuring partial productivities would be of no value." Do you agree? Comment briefly.

Exercises

13-16 Balanced scorecard. La Quinta Corporation manufactures corrugated cardboard boxes. It competes and plans to grow by producing high-quality boxes at a low cost and by delivering them to customers in a timely manner. There are many other manufacturers who produce similar boxes. La Quinta believes that continuously improving its manufacturing processes and having satisfied employees are critical to implementing its strategy in 2007.

Required

1. Is La Quinta's 2007 strategy one of product differentiation or cost leadership? Explain briefly.
2. Indicate two measures you would expect to see under each perspective in La Quinta's balanced scorecard for 2007. Explain your answer briefly.

13-17 Analysis of growth, price-recovery, and productivity components (continuation of 13-16). An analysis of La Quinta's operating-income changes between 2006 and 2007 shows the following:

Operating income for 2006	$1,600,000
Add growth component	60,000
Deduct price-recovery component	(50,000)
Add productivity component	180,000
Operating income for 2007	$1,790,000

The industry market size for corrugated cardboard boxes did not grow in 2007, input prices did not change, and La Quinta reduced the prices of its boxes.

Required

1. Was La Quinta's gain in operating income in 2007 consistent with the strategy you identified in requirement 1 of Exercise 13-16?
2. Explain the productivity component. In general, does it represent savings in only variable costs, only fixed costs, or both variable and fixed costs?

13-18 Strategy, balanced scorecard, merchandising operation. Oceano & Sons buys T-shirts in bulk, applies its own trendsetting silk-screen designs, and then sells the T-shirts to a number of retailers. Oceano wants to be known for its trendsetting designs, and it wants every teenager to be seen in a distinctive Oceano T-shirt. Oceano presents the following data for its first two years of operations, 2006 and 2007.

	A	B	C
1		**2006**	**2007**
2	Number of T-shirts purchased	200,000	250,000
3	Number of T-shirts discarded	2,000	3,300
4	Number of T-shirts sold	198,000	246,700
5	Average selling price	$ 25.00	$ 26.00
6	Average cost per T-shirt	$ 10.00	$ 8.50
7	Administrative capacity (number of customers)	4,000	3,750
8	Administrative costs	$1,200,000	$1,162,500
9	Administrative cost per customer	$ 300	$ 310
10	Design staff	5	5
11	Total design costs	$ 250,000	$ 275,000
12	Design cost per employee	$ 50,000	$ 55,000

Administrative costs depend on the number of customers that Oceano has created capacity to support, not on the actual number of customers served. Oceano had 3,600 customers in 2006 and 3,500 customers in 2007. At the start of each year, management uses its discretion to determine the number of employees on the design staff for the year. The design staff and its costs have no direct relationship with the number of T-shirts purchased and sold or the number of customers to whom T-shirts are sold.

Required

1. Is Oceano's strategy product differentiation or cost leadership? Explain briefly.
2. Describe briefly the key elements Oceano should include in its balanced scorecard and the reasons it should do so.

13-19 Strategic analysis of operating income (continuation of 13-18). Refer to Exercise 13-18.

If you want to use Excel to solve this exercise, go to the Excel Lab at **www.prenhall.com/horngren/cost12e** and download the template for Exercise 13-18.

Excel Lab
www.prenhall.com/horngren/cost12e

Required

1. Calculate Oceano's operating income in both 2006 and 2007.
2. Calculate the growth, price-recovery, and productivity components that explain the change in operating income from 2006 to 2007.
3. Comment on your answers in requirement 2. What do each of these components indicate?

Excel Lab
www.prenhall.com/horngren/cost12e

13-20 Analysis of growth, price-recovery, and productivity components (continuation of 13-19). Refer to Exercise 13-19. Suppose that the market for silk-screened T-shirts grew by 10% during 2007. All other increases in Oceano's sales were the result of its own strategic actions.

If you want to use Excel to solve this exercise, go to the Excel Lab at **www.prenhall.com/horngren/cost12e** and download the template for Exercise 13-18.

Required

Calculate the change in operating income from 2006 to 2007 due to growth in market size, cost leadership, and product differentiation. How successful has Oceano been in implementing its strategy? Explain.

Excel Lab
www.prenhall.com/horngren/cost12e

13-21 Identifying and managing unused capacity (continuation of 13-18). Refer to Exercise 13-18.

If you want to use Excel to solve this exercise, go to the Excel Lab at **www.prenhall.com/horngren/cost12e** and download the template for Exercise 13-18.

Required

1. Calculate the amount and cost of (a) unused administrative capacity and (b) unused design capacity at the beginning of 2007, based on information for 2007. If you are unable to calculate the amount and cost of a particular unused capacity, indicate why not.
2. Suppose Oceano can only add or reduce administrative capacity in increments of 200 customers. What is the maximum amount of costs that Oceano can save in 2007 by downsizing administrative capacity?
3. What factors other than cost should Oceano consider before it downsizes administrative capacity?

13-22 Strategy, balanced scorecard. Meredith Corporation makes a special-purpose machine, D4H, used in the textile industry. Meredith has designed the D4H machine for 2006 to be distinct from its competitors. It has been generally regarded as a superior machine. Meredith presents the following data for 2005 and 2006.

	2005	2006
1. Units of D4H produced and sold	200	210
2. Selling price	$40,000	$42,000
3. Direct materials (kilograms)	300,000	310,000
4. Direct material cost per kilogram	$8	$8.50
5. Manufacturing capacity in units of D4H	250	250
6. Total conversion costs	$2,000,000	$2,025,000
7. Conversion cost per unit of capacity	$8,000	$8,100
8. Selling and customer-service capacity	100 customers	95 customers
9. Total selling and customer-service costs	$1,000,000	$940,500
10. Selling and customer-service capacity cost per customer	$10,000	$9,900
11. Design staff	12	12
12. Total design costs	$1,200,000	$1,212,000
13. Design cost per employee	$100,000	$101,000

Meredith produces no defective machines, but it wants to reduce direct materials usage per D4H machine in 2006. Conversion costs in each year depend on production capacity defined in terms of D4H units that can be produced, not the actual units produced. Selling and customer-service costs depend on the number of customers that Meredith can support, not the actual number of customers it serves. Meredith has 75 customers in 2005 and 80 customers in 2006. At the start of each year, management uses its discretion to determine the number of design staff for the year. The design staff and its costs have no direct relationship with the quantity of D4H produced or the number of customers to whom D4H is sold.

Required

1. Is Meredith's strategy one of product differentiation or cost leadership? Explain briefly.
2. Describe briefly key elements that you would include in Meredith's balanced scorecard and the reasons for doing so.

13-23 Strategic analysis of operating income (continuation of 13-22). Refer to Exercise 13-22.

Required

1. Calculate the operating income of Meredith Corporation in 2005 and 2006.
2. Calculate the growth, price-recovery, and productivity components that explain the change in operating income from 2005 to 2006.
3. Comment on your answer in requirement 2. What do these components indicate?

13-24 Analysis of growth, price-recovery, and productivity components (continuation of 13-23). Suppose that during 2006, the market for Meredith's special-purpose machines grew by 3%. All increases in market share (that is, sales increases greater than 3%) are the result of Meredith's strategic actions.

Required

Calculate how much of the change in operating income from 2005 to 2006 is due to the industry-market-size factor, cost leadership, and product differentiation. How successful has Meredith been in implementing its strategy? Explain.

13-25 Identifying and managing unused capacity (continuation of 13-22). Refer to Exercise 13-22.

Required

1. Where possible, calculate the amount and cost of (a) unused manufacturing capacity, (b) unused selling and customer-service capacity, and (c) unused design capacity at the beginning of 2006, based on 2006 production. If you are unable to calculate the amount and cost of unused capacity, indicate why not.
2. Suppose Meredith can add or reduce its manufacturing capacity in increments of 30 units. What is the maximum amount of costs that Meredith could save in 2006 by downsizing manufacturing capacity?
3. Meredith, in fact, does not eliminate any of its unused manufacturing capacity. Why might Meredith not downsize?

13-26 Strategy, balanced scorecard, service company. Snyder Corporation is a small information-systems consulting firm that specializes in helping companies implement sales-management software. The market for Snyder's products is very competitive. To compete, Snyder must deliver quality service at a low cost. Snyder bills clients in terms of units of work performed, which depends on the size and complexity of the sales-management system. Snyder presents the following data for 2005 and 2006.

	2005	2006
1. Units of work performed	60	70
2. Selling price	$50,000	$48,000
3. Software-implementation labor-hours	30,000	32,000
4. Cost per software-implementation labor-hour	$60	$63
5. Software-implementation support capacity (in units of work)	90	90
6. Total cost of software-implementation support	$360,000	$369,000
7. Software-implementation support-capacity cost per unit of work	$4,000	$4,100
8. Number of employees doing software-development	3	3
9. Total software-development costs	$375,000	$390,000
10. Software-development cost per employee	$125,000	$130,000

Software-implementation labor-hour costs are variable costs. Software-implementation support costs for each year depend on the software-implementation support capacity (defined in terms of units of work) that Snyder chooses to maintain each year. It does not vary with the actual units of work performed that year. At the start of each year, management uses its discretion to determine the number of software-development employees. The software-development staff and costs have no direct relationship with the number of units of work performed.

Required

1. Is Snyder Corporation's strategy one of product differentiation or cost leadership? Explain briefly.
2. Describe key elements you would include in Snyder's balanced scorecard and your reasons for doing so.

13-27 Strategic analysis of operating income (continuation of 13-26). Refer to Exercise 13-26.

Required

1. Calculate the operating income of Snyder Corporation in 2005 and 2006.
2. Calculate the growth, price-recovery, and productivity components that explain the change in operating income from 2005 to 2006.
3. Comment on your answer in requirement 2. What do these components indicate?

13-28 Analysis of growth, price-recovery, and productivity components (continuation of 13-27). Suppose that during 2006 the market for implementing sales-management software increases by 5% and that Snyder experiences a 1% decline in selling prices. Assume that any further decreases in selling price and increases in market share are strategic choices by Snyder's management to implement their strategy.

Required

Calculate how much of the change in operating income from 2005 to 2006 is due to the industry-market-size factor, cost leadership, and product differentiation. How successful has Snyder been in implementing its strategy? Explain.

13-29 Identifying and managing unused capacity (continuation of 13-26). Refer to Exercise 13-26.

Required

1. Where possible, calculate the amount and cost of (a) unused software-implementation support capacity and (b) unused software-development capacity at the beginning of 2006, based on units of work performed in 2006. If you are unable to calculate the amount and cost of unused capacity, indicate why not.
2. Suppose Snyder can add or reduce its software-implementation support capacity in increments of 15 units. What is the maximum amount of costs that Snyder could save in 2006 by downsizing software-implementation support capacity?
3. Snyder, in fact, does not eliminate any of its unused software-implementation support capacity. Why might Snyder not downsize?

Problems

13-30 Balanced scorecard. Following is a random-order listing of perspectives, strategic objectives, and performance measures for the balanced scorecard.

Perspectives

Internal business process
Customer
Learning and growth
Financial

Strategic Objectives

Acquire new customers
Increase shareholder value
Retain customers
Improve manufacturing quality
Develop profitable customers
Increase proprietary products
Increase information-system capabilities
Enhance employee skills
On-time delivery by suppliers
Increase profit generated by each salesperson
Introduce new products
Minimize invoice-error rate

Performance Measures

Percentage of defective-product units
Return on assets
Number of patents
Employee turnover rate
Net income
Customer profitability
Percentage of processes with real-time feedback
Return on sales
Average job-related training-hours per employee
Return on equity
Percentage of on-time deliveries by suppliers
Product cost per unit
Profit per salesperson
Percentage of error-free invoices
Customer cost per unit
Earnings per share
Number of new customers
Percentage of customers retained

Required For each perspective, select those strategic objectives from the list that best relate to it. For each strategic objective, select the most appropriate performance measure(s) from the list.

13-31 Balanced scorecard. (R. Kaplan, adapted) Caltex, Inc., refines gasoline and sells it through its own Caltex Gas Stations. On the basis of market research, Caltex determines that 60% of the overall gasoline market consists of "service-oriented customers," medium- to high-income individuals who are willing to pay a higher price for gas if the gas stations can provide excellent customer service, such as a clean facility, a convenience store, friendly employees, a quick turnaround, the ability to pay by credit card, and high-octane premium gasoline. The remaining 40% of the overall market are "price shoppers" who look to buy the cheapest gasoline available. Caltex's strategy is to focus on the 60% of service-oriented customers. Caltex's balanced scorecard for 2006 follows. For brevity, the initiatives taken under each objective are omitted.

Objectives	Measures	Target Performance	Actual Performance
Financial Perspective			
Increase shareholder value	Operating-income changes from price recovery	$90,000,000	$95,000,000
	Operating-income changes from growth	$65,000,000	$67,000,000
Customer Perspective			
Increase market share	Market share of overall gasoline market	10%	9.8%
Internal-Business-Process Perspective			
Improve gasoline quality	Quality index	94 points	95 points
Improve refinery performance	Refinery-reliability index (%)	91%	91%
Ensure gasoline availability	Product-availability index (%)	99%	100%
Learning-and-Growth Perspective			
Increase refinery process capability	Percentage of refinery processes with advanced controls	88%	90%

Required

1. Was Caltex successful in implementing its strategy in 2006? Explain your answer.
2. Would you have included some measure of employee satisfaction and employee training in the learning-and-growth perspective? Are these objectives critical to Caltex for implementing its strategy? Why or why not? Explain briefly.
3. Explain how Caltex did not achieve its target market share in the total gasoline market but still exceeded its financial targets. Is "market share of overall gasoline market" the correct measure of market share? Explain briefly.
4. Is there a cause-and-effect linkage between improvements in the measures in the internal business-process perspective and the measure in the customer perspective? That is, would you add other measures to the internal-business-process perspective or the customer perspective? Why or why not? Explain briefly.
5. Do you agree with Caltex's decision not to include measures of changes in operating income from productivity improvements under the financial perspective of the balanced scorecard? Explain briefly.

13-32 Balanced scorecard. Lee Corporation manufactures various types of color laser printers in a highly automated facility with high fixed costs. The market for laser printers is competitive. The various color laser printers on the market are comparable in terms of features and price. Lee believes that satisfying customers with products of high quality at low costs is key to achieving its target profitability. For 2006, Lee plans to achieve higher quality and lower costs by improving yields and reducing defects in its manufacturing operations. Lee will train workers and encourage and empower them to take the necessary actions. Currently, a significant amount of Lee's capacity is used to produce products that are defective and cannot be sold. Lee expects that higher yields will reduce the capacity that Lee needs to manufacture products. Lee does not anticipate that improving manufacturing will automatically lead to lower costs because Lee has high fixed costs. To reduce fixed costs per unit, Lee could lay off employees and sell equipment, or it could use the capacity to produce and sell more of its current products or improved models of its current products.

Lee's balanced scorecard (initiatives omitted) for the just-completed fiscal year 2006 follows:

Objectives	Measures	Target Performance	Actual Performance
Financial Perspective			
Increase shareholder value	Operating-income changes from productivity improvements	$1,000,000	$400,000
	Operating-income changes from growth	$1,500,000	$600,000
Customer Perspective			
Increase market share	Market share in color laser printers	5%	4.6%
Internal-Business-Process Perspective			
Improve manufacturing quality	Yield	82%	85%
Reduce delivery time to customers	Order-delivery time	25 days	22 days
Learning-and-Growth Perspective			
Develop process skills	Percentage of employees trained in process and quality management	90%	92%
Enhance information-system capabilities	Percentage of manufacturing processes with real-time feedback	85%	87%

Required

1. Was Lee successful in implementing its strategy in 2006? Explain.
2. Is Lee's balanced scorecard useful in helping the company understand why it did not reach its target market share in 2006? If it is, explain why. If it is not, explain what other measures you might want to add under the customer perspective and why.
3. Would you have included some measure of employee satisfaction in the learning-and-growth perspective and new-product development in the internal-business-process perspective? That is, do you think employee satisfaction and development of new products are critical for Lee to implement its strategy? Why or why not? Explain briefly.
4. What problems, if any, do you see in Lee improving quality and significantly downsizing to eliminate unused capacity?

PH Grade Assist

13-33 Strategic analysis of operating income. Halsey Company sells women's clothing. Halsey's strategy is to offer a wide selection of clothes and excellent customer service and to charge a premium price. Halsey presents the following data for 2007 and 2008. For simplicity, assume that each customer purchases one piece of clothing.

	2007	2008
1. Pieces of clothing purchased and sold	40,000	40,000
2. Average selling price	$60	$59
3. Average cost per piece of clothing	$40	$41
4. Selling and customer-service capacity	51,000 customers	43,000 customers
5. Selling and customer-service costs	$357,000	$296,700
6. Selling and customer-service capacity cost per customer (Line 5 ÷ Line 4)	$7 per customer	$6.90 per customer
7. Purchasing and administrative capacity	980 designs	850 designs
8. Purchasing and administrative costs	$245,000	$204,000
9. Purchasing and administrative capacity cost per distinct design	$250 per design	$240 per design

Total selling and customer-service costs depend on the number of customers that Halsey has created capacity to support, not the actual number of customers that Halsey serves. Total purchasing and administrative costs depend on purchasing and administrative capacity that Halsey has created (defined in terms of the number of distinct clothing designs that Halsey can purchase and administer). Purchasing and administrative costs do not depend on the actual number of distinct clothing designs purchased. Halsey purchased 930 distinct designs in 2007 and 820 distinct designs in 2008.

At the start of 2008, Halsey planned to increase operating income by 10% over operating income in 2007.

Required

1. Is Halsey's strategy one of product differentiation or cost leadership? Explain.
2. Calculate Halsey's operating income in 2007 and 2008.
3. Calculate the growth, price-recovery, and productivity components of changes in operating income between 2007 and 2008.
4. Does the strategic analysis of operating income indicate Halsey was successful in implementing its strategy in 2008? Explain.

13-34 Analysis of growth, price-recovery, and productivity components. Winchester Corporation manufactures special ball bearings. In 2007, it plans to grow and increase operating-income by capitalizing on its reputation for manufacturing a product that is superior to its competitors. An analysis of Winchester's operating-income changes between 2006 and 2007 shows the following:

Operating income for 2006	$3,450,000
Add growth component	300,000
Add price-recovery component	400,000
Add productivity component	350,000
Operating income for 2007	$4,500,000

Further analysis of these components indicates that had the growth in Winchester's sales kept up with market growth, the growth component in 2007 would have been $750,000. All decreases in market share (that is, sales increases less than the market growth) are attributable to Winchester not implementing its strategy.

Required

1. Is Winchester's 2007 strategy one of product differentiation or cost leadership? Explain briefly.
2. Provide a brief explanation of why the growth, price-recovery, and productivity components are favorable.
3. Was Winchester's gain in operating income in 2007 consistent with the strategy you identified in requirement 1? Explain briefly.

13-35 Engineered and discretionary overhead costs, unused capacity, customer help desk. Cable Galore, a large cable television operator, had 750,000 subscribers in 2005. Cable Galore employs five customer-help-desk representatives to respond to customer questions and problems. During 2005, each customer-help-desk representative worked 8 hours per day for 250 days at a fixed annual salary of $36,000. Cable Galore received 45,000 telephone calls from its customers in 2005. Each call took an average of 10 minutes.

Required

1. Do you think customer-help-desk costs at Cable Galore are engineered costs or discretionary costs? Explain your answer.
2. Where possible, calculate the cost of unused customer-help-desk capacity in 2005 under each of the following assumptions: (a) customer-help-desk costs are engineered costs, and (b) customer-help-desk costs are discretionary costs. If you are unable to calculate the amount and cost of unused capacity, indicate why not.
3. Assume that Cable Galore had 900,000 subscribers in 2006 and that the 2005 percentage of telephone calls received to total subscribers continued in 2006. Customer-help-desk capacity in 2006 was the same as it was in 2005. Where possible, calculate the cost of unused customer-help-desk capacity in

2006 under each of the following assumptions: (a) customer-service costs are engineered costs, and (b) customer-service costs are discretionary costs. If you are unable to calculate the amount and cost of unused capacity, indicate why not.

13-36 Partial productivity measurement. (Chapter appendix) Berkshire Corporation makes small steel parts. Berkshire management has the option, within limits, to substitute direct materials for direct manufacturing labor. If workers cut the steel carefully, Berkshire can manufacture more parts out of a metal sheet, but this approach will require more direct manufacturing labor-hours. Alternatively, Berkshire can use fewer direct manufacturing labor-hours if it is willing to tolerate a larger quantity of direct materials waste. Berkshire operates in a very competitive market. Its strategy is to produce a quality product at a low cost. Berkshire produces no defective products. Berkshire reports the following data for the past two years of operations:

PH Grade Assist

Excel Lab www.prenhall.com/horngren/cost12e

	A	B	C
1		**2007**	**2008**
2	Output units produced and sold	400,000	550,000
3	Direct materials used, in kilograms	450,000	630,000
4	Direct material cost per kilogram	$ 1.20	$ 1.25
5	Direct manurfacturing labor-hours used	7,500	10,100
6	Wages per hour	$ 20.00	$ 25.00
7	Manufacturing capacity in output units	600,000	582,000
8	Manufacturing capacity-related fixed costs	$1,038,000	$1,018,500
9	Fixed manufacturing cost per unit of capacity	$ 1.73	$ 1.75

If you want to use Excel to solve this problem, go to the Excel Lab at **www.prenhall.com/horngren/cost12e** and download the template for Problem 13-36.

Required

1. Compute the partial-productivity ratios for 2008. Compare the partial-productivity ratios in 2008 with partial-productivity ratios for 2007 calculated based on 2008 output produced.
2. On the basis of the partial-productivity ratios alone, can you conclude whether and by how much productivity improved overall in 2008 relative to 2007? Explain.
3. How might the management of Berkshire Corporation use the partial-productivity analysis?

13-37 Total factor productivity (continuation of 13-36). Refer to the information in Problem 13-36.

If you want to use Excel to solve this problem, go to the Excel Lab at **www.prenhall.com/horngren/cost12e** and download the template for Problem 13-36.

PH Grade Assist

Excel Lab www.prenhall.com/horngren/cost12e

Required

1. Compute Berkshire Corporation's total factor productivity (TFP) in 2008.
2. Compare Berkshire Corporation's TFP performance in 2008 relative to a benchmark TFP for 2007 based on cost of inputs that would have been used in 2007 to produce 2008 output at 2008 input prices.
3. What does TFP tell you that partial-productivity measures do not?

13-38 Balanced scorecard, ethics. John Emburey, division manager of the Household Products Division, a maker of kitchen dishwashers, has just seen the balanced scorecard for his division for 2007. He immediately calls Patricia Conley, the division's management accountant, into his office for a meeting. "I think the employee-satisfaction and customer-satisfaction numbers are way too low. These numbers are based on a random sample of subjective assessments made by individual managers and customer representatives. My own experience indicates that we are doing well on both these dimensions. Until we do a formal survey of employees and customers sometime next year, I think we are doing a disservice to ourselves and this company by reporting such low scores for employee and customer satisfaction. These scores will be an embarrassment for us at the division managers' meeting next month. We need to get these numbers up."

Conley knows that the employee- and customer-satisfaction scores are subjective, but the procedure she used this year is identical to the procedures she has used in the past. She knows from the comments she had asked for that the scores represent the unhappiness of employees with the latest work rules and the unhappiness of customers with late deliveries. She also knows that these problems will be corrected in time.

Required

1. Do you think that the Household Products Division should include subjective measures of employee satisfaction and customer satisfaction in its balanced scorecard? Explain.
2. What should Conley do?

Collaborative Learning Problem

13-39 Downsizing. (CMA, adapted) Mayfair Corporation, which currently subsidizes cafeteria services for its employees, has to reduce its costs to stay competitive. It is considering two alternatives for the 250 days of cafeteria service that it needs to provide annually: downsize the current cafeteria operation and offer a reduced menu, or contract with Wilco Foods, an outside vendor, to provide cafeteria services.

Excel Lab www.prenhall.com/horngren/cost12e

The downsizing plan includes reducing the number of cafeteria employees and eliminating entrees from the menu. This plan would be acceptable to Mayfair if the subsidy it has to provide is less than 20% of the current cafeteria subsidy.

If Wilco Foods takes over the cafeteria operation, it would pay rent to Mayfair for the use of the cafeteria and, at the end of each year, pay a percentage of revenues over breakeven. Wilco expects that all its other costs to provide cafeteria service, including employee wages, will be variable at 70% of revenues. Mayfair would be responsible for utilities and maintenance costs. The three alternatives are summarized here:

	A	B	C	D	E	F	G	H	I	J	K	L	M
1		Current Operation				Downsized Operation				Wilco Foods' Proposal			
2	Cafeteria employees' annual wages	$150,000				$75,000							
3	Additional benefits (% of salary)	25%				25%							
4	Days of cafeteria operation	250				250				250			
5	Annual cost of utilities and maintainance (paid by Mayfair)	$ 40,000				$40,000				$40,000			
6													
7	**Daily sales:**									Wilco's revenues and costs:			
8	Entrees	120	at	$4.00	each					75	at	$5.00	each
9	Sandwiches	100	at	$3.00	each	150	at	$3.50	each	95	at	$4.00	each
10	Beverages/desserts	250	at	$1.00	each	280	at	$1.50	each	230	at	$1.50	each
11													
12	Cost of supplies (% of revenues)	60%				50%				70%			
13	Annual rent (paid to Mayfair)									$18,000			
14	Percent of revenues above breakeven (paid to Mayfair)									5.00%			

If you want to use Excel to solve this problem, go to the Excel Lab at **www.prenhall.com/horngren/cost12e** and download the template for Problem 13-39.

Required

1. Determine whether the plan for downsizing the current cafeteria operation would be acceptable to Mayfair Corporation. Show your calculations.
2. What is Wilco's expected breakeven level of revenues? If cost is the only decision criterion, would Mayfair prefer to downsize or let Wilco operate the cafeteria? Show your calculations.
3. If you were the operations manager at Mayfair, what other factors might you consider before choosing to downsize or outsource?

Get Connected: Cost Accounting in the News

WWW

Go to www.prenhall.com/horngren/cost12e for additional online exercise(s) that explore issues affecting the accounting world today. These exercises offer you the opportunity to analyze and reflect on how cost accounting helps managers make better decisions and handle the challenges of strategic planning and implementation.

CHAPTER 13 Video Case

McDONALD'S CORPORATION: The Balanced Scorecard

The challenge for McDonald's Corporation is global: to be the world's best quick-service restaurant experience. This vision is supported by five global strategies:

1. Develop the organization's people—its workers—beginning in its restaurants
2. Foster innovation in menus, facilities, marketing, operations, and technology
3. Share best practices and leverage best-people resources around the world
4. Continue to implement change in the McDonald's organization
5. Reinvent the quick-service-restaurant category and develop other business and growth opportunities

Decades ago, McDonald's revolutionized the restaurant business with its emphasis on quality food, good prices, and fast service in a clean store environment. Founder Ray Kroc believed that this type of setting would be a big hit with the American public and eventually throughout the world. He was right. With more than 28,000 stores in 120 countries, the McDonald's store operating model set the standard in the industry.

Realizing that its position is challenged daily, management at McDonald's has placed its stores in convenient locations. When people are hungry, McDonald's wants to be there when the first hunger pangs strike. Once customers are in the restaurant, employee focus is directed at making each customer's experience one of quality, all the way from hassle-free service to the perception of value and store cleanliness.

There are many factors that affect the company's ability to maintain its position in the industry and fulfill its vision. These factors focus on four areas: financial performance, customers, employees, and store operations. Success in all areas is critical because they are all interrelated. If performance is poor in one area, such as customer satisfaction, it could trigger poor performance in another, such as lower sales. Likewise, if employees are not committed or satisfied, this could result in poor customer satisfaction.

Performance results are provided to store managers on a monthly report card called the "Store Manager Scorecard." This one-page report focuses on the four areas: financial performance, customers, employees, and store operations. These categories are linked to McDonald's vision and strategies, and they contain items that store managers can control and attain. For example, customer- and employee-satisfaction ratings are linked to developing the organization's people. The reasoning is that employees who are trained and treated well will stay with the job. Those same well-trained employees will also pay closer attention to product-preparation standards, so that costs are more tightly controlled. When taking customers' orders, the well-trained employee can attempt to upsell customers on dessert items or larger portion sizes to boost sales. Every customer interaction affects store performance.

From the perspective of McDonald's management, the following guidelines are used to develop and use its scorecard systems. First, link performance measures to the key drivers of the business and the corporate vision. Second, create objective measures that cannot be manipulated at the store level to make the store's performance look better than it really is. Third, make sure any measurements are within the control of the person being evaluated and that they are attainable. For example, a target of zero employee turnover for a store that has been historically experiencing 100% turnover is not realistic.

Other considerations for McDonald's include making sure the information collected and reported on the scorecard is accurate and that any discussions about performance center on actual performance. The number of areas measured also needs to be manageable, so that personnel can focus on being effective in the areas of greatest importance. Finally, McDonald's management has learned that once scorecard results are provided, managers must be given time to resolve problems.

McDonald's managers are confident that the current balanced scorecard approach is appropriate for their business, but they aren't complacent. Because the business is changing, the scorecard also must change. As the vision and strategies are updated, so are the scorecard's measures.

QUESTIONS

1. Evaluate McDonald's using the five forces industry-analysis tool (p. 456). Which force appears strongest? Weakest? How could McDonald's management use this analysis?
2. What strategy is McDonald's pursuing: cost leadership or product differentiation?
3. Think about the four areas in McDonald's scorecard. If you were a store manager, what would you want included in each area and why?

CHAPTER 14

COST ALLOCATION, CUSTOMER-PROFITABILITY ANALYSIS, AND SALES-VARIANCE ANALYSIS

LEARNING OBJECTIVES

1. **Identify four purposes for allocating costs to cost objects**
2. **Understand criteria to guide cost-allocation decisions**
3. **Discuss decisions faced when collecting costs in indirect-cost pools**
4. **Discuss why a company's revenues can differ across customers purchasing the same product**
5. **Apply the concept of cost hierarchy to customer costing**
6. **Discuss why customer-level costs differ across customers**
7. **Subdivide the sales-volume variance into the sales-mix variance and the sales-quantity variance**
8. **Subdivide the sales-quantity variance into the market-share variance and the market-size variance**

Companies are increasingly making distinctions among their customers—providing more support for and allocating more resources to their regular and most profitable customers, and reducing resources spent on customers who do little business with the company or who are unprofitable. For example, airlines such as Lufthansa provide special services (preferred seat assignments and baggage handling) for their most frequent fliers, and hotels such as Hilton offer special vacation packages for their most frequent guests. Building the loyalty of their most profitable customers is a strategy for a range of other industries, including banking, retail, and construction.

Mike Nixon is the CFO of Winona Holding Company. Winona owns two companies: Consumer Appliances, Inc. (CAI), which manufactures and sells refrigerators and clothes dryers, and Spring Distribution Company, which sells bottled water. Winona operates these companies as independent businesses. Nixon has challenged the CFOs of both companies to examine their costing systems. He is meeting with Jim Lin, CFO of CAI, and Christine Weld, CFO of Spring, to review the changes they've made and the resulting effects on operations.

Mike: Good morning, Jim and Christine. Thanks for coming. Let's get right to work, shall we? Jim, what's the status of your cost-allocation initiative?

Jim: My team and I have analyzed the cost structures of both our divisions. We've decided to allocate all the corporate costs of CAI's headquarters to the two divisions: the Refrigerator Division and the Clothes Dryer Division. Our rationale is that we want divisions to recognize the costs of all the services that headquarters provides them when making strategic and operating decisions.

Mike: How did the division managers react to this? They couldn't be too happy to have corporate costs charged to them, especially when they have no control over these costs.

Jim: No, they weren't too thrilled with the change, but we were able to identify cost-allocation bases that had a cause-and-effect relationship with corporate costs, so at least we could demonstrate how we made our decision.

Mike: Great. How about you, Christine, what changes have you made?

Christine: We've begun to identify and allocate costs to customers instead of products. In our business, calculating profitability by products is not particularly helpful because we have essentially only one product. We've discovered that some customers are very profitable and others are unprofitable. We may want to take a closer look at whether some of them are even worth our time if we plan to meet our aggressive growth targets this year.

Mike: Good idea. What approach are you using to determine what it costs to support each customer?

Christine: We use activity-based costing to calculate the cost of resources demanded by each customer for activities such as purchase orders, deliveries, and sales visits. The results have been pretty revealing.

Mike: Tell me more. How are you using the customer-profitability information you generate?

Christine: Well, for one, we're trying to reduce the services we provide to customers who are unprofitable and trying to increase sales to customers who are profitable. We're even thinking about offering preferred or enhanced service levels to those who meet our profitability thresholds.

Mike: That's excellent. What else?

Christine: As you know, we sell through wholesalers as well as directly to retailers. We've done some sales-variance analysis to see how the shift in our business toward wholesalers has affected our profits. We've also tried to evaluate how much of the increase in our sales is because of a change in market size and how much is because of a change in market share. I sent a copy of this report to you via e-mail before I came to the meeting. The customer-profitability information and sales-variance analysis together give us great insight into our individual customers and our overall market.

Mike: Good job, both of you. I'd like you to prepare a short presentation of these important changes for our next board meeting to be sure the board understands how these changes will help us all achieve our strategic goals, both in the short run and the long run.

As the Winona Company example suggests, cost allocation, which is a challenge in nearly every organization and nearly every facet of accounting, provides information needed for both strategic and operating decisions. For example, how should Stanford University allocate costs among undergraduate programs, graduate programs, and research? How should Boston's Children's Hospital allocate the costs of expensive medical equipment, facilities, and staff among its departments? How should Heinz allocate manufacturing overhead to individual products?

Television and newspaper stories about questionable cost-charging practices frequently focus on cost-allocation issues. In one case, a patient in a hospital was charged $17 for a quart of distilled water—$3.40 of direct costs and $13.60 of allocated costs. Much of the $13.60 was questionably related to the services provided to the patient. Cost-allocation issues also arise in disputes over large cost overruns on construction projects such as the Big Dig project in Boston and even Hollywood movies. One such well-publicized dispute arose in the case of the highly successful film "Forrest Gump." A writer, whose royalty depended on the film's profits, disputed the costs allocated to the film.

Chapters 4 and 5 examined topics related largely to the allocation of indirect costs to individual products. As we saw then, finding answers to cost-allocation questions is often difficult. The answers are seldom clearly right or wrong. Nevertheless, in this chapter and the next, we provide insight into cost allocation and the different issues that arise, even if the answers seem elusive. The emphasis in this chapter is on macro issues in cost allocation: allocation of costs to divisions, plants, and customers. We describe customer-profitability analysis, in which the customer rather than the product is the cost object and revenues and costs are assigned to each customer. We also show how the sales-volume variance introduced in Chapter 7 can be further analyzed when there are multiple customers and multiple products. Chapter 15 describes micro issues in cost allocation—allocating support-department costs to operating departments and allocating common costs to various cost objects—as well as revenue allocations.

There is rarely one "best" way to allocate costs. Cost allocation requires judgment, and managers may differ in their judgments.

Purposes of Cost Allocation

1

Identify four purposes for allocating costs to cost objects

. . . to provide information for decisions, motivate managers, justify costs, and measure income

Indirect costs of a particular cost object are costs that are related to that cost object but cannot be traced to it in an economically feasible (cost-effective) way. These costs often comprise a large percentage of the overall costs assigned to such cost objects as products, customers, and distribution channels. Why do managers allocate indirect costs to these cost objects? Exhibit 14-1 illustrates four purposes of cost allocation.

Different costs are appropriate for different purposes. Consider costs of a product in terms of the business functions in the value chain.

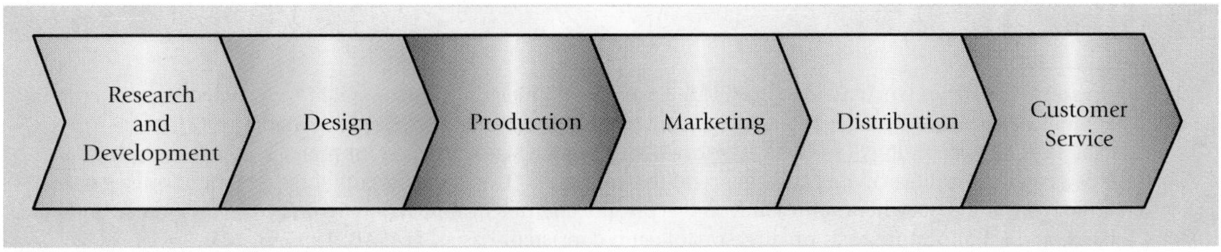

EXHIBIT 14-1

Purposes of Cost Allocation

Purpose	Illustrations
1. To provide information for economic decisions	To decide whether to add a new airline flight To decide whether to manufacture a component part of a television set or to purchase it from another manufacturer To decide on the selling price for a customized product or service To evaluate the cost of available capacity used to support different products
2. To motivate managers and other employees	To encourage the design of products that are simpler to manufacture or less costly to service To encourage sales representatives to emphasize high-margin products or services
3. To justify costs or compute reimbursement amounts	To cost products at a "fair" price, often required by government defense contracts To compute reimbursement for a consulting firm based on a percentage of the cost savings resulting from the implementation of its recommendations
4. To measure income and assets	To cost inventories for financial reporting for reporting to external parties To cost inventories for reporting to tax authorities

Cost allocations can be made to motivate managers to *liberally use* a department's services (for example, internal auditing). In this case, top management (1) might not allocate the costs of internal auditing to departments using the services or (2) might allocate a fixed amount of the costs of internal auditing to departments using the services regardless of how much they consume. Cost allocations also can be made to motivate managers to *prudently use* a department's services (for example, R&D). In this case, top management might allocate all costs of R&D to departments using the services.

The same set of costs in these six business functions typically will not satisfy each of the four purposes in Exhibit 14-1.

For some decisions related to the economic-decision purpose (for example, long-run product pricing), the costs in all six functions are relevant. For other decisions, particularly short-run economic decisions (for example, make or buy decisions), costs from only one or two functions (for example, design and manufacturing) might be relevant.

For the motivation purpose, costs from more than one business function are often included to emphasize to decision makers how costs in different functions are related to one another. For example, product designers at some Japanese companies such as Hitachi and Toshiba incorporate costs of other functions in the value chain—for example, production, distribution, and customer service—into their product-cost estimates. The aim is to focus designers' attention on how different product-design alternatives affect total costs.

For the cost-reimbursement purpose, the particular contract will often stipulate whether all six of the business functions or only a subset of them are to be reimbursed. For instance, cost-reimbursement rules for U.S.-government contracts explicitly exclude marketing costs.

For the purpose of income and asset measurement for reporting to external parties, inventoriable costs under GAAP include only manufacturing costs (and product-design costs in some cases). In the United States, R&D costs in most industries are a period cost when they are incurred, as are marketing, distribution, and customer-service costs.[1]

Criteria to Guide Cost-Allocation Decisions

2

Understand criteria to guide cost-allocation decisions

. . . such as identifying factors that cause resources to be consumed

After identifying the purposes of cost allocation, managers and management accountants must decide how to allocate costs. This section describes the different criteria companies use to allocate costs.

Exhibit 14-2 presents four criteria used to guide cost-allocation decisions. These decisions affect both the number of indirect-cost pools and the cost-allocation base for each indirect-cost pool. We emphasize the superiority of the cause-and-effect and the benefits-received criteria, especially when the purpose of cost allocation is to provide information for economic decisions or to motivate managers and employees.[2] Cause and effect is the

Using the cause-and-effect criterion to choose a cost-allocation base means that the base is a cost driver of the indirect-cost pool.

[1]In some industries (such as software), U.S.-based companies can capitalize R&D costs when certain criteria are met (such as the R&D leads to a product that is believed to be commercially viable).

[2]The Federal Accounting Standards Advisory Board (which sets standards for management accounting for U.S.-government departments and agencies) recommends: "Cost assignments should be performed by: (a) directly tracing costs whenever feasible and economically practicable, (b) assigning costs on a cause-and-effect basis, and (c) allocating costs on a reasonable and consistent basis." (*FASAB*, 1995, p. 12).

1. Cause and Effect. Using this criterion, managers identify the variables that cause resources to be consumed. For example, managers may use hours of testing as the variable when allocating the costs of a quality-testing area to products. Cost allocations based on the cause-and-effect criterion are likely to be the most credible to operating personnel.
2. Benefits Received. Using this criterion, managers identify the beneficiaries of the outputs of the cost object. The costs of the cost object are allocated among the beneficiaries in proportion to the benefits each receives. Consider a corporatewide advertising program that promotes the general image of the corporation rather than any individual product. The costs of this program may be allocated on the basis of division revenues; the higher the revenues, the higher the division's allocated cost of the advertising program. The rationale behind this allocation is that divisions with higher revenues apparently benefited from the advertising more than divisions with lower revenues and, therefore, ought to be allocated more of the advertising costs.
3. Fairness or Equity. This criterion is often cited in government contracts when cost allocations are the basis for establishing a price satisfactory to the government and its suppliers. Cost allocation here is viewed as a "reasonable" or "fair" means of establishing a selling price in the minds of the contracting parties. For most allocation decisions, fairness is a difficult-to-achieve objective rather than an operational criterion.
4. Ability to Bear. This criterion advocates allocating costs in proportion to the cost object's ability to bear costs allocated to it. An example is the allocation of corporate executive salaries on the basis of division operating income. The presumption is that the more-profitable divisions have a greater ability to absorb corporate headquarters' costs.

EXHIBIT 14-2

Criteria for Cost-Allocation Decisions

The following outline provides an overview of cost allocation:

Step 1: Determine the purpose of the allocation, because the purpose defines *what costs* will be allocated.
Step 2: Decide *how* to allocate the costs from step 1. To do so,
- a. Decide *how many indirect-cost pools* to form, and then
- b. Identify an *allocation base* (preferably a cost driver) *for each cost pool.*

primary criterion used in activity-based costing (ABC) applications. ABC systems use the concept of a cost hierarchy to identify the cost drivers that best demonstrate the cause-and-effect relationship between each activity and the costs in the related cost pool. The cost drivers are then chosen as cost-allocation bases.

Fairness and ability to bear are less-frequently-used criteria than cause and effect or benefits received. Fairness is a difficult criterion on which to obtain agreement. What one party views as fair, another party may view as unfair.[3] For example, a university may view allocating a share of general administrative costs to government contracts as fair because general administrative costs are incurred to support all activities of the university. The government may view the allocation of such costs as unfair because the general administrative costs would have been incurred by the university regardless of whether the government contract existed. To get a sense of the issues that arise when using the ability-to-bear criterion, consider a product that consumes a large amount of indirect costs but whose selling price is currently below its direct costs. This product has no ability to bear any of the indirect costs it uses. If the indirect costs it consumes are allocated to other products, these other products are subsidizing the product that is losing money.

Most importantly, companies must weigh the costs and benefits when designing and implementing their cost allocations. Companies incur costs not only in collecting data but also in taking the time to educate managers about cost allocations. In general, the more complex the cost allocations, the higher these education costs.

The costs of designing and implementing complex cost allocations are highly visible. Unfortunately, the benefits from using well-designed cost allocations—enabling managers to make better-informed sourcing decisions, pricing decisions, cost-control decisions, and so on—are difficult to measure. Still, when making cost allocations, managers should consider the benefits as well as the costs.

Spurred by rapid reductions in the costs of collecting and processing information, companies are now moving toward more-detailed cost allocations. Many companies have developed manufacturing- or distribution-overhead costing systems that use multiple (in some cases more than 10) cost-allocation bases. Also, some businesses already have state-of-the-art information technology in place for operating their plants or distribution networks. Applying this technology to allocate costs is less expensive—and more inviting—than developing cost allocations from scratch.

[3]Kaplow and Shavell, for example, in a review of the legal literature, note that "notions of fairness are many and varied. They are analyzed and rationalized by different writers in different ways, and they also typically depend upon the circumstances under consideration. Accordingly, it is not possible to identify a consensus view on these notions. . . . " See L. Kaplow and S. Shavell, "Fairness Versus Welfare," *Harvard Law Review*, February 2001.

Cost Allocation and Costing Systems

In this section, we focus on the first purpose of cost allocation: to provide information for economic decisions such as pricing by measuring the full costs of delivering products based on an ABC system.

Chapter 5 described how ABC systems define indirect-cost pools for different activities and use cost drivers as allocation bases to assign costs of indirect-cost pools to products. In this section, we focus on how costs are assigned to the indirect-cost pools.

We will use Consumer Appliances, Inc. (CAI), to illustrate how costs incurred in different parts of a company can be assigned, and then reassigned, for costing products, services, customers, or contracts. Recall, CAI has two divisions and each has its own manufacturing plant—the Refrigerator Division with a plant in Minneapolis and the Clothes Dryer Division with a plant in St. Paul. CAI's headquarters is in a separate location in Minneapolis. In each division, CAI manufactures and sells multiple products that differ in size and complexity.

CAI's management team collects costs at the following levels:

- **Corporate costs** —there are three major categories of corporate costs:
  1. **Treasury costs** —interest of $900,000 on debt used to finance the construction of new assembly equipment in the two divisions. The cost of new assembly equipment is $5,200,000 in the Refrigerator Division and $3,800,000 in the Clothes Dryer Division.
  2. **Human-resource-management costs** —recruitment and ongoing employee training and development, $1,600,000.
  3. **Corporate-administration costs** —executive salaries, rent, and general administration costs, $5,400,000.
- **Division costs** —for each division, there are two direct-cost categories (direct materials and direct manufacturing labor) and seven indirect-cost pools—one cost pool each for the five activities (design, setup, manufacturing, distribution, and administration), one cost pool to accumulate facility costs, and one cost pool for the allocated corporate treasury costs. Exhibit 14-3 presents data for six of the division indirect-cost pools and cost-allocation bases. (In a later section, we describe how corporate treasury costs are allocated to each division to create the seventh division indirect-cost pool.) CAI identifies the cost hierarchy category for each cost pool—output-unit level, batch level, product-sustaining level, and facility- sustaining level (as described in Chapter 5, pp. 147–148).

EXHIBIT 14-3 **Division Indirect-Cost Pools and Cost-Allocation Bases, CAI, Inc., for Refrigerator Division (R) and Clothes Dryer Division (CD)**

Division Indirect-Cost Pools	Example of Costs	Total Indirect Costs	Cost Hierarchy Category	Cost-Allocation Base	Cause-and-Effect Relationship That Motivates Management's Choice of Allocation Base
Design	Design engineering salaries	(R) $6,000,000 (CD) 4,250,000	Product sustaining	Parts times cubic feet	Complex products (more parts and larger size) require greater design resources.
Setups of machines	Setup labor and equipment cost	(R) $3,000,000 (CD) 2,400,000	Batch level	Setup-hours	Overhead costs of the setup activity increase as setup-hours increase.
Manufacturing operations	Plant and equipment, energy	(R) $25,000,000 (CD) 18,750,000	Output unit level	Machine-hours	Manufacturing-operations overhead costs support machines and, hence, increase with machine usage.
Distribution	Shipping labor and equipment	(R) $8,000,000 (CD) 5,500,000	Output unit level	Cubic feet	Distribution-overhead costs increase with cubic feet of product shipped.
Administration	Division executive salaries	(R) $1,000,000 (CD) 800,000	Facility sustaining	Revenues	Weak relationship between division executive salaries and revenues, but justified by CAI on a benefits-received basis.
Facility	Annual building and space costs	(R) $4,500,000 (CD) 3,500,000	All	Square feet	Facility costs increase with square feet of space.

Exhibit 14-4 presents an overview diagram of the allocation of corporate and division indirect costs to products of the Refigerator Division. Note: The Clothes Dryer Division has its own seven indirect-cost pools used to allocate costs to products. These cost pools and cost-allocation bases parallel the indirect-cost pools and allocation bases for the Refrigerator Division.

Look first at the middle row of the exhibit, where you see "Division Indirect-Cost Pools," and scan the lower half. It is similar to Exhibit 5-3, (p. 150), which illustrates ABC systems using indirect-cost pools and cost drivers for different activities. A major difference in the lower half of Exhibit 14-4 is the cost pool called Facility Costs (far right, middle row), which accumulates all annual costs of buildings and furnishings (such as depreciation) incurred in the division. The arrows in Exhibit 14-4 indicate that

In practice, costing systems are usually much more complex than most textbook examples. Although we use simplified examples to aid learning, the underlying concepts apply equally in more-complex, real-world costing systems.

EXHIBIT 14-4 **Overview Diagram of Allocation of Corporate Costs and Division Indirect Costs to Products of the Refrigerator Division, CAI, Inc.**

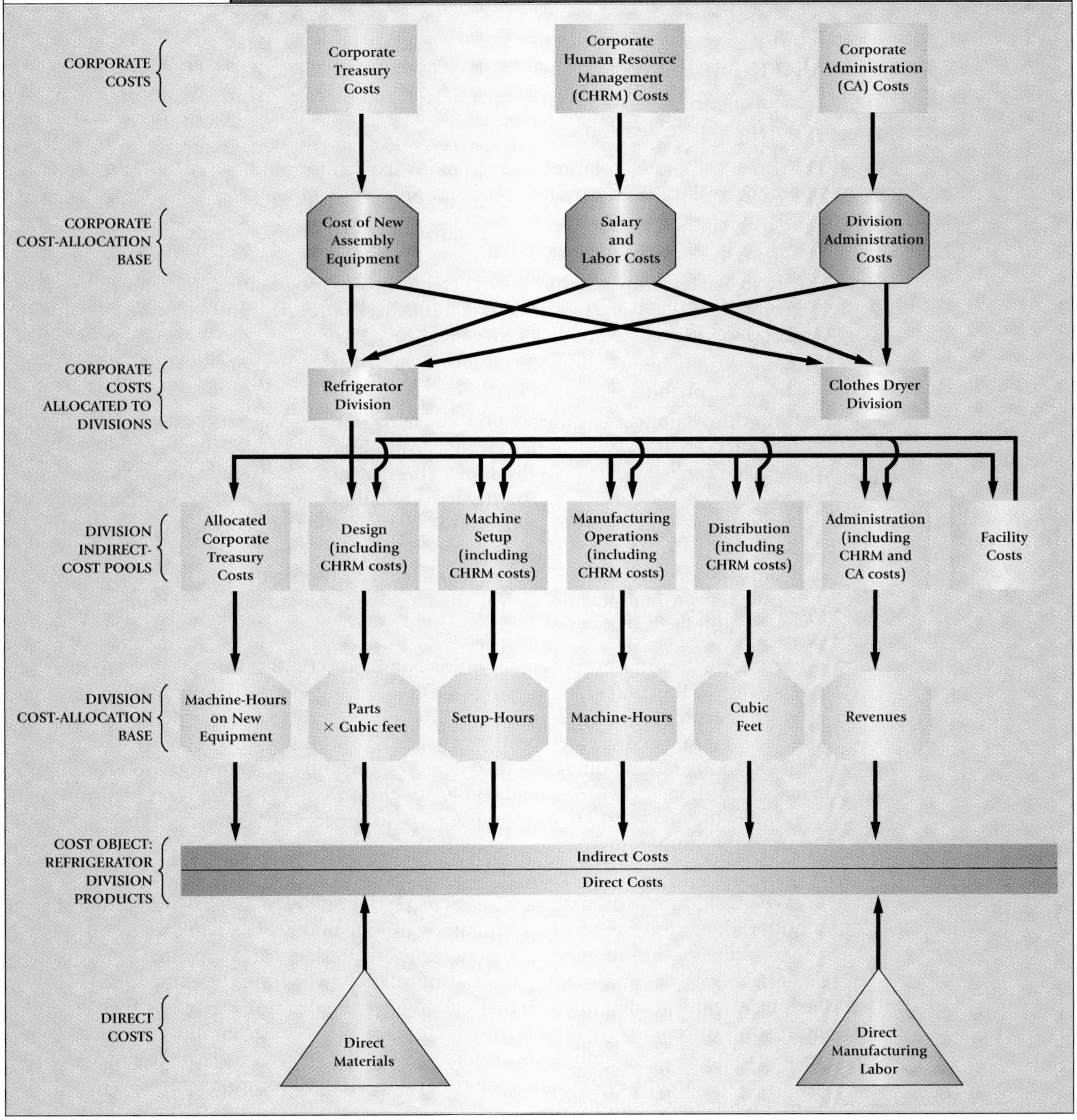

CAI allocates facility costs to the five activity-cost pools. Recall from Exhibit 14-3 that CAI uses square feet area required for various activities (design, setup, manufacturing, distribution, and administration) to allocate these facility costs. These activity-cost pools then include the costs of the building and facilities needed to perform the various activities.

The costs in the six remaining indirect-cost pools (that is, after costs of the facility cost pool have been allocated to other cost pools) are allocated to products on the basis of cost drivers described in Exhibit 14-3. These cost drivers are chosen as the cost-allocation bases because there is a cause-and-effect relationship between the cost drivers and the costs in the indirect-cost pool. A cost rate per unit is calculated for each cost-allocation base. Indirect costs are allocated to products on the basis of the total quantity of the cost-allocation base for each activity used by the product.

Next focus on the upper half of Exhibit 14-4: how corporate costs are allocated to divisions and then to indirect-cost pools. Before getting into the details of the allocations, let's first consider some broader choices that CAI faces regarding the allocation of corporate costs.

3

Discuss decisions faced when collecting costs in indirect-cost pools

. . . determining the number of cost pools and the costs to be included in each cost pool

Allocating Corporate Costs to Divisions and Products

CAI's management team has several choices to make when accumulating and allocating corporate costs to divisions.

1. Which corporate-cost categories should CAI allocate as indirect costs of the divisions? Should CAI allocate all corporate costs or only some of them?

- Some companies allocate all corporate costs to divisions because corporate costs are incurred to support division activities. Allocating all corporate costs motivates division managers to examine how corporate costs are planned and controlled. Also, companies that want to calculate the full cost of products must allocate all corporate costs to indirect-cost pools of divisions.
- Other companies do not allocate corporate costs to divisions because these costs are not controllable by division managers.
- Still other companies allocate only those corporate costs, such as corporate human resources, that are widely perceived as causally related to division activities or that provide explicit benefits to divisions. These companies exclude corporate costs such as corporate donations to charitable foundations because division managers often have no say in making these decisions and because the benefits to the divisions are less evident or too remote (see Global Surveys of Company Practice, p. 499). If a company decides not to allocate some or all corporate costs, this results in total company profitability being less than the sum of individual division or product profitabilities.

For some decision purposes, allocating some but not all corporate costs to divisions may be the preferred alternative. Consider the performance evaluation of division managers. The controllability notion (see p. 198) is frequently used to justify excluding some corporate costs from division reports. For example, salaries of the top management at corporate headquarters are often excluded from responsibility accounting reports of division managers. Although divisions tend to benefit from these corporate costs, division managers argue they have no say in ("are not responsible for") how much of these corporate resources they use or how much they cost. The contrary argument is that full allocation is justified because the divisions receive benefits from all corporate costs.

2. When allocating corporate costs to divisions, should CAI allocate only variable costs or both variable and fixed costs? Companies allocate both variable and fixed costs to divisions and then to products because they use these product costs to make long-run strategic decisions. For example, companies want to know which products they should sell in the long run and at what price. To make good long-run decisions, managers need to know the cost of all resources (whether variable or fixed) needed to produce products. Why? Because in the long run, more costs can be managed and fewer costs are regarded as fixed, and to survive and prosper in the long run, prices charged for products must exceed total costs (both variable and fixed).

GLOBAL SURVEYS OF COMPANY PRACTICE

Allocation of Corporate and Other Support Costs to Divisions and Departments

Recent surveys confirm the continued importance that companies place on allocating corporate and other support costs to divisions and departments. For example, 70% of U.S. companies allocate corporate and support costs (which typically comprise 34% to 42% of all costs incurred).[a] In the United Kingdom and Sweden, 77% and 90% respectively of companies allocate corporate and support costs.[b,c]

Managers across the globe cite very similar reasons for allocating corporate and other support costs to divisions and departments. For example, Australian managers identified the following reasons for allocating corporate costs to divisions (in order of importance): (1) to acknowledge that divisions would incur such costs if they were independent units or if the services were not provided internally; (2) to make division managers aware that corporate costs exist; (3) to stimulate division managers to put pressure on corporate managers to control costs; and (4) to stimulate division managers to use corporate services economically.[d]

Similar to U.S. companies, Swedish respondents consider overhead-cost allocation a high priority, so they have significantly changed their cost accounting systems to more accurately allocate overhead costs. These changes include the establishment of more-homogeneous cost pools, the development of allocation bases, and a switch from allocating overhead on the basis of direct labor and direct materials to using separate machine-related overhead cost pools and machine-hours. However, despite these efforts, overhead-related cost distortions remain a significant problem for managers. Among the 98% of U.S. survey respondents who identified at least some cost distortion within their organizations, the most-frequently-cited distortion factor reported was overhead allocations (30%).

In general, executives cite the following difficulties in implementing their cost-allocation programs: allocations resulting in profit-center losses, friction among managers, unstable market prices, allocations perceived as arbitrary, usage hard to monitor, agreement on the allocation method difficult to obtain, and time-consuming allocation process.

---

[a]Ernst & Young, "2003 Survey."

[b]C. Drury and M. Tayles, "Product Costing."

[c]U. Ask, C. Ax, and S. Jönsson, "Cost Management."

[d]G. Dean, M. Joye, and P. Blayney, *Strategic Management.*

Full citations are in Appendix A at the end of the book.

3. If CAI allocates corporate costs to divisions, how many cost pools should it use? One extreme is to aggregate all corporate costs into a single cost pool. The other extreme is to have numerous individual corporate cost pools. A variety of factors may prompt managers to consider using multiple cost pools. A major factor is the concept of homogeneous cost pools.

In a **homogeneous cost pool**, all of the costs in the cost pool have the same or a similar cause-and-effect or benefits-received relationship with the cost-allocation base. Homogeneity of costs is important because creating homogeneous cost pools leads to more-accurate costs of a given cost object. If a homogeneous cost pool exists, cost allocations using that pool will be the same as they would be if costs of each individual activity in that pool were allocated separately. The greater the degree of homogeneity, the fewer the number of cost pools required to explain accurately differences in how divisions or products use resources of the company.

For example, when allocating corporate costs to divisions, CAI can combine corporate administration costs and corporate human-resource-management costs into a single cost pool if both cost categories have the same or a similar cause-and-effect relationship with the same cost-allocation base (say, number of employees in each division). If, however, each cost category has a cause-and-effect relationship with a different cost-allocation base (for example, number of employees in each division affects corporate human-resource-management costs, whereas revenues of each division affect corporate administration costs), CAI will prefer to maintain separate cost pools for each of these costs. Determining homogeneous cost pools requires judgment and should be revisited on a regular basis to evaluate whether the cause-and-effect relationship between the cost-allocation base and the different cost categories in a cost pool has changed.

Another factor in deciding on the number of cost pools is the views of managers. Do they believe that aggregating corporate costs into a single cost pool ignores important differences in how divisions use corporate resources? A final factor is the costs of implementing a multiple-cost-pool system. Improvements in information-gathering technology are enhancing the capability of companies and reducing the cost of using multiple cost pools. In deciding the number of cost pools to use, management must weigh the costs of implementation against the benefits of better information.

4. If CAI allocates corporate costs to divisions, which allocation bases should it use? Generally, it should use the ones that have the best cause-and-effect relationship with corporate costs.

Implementing Corporate Cost Allocations

This section links the cost-allocation material in this chapter with the ABC material in Chapter 5.

After much discussion and debate, CAI's management team chooses to allocate all corporate costs to divisions. We now illustrate the allocation of corporate costs to divisions in CAI's ABC system.

The demands for corporate resources by the Refrigerator Division and the Clothes Dryer Division depend on the demands that each division's products place on these resources. The top half of Exhibit 14-4 graphically represents the allocations.

1. CAI allocates treasury costs to each division on the basis of the cost of new assembly equipment installed in each division (the cost driver of treasury costs). It allocates the \$900,000 of treasury costs as follows (using information from p. 496):

$$\text{Refrigerator Division:} \quad \$900{,}000 \times \frac{\$5{,}200{,}000}{\$5{,}200{,}000 + \$3{,}800{,}000} = \$520{,}000$$

$$\text{Clothes Dryer Division:} \quad \$900{,}000 \times \frac{\$3{,}800{,}000}{\$5{,}200{,}000 + \$3{,}800{,}000} = \$380{,}000$$

Each division then creates a separate cost pool consisting of the allocated corporate treasury costs and reallocates these costs to products on the basis of machine-hours used on the new equipment. Treasury costs are an output unit-level cost because they represent resources used on activities performed on each individual unit of a product.

2. CAI's analysis indicates that the demand for corporate human-resource-management (CHRM) costs for recruitment and training varies with total salary and labor costs. As a result, these costs are allocated to divisions on the basis of the total salary and labor costs incurred in each division. Suppose salary and labor costs are \$44,000,000 in the Refrigerator Division and \$36,000,000 in the Clothes Dryer Division. Then CHRM costs are allocated to the divisions as follows:

$$\text{Refrigerator Division:} \quad \$1{,}600{,}000 \times \frac{\$44{,}000{,}000}{\$44{,}000{,}000 + \$36{,}000{,}000} = \$880{,}000$$

$$\text{Clothes Dryer Division:} \quad \$1{,}600{,}000 \times \frac{\$36{,}000{,}000}{\$44{,}000{,}000 + \$36{,}000{,}000} = \$720{,}000$$

Each division reallocates the CHRM costs allocated to it to the indirect-cost pools on the basis of total salary and labor costs of each indirect-cost pool. As a result, CHRM costs are allocated to the activity cost pools of design, machine setup, manufacturing operations, distribution, and division administration (the allocated-corporate-treasury cost pool and the facility costs pool have no salary and labor costs, so no CHRM costs are allocated to them). CHRM costs that are added to division indirect-cost pools are then allocated to products using the cost driver for the respective cost pool. Therefore, CHRM costs are product-sustaining costs (for the portion of CHRM costs allocated to the design cost pool), batch-level costs (for the portion of CHRM costs allocated to the machine-setup cost pool), output unit-level costs (for the portions of CHRM costs allocated to the manufacturing-operations and distribution cost pools), and facility-sustaining costs (for the portion of CHRM costs allocated to the division-administration cost pool).

3. CAI allocates corporate administration costs to each division on the basis of division administration costs (see Exhibit 14-3) because corporate administration's main role is to support division management.

$$\text{Refrigerator Division:} \quad \$5{,}400{,}000 \times \frac{\$1{,}000{,}000}{\$1{,}000{,}000 + \$800{,}000} = \$3{,}000{,}000$$

$$\text{Clothes Dryer Division:} \quad \$5{,}400{,}000 \times \frac{\$800{,}000}{\$1{,}000{,}000 + \$800{,}000} = \$2{,}400{,}000$$

Each division adds the allocated corporate-administration costs to the division-administration cost pool. The costs in this cost pool are facility-sustaining costs and do not have a cause-and-effect relationship with individual products produced and sold by each division. CAI's policy, however, is to allocate all costs to products so that CAI's division managers become aware of all costs incurred at CAI in their pricing and other decisions. It allocates the division-administration costs (including allocated corporate-administration costs) to products on the basis of product revenues (a benefits-received criterion).

Exhibit 14-4 highlights the different ways CAI allocates corporate costs to divisions and then to products. The company

- Establishes a separate indirect-cost pool at the division level to allocate corporate treasury costs to products.
- Allocates CHRM costs to divisions on the basis of division salary and labor costs and then reallocates the CHRM costs allocated to divisions to multiple indirect-cost pools on the basis of total salary and labor costs in each cost pool. Therefore, some of the indirect-cost pools of each division include an allocation of CHRM costs, as shown in Exhibit 14-4.
- Allocates corporate-administration costs to divisions on the basis of division-administration costs and adds these costs to a single indirect-cost pool (division administration) as shown in Exhibit 14-4.

As we described in Chapter 5, focusing on activities and the hierarchy of costs promotes cost management. The set of activities and the actions necessary to manage costs are different if a cost is an output unit-level cost, a batch-level cost, a product-sustaining cost, or a facility-sustaining cost. For example, to manage setup cost, which is a batch-level cost, CAI must focus on batch-level activities, such as ways to reduce setup-hours and the cost per setup-hour.

The issues discussed in this section regarding divisions and products apply nearly identically to customers, as we shall show next. *Instructors and students who, at this point, want to explore more-detailed issues in cost allocation rather than focusing on how activity-based costing extends to customer profitability can skip ahead to Chapter 15.*

Customer Revenues and Customer Costs

Customer-profitability analysis is the reporting and analysis of revenues earned from customers and the costs incurred to earn those revenues. An analysis of customer differences in revenues and costs can provide insight into why differences exist in the operating income earned from different customers. With this information, managers can ensure that customers making large contributions to the operating income of a company receive a level of attention from the company matching their contribution to the company's profitability.

Customer-profitability analysis is management accounting's response to the notion that "the customer is priority one" from marketing and management courses. In particular, this section shows how accounting can provide marketing personnel with useful information.

Consider Spring Distribution Company, which sells bottled water. It has two distribution channels: (1) a wholesale distribution channel, in which the wholesaler sells to supermarkets, drugstores, and other stores, and (2) a retail distribution channel for a small number of business customers. We focus mainly on customer-profitability analysis in Spring's retail distribution channel. The list selling price in this channel is $14.40 per case (24 bottles). The full cost to Spring is $12 per case. If every case is sold at list price in this distribution channel, Spring would earn a gross margin of $2.40 per case.

4

Discuss why a company's revenues can differ across customers purchasing the same product

. . . revenues can differ because of differences in the quantity purchased and the price discounts given

Customer-Revenue Analysis

Consider revenues from 4 of Spring's 10 retail customers in June 2007:

	A	B	C	D	E
1		CUSTOMER			
2		A	B	G	J
3	Cases sold	42,000	33,000	2,900	2,500
4	List selling price	$ 14.40	$ 14.40	$ 14.40	$ 14.40
5	Price discount	$ 0.96	$ 0.24	$ 1.20	$ 0.00
6	Invoice price	$ 13.44	$ 14.16	$ 13.20	$ 14.40
7	Revenues (Row 3 x Row 6)	$564,480	$467,280	$38,280	$36,000

Two variables explain revenue differences across these four customers: (1) the number of cases they purchased and (2) the magnitude of price discounting.

A **price discount** is the reduction in selling price below list selling price to encourage increases in customer purchases. Companies that record only the final invoice price in their information system cannot readily track the magnitude of their price discounting.[4]

Price discounts are a function of multiple factors, including the volume of product purchased (higher-volume customers receive higher discounts) and the desire to sell to a customer who might help promote sales to other customers. Discounts could also be because of poor negotiating by a salesperson or the unwanted effect of an incentive plan based only on revenues. At no time should price discounts run afoul of the law by way of price discrimination, predatory pricing, or collusive pricing (pp. 438–440). Price discounts can also be unethical, for example, when discounts are given by pharmaceutical representatives to doctors to encourage them to prescribe a particular drug.

Tracking price discounts by customer and by salesperson helps improve customer profitability. For example, Spring Distribution may decide to strictly enforce its volume-based price discounting policy. It may also require its salespeople to obtain approval for giving large discounts to customers who do not normally qualify for such discounts. In addition, Spring could track the future sales of customers who its salespeople have given sizable price discounts to because of their "high growth potential." For example, Spring should track future sales to customer G to see if the $1.20-per-case discount translates into higher future sales. Training in sales forecasting should be given to salespeople to help them accurately predict future growth in sales of customers.

Customer revenues are one element of customer profitability. The other element is customer costs.

5

Apply the concept of cost hierarchy to customer costing

. . . such as assigning some costs to individual customers and other costs to distribution channels or to corporatewide efforts

Customer-Cost Analysis

We apply to customers the cost hierarchy discussed in the previous section and in Chapter 5. A **customer-cost hierarchy** categorizes costs related to customers into different cost pools on the basis of different types of cost drivers, or cost-allocation bases, or different degrees of difficulty in determining cause-and-effect or benefits-received relationships. Spring's ABC system focuses on customers rather than products. It has one direct cost—the cost of bottled water—and multiple indirect-cost pools. Spring identifies five categories of indirect costs in its customer cost hierarchy:

1. **Customer output unit-level costs** —costs of activities to sell each unit (case) to a customer. An example is product-handling costs of each case sold.
2. **Customer batch-level costs** —costs of activities that are related to a group of units (cases) sold to a customer. Examples are costs incurred to process orders or to make deliveries.
3. **Customer-sustaining costs** —costs of activities to support individual customers, regardless of the number of units or batches of product delivered to the customer. Examples are costs of visits to customers or costs of displays at customer sites.

[4]Further analysis of customer revenues could distinguish gross revenues from net revenues. This approach highlights differences across customers in sales returns. Additional discussion of ways to analyze revenue differences across customers is in R. S. Kaplan and R. Cooper, *Cost and Effect* (Boston, MA: Harvard Business School Press, 1998, Chapter 10); and G. Cokins, *Activity-Based Cost Management: An Executive's Guide* (New York, NY: John Wiley & Sons, 2001, Chapter 3).

4. **Distribution-channel costs** —costs of activities related to a particular distribution channel rather than to each unit of product, each batch of product, or specific customers. An example is the salary of the manager of Spring's retail distribution channel.
5. **Corporate-sustaining costs** —costs of activities that cannot be traced to individual customers or distribution channels. Examples are top-management and general-administration costs.

Note from these descriptions that four of the five levels of Spring's cost hierarchy closely parallel the cost hierarchy described in Chapter 5, except that Spring focuses on *customers* whereas the cost hierarchy in Chapter 5 focused on *products*. Spring has one additional cost hierarchy category—distribution-channel costs—for the costs it incurs to support its wholesale and retail distribution channels.

Customer-Level Costs

6

Discuss why customer-level costs differ across customers

. . . because different customers place different demands on a company's resources

Spring is particularly interested in analyzing customer-level indirect costs that are incurred in the first three categories of the customer-cost hierarchy: customer output-unit-level costs, customer batch-level costs, and customer-sustaining costs. Spring believes that it can work with customers to reduce these costs. It believes that customer actions will have less impact on distribution-channel and corporate-sustaining costs. The following table shows five activities (in addition to cost of goods sold) that Spring identifies as resulting in customer-level costs. The table indicates the cost drivers and cost-driver rates for each activity, as well as the cost-hierarchy category for each activity.

	G	H	I	J
1	**Activity Area**	**Cost Driver and Rate**		**Cost-Hierarchy Category**
2	Product handling	$0.50	per case sold	Customer output-unit-level costs
3	Order taking	$ 100	per purchase order	Customer batch-level costs
4	Delivery vehicles	$ 2	per delivery mile traveled	Customer batch-level costs
5	Rush deliveries	$ 300	per expedited delivery	Customer batch-level costs
6	Visits to customers	$ 80	per sales visit	Customer-sustaining costs

Information on the quantity of cost drivers used by each of four customers is:

	A	B	C	D	E
10		**CUSTOMER**			
11		**A**	**B**	**G**	**J**
12	Number of purchase orders	30	25	15	10
13	Number of deliveries	60	30	20	15
14	Miles traveled per delivery	5	12	20	6
15	Number of rush deliveries	1	0	2	0
16	Number of visits to customers	6	5	4	3

Exhibit 14-5 shows a customer-profitability analysis for the four retail customers using information on customer revenues previously presented (p. 502) and customer-level costs from the ABC system.

Spring Distribution can use the information in Exhibit 14-5 to work with customers to reduce the quantity of activities needed to support them. (See also the Focus on Values and Behaviors feature, p. 505) Consider a comparison of Customer G and Customer A. Customer G purchases only 7% of the cases that customer A purchases (2,900 versus 42,000). Yet, compared with Customer A, Customer G uses one-half as many purchase orders, two-thirds as many visits to customers, one-third as many deliveries, and twice as many rush deliveries. By implementing charges for each of these services, Spring might be able to induce Customer G to make fewer but larger purchase orders, customer visits, deliveries and rush deliveries while looking to increase sales in the future.

Consider Owens and Minor, a distributor of medical supplies to hospitals. It strategically prices each of its services separately. For example, if a hospital wants a rush delivery or special packaging, Owens and Minor charges the hospital an additional price for each particular service. How have Owens and Minor's customers reacted? Hospitals that

EXHIBIT 14-5 Customer-Profitability Analysis for Four Retail Channel Customers of Spring Distribution for June 2007

	A	B	C	D	E
1		CUSTOMER			
2		A	B	G	J
3	Revenues at list price: $14.40 x 42,000; 33,000; 2,900; 2,500	$604,800	$475,200	$41,760	$36,000
4	Price discount: $0.96 x 42,000; $0.24 x 33,000; $1.20 x 2,900; $0 x 2,500	40,320	7,920	3,480	0
5	Revenues (at actual price)	564,480	467,280	38,280	36,000
6	Cost of goods sold: $12 x 42,000; 33,000; 2,900; 2,500	504,000	396,000	34,800	30,000
7	Gross margin	60,480	71,280	3,480	6,000
8	Customer-level operating costs				
9	Product handling $0.50 x 42,000; 33,000; 2,900; 2,500	21,000	16,500	1,450	1,250
10	Order taking $100 x 30; 25; 15; 10	3,000	2,500	1,500	1,000
11	Delivery vehicles $2 x (5 x 60); (12 x 30); (20 x 20); (6 x 15)	600	720	800	180
12	Rush deliveries $300 x 1; 0; 2; 0	300	0	600	0
13	Visits to customers $80 x 6; 5; 4; 3	480	400	320	240
14	Total customer-level operating costs	25,380	20,120	4,670	2,670
15	Customer-level operating income	$ 35,100	$ 51,160	$ (1,190)	$ 3,330

value these services continue to demand them and pay for them while hospitals that do not value these services drop them, saving Owens and Minor some costs. Owens and Minor's pricing strategy influences customer behavior in a way that increases its revenues or decreases its costs. (See the Concepts in Action feature, p. 506.)

The ABC system also highlights a second opportunity for cost reduction: Spring can seek to reduce costs of each activity. For example, improving the efficiency of the ordering process (such as by having customers order electronically) can reduce costs even if customers place the same number of orders.

Exhibit 14-6 shows a monthly operating income statement for Spring Distribution. The customer-level operating income of customers A and B in Exhibit 14-5 are shown in columns 8 and 9 of Exhibit 14-6. The format of Exhibit 14-6 is based on Spring's cost hierarchy. All costs incurred to serve customers are not included in customer-level costs and therefore are not allocated to customers in Exhibit 14-6. For example, distribution-channel costs such as the salary of the manager of the retail distribution channel are not included in customer-level costs and are not allocated to customers. Instead, these costs are identified as costs of the retail channel as a whole. That's because Spring's management believes that changes in customer behavior will not affect distribution-channel costs. Distribution-channel costs will be affected only by decisions pertaining to the whole channel, such as a decision to discontinue retail distribution. Another reason Spring does not allocate distribution-channel costs to customers is motivation. Spring's managers contend that salespersons responsible for managing individual customer

EXHIBIT 14-6 Income Statement of Spring Distribution for June 2007

	A	B	C	D	E	F	G	H	I	J	K	L	M
1		CUSTOMER DISTRIBUTION CHANNELS											
2			Wholesale Customers						Retail Customers				
3		Total	Total	A1	A2	A3	•		Total	A[a]	B[a]	C	•
4		(1) = (2) + (7)	(2)	(3)	(4)	(5)	(6)		(7)	(8)	(9)	(10)	(11)
5	Revenues (at actual prices)	$12,138,120	$10,107,720	$1,946,000	$1,476,000	•	•		$2,030,400	$564,480	$467,280	•	•
6	Customer-level costs	11,633,760	9,737,280	1,868,000	1,416,000	•	•		1,896,480	529,380[b]	416,120[b]	•	•
7	Customer-level operating income	504,360	370,440	$ 78,000	$ 60,000	•	•		133,920	$ 35,100	$ 51,160	•	•
8	Distribution-channel costs	160,500	102,500						58,000				
9	Distribution-channel-level operating income	343,860	$ 267,940						$ 75,920				
10	Corporate-sustaining costs	263,000											
11	Operating income	$ 80,860											
12													
13	[a] Full details are presented in Exhibit 14-5.												
14	[b] Cost of goods sold + Total customer-level operating costs from Exhibit 14-5.												

FOCUS ON VALUES AND BEHAVIORS

SO IS THE CUSTOMER ALWAYS RIGHT?

What are some of the most important aspects of a business? The bottom line? Shareholders' perception of a company? The quality of a product or service offered? What about customers? Customers are essential to any business, but unfortunately some customers are not always profitable, which makes customer-profitability analysis a complex issue for management accountants.

Once an organization decides to measure customer profitability, management accountants are responsible for articulating the benefits of such measurements. This can be problematic for management accountants because the sales organizations in most companies are compensated on the basis of revenues, not customer profits. Therefore, the sales force may be reluctant to follow a strategy of serving only profitable customers and taking actions to change the behavior and buying patterns of those that are unprofitable. Management accountants need to communicate to the sales force why measuring customer profits is critical to the organization. For example, they need to explain what might happen if change does not occur and how customer-profitability analysis can help the company reallocate resources to increase both revenues and profits.

When it comes to customer-profitability analysis, the sales force is not the only part of an organization that may pose challenges for management accountants. Line managers are sometimes surprised by which customers are profitable and which are not because they may assume a company's largest customer is profitable. However, this customer may consume high levels of customer support and actually be unprofitable. For this reason, management accountants must make it a point to team up with line managers when designing the system to calculate customer profitability. Customer-profitability analysis should always be based on a thorough understanding of business processes so that it correctly represents the costs incurred to support different customers.

Consider Fidelity Investments. Fidelity's customer-profitability analysis revealed that some of its customers were unprofitable because of the ways they communicated with the company. Armed with this information, managers made changes to the company's processes. For example, telephone calls from unprofitable customers were placed in a long waiting queue, which was intended to discourage these customers from calling service representatives and to encourage them to instead use less-costly Internet and automated phone-line services. Fidelity's management was concerned that, unhappy with these changes, customers would leave; however, 96% of the targeted customers stayed, switched to lower-cost channels, and became profitable.[a] These short-term successes were shared with other managers, and the company grew more confident about the actions it needed to take. Teamwork, communication, and careful management of the changes were critical to the success of the customer-profitability implementation and the positive results that followed.

[a] *See L. Selden and G. Colvin, "Will This Customer Sink Your Stock?"* Fortune, *September 30, 2003.*

accounts would lose motivation if their bonuses were affected by the allocation to customers of distribution-channel costs over which they had minimal influence.

Next, consider corporate-sustaining costs such as top-management and general-administration costs. Spring's managers have concluded that there is no cause-and-effect or benefits-received relationship between any cost-allocation base and corporate-sustaining costs. Consequently, allocation of corporate-sustaining costs serves no useful purpose in decision making, performance evaluation, or motivation. For example, suppose Spring allocated the \$263,000 of corporate-sustaining costs to its distribution channels: \$173,000 to the wholesale channel and \$90,000 to the retail channel. Using information from Exhibit 14-6, the retail channel would then show a loss of \$14,080 (\$75,920 − \$90,000). If this same situation persisted in subsequent months, should Spring shut down the retail distribution channel? No, because if retail distribution were discontinued, corporate-sustaining costs would be unaffected. Allocating corporate-sustaining costs to distribution channels could give the misleading impression that the potential cost savings from discontinuing a distribution channel would be greater than the likely amount.

Some managers and management accountants advocate fully allocating all costs to customers and distribution channels so that (1) the sum of operating incomes of all customers in a distribution channel (segment) equals the operating income of the distribution channel and (2) the sum of the distribution-channel operating incomes equals companywide operating income. These managers and management accountants argue that customers and products must eventually be profitable on a full-cost basis. In the previous example, CAI allocated all corporate and division-level costs to its refrigerator and clothes dryer products (see pp. 500–501). For some decisions, such as pricing,

CONCEPTS IN ACTION

Customer Profitability at Nextel

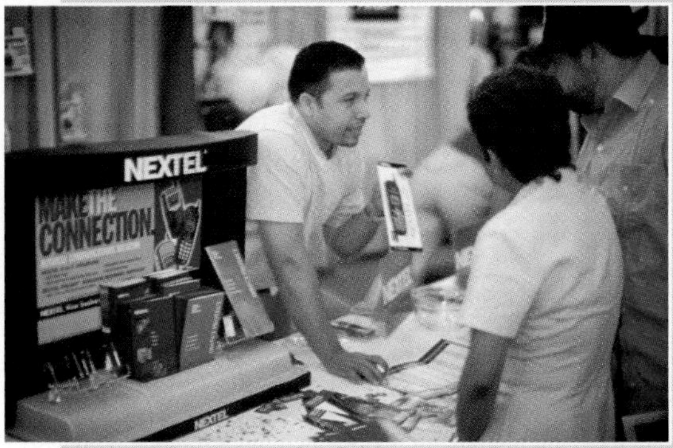

Nextel, a leading wireless-communications service provider, offers cellular telephone service and wireless-data access to a broad range of businesses, government agencies, and individuals. Nextel uses cost accounting to price its various wireless service plans and to calculate customer profitability.

The costs of serving different wireless customers vary. Most business customers, for example, require reliable service during peak network usage periods (that is, standard business hours), on-demand two-way messaging, and large amounts of wireless data bandwidth to run PDA and BlackBerry handheld devices. In contrast, many individuals use their wireless phones extensively at night and on weekends and also use features such as text messaging, digital pictures, music ringtones, and video games. Within each segment, each customer differs in their amount of overall usage and geographic location (urban versus rural).

Nextel considers the costs for each of these services when developing their pricing plans and calculating customer profitability. Therefore, individuals using their phone service sparingly can select a less-expensive plan with limited minutes, for use mostly at night and on weekends, whereas more-demanding individuals and lucrative business customers can choose plans with unlimited telephone minutes, secure wireless data bandwidth access, and guaranteed service reliability . . . for a price. In 2004, Nextel's base wireless plans ranged from $15.00 to $199.99 per month, with additional charges for data services and rural-area roaming. Business and government customers who use Nextel services extensively are eligible for negotiated volume discounts.

Because of the range in prices, Nextel analyzes customer profitability to ensure that its prices cover the costs it incurs to provide services to its different customers. Nextel then uses customer-profitability analysis to determine where and how to expand its service network, design new pricing plans, manage costs, and develop strategies to ensure that the company acquires and retains the most profitable customers. The result has been record profitability and a soaring stock price.

Sources: A. Lagocre, "Nextel's Direct Connection to Profits," *Forbes* (February 6, 2004); C. Osborn, "Customer Retention: Can Wireless Data Make 'Em Stay Put?" in *The Future of Wireless: Business Strategies, Broadband Technologies, and Network Operations* (Chicago: International Engineering Consortium, 2004); R. Prentiss and T. Nelson, *Nextel Communications, Inc.* (Raymond James, February 9, 2004); Nextel Communications, Inc., March 11, 2004, 10-K (Reston, VA: Nextel Communications, 2003); Nextel Communications (Multiple pages). Nextel Communications Web site, **http://www.nextel.com**, accessed July 25, 2004.

allocating all costs ensures that long-run prices are set at a level to cover the cost of all resources used to produce and sell products. Nevertheless, the value of the hierarchical format in Exhibit 14-6 is that it distinguishes among various degrees of objectivity when allocating costs, and it dovetails with the different levels at which decisions are made and performance is evaluated. The issue of when and what costs to allocate is another example of the "different costs for different purposes" theme emphasized throughout the book.

Customer-Profitability Profiles

Customer-profitability profiles are a useful tool for managers. Exhibit 14-7 ranks Spring's 10 retail customers based on customer-level operating income. (Four of these customers are analyzed in Exhibit 14-5.)

Column 4, computed by adding the individual amounts in column 1, shows the cumulative customer-level operating income. For example, customer C has a cumulative income of $107,330 in column 4. This $107,330 is the sum of $51,160 for customer B, $35,100 for customer A, and $21,070 for customer C.

Column 5 shows what percentage the $107,330 *cumulative* total for customers B, A, and C is of the total customer-level operating income of $133,920 earned in the retail-distribution channel from all 10 customers. The three most profitable customers con-

	A	B	C	D	E	F
1	**Customers Ranked on Customer-Level Operating Income**					
2						**Cumulative**
3						**Customer-Level**
4		**Customer-**				**Operating Income**
5		**Level**		**Customer-Level**	**Cumulative**	**as a % of Total**
6		**Operating**	**Customer**	**Operating Income**	**Customer-Level**	**Customer-Level**
7	**Customer**	**Income**	**Revenue**	**Divided by Revenue**	**Operating Income**	**Operating Income**
8	**Code**	**(1)**	**(2)**	**(3) = (1) ÷ (2)**	**(4)**	**(5) = (4) ÷ $133,920**
9	B	$ 51,160	$ 467,280	10.9%	$ 51,160	38%
10	A	35,100	564,480	6.2%	86,260	64%
11	C	21,070	255,640	8.2%	107,330	80%
12	D	17,580	277,000	6.3%	124,910	93%
13	F	7,504	123,500	6.1%	132,414	99%
14	J	3,330	36,000	9.3%	135,744	101%
15	E	3,176	193,000	1.6%	138,920	104%
16	G	-1,190	38,280	-3.1%	137,730	103%
17	H	-1,690	38,220	-4.4%	136,040	102%
18	I	-2,120	37,000	-5.7%	133,920	100%
19		$133,920	$2,030,400			
20						

EXHIBIT 14-7

Customer-Profitability Analysis for Retail Channel Customers: Spring Distribution, June 2007

Note that cumulative customer-level operating income for customer I (the least-profitable customer) in column 4 ($133,920) equals the total customer-level operating income in column 1.

tribute 80% of total customer-level operating income. This high percentage of operating income contributed by a small number of customers is common. It highlights how vital a small set of customers is to Spring's retail profitability. These customers should receive the highest service and priority. Microsoft uses the phrase "not all revenue dollars are endowed equally in profitability" to stress this point.

Column 3 shows the profitability per dollar of revenue by customer. This measure of customer profitability indicates that, although customer A contributes the second-highest operating income, the profitability per dollar of revenue is lower because of high price discounts. Spring's goal is to increase profit margins for Customer A by decreasing the price discounts or saving customer-level costs while maintaining sales. Customer J has a higher profit margin but has lower total sales. Spring's challenge with Customer J is to maintain margins while increasing sales.

Managers often find the bar chart presentation in Exhibit 14-8 to be the most intuitive way to visualize customer profitability. The highly profitable customers clearly stand out. Moreover, the number of "unprofitable" customers and the magnitude of their losses are apparent. Spring's managers must explore ways to make unprofitable customers profitable.

The "80-20 rule" also applies to customers: 80% of a company's profits often come from 20% of its customers. Customer-profitability information can help marketing and customer-service personnel (1) focus on maintaining the best-possible relations with those 20% of customers and (2) transform the other 80% into more-profitable customers.

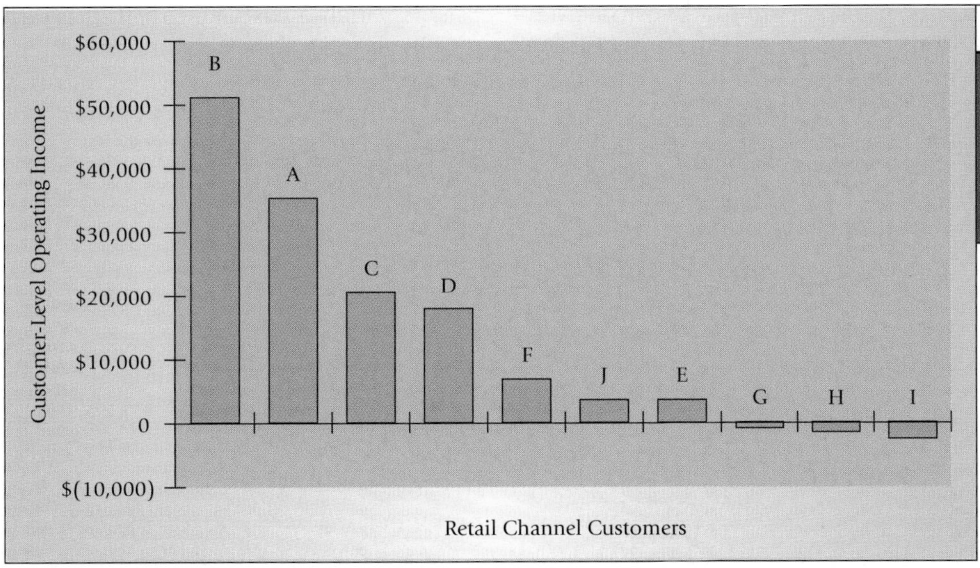

EXHIBIT 14-8

Bar Chart of Customer-Level Operating Income for Spring Distribution's Retail Channel Customers in June 2007

The idea that "a picture is worth a thousand words" is supported by research findings. Graphs and charts help managers make faster and better-informed decisions. Software such as Excel makes it easier for management accountants to provide information in pictorial form.

Exhibits 14-5 to 14-8 emphasize short-run customer profitability. Other factors managers should consider in deciding how to allocate resources among customers include:

- **Likelihood of customer retention.** The more likely a customer will continue to do business with a company, the more valuable the customer. Customers differ in their loyalty and their willingness to frequently "shop their business."
- **Potential for sales growth.** The higher the likely growth of the customer's industry and the customer's sales, the more valuable the customer. Customers to whom a company can cross-sell other products are more desirable.
- **Long-run customer profitability.** This factor will be influenced by the first two factors specified and the cost of customer-support staff and special services required to retain customer accounts.
- **Increases in overall demand from having well-known customers.** Customers with established reputations help generate sales from other customers through product endorsements.
- **Ability to learn from customers.** Customers who provide ideas about new products or ways to improve existing products are especially valuable.

Managers should be cautious when deciding to discontinue customers in the short run. Consider customer G in Exhibit 14-7. The long-run unprofitability of customer G may provide misleading signals about customer G's short-run profitability. Not all costs assigned to customer G are variable in the short run. Discontinuing customer G will not eliminate all the costs assigned to that customer in the short run.

Sales Variances

The customer-profitability analysis in the previous section focused on the actual profitability of individual customers within a distribution channel (retail, for example) and their impact on Spring Distribution's profitability for June 2007. At a more-strategic level, however, recall that Spring operates in two different markets: wholesale and retail. The operating margins in the retail market are much higher than the operating margins in the wholesale market. In June 2007, Spring had budgeted to sell 80% of its cases to wholesalers and 20% to retailers. It actually sold more cases in total than it had budgeted, but its actual sales mix (in cases) was 84% to wholesalers and 16% to retailers. Regardless of the profitability of sales to individual customers within each of the retail and wholesale channels, Spring's actual operating income, relative to the master budget, is likely to be positively affected by the higher sales of cases and negatively affected by the shift in mix away from the more-profitable retail customers. Sales-quantity and sales-mix variances can identify the effect of each of these factors on Spring's profitability. Companies such as Cisco, GE, and Hewlett-Packard perform similar analyses because they sell their products through multiple distribution channels, for example, via the Internet, over the telephone, or in retail stores.

Spring classifies all customer-level costs as variable costs and distribution-channel and corporate-sustaining costs as fixed costs. To simplify the sales-variances analysis and calculations, we assume that all these variable costs are variable with respect to units (cases) sold. (This means, for example, that average batch sizes remain the same as the total cases sold vary.) Without this assumption, the analysis would become more complex and would have to be done using the ABC-variance analysis approach described in Chapter 7, pp. 239–240. The basic insights, however, would not change.

Budgeted and actual operating data for June 2007 are:

"Unit" in the column headings refers to a case of 24 bottles.

Budget Data for June 2007

	Selling Price per Unit (1)	Variable Cost per Unit (2)	Contribution Margin per Unit (3) = (1) − (2)	Sales Volume in Units (4)	Sales Mix (Based on Units) (5)	Contribution Margin (6) = (3) × (4)
Wholesale channel	$13.37	$12.88	$0.49	712,000	80%[a]	$348,880
Retail channel	14.10	13.12	0.98	178,000	20	174,440
Total				890,000	100%	$523,320

[a]Percentage of unit sales to wholesale channel = 712,000 units ÷ 890,000 total units = 80%.

Actual Results for June 2007

	Selling Price per Unit (1)	Variable Cost per Unit (2)	Contribution Margin per Unit (3) = (1) – (2)	Sales Volume in Units (4)	Sales Mix (Based on Units) (5)	Contribution Margin (6) = (3) × (4)
Wholesale channel	$13.37	$12.88	$0.49	756,000	84%	$370,440
Retail channel	14.10	13.17	0.93	144,000	16	133,920
Total				900,000	100%	$504,360

The budgeted and actual fixed distribution-channel costs and corporate-sustaining costs are $160,500 and $263,000, respectively (see Exhibit 14-6, p. 504).

Recall that the levels of detail introduced in Chapter 7 included the static-budget variance (level 1), the flexible-budget variance (level 2), and the sales-volume variance (level 2). The sales-quantity and sales-mix variances are level 3 variances that subdivide the sales-volume variance.[5]

Static-Budget Variance

The *static-budget variance* is the difference between an actual result and the corresponding budgeted amount in the static budget. Our analysis focuses on the difference between actual and budgeted contribution margins (column 6 in the preceding tables). The total static-budget variance is $18,960 U (actual contribution margin of $504,360 – budgeted contribution margin of $523,320). Exhibit 14-9 (columns 1 and 3) uses the columnar format introduced in Chapter 7 to show detailed calculations of the static-budget variance. Managers can gain more insight about the static-budget variance by subdividing it into the flexible-budget variance and the sales-volume variance.

Flexible-Budget Variance and Sales-Volume Variance

The *flexible-budget variance* is the difference between an actual result and the corresponding flexible-budget amount based on actual output level in the budget period. The flexible-budget contribution margin is equal to budgeted contribution margin per unit times actual units sold of each product. Exhibit 14-9, column 2, shows the flexible-budget calculations. The flexible budget measures the contribution margin that Spring would have

EXHIBIT 14-9 **Flexible-Budget and Sales-Volume Variance Analysis of Spring Distribution for June 2007**

	Actual Results: Actual Units of All Products Sold × Actual Sales Mix × Actual Contribution Margin per Unit (1)	Flexible Budget: Actual Units of All Products Sold × Actual Sales Mix × Budgeted Contribution Margin per Unit (2)	Static Budget: Budgeted Units of All Products Sold × Budgeted Sales Mix × Budgeted Contribution Margin per Unit (3)
Wholesale	900,000 × 0.84 × $0.49 = $370,440	900,000 × 0.84 × $0.49 = $370,440	890,000 × 0.80 × $0.49 = $348,880
Retail	900,000 × 0.16 × $0.93 = 133,920	900,000 × 0.16 × $0.98 = 141,120	890,000 × 0.20 × $0.98 = 174,440
	$504,360	$511,560	$523,320

Level 2: $7,200 U Flexible-budget variance (between columns 1 and 2); $11,760 U Sales-volume variance (between columns 2 and 3)

Level 1: $18,960 U Static-budget variance (between columns 1 and 3)

F = favorable effect on operating income; U = unfavorable effect on operating income.

[5]The presentation of the variances in this chapter and the appendix draws on teaching notes prepared by J. K. Harris.

budgeted for the actual quantities of cases sold. The flexible-budget variance is the difference between columns 1 and 2 in Exhibit 14-9. The only difference between columns 1 and 2 is that actual units sold of each product is multiplied by actual contribution margin per unit in column 1 and budgeted contribution margin per unit in column 2. The \$7,200 U flexible-budget variance arises because actual contribution margin on retail sales of \$0.93 per case is lower than the budgeted amount of \$0.98 per case. Spring's management is aware that this difference of \$0.05 per case resulted from excessive price discounts, and they have put in place controls to reduce discounts in the future.

The *sales-volume variance* is the difference between a flexible-budget amount and the corresponding static-budget amount. In Exhibit 14-9, the sales-volume variance shows the effect on budgeted contribution margin of the difference between actual quantity of units sold and budgeted quantity of units sold. The sales-volume variance of \$11,760 U is the difference between columns 2 and 3 in Exhibit 14-9. Spring's managers can gain substantial insight into the sales-volume variance by subdividing it into the sales-mix variance and the sales-quantity variance.

7

Subdivide the sales-volume variance into the sales-mix variance

. . . this variance arises because actual sales mix differs from budgeted sales mix

and the sales-quantity variance

. . . this variance arises because actual total unit sales differ from budgeted total unit sales

The variances described here—the sales-mix variance, sales-quantity variance, market-share variance, and market-size variance—provide information on why sales differed from expectations, which is especially helpful to marketing managers in planning and controlling their activities.

Sales-Mix and Sales-Quantity Variances

Exhibit 14-10 uses the columnar format to calculate the sales-mix variance and the sales-quantity variance. Refer to this exhibit when reading the following discussion of these two variances.

Sales-Mix Variance

The **sales-mix variance** is the difference between (1) budgeted contribution margin for the *actual sales mix* and (2) budgeted contribution margin for the *budgeted sales mix*. The formula and computations (using data from pp. 508–509) are:

	Actual Units of All Products Sold	×	(Actual Sales-Mix Percentage − Budgeted Sales-Mix Percentage)	×	Budgeted Contribution Margin per Unit	=	Sales-Mix Variance
Wholesale	900,000 units	×	(0.84 − 0.80)	×	\$0.49 per unit	=	\$17,640 F
Retail	900,000 units	×	(0.16 − 0.20)	×	\$0.98 per unit	=	35,280 U
Total sales-mix variance							\$17,640 U

EXHIBIT 14-10 **Sales-Mix and Sales-Quantity Variance Analysis of Spring Distribution for June 2007**

	Flexible Budget: Actual Units of All Products Sold × Actual Sales Mix × Budgeted Contribution Margin per Unit (1)	Actual Units of All Products Sold × Budgeted Sales Mix × Budgeted Contribution Margin per Unit (2)	Static Budget: Budgeted Units of All Products Sold × Budgeted Sales Mix × Budgeted Contribution Margin per Unit (3)
Wholesale	900,000 × 0.84 × \$0.49 = \$370,440	900,000 × 0.80 × \$0.49 = \$352,800	890,000 × 0.80 × \$0.49 = \$348,880
Retail	900,000 × 0.16 × \$0.98 = 141,120	900,000 × 0.20 × \$0.98 = 176,400	890,000 × 0.20 × \$0.98 = 174,440
	\$511,560	\$529,200	\$523,320

Level 3: \$17,640 U Sales-mix variance (between columns 1 and 2); \$5,880 F Sales-quantity variance (between columns 2 and 3)

Level 2: \$11,760 U Sales-volume variance (between columns 1 and 3)

F = favorable effect on operating income; U = unfavorable effect on operating income.

A favorable sales-mix variance arises for the wholesale channel because the 84% actual sales-mix percentage exceeds the 80% budgeted sales-mix percentage. In contrast, the retail channel has an unfavorable variance because the 16% actual sales-mix percentage is less than the 20% budgeted sales-mix percentage. The sales-mix variance is unfavorable because actual sales mix shifted toward the less-profitable wholesale channel relative to budgeted sales mix.

The concept underlying the sales-mix variance is best explained in terms of budgeted contribution margin per composite unit of the sales mix. A **composite unit** is a hypothetical unit with weights based on the mix of individual units. For actual sales mix, the composite unit consists of 0.84 units of sales to the wholesale channel and 0.16 units of sales to the retail channel. For budgeted sales mix, the composite unit consists of 0.80 units of sales to the wholesale channel and 0.20 units of sales to the retail channel. In the following table, budgeted contribution margin per composite unit is computed in column 3 for actual mix and in column 5 for budgeted mix:

Actual contribution margins per unit are not used in calculating the sales-volume variance or any of the variances that are subdivided from it. That's why Exhibits 14-10 and 14-11 use budgeted contribution margins per unit.

	Budgeted Contribution Margin per Unit (1)	Actual Sales-Mix Percentage (2)	Budgeted Contribution Margin per Composite Unit for Actual Mix (3) = (1) × (2)	Budgeted Sales-Mix Percentage (4)	Budgeted Contribution Margin per Composite Unit for Budgeted Mix (5) = (1) × (4)
Wholesale	$0.49	0.84	$0.4116	0.80	$0.3920
Retail	0.98	0.16	0.1568	0.20	0.1960
			$0.5684		$0.5880

Actual sales mix has a budgeted contribution margin per composite unit of $0.5684. Budgeted sales mix has a budgeted contribution margin per composite unit of $0.5880. Budgeted contribution margin per composite unit can be computed in another way by dividing total budgeted contribution margin of $523,320 by total budgeted units of 890,000 (p. 508): $523,320 ÷ 890,000 units = $0.5880 per unit. The effect of the sales-mix shift for Spring is to decrease budgeted contribution margin per composite unit by $0.0196 ($0.5880 – $0.5684). For the 900,000 units actually sold, this decrease translates to a $17,640 U sales-mix variance ($0.0196 per unit × 900,000 units).

The intuition for the sales-mix variance is that there is a composite unit at the *budgeted mix* and a different composite unit at the *actual mix*. Accordingly, the sales-mix variance (per composite unit) is the difference between the budgeted contribution margins of these two composite units.

Managers should probe why the $17,640 U sales-mix variance occurred in June 2007. Is the shift in sales mix because, as the analysis in the previous section showed, profitable retail customers proved to be more difficult to find? Is it because of a competitor in the retail channel providing better service at a lower price? Or is it because the initial sales-volume estimates were made without adequate analysis of the potential market?

Sales-Quantity Variance

The **sales-quantity variance** is the difference between (1) budgeted contribution margin based on *actual units sold of all products* at the budgeted mix and (2) contribution margin in the static budget (which is based on *budgeted units of all products to be sold* at budgeted mix). The formula and computations (using data from pp. 508–509) are

	(Actual Units of All Products Sold – Budgeted Units of All Products Sold)	×	Budgeted Sales-Mix Percentage	×	Budgeted Contribution Margin per Unit	=	Sales-Quantity Variance
Wholesale	(900,000 units – 890,000 units)	×	0.80	×	$0.49 per unit	=	$3,920 F
Retail	(900,000 units – 890,000 units)	×	0.20	×	$0.98 per unit	=	1,960 F
Total sales-quantity variance							$5,880 F

This variance is favorable when actual units of all products sold exceed budgeted units of all products sold. Spring sold 10,000 more cases than were budgeted, resulting in a $5,880 F sales-quantity variance (also equal to budgeted contribution margin per composite unit for the budgeted sales mix times additional cases sold, $0.5880 × 10,000). Managers would want to probe the reasons for the increase in sales. Did higher sales come as a result of a competitor's distribution problems? Better customer service? Or growth in the overall market? Further insight into the causes of the sales-quantity variance can be gained by analyzing changes in Spring's share of the total industry market and in the size of that market.

8

Subdivide the sales-quantity variance into the market-share variance

. . . this variance arises because actual market share differs from budgeted market share

. . . and the market-size variance

. . . this variance arises because actual market size differs from budgeted market size

Market-Share and Market-Size Variances

Sales depend on overall demand for bottled water, as well as Spring's share of the market. Assume that Spring derived its total unit sales budget for June 2007 from a management estimate of a 25% market share and a budgeted industry market size of 3,560,000 units (0.25 × 3,560,000 units = 890,000 units). For June 2007, actual market size was 4,000,000 units and actual market share was 22.5% (900,000 units ÷ 4,000,000 units = 0.225 or 22.5%). Exhibit 14-11 shows the columnar presentation of how Spring's sales-quantity variance can be further subdivided into market-share and market-size variances.

Market-Share Variance

The **market-share variance** is the difference in budgeted contribution margin for actual market size in units caused solely by *actual market share* being different from *budgeted market share*. The formula for computing the market-share variance is:

$$\text{Market-share variance} = \begin{matrix}\text{Actual}\\ \text{market size}\\ \text{in units}\end{matrix} \times \left(\begin{matrix}\text{Actual}\\ \text{market}\\ \text{share}\end{matrix} - \begin{matrix}\text{Budgeted}\\ \text{market}\\ \text{share}\end{matrix}\right) \times \begin{matrix}\text{Budgeted}\\ \text{contribution margin}\\ \text{per composite unit}\\ \text{for budgeted mix}\end{matrix}$$

$$= 4{,}000{,}000 \text{ units} \times (0.225 - 0.25) \times \$0.5880 \text{ per unit}$$

$$= \$58{,}800 \text{ U}$$

Budgeted contribution margin per composite unit for budgeted mix (also called budgeted average contribution margin per unit) is computed using the approach outlined earlier in this chapter (p. 511).

Spring lost 2.5 market-share percentage points—from the 25% budgeted share to the actual share of 22.5%. The $58,800 U market-share variance is the effect of the decline on contribution margin.

EXHIBIT 14-11 **Market-Share and Market-Size Variance Analysis of Spring Distribution for June 2007**

Actual Market Size × Actual Market Share × Budgeted Average Contribution Margin per Unit	Actual Market Size × Budgeted Market Share × Budgeted Average Contribution Margin per Unit	Static Budget: Budgeted Market Size × Budgeted Market Share × Budgeted Average Contribution Margin per Unit
4,000,000 × 0.225[a] × $0.5880[b]	4,000,000 × 0.25[c] × $0.5880[b]	3,560,000 × 0.25[c] × $0.5880[b]
$529,200	$588,000	$523,320

Level 4: $58,800 U Market-share variance; $64,680 F Market-size variance

Level 3: $5,880 F Sales-quantity variance

F = favorable effect on operating income; U = unfavorable effect on operating income.

[a]Actual market share: 900,000 units ÷ 4,000,000 units = 0.225, or 22.5%.

[b]Budgeted average contribution margin per unit: $523,320 ÷ 890,000 units = $0.5880 per unit.

[c]Budgeted market share: 890,000 units ÷ 3,560,000 units = 0.25, or 25%.

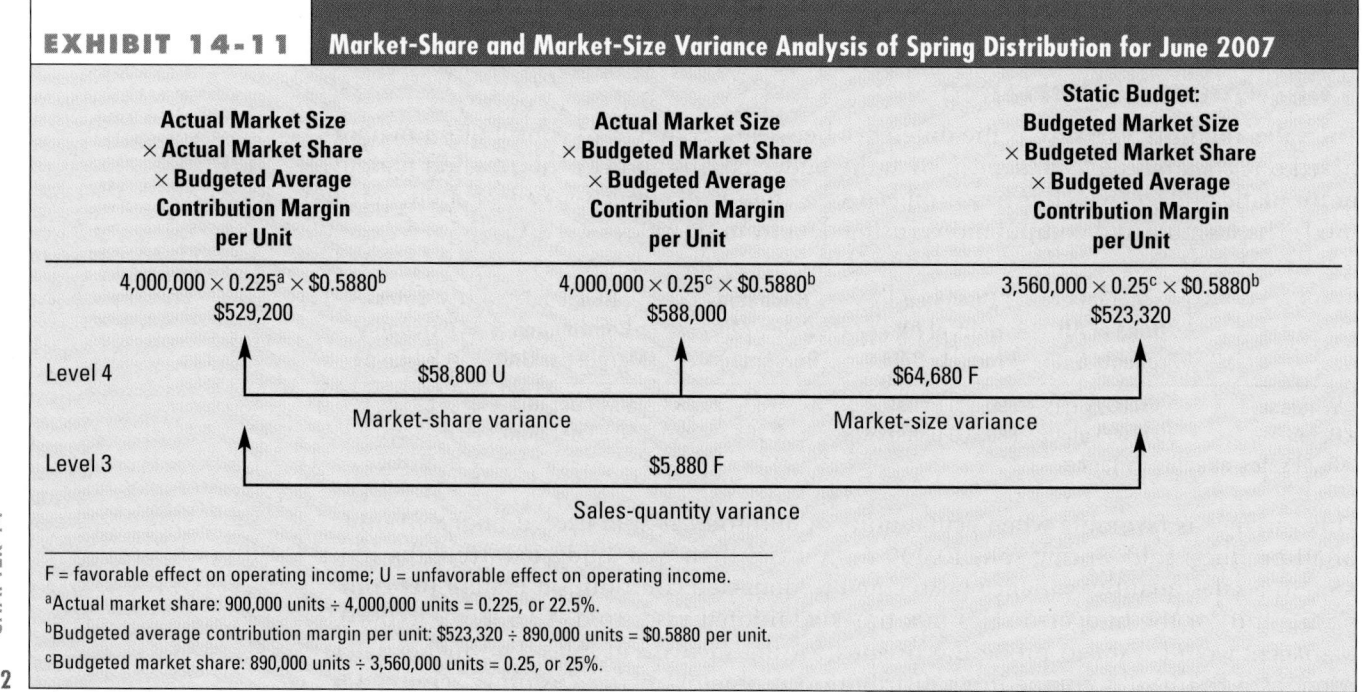

Market-Size Variance

The **market-size variance** is the difference in budgeted contribution margin at budgeted market share caused solely by *actual market size in units* being different from *budgeted market size in units*. The formula for computing the market-size variance is:

$$\text{Market-size variance} = \left(\begin{array}{c}\text{Actual}\\ \text{market}\\ \text{size}\end{array} - \begin{array}{c}\text{Budgeted}\\ \text{market}\\ \text{size}\end{array}\right) \times \begin{array}{c}\text{Budgeted}\\ \text{market}\\ \text{share}\end{array} \times \begin{array}{c}\text{Budgeted}\\ \text{contribution margin}\\ \text{per composite unit}\\ \text{for budgeted mix}\end{array}$$

$$= (4{,}000{,}000 \text{ units} - 3{,}560{,}000 \text{ units}) \times 0.25 \times \$0.5880 \text{ per unit}$$

$$= \$64{,}680 \text{ F}$$

The market-size variance is favorable because actual market size increased 12.4% [(4,000,000 − 3,560,000) ÷ 3,560,000 = 0.124, or 12.4%] compared to budgeted market size.

Managers should probe the reasons for the market-share and market-size variances for June 2007. Was the $58,800 unfavorable market-share variance because of competitors providing better service and offering a lower price? Did Spring's products experience quality-control problems that were the subject of negative media coverage? Is the $64,680 F market-size variance because of an increase in market size that can be expected to continue in the future? If yes, Spring has much to gain by attaining or exceeding its budgeted 25% market share. Some companies place more emphasis on the market-share variance than the market-size variance when evaluating their managers. That's because they believe the market-size variance is influenced by economywide factors and shifts in consumer preferences that are outside the managers' control, whereas the market-share variance measures how well managers performed relative to their peers.

Be cautious when computing the market-size variance and the market-share variance. Reliable information on market size and market share is available for some, but not all, industries. The automobile, computer, and television industries are cases in which market-size and market-share statistics are widely available. In other industries, such as management consulting and personal financial planning, information about market size and market share is far less reliable.

Exhibit 14-12 presents an overview of the level 1 to level 4 variances. The appendix to this chapter describes mix and quantity variances for production inputs.

The concepts of market size and market share are also important to TV networks. A network's advertising revenues increase when the aggregate market (viewers) increases or when the network's share of the market increases. The measures used to calculate market size and market share are debated intensively in the TV industry.

Study Tip: To check your understanding of the material in the body of this chapter, see the Featured Exercise, true–false statements 3 and 8, multiple-choice questions 3 through 5, and Review Exercises 1 and 2 (*Student Guide*, beginning p. 186). Fully explained answers begin on p. 193.

We calculated market-share and market-size variances (as subdivisions of the *sales-quantity variance*) based on the overall market for bottled water, regardless of whether the water was sold through wholesale or retail channels. However, if a company has products that it sells in different markets (for example, consumer products and pharmaceuticals), the company may decide to calculate market-share and market-size variances for each product separately as an alternative way of subdividing the *sales-volume variance.*

EXHIBIT 14-12 Overview of Variances for Spring Distribution for June 2007

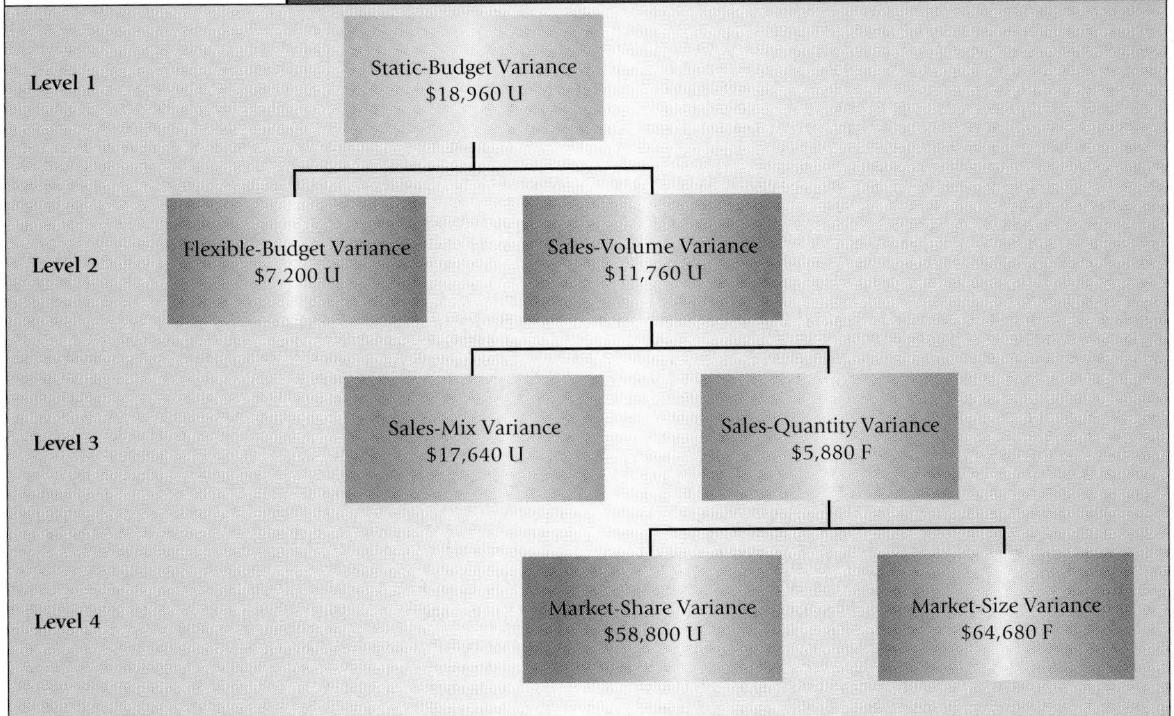

F = favorable effect on operating income; U = unfavorable effect on operating income

The sales-mix variance, sales-quantity variance, market-share variance, and market-size variance can also be calculated in a multiproduct company, in which each individual product has a different contribution margin per unit. The Problem for Self-Study calculates these level 3 and level 4 sales variances in a multiproduct company.

PROBLEM FOR SELF-STUDY

The Payne Company manufactures two types of vinyl flooring. Budgeted and actual operating data for 2006 are:

	Static Budget			Actual Results		
	Commercial	Residential	Total	Commercial	Residential	Total
Unit sales in rolls	20,000	60,000	80,000	25,200	58,800	84,000
Contribution margin	$10,000,000	$24,000,000	$34,000,000	$11,970,000	$24,696,000	$36,666,000

In late 2005, a marketing research firm estimated industry volume for commercial and residential vinyl flooring for 2006 at 800,000 rolls. Actual industry volume for 2006 was 700,000 rolls.

Required

1. Compute the sales-mix variance and the sales-quantity variance by type of vinyl flooring and in total. (Compute all variances in terms of contribution margins.)
2. Compute the market-share variance and the market-size variance.
3. What insights do the variances calculated in 1 and 2 provide about Payne Company's performance in 2006?

SOLUTION

1. Actual sales-mix percentage:

$$\text{Commercial} = 25{,}200 \div 84{,}000 = 0.30, \text{ or } 30\%$$
$$\text{Residential} = 58{,}800 \div 84{,}000 = 0.70, \text{ or } 70\%$$

Budgeted sales-mix percentage:

$$\text{Commercial} = 20{,}000 \div 80{,}000 = 0.25, \text{ or } 25\%$$
$$\text{Residential} = 60{,}000 \div 80{,}000 = 0.75, \text{ or } 75\%$$

Budgeted contribution margin per unit:

$$\text{Commercial} = \$10{,}000{,}000 \div 20{,}000 \text{ units} = \$500 \text{ per unit}$$
$$\text{Residential} = \$24{,}000{,}000 \div 60{,}000 \text{ units} = \$400 \text{ per unit}$$

	Actual Units of All Products Sold	×	(Actual Sales-Mix Percentage – Budgeted Sales-Mix Percentage)	×	Budgeted Contribution Margin per Unit	=	Sales-Mix Variance
Commercial	84,000 units	×	(0.30 – 0.25)	×	$500 per unit	=	$2,100,000 F
Residential	84,000 units	×	(0.70 – 0.75)	×	$400 per unit	=	1,680,000 U
Total sales-mix variance							$ 420,000 F

	(Actual Units of All Products Sold – Budgeted Units of All Products Sold)	×	Budgeted Sales-Mix Percentage	×	Budgeted Contribution Margin per Unit	=	Sales-Quantity Variance
Commercial	(84,000 units – 80,000 units)	×	0.25	×	$500 per unit	=	$ 500,000 F
Residential	(84,000 units – 80,000 units)	×	0.75	×	$400 per unit	=	1,200,000 F
Total sales-quantity variance							$ 1,700,000 F

2. Actual market share = 84,000 ÷ 700,000 = 0.12, or 12%
Budgeted market share = 80,000 ÷ 800,000 = 0.10, or 10%
Budgeted contribution margin per composite unit of budgeted mix = \$34,000,000 ÷ 80,000 units = \$425 per unit

Budgeted contribution margin per composite unit of budgeted mix can also be calculated as:

Commercial:	\$500 per unit × 0.25 =	\$125 per unit
Residential:	\$400 per unit × 0.75 =	300 per unit
		\$425 per unit

$$\text{Market-share variance} = \text{Actual market size in units} \times \left(\text{Actual market share} - \text{Budgeted market share}\right) \times \text{Budgeted contribution margin per composite unit for budgeted mix}$$

$$= 700{,}000 \text{ units} \times (0.12 - 0.10) \times \$425 \text{ per unit}$$

$$= \$5{,}950{,}000 \text{ F}$$

$$\text{Market-size variance} = \left(\text{Actual market size in units} - \text{Budgeted market size in units}\right) \times \text{Budgeted market share} \times \text{Budgeted contribution margin per composite unit for budgeted mix}$$

$$= (700{,}000 \text{ units} - 800{,}000 \text{ units}) \times 0.10 \times \$425 \text{ per unit}$$

$$= \$4{,}250{,}000 \text{ U}$$

Note that the algebraic sum of the market-share variance and the market-size variance is equal to the sales-quantity variance: \$5,950,000 F + \$4,250,000 U = \$1,700,000 F.

3. Both the sales-mix variance and the sales-quantity variance are favorable. The favorable sales-mix variance occurred because the actual mix comprised more of the higher-margin commercial vinyl flooring. The favorable sales-quantity variance occurred because the actual total quantity of rolls sold exceeded the budgeted amount.

The company's large favorable market-share variance is due to a 12% actual market share compared with a 10% budgeted market share. The market-size variance is unfavorable because the actual market size was 100,000 rolls less than the budgeted market size. Payne's performance in 2006 appears to be very good. Although overall market size declined, the company sold more units than budgeted by gaining market share.

DECISION POINTS

The following question-and-answer format summarizes the chapter's learning objectives. Each decision presents a key question related to a learning objective. The guidelines are the answer to that question.

Decision	**Guidelines**
1. What are four purposes for allocating costs to cost objects?	Four purposes of cost allocation are (a) to provide information for economic decisions, (b) to motivate managers and other employees, (c) to justify costs or compute reimbursement amounts, and (d) to measure income and assets for reporting to external parties. Different cost allocations are appropriate for different purposes.
2. What criteria should managers use to guide cost-allocation decisions?	Managers should use the cause-and-effect and the benefits-received criteria to guide most cost-allocation decisions. Other criteria are fairness or equity and ability to bear.
3. What are two key decisions managers must make when collecting costs in indirect-cost pools?	Two key decisions related to indirect-cost pools are the number of indirect-cost pools to form and the individual cost items to be included in each cost pool to make homogeneous cost pools.

4. Why can revenues differ across customers purchasing the same product?	Revenues can differ because of differences in the quantity purchased and price discounts given from the list selling price.
5. What is the advantage of using a customer-cost hierarchy?	Customer-cost hierarchies highlight how different cost pools have different types of cost drivers and how some costs can be reliably assigned to individual customers whereas other costs can be reliably assigned only to distribution channels or to companywide activities.
6. Why do customer-level costs differ across customers?	Different customers place different demands on a company's resources in terms of processing purchase orders, making deliveries, and customer support. Companies should be aware of and devote sufficient resources to maintaining and expanding relationships with customers who contribute significantly to profitability. Customer-profitability reports often highlight that a small percentage of customers contributes a large percentage of operating income.
7. What are the two components of the sales-volume variance?	The two components are (a) the difference between actual sales mix and budgeted sales mix (the sales-mix variance) and (b) the difference between actual unit sales and budgeted unit sales (the sales-quantity variance).
8. What are the two components of the sales-quantity variance?	The two components are (a) the difference between actual share of the market attained and budgeted share (the market-share variance) and (b) the difference between actual market size in units and budgeted market size (the market-size variance).

APPENDIX: MIX AND YIELD VARIANCES FOR SUBSTITUTABLE INPUTS

The framework for calculating the sales-mix variance and the sales-quantity variance can also be used to analyze production-input variances in cases where managers have some leeway in combining and substituting inputs. For example, Del Monte can combine material inputs (such as pineapples, cherries, and grapes) in varying proportions for its cans of fruit cocktail. Within limits, these individual fruits are *substitutable inputs* in making the fruit cocktail.

We illustrate how the efficiency variance discussed in Chapter 7 (pp. 231–232) can be subdivided into variances that highlight the financial impact of input mix and input yield when inputs are substitutable. Consider Delpino Corporation, which makes tomato ketchup. Our example focuses on direct material inputs and substitution among three of these inputs. The same approach can also be used to examine substitutable direct manufacturing labor inputs.

To produce ketchup of a specified consistency, color, and taste, Delpino mixes three types of tomatoes grown in different regions: Latin American tomatoes (Latoms), California tomatoes (Caltoms), and Florida tomatoes (Flotoms). Delpino's production standards require 1.60 tons of tomatoes to produce 1 ton of ketchup; 50% of the tomatoes are budgeted to be Latoms, 30% Caltoms, and 20% Flotoms. The direct material inputs budgeted to produce 1 ton of ketchup are:

0.80 (50% of 1.6) ton of Latoms at $70 per ton	$ 56.00
0.48 (30% of 1.6) ton of Caltoms at $80 per ton	38.40
0.32 (20% of 1.6) ton of Flotoms at $90 per ton	28.80
Total budgeted cost of 1.6 tons of tomatoes	$123.20

Budgeted average cost per ton of tomatoes is $123.20 ÷ 1.60 tons = $77 per ton.

Because Delpino uses fresh tomatoes to make ketchup, no inventories of tomatoes are kept. Purchases are made as needed, so all price variances relate to tomatoes purchased and used. Actual results for June 2007 show that a total of 6,500 tons of tomatoes were used to produce 4,000 tons of ketchup:

3,250 tons of Latoms at actual cost of $70 per ton	$227,500
2,275 tons of Caltoms at actual cost of $82 per ton	186,550
975 tons of Flotoms at actual cost of $96 per ton	93,600
6,500 tons of tomatoes	507,650
Budgeted cost of 4,000 tons of ketchup at $123.20 per ton	492,800
Flexible-budget variance for direct materials	$ 14,850 U

Given the standard ratio of 1.60 tons of tomatoes to 1 ton of ketchup, 6,400 tons of tomatoes should be used to produce 4,000 tons of ketchup. At standard mix, quantities of each type of tomato required are:

Latoms: $0.50 \times 6{,}400 = 3{,}200$ tons

Caltoms: $0.30 \times 6{,}400 = 1{,}920$ tons

Flotoms: $0.20 \times 6{,}400 = 1{,}280$ tons

Direct Materials Price and Efficiency Variances

Exhibit 14-13 presents in columnar format the analysis of the flexible-budget variance for direct materials discussed in Chapter 7. The materials price and efficiency variances are calculated separately for each input material and then added together. The variance analysis prompts Delpino to investigate the unfavorable price and efficiency variances. Why did they pay more for tomatoes and use greater quantities than they had budgeted? Were actual market prices of tomatoes higher, in general, or could the Purchasing Department have negotiated lower prices? Did the inefficiencies result from inferior tomatoes or from problems in processing?

Direct Materials Mix and Direct Materials Yield Variances

Managers sometimes have discretion to substitute one material for another. The manager of Delpino's ketchup plant has some leeway in combining Latoms, Caltoms, and Flotoms without affecting the ketchup's quality. We will assume that to maintain quality, mix percentages of each type of tomato can only vary up to 5% from standard mix. For example, the percentage of Caltoms in the mix can vary between 25% and 35% (30% ± 5%). When inputs are substitutable, direct materials efficiency improvement relative to budgeted costs can come from two sources: (1) using a cheaper mix to produce a given quantity of output, measured by the direct materials mix variance, and (2) using less input to achieve a given quantity of output, measured by the direct materials yield variance.

The materials mix variance arises only when materials are substitutable. If there can be no substitutions, the mix of materials is constant, the mix variance is zero, and the entire efficiency variance is attributable to the yield variance.

Holding actual total quantity of all direct materials inputs used constant, the total **direct materials mix variance** is the difference between (1) budgeted cost for actual mix of actual total quantity of direct materials used and (2) budgeted cost of budgeted mix of actual total quantity of direct materials used. Holding budgeted input mix constant, the **direct materials yield variance** is the difference between (1) budgeted cost of direct materials based on actual total quantity of direct materials used and (2) flexible-budget cost of direct materials based on budgeted total quantity of direct materials allowed for actual output produced. Exhibit 14-14 presents the direct materials mix and yield variances for the Delpino Corporation.

Budgeted price per unit of each type of material (or labor) is used to calculate the mix and yield variances. Keeping prices constant at budgeted amounts allows us to compare for an input category (1) actual quantity used with budgeted quantity allowed and (2) actual mix with budgeted mix.

Direct materials mix variance The direct materials mix variance is the sum of the direct materials mix variances for each input:

$$\text{Direct materials mix variance for each input} = \text{Actual total quantity of all direct materials inputs used} \times \left(\text{Actual direct materials input mix percentage} - \text{Budgeted direct materials input mix percentage}\right) \times \text{Budgeted price of direct materials input}$$

EXHIBIT 14-13 Direct Materials Price and Efficiency Variances for the Delpino Corporation for June 2007

	Actual Costs Incurred: Actual Input Quantity × Actual Price (1)	Actual Input Quantity × Budgeted Price (2)	Flexible Budget: Budgeted Input Quantity Allowed for Actual Output × Budgeted Price (3)
Latoms:	3,250 × $70 = $227,500	3,250 × $70 = $227,500	3,200 × $70 = $224,000
Caltoms:	2,275 × $82 = 186,550	2,275 × $80 = 182,000	1,920 × $80 = 153,600
Flotoms:	975 × $96 = 93,600	975 × $90 = 87,750	1,280 × $90 = 115,200
	$507,650	$497,250	$492,800
Level 3	$10,400 U Price variance		$4,450 U Efficiency variance
Level 2		$14,850 U Flexible-budget variance	

F = favorable effect on operating income; U = unfavorable effect on operating income.

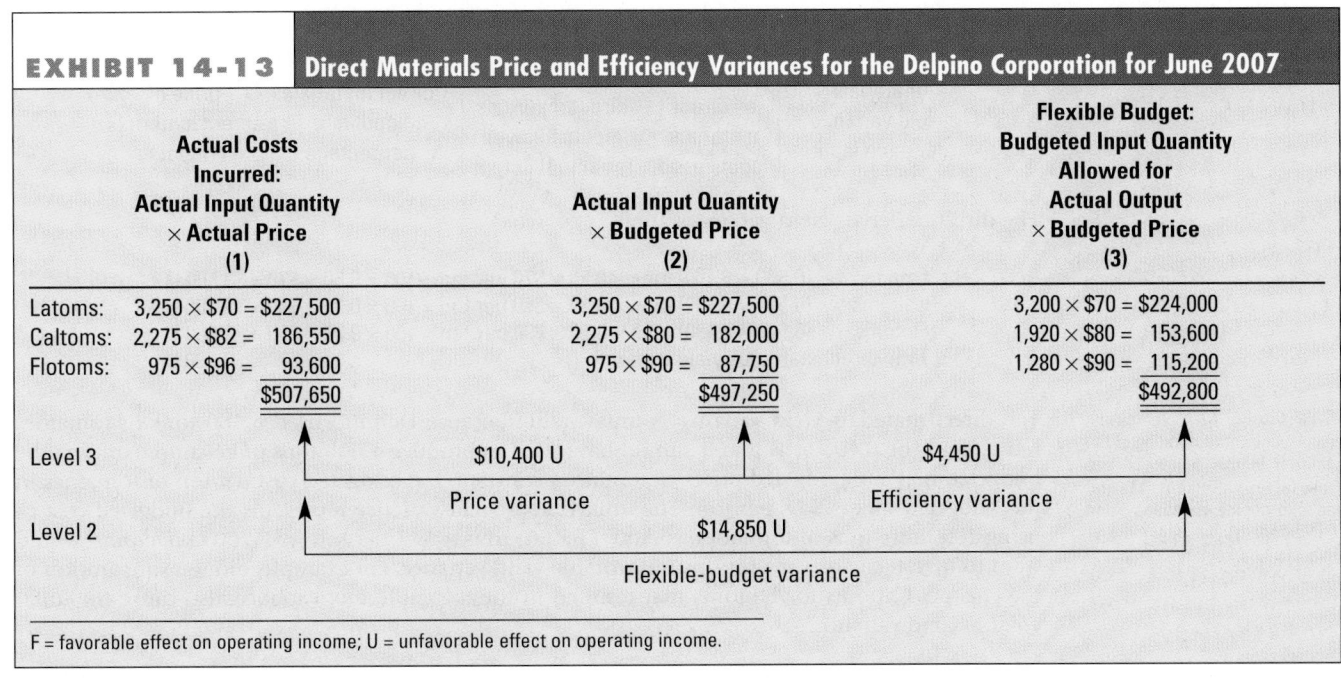

EXHIBIT 14-14 Total Direct Materials Yield and Mix Variances for the Delpino Corporation for June 2007

	Actual Total Quantity of All Inputs Used × Actual Input Mix × Budgeted Price (1)	Actual Total Quantity of All Inputs Used × Budgeted Input Mix × Budgeted Price (2)	Flexible Budget: Budgeted Total Quantity of All Inputs Allowed for Actual Output × Budgeted Input Mix × Budgeted Price (3)
Latoms:	6,500 × 0.50 × $70 = $227,500	6,500 × 0.50 × $70 = $227,500	6,400 × 0.50 × $70 = $224,000
Caltoms:	6,500 × 0.35 × $80 = 182,000	6,500 × 0.30 × $80 = 156,000	6,400 × 0.30 × $80 = 153,600
Flotoms:	6,500 × 0.15 × $90 = 87,750	6,500 × 0.20 × $90 = 117,000	6,400 × 0.20 × $90 = 115,200
	$497,250	$500,500	$492,800
Level 4	$3,250 F Mix variance (1)–(2)	$7,700 U Yield variance (2)–(3)	
Level 3	$4,450 U Efficiency variance (1)–(3)		

F = favorable effect on operating income; U = unfavorable effect on operating income.

The direct materials mix variances are:

Latoms:	6,500 tons × (0.50 – 0.50) × $70 per ton = 6,500 × 0.00 × $70 =	$ 0
Caltoms:	6,500 tons × (0.35 – 0.30) × $80 per ton = 6,500 × 0.05 × $80 =	26,000 U
Flotoms:	6,500 tons × (0.15 – 0.20) × $90 per ton = 6,500 × –0.05 × $90 =	29,250 F
Total direct materials mix variance		$ 3,250 F

The direct materials mix variance is favorable because relative to the budgeted mix, Delpino substitutes 5% of the cheaper Caltoms for 5% of the more-expensive Flotoms.

Direct Materials Yield Variance The direct materials yield variance is the sum of the direct materials yield variances for each input:

$$\text{Direct materials yield variance for each input} = \left(\text{Actual total quantity of all direct materials inputs used} - \text{Budgeted total quantity of all direct materials inputs allowed for actual output}\right) \times \text{Budgeted direct materials input mix percentage} \times \text{Budgeted price of direct materials input}$$

The direct materials yield variances are:

Latoms:	(6,500 – 6,400) tons × 0.50 × $70 per ton = 100 × 0.50 × $70 =	$3,500 U
Caltoms:	(6,500 – 6,400) tons × 0.30 × $80 per ton = 100 × 0.30 × $80 =	2,400 U
Flotoms:	(6,500 – 6,400) tons × 0.20 × $90 per ton = 100 × 0.20 × $90 =	1,800 U
Total direct materials yield variance		$7,700 U

Study Tip: To check your understanding of the material in this appendix, see true–false statement 11 and multiple-choice questions 6 and 7 (*Student Guide*, beginning p. 188). Fully explained answers begin on p. 193.

The direct materials yield variance is unfavorable because Delpino used 6,500 tons of tomatoes rather than the 6,400 tons that it should have used to produce 4,000 tons of ketchup. Holding the budgeted mix and budgeted prices of tomatoes constant, the budgeted cost per ton of tomatoes in the budgeted mix is $77 per ton. The unfavorable yield variance represents the budgeted cost of using 100 more tons of tomatoes, (6,500 – 6,400) tons × $77 per ton = $7,700 U. Delpino would want to investigate reasons for this unfavorable yield variance. For example, did the substitution of the cheaper Caltoms for Flotoms that resulted in the favorable mix variance also cause the unfavorable yield variance?

The direct materials variances computed in Exhibits 14-13 and 14-14 can be summarized as follows:

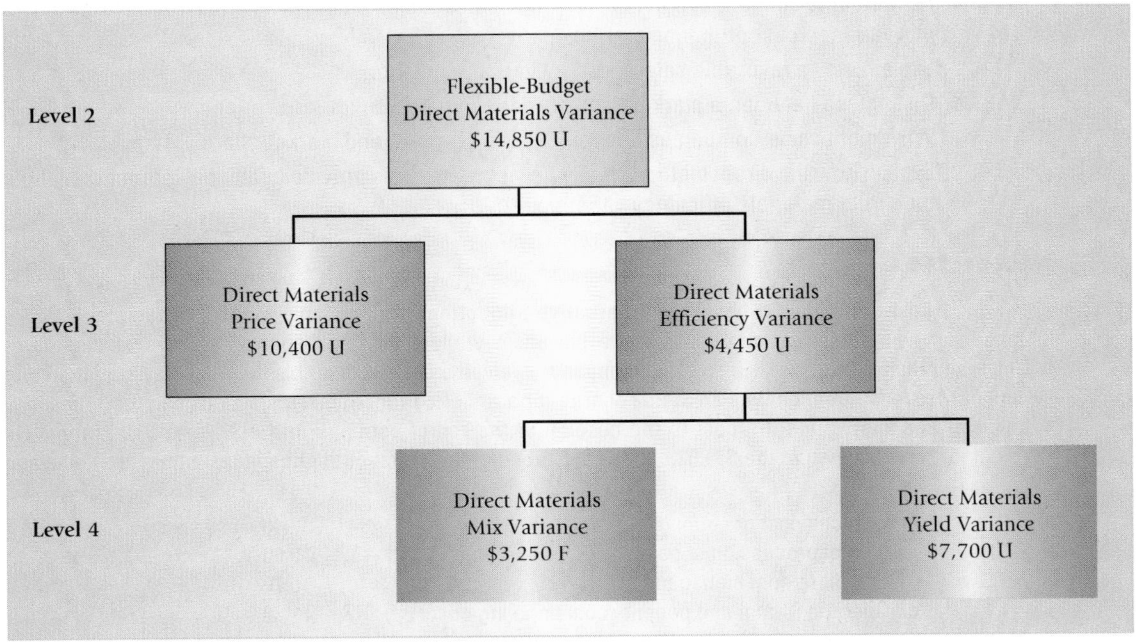

TERMS TO LEARN

This chapter and the Glossary at the end of the book contain definitions of:

composite unit (p. 511)
customer-cost hierarchy (p. 502)
customer-profitability analysis (p. 501)
direct materials mix variance (p. 517)
direct materials yield variance (p. 517)
homogeneous cost pool (p. 499)
market-share variance (p. 512)
market-size variance (p. 513)
price discount (p. 502)
sales-mix variance (p. 510)
sales-quantity variance (p. 511)

PH Grade Assist	**Prentice Hall Grade Assist (PHGA)** Your professor may ask you to complete selected exercises and problems in Prentice Hall Grade Assist (PHGA). PHGA is an online tool that can help you master the chapter's topics. It provides you with multiple variations of exercises and problems designated by the PHGA icon. You can rework these exercises and problems—each time with new data—as many times as you need. You also receive immediate feedback and grading.

ASSIGNMENT MATERIAL

Questions

14-1 "I am going to focus on the customers of my business and leave cost-allocation issues to my accountant." Do you agree with this comment by a division president? Why?

14-2 A given cost may be allocated for one or more purposes. List four purposes.

14-3 What criteria might be used to guide cost-allocation decisions? Which are the dominant criteria?

14-4 "A company should not allocate all of its corporate costs to its divisions." Do you agree? Explain.

14-5 "Once a company allocates corporate costs to divisions, these costs should not be reallocated to the indirect-cost pools of the division." Do you agree? Explain.

14-6 Why is customer-profitability analysis a vitally important topic to managers?

14-7 How can the extent of price discounting be tracked on a customer-by-customer basis?

14-8 "A customer-profitability profile highlights those customers who should be dropped to improve profitability." Do you agree? Explain.

14-9 Give examples of three different levels of costs in a customer-cost hierarchy.

14-10 Show how managers can gain insight into the causes of a sales-volume variance by subdividing the components of this variance.

14-11 How can the concept of a composite unit be used to explain why an unfavorable total sales-mix variance of contribution margin occurs?

14-12 Explain why a favorable sales-quantity variance occurs.

14-13 Distinguish between a market-share variance and a market-size variance.

14-14 Why might some companies not compute market-size and market-share variances?

14-15 Explain how the direct materials mix and yield variances provide additional information about the direct materials efficiency variance.

Exercises

PH Grade Assist

14-16 Cost allocation in hospitals, alternative allocation criteria. Dave Meltzer vacationed at Lake Tahoe last winter. Unfortunately, he broke his ankle while skiing and spent two days at the Sierra University Hospital. Meltzer's insurance company received a $4,800 bill for his two-day stay. One item that caught Meltzer's attention was an $11.52 charge for a roll of cotton. Meltzer is a salesman for Johnson & Johnson and knows that the cost to the hospital of the roll of cotton is in the $2.20 to $3.00 range. He asked for a breakdown of the $11.52 charge. The accounting office of the hospital sent him the following information:

a. Invoiced cost of cotton roll	$ 2.40
b. Cost of processing of paperwork for purchase	0.60
c. Supplies-room management fee	0.70
d. Operating-room and patient-room handling costs	1.60
e. Administrative hospital costs	1.10
f. University teaching–related costs	0.60
g. Malpractice insurance costs	1.20
h. Cost of treating uninsured patients	2.72
i. Profit component	0.60
Total	$11.52

Meltzer believes the overhead charge is obscene. He comments, "There was nothing I could do about it. When they come in and dab your stitches, it's not as if you can say, 'Keep your cotton roll. I brought my own.'"

Required

1. Compute the overhead rate Sierra University Hospital charged on the cotton roll.
2. What criteria might Sierra use to justify allocation of the overhead items b through i in the preceding list? Examine each item separately and use the allocation criteria listed in Exhibit 14-2 (p. 495) in your answer.
3. What should Meltzer do about the $11.52 charge for the cotton roll?

14-17 Cost allocation and motivation. Environ Petroleum Company is engaged in all phases of the exploring, refining, and marketing of oil and petrochemical products. To ensure full compliance with all applicable laws, the company has a legal department staffed by lawyers who have expertise in a variety of legal areas. The top management of Environ wants to motivate all operating managers to seek legal counsel from the in-house lawyers whenever necessary to avoid violation of any laws during the course of its operations.

Currently, users of the Legal Department are allocated cost at a $400 standard hourly rate based on actual usage. The chief financial officer has suggested that department managers would make more use of the Legal Department services, and thus avoid potential legal pitfalls, if the service was provided free of cost to their departments.

Required

Comment on the proposal of the chief financial officer. Do you have any alternative suggestion(s)?

14-18 Cost allocation to divisions. Rembrandt Hotel & Casino is situated on beautiful Lake Tahoe in Nevada. The complex includes a 300-room hotel, a casino, and a restaurant. As Rembrandt's new controller, you are asked to recommend the basis to be used for allocating fixed overhead costs to the three divisions in 2007. You are presented with the following income statement information for 2006:

	Hotel	Restaurant	Casino
Revenues	$16,425,000	$5,256,000	$12,340,000
Direct costs	9,819,260	3,749,172	4,248,768
Segment margin	$ 6,605,740	$1,506,828	$ 8,091,232

You are also given the following data on the three divisions:

	Hotel	Restaurant	Casino
Floor space (square feet)	80,000	16,000	64,000
Number of employees	200	50	250

You may choose to allocate indirect costs based on direct costs, square feet, or the number of employees. Total fixed overhead for 2006 was $14,550,000.

Required

1. Calculate division margins in percentage terms prior to allocating fixed overhead costs.
2. Allocate indirect costs to the three divisions using each of the three allocation bases suggested. Calculate division margins in dollar and percentage terms with each allocation base.
3. Discuss the results. How would you decide how to allocate indirect costs to the divisions? Why?
4. Would you recommend closing any of the three divisions (and possibly reallocating resources to other divisions) as a result of your analysis? If so, which division would you close and why?

14-19 Cost allocation to divisions. Lenzig Corporation has three divisions: Pulp, Paper, and Fibers. Lenzig's new controller, Ari Bardem, is reviewing the allocation of fixed corporate-overhead costs to the three divisions. He is presented with the following information for each division for 2006:

PH Grade Assist

Excel Lab www.prenhall.com/horngren/cost12e

	A	B	C	D
1		**Pulp**	**Paper**	**Fibers**
2	Revenues	$8,500,000	$17,500,000	$24,000,000
3	Direct manufacturing costs	4,100,000	8,600,000	11,300,000
4	Division administrative costs	2,000,000	1,800,000	3,200,000
5	Division margin	$2,400,000	$ 7,100,000	$ 9,500,000
6				
7	Number of employees	350	250	400
8	Floor space (square feet)	35,000	24,000	66,000

Until now, Lenzig Corporation has allocated fixed corporate-overhead costs to the divisions on the basis of division margins. Bardem asks for a list of costs that comprise fixed corporate overhead and suggests the following new allocation bases:

	F	G	H
1	**Fixed Corporate Overhead Costs**		**Suggested Allocation Bases**
2	Human resource management	$1,800,000	Number of employees
3	Facility	2,700,000	Floor space (square feet)
4	Corporate Administration	4,500,000	Division administrative costs
5	Total	$9,000,000	

If you want to use Excel to solve this exercise, go to the Excel Lab at **www.prenhall.com/horngren/cost12e** and download the template for Exercise 14-19.

Required

1. Allocate 2006 fixed corporate-overhead costs to the three divisions using division margin as the allocation base. What is each division's operating margin percentage (division margin minus allocated fixed corporate-overhead costs as a percentage of revenues)?
2. Allocate 2006 fixed costs using the allocation bases suggested by Bardem. What is each division's operating margin percentage under the new allocation scheme?
3. Compare and discuss the results of requirements 1 and 2. If division performance is linked to operating margin percentage, which division would be most receptive to the new allocation scheme? Which division would be the least receptive? Why?
4. Which allocation scheme should Lenzig Corporation use? Why? How might Bardem overcome any objections that may arise from the divisions?

14-20 Customer profitability, customer-cost hierarchy. Ramish Electronics has only two retail and two wholesale customers. Information relating to each customer for 2006 follows (in thousands):

Excel Lab www.prenhall.com/horngren/cost12e

	A	B	C	D	E
1		**Wholesale Customers**		**Retail Customers**	
2		**North America**	**South America**	**Big Sam**	**World**
3		**Wholesaler**	**Wholesaler**	**Stereo**	**Market**
4	Revenues at list price	$420,000	$580,000	$130,000	$100,000
5	Discounts from list prices	30,000	40,000	7,000	500
6	Cost of goods sold	325,000	455,000	118,000	90,000
7	Delivery costs	450	650	200	125
8	Order processing costs	800	1,000	200	130
9	Cost of sales visits	5,600	5,500	2,300	1,350

Ramish's annual distribution-channel costs are $35 million for wholesale customers and $8 million for retail customers. Its annual corporate-sustaining costs, such as salary for top management and general-administration costs, are $60 million. There is no cause-and-effect or benefits-received relationship between any cost-allocation base and corporate-sustaining costs. That is, corporate-sustaining costs could be saved only if Ramish Electronics were to completely shut down.

If you want to use Excel to solve this exercise, go to the Excel Lab at **www.prenhall.com/horngren/cost12e** and download the template for Exercise 14-20.

Required

1. Calculate customer-level operating income using the format in Exhibit 14-5.
2. Prepare a customer-cost hierarchy report, using the format in Exhibit 14-6.
3. Ramish's management decides to allocate all corporate-sustaining costs to distribution channels: $48 million to the wholesale channel and $12 million to the retail channel. As a result, distribution-channel costs are now $83 million ($35 million + $48 million) for the wholesale channel and $20 million ($8 million + $12 million) for the retail channel. Calculate the distribution-channel-level operating income. On the basis of these calculations, what actions, if any, should Ramish's managers take? Explain.

Excel Lab
www.prenhall.com/horngren/cost12e

14-21 Customer profitability, service company. Instant Service (IS) repairs printers and photocopiers for five multisite companies in a tristate area. IS's costs consist of the cost of technicians and equipment that are directly traceable to the customer site and a pool of office overhead. Until recently, IS estimated customer profitability by allocating the office overhead to each customer based on share of revenues. For 2007, IS reported the following results:

	A	B	C	D	E	F	G
1		**Avery**	**Okie**	**Wizard**	**Grainger**	**Duran**	**Total**
2	Revenues	$260,000	$200,000	$322,000	$122,000	$212,000	$1,116,000
3	Technician and equipment cost	182,000	175,000	225,000	107,000	178,000	867,000
4	Office overhead allocated	31,859	24,507	39,457	14,949	25,978	136,750
5	Operating income	$ 46,141	$ 493	$ 57,543	$ 51	$ 8,022	$ 112,250

Tina Sherman, IS's new controller, notes that office overhead is more than 10% of total costs, so she spends a couple of weeks analyzing the consumption of office overhead resources by customers. She collects the following information:

	I	J	K
1	**Activity Area**	**Cost Driver Rate**	
2	Service call handling	$75	per service call
3	Parts ordering	$80	per web-based parts order
4	Billing and collection	$50	per bill (or reminder)
5	Customer database maintenance	$10	per service call

	A	B	C	D	E	F
8		**Avery**	**Okie**	**Wizard**	**Grainger**	**Duran**
9	Number of service calls	150	240	40	120	180
10	Number of web-based parts orders	120	210	60	150	150
11	Number of bills (or reminders)	30	90	90	60	120

If you want to use Excel to solve this exercise, go to the Excel Lab at **www.prenhall.com/horngren/cost12e** and download the template for Exercise 14-21.

Required

1. Compute customer-level operating income using the new information that Sherman has gathered.
2. Prepare exhibits for IS similar to Exhibits 14-7 and 14-8. Comment on the results.
3. What options should IS consider, with regard to individual customers, in light of the new data and analysis of office overhead?

14-22 Customer profitability, distribution. Figure Four is a distributor of pharmaceutical products. Its ABC system has five activities:

Activity Area	Cost Driver Rate in 2006
1. Order processing	$40 per order
2. Line-item ordering	$3 per line item
3. Store deliveries	$50 per store delivery
4. Carton deliveries	$1 per carton
5. Shelf-stocking	$16 per stocking-hour

Rick Flair, the controller of Figure Four, wants to use this ABC system to examine individual customer profitability within each distribution market. He focuses first on the Ma and Pa single-store distribution market. Two customers are used to exemplify the insights available with the ABC approach. Data pertaining to these two customers in August 2006 are as follows:

	Charleston Pharmacy	Chapel Hill Pharmacy
Total orders	12	10
Average line items per order	10	18
Total store deliveries	6	10
Average cartons shipped per store delivery	24	20
Average hours of shelf-stocking per store delivery	0	0.5
Average revenue per delivery	$2,400	$1,800
Average cost of goods sold per delivery	$2,100	$1,650

Required

1. Use the ABC information to compute the operating income of each customer in August 2006. Comment on the results.
2. Flair ranks the individual customers in the Ma and Pa single-store distribution market on the basis of monthly operating income. The cumulative operating income of the top 20% of customers is $55,680. Figure Four reports operating losses of $21,247 for the bottom 40% of its customers. Make four recommendations that you think Figure Four should consider in light of this new customer-profitability information.

14-23 Variance analysis, multiple products. The Detroit Penguins play in the American Ice Hockey League. The Penguins play in the Downtown Arena (owned and managed by the City of Detroit), which has a capacity of 15,000 seats (5,000 lower-tier seats and 10,000 upper-tier seats). The Downtown Arena charges the Penguins a per-ticket charge for use of their facility. All tickets are sold by the Reservation Network, which charges the Penguins a reservation fee per ticket. The Penguins' budgeted contribution margin for each type of ticket in 2007 is computed as follows:

PH Grade Assist

	Lower-Tier Tickets	Upper-Tier Tickets
Selling price	$35	$14
Downtown Arena fee	10	6
Reservation Network fee	5	3
Contribution margin per ticket	$20	$ 5

The budgeted and actual average attendance figures per game in the 2007 season are:

	Budgeted Seats Sold	Actual Seats Sold
Lower tier	4,000	3,300
Upper tier	6,000	7,700
Total	10,000	11,000

There was no difference between the budgeted and actual contribution margin for lower-tier or upper-tier seats.

The manager of the Penguins was delighted that actual attendance was 10% above budgeted attendance per game, especially given the depressed state of the local economy in the past six months.

Required

1. Compute the sales-volume variance for each type of ticket and in total for the Detroit Penguins in 2007. (Calculate all variances in terms of contribution margins.)
2. Compute the sales-quantity and sales-mix variances for each type of ticket and in total in 2007.
3. Present a summary of the variances in requirements 1 and 2. Comment on the results.

14-24 Variance analysis, working backward. The Jinwa Corporation sells two brands of wine glasses: Plain and Chic. Jinwa provides the following information for sales in the month of June 2006:

PH Grade Assist

Static-budget total contribution margin	$5,600
Budgeted units to be sold of all glasses	2,000 units
Budgeted contribution margin per unit of Plain	$2 per unit
Budgeted contribution margin per unit of Chic	$6 per unit
Total sales-quantity variance	$1,400 U
Actual sales-mix percentage of Plain	60%

All variances are to be computed in contribution-margin terms.

Required

1. Calculate the sales-quantity variances for each product for June 2006.
2. Calculate the individual-product and total sales-mix variances for June 2006. Calculate the individual-product and total sales-volume variances for June 2006.
3. Briefly describe the conclusions you can draw from the variances.

14-25 Variance analysis, multiple products. Soda-King manufactures and sells three soft drinks: Kola, Limor, and Orlem. Budgeted and actual results for 2006 are as follows:

	Budget for 2006			Actual for 2006		
Product	**Selling Price per Carton**	**Variable Cost per Carton**	**Cartons Sold**	**Selling Price per Carton**	**Variable Cost per Carton**	**Cartons Sold**
Kola	$6.00	$4.00	400,000	$6.20	$4.50	480,000
Limor	$4.00	$2.80	600,000	$4.25	$2.75	900,000
Orlem	$7.00	$4.50	1,500,000	$6.80	$4.60	1,620,000

Required

1. Compute the total sales-volume variance, the total sales-mix variance, and the total sales-quantity variance. (Calculate all variances in terms of contribution margin.) Show results for each product in your computations.
2. What inferences can you draw from the variances computed in requirement 1?

14-26 Market-share and market-size variances (continuation of 14-25). Soda-King prepared the budget for 2006 assuming a 10% market share based on total sales in the western region of the United States. The total soft drinks market was estimated to reach sales of 25 million cartons in the region. However, actual total sales volume in the western region was 24 million cartons.

Required

Calculate the market-share and market-size variances for Soda-King in 2006. (Calculate all variances in terms of contribution margin.) Comment on the results.

Problems

Excel Lab
www.prenhall.com/horngren/cost12e

14-27 Allocation of corporate costs to divisions. Dusty Rhodes, controller of Richfield Oil Company, is preparing a presentation to senior executives about the performance of its four divisions. Summary data (dollar amounts in millions) related to the four divisions for the most recent year are:

	A	B	C	D	E	F
1		DIVISIONS				
2		**Oil & Gas Upstream**	**Oil & Gas Downstream**	**Chemical Products**	**Copper Mining**	**Total**
3	Revenues	$ 8,000	$16,000	$4,800	$3,200	$32,000
4	Operating Costs	3,000	15,000	3,800	3,500	25,300
5	Operating Income	$ 5,000	$ 1,000	$1,000	$ (300)	$ 6,700
6						
7	Identifiable assets	$14,000	$ 6,000	$3,000	$2,000	$25,000
8	Number of employees	9,000	12,000	6,000	3,000	30,000

Under the existing accounting system, costs incurred at corporate headquarters are collected in a single cost pool ($3,228 million in the most recent year) and allocated to each division on the basis of its actual revenues. The top managers in each division share in a division-income bonus pool. Division income is defined as operating income less allocated corporate costs.

Rhodes has analyzed the components of corporate costs and proposes that corporate costs be collected in four cost pools. The components of corporate costs for the most recent year (dollar amounts in millions) and Rhodes' suggested cost pools and allocation bases are:

	A	B	C	D	E	F
11	**Corporate Cost Category**	**Amount**	**Suggested Cost Pool**	**Suggested Allocation Base**		
12	Interest on debt	$2,000	Cost Pool 1	Identifiable assets		
13	Corporate salaries	150	Cost Pool 2			
14	Accounting and control	110	Cost Pool 2			
15	General marketing	200	Cost Pool 2	Division Revenues		
16	Legal	140	Cost Pool 2			
17	Research and Development	200	Cost Pool 2			
18	Public affairs	203	Cost Pool 3	Positive Operating Income*		
19	Personnel and payroll	225	Cost Pool 4	Number of employees		
20	Total	$3,228				
21						
22	*Since Public Affairs cost includes the cost of public relations staff, lobbyists, and donations to					
23	environmental charities, Rhodes proposes that this cost be allocated using operating income (if positive)					
24	of divisions, with only divisions with positive operating income included in the allocation base.					

If you want to use Excel to solve this problem, go to the Excel Lab at **www.prenhall.com/horngren/cost12e** and download the template for Problem 14-27.

Required

1. Discuss two reasons why Richfield Oil should allocate corporate costs to each division.
2. Calculate the operating income of each division when all corporate costs are allocated based on revenues of each division.
3. Calculate the operating income of each division when all corporate costs are allocated using the four cost pools.
4. How do you think the new proposal will be received by the division managers? What are the strengths and weaknesses of Rhodes' proposal relative to the existing single-cost-pool method?

14-28 Allocation of central corporate costs to divisions. Legarde has four geographically dispersed divisions:

- Book publishing
- Broadcasting
- Print media
- Multimedia

Under the current allocation system, costs incurred at Legarde corporate headquarters are collected in a single pool and allocated to each division on the basis of its revenues. The central corporate costs for 2006 (in millions) are:

Interest on debt	$ 10
Human resource management	150
Corporate administration	50
Research and development	100
Advertising	200
	$510

Summary data (in millions) related to the divisions for 2006 are:

	Multimedia	Broadcasting	Print Media	Book Publishing
Revenues	$1,400	$4,500	$2,500	$1,600
Direct costs	750	3,500	2,000	1,000
Division margin	$ 650	$1,000	$ 500	$ 600

The following information on the four divisions is also available.

	Multimedia	Broadcasting	Print Media	Book Publishing
Floor space (square feet)	40,000	160,000	200,000	100,000
Number of employees	1,000	3,000	2,500	1,500
Division administrative costs (in millions)	$150	$400	$250	$200

A review of the central corporate costs for divisions reveals the following:

- Out of the total $10 million interest on debt, $6.5 million is for the debt to purchase a building for the Broadcasting division. The remaining $3.5 million interest cost is on the borrowings for the purchase of equipment for the Multimedia division.
- The resources expended by human resource management on recruiting, training, and so forth for the divisions are approximately in proportion to the number of employees.
- Corporate administration supports division managers. The division administrative costs are a good indicator of the relative size of each division's management team.
- No research and development work is done for the Print Media division. The director of research and development estimates that 40% of the work in her responsibility area is done for the Multimedia division, and the remaining 60% is done equally for the Broadcasting and Book Publishing divisions.
- Advertising campaigns sponsored at the central corporate level are to boost the overall corporate image. It is assumed that the benefits to the divisions are in proportion to their revenues.

Required

Allocate the central corporate costs to divisions that are consistent with cause-and-effect or benefits-received criteria.

14-29 Customer-profitability analysis, customer-cost hierarchy. Zoot's Suits is a ready-to-wear suit manufacturer. Zoot's has two wholesale-channel customers (Arvin Outfitters and Madison Brothers) and two retail-channel customers (Suitors Men's Store and LuxTux Clothing Store). Al Sims, Zoot's owner and CEO, has developed an ABC system with four activities related to customer service and order fulfillment. List selling price is $250, and cost per suit is $150. Hoping to better understand the relative profitability of Zoot's customers and to find ways to improve overall profitability, Sims compiles the following data for 2007:

Excel Lab
www.prenhall.com/horngren/cost12e

	A	B	C	D	E	F	G	H	I
1			WHOLESALE CUSTOMERS			RETAIL CUSTOMERS			
2	Item		Arvin	Madison		Suitors	LuxTux		
3	Average number of suits per order		380	660		40	30		
4	Average selling price per suit		$190	$210		$220	$230		
5	Activity	Cost Driver						Cost Driver Rate	
6	Order processing	Total number of orders	52	30		220	280	$ 250	per order
7	Sales visits	Total number of sales visits	12	15		35	20	$1,150	per sales visit
8	Regular deliveries	Number of regular deliveries	45	18		150	245	$ 300	per regular delivery
9	Rush deliveries	Number of rush deliveries	7	12		70	35	$ 850	per rush delivery

If you want to use Excel to solve this problem, go to the Excel Lab at **www.prenhall.com/horngren/cost12e** and download the template for Problem 14-29.

Required

1. Calculate customer-level operating income in 2007 using the format in Exhibit 14-5. What is the operating income per suit sold to each customer?
2. Based on the calculations in requirement 1, what should Al Sims do to increase Zoot's profitability in 2008?
3. Assume Zoot's distribution-channel costs are $800,000 for its wholesale customers and $680,000 for its retail customers. Its corporate-sustaining costs are $600,000. There is no cause-and-effect or benefits-received relationship between any cost-allocation base and corporate-sustaining costs. That is, corporate-sustaining costs would be saved only if Zoot's Suits were to shut down. Prepare a customer-cost hierarchy report for Zoot's, using the format in Exhibit 14-6.
4. Sims decides to allocate all corporate-sustaining costs to the distribution channels: $330,000 to the wholesale channel and $270,000 to the retail channel. As a result, distribution-channel costs are $1,130,000 ($800,000 + $330,000) for the wholesale channel and $950,000 ($680,000 + $270,000) for the retail channel. Calculate the distribution-channel-level operating income. On the basis of these calculations, what actions, if any, should Sims take? Explain.

14-30 Customer profitability, distribution. Spring Distribution has decided to analyze the profitability of five new customers (see pp. 501–508). It buys bottled water at $12 per case and sells to retail customers at a list price of $14.40 per case. Data pertaining to the five customers are:

	Customer				
	P	Q	R	S	T
Cases sold	2,080	8,750	60,800	31,800	3,900
List selling price	$14.40	$14.40	$14.40	$14.40	$14.40
Actual selling price	$14.40	$14.16	$13.20	$13.92	$12.96
Number of purchase orders	15	25	30	25	30
Number of customer visits	2	3	6	2	3
Number of deliveries	10	30	60	40	20
Miles traveled per delivery	14	4	3	8	40
Number of expedited deliveries	0	0	0	0	1

Its five activities and their cost drivers are:

Activity	Cost Driver Rate
Order taking	$100 per purchase order
Customer visits	$80 per customer visit
Deliveries	$2 per delivery mile traveled
Product handling	$0.50 per case sold
Expedited deliveries	$300 per expedited delivery

Required

1. Compute the customer-level operating income of each of the five retail customers now being examined (P, Q, R, S, and T). Comment on the results.
2. What insights are gained by reporting both the list selling price and the actual selling price for each customer?
3. What factors should Spring Distribution consider in deciding whether to drop one or more of the five customers?

14-31 Customer loyalty clubs and profitability analysis. The Sherriton Hotels chain embarked on a new customer-loyalty program in 2006. The 2006 year-end data have been collected, and it is now time for you to determine whether the loyalty program should be continued, discontinued, or perhaps altered to improve loyalty and profitability levels at Sherriton.

Sherriton's loyalty program consists of three different customer-loyalty levels. All new customers can sign up for the Sherriton Bronze Card. This card provides guests with a complimentary bottle of wine per night (cost to the chain is $5 per bottle) and $20 in restaurant coupons each night (cost to the chain is $10). Bronze customers also receive a 10% discount off the nightly rate. The program enables the chain to track a member's stays and activities. Once customers have stayed and paid for 20 nights at any of the chain's locations worldwide, they are upgraded to Silver Customer status. Silver benefits include the bottle of wine (cost to the chain is $5 per bottle per night), $30 in restaurant coupons per night (cost to the chain is $15), and 20% off every night from the 21st night on. A customer who reaches the 50-night level is upgraded to Gold Customer status. Gold status increases the nightly discount to 30% and replaces the $5 bottle of wine with a bottle of champagne per night (cost to the chain is $20 per bottle). As well, $40 in restaurant coupons per night are granted (cost to the chain is $20). Assume all bottles and coupons offered are used.

The average full price for one night's stay is $200. The chain incurs variable costs of $65 per night, exclusive of loyalty-program costs. Total fixed costs for the chain are $140,580,000. Sherriton operates 10 hotels, with, on average, 500 rooms each. All hotels are open for business 365 days a year, and average occupancy rates are around 80%. Following are some loyalty-program characteristics for 2006:

Loyalty Program	Number of Customers	Average Number of Nights per Customer
Gold	2,430	60
Silver	8,340	35
Bronze	80,300	10
No program	219,000	1

Note that an average Gold Customer would have received the 10% discount for his or her first 20 stays, received the 20% discount for the next 30 stays, and the 30% discount only for the last 10 nights. Assume that all program members signed on to the program the first time they stayed with one of the chain's hotels. Also, assume the restaurants are managed by a 100%-owned subsidiary of Sherriton.

Required

1. Calculate the contribution margin for each of the three programs, as well as for the customers not subscribing to the loyalty program. Which of the programs is the most profitable? Which is the least profitable? Do not allocate fixed costs to individual rooms or specific loyalty programs.
2. Prepare a contribution income statement for Sherriton for the year ended December 31, 2006.
3. What is the average room rate per night? What are average variable costs per night inclusive of the loyalty program?
4. Explain what drives the profitability (or lack thereof) of Sherriton's loyalty program.

14-32 Variance analysis, sales-mix and sales-quantity variances. Aussie Infonautics, Inc., produces handheld Windows CE™–compatible organizers. Aussie Infonautics markets three different handheld models. PalmPro is a souped-up version for the executive on the go; PalmCE is a consumer-oriented version; and PalmKid is a stripped-down version for the young adult market. You are Aussie Infonautics' senior vice president of marketing. The CEO has discovered that the total contribution margin came in lower than budgeted, and it is your responsibility to explain to him why actual results are different from the budget. Budgeted and actual operating data for the company's third quarter (2007) are as follows:

Budgeted Operating Data, Third Quarter 2007

	Selling Price	Variable Cost per Unit	Contribution Margin per Unit	Sales Volume in Units
PalmPro	$379	$182	$197	12,500
PalmCE	269	98	171	37,500
PalmKid	149	65	84	50,000
				100,000

Actual Operating Data, Third Quarter 2007

	Selling Price	Variable Cost per Unit	Contribution Margin per Unit	Sales Volume in Units
PalmPro	$349	$178	$171	11,000
PalmCE	285	92	193	44,000
PalmKid	102	73	29	55,000
				110,000

Required

1. Compute the actual and budgeted contribution margins in dollars for each product and in total for the third quarter of 2007.
2. Calculate the actual and budgeted sales mixes for the three products for the third quarter of 2007.
3. Calculate total sales-volume, sales-mix, and sales-quantity variances for the third quarter of 2007. (Calculate all variances in terms of contribution margins.)
4. Given that your CEO is known to have temper tantrums, you want to be well prepared for this meeting. In order to prepare, write a paragraph or two comparing actual results to budgeted amounts.

14-33 Market-share and market-size variances (continuation of 14-32). Aussie Infonautics' senior vice president of marketing prepared his budget at the beginning of the third quarter assuming a 25% market share based on total sales. The total handheld-organizer market was estimated by Foolinstead Research to reach sales of 400,000 units worldwide in the third quarter. However, actual sales in the third quarter were 500,000 units.

Required

1. Calculate the market-share and market-size variances for Aussie Infonautics in the third quarter of 2007 (calculate all variances in terms of contribution margins).
2. Explain what happened based on the market-share and market-size variances.
3. Calculate the actual market size, in units, that would have led to no market-size variance (again using budgeted contribution margin per unit). Use this market-size figure to find the actual market share that would have led to a zero market-share variance.

PH Grade Assist

14-34 Variance analysis, multiple products. Debbie's Delight, Inc., operates a chain of cookie stores. Budgeted and actual operating data of its three Chicago stores for August 2006 are as follows:

Budget for August 2006

	Selling Price per Pound	Variable Cost per Pound	Contribution Margin per Pound	Sales Volume in Pounds
Chocolate chip	$4.50	$2.50	$2.00	45,000
Oatmeal raisin	5.00	2.70	2.30	25,000
Coconut	5.50	2.90	2.60	10,000
White chocolate	6.00	3.00	3.00	5,000
Macadamia nut	6.50	3.40	3.10	15,000
				100,000

Actual for August 2006

	Selling Price per Pound	Variable Cost per Pound	Contribution Margin per Pound	Sales Volume in Pounds
Chocolate chip	$4.50	$2.60	$1.90	57,600
Oatmeal raisin	5.20	2.90	2.30	18,000
Coconut	5.50	2.80	2.70	9,600
White chocolate	6.00	3.40	2.60	13,200
Macadamia nut	7.00	4.00	3.00	21,600
				120,000

Debbie's Delight focuses on contribution margin in its variance analysis.

Required

1. Compute the total sales-volume variance for August 2006.
2. Compute the total sales-mix variance for August 2006.
3. Compute the total sales-quantity variance for August 2006.
4. Comment on your results in requirements 1, 2, and 3.

PH Grade Assist

14-35 Market-share and market-size variances (continuation of 14-34). Debbie's Delight attains a 10% market share based on total sales of the Chicago market. The total Chicago market is expected to be 1,000,000 pounds in sales volume for August 2006. The actual total Chicago market for August 2006 was 960,000 pounds in sales volume.

Required

Compute the market-share and market-size variances for Debbie's Delight in August 2006. Calculate all variances in contribution-margin terms. Comment on the results.

Excel Lab www.prenhall.com/horngren/cost12e

14-36 Direct materials efficiency, mix, and yield variances. (Chapter appendix, CMA adapted) The Energex Company produces a gasoline additive, Gas Gain, that increases engine efficiency and improves gasoline mileage. The actual and budgeted quantities and the budgeted prices in August 2007 of the two petroleum products required to produce 50,000 gallons of Gas Gain are as follows:

	A	B	C	D
1		Actual Quantity	Budgeted Quantity	Budgeted Price
2	Chemical	(gallons)	(gallons)	(per gallon)
3	Protex	16,200	20,800	$0.40
4	Benz	37,800	31,200	$0.25

If you want to use Excel to solve this problem, go to the Excel Lab at **www.prenhall.com/horngren/cost12e** and download the template for Problem 14-36.

Required

1. Calculate the total direct materials efficiency variance for August 2007.
2. Calculate the total direct materials mix and yield variances for August 2007.
3. What conclusions can you draw from the variance analysis?

14-37 Direct materials price, efficiency, mix, and yield variances. (Chapter appendix) Greenwood, Inc., processes apples into applesauce and apple butter. Greenwood's applesauce is made with a blend of Tolman, Golden Delicious, and Ribston apples. Budgeted and actual costs to produce 150,000 pounds of applesauce in November 2006 are as follows:

Excel Lab
www.prenhall.com/horngren/cost12e

	A	B	C	D	E	F	G	H
1		BUDGETED				ACTUAL		
2		Quantity (pounds)	Price per Pound	Total Costs		Quantity (pounds)	Price per Pound	Total Costs
3	Tolman	52,500	$0.40	$21,000		72,000	$0.35	$25,200
4	Golden Delicious	210,000	$0.30	$63,000		180,000	$0.29	$52,200
5	Ribston	87,500	$0.20	$17,500		108,000	$0.22	$23,760
6		350,000				360,000		

If you want to use Excel to solve this problem, go to the Excel Lab at **www.prenhall.com/horngren/cost12e** and download the template for Problem 14-37.

Required

1. Calculate the total direct materials price and efficiency variances for November 2006.
2. Calculate the total direct materials mix and yield variances for November 2006.
3. Comment on your results in requirements 1 and 2.

14-38 Customer profitability, responsibility for environmental cleanup, ethics. Industrial Fluids, Inc. (IF), manufactures and sells fluids used by metal-cutting plants. These fluids enable metal cutting to be done more accurately and more safely.

IF has more than 1,000 customers. It is currently undertaking a customer-profitability analysis. Ariana Papandopolis, a newly hired MBA, is put in charge of the project. One issue in this analysis is IF's liability for its customers' fluid disposal.

Papandopolis discovers that IF may have a responsibility under U.S. environmental legislation for the disposal of toxic waste by its customers. Moreover, she visits 10 customer sites and finds dramatic differences in their toxic-waste-handling procedures. She describes one site owned by Acme Metal as an "environmental nightmare about to become a reality." She tells the IF controller that even if they have only one-half of the responsibility for the cleanup at Acme's site, they will still be facing very high damages. He is displeased that Acme Metal has not paid its account to IF for the past three months and has formally sought protection from its creditors. He cautions Papandopolis to be careful in her written report. He notes that, "IF does not want any smoking guns in its files in case of subsequent litigation."

Required

1. As Papandopolis prepares IF's customer-profitability analysis, how should she handle any estimates of litigation and cleanup costs that IF may be held responsible for?
2. How should Papandopolis handle the Acme Metal situation when she prepares a profitability report for that customer?

Collaborative Learning Problem

14-39 Customer profitability, credit-card operations. The Freedom Card is a credit card that competes with national credit cards such as Visa and MasterCard. Freedom Card is marketed by the Bay Bank. Mario Verdolini is manager of the Freedom Card division. He is seeking to develop a customer-profitability reporting system. He collects the following information on four users of the Freedom Card during 2006:

	A	B	C	D
Annual purchases at retail merchants	$80,000	$26,000	$34,000	$8,000
Number of customer transactions at retail merchant	800	520	272	200
Annual fee	$50	$0	$50	$0
Average annual outstanding balance on credit card on which interest is paid to Bay Bank	$6,000	$0	$2,000	$100
Number of inquiries to Bay Bank	6	12	8	2
Number of credit-card replacement due to loss or theft	0	2	1	0

Customer B pays no membership fee because his card was issued under a special "lifetime promotion program," in which annual fees are waived as long as the card is used at least once a year. Customer D is a student. Bay Bank does not charge an annual fee to student credit-card holders at select universities.

Bay Bank has an ABC system that Verdolini can use in his analysis. The following data are for 2006:

a. Each customer transaction with a retail merchant costs Bay Bank $0.50 to process.
b. Each customer inquiry to Bay Bank costs $5.
c. Replacing a lost card costs $120.
d. Annual cost to Bay Bank of maintaining a credit-card account is $108 (includes sending out monthly statements).

Bay Bank receives 2.0% of the purchase amount from retail merchants when the Freedom Card is used. Bad debts of the Freedom Card in 2006 were 0.5% of the total purchases at retail merchants. Thus, Bay Bank nets 1.5% of the total purchases made using the Freedom Card.

Bay Bank had an interest spread of 9% in 2006 on the average outstanding balances on which interest is paid by its credit-card holders. An interest spread is the difference between what Bay Bank receives from card holders on outstanding balances and what it pays to obtain the funds so used. Thus, on a $500 average annual outstanding balance in 2006, Bay Bank would receive a net amount of $45 in interest (9% × $500).

Required

1. Compute the customer profitability of the four representative credit-card users of the Freedom Card for 2006.
2. Develop profiles of (a) profitable card holders and (b) unprofitable card holders for Bay Bank.
3. Should Bay Bank charge its card holders for making inquiries (such as outstanding balances or disputed charges) or for replacing lost or stolen cards?
4. Verdolini has an internal proposal that Bay Bank discontinue a sizable number of the low-volume credit-card customers. What factors should he consider in evaluating and responding to this proposal?
5. Verdolini seeks your group's advice on an ethical issue he is facing. A chain of gambling casinos (Lucky Roller) has offered to provide Freedom Card holders with money advances of up to $500 at its casinos. Verdolini observes that from a strictly financial perspective, providing money advances to its customers would be highly profitable. Should Freedom Card holders be able to obtain money advances at Lucky Roller gambling casinos? Explain.

WWW

Get Connected: Cost Accounting in the News

Go to www.prenhall.com/horngren/cost12e for additional online exercise(s) that explore issues affecting the accounting world today. These exercises offer you the opportunity to analyze and reflect on how cost accounting helps managers to make better decisions and handle the challenges of strategic planning and implementation.

CHAPTER 14 Video Case

NANTUCKET NECTARS: Cost Allocation

Tom First and Tom Scott knew they didn't want corporate "suit and tie" jobs when they graduated from Brown University. Tom First suggested they concoct a peach-juice beverage reminiscent of one he had sampled in Spain on a recent trip. One blender and lots of peaches later, the two Toms emerged with their first "Nantucket Nectar" beverage, named after their beloved harbor home. Today, their Cambridge, Massachusetts–based, company makes close to 50 flavors of juice drinks. Sales hover around $70 million annually.

The company partners with a number of juice bottlers, called "co-packers," to produce the juice. Recipes are created in the company's central test kitchen, with detailed specifications for winning flavors communicated to both the internal Purchasing function and each co-packer.

The ingredients are combined at the plant in 5,000-gallon batches. Each batch feeds the production line, which is set to fill 550 bottles per minute. As bottles come off the line, they are packed into cases of 20 bottles each. Cases are shrink-wrapped and stacked onto pallets. Full pallets are transported via forklift to trucks waiting to travel to distributor warehouses. Distributors pull products from the warehouses for delivery to retail outlets such as restaurants and grocery stores.

Ninety sales representatives are scattered throughout four regions: Central, Pacific Northwest, East, and Northeast. Each region is supplied by its own set of co-packers. Each region's sales representatives have responsibility for opening new customer accounts and securing local distributors for the company's single-serve juice bottles and cans, and multiserve juice cartons. To help boost sales in their regions, regional managers can request promotional support from headquarters' Mobile Juice Guy Team. This team of four full-time employees roves the United States, from region to region as requested by regional managers, in a dedicated full-size van to help promote Nantucket Nectars at charitable events, local festivals, community sports events, and so on. The mobile team takes banners, display tables, and plenty of coupons and products for sampling by a crowd. Regional managers expect to see a boost in new-customer accounts and sales as a result of incurring the expense to bring in the team.

Initially Mobile Team costs were not allocated to the regions that used the services of the Mobile Juice Guy Team. Top management is now interested in allocating the Mobile Team's costs to the regions.

These questions focus on the four purposes of cost allocation (pp. 493–494).

QUESTIONS

1. What types of economic decisions that involve cost allocation might Nantucket Nectars face with respect to the Mobile Juice Guy Team?
2. Give an example of how cost allocation can help motivate regional managers to use the Mobile Juice Guy Team.
3. Give an example of how cost allocation can be used to justify costs or compute reimbursement amounts for the Mobile Juice Guy Team.
4. Give examples of how cost allocations can help in measuring income and assets for reporting to external parties.

CHAPTER 15

ALLOCATION OF SUPPORT-DEPARTMENT COSTS, COMMON COSTS, AND REVENUES

LEARNING OBJECTIVES

1. **Distinguish the single-rate method from the dual-rate method**
2. **Understand how the uncertainty user managers face is affected by the choice between budgeted and actual cost-allocation rates**
3. **Allocate support-department costs using the direct method, the step-down method, and the reciprocal method**
4. **Allocate common costs using the stand-alone method and the incremental method**
5. **Explain the importance of explicit agreement between contracting parties when the reimbursement amount is based on costs incurred**
6. **Understand how bundling of products gives rise to revenue-allocation issues**
7. **Allocate the revenues of a bundled product to the individual products in that bundle**

Pamela Marbury has just returned from the annual Global Technology Summit (GTS) in London. As CEO of Sand Hill Company (SHC), a manufacturer of electronic products, she always finds the conference valuable for keeping in touch with her peers, gathering intelligence about current market conditions and her competitors, and learning about new practices and techniques. One of the speakers at the GTS highlighted how the relatively simple cost-allocation systems employed throughout the industry may not provide sufficiently accurate information for complex decisions. Pamela decides to meet with Annette Knoll, her CFO, to discuss whether their current system of allocating the costs of the Central Computer Department to SHC's two operating divisions—the Microcomputer Division and the Peripheral Equipment Division—needs an overhaul.

Pamela: As I mentioned in my e-mail, Annette, there was a lot of discussion at the GTS this year about cost-allocation techniques. I gather from the message you sent back that our approach for allocating computer-department costs is fairly straightforward. We use budgeted costs of the computer department and budgeted hours of service provided to calculate a budgeted rate. We use this rate to allocate computer-department costs to the operating divisions based on the actual hours of service used by the divisions. Is this our best option, or are there other approaches we should be considering?

Annette: Well, there are several alternatives. For example, we could use different methods for allocating fixed and variable costs. We could use actual rates rather than budgeted rates. We could allocate costs based on the budgeted hours of service provided to operating divisions rather than the actual hours of service provided.

Pamela: Okay, but is one of these approaches superior to the others?

Annette: No, there are pros and cons to each. Let me send you a memo explaining our choices and we can meet in a month or so to decide whether a change is in order.

Pamela: That will be a big help. Are there any other related issues for us to review?

Annette: We are increasingly finding that our support departments are providing a fair amount of service to each other. For example, the computer department and the human resources department are doing work for each other in addition to serving the operating divisions. I'll add a separate section to my memo about the choices we have for allocating costs when multiple support departments provide service to each other.

Pamela: That would be terrific.

Annette: One final issue. Our Peripheral Equipment Division is planning to bundle some of its products together. For example, if our customers buy a scanner and printer together, it will cost them less than purchasing each item from us separately. We have to decide how to allocate the revenues from the bundle to each product. In my memo, I'll provide a bit more background as well as explain our alternatives for allocating this new revenue bundle.

Pamela: Thank you, Annette. I'll look forward to reading it.

The issues Pamela Marbury is facing are common to managers at manufacturing companies such as Nestle, merchandising companies such as Staples, service companies such as Verizon, and universities such as New York University (NYU). This chapter focuses on several issues that arise in cost and revenue allocations.

1
Distinguish the single-rate method
... one rate for allocating costs in a cost pool
from the dual-rate method
... two rates for allocating costs in a cost pool—one for variable costs and one for fixed costs

Allocating Costs of a Support Department to Operating Departments

Companies distinguish operating departments (and operating divisions) from support departments. An **operating department**, which is also called a **production department** in manufacturing companies, directly adds value to a product or service. A **support department**, which is also called a **service department**, provides the services that assist other internal departments (operating departments and other support departments) in the company. Examples of support departments are information systems and plant maintenance. Managers face two questions when allocating the costs of a support department to operating departments or divisions: (1) Should fixed costs of support departments be allocated to operating divisions? (2) If fixed costs are allocated, should variable and fixed costs be allocated in the same way? Most companies believe that fixed costs of support departments should be allocated because the support department needs to incur fixed costs to provide operating divisions with the services they require. Managers use two basic methods to allocate support-department costs: the *single-rate cost-allocation method* and the *dual-rate cost-allocation method*.

Single-Rate and Dual-Rate Methods

The **single-rate method**—also called the **single-rate cost-allocation method**—allocates costs in each cost pool (support department in this section) to cost objects (operating divisions in this section) using the same rate per unit of a single allocation base. No distinction is made between fixed and variable costs in the cost pool. The **dual-rate method**—also called the **dual-rate cost-allocation method**—classifies costs in each cost pool into two pools—a variable-cost pool and a fixed-cost pool—with each pool using a different cost-allocation base. When using the single-rate method and the dual-rate method, managers can allocate support-department costs to operating divisions based on (a) *budgeted* rate and hours *budgeted* to be used by operating divisions, (b) *budgeted* rate and *actual* hours used by operating divisions, and (c) *actual* rate and *actual* hours used by operating divisions.

Consider Sand Hill Company's Central Computer Department (support department), which was introduced at the beginning of this chapter. This department has only two users: the Microcomputer Division and the Peripheral Equipment Division. The following data relate to the 2007 budget:

Fixed costs of operating the computer facility in the 6,000-hour to 18,750-hour relevant range	$ 3,000,000
Practical capacity	18,750 hours
Budgeted long-run usage (quantity) in hours:	
Microcomputer Division	8,000 hours
Peripheral Equipment Division	4,000 hours
Total	12,000 hours
Budgeted variable cost per hour in the 6,000-hour to 18,750-hour relevant range	$ 200 per hour used
Actual usage in 2007 in hours:	
Microcomputer Division	9,000 hours
Peripheral Equipment Division	3,000 hours
Total	12,000 hours

Let's consider the allocation of Central Computer Department costs based first on the demand for or usage of computer services and then on the supply of computer services.

Allocation Based on the Demand for or Usage of Computer Services

We present the single-rate method followed by the dual-rate method.

Chapter 9 (pp. 309–310) described similar denominator choices—normal capacity utilization and master-budget capacity utilization as measures of *capacity demanded*, and theoretical capacity and practical capacity as measures of *capacity supplied*—for allocating manufacturing costs to products.

Single-rate method In this section, we illustrate how SHC allocates Central Computer Department costs based on the budgeted rate and actual hours used by the operating divisions.

Budgeted usage	12,000 hours
Budgeted total cost pool: $3,000,000 + (12,000 hours × $200/hour)	$5,400,000
Budgeted total rate per hour: $5,400,000 ÷ 12,000 hours	$450 per hour used
Allocation rate for Microcomputer Division	$450 per hour used
Allocation rate for Peripheral Equipment Division	$450 per hour used

Note that the budgeted rate of $450 per hour differs significantly from the $200 budgeted *variable* cost per hour. That's because the $450 rate includes an allocated amount of $250 per hour (budgeted fixed costs, $3,000,000, ÷ budgeted usage, 12,000 hours) for the *fixed* costs of operating the facility. These fixed costs will be incurred whether the computer runs at its practical capacity of 18,750 hours, or, say, at its 12,000-hour budgeted usage. The Central Computer Department costs are allocated to the two divisions on the basis of *actual* hours used:

Microcomputer Division: 9,000 hours × $450 per hour	$4,050,000
Peripheral Equipment Division: 3,000 hours × $450 per hour	$1,350,000

A problem with the single-rate method is that it makes the $250 allocated fixed cost per hour of the Central Computer Department appear as a variable cost to users of the Central Computer Department. This could lead operating divisions to take actions that could harm SHC as a whole. For example, suppose an external vendor offers the Microcomputer Division computer services at a rate of $340 per hour when the Central Computer Department has unused capacity. The Microcomputer Division's managers may be tempted to use this vendor because it would appear to decrease costs ($340 per hour instead of $450 per hour if it uses the Central Computer Department). In the short run, however, SHC would actually incur an extra $140 per hour—$340 external purchase price per hour minus the savings of $200 in internal variable cost per hour from not using the Central Computer Department—because the fixed costs of the Central Computer Department will remain the same.

Dual-rate method When the dual-rate method is used, allocation bases must be chosen for both the variable and fixed cost pools of the Central Computer Department. SHC allocates variable costs to each division based on *budgeted* variable cost per hour of $200 for *actual* hours used by each division. SHC allocates fixed costs based on *budgeted* fixed costs per hour and *budgeted* number of hours for each division. The Central Computer Department budgets usage of 12,000 hours: 8,000 hours for the Microcomputer Division and 4,000 hours for the Peripheral Equipment Division. The budgeted fixed-cost rate is $250 per hour ($3,000,000 ÷ 12,000 hours). The costs allocated to the Microcomputer Division in 2007 would be:

Fixed costs: $250 per hour × 8,000 (budgeted) hours	$2,000,000
Variable costs: $200 per hour × 9,000 (actual) hours	1,800,000
Total costs	$3,800,000

The costs allocated to the Peripheral Equipment Division in 2007 would be:

Fixed costs: $250 per hour × 4,000 (budgeted) hours	$1,000,000
Variable costs: $200 per hour × 3,000 (actual) hours	600,000
Total costs	$1,600,000

If actual costs of the Central Computer Department differ from allocated costs of $5,400,000 ($3,800,000 + $1,600,000), SHC would have to dispose of the overallocated or underallocated costs using methods described in Chapter 4 (pp. 118–122).

We next consider the allocation of Central Computer Department costs based on the capacity of computer services supplied.

Allocation Based on the Supply of Capacity

We illustrate this alternative approach using the 18,750 hours of practical capacity of the Central Computer Department.

Budgeted fixed-cost rate per hour, $3,000,000 ÷ 18,750 hours	$160 per hour
Budgeted variable-cost rate per hour	200 per hour
Budgeted total-cost rate per hour	$360 per hour

The costs are allocated to the two divisions as follows:

Single-rate method	
Microcomputer Division: $360 per hour × 9,000 (actual) hours	$3,240,000
Peripheral Equipment Division: $360 per hour × 3,000 (actual) hours	1,080,000
Fixed costs of unused computer capacity:	
$160 per hour × 6,750[a] hours	1,080,000

[a]6,750 hours = Practical capacity of 18,750 – (9,000 hours used by Microcomputer Division + 3,000 hours used by Peripheral Equipment Division).

Dual-rate method	
Microcomputer Division	
Fixed costs: $160 per hour × 8,000 (budgeted) hours	$1,280,000
Variable costs: $200 per hour × 9,000 (actual) hours	1,800,000
Total costs	$3,080,000
Peripheral Equipment Division	
Fixed costs: $160 per hour × 4,000 (budgeted) hours	$ 640,000
Variable costs: $200 per hour × 3,000 (actual) hours	600,000
Total costs	$1,240,000
Fixed costs of unused computer capacity:	
$160 per hour × 6,750[b] hours	$1,080,000

[b]6,750 hours = Practical capacity of 18,750 hours – (8,000 hours budgeted to be used by Microcomputer Division + 4,000 hours budgeted to be used by Peripheral Equipment Division).

Companies using the dual-rate method allocate their fixed costs in various ways. For example, if the capacity of the Central Computer Department had been chosen based on the Microcomputer Division needing 60% of the capacity and the Peripheral Equipment Division needing 40% of the capacity, all $3,000,000 of fixed costs would be allocated to the divisions in the 60:40 ratio.

Note that the difference between the single-rate and dual-rate methods in the SHC example arises because the single-rate method allocates fixed costs of the support department based on actual usage of computer resources by the user divisions, whereas the dual-rate method allocates fixed costs based on budgeted usage. When practical capacity is used to allocate costs, both the single-rate and the dual-rate methods allocate only the actual fixed-cost resources used or the budgeted fixed-cost resources to be used by the Microcomputer and Peripheral Equipment Divisions. Unused Central Computer Department resources are highlighted but usually not allocated to the divisions. If, however, the unused Central Computer Department resources were caused by one of the divisions—say, the Microcomputer Division, wanting Central Computer Department resources that it later did not need—the unused Central Computer Department resources would be allocated to the Microcomputer Division. The advantage of using practical capacity to allocate costs is that it focuses management's attention on managing unused capacity (described in Chapter 9, pp. 311–312, and Chapter 13, pp. 474–476). Using practical capacity also avoids burdening the user divisions with the cost of unused capacity of the Central Computer Department. In contrast, when costs are allocated on the basis of budgeted or actual usage, all $3,000,000 of fixed costs, including the cost of unused capacity, are allocated to user divisions. If costs are used as a basis for pricing, then charging user divisions for unused capacity could result in the downward demand spiral (see p. 312).

There are benefits and costs of both the single-rate and dual-rate methods. One benefit of the single-rate method is the low cost to implement it. The single-rate method avoids the often-expensive analysis necessary to classify the individual cost items of a department into fixed and variable categories. However, the single-rate method makes allocated fixed costs of the support department appear as variable costs to the operating divisions. Consequently, the single-rate method may lead division managers to make outsourcing decisions that are in their own best interest but not in the best interest of the organization as a whole.

A big benefit of the dual-rate method is that it signals to division managers how variable costs and fixed costs behave differently. This information guides division managers to make decisions that benefit the organization as a whole, as well as each division. For example, using a third-party computer provider that charges more than $200 per hour would result in SHC and each division being worse off than if SHC's own Central Computer Department, were used, because it has a variable cost of $200 per hour. That's because fixed costs of resources budgeted to be used by the divisions would be charged to each division, regardless of whether a division bought the service inside or outside the company.

Budgeted versus Actual Rates

The decision whether to use budgeted or actual cost rates affects the level of uncertainty faced by user divisions. When cost allocations are made using budgeted rates, managers of divisions to which costs are allocated know with certainty about the rates to be used in that budget period. Users can then determine the amount of the service to request and—if company policy allows—whether to use the internal-department source or an external vendor. In contrast, when actual rates are used for cost allocation, user divisions will not know the rates to be used until the end of the budget period.

Budgeted rates also help motivate the manager of the supplier (support) department (for example, the Central Computer Department) to improve efficiency. During the budget period, the supplier department, not the user divisions, bears the risk of any unfavorable cost variances. That's because user divisions do not pay for any costs or inefficiencies of the supplier department that cause actual rates to exceed budgeted rates.

The manager of the supplier department likely would view the budgeted rates negatively, if unfavorable cost variances occur due to price increases outside of his or her control. Some organizations try to identify these uncontrollable factors and relieve the supplier-department manager of responsibility for these variances. In other organizations, the supplier department and the user division agree to share the risk (through an explicit formula) of a large, uncontrollable increase in the prices of inputs used by the supplier department rather than impose this risk completely on the supplier department (by using budgeted rates) or completely on the user division (by using actual rates). The Focus on Values and Behaviors feature (p. 536) describes the role of judgment in cost allocations and the challenges management accountants face.

2

Understand how the uncertainty user managers face is affected by the choice between budgeted cost-allocation rates

. . . there is no uncertainty when using budgeted rates because users know the rates at the start of the period

and actual cost-allocation rates

. . . there is uncertainty when using actual rates because users don't know the rates until the end of the period

If the costs of the supplier department's inefficiency were passed to the user divisions, the supplier department would have no incentive to work efficiently.

Budgeted Usage, Actual Usage, and Capacity-Level Allocation Bases

Under the dual-rate method, the choice between actual usage and budgeted usage for allocating fixed costs also can affect a manager's behavior. Consider the budget of $3,000,000 fixed costs at the Central Computer Department of SHC. Assume that actual fixed costs and budgeted fixed costs are equal and that actual usage by the Microcomputer Division is always equal to budgeted usage. We consider three cases: when actual usage by the Peripheral Equipment Division equals (Case 1), is greater than (Case 2), and is less than (Case 3) budgeted usage. Recall that budgeted usage is 8,000 hours for the Microcomputer Division and 4,000 hours for the Peripheral Equipment Division.

Allocation based on budgeted usage When budgeted usage is the allocation base, user divisions will know in advance their allocated costs regardless of actual usage in the three cases (Exhibit 15-1, column 2). This information helps the user divisions with both short-run and long-run planning. Companies commit to infrastructure costs (such as the fixed costs of a support department) on the basis of a long-run planning horizon; budgeted usage measures the long-run demands of the user divisions for support-department services.

Allocating fixed costs on the basis of budgeted long-run usage may tempt some managers to underestimate their planned usage. Underestimating will result in their divisions bearing a lower percentage of fixed costs (assuming all other managers do not similarly underestimate their usage). To discourage such underestimates, some companies offer bonuses or other rewards—the carrot approach—to managers who make accurate forecasts of long-run usage. Other companies impose cost penalties—the stick approach—for underestimating long-run usage. For instance, a higher cost rate is charged after a division exceeds its budgeted usage.

Question: Under the dual-rate method, why shouldn't fixed costs be allocated according to divisions' actual usage?

Answer: Because (1) fixed costs would be treated as if they were variable costs, so (2) the allocation wouldn't capture the cause and effect of cost incurrence (fixed costs are "caused" by long-run expected usage), and (3) changes in one division's usage would affect another division's allocation (illustrated in Exhibit 15-1).

FOCUS ON VALUES AND BEHAVIORS

FINANCE EXECUTIVES AT BOEING: SETTING THE WRONG EXAMPLE

Cost allocations invariably require judgment. For example, which method should be used for allocating support-department costs to operating divisions? When working to determine the appropriate method, management accountants should seek to understand the facts, ask tough questions, and propose cost-allocation methods that will help improve decision making within the organization. Because cost allocations to operating divisions will differ according to the method used, division managers may try to convince management accountants to recommend a cost-allocation method that is most favorable to their division. Management accountants must be able to confidently explain how costs will be allocated, why a method was chosen, and how managers should and should not use this information. If management accountants do not resist pressure from managers, they could put the welfare of the company at risk.

As management accountants rise to senior levels in the finance area, their ethical responsibilities increase. Unethical decisions can have even more detrimental consequences. Consider the recent events at Boeing. In October 2002, Darleen Druyun, a senior Air Force acquisition officer, negotiated a multimillion-dollar NATO aircraft order that Boeing won. She had also been working on a multibillion-dollar contract to lease and buy Boeing aircraft that would serve as refueling planes. In November 2002, as Ms. Druyun prepared for retirement from the Air Force, she removed herself from discussions involving Boeing, and in January 2003, she joined Boeing as an executive in its defense business operations.

In December 2003, *The Wall Street Journal* reported, "Actions related to Ms. Druyun's hiring in January 2003 are now the subject of Pentagon and Justice Department probes as well as Congressional scrutiny into the nation's No. 2 defense contractor. Boeing fired both Mr. Sears (Boeing's chief financial officer who had allegedly discussed employment opportunities at Boeing with Ms. Druyun while she still had authority over contracts in which Boeing had an interest) and Ms. Druyun for what it called "unethical" conduct in late November [2002]. Their dealings were a major factor in the resignation a week later of the company's chairman and chief executive, Phil Condit.

. . . In an October interview that predated Ms. Druyun's firing, her attorney defended her career as beyond reproach . . . after the firing, Mr. Sears in a statement said he had done nothing wrong."

Source: *A. M. Squeo and J. L. Lunsford, "How Two Officials Got Caught by Pentagon's Revolving Door,"* The Wall Street Journal, *December 18, 2003, p. A1.*

Allocation based on actual usage Exhibit 15-1, column 3, presents the allocation of total fixed costs of \$3,000,000 to each division for the three cases. Compare columns 2 and 3 in Exhibit 15-1. In Case 1, the fixed-cost allocation equals the budgeted amount. In Case 2, the fixed-cost allocation is \$400,000 less to the Microcomputer Division than the amount based on budgeted usage (\$1,600,000 versus \$2,000,000). In Case 3, the fixed-cost allocation is \$400,000 more to the Microcomputer Division than the amount based on budgeted usage (\$2,400,000 versus \$2,000,000). Why this increase of \$400,000 to the Microcomputer Division in Case 3, even though its actual usage equals its budgeted usage? Because fixed costs are spread over fewer hours of actual usage. That is, variations in usage in the Peripheral Equipment Division affect

EXHIBIT 15-1 Effect of Variations in Actual Usage on Division Cost Allocations

	(1) Actual Usage		(2) Budgeted Usage as Allocation Base		(3) Actual Usage as Allocation Base		(4) Practical Capacity–Based Allocations	
Case	Micro. Div.	Perif. Div.	Micro. Div.	Perif. Div.	Micro. Div.	Perif. Div.	Micro. Div.	Perif. Div.
1	8,000 hours	4,000 hours	\$2,000,000[a]	\$1,000,000[b]	\$2,000,000[a]	\$1,000,000[b]	\$1,280,000[g]	\$ 640,000[h]
2	8,000 hours	7,000 hours	\$2,000,000[a]	\$1,000,000[b]	\$1,600,000[c]	\$1,400,000[d]	\$1,280,000[g]	\$1,120,000[i]
3	8,000 hours	2,000 hours	\$2,000,000[a]	\$1,000,000[b]	\$2,400,000[e]	\$ 600,000[f]	\$1,280,000[g]	\$ 320,000[j]

[a] $\frac{8,000}{(8,000+4,000)} \times \$3,000,000$

[b] $\frac{4,000}{(8,000+4,000)} \times \$3,000,000$

[c] $\frac{8,000}{(8,000+7,000)} \times \$3,000,000$

[d] $\frac{7,000}{(8,000+7,000)} \times \$3,000,000$

[e] $\frac{8,000}{(8,000+2,000)} \times \$3,000,000$

[f] $\frac{2,000}{(8,000+2,000)} \times \$3,000,000$

[g] $8,000 \times \$160$

[h] $4,000 \times \$160$

[i] $7,000 \times \$160$

[j] $2,000 \times \$160$

the fixed costs allocated to the Microcomputer Division. When actual usage is the allocation base, user divisions will not know how much fixed cost is allocated to them until the end of the budget period.

Allocation based on practical capacity As we have seen, an alternative to using measures of capacity demanded—budgeted usage or actual usage—is to allocate fixed costs of the Central Computer Department on the basis of the practical capacity supplied. The budgeted fixed-cost rate is $160 per hour (budgeted fixed costs, $3,000,000, ÷ practical capacity, 18,750 hours). Exhibit 15-1, column 4, shows the fixed costs allocated to the Microcomputer and Peripheral Equipment Divisions using this approach.

There are three features of this approach: (1) each division is charged only for the computer-facility services it actually uses; (2) variations in actual usage in one division (the Peripheral Equipment Division) do not affect the costs allocated to the other division (the Microcomputer Division is allocated $1,280,000 in all three cases); and (3) the costs of unused capacity of the Central Computer Department are highlighted and are not allocated to user divisions. In all three cases, the total amount of fixed costs allocated to the user divisions is less than the $3,000,000 fixed costs of the Central Computer Department.

3

Allocate support-department costs using the direct method,

. . . allocates support-department costs directly to operating departments

the step-down method,

. . . partially allocates support-department costs to other support departments

and the reciprocal method

. . . fully allocates support-department costs to other support departments

Allocating Costs of Multiple Support Departments

We just examined general issues that arise when allocating costs from one support department to operating divisions. In this section, we examine the special cost-allocation problems that arise when two or more of the support departments whose costs are being allocated provide reciprocal support to each other as well as to operating departments. An example of reciprocal support is a Corporate Human Resource (HR) Department providing services to a Corporate Legal Department (such as advice about hiring attorneys) while the Corporate Legal Department provides services to the HR department (such as advice on compliance with labor laws). More-accurate support-department cost allocations result in more-accurate product, service, and customer costs.

Consider Castleford Engineering, which operates at practical capacity to manufacture engines used in electric-power generating plants. Castleford has two support departments and two operating departments in its manufacturing facility:

Support Departments	Operating Departments
Plant (and equipment) maintenance	Machining
Information systems	Assembly

The two support departments at Castleford provide reciprocal support to each other as well as support to the two operating departments. Costs are accumulated in each department for planning and control purposes. Exhibit 15-2 displays the data for our example. We

Reciprocal support-department allocations can also arise when there are two or more central support departments and two or more operating divisions. In the previous section, Sand Hill Company could also have had a Central Human Resources Department in addition to the Central Computer Department to support the two operating divisions—the Microcomputer Division and the Peripheral Equipment Division.

EXHIBIT 15-2 **Data for Allocating Support-Department Costs at Castleford Engineering for 2007**

	A	B	C	D	E	F	G
1		SUPPORT DEPARTMENTS			OPERATING DEPARTMENTS		
2		Plant Maintenance	Information Systems		Machining	Assembly	Total
3	Budgeted manufacturing overhead costs						
4	before any interdepartment cost allocations	$600,000	$116,000		$400,000	$200,000	$1,316,000
5	Support work furnished:						
6	By Plant Maintenance						
7	Budgeted labor-hours	-	1,600		2,400	4,000	8,000
8	Percentage	-	20%		30%	50%	100%
9	By Information Systems						
10	Budgeted computer hours	200	-		1,600	200	2,000
11	Percentage	10%	-		80%	10%	100%

explain the percentages in this exhibit using the Plant Maintenance Department. This support department provides a total of 8,000 hours of support work: 20% (1,600 ÷ 8,000 = 0.20) for the Information Systems Department, 30% (2,400 ÷ 8,000 = 0.30) for the Machining Department, and 50% (4,000 ÷ 8,000 = 0.50) for the Assembly Department.

In terms of computational detail, the direct method is the simplest, the step-down method adds complexity, and the reciprocal method is the most complex.

We now examine three methods of allocating the costs of reciprocal support departments: *direct, step-down*, and *reciprocal*. To simplify the exposition and to focus on concepts, we use the single-rate method to allocate the costs of each support department using budgeted rates and budgeted hours used by the other departments. (The Problem for Self-Study illustrates the dual-rate method for allocating reciprocal support-department costs.)

Direct Method

The **direct method**—also called the **direct allocation method**—allocates each support-department's costs to operating departments only. The direct method does not allocate support department costs to other support departments. Exhibit 15-3 illustrates this method using the data in Exhibit 15-2. The base used to allocate Plant Maintenance costs to the operating departments is the budgeted total maintenance labor-hours worked in the operating departments: 2,400 + 4,000 = 6,400 hours. This amount excludes the 1,600 hours of budgeted support time provided by Plant Maintenance to Information Systems. Similarly, the base used for allocation of Information Systems costs to the operating departments is 1,600 + 200 = 1,800 budgeted hours of computer time, which excludes the 200 hours of budgeted support time provided by Information Systems to Plant Maintenance.

The direct method is widely accepted because of its ease of use. The benefit of the direct method is simplicity. There is no need to predict the usage of support department services

EXHIBIT 15-3 **Direct Method of Allocating Support-Department Costs at Castleford Engineering for 2007**

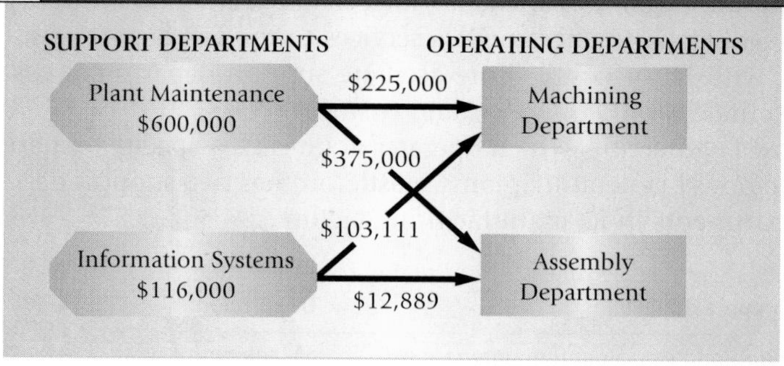

	A	B	C	D	E	F	G
1		SUPPORT DEPARTMENTS			OPERATING DEPARTMENTS		
2		Plant Maintenance	Information Systems		Machining	Assembly	Total
3	Budgeted manufacturing overhead costs						
4	before any interdepartment cost allocations	$600,000	$116,000		$400,000	$200,000	$1,316,000
5	Allocation of Plant Maintenance (3/8, 5/8)[a]	(600,000)			225,000	375,000	
6	Allocation of Information Systems (8/9, 1/9)[b]		(116,000)		103,111	12,889	
7	Total budgeted manufacturing overhead of						
8	operating departments	$ 0	$ 0		$728,111	$587,889	$1,316,000
9							
10	[a]Base is (2,400 + 4,000), or 6,400 hours; 2,400 ÷ 6,400 = 3/8; 4,000 ÷ 6,400 = 5/8. An equivalent approach is to calculate						
11	a budgeted rate for allocating Plant Maintenance Department costs, $600,000 ÷ 6,400 hours = $93.75 per hour. The						
12	Machining Department would then be allocated $225,000 ($93.75 per hour × 2,400 hours) and the Assembly Department						
13	$375,000 ($93.75 per hour × 4,000 hours).						
14	[b]Base is (1,600 + 200), or 1,800 hours; 1,600 ÷ 1,800 = 8/9; 200 ÷ 1,800 = 1/9. An equivalent approach is to calculate a						
15	budgeted rate for allocating Information Systems Department costs, $116,000 ÷ 1,800 hours = $64.444 per hour. The						
16	Machining Department would then be allocated $103,111 ($64.444 per hour × 1,600 hours) and the Assembly Department						
17	$12,889 ($64.444 per hour × 200 hours). For ease of exposition throughout this section, we will use the fraction of the						
18	support department services used by other departments to allocate support department costs to other departments rather						
19	than calculate budgeted rates to allocate costs.						

by other support departments. A disadvantage of the direct method is that it ignores reciprocal services provided among support departments. We now examine a straightforward approach to partially recognize the services provided among support departments.

Step-Down Method

Some organizations use the **step-down method**—also called the **step-down allocation method** or the **sequential allocation method**—which allocates support-department costs to other support departments and to operating departments in a sequential manner that partially recognizes the mutual services provided among all support departments.

Exhibit 15-4 shows the step-down method. The Plant Maintenance costs of \$600,000 are allocated first. Exhibit 15-2 shows that Plant Maintenance provides 20% of its services to Information Systems, 30% to Machining, and 50% to Assembly. Therefore, \$120,000 is allocated to Information Systems (20% of \$600,000), \$180,000 to Machining (30% of \$600,000), and \$300,000 to Assembly (50% of \$600,000). The Information Systems costs now total \$236,000: budgeted costs of the Information Systems Department before any interdepartmental cost allocations (from Exhibit 15-2), \$116,000, plus \$120,000 from the allocation of Plant Maintenance costs to the Information Systems Department. The \$236,000 is then only allocated between the two operating departments based on the proportion of the Information Systems Department services provided to Machining and Assembly. From Exhibit 15-2, the Information Systems Department provides 80% of its services to Machining and 10% to Assembly, so \$209,778 (8/9 × \$236,000) is allocated to Machining and \$26,222 (1/9 × \$236,000) is allocated to Assembly.

Note that this method requires the support departments to be ranked (sequenced) in the order that the step-down allocation is to proceed. In our example, the costs of the Plant Maintenance Department were allocated first to all other departments, including the Information Systems Department. The costs of the Information Systems support department were allocated second, but only to the two operating departments. Different sequences will result in different allocations of support-department costs to operating

EXHIBIT 15-4 **Step-Down Method of Allocating Support-Department Costs at Castleford Engineering for 2007**

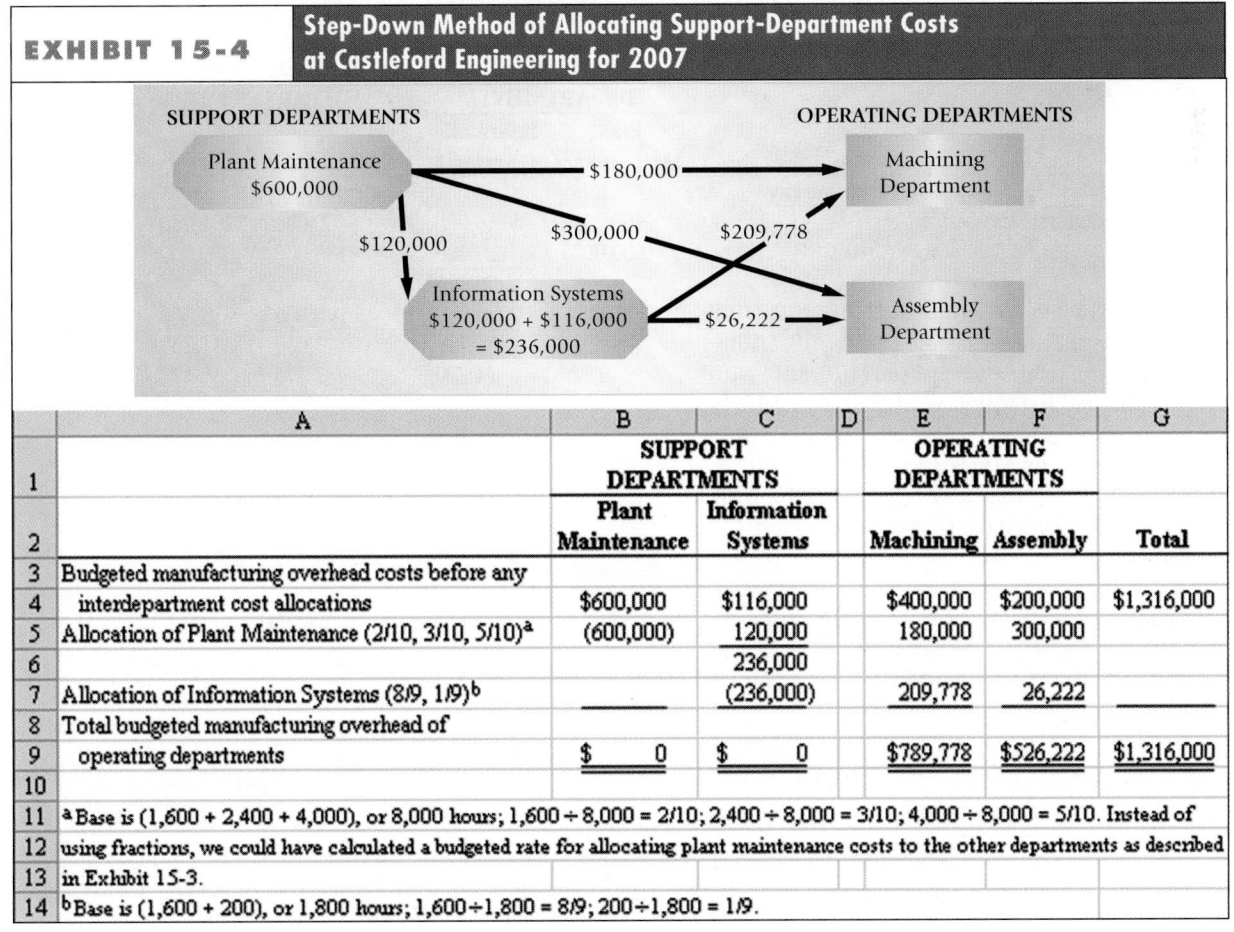

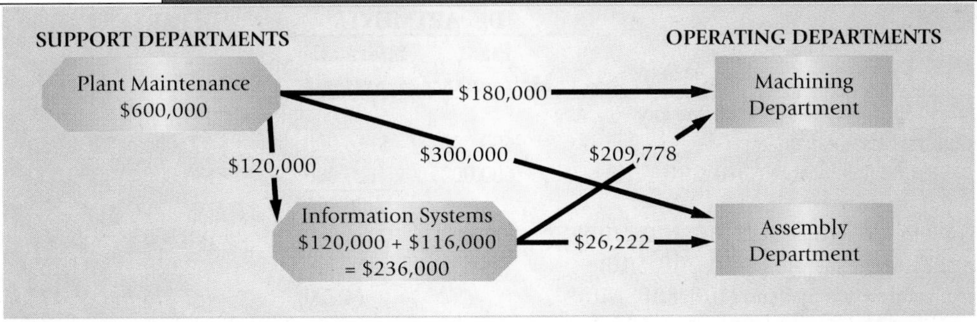

	A	B	C	D	E	F	G
1		SUPPORT DEPARTMENTS			OPERATING DEPARTMENTS		
2		Plant Maintenance	Information Systems		Machining	Assembly	Total
3	Budgeted manufacturing overhead costs before any						
4	interdepartment cost allocations	\$600,000	\$116,000		\$400,000	\$200,000	\$1,316,000
5	Allocation of Plant Maintenance (2/10, 3/10, 5/10)[a]	(600,000)	120,000		180,000	300,000	
6			236,000				
7	Allocation of Information Systems (8/9, 1/9)[b]		(236,000)		209,778	26,222	
8	Total budgeted manufacturing overhead of						
9	operating departments	\$ 0	\$ 0		\$789,778	\$526,222	\$1,316,000
10							
11	[a]Base is (1,600 + 2,400 + 4,000), or 8,000 hours; 1,600 ÷ 8,000 = 2/10; 2,400 ÷ 8,000 = 3/10; 4,000 ÷ 8,000 = 5/10. Instead of						
12	using fractions, we could have calculated a budgeted rate for allocating plant maintenance costs to the other departments as described						
13	in Exhibit 15-3.						
14	[b]Base is (1,600 + 200), or 1,800 hours; 1,600÷1,800 = 8/9; 200÷1,800 = 1/9.						

departments—for example, if the Information Systems Department costs had been allocated first and the Plant Maintenance Department costs second. A popular step-down sequence begins with the support department that renders the highest percentage of its total services to *other support departments*. The sequence continues with the department that renders the next-highest percentage, and so on, ending with the support department that renders the lowest percentage.[1] In our example, costs of the Plant Maintenance Department were allocated first because it provides 20% of its services to the Information Systems Department, whereas the Information Systems Department provides only 10% of its services to the Plant Maintenance Department (see Exhibit 15-2).

Under the step-down method, once a support department's costs have been allocated, no subsequent support-department costs are allocated back to it. Once the Plant Maintenance Department costs are allocated, it receives no further allocation from other (lower-ranked) support departments. The result is that the step-down method does not recognize the total services that support departments provide to each other. The reciprocal method fully recognizes all such services, as you will see next.

Reciprocal Method

The **reciprocal method**—also called the **reciprocal allocation method**—allocates support-department costs to operating departments by fully recognizing the mutual services provided among all support departments. For example, the Plant Maintenance Department maintains all the computer equipment in the Information Systems Department. Similarly, Information Systems provides database support for Plant Maintenance. The reciprocal method fully incorporates interdepartmental relationships into the support-department cost allocations.

Exhibit 15-5 presents a simple way to understand the reciprocal method. First, Plant Maintenance costs are allocated to all other departments, including the Information

EXHIBIT 15-5 Reciprocal Method of Allocating Support-Department Costs Using Repeated Iterations at Castleford Engineering for 2007

	A	B	C	D	E	F	G
1		SUPPORT DEPARTMENTS			OPERATING DEPARTMENTS		
2		Plant Maintenance	Information Systems		Machining	Assembly	Total
3	Budgeted manufacturing overhead costs before any						
4	interdepartment cost allocations	$600,000	$116,000		$400,000	$200,000	$1,316,000
5	1st Allocation of Plant Maintenance (2/10, 3/10, 5/10)[a]	(600,000)	120,000		180,000	300,000	
6			236,000				
7	1st Allocation of Information Systems (1/10, 8/10, 1/10)[b]	23,600	(236,000)		188,800	23,600	
8	2nd Allocation of Plant Maintenance (2/10, 3/10, 5/10)[a]	(23,600)	4,720		7,080	11,800	
9	2nd Allocation of Information Systems (1/10, 8/10, 1/10)[b]	472	(4,720)		3,776	472	
10	3rd Allocation of Plant Maintenance (2/10, 3/10, 5/10)[a]	(472)	94		142	236	
11	3rd Allocation of Information Systems (1/10, 8/10, 1/10)[b]	9	(94)		75	10	
12	4th Allocation of Plant Maintenance (2/10, 3/10, 5/10)[a]	(9)	2		2	5	
13	4th Allocation of Information Systems (1/10, 8/10, 1/10)[b]	0	(2)		2	0	
14	Total budgeted manufacturing overhead of operating						
15	departments	$ 0	$ 0		$779,877	$536,123	$1,316,000
16							
17	Total support department amounts allocated and reallocated (the numbers in parentheses in first two columns)						
18	Plant Maintenance: $600,000 + $23,600 + $472 + $9 = $624,081						
19	Information Systems: $236,000 + $4,720 + $94 + $2 = $240,816						
20							
21	[a]Base is (1,600 + 2,400 + 4,000) or 8,000 hours; 1,600 ÷ 8,000 = 2/10; 2,400 ÷ 8,000 = 3/10; 4,000 ÷ 8,000 = 5/10.						
22	[b]Base is (200 + 1,600 + 200) or 2,000 hours; 200 ÷ 2,000 = 1/10; 1,600 ÷ 2,000 = 8/10; 200 ÷ 2,000 = 1/10.						

[1]An alternative approach to selecting the sequence of allocations is to begin with the support department that renders the highest dollar amount of services to other support departments. The sequence ends with the allocation of the costs of the department that renders the lowest dollar amount of services to other support departments.

Systems support department (Information Systems, 20%; Machining, 30%; Assembly, 50%). The costs in the Information Systems Department then total $236,000 ($116,000 + $120,000 from the first-round allocation), as in Exhibit 15-4. The $236,000 is then allocated to all other departments, including the Plant Maintenance support department, that the Information Systems Department supports—Plant Maintenence, 10%; Machining, 80%; Assembly, 10% (see Exhibit 15-2). The Plant Maintenance costs that had been brought down to $0 now again have $23,600 from the Information Systems Department allocation. These costs are again reallocated to all other departments, including Information Systems, in the same ratio that the Plant Maintenance costs were previously allocated. Now the Information Systems Department costs that had been brought down to $0 have $4,720 from the Plant Maintenance Department allocations. These costs are again reallocated in the same ratio that the Information Systems Department costs were previously allocated. Successive rounds result in smaller and smaller amounts being allocated to and reallocated from the support departments until eventually all support department costs are allocated to the operating departments.

An alternative way to implement the reciprocal method is to formulate and solve linear equations. This requires three steps.

Step 1: Express Support-Department Costs and Support-Department Reciprocal Relationships in the Form of Linear Equations. Let *PM* be the *complete reciprocated costs* of Plant Maintenance and *IS* be the complete reciprocated costs of Information Systems. We then express the data in Exhibit 15-2 as follows:

$$PM = \$600{,}000 + 0.1IS \qquad (1)$$

$$IS = \$116{,}000 + 0.2PM \qquad (2)$$

The $0.1IS$ term in equation (1) is the percentage of the Information Systems services *used by* Plant Maintenance. The $0.2PM$ term in equation (2) is the percentage of Plant Maintenance services *used by* Information Systems. By **complete reciprocated costs** in equations (1) and (2), we mean the support department's own costs plus any interdepartmental cost allocations. This complete-reciprocated-costs figure is sometimes called the **artificial costs** of the support department.

Step 2: Solve the Set of Linear Equations to Obtain the Complete Reciprocated Costs of Each Support Department. Substituting equation (2) into (1):

$$\begin{aligned} PM &= \$600{,}000 + [0.1(\$116{,}000 + 0.2PM)] \\ PM &= \$600{,}000 + \$11{,}600 + 0.02PM \\ 0.98PM &= \$611{,}600 \\ PM &= \$624{,}082 \end{aligned}$$

Substituting into equation (2):

$$\begin{aligned} IS &= \$116{,}000 + 0.2(\$624{,}082) \\ IS &= \$116{,}000 + \$124{,}816 = \$240{,}816 \end{aligned}$$

When there are more than two support departments with reciprocal relationships, software such as Excel can be used to calculate the complete reciprocated costs of each support department. The complete-reciprocated-cost figures also appear at the bottom of Exhibit 15-5 as the total amounts allocated and reallocated (subject to minor rounding differences).

Step 3: Allocate the Complete Reciprocated Costs of Each Support Department to All Other Departments (Both Support Departments and Operating Departments) on the Basis of the Usage Percentages (Based on Total Units of Service Provided to All Departments). Consider the Information Systems Department. The complete reciprocated costs of $240,816 are allocated as follows:

To Plant Maintenance (1/10) × $240,816	=	$ 24,082
To Machining (8/10) × $240,816	=	192,652
To Assembly (1/10) × $240,816	=	24,082
Total		$240,816

Exhibit 15-6 presents summary data pertaining to the reciprocal method.

EXHIBIT 15-6 **Reciprocal Method of Allocating Support-Department Costs Using Linear Equations at Castleford Engineering for 2007**

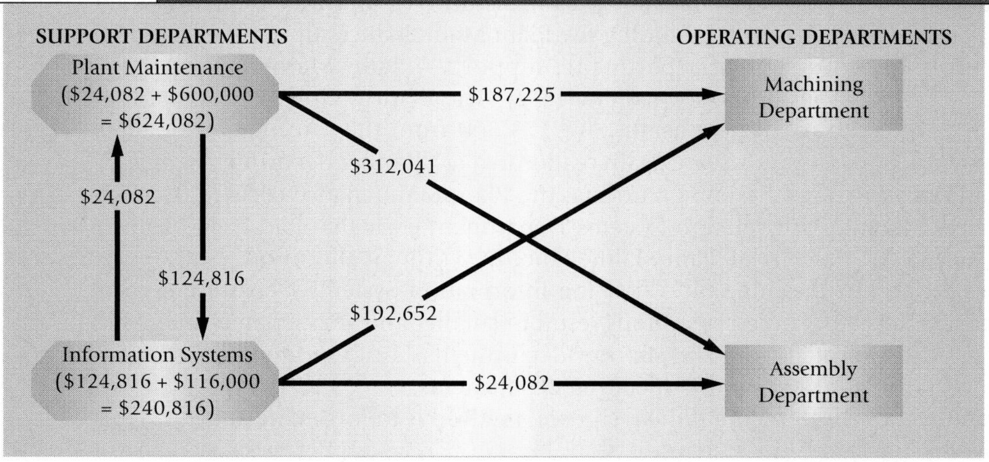

	A	B	C	D	E	F	G
1		SUPPORT DEPARTMENTS			OPERATING DEPARTMENTS		
2		Plant Maintenance	Information Systems		Machining	Assembly	Total
3	Budgeted manufacturing overhead costs before any						
4	interdepartment cost allocations	$600,000	$116,000		$400,000	$200,000	$1,316,000
5	Allocation of Plant Maintenance (2/10, 3/10, 5/10)[a]	(624,082)	124,816		187,225	312,041	
6	Allocation of Information Systems (1/10, 8/10, 1/10)[b]	24,082	(240,816)		192,652	24,082	
7	Total budgeted manufacturing overhead of operating						
8	departments	$ 0	$ 0		$779,877	$536,123	$1,316,000
9							
10	[a]Base is (1,600 + 2,400 + 4,000), or 8,000 hours; 1,600 ÷ 8,000 = 2/10; 2,400 ÷ 8,000 = 3/10; 4,000 ÷ 8,000 = 5/10.						
11	[b]Base is (200 + 1,600 + 200), or 2,000 hours; 200 ÷ 2,000 = 1/10; 1,600 ÷ 2,000 = 8/10; 200 ÷ 2,000 = 1/10.						

Castleford's $864,898 complete reciprocated costs of the support departments exceed the budgeted amount of $716,000.

Support Department	Complete Reciprocated Costs	Budgeted Costs	Difference
Plant Maintenance	$624,082	$600,000	$ 24,082
Information Systems	240,816	116,000	124,816
Total	$864,898	$716,000	$148,898

Each support department's complete reciprocated cost is greater than the budgeted amount to take into account that the allocation of support costs will be made to all departments using its services and not just to operating departments. It is this step that ensures that the reciprocal method fully recognizes all interrelationships among support departments, as well as relationships between support and operating departments. The difference between complete reciprocated costs and budgeted costs for each support department is the total costs that are allocated among support departments. The total costs allocated to the operating departments under the reciprocal method are still only $716,000.

Overview of Methods

Assume that Castleford reallocates the total budgeted overhead costs of each operating department in Exhibits 15-3 through 15-6 to individual products on the basis of budgeted machine-hours for the Machining Department (4,000 hours) and budgeted direct manufacturing labor-hours for the Assembly Department (3,000 hours). The budgeted overhead allocation rates (to the nearest dollar) for each operating department by allocation method are:

Support Department Cost-Allocation Method	Total Budgeted Overhead Costs After Allocation of All Support-Department Costs		Budgeted Overhead Rate per Hour for Product-Costing Purposes	
	Machining	Assembly	Machining (4,000 machine-hours)	Assembly (3,000 labor-hours)
Direct	$728,111	$587,889	$182	$196
Step-down	789,778	526,222	197	175
Reciprocal	779,877	536,123	195	179

Differences among the three methods' allocations increase (1) as the magnitude of the reciprocal services increases and (2) as the differences across operating departments' usage of each support department's services increase.

These differences in budgeted overhead rates under the three support-department cost-allocation methods can, for example, affect the amount of costs Castleford is reimbursed for engines it manufactures under cost-reimbursement contracts. Consider a cost-reimbursement contract that uses 100 machine-hours in the Machining Department and 15 direct manufacturing labor-hours in the Assembly Department. The support-department costs allocated to this contract under the three methods would be:

Direct:	\$21,140 (\$182 per hour × 100 hours + \$196 per hour × 15 hours)
Step-down:	22,325 (\$197 per hour × 100 hours + \$175 per hour × 15 hours)
Reciprocal:	22,185 (\$195 per hour × 100 hours + \$179 per hour × 15 hours)

The amount of cost reimbursed to Castleford will be different depending on the method used to allocate support-department costs to the contract. To avoid disputes in cost-reimbursement contracts that require allocation of support-department costs, managers should always clarify the method to be used for allocation.

The reciprocal method is conceptually the most precise method because it considers the mutual services provided among all support departments. The advantage of the direct and step-down methods is that they are simple to compute and understand relative to the reciprocal method. The direct method is widely used (see Global Surveys of Company Practice, p. 544). However, as computing power to do repeated iterations (as in Exhibit 15-5) or to solve sets of simultaneous equations (as on pp. 541–542) increases, more companies find the reciprocal method easier to implement.

Another advantage of the reciprocal method is that it highlights the complete reciprocated costs of support departments and how these costs differ from budgeted or actual costs of the departments. Knowing the complete reciprocated costs of a support department is a key input for decisions about whether to outsource all the services that the support department provides.

Suppose all of Castleford's support-department costs are variable over the period of a possible outsourcing contract. Consider a third party's bid to provide, say, all the information systems services currently provided by Castleford's Information Systems Department. Do not compare the bid to the \$116,000 costs reported for the Information Systems Department. The complete reciprocated costs of the Information Systems Department, which include the services the Plant Maintenance Department provides the Information Systems Department, are \$240,816 to deliver 2,000 hours of computer time to all other departments at Castleford. The complete reciprocated costs for computer time are \$120.408 per hour (\$240,816 ÷ 2,000 hours). Other things being equal, a third party's bid to provide the same information services as Castleford's internal department at less than \$240,816, or \$120.408 per hour (even if much greater than \$116,000) would improve Castleford's operating income. To see this point, note that the relevant savings from shutting down the Information Systems Department are \$116,000 of Information Systems Department costs *plus* \$124,816 of Plant Maintenance Department costs. By closing down the Information Systems Department, Castleford will no longer incur the 20% of Plant Maintenance Department costs (equal to \$124,816) that were incurred to support the Information Systems Department. Therefore, the total relevant-cost savings are \$240,816 (\$116,000 + \$124,816).[2] Neither the direct nor the step-down methods can provide this relevant information for outsourcing decisions.

[2]Technical issues when using the reciprocal method in outsourcing decisions are discussed in R. S. Kaplan and A. A. Atkinson, *Advanced Management Accounting*, 3rd ed. (Upper Saddle River, NJ: Prentice Hall, 1998, pp. 73–81).

GLOBAL SURVEYS OF COMPANY PRACTICE

Allocation of Support-Department Costs

Use of the direct method of allocating support-department costs is widespread in many nations, whereas the step-down and reciprocal methods are gaining popularity in others. Surveys of support-department cost-allocation methods are available for Australia, Japan, the United Kingdom, and Poland.[a,b]

Support Department Cost-Allocation Method	Australia	Japan	United Kingdom	Poland
1. Direct method	43%	58%	64%	19%
2. Step-down method	3%	27%	6%	39%
3. Reciprocal method	5%	10%	14%	33%
4. Other method	15%	1%	8%	6%
5. Not allocated	34%	4%	8%	3%

[a]P. Blayney, and I. Yokohama, "Comparative Analysis."
[b]A. Szychta, "The Scope and Application."
Full citations are in Appendix A at the end of the book.

We now consider common costs, another special class of costs for which management accountants have developed specific allocation methods.

4

Allocate common costs using the stand-alone method

. . . uses cost information of each user as a separate entity to allocate common costs in a more-balanced way

and the incremental method

. . . allocates common costs primarily to one user and the remainder to other users

Allocating Common Costs

A **common cost** is a cost of operating a facility, activity, or like cost object that is shared by two or more users. The common cost is lower than the individual cost to each user. The goal is to allocate common costs to each user in an equitable way on the basis of the individual costs of the cost object. Consider Jason Stevens, a graduating senior in Seattle who has been invited to a job interview with an employer in Albany. The round-trip Seattle–Albany airfare costs $1,200. A week later, Stevens is also invited to an interview with an employer in Chicago. The Seattle–Chicago round-trip airfare costs $800. Stevens decides to combine the two recruiting trips into a Seattle–Albany–Chicago–Seattle trip that will cost $1,500 in airfare. The $1,500 is a common cost that benefits both prospective employers. Two methods of allocating this common cost between the two prospective employers are the stand-alone method and the incremental method.

Stand-Alone Cost-Allocation Method

The **stand-alone cost-allocation method** uses information pertaining to each user of a cost object as a separate entity to determine the cost-allocation weights. For the common-cost airfare of $1,500, information about the separate (stand-alone) round-trip airfares ($1,200 and $800) is used to determine the allocation weights:

$$\text{Albany employer: } \frac{\$1{,}200}{\$1{,}200 + \$800} \times \$1{,}500 = 0.60 \times \$1{,}500 = \$900$$

$$\text{Chicago employer: } \frac{\$800}{\$800 + \$1{,}200} \times \$1{,}500 = 0.40 \times \$1{,}500 = \$600$$

Advocates of this method often emphasize the fairness or equity criterion described in Exhibit 14-2 (p. 495). The method is viewed as fair because each employer bears a proportionate share of total costs in relation to the individual stand-alone costs.

Incremental Cost-Allocation Method

The **incremental cost-allocation method** ranks the individual users of a cost object in the order of users most responsible for common cost and then uses this ranking to allocate cost among those users. The first-ranked user of the cost object is the *primary user* (also called the *primary party*) and is allocated costs up to the costs of the primary user as a stand-alone user. The second-ranked user is the *first incremental user* (*first incremental party*) and is allocated the additional cost that arises from two users instead of only the primary user. The third-ranked user is the *second incremental user* (*second incremental party*) and is allocated the additional cost that arises from three users instead of two users, and so on.

The incremental cost-allocation method allocates the most costs to the first-ranked user, creating the incentive for users of the cost object to not want to be the first-ranked user.

To see how this method works, consider again Jason Stevens and his $1,500 airfare cost. Assume the Albany employer is viewed as the primary party. Stevens' rationale is that he had already committed to go to Albany before accepting the invitation to interview in Chicago. The cost allocations would be:

Party	Costs Allocated	Cumulative Costs Allocated
Albany (primary)	$1,200	$1,200
Chicago (incremental)	300 ($1,500 – $1,200)	$1,500
Total	$1,500	

The Albany employer is allocated the full Seattle–Albany airfare. The unallocated part of the total airfare is then allocated to the Chicago employer. If the Chicago employer had been chosen as the primary party, the cost allocations would have been Chicago $800 (the stand-alone round-trip Seattle–Chicago airfare) and Albany $700 ($1,500 – $800). When there are more than two parties, this method requires them to be ranked from first to last (say, based on the date on which each employer invited the candidate to interview).

Under the incremental method, the primary party typically receives the highest allocation of the common costs. No surprise that most users in common-cost situations prefer to be an incremental party! In some cases, the incremental users are newly formed companies or a company's new subunits, such as a new product line or a new sales territory. Chances for their short-run survival may be enhanced if they bear a low allocation of the common costs.

When both parties are viewed as primary parties, there is no incremental party. If there is a large common cost that must be incurred, using the incremental method can cause the parties to dispute who is the incremental party. One approach in such situations is to use the stand-alone cost-allocation method. Another approach is to use the *Shapley value*, which considers each party as first the primary party and then the incremental party. From the calculations shown earlier, the Albany employer is allocated $1,200 as the primary party and $700 as the incremental party, for an average of $950 [($1,200 + $700) ÷ 2]. The Chicago employer is allocated $800 as the primary party and $300 as the incremental party, for an average of $550 [($800 + 300) ÷ 2]. The Shapley value method would allocate, to each employer, the average of the costs allocated as the primary party and as the incremental party—that is, $950 to the Albany employer and $550 to the Chicago employer.[3]

A caution regarding Stevens' cost-allocation options: His chosen method must be acceptable to each prospective employer—for example, he should not exceed the maximum reimbursable amount of airfare.

As our discussion suggests, allocating common costs is not clear-cut. That is why managers should always exercise judgment when allocating common costs rather than blindly follow one method or another. Disputes over how to allocate common costs are often encountered. The next section discusses the role of cost data in various types of contracts. This is also an area in which disputes about cost allocation frequently arise.

[3]For further discussion of the Shapley value, see J. Demski, "Cost Allocation Games," in S. Moriarity (Ed.), *Joint Cost Allocations* (University of Oklahoma Center for Economic and Management Research, 1981); L. Kruz and P. Bronisz, "Cooperative Game Solution Concepts to a Cost Allocation Problem," *European Journal of Operations Research* (vol. 122: 2000, 258–271).

5

Explain the importance of explicit agreement between contracting parties when the reimbursement amount is based on costs incurred

. . . to avoid disputes regarding allowable cost items and how indirect costs should be allocated

Cost Allocations and Contracts

Many commercial contracts include clauses based on cost accounting information. For example:

- A contract between the Department of Defense and a company designing and assembling a new fighter plane specifies that the price paid for the plane is to be based on the contractor's direct and overhead costs plus a fixed fee.
- A contract between an energy-consulting firm and a hospital specifies that the consulting firm is to receive a fixed fee plus a share of the energy-cost savings arising from implementing the consulting firm's recommendations.

Contract disputes arise often, usually with respect to cost allocation. The areas of dispute between the contracting parties can be reduced by making the "rules of the game" explicit and in writing at the time the contract is signed. Such rules of the game include the definition of allowable cost items; the definitions of terms used, such as what constitutes direct labor; the permissible cost-allocation bases; and how differences between budgeted and actual costs are to be accounted for.

Contracting with the U.S. Government

Boeing builds standard planes for commercial customers and specialized fighter planes for the U.S. armed services. Boeing has fixed-price contracts with commercial customers and cost-plus contracts with the U.S. armed services. If Boeing were to shift indirect costs away from its commercial customers to its cost-plus contracts, Boeing would increase its revenues. Management accountants have a responsibility to monitor this type of illegal behavior.

The U.S. government reimburses most contractors in one of two main ways:

1. **The contractor is paid a set price without analysis of actual contract cost data.** This approach is used, for example, when there is competitive bidding, when there is adequate price competition, or when there is an established catalog with prices quoted for items sold in substantial quantities to the general public.
2. **The contractor is paid after analysis of actual contract cost data.** In some cases, the contract will explicitly state that the reimbursement amount is based on actual allowable costs plus a fixed fee.[4] This arrangement is called a *cost-plus contract.*

All contracts with U.S. government agencies must comply with cost accounting standards issued by the **Cost Accounting Standards Board (CASB)**. For government contracts, the CASB has the exclusive authority to make, put into effect, amend, and rescind cost accounting standards and interpretations. The standards are designed to achieve *uniformity and consistency* in regard to measurement, assignment, and allocation of costs to contracts within the United States.[5]

In government contracting, there is a complex interplay of political considerations and accounting principles. Terms such as "fairness" and "equity," as well as cause and effect and benefits received, are often used in government contracts.

Fairness of Pricing

In many defense contracts involving new weapons and equipment, the uncertainty is high about what it will cost to produce the weapon or equipment. Such contracts are rarely subject to competitive bidding. That's because no contractor is willing to assume

---

[4]The Federal Acquisition Regulation (FAR) includes the following definition of "allocability" (in FAR 31.201-4):

> A cost [is] allocable if it is assignable or chargeable to one or more cost objectives in accordance with the relative benefits received or other equitable relationship. Subject to the foregoing, a cost is allocable to a government contract if it:
>
> - Is incurred specifically for the contract;
> - Benefits both the contract and other work, . . . and can be distributed to them in reasonable proportion to the benefits received; or
> - Is necessary to the overall operation of the business, although a direct relationship to any particular cost objective cannot be shown.

AcqNet, "Federal Acquisition Regulation," AcqNet Web site, **www.acqnet.gov/far**; F. Alston, M. Worthington, and L. Goldsman, *Contracting with the Federal Government,* 3rd ed. (New York: Wiley, 1993, p. 136). This book contains extensive discussion of the use of cost data in government contracting.

[5]Details on the Cost Accounting Standards Board are available at **www.whitehouse.gov/omb/procurement/casb.html**. The CASB is part of the Office of Federal Procurement Policy, U.S. Office of Management and Budget.

all the risk of receiving a fixed price for the contract and subsequently incurring high costs to fulfill the contract. Hence, setting a market-based fixed price for the contract fails to attract contractors, or the contract price is too high from the government's standpoint. Therefore, the government assumes a major share of the risk of the potentially high costs of completing the contract. It negotiates contracts by using *costs plus a fixed fee* as a substitute for selling prices as ordinarily set by suppliers in the marketplace. In costs-plus-fixed-fee contracts, which often involve billions of dollars, a cost allocation may be difficult to defend on the basis of any cause-and-effect reasoning. Nonetheless, the contracting parties may still view it as a "reasonable" or "fair" means to help establish a contract amount.

Some costs are "allowable"; others are "unallowable." An **allowable cost** is a cost that the contract parties agree to include in the costs to be reimbursed. Some contracts specify how allowable costs are to be determined. For example, only economy-class airfares are allowable in many U.S. government contracts. Other contracts identify cost categories that are unallowable. For example, the costs of lobbying activities and alcoholic beverages are not allowable costs in U.S. government contracts. However, what costs are allowable is not always clear-cut. Contract disputes and allegations about overcharging the government arise from time to time (see Concepts in Action, p. 548).

Cost-based prices are one way of setting prices for products when no market price exists. One problem with a cost-plus contract is that the producer has less incentive to control costs because cost increases can be passed on to the buyer. Cost-reimbursement contracts must be specific and, if possible, should include incentives to prevent such abuses.

Study Tip: To check your understanding of the cost-allocation material in this chapter, see the Featured Exercise, true–false statements 1 and 4, multiple-choice questions 2 through 4, and Review Exercises 1 and 2 (*Student Guide*, beginning p. 202.). Fully explained answers begin on p. 208.

Revenue Allocation and Bundled Products

6

Understand how bundling of products

. . . two or more products sold for a single price

gives rise to revenue-allocation issues

. . . allocating revenues to each product in the bundle to evaluate managers of individual products

Allocation issues can also arise when revenues from multiple products (for example, different software programs) are bundled together and sold at a single price. The methods for revenue allocation parallel those described for common-cost allocations.

Revenues are inflows of assets (almost always cash or accounts receivable) received for products or services provided to customers. Analogous to cost allocation, **revenue allocation** occurs when revenues are related to a particular *revenue object* but cannot be traced to it in an economically feasible (cost-effective) way. A **revenue object** is anything for which a separate measurement of revenue is desired. Examples of revenue objects include products, customers, and divisions. We illustrate revenue-allocation issues for Supersoft Corporation, which develops, sells, and supports three software programs:

1. WordMaster, a word-processing program—current version is WordMaster 5.0, released 36 months ago (January 2004).
2. SpreadMaster, a spreadsheet program—current version is SpreadMaster 3.0, released 18 months ago (July 2005).
3. FinanceMaster, a budgeting and cash-management program—current version is FinanceMaster 1.0, released 6 months ago (July 2006) with a lot of favorable media attention.

When a manager is deciding whether to keep or discontinue a product line, the product line is both the revenue object and the cost object.

Supersoft sells these three products individually as well as together as bundled products.

A **bundled product** is a package of two or more products (or services) that is sold for a single price but whose individual components may be sold as separate items at their own "stand-alone" prices. The price of a bundled product is typically less than the sum of the prices of the individual products sold separately. For example, banks often provide individual customers with a bundle of services from different departments (checking, safety-deposit box, and investment advisory) for a single fee. A resort hotel may offer, for a single amount per customer, a weekend package that includes services from its Lodging (the room), Food (the restaurant), and Recreational (golf and tennis) Departments. When department managers have revenue or profit responsibilities for individual products, the bundled revenue must be allocated among the individual products in the bundle.[6]

[6]Revenue-allocation issues also arise in external reporting. Statement of Position 97-2 (Software Revenue Recognition) states that with bundled products, revenue allocation "based on vendor-specific objective evidence of fair value" is required. The "price charged when the element is sold separately" is said to be "objective evidence of fair value." See American Institute of Certified Public Accountants, "Statement of Position 97-2" (Jersey City, NJ: AICPA, 1998).

CONCEPTS IN ACTION

Contract Disputes over Reimbursable Costs for U.S. Government Agencies

Allegations about a contractor overcharging a government agency invariably make interesting copy for the media. The following four examples are from cases in which contractors "settled with the government without admitting wrongdoing with respect to the charges." The U.S. Department of Justice's Civil Division pursued these cases and negotiated the settlements on behalf of the federal government. These recent examples illustrate several types of cost disputes that arise in practice:

1. Ogilvy & Mather North America, one of the largest advertising agencies in the world, agreed to pay $1.8 million to resolve claims that the company overcharged the Office of National Drug Control Policy for labor costs on a contract to provide advertising services. Ogilvy & Mather had a cost-plus-fixed-fee contract in which the labor-hours were charged on the basis of time records reflecting the proportion of an employee's time spent on the contract. It was alleged that Ogilvy's labor charges were based on inaccurate timesheets submitted by employees and that the company's management did not exercise reasonable control to ensure that billings for labor were accurate.
2. Johnson & Johnson Medical, a division of the diversified-health-care-products supplier, paid $3.8 million in damages to settle claims that it overcharged the U.S. Department of Veterans Affairs (VA). The settlement resolved allegations that the company failed to disclose, as required by law, full and accurate pricing information to VA negotiators on a contract for the purchase of medical supplies, and that, as a result, the VA was overcharged.
3. Lockheed Martin, a leading defense contractor, agreed to pay the federal government $37.9 million to settle allegations that it inflated the cost of performing several Air Force contracts. The complaint alleged that a Lockheed Martin program-management team deliberately inflated costs in four cost-plus contract proposals for the purchase of navigation and targeting pods for military jets.
4. Northrop Grumman, another large defense contractor, paid $60 million to resolve allegations that it overcharged the government on Navy shipbuilding contracts. It was alleged that from 1994 to 1999, Newport News Shipbuilding (at the time an independent company, now a Northrop Grumman subsidiary) mischarged as Independent Research and Development (IR&D) its cost for the design and development of double-hulled tankers that the shipbuilder had already designed for commercial customers. Under federal regulations, costs may be charged only as IR&D to government contracts if the R&D is specifically incurred for the contract.

Source: Press releases from the U.S. Department of Justice, Civil Division.

Supersoft allocates revenues from its bundled product sales (called "suite sales") to individual products. Individual-product profitability is used to compensate software engineers, outside developers, and product managers responsible for developing and managing each product.

Revenue-Allocation Methods

7

Allocate the revenues of a bundled product to the individual products in that bundle

. . . using the stand-alone method, the incremental method, or management judgment

How should Supersoft allocate suite revenues to individual products? Consider information pertaining to the three "stand-alone" and "suite" products in 2006:

	Selling Price	Manufacturing Cost per Unit
Stand-alone		
WordMaster	$125	$18
SpreadMaster	150	20
FinanceMaster	225	25
Suite		
Word + Spread	$220	
Word + Finance	280	
Finance + Spread	305	
Word + Finance + Spread	380	

Just as we saw in the section on common-cost allocations, the two main revenue-allocation methods are the stand-alone method and the incremental method.

Stand-Alone Revenue-Allocation Method

The **stand-alone revenue-allocation method** uses product-specific information on the products in the bundle as weights for allocating the bundled revenues to the individual products. The term *stand-alone* refers to the product as a separate (nonsuite) item. Consider the Word + Finance suite, which sells for \$280. Three types of weights for the stand-alone method are as follows:

Conceptually, it is preferable to allocate common revenues based on unit revenues or stand-alone revenues because they best reflect customers' willingness to pay for the different products. If the products are never sold separately, however, individual selling prices and revenues are unavailable, so revenues are allocated based on unit costs or number of units.

1. **Selling prices.** Using the individual selling prices of \$125 for WordMaster and \$225 for FinanceMaster, the weights for allocating the \$280 suite revenues between the products are:

$$\text{WordMaster: } \frac{\$125}{\$125 + \$225} \times \$280 = 0.357 \times \$280 = \$100$$

$$\text{FinanceMaster: } \frac{\$225}{\$125 + \$225} \times \$280 = 0.643 \times \$280 = \$180$$

2. **Unit costs.** This method uses the costs of the individual products (in this case, manufacturing cost per unit) to determine the weights for the revenue allocations.

$$\text{WordMaster: } \frac{\$18}{\$18 + \$25} \times \$280 = 0.419 \times \$280 = \$117$$

$$\text{FinanceMaster: } \frac{\$25}{\$18 + \$25} \times \$280 = 0.581 \times \$280 = \$163$$

Using unit costs will make the different products appear equally profitable in terms of gross margin %. In the Supersoft example:

	Word	Finance
Revenues	\$117	\$163
Manuf. costs	18	25
Gross margin	\$ 99	\$138
Gross margin %	84.6%	84.7%

3. **Physical units.** This method gives each product unit in the suite the same weight when allocating suite revenue to individual products. Therefore, with two products in the Word + Finance suite, each product is allocated 50% of the suite revenues.

$$\text{WordMaster: } \frac{1}{1+1} \times \$280 = 0.50 \times \$280 = \$140$$

$$\text{FinanceMaster: } \frac{1}{1+1} \times \$280 = 0.50 \times \$280 = \$140$$

It is most appropriate to use physical units when the sales values of the individual products in the bundle are approximately equal. Using physical units for, say, a bundle that includes a washing machine and a box of detergent would be inappropriate because it makes no sense to allocate half of the revenue to the box of detergent.

These three approaches to determining weights for the stand-alone method result in very different revenue allocations to the individual products:

Revenue-Allocation Weights	WordMaster	FinanceMaster
Selling prices	\$100	\$180
Unit costs	117	163
Physical units	140	140

Which method is preferred? The selling-price weights explicitly consider the prices customers are willing to pay for the individual products. Weighting approaches that use revenue information better capture "benefits received" by customers than unit costs or physical units. The physical-units revenue-allocation method is used when any of the other methods cannot be used (such as when selling prices are unstable or unit costs are difficult to calculate for individual products).

Incremental Revenue-Allocation Method

The **incremental revenue-allocation method** ranks individual products in a bundle according to criteria determined by management—such as the product in the bundle with the most sales—and then uses this ranking to allocate bundled revenues to individual

Under the incremental revenue-allocation method, all users of the revenue object want to be the first-ranked user. That's because the first-ranked user will be allocated a larger portion of the revenues.

products. The first-ranked product is the *primary product* in the bundle. The second-ranked product is the *first incremental product*, the third-ranked product is the *second incremental product*, and so on.

How do companies decide on product rankings under the incremental revenue-allocation method? One way is to survey customers on how important each of the individual products was in their decisions to purchase the bundled product. Another way is to use data on the recent stand-alone sales performance of the individual products in the bundle. A third way is for top managers to use their knowledge or intuition to decide the rankings.

Consider again the Word + Finance suite. Assume WordMaster is designated as the primary product. If the suite selling price exceeds the stand-alone price of the primary product, the primary product is allocated 100% of its *stand-alone* revenue. Because the suite price of $280 exceeds the stand-alone price of $125 for WordMaster, WordMaster is allocated revenues of $125, with the remaining revenue of $155 ($280 – $125) allocated to FinanceMaster:

Product	Revenue Allocated	Cumulative Revenue Allocated
WordMaster	$125	$125
FinanceMaster	155 ($280 – $125)	$280
Total	$280	

If the suite price is less than or equal to the stand-alone price of the primary product, the primary product is allocated 100% of the *suite* revenue. All other products in the suite receive no allocation of revenue.

Now suppose FinanceMaster is designated as the primary product and WordMaster as the first incremental product, then the incremental revenue-allocation method allocates revenues of the Word + Finance suite as:

Product	Revenue Allocated	Cumulative Revenue Allocated
FinanceMaster	$225	$225
WordMaster	55 ($280 – $225)	$280
Total	$280	

If Supersoft sells equal quantities of WordMaster and FinanceMaster, then the Shapley value method allocates to each product the average of the revenues allocated as the primary and first incremental products:

WordMaster:	($125 + $ 55) ÷ 2 = $180 ÷ 2 =	$ 90
FinanceMaster:	($225 + $155) ÷ 2 = $380 ÷ 2 =	190
Total		$280

But what if, in the most recent quarter, Supersoft sells 80,000 units of WordMaster and 20,000 units of FinanceMaster. Because Supersoft sells four times as many units of WordMaster, its managers believe that the sales of the Word + Finance suite are four times more likely to be driven by WordMaster as the primary product. The *weighted Shapley value method* takes this into account by weighting the revenue allocations when WordMaster is the primary product four times as much as when FinanceMaster is the primary product:

WordMaster:	($125 × 4 + $ 55 × 1) ÷ (4 + 1) = $555 ÷ 5 =	$111
FinanceMaster:	($225 × 1 + $155 × 4) ÷ (4 + 1) = $845 ÷ 5 =	169
Total		$280

When there are more than two products in the suite, the incremental revenue-allocation method allocates suite revenues sequentially. Assume WordMaster is the primary product in Supersoft's three-product suite (Word + Finance + Spread). FinanceMaster is the first incremental product, and SpreadMaster is the second incremental product. This suite sells for $380. The allocation of the $380 suite revenues proceeds as follows:

Product	Revenue Allocated	Cumulative Revenue Allocated
WordMaster	$125	$125
FinanceMaster	155 ($280 – $125)	$280 (price of Word + Finance suite)
SpreadMaster	100 ($380 – $280)	$380 (price of Word + Finance + Spread suite)
Total	$380	

Now suppose WordMaster is the primary product, SpreadMaster is the first incremental product, and FinanceMaster is the second incremental product.

Product	Revenue Allocated	Cumulative Revenue Allocated
WordMaster	$125	$125
SpreadMaster	95 ($220 – $125)	$220 (price of Word + Spread suite)
FinanceMaster	160 ($380 – $220)	$380 (price of Word + Spread + Finance suite)
Total	$380	

The ranking of the individual products in the suite determines the revenues allocated to them. Product managers at Supersoft likely would differ on how they believe their individual products contribute to sales of the suite products. It is possible that each product manager would claim to be responsible for the primary product in the Word + Finance + Spread suite![7] Because the stand-alone revenue-allocation method does not require rankings of individual products in the suite, this method is less likely to cause debates among product managers.

Other Revenue-Allocation Methods

Management judgment not explicitly based on a specific formula is another method of revenue allocation. In one case, the president of a software company decided to issue a set of revenue-allocation weights after the managers of the three products in a bundled product could not agree among themselves on a set of weights. The weights chosen by the president were 45% for product A, 45% for product B, and 10% for product C. Factors the president considered included stand-alone selling prices (all three were very similar), stand-alone unit sales (A and B were over 10 times more than C), product ratings by independent experts, and consumer awareness. The product C manager complained that his 10% weighting drastically shortchanged the contribution of product C to suite revenues. The president responded that its inclusion in the suite greatly

[7]Calculating the Shapley value mitigates this problem because each product is considered as a primary, first-incremental, and second-incremental product. Assuming equal weights on all products, the revenue allocated to each product is an average of the revenues calculated for each product under these different assumptions: FinanceMaster, $180; WordMaster, $87.50; and SpreadMaster, $112.50.

Order			Revenues Allocated to Each Product		
Primary	First Incremental	Second Incremental	FinanceMaster	WordMaster	SpreadMaster
FinanceMaster	WordMaster	SpreadMaster	$225	$ 55 ($280 – $225)	$100 ($380 – $225 – $55)
FinanceMaster	SpreadMaster	WordMaster	$225	$ 75 ($380 – $225 – $80)	$ 80 ($305 – $225)
WordMaster	FinanceMaster	SpreadMaster	$155 ($280 – $125)	$125	$100 ($380 – $125 – $155)
WordMaster	SpreadMaster	FinanceMaster	$160 ($380 – $125 – $95)	$125	$ 95 ($220 – $125)
SpreadMaster	FinanceMaster	WordMaster	$155 ($305 – $150)	$ 75 ($380 – $150 – $155)	$150
SpreadMaster	WordMaster	FinanceMaster	$160 ($380 – $150 – $70)	$ 70 ($220 – $150)	$150
Total:			$1,080	$525	$675
Average Revenue Allocated:			$1,080 ÷ 6 = $180	$525 ÷ 6 = $87.50	$675 ÷ 6 = $112.50

increased consumer exposure to product C, with the result that product C's total revenues would be far larger (even with only 10% of suite revenues) than if it had not been included in the suite.

PROBLEM FOR SELF-STUDY

This problem illustrates how costs of two corporate support departments are allocated to operating divisions using the dual-rate method. Fixed costs are allocated using budgeted costs and budgeted hours used by other departments. Variable costs are allocated using actual costs and actual hours used by other departments.

Computer Horizons budgets the following amounts for its two central corporate support departments (legal and personnel) in supporting each other and the two manufacturing divisions, the Laptop Division (LTD) and the Work Station Division (WSD):

	A	B	C	D	E	F	G
1		SUPPORT			OPERATING		
2		Legal Department	Personnel Department		LTD	WSD	Total
3	**BUDGETED USAGE**						
4	Legal (hours)	-	250		1,500	750	2,500
5	(Percentages)	-	10%		60%	30%	100%
6	Personnel (hours)	2,500	-		22,500	25,000	50,000
7	(Percentages)	5%	-		45%	50%	100%
8							
9	**ACTUAL USAGE**						
10	Legal (hours)	-	400		400	1,200	2,000
11	(Percentages)	-	20%		20%	60%	100%
12	Personnel (hours)	2,000	-		26,600	11,400	40,000
13	(Percentages)	5%	-		66.5%	28.5%	100%
14	Budgeted fixed overhead costs before any						
15	interdepartment cost allocations	$360,000	$475,000		-	-	$835,000
16	Actual variable overhead costs before any						
17	interdepartment cost allocations	$200,000	$600,000		-	-	$800,000

Required

What amount of support-department costs for legal and personnel will be allocated to LTD and WSD using (a) the direct method, (b) the step-down method (allocating the Legal Department costs first), and (c) the reciprocal method using linear equations?

SOLUTION

Exhibit 15-7 presents the computations for allocating the fixed and variable support-department costs. A summary of these costs follows:

	Laptop Division (LTD)	Work Station Division (WSD)
(a) Direct Method		
Fixed costs	$465,000	$370,000
Variable costs	470,000	330,000
	$935,000	$700,000
(b) Step-Down Method		
Fixed costs	$458,053	$376,947
Variable costs	488,000	312,000
	$946,053	$688,947
(c) Reciprocal Method		
Fixed costs	$462,513	$372,487
Variable costs	476,364	323,636
	$938,877	$696,123

EXHIBIT 15-7 **Alternative Methods of Allocating Corporate Support-Department Costs to Operating Divisions of Computer Horizons: Dual-Rate Method**

	A	B	C	D	E	F	G
20		CORPORATE SUPPORT DEPARTMENTS			OPERATING DIVISIONS		
21	**Allocation Method**	**Legal Department**	**Personnel Department**		**LTD**	**WSD**	**Total**
22	**A. DIRECT METHOD**						
23	Fixed Costs	$360,000	$475,000				
24	Legal (1,500 ÷ 2,250; 750 ÷ 2,250)	(360,000)			$240,000	$120,000	
25	Personnel (22,500 ÷ 47,500; 25,000 ÷ 47,500)		(475,000)		225,000	250,000	
26	Corporate support dept. costs allocated to operating divisions	$ 0	$ 0		$465,000	$370,000	$835,000
27	Variable Costs	$200,000	$600,000				
28	Legal (400 ÷ 1,600; 1,200 ÷ 1,600)	(200,000)			$ 50,000	$150,000	
29	Personnel (26,600 ÷ 38,000; 11,400 ÷ 38,000)		(600,000)		420,000	180,000	
30	Corporate support dept. costs allocated to operating divisions	$ 0	$ 0		$470,000	$330,000	$800,000
31	**B. STEP-DOWN METHOD**						
32	(Legal Department First)						
33	Fixed Costs	$360,000	$475,000				
34	Legal (250 ÷ 2,500; 1,500 ÷ 2,500; 750 ÷ 2,500)	(360,000)	36,000		$216,000	$108,000	
35	Personnel (22,500 ÷ 47,500; 25,000 ÷ 47,500)		(511,000)		242,053	268,947	
36	Corporate support dept. costs allocated to operating divisions	$ 0	$ 0		$458,053	$376,947	$835,000
37	Variable Costs	$200,000	$600,000				
38	Legal (400 ÷ 2,000; 400 ÷ 2,000; 1,200 ÷ 2,000)	(200,000)	40,000		$ 40,000	$120,000	
39	Personnel (26,600 ÷ 38,000; 11,400 ÷ 38,000)		(640,000)		448,000	192,000	
40	Corporate support dept. costs allocated to operating divisions	$ 0	$ 0		$488,000	$312,000	$800,000
41	**C. RECIPROCAL METHOD**						
42	Fixed Costs	$360,000	$475,000				
43	Legal (250 ÷ 2,500; 1,500 ÷ 2,500; 750 ÷ 2,500)	(385,678)[a]	38,568		$231,407	$115,703	
44	Personnel (2,500 ÷ 50,000; 22,500 ÷ 50,000; 25,000 ÷ 50,000)	25,678	(513,568)[a]		231,106	256,784	
45	Corporate support dept. costs allocated to operating divisions	$ 0	$ 0		$462,513	$372,487	$835,000
46	Variable Costs	$200,000	$600,000				
47	Legal (400 ÷ 2,000; 400 ÷ 2,000; 1,200 ÷ 2,000)	(232,323)[b]	46,465		$ 46,465	$139,393	
48	Personnel (2,000 ÷ 40,000; 26,600 ÷ 40,000; 11,400 ÷ 40,000)	32,323	(646,465)[b]		429,899	184,243	
49	Corporate support dept. costs allocated to operating divisions	$ 0	$ 0		$476,364	$323,636	$800,000
50							
51	[a]FIXED COSTS	[b]VARIABLE COSTS					
52	Letting *LF* = Legal Department Fixed Costs, and *PF* = Personnel Department Fixed Costs, the simultaneous equations for the reciprocal method for fixed costs are	Letting *LV* =Legal Department Variable Costs, and *PV* = Personnel Department Variable Costs, the simultaneous equations for the reciprocal method for variable costs are					
53	$LF = \$360,000 + 0.05\ PF$	$LV = \$200,000 + 0.05\ PV$					
54	$PF = \$475,000 + 0.10\ LF$	$PV = \$600,000 + 0.20\ LV$					
55	$LF = \$360,000 + 0.05\ (\$475,000 + 0.10\ LF)$	$LV = \$200,000 + 0.05\ (\$600,000 + 0.20\ LV)$					
56	$LF = \$385,678$	$LV = \$232,323$					
57	$PF = \$475,000 + 0.10\ (\$385,678) = \$513,568$	$PV = \$600,000 + 0.20\ (\$232,323) = \$646,465$					

DECISION POINTS

The following question-and-answer format summarizes the chapter's learning objectives. Each decision presents a key question related to a learning objective. The guidelines are the answer to that question.

Decision	**Guidelines**
1. Should managers use the single-rate or the dual-rate method?	The single-rate method allocates costs in each cost pool to cost objects using the same rate per unit of a single allocation base. Under the dual-rate method, costs are grouped into a variable cost pool and a fixed cost pool; each pool uses a different cost-allocation base. If costs can be easily separated into variable and fixed costs, the dual-rate method should be used because it provides better information for making decisions.

2. What factors should managers consider when deciding whether to use budgeted or actual cost-allocation rates?	When cost allocations are made using budgeted rates, managers of divisions to which costs are allocated face no uncertainty about the rates to be used in that budget period. In contrast, when actual rates are used for cost allocation, managers do not know the rates until the end of the budget period. If actual rates are used, the efficiency of the supplier department affects the costs allocated to the user departments.
3. What methods can managers use to allocate costs of multiple support departments to operating departments?	The three methods managers can use are the direct, the step-down, and the reciprocal methods. The direct method allocates each support department's costs to operating departments without allocating a support department's costs to other support departments. The step-down method allocates support-department costs to other support departments and to operating departments in a sequential manner that partially recognizes the mutual services provided among all support departments. The reciprocal method fully recognizes mutual services provided among all support departments, but it is more complex than the direct or step-down methods.
4. What methods can managers use to allocate common costs to two or more users?	Common costs are the costs of a cost object (such as operating a facility or performing an activity) that are shared by two or more users. The stand-alone cost-allocation method uses information pertaining to each user of the cost object to determine cost-allocation weights. The incremental cost-allocation method ranks individual users of the cost object and allocates common costs first to the primary user and then to the other incremental users. The Shapely value method considers each user, in turn, as the primary and the incremental user.
5. How can contract disputes over reimbursement amounts based on costs be reduced?	Disputes can be reduced by making the cost-allocation rules as explicit as possible and in writing at the time the contract is signed. These rules should include details such as the allowable cost items, the acceptable cost-allocation bases, and how differences between budgeted and actual costs are to be accounted for.
6. What is product bundling and why does it give rise to revenue-allocation issues?	Bundling occurs when a package of two or more products (or services) is sold for a single price. Revenue allocation of the bundled price is required when managers of the individual products in the bundle are evaluated on product revenue or product operating income.
7. What methods can managers use to allocate revenues of a bundled product to individual products in the package?	Revenues can be allocated for a bundled product using the stand-alone method, the incremental method, the Shapely value method, or management judgment.

TERMS TO LEARN

This chapter and the Glossary at the end of the book contain definitions of:

allowable cost (p. 547)
artificial costs (p. 541)
bundled product (p. 547)
common cost (p. 544)
complete reciprocated costs (p. 541)
Cost Accounting Standards Board (CASB) (p. 546)
direct allocation method (p. 538)
direct method (p. 538)
dual-rate cost-allocation method (p. 532)
dual-rate method (p. 532)
incremental cost-allocation method (p. 545)
incremental revenue-allocation method (p. 549)
operating department (p. 532)
production department (p. 532)
reciprocal allocation method (p. 540)
reciprocal method (p. 540)
revenue allocation (p. 547)
revenue object (p. 547)
service department (p. 532)
single-rate cost-allocation method (p. 532)
single-rate method (p. 532)
sequential allocation method (p. 539)
stand-alone cost-allocation method (p. 544)
stand-alone revenue-allocation method (p. 549)
step-down allocation method (p. 539)
step-down method (p. 539)
support department (p. 532)

PH Grade Assist

Prentice Hall Grade Assist (PHGA)
Your professor may ask you to complete selected exercises and problems in Prentice Hall Grade Assist (PHGA). PHGA is an online tool that can help you master the chapter's topics. It provides you with multiple variations of exercises and problems designated by the PHGA icon. You can rework these exercises and problems—each time with new data—as many times as you need. You also receive immediate feedback and grading.

ASSIGNMENT MATERIAL

Questions

15-1 Distinguish between the single-rate and the dual-rate methods.

15-2 Describe how the dual-rate method is useful to division managers in decision making.

15-3 How do budgeted cost rates motivate the manager of the support department to improve efficiency?

15-4 Give examples of allocation bases used to allocate support-department cost pools to operating departments.

15-5 Why might a manager prefer that budgeted rather than actual cost-allocation rates be used for costs being allocated to her department from another department?

15-6 "To ensure unbiased cost allocations, fixed costs should be allocated on the basis of estimated long-run use by user department managers." Do you agree? Why?

15-7 Distinguish among the three methods of allocating the costs of support departments to operating departments.

15-8 What is conceptually the most defensible method for allocating support-department costs? Why?

15-9 Distinguish between two methods of allocating common costs.

15-10 What role does the Cost Accounting Standards Board play when companies contract with the U.S. government?

15-11 What is one key way to reduce cost-allocation disputes that arise with government contracts?

15-12 Describe how companies are increasingly facing revenue-allocation decisions.

15-13 Distinguish between the stand-alone and the incremental revenue-allocation methods.

15-14 Identify and discuss arguments individual product managers may put forward to support their preferred revenue-allocation method.

15-15 How might a dispute over the allocation of revenues of a bundled product be resolved?

Exercises

PH Grade Assist

15-16 Single-rate versus dual-rate methods, support department. The Chicago power plant that services all manufacturing departments of MidWest Engineering has a budget for the coming year. This budget has been expressed in the following monthly terms:

Manufacturing Department	Needed at Practical Capacity Production Level (Kilowatt-Hours)	Average Expected Monthly Usage (Kilowatt-Hours)
Rockford	10,000	8,000
Peoria	20,000	9,000
Hammond	12,000	7,000
Kankakee	8,000	6,000
Total	50,000	30,000

The expected monthly costs for operating the power plant during the budget year are $15,000: $6,000 variable and $9,000 fixed.

Required

1. Assume that a single cost pool is used for the power plant costs. What budgeted amounts will be allocated to each manufacturing department if (a) the rate is calculated based on practical capacity and costs are allocated based on practical capacity and (b) the rate is calculated based on expected monthly usage and costs are allocated based on expected monthly usage.
2. Assume the dual-rate method is used with separate cost pools for the variable and fixed costs. Variable costs are allocated on the basis of expected monthly usage. Fixed costs are allocated on the basis of practical capacity. What budgeted amounts will be allocated to each manufacturing department? Why might you prefer the dual-rate method?

PH Grade Assist

Excel Lab
www.prenhall.com/horngren/cost12e

15-17 Single-rate method, budgeted versus actual costs and quantities. Sunrise, Inc., processes fruit at its Orlando plant and sells fruit juice and preserves (jams and jellies). It purchases oranges from a grower in East Miami for its Juices Division and from a grower in West Miami for its Preserves Division. Both of its Miami orange growers are the same distance from the Orlando plant.

Sunrise operates a trucking fleet as a cost center that charges the divisions for variable costs (drivers, fuel, and tolls) and fixed costs (vehicle depreciation, insurance, and registration fees) of operating the trucks. Each division is evaluated on the basis of division operating income. For 2007, the trucking fleet had a practical capacity of 250 round-trips between the Orlando plant and the Miami orange growers. It recorded the following information:

	A	B	C
1		**Budgeted**	**Actual**
2	Costs of trucking fleet	$575,000	$483,750
3	Number of round-trips for Juices Division (Orlando plant -- East Miami grower)	150	150
4	Number of round-trips for Preserves Division (Orlando plant -- West Miami grower)	100	75

If you want to use Excel to solve this exercise, go to the Excel Lab at **www.prenhall.com/horngren/cost12e** and download the template for Exercise 15-17.

Required

1. Using the single-rate method, allocate costs to the Juices Division and the Preserves Division in these three ways. (a) Calculate the budgeted rate per round-trip and allocate costs based on round-trips budgeted for each division. (b) Calculate the budgeted rate per round-trip and allocate costs based on actual round-trips used by each division. (c) Calculate the actual rate per round-trip and allocate costs based on actual round-trips used by each division.
2. Describe the advantages and disadvantages of using each of the three methods in requirement 1. Would you encourage Sunrise to use one of these methods? Explain and indicate any assumptions you made.

Excel Lab www.prenhall.com/horngren/cost12e PH Grade Assist

15-18 Dual-rate method, budgeted versus actual costs, and practical capacity versus actual quantities (continuation of 15-17). Sunrise, Inc., decides to examine the effect of using the dual-rate method for allocating trucking costs to each round-trip. At the start of 2007, the budgeted costs were:

Variable cost per round-trip	$1,500
Fixed costs	$200,000

The actual results for the 225 round-trips made in 2007 were:

Variable costs	$303,750
Fixed costs	180,000
	$483,750

Assume all other information to be the same as in Exercise 15-17.

If you want to use Excel to solve this exercise, go to the Excel Lab at **www.prenhall.com/horngren/cost12e** and download the template for Exercise 15-17.

Required

1. Using the dual-rate method, what are the costs allocated to the Juices Division and the Preserves Division when (a) variable costs are allocated using the budgeted rate per round-trip and actual round-trips used by each division and when (b) fixed costs are allocated based on the budgeted rate per round-trip and round-trips budgeted for each division?
2. From the viewpoint of the Juices Division, what are the effects of using the dual-rate method rather than the single-rate methods?

Excel Lab www.prenhall.com/horngren/cost12e PH Grade Assist

15-19 Support-department cost allocation; direct and step-down methods. Phoenix Partners provides management consulting services to government and corporate clients. Phoenix has two support departments—Administrative Services (AS) and Information Systems (IS)—and two operating departments—Government Consulting (GOVT) and Corporate Consulting (CORP). For the first quarter of 2006, Phoenix's cost records indicate the following:

	A	B	C	D	E	F	G
1		SUPPORT			OPERATING		
2		AS	IS		GOVT	CORP	Total
3	Budgeted overhead costs before any						
4	interdepartment cost allocations	$600,000	$2,400,000		$8,756,000	$12,452,000	$24,208,000
5	Support work supplied by AS (Budgeted head count)	-	25%		40%	35%	100%
6	Support work supplied by IS (Budgeted computer time)	10%	-		30%	60%	100%

If you want to use Excel to solve this exercise, go to the Excel Lab at **www.prenhall.com/horngren/cost12e** and download the template for Exercise 15-19.

Required

1. Allocate the two support departments' costs to the two operating departments using the following methods:
   a. Direct method
   b. Step-down method (allocate AS first)
   c. Step-down method (allocate IS first)
2. Compare and explain differences in the support-department costs allocated to each operating department.
3. What approaches might be used to decide the sequence in which to allocate support departments when using the step-down method?

Excel Lab www.prenhall.com/horngren/cost12e PH Grade Assist

15-20 Support-department cost allocation, reciprocal method (continuation of 15-19). Refer to the data given in Exercise 15-19.

If you want to use Excel to solve this exercise, go to the Excel Lab at **www.prenhall.com/horngren/cost12e** and download the template for Exercise 15-19.

Required

1. Allocate the two support departments' costs to the two operating departments using the reciprocal method. Use (a) linear equations and (b) repeated iterations.
2. Compare and explain differences in requirement 1 with those in requirement 1 of Exercise 15-19. Which method do you prefer? Why?

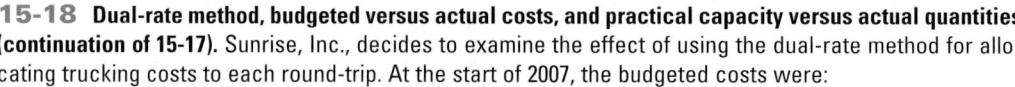

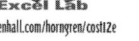

15-21 Direct and step-down allocation. E-books, an online book retailer, has two operating departments—Corporate Sales and Consumer Sales—and two support departments—Human Resources and Information Systems. Each of the sales departments conducts merchandising and marketing operations independently. E-books uses number of employees to allocate Human Resources costs and processing time to allocate Information Systems costs. The following data are available for September 2007:

Excel Lab
www.prenhall.com/horngren/cost12e

	A	B	C	D	E	F
1		SUPPORT DEPARTMENTS			OPERATING DEPARTMENTS	
2		Human Resources	Information Systems		Corporate Sales	Consumer Sales
3	Budgeted costs incurred before any					
4	interdepartment cost allocations	$72,700	$234,400		$998,270	$489,860
5	Support work supplied by Human Resources Department					
6	Budgeted number of employees	-	21		42	28
7	Support work supplied by Information Systems Department					
8	Budgeted processing time (in minutes)	320	-		1,920	1,600

If you want to use Excel to solve this exercise, go to the Excel Lab at **www.prenhall.com/horngren/cost12e** and download the template for Exercise 15-21.

Required

1. Allocate the support-departments' costs to the operating departments using the direct method.
2. Rank the support departments based on the percentage of their services provided to other support departments. Use this ranking to allocate support departments' costs to the operating departments based on the step-down method.
3. How could you have ranked the support departments differently?

15-22 Reciprocal cost allocation (continuation of 15-21). Consider E-books again. The controller of E-books reads a widely used textbook that states that "the reciprocal method is conceptually the most defensible." He seeks your assistance.

Excel Lab
www.prenhall.com/horngren/cost12e

If you want to use Excel to solve this exercise, go to the Excel Lab at **www.prenhall.com/horngren/cost12e** and download the template for Exercise 15-21.

Required

1. Describe the key features of the reciprocal method.
2. Allocate the support-departments' costs (Human Resources and Information Systems) to the two operating departments using the reciprocal method.
3. In the case presented in this exercise, which method (direct, step-down, or reciprocal) would you recommend? Why?

15-23 Allocation of common costs. Sam and Tony work as skilled machinists at Bedford Engineering. They share a penthouse apartment that has a lounge room with the latest 50-inch TV. Tony owns the apartment, its furniture, and the TV. He can subscribe to a cable television company that has the following packages available:

Package	Per Month
A. Basic news	$40
B. Premium sports	20
C. Basic news + Premium sports	48

Sam is a TV news junkie who has less interest in sports ("they are overpaid jocks"). Tony is into sports in a big way and has less interest in news ("it's all depressing anyway"). They agree that the purchase of the $48 total package is a "win–win" situation.

Each of the roommates works on a different eight-hour shift at Bedford, so conflicts in viewing are minimal.

Required

1. Allocate the $48 between Sam and Tony using (a) the stand-alone cost-allocation method, (b) the incremental cost-allocation method, and (c) the Shapely value method.
2. Which method would you recommend they use and why?

15-24 Allocation of common costs. Joan Ernst, a graduating senior at a university near Sacramento, received an invitation to visit a prospective employer in Baltimore. A few days later, she received an invitation from a prospective employer in Chicago. She decided to combine her visits, traveling from Sacramento to Baltimore, Baltimore to Chicago, and Chicago to Sacramento.

Ernst received job offers from both companies. Upon her return, she decided to accept the offer in Chicago. She is puzzled over how to allocate her travel costs between the two employers. She has collected the following data for regular round-trip fares with no stopovers:

Sacramento to Baltimore	$1,400
Sacramento to Chicago	$1,100

Ernst paid $1,800 for her three-leg flight (Sacramento–Baltimore, Baltimore–Chicago, Chicago–Sacramento). In addition, she paid $30 each way for limousines from her home to Sacramento Airport and back when she returned.

Required

1. How should Ernst allocate the $1,800 airfare between the employers in Baltimore and Chicago using (a) the stand-alone cost-allocation method, (b) the incremental cost-allocation method, and (c) the Shapely value method?
2. Which method would you recommend Ernst use and why?
3. How should Ernst allocate the $60 limousine charges between the employers in Baltimore and Chicago?

Excel Lab www.prenhall.com/horngren/cost12e

PH Grade Assist

15-25 Revenue allocation, bundled products. Yves Parfum Company blends and sells designer fragrances. It has a Men's Fragrances Division and a Women's Fragrances Division, each with different sales strategies, distribution channels, and product offerings. Yves is now considering the sale of a bundled product consisting of a men's cologne and a women's perfume. For the most recent year, Yves reported the following:

	A	B
1	**Product**	**Retail Price**
2	Monaco (men's cologne)	$ 80
3	Innocence (women's perfume)	120
4	L'Amour (Monaco + Innocence)	180

If you want to use Excel to solve this exercise, go to the Excel Lab at **www.prenhall.com/horngren/cost12e** and download the template for Exercise 15-25.

Required

1. Allocate revenue from the sale of each unit of L'Amour to Monaco and Innocence using:
   a. The stand-alone revenue-allocation method based on selling price of each product
   b. The incremental revenue-allocation method, with Monaco ranked as the primary product
   c. The incremental revenue-allocation method, with Innocence ranked as the primary product
   d. The Shapely value method, assuming equal unit sales of Monaco and Innocence.
2. Of the four methods in requirement 1, which one would you recommend for allocating L'Amour's revenues to Monaco and Innocence? Explain.

Excel Lab www.prenhall.com/horngren/cost12e

15-26 Units sold, revenue allocation (continuation of 15-25). Refer to the information in Exercise 15-25. Further assume units sold of Monaco and Innocence in the most recent year are:

Monaco	30,000 units
Innocence	10,000 units

L'Amour's managers believe that, because Monaco sells three times as many units as Innocence, L'Amour's sales are three times more likely to be driven by Monaco as the primary product.

If you want to use Excel to solve this exercise, go to the Excel Lab at **www.prenhall.com/horngren/cost12e** and download the template for Exercise 15-25.

Required

1. Allocate revenues from the sales of L'Amour to Monaco and Innocence using the weighted Shapely value method.
2. What is the advantage of using the weighted Shapely value method relative to the methods used in Exercise 15-25?

Problems

Excel Lab www.prenhall.com/horngren/cost12e

15-27 Single-rate, dual-rate, and practical capacity allocation. Quentin's Department Store offers a free gift-wrapping service for its customers. Quentin's customer-service department has practical capacity to wrap 10,000 gifts at a budgeted fixed cost of $9,000 each month. Average budgeted variable cost to gift wrap an item is $0.50. Although the service is free to customers, a gift-wrapping service cost allocation is made to the department where the item was purchased. The customer-service department reported the following for the most recent month:

	A	B	C	D
1	**Department**	**Actual Number of Gifts Wrapped**	**Budgeted Number of Gifts to be Wrapped**	**Practical Capacity Available for Gift-Wrapping**
2	Children's Wear	2,800	3,300	3,500
3	Men's Wear	1,000	1,100	1,250
4	Women's Wear	2,100	2,400	2,625
5	Gourmet Foods	700	600	875
6	Housewares	1,400	1,600	1,750
7	Total	8,000	9,000	10,000

If you want to use Excel to solve this problem, go to the Excel Lab at **www.prenhall.com/horngren/cost12e** and download the template for Problem 15-27.

Required

1. Using the single-rate method, allocate gift-wrapping costs to the different departments in these three ways. (a) Calculate the budgeted rate based on the budgeted number of gifts to be wrapped and allocate costs based on the budgeted use (of gift-wrapping services). (b) Calculate the budgeted rate based on the bud-

geted number of gifts to be wrapped and allocate costs based on actual usage. (c) Calculate the budgeted rate based on the practical gift-wrapping capacity available and allocate costs based on actual usage.

2. Using the dual-rate method, compute the amount allocated to each department when (a) the fixed-cost rate is calculated using budgeted costs and the practical gift-wrapping capacity, (b) fixed-costs are allocated based on budgeted usage of gift-wrapping services, and (c) variable costs are allocated using the budgeted variable-cost rate and actual usage.
3. Comment on your results in requirements 1 and 2.

15-28 Single-rate versus dual-rate methods. (W. Crum, adapted) Carolina Company has designed and built a power plant to serve its three plants. Data for 2006 are as follows:

	Usage in Kilowatt-Hours		
Plant	**Needed at Practical Capacity Production Level**	**Budgeted Usage**	**Actual Usage**
Durham	100,000	80,000	85,000
Charlotte	60,000	50,000	40,000
Raleigh	40,000	30,000	35,000
Total	200,000	160,000	160,000

Budgeted fixed costs of the power plant were \$1 million in 2006; budgeted variable-cost rate is \$12.50 per kilowatt hour.

Required

1. Allocate the power plant's costs to Durham, Charlotte, and Raleigh using the single-rate method in which the budgeted rate is calculated using practical capacity and costs are allocated to Durham, Charlotte, and Raleigh based on actual usage.
2. Allocate the power plant's costs to Durham, Charlotte, and Raleigh using the single-rate method in which the budgeted rate is based on budgeted usage and costs are allocated to Durham, Charlotte, and Raleigh based on actual usage.
3. Allocate the power plant's costs to Durham, Charlotte, and Raleigh using the dual-rate method in which the budgeted fixed-cost rate is calculated using practical capacity and fixed costs are allocated to Durham, Charlotte, and Raleigh based on practical capacity. Variable costs are allocated to Durham, Charlotte, and Raleigh based on the budgeted variable-cost rate and actual usage.
4. Allocate the power plant's costs to Durham, Charlotte, and Raleigh using the dual-rate method in which the budgeted fixed-cost rate is calculated using budgeted usage and fixed costs are allocated to Durham, Charlotte, and Raleigh based on budgeted usage. Variable costs are allocated to Durham, Charlotte, and Raleigh based on the budgeted variable-cost rate and actual usage.
5. Comment briefly on your results in requirements 1 through 4.

15-29 Single-rate, dual-rate, practical capacity allocations. Teradome, Inc., has its own water-processing plant, which is used by its Chemicals Division and Cosmetics Division. The water-processing plant was designed for a practical capacity of 200,000 gallons per year. Budgeted variable cost is \$5 per gallon processed. The following table presents the data for 2007:

Excel Lab
www.prenhall.com/horngren/cost12e

	A	B	C	D
1		Chemicals	Cosmetics	
2		Division	Division	Total
3	Practical capacity for each department (gallons)	120,000	80,000	200,000
4	Actual usage in 2007 (gallons)	80,000	60,000	140,000
5	Annual budgeted practical capacity fixed costs			\$600,000

If you want to use Excel to solve this problem, go to the Excel Lab at **www.prenhall.com/horngren/cost12e** and download the template for Problem 15-29.

Required

1. Allocate the water-processing plant's costs to the Chemicals and Cosmetics Divisions using a single-rate method in which the budgeted rate is calculated using practical capacity and costs are allocated based on actual usage.
2. Using the dual-rate method, allocate the water-processing plant's costs to the Chemicals and Cosmetics Divisions when (a) the fixed-cost rate is calculated based on budgeted costs and practical capacity, (b) fixed costs are allocated based on practical capacity, and (c) variable costs are allocated using the budgeted variable-cost rate and actual usage.
3. Using the dual-rate method, allocate the water-processing plant's costs to the Chemicals and Cosmetics Divisions when (a) the fixed-cost rate is calculated using budgeted costs and practical capacity, (b) fixed costs are allocated based on actual usage, and (c) variable costs are allocated using the budgeted variable-cost rate and actual usage.
4. Comment on your results in requirements 1, 2 and 3.

15-30 Cost allocation, actual versus budgeted usage. (CMA, adapted) Bulldog, Inc., is a large manufacturing company that runs its own electrical power plant from the excess steam produced in its manufacturing process. Power is provided to two production departments: Department A and Department B. The capacity of the power plant was originally determined by the expected peak demands of the two production departments. The expected normal usages are, respectively, 60,000,000 kilowatt-hours (kWh) for Department A and 40,000,000 kWh for Department B.

The budgeted monthly costs of producing power, based on normal usage of 100,000,000 kWh, are $30,000,000 in fixed costs and $7,500,000 in variable costs. For November, the actual kilowatt-hours used were 60,000,000 by Department A and 20,000,000 by Department B. Actual fixed costs were $30,000,000, and actual variable costs were $7,500,000.

Terry Lamb, the controller, prepared the following monthly report:

Bulldog, Inc.
Monthly Allocation Report
November 2006

Power plant usage	80,000,000 kWh
Actual costs:	
Variable	$ 7,500,000
Fixed	30,000,000
Total	$37,500,000
Rate per kWh ($37,500,000 ÷ 80,000,000 kWh)	$0.46875
Allocations:	
To Department A (60,000,000 kWh × $0.46875)	$28,125,000
To Department B (20,000,000 kWh × $0.46875)	9,375,000
Total allocated	$37,500,000

Lamb fully allocated all power-plant costs on the basis of actual kilowatt-hours used by each production department. This report will be submitted to the two production-department operating managers.

Required

1. Discuss at least two problems with the monthly allocation report prepared by Lamb for November 2006.
2. Prepare a revised monthly allocation report for November 2006 using a budgeted rate times actual usage for variable costs and a budgeted rate assuming budgeted (normal) usage for fixed costs.
3. Discuss the behavioral implication of Lamb's monthly allocation report for November 2006 on the production manager of Department B.

15-31 Allocating costs of support departments; step-down and direct methods. The Central Valley Company has prepared department overhead budgets for budgeted-volume levels before allocations as follows:

Support departments:		
Building and grounds	$10,000	
Personnel	1,000	
General plant administration	26,090	
Cafeteria: operating loss	1,640	
Storeroom	2,670	
Total for support departments		$ 41,400
Operating departments:		
Machining	$34,700	
Assembly	48,900	
Total for operating departments		83,600
Total for support and operating departments		$125,000

Management has decided that the most appropriate inventory costs are achieved by using individual-department overhead rates. These rates are developed after support-department costs are allocated to operating departments.

Bases for allocation are to be selected from the following:

Department	Direct Manufacturing Labor-Hours	Number of Employees	Square Feet of Floor Space Occupied	Manufacturing Labor-Hours	Number of Requisitions
Building and grounds	0	0	0	0	0
Personnel[a]	0	0	2,000	0	0
General plant administration	0	35	7,000	0	0
Cafeteria: operating loss	0	10	4,000	1,000	0
Storeroom	0	5	7,000	1,000	0
Machining	5,000	50	30,000	8,000	2,000
Assembly	15,000	100	50,000	17,000	1,000
Total	20,000	200	100,000	27,000	3,000

[a]Basis used is number of employees.

Required

1. Using the step-down method, allocate support-department costs. Develop overhead rates per direct manufacturing labor-hour for machining and assembly. Allocate the costs of the support departments in the order given in this problem. Use the allocation base for each support department you think is most appropriate.
2. Using the direct method, rework requirement 1.
3. Based on the following information about two jobs, determine the total overhead costs for each job by using rates developed in (a) requirement 1 and (b) requirement 2.

	Direct Manufacturing Labor-Hours	
	Machining	**Assembly**
Job 88	18	2
Job 89	3	17

4. The company evaluates the performance of the operating department managers on the basis of how well they managed their total costs, including allocated costs. As the manager of the Machining Department, which allocation method would you prefer from the results obtained in requirements 1 and 2? Explain.

15-32 Support-department cost allocations; single-department cost pools; direct, step-down, and reciprocal methods. The Manes Company has two products. Product 1 is manufactured entirely in Department X. Product 2 is manufactured entirely in Department Y. To produce these two products, the Manes Company has two support departments: A (a materials-handling department) and B (a power-generating department).

An analysis of the work done by departments A and B in a typical period follows:

	Used By			
Supplied By	**A**	**B**	**X**	**Y**
A	—	100	250	150
B	500	—	100	400

The work done in Department A is measured by the direct labor-hours of materials-handling time. The work done in Department B is measured by the kilowatt-hours of power. The budgeted costs of the support departments for the coming year are:

	Department A (Materials Handling)	**Department B (Power Generation)**
Variable indirect labor and indirect materials costs	$ 70,000	$10,000
Supervision	10,000	10,000
Depreciation	20,000	20,000
	$100,000	$40,000
	+ Power costs	+ Materials-handling costs

The budgeted costs of the operating departments for the coming year are $1,500,000 for Department X and $800,000 for Department Y.

Supervision costs are salary costs. Depreciation in Department B is the straight-line depreciation of power-generation equipment in its nineteenth year of an estimated 25-year useful life; it is old, but well-maintained, equipment.

Required

1. What are the allocations of costs of support departments A and B to operating departments X and Y using (a) the direct method, (b) the step-down method (allocate Department A first), (c) the step-down method (allocate Department B first), and (d) the reciprocal method?
2. An outside company has offered to supply all the power needed by the Manes Company and to provide all the services of the present power department. The cost of this service will be $40 per kilowatt-hour of power. Should Manes accept? Explain.

15-33 Common costs. Jason Miller and Eric Jackson would like to lease an office building to open their separate law offices. The building has a total of 1,500 square feet of office space. Miller and Jackson need 900 square feet and 600 square feet, respectively. If each rents the space on his own, the rent will be $1 per square foot. If they rent the space together, the rent will decrease to $0.80 per square foot.

Required

1. Calculate Miller and Jackson's respective share of rent under the stand-alone cost-allocation method.
2. Calculate Miller and Jackson's respective share of rent using the incremental cost-allocation method. Assume Miller to be the primary party.
3. Calculate Miller and Jackson's respective share of rent using the Shapely value method.
4. Which method would you recommend Miller and Jackson use to share the rent?

15-34 Revenue allocation, bundled products. Pebble Resorts operates a five-star hotel with a world-recognized championship golf course. It has a decentralized management structure. There are three divisions:

- Lodging (rooms, conference facilities)
- Food (restaurants and in-room service)
- Recreation (golf course, tennis courts, and so on)

Starting next month, Pebble Resorts will offer a two-day, two-person "getaway package" deal for $700. This deal includes:

- Two nights' stay for two in an ocean-view room—separately priced at $640 ($320 per night for two).
- Two rounds of golf—separately priced at $300 ($150 per round). One person can do two rounds, or two people can do one round each.
- Candlelight dinner for two at the exclusive Pebble Pacific Restaurant—separately priced at $160 ($80 per person).

Samantha Lee, president of the Recreation Division, recently asked the CEO of Pebble Resorts how her division would share in the $700 revenue from the package. The golf course was operating at 100% capacity. Under the getaway-package rules, participants who booked one week in advance were guaranteed access to the golf course. Lee noted that every "getaway" booking would displace $300 of golf bookings. She emphasized that the high demand reflected the devotion of her team to keeping the golf course rated in the "Best 10 Courses in the World" listings in *Golf Monthly*. As an aside, she also noted that the Lodging and Food divisions only had to turn away customers on "peak-season events such as the New Year's period."

Required

1. Using selling prices, allocate the $700 getaway-package revenue to the three divisions using:
   a. The stand-alone revenue-allocation method
   b. The incremental revenue-allocation method (with Recreation first, then Lodging, and then Food)
2. What are the pros and cons of the two methods in requirement 1?

15-35 Revenue allocation, bundled products, additional complexities (continuation of 15-34). The individual items in the getaway-package deal at Pebble Resorts are not fully used by each guest. Assume that in the first month 10% of the getaway-package users do not use the golfing option, and 5% do not use the food option. The lodging option has a 100% usage rate.

Required

How should Pebble Resorts recognize this nonuse factor in its revenue sharing of the $700 package across the Lodging, Food, and Recreation divisions? Explain.

15-36 Overhead-allocation disputes, ethics. (Suggested by Howard Wright) American Dynamics is a contractor that builds U.S. Navy vessels and commercial vessels on a cost-plus-fixed-fee basis. Its costing system contains two direct-cost categories—direct materials and direct labor—and one indirect-cost category—General Yard overhead—which includes the cost of purchasing activities. Indirect costs are allocated on the basis of direct labor costs. Government auditors periodically examine all defense contractors' records.

In 2007, American Dynamics reported a total direct-labor cost of $150 million: $50 million for Navy contracts and $100 million for commercial contracts. General Yard overhead was $30 million. The $50 million of the Navy's direct labor costs included the $5 million cost of a special expediting (SE) group within the central purchasing group; the SE group worked exclusively on a nuclear submarine contract for the U.S. Navy. Upon examination of the records for that year, the government auditors demanded a refund of $689,658. They pointed to the following provision in the naval contract:

> Par. 15-202. Direct Costs
>
> (a) A direct cost is any cost that can be identified specifically with a particular cost object. Direct costs are not limited to items that are incorporated in the end product such as material or labor. Costs identified specifically with the contract are direct costs of the contract and are to be charged directly thereto. Costs identified specifically with other work of the contractor are direct costs of that work and are not to be charged to the contract directly or indirectly. When items ordinarily chargeable as indirect costs are charged to the contract as direct costs, the cost of like items applicable to other work must be eliminated from indirect costs allocated to the contract.

The SE cost of $5 million was not included in the General Yard overhead. The auditors claimed that SE costs were direct costs but not part of direct labor costs and, therefore, no overhead should have been allocated to the SE costs.

Required

1. Show calculations to explain how the auditors arrived at a refund of $689,658 on Naval contracts.
2. Suppose that Roxy Marden, manager of the Commercial Division, also knows that $4 million of the General Yard overhead was caused exclusively by purchasing activities related to commercial vessels. Marden knows that if the government auditors discover this, they will insist that it be reclassified as a direct cost of commercial contracts, but not as direct labor.
   a. Compute the additional refund that the government auditors could claim.
   b. Commercial-vessel construction is a very competitive industry. Marden's performance as a manager is partly dependent on her ability to meet agreed-upon cost targets and, hence, to retain commercial customers. What should Marden do?

Collaborative Learning Exercise

15-37 Allocating costs of support departments; dual rates; direct, step-down, and reciprocal methods. Magnum T.A., Inc., specializes in the assembly and installation of high-quality security systems for the home and business segments of the market. The four departments at its highly automated state-of-the-art assembly plant are:

Service Departments	Assembly Departments
Engineering Support	Home Security Systems
Information Systems Support	Business Security Systems

The budgeted level of service relationships, which is at practical capacity, for 2007 is:

	Used By			
Supplied By	**Engineering Support**	**Information Systems Support**	**Home Security Systems**	**Business Security Systems**
Engineering Support	—	10%	40%	50%
Information Systems Support	20%	—	30%	50%

The actual level of service relationships for 2007 is:

	Used By			
Supplied By	**Engineering Support**	**Information Systems Support**	**Home Security Systems**	**Business Security Systems**
Engineering Support	—	15%	30%	55%
Information Systems Support	25%	—	15%	60%

Magnum collects fixed costs and variable costs for each department in separate cost pools. The actual costs in each pool for 2007 are:

	Fixed Cost Pool	Variable Cost Pool
Engineering Support	$2,700,000	$8,500,000
Information Systems Support	8,000,000	3,750,000

Fixed costs are allocated on the basis of budgeted level of service. Variable costs are allocated on the basis of the actual level of service.

The support-department costs allocated to each assembly department are allocated to products on the basis of units assembled. The units assembled in each department during 2007 are:

Home Security Systems	7,950 units
Business Security Systems	3,750 units

Required

1. Allocate the support-department costs to the assembly departments using the dual-rate method and (a) the direct method, (b) the step-down method (allocate Information Systems Support first), (c) the step-down method (allocate Engineering Support first), (d) the reciprocal method (use linear equations), and (e) the reciprocal method (use repeated iterations). Present results in a format similar to Exhibit 15-7 (p. 553).
2. Compare the support-department costs allocated to each Home Security System unit assembled and each Business Security System unit assembled under (a), (b), (c), (d), and (e) in requirement 1.
3. What factors might explain why the reciprocal method is not more widely used in practice?
4. Refer to the results obtained in requirements 1 and 2. Which alternative would be preferred by the manager of Home Security Systems? Explain.

WWW

Get Connected: Cost Accounting in the News

Go to www.prenhall.com/horngren/cost12e for additional online exercise(s) that explore issues affecting the accounting world today. These exercises offer you the opportunity to analyze and reflect on how cost accounting helps managers to make better decisions and handle the challenges of strategic planning and implementation.

CHAPTER 15 Case

STANFORD UNIVERSITY: Indirect-Cost Allocation, Indirect-Cost Recovery[a]

In 1990, an extensive audit was conducted on Stanford University's cost allocations for federally funded research. The federal government follows a policy of reimbursing universities for the full costs of conducting federally sponsored research. In a statement to investigators, Stanford President Donald Kennedy provided some historical perspective:

> After WWII, the United States made the decision to convert its wartime research efforts into a greatly expanded basic research program located in our universities, where the training of the next generation of scientists takes place. Originally, federal support of basic research in universities developed along the lines of an "assistance model"; academic scientists wanted to work on fundamental problems and the government (in the first instance, the Office of Naval Research) wanted to get it done. . . . Federal support for university research has made possible an extraordinarily broad array of valuable advances in fields from microbiology to engineering, from particle physics to genetics. At Stanford, federal research support has played a critical role in stunning advances, including such non-invasive technologies as magnetic resonance imaging; the discovery of the first reliable cure for Hodgkin's disease; . . . and a series of basic discoveries essential to modern genetic engineering.[b]

Indirect Cost Recovery

Specific governmental guidelines existed for determination of costs eligible for indirect-cost recovery for research activities. Office of Management and Budget (OMB) Circular A-21, titled "Cost Principles for Educational Institutions," establishes:

> . . . principles for determining the costs applicable to research and development, training, and other sponsored work performed by colleges and universities under grants, contracts, and other agreements with the federal government. The cost of a sponsored agreement is comprised of the allowable direct costs incident to its performance, plus the allocable portion of the allowable indirect costs of the institution.
>
> Direct costs are those costs that can be identified specifically with a particular sponsored project, an instructional activity, or any other institutional activity; or that can be directly assigned to such activities relatively easily with a high degree of accuracy. Indirect costs are those that are incurred for common or joint objectives and therefore cannot be identified readily and specifically with a particular sponsored project. Identification with the sponsored work rather than the nature of the goods or services involved is the determining factor in distinguishing direct from indirect costs of a sponsored project. At educational institutions, such [indirect] costs normally are classified under the following indirect cost categories: depreciation and use allowances, general administration and general expenses, sponsored projects administration expenses, operations and maintenance expenses, library expenses, departmental administration expenses, and student administration and services.
>
> A cost is allocable to a particular cost objective . . . if the goods or services involved are chargeable or assignable to such cost objective in accordance with relative benefits received or other equitable relationship. The test of allowability of costs under these principles are: (a) they must be reasonable; (b) they must be allocable to sponsored agreements under the principles and methods provided herein; (c) they must be given consistent treatment through application of those generally accepted accounting principles appropriate to the circumstances; and (d) they must conform to any limitations or exclusions set forth in these principles or in the sponsored agreement as to types or amounts of cost items.[c]

Unless a university and its cognizant government agency agree on a different method of cost determination, the methodology in the circular applies. Indirect-cost rates are negotiated each year between universities and their cognizant federal agencies, such as the National Institutes of Health and the National Science Foundation. The agencies are also responsible for auditing university contracts. The Department of Defense (DoD) is the cognizant agency for Stanford, with its Office of Naval Research (ONR) negotiating cost rates and the Defense Contract Audit Agency (DCAA) conducting audits.

Stanford's 1988–1989 operating expenses were about $355 million. In that year, Stanford received $78 million in indirect-cost reimbursement from the government. Some of the indirect-cost pools included for reimbursement were economy-class air travel related to a specific research project; depreciation on the university's yacht *Victoria*; alcoholic beverages and entertainment costs; advertising; organized fund-raising costs; costs of books and periodicals purchased for campus libraries; alumni activities; investment management; operation, renovation, and depreciation of university-owned houses; and public relations.

Stanford deducted a certain percentage (say, 20%) from the indirect-cost pools to adjust for the amounts included in the cost pools that are unallowable or unallocable to government contracts. It then allocated the remaining amount in the indirect-cost pool to government-sponsored research contracts on the basis of its agreement with the government.

QUESTIONS

1. Why does the federal government engage in cost-plus contracting rather than seek competitive bids for sponsored research?
2. During the audit, there was a review of the costs that fall under Circular A-21. As defined in this case, distinguish between:
   a. Direct and indirect costs
   b. Allocable and unallocable costs
3. There are four possible combinations of the terms above (for example, indirect, allocable costs). Use the table column layout below to categorize the costs given in the next-to-last paragraph in the case.

Example	Direct or Indirect	Allocable or Unallocable	Explanation

4. Why does the federal government pay indirect costs of sponsored research?

[a]Case summary prepared from the entire case on Stanford University by Steven Huddart, copyright 1992 by the Board of Trustees of the Leland Stanford Junior University.

[b]Donald Kennedy, in a statement to the Congressional Subcommittee on Oversight and Investigations (March 13, 1991).

[c]Excerpts from Office of Management and Budget Circular A-21, "Cost Principles for Educational Institutions" (March, 1979).

CHAPTER 16

COST ALLOCATION: JOINT PRODUCTS AND BYPRODUCTS

LEARNING OBJECTIVES

1. Identify the splitoff point in a joint-cost situation
2. Distinguish joint products from byproducts
3. Explain why joint costs are allocated to individual products
4. Allocate joint costs using four methods
5. Explain why the sales value at splitoff method is preferred when allocating joint costs
6. Explain why joint costs are irrelevant in a sell-or-process-further decision
7. Account for byproducts using two methods

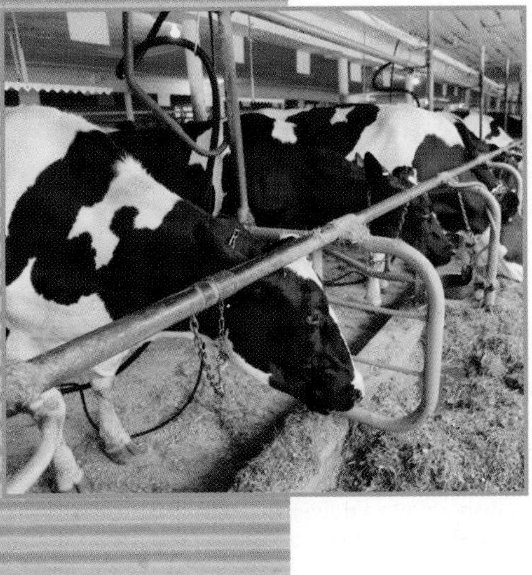

Jessica Brady is proud of the dairy-milk farm her family had been successfully running since 1967. Jessica recently took over as CEO of Farmers' Dairy from her father, and she is intent on managing and growing the commercial operation.

As Jessica studied the May 2007 financial statements, she wondered if something was amiss. Profits had declined from the previous month. Concerned, she called her management accountant, Troy Allen, and asked to meet with him.

Jessica: Troy, as I was looking over these statements, I noticed that the value of the liquid skim inventory declined even though the quantity of that inventory had not declined. Did this contribute to the lower profits we earned in May?

Troy: As a matter of fact, it did. As we process raw milk to jointly produce cream and liquid skim, we allocate joint costs of production to the two products using the sales value of the two products produced. The price of liquid skim dropped in May, and unfortunately we had a lot of inventory on hand. As a result, we earned less on the liquid skim we sold, but we also carried forward lower joint costs in the liquid-skim inventory.

Jessica: I recall you once telling me that there are other methods we could use to allocate joint production costs but that you like our current method best. Does our choice of method affect any of the decisions we make?

Troy: No, the allocation of joint costs to cream and liquid skim is irrelevant for all the decisions we make but we need to ensure that the evaluation of a manager's performance is consistent with the manager's decision model. Otherwise, managers may not make the desired decisions.

Jessica: Good. I was just reading an article about how companies sometimes treat one of their products as a byproduct in their accounting system. What's that all about?

Troy: For a product to be a byproduct, it must have a low total sales value compared with the main product. This is not the case for our products. Accounting for byproducts differs from what we do. How about this—I'll put together a brief memo explaining these issues if you'd like.

Jessica: I would really like that. Thanks, Troy.

Many companies such as Dole, Nally & Gibson Georgetown Quarries, and ExxonMobil produce two or more products simultaneously, using the same processes. For example, in its pineapple-processing plant, Dole produces multiple products, such as rings, juice, and crushed pineapple, from each pineapple processed. Nally & Gibson mines limestone rock to produce crushed rock for athletic track beds, small stones for highway construction, and larger rocks for landscaping use. ExxonMobil produces crude oil, natural gas, and raw liquified petroleum gas (LPG) from petroleum. This chapter examines methods for allocating costs to joint products. We also examine how cost numbers appropriate for one purpose, such as external reporting, may not be appropriate for other purposes, such as decisions about the further processing of joint products. This chapter provides yet another illustration of the different-costs-for-different purposes theme that underlies cost accounting.

Joint-Cost Basics

1

Identify the splitoff point in a joint-cost situation

... the point at which two or more products become separately identifiable

Joint costs are the costs of a production process that yields multiple products simultaneously. Consider the distillation of coal, which yields coke, natural gas, and other products. The cost of this distillation is a joint cost. The **splitoff point** is the juncture in a joint production process when two or more products become separately identifiable. An example is the point at which coal becomes coke, natural gas, and other products. **Separable costs** are all costs—manufacturing, marketing, distribution, and so on—incurred beyond the splitoff point that are assignable to each of the specific products identified at the splitoff point. At or beyond the splitoff point, decisions relating to the sale or further processing of each identifiable product can be made independently of decisions about the other products.

Industries abound in which a production process simultaneously yields two or more products, either at the splitoff point or after further processing. Exhibit 16-1 presents examples of joint-cost situations in diverse industries. In each of these examples, no individual product can be produced without the accompanying products appearing, although in some cases the proportions can be varied. The focus of joint costing is on allocating costs to individual products at the splitoff point. In preceding chapters we emphasized allocating costs to individual products as assembly occurs.

Main Products, Joint Products, and Byproducts

2

Distinguish joint products

... products with high sales values

from byproducts

... products with low sales values

The outputs of a joint production process can be classified into two general categories: outputs with a positive sales value and outputs with a zero sales value.[1] For example, offshore processing of hydrocarbons yields oil and natural gas, which have positive sales value, and it also yields water, which has zero sales value and is recycled back into the ocean. The term **product** describes any output that has a positive total sales value (or an output that enables a company to avoid incurring costs, such as an intermediate chemical product used as input in another process). The total sales value can be high or low.

EXHIBIT 16-1

Examples of Joint-Cost Situations

Industry	Separable Products at the Splitoff Point
Agriculture and Food Processing	
Cocoa beans	Cocoa butter, cocoa powder, cocoa drink mix, tanning cream
Lambs	Lamb cuts, tripe, hides, bones, fat
Hogs	Bacon, ham, spare ribs, pork roast
Raw milk	Cream, liquid skim
Lumber	Lumber of varying grades and shapes
Turkeys	Breast, wings, thighs, drumsticks, digest, feather meal, and poultry meal
Extractive Industries	
Coal	Coke, gas, benzol, tar, ammonia
Copper ore	Copper, silver, lead, zinc
Petroleum	Crude oil, natural gas, raw LPG
Salt	Hydrogen, chlorine, caustic soda
Chemical Industries	
Raw LPG (liquefied petroleum gas)	Butane, ethane, propane
Crude oil	Gasoline, kerosene, benzene, naphtha
Semiconductor Industry	
Fabrication of silicon-wafer chips	Memory chips of different quality (as to capacity), speed, life expectancy, and temperature tolerance

[1]Some outputs of a joint production process have "negative" revenue when their disposal costs (such as the costs of handling nonsalable toxic substances that require special disposal procedures) are considered. These disposal costs should be added to the joint production costs that are allocated to joint or main products.

When a joint production process yields one product with a high total sales value, compared with total sales values of other products of the process, that product is called a **main product**. When a joint production process yields two or more products with high total sales values compared with the total sales values of other products, if any, those products are called **joint products**. The products of a joint production process that have low total sales values compared with the total sales value of the main product or of joint products are called **byproducts**.

Consider some examples. If timber (logs) is processed into standard lumber and wood chips, standard lumber is a main product and wood chips are the byproduct. That's because standard lumber has a high total sales value compared with wood chips. If, however, logs are processed into fine-grade lumber, standard lumber, and wood chips, fine-grade lumber and standard lumber are joint products, and wood chips are the byproduct. That's because both fine-grade lumber and standard lumber have high total sales values when compared with wood chips.

Distinctions among main products, joint products, and byproducts are not so definite in practice. For example, some companies may classify kerosene obtained when refining crude oil as a byproduct because they believe kerosene has a low total sales value relative to the total sales values of gasoline and other products. Other companies may classify kerosene as a joint product because they believe kerosene has a high total sales value relative to the total sales values of gasoline and other products. Moreover, the classification of products—main, joint, or byproduct—can change over time, especially for products such as lower-grade semiconductor chips, whose market prices can increase or decrease by, say, 30% or more in a year. When prices of lower-grade chips are high, they are considered joint products together with higher-grade chips; when prices of lower-grade chips fall considerably, they are considered byproducts. Be sure you understand how a specific company classifies products and uses terms.

Why Allocate Joint Costs?

3

Explain why joint costs are allocated to individual products

. . . to calculate cost of goods sold and inventory, and for reimbursements under cost-plus contracts and other types of claims

Some of the contexts that require joint costs to be allocated to individual products or services are:

- Computation of inventoriable costs and cost of goods sold for financial accounting purposes and reports for income tax authorities
- Computation of inventoriable costs and cost of goods sold for internal reporting purposes (Such reports are used in division-profitability analysis, and they affect evaluation of division managers' performance.)
- Cost reimbursement for companies that have a few, but not all, of their products or services reimbursed under cost-plus contracts with, say, a government agency
- Insurance-settlement computations for damage claims made on the basis of cost information of jointly produced products
- Rate regulation for one or more of the jointly produced products or services that are subject to price regulation[2]
- Litigation in which costs of joint products are key inputs

Approaches to Allocating Joint Costs

4

Allocate joint costs using four methods

. . . sales value at splitoff, physical measure, net realizable value (NRV), and constant gross-margin percentage NRV

Two approaches are used to allocate joint costs.

- **Approach 1.** Allocate joint costs using *market-based* data such as revenues. This chapter illustrates three methods that use this approach:
  1. Sales value at splitoff method
  2. Net realizable value (NRV) method
  3. Constant gross-margin percentage NRV method
- **Approach 2.** Allocate joint costs using *physical measures,* such as the weight (say, kilograms) or volume (say, cubic feet) of the joint products.

[2]See J. Crespi and J. Harris, "Joint Cost Allocation Under the Natural Gas Act: An Historical Review," *Journal of Extractive Industries Accounting 2* (2): 133–142. Also see International Accounting Standards Committee Foundation, *IASC Issues Paper: Extractive Industries* (London, United Kingdom: IASB, 2000).

In preceding chapters, we used the cause-and-effect and benefits-received criteria for guiding cost-allocation decisions (see Exhibit 14-2, p. 495). Joint costs do not have a cause-and-effect relationship with individual products because the production process simultaneously yields multiple products. Using the benefits-received criterion leads to a preference for methods under approach 1 because revenues are, in general, a better indicator of benefits received than physical measures. Mining companies, for example, receive more benefits from 1 ton of gold than they do from 10 tons of coal.

In the simplest joint production process, the joint products are sold at the splitoff point without further processing. Example 1 illustrates the two methods that apply in this case: the sales value at splitoff method and the physical-measure method. Then we introduce joint production processes that yield products that require further processing beyond the splitoff point. Example 2 illustrates the NRV method and the constant-gross margin percentage NRV method. To help you focus on key concepts, we use numbers and amounts in all examples in this chapter that are much smaller than the numbers that are typically found in practice.

The exhibits in this chapter use the following symbols to distinguish a joint or main product from a byproduct:

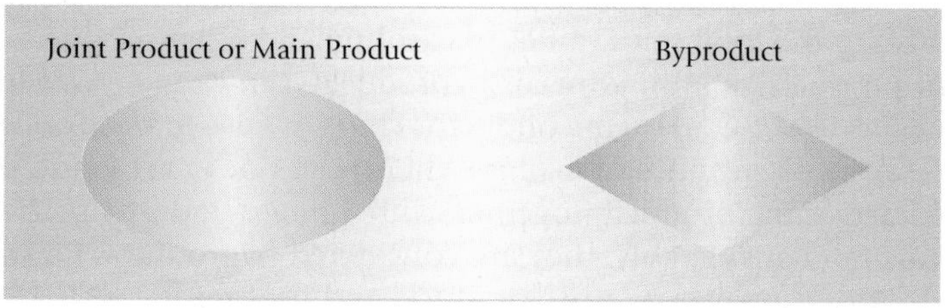

To compare methods, we report gross-margin percentages for individual products under each method.

Example 1: Farmers' Dairy purchases raw milk from individual farms and processes it until the splitoff point, when two products—cream and liquid skim—emerge. These two products are sold to an independent company, which markets and distributes them to supermarkets and other retail outlets.

In May 2007, Farmers' processes 110,000 gallons of raw milk. During processing, 10,000 gallons are lost due to evaporation, spillage, and the like, yielding 25,000 gallons of cream and 75,000 gallons of liquid skim. Summary data follow.

	A	B	C
1		**Joint Costs**	
2	Joint costs (costs of 110,000 gallons raw milk and processing to splitoff point)	$400,000	
3			
4		**Cream**	**Liquid Skim**
5	Beginning inventory (gallons)	0	0
6	Production (gallons)	25,000	75,000
7	Sales (gallons)	20,000	30,000
8	Ending inventory (gallons)	5,000	45,000
9	Selling price per gallon	$ 8	$ 4

Exhibit 16-2 depicts the basic relationships in this example.

How much of the $400,000 joint costs should be allocated to the cost of goods sold of 20,000 gallons of cream and 30,000 gallons of liquid skim, and how much should be allocated to the ending inventory of 5,000 gallons of cream and 45,000 gallons of liquid skim? In the following sections we illustrate how the sales value at splitoff method and the physical-measure method allocate the $400,000 in joint costs to joint products.

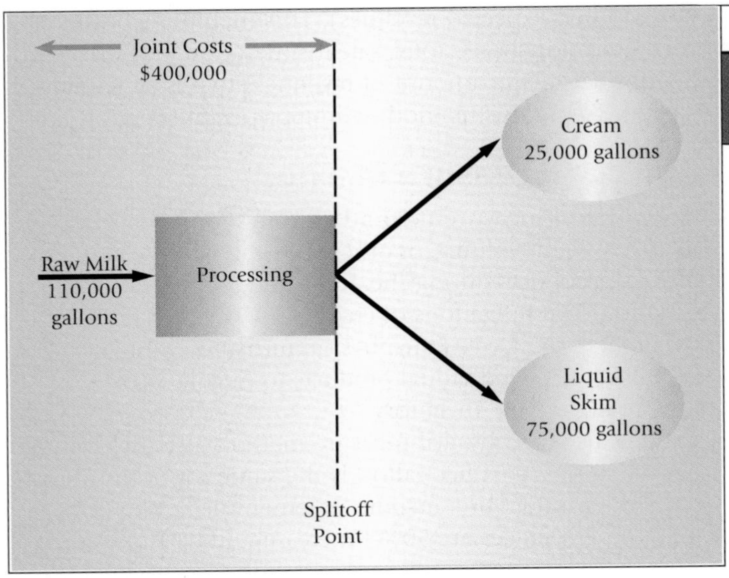

EXHIBIT 16-2

Example 1: Overview of Farmers' Dairy

Sales Value at Splitoff Method

The **sales value at splitoff method** allocates joint costs to joint products on the basis of the relative total sales value at the splitoff point of the total production of these products during the accounting period. Using this method for Example 1, Exhibit 16-3, Panel A, shows how joint costs are allocated to individual products to calculate cost per gallon of cream and liquid skim for valuing ending inventory. This method uses the sales value of the *entire production of the accounting period* (25,000 gallons of cream and 75,000 gallons of liquid skim), not just the quantity sold (20,000 gallons of cream and 30,000 gallons of liquid skim). The reason is that the joint costs were incurred on all units produced, not just the portion sold during the current period. Exhibit 16-3, Panel B, presents the product-line income statement using the sales value at splitoff method. Note that the sales value at splitoff method allocates joint costs to each product in proportion to sales value of total production (cream: $160,000 ÷ $200,000 = 80%; liquid skim: $240,000 ÷ $300,000 = 80%). Therefore, the gross-margin percentage for each product manufactured in May 2007 is the same: 20%.[3]

Note how the sales value at splitoff method follows the benefits-received criterion of cost allocation: Costs are allocated to products in proportion to their revenue-generating

The gross-margin percentages of the individual products are always equal under the sales value at splitoff method when (1) there are no beginning inventories and (2) all products are sold at the splitoff point.

EXHIBIT 16-3 **Joint-Cost Allocation and Product-Line Income Statement Using Sales Value at Splitoff Method: Farmers' Dairy for May 2007**

	A	B	C	D
1	**PANEL A: Allocation of Joint Costs Using Sales Value at Splitoff Method**	**Cream**	**Liquid Skim**	**Total**
2	Sales value of total production at splitoff point			
3	(25,000 gallons x $8 per gallon; 75,000 gallons x $4 per gallon)	$200,000	$300,000	$500,000
4	Weighting ($200,000 ÷ $500,000; $300,000 ÷ $500,000)	0.40	0.60	
5	Joint costs allocated (0.40 x $400,000; 0.60 x $400,000)	$160,000	$240,000	$400,000
6	Joint production cost per gallon			
7	($160,000 ÷ 25,000 gallons; $240,000 ÷ 75,000 gallons)	$ 6.40	$3.20	
8				
9	**PANEL B: Product-Line Income Statement Using Sales Value at Splitoff Method for May 2007**	**Cream**	**Liquid Skim**	**Total**
10	Revenues (20,000 gallons x $8 per gallon; 30,000 gallons x $4 per gallon)	$160,000	$120,000	$280,000
11	Cost of goods sold (joint costs)			
12	Production costs (0.40 x $400,000; 0.60 x $400,000)	160,000	240,000	400,000
13	Deduct ending inventory (5,000 gallons x $6.40 per gallon; 45,000 gallons x $3.20 per gallon)	32,000	144,000	176,000
14	Cost of goods sold (joint costs)	128,000	96,000	224,000
15	Gross margin	$ 32,000	$ 24,000	$ 56,000
16	Gross margin percentage ($32,000 ÷ $160,000; $24,000 ÷ $120,000; $56,000 ÷ $280,000)	20%	20%	20%

[3]Suppose Farmers' Dairy has beginning inventory of cream and liquid milk in May 2007. Suppose further that when this inventory is sold, Farmers' earns a gross margin different from 20%. Then the gross-margin percentage for cream and liquid skim will not be the same. The gross-margin percentage will depend on how much of the sales of each product came from beginning inventory and how much came from current-period production.

power (their expected revenues). This method is both straightforward and intuitive. The cost-allocation base (total sales value at splitoff) is expressed in terms of a common denominator (the amount of revenues) that is systematically recorded in the accounting system. To use this method, selling prices must exist for all products at the splitoff point.

Physical-Measure Method

The **physical-measure method** allocates joint costs to joint products on the basis of the relative weight, volume, or other physical measure at the splitoff point of total production of these products during the accounting period. In Example 1, the $400,000 joint costs produced 25,000 gallons of cream and 75,000 gallons of liquid skim. Using the number of gallons produced as the physical measure, Exhibit 16-4, Panel A, shows how joint costs are allocated to individual products to calculate cost per gallon of cream and liquid skim for valuing ending inventory.

Alternatively, Farmers' Dairy could have calculated cost per gallon as total joint costs of $400,000 ÷ 100,000 gallons of total production = $4 per gallon and then allocated $100,000 to cream ($4 per gallon × 25,000 gallons) and $300,000 to liquid skim ($4 per gallon × 75,000 gallons).

The physical-measure method doesn't meet any of the cost-allocation criteria—cause and effect, benefits received, fairness, or ability to bear—described in Exhibit 14-2, p. 495.

Because the physical-measure method allocates joint costs on the basis of the number of gallons, cost per gallon is the same for both products. Exhibit 16-4, Panel B, presents the product-line income statement using the physical-measure method. The gross-margin percentages are 50% for cream and 0% for liquid skim.

Under the benefits-received criterion, the physical-measure method is much less desirable than the sales value at splitoff method. That's because the physical measure of the individual products has no relationship to the revenue-generating power of the individual products. Consider a gold mine that extracts ore containing gold, silver, and lead. Use of a common physical measure (tons) would result in almost all costs being allocated to lead—the product that weighs the most but has the lowest revenue-generating power. In this case, the method of cost allocation is inconsistent with the main reason that the mining company is incurring mining costs—to earn revenues from gold and silver, not lead. When a company uses the physical-measure method in a product-line income statement, products that have a high sales value per ton—for example, gold and silver—would show a large "profit," and products that have a low sales value per ton—for example, lead—would show sizable losses.

Obtaining comparable physical measures for all products is not always straightforward. Consider the joint costs of producing oil and natural gas; oil is a liquid and gas is a vapor. To use a physical measure, the oil and gas need to be converted to the energy equivalent for oil and gas, British thermal units (BTUs). Using some physical measures to allocate joint costs may require assistance from technical personnel outside of accounting.

Determining which products of a joint process to include in a physical-measure computation can greatly affect the allocations to those products. Outputs with no sales value (such as dirt in gold mining) are always excluded. Although many more tons of dirt than gold are produced, costs are not incurred to produce outputs that have zero sales value. Byproducts are also often excluded from the denominator used in the physical-measure method because of their low sales values relative to the joint products or the main product. The general guideline for the physical-measure method is to include only the joint-product outputs in the weighting computations.

EXHIBIT 16-4 **Joint-Cost Allocation and Product-Line Income Statement Using Physical-Measure Method: Farmers' Dairy for May 2007**

	A	B	C	D
1	**PANEL A: Allocation of Joint Costs Using Physical-Measure Method**	**Cream**	**Liquid Skim**	**Total**
2	Physical measure of total production (gallons)	25,000	75,000	100,000
3	Weighting (25,000 gallons ÷ 100,000 gallons; 75,000 gallons ÷ 100,000 gallons)	0.25	0.75	
4	Joint costs allocated (0.25 x $400,000; 0.75 x $400,000)	$100,000	$300,000	$400,000
5	Joint production cost per gallon ($100,000 ÷ 25,000 gallons; $300,000 ÷ 75,000 gallons)	$ 4.00	$ 4.00	
6				
7	**PANEL B: Product-Line Income Statement Using Physical-Measure Method for May 2007**	**Cream**	**Liquid Skim**	**Total**
8	Revenues (20,000 gallons x $8 per gallon; 30,000 gallons x $4 per gallon)	$160,000	$120,000	$280,000
9	Cost of goods sold (joint costs)			
10	Production costs (0.25 x $400,000; 0.75 x $400,000)	100,000	300,000	400,000
11	Deduct ending inventory (5,000 gallons x $4 per gallon; 45,000 gallons x $4 per gallon)	20,000	180,000	200,000
12	Cost of goods sold (joint costs)	80,000	120,000	200,000
13	Gross margin	$ 80,000	$ 0	$ 80,000
14	Gross margin percentage ($80,000 ÷ $160,000; $0 ÷ $120,000; $80,000 ÷ $280,000)	50%	0%	28.6%

Net Realizable Value (NRV) Method

In many cases, products are processed beyond the splitoff point to bring them to a marketable form or to increase their value above their selling price at the splitoff point. For example, when crude oil is refined, the gasoline, kerosene, benzene, and naphtha need to be processed further before they can be sold. To illustrate, let's extend the Farmers' Dairy example.

Example 2: Assume the same data as in Example 1 except that both cream and liquid skim can be processed further:

- Cream → Buttercream: 25,000 gallons of cream are further processed to yield 20,000 gallons of buttercream at additional processing costs of $280,000. Buttercream, which sells for $25 per gallon, is used in the manufacture of butter-based products.
- Liquid Skim → Condensed Milk: 75,000 gallons of liquid skim are further processed to yield 50,000 gallons of condensed milk at additional processing costs of $520,000. Condensed milk sells for $22 per gallon.
- Sales during May 2007 were 12,000 gallons of buttercream and 45,000 gallons of condensed milk.

Exhibit 16-5, Panel A, depicts the basic relationships of how raw milk is converted into cream and liquid skim in the joint production process, and how cream is separately processed into buttercream and liquid skim is separately processed into condensed milk. Panel B shows the data for Example 2.

EXHIBIT 16-5 **Example 2: Overview of Farmers' Dairy**

PANEL A: Graphical Presentation of Process for Example 2

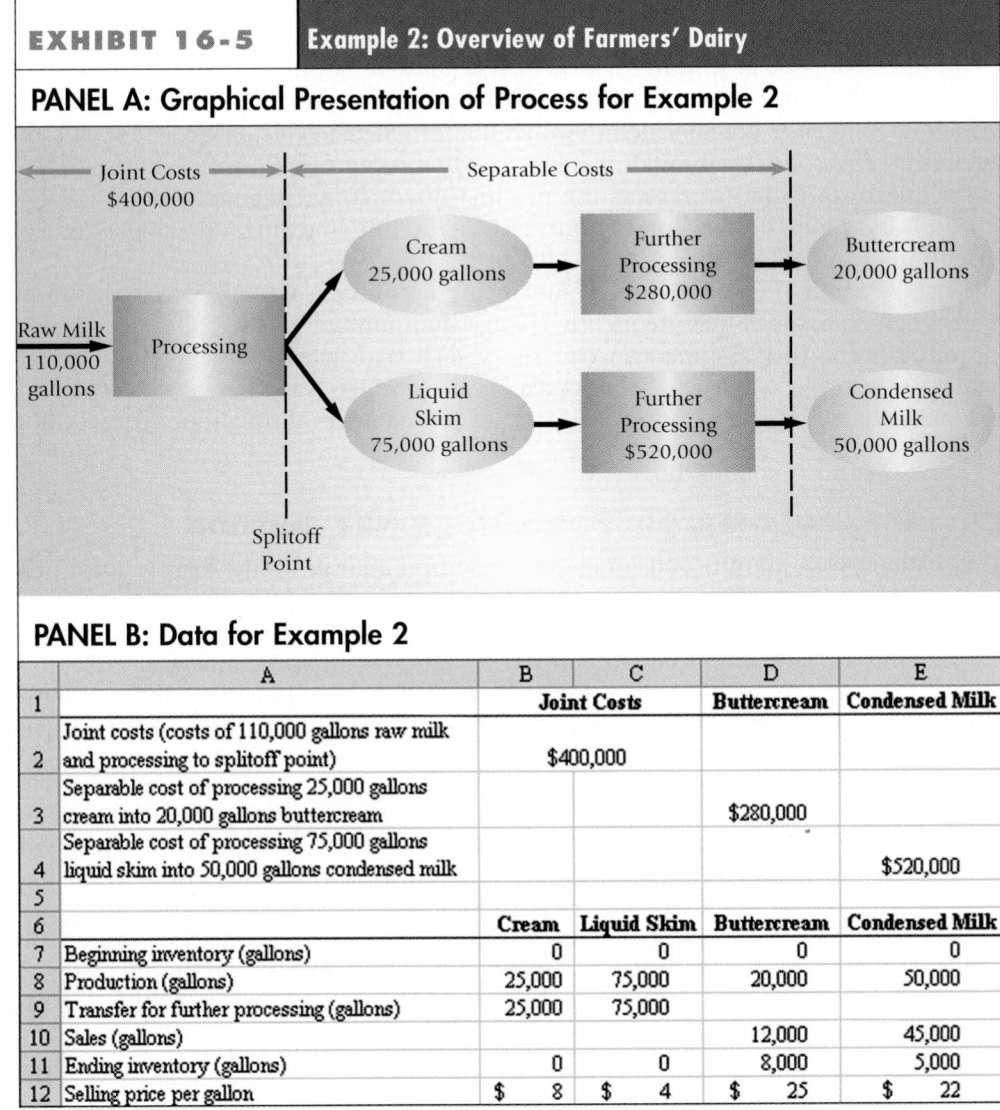

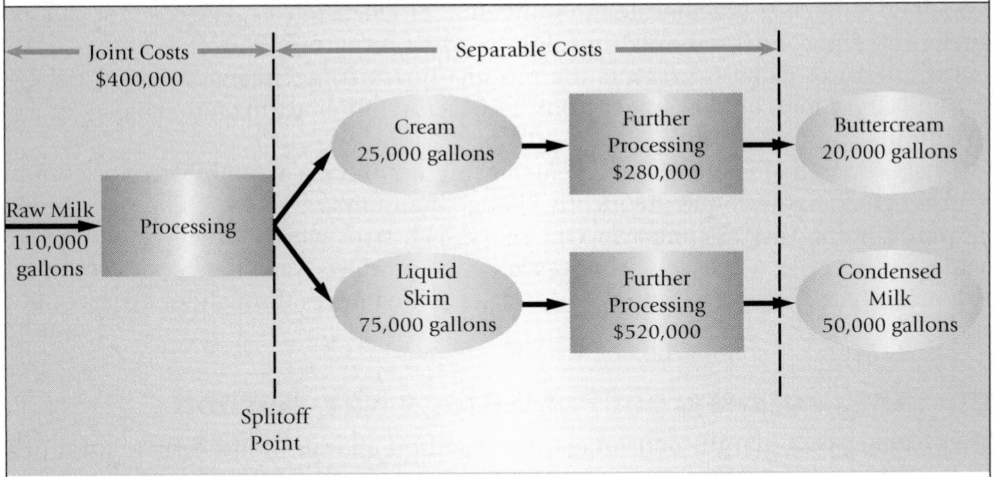

PANEL B: Data for Example 2

	A	B	C	D	E
1		Joint Costs		Buttercream	Condensed Milk
2	Joint costs (costs of 110,000 gallons raw milk and processing to splitoff point)	$400,000			
3	Separable cost of processing 25,000 gallons cream into 20,000 gallons buttercream			$280,000	
4	Separable cost of processing 75,000 gallons liquid skim into 50,000 gallons condensed milk				$520,000
5					
6		Cream	Liquid Skim	Buttercream	Condensed Milk
7	Beginning inventory (gallons)	0	0	0	0
8	Production (gallons)	25,000	75,000	20,000	50,000
9	Transfer for further processing (gallons)	25,000	75,000		
10	Sales (gallons)			12,000	45,000
11	Ending inventory (gallons)	0	0	8,000	5,000
12	Selling price per gallon	$ 8	$ 4	$ 25	$ 22

EXHIBIT 16-6 **Joint-Cost Allocation and Product-Line Income Statement Using NRV Method: Farmers' Dairy for May 2007**

	A	B	C	D
1	**PANEL A: Allocation of Joint Costs Using Net Realizable Value Method**	**Buttercream**	**Condensed Milk**	**Total**
2	Final sales value of total production during accounting period			
3	(20,000 gallons x $25 per gallon; 50,000 gallons x $22 per gallon)	$500,000	$1,100,000	$1,600,000
4	Deduct separable costs	280,000	520,000	800,000
5	Net realizable value at splitoff point	$220,000	$ 580,000	$ 800,000
6	Weighting ($220,000 ÷ $800,000; $580,000 ÷ $800,000)	0.275	0.725	
7	Joint costs allocated (0.275 x $400,000; 0.725 x $400,000)	$110,000	$ 290,000	$ 400,000
8	Production cost per gallon			
9	([$110,000 + $280,000] ÷ 20,000 gallons; [$290,000 + $520,000] ÷ 50,000 gallons)	$ 19.50	$ 16.20	
10				
11	**PANEL B: Product-Line Income Statement Using Net Realizable Value Method for May 2007**	**Buttercream**	**Condensed Milk**	**Total**
12	Revenues (12,000 gallons x $25 per gallon; 45,000 gallons x $22 per gallon)	$300,000	$ 990,000	$1,290,000
13	Cost of goods sold			
14	Joint costs (0.275 x $400,000; 0.725 x $400,000)	110,000	290,000	400,000
15	Separable costs	280,000	520,000	800,000
16	Production costs	390,000	810,000	1,200,000
17	Deduct ending inventory (8,000 gallons x $19.50 per gallon; 5,000 gallons x $16.20 per gallon)	156,000	81,000	237,000
18	Cost of goods sold	234,000	729,000	963,000
19	Gross margin	$ 66,000	$ 261,000	$ 327,000
20	Gross margin percentage ($66,000 ÷ $300,000; $261,000 ÷ $990,000; $327,000 ÷ $1,290,000)	22.0%	26.4%	25.3%

The NRV method is often used for joint products that have no market value at splitoff. This method, however, requires assumptions about events occurring beyond splitoff. In what quantities will products be produced? What will be the selling prices? How much will separable costs be?

The **net realizable value (NRV) method** allocates joint costs to joint products on the basis of relative NRV—final sales value minus separable costs—of total production of the joint products during the accounting period. The NRV method is typically used in preference to the sales value at splitoff method only when selling prices for one or more products at splitoff do not exist. Using this method for Example 2, Exhibit 16-6, Panel A, shows how joint costs are allocated to individual products to calculate cost per gallon of buttercream and condensed milk for valuing ending inventory.

Exhibit 16-6, Panel B presents the product-line income statement using the NRV method. Gross-margin percentages are 22.0% for buttercream and 26.4% for condensed milk.

The NRV method is often implemented using simplifying assumptions. For example, even though companies may frequently change the number of processing steps beyond the splitoff point, they assume a specific set of such steps when implementing the NRV method. Also, even when selling prices of joint products vary frequently, companies implement the NRV method using a given set of selling prices throughout the accounting period.

The constant gross-margin percentage NRV method works backward. For each product, the gross margin (based on the overall gross-margin percentage) and separable costs are deducted from the final sales value of units produced. The resulting dollar amount for each product is its allocation of joint costs.

Under the constant gross-margin NRV method, the gross-margin percentage for each product is the same, regardless of its separable costs. This method, in effect, "subsidizes" products with relatively high separable costs by assigning fewer joint costs to them. That's why in the Farmers' Dairy example, buttercream has a 25% gross margin under the constant gross-margin percentage NRV method (in Exhibit 16-7) but has a 22% gross-margin percentage under the NRV method (in Exhibit 16-6).

Constant Gross-Margin Percentage NRV Method

The **constant gross-margin percentage NRV method** allocates joint costs to joint products in such a way that the overall gross-margin percentage is identical for the individual products. This method entails three steps. Exhibit 16-7, Panel A, shows these three steps for allocating the $400,000 joint costs between buttercream and condensed milk in the Farmers' Dairy example to calculate the cost per gallon of buttercream and condensed milk for valuing ending inventory. As we describe each step, refer to Exhibit 16-7, Panel A, for an illustration of the step.

Step 1: Compute the overall gross-margin percentage for all joint products together. Note, Exhibit 16-7, Panel A, uses final sales value of *total production* during the accounting period—$1,600,000—*not total revenues* of the period, to calculate the overall gross-margin percentage of 25%.

Step 2: Multiply the overall gross-margin percentage by final sales values of total production for each product to calculate gross margin for each product. Subtract gross margin for each product from final sales value of production for each product to obtain total costs that each product will bear.

Step 3: Deduct separable costs from total costs that each product will bear to obtain the joint-cost allocation.

EXHIBIT 16-7 **Joint-Cost Allocation and Product-Line Income Statement Using Constant Gross-Margin Percentage NRV Method: Farmers' Dairy for May 2007**

	A	B	C	D
1	**PANEL A: Allocation of Joint Costs Using Constant Gross Margin Percentage NRV Method**			
2	**Step 1**			
3	Final sales value of total production during accounting period: (20,000 gallons x $25 per gallon) + (50,000 gallons x $22 per gallon)	$1,600,000		
4	Deduct joint and separable costs ($400,000 + $280,000 + $520,000)	1,200,000		
5	Gross margin	$ 400,000		
6	Gross margin percentage ($400,000 ÷ $1,600,000)	25%		
7		**Buttercream**	**Condensed Milk**	**Total**
8	**Step 2**			
9	Final sales value of total production during accounting period: (20,000 gallons x $25 per gallon; 50,000 gallons x $22 per gallon)	$ 500,000	$1,100,000	$1,600,000
10	Deduct gross margin, using overall gross-margin percentage (25% x $500,000; 25% x $1,100,000)	125,000	275,000	400,000
11	Total production costs	375,000	825,000	1,200,000
12	**Step 3**			
13	Deduct separable costs	280,000	520,000	800,000
14	Joint costs allocated	$ 95,000	$ 305,000	$ 400,000
15				
16	**PANEL B: Product-Line Income Statement Using Constant Gross Margin Percentage NRV Method for May 2007**	**Buttercream**	**Condensed Milk**	**Total**
17	Revenues (12,000 gallons x $25 per gallon; 45,000 gallons x $22 per gallon)	$ 300,000	$ 990,000	$1,290,000
18	Cost of goods sold			
19	Joint costs (from Panel A)	95,000	305,000	400,000
20	Separable costs	280,000	520,000	800,000
21	Production costs	375,000	825,000	1,200,000
22	Deduct ending inventory			
23	(8,000 gallons x $18.75 per gallon[a]; 5,000 gallons x $16.50 per gallon[b])	150,000	82,500	232,500
24	Cost of goods sold	225,000	742,500	967,500
25	Gross margin	$ 75,000	$ 247,500	$ 322,500
26	Gross margin percentage ($75,000 ÷ 300,000; $247,500 ÷ $990,000; $322,500 ÷ $1,290,000)	25%	25%	25%
27				
28	[a]Total production costs of buttercream ÷ Total production of buttercream = $375,000 ÷ 20,000 gallons = $18.75 per gallon.			
29	[b]Total production costs of condensed milk ÷ Total production of condensed milk = $825,000 ÷ 50,000 gallons = $16.50 per gallon.			

Some products may receive negative allocations of joint costs to bring their gross-margin percentages up to the overall average. Exhibit 16-7, Panel B, presents the product-line income statement for the constant gross-margin percentage NRV method.

The constant gross-margin percentage NRV method is different in one fundamental way from the two other market-based joint-cost-allocation methods described earlier. Recall that the sales value at splitoff method and the NRV method allocate only the joint costs to the joint products. Neither method takes account of profits earned either before or after the splitoff point when allocating the joint costs. In contrast, the constant gross-margin percentage NRV method is both a joint-cost-allocation method and a profit-allocation method. The total difference between sales value of production of all products and separable costs of all products includes both (a) joint costs and (b) total gross margin. Gross margin is allocated to the joint products under the constant gross-margin percentage NRV method to determine the joint-cost allocations so that each product has the same gross-margin percentage.

Choosing a Method

Which method of allocating joint costs should be used? Use the sales value at splitoff method when selling-price data exist at splitoff (even if further processing is done). Reasons for using the sales value at splitoff method include:

5

Explain why the sales value at splitoff method is preferred when allocating joint costs

. . . because it objectively measures the benefits received by each product

1. **Measurement of the value of the joint products at the splitoff point.** Sales value at splitoff is the best measure of the benefits received as a result of joint processing relative to all other methods of allocating joint costs. It is a meaningful basis for allocating joint costs because generating revenues is the reason why a company incurs joint costs in the first place.

2. **No anticipation of subsequent management decisions.** The sales value at splitoff method does not require information on the processing steps after splitoff, if there is further processing. In contrast, the NRV and constant gross-margin percentage NRV methods require information on (a) the specific sequence of further processing decisions, (b) the separable costs of further processing, and (c) the point at which individual products are sold.
3. **Availability of a common basis to allocate joint costs to products.** The sales value at splitoff method (as well as other market-based methods) has a common basis to allocate joint costs to products, which is revenues. In contrast, the physical-measure method may lack an easily identifiable common basis that can be used to allocate joint costs to individual products.
4. **Simplicity.** The sales value at splitoff method is simple. In contrast, the NRV and constant gross-margin percentage NRV methods can be complex for processing operations having multiple products and multiple splitoff points. This complexity is increased when management makes frequent changes in the specific sequence of post-splitoff processing decisions or in the point at which individual products are sold.

When selling prices of all products at the splitoff point are not available, the NRV method is commonly used because it attempts to approximate sales value at splitoff by subtracting separable costs incurred after the splitoff point on each product from selling prices. The NRV method assumes that all the markup or profit margin is attributable to the joint process and none of the markup is attributable to the separable costs. Profit, however, is attributable to all phases of production and marketing, not just the joint process. More of the profit may be attributable to the joint process if the separable process is relatively routine, whereas more of the profit may be attributable to the separable process if the separable process uses a special patented technology. Despite its complexities, the NRV method is used when selling prices at splitoff are not available. It is a better measure of benefits received compared with the constant gross-margin percentage NRV method or the physical-measure method (see Global Surveys of Company Practice, p. 575).

The main advantage of the constant gross-margin percentage NRV method is that it is relatively easy to implement. This method treats the joint products as though they comprise a single product by calculating an aggregate gross-margin percentage, applying this gross-margin percentage to each product, and backing into the joint costs allocated to each product. This method avoids the complexities inherent in the NRV method to measure the benefits received by each of the joint products at the splitoff point. The main issue with the constant gross-margin percentage NRV method is the assumption that all products have the same ratio of cost to sales value. A constant ratio of cost to sales value across products is very uncommon in companies that produce multiple products that do not involve joint costs.

Although there are difficulties in using the physical-measure method—such as lack of congruence with the benefits-received criterion—there are instances when it may be preferred. Consider rate regulation. Market-based measures are difficult to use in the context of rate or price regulation. It is circular reasoning to use selling prices as a basis for setting prices (rates) and at the same time use selling prices to allocate the costs on which prices (rates) are based. To avoid this circular reasoning, the physical-measure method is useful in rate regulation.

Not Allocating Joint Costs

The preceding methods for allocating joint costs to individual products are somewhat arbitrary, so some companies do not allocate joint costs to products. Instead, they carry their inventories at NRV. Income on each product is recognized when production is completed. Some industries that use variations of this no-allocation approach include meat-packing, canning, and mining.

Accountants do not ordinarily record inventories at NRV. That's because by carrying inventory at NRV, income is recognized *before* sales are made. In response, some companies using this no-allocation approach carry their inventories at NRV minus an estimated operating income margin. When any end-of-period inventories are sold in the next period, cost of goods sold will be NRV minus the estimated operating income margin on these products shown for ending inventory of the previous accounting period.

GLOBAL SURVEYS OF COMPANY PRACTICE

Joint-Cost Allocation in the Oil Patch

The petroleum industry is an example of an industry with joint costs. Petroleum mining and processing starts with hydrocarbons being extracted from either onshore or offshore fields. During this process, petroleum companies frequently obtain multiple products from the same field, such as crude oil, natural gas, and raw liquefied petroleum gas (LPG). One survey of European petroleum-producing companies found that 46% allocate joint costs to gas and oil extracted from the same field.[a] Of those companies, 33% use market-based methods, 50% use the physical-measure method, and 17% use other methods.

When LPG is extracted, it is often further processed into butane, ethane, and propane. How are these joint refining costs, which include raw LPG and processing costs, allocated to the separately marketable products produced at the refinery? A survey of American companies focused on joint-cost-allocation methods chosen by refiners for external reporting purposes:[b]

Market-based methods	
Net realizable value	46%
Other	20%
Physical-measure method	
Volume (barrels, gallons, or cubic feet)	27%
Mass (weight or molecular mass)	2%
Other	5%
	100%

Among market-based methods, the NRV method was the predominant choice. The most common other market-based choice was a variation of the NRV method in which the final sales value of each product was used as the allocation base without any deduction for the expected separable costs. This variation illustrates how companies make adjustments to the basic methods described in this chapter, often on the grounds of a perceived cost-benefit basis.

[a] Coopers & Lybrand, "Survey of Accounting Practices."
[b] R. Koester and D. Barnett, "Petroleum Refinery."
Full citations are in Appendix A at the end of the book.

Irrelevance of Joint Costs for Decision Making

6 **Explain why joint costs are irrelevant in a sell-or-process-further decision**
. . . because joint costs are the same whether or not further processing occurs

Chapter 11 introduced the concepts of *relevant revenues*—expected future revenues that differ among alternative courses of action—and *relevant costs*—expected future costs that differ among alternative courses of action. We apply these concepts to decisions on whether a joint product or main product should be sold at the splitoff point or processed further.

Sell-or-Process-Further Decisions

Consider Farmers' Dairy's decision to sell the joint products, cream and liquid skim, at the splitoff point or to further process them into buttercream and condensed milk. The decision to incur additional costs for further processing should be based on the incremental operating income attainable beyond the splitoff point. Example 2 assumed it was profitable for both cream and liquid skim to be further processed into buttercream and condensed milk, respectively. The incremental analysis for the decision to process further is:

Further Processing Cream into Buttercream	
Incremental revenues	
($25/gallon × 20,000 gallons) − ($8/gallon × 25,000 gallons)	$300,000
Deduct incremental processing costs	280,000
Increase in operating income from buttercream	$ 20,000

Further Processing Liquid Skim into Condensed Milk	
Incremental revenues	
($22/gallon × 50,000 gallons) – ($4/gallon × 75,000 gallons)	$800,000
Deduct incremental processing costs	520,000
Increase in operating income from condensed milk	$280,000

In this example, operating income increases for both products, so the manager decides to process cream into buttercream and liquid skim into condensed milk. *The $400,000 joint costs incurred before the splitoff point are irrelevant in deciding whether to process further.* That's because the joint costs of $400,000 are the same whether the products are sold at the splitoff point or processed further. The decision whether to process further should not be influenced by the total amount of joint costs; nor should it be influenced by the portion of joint costs allocated to individual products.

Incremental costs are the additional costs incurred for an activity, such as process further. *Do not assume all separable costs in joint-cost allocations are always incremental costs.* Some separable costs may be fixed costs, such as lease costs on buildings where the further processing is done; some separable costs may be sunk costs, such as depreciation on the equipment that converts cream into buttercream; and some separable costs may be allocated costs, such as corporate costs allocated to the condensed milk operations. None of these costs will differ between the alternatives of selling products at the splitoff point or processing further, therefore they are irrelevant.

Joint-Cost Allocation and Performance Evaluation

The potential conflict between cost concepts used for decision making and cost concepts used for evaluating the performance of managers could also arise in sell-or-process-further decisions. To see how, let's continue with Example 2. Suppose *allocated* fixed corporate and administrative costs of further processing cream into buttercream equal $30,000 and that these costs will be allocated only to buttercream and to the manager's product-line income statement if buttercream is produced. How might this affect the decision to process further?

As we have seen, on the basis of incremental revenues and incremental costs, Farmers' operating income will increase by $20,000 if it processes cream into buttercream. However, producing the buttercream also results in an additional charge for allocated fixed costs of $30,000. If the manager is evaluated on a full-cost basis (that is, after allocating all costs), processing cream into buttercream will lead to the manager's performance-evaluation measure being lower by $10,000 (incremental operating income, $20,000 – allocated fixed costs, $30,000). Therefore, the manager may be tempted to sell cream at splitoff and not process it into buttercream.

A similar conflict can also arise with respect to production of joint products. Consider again Example 1. Suppose Farmers' Dairy has the option of selling raw milk at a profit of $20,000. From a decision-making standpoint, Farmers' would maximize operating income by processing raw milk into cream and liquid skim because the total revenues from selling both joint products ($500,000, p. 569) exceed the joint costs ($400,000, p. 569) by $100,000. (This is greater than the $20,000 Farmers' Dairy would make if it sold the raw milk instead of processing it.) Suppose, however, the cream and liquid-skim product lines are managed by different managers, each of whom is evaluated based on a product-line income statement. If the physical-measure method of joint-cost allocation is used and the selling price per gallon of liquid skim falls below $4.00 per gallon, the liquid-skim product line will show a loss (from Exhibit 16-4, p. 570, revenues will be less than $120,000, but cost of goods sold will be unchanged at $120,000). The manager of the liquid-skim line will prefer, from his performance-evaluation standpoint, to not produce liquid skim and to sell the raw milk instead.

This conflict between decision making and performance evaluation is less severe if Farmers' uses any of the market-based methods of joint-cost allocations—sales value at splitoff, NRV, or constant gross-margin percentage NRV. That's because each of these methods allocates costs using revenues, which generally leads to a positive income for each joint product. The Focus on Values and Behaviors feature (p. 577) describes the challenges management accountants face when product managers are evaluated on product profitability after allocating joint costs.

FOCUS ON VALUES AND BEHAVIORS

MANAGEMENT ACCOUNTANTS: OVERCOMING THE PITFALLS OF ALLOCATING JOINT COSTS

When you think of companies such as Hershey Food Corporation, Oscar Mayer, ExxonMobil, and British Petroleum, perhaps the first thing that comes to mind is a chocolate bar, or a hot dog at a baseball game, or the high cost of gasoline. Chances are you don't think about the accounting challenges the management accountants at these companies face on a daily basis.

But what are the challenges? Consider the process of allocating joint costs to products. Unfortunately, this process is somewhat arbitrary, which means product managers, who are evaluated on product profitability, invariably favor joint-cost allocations that assign the lowest joint costs to their department. However, allocating joint costs in the way that product managers want may not be in the best interests of the company as a whole. Management accountants' decisions should never be influenced by product managers who might be more concerned with their own performance. Therefore, management accountants must diplomatically convey how and why joint costs are allocated and must apply these policies consistently over time.

Challenges with joint-cost allocations can also arise when two separate companies, such as British Petroleum and ExxonMobil, enter into a joint venture to produce crude oil and natural gas from petroleum, with one company processing primarily the crude oil and the other company processing primarily the natural gas. The contract terms often spell out how joint costs—such as labor and manufacturing overhead—are to be allocated. It is the responsibility of the management accountants to ensure that both sides adhere to the terms of the contract when allocating joint costs to the two companies. When circumstances arise that are not specifically covered by the contract clauses, management accountants must have the integrity to make decisions in a fair and unbiased manner.

Pricing Decisions

Should the joint costs allocated to the joint products be used in making pricing decisions for joint products? No. Why? Because there is no cause-and-effect relationship that identifies the resources demanded by each joint product that can then be used as a basis for pricing. The way it is in much of joint-costing, selling prices (through their effects on benefits received) drive joint-cost allocations. Cost allocations do not drive pricing.

Accounting for Byproducts

7

Account for byproducts using two methods

. . . recognize in financial statements at time of production or at time of sale

Distinguishing joint products from byproducts is based on the relative amounts of their total sales values, but this can be a gray area requiring the accountant's judgment.

Joint production processes may yield not only joint products and main products but byproducts as well. Although byproducts have low total sales values compared with total sales values of joint or main products, the presence of byproducts in a joint production process can affect the allocation of joint costs. Let's consider a two-product example consisting of a main product and a byproduct.

Example 3: The Westlake Corporation processes timber into fine-grade lumber and wood chips that are used as mulch in gardens and lawns. Information about these products follows:

- Fine-grade lumber (the main product)—sells for $6 per board foot (b.f.)
- Wood chips (the byproduct)—sells for $1 per cubic foot (c.f.)

Data for July 2007 are:

	Beginning Inventory	Production	Sales	Ending Inventory
Fine-grade lumber (b.f.)	0	50,000	40,000	10,000
Wood chips (c.f.)	0	4,000	1,200	2,800

Joint manufacturing costs for these products in July 2007 were $250,000, comprising $150,000 for direct materials and $100,000 for conversion costs. Both products are sold at the splitoff point without further processing, as Exhibit 16-8 shows.

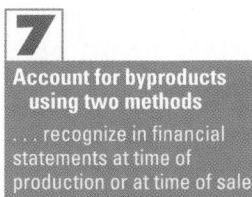

EXHIBIT 16-8

Example 3: Overview of Westlake Corporation

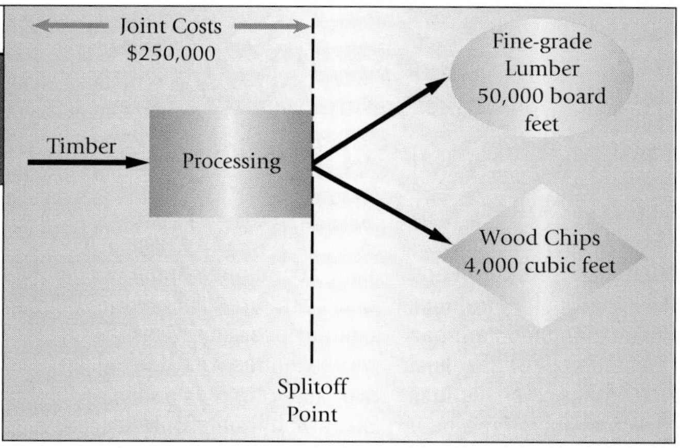

Keep in mind that both methods of accounting for byproducts satisfy GAAP because the dollar amounts of byproducts are (by definition) immaterial.

We present two byproduct accounting methods: the production method and the sales method. The production method recognizes byproducts in the financial statements at the time production is completed. The sales method delays recognition of byproducts until the time of sale.[4] Exhibit 16-9 presents the income statement of Westlake Corporation under both methods.

Production Method: Byproducts Recognized at Time Production Is Completed

This method recognizes the byproduct in the financial statements—the 4,000 cubic feet of wood chips—in the month it is produced, July 2007. The NRV from the byproduct produced is offset against the costs of the main product (see Concepts in Action, p. 580). The following journal entries illustrate the production method:

1. Work in Process	150,000	
Accounts Payable Control		150,000
To record direct materials purchased and used in production during July.		

EXHIBIT 16-9

Income Statements of Westlake Corporation for July 2007 Using the Production and Sales Methods for Byproduct Accounting

	Production Method	Sales Method
Revenues		
Main product: Fine-grade lumber (40,000 b.f. × $6 per b.f.)	$240,000	$240,000
Byproduct: Wood chips (1,200 c.f. × $1 per c.f.)	—	1,200
Total revenues	240,000	241,200
Cost of goods sold		
Total manufacturing costs	250,000	250,000
Deduct byproduct revenue (4,000 c.f. × $1 per c.f.)	4,000	—
Net manufacturing costs	246,000	250,000
Deduct main-product inventory	49,200[a]	50,000[b]
Cost of goods sold	196,800	200,000
Gross margin	$ 43,200	$ 41,200
Gross-margin percentage ($43,200 ÷ $240,000; $41,200 ÷ $241,200)	18.00%	17.08%
Inventoriable costs (end of period):		
Main product: Fine-grade lumber	$ 49,200	$ 50,000
Byproduct: Wood chips (2,800 c.f. × $1 per c.f.)[c]	2,800	0

[a](10,000 ÷ 50,000) × net manufacturing cost = (10,000 ÷ 50,000) × $246,000 = $49,200.
[b](10,000 ÷ 50,000) × total manufacturing cost = (10,000 ÷ 50,000) × $250,000 = $50,000.
[c]Recorded at selling prices.

[4]Further discussion on byproduct accounting methods is in C. Cheatham and M. Green, "Teaching Accounting for Byproducts," *Management Accounting News & Views* (Spring, 1988): 14–15; and D. Stout and D.Wygal, "Making Byproducts a Main Product of Discussion: A Challenge to Accounting Educators," *Journal of Accounting Education* (1989): 219–233. See also P. D. Marshall and R. F. Dombrowski, "A Small Business Review of Accounting for Primary Products, Byproducts and Scrap," *The National Public Accountant* (February/March 2003): 10–13.

		Dr.	Cr.
2.	Work in Process	100,000	
	Various accounts such as Wages Payable Control and Accumulated Depreciation		100,000
	To record conversion costs in the production process during July; examples include energy, manufacturing supplies, all manufacturing labor, and plant depreciation.		
3.	Byproduct Inventory—Wood Chips (4,000 c.f. × $1 per c.f.)	4,000	
	Finished Goods—Fine-grade Lumber ($250,000 – $4,000)	246,000	
	Work in Process ($150,000 + $100,000)		250,000
	To record cost of goods completed during July.		
4a.	Cost of Goods Sold [(40,000 b.f. ÷ 50,000 b.f.) × $246,000]	196,800	
	Finished Goods—Fine-grade Lumber		196,800
	To record the cost of the main product sold during July.		
4b.	Cash or Accounts Receivable (40,000 b.f. × $6 per b.f.)	240,000	
	Revenues—Fine-grade Lumber		240,000
	To record the sales of the main product during July.		
5.	Cash or Accounts Receivable (1,200 c.f. × $1 per c.f.)	1,200	
	Byproduct Inventory—Wood Chips		1,200
	To record the sales of the byproduct during July.		

The production method reports the byproduct inventory of wood chips in the balance sheet at its $1 per cubic foot selling price [(4,000 cubic feet – 1,200 cubic feet) × $1 per cubic foot = $2,800].

One variation of this method would be to report byproduct inventory at its NRV reduced by a normal profit margin ($4,000 – 20% × $4,000 = $3,200, assuming a normal profit margin of 20%[5]). When byproduct inventory is sold in a subsequent period, the income statement will match the selling price, $1,200, with the "cost" reported for the byproduct inventory, $960 (1,200 c.f./4,000 c.f. × $3,200), resulting in a byproduct operating income of $240 ($1,200 – $960).

Sales Method: Byproducts Recognized at Time of Sale

This method makes no journal entries until sale of the byproduct occurs. Revenues of the byproduct are reported as a revenue item in the income statement at the time of sale. These revenues are either grouped with other sales, included as other income, or are deducted from cost of goods sold. In the Westlake Corporation example, byproduct revenues in July 2007 are $1,200 (1,200 cubic feet × $1 per cubic foot) because only 1,200 cubic feet of wood chips are sold in July (of the 4,000 cubic feet produced). The journal entries are:

You may find that contrasting the journal entries under the two methods of accounting for byproducts is helpful in understanding the differences between the methods.

Study Tip: To check your understanding of the material in this chapter, see the Featured Exercise, true–false statements 4 and 5, multiple-choice questions 1 through 6, and Review Exercises 1 and 2 (*Student Guide*, beginning p. 213). Fully explained answers begin on p. 218.

		Dr.	Cr.
1. and 2.	Same as for the production method.		
	Work in Process	150,000	
	Accounts Payable		150,000
	Work in Process	100,000	
	Various accounts such as Wages Payable and and Accumulated Depreciation		100,000
3.	Finished Goods—Fine-grade Lumber	250,000	
	Work in Process		250,000
	To record cost of main product completed during July.		
4a.	Cost of Goods Sold [(40,000 b.f. ÷ 50,000 b.f.) × $250,000]	200,000	
	Finished Goods—Fine-grade Lumber		200,000
	To record the cost of the main product sold during July.		
4b.	Same as for the production method.		
	Cash or Accounts Receivable (40,000 b.f. × $6 per b.f.)	240,000	
	Revenues—Fine-grade lumber		240,000
5.	Cash or Accounts Receivable	1,200	
	Revenues—Wood Chips		1,200
	To record the sales of the byproduct during July.		

[5]One way to make this calculation is to assume all products have the same "normal" profit margin like the constant gross-margin percentage NRV method. Alternatively, the company might allow products to have different profit margins based on an analysis of the margins earned by other companies that sell these products individually.

CONCEPTS IN ACTION

Chicken Processing: Costing of Joint Products and Byproducts

Chicken-processing operations provide examples in which joint and byproduct costing issues arise. White breast meat, the highest revenue-generating product, is obtained from the front end of the bird; dark meat from the back end. Other edible products include chicken wings and giblets. There are many inedible products that have a diverse set of uses. For example, poultry feathers are used in bedding and sporting goods.

Poultry companies use individual-product cost information for several purposes. One purpose is in customer-profitability analysis. Customers (such as supermarkets and fast-food restaurants) differ greatly in the mix of products they purchase. Individual-product cost data enable companies to determine differences in individual-customer profitability. A subset of products is placed into frozen storage, which creates a demand for individual-product cost information for inventory valuation.

Companies differ in how they cost individual products. Consider two of the largest U.S. companies: Southern Poultry and Golden State Poultry (disguised names).

Southern Poultry classifies white breast meat as the single main product in its costing system. All other products are classified as byproducts. Selling prices of the many byproducts are used to reduce the chicken-processing costs that are allocated to the main product. White breast meat is often further processed into many individual products (such as trimmed chicken and marinated chicken). The separable cost of this further processing is added to the cost per pound of deboned white breast meat to obtain the cost of further-processed products.

Golden State Poultry classifies any product sold to a retail outlet as a joint product. Such products include breast fillets, half-breasts, thighs, whole legs, and wings. Products not sold to a retail outlet are classified as byproducts. Revenue that will be earned from byproducts is offset against the chicken-processing cost before that cost is allocated among the joint products. Average selling prices of products sold to retail outlets are used to allocate net chicken-processing cost to the individual joint products. Distribution costs of transporting the chicken products from the processing plants to retail outlets are not taken into account when determining weights for joint-cost allocation.

Source: Adapted from conversations with executives of Southern Poultry and Golden State Poultry.

Which method should a company use? The production method is the conceptually correct method. That's because it recognizes byproduct inventory in the accounting period in which it is produced and simultaneously reduces the cost of manufacturing the main or joint products. The production method better matches the revenues and expenses from selling the main product. However, the sales method is simpler and is often used in practice, primarily on the grounds that the dollar amounts of byproducts are immaterial. However, the sales method permits managers to "manage" reported earnings by timing when they sell byproducts. Managers may store byproducts for several periods and give revenues and income a "small boost" by selling byproducts accumulated over several periods when revenues and profits from the main product or joint products are low.

PROBLEM FOR SELF-STUDY

Inorganic Chemicals (IC) processes salt into various industrial products. In July 2006, IC incurred joint costs of $100,000 to purchase salt and convert it into two saleable products: caustic soda and chlorine. Although there is an active outside market for chlorine, IC processes all 800 tons of chlorine it produces into 500 tons of PVC (polyvinyl chloride), which is then sold. There were no beginning or ending inventories of salt, caustic soda, chlorine, or PVC in July. Information for July 2006 production and sales follows:

	A	B	C	D
1		Joint Costs		PVC
2	Joint costs (costs of salt and processing to split-off point)	$100,000		
3	Separable cost of processing 800 tons chlorine into 500 tons PVC			$20,000
4				
5		Caustic Soda	Chlorine	PVC
6	Beginning inventory (tons)	0	0	0
7	Production (tons)	1,200	800	500
8	Transfer for further processing (tons)		800	
9	Sales (tons)	1,200		500
10	Ending inventory (tons)	0	0	0
11	Selling price per ton in active outside market (for products not actually sold)		$ 75	
12	Selling price per ton for products sold	$ 50		$ 200

Required

1. Allocate the joint costs of $100,000 between caustic soda and chlorine under (a) the sales value at splitoff method and (b) the physical-measure method.
2. Allocate the joint costs of $100,000 between caustic soda and PVC under the NRV method.
3. What is the gross-margin percentage of (a) caustic soda and (b) PVC under the three allocation methods?
4. Lifetime Swimming Pool Products offers to purchase 800 tons of chlorine in August 2006 at $75 per ton. Assume all other production and sales data are the same for August as they were for July. This sale of chlorine to Lifetime would mean that no PVC would be produced by IC in August. How would accepting this offer affect IC's August 2006 operating income?

SOLUTION

1a. Sales value at splitoff method

	A	B	C	D
1	Allocation of Joint Costs using Sales Value at Splitoff Method	Caustic Soda	Chlorine	Total
2	Sales value of total production at splitoff point			
3	(1,200 tons x $50 per ton; 800 x $75 per ton)	$ 60,000	$ 60,000	$120,000
4	Weighting ($60,000 ÷ $120,000; $60,000 ÷ $120,000)	0.50	0.50	
5	Joint costs allocated (0.50 x $100,000; 0.50 x $100,000)	$ 50,000	$ 50,000	$100,000

1b. Physical-measure method

	A	B	C	D
8	Allocation of Joint Costs using Physical Measure Method	Caustic Soda	Chlorine	Total
9	Physical measure of total production (tons)	1,200	800	2,000
10	Weighting (1,200 tons ÷ 2,000 tons; 800 tons ÷ 2,000 tons)	0.60	0.40	
11	Joint costs allocated (0.60 x $100,000; 0.40 x $100,000)	$ 60,000	$ 40,000	$100,000

2. Net realizable value (NRV) method

	A	B	C	D
14	Allocation of Joint Costs using Net Realizable Value Method	Caustic Soda	PVC	Total
15	Final sales value of total production during accounting period			
16	(1,200 tons x $50 per ton; 500 tons x $200 per ton)	$ 60,000	$100,000	$160,000
17	Deduct separable costs to complete and sell	0	20,000	20,000
18	Net realizable value at splitoff point	$ 60,000	$ 80,000	$140,000
19	Weighting ($60,000 ÷ $140,000; $80,000 ÷ $140,000)	3/7	4/7	
20	Joint costs allocated (3/7 x $100,000; 4/7 x $100,000)	$ 42,857	$ 57,143	$100,000

3a. Gross-margin percentage of caustic soda

	A	B	C	D
23	Caustic Soda	Sales Value at Splitoff Point	Physical Measure	NRV
24	Revenues (1,200 tons x $50 per ton)	$ 60,000	$ 60,000	$ 60,000
25	Cost of goods sold (joint costs)	50,000	60,000	42,857
26	Gross margin	$ 10,000	$ 0	$ 17,143
27	Gross margin percentage ($10,000 ÷ $60,000; $0 ÷ $60,000; $17,143 ÷ $60,000)	16.67%	0.00%	28.57%

3b. Gross-margin percentage of PVC

	A	B	C	D
30	PVC	Sales Value at Splitoff Point	Physical Measure	NRV
31	Revenues (500 tons x $200 per ton)	$100,000	$100,000	$100,000
32	Cost of goods sold			
33	Joint costs	50,000	40,000	57,143
34	Separable costs	20,000	20,000	20,000
35	Cost of goods sold	70,000	60,000	77,143
36	Gross margin	$ 30,000	$ 40,000	$ 22,857
37	Gross margin percentage ($30,000 ÷ $100,000; $40,000 ÷ $100,000; $22,857 ÷ $100,000)	30.00%	40.00%	22.86%

4.

	A	B
40	Incremental revenue from processing 800 tons of chlorine into 500 tons of PVC	
41	(500 tons x $200 per ton) - (800 tons x $75 per ton)	$ 40,000
42	Incremental cost of processing 800 tons of chlorine into 500 tons of PVC	20,000
43	Incremental operating income from further processing	$ 20,000

If IC sells 800 tons of chlorine to Lifetime Swimming Pool instead of further processing it into PVC, its August 2006 operating income will be reduced by $20,000.

DECISION POINTS

The following question-and-answer format summarizes the chapter's learning objectives. Each decision presents a key question related to a learning objective. The guidelines are the answer to that question.

Decision	**Guidelines**
1. What are a joint cost and a splitoff point?	A joint cost is the cost of a single production process that yields multiple products simultaneously. The splitoff point is the juncture in a joint production process when the products become separately identifiable.
2. How do joint products differ from byproducts?	Joint products have high total sales values at the splitoff point. A byproduct has a low total sales value at the splitoff point compared with the total sales value of a joint or main product. Products can change from byproducts to joint products when their total sales values significantly increase or change from joint products to byproducts when their total sales values significantly decrease.
3. Why are joint costs allocated to individual products?	The purposes for allocating joint costs to products include inventory costing for financial accounting and internal reporting, cost reimbursement, insurance settlements, rate regulation, and product-cost litigation.

4. What methods can be used to allocate joint costs to individual products?

The methods to allocate joint costs to products are the sales value at splitoff, NRV, constant gross-margin percentage NRV, and physical-measure methods.

5. When is the sales value at splitoff method used for allocating joint costs to individual products and why?

The sales value at splitoff method is used when market prices exist at splitoff because using revenues is consistent with the benefits-received criterion, it does not anticipate subsequent management decisions on further processing, and it is simple.

6. Are joint costs relevant in a sell-or-process-further decision?

No, joint costs and how they are allocated are irrelevant in deciding whether to process further because joint costs are the same regardless of whether further processing occurs.

7. What methods can be used to account for byproducts?

The production method recognizes byproducts in financial statements at the time of production, whereas the sales method recognizes byproducts in financial statements at the time of sale. The production method is conceptually superior, but the sales method is often used in practice because dollar amounts of byproducts are immaterial.

TERMS TO LEARN

This chapter and the Glossary at the end of the book contain definitions of:

byproducts (p. 567)
constant gross-margin percentage NRV method (p. 572)
joint costs (p. 566)
joint products (p. 567)
main product (p. 567)
net realizable value (NRV) method (p. 572)
physical-measure method (p. 570)
product (p. 566)
sales value at splitoff method (p. 569)
separable costs (p. 566)
splitoff point (p. 566)

PH Grade Assist

Prentice Hall Grade Assist (PHGA)
Your professor may ask you to complete selected exercises and problems in Prentice Hall Grade Assist (PHGA). PHGA is an online tool that can help you master the chapter's topics. It provides you with multiple variations of exercises and problems designated by the PHGA icon. You can rework these exercises and problems—each time with new data—as many times as you need. You also receive immediate feedback and grading.

ASSIGNMENT MATERIAL

Questions

16-1 Give two examples of industries in which joint costs are found. For each example, what are the individual products at the splitoff point?

16-2 What is a joint cost? What is a separable cost?

16-3 Distinguish between a joint product and a byproduct.

16-4 Why might the number of products in a joint-cost situation differ from the number of outputs? Give an example.

16-5 Provide three reasons for allocating joint costs to individual products or services.

16-6 Why does the sales value at splitoff method use the sales value of the total production in the accounting period and not just the revenues from the products sold?

16-7 Describe a situation in which the sales value at splitoff method cannot be used but the NRV method can be used for joint-cost allocation.

16-8 Distinguish between the sales value at splitoff method and the NRV method.

16-9 Give two limitations of the physical-measure method of joint-cost allocation.

16-10 How might a company simplify its use of the NRV method when final selling prices can vary sizably in an accounting period and management frequently changes the point at which it sells individual products?

16-11 Why is the constant gross-margin percentage NRV method sometimes called a "joint-cost-allocation and a profit-allocation" method?

16-12 "Managers must decide whether a product should be sold at splitoff or processed further. The sales value at splitoff method of joint-cost allocation is the best method for generating the information managers need for this decision." Do you agree? Explain.

16-13 "Managers should consider only additional revenues and separable costs when making decisions about selling at splitoff or processing further." Do you agree? Explain.

16-14 Describe two major methods to account for byproducts.

16-15 Why might managers seeking a monthly bonus based on attaining a target operating income prefer the sales method of accounting for byproducts rather than the production method?

Exercises

PH Grade Assist

16-16 Joint-cost allocation, insurance settlement. Chicken Little grows and processes chickens. Each chicken is disassembled into five main parts. Information pertaining to production in July 2007 is:

Parts	Pounds of Product	Wholesale Selling Price per Pound When Production Is Complete
Breasts	100	$1.10
Wings	20	0.40
Thighs	40	0.70
Bones	80	0.20
Feathers	10	0.10

Joint cost of production in July 2007 was $100.

A special shipment of 20 pounds of breasts and 10 pounds of wings has been destroyed in a fire. Chicken Little's insurance policy provides reimbursement for the cost of the items destroyed. The insurance company permits Chicken Little to use a joint-cost-allocation method. The splitoff point is assumed to be at the end of the production process.

Required

1. Compute the cost of the special shipment destroyed using
   a. Sales value at splitoff method
   b. Physical-measure method (pounds of finished product)
2. What joint-cost-allocation method would you recommend Chicken Little use? Explain.

PH Grade Assist

16-17 Joint products and byproducts (continuation of 16-16). Chicken Little is computing the ending inventory values for its July 31, 2007, balance sheet. Ending inventory amounts on July 31 are 10 pounds of breasts, 4 pounds of wings, 3 pounds of thighs, 5 pounds of bones, and 2 pounds of feathers.

Chicken Little's management wants to use the sales value at splitoff method. However, they want you to explore the effect on ending inventory values of classifying one or more products as a byproduct rather than a joint product.

Required

1. Assume Chicken Little classifies all five products as joint products. What are the ending inventory values of each product on July 31, 2007?
2. Assume Chicken Little uses the production method of accounting for byproducts. What are the ending inventory values for each joint product on July 31, 2007, assuming breasts and thighs are the joint products and wings, bones, and feathers are byproducts?
3. Comment on differences in the results in requirements 1 and 2.

Excel Lab www.prenhall.com/horngren/cost12e

PH Grade Assist

16-18 Net realizable value method. Illana, Inc., produces two joint products—cooking oil and soap oil—from a single vegetable-oil refining process. In July 2007, Illana reported the following production and selling-price information:

	A	B	C	D
1		**Cooking Oil**	**Soap Oil**	**Joint Costs**
2	Joint costs (costs of vegetable oil and processing to splitoff point)			$24,000,000
3	Separable cost of processing beyond splitoff point	$30,000,000	$7,500,000	
4				
5	Beginning inventory (drums)	0	0	
6	Production (drums)	1,000,000	500,000	
7	Sales (drums)	1,000,000	500,000	
8	Ending inventory (drums)	0	0	
9	Selling price per drum	$ 50	$ 25	

If you want to use Excel to solve this exercise, go to the Excel Lab at **www.prenhall.com/horngren/cost12e** and download the template for Exercise 16-18.

Required

Allocate the $24,000,000 joint costs using the NRV method.

16-19 Alternative joint-cost-allocation methods, further-process decision. The Wood Spirits Company produces two products—turpentine and methanol (wood alcohol)—by a joint process. Joint costs amount to $120,000 per batch of output. Each batch totals 10,000 gallons: 25% methanol and 75% turpentine. Both products are processed further without gain or loss in volume. Separable processing costs are methanol, $3 per gallon; turpentine, $2 per gallon. Methanol sells for $21 per gallon. Turpentine sells for $14 per gallon.

Required

1. How much of the joint costs per batch will be allocated to turpentine and to methanol, assuming that joint costs are allocated on a physical-measure (number of gallons at splitoff point) basis?
2. If joint costs are allocated on an NRV basis, how much of the joint costs will be allocated to turpentine and to methanol?
3. Prepare product-line income statements per batch for requirements 1 and 2. Assume no beginning or ending inventories.
4. The company has discovered an additional process by which the methanol (wood alcohol) can be made into a pleasant-tasting alcoholic beverage. The selling price of this beverage would be $60 a gallon. Additional processing would increase separable costs $9 per gallon (in addition to the $3 per gallon separable cost required to yield methanol). The company would have to pay excise taxes of 20% on the selling price of the beverage. Assuming no other changes in cost, what is the joint cost applicable to the wood alcohol (using the NRV method)? Should the company produce the alcoholic beverage? Show your computations.

16-20 Alternative methods of joint-cost allocation, ending inventories. The Darl Company operates a simple chemical process to convert a single material into three separate items, referred to here as X, Y, and Z. All three end products are separated simultaneously at a single splitoff point.

PH Grade Assist

Products X and Y are ready for sale immediately upon splitoff without further processing or any other additional costs. Product Z, however, is processed further before being sold. There is no available market price for Z at the splitoff point.

The selling prices quoted here are expected to remain the same in the coming year. During 2007, the selling prices of the items and the total amounts sold were:

- X—120 tons sold for $1,500 per ton
- Y—340 tons sold for $1,000 per ton
- Z—475 tons sold for $700 per ton

The total joint manufacturing costs for the year were $400,000. Darl spent an additional $200,000 to finish product Z.

There were no beginning inventories of X, Y, or Z. At the end of the year, the following inventories of completed units were on hand: X, 180 tons; Y, 60 tons; Z, 25 tons. There was no beginning or ending work in process.

Required

1. Compute the cost of inventories of X, Y, and Z for balance sheet purposes and the cost of goods sold for income statement purposes as of December 31, 2007, using
   a. NRV method of joint-cost allocation
   b. Constant gross-margin percentage NRV method of joint-cost allocation
2. Compare the gross-margin percentages for X, Y, and Z using the two methods given in requirement 1.

16-21 Joint-cost allocation, process further. Sinclair Oil & Gas, a large energy conglomerate, jointly processes purchased hydrocarbons to generate three nonsaleable intermediate products: ICR8, ING4, and XGE3. These intermediate products are further processed separately to produce Crude Oil, Natural Gas Liquids (NGL) and Natural Gas (measured in liquid equivalents). An overview of the process and results for August 2007 are shown here (Note: The numbers are small to keep the focus on key concepts):

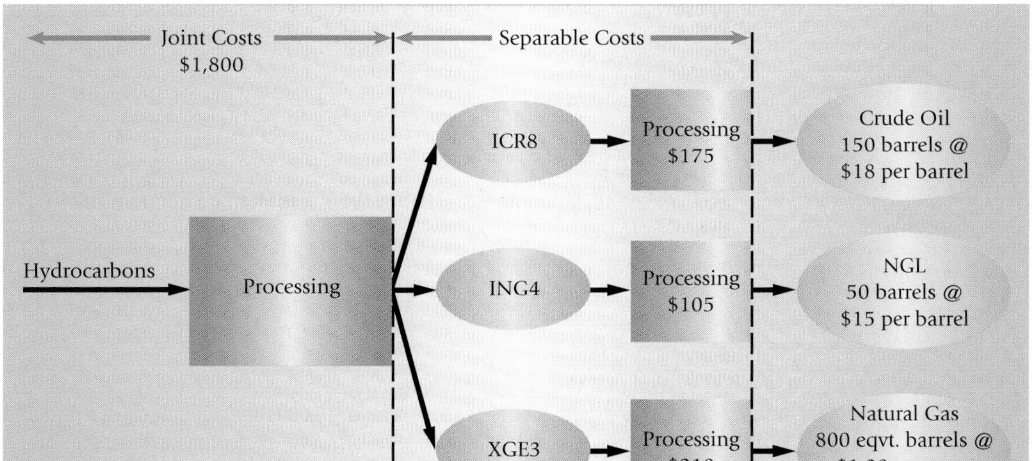

A new federal law has recently been passed that taxes crude oil at 30% of operating income. No new tax is to be paid on natural gas liquid or natural gas. Starting August 2007, Sinclair Oil & Gas must report a separate product-line income statement for crude oil. One challenge facing Sinclair Oil & Gas is how to allocate the joint cost of producing the three separate saleable outputs. Assume no beginning or ending inventory.

Required

1. Allocate the August 2007 joint cost among the three products using
   a. Physical-measure method
   b. NRV method
2. Show the operating income for each product using the methods in requirement 2.
3. Discuss the pros and cons of the two methods to Sinclair Oil & Gas for product emphasis decisions.
4. Draft a letter to the taxation authorities on behalf of Sinclair Oil & Gas that justifies the joint-cost-allocation method you recommend Sinclair use.

Excel Lab
www.prenhall.com/horngren/cost12e

16-22 Joint-cost allocation, sales value, physical measure, NRV methods. Armstrong Foods produces two rice-based instant-food products—Ricito (small rice grains) and Pancito (large rice grains)—from common inputs (rice, cheese, and spices) and sells them to food companies who package and sell these products under their own brand names. A waste product referred to as sludge results from the production of Ricito and Pancito, and until now, Armstrong has dumped the sludge at negligible cost in a local landfill. In June 2006, the following data were reported for the production and sales of Ricito and Pancito:

	A	B	C
1		**Joint Costs**	
2	Joint costs (costs of rice and other inputs and processing to splitoff point)	$600,000	
3			
4		**Ricito**	**Pancito**
5	Beginning inventory (tons)	0	0
6	Production (tons)	25,000	50,000
7	Sales (tons)	25,000	50,000
8	Selling price per ton	$ 10	$ 15

With the rising popularity of meals-in-a-cup, Armstrong's Marketing Department urges that they should add bits of preprocessed vegetables to Ricito and Pancito, package them, and sell them under the brand names Rilaf and Pilaf. Their analysis yields the following monthly data for all the products:

	A	B	C	D	E
11		**Joint Costs**		**Rilaf**	**Pilaf**
12	Joint costs (costs of rice and other inputs and processing to splitoff point)	$600,000			
13	Separable costs of processing 25,000 tons of Ricito into 30,000 tons of Rilaf			$120,000	
14	Separable costs of processing 50,000 tons of Pancito into 60,000 tons of Pilaf				$420,000
15					
16		**Ricito**	**Pancito**	**Rilaf**	**Pilaf**
17	Beginning inventory (tons)	0	0	0	0
18	Production (tons)	25,000	50,000	30,000	60,000
19	Transfer for further processing (tons)	25,000	50,000		
20	Sales (tons)			30,000	60,000
21	Selling price per ton	$ 10	$ 15	$ 18	$ 25

If you want to use Excel to solve this exercise, go to the Excel Lab at **www.prenhall.com/horngren/cost12e** and download the template for Exercise 16-22.

Required

1. Calculate Armstrong's gross-margin percentage for Rilaf and Pilaf when joint costs are allocated using:
   a. Sales value at splitoff method
   b. Physical-measure method
   c. Net realizable value method
2. Recently, Armstrong has discovered that the sludge it is dumping can be sold to cattle ranchers at $5 per ton. In a typical month with the production levels shown above, 10,000 tons of sludge are produced and can be sold by incurring marketing costs of $27,000. Shel Brown, a management accountant, points out that treating the sludge as a joint product and using the sales value at splitoff method, the sludge product would lose about $5,571 each month, so it should not be sold. How did Brown arrive at that final number, and what do you think of his analysis? Should Armstrong sell the sludge?

16-23 Process further or sell. (R. Capettini, adapted) Henley Company produces joint products A, B, and C from a single joint process with a fixed cost of $5,000 and a variable cost of $2.00 per input unit. Each product can be either processed further or, at the splitoff point, it can be sold or disposed of at a cost. Out of each input unit, Henley Company produces one unit of product A, three units of product B, and two units of product C.

Required

1. Use the following data to decide whether Henley Company should process each product further or dispose of it (or sell it) at the splitoff point if Henley inputs 5,000 units. For each product, show how much better off Henley would be if it followed your advice versus making the alternative decision. Assume that if Henley does not further process a product, it does not incur any of the further processing costs.

Product	Selling Price per Unit at Splitoff Point	Cost per Unit to Dispose of Product at Splitoff Point	Further Processing Costs: Fixed	Further Processing Costs: Variable per Unit	Selling Price per Unit After Further Processing
A	$ 0	$0.20	$ 6,000	$0.90	$1.50
B	0.50	0	1,000	1.00	1.50
C	0	0.90	10,000	1.10	5.40

2. Assuming Henley follows your advice in requirement 1, what is Henley's gross margin at the 5,000-unit input level?

16-24 Accounting for a main product and a byproduct. (Cheatham and Green, adapted) Bill Dundee is the owner and operator of Louisiana Bottling, a bulk soft-drink producer. A single production process yields two bulk soft drinks: Rainbow Dew (the main product) and Resi-Dew (the byproduct). Both products are fully processed by the splitoff point, and there are no separable costs.

PH Grade Assist

For September 2006, the cost of the soft-drink operations is $120,000. Production and sales data are as follows:

	Production (in Gallons)	Sales (in Gallons)	Selling Price per Gallon
Main product: Rainbow Dew	10,000	8,000	$20
Byproduct: Resi-Dew	2,000	1,400	2

There were no beginning inventories on September 1, 2006.

Required

1. What is the gross margin for Louisiana Bottling under the production method and the sales method of byproduct accounting?
2. What are the inventory costs reported in the balance sheet on September 30, 2006, for Rainbow Dew and Resi-Dew under the two methods of byproduct accounting in requirement 1?

16-25 Joint costs and byproducts. (W. Crum) Caldwell Company processes 600,000 pounds of an ore in Department 1 at a cost of $800,000 to yield 50,000 pounds of product L, 300,000 pounds of product W, and 100,000 pounds of product X.

- Product L is processed further in Department 2 at a cost of $100,000 and sold for $10 per pound.
- Product W is sold without further processing at $2 per pound.
- Product X is considered a byproduct and is processed further in Department 3 at a cost of $50,000 and sold for $3 per pound.

The company wants to make a gross margin of 10% of revenues on product X and needs to allow 25% of revenues for marketing costs on product X.

An overview of operations follows:

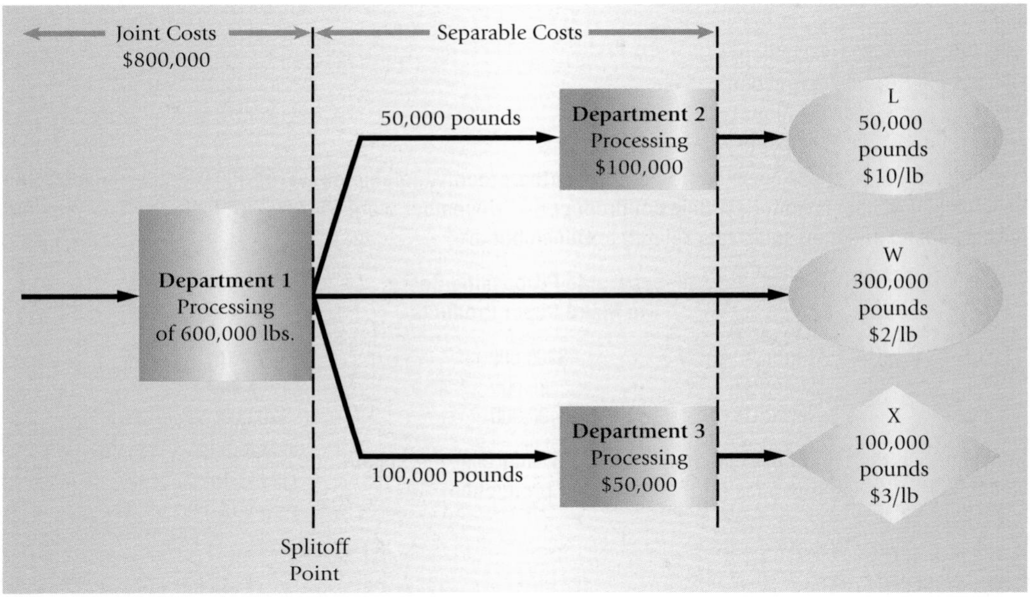

Required

1. Compute unit costs per pound for products L, W, and X, treating X as a byproduct. Use the NRV method for allocating joint costs. Deduct the NRV of the byproduct produced from the joint cost of products L and W.
2. Compute unit costs per pound for products L, W, and X, treating all three as joint products and allocating costs by the NRV method.

Problems

16-26 Alternative methods of joint-cost allocation, product-mix decision. Pacific Lumber processes lumber products for sale to lumber wholesalers. Its most popular line is oak products. Oak tree growers sell Pacific Lumber whole trees. These trees are jointly processed up to the splitoff point at which raw select oak, raw white oak, and raw knotty oak become separable products. Each raw product is then separately further processed by Pacific Lumber into finished products (select oak, white oak, and knotty oak) that are sold to lumber wholesalers. Data for August 2007 are:

a. Joint processing costs (including cost of oak trees)—$300,000

b. Separable products at splitoff point

- Raw select oak, 30,000 board-feet
- Raw white oak, 50,000 board-feet
- Raw knotty oak, 20,000 board-feet

c. Final products produced and sold

- Select oak, 25,000 board feet at $16 per board-foot
- White oak, 40,000 board feet at $9 per board-foot
- Knotty oak, 15,000 board feet at $7 per board-foot

d. Separable processing costs

- For select oak, $60,000
- For white oak, $90,000
- For knotty oak, $15,000

There is an active market for raw oak products. Selling prices available in August 2007 were raw select oak, $8 per board-foot; raw white oak, $4 per board-foot; and raw knotty oak, $3 per board-foot.

There were no beginning or ending inventories for August 2007.

Required

1. Allocate the joint costs to the three products using
   a. Sales value at splitoff method
   b. Physical-measure method
   c. NRV method
2. Assume that not all final products produced in August 2007 were sold. Ending inventory for August 2007 was select oak, 1,000 board-feet; white oak, 2,000 board-feet; and knotty oak, 500 board-feet. What would be the ending inventory values in the August 31 balance sheet under each product for the three methods in requirement 1?
3. Is Pacific Lumber maximizing its total August 2007 operating income by fully processing each raw-oak product into its finished-product form? Show your computations.

16-27 Alternative methods of joint-cost allocation, product-mix decisions. The Sunshine Oil Company buys crude vegetable oil. Refining this oil results in four products at the splitoff point: A, B, C, and D. Product C is fully processed by the splitoff point. Products A, B, and D can individually be further refined into Super A, Super B, and Super D. In the most recent month (December), the output at the splitoff point was:

- Product A, 300,000 gallons
- Product B, 100,000 gallons
- Product C, 50,000 gallons
- Product D, 50,000 gallons

The joint costs of purchasing and processing the crude vegetable oil were $100,000. Sunshine had no beginning or ending inventories. Sales of product C in December were $50,000. Products A, B, and D were further refined and then sold. Data related to December are:

	Separable Processing Costs to Make Super Products	Revenues
Super A	$200,000	$300,000
Super B	80,000	100,000
Super D	90,000	120,000

Sunshine had the option of selling products A, B, and D at the splitoff point. This alternative would have yielded the following revenues for the December production:

- Product A, $50,000
- Product B, $30,000
- Product D, $70,000

Required

1. Compute the gross-margin percentage for each product sold in December, using the following methods for allocating the $100,000 joint costs:
   a. Sales value at splitoff
   b. Physical measure
   c. NRV
2. Could Sunshine have increased its December operating income by making different decisions about the further processing of products A, B, or D? Show the effect on operating income of any changes you recommend.

16-28 Comparison of alternative joint-cost-allocation methods, further-processing decision, chocolate products. Roundtree Chocolates manufactures and distributes chocolate products. It purchases cocoa beans and processes them into two intermediate products:

- Chocolate-powder liquor base
- Milk-chocolate liquor base

These two intermediate products become separately identifiable at a single splitoff point. Every 500 pounds of cocoa beans yields 20 gallons of chocolate-powder liquor base and 30 gallons of milk-chocolate liquor base.

The chocolate-powder liquor base is further processed into chocolate powder. Every 20 gallons of chocolate-powder liquor base yield 200 pounds of chocolate powder. The milk-chocolate liquor base is further processed into milk chocolate. Every 30 gallons of milk-chocolate liquor base yield 340 pounds of milk chocolate.

Production and sales data for August 2006 are:

- Cocoa beans processed, 5,000 pounds
- Costs of processing cocoa beans to splitoff point (including purchase of beans, $10,000

	Production	Sales	Selling Price	Separable Processing Costs
Chocolate powder	2,000 pounds	2,000 pounds	$4 per pound	$4,250
Milk chocolate	3,400 pounds	3,400 pounds	$5 per pound	$8,750

Roundtree fully processes both of its intermediate products into chocolate powder or milk chocolate. There is an active market for these intermediate products. In August 2006, Roundtree could have sold the chocolate-powder liquor base for $21 a gallon and the milk-chocolate liquor base for $26 a gallon.

Required

1. Calculate how the joint costs of $10,000 would be allocated between the chocolate-powder and milk-chocolate liquor bases under the following methods:
   a. Sales value at splitoff
   b. Physical measure (gallons)
   c. NRV
   d. Constant gross-margin percentage NRV
2. What are the gross-margin percentages of the chocolate-powder and milk-chocolate liquor bases under each of the methods in requirement 1?
3. Could Roundtree Chocolates have increased its operating income by a change in its decision to fully process both of its intermediate products? Show your computations.

16-29 Joint-cost allocation, process further or sell. (CMA, adapted) Sonimad Sawmill, Inc. (SSI), purchases logs from independent timber contractors and processes the logs into three types of lumber products:

- Studs for residential buildings (walls, ceilings)
- Decorative pieces (fireplace mantels, beams for cathedral ceilings)
- Posts used as support braces (mine support braces, braces for exterior fences on ranch properties)

These products are the result of a joint sawmill process that involves removal of bark from the logs, cutting the logs into a workable size (ranging from 8 to 16 feet in length), and then cutting the individual products from the logs.

The joint process results in the following costs of products for a typical month:

Direct materials (rough timber logs)	$ 500,000
Debarking (labor and overhead)	50,000
Sizing (labor and overhead)	200,000
Product cutting (labor and overhead)	250,000
Total joint costs	$1,000,000

Product yields and average sales values on a per-unit basis from the joint process are as follows:

Product	Monthly Output of Materials at Splitoff Point	Fully Processed Selling Price
Studs	75,000 units	$ 8
Decorative pieces	5,000 units	100
Posts	20,000 units	20

The studs are sold as rough-cut lumber after emerging from the sawmill operation without further processing by SSI. Also, the posts require no further processing beyond the splitoff point. The decorative pieces must be planed and further sized after emerging from the sawmill. This additional processing costs $100,000 per month and normally results in a loss of 10% of the units entering the process. Without this planing and sizing process, there is still an active intermediate market for the unfinished decorative pieces in which the selling price averages $60 per unit.

Required

1. Based on the information given for Sonimad Sawmill, allocate the joint processing costs of $1,000,000 to the three products using:
   a. Sales value at splitoff method
   b. Physical-measure method (volume in units)
   c. NRV method
2. Prepare an analysis for Sonimad Sawmill that compares processing the decorative pieces further, as they currently do, with selling them as a rough-cut product immediately at splitoff.
3. Assume Sonimad Sawmill announced that in six months it will sell the unfinished decorative pieces at splitoff due to increasing competitive pressure. Identify at least three types of likely behavior that will be demonstrated by the skilled labor in the planing-and-sizing process as a result of this announcement. Include in your discussion how this behavior could be influenced by management.

16-30 Joint-cost allocation, relevant costs. (R. Capettini, adapted) Consider the following scenario: Each day a butcher buys a 200-pound pig for $300. The pig can be processed to yield the following three products:

	Selling Price per Pound	Weight (Pounds)
Pork chops	$4.00	30
Ham	$3.00	50
Bacon	$1.20	120
		200

Day 1 The butcher buys a pig. The $300 joint cost of the pig is allocated to individual products based on the relative weights of the products.

	Selling Price	Weight (Pounds)	Revenues	–	Joint Costs Allocated	=	Operating Income
Pork chops	$4.00	30	$120	–	$ 45.00	=	$ 75.00
Ham	3.00	50	150	–	75.00	=	75.00
Bacon	1.20	120	144	–	180.00	=	(36.00)
			$414	–	$300.00	=	$114.00

Day 2 The butcher buys an identical pig and throws out the bacon because the previous day's analysis showed that it lost money. She now has 80 pounds of "good output."

	Selling Price	Weight (Pounds)	Revenues	–	Joint Costs Allocated	=	Operating Income
Pork chops	$4.00	30	$120	–	$112.50	=	$ 7.50
Ham	3.00	50	150	–	187.50	=	(37.50)
			$270	–	$300.00	=	$(30.00)

Day 3 The butcher buys an identical pig and throws out the ham and the bacon because the previous days' analyses showed that they lost money. She now has 30 pounds of "good output."

	Selling Price	Weight (Pounds)	Revenues	–	Joint Costs Allocated	=	Operating Income
Pork chops	$4.00	30	$120	–	$300.00	=	$(180.00)
			$120	–	$300.00	=	$(180.00)

Day 4 The butcher buys an identical pig and throws out the whole pig because the previous days' analyses showed that it lost money. Therefore, she loses $300.

Required

1. Comment on the day-by-day decisions.
2. How would the joint costs be allocated to all three products using the sales value at splitoff method?
3. Should the operating-income numbers from requirement 2 be used to determine if the butcher is better off selling or not selling individual products? Explain briefly.

16-31 Joint and byproducts, NRV method. (CPA) The Harrison Corporation produces three products: Alpha, Beta, and Gamma. Alpha and Gamma are joint products, and Beta is a byproduct of Alpha. No joint costs are to be allocated to the byproduct. The production processes for a given year are as follows:

a. In Department 1, 110,000 pounds of direct material, Rho, are processed at a total cost of $120,000. After processing in Department 1, 60% of the pounds are transferred to Department 2, and 40% of the pounds (now Gamma) are transferred to Department 3.

b. In Department 2, the material is further processed at a total additional cost of $38,000. Then 70% of the pounds (now Alpha) are transferred to Department 4; and 30% emerge as Beta, the byproduct, to be sold at $1.20 per pound. Separable marketing costs for Beta are $8,100.

c. In Department 4, Alpha is processed at a total additional cost of $23,660. After this processing, Alpha is ready for sale at $5 per pound.

d. In Department 3, Gamma is processed at a total additional cost of $165,000. In this department, a normal loss of Gamma occurs, which equals 10% of the good pounds of output. The remaining good pounds of output are then sold for $12 per pound.

Required

1. Prepare a schedule showing the allocation of the $120,000 joint costs between Alpha and Gamma using the NRV method. The NRV of Beta should be treated as an addition to the sales value of Alpha.
2. Independent of your answer to requirement 1, assume that $102,000 of total joint costs were appropriately allocated to Alpha. Assume also that there were 48,000 pounds of Alpha and 20,000 pounds of Beta available to sell. Prepare an income statement through the gross-margin line item for Alpha using the following facts:
   - **a.** During the year, sales of Alpha were 80% of the pounds available for sale. There was no beginning inventory.
   - **b.** The NRV of Beta available for sale is to be deducted from the cost of producing Alpha. The ending inventory of Alpha is to be based on the net costs of production.
   - **c.** All other cost and selling-price data are listed in a through d above.

16-32 NRV method, byproducts. (CMA, adapted) Purity Corporation processes, packages, and sells three apple products: frozen slices, applesauce, and juice. Apple peel is treated as a byproduct and is sold as animal feed.

Excel Lab
www.prenhall.com/horngren/cost12e

Purity uses the NRV method to allocate joint production costs to its products. The byproduct is inventoried at its estimated selling price and reduces the joint production costs allocated to the other products. Purity's production process consists of the following departments:

- Preparation Department (joint): Apples are washed, peeled, cored, and trimmed. The three joint products and the byproduct emerge at the end of this stage, and each is transferred to a separate department for final processing.
- Slicing Department: Trimmed apples are sliced. The slices and accumulated juices are frozen and ready for sale.
- Crushing Department: Trimmings generated in the Preparation Department are processed into applesauce ready for sale. Accumulated juices are included in the applesauce.
- Juicing Department: Cores and surplus apple pieces from the Preparation Department are processed into apple juice. There is a loss of 8% of weight of good output in this department.
- Feed Processing Department: The peels generated in the preparation of the apples are chopped and frozen for storage and sale as animal feed.

During November 2006, 270,000 pounds of apples were put into production in the Preparation Department. The following table provides cost, selling-price, and other information for that period:

	A	B	C	D
1	Departments	Costs Incurred	Proportion of Product by Weight Transferred from Preparation Department to Other Departments	Selling Price per Pound of Final Product
2	Preparation	$120,000		
3	Slicing	22,560	33%	$1.60
4	Crushing	17,100	30%	1.10
5	Juicing	6,000	27%	0.80
6	Feed Processing	1,400	10%	0.20
7	Total	$167,060	100%	

If you want to use Excel to solve this problem, go to the Excel Lab at **www.prenhall.com/horngren/cost12e** and download the template for Problem 16-32.

Required

1. For the month of November 2006, calculate:
   a. The output of apple slices, applesauce, apple juice, and animal feed, in pounds
   b. The NRV at the splitoff point of each joint product
   c. The amount of Preparation Department costs allocated to each joint product and the amount allocated to the byproduct following Purity's cost-allocation method described earlier.
   d. The gross margin in dollars for each joint product
2. Comment on the significance to management of the gross-margin dollar information by joint product for planning-and-control purposes, as distinguished from inventory-costing purposes.

Excel Lab www.prenhall.com/horngren/cost12e

16-33 Process further or sell, byproduct. (CMA, adapted) Newcastle Mining Company (NMC) mines coal, puts it through a one-step crushing process, and loads the bulk raw coal onto river barges for shipment to customers.

NMC's management is currently evaluating the possibility of further processing the raw coal by sizing and cleaning it and selling it to an expanded set of customers at higher prices. The option of building a new sizing and cleaning plant is ruled out as being financially infeasible. Instead, Amy Kimbell, a mining engineer, is asked to explore outside-contracting arrangements for the cleaning and sizing process. Kimbell puts together the following summary:

	A	B	C
1	Selling price of raw coal	$27	per ton
2	Cost of producing raw coal	$22	per ton
3	Selling price of sized and cleaned coal	$36	per ton
4	Annual raw coal output	10,000,000	tons
5	Percentage of material weight loss in sizing/cleaning coal	6%	
6			
7		Incremental Costs of Sizing & Cleaning Processes	
8	Direct labor	$800,000	per year
9	Supervisory personnel	$200,000	per year
10	Heavy equipment: rental, operating, maintenance costs	$25,000	per month
11	Contract sizing and cleaning	$3.50	per ton of raw coal
12	Outbound rail freight	$240	per 60-ton rail car

Kimbell also learns that 75% of the material loss that occurs in the cleaning and sizing process can be salvaged as coal fines, which can be sold to steel manufacturers for their furnaces. The sale of coal fines is erratic and NMC may need to stockpile it in a protected area for up to one year. The selling price of coal fine ranges from $15 to $24 per ton and costs of preparing coal fines for sale range from $2 to $4 per ton.

If you want to use Excel to solve this problem, go to the Excel Lab at **www.prenhall.com/horngren/cost12e** and download the template for Problem 16-33.

Required

1. Prepare an analysis to show whether it is more profitable for NMC to continue selling raw bulk coal or to process it further through sizing and cleaning. (Ignore coal fines in your analysis.)
2. How would your analysis be affected if the cost of producing raw coal could be held down to $20 per ton?
3. Now consider the potential value of the coal fines and prepare an addendum that shows how their value affects the results of your analysis prepared in requirement 1.

Excel Lab www.prenhall.com/horngren/cost12e

16-34 Byproduct, disposal costs, ethics. Dupree Chemicals is a multinational company. One of its subsidiaries, Shanto Company, is located in a small developing nation, which, in its rush to industrialize, maintains and enforces few environmental laws.

Shanto's three major products emerge at a splitoff point from a common input, and joint costs are allocated to each product using the sales value at splitoff method. In addition to the three joint products, another product that emerges at the splitoff point is a hazardous chemical TXT45. TXT45 can either be dumped into the ocean at zero cost to Shanto, or it can be processed further and sold as a cleaning fluid. Dupree's management accountant presents the following analysis:

	A	B	C
1		TXT45: Alternatives	
2		Dump into Ocean	Process Further
3	Revenue	$0	$ 600,000
4	Costs:		
5	Further processing	0	400,000
6	Allocated joint costs	0	250,000
7	Marketing and distribution	0	50,000
8	Total costs	0	700,000
9	Net realizable value	$0	$(100,000)

If you want to use Excel to solve this problem, go to the Excel Lab at **www.prenhall.com/horngren/cost12e** and download the template for Problem 16-34.

Required

1. Using a purely financial perspective, comment on the analysis prepared by the management accountant. Show any supporting calculations.
2. Regardless of your conclusions in requirement 1, assume that adopting the process-further alternative would lead to a decrease in Dupree's operating income. Disposal of TXT45 in a manner different from dumping it into the ocean would also be costly. Discuss the legal and ethical implications of dumping TXT45 into the ocean.

Collaborative Learning Exercise

16-35 Joint-cost allocation, process further or sell. (CMA, adapted) Goodson Pharmaceutical Company manufactures three joint products from a joint process: Altox, Lorex, and Hycol. Data regarding these products for the fiscal year ended May 31, 2006, are as follows:

	Altox	Lorex	Hycol
Units produced	170,000	500,000	330,000
Selling price per unit at splitoff	\$3.50	—	\$2.00
Separable costs	—	\$1,400,000	—
Final selling price per unit	—	\$5.00	—

The joint production cost up to the splitoff point at which Altox, Lorex, and Hycol become separable products is \$1,800,000.

The president of Goodson, Arlene Franklin, is reviewing an opportunity to change the way in which these three products are processed and sold. Proposed changes for each product are as follows:

- Altox can be processed into a blood pressure medication. However, this additional processing causes a loss of 20,000 units of Altox. The separable costs to further process Altox are estimated to be \$250,000 annually. The blood pressure medication sells for \$5.50 per unit.
- Lorex is currently processed further after the splitoff point and is sold by Goodson as a cold remedy. A pharmaceutical company has offered to purchase Lorex at the splitoff point for \$2.25 per unit.
- Goodson's Research Department has recommended that the company process Hycol further and sell it as an ointment to relieve muscle pain. The additional processing would cost \$75,000 annually and would result in 25% more units of product. The ointment sells for \$1.80 per unit.

Required

1. Allocate the \$1,800,000 joint production cost to Altox, Lorex, and Hycol using the NRV method.
2. Identify which of the three joint products Goodson should sell at the splitoff point in the future and which of the three the company should process further to maximize operating income. Support your decisions with appropriate computations.

Get Connected: Cost Accounting in the News

Go to www.prenhall.com/horngren/cost12e for additional online exercise(s) that explore issues affecting the accounting world today. These exercises offer you the opportunity to analyze and reflect on how cost accounting helps managers to make better decisions and handle the challenges of strategic planning and implementation.

CHAPTER 16 Caselet

MEMORY MANUFACTURING COMPANY (MMC): Joint-Cost Allocation

MMC manufactures memory modules in a two-step process: chip fabrication and module assembly.

In chip fabrication, each batch of raw silicon wafers yields 500 "standard" chips and 500 "deluxe" chips. Chips are classified as standard and deluxe on the basis of their density (the number of memory bits on each chip). Standard chips have 500 memory bits per chip and deluxe chips have 1,000 memory bits per chip. Joint costs to process each batch are \$24,000.

In module assembly, each batch of standard chips is converted into standard memory modules at a separately identified cost of \$1,000 and then sold for \$8,500. Each batch of deluxe chips is converted into deluxe memory modules at a separately identified cost of \$1,500 and then sold for \$25,000.

QUESTIONS

1. Allocate joint costs of each batch to deluxe modules and standard modules using (a) the NRV method, (b) the constant gross-margin percentage NRV method, and (c) the physical-measure method, based on the number of memory bits. Which method should MMC use?
2. MMC can process each batch of 500 standard memory modules to yield 400 DRAM modules at an additional cost of \$1,600. The selling price per DRAM module would be \$26. Assume MMC uses the physical-measure method. Should MMC sell the standard memory modules or the DRAM modules?

CHAPTER 17

PROCESS COSTING

LEARNING OBJECTIVES

1. **Identify the situations in which process-costing systems are appropriate**
2. **Describe the five steps in process costing**
3. **Calculate equivalent units and understand how to use them**
4. **Prepare journal entries for process-costing systems**
5. **Use the weighted-average method of process costing**
6. **Use the first-in, first-out (FIFO) method of process costing**
7. **Incorporate standard costs into process-costing systems**
8. **Apply process-costing methods to situations with transferred-in costs**

Global Defense manufactures complex electronic components for missiles and military equipment. All units of a particular component are identical and are mass-produced. Global Defense uses a process-costing system to determine the cost of each component. Bill Suhara, CEO, is meeting with Global Defense's management accountant, Maria Havel, to discuss the company's performance for the first quarter of 2007.

Bill: For me to understand our inventory situation, can you explain the computations for equivalent units?

Maria: Equivalent units arise because there are some units of output that are 100% processed, but there are also units in ending inventory that are, say, only 60% complete. If there are 50 units in ending inventory, we convert them into the equivalent of 60% × 50, which would equal 30 units that are 100% complete. Based on equivalent units, we compare how unit costs have changed from one month to the next—important information, given our strategy to continuously reduce our costs.

Bill: Okay. I also wanted to ask you about one of the notes to our financial statements—the one that says we assume the first-in, first-out inventory cost-flow assumption. What other choices could we have made?

Maria: We've always used FIFO but, just as in all other inventory costing, we could have used the weighted-average method or the standard costing method. Accounting rules allow us to choose any one of these methods, but we then have to apply that method consistently over time. For us, it's been FIFO.

Bill: Just out of curiosity, would our operating income have been higher this quarter if we'd used the weighted-average method?

Maria: Good question. Yes, it would have. Any time you are successful in reducing costs from one period to the next, the operating income reported under the weighted-average method will be higher than the operating income reported under FIFO.

Bill: I am curious how the choice of accounting method has affected the operating income we have reported in the past. Could you compile a report comparing operating incomes over the last few quarters using the FIFO and weighted-average methods.

Maria: Certainly. I'll e-mail it to you by the end of the week.

Companies such as semiconductor manufacturer Intel, pharmaceutical-products maker GlaxoSmithKline, juice producer Nantucket Nectars, and chemical manufacturer Ciba Specialty produce many identical or similar units, so they face the same accounting and inventory issues as Global Defense. These companies use process costing, in which each individual process forms the basis of the costing system.

Job-costing systems, which were described in Chapter 4, serve three functions: (1) determining the costs of products or services, which aids in planning decisions such as pricing and product mix; (2) valuing inventory and cost of goods sold for external reporting; and (3) managing costs and evaluating performance. As we examine process costing in this chapter, we will emphasize the first two functions. We will be concerned only incidentally with the third function—cost management and performance evaluation—which is discussed in other chapters (see, for example, Chapters 6, 7, and 8). The ideas described in Chapters 6, 7, and 8 apply to process-costing systems as well.

Illustrating Process Costing

1

Identify the situations in which process-costing systems are appropriate

. . . when masses of identical or similar units are produced

Before we examine process costing in more detail, let's briefly compare job costing and process costing. Job-costing and process-costing systems are best viewed as ends of a continuum:

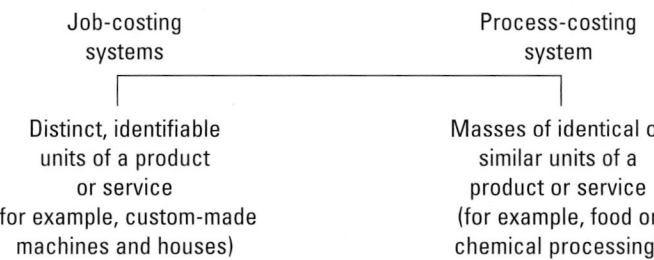

Job-costing systems	Process-costing system
Distinct, identifiable units of a product or service (for example, custom-made machines and houses)	Masses of identical or similar units of a product or service (for example, food or chemical processing)

In a *process-costing system,* unit cost of a product or service is obtained by assigning total costs to many identical or similar units. In a manufacturing process-costing setting, each unit receives the same or similar amounts of direct material costs, direct manufacturing labor costs, and indirect manufacturing costs (manufacturing overhead). Unit costs are then computed by dividing total costs incurred by the number of units of output from the production process.

The main difference between process costing and job costing is the *extent of averaging* used to compute unit costs of products or services. In a job-costing system, individual jobs use different quantities of production resources, so it would be incorrect to cost each job at the same average production cost. In contrast, when identical or similar units of products or services are mass-produced, not processed as individual jobs, process costing is used to calculate an average production cost for all units produced (see Global Surveys of Company Practice, p. 600). Some processes such as clothes manufacturing have aspects of both process costing (cost per unit of each operation, such as cutting or sewing, is identical) and job costing (different materials are used in different batches of clothing, say, wool versus cotton). The appendix to this chapter describes costing systems that combine process costing and job costing.

Consider the following illustration of process costing: Recall that Global Defense, the company introduced at the beginning of the chapter, manufactures thousands of components for missiles and military equipment. These components are assembled in the Assembly Department. Upon completion, units are transferred to the Testing Department. We focus on the Assembly Department process for one component, DG-19. All units of DG-19 are identical and must meet a set of demanding performance specifications. The process-costing system for DG-19 in the Assembly Department has a single direct-cost category—direct materials—and a single indirect-cost category—conversion costs. Conversion costs are all manufacturing costs other than direct material costs, including manufacturing labor, energy, plant depreciation, and so on. Direct materials are added at the beginning of the Assembly process. Conversion costs are added evenly during assembly.

The following graphic represents these facts:

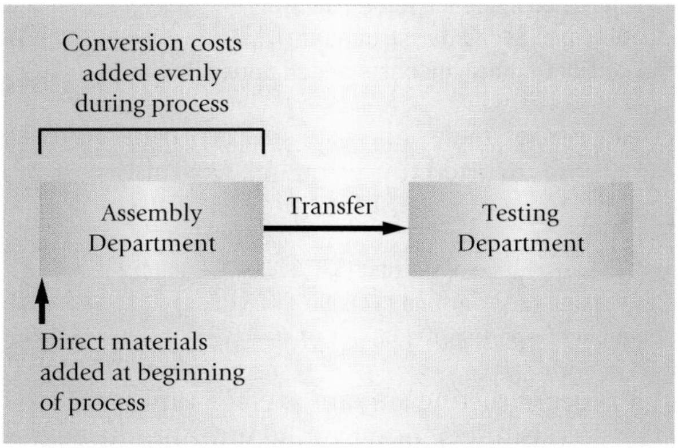

Process-costing systems separate costs into cost categories according to *when costs are introduced into the process*. Often, as in our Global Defense example, only two cost classifications, direct materials and conversion costs, are necessary to assign costs to products. Why only two? Because *all* direct materials are added to the process at one time and all conversion costs generally are added to the process evenly through time. If, however, two different direct materials were added to the process at different times, two different direct-materials categories would be needed to assign these costs to products. Similarly, if manufacturing labor costs were added to the process at a different time than when the other conversion costs were added, an additional cost category—direct manufacturing labor costs—would be needed to separately assign these costs to products.

We will use the production of the DG-19 component in the Assembly Department to illustrate process costing in three cases, starting with the simplest case and introducing additional complexities in subsequent cases:

- **Case 1**—Process costing with zero beginning and zero ending work-in-process inventory of DG-19 (that is, all units are started and fully completed within the accounting period). *This case presents the most basic concepts of process costing and illustrates the feature of averaging of costs.*
- **Case 2**—Process costing with zero beginning work-in-process inventory but some ending work-in-process inventory of DG-19 (that is, some units of DG-19 started during the accounting period are incomplete at the end of the period). *This case introduces the concept of equivalent units.*
- **Case 3**—Process costing with both some beginning and some ending work-in-process inventory of DG-19. *This case adds more complexity and illustrates the effect of weighted-average and first-in, first-out (FIFO) cost flow assumptions on cost of units completed and cost of work-in-process inventory.*

Choosing between the weighted-average method and the FIFO method is unnecessary for cases 1 and 2 because beginning work-in-process inventory is zero. Differences between weighted average and FIFO arise only when there is beginning work-in-process inventory *and* the manufacturing cost per unit changes from period to period.

Case 1: Process Costing with Zero Beginning and Zero Ending Work-in-Process Inventory

On January 1, 2007, there was no beginning inventory of DG-19 units in the Assembly Department. During January, Global Defense started, completely assembled, and transferred out to the Testing Department 400 units.

Data for the Assembly Department for January 2007 are:

Physical Units for January 2007	
Work in process, beginning inventory (January 1)	0 units
Started during January	400 units
Completed and transferred out during January	400 units
Work in process, ending inventory (January 31)	0 units

Physical units refers to the number of output units, whether complete or incomplete. In January 2007, all 400 physical units started were completed.

Total Costs for January 2007	
Direct material costs added during January	$32,000
Conversion costs added during January	24,000
Total Assembly Department costs added during January	$56,000

Global Defense records direct material costs and conversion costs in the Assembly Department as these costs are incurred. By averaging, assembly cost of DG-19 is $56,000 ÷ 400 units = $140 per unit, itemized as follows:

Direct material cost per unit ($32,000 ÷ 400 units)	$ 80
Conversion cost per unit ($24,000 ÷ 400 units)	60
Assembly Department cost per unit	$140

Case 1 shows that in a process-costing system, average unit costs are calculated by dividing total costs in a given accounting period by total units produced in that period. Because each unit is identical, we assume all units receive the same amount of direct material costs and conversion costs. Case 1 applies whenever a company produces a homogeneous product or service but has no incomplete units when each accounting period ends, which is a common situation in service-sector organizations. For example, a bank can adopt this process-costing approach to compute the unit cost of processing 100,000 customer deposits, each similar to the other, made in a month.

Case 2: Process Costing with Zero Beginning but Some Ending Work-in-Process Inventory

In February 2007, Global Defense places another 400 units of DG-19 into production. Because all units placed into production in January were completely assembled, there is no beginning inventory of partially completed units in the Assembly Department on February 1. Some customers order late, so not all units started in February are completed by the end of the month. Only 175 units are completed and transferred to the Testing Department.

Data for the Assembly Department for February 2007 are:

	A	B	C	D	E
1		Physical Units (DG-19s) (1)	Direct Materials (2)	Conversion Costs (3)	Total Costs (4) = (2) + (3)
2	Work in process, beginning inventory (February 1)	0			
3	Started during February	400			
4	Completed and transferred out during February	175			
5	Work in process, ending inventory (February 28)	225			
6	Degree of completion of ending work in process		100%	60%	
7	Total costs added during February		$32,000	$18,600	$50,600

The 225 partially assembled units as of February 28, 2007, are fully processed with respect to direct materials. That's because all direct materials in the Assembly Department are added at the beginning of the assembly process. Conversion costs, however, are added evenly during assembly. Based on the work completed relative to the total work required to complete the DG-19 units still in process at the end of February, an Assembly Department supervisor estimates that the partially assembled units are, on average, 60% complete with respect to conversion costs.

The accuracy of the completion estimate of conversion costs depends on the care, skill, and experience of the estimator and the nature of the conversion process. Estimating the degree of completion is usually easier for direct material costs than for conversion costs. That's because the quantity of direct materials needed for a completed unit and the quantity of direct materials in a partially completed unit can be measured more accurately. In contrast, the conversion sequence usually consists of a number of basic operations for a specified number of hours, days, or weeks for various steps in the production process. The degree of completion for conversion costs depends on what proportion of the total conversion costs needed to complete one unit or one batch of production has already been incurred on units still in process. This estimate is more difficult to make accurately. Because of these uncertainties, department supervisors and line managers—individuals most familiar with the process—often make conversion cost estimates. Still, in some industries, such as semiconductor manufacturing, no exact estimate is possible or, as in the textile industry, vast quantities in process make the task of estimation costly. In these cases, it is necessary to assume that all work in process in a department is complete to some degree with respect to conversion costs (for example, one-third, one-half, or two-thirds complete). The Focus on Values and Behaviors describes the challenges management accountants face when making these estimates (p. 605).

The point to understand here is that a partially assembled unit is not the same as a fully assembled unit. Faced with some fully assembled units and some partially assembled units,

The accuracy of product costs in process-costing systems hinges on the accuracy of the estimate of percentage of completion, particularly when work in process is large.

2

Describe the five steps in process costing

. . . to assign total costs to units completed and to units in work in process

Global Defense calculates in five steps (1) the cost of fully assembled units in February 2007 and (2) the cost of partially assembled units still in process at the end of that month:

Step 1: Summarize the flow of physical units of output.
Step 2: Compute output in terms of equivalent units.
Step 3: Compute cost per equivalent unit.
Step 4: Summarize total costs to account for.
Step 5: Assign total costs to units completed and to units in ending work in process.

3

Calculate equivalent units

. . . output units adjusted for incomplete units

and understand how to use them

. . . to assign costs to units completed and to units in ending work in process

Physical Units and Equivalent Units (Steps 1 and 2)

Step 1 tracks physical units of output. Recall that physical units are the number of output units, whether complete or incomplete. Where did physical units come from? Where did they go? The physical-units column of Exhibit 17-1 tracks where the physical units came from (400 units started) and where they went (175 units completed and transferred out and 225 units in ending inventory).

Because not all 400 physical units are fully completed, output in step 2 is computed in *equivalent units*, not in *physical units*. To see what we mean by equivalent units, let's say that during a month, 50 physical units were started but not completed by the end of the month. These 50 units in ending inventory are estimated to be 70% complete with respect to conversion costs. Let's examine those units from the perspective of the conversion costs already incurred to get the units to be 70% complete. Suppose we put all the conversion costs represented in the 70% into making fully completed units. How many units could have been 100% complete by the end of the month? The answer: 35 units. Why? Because 70% of conversion costs incurred on 50 incomplete units could have been incurred to make 35 (0.70×50) complete units by the end of the month. That is, if all the conversion-cost input in the 50 units in inventory had been used to make completed output units, the company would have produced 35 completed units (also called *equivalent units*) of output.

Equivalent units is a derived amount of output units that (1) takes the quantity of each input (factor of production) in units completed and in incomplete units of work in process and (2) converts the quantity of input into the amount of completed output units that could be produced with that quantity of input. Note that equivalent units are calculated separately for each input (such as direct materials and conversion costs). This chapter focuses on equivalent-unit calculations in manufacturing settings. Equivalent-unit concepts are also found in nonmanufacturing settings. For example, universities convert their part-time student enrollments into "full-time student equivalents."

Whenever a factor of production is added at a different stage in the production process, a separate equivalent-unit computation is required. In the Global Defense example, suppose steel is added at the beginning of Assembly and electronics are added 75% of the way through Assembly. Ending work in process that is 60% complete would have had 100% of the steel added but 0% of the electronics added. Therefore, we need separate equivalent-unit calculations for steel and electronics—even though both are elements of direct materials.

When calculating equivalent units in step 2, focus on quantities. Disregard dollar amounts until after equivalent units are computed. In the Global Defense example, all 400 physical units—the 175 fully assembled units and the 225 partially assembled units—are 100% complete with respect to direct materials because all direct materials are added in the Assembly Department at the start of the process. Therefore, Exhibit 17-1 shows output as 400 *equivalent units* for direct materials: 175 equivalent units for the 175 physical units assembled and transferred out, and 225 equivalent units for the 225 physical units in ending work-in-process inventory.

EXHIBIT 17-1

Steps 1 and 2: Summarize Output in Physical Units and Compute Output in Equivalent Units for Assembly Department of Global Defense for February 2007

	A	B	C	D
1		(Step 1)	(Step 2)	
2			Equivalent Units	
3	Flow of Production	Physical Units	Direct Materials	Conversion Costs
4	Work in process, beginning	0		
5	Started during current period	400		
6	To account for	400		
7	Completed and transferred out during current period	175	175	175
8	Work in process, ending [a]	225		
9	(225 x 100%; 225 x 60%)		225	135
10	Accounted for	400		
11	Work done in current period only		400	310
12				
13	[a]Degree of completion in this department: direct materials, 100%; conversion costs, 60%.			

EXHIBIT 17-2 **Steps 3, 4, and 5: Compute Cost per Equivalent Unit, Summarize Total Costs to Account for and Assign Total Costs to, Units Completed and to Units in Ending Work in Process for Assembly Department of Global Defense for February 2007**

	A	B	C	D	E
1			**Total Production Costs**	**Direct Materials**	**Conversion Costs**
2	**(Step 3)**	Costs added during February	$50,600	$32,000	$18,600
3		Divide by equivalent units of work done in current period (Exhibit 17-1)		÷ 400	÷ 310
4		Cost per equivalent unit		$ 80	$ 60
5	**(Step 4)**	Total costs to account for	$50,600		
6	**(Step 5)**	Assignment of costs:			
7		Completed and transferred out (175 units)	$24,500	(175[a] x $80)	+ (175[a] x $60)
8		Work in process, ending (225 units):	26,100	(225[b] x $80)	+ (135[b] x $60)
9		Total costs accounted for	$50,600		
10					
11	[a]Equivalent units completed and transferred out from Exhibit 17-1, step 2.				
12	[b]Equivalent units in ending work in process from Exhibit 17-1, step 2.				

The 175 fully assembled units are also completely processed with respect to conversion costs. The partially assembled units in ending work in process are 60% complete (on average). Therefore, conversion costs in the 225 partially assembled units are *equivalent* to conversion costs in 135 (60% of 225) fully assembled units. Hence, Exhibit 17-1 shows output as 310 *equivalent units* with respect to conversion costs: 175 equivalent units for the 175 physical units assembled and transferred out and 135 equivalent units for the 225 physical units in ending work-in-process inventory.

Calculation of Product Costs (Steps 3, 4, and 5)

Exhibit 17-2 shows steps 3, 4, and 5. Together, they are called the *production cost worksheet.* Step 3 calculates cost per equivalent unit separately for direct materials and for conversion costs by dividing direct material costs and conversion costs added during February by the related quantity of equivalent units of work done in February (as calculated in Exhibit 17-1).

To see the importance of using equivalent units in unit-cost calculations, compare conversion costs for January and February 2007. Total conversion costs of $18,600 for the 400 units worked on during February are lower than the conversion costs of $24,000 for the 400 units worked on in January. However, in this example, the conversion costs to fully assemble a unit are $60 in both January and February. Total conversion costs are lower in February because fewer equivalent units of conversion-costs work were completed in February (310) than in January (400). Using physical units instead of equivalent units in the per-unit calculation would have led to the erroneous conclusion that conversion costs per unit declined from $60 in January to $46.50 ($18,600 ÷ 400 units) in February. This incorrect costing might have prompted Global Defense, for example, to lower the price of DG-19 when, in fact, costs had not declined.

Step 4 in Exhibit 17-2 summarizes total costs to account for. Because the beginning balance of work-in-process inventory is zero on February 1, total costs to account for (that is, the total charges or debits to the Work in Process—Assembly account) consist only of costs added during February: direct materials of $32,000 and conversion costs of $18,600, for a total of $50,600.

Step 5 in Exhibit 17-2 assigns these costs to units completed and transferred out and to units still in process at the end of February 2007. The idea is to attach dollar amounts to the equivalent output units for direct materials and conversion costs of (a) units completed and (b) ending work in process, as calculated in Exhibit 17-1, step 2. *Equivalent output units for each input are multiplied by cost per equivalent unit, as calculated in step 3 of Exhibit 17-2.* For example, costs assigned to the 225 physical units in ending work-in-process inventory are:

If you remember where the units go in step 1, there is no need to memorize where the costs go in step 5, because the costs attach to the units. In Exhibits 17-1 and 17-2, the costs are attached (1) to units completed and transferred out of Assembly and (2) to units in ending work in process.

To see the big picture in process costing, tie the numbers in the production-cost worksheet (Exhibit 17-2) to the related Work in Process T-account (Exhibit 17-3).

Direct material costs of 225 equivalent units (Exhibit 17-1, step 2) × $80 cost per equivalent unit of direct materials calculated in step 3	$18,000
Conversion costs of 135 equivalent units (Exhibit 17-1, step 2) × $60 cost per equivalent unit of conversion costs calculated in step 3	8,100
Total cost of ending work-in-process inventory	$26,100

Note that total costs to account for in step 4 ($50,600) equal total costs accounted for in step 5.

4

Prepare journal entries for process-costing systems

. . . they are similar to those in job costing, but separate entries are made for each process

Journal Entries

Journal entries in process-costing systems are similar to the entries made in job-costing systems with respect to direct materials and conversion costs. The main difference is that, in process costing, there is one Work-in-Process account for each process—in our example, Work in Process—Assembly and Work in Process—Testing. Global Defense purchases direct materials as needed. These materials are delivered directly to the Assembly Department. Using amounts from Exhibit 17-2, summary journal entries for February (on facing page) are:

GLOBAL SURVEYS OF COMPANY PRACTICE

Process Costing in Different Industries

Recent surveys indicate that process costing is used extensively at corporations around the world. One survey noted that 52% of Australian companies and 46% of Japanese companies use process costing, making it the most popular product-costing system in both countries.[a] Additional findings from Eastern Europe show that 66% of all Estonian manufacturing companies also use process costing.[b]

Another Australian survey examines the widespread use of process costing across a variety of industries.[c] (The reported percentages exceed 100% because several companies surveyed use more than one product-costing system.)

	Food	Textiles	Metals	Chemicals	Refining
Process costing	96%	91%	92%	75%	100%
Job costing	4	18	25	25	25
Other	—	—	8	12	—

Process costing is widely used in mass-production industries that manufacture homogeneous products, including food, textiles, primary metals, chemicals, and refining. In contrast, job costing is favored over process costing in industries that produce many distinct products—for example, in printing and publishing, furniture and fixtures, machinery and computers, and electronics.

	Printing and Publishing	Furniture and Fixtures	Machinery and Computers	Electronics
Process costing	20%	38%	43%	55%
Job costing	73	63	65	58
Other	13	—	9	10

Among artisan-based enterprises in Nigeria, 49% of respondents use job costing, whereas only 10% rely on process costing for product-costing purposes.[d]

[a] H. Wijewardena and A. De Zoysa, "A Comparative Analysis."
[b] T. Haldma and K. Lääts, "Contingencies."
[c] M. Joye and P. Blayney, "Cost and Management."
[d] L. Obara and N. Ukpai, "Cost Accounting Practice."
Full citations are in Appendix A at the end of the book.

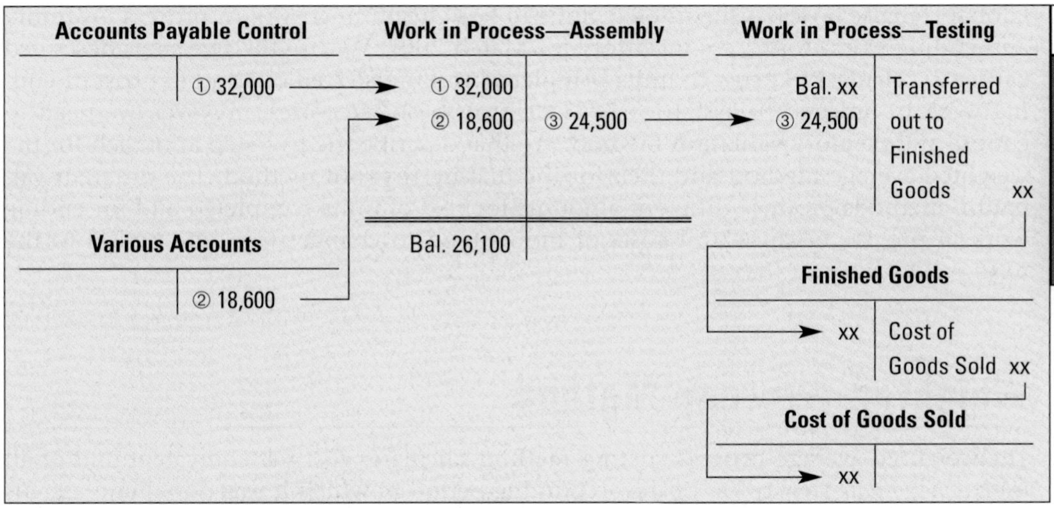

EXHIBIT 17-3

Flow of Costs in a Process-Costing Sytem for Assembly Department of Global Defense for February 2007

1. Work in Process—Assembly	32,000	
Accounts Payable Control		32,000
To record direct materials purchased and used in production during February.		
2. Work in Process—Assembly	18,600	
Various accounts such as Wages Payable Control and Accumulated Depreciation		18,600
To record conversion costs for February; examples include energy, manufacturing supplies, all manufacturing labor, and plant depreciation.		
3. Work in Process—Testing	24,500	
Work in Process—Assembly		24,500
To record cost of goods completed and transferred from Assembly to Testing during February.		

Exhibit 17-3 shows a general framework for the flow of costs through T-accounts. Notice how entry 3 for $24,500 follows the physical transfer of goods from Assembly to the Testing Department. The T-account Work in Process—Assembly shows February 2007's ending balance of $26,100, which is the beginning balance of Work in Process—Assembly in March 2007.

Case 3: Process Costing with Some Beginning and Some Ending Work-in-Process Inventory

At the beginning of March 2007, Global Defense had 225 partially assembled DG-19 units in the Assembly Department. It started production of another 275 units in March. Data for the Assembly Department for March are:

	A	B	C	D	E
1		Physical Units (DG-19s) (1)	Direct Materials (2)	Conversion Costs (3)	Total Costs (4) = (2) + (3)
2	Work in process, beginning inventory (March 1)	225	$18,000[a]	$ 8,100[a]	$26,100
3	Degree of completion of beginning work in process		100%	60%	
4	Started during March	275			
5	Completed and transferred out during March	400			
6	Work in process, ending inventory (March 31)	100			
7	Degree of completion of ending work in process		100%	50%	
8	Total costs added during March		$19,800	$16,380	$36,180
9					
10	[a]Work in process, beginning inventory (equals work in process, ending inventory for February)				
11	Direct materials: 225 physical units x 100% completed x $80 per unit = $18,000				
12	Conversion costs: 225 physical units x 60% completed x $60 per unit = $8,100				

Global Defense now has incomplete units in both beginning work-in-process inventory and ending work-in-process inventory for March 2007. We use the five steps described earlier to calculate (1) cost of units completed and transferred out and (2) cost of ending work in process. To assign costs to each of these categories, however, we need to choose an inventory-valuation method. We first describe the five-step approach for the weighted-average method and then for the first-in, first-out method. The different valuation methods produce different amounts for cost of units completed and for ending work in process because unit costs of inputs tend to change from one period to the next.

Weighted-Average Method

5

Use the weighted-average method of process costing

. . . assigns costs based on total costs and equivalent units completed to date

The **weighted-average process-costing method** calculates cost per equivalent unit of all *work done to date* (regardless of the accounting period in which it was done) and assigns this cost to equivalent units completed and transferred out of the process and to equivalent units in ending work-in-process inventory. The weighted-average cost is the total of all costs entering the Work in Process account (whether they are from beginning work in process or from work started during the current period) divided by total equivalent units of work done to date. We now describe the weighted-average method using the five-step procedure introduced earlier.

Step 1: **Summarize the Flow of Physical Units.** The physical-units column of Exhibit 17-4 shows where the units came from—225 units from beginning inventory and 275 units started during the current period—and where they went—400 units completed and transferred out and 100 units in ending inventory.

Step 2: **Compute Output in Terms of Equivalent Units.** The weighted-average cost of inventory is calculated by merging together the costs of beginning inventory and the manufacturing costs of a period and dividing by the total number of units in beginning inventory and units produced during the accounting period. We apply the same concept here except that calculating the units—in this case equivalent units—is done differently. We use the relationship shown in the equation below.

$$\begin{array}{c}\text{Equivalent units}\\\text{in beginning}\\\text{work in process}\end{array} + \begin{array}{c}\text{Equivalent units}\\\text{of work done in}\\\text{current period}\end{array} = \begin{array}{c}\text{Equivalent units}\\\text{completed and}\\\text{transferred out}\\\text{in current period}\end{array} + \begin{array}{c}\text{Equivalent units}\\\text{in ending}\\\text{work in process}\end{array}$$

EXHIBIT 17-4

Steps 1 and 2: Summarize Output in Physical Units and Compute Output in Equivalent Units Using Weighted-Average Method of Process Costing for Assembly Department of Global Defense for March 2007

	A	B	C	D
1		**(Step 1)**	**(Step 2)**	
2			**Equivalent Units**	
3	**Flow of Production**	**Physical Units**	**Direct Materials**	**Conversion Costs**
4	Work in process, beginning (given, p. 601)	225		
5	Started during current period (given, p. 601)	275		
6	To account for	500		
7	Completed and transferred out during current period	400	400	400
8	Work in process, ending[a] (given, p. 601)	100		
9	(100 x 100%; 100 x 50%)		100	50
10	Accounted for	500		
11	Work done to date		500	450
12				
13	[a]Degree of completion in this department: direct materials, 100%; conversion costs, 50%.			

Although we are interested in calculating the sum of equivalent units in beginning work in process and equivalent units of work done in the current period, it is easier to calculate this sum using the right-hand side of the preceding equation: (1) equivalent units completed and transferred out in the current period plus (2) equivalent units in ending work in process. *Note that the stage of completion of the current-period beginning work in process is not used in this computation.*

The equivalent-units columns in Exhibit 17-4 show equivalent units of work done to date: 500 equivalent units of direct materials and 450 equivalent units of conversion costs. All completed and transferred-out units are 100% complete as to both direct materials and conversion costs. Partially completed units in ending work in process are 100% complete as to direct materials, because direct materials are introduced at the beginning of the process, and 50% complete as to conversion costs, based on estimates made by the Assembly Department manager.

Step 3: Compute Cost per Equivalent Unit. Exhibit 17-5, step 3, shows the computation of weighted-average cost per equivalent unit for direct materials and conversion costs. Weighted-average cost per equivalent unit is obtained by dividing the sum of costs for beginning work in process plus costs for work done in the current period by total equivalent units of work done to date. When calculating weighted-average conversion cost per equivalent unit in Exhibit 17-5, for example, we divide total conversion costs, \$24,480 (beginning work in process, \$8,100, plus work done in current period, \$16,380), by total equivalent units of work done to date, 450 (equivalent units of conversion costs in beginning work in process and in work done in current period), to obtain weighted-average cost per equivalent unit of \$54.40.

Step 4: Summarize Total Costs to Account For. Total costs to account for in March 2007 are described in the example data on page 601: beginning work in process, \$26,100 (direct materials, \$18,000, plus conversion costs, \$8,100), plus costs added during March, \$36,180 (direct materials, \$19,800, plus conversion costs, \$16,380). The total of these costs is \$62,280.

EXHIBIT 17-5 **Steps 3, 4, and 5: Compute Cost per Equivalent Unit, Summarize Total Costs to Account for, and Assign Total Costs to Units Completed and to Units in Ending Work in Process Using Weighted-Average Method of Process Costing for Assembly Department of Global Defense for March 2007**

	A	B	C	D	E
1			**Total Production Costs**	**Direct Materials**	**Conversion Costs**
2	**(Step 3)**	Work in process, beginning (given, p. 601)	\$26,100	\$18,000	\$ 8,100
3		Costs added in current period (given, p. 601)	36,180	19,800	16,380
4		Costs incurred to date		\$37,800	\$24,480
5		Divide by equivalent units of work done to date (Exhibit 17-4)		÷ 500	÷ 450
6		Cost per equivalent unit of work done to date		\$ 75.60	\$ 54.40
7	**(Step 4)**	Total costs to account for	\$62,280		
8	**(Step 5)**	Assignment of costs:			
9		Completed and transferred out (400 units)	\$52,000	(400[a] x \$75.60)+(400[a] x \$54.40)	
10		Work in process, ending (100 units):	10,280	(100[b] x \$75.60)+ (50[b] x \$54.40)	
11		Total costs accounted for	\$62,280		
12					
13	[a]Equivalent units completed and transferred out from Exhibit 17-4, step 2.				
14	[b]Equivalent units in ending work in process from Exhibit 17-4, step 2.				

Step 5: Assign Total Costs to Units Completed and to Units in Ending Work in Process. Step 5 in Exhibit 17-5 takes the equivalent units completed and transferred out and equivalent units in ending work in process calculated in Exhibit 17-4, step 2, and assigns dollar amounts to them using the weighted-average cost per equivalent unit for direct materials and conversion costs calculated in step 3. For example, total costs of the 100 physical units in ending work in process are:

Direct materials:	
100 equivalent units × weighted-average cost per equivalent unit of $75.60	$ 7,560
Conversion costs:	
50 equivalent units × weighted-average cost per equivalent unit of $54.40	2,720
Total costs of ending work in process	$10,280

The following table summarizes total costs to account for ($62,280) and how they are accounted for in Exhibit 17-5. The arrows indicate that the costs of units completed and transferred out and units in ending work in process are calculated using weighted-average total costs obtained after merging costs of beginning work in process and costs added in the current period.

Costs to Account For		Costs Accounted for Calculated on a Weighted-Average Basis	
Beginning work in process	$26,100	Completed and transferred out	$52,000
Costs added in current period	36,180	Ending work in process	10,280
Total costs to account for	$62,280	Total costs accounted for	$62,280

Before proceeding, review Exhibits 17-4 and 17-5 to check your understanding of the weighted-average method. Note: Exhibit 17-4 deals only with physical and equivalent units, not costs. Exhibit 17-5 shows the cost amounts.

Using amounts from Exhibit 17-5, the summary journal entries under the weighted-average method for March 2007 at Global Defense, are:

The purpose of Exhibits 17-4 and 17-5 (weighted average), 17-6 and 17-7 (FIFO), and 17-8 and 17-9 (standard costing) is to calculate the costs of the units completed and transferred out during March 2007 to record the journal entry debiting Work in Process—Testing and crediting Work in Process—Assembly.

1. Work in Process—Assembly	19,800	
Accounts Payable Control		19,800
To record direct materials purchased and used in production during March.		
2. Work in Process—Assembly	16,380	
Various accounts such as Wages Payable Control and Accumulated Depreciation		16,380
To record conversion costs for March; examples include energy, manufacturing supplies, all manufacturing labor, and plant depreciation.		
3. Work in Process—Testing	52,000	
Work in Process—Assembly		52,000
To record cost of goods completed and transferred from Assembly to Testing during March.		

The T-account Work in Process—Assembly, under the weighted-average method, shows:

Work in Process—Assembly

Beginning inventory, March 1	26,100	③ Completed and transferred out to Work in Process—Testing	52,000
① Direct materials	19,800		
② Conversion costs	16,380		
Ending inventory, March 31	10,280		

6 **Use the first-in, first-out (FIFO) method of process costing**

. . . to assign costs based on costs and equivalent units of work done in the current period

First-In, First-Out Method

The **first-in, first-out (FIFO) process-costing method** (1) assigns the cost of the previous accounting period's equivalent units in beginning work-in-process inventory to the first units completed and transferred out of the process; and (2) assigns the cost of equivalent units worked on during the *current* period first to complete beginning inventory, next to start and

FOCUS ON VALUES AND BEHAVIORS

ROYAL DUTCH/SHELL: MAKING ESTIMATIONS FOR ALL THE WRONG REASONS

A key input into process-costing calculations is the degree of completion of inventory, particularly with respect to conversion costs—that is, how much of the total conversion costs needed to complete one unit have been used for units still in process. Process-costing calculations pose many challenges for a company's management accountants because it is difficult to estimate conversion costs accurately. Management accountants must therefore work with department managers to get the best possible information when making these estimates. At the same time, management accountants must recognize the incentives department managers may have to bias estimates in favor of showing higher percentages of completion, resulting in higher inventory valuations and profits. If management accountants want their estimations to be sound, they must act sensitively and thoughtfully but also ask critical, tough-minded questions.

But what happens when management accountants and department managers do not make estimations responsibly? Consider Royal Dutch/Shell. Similar to conversion-cost estimations, oil companies must make many engineering and geological estimates and judgments to calculate their proven oil and natural gas reserves. In January 2004, Royal Dutch/Shell cut by 20%, or 3.9 billion barrels, its estimates of proven oil and gas reserves. Later on in 2004, *The New York Times* reported:

> *Internal corporate documents and interviews with oil executives and industry analysts describe a company that in the go-go period of the 1990s tried to manage its reserve figures much the way other companies managed their earnings—to satisfy investors.*
>
> *The documents show that worried executives felt compelled to increase the reserves, which throughout the first half of the 1990s were declining because discoveries did not keep pace with production.*
>
> *According to a confidential internal review . . . senior company executives ignored warnings over several years of the possible inflation of reserves. . . . The review also suggested that there may have been financial incentives for some executives to overstate reserves, although it provided few details. . . . Company officials have said in recent days that there is a minimal connection between increasing reserves and performance-related pay.*

As a result of these disclosures, Royal Dutch/Shell ousted its chairman, Sir Philip Watts, and another senior executive in March 2004. The Securities and Exchange Commission is investigating the company's accounting for reserves. Though the role played by the management accountants in this situation is still unclear, the Royal Dutch/Shell story serves as a reminder of the importance of acting with integrity.

Source: *S. Labaton and J. Gerth, "At Shell, New Accounting and Rosier Oil Outlook,"* The New York Times, *March 12, 2004, p. A1.*

complete new units, and finally to units in ending work-in-process inventory. The FIFO method assumes that the earliest equivalent units in work in process are completed first.

A distinctive feature of the FIFO process-costing method is that work done on beginning inventory before the current period is kept separate from work done in the current period. Costs incurred and units produced in the current period are used to calculate cost per equivalent unit of work done in the current period. In contrast, equivalent-unit and cost-per-equivalent-unit calculations under the weighted-average method *merge* units and costs in beginning inventory with units and costs of work done in the current period.

We now describe the FIFO method using the five-step procedure introduced earlier.

Step 1: **Summarize the Flow of Physical Units.** Exhibit 17-6, step 1, traces the flow of physical units of production. The following observations help explain the calculation of physical units under the FIFO method for Global Defense.

- The first physical units assumed to be completed and transferred out during the period are 225 units from beginning work-in-process inventory.
- The March data on page 601 indicate that 400 physical units were completed during March. The FIFO method assumes that of these 400 units, 175 units (400 units − 225 units from beginning work-in-process inventory) must have been started and completed during March.
- Ending work-in-process inventory consists of 100 physical units—the 275 physical units started minus the 175 units that were started and completed.
- The physical units "to account for" equal the physical units "accounted for" (500 units).

EXHIBIT 17-6

Steps 1 and 2: Summarize Output in Physical Units and Compute Output in Equivalent Units Using FIFO Method of Process Costing for Assembly Department of Global Defense for March 2007

During March 2007, beginning work in process had 0% direct materials and 40% conversion costs added to it. That's because at the start of March, beginning work in process was 100% complete with respect to direct materials and 60% complete with respect to conversion costs. This same concept applies to Exhibits 17-8 and 17-13.

	A	B	C	D
1		**(Step 1)**	**(Step 2)**	
2			**Equivalent Units**	
3	**Flow of Production**	**Physical Units**	**Direct Materials**	**Conversion Costs**
4	Work in process, beginning (given, p. 601)	225	(work done before current period)	
5	Started during current period (given, p. 601)	275		
6	To account for	500		
7	Completed and transferred out during current period:			
8	From beginning work in process[a]	225		
9	[225 x (100% - 100%); 225 x (100% - 60%)]		0	90
10	Started and completed	175[b]		
11	(175 x 100%;175 x 100%)		175	175
12	Work in process, ending[c] (given, p. 601)	100		
13	(100 x 100%; 100 x 50%)		100	50
14	Accounted for	500		
15	Work done in current period only		275	315
16				
17	[a]Degree of completion in this department: direct materials, 100%; conversion costs, 60%.			
18	[b]400 physical units completed and transferred out minus 225 physical units completed and			
19	transferred out from beginning work-in-process inventory.			
20	[c]Degree of completion in this department: direct materials, 100%; conversion costs, 50%.			

Step 2: Compute Output in Terms of Equivalent Units. Exhibit 17-6 also presents the computations for step 2 under the FIFO method. *The equivalent-unit calculations for each cost category focus on equivalent units of work done in the current period (March) only.*

Under the FIFO method, equivalent units of work done in March on the beginning work-in-process inventory equal 225 physical units times *the percentage of work remaining to be done in March to complete these units*: 0% for direct materials, because beginning work in process is 100% complete with respect to direct materials, and 40% for conversion costs, because beginning work in process is 60% complete with respect to conversion costs. The results are 0 (0% × 225) equivalent units of work for direct materials and 90 (40% × 225) equivalent units of work for conversion costs.

The equivalent units of work done on the 175 physical units started and completed equals 175 units times 100% for both direct materials and conversion costs, because all work on these units is done in the current period.

The equivalent units of work done on the 100 units of ending work in process equal 100 physical units times 100% for direct materials (because all direct materials for these units are added in the current period) and 50% for conversion costs (because 50% of conversion-costs work on these units is done in the current period).

Step 3: Compute Cost per Equivalent Unit. Exhibit 17-7 shows the step 3 computation of cost per equivalent unit for *work done in the current period only* for direct materials and conversion costs. For example, conversion cost per equivalent unit of $52 is obtained by dividing current-period conversion costs of $16,380 by current-period conversion-costs equivalent units of 315.

Step 4: Summarize Total Costs to Account For. The "Total Production Costs" column in Exhibit 17-7 presents step 4 and summarizes total costs to account for in March 2007 (beginning work in process and costs added in the current period) of $62,280, as described in the example data (p. 601).

Step 5: Assign Total Costs to Units Completed and to Units in Ending Work in Process. Exhibit 17-7 shows the assignment of costs under the FIFO method. Costs of work done in the current period are assigned (1) first to the additional work done to complete the beginning work in process, then (2) to work done on units started and completed during the current period, and finally (3) to

EXHIBIT 17-7 **Steps 3, 4, and 5: Compute Cost per Equivalent Unit, Summarize Total Costs to Account for, and Assign Total Costs to Units Completed and to Units in Ending Work in Process Using FIFO Method of Process Costing for Assembly Department of Global Defense for March 2007**

	A	B	C	D	E
1			**Total Production Costs**	**Direct Materials**	**Conversion Costs**
2		Work in process, beginning (given, p. 601)	$26,100	(costs of work done before current period)	
3	**(Step 3)**	Costs added in current period (given, p. 601)	36,180	$19,800	$16,380
4		Divide by equivalent units of work done in current period (Exhibit 17-6)		÷ 275	÷ 315
5		Cost per equivalent unit of work done in current period		$ 72	$ 52
6	**(Step 4)**	Total costs to account for	$62,280		
7	**(Step 5)**	Assignment of costs:			
8		Completed and transferred out (400 units)			
9		Work in process, beginning (225 units)	$26,100		
10		Costs added to beginning work in process in current period	4,680	(0[a] × $72) +	(90[a] × $52)
11		Total from beginning inventory	30,780		
12		Started and completed (175 units)	21,700	(175[b] × $72) +	(175[b] × $52)
13		Total costs of units completed and transferred out	52,480		
14		Work in process, ending (100 units):	9,800	(100[c] × $72) +	(50[c] × $52)
15		Total costs accounted for	$62,280		
16					
17	[a]Equivalent units used to complete beginning work in process from Exhibit 17-6, step 2.				
18	[b]Equivalent units started and completed from Exhibit 17-6, step 2.				
19	[c]Equivalent units in ending work in process from Exhibit 17-6, step 2.				

ending work in process. *Step 5 takes each quantity of equivalent units calculated in Exhibit 17-6, step 2, and assigns dollar amounts to them (using the cost-per-equivalent-unit calculations in step 3).* The goal is to use the cost of work done in the current period to determine total costs of all units completed from beginning inventory and from work started and completed in the current period, and costs of ending work in process.

Of the 400 completed units, 225 units are from beginning inventory and 175 units are started and completed during March. The FIFO method starts by assigning the costs of beginning work-in-process inventory of $26,100 to the first units completed and transferred out. As we saw in step 2, an additional 90 equivalent units of conversion costs are needed to complete these units in the current period. Current-period conversion cost per equivalent unit is $52, so $4,680 (90 equivalent units × $52 per equivalent unit) of additional costs are incurred to complete beginning inventory. Total production costs for units in beginning inventory are $26,100 + $4,680 = $30,780. The 175 units started and completed in the current period consist of 175 equivalent units of direct materials and 175 equivalent units of conversion costs. These units are costed at the cost per equivalent unit in the current period (direct materials, $72, and conversion costs, $52) for a total production cost of $21,700 [175 × ($72 + $52)].

Under FIFO, ending work-in-process inventory comes from units that were started but not fully completed during the current period. Total costs of the 100 partially assembled physical units in ending work in process are:

Direct materials:	
100 equivalent units × $72 cost per equivalent unit in March	$7,200
Conversion costs:	
50 equivalent units × $52 cost per equivalent unit in March	2,600
Total cost of work in process on March 31	$9,800

The following table summarizes total costs to account for and costs accounted for of $62,280 in Exhibit 17-7. Notice how under the FIFO method, the layers of beginning work in process and costs added in the current period are kept separate. The arrows indicate where the costs in each layer go—that is, to units completed and transferred out or to ending work in process. Be sure to include costs of beginning work in process ($26,100) when calculating costs of units completed from beginning inventory.

Costs to Account for			Costs Accounted for Calculated on a FIFO Basis	
			Completed and transferred out	
Beginning work in process	$26,100	→	Beginning work in process	$26,100
Costs added in current period	36,180	→	Used to complete beginning work in process	4,680
		→	Started and completed	21,700
			Completed and transferred out	52,480
		→	Ending work in process	9,800
Total costs to account for	$62,280		Total costs accounted for	$62,280

Before proceeding, review Exhibits 17-6 and 17-7 to check your understanding of the FIFO method. Note: Exhibit 17-6 deals only with physical and equivalent units, not costs. Exhibit 17-7 shows the cost amounts.

The journal entries under the FIFO method are identical to the journal entries under the weighted-average method except for one difference. The entry to record the cost of goods completed and transferred out would be $52,480 under the FIFO method instead of $52,000 under the weighted-average method.

Only rarely is an application of pure FIFO ever encountered in process costing. That's because FIFO is applied within a department to compile the cost of units *transferred out*, but as a practical matter, units *transferred in* during a given period usually are carried at a single average unit cost. For example, average cost of units transferred out of the Assembly Department is $52,480 ÷ 400 units = $131.20 per DG-19 unit. The Assembly Department uses FIFO to distinguish between monthly batches of production. The succeeding department, Testing, however, costs these units (which consist of costs incurred in both February and March) at one average unit cost ($131.20 in this illustration). If this averaging were not done, the attempt to track costs on a pure FIFO basis throughout a series of processes would be cumbersome. As a result, the FIFO method should really be called a *modified* or *department* FIFO method.

Comparison of Weighted-Average and FIFO Methods

Consider the summary of the costs assigned to units completed and to units still in process under the weighted-average and FIFO process-costing methods in our example for March 2007:

	Weighted Average (from Exhibit 17-5)	FIFO (from Exhibit 17-7)	Difference
Cost of units completed and transferred out	$52,000	$52,480	+$480
Work in process, ending	10,280	9,800	–$480
Total costs accounted for	$62,280	$62,280	

The weighted-average ending inventory is higher than the FIFO ending inventory by $480, or 4.9% ($480 ÷ $9,800 = 0.049, or 4.9%). This would be a significant difference when aggregated over the many thousands of products that Global Defense makes. When completed units are sold, the weighted-average method in our example leads to a lower cost of goods sold and, therefore, higher operating income and higher income taxes than the FIFO method. To see why the weighted-average method yields a lower cost of units completed, recall the data on page 601. Direct material cost per equivalent unit in beginning work-in-process inventory is $80, and conversion cost per equivalent unit in beginning work-in-process inventory is $60. These costs are greater, respectively, than the $72 direct materials cost and the $52 conversion cost per equivalent unit of work done during the current period. The current-period costs could be lower due to a decline in the prices of direct materials and conversion-cost inputs, and/or they could be lower as a result of Global Defense becoming more efficient in its processes by using smaller quantities of inputs per unit of output.

For the Assembly Department, FIFO assumes that (1) all the higher-cost units from the previous period in beginning work in process are the first to be completed and transferred out of the process and (2) ending work in process consists of only the lower-cost current-period units. The weighted-average method, however, smooths out cost per equivalent unit by assuming that (1) more of the lower-cost units are completed and transferred out and (2) some of the higher-cost units are placed in ending work in process. The decline in the current-period cost per equivalent unit results in a lower cost of units completed and transferred out and a higher ending work-in-process inventory under the weighted-average method compared with FIFO.

Cost of units completed and, hence, operating income can differ materially between the weighted-average and FIFO methods when (1) direct material or conversion cost per equivalent unit varies significantly from period to period and (2) physical-inventory levels of work in process are large in relation to the total number of units transferred out of the process. As companies move toward long-term procurement contracts that reduce differences in unit costs from period to period and reduce inventory levels, the difference in cost of units completed under the weighted-average and FIFO methods will decrease.[1]

Managers use information from process-costing systems to aid them in pricing and product-mix decisions and to provide them with feedback about their performance. FIFO provides managers with information about changes in costs per unit from one period to the next. Managers can use this information to adjust selling prices (for example, based on the $72 direct material cost and $52 conversion cost in March) and to evaluate performance in the current period compared with a budget or relative to performance in the previous period. By focusing on work done and costs of work done during the current period, the FIFO method provides useful information for these planning and control purposes.

The weighted-average method merges unit costs from different accounting periods, obscuring period-to-period comparisons. For example, the weighted-average method would lead managers at Global Defense to make decisions based on the $75.60 direct materials and $54.40 conversion costs, rather than the costs of $72 and $52 prevailing in the current period. Advantages of the weighted-average method, however, are its relative computational simplicity and its reporting of a more-representative average unit cost when input prices fluctuate markedly from month to month.

Activity-based costing plays a significant role in our study of job costing, but how is activity-based costing related to process costing? Each process—assembly, testing, and so on—can be considered a different (production) activity. However, no additional activities need to be identified within each process. That's because products are homogeneous and use resources of each process in a uniform way. The bottom line: activity-based costing has less applicability in process-costing environments.

Standard-Costing Method of Process Costing

7

Incorporate standard costs into process-costing systems

. . . use standard costs as the cost per equivalent unit

This section assumes that you have studied Chapters 7 and 8. Instructors and students who wish to skip this section can go directly to the section on Transferred-In Costs in Process Costing, page 612, without any loss of continuity.

Companies that use process-costing systems produce masses of identical or similar units of output. In such companies, it is fairly easy to set standards for quantities of inputs needed to produce output. Standard cost per input unit can then be multiplied by input quantity standards to develop standard cost per output unit.

The weighted-average and FIFO methods become very complicated when used in process industries that produce a wide variety of similar products. For example, a steel-

One reason for using the standard-costing method is that it simplifies record keeping.

[1]For example, suppose beginning work-in-process inventory for March were 125 physical units (instead of 225), and suppose costs per equivalent unit of work done in the current period (March) were direct materials, $75, and conversion costs, $55. Assume all other data for March are the same as in our example. In this case, the cost of units completed and transferred out would be $52,833 under the weighted-average method and $53,000 under the FIFO method. The work-in-process ending inventory would be $10,417 under the weighted-average method and $10,250 under the FIFO method (calculations not shown). These differences are much smaller than in the chapter example. The weighted-average ending inventory is higher than the FIFO ending inventory by only $167 ($10,417 – $10,250), or 1.6% ($167 ÷ $10,250 = 0.016, or 1.6%), compared with 4.9% higher in the chapter example.

rolling mill uses various steel alloys and produces sheets of various sizes and finishes. The different types of direct materials used and the operations performed are few, but used in various combinations, they yield a wide variety of products. Similarly, complex conditions are frequently found, for example, in plants that manufacture rubber products, textiles, ceramics, paints, and packaged food products. In each of these cases, if the broad averaging procedure of *actual* process costing were used, the result would be inaccurate costs for each product. Therefore, the standard-costing method of process costing is widely used in these industries.

Under the standard-costing method, teams of design and process engineers, operations personnel, and management accountants work together to determine *separate* standard costs per equivalent unit on the basis of different technical processing specifications for each product. Identifying standard costs for each product overcomes the disadvantage of costing all products at a single average amount, as under actual costing.

Computations Under Standard Costing

We return to the Assembly Department of Global Defense, but this time we use standard costs. Assume the same standard costs apply in February and March of 2007. Data for the Assembly Department are:

	A	B	C	D	E
1		Physical Units (DG-19s) (1)	Direct Materials (2)	Conversion Costs (3)	Total Costs (4) = (2) + (3)
2	Standard cost per unit		$ 74	$ 54	
3	Work in process, beginning inventory (March 1)	225			
4	Degree of completion of beginning work in process		100%	60%	
5	Beginning work in process inventory at standard costs		$16,650[a]	$ 7,290[a]	$23,940
6	Started during March	275			
7	Completed and transferred out during March	400			
8	Work in process, ending inventory (March 31)	100			
9	Degree of completion of ending work in process		100%	50%	
10	Actual total costs added during March		$19,800	$16,380	$36,180
11					
12	[a]Work in process, beginning inventory at standard costs				
13	Direct materials: 225 physical units x 100% completed x $74 per unit = $16,650				
14	Conversion costs: 225 physical units x 60% completed x $54 per unit = $7,290				

We illustrate the standard-costing method of process costing using the five-step procedure introduced earlier (p. 598).

Exhibit 17-8 presents steps 1 and 2. These steps are identical to the steps described for the FIFO method in Exhibit 17-6 because, as in FIFO, the standard-costing method also assumes that the earliest equivalent units in beginning work in process are completed first. Work done in the current period for direct materials is 275 equivalent units. Work done in the current period for conversion costs is 315 equivalent units.

Exhibit 17-9 describes steps 3, 4, and 5. In step 3, costs per equivalent unit are standard costs: direct materials, $74, and conversion costs, $54. *Therefore, costs per equivalent unit do not have to be computed as they were for the weighted-average and FIFO methods.*

Total costs to account for in Exhibit 17-9, step 4 (that is, the total debits to Work in Process—Assembly) differ from total debits to Work in Process—Assembly under the actual-cost-based weighted-average and FIFO methods. That's because, as in all standard-costing systems, the debits to the Work-in-Process account are at standard costs, rather than actual costs. These standard costs total $61,300 in Exhibit 17-9.

Exhibit 17-9, step 5, assigns total costs to units completed and transferred out and to units in ending work-in-process inventory, as in the FIFO method. Step 5 assigns amounts of standard costs to equivalent units calculated in Exhibit 17-8. These costs are assigned (1) first to complete beginning work-in-process inventory, (2) next to start and complete

EXHIBIT 17-8

Steps 1 and 2: Summarize Output in Physical Units and Compute Output in Equivalent Units Using Standard-Costing Method of Process Costing for Assembly Department of Global Defense for March 2007

	A	B	C	D
1		(Step 1)	(Step 2)	
2			Equivalent Units	
3	Flow of Production	Physical Units	Direct Materials	Conversion Costs
4	Work in process, beginning (given, p. 610)	225		
5	Started during current period (given, p. 610)	275		
6	To account for	500		
7	Completed and transferred out during current period:			
8	From beginning work in process[a]	225		
9	[225 x (100% - 100%); 225 x (100% - 60%)]		0	90
10	Started and completed	175[b]		
11	(175 x 100%, 175 x 100%)		175	175
12	Work in process, ending[c] (given, p. 610)	100		
13	(100 x 100%; 100 x 50%)		100	50
14	Accounted for	500		
15	Work done in current period only		275	315
16				
17	[a]Degree of completion in this department: direct materials, 100%; conversion costs, 60%.			
18	[b]400 physical units completed and transferred out minus 225 physical units completed and transferred out from beginning work-in-process inventory.			
19	[c]Degree of completion in this department: direct materials, 100%; conversion costs, 50%.			

EXHIBIT 17-9

Steps 3, 4, and 5: Compute Cost per Equivalent Unit, Summarize Total Costs to Account For, and Assign Total Costs to Units Completed and to Units in Ending Work in Process Using Standard-Costing Method of Process Costing for Assembly Department of Global Defense for March 2007

	A	B	C	D	E	F	G
1			Total Production Costs	Direct Materials		Conversion Costs	
2	(Step 3)	Standard cost per equivalent unit (given, p. 610)		$ 74		$ 54	
3		Work in process, beginning (given, p. 610)					
4		Direct materials, 225 x $74; Conversion costs, 135 x $54	$23,940	$16,650		$ 7,290	
5		Costs added in current period at standard costs					
6		Direct materials, 275 x $74; Conversion costs, 315 x $54	37,360	$20,350		$17,010	
7	(Step 4)	Total costs to account for	$61,300				
8	(Step 5)	Assignment of costs at standard costs:					
9		Completed and transferred out (400 units)					
10		Work in process, beginning (225 units)	$23,940				
11		Costs added to beginning work in process in current period	4,860	(0[a] x $74)	+	(90[a] x $54)	
12		Total from beginning inventory	28,800				
13		Started and completed (175 units)	22,400	(175[b] x $74)	+	(175[b] x $54)	
14		Total costs of units completed and transferred out	51,200				
15		Work in process, ending (100 units):	10,100	(100[c] x $74)	+	(50[c] x $54)	
16		Total costs accounted for	$61,300				
17	Summary of variances for current performance:						
18	Costs added in current period at standard costs (see step 3 above)			$20,350		$17,010	
19	Actual costs incurred (given, p. 610)			$19,800		$16,380	
20	Variance			$ 550	F	$ 630	F
21							
22	[a]Equivalent units to complete beginning work in process from Exhibit 17-8, step 2.						
23	[b]Equivalent units started and completed from Exhibit 17-8, step 2.						
24	[c]Equivalent units in ending work in process from Exhibit 17-8, step 2.						

new units, and (3) finally to start new units that are in ending work-in-process inventory. Note how the $61,300 total costs accounted for in step 5 of Exhibit 17-9 equal total costs to account for.

Accounting for Variances

For control purposes, variances for direct materials and conversion costs should be based on work done *in the current period only.*

Process-costing systems using standard costs record actual direct material costs in Direct Materials Control and actual conversion costs in Conversion Costs Control (analogous to Manufacturing Overhead Control in Chapter 8). In the journal entries that follow, the first two journal entries record these *actual costs*. In entries 3 and 4a, the Work-in-Process—Assembly account accumulates direct material costs and conversion costs at *standard costs*. Entries 3 and 4b isolate total variances. The final entry transfers out completed goods at standard costs.

1.	Assembly Department Direct Materials Control (at actual costs)	19,800	
	Accounts Payable Control		19,800
	To record direct materials purchased and used in production during March. This cost control account is debited with actual costs.		
2.	Assembly Department Conversion Costs Control (at actual costs)	16,380	
	Various accounts such as Wages Payable Control and Accumulated Depreciation		16,380
	To record Assembly Department conversion costs for March. This cost control account is debited with actual costs.		
	Entries 3, 4, and 5 use standard cost amounts from Exhibit 17-9.		
3.	Work in Process—Assembly (at standard costs)	20,350	
	Direct Materials Variances		550
	Assembly Department Direct Materials Control		19,800
	To record standard costs of direct materials assigned to units worked on and total direct materials variances.		
4a.	Work in Process—Assembly (at standard costs)	17,010	
	Assembly Department Conversion Costs Allocated		17,010
	To record conversion costs allocated at standard rates to the units worked on during March.		
4b.	Assembly Department Conversion Costs Allocated	17,010	
	Conversion Costs Variances		630
	Assembly Department Conversion Costs Control		16,380
	To record total conversion costs variances.		
5.	Work in Process—Testing (at standard costs)	51,200	
	Work in Process—Assembly (at standard costs)		51,200
	To record standard costs of units completed and transferred out from Assembly to Testing.		

Variances arise under standard costing, as in entries 3 and 4b. That's because the standard costs assigned to products on the basis of work done in the current period do not equal actual costs incurred in the current period. Variances can be analyzed in little or great detail for planning and control purposes, as described in Chapters 7 and 8. Sometimes direct materials price variances are isolated at the time direct materials are purchased and only efficiency variances are computed in entry 3. Exhibit 17-10 shows how the costs flow through the general-ledger accounts under standard costing.

8

Apply process-costing methods to situations with transferred-in costs

. . . using weighted-average and FIFO methods

Transferred-In Costs in Process Costing

Many process-costing systems have two or more departments or processes in the production cycle. As units move from department to department, the related costs are also transferred by monthly journal entries. **Transferred-in costs** (also called **previous-department costs**) are costs incurred in previous departments that are carried forward as the product's cost when it moves to a subsequent process in the production cycle. If standard costs are

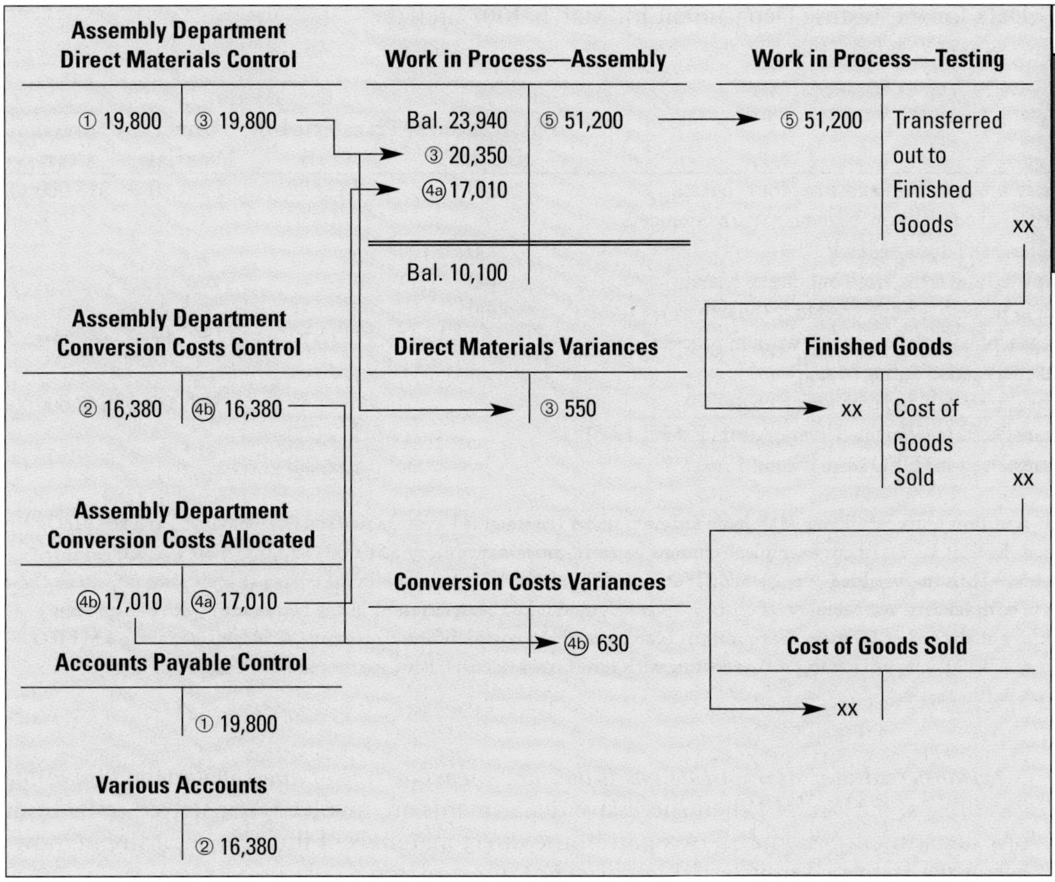

EXHIBIT 17-10

Flow of Standard Costs in a Process-Costing System for Assembly Department of Global Defense for March 2007

used, accounting for such transfers is simple. However, if the weighted-average or FIFO method is used, the accounting becomes more complex.

We now extend our Global Defense example to the Testing Department. As the assembly process is completed, the Assembly Department of Global Defense immediately transfers DG-19 units to the Testing Department. In Testing, units receive additional direct materials at the *end* of the process, crating and other packing materials to prepare units for shipment. Conversion costs are added evenly during the Testing Department's process. As units are completed in Testing, they are immediately transferred to Finished Goods. Computation of Testing Department costs consists of transferred-in costs, as well as direct materials and conversion costs that are added in Testing.

The following diagram represents these facts:

This graphic provides a helpful overview of costing units in the Testing Department.

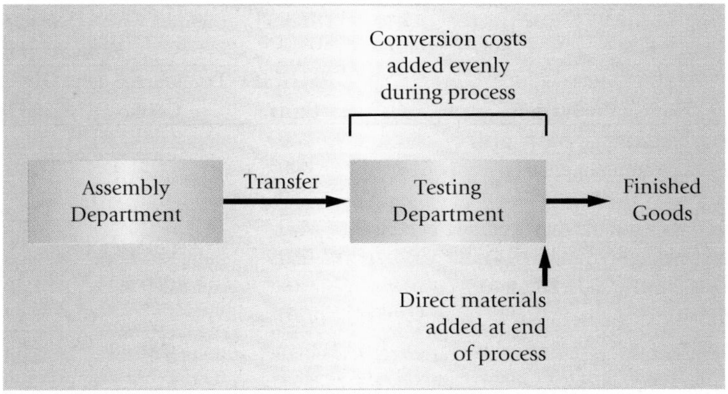

Data for the Testing Department for March 2007 are:

	A	B	C	D	E
1		Physical Units (DG-19s)	Transferred-in Costs	Direct Materials	Conversion Costs
2	Work in process, beginning inventory (March 1)	240	$33,600	$ 0	$18,000
3	Degree of completion, beginning work in process		100%	0%	62.5%
4	Transferred-in during March	400			
5	Completed and transferred out during March	440			
6	Work in process, ending inventory (March 31)	200			
7	Degree of completion,ending work in process		100%	0%	80%
8	Total costs added during March				
9	Direct materials and conversion costs			$13,200	$48,600
10	Transferred-in (Weighted-average from Exhibit 17-5)[a]		$52,000		
11	Transferred-in (FIFO from Exhibit 17-7)[a]		$52,480		
12					
13	[a] The transferred-in costs during March are different under the weighted-average method (Exhibit 17-5) and the FIFO method (Exhibit 17-7). In our example, beginning work-in-process inventory $51,600 ($33,600 + $0 + $18,000) is the same under both the weighted-average and FIFO inventory methods because we assume costs per equivalent unit to be the same in both January and February. If costs per equivalent unit had been different in the two months, work-in-process inventory at the end of February (beginning of March) would be costed differently under the weighted-average and FIFO methods. The basic approach to process costing with transferred-in costs, however, would still be the same as what we describe in this section.				

Transferred-in costs are treated as if they are a separate type of direct material added at the beginning of the process. When successive departments are involved, transferred units from one department become all or a part of the direct materials of the next department; however, they are called transferred-in costs, not direct material costs.

Transferred-In Costs and the Weighted-Average Method

To examine the weighted-average process-costing method with transferred-in costs, we use the five-step procedure described earlier (p. 598) to assign costs of the Testing Department to units completed and transferred out and to units in ending work in process.

Exhibit 17-11 shows steps 1 and 2. The computations are similar to the calculations of equivalent units under the weighted-average method for the Assembly Department in Exhibit 17-4, but here we also have transferred-in costs as an additional input. All units, whether completed and transferred out during the period or in ending work in process, are fully completed as to transferred-in costs carried forward from the previous process. But direct material costs have a zero degree of completion in both beginning and ending work-in-process inventories because, in Testing, direct materials are introduced at the *end* of the process.

Exhibit 17-12 describes steps 3, 4, and 5 for the weighted-average method. Beginning work in process and work done in the current period are combined for purposes of computing cost per equivalent unit for transferred-in costs, direct material costs, and conversion costs.

EXHIBIT 17-11

Steps 1 and 2: Summarize Output in Physical Units and Compute Output in Equivalent Units Using Weighted-Average Method of Process Costing for Testing Department of Global Defense for March 2007

	A	B	C	D	E
1		(Step 1)	(Step 2)		
2			Equivalent Units		
3	Flow of Production	Physical Units	Transferred-in Costs	Direct Materials	Conversion Costs
4	Work in process, beginning (given, p. 614)	240			
5	Transferred-in during current period (given, p. 614)	400			
6	To account for	640			
7	Completed and transferred out during current period:	440	440	440	440
8	Work in process, ending[a] (given, p. 614)	200			
9	(200 x 100%; 200 x 0%; 200 x 80%)		200	0	160
10	Accounted for	640			
11	Work done to date		640	440	600
12					
13	[a]Degree of completion in this department: transferred-in costs, 100%; direct materials, 0%; conversion costs, 80%.				

EXHIBIT 17-12 **Steps 3, 4, and 5: Compute Cost per Equivalent Unit, Summarize Total Costs to Account for, and Assign Total Costs to Units Completed and to Units in Ending Work in Process Using Weighted-Average Method of Process Costing for Testing Department of Global Defense for March 2007**

	A	B	C	D	E	F
1			Total Production Costs	Transferred-in Costs	Direct Materials	Conversion Costs
2	(Step 3)	Work in process, beginning (given, p. 614)	$ 51,600	$ 33,600	$ 0	$18,000
3		Costs added in current period (given, p. 614)	113,800	52,000	13,200	48,600
4		Costs incurred to date		$ 85,600	$13,200	$66,600
5		Divide by equivalent units of work done to date (Exhibit 17-11)		÷ 640	÷ 440	÷ 600
6		Cost per equivalent unit of work done to date		$ 133.75	$ 30	$ 111
7	(Step 4)	Total costs to account for	$165,400			
8	(Step 5)	Assignment of costs:				
9		Completed and transferred out (440 units)	$120,890	(440[a] x $133.75)	+ (440[a] x $30)	+ (440[a] x $111)
10		Work in process, ending (200 units):	44,510	(200[b] x $133.75)	+ (0[b] x $30)	+ (160[b] x $111)
11		Total costs accounted for	$165,400			
12						
13	[a]Equivalent units completed and transferred out from Exhibit 17-11, step 2.					
14	[b]Equivalent units in ending work in process from Exhibit 17-11, step 2.					

The journal entry for the transfer from Testing to Finished Goods (see Exhibit 17-12) is:

Finished Goods Control	120,890	
Work in Process—Testing		120,890
To record cost of goods completed and transferred from Testing to Finished Goods.		

Entries in the Work in Process—Testing account (see Exhibit 17-12) are:

Work in Process—Testing

Beginning inventory, March 1	51,600	Transferred out	120,890
Transferred-in costs	52,000		
Direct materials	13,200		
Conversion costs	48,600		
Ending inventory, March 31	44,510		

Transferred-In Costs and the FIFO Method

To examine the FIFO process-costing method with transferred-in costs, we again use the five-step procedure. Exhibit 17-13 shows steps 1 and 2. Other than considering transferred-in costs, computations of equivalent units are the same as under the FIFO method for the Assembly Department shown in Exhibit 17-6.

Exhibit 17-14 describes steps 3, 4, and 5. Cost per equivalent unit for the current period in step 3 is calculated on the basis of costs transferred in and work done in the current period only. In steps 4 and 5, total costs to account for and accounted for of $165,880 under the FIFO method differ from the corresponding amounts under the weighted-average method of $165,400. That's because of different costs of completed units transferred in from the Assembly Department under the two methods—$52,480 under FIFO and $52,000 under weighted average.

The journal entry for the transfer from Testing to Finished Goods (see Exhibit 17-14) is:

Finished Goods Control	122,360	
Work in Process—Testing		122,360
To record cost of goods completed and transferred from Testing to Finished Goods.		

EXHIBIT 17-13 Steps 1 and 2: Summarize Output in Physical Units and Compute Output in Equivalent Units Using FIFO Method of Process Costing for Testing Department of Global Defense for March 2007

	A	B	C	D	E
1		(Step 1)	(Step 2)		
2			Equivalent Units		
3	Flow of Production	Physical Units	Transferred-in Costs	Direct Materials	Conversion Costs
4	Work in process, beginning (given, p. 614)	240	(work done before current period)		
5	Transferred-in during current period (given, p. 614)	400			
6	To account for	640			
7	Completed and transferred out during current period:				
8	From beginning work in process[a]	240			
9	[240 x (100% - 100%); 240 x (100% - 0%); 240 x (100% - 62.5%)]		0	240	90
10	Started and completed	200[b]			
11	(200 x 100%; 200 x 100%; 200 x 100%)		200	200	200
12	Work in process, ending[c] (given, p. 614)	200			
13	(200 x 100%; 200 x 0%; 200 x 80%)		200	0	160
14	Accounted for	640			
15	Work done in current period only		400	440	450
16					
17	[a]Degree of completion in this department: Transferred-in costs, 100%; direct materials, 0%; conversion costs, 62.5%.				
18	[b]440 physical units completed and transferred out minus 240 physical units completed and transferred out from beginning				
19	work-in-process inventory.				
20	[c]Degree of completion in this department: transferred-in costs, 100%; direct materials, 0%; conversion costs, 80%.				

EXHIBIT 17-14 Steps 3, 4, and 5: Compute Cost per Equivalent Unit, Summarize Total Costs to Account for, and Assign Total Costs to Units Completed and to Units in Ending Work in Process Using FIFO Method of Process Costing for Testing Department of Global Defense for March 2007

	A	B	C	D	E	F
1			Total Production Costs	Transferred-in Costs	Direct Materials	Conversion Costs
2		Work in process, beginning (given, p. 614)	$ 51,600	(costs of work done before current period)		
3	(Step 3)	Costs added in current period (given, p. 614)	114,280	$52,480	$13,200	$48,600
4		Divide by equivalent units of work done in current period (Exhibit 17-13)		÷ 400	÷ 440	÷ 450
5		Cost per equivalent unit of work done in current period		$131.20	$ 30	$ 108
6	(Step 4)	Total costs to account for	$165,880			
7	(Step 5)	Assignment of costs:				
8		Completed and transferred out (440 units)				
9		Work in process, beginning (240 units)	$ 51,600			
10		Costs added to beginning work in process in current period	16,920	(0[a] x $131.20) +	(240[a] x $30) +	(90[a] x $108)
11		Total from beginning inventory	68,520			
12		Started and completed (200 units)	53,840	(200[b] x $131.20) +	(200[b] x $30) +	(200[b] x $108)
13		Total costs of units completed and transferred out	122,360			
14		Work in process, ending (200 units):	43,520	(200[c] x $131.20) +	(0[c] x $30) +	(160[c] x $108)
15		Total costs accounted for	$165,880			
16						
17	[a]Equivalent units used to complete beginning work in process from Exhibit 17-13, step 2.					
18	[b]Equivalent units started and completed from Exhibit 17-13, step 2.					
19	[c]Equivalent units in ending work in process from Exhibit 17-13, step 2.					

Entries in the Work in Process—Testing account (see Exhibit 17-14) are:

Work in Process—Testing

Beginning inventory, March 1	51,600	Transferred out	122,360
Transferred-in costs	52,480		
Direct materials	13,200		
Conversion costs	48,600		
Ending inventory, March 31	43,520		

Remember that in a series of interdepartmental transfers, each department is regarded as separate and distinct for accounting purposes. All costs transferred in during a given accounting period are carried at the same unit cost, as described when discussing modified FIFO (p. 608), whether previous departments used the weighted-average method or the FIFO method.

Points to Remember About Transferred-In Costs

Some points to remember when accounting for transferred-in costs are:

1. Be sure to include transferred-in costs from previous departments in your calculations.
2. In calculating costs to be transferred on a FIFO basis, do not overlook costs assigned in the previous period to units that were in process at the beginning of the current period but are now included in the units transferred. For example, do not overlook the $51,600 in Exhibit 17-14.
3. Unit costs may fluctuate between periods. Therefore, transferred units may contain batches accumulated at different unit costs. For example, the 400 units transferred in at $52,480 in Exhibit 17-14 using the FIFO method consist of units that have different unit costs of direct materials and conversion costs when these units were worked on in the Assembly Department (see Exhibit 17-7). Remember, however, that when these units are transferred to the Testing Department, they are costed at *one average unit cost* of $131.20 ($52,480 ÷ 400 units), as in Exhibit 17-14.
4. Units may be measured in different denominations in different departments. Consider each department separately. For example, unit costs could be based on kilograms in the first department and liters in the second department. Accordingly, as units are received in the second department, their measurements must be converted to liters.

Study Tip: To check your understanding of the material in this chapter, see the Featured Exercise, true–false statements 6 and 9, and multiple-choice questions 1 through 9 (*Student Guide*, beginning p. 227). Fully explained answers begin on page 236.

Hybrid Costing Systems

Product-costing systems do not always fall neatly into either job-costing or process-costing categories. Consider Ford Motor Company. Automobiles may be manufactured in a continuous flow (suited to process costing), but individual units may be customized with a special combination of engine size, transmission, music system, and so on (which requires job costing). A **hybrid-costing system** blends characteristics from both job-costing and process-costing systems. Product-costing systems must often be designed to fit the particular characteristics of different production systems. Many production systems are a hybrid: They have some features of custom-order manufacturing and other features of mass-production manufacturing. Manufacturers of a relatively wide variety of closely related standardized products (for example, televisions, dishwashers, and washing machines) tend to use hybrid-costing systems. The Concepts in Action feature (p. 618) describes a hybrid-costing system at Adidas. The appendix to this chapter explains *operation costing,* a common type of hybrid-costing system.

CONCEPTS IN ACTION

Hybrid Costing for Customized Shoes at Adidas

Adidas has been designing and manufacturing athletic footwear for more than 80 years. While shoemakers have long individually crafted shoes for professional athletes, Adidas took this concept a step further when it initiated the *mi adidas* program. *Mi adidas* allows customers throughout North America, Europe, and Asia the opportunity to create shoes to their exact personal specifications for function, fit, and aesthetics. *Mi adidas* is available in 100 U.S. retail stores and at specialized mobile units that travel to major sporting events, such as the Boston Marathon.

The process works as follows: The customer goes to a *mi adidas* station, where a salesperson develops an in-depth customer profile, a 3-D computer scanner develops a scan of the customer's feet, and the customer selects from among 90 to 100 different styles and colors for his/her modularly designed shoe. The resulting data are transferred to an Adidas plant, where small, multiskilled teams produce the customized shoe.

Historically, costs associated with individually customized products have generally fallen into the domain of job costing. Adidas, however, uses a hybrid-costing system—job costing for the material and customizable components that customers choose and process costing to account for the conversion costs of production. The cost of making each pair of shoes is calculated by accumulating all production costs and dividing by the number of shoes made. Even though each pair of shoes is different, the cost of making each pair is the same.

The combination of customization with certain features of mass production is called mass customization. It is the consequence of being able to digitize information that individual customers indicate is important to them. Various products that companies are now able to customize within a mass-production setting (for example, personal computers, blue jeans, bicycles) still require job costing of materials and considerable human intervention. However, as manufacturing systems become flexible, companies are also using process costing to account for the standardized conversion costs.

Sources: "The 'mi adidas' Mass Customization Initiative," IMD case number IMD159; N. Tait, "How 'mi adidas' Provides Personalized Style, Fit," *Apparel* (January 1, 2004); "Adidas America to Introduce Running Customization Shoe at 2002 LaSalle Bank Chicago Marathon," *Chicago Athlete* (October 2, 2002).

PROBLEM FOR SELF-STUDY

Allied Chemicals operates a thermo-assembly process as the second of three processes at its plastics plant. Direct materials in thermo-assembly are added at the end of the process. Conversion costs are added evenly during the process. The following data pertain to the Thermo-Assembly Department for June 2007:

	A	B	C	D	E
1		Physical Units	Transferred-in Costs	Direct Materials	Conversion Costs
2	Work in process, beginning inventory	50,000			
3	Degree of completion, beginning work in process		100%	0%	80%
4	Transferred-in during current period	200,000			
5	Completed and transferred out during current period	210,000			
6	Work in process, ending inventory	?			
7	Degree of completion, ending work in process		100%	0%	40%

Required

Compute equivalent units under (1) the weighted-average method and (2) the FIFO method.

SOLUTION

1. The weighted-average method uses equivalent units of work done to date to compute cost per equivalent unit. The calculations of equivalent units follow:

	A	B	C	D	E
1		(Step 1)	(Step 2)		
2			Equivalent Units		
3	Flow of Production	Physical Units	Transferred-in Costs	Direct Materials	Conversion Costs
4	Work in process, beginning (given)	50,000			
5	Transferred-in during current period (given)	200,000			
6	To account for	250,000			
7	Completed and transferred out during current period:	210,000	210,000	210,000	210,000
8	Work in process, ending [a]	40,000[b]			
9	(40,000 x 100%; 40,000 x 0%; 40,000 x 40%)		40,000	0	16,000
10	Accounted for	250,000			
11	Work done to date		250,000	210,000	226,000
12					
13	[a]Degree of completion in this department: transferred-in costs, 100%; direct materials, 0%; conversion costs, 40%.				
14	[b]250,000 physical units to account for minus 210,000 physical units completed and transferred out.				

2. The FIFO method uses equivalent units of work done in the current period only to compute cost per equivalent unit. The calculations of equivalent units follow:

	A	B	C	D	E	F
1		(Step 1)	(Step 2)			
2			Equivalent Units			
3	Flow of Production	Physical Units	Transferred-in Costs	Direct Materials	Conversion Costs	
4	Work in process, beginning (given)	50,000				
5	Transferred-in during current period (given)	200,000				
6	To account for	250,000				
7	Completed and transferred out during current period:					
8	From beginning work in process [a]	50,000				
9	[50,000 x (100% - 100%); 50,000 x (100% - 0%); 50,000 x (100% - 80%)]		0	50,000	10,000	
10	Started and completed	160,000[b]				
11	(160,000 x 100%; 160,000 x 100%; 160,000 x 100%)		160,000	160,000	160,000	
12	Work in process, ending [c]	40,000[d]				
13	(40,000 x 100%; 40,000 x 0%; 40,000 x 40%)		40,000	0	16,000	
14	Accounted for	250,000				
15	Work done in current period only		200,000	210,000	186,000	
16						
17	[a]Degree of completion in this department: transferred-in costs, 100%; direct materials, 0%; conversion costs, 80%.					
18	[b]210,000 physical units completed and transferred out minus 50,000 physical units completed and transferred out from beginning work-in-process inventory.					
19	[c]Degree of completion in this department: transferred-in costs, 100%; direct materials, 0%; conversion costs, 40%.					
20	[d]250,000 physical units to account for minus 210,000 physical units completed and transferred out.					

DECISION POINTS

The following question-and-answer format summarizes the chapter's learning objectives. Each decision presents a key question related to a learning objective. The guidelines are the answer to that question.

Decision	Guidelines
1. Under what conditions is a process-costing system used?	A process-costing system is used to determine cost of a product or service when masses of identical or similar units are produced. Industries using process-costing systems include food, textiles, and oil refining.

2. What are the five steps in a process-costing system to assign costs to units completed and to units in ending work in process?

The five steps in a process-costing system are (a) summarize the flow of physical units of output, (b) compute output in terms of equivalent units, (c) compute cost per equivalent unit, (d) summarize total costs to account for, and (e) assign total costs to units completed and to units in ending work in process.

3. What are equivalent units and why is it necessary to calculate them?

Equivalent units is a derived amount of output units that (a) takes the quantity of each input (factor of production) in units completed or in incomplete units in work in process and (b) converts the quantity of input into the amount of completed output units that could be made with that quantity of input. Equivalent-unit calculations are necessary when all physical units of output are not uniformly completed during an accounting period.

4. Are journal entries in process-costing systems similar to journal entries in job-costing systems?

Journal entries in a process-costing system are similar to journal entries in a job-costing system. The main difference is that in a process-costing system, there is a separate Work-in-Process account for each process.

5. What is the weighted-average method of process costing?

The weighted-average method computes unit costs by dividing total costs in the work-in-process account (whether from beginning work in process or from work started during the period) by total equivalent units completed to date, and it assigns this average cost to units completed and to units in ending work-in-process inventory.

6. What is the first-in, first-out method of process costing?

The first-in, first-out (FIFO) method computes unit costs based on costs incurred during the current period and equivalent units of work done in the current period. It assigns the costs of beginning work-in-process inventory to the first units completed, and it assigns costs of the equivalent units worked on during the current period first to complete beginning inventory, next to start and complete new units, and finally to units in ending work-in-process inventory.

7. How does the standard-costing method simplify process costing?

Under this method, standard costs serve as the cost per equivalent unit for assigning cost to units completed and to units in ending work-in-process inventory.

8. How are the weighted-average and FIFO process-costing methods applied to transferred-in costs?

The weighted-average method computes transferred-in costs per unit by dividing total transferred-in costs to date by total equivalent transferred-in units completed to date, and it assigns this average cost to units completed and to units in ending work-in-process inventory. The FIFO method computes transferred-in costs per unit based on costs transferred in during the current period and equivalent units of transferred-in costs of work done in the current period. The FIFO method assigns transferred-in costs in beginning work in process to units completed and costs transferred in during the current period first to complete beginning inventory, next to start and complete new units, and finally to units in ending work-in-process inventory.

APPENDIX: OPERATION COSTING

This appendix describes operation costing and uses an example to illustrate operation costing.

Overview of Operation-Costing Systems

An **operation** is a standardized method or technique that is performed repetitively, often on different materials, resulting in different finished goods. Multiple operations are usually conducted within a department. For instance, a suit maker may have a cutting operation and a hemming operation within a single department. The term *operation*, however, is often used loosely. It may be a synonym for a department or process. For example, some companies may call their finishing department a finishing process or a finishing operation.

An **operation-costing system** is a hybrid-costing system applied to batches of similar, but not identical, products. Each batch of products is often a variation of a single design, and it proceeds through a sequence of operations, but each batch does not necessarily move through the same operations as other batches. Within each operation, all product units are treated exactly alike, using identical amounts of the operation's resources. Batches are also called production runs.

Consider a company that makes suits. Management may select a single basic design for every suit to be made. Depending on specifications, each batch of suits varies somewhat from other batches. One batch may use wool; another batch, cotton. One batch may require special hand stitching; another batch, machine stitching. Other products manufactured in batches are semiconductors, textiles, and shoes.

An operation-costing system uses work orders that specify the needed direct materials and step-by-step operations. Product costs are compiled for each work order. Direct materials that are unique to different work orders are specifically identified with the appropriate work order, as in job costing. Each unit uses an identical amount of conversion costs for a given operation. For each operation, a single average conversion cost per unit is calculated, as in process costing, by dividing total conversion costs by all units passing through that operation. Average conversion cost is assigned to each unit passing through a given operation. Units that do not pass through an operation are not allocated any costs of that operation. Our examples assume only two cost categories—direct materials and conversion costs—but operation costing can have more than two cost categories. Costs in each category are identified with specific work orders using job-costing or process-costing methods as appropriate.

Managers find operation costing useful in cost management because operation costing focuses on control of physical processes, or operations, of a given production system. For example, in clothing manufacturing, managers are concerned with fabric waste, how many fabric layers that can be cut at one time, and so on. Operation costing measures in financial terms how well managers have controlled physical processes.

Illustration of an Operation-Costing System

Baltimore Company, a clothing manufacturer, produces two lines of blazers for department stores. Wool blazers use better-quality materials and undergo more operations than polyester blazers. Operations information on work order 423 for 50 wool blazers and work order 424 for 100 polyester blazers is:

	Work Order 423	Work Order 424
Direct materials	Wool Satin full lining Bone buttons	Polyester Rayon partial lining Plastic buttons
Operations		
1. Cutting cloth	Use	Use
2. Checking edges	Use	Do not use
3. Sewing body	Use	Use
4. Checking seams	Use	Do not use
5. Machine sewing of collars and lapels	Do not use	Use
6. Hand sewing of collars and lapels	Use	Do not use

Cost data for these work orders, started and completed in March 2006, are:

	Work Order 423	Work Order 424
Number of blazers	50	100
Direct material costs	$ 6,000	$3,000
Conversion costs allocated:		
Operation 1	580	1,160
Operation 2	400	—
Operation 3	1,900	3,800
Operation 4	500	—
Operation 5	—	875
Operation 6	700	—
Total manufacturing costs	$10,080	$8,835

As in process costing, all product units in any work order are assumed to consume identical amounts of conversion costs of a particular operation. Baltimore's operation-costing system uses a budgeted rate to calculate the conversion costs of each operation. The budgeted rate for Operation 1 (amounts assumed) is:

$$\begin{aligned}\text{Operation 1 budgeted conversion-cost rate for 2006} &= \frac{\text{Operation 1 budgeted conversion costs for 2006}}{\text{Operation 1 budgeted product units for 2006}}\\ &= \frac{\$232{,}000}{20{,}000\text{ units}}\\ &= \$11.60\text{ per unit}\end{aligned}$$

In the Baltimore Company example, the 20,000-unit denominator level is the sum of wool jackets and polyester jackets that managers expect to be processed in Operation 1. It's appropriate to use this sum of the two types of jackets because each jacket requires the same amount of conversion costs.

Budgeted conversion costs of Operation 1 include labor, power, repairs, supplies, depreciation, and other overhead of this operation. If some units have not been completed (so all units in Operation 1 have not received the same amounts of conversion costs), the conversion-cost rate is computed by dividing budgeted conversion costs by *equivalent units* of conversion costs, as in process costing.

As goods are manufactured, conversion costs are allocated to the work orders processed in Operation 1 by multiplying the $11.60 conversion cost per unit by the number of units processed. Conversion costs of Operation 1 for 50 wool blazers (work order 423) are $11.60 per blazer × 50 blazers = $580; and for 100 polyester blazers (work order 424) are $11.60 per blazer × 100 blazers = $1,160. If work order 424 had contained 75 blazers, its total costs in Operation 1 would be $870 ($11.60 per blazer × 75 blazers). When equivalent units are used to calculate the conversion-cost rate, costs are allocated to work orders by multiplying conversion cost per equivalent unit by number of equivalent units in the work order. Direct material costs of $6,000 for the 50 wool blazers (work order 423) and $3,000 for the 100 polyester blazers (work order 424) are specifically identified with each order, as in job costing. Remember the basic point in operation costing: Operation unit costs are assumed to be the same regardless of the work order, but direct material costs vary across orders when the materials for each work order vary.

Journal Entries

Actual conversion costs for Operation 1 in March 2006—assumed to be $24,400, of which $580 are on work order 423 and $1,160 are on work order 424—are entered into a Conversion Costs Control account:

1. Conversion Costs Control	24,400	
Various accounts (such as Wages Payable Control and Accumulated Depreciation)		24,400

Summary journal entries for assigning costs to polyester blazers (work order 424) follow. Entries for wool blazers would be similar. Of the $3,000 of direct materials for work order 424, $2,975 are used in Operation 1. The journal entry to record direct materials used for the 100 polyester blazers in March 2006 is:

2. Work in Process, Operation 1	2,975	
Materials Inventory Control		2,975

The journal entry to record the allocation of conversion costs to products uses the budgeted rate of $11.60 per blazer times the 100 polyester blazers processed, or $1,160:

3. Work in Process, Operation 1	1,160	
Conversion Costs Allocated		1,160

The journal entry to record the transfer of the 100 polyester blazers (at a cost of $2,975 + $1,160) from Operation 1 to Operation 3 (polyester blazers do not go through Operation 2) is:

4. Work in Process, Operation 3	4,135	
Work in Process, Operation 1		4,135

After posting these entries, the Work in Process, Operation 1, account appears as follows:

Work in Process, Operation 1

② Direct materials	2,975	④ Transferred to Operation 3	4,135
③ Conversion costs allocated	1,160		
Ending inventory, March 31	0		

Costs of the blazers are transferred through the operations in which blazers are worked on and then to finished goods in the usual manner. Costs are added throughout the fiscal year in the Conversion Costs Control account and the Conversion Costs Allocated account. Any overallocation or underallocation of conversion costs is disposed of in the same way as overallocated or underallocated manufacturing overhead in a job-costing system. (See pp. 118–122.)

TERMS TO LEARN

This chapter and the Glossary at the end of the book contain definitions of:

equivalent units (p. 598)
first-in, first-out (FIFO) process-costing method (p. 604)
hybrid-costing system (p. 617)
operation (p. 620)
operation-costing system (p. 620)
previous-department costs (p. 612)
transferred-in costs (p. 612)
weighted-average process-costing method (p. 602)

PH Grade Assist

Prentice Hall Grade Assist (PHGA)

Your professor may ask you to complete selected exercises and problems in Prentice Hall Grade Assist (PHGA). PHGA is an online tool that can help you master the chapter's topics. It provides you with multiple variations of exercises and problems designated by the PHGA icon. You can rework these exercises and problems—each time with new data—as many times as you need. You also receive immediate feedback and grading.

ASSIGNMENT MATERIAL

Questions

17-1 Give three examples of industries that use process-costing systems.

17-2 In process costing, why are costs often divided into two main classifications?

17-3 Explain equivalent units. Why are equivalent-unit calculations necessary in process costing?

17-4 What problems might arise in estimating the degree of completion of semiconductor chips in a semiconductor plant?

17-5 Name the five steps in process costing when equivalent units are computed.

17-6 Name the three inventory methods commonly associated with process costing.

17-7 Describe the distinctive characteristic of weighted-average computations in assigning costs to units completed and to units in ending work in process.

17-8 Describe the distinctive characteristic of FIFO computations in assigning costs to units completed and to units in ending work in process.

17-9 Why should the FIFO method be called a modified or department FIFO method?

17-10 Identify a major advantage of the FIFO method for purposes of planning and control.

17-11 Identify the main difference between journal entries in process costing and job costing.

17-12 "The standard-costing method is particularly applicable to process-costing situations." Do you agree? Why?

17-13 Why should the accountant distinguish between transferred-in costs and additional direct material costs for each subsequent department in a process-costing system?

17-14 "Transferred-in costs are those costs incurred in the preceding accounting period." Do you agree? Explain.

17-15 "There's no reason for me to get excited about the choice between the weighted-average and FIFO methods in my process-costing system. I have long-term contracts with my materials suppliers at fixed prices." Do you agree with this statement made by a plant controller. Explain.

Exercises

PH Grade Assist

17-16 Equivalent units, zero beginning inventory. International Electronics manufactures microchips in large quantities. Each microchip undergoes assembly and testing. The total assembly costs during January 2007 were:

Direct materials used	$ 720,000
Conversion costs	760,000
Total manufacturing costs	$1,480,000

Required

1. Assume there was no beginning inventory on January 1, 2007. During January, 10,000 microchips were placed into production and all 10,000 were fully completed at the end of the month. What is the unit cost of an assembled microchip in January?
2. Assume that during February 10,000 microchips are placed into production. Further assume the same total assembly costs for January are also incurred in February, but only 9,000 microchips are fully completed at the end of the month. All direct materials have been added to the remaining 1,000

microchips. However, on average, these remaining 1,000 microchips are only 50% complete as to conversion costs. (a) What are the equivalent units for direct materials and conversion costs and their respective costs per equivalent unit for February? (b) What is the unit cost of an assembled microchip in February 2007?

3. Explain the difference in your answers to requirements 1 and 2.

17-17 Journal entries (continuation of 17-16). Refer to requirement 2 of Exercise 17-16.

Required

Prepare summary journal entries for the use of direct materials and incurrence of conversion costs. Also prepare a journal entry to transfer out the cost of goods completed. Show the postings to the Work-in-Process account.

PH Grade Assist

17-18 Zero beginning inventory, materials introduced in middle of process. Vaasa Chemicals has a Mixing Department and a Refining Department. Its process-costing system in the Mixing Department has two direct materials cost categories (Chemical P and Chemical Q) and one conversion costs pool. The following data pertain to the Mixing Department for July 2007:

Units	
Work in process, July 1	0
Units started	50,000
Completed and transferred to Refining Department	35,000
Costs	
Chemical P	$250,000
Chemical Q	70,000
Conversion costs	135,000

Chemical P is introduced at the start of operations in the Mixing Department, and chemical Q is added when the product is three-fourths completed in the Mixing Department. Conversion costs are added evenly during the process. The ending work in process in the Mixing Department is two-thirds complete.

Required

1. Compute the equivalent units in the Mixing Department for July 2007 for each cost category.
2. Compute (a) the cost of goods completed and transferred to the Refining Department during July and (b) the cost of work in process as of July 31, 2007.

PH Grade Assist

17-19 Weighted-average method, equivalent units. Consider the following data for the Satellite Assembly Division of Aerospatiale:

The Satellite Assembly Division uses the weighted-average method of process costing.

	Physical Units (Satellites)	Direct Materials	Conversion Costs
Beginning work in process (May 1)[a]	8	$ 4,933,600	$ 910,400
Started in May 2007	50		
Completed during May 2007	46		
Ending work in process (May 31)[b]	12		
Total costs added during May 2007		$32,200,000	$13,920,000

[a]Degree of completion: direct materials, 90%; conversion costs, 40%.

[b]Degree of completion: direct materials, 60%; conversion costs, 30%.

Required

Compute equivalent units for direct materials and conversion costs. Show physical units in the first column of your schedule.

PH Grade Assist

17-20 Weighted-average method, assigning costs (continuation of 17-19).

Required

For the data in Exercise 17-19, calculate cost per equivalent unit for direct materials and conversion costs, summarize total costs to account for, and assign total costs to units completed and transferred out and to units in ending work in process.

PH Grade Assist

17-21 FIFO method, equivalent units. Refer to the information in Exercise 17-19. Suppose the Satellite Assembly Division uses the FIFO method of process costing instead of the weighted-average method.

Required

Compute equivalent units for direct materials and conversion costs. Show physical units in the first column of your schedule.

PH Grade Assist

17-22 FIFO method, assigning costs (continuation of 17-21).

Required

For the data in Exercise 17-19, use the FIFO method to calculate cost per equivalent unit for direct materials and conversion costs, summarize total costs to account for, and assign total costs to units completed and transferred out and to units in ending work in process.

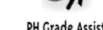

17-23 Standard-costing method, assigning costs. Refer to the information in Exercise 17-19. Suppose the Satellite Assembly Division uses the standard-costing method of process costing. Suppose further that the Satellite Assembly Division determines standard costs of $695,000 per equivalent unit for direct materials and $295,000 per equivalent unit for conversion costs for both beginning work in process and work done in the current period.

Required

1. Compute equivalent units for direct materials and conversion costs. Show physical units in the first column of your schedule.
2. Summarize total costs to account for, and assign total costs to units completed and transferred out and to units in ending work in process.
3. Compute the total direct materials and conversion costs variances for May 2007.

17-24 Weighted-average method, assigning costs. The Chatham Company makes a water-treatment chemical in a single processing department. Direct materials are added at the start of the process. Conversion costs are added evenly during the process. Chatham uses the weighted-average method of process costing. The following information for July 2007 is available.

		Equivalent Units	
	Physical Units	**Direct Materials**	**Conversion Costs**
Work in process, July 1	10,000[a]	10,000	7,000
Started during July	40,000		
Completed and transferred out during July	34,000	34,000	34,000
Work in process, July 31	16,000[b]	16,000	8,000

[a]Degree of completion: direct materials, 100%; conversion costs, 70%.
[b]Degree of completion: direct materials, 100%; conversion costs, 50%.

Total Costs for July 2007		
Work in process, beginning		
Direct materials	$60,000	
Conversion costs	70,000	$130,000
Direct materials added during July		280,000
Conversion costs added during July		371,000
Total costs to account for		$781,000

Required

1. Calculate cost per equivalent unit for direct materials and conversion costs.
2. Summarize total costs to account for, and assign total costs to units completed (and transferred out) and to units in ending work in process.

17-25 FIFO method, assigning costs.

Required

Do Exercise 17-24 using the FIFO method. Note that you first need to calculate the equivalent units of work done in the current period (for direct materials and conversion costs) to complete beginning work in process, to start and complete new units, and to produce ending work in process.

17-26 Standard-costing method, assigning costs. Refer to the information in Exercise 17-24. Suppose Chatham determines standard costs of $6.60 per equivalent unit for direct materials and $10.40 per equivalent unit for conversion costs for both beginning work in process and work done in the current period.

Required

1. Do Exercise 17-24 using the standard-costing method. Note that you first need to calculate the equivalent units of work done in the current period (for direct materials and conversion costs) to complete beginning work in process, to start and complete new units, and to produce ending work in process.
2. Compute the total direct materials and conversion costs variances for July 2007.

17-27 Transferred-in costs, weighted-average method. Aragon Industrials manufactures an industrial solvent in two departments: blending and finishing. This exercise focuses on the Finishing Department. Direct materials are added at the end of the process. Conversion costs are added evenly during the process. Aragon uses the weighted-average method of process costing. The following information for June 2007 is available.

Excel Lab www.prenhall.com/horngren/cost12e

	A	B	C	D	E
1		**Physical Units (tons)**	**Transferred-in Costs**	**Direct Materials**	**Conversion Costs**
2	Work in process, beginning inventory (June 1)	50	$50,000	$ 0	$20,000
3	Degree of completion, beginning work in process		100%	0%	60%
4	Transferred-in during June	90			
5	Completed and transferred out during June	100			
6	Work in process, ending inventory (June 30)	40			
7	Degree of completion, ending work in process		100%	0%	75%
8	Total costs added during June		$95,000	$25,000	$52,000

If you want to use Excel to solve this exercise, go to the Excel Lab at **www.prenhall.com/horngren/cost12e** and download the template for Exercise 17-27.

Required

1. Calculate equivalent units of transferred-in costs, direct materials, and conversion costs.
2. Calculate cost per equivalent unit for transferred-in costs, direct materials, and conversion costs.
3. Summarize total costs to account for, and assign total costs to units completed (and transferred out) and to units in ending work in process.

Excel Lab
www.prenhall.com/horngren/cost12e

17-28 Transferred-in costs, FIFO method. Refer to the information in Exercise 17-27. Suppose that Aragon uses the FIFO method instead of the weighted-average method in all its departments. The only changes to Exercise 17-27 under the FIFO method are that total transferred-in costs of beginning work in process on June 1 are $40,000 (instead of $50,000) and total transferred-in costs added during June are $87,200 (instead of $95,000).

If you want to use Excel to solve this exercise, go to the Excel Lab at **www.prenhall.com/horngren/cost12e** and download the template for Exercise 17-27.

Required

Do Exercise 17-27 using the FIFO method. Note that you first need to calculate equivalent units of work done in the current period (for transferred-in costs, direct materials, and conversion costs) to complete beginning work in process, to start and complete new units, and to produce ending work in process.

17-29 Operation costing (chapter appendix). Feather Light Shoe Company manufactures two styles of men's shoes: Designer and Regular. Designer style is made from leather, and Regular style uses synthetic materials. Three operations—cutting, sewing and packing—are common to both styles, but only Designer style passes through a lining operation. The conversion cost rates for 2007 are:

	Cutting	Sewing	Lining	Packing
Rate per unit (pair)	$10	$15	$8	$2

Details of two work orders processed in August are:

	Work Order 815	Work Order 831
Number of units (pairs)	1,000	5,000
Direct material costs	$30,000	$50,000
Style	Designer	Regular

Required

Calculate the total costs and the total cost per unit of work order 815 and work order 831.

Problems

17-30 Weighted-average method. Global Defense is a manufacturer of military equipment. Its Santa Fe plant manufactures the Interceptor Missile under contract to the U.S. government and friendly countries. All Interceptors go through an identical manufacturing process. Every effort is made to ensure that all Interceptors are identical and meet many demanding performance specifications. The process-costing system at the Santa Fe plant has a single direct-cost category (direct materials) and a single indirect-cost category (conversion costs). Each Interceptor passes through two departments: the Assembly Department and the Testing Department. Direct materials are added at the beginning of the process in Assembly. Conversion costs are added evenly during the Assembly Department's process. When the Assembly Department finishes work on each Interceptor, it is immediately transferred to Testing.

Global Defense uses the weighted-average method of process costing. Data for the Assembly Department for October 2007 are:

	Physical Units (Missiles)	Direct Materials	Conversion Costs
Work in process, October 1[a]	20	$ 460,000	$120,000
Started during October 2007	80		
Completed during October 2007	90		
Work in process, October 31[b]	10		
Total costs added during October 2007		$2,000,000	$935,000

[a]Degree of completion: direct materials, ?%; conversion costs, 60%.
[b]Degree of completion: direct materials, ?%; conversion costs, 70%.

Required

1. For each cost category, compute equivalent units in the Assembly Department. Show physical units in the first column of your schedule.
2. For each cost category, calculate cost per equivalent unit.
3. Summarize total Assembly Department costs for October 2007, and assign total costs to units completed and transferred out and to units in ending work in process.

17-31 Journal entries (continuation of 17-30).

Required

Prepare a set of summarized journal entries for all October 2007 transactions affecting Work in Process—Assembly. Set up a T-account for Work in Process—Assembly, and post your entries to it.

17-32 FIFO method (continuation of 17-30).

Do Problem 17-30 using the FIFO method of process costing. Explain any difference between the cost per equivalent unit in the Assembly Department under the weighted-average method and the FIFO method.

Required

17-33 Transferred-in costs, weighted average method (related to 17-30 to 17-32). Global Defense, as you know, manufactures the Interceptor Missile at its Santa Fe plant. It has two departments: Assembly Department and Testing Department. This problem focuses on the Testing Department. (Problems 17-30 to 17-32 focused on the Assembly Department.) Direct materials are added when the Testing Department process is 90% complete. Conversion costs are added evenly during the Testing Department's process. As work in Assembly is completed, each unit is immediately transferred to Testing. As each unit is completed in Testing, it is immediately transferred to Finished Goods.

Global Defense uses the weighted-average method of process costing. Data for the Testing Department for October 2007 are:

	Physical Units (Missiles)	Transferred-In Costs	Direct Materials	Conversion Costs
Work in process, October 1[a]	30	$ 985,800	$ 0	$ 331,800
Transferred in during October 2007	?			
Completed during October 2007	105			
Work in process, October 31[b]	15			
Total costs added during October 2007		$3,192,866	$3,885,000	$1,581,000

[a]Degree of completion: transferred-in costs, ?%; direct materials, ?%; conversion costs, 70%.
[b]Degree of completion: transferred-in costs, ?%; direct materials, ?%; conversion costs, 60%.

Required

1. What is the percentage of completion for (a) transferred-in costs and direct materials in beginning work-in-process inventory, and (b) transferred-in costs and direct materials in ending work-in-process inventory?
2. For each cost category, compute equivalent units in the Testing Department. Show physical units in the first column of your schedule.
3. For each cost category, calculate the cost per equivalent unit, summarize total Testing Department costs for October 2007, and assign total costs to units completed (and transferred out) and to units in ending work in process.
4. Prepare journal entries for October transfers from the Assembly Department to the Testing Department and from the Testing Department to Finished Goods.

17-34 Transferred-in costs, FIFO method (continuation of 17-33). Refer to the information in Problem 17-33. Suppose that Global Defense uses the FIFO method instead of the weighted-average method in all its departments. The only changes to Problem 17-33 under the FIFO method are that total transferred-in costs of beginning work in process on October 1 are $980,060 (instead of $985,800) and that total transferred-in costs added during October are $3,188,000 (instead of $3,192,866).

Required

Using the FIFO process-costing method, do Problem 17-33.

17-35 Weighted-average method. Star Toys manufactures one type of wooden toy figure. It buys wood as its direct material for the Forming Department of its Madison plant. The toys are transferred to the Finishing Department, where they are hand-shaped and metal is added to them. The process-costing system at Star Toys has a single direct-cost category (direct materials) and a single indirect-cost category (conversion costs). Direct materials are added when the Forming Department process is 10% complete. Conversion costs are added evenly during the Forming Department's process.

Star Toys uses the weighted-average method of process costing. Consider the following data for the Forming Department in April 2007:

	Physical Units (Toys)	Direct Materials	Conversion Costs
Work in process, April 1[a]	300	$ 7,500	$ 2,125
Started during April 2007	2,200		
Completed during April 2007	2,000		
Work in process, April 30[b]	500		
Total costs added during April 2007		$70,000	$42,500

[a]Degree of completion: direct materials, 100%; conversion costs, 40%.
[b]Degree of completion: direct materials, 100%; conversion costs, 25%.

Required

Summarize total Forming Department costs for April 2007, and assign total costs to units completed (and transferred out) and to units in ending work in process.

17-36 Journal entries (continuation of 17-35).

Required Prepare a set of summarized journal entries for all April transactions affecting Work in Process—Forming. Set up a T-account for Work in Process—Forming, and post your entries to it.

17-37 FIFO method (continuation of 17-35).

Required Do Problem 17-35 using FIFO and three decimal places for unit costs. If you did Problem 17-35, explain any difference between the cost of work completed and transferred out and the cost of ending work in process in the Forming Department under the weighted-average method and the FIFO method.

Excel Lab
www.prenhall.com/horngren/cost12e

17-38 Transferred-in costs, weighted-average method. Jhirmack Woolen Mills produces 100% wool yarn at its St. John's plant. It has two departments: drawing and spinning. Each department has one direct-cost category (direct materials) and one indirect-cost category (conversion costs).

Consider the Spinning Department, which takes as input drawn yarn from the Drawing Department, spins it, and produces bundles of wool yarn, ready to be sold to specialty dyeing and printing businesses. A softening agent (direct material) is added to the yarn when the spinning process is 80% complete. Conversion costs are added evenly during spinning operations. When those operations are done, the yarn is immediately transferred to Finished Goods. Jhirmack uses the weighted-average method of process costing. The following is a summary of the April 2007 operations of the Spinning Department:

	A	B	C	D	E
1		**Physical Units (tons of yarn)**	**Transferred-in Costs**	**Direct Materials**	**Conversion Costs**
2	Beginning work in process (April 1)	600	$21,850	$ 0	$10,000
3	Degree of completion, beginning work in process		100%	0%	40%
4	Transferred-in during April 2007	1,800			
5	Completed and transferred out during April	2,000			
6	Ending work in process (April 30)	400			
7	Degree of completion,ending work in process		100%	0%	60%
8	Total costs added during April		$96,000	$17,800	$46,000

If you want to use Excel to solve this problem, go to the Excel Lab at **www.prenhall.com/horngren/cost12e** and download the template for Problem 17-38.

Required

1. Summarize total Spinning Department costs for April 2007, and assign these costs to units completed (and transferred out) and to units in ending work in process.
2. Prepare journal entries for April transfers from the Drawing Department to the Spinning Department and from the Spinning Department to Finished Goods.

Excel Lab
www.prenhall.com/horngren/cost12e

17-39 Transferred-in costs, FIFO method. Refer to the information in Problem 17-38. Suppose that Jhirmack uses the FIFO method instead of the weighted-average method in all its departments. The only changes to Problem 17-38 under the FIFO method are that total transferred-in costs of beginning work in process on April 1 are $18,320 (instead of $21,850) and that total transferred-in costs added during April are $94,500 (instead of $96,000).

If you want to use Excel to solve this problem, go to the Excel Lab at **www.prenhall.com/horngren/cost12e** and download the template for Problem 17-38.

Required

1. Using the FIFO process-costing method, do Problem 17-38.
2. If you did Problem 17-38, explain any difference between the cost of work completed and transferred out and the cost of ending work in process in the Spinning Department under the weighted-average method and the FIFO method.

17-40 Transferred-in costs, weighted-average and FIFO methods. Frito-Lay, Inc., manufactures convenience foods, including potato chips and corn chips. Production of corn chips occurs in four departments: cleaning, mixing, cooking, and drying and packaging. Consider the Drying and Packaging Department, where direct materials (packaging) are added at the end of the process. Conversion costs are added evenly during the process. The accounting records of a Frito-Lay plant provide the following information for corn chips in its Drying and Packaging Department during a weekly period (week 37):

	Physical Units (Cases)	Transferred-In Costs	Direct Materials	Conversion Costs
Beginning work in process[a]	1,250	$29,000	$ 0	$ 9,060
Transferred in during week 37 from Cooking Department	5,000			
Completed during week 37	5,250			
Ending work in process, week 37[b]	1,000			
Total costs added during week 37		$96,000	$25,200	$38,400

[a]Degree of completion: transferred-in costs, 100%; direct materials, ?%; conversion costs, 80%.
[b]Degree of completion: transferred-in costs, 100%; direct materials, ?%; conversion costs, 40%.

Required

1. Using the weighted-average method, summarize the total Drying and Packaging Department costs for week 37, and assign total costs to units completed (and transferred out) and to units in ending work in process.
2. Assume that the FIFO method is used for the Drying and Packaging Department. Under FIFO, the transferred-in costs for work-in-process beginning inventory in week 37 are $28,920 (instead of $29,000 under the weighted-average method), and the transferred-in costs during week 37 from the Cooking Department are $94,000 (instead of $96,000 under the weighted-average method). All other data are unchanged. Summarize the total Drying and Packaging Department costs for week 37, and assign total costs to units completed and transferred out and to units in ending work in process using the FIFO method.

17-41 Standard costing with beginning and ending work in process. The Victoria Corporation uses the standard-costing method for its process-costing system. Standard costs for the Cooking Process are $6 per equivalent unit for direct materials and $3 per equivalent unit for conversion costs. All direct materials are introduced at the beginning of the process, and conversion costs are added evenly during the process. The operating summary for May 2007 includes the following data for the Cooking Process.

Excel Lab
www.prenhall.com/horngren/cost12e

	A	B	C	D
1		Physical Units	Direct Materials	Conversion Costs
2	Work in process, beginning inventory (May 1)	3,000	$ 18,000	$ 5,400
3	Degree of completion of beginning work in process		100%	60%
4	Started during May	20,000		
5	Completed and transferred out during May	18,000		
6	Work in process, ending inventory (May 31)	5,000		
7	Degree of completion of ending work in process		100%	50%
8	Total costs added during May		$125,000	$57,000

If you want to use Excel to solve this problem, go to the Excel Lab at **www.prenhall.com/horngren/cost12e** and download the template for Problem 17-41.

Required

1. Compute the total standard costs of units transferred out in May and the total standard costs of the May 31 inventory of work in process.
2. Compute the total May variances for direct materials and conversion costs.

17-42 Operation costing, equivalent units. (Chapter appendix, CMA, adapted) Gregg Industries manufactures plastic molded chairs. The three models of molded chairs, all variations of the same design, are Standard, Deluxe, and Executive. The company uses an operation-costing system.

Gregg has extrusion, form, trim, and finish operations. Plastic sheets are produced by the extrusion operation. During the forming operation, the plastic sheets are molded into chair seats and the legs are added. The Standard model is sold after this operation. During the trim operation, the arms are added to the Deluxe and Executive models and the chair edges are smoothed. Only the Executive model enters the finish operation, in which padding is added. All of the units produced receive the same steps within each operation.

The May units of production and direct material costs incurred are as follows:

	Units Produced	Extrusion Materials	Form Materials	Trim Materials	Finish Materials
Standard model	6,000	$ 72,000	$24,000	$ 0	$ 0
Deluxe model	3,000	36,000	12,000	9,000	0
Executive model	2,000	24,000	8,000	6,000	12,000
	11,000	$132,000	$44,000	$15,000	$12,000

The total conversion costs for the month of May are:

	Extrusion Operation	Form Operation	Trim Operation	Finish Operation
Total conversion costs	$269,500	$132,000	$69,000	$42,000

Required

1. For each product produced by Gregg Industries during May, determine (a) the unit cost and (b) the total cost. Support your answer with appropriate calculations.
2. Now consider the following information for June. All unit costs in June are identical to the May unit costs calculated in requirement 1a. At the end of June, 1,000 units of the Deluxe model remained in work in process. These units were 100% complete as to material costs and 60% complete in the trim operation. Determine the cost of the Deluxe model work-in-process inventory at the end of June.

17-43 Equivalent-unit computations, benchmarking, ethics. Margaret Major is the corporate controller of Leisure Suits. Leisure Suits has 20 plants that manufacture suits for retail stores. Each plant uses a process-costing system. At the end of each month, each plant manager submits a production report and a production-cost report. The production report includes the plant manager's estimate of the percentage of completion of the ending work in process as to direct materials and conversion costs. Major uses these estimates to compute the equivalent units of work done in each plant and the cost per equivalent unit of work done for both direct materials and conversion costs in each month. Plants are ranked from 1 to 20 in terms of (a) cost per equivalent unit of direct materials and (b) cost per equivalent unit of conversion costs. The three top-ranked plants in each category receive a bonus and are written up as the best in their class in the company newsletter.

Major has been pleased with the success of her benchmarking program. However, she has just received some unsigned letters stating that two plant managers have been manipulating their monthly estimates of percentage of completion in an attempt to obtain best-in-class status.

Required

1. Why and how might plant managers "manipulate" their monthly estimates of percentage of completion?
2. Major's first reaction is to contact each plant controller and discuss the problem raised by the unsigned letters. Is that a good idea?
3. Assume that the plant controller's primary reporting responsibility is to the plant manager and that each plant controller receives the phone call from Major mentioned in requirement 2. What is the ethical responsibility of each plant controller (a) to Margaret Major and (b) to Leisure Suits in relation to the equivalent-unit information each plant provides?
4. How might Major gain some insight into whether the equivalent-unit figures provided by particular plants are being manipulated?

Collaborative Learning Problem

17-44 Transferred-in costs, cost per equivalent unit, working backward. Lennox Plastics has two processes: extrusion and thermo-assembly. Consider the June 2007 data for physical units in the thermo-assembly process: beginning work in process, 15,000 units; transferred in from the Extruding Department during June, 9,000 units; ending work in process, 5,000 units. Direct materials are added when the process in the Thermo-Assembly Department is 80% complete. Conversion costs are added evenly during the process. Lennox Plastics uses the FIFO method of process costing. The following information is available.

	Transferred-In Costs	Direct Materials	Conversion Costs
Beginning work in process	$90,000	—	$45,000
Percentage completion of beginning work in process	100%	—	60%
Costs added in current period	$58,500	$57,000	$57,200
Cost per equivalent unit of work done in current period	$ 6.50	$ 3	$ 5.20

Required

1. For each cost category, compute equivalent units of work done in the current period.
2. For each cost category, compute separately the equivalent units of work done to complete beginning work-in-process inventory, to start and complete new units, and to produce ending work in process.
3. For each cost category, calculate the percentage of completion of ending work-in-process inventory.
4. Summarize total costs to account for, and assign total costs to units completed (and transferred out) and to units in ending work in process.

Get Connected: Cost Accounting in the News

WWW

Go to www.prenhall.com/horngren/cost12e for additional online exercise(s) that explore issues affecting the accounting world today. These exercises offer you the opportunity to analyze and reflect on how cost accounting helps managers to make better decisions and handle the challenges of strategic planning and implementation.

CHAPTER 17 Video Case[a]

NANTUCKET NECTARS: Process Costing

"Juice Guys" Tom First and Tom Scott started Nantucket Nectars in 1989 with a blender and the idea for a peach nectar drink. With a booming summer business servicing boats visiting the harbor off Nantucket Island, the two founders knew they wanted to find a way to keep their connection to the island after college graduation. What they didn't know was how big their simple juice-drink idea would become. Today, Nantucket Nectars makes close to 50 different juice drinks and flavored teas with all-natural ingredients and no preservatives. There must be something to those beverages, because sales in a recent year topped $70 million.

The process of converting fruit into juice blends starts with a recipe. The company's test kitchen develops the specifications for each drink and then gives those details to the company's buyers. The buyers secure the necessary quantities of ingredients, such as cane sugar and fruit juice concentrates, for delivery to one of five bottling plants around the country. The bottling plants, called "co-packers," are experts at producing large batches of bottled beverages, and they play a role in finalizing the specifications for each new drink recipe.

Inside the plant, beverage production is scheduled to achieve maximum efficiency. Ingredients are timed to arrive by the first of the month. Some materials, such as single-serve glass bottles, arrive throughout the day at the plant. The ingredients are mixed in 5,000-gallon batches, according to recipe specifications. Each batch makes about 36,000 bottles of finished juice. Every blended-juice batch is checked for quality to be sure the correct levels of acidity and sweetness are present before the batch is released to the production line.

From ingredient batching, the juice is pumped into storage tanks that feed the production line. The tank contents are heated to 190 degrees to inhibit bacteria growth. Empty glass bottles are removed from their shipping pallets and travel by automated conveyer through a 220-degree steam bath that tempers the glass before filling. Without this step, the cold glass would shatter when filled with hot juice. The conveyer line speed is set to fill 550 bottles per minute. The entire line shuts down if there is a problem at any point.

Once bottles are filled, they are capped and sprayed with ID codes on both cap and bottle shoulder. The codes contain bottling plant ID, date, and time. Then the bottles travel through a large cooling tunnel. The tunnel draws a vacuum in each bottle by lowering the liquid temperature to 100 to 105 degrees. This quick-cooling process also helps maintain juice color because Nantucket Nectars adds no preservatives for this purpose. The conveyer then moves through a check station to verify that each bottle has sealed properly and has cooled to the correct temperature. Each bottle will also pass by an electronic eye that checks to be sure it is filled to the right level. Those bottles that don't pass are mechanically taken off the line.

After this stage, the juice bottles are ready for labeling. An automated labeling machine glues a label to each bottle, then the bottles are moved via conveyer to a final quality checkpoint. Here, the bottles are inspected for proper labeling and spray codes. If problems are detected, the production line is halted until the problem is corrected. After passing inspection, the bottles are ready for tray packaging. Each full tray is called a "case," and it holds 20 bottles. Trays are inspected to be sure the correct amount of glue holds the ends securely so cases don't break open later. As full trays come off the production line, they are shrink-wrapped and bundled into pallets of 60 cases each. The pallets are wrapped in plastic and prepared for transport to a distribution warehouse. From there, distributors pick up their orders and deliver the juices to retail outlets for customer sale. About 20,000 cases, or 400,000 bottles, come off the production line each day.

QUESTIONS

1. Why is process costing an appropriate system of accounting for the costs of Nantucket Nectars' juice-beverage production?
2. What are the direct material costs associated with the production of juices, and when would those costs be added to the production process (beginning, middle, or end)?
3. What items would be considered "conversion costs"?
4. Think about the production process and the daily production of juice. How important are equivalent-unit calculations for costing units in ending inventory? Would you expect there to be significant differences in the inventory costs under the weighted-average and FIFO methods?

[a] *There is an additional video case on Process Costing at Jelly Belly available in the Instructor's Resource Manual.*

CHAPTER 18

SPOILAGE, REWORK, AND SCRAP

LEARNING OBJECTIVES

1. **Distinguish among spoilage, rework, and scrap**
2. **Describe the accounting procedures for normal and abnormal spoilage**
3. **Account for spoilage in process costing using the weighted-average method**
4. **Account for spoilage in process costing using the first-in, first-out (FIFO) method**
5. **Account for spoilage in process costing using the standard-costing method**
6. **Account for spoilage in job costing**
7. **Account for rework in job costing**
8. **Account for scrap**

John Shanahan, the CEO of Anzio Company, which manufactures recycling containers, has always been proud of his company's culture and longtime commitment to environmental responsibility. The company's halls are lined with numerous awards for its leadership, and employees take great pride in working there. So when the July 2006 financial statements became available, he was more than a little surprised to see a significant rise in spoiled units relative to prior periods. He wasted no time in calling Brad Foley, manufacturing manager, and Lillian Makhoul, management accountant, to his office.

John: The larger-than-usual number of spoiled units concerns me quite a bit. As you know, our margins are quite small, so even a small increase in spoilage can lead to a loss.

Brad: You're right, John. Lillian and I have already begun looking into the reasons for the excessive spoilage. We're very close to identifying the causes and making the changes necessary so this doesn't happen again.

John: I'd like to see a report on what you've found as soon as possible. Have you been involving our design and process engineers in your investigation? Working together as a team is critical, especially if significant improvements or changes need to be made.

Brad: Yes, they're all on board, and I've also brought the quality control staff and line workers into the discussion.

John: I knew you'd already be working on this. I'd like to see your team set some ambitious targets for reducing spoilage in the next couple of months.

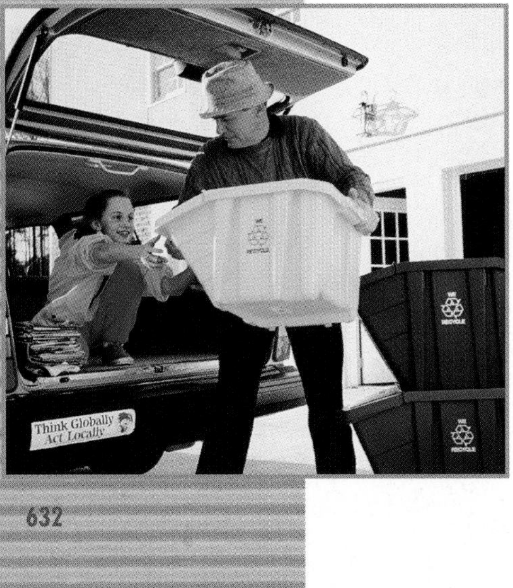

Managing spoilage, rework, and scrap is a challenge for many companies, regardless of a company's size or the products it manufactures. Managers are focusing increasingly on improving the quality of and reducing the defects in their products, services, and activities. A rate of defects regarded as normal in the past is no longer tolerable. Jack Welch, the former chairman and chief executive officer of General Electric (GE), considers emphasis on reducing defects in all of GE's operations as one of the reasons for the company's success. Welch describes GE's quality efforts as "the most challenging and potentially rewarding initiative we have ever undertaken." Highlighting and recording the costs of defects as they occur help managers better determine what to do about defects and their costs.

In this chapter, we focus on three types of costs that arise as a result of defects—spoilage, rework, and scrap—and ways to account for them. We also describe how to determine (1) cost of products, (2) cost of goods sold, and (3) inventory values when spoilage, rework, and scrap occur.

Terminology

The terms used in this chapter may seem familiar, but be sure you understand them in the context of management accounting.

Spoilage is units of production—whether fully or partially completed—that do not meet the specifications required by customers for good units and that are discarded or sold at reduced prices. Some examples of spoilage are defective shirts, jeans, shoes, and carpeting sold as "seconds," or defective aluminum cans sold to aluminum manufacturers for remelting to produce other aluminum products.

Rework is units of production that do not meet the specifications required by customers but which are subsequently repaired and sold as good finished units. For example, defective units of products (such as pagers, computers, and telephones) detected during or after the production process but before units are shipped to customers can sometimes be reworked and sold as good products.

Scrap is residual material that results from manufacturing a product. It has low total sales value compared with the total sales value of the product. Examples are short lengths from woodworking operations, edges from plastic molding operations, and frayed cloth and end cuts from suit-making operations.

Some amounts of spoilage, rework, or scrap are inherent in many production processes. For example, semiconductor manufacturing is so complex and delicate that some spoiled units are commonly produced; and usually, the spoiled units cannot be reworked. In the manufacture of high-precision machine tools, spoiled units can be reworked to meet standards, but only at a considerable cost. And in the mining industry, companies process ore that contains varying amounts of valuable metals and rock. Some amount of rock, which is scrap, is inevitable. The Global Surveys of Company Practice, page 638, describes spoilage (rejects), rework, and scrap in the U.S. electronics industry.

1

Distinguish among spoilage,

. . . unacceptable units of production

rework,

. . . unacceptable units of production subsequently repaired

and scrap

. . . leftover material

Spoilage, rework, and scrap are often locked in during R&D and product design when the products and production processes are developed.

Different Types of Spoilage

Accounting for spoilage aims to determine the magnitude of spoilage costs and to distinguish between costs of normal and abnormal spoilage.[1] To manage, control, and reduce spoilage costs, companies need to highlight them, not bury them as an unidentified part of the costs of good units manufactured.

To illustrate normal and abnormal spoilage, consider Mendonza Plastics, which makes plastic casings for the iMac computer using plastic injection molding. In October 2005, Mendonza incurs costs of $615,000 to produce 20,500 units. Of these 20,500 units, 20,000 are good units and 500 are spoiled units. Mendonza has no beginning inventory and no ending inventory that month. Of the 500 spoiled units, 400 units are spoiled because the injection molding machines are unable to manufacture good casings 100% of the time. That is, these units are spoiled even though the machines were run carefully and efficiently. The remaining 100 units are spoiled because of machine breakdowns and operator errors.

2

Describe the accounting procedures for normal spoilage

. . . spoilage inherent in the production process, included as part of the cost of good output

and abnormal spoilage

. . . spoilage that should not arise, recorded as a loss of the period

Normal Spoilage

Normal spoilage is spoilage inherent in a particular production process that arises even under efficient operating conditions. Management decides the spoilage rate it considers normal depending on the production process. At Mendonza Plastics, the 400 units spoiled because of the limitations of injection molding machines and despite efficient operating conditions are normal spoilage. Costs of normal spoilage are typically included as a component of the costs of good units manufactured because good units cannot be made without also making some units that are spoiled. At Mendonza,

Manufacturing cost per unit, $615,000 ÷ 20,500 units = $30	
Manufacturing costs of good units themselves, $30/unit × 20,000 units	$600,000
Normal spoilage costs, $30/unit × 400 units	12,000
Manufacturing costs of good units completed (includes normal spoilage)	$612,000

$$\text{Manufacturing cost per good unit} = \frac{\$612{,}000}{20{,}000 \text{ units}} = \$30.60$$

[1]The helpful suggestions of Samuel Laimon, University of Saskatchewan, are gratefully acknowledged.

Normal spoilage rates are computed by dividing units of normal spoilage by total *good units completed*, not total *actual units started* in production. (At Mendonza Plastics, the normal spoilage rate is 400 ÷ 20,000 = 0.02, or 2%, not 400 ÷ 20,500 = 0.0195, or 1.95%.) Why? Because normal spoilage is the spoilage related to the good units produced.

Abnormal Spoilage

Abnormal spoilage is spoilage that is not inherent in a particular production process and would not arise under efficient operating conditions. At Mendonza, the 100 units spoiled because of machine breakdowns and operator errors are abnormal spoilage. Abnormal spoilage is usually regarded as avoidable and controllable. Line operators and other plant personnel generally can decrease or eliminate abnormal spoilage by identifying the reasons for machine breakdowns, operator errors, and the like, and by taking steps to prevent their recurrence. To highlight the effect of abnormal spoilage costs, companies calculate the units of abnormal spoilage and record the cost in the Loss from Abnormal Spoilage account, which appears as a separate line item in the income statement. At Mendonza, the loss from abnormal spoilage is $3,000 ($30 per unit × 100 units).

Issues about accounting for spoilage arise in both process-costing and job-costing systems. We first present the accounting for spoilage in process-costing systems.

Process Costing and Spoilage

How do process-costing systems account for spoiled units? We have already said that units of abnormal spoilage should be counted and recorded separately in a Loss from Abnormal Spoilage account. But what about units of normal spoilage? These units can either be counted (approach A) or not counted (approach B) when computing output units—physical or equivalent—in a process-costing system. The following example and discussion illustrate the superiority of approach A over approach B.

Count All Spoilage

Example 1: Chipmakers, Inc., manufactures computer chips for television sets. All direct materials are added at the beginning of the production process. To highlight issues that arise with normal spoilage, we assume no beginning inventory and focus only on direct material costs. The following data are available for May 2006.

	A	B	C
1		Physical Units	Direct Materials
2	Work in process, beginning inventory (May 1)	0	
3	Started during May	10,000	
4	Good units completed and transferred out during May	5,000	
5	Units spoiled (all normal spoilage)	1,000	
6	Work in process, ending inventory (May 31)	4,000	
7	Degree of completion of ending work in process		100%
8	Direct material costs added in May		$270,000

Spoilage is detected upon completion of the process and has zero net disposal value.

An **inspection point** is the stage of the production process at which products are examined to determine whether they are acceptable or unacceptable units. Spoilage is typically assumed to occur at the stage of completion where inspection takes place. That's because spoilage is not detected until inspection. In our example, the inspection point is at the end of the process. As a result, the spoiled units are assumed to be 100% complete with respect to direct materials.

Exhibit 18-1 calculates and assigns cost per unit of direct materials using approach A and approach B. Approach A shows 10,000 equivalent units of output: 5,000 equivalent units in good units completed (5,000 physical units × 100%), 4,000 units in ending work in process (4,000 physical units × 100%), and 1,000 equivalent units in normal spoilage (1,000 physical units × 100%). Approach B shows 9,000 equivalent units of output: 5,000 equivalent units in good units completed and 4,000 equivalent units in ending work in process. Not counting the equivalent units for normal spoilage in approach B decreases equivalent units,

EXHIBIT 18-1 **Effect of Recognizing Equivalent Units in Spoilage for Direct Material Costs Chipmakers, Inc., for May 2006**

	A	B	C
1		Approach A: Counting Spoiled Units When Computing Output in Equivalent Units	Approach B: Not Counting Spoiled Units When Computing Output in Equivalent Units
2	Costs to account for	$270,000	$270,000
3	Divide by equivalent units of output	÷ 10,000	÷ 9,000
4	Cost per equivalent unit of output	$ 27	$ 30
5	Assignment of costs:		
6	Good units completed (5,000 units x $27 per unit; 5,000 units x $30 per unit)	$135,000	$150,000
7	Add normal spoilage (1,000 units x $27 per unit)	27,000	0
8	Total costs of good units completed and transferred out	162,000	150,000
9	Work in process, ending (4,000 units x $27 per unit; 4,000 units x $30 per unit)	108,000	120,000
10	Costs accounted for	$270,000	$270,000

resulting in a higher cost of each good unit. A $30 equivalent-unit cost in approach B (by not counting spoiled units), instead of a $27 equivalent-unit cost in approach A (by counting spoiled units), is assigned to work in process that has not reached the inspection point.

Under approach B, the direct material costs assigned to good units completed and transferred out, which include the costs of normal spoilage, are understated by $12,000—$150,000 instead of $162,000. The 4,000 units in ending work in process contain costs of normal spoilage of $12,000 ($120,000 – $108,000) that do not pertain to the 4,000 units in ending work in process because they have not yet been inspected. That $12,000 belongs with the good units completed and transferred out. The 4,000 units in ending work in process undoubtedly include some units that will be detected as spoiled when they are inspected upon completion in the subsequent accounting period. Under approach B, the ending work in process is being charged for spoilage in the current period, and it will be charged again in the next period when inspection occurs as the units are completed. That is, approach B charges these units twice for spoilage. Such cost distortions do not occur under approach A, when spoiled units are recognized in the computation of equivalent units, because the costs of normal spoilage are assigned only to the good units produced. Approach A has a further advantage. It highlights the cost of normal spoilage as $27,000. Approach B shows no cost for normal spoilage (see Exhibit 18-1). The $27,000 cost focuses management's attention on reducing spoilage. Therefore, we will use approach A to present process costing when spoilage exists.

Five-Step Procedure for Process Costing with Spoilage

Example 2: Anzio Company manufactures a recycling container in its Forming Department. Direct materials are added at the beginning of the production process. Conversion costs are added evenly during the production process. Some units of this product are spoiled as a result of defects, which are detectable only upon inspection of finished units. Normally, spoiled units are 10% of the finished output of good units. That is, for every 10 good units produced, there is 1 unit of normal spoilage. Summary data for July 2006 are:

	A	B	C	D	E
1		Physical Units (1)	Direct Materials (2)	Conversion Costs (3)	Total Costs (4) = (2) + (3)
2	Work in process, beginning inventory (July 1)	1,500	$12,000	$ 9,000	$ 21,000
3	Degree of completion of beginning work in process		100%	60%	
4	Started during July	8,500			
5	Good units completed and transferred out during July	7,000			
6	Work in process, ending inventory (July 31)	2,000			
7	Degree of completion of ending work in process		100%	50%	
8	Total costs added during July		$76,500	$89,100	$165,600
9	Normal spoilage as a percentage of good units	10%			
10	Degree of completion of normal spoilage		100%	100%	
11	Degree of completion of abnormal spoilage		100%	100%	

The five-step procedure for process costing used in Chapter 17 needs only slight modification to accommodate spoilage.

Step 1: Summarize the Flow of Physical Units of Output. Identify units of both normal and abnormal spoilage.

$$\text{Total Spoilage} = \left(\begin{array}{c}\text{Units in beginning}\\ \text{work-in-process inventory}\end{array} + \begin{array}{c}\text{Units}\\ \text{started}\end{array}\right) - \left(\begin{array}{c}\text{Good units}\\ \text{completed and}\\ \text{transferred out}\end{array} + \begin{array}{c}\text{Units in ending}\\ \text{work-in-process inventory}\end{array}\right)$$

$$= (1{,}500 + 8{,}500) - (7{,}000 + 2{,}000)$$

$$= 10{,}000 - 9{,}000$$

$$= 1{,}000 \text{ units}$$

Recall that normal spoilage is 10% of good output at Anzio Corporation. Therefore, normal spoilage = 10% of the 7,000 units of *good* output = 700 units.

$$\text{Abnormal spoilage} = \text{Total spoilage} - \text{Normal spoilage}$$

$$= 1{,}000 \text{ units} - 700 \text{ units}$$

$$= 300 \text{ units}$$

Step 2: Compute Output in Terms of Equivalent Units. Compute equivalent units for spoilage in the same way we compute equivalent units for good units. Following approach A, all spoiled units are included in the computation of output units. Because Anzio's inspection point is at the completion of production, the same amount of work will have been done on each spoiled and each completed good unit.

Step 3: Compute Cost per Equivalent Unit. This step is similar to step 3 in Chapter 17.

Step 4: Summarize Total Costs to Account For. The total costs to account for are all the costs debited to Work in Process. The details for this step are similar to step 4 in Chapter 17.

Step 5: Assign Total Costs to Units Completed, to Spoiled Units, and to Units in Ending Work in Process. This step now includes computation of the cost of spoiled units and the cost of good units.

We illustrate these five steps of process costing for the weighted-average, FIFO, and standard-costing methods.

3

Account for spoilage in process costing using the weighted-average method

. . . spoilage cost based on total costs and equivalent units completed to date

Weighted-Average Method and Spoilage

Exhibit 18-2, Panel A, presents steps 1 and 2 to calculate equivalent units of work done to date and includes calculations of equivalent units of normal and abnormal spoilage. Exhibit 18-2, Panel B, presents steps 3, 4, and 5 (together called the production-cost worksheet).

Step 3 presents cost-per-equivalent-unit calculations using the weighted-average method. Note how, for each cost category, costs of beginning work in process and costs of work done in the current period are totaled and divided by equivalent units of all work done to date to calculate the weighted-average cost per equivalent unit. Step 4 summarizes total costs to account for. Step 5 assigns costs to completed units, normal and abnormal spoiled units, and ending inventory by multiplying the equivalent units calculated in step 2 by the cost per equivalent unit calculated in step 3. Also note that the $13,825 costs of normal spoilage are added to the costs of the related good units completed and transferred out.

In Panel B, Exhibit 18-2, total costs to account for in step 4 represent the debits to the Work in Process account. Step 5 represents the credits to the Work in Process account, with debits (1) to the Loss from Abnormal Spoilage account for $5,925 and (2) to Finished Goods for $152,075 (the cost of units completed and transferred out). Step 5 also shows the ending balance of work in process, $28,600.

$$\begin{array}{c}\text{Cost per good unit}\\ \text{completed and transferred}\\ \text{out of the process}\end{array} = \frac{\text{Total costs transferred out (including normal spoilage)}}{\text{Number of good units produced}}$$

$$= \$152{,}075 \div 7{,}000 \text{ good units} = \$21.725 \text{ per good unit}$$

This amount is not equal to $19.75 per good unit, the sum of the $8.85 cost per equivalent unit of direct materials plus the $10.90 cost per equivalent unit of conversion costs. That's because the cost per good unit equals the total cost of direct materials and con-

EXHIBIT 18-2	Weighted-Average Method of Process Costing with Spoilage Forming Department of the Anzio Company for July 2006

PANEL A: Steps 1 and 2—Summarize Output in Physical Units and Compute Equivalent Units

	A	B	C	D	E
1			(Step 1)	(Step 2)	
2				Equivalent Units	
3		Flow of Production	Physical Units	Direct Materials	Conversion Costs
4		Work in process, beginning (given, p. 635)	1,500		
5		Started during current period (given, p. 635)	8,500		
6		To account for	10,000		
7		Good units completed and transferred out during current period:	7,000	7,000	7,000
8		Normal spoilage[a]	700		
9		(700 x 100%; 700 x 100%)		700	700
10		Abnormal spoilage[b]	300		
11		(300 x 100%; 300 x 100%)		300	300
12		Work in process, ending[c] (given, p. 635)	2,000		
13		(2,000 x 100%; 2,000 x 50%)		2,000	1,000
14		Accounted for	10,000		
15		Work done to date		10,000	9,000
16					
17	[a]Normal spoilage is 10% of good units transferred out: 10% × 7,000 = 700 units. Degree of completion of normal spoilage				
18	in this department: direct materials, 100%; conversion costs, 100%.				
19	[b]Abnormal spoilage = Total spoilage – Normal spoilage = 1,000 – 700 = 300 units. Degree of completion of abnormal spoilage				
20	in this department: direct materials, 100%; conversion costs, 100%.				
21	[c]Degree of completion in this department: direct materials, 100%; conversion costs, 50%.				

PANEL B: Steps 3, 4, and 5—Compute Cost per Equivalent Unit, Summarize Total Costs to Account for, and Assign Total Costs to Units Completed, to Spoiled Units, and to Units in Ending Work in Process

	A	B	C	D	E
23			Total Production Costs	Direct Materials	Conversion Costs
24	(Step 3)	Work in process, beginning (given, p. 635)	$ 21,000	$12,000	$ 9,000
25		Costs added in current period (given, p. 635)	165,600	76,500	89,100
26		Costs incurred to date		$88,500	$98,100
27		Divide by equivalent units of work done to date		÷10,000	÷ 9,000
28		Cost per equivalent unit		$ 8.85	$ 10.90
29	(Step 4)	Total costs to account for	$186,600		
30	(Step 5)	Assignment of costs:			
31		Good units completed and transferred out (7,000 units)			
32		Costs before adding normal spoilage	$138,250	(7,000[d] x $8.85)+(7,000[d] x $10.90)	
33		Normal spoilage (700 units)	13,825	(700[d] x $8.85) + (700[d] x $10.90)	
34	(A)	Total costs of good units completed and transferred out	152,075		
35	(B)	Abnormal spoilage (300 units)	5,925	(300[d] x $8.85) + (300[d] x $10.90)	
36	(C)	Work in process, ending (2,000 units):	28,600	(2,000[d] x $8.85)+(1,000[d] x $10.90)	
37	(A) + (B) + (C)	Total costs accounted for	$186,600		
38					
39	[d]Equivalent units of direct materials and conversion costs calculated in step 2 in Panel A.				

version costs per equivalent unit, $19.75, plus a share of normal spoilage, $1.975 ($13,825 ÷ 7,000 good units), = $21.725 per good unit. The $5,925 costs of abnormal spoilage are charged to the Loss from Abnormal Spoilage account and do not appear in the costs of good units.[2]

[2]The actual costs of spoilage (and rework) are often greater than the costs recorded in the accounting system because the opportunity costs of disruption of the production line, storage, and lost contribution margins are not recorded in accounting systems. Chapter 19 discusses these opportunity costs from the perspective of cost management.

GLOBAL SURVEYS OF COMPANY PRACTICE

Rejection in the Electronics Industry

From country to country and from industry to industry, the rates of spoilage and rework vary tremendously. The data in the following table focus on different segments of the U.S. electronics industry. The data reported are median numbers drawn from companies that are members of the American Electronics Association. The spoilage rate is spoilage as a percentage of units inspected. The rework rate is rework as a percentage of units inspected. The scrap rate reports scrap as a percentage of all materials and products purchased. Also reported is the operating-income-to-revenues percentage for each segment of the electronics industry.

Segment of Electronics Industry	Spoilage Rate (% Rejects)	Rework Rate (% Rework)	Scrap Rate (% Scrap)	Operating Income to Revenues
1. Computers and office equipment (includes mainframes, minicomputers, microcomputers, printers, and point-of-sale equipment)	2.6%	6.5%	0.6%	5.3%
2. Electronic components and accessories (includes printed circuit boards and semiconductors)	1.6	2.0	1.6	4.5
3. Specialized production equipment (includes semiconductor production equipment)	7.5	10.0	0.4	5.7
4. Telecommunications equipment (includes telephone, radio, and TV apparatus)	1.0	2.0	1.3	4.7
5. Aerospace, nautical, and military equipment (includes aircraft manufacture and guided missiles)	—	1.5	0.5	6.5
6. Laboratory and measurement devices (includes optical instruments and process-control equipment)	4.9	3.3	0.7	3.9
7. Prepackaged software	1.0	0.8	0.1	4.0

The spoilage rate for specialized production equipment is almost five times greater than the spoilage rate for electronic components and accessories. Electronic components and accessories show a low percentage of rework (in part because rework is not always possible when defects arise). Scrap rates are reasonably small across all industry segments. Operating-income-to-revenues percentage ranges from 3.9% for laboratory and measurement devices to 6.5% for aerospace, nautical, and military equipment. Given these profitability percentages, reductions in spoilage and rework rates can markedly increase the profitability of many companies in the electronics industry.

Source: Adapted from American Electronics Association, Operating Ratios Survey. Full citation is in Appendix A at the end of the book.

4

Account for spoilage in process costing using the first-in, first-out (FIFO) method

. . . spoilage cost based on costs of current period and equivalent units of work done in current period

FIFO Method and Spoilage

Exhibit 18-3, Panel A, presents steps 1 and 2 using the FIFO method, which focuses on equivalent units of work done in the current period. Exhibit 18-3, Panel B, presents steps 3, 4, and 5. Note how when assigning costs, the FIFO method keeps the costs of the beginning work in process separate and distinct from the costs of work done in the current period. All spoilage costs are assumed to be related to units completed during this period, using the unit costs of the current period.[3]

[3]To simplify calculations under FIFO, spoiled units are accounted for *as if* they were started in the current period. Although some of the beginning work in process probably did spoil, all spoilage is treated as if it came from current production.

EXHIBIT 18-3 First-In, First-Out (FIFO) Method of Process Costing with Spoilage Forming Department of the Anzio Company for July 2006

PANEL A: Steps 1 and 2—Summarize Output in Physical Units and Compute Equivalent Units

	A	B	C	D	E
1			**(Step 1)**	**(Step 2)**	
2				**Equivalent Units**	
3		**Flow of Production**	**Physical Units**	**Direct Materials**	**Conversion Costs**
4		Work in process, beginning (given, p. 635)	1,500		
5		Started during current period (given, p. 635)	8,500		
6		To account for	10,000		
7		Good units completed and transferred out during current period:			
8		From beginning work in process[a]	1,500		
9		[1,500 × (100% – 100%); 1,500 × (100% – 60%)]		0	600
10		Started and completed	5,500[b]		
11		(5,500 × 100%; 5,500 × 100%)		5,500	5,500
12		Normal spoilage[c]	700		
13		(700 × 100%; 700 × 100%)		700	700
14		Abnormal spoilage[d]	300		
15		(300 × 100%; 300 × 100%)		300	300
16		Work in process, ending[e] (given, p. 635)	2,000		
17		(2,000 × 100%; 2,000 × 50%)		2,000	1,000
18		Accounted for	10,000		
19		Work done in current period only		8,500	8,100
20					
21	[a] Degree of completion in this department: direct materials, 100%; conversion costs, 60%.				
22	[b] 7,000 physical units completed and transferred out minus 1,500 physical units completed and transferred out from beginning				
23	work-in-process inventory.				
24	[c] Normal spoilage is 10% of good units transferred out: 10% × 7,000 = 700 units. Degree of completion of normal spoilage in this				
25	department: direct materials, 100%; conversion costs, 100%.				
26	[d] Abnormal spoilage = Actual spoilage – Normal spoilage = 1,000 – 700 = 300 units. Degree of completion of abnormal spoilage				
27	in this department: direct materials, 100%; conversion costs, 100%.				
28	[e] Degree of completion in this department: direct materials, 100%; conversion costs, 50%.				

PANEL B: Steps 3, 4, and 5—Compute Cost per Equivalent Unit, Summarize Total Costs to Account for, and Assign Total Costs to Units Completed, to Spoiled Units, and to Units in Ending Work in Process

	A	B	C	D	E
30			**Total Production Costs**	**Direct Materials**	**Conversion Costs**
31	**(Step 3)**	Work in process, beginning (given, p. 635)	$ 21,000		
32		Costs added in current period (given, p. 635)	165,600	$76,500	$89,100
33		Divide by equivalent units of work done in current period		÷ 8,500	÷ 8,100
34		Cost per equivalent unit		$ 9	$ 11
35	**(Step 4)**	Total costs to account for	$186,600		
36	**(Step 5)**	Assignment of costs:			
37		Good units completed and transferred out (7,000 units)			
38		Work in process, beginning (1,500 units)	$ 21,000		
39		Costs added in current period	6,600	(0[f] × $9) +	(600[f] × $11)
40		Total from beginning inventory before normal spoilage	27,600		
41		Started and completed before normal spoilage (5,500 units)	110,000	(5,500[f] × $9)+	(5,500[f] × $11)
42		Normal spoilage (700 units)	14,000	(700[f] × $9) +	(700[f] × $11)
43	(A)	Total costs of good units completed and transferred out	151,600		
44	(B)	Abnormal spoilage (300 units)	6,000	(300[f] × $9) +	(300[f] × $11)
45	(C)	Work in process, ending (2,000 units):	29,000	(2,000[f] × $9)+	(1,000[f] × $11)
46	(A) + (B) + (C)	Total costs accounted for	$186,600		
47					
48	[f] Equivalent units of direct materials and conversion costs calculated in step 2 in Panel A.				

Standard-Costing Method and Spoilage

This section assumes you have studied the standard-costing method in Chapter 17(pp. 609–612). Instructors and students who wish to skip this section can go directly to the section on Job Costing and Spoilage, page 642, without any loss of continuity.

5 **Account for spoilage in process costing using the standard-costing method** . . . spoilage cost based on standard cost as the cost per equivalent unit

The standard-costing method simplifies the computations for normal and abnormal spoilage. To illustrate, suppose Anzio Company develops the following standard costs per unit for work done in the Forming Department in July 2006:

Direct materials	$ 8.50
Conversion costs	10.50
Total manufacturing cost	$19.00

Assume the same standard costs per unit also apply to the beginning inventory: 1,500 (1,500 × 100%) equivalent units of direct materials and 900 (1,500 × 60%) equivalent units of conversion costs. Hence, the beginning inventory at standard costs is:

Direct materials, 1,500 units × $8.50/unit	$12,750
Conversion costs, 900 units × $10.50/unit	9,450
Total manufacturing costs	$22,200

Exhibit 18-4, Panel A, presents steps 1 and 2 for calculating physical and equivalent units. These steps are the same as for the FIFO method described in Exhibit 18-3. Exhibit 18-4, Panel B, presents steps 3, 4, and 5.

In Step 3, cost per equivalent unit is simply the standard cost: $8.50 per unit for direct materials and $10.50 per unit for conversion costs. The standard-costing method makes calculating equivalent-unit costs unnecessary, so it simplifies process costing. The costs to account for in step 4 are at standard costs and, hence, they differ from the costs to account for under the weighted-average and FIFO methods, which are at actual costs. Step 5 assigns standard costs to units completed (including normal spoilage), to abnormal spoilage, and to ending work-in-process inventory by multiplying the equivalent units calculated in step 2 by the standard costs per equivalent unit presented in step 3. Variances can then be measured and analyzed in the manner described in Chapter 17 (p. 612).[4]

Journal Entries

The information from Panel B in Exhibits 18-2, 18-3, and 18-4 supports the following journal entries to transfer good units completed to finished goods and to recognize the loss from abnormal spoilage.

	Weighted Average		FIFO		Standard Costs	
Finished Goods	152,075		151,600		146,300	
Work in Process—Forming		152,075		151,600		146,300
To record transfer of good units completed in July.						
Loss from Abnormal Spoilage	5,925		6,000		5,700	
Work in Process—Forming		5,925		6,000		5,700
To record abnormal spoilage detected in July.						

[4]For example, from Exhibit 18-4, Panel B, the standard costs for July are direct materials used, 8,500 × $8.50 = $72,250, and conversion costs, 8,100 × $10.50 = $85,050. From page 635, the actual costs added during July are direct materials, $76,500, and conversion costs, $89,100, resulting in a direct materials variance of $72,250 – $76,500 = $4,250 U and a conversion costs variance of $85,050 – $89,100 = $4,050 U. These variances could then be subdivided further as in Chapters 7 and 8; the abnormal spoilage would be part of the efficiency variance.

EXHIBIT 18-4 **Standard-Costing Method of Process Costing with Spoilage Forming Department of the Anzio Company for July 2006**

PANEL A: Steps 1 and 2—Summarize Output in Physical Units and Compute Equivalent Units

	A	B	C	D	E
1			**(Step 1)**	**(Step 2)**	
2				**Equivalent Units**	
3		**Flow of Production**	**Physical Units**	**Direct Materials**	**Conversion Costs**
4		Work in process, beginning (given, p. 635)	1,500		
5		Started during current period (given, p. 635)	8,500		
6		To account for	10,000		
7		Good units completed and transferred out during current period:			
8		From beginning work in process[a]	1,500		
9		[1,500 × (100% - 100%); 1,500 × (100% - 60%)]		0	600
10		Started and completed	5,500[b]		
11		(5,500 × 100%; 5,500 × 100%)		5,500	5,500
12		Normal spoilage[c]	700		
13		(700 × 100%; 700 × 100%)		700	700
14		Abnormal spoilage[d]	300		
15		(300 × 100%; 300 × 100%)		300	300
16		Work in process, ending[e] (given, p. 635)	2,000		
17		(2,000 × 100%; 2,000 × 50%)		2,000	1,000
18		Accounted for	10,000		
19		Work done in current period only		8,500	8,100
20					
21	[a]Degree of completion in this department: direct materials, 100%; conversion costs, 60%.				
22	[b]7,000 physical units completed and transferred out minus 1,500 physical units completed and transferred out from beginning				
23	work-in-process inventory.				
24	[c]Normal spoilage is 10% of good units transferred out: 10% × 7,000 = 700 units. Degree of completion of normal spoilage in this				
25	department: direct materials, 100%; conversion costs, 100%.				
26	[d]Abnormal spoilage = Actual spoilage – Normal spoilage = 1,000 – 700 = 300 units. Degree of completion of abnormal spoilage in this				
27	department: direct materials, 100%; conversion costs, 100%.				
28	[e]Degree of completion in this department: direct materials, 100%; conversion costs, 50%.				

PANEL B: Steps 3, 4, and 5—Compute Cost per Equivalent Unit, Summarize Total Costs to Account for, and Assign Total Costs to Units Completed, to Spoiled Units, and to Units in Ending Work in Process

30			**Total Production Costs**	**Direct Materials**	**Conversion Costs**
31	**(Step 3)**	Standard cost per equivalent unit (given, p. 640)	$ 19.00	$8.50	$10.50
32		Work in process, beginning (given, p. 640)	$ 22,200		
33		Costs added in current period at standard prices	157,300	(8,500 x $8.50) +	(8,100 x $10.50)
34	**(Step 4)**	Total costs to account for	$179,500		
35	**(Step 5)**	Assignment of costs at standard costs:			
36		Good units completed and transferred out (7,000 units)			
37		Work in process, beginning (1,500 units)	$ 22,200		
38		Costs added in current period	6,300	(0[f] × $8.50) +	(600[f] × $10.50)
39		Total from beginning inventory before normal spoilage	28,500		
40		Started and completed before normal spoilage (5,500 units)	104,500	(5,500[f] × $8.50) +	(5,500[f] × $10.50)
41		Normal spoilage (700 units)	13,300	(700[f] × $8.50) +	(700[f] × $10.50)
42	(A)	Total costs of good units completed and transferred out	146,300		
43	(B)	Abnormal spoilage (300 units)	5,700	(300[f] × $8.50) +	(300[f] × $10.50)
44	(C)	Work in process, ending (2,000 units):	27,500	(2,000[f] × $8.50) +	(1,000[f] × $10.50)
45	(A) + (B) + (C)	Total costs accounted for	$179,500		
46					
47	[f]Equivalent units of direct materials and conversion costs calculated in step 2 in Panel A.				

Inspection Points and Allocating Costs of Normal Spoilage

Our Anzio Company example assumes inspection upon completion of the units. However, spoilage might actually occur at various stages of the production process, although it is typically detected only at one or more inspection points. The cost of spoiled units is assumed to equal all costs incurred in producing spoiled units up to the point of inspection. When spoiled goods have a disposal value (for example, carpeting sold as "seconds"), the net cost of spoilage is computed by deducting the disposal value from the costs of the spoiled goods that have been accumulated up to the inspection point. The unit costs of normal and abnormal spoilage are the same when the two are detected at the same inspection point. However, situations may arise when abnormal spoilage is detected at a different point than normal spoilage. Consider shirt manufacturing. Normal spoilage in the form of defective shirts is identified upon inspection at the end of the production process. Now suppose a faulty machine causes many defective shirts to be produced at the halfway point of the production process. These defective shirts are abnormal spoilage and occur at a different point in the production process than normal spoilage. In such cases, the unit cost of abnormal spoilage, which is based on costs incurred up to the halfway point of the production process, differs from the unit cost of normal spoilage, which is based on costs incurred through the end of the production process.

Consider another example of how abnormal spoilage may occur other than at the inspection point. If a foreman at a glass plant discovers a furnace has been contaminated with foreign matter, abnormal spoilage is detected and recorded in the accounting system at that time—well before completed glass products are inspected.

Costs of abnormal spoilage are separately accounted for as losses of the accounting period in which they are detected. However, recall that normal spoilage costs are added to the costs of good units, which raises an additional issue: Should normal spoilage costs be allocated between completed units and ending work-in-process inventory? *The common approach is to presume that normal spoilage occurs at the inspection point in the production cycle and to allocate its cost over all units that have passed that point during the accounting period.* In the Anzio Company example, spoilage is assumed to occur when units are inspected at the end of the production process, so no costs of normal spoilage are allocated to ending work in process.

The costs of normal spoilage are allocated to units in ending work in process—in addition to completed units—if the units in ending work in process have passed the inspection point. For example, if the inspection point is at the halfway point of production, then any work in process that is at least 50% complete would be allocated a full measure of normal spoilage costs, and those spoilage costs would be calculated on the basis of all costs incurred up to the inspection point. But if work in process is less than 50% complete, no normal spoilage costs would be allocated to it. The appendix to this chapter contains a discussion of spoilage when units are inspected at different points in the production process.

Early and frequent inspections prevent any further direct materials and conversion costs being wasted on units that are already spoiled. If inspection can occur when units are 80% (rather than 100%) complete as to conversion costs and spoilage occurs prior to the 80% point, a company can avoid incurring the final 20% of conversion costs on the spoiled units.

Job Costing and Spoilage

6

Account for spoilage in job costing

. . . normal spoilage assigned directly or indirectly to job; abnormal spoilage written off as a loss of the period

The concepts of normal and abnormal spoilage also apply to job-costing systems. Abnormal spoilage is separately identified so companies can work to eliminate it altogether. Costs of abnormal spoilage are not considered to be inventoriable costs and are written off as costs of the accounting period in which the abnormal spoilage is detected. Normal spoilage costs in job-costing systems—as in process-costing systems—are inventoriable costs, although increasingly companies are tolerating only small amounts of spoilage as normal. When assigning costs, job-costing systems generally distinguish *normal spoilage attributable to a specific job from normal spoilage common to all jobs.*

We describe accounting for spoilage in job costing using the following example.

Example 3: In the Hull Machine Shop, 5 aircraft parts out of a job lot of 50 aircraft parts are spoiled. Costs assigned prior to the inspection point are $2,000 per part. Our presentation here and in subsequent sections focuses on how the $2,000 cost per part is accounted for. When the spoilage is detected, the spoiled goods are inventoried at $600 per part, the net disposal value.

Although not the focus of this example, Hull calculates the $2,000 cost per part based on its inventory-costing method (weighted average, FIFO, or standard costing).

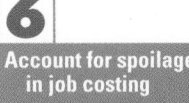

Normal spoilage attributable to a specific job When normal spoilage occurs because of the specifications of a particular job, that job bears the cost of the spoilage minus the disposal value of the spoilage. The journal entry to recognize disposal value (items in parentheses indicate subsidiary ledger postings) is:

Materials Control (spoiled goods at current net disposal value):		
5 units × $600 per unit	3,000	
Work-in-Process Control (specific job): 5 units × $600 per unit		3,000

Note, the Work-in-Process Control (specific job) has already been debited (charged) $10,000 for the spoiled parts (5 spoiled parts × $2,000 per part). The net cost of normal spoilage = $7,000 ($10,000 – $3,000), which is an additional cost of the 45 (50 – 5) good units produced. Therefore, total cost of the 45 good units is $97,000: $90,000 (45 units × $2,000 per unit) incurred to produce the good units plus the $7,000 net cost of normal spoilage. Cost per good unit is $2,155.56 ($97,000 ÷ 45 good units).

Because the costs of normally spoiled units attributable to a specific job are in the Work in Process account, the cost of both good units and normally spoiled units will be spread over the good units, which increases the cost per unit of the good units. No journal entry is necessary for normal spoilage, except to reduce (credit) the Work in Process account for any disposal value of the normal spoilage.

Normal spoilage common to all jobs In some cases, spoilage may be considered a normal characteristic of the production process. The spoilage inherent in production will, of course, occur when a specific job is being worked on. But the spoilage is not attributable to, and hence is not charged directly to, the specific job. Instead, the spoilage is allocated indirectly to the job as manufacturing overhead because the spoilage is common to all jobs. The journal entry is:

Materials Control (spoiled goods at current disposal value):		
5 units × $600 per unit	3,000	
Manufacturing Overhead Control (normal spoilage):		
($10,000 – $3,000)	7,000	
Work-in-Process Control (specific job): 5 units × $2,000 per unit		10,000

When normal spoilage is common to all jobs, the budgeted manufacturing overhead rate includes a provision for normal spoilage cost. Normal spoilage cost is spread, through overhead allocation, over all jobs rather than allocated to a specific job.[5] For example, if Hull produced 140 good units from all jobs in a given month, the $7,000 of normal spoilage overhead costs would be allocated at the rate of $50 per good unit ($7,000 ÷ 140 good units). Normal spoilage overhead costs allocated to the 45 good units in the job would be $2,250 ($50 × 45 good units). Total cost of the 45 good units is $92,250: $90,000 (45 units × $2,000 per unit) incurred to produce the good units plus $2,250 of normal spoilage overhead costs. Cost per good unit is $2,050 ($92,250 ÷ 45 good units).

Abnormal spoilage If the spoilage is abnormal, the net loss is charged to the Loss from Abnormal Spoilage account. Unlike normal spoilage costs, abnormal spoilage costs are not included as a part of the cost of good units produced. Total cost of the 45 good units is $90,000 (45 units × $2,000 per unit). Cost per good unit is $2,000 ($90,000 ÷ 45 good units).

Materials Control (spoiled goods at current disposal value):		
5 units × $600 per unit	3,000	
Loss from Abnormal Spoilage: ($10,000 – $3,000)	7,000	
Work-in-Process Control (specific job): 5 units × $2,000 per unit		10,000

[5]Note that costs *already assigned to products* are charged back to Manufacturing Overhead Control, which generally accumulates only *costs incurred*, not both costs incurred and costs already assigned.

Even though, for external reporting purposes, abnormal spoilage costs are written off in the accounting period and are not linked to specific jobs or units, companies often identify the particular reasons for abnormal spoilage, and, when appropriate, link abnormal spoilage with specific jobs or units for cost management purposes.

7

Account for rework in job costing

. . . normal rework assigned directly or indirectly to job; abnormal rework written off as a loss of the period

Job Costing and Rework

Rework is units of production that are inspected, determined to be unacceptable, repaired, and sold as acceptable finished goods. We again distinguish (1) normal rework attributable to a specific job, (2) normal rework common to all jobs, and (3) abnormal rework.

Consider the Hull Machine Shop data in Example 3 on page 642. Assume the five spoiled parts are reworked. The journal entry for the $10,000 of total costs (the details of these costs are assumed) assigned to the five spoiled units before considering rework costs is:

Work-in-Process Control (specific job)	10,000	
Materials Control		4,000
Wages Payable Control		4,000
Manufacturing Overhead Allocated		2,000

Assume the rework costs equal $3,800 (comprising $800 direct materials, $2,000 direct manufacturing labor, and $1,000 manufacturing overhead).

Normal rework attributable to a specific job If the rework is normal but occurs because of the requirements of a specific job, the rework costs are charged to that job. The journal entry is:

Work-in-Process Control (specific job)	3,800	
Materials Control		800
Wages Payable Control		2,000
Manufacturing Overhead Allocated		1,000

Normal rework common to all jobs When rework is normal and not attributable to a specific job, the costs of rework are charged to manufacturing overhead and are spread, through overhead allocation, over all jobs.

Question: Why are both Manufacturing Overhead (MOH) Control and MOH Allocated in the same journal entry?

Answer: MOH Control is debited because the normal rework is common to all jobs (rather than attributable to a specific job). In such cases, the additional MOH costs incurred to rework the units (such as electricity and materials handling) are spread over all jobs by including an allowance for estimated rework in the budgeted MOH (accounted for by the credit to MOH Allocated).

Manufacturing Overhead Control (rework costs)	3,800	
Materials Control		800
Wages Payable Control		2,000
Manufacturing Overhead Allocated		1,000

Abnormal rework If the rework is abnormal, it is recorded by charging abnormal rework to a loss account.

Loss from Abnormal Rework	3,800	
Materials Control		800
Wages Payable Control		2,000
Manufacturing Overhead Allocated		1,000

Accounting for rework in a process-costing system also requires abnormal rework to be distinguished from normal rework. Process costing accounts for abnormal rework in the same way as job costing. Accounting for normal rework follows the accounting described for normal rework common to all jobs (units) because masses of identical or similar units are being manufactured.

Costing rework focuses managers' attention on the resources wasted on activities that would not have to be undertaken if the product had been made correctly. The cost of rework prompts managers to seek ways to reduce rework, for example, by designing new products or processes, training workers, or investing in new machines. To eliminate rework and to simplify the accounting, some companies set a standard of zero rework. All rework is then treated as abnormal and is written off as a cost of the current period.

Accounting for Scrap

Scrap is residual material that results from manufacturing a product; it has low total sales value compared with the total sales value of the product. No distinction is made between normal and abnormal scrap because no cost is assigned to scrap. The only distinction made is between scrap attributable to a specific job and scrap common to all jobs.

There are two aspects of accounting for scrap:

1. Planning and control, including physical tracking
2. Inventory costing, including when and how scrap affects operating income

8 **Account for scrap** . . . reduces cost of job either at time of sale or at time of production

Initial entries to scrap records are commonly in physical terms. In various industries, companies quantify items such as stamped-out metal sheets or edges of molded plastic parts by weighing, counting, or some other measure. Scrap records not only help measure efficiency, but also help keep track of scrap, and so reduce the chances of theft. Companies use scrap records to prepare periodic summaries of the amounts of actual scrap compared with budgeted or standard amounts. Scrap is either sold or disposed of quickly, or it is stored for later sale, disposal, or reuse.

Careful tracking of scrap often extends into the accounting records. Many companies maintain a distinct account for scrap costs somewhere in their accounting system. The issues here are similar to the issues in Chapter 16 regarding the accounting for byproducts:

- When should the value of scrap be recognized in the accounting records—at the time scrap is produced or at the time scrap is sold?
- How should revenues from scrap be accounted for?

To illustrate, we extend our Hull example. Assume the manufacture of aircraft parts generates scrap and that the scrap from a job has a net sales value of $900.

Recognizing Scrap at the Time of Its Sale

When the dollar amount of scrap is immaterial, the simplest accounting is to record the physical quantity of scrap returned to the storeroom and to regard scrap sales as a separate line item in the income statement. In this case, the only journal entry is:

Rework costs are recorded when incurred because they tend to be material in amount. Because scrap is immaterial in amount, it may not be recorded until the time of sale (rather than at the time of production).

Sale of scrap:	Cash or Accounts Receivable	900	
	Scrap Revenues		900

When the dollar amount of scrap is material and the scrap is sold quickly after it is produced, the accounting depends on whether the scrap is attributable to a specific job or is common to all jobs.

Scrap attributable to a specific job Job-costing systems sometimes trace scrap revenues to the jobs that yielded the scrap. This method is used only when the tracing can be done in an economically feasible way. For example, the Hull Machine Shop and its customers, such as the U.S. Department of Defense, may reach an agreement that provides for charging specific jobs with all rework or spoilage costs and then crediting these jobs with all scrap revenues that arise from the jobs. The journal entry is:

Scrap returned to storeroom:	No journal entry. [Notation of quantity received and related job entered in the inventory record]		
Sale of scrap:	Cash or Accounts Receivable	900	
	Work-in-Process Control		900
	Posting made to specific job cost record.		

In job costing, the cost of scrap is already in the Work in Process account of the job generating the scrap. If the scrap is attributable to that job, the costs are already accounted for and no journal entry is necessary. When the scrap is sold, the Work in Process account is decreased (credited) to reduce the cost of the job by the amount of the scrap's disposal value.

Unlike spoilage and rework, there is no cost assigned to the scrap, so no distinction is made between normal and abnormal scrap. All scrap revenues, whatever the amount, are credited to the specific job. Scrap revenues reduce the costs of the job.

Scrap common to all jobs The journal entry in this case is:

Scrap returned to storeroom:	No journal entry. [Notation of quantity received and related job entered in the inventory record]		
Sale of scrap:	Cash or Accounts Receivable	900	
	Manufacturing Overhead Control		900
	Posting made to subsidiary ledger—"Sales of Scrap" column on department cost record.		

Scrap is not linked with any particular job or product. Instead, all products bear production costs without any credit for scrap revenues except in an indirect manner: Expected scrap revenues are considered when setting the budgeted manufacturing overhead rate. Thus, the budgeted overhead rate is lower than it would be if the overhead budget had not been reduced by expected scrap revenues. This method of accounting for scrap is also used in process costing when the dollar amount of scrap is immaterial. That's because the scrap in process costing is common to the manufacture of all the identical or similar units produced (and cannot be identified with specific units).

Recognizing Scrap at the Time of Its Production

Our preceding illustrations assume that scrap returned to the storeroom is sold quickly, so it is not assigned an inventory cost figure. Sometimes, as in the case with edges of molded plastic parts, the value of scrap is not immaterial, and the time between storing it and selling or reusing it can be long. In these situations, the company assigns an inventory cost to scrap at a conservative estimate of its net realizable value so that production costs and related scrap revenues are recognized in the same accounting period. Some companies tend to delay sales of scrap until its market price is considered attractive. Volatile price fluctuations are typical for scrap metal. In these cases, it's not easy to determine some "reasonable inventory value."

Scrap attributable to a specific job The journal entry in the Hull example is:

Scrap returned to storeroom:	Materials Control	900	
	Work-in-Process Control		900

Scrap common to all jobs The journal entry in this case is:

Scrap returned to storeroom:	Materials Control	900	
	Manufacturing Overhead Control		900

Observe that the Materials Control account is debited in place of Cash or Accounts Receivable. When the scrap is sold, the journal entry is:

Sale of scrap:	Cash or Accounts Receivable	900	
	Materials Control		900

Scrap is sometimes reused as direct material rather than sold as scrap. In this case, Materials Control is debited at its estimated net realizable value and then credited when the scrap is reused. For example, the entries when the scrap is common to all jobs are:

Scrap returned to storeroom:	Materials Control	900	
	Manufacturing Overhead Control		900
Reuse of scrap:	Work-in-Process Control	900	
	Materials Control		900

CONCEPTS IN ACTION

Managing Waste and Environmental Costs at Toyota

Toyota Motor Corporation, the world's third-largest automotive manufacturer, builds and sells a wide range of vehicles under the Toyota, Lexus, and Scion brands. Toyota has done a wonderful job of reducing waste and environmental costs. Fujio Cho, Toyota's president, defines waste as "anything other than the minimum amount of equipment, materials, parts, space, and workers' time which are absolutely essential to add value to the product." Scrap, generated from wasted materials and parts, poses additional problems because of its impact on the environment. Domestic and international environmental laws dictate that scrap materials be disposed of in an environmentally friendly way; therefore they add to the cost of generating waste.

Toyota regards environmental preservation and improvement as a top-priority management issue. The company seeks to reduce the environmental burden at every stage of a car's lifecycle, from production, distribution, and use to disposal and recycling. Consistent with its corporate culture and the recommendations of the U.S. Environmental Protection Agency and Japanese Ministry of the Environment, Toyota focuses on source reduction (avoidance of waste altogether, rather than disposal and treatment of waste) as the best way to achieve profitability and environmental performance. For example, Toyota reduced the chemical solvents used to clean paint robots by 25%. Toyota and its subsidiary companies have crafted environmental-action guidelines, which include the following:

- Develop and provide clean products with minimal environmental impact
- Promote manufacturing that strives for zero landfill waste
- Expand environmental management systems
- Actively participate in public environmental-waste reduction efforts as a responsible corporate citizen

Thus far, the results have been remarkable. Currently, 99% of all scrap metal generated by Toyota plants is recycled; Toyota vehicles are 85% recyclable; hazardous waste has been reduced 40% since 2000; and two U.S. plants do not produce any landfill waste. Overall, these efforts resulted in more than $38 million of cost savings during 2002. Not satisfied with these results, Toyota plans to further reduce costs by eliminating landfill waste from all plants, by reducing hazardous waste by 95%, and by achieving the highest fuel-efficiency performance in all vehicle classes by the end of 2006.

Sources: J. Newberry, "A Goal of Zero," *Cincinnati Post* (June 30, 2003).

Toyota Industries Corporation. *Annual Report 2003.* (Kariya, Japan: Toyota Industries Corporation, 2004).

Toyota Motor Corporation. *Environmental & Social Report 2003.* (Toyota-shi, Japan: Toyota Motor Corporation, 2003).

Toyota Motor Corporation. "About Toyota: Environmental Commitment—Manufacturing—How Does Toyota Help the Environment." Toyota Motor Corporation Web site, **http://www.toyota.com/about/environment/manufacturing/help_environment.html**, accessed August 8, 2004.

Toyota Motor Corporation. "Toyota Strives to Be a 'Solution to Pollution'—New Report Chronicles the Company's Progress in North America," press release (Long Beach, CA: November 16, 2003).

Accounting for scrap under process costing is like the accounting under job costing when scrap is common to all jobs. That's because the scrap in process costing is common to the manufacture of masses of identical or similar units.

Managers focus their attention on ways to reduce scrap and to use it more profitably, especially when the cost of scrap is high (see Concepts in Action above). General Motors has redesigned its plastic injection molding processes to reduce the scrap plastic that must be broken away from its molded products. General Motors also regrinds and reuses the plastic scrap as direct material, saving substantial input costs.

Study Tip: To check your understanding of the material in this chapter, see true–false statement 5, multiple-choice questions 1 through 8, and Review Exercise 1 (*Student Guide*, beginning p. 248). Fully explained answers begin on page 253.

PROBLEM FOR SELF-STUDY

Burlington Textiles has some spoiled goods that had an assigned cost of $40,000 and zero net disposal value.

Required

Prepare a journal entry for each of the following conditions under (a) process costing (Department A) and (b) job costing:

1. Abnormal spoilage of $40,000
2. Normal spoilage of $40,000 regarded as common to all operations
3. Normal spoilage of $40,000 regarded as attributable to specifications of a particular job

SOLUTION

(a) Process Costing			(b) Job Costing		
1. Loss from Abnormal Spoilage	40,000		Loss from Abnormal Spoilage	40,000	
Work in Process—Dept. A		40,000	Work-in-Process Control (specific job)		40,000
2. No entry until units are completed and transferred out. Then the normal spoilage costs are transferred as part of the cost of good units.			Manufacturing Overhead Control	40,000	
			Work-in-Process Control (specific job)		40,000
Work in Process—Dept. B	40,000				
Work in Process—Dept. A		40,000			
3. Not applicable			No entry. Normal spoilage cost remains in Work-in-Process Control (specific job).		

DECISION POINTS

The following question-and-answer format summarizes the chapter's learning objectives. Each decision presents a key question related to a learning objective. The guidelines are the answer to that question.

Decision	Guidelines
1. What are spoilage, rework, and scrap?	Spoilage is units of production that do not meet the specifications required by customers for good units and that are discarded or sold at reduced prices. Rework is unacceptable units that are subsequently repaired and sold as acceptable finished goods. Scrap is residual material that results from manufacturing a product; it has low total sales value compared with the total sales value of the product.
2. What are normal and abnormal spoilage, and how are they accounted for?	Normal spoilage is inherent in a particular production process and arises under efficient operating conditions. Abnormal spoilage would not arise under efficient operating conditions. Generally, accounting systems explicitly recognize both types of spoilage when computing the number of output units. Normal spoilage is typically included in the cost of good output units; abnormal spoilage is recorded as a loss for the accounting period in which it is detected.
3. How does the weighted-average method of process costing calculate the costs of good units and spoilage?	The weighted-average method combines costs in beginning inventory with costs of the current period when determining the costs of good units (which includes normal spoilage) and the costs of abnormal spoilage.

4. How does the FIFO method of process costing calculate the costs of good units and spoilage?

The FIFO method keeps separate the costs in beginning inventory from the costs of the current period when determining the costs of good units (which include a normal spoilage amount) and the costs of abnormal spoilage.

5. How does the standard-costing method of process costing calculate the costs of good units and spoilage?

The standard-costing method uses standard costs to determine the costs of good units (which include a normal spoilage amount) and the costs of abnormal spoilage.

6. How do job-costing systems account for spoilage?

Normal spoilage specific to a job is assigned to that job, or when common to all jobs, it is allocated as part of manufacturing overhead. Loss from abnormal spoilage is recorded as a cost of the accounting period in which it is detected.

7. How do job-costing systems account for rework?

Completed reworked units should be indistinguishable from non-reworked good units. Normal rework can be assigned to a specific job, or when common to all jobs, as part of manufacturing overhead. Abnormal rework is written off as a cost of the accounting period in which it is detected.

8. How is scrap accounted for?

Scrap is recognized in the accounting records either at the time of its sale or at the time of its production. Sale of scrap, if immaterial, is often recognized as other revenue. If not immaterial, sale of scrap or its net realizable value reduces the cost of a specific job or, when common to all jobs, it reduces Manufacturing Overhead Control.

APPENDIX: INSPECTION AND SPOILAGE AT VARIOUS STAGES OF COMPLETION IN PROCESS COSTING

How does inspection at various stages of completion affect the amount of normal and abnormal spoilage? Consider the Forging Department of Dana Corporation, a manufacturer of automobile parts. Direct materials are added at the start of production in the Forging Department. Conversion costs are added evenly during the process.

Consider three different cases: Inspection occurs at (1) the 20%, (2) the 50%, or (3) the 100% completion stage. A total of 8,000 units are spoiled in all three cases. Normal spoilage is computed on the basis of the number of *good units* that pass the inspection point *during the current period.* Assume that normal spoilage is 10% of the good units passing inspection. The following data are for October 2007. Note how the number of units of normal and abnormal spoilage change, depending on when inspection occurs.

	Physical Units: Stage of Completion at Which Inspection Occurs		
Flow of Production	**20%**	**50%**	**100%**
Work in process, beginning[a]	11,000	11,000	11,000
Started during October	74,000	74,000	74,000
To account for	85,000	85,000	85,000
Good units completed and transferred out (85,000 – 8,000 spoiled – 16,000 ending)	61,000	61,000	61,000
Normal spoilage	6,600[b]	7,700[c]	6,100[d]
Abnormal spoilage (8,000 – normal spoilage)	1,400	300	1,900
Work in process, ending[e]	16,000	16,000	16,000
Accounted for	85,000	85,000	85,000

[a]Degree of completion in this department: direct materials, 100%; conversion costs, 25%.
[b]10% × (74,000 units started – 8,000 units spoiled), because only the units started passed the 20% completion inspection point in the current period. Beginning work in process is excluded from this calculation because, being 25% complete at the start of the period, it passed the inspection point in the previous period.
[c]10% × (85,000 units – 8,000 units spoiled), because all units passed the 50% completion inspection point in the current period.
[d]10% × 61,000, because 61,000 units are fully completed and inspected in the current period.
[e] Degree of completion in this department: direct materials, 100%; conversion costs, 75%.

The following diagram shows the flow of physical units for October and illustrates the normal spoilage numbers in the table. Note that 61,000 good units are completed and transferred out—

11,000 from beginning work in process and 50,000 started and completed during the period—and 16,000 units are in ending work in process.

This time line is helpful in calculating the amount of normal spoilage in the current period.

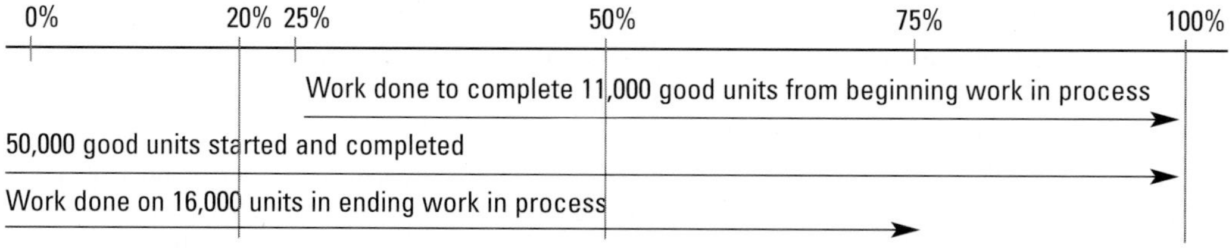

To see the number of units passing each inspection point, consider in the diagram the vertical lines at the 20%, 50%, and 100% inspection points. Note that the vertical line at 20% crosses two horizontal lines—50,000 good units started and completed and 16,000 units in ending work in process—for a total of 66,000 good units. (The 20% vertical line does not cross the line representing work done on the 11,000 good units completed from beginning work in process because these units are already 25% complete at the start of the period and, hence, are not inspected this period.) Normal spoilage equals 10% of 66,000 = 6,600 units. Similarly, the vertical line at the 50% point crosses all three horizontal lines, indicating that 11,000 + 50,000 + 16,000 = 77,000 good units pass this point. Normal spoilage in this case is 10% of 77,000 = 7,700 units. At the 100% point, normal spoilage = 10% of 61,000 (11,000 + 50,000) good units = 6,100 units.

Exhibit 18-5 shows the computation of equivalent units under the weighted-average method, assuming inspection at the 50% completion stage. The calculations depend on the direct materials and conversion costs incurred to get the units to this inspection point. The spoiled units have a full measure of direct materials and a 50% measure of conversion costs. Calculations of costs per equivalent unit and the assignment of total costs to units completed and to ending work in process are similar to calculations in previous illustrations in this chapter. Because ending work in process has passed the inspection point in this example, these units bear normal spoilage costs, just like the units that have been completed and transferred out. For example, conversion costs for units completed and transferred out include conversion costs for 61,000 good units produced plus 50% × (10% × 61,000) = 0.50 × 6,100 = 3,050 equivalent units of normal spoilage. *We multiply by 50% to obtain equivalent units of normal spoilage because conversion costs are only 50% complete at the inspection point.* Conversion costs of equivalent units in ending work in process include conversion costs of 75% of 16,000 = 12,000 equivalent good units plus 50% × (10% × 16,000) = 0.50 × 1,600 = 800 equivalent units of normal spoilage. We take 10% of 16,000 because 16,000 good units currently in ending work in process passed the inspection point. Thus, the equivalent units of normal spoilage accounted for are 3,050 equivalent units related to units completed and transferred out plus 800 equivalent units related to units in ending work in process, for a total of 3,850 equivalent units, as shown in Exhibit 18-5.

Question: If ending work in process is 70% complete, should it get a "full dose" of normal spoilage when inspection is at the 50%-completion point?

Answer: Yes, because spoilage is recognized at the inspection point. Even though these units are only 70% of the way through the production process, they are nevertheless complete in terms of normal spoilage at the 50%-completion point.

EXHIBIT 18-5

Steps 1 and 2: Computing Equivalent Units with Spoilage Using Weighted-Average Method of Process Costing with Inspection at 50% of Completion for Forging Department of the Dana Corporation for October 2007

Flow of Production	(Step 1) Physical Units	(Step 2) Equivalent Units: Direct Materials	(Step 2) Equivalent Units: Conversion Costs
Work in process, beginning[a]	11,000		
Started during current period	74,000		
To account for	85,000		
Good units completed and transferred out	61,000	61,000	61,000
Normal spoilage	7,700		
(7,700 × 100%; 7,700 × 50%)		7,700	3,850
Abnormal spoilage	300		
(300 × 100%; 300 × 50%)		300	150
Work in process, ending[b]	16,000		
(16,000 × 100%; 16,000 × 75%)		16,000	12,000
Accounted for	85,000		
Total work done to date		85,000	77,000

[a]Degree of completion: direct materials, 100%; conversion costs, 25%.
[b]Degree of completion: direct materials, 100%; conversion costs, 75%.

TERMS TO LEARN

This chapter and the Glossary at the end of the book contain definitions of:

abnormal spoilage (p. 634)	normal spoilage (p. 633)	scrap (p. 633)
inspection point (p. 634)	rework (p. 633)	spoilage (p. 633)

PH Grade Assist

Prentice Hall Grade Assist (PHGA)
Your professor may ask you to complete selected exercises and problems in Prentice Hall Grade Assist (PHGA). PHGA is an online tool that can help you master the chapter's topics. It provides you with multiple variations of exercises and problems designated by the PHGA icon. You can rework these exercises and problems—each time with new data—as many times as you need. You also receive immediate feedback and grading.

ASSIGNMENT MATERIAL

Questions

18-1 Why is there an unmistakable trend in manufacturing to improve quality?

18-2 Distinguish among spoilage, rework, and scrap.

18-3 "Normal spoilage is planned spoilage." Discuss.

18-4 "Costs of abnormal spoilage are losses." Explain.

18-5 "What has been regarded as normal spoilage in the past is not necessarily acceptable as normal spoilage in the present or future." Explain.

18-6 "Units of abnormal spoilage are inferred rather than identified." Explain.

18-7 "In accounting for spoiled units, we are dealing with cost assignment rather than cost incurrence." Explain.

18-8 "Total input includes abnormal as well as normal spoilage and is, therefore, inappropriate as a basis for computing normal spoilage." Do you agree? Explain.

18-9 "The inspection point is the key to the allocation of spoilage costs." Do you agree? Explain.

18-10 "The unit cost of normal spoilage is the same as the unit cost of abnormal spoilage." Do you agree? Explain.

18-11 "In job costing, the costs of normal spoilage that occur while a specific job is being done are charged to the specific job." Do you agree? Explain.

18-12 "The costs of rework are always charged to the specific jobs in which the defects were originally discovered." Do you agree? Explain.

18-13 "Abnormal rework costs should be charged to a loss account, not to manufacturing overhead." Do you agree? Explain.

18-14 When is a company justified in inventorying scrap?

18-15 How do managers use information about scrap?

Exercises

18-16 Normal and abnormal spoilage in units. The following data, in physical units, describe a grinding process for January:

PH Grade Assist

Work in process, beginning	19,000
Started during current period	150,000
To account for	169,000
Spoiled units	12,000
Good units completed and transferred out	132,000
Work in process, ending	25,000
Accounted for	169,000

Inspection occurs at the 100% completion stage. Normal spoilage is 5% of the good units passing inspection.

Required

1. Compute the normal and abnormal spoilage in units.
2. Assume that the equivalent-unit cost of a spoiled unit is $10. Compute the amount of potential savings if all spoilage were eliminated, assuming that all other costs would be unaffected. Comment on your answer.

PH Grade Assist

18-17 Weighted-average method, spoilage, equivalent units. (CMA, adapted) Consider the following data for November 2006 from Gray Manufacturing Company, which makes silk pennants and uses a process-costing system. All direct materials are added at the beginning of the process, and conversion costs are added evenly during the process. Spoilage is detected upon inspection at the completion of the process. Spoiled units are disposed of at zero net disposal value. Gray Manufacturing Company uses the weighted-average method of process costing.

	Physical Units (Pennants)	Direct Materials	Conversion Costs
Work in process, November 1[a]	1,000	$ 1,423	$ 1,110
Started in November 2006	?		
Good units completed and transferred out during November 2006	9,000		
Normal spoilage	100		
Abnormal spoilage	50		
Work in process, November 30[b]	2,000		
Total costs added during November 2006		$12,180	$27,750

[a]Degree of completion: direct materials, 100%; conversion costs, 50%.
[b]Degree of completion: direct materials, 100%; conversion costs, 30%.

Required Compute equivalent units for direct materials and conversion costs. Show physical units in the first column of your schedule.

PH Grade Assist

18-18 Weighted-average method, assigning costs (continuation of 18-17).

Required For the data in Exercise 18-17, calculate the cost per equivalent unit for direct materials and conversion costs, summarize total costs to account for, and assign total costs to units completed and transferred out (including normal spoilage), to abnormal spoilage, and to units in ending work in process.

PH Grade Assist

18-19 FIFO method, spoilage, equivalent units. Refer to the information in Exercise 18-17. Suppose Gray Manufacturing Company uses the FIFO method of process costing instead of the weighted-average method.

Required Compute equivalent units for direct materials and conversion costs. Show physical units in the first column of your schedule.

PH Grade Assist

18-20 FIFO method, assigning costs (continuation of 18-19).

Required For the data in Exercise 18-17, use the FIFO method to calculate the cost per equivalent unit for direct materials and conversion costs, summarize total costs to account for, and assign total costs to units completed and transferred out (including normal spoilage), to abnormal spoilage, and to units in ending work in process.

Excel Lab
www.prenhall.com/horngren/cost12e

18-21 Weighted-average method, spoilage. Appleton Company makes wooden toys in its Forming Department, and it uses the weighted-average method of process costing. All direct materials are added at the beginning of the process, and conversion costs are added evenly during the process. Spoiled units are detected upon inspection at the end of the process and are disposed of at zero net disposal value. Summary data for August 2006 are:

	A	B	C	D
1		Physical Units	Direct Materials	Conversion Costs
2	Work in process, beginning inventory (August 1)	2,000	$17,700	$10,900
3	Degree of completion of beginning work in process		100%	50%
4	Started during August	10,000		
5	Good units completed and transferred out during August	9,000		
6	Work in process, ending inventory (August 31)	1,800		
7	Degree of completion of ending work in process		100%	75%
8	Total costs added during August		$81,300	$93,000
9	Normal spoilage as a percentage of good units	10%		
10	Degree of completion of normal spoilage		100%	100%
11	Degree of completion of abnormal spoilage		100%	100%

If you want to use Excel to solve this exercise, go to the Excel Lab at **www.prenhall.com/horngren/cost12e** and download the template for Exercise 18-21.

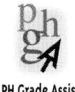

1. For each cost category, calculate equivalent units. Show physical units in the first column of your schedule.
2. For each cost category, calculate cost per equivalent unit.
3. Summarize total costs to account for and assign total costs to units completed and transferred out (including normal spoilage), to abnormal spoilage, and to units in ending work in process.

Required

18-22 FIFO method, spoilage. Refer to the information in Exercise 18-21. If you want to use Excel to solve this exercise, go to the Excel Lab at **www.prenhall.com/horngren/cost12e** and download the template for Exercise 18-21.

Excel Lab www.prenhall.com/horngren/cost12e

Required

Do Exercise 18-21 using the FIFO method. Note that you first need to calculate the equivalent units of work done in the current period (for direct materials and conversion costs) to complete beginning work in process, to start and complete new units and normal and abnormal spoilage units, and to produce ending work in process.

18-23 Standard-costing method, spoilage. Refer to the information in Exercise 18-21. Suppose Appleton determines standard costs of $8 per equivalent unit for direct materials and $9.50 per equivalent unit for conversion costs for both beginning work in process and work done in the current period.

If you want to use Excel to solve this exercise, go to the Excel Lab at **www.prenhall.com/horngren/cost12e** and download the template for Exercise 18-21.

Excel Lab www.prenhall.com/horngren/cost12e

Required

Do Exercise 18-21 using the standard-costing method. Note that you first need to calculate the equivalent units of work done in the current period (for direct materials and conversion costs) to complete beginning work in process, to start and complete new units and normal and abnormal spoilage units, and to produce ending work in process.

18-24 Weighted-average method, spoilage. Superchip specializes in the manufacture of microchips for aircraft. Direct materials are added at the start of the production process. Conversion costs are added evenly during the process. Some units of this product are spoiled as a result of defects not detectable before inspection of finished goods. Spoiled units are disposed of at zero net disposal value. Superchip uses the weighted-average method of process costing.

Excel Lab www.prenhall.com/horngren/cost12e

Summary data for September 2006 are:

	A	B	C	D
1		Physical Units (Microchips)	Direct Materials	Conversion Costs
2	Work in process, beginning inventory (September 1)	400	$64,000	$10,200
3	Degree of completion of beginning work in process		100%	30%
4	Started during September	1,700		
5	Good units completed and transferred out during September	1,400		
6	Work in process, ending inventory (September 30)	300		
7	Degree of completion of ending work in process		100%	40%
8	Total costs added during September		$378,000	$153,600
9	Normal spoilage as a percentage of good units	15%		
10	Degree of completion of normal spoilage		100%	100%
11	Degree of completion of abnormal spoilage		100%	100%

If you want to use Excel to solve this exercise, go to the Excel Lab at **www.prenhall.com/horngren/cost12e** and download the template for Exercise 18-24.

Required

1. For each cost category, compute equivalent units. Show physical units in the first column of your schedule.
2. For each cost category, calculate cost per equivalent unit.
3. Summarize total costs to account for, and assign total costs to units completed and transferred out (including normal spoilage), to abnormal spoilage, and to units in ending work in process.

18-25 FIFO method, spoilage. Refer to the information in Exercise 18-24. If you want to use Excel to solve this exercise, go to the Excel Lab at **www.prenhall.com/horngren/cost12e** and download the template for Exercise 18-24.

Excel Lab www.prenhall.com/horngren/cost12e

Required

Do Exercise 18-24 using the FIFO method of process costing.

18-26 Standard-costing method, spoilage. Refer to the information in Exercise 18-24. Suppose Superchip determines standard costs of $210 per equivalent unit for direct materials and $80 per equivalent unit for conversion costs for both beginning work in process and work done in the current period.

If you want to use Excel to solve this exercise, go to the Excel Lab at **www.prenhall.com/horngren/cost12e** and download the template for Exercise 18-24.

Excel Lab www.prenhall.com/horngren/cost12e

Required

Do Exercise 18-24 using the standard-costing method.

18-27 Spoilage and job costing. (L. Bamber) Bamber Kitchens produces a variety of items in accordance with special job orders from hospitals, plant cafeterias, and university dormitories. An order for 2,500 cases of mixed vegetables costs $6 per case: direct materials, $3; direct manufacturing labor, $2; and manufacturing overhead allocated, $1. The manufacturing overhead rate includes a provision for normal spoilage. Consider each requirement independently.

Required

1. Assume that a laborer dropped 200 cases. Suppose part of the 200 cases could be sold to a nearby prison for $200 cash. Prepare a journal entry to record this event. Calculate and explain briefly the unit cost of the remaining 2,300 cases.
2. Refer to the original data. Tasters at the company reject 200 of the 2,500 cases. The 200 cases are disposed of for $400. Assume that this rejection rate is considered normal. Prepare a journal entry to record this event, and:
   a. Calculate the unit cost if the rejection is attributable to exacting specifications of this particular job.
   b. Calculate the unit cost if the rejection is characteristic of the production process and is not attributable to this specific job.
   c. Are unit costs the same in requirements 2a and 2b? Explain your reasoning briefly.
3. Refer to the original data. Tasters rejected 200 cases that had insufficient salt. The product can be placed in a vat, salt can be added, and the product can be reprocessed into jars. This operation, which is considered normal, will cost $200. Prepare a journal entry to record this event and:
   a. Calculate the unit cost of all the cases if this additional cost was incurred because of the exacting specifications of this particular job.
   b. Calculate the unit cost of all the cases if this additional cost occurs regularly because of difficulty in seasoning.
   c. Are unit costs the same in requirements 3a and 3b? Explain your reasoning briefly.

18-28 Reworked units, costs of rework. White Goods assembles washing machines at its Auburn plant. In February 2007, 60 tumbler units that cost $44 each (from a new supplier who subsequently went bankrupt) were defective and had to be disposed of at zero net disposal value. White Goods was able to rework all 60 washing machines by substituting new tumbler units purchased from one of its existing suppliers. Each replacement tumbler cost $50.

Required

1. What alternative approaches are there to account for the material cost of reworked units?
2. Should White Goods use the $44 tumbler or the $50 tumbler to calculate the cost of materials reworked? Explain.
3. What other costs might White Goods include in its analysis of the total costs of rework due to the tumbler units purchased from the (now) bankrupt supplier?

18-29 Scrap, job costing. The Mendoza Company has an extensive job-costing facility that uses a variety of metals. Consider each requirement independently.

Required

1. Job 372 uses a particular metal alloy that is not used for any other job. Assume that scrap is material in amount and sold for $490 quickly after it is produced. Prepare the journal entry.
2. The scrap from Job 372 consists of a metal used by many other jobs. No record is maintained of the scrap generated by individual jobs. Assume that scrap is accounted for at the time of its sale. Scrap totaling $4,000 is sold. Prepare two alternative journal entries that could be used to account for the sale of scrap.
3. Suppose the scrap generated in requirement 2 is returned to the storeroom for future use and a journal entry is made to record the scrap. A month later, the scrap is reused as direct material on a subsequent job. Prepare the journal entries to record these transactions.

Problems

Excel Lab
www.prenhall.com/horngren/cost12e

18-30 Weighted-average method, spoilage. The Alston Company operates under the weighted-average method of process costing. It has two departments: Cleaning and Milling. For the Cleaning Department, conversion costs are added evenly during the process and direct materials are added at the beginning of the process. Spoiled units are detected upon inspection at the end of the process and are disposed of at zero net disposal value. All completed work is transferred to the Milling Department. Summary data for May follow:

	A	B	C	D
1	**Alston Company: Cleaning Department**	**Physical Units**	**Direct Materials**	**Conversion Costs**
2	Work in process, beginning inventory (May 1)	1,000	$1,000	$ 800
3	Degree of completion of beginning work in process		100%	80%
4	Started during May	9,000		
5	Good units completed and transferred out during May	7,400		
6	Work in process, ending inventory (May 31)	1,600		
7	Degree of completion of ending work in process		100%	25%
8	Total costs added during May		$9,000	$8,000
9	Normal spoilage as a percentage of good units	10%		
10	Degree of completion of normal spoilage		100%	100%
11	Degree of completion of abnormal spoilage		100%	100%

If you want to use Excel to solve this problem, go to the Excel Lab at **www.prenhall.com/horngren/cost12e** and download the template for Problem 18-30.

Required

For the Cleaning Department, summarize total costs to account for, and assign total costs to units completed and transferred out (including normal spoilage), to abnormal spoilage, and to units in ending work in process. Carry unit-cost calculations to four decimal places when necessary. Calculate final totals to the nearest dollar. (Problem 18-32 explores additional facets of this problem.)

18-31 FIFO method, spoilage. Refer to the information in Problem 18-30. If you want to use Excel to solve this problem, go to the Excel Lab at **www.prenhall.com/horngren/cost12e** and download the template for Problem 18-30.

Excel Lab
www.prenhall.com/horngren/cost12e

Required

Do Problem 18-30 using the FIFO method of process costing. (Problem 18-33 explores additional facets of this problem.)

18-32 Weighted-average method, Milling Department (continuation of 18-30). In Alston Company's Milling Department, conversion costs are added evenly during the process, and direct materials are added at the end of the process. Spoiled units are detected upon inspection at the end of the process and are disposed of at zero net disposal value. All completed work is transferred to the next department. The transferred-in costs for May equal the total cost of good units completed and transferred out in May from the Cleaning Department, which were calculated in Problem 18-30 using the weighted-average method of process costing. Summary data for May follow.

Excel Lab
www.prenhall.com/horngren/cost12e

	A	B	C	D	E
1	**Alston Company: Milling Department**	**Physical Units**	**Transferred-in Costs**	**Direct Materials**	**Conversion Costs**
2	Work in process, beginning inventory (May 1)	3,000	$6,450	$ 0	$2,450
3	Degree of completion of beginning work in process		100%	0%	80%
4	Started during May	7,400			
5	Good units completed and transferred out during May	6,000			
6	Work in process, ending inventory (May 31)	4,000			
7	Degree of completion of ending work in process		100%	0%	25%
8	Total costs added during May		?	$640	$4,950
9	Normal spoilage as a percentage of good units	5%			
10	Degree of completion of normal spoilage			100%	100%
11	Degree of completion of abnormal spoilage			100%	100%

If you want to use Excel to solve this problem, go to the Excel Lab at **www.prenhall.com/horngren/cost12e** and download the template for Problem 18-32.

Required

For the Milling Department, use the weighted-average method to summarize total costs to account for and assign total costs to units completed and transferred out (including normal spoilage), to abnormal spoilage, and to units in ending work in process.

18-33 FIFO method, Milling Department (continuation of 18-31). Refer to the information in Problem 18-32 except for the transferred-in costs for May, which equal the total cost of good units completed and transferred out in May from the Cleaning Department, which were calculated in Problem 18-31 using the FIFO method of process costing.

Excel Lab
www.prenhall.com/horngren/cost12e

If you want to use Excel to solve this problem, go to the Excel Lab at **www.prenhall.com/horngren/cost12e** and download the template for Problem 18-32.

Required

For the Milling Department, use the FIFO method to summarize total costs to account for, and assign total costs to units completed and transferred out (including normal spoilage), to abnormal spoilage, and to units in ending work in process.

18-34 Job-costing spoilage and scrap. (F. Mayne) Santa Cruz Metal Fabricators, Inc., has a large job, No. 2734, that calls for producing various ore bins, chutes, and metal boxes for enlarging a copper concentrator. The following charges were made to the job in November 2007:

Direct materials	$26,951
Direct manufacturing labor	15,076
Manufacturing overhead	7,538

The contract with the customer called for the total price to be based on a cost-plus approach. The contract defined cost to include direct materials, direct manufacturing labor costs, and manufacturing overhead to be allocated at 50% of direct manufacturing labor costs. The contract also provided that the total costs of all work spoiled were to be removed from the billable cost of the job and that the benefits from scrap sales were to reduce the billable cost of the job.

Required

1. In accordance with the stated terms of the contract, prepare journal entries for the following two items:
   a. A cutting error was made in production. The up-to-date job cost record for this batch of work showed materials of $650, direct manufacturing labor of $500, and allocated overhead of $250. Because fairly large pieces of metal were recoverable, the company believed their value was $600 and that the materials recovered could be used on other jobs. The spoiled work was sent to the warehouse.
   b. Small pieces of metal cuttings and scrap in November 2007 amounted to $1,250, which was the price quoted by a scrap dealer. No journal entries were made with regard to the scrap until the price was quoted by the scrap dealer. The scrap dealer's offer was immediately accepted.
2. Consider normal and abnormal spoilage. Suppose the contract described above had contained the clause "a normal spoilage allowance of 1% of the job costs will be included in the billable costs of the job."
   a. Is this clause specific enough to define exactly how much spoilage is normal and how much is abnormal? Explain.
   b. Repeat requirement 1a with this "normal spoilage of 1%" clause in mind. You should be able to provide two slightly different journal entries.

18-35 Job costing, rework. Bristol Corporation manufactures two brands of motors, SM-5 and RW-8. The costs of manufacturing each SM-5 motor, excluding rework costs, are direct materials, $300; direct manufacturing labor, $60; and manufacturing overhead, $190. Defective units are sent to a separate rework area. Rework costs per SM-5 motor are direct materials, $60; direct manufacturing labor, $45; and manufacturing overhead, $75.

In February 2007, Bristol manufactured 1,000 SM-5 and 500 RW-8 motors. Eighty of the SM-5 motors and none of the RW-8 motors required rework. Bristol classifies 50 of the SM-5 motors reworked as normal rework caused by inherent problems in its production process that only coincidentally occurred during the production of SM-5. Hence the rework costs for these 50 SM-5 motors are normal rework costs not specifically attributable to the SM-5 product. Bristol classifies the remaining 30 units of SM-5 motors reworked as abnormal rework. Bristol allocates manufacturing overhead on the basis of machine-hours required to manufacture SM-5 and RW-8. Each SM-5 or RW-8 motor requires the same number of machine-hours.

Required

1. Prepare journal entries to record the accounting for the cost of the spoiled motors and for rework.
2. What were the total rework costs of SM-5 motors in February 2007?

18-36 Job costing, scrap. Wong Corporation makes two different types of hubcaps for cars: models HM3 and JB4. Circular pieces of metal are stamped out of steel sheets (leaving the edges as scrap), formed, and finished. The stamping operation is identical for both types of hubcaps. During March, Wong manufactured 20,000 units of HM3 and 10,000 units of JB4. In March, manufacturing costs of HM3 and JB4 before accounting for the scrap were as follows:

	HM3	JB4
Direct materials	$200,000	$150,000
Direct manufacturing labor	60,000	40,000
Manufacturing overhead	120,000	80,000
Total manufacturing costs	$380,000	$270,000

Manufacturing overhead is allocated to products at 200% of direct manufacturing labor costs. Because the same metal sheets are used to make both types of hubcaps, Wong maintains no records of the scrap generated by individual products. Scrap generated during manufacturing is accounted for at the time it is returned to the storeroom as an offset to manufacturing overhead. The value of scrap generated during March and returned to the storeroom was $10,000.

Required

1. Prepare a journal entry to summarize the accounting for scrap during March.
2. Suppose the scrap generated in March is sold in April for $10,000. Prepare a journal entry to account for this transaction.
3. Calculate the manufacturing cost per unit of HM3 and JB4 in March after accounting for scrap?

18-37 Physical units, inspection at various stages of completion (chapter appendix). Normal spoilage is 6% of the good units passing inspection in a forging process. In March, a total of 10,000 units were spoiled. Other data include units started during March, 120,000; work in process, beginning, 14,000 units (20% completed for conversion costs); and work in process, ending, 11,000 units (70% completed for conversion costs).

Required

Using the format on page 649, compute the normal and abnormal spoilage in units, assuming the inspection point is at (a) the 15% stage of completion, (b) the 40% stage of completion, and (c) the 100% stage of completion.

18-38 Weighted-average method, inspection at 80% completion (chapter appendix). (A. Atkinson) Ottawa Manufacturing produces a plastic toy in a two-stage molding and finishing operation. The company uses the weighted-average method of process costing. During June, the following data were recorded for the Finishing Department:

Units of beginning inventory	10,000
Percentage completion of beginning units	25%
Cost of direct materials in beginning work in process	$0
Units started	70,000
Units completed	50,000
Units in ending inventory	20,000
Percentage completion of ending units	95%
Spoiled units	10,000
Total costs added during current period:	
Direct materials	$655,200
Direct manufacturing labor	$635,600
Manufacturing overhead	$616,000
Work in process, beginning:	
Transferred-in costs	$82,900
Conversion costs	$42,000
Cost of units transferred in during current period	$647,500

Conversion costs are added evenly during the process. Direct material costs are added when production is 90% complete. The inspection point is at the 80% stage of production. Normal spoilage is 10% of all good units that pass inspection. Spoiled units are disposed of at zero net disposal value.

Required

For June, summarize total costs to account for, and assign these costs to units completed and transferred out (including normal spoilage), to abnormal spoilage, and to units in ending work in process.

18-39 Job costing, spoilage, ethics. (CMA, adapted) Richport Company has a normal spoilage rate of 2.5% of normal input. Normal spoilage is recognized during the budgeting process and is classified as a component of manufacturing overhead when determining the overhead rate. Rose Duncan, one of Richport's inspection managers, obtains the following information for Job No. N1192-122, which was recently completed, just before the end of Richport's current accounting year. The units will be delivered early in the next accounting year. A total of 122,000 units were started, and 5,000 spoiled units were rejected at final inspection, yielding 117,000 good units. Spoiled units were sold at $7 per unit. Duncan indicates that all spoilage was related to this specific job.

The total costs for all 122,000 units of Job No. N1192-122 follow. The job has been completed, but the costs are yet to be transferred to Finished Goods.

Direct materials	$2,196,000
Direct manufacturing labor	1,830,000
Manufacturing overhead	2,928,000
Total manufacturing costs	$6,954,000

Required

1. Calculate the unit quantities of normal and abnormal spoilage.
2. Prepare the journal entry (or entries) to account for Job No. N1192-122, including spoilage, disposal of spoiled units, and transfer of costs to the Finished Goods account.
3. Richport's controller, Thomas Rutherford, tells Martha Gonzales, the management accountant responsible for Job No. N1192-122, the following: "This was an unusual job. I think all 5,000 spoiled units should be considered normal." Gonzales knows that Richport's normal spoilage rate is a good measure of normal spoilage for Job N1192-122 and that actual spoilage levels were much greater. She feels Rutherford made these comments because he wants to show higher operating income for the year.
   a. Prepare journal entries, similar to requirement 2, to account for Job No. N1192-122 if all spoilage were considered normal. How will operating income be affected if all spoilage is considered normal?
   b. What should Gonzales do in response to Rutherford's comment?

Collaborative Learning Problem

18-40 Weighted-average method, spoilage, working backward. Ferguson, Inc., uses the weighted-average method of process costing. Direct materials are added at the beginning of the process. Conversion costs are added evenly during the process. Inspection occurs when production is 100% complete. Normal spoilage is 10% of good units completed and transferred out during the current period. Consider the following data for January:

	Physical Units	Direct Materials	Conversion Costs
Work in process, January 1	10,000	$220,000	$30,000
Started in January	74,000		
Good units completed and transferred out during January	61,000		
Spoiled units	8,000		
Work in process, January 31	15,000		
Total costs added during January		$1,460,000	$942,000
Cost per equivalent unit of work done to date		$20	$12

Required

1. For each cost category, calculate equivalent units of work done to date.
2. For each cost category, lay out a table as in Exhibit 18-2, Panel A, steps 1 and 2, and calculate the equivalent units of ending work-in-process inventory.
3. Summarize total costs to account for, and assign total costs to units completed and transferred out (including normal spoilage), to abnormal spoilage, and to units in ending work in process.

Get Connected: Cost Accounting in the News

Go to www.prenhall.com/horngren/cost12e for additional online exercise(s) that explore issues affecting the accounting world today. These exercises offer you the opportunity to analyze and reflect on how cost accounting helps managers to make better decisions and handle the challenges of strategic planning and implementation.

CHAPTER 18 Case

THE UNITED LIBBEY-NIPPON PLANT: Responsibility and Accounting for Spoilage

Libbey-Owens-Ford Co., (L-O-F), is a major producer of glass products in the United States. Its newest plant, United L/N, is a joint venture between L-O-F and a Japanese company, Nippon Sheet Glass.

The management of the United L/N plant is evaluated on the basis of profit goals established by the board of directors. The production process is fully automated, requiring no human intervention from beginning to end. High quality and minimal spoilage are the norm.

The fabrication process has the following steps: (1) United L/N obtains raw glass, the direct material, from the Rossford plant of L-O-F; the raw glass is cut to the basic shape of the "lite" (a lite is a unit such as a rear window, called a "back lite," or a side window, a "side lite"); (2) the cut pattern is edged; (3) the edged pattern goes through a furnace where it is formed (bent to shape) and tempered; and (4) the final product is inspected, packed, and shipped. A small team of operators monitors and maintains all steps in the process.

United L/N's costs consist of short-term fixed operating costs, labor costs of the operating teams, and the cost of raw glass from the Rossford plant priced at standard manufacturing cost. Because the entire process is automated, the feed rate is constant across all subprocesses for each individual lite being fabricated. The costing system accumulates conversion costs in one large cost pool, assigns conversion costs to units based on standard feed rates, and traces direct material costs based on standard costs of individual lites. The system allows for standard levels of downtime and anticipated yields.

"A couple of months ago we began experiencing problems with our yields at United L/N," remarked Ken Marvin, planning and control director. "Our problem was keeping the furnaces on the two production lines working efficiently. Each furnace was designed to work perfectly when a certain number of glass pieces were being fired, a certain number were on the threshold entering the furnace, and a certain number were leaving it. In our traditional plants, we stockpile pieces in front of the furnaces so that we can keep them filled to their optimal levels when forming and tempering. However, the United L/N production lines were designed so that inventories did not have to be maintained in front of the furnaces to keep the furnaces running efficiently at all times. Unfortunately, for reasons such as problems during pattern cutting or edging, there might have been gaps in the lines as they entered the furnaces. Partly because of these gaps and the resulting inefficient furnace operations, we have had unacceptably high spoilage rates that have decreased the plant's yield. Furthermore, the plant incurs opportunity costs associated with having an empty tempering furnace and with having to rest the furnace after it has been empty during periods of time when it was programmed to be full.

"We believe the problem of spoilage is caused by imperfections in the raw glass rather than by problems in the process," and that spoilage costs (the cost of raw glass plus United L/N's manufacturing costs) should therefore be charged to the Rossford Plant. The Rossford plant manager believes that the charge-back cost, even if appropriate (which remains an issue), is much too high. Because units are only inspected upon completion, United L/N's costing system costs spoiled units as all costs incurred throughout the entire process even if spoilage occurs, for example, at the pattern-cutting or edging stages."

QUESTIONS

1. As the manager of the Rossford plant, what would be your position regarding the treatment of the United L/N scrap cost?
2. What would United L/N's position be regarding the treatment of the United L/N scrap?
3. How could United L/N's management determine the specific causes of defects (for example, bad glass or defective cutting, edging, or tempering) in scrapped units? What are the implications for the process-costing system?
4. What could be done to reduce the problems of furnace inefficiency and ineffectiveness?

CHAPTER 19

BALANCED SCORECARD: QUALITY, TIME, AND THE THEORY OF CONSTRAINTS

LEARNING OBJECTIVES

1. **Explain the four cost categories in a costs-of-quality program**
2. **Provide examples of nonfinancial quality measures of customer satisfaction in the balanced scorecard**
3. **Use three methods to identify quality problems**
4. **Identify relevant costs and benefits of quality improvement programs**
5. **Describe the benefits of financial and nonfinancial measures of quality**
6. **Describe customer-response time and explain why delays happen and their costs**
7. **Apply the three measures in the theory of constraints**
8. **Explain how to manage bottlenecks**

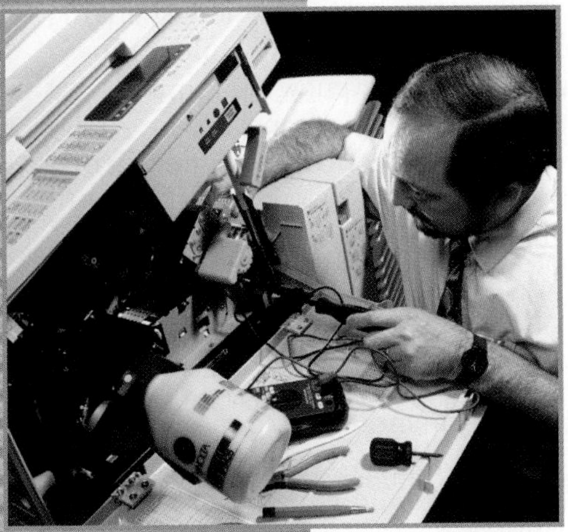

Jessica Sharpe, the CEO of Photon Corporation, couldn't believe the report she had just received. She had always thought that Photon made the highest quality photocopiers on the market. But now she wasn't so sure. The report indicated that quality-related costs (mostly the costs of poor quality) were 17.3% of revenues. She immediately called the CFO, Charles Jordan, to her office.

Jessica: Charles, I just can't believe these numbers. I never realized they were this high.

Charles: Well, that was one of the reasons why I was insisting on measuring the costs of quality. It certainly has gotten everyone's attention. You can't manage what you don't measure.

Jessica: How confident are you about these numbers?

Charles: I'm confident that they are reasonably correct. As you know, these numbers include profits forgone from lost sales because of poor quality. We had to use estimates, but I think those numbers represent our situation quite accurately.

Jessica: What are we going to do about this? We'll be in big trouble if we continue to lose money at this rate because of poor quality.

Charles: I've had several calls from managers who've received this report. We are thinking about this situation in the context of our balanced scorecard, and we've already scheduled a meeting for later today to talk about how we're going to make quality improvements. It will require a team effort, but everybody is up for it.

Jessica: Okay, this is a step in the right direction, but poor quality also hurts our ability to make timely deliveries to our customers, and we must keep our commitments.

Charles: Absolutely, and that is why I've also collected some nonfinancial measures regarding customer satisfaction, defect rates, and employee training. If we do not take these nonfinancial measures into consideration, we simply cannot improve.

Jessica: Keep me informed, Charles. I would like to see some improvements soon.

Achieving a high level of quality is hard work. Companies the world over strive to make high-quality products or to provide high-quality services. For example, the Ritz-Carlton's ongoing commitment to furthering its quality is evident in every department, from housekeeping to room service. Inefficiencies, breakdowns, and variations from expected levels of quality are tracked. Anything that misses target service standards is analyzed and discussed at weekly staff meetings in an effort to be sure that it doesn't happen again. All staff, from the general manager to the newest front-desk clerk, realize that a failure to meet a guest's quality expectations could mean the guest will check out, not come back, and inform others of his or her dissatisfaction.

Customers are becoming more intolerant of poor quality and long delivery times. To satisfy customers, managers need to find cost-effective ways to continuously improve the quality of their products and to shorten delivery times. This chapter describes how managers can identify what blocks an organization from producing higher-quality products and making products faster and how to remove these constraints. We'll explain how management accountants can help managers to take strategic initiatives toward improving quality and reducing delays and to make decisions when faced with multiple constraints.

We build on the discussion of the balanced scorecard introduced in Chapter 13. Recall that the balanced scorecard translates an organization's mission and strategy into a set of performance measures that provides the framework for implementing the strategy. We will focus specifically on those parts of a scorecard that relate to using quality, time, and increased throughput to satisfy customers and gain competitive advantage.

We present this chapter in three parts. Part One is Quality as a Competitive Tool, Part Two is Time as a Competitive Tool, and Part Three is Theory of Constraints and Throughput Contribution Analysis. The presentation is modular so you can omit a part or explore these topics in any order.

PART ONE: QUALITY AS A COMPETITIVE TOOL

We begin by introducing different aspects of quality and then describe how quality measures appear on the balanced scorecard. The American Society for Quality Control defines **quality** as the total features and characteristics of a product or a service made or performed according to specifications to satisfy customers at the time of purchase and during use. Many companies throughout the world—for example, Cisco Systems and Motorola in the United States and Canada, British Telecom in the United Kingdom, Fujitsu and Toyota in Japan, Crysel in Mexico, and Samsung in South Korea—have emphasized quality as an important strategic initiative. That's because a quality focus reduces costs and increases customer satisfaction. Several high-profile awards—the Malcolm Baldrige Quality Award in the United States, the Deming Prize in Japan, and the Premio Nacional de Calidad in Mexico—are given to companies that have produced high-quality products.

International quality standards have also emerged. ISO 9000, developed by the International Organization for Standardization, is a set of five international standards for quality management adopted by more than 85 countries. ISO 9000 enables companies to effectively document and certify the elements of their production processes that lead to quality. To ensure that their suppliers deliver high-quality products at competitive costs, companies such as DuPont and General Electric require their suppliers to obtain ISO 9000 certification. Documenting evidence of quality through ISO 9000 has become a necessary condition for competing in the global marketplace.

Focusing on the quality of a product will generally build expertise in producing it, lower the costs of making it, create higher satisfaction for customers using it, and generate higher future revenues for the company selling it. Dell Computer's quality initiatives increased customer satisfaction and fueled its 1,912% increase in revenues, 1,884% increase in profits, and 8,015% increase in stock price for the 10 years ending September 2003. In some cases, the benefit of better quality is in preserving revenues, not generating higher revenues. A company that does not invest in quality improvement while competitors are doing so will likely suffer a decline in its market share, revenues, and profits.

As corporations' responsibilities toward the environment grow, managers are applying ideas of quality management to find cost-effective ways to reduce the environmental and economic costs of air pollution, wastewater, oil spills, and hazardous waste disposal. Under the U.S. Clean Air Act, costs of environmental damage can be extremely high. Exxon paid $125 million in fines and restitution on top of $1 billion in civil payments for the Exxon Valdez oil spill, which harmed the Alaskan coast. An environmental management standard, ISO 14000, encourages organizations to pursue environmental goals vigorously by developing (1) environmental management systems to reduce environmental costs and (2) environmental auditing and performance-evaluation systems to review and provide feedback on environmental goals.

We focus on two basic aspects of quality: design quality and conformance quality. **Design quality** refers to how closely the characteristics of a product or service meet the needs and wants of customers. Suppose customers of photocopying machines want copiers that combine copying, faxing, scanning, and electronic printing. Photocopying machines that fail to meet these customer needs fail in the quality of their designs. If customers of a bank want online banking services, then not providing these services would be a design-quality failure.

Conformance quality refers to the performance of a product or service relative to its design and product specifications. For example, if a photocopying machine mishandles paper or breaks down, it fails to satisfy conformance quality. A bank that deposits a customer's check into the wrong account fails on conformance quality.

Even if a product meets manufacturing specifications (good conformance quality), it can still be of poor overall quality if it fails to satisfy customer needs and wants (poor design quality).

To ensure that performance will achieve customer satisfaction, companies must first design products to satisfy customers through design quality. They must then meet design specifications through conformance quality. The following diagram illustrates that actual performance can fall short of customer satisfaction because of quality-of-design failure and because of conformance-quality failure.

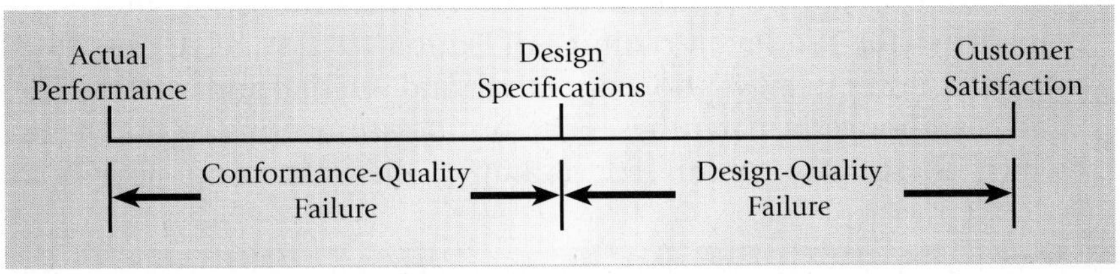

We illustrate the issues in managing quality—computing the costs of quality, identifying quality problems, and taking actions to improve quality—using Photon Corporation. Photon makes many products; however, we'll focus on Photon's photocopying machines, which earned an operating income of $24 million on revenues of $300 million (from sales of 20,000 copiers) in 2006.

Recall from Chapter 13, Exhibit 13-1 (p. 460), the four perspectives of the balanced scorecard: financial, customer, internal business process, and learning and growth. We now present the financial measures of quality and, in particular, the costs of conformance quality. The (financial) costs of poor design quality are mainly the opportunity costs of future sales lost if Photon does not design a product that customers want. These opportunity costs are difficult to measure objectively. Photon measures design quality only in its customer perspective.

The Financial Perspective: Costs of Quality

1

Explain the four cost categories in a costs-of-quality program

. . . prevention, appraisal, internal failure, and external failure costs

The financial perspective of Photon's balanced scorecard includes measures such as revenue growth and operating income—financial measures that are likely to be affected by quality improvement programs. In addition, Photon measures costs of quality. **Costs of quality (COQ)** refer to the costs incurred to prevent, or the costs arising as a result of, the production of a low-quality product. Costs of quality are classified into four categories; examples for each category are listed in Exhibit 19-1.

1. **Prevention costs**—costs incurred to preclude the production of products that do not conform to specifications.
2. **Appraisal costs**—costs incurred to detect which of the individual units of products do not conform to specifications.

EXHIBIT 19-1

Items Pertaining to Costs-of-Quality Reports

Prevention Costs	Appraisal Costs	Internal Failure Costs	External Failure Costs
Design engineering	Inspection	Spoilage	Customer support
Process engineering	Online product manufacturing and process inspection	Rework	Manufacturing/process engineering for external failures
Supplier evaluations	Product testing	Scrap	Warranty repair costs
Preventive equipment maintenance		Machine repairs	Liability claims
Quality training		Manufacturing/process engineering on internal failures	
Testing of new materials			

3. **Internal failure costs**—costs incurred on defective products before they are shipped to customers.
4. **External failure costs**—costs incurred on defective products after they are shipped to customers.

The items in Exhibit 19-1 come from all business functions of the value chain, and they are broader than the internal failure costs of spoilage, rework, and scrap described in Chapter 18.

An important role of management accounting is to prepare costs-of-quality (COQ) reports for managers (see Exhibit 19-2).

Photon determines the costs of quality of its photocopying machines by adapting the seven-step activity-based costing approach described in Chapter 5.

Step 1: Identify the Chosen Product. The product is the 20,000 photocopying machines that Photon made and sold in 2006. Photon's goal is to calculate the total costs of quality of these machines.

Step 2: Identify the Product's Direct Costs of Quality. The photocopying machines have no direct costs of quality.

In the Photon example, all the costs of quality are indirect costs of the photocopying machines.

Step 3: Select the Cost-Allocation Bases to Use for Allocating Indirect Costs of Quality to the Product. Column 1 of Exhibit 19-2, Panel A, classifies the activities that result in prevention, appraisal, and internal and external failure costs, and it indicates in parentheses the business functions of the value chain in which these costs occur. For example, the inspection activity results in

EXHIBIT 19-2 **Analysis of Activity-Based Costs of Quality (COQ) for Photocopying Machines at Photon Corporation**

	A	B	C	D	E	F	G
1	**PANEL A: COQ REPORT**						**Percentage of**
2		**Cost Allocation**		**Quantity of Cost**		**Total**	**Revenues**
3	**Cost of Quality and Value-Chain Category**	**Rate**[a]		**Allocation Base**		**Costs**	**(5) = (4) ÷**
4	**(1)**	**(2)**		**(3)**		**(4) = (2) x (3)**	**$300,000,000**
5	*Prevention costs*						
6	Design engineering (R&D/Design)	$ 80	per hour	40,000	hours	$ 3,200,000	1.1%
7	Process engineering (R&D/Design)	$ 60	per hour	45,000	hours	2,700,000	0.9%
8	Total prevention costs					5,900,000	2.0%
9	*Appraisal costs*						
10	Inspection (Manufacturing)	$ 40	per hour	240,000	hours	9,600,000	3.2%
11	Total appraisal costs					9,600,000	3.2%
12	*Internal failure costs*						
13	Rework (Manufacturing)	$100	per hour	100,000	hours	10,000,000	3.3%
14	Total internal failure costs					10,000,000	3.3%
15	*External failure costs*						
16	Customer support (Marketing)	$ 50	per hour	12,000	hours	600,000	0.2%
17	Transportation (Distribution)	$240	per load	3,000	loads	720,000	0.2%
18	Warranty repair (Customer service)	$110	per hour	120,000	hours	13,200,000	4.4%
19	Total external failure costs					14,520,000	4.8%
20	Total costs of quality					$40,020,000	13.3%
21							
22	[a]Amounts assumed.						
23							
24	**PANEL B: OPPORTUNITY COST ANALYSIS**						
25						**Total Estimated**	**Percentage**
26						**Contribution**	**of Revenues**
27	**Cost of Quality Category**					**Margin Lost**	**(3) = (2) ÷**
28	**(1)**					**(2)**	**$300,000,000**
29	*External failure costs*						
30	Estimated forgone contribution margin						
31	and income on lost sales					$12,000,000[b]	4.0%
32	Total external failure costs					$12,000,000	4.0%
33							
34	[b]Calculated as total revenues minus all variable costs (whether output-unit, batch, product-sustaining, or facility-sustaining) on						
35	lost sales in 2006. If poor quality causes Photon to lose sales in subsequent years as well, the opportunity costs will be						
36	even greater.						

appraisal costs and occurs in the manufacturing function. Photon identifies the number of inspection-hours as the cost-allocation base for the inspection activity. (To avoid details not needed to explain the concepts here, we do not provide information on the total quantities of each cost-allocation base.)

Step 4: **Identify the Indirect Costs of Quality Associated with Each Cost-Allocation Base.** These are the total costs (variable and fixed) incurred for each of the costs-of-quality activities, such as inspections, in all of Photon's operations. (To avoid details not needed to understand the points described here, we do not provide information about these total costs.)

Step 5: **Compute the Rate per Unit of Each Cost-Allocation Base Used to Allocate Indirect Costs of Quality to the Product.** For each activity, total costs (identified in step 4) are divided by total quantity of the cost-allocation base (calculated in step 3) to compute rate per unit of each cost-allocation base. Column 2 of Exhibit 19-2, Panel A, shows these rates (without supporting calculations).

Step 6: **Compute the Indirect Costs of Quality Allocated to the Product.** Photon first determines the quantity of each cost-allocation base used by the photocopying machines (column 3 of Panel A). For example, photocopying machines use 240,000 inspection-hours. The indirect costs of quality of the photocopying machines, shown in column 4, Panel A, equal the total quantity of the cost-allocation base used by the photocopying machines for each activity (column 3) multiplied by the cost-allocation rate from step 5 (column 2). For example, quality-related inspection costs for the photocopying machines are $9,600,000 ($40 per hour × 240,000 inspection-hours).

Step 7: **Compute the Total Costs of Quality by Adding All Direct and Indirect Costs of Quality Assigned to the Product.** Photon's total cost of quality in the COQ report for photocopying machines is $40.02 million (bottom of column 4, Panel A), or 13.3% of current revenues (bottom of column 5).

The total costs of quality typically shown in COQ reports exclude costs-of-quality items such as the opportunity cost of the contribution margin and income forgone from lost sales, lost production, and lower prices that result from poor quality. Why are opportunity costs usually excluded? Because they are not recorded in financial accounting systems and are difficult to estimate. Photon's Market Research Department estimates lost sales of 2,000 photocopying machines in 2006 because of external failures. The forgone contribution margin and operating income of $12 million (Exhibit 19-2, Panel B) measures the financial costs of estimated sales lost because of quality problems. Total costs of quality, including opportunity costs, equal $52.02 million ($40.02 million in Panel A + $12 million in Panel B), or 17.3% of current revenues. Opportunity costs account for 23% ($12 million ÷ $52.02 million) of Photon's total costs of quality.

The COQ report and the opportunity-cost analysis highlight Photon's high internal and external failure costs. But even before the opportunity cost of lost sales appears in the financial perspective of its balanced scorecard, Photon uses nonfinancial measures to determine how its customers are reacting to the quality of its photocopiers. Without completing both analyses (financial and nonfinancial), Photon would limit the potential to reduce its high internal and external failure costs.

Spoilage and rework discussed in Chapter 18 considered only some elements of internal failure costs.

The Customer Perspective: Nonfinancial Measures of Customer Satisfaction

2

Provide examples of nonfinancial quality measures of customer satisfaction in the balanced scorecard

. . . market share, number of customer complaints, on-time delivery rate

Nonfinancial measures of customer satisfaction relating to quality in a balanced scorecard include measures of both design quality and conformance quality. Management accountants are usually responsible for maintaining and presenting these nonfinancial measures.

Similar to Unilever, Federal Express, and TiVo, Photon measures customer satisfaction over time. Some measures are:

- Market research information on customer preferences for and customer satisfaction with specific product features (to measure design quality)
- Market share
- Percentage of customers that give high ratings for customer satisfaction

- Number of defective units shipped to customers as a percentage of total units shipped
- Number of customer complaints (Companies estimate that for every customer who actually complains, there are 10 to 20 others who have had bad experiences with the product or service but did not complain.)
- Percentage of products that fail soon after delivery
- Delivery delays (difference between the scheduled delivery date and the date requested by the customer)
- On-time delivery rate (percentage of shipments made on or before the scheduled delivery date)

Photon's management monitors whether these numbers improve or deteriorate over time. If improvement occurs, management can be more confident about operating income being strong in future years. For example, improvements in design quality should lead to future revenue growth; reducing defects and improving conformance quality should decrease costs of quality. If, however, customer-satisfaction numbers deteriorate, costs of quality will be higher in the future.

In addition to these nonfinancial measures, many companies such as Procter & Gamble and Porsche use surveys to gain a deeper perspective into customer experiences and preferences about products. Surveys also provide a glimpse of features that customers may like to see in future products. To satisfy its customers and to achieve better financial performance, Photon must improve its internal business processes.

The Internal-Business-Process Perspective: Analyzing Quality Problems and Improving Quality

3

Use three methods to identify quality problems

. . . control charts, Pareto diagrams, and cause-and-effect diagrams

To enhance the quality of work done inside the company, Photon's managers analyze and identify quality problems with the goal of reducing failures. Three techniques we consider for identifying and analyzing quality problems are control charts, Pareto diagrams, and cause-and-effect diagrams.

Control Charts

Statistical quality control (SQC), which is also called statistical process control (SPC), is a formal means of distinguishing between random and nonrandom variations in an operating process. Random variations occur, for example, when power surges or chance fluctuations in temperature cause defective products to be produced in a chemical process. Nonrandom variations occur when defective products are produced as a result of a systematic problem such as inaccurate temperature readings. A **control chart**, one of the tools in SQC, is a graph of a series of successive observations of a particular step, procedure, or operation taken at regular intervals of time. Each observation is plotted relative to specified ranges that represent the limits within which observations are expected to fall. Only those observations outside the control limits are ordinarily regarded as nonrandom and worth investigating.

The arithmetic mean is the sum of the observations divided by the number of observations. The standard deviation measures how much the observations differ from the mean. If the observations are clustered around the mean, the standard deviation is small. If the observations are widely dispersed around the mean, the standard deviation is large.

If you have taken a statistics course, you understand the meaning of the 2-sigma rule in control charts. If the defect rates are normally distributed and the production process is "in control," then a defect rate of more than 2 sigma from the mean is due to random variations only about 5% of the time.

Exhibit 19-3 presents control charts for the daily defect rates observed at Photon's three photocopying-machine production lines. Defect rates in the prior 60 days for each production line were assumed to provide a good basis from which to calculate the distribution of daily defect rates. The arithmetic mean (μ, read mu) and standard deviation (σ, read sigma) are the two parameters of the distribution that are used in the control charts in Exhibit 19-3. On the basis of experience, the company decides that any observation outside the $\mu \pm 2\sigma$ range should be investigated.

For production line A, all observations are within the range of $\mu \pm 2\sigma$, so management believes no investigation is necessary. For production line B, the last two observations signal that an out-of-control occurrence is highly likely. Given the $\pm 2\sigma$ rule, both observations would be investigated. Production line C illustrates a process that would not prompt an investigation under the $\pm 2\sigma$ rule but that may well be out of control. That's because the last eight observations show a clear direction, and the last six are getting further and further away from the mean. Statistical procedures have been developed using the trend as well as the variation to evaluate whether a process is out of control.

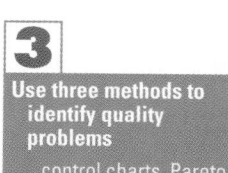

EXHIBIT 19-3 **Statistical Quality Control Charts: Daily Defect Rate for Photocopying Machines at Photon Corporation**

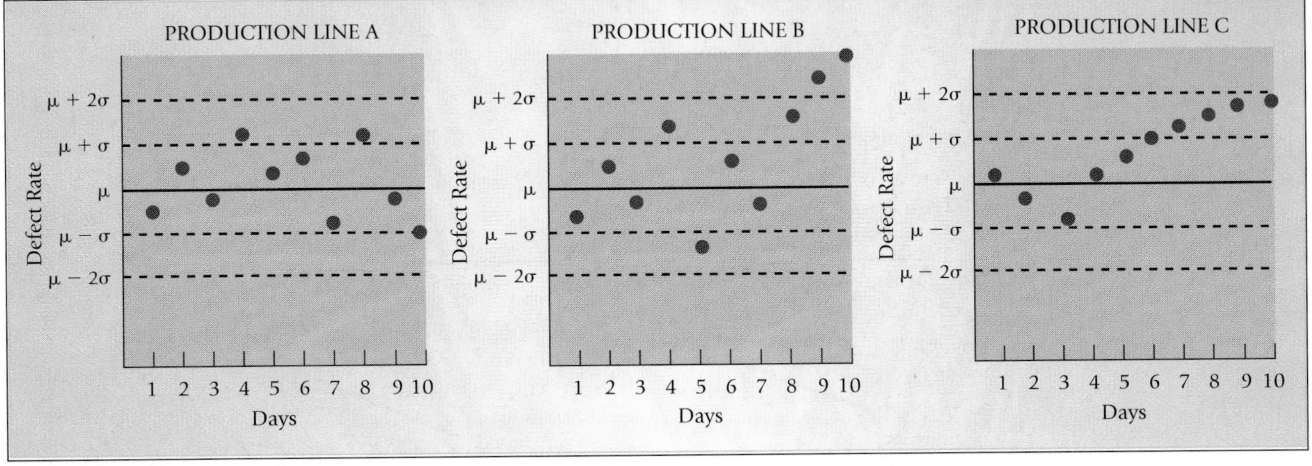

Pareto Diagrams

Observations outside control limits serve as inputs for Pareto diagrams. A **Pareto diagram** is a chart that indicates how frequently each type of defect occurs, ordered from the most frequent to the least frequent. Exhibit 19-4 presents a Pareto diagram of quality problems with respect to Photon's photocopying machines. Fuzzy and unclear copies are the most frequently recurring problem. Fuzzy and unclear copies result in high rework costs. Sometimes fuzzy and unclear copies occur at customer sites and result in high warranty and repair costs.

Cause-and-Effect Diagrams

The most frequently recurring and costly problems identified by the Pareto diagram are analyzed using cause-and-effect diagrams. A **cause-and-effect diagram** identifies potential causes of defects. Exhibit 19-5 presents the cause-and-effect diagram describing potential reasons why fuzzy and unclear copies occur. The exhibit identifies four categories of potential causes of failure: human factors, methods and design factors, machine-related factors, and materials and components factors. As additional arrows are added providing more-detailed reasons for each cause of defect, this diagram begins to resemble the bone structure of a fish (hence, cause-and-effect diagrams are also called *fishbone diagrams*).[1]

Combinations of methods can help identify quality problems. For example, Photon's managers first used the Pareto diagram to identify the most frequently encountered defect (fuzzy and unclear copies), and then they used the cause-and-effect diagram to identify specific causes of the defect.

EXHIBIT 19-4 **Pareto Diagram for Photocopying Machines at Photon Corporation**

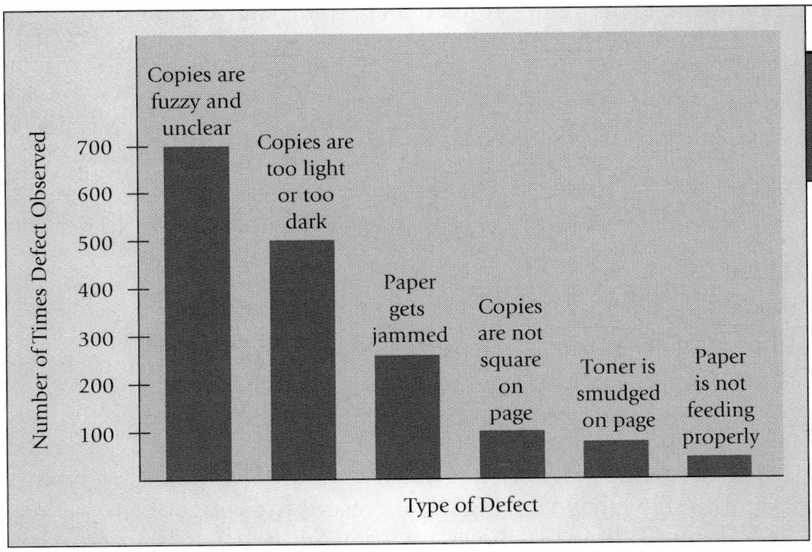

[1]See P. Clark, "Getting the Most from Cause-and-Effect Diagrams," *Quality Progress* (June 2000).

EXHIBIT 19-5 Cause-and-Effect Diagram for Fuzzy and Unclear Photocopies at Photon Corporation

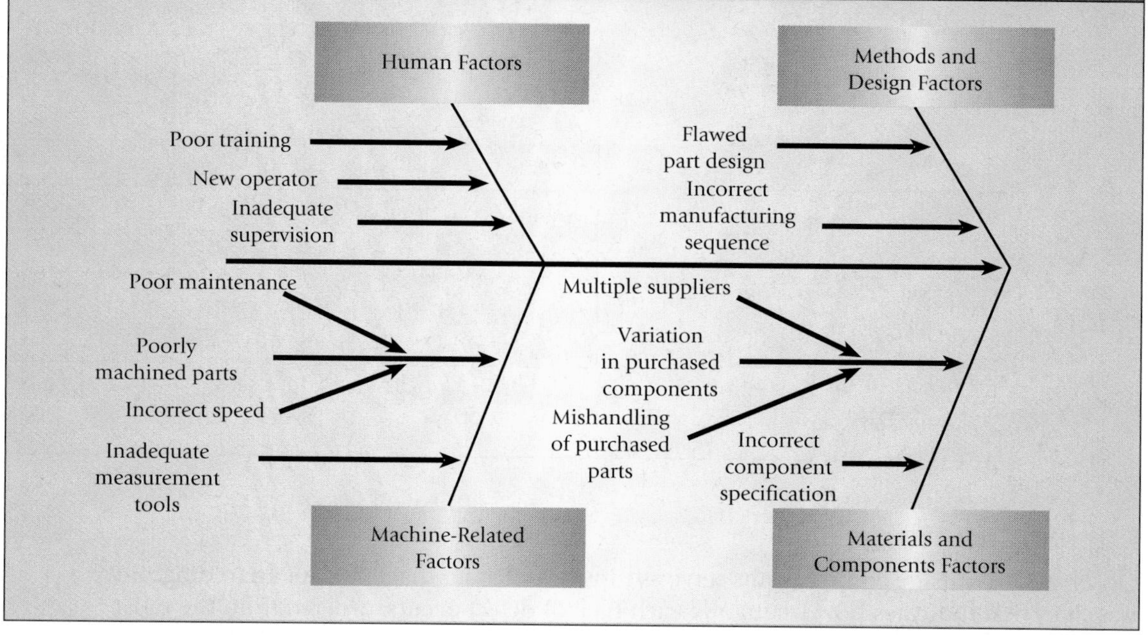

The analysis of quality problems is aided by automated equipment and computers that record the number and types of defects and the operating conditions that existed at the time the defects occurred. Using these inputs, computer programs simultaneously prepare control charts, Pareto diagrams, and cause-and-effect diagrams.

4

Identify relevant costs
. . . incremental costs
and benefits of quality improvement programs
. . . cost savings and increase in contribution margin

Relevant Costs and Benefits of Evaluating Quality Improvement

Analysis of Photon's cause-and-effect diagram reveals that the steel frame (or chassis) of the copier is often mishandled as it travels from a supplier's warehouse to Photon's plant. The frame must be produced to within very precise specifications or else copier components (such as drums, mirrors, and lenses) will not fit exactly on the frame. Mishandling during transport causes the frame to vary from manufacturing specifications, which results in the copier producing fuzzy and unclear copies.

The team of engineers working to solve this problem offers two solutions: (1) further inspect the frames immediately upon delivery or (2) redesign and strengthen the frames and the containers used to transport them to better withstand mishandling during transportation.

To evaluate each alternative versus the status quo, management identifies the relevant costs and benefits for each solution. The key question is *how total costs and total revenues will change under each alternative solution*. Remember, relevant-cost and relevant-revenue analysis ignores allocated amounts, as explained in Chapter 11.

Photon considers only a one-year time horizon over which to analyze each solution because it plans to introduce a completely new line of copiers at the end of the year. The new line will be so different that the choice of either the inspection or the redesign alternative will have no effect on the sales of copiers in future years.

Exhibit 19-6 shows the relevant costs and benefits for each alternative.

1. **Estimated incremental costs:** $400,000 for the inspection alternative; $460,000 for the redesign alternative.

2. **Cost savings from less rework, customer support, and repairs.** Exhibit 19-6, lines 9 and 10 show that reducing rework results in savings of $40 per hour. Exhibit 19-2, Panel A, column 2, line 13, shows total rework cost per hour of $100. Why the difference? Because Photon concludes that as it improves quality, it will only save the $40 variable cost per rework-hour, not the $60 fixed cost per rework-hour.

The largest single line item in Exhibit 19-6 is contribution margin from additional sales generated by improved quality.

EXHIBIT 19-6 **Estimated Effect of Quality-Improvement Actions on Costs of Quality for Photocopying Machines at Photon Corporation**

	A	B	C	D
1		Relevant Costs and Benefits of		
2		Further Inspecting		Redesigning
3	Relevant Items	Incoming Frames		Frames
4	(1)	(2)		(3)
5	Additional inspection and testing costs	$(400,000)		-
6	Additional process engineering costs	-		$(300,000)
7	Additional design engineering costs	-		(160,000)
8	Savings in rework costs			
9	($40 per hour x 24,000 fewer rework hours)	960,000		
10	($40 per hour x 32,000 fewer rework hours)			1,280,000
11	Savings in customer-support costs			
12	($20 per hour x 2,000 fewer customer-support hours)	40,000		
13	($20 per hour x 2,800 fewer customer support hours)			56,000
14	Savings in transportation costs for repair parts			
15	($180 per load x 500 fewer loads moved)	90,000		
16	($180 per hour x 700 fewer loads moved)			126,000
17	Savings in warranty repair costs			
18	($45 per hour x 20,000 fewer repair-hours)	900,000		
19	($45 per hour x 28,000 fewer repair-hours)			1,260,000
20	Total contribution margin from additional sales			
21	(250 additional copiers x $6,000 per copier)	1,500,000		
22	(300 additional copiers x $6,000 per copier)			1,800,000
23	Net cost savings and additional contribution margin	$3,090,000		$4,062,000
24	Difference in favor of redesigning frame	↑	$972,000	↑

Exhibit 19-6, line 9, shows the inspection alternative is expected to eliminate 24,000 rework-hours and therefore save variable costs of $960,000 ($40 per hour × 24,000 rework-hours). The redesign alternative (Exhibit 19-6, line 10) is expected to eliminate 32,000 rework-hours and therefore save variable costs of $1,280,000 ($40 per rework-hour × 32,000 rework-hours). Exhibit 19-6 also shows expected variable-cost savings in customer support, transportation, and warranty repair for the two alternatives.

3. Increased contribution margin from higher sales as a result of building a reputation for quality and performance (Exhibit 19-6, lines 21 and 22): $1,500,000 for 250 copiers under the inspection alternative and $1,800,000 for 300 copiers under the redesign alternative. This benefit is important because quality improvements cannot always be translated into lower costs. For example, laying off workers (as a result of quality improvements) to reduce costs can adversely affect the morale of employees and limit future quality initiatives. Management should always look for opportunities to generate higher revenues from quality improvements. (The Focus on Values and Behaviors feature on p. 668 illustrates how quality problems can lead to revenues losses.)

Exhibit 19-6 shows that both the inspection and the redesign alternatives yield net benefits relative to the status quo. However, the net benefits from the redesign alternative are expected to be $972,000 greater.

Note how making improvements in internal business processes affects the COQ numbers reported in the financial perspective of the balanced scorecard. In our example, redesigning the frame increases prevention costs (design and process engineering), decreases internal failure costs (rework), and decreases external failure costs (warranty repairs). COQ reports provide more insight about quality improvements when managers compare trends over time. In successful quality programs, companies decrease costs of quality as a percentage of revenues and the sum of internal and external failure costs as a percentage of total costs of quality. Many companies, such as Hewlett-Packard, believe they should eliminate all failure costs and have zero defects.

We now describe the nonfinancial quality-related measures Photon uses for the internal-business-process perspective in its balanced scorecard.

FOCUS ON VALUES AND BEHAVIORS

THE COST OF QUALITY FAILURE AT FIRESTONE

Company and division managers undoubtedly feel pressure to meet quarterly and annual financial performance targets, but these measures should never be pursued without regard to product or service quality. Although quality-control and assurance activities carry significant costs, quality failures are even more costly. As Bridgestone/Firestone, Inc., makers of Firestone tires, learned during a widely publicized recall of 6.5 million tires in 2000, the financial, public-relations, and legal effects of quality failure can be disastrous.

In August 2000, Firestone announced a national recall of its Radial ATX, ATXII, and Wilderness AT tires. Prior to announcing the recall, Firestone had received more than 1,500 claims for property damage, injuries, and even deaths related to tread separation in those tires. Ford Motor Company—Firestone's largest U.S. customer—conducted an analysis that indicated that tires from Firestone's Decatur, Illinois, plant exhibited tendencies to come apart at high speeds, which caused vehicles, especially Ford's popular Explorer sports utility vehicle, to roll over. Although both companies displayed public remorse and began working together in handling the recall, Firestone responded to Ford's study by stating:

> *We are confident in the quality of our tires and in the effectiveness of our inspection processes at the Decatur, Illinois, plant and at all of our plants. . . . Like all Bridgestone/Firestone production facilities, the Decatur plant adheres to stringent standards of quality control where every tire is subject to strict inspection by both people and machines at every step of the manufacturing process, from raw material through finished tire. And, every production employee, at each of our plants, receives substantial training before they work on the line. . . . The plant also has received quality awards from our customers, including Ford, General Motors, and Nissan.*

In the subsequent weeks, however, the increasing scrutiny of quality practices at Firestone told a different story. In late 1999, after tread separation among light-truck tires rose 18.6% during the previous year, Firestone engineers identified tread separation as a "critical performance issue" at their October 2000 quarterly quality meeting. Another study found that the number of warranty claims for ATX and ATXII tires made at the Decatur facility between 1994 and 1996 were three to six times higher than claims for tires made at all other domestic Firestone plants. And, although overall quality improved after 1996, claim rates remained significantly higher for the Decatur plant than those at all other facilities. These findings—coupled with news that tread separation caused Ford to replace the same, or similar, tires on nearly 50,000 of its vehicles in 16 South American and Asian countries starting in 1999—led most observers to conclude that the rollovers were being caused by Firestone tire defects.

Numerous factors contributed to the quality defects and subsequent lack of action by Firestone, but alert management accountants and financial managers could have called attention to the problem years earlier. A failure to share information among functional units left executives in the dark about how quality defects were harming the company. A Harvard Business School case notes:

> *Although the rising cost of claims and lawsuits regarding the Firestone ATX tire was apparently discussed at some quarterly financial meetings beginning in 1997, the matter did not go beyond the finance area which maintained information on claims costs. As [Vice President Gary] Crigger explained: "Claims and lawsuits are not considered to be representative throughout a line. They are considered to be individual cases that occur for a variety of reasons. So they have never been part of [tire] performance evaluation."*

This narrow view, a culture in which individuals did not speak up, and inaction cost Firestone dearly. As the recall proceeded, Firestone received thousands of unfavorable news stories, more than 200 lawsuits from angry customers, and high-profile congressional inquiries. On May 22, 2001, Ford announced the further recall of another 13 million tires. Ultimately, Ford ended its relationship with Firestone. Firestone suffered 40% revenue declines in key segments and a $510 million loss in 2000. It also paid out over $1 billion in recall-related costs (including new tires, claim settlements, and lawsuits), lost $10 billion in stock market capitalization, and dismissed most Bridgestone/Firestone corporate executives in the United States and Japan.

Sources: *L. S. Payne, "Recall 2000: Bridgestone Corp. (A)," HBS Case No. 9-302-013 (Boston: Harvard Business School Publishing, 2003); S. Govindaraj and B. Jaggi, "Market Overreaction to Product Recall Revisited—The Case of Firestone Tires and the Ford Explorer,"* Review of Quantitative Finance and Accounting *(July 2004); D. Welch, "Firestone: Is This Brand Beyond Repair?"* Business Week, *June 11, 2001; "Firestone Decatur Tire Plant Inspection—Defective Tires," Bridgestone America Holdings press release (Nashville, TN: August 13, 2001).*

Nonfinancial Measures of Internal-Business-Process Quality

Photon measures internal-business-process quality using the following nonfinancial measures:

- Percentage of defective products
- Average time taken to repair photocopying machines at customer sites
- Percentage of reworked products

- Number of different types of defects analyzed using control charts, Pareto diagrams, and cause-and-effect diagrams
- Number of design and process changes made

Photon's managers believe that improving these measures will lead to greater customer satisfaction, lower costs of quality, and better financial performance.

The Learning-and-Growth Perspective for Quality Improvements

What are the drivers of internal-business-process quality? Photon measures the following factors in the learning-and-growth perspective in the balanced scorecard:

- Employee turnover (ratio of number of employees who leave the company to the average total number of employees).
- Employee empowerment (ratio of the number of processes in which employees have the right to make decisions without consulting supervisors to the total number of processes).
- Employee satisfaction (ratio of employees indicating high satisfaction ratings to the total number of employees surveyed).
- Employee training (percentage of employees trained in different quality-enhancing methods).

These quality-related balanced scorecard measures are particularly informative when managers examine trends and relationships (across the learning and growth, the internal business process, and the customer and financial perspectives) over time as they seek to improve performance. To provide information on trends, management accountants must review the nonfinancial measures for accuracy and consistency.

Evaluating Quality Performance

5

Describe the benefits of financial measures of quality

. . . evaluate trade-offs among different categories of costs of quality

and nonfinancial measures of quality

. . . identify problem areas, highlight leading indicators of future performance

Financial (COQ) and nonfinancial measures of quality in the balanced scorecard have different advantages.

Advantages of COQ Measures

- Consistent with the attention-directing role of management accounting, COQ measures focus managers' attention on the costs of poor quality.
- Total COQ provides a measure of quality performance for evaluating trade-offs among prevention costs, appraisal costs, internal failure costs, and external failure costs.
- COQ measures assist in problem solving by comparing costs and benefits of different quality-improvement programs and setting priorities for cost reduction.

Advantages of Nonfinancial Measures of Quality

- Nonfinancial measures of quality are often easy to quantify and understand.
- Nonfinancial measures direct attention to physical processes and hence help managers identify the precise problem areas that need improvement.
- Nonfinancial measures, such as number of defects, provide immediate short-run feedback on whether quality-improvement efforts are succeeding.
- Nonfinancial measures such as measures of customer satisfaction and employee satisfaction are useful indicators of long-run future performance.

COQ measures and nonfinancial measures supplement each other. In its balanced scorecard, Photon evaluates whether improvements in various nonfinancial quality measures eventually lead to improvements in financial measures. Most organizations use both types of measures to gauge quality performance. Some corporations, such as McDonald's, evaluate employees and individual franchisees on multiple measures of quality and customer satisfaction. A mystery shopper—an outside party contracted by McDonald's to evaluate restaurant performance—scores individual restaurants on quality, cleanliness,

Study Tip: To check your understanding of quality as a competitive tool, see the Featured Exercise, true–false statement 5, and multiple-choice question 4 (*Student Guide*, beginning p. 261). Fully explained answers begin on page 265.

service, and value. A restaurant's performance on these dimensions is evaluated over time and against other restaurants.

PART TWO: TIME AS A COMPETITIVE TOOL

Companies increasingly view time as a driver of strategy.[2] Conducting business correctly and quickly helps increase revenues and decrease costs. A moving company such as United Van Lines will be able to generate more revenues if it can move items in good condition from one place to another faster and on time. Companies such as AT&T, General Electric, and Wal-Mart attribute not only higher revenues but also lower costs to doing things faster and on time. They cite, for example, the need to carry less inventory because of their ability to respond rapidly to customer demands.

Companies need to measure time to manage it properly. In this section, we focus on *operational measures of time,* which reveal how quickly companies respond to customers' demands for their products and services and their reliability in meeting scheduled delivery dates. Two common operational measures of time are customer-response time and on-time performance. We will also show how companies can measure the causes and costs of delays.

6

Describe customer-response time

. . . time between receipt of customer order and product delivery

and explain why delays happen and their costs

. . . uncertainty about the timing of customer orders and limited capacity lead to lower revenues and higher inventory carrying costs

Customer-response time is particularly important in mail-order catalog companies. These companies often learn that their customers are willing to pay a higher price for faster delivery. Therefore, to compete more effectively with stores (as well as with other mail-order companies), mail-order companies promise delivery of their products in a week or less. For example, second-day express delivery is standard for companies such as Neiman Marcus.

Customer-Response Time and On-Time Performance

Customer-response time is how long it takes from the time a customer places an order for a product or service to the time the product or service is delivered to the customer. Fast responses to customers are of strategic importance in industries such as construction, banking, car rental, and fast food. Some companies, such as Boeing, have to pay penalties to compensate their customers for lost revenues and profits (such as from being unable to operate flights) as a result of delays in delivering products to them.

Exhibit 19-7 describes the components of customer-response time. In the case of Boeing, *receipt time* is how long it takes the Marketing Department to specify to the Manufacturing Department the exact requirements in the customer's order. **Manufacturing lead time** (also called **manufacturing cycle time**) is how long it takes from the time an order is received by Manufacturing to the time a finished good is produced. Manufacturing lead time is the sum of waiting time and manufacturing time for an order. An aircraft order received by Boeing may need to wait because the required equipment is busy processing earlier orders. *Delivery time* is how long it takes to deliver a completed order to a customer.

Several companies have adopted manufacturing lead time as the base for allocating manufacturing overhead costs to products. They believe that using manufacturing lead time as a cost-allocation base motivates managers to reduce the time it takes to manufacture products. Over time, total overhead costs decrease and operating income rises.

On-time performance refers to delivering a product or service by the time it is scheduled to be delivered. Consider Federal Express, which specifies a price per package and a next-day delivery time of 10:30 A.M. for its overnight courier service. Federal Express mea-

EXHIBIT 19-7

Components of Customer-Response Time

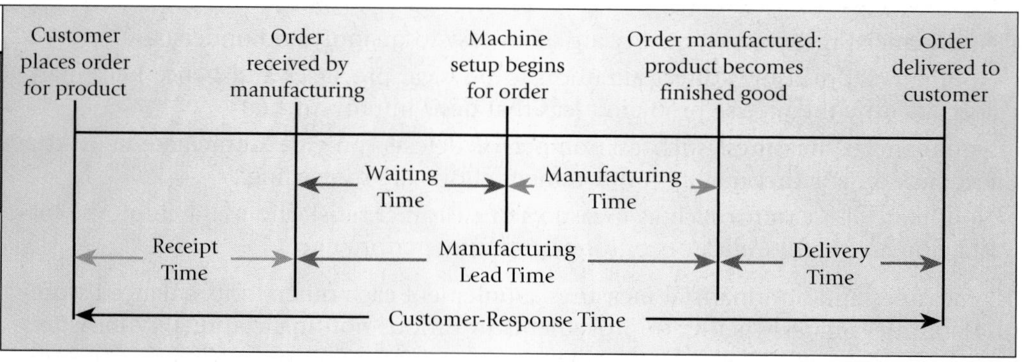

[2]See G. Stalk and T. Hout, *Competing Against Time* (New York: Free Press, 1990); K. Eisenhardt and S. Brown, "Time Pacing: Competing in Strategic Markets That Won't Stand Still," *Harvard Business Review* (March-April 1998); and T. Willis and A. Jurkus, "Product Development: An Essential Ingredient of Time-Based Competition," *Review of Business* (2001).

sures on-time performance by how often it meets its stated delivery time of 10:30 A.M. On-time performance increases customer satisfaction. Commercial airlines gain loyal passengers as a result of consistent on-time service. But there is a trade-off between customer-response time and on-time performance. Deliberately scheduling longer customer-response times, such as airlines lengthening scheduled arrival times, makes achieving on-time performance easier—but it could displease customers!

Time Drivers and Costs of Time

Managing customer-response time and on-time performance requires understanding the causes and costs of delays. Delays can occur, for example, at a machine in a manufacturing plant or at a checkout counter in a store.

Uncertainty and Bottlenecks as Drivers of Time

A **time driver** is any factor that causes a change in the speed of an activity when the factor changes. Two time drivers we consider are:

1. **Uncertainty about when customers will order products or services.** For example, the more randomly Boeing receives orders for its airplanes, the more likely queues will form and delays will occur.
2. **Bottlenecks due to limited capacity.** A **bottleneck** occurs in an operation when the work to be performed approaches or exceeds the capacity available to do it. For example, a bottleneck results and causes delays when products that must be processed at a particular machine arrive while the machine is being used to process other products. Bottlenecks also occur when many people try to view a company's Web site at the same time (see Concepts in Action, p. 672).

Consider Falcon Works (FW), which uses one turning machine to convert steel bars into a special gear for pumps. FW makes this gear, which is its only product, only after customers have ordered it. To focus on manufacturing lead time, we assume FW's receipt time and delivery time are minimal.

FW expects to receive 30 orders for gears, but it could receive 10, 30, or 50 orders. Each order is for 1,000 units and will take 100 hours of manufacturing time (8 hours of setup time to clean and prepare the machine, and 92 hours of processing time). Annual capacity of the machine is 4,000 hours. If FW receives the 30 orders it expects, the total amount of manufacturing time required on the machine will be 3,000 hours (100 hours per order × 30 orders), which is within the available machine capacity of 4,000 hours. Even though expected capacity utilization is not strained, queues and delays can still occur. That's because uncertainty about when FW's customers will place their orders can cause an order to be received while the machine is processing an earlier order.

In the single-product case, under certain assumptions about the pattern of customer orders and how orders will be processed, **average waiting time**, the average amount of time that an order will wait in line before the machine is set up and the order is processed, equals:[3]

$$\frac{\begin{matrix}\text{Annual average} \\ \text{number of} \\ \text{orders for gears}\end{matrix} \times \begin{pmatrix}\text{Manufacturing} \\ \text{time per order} \\ \text{for gears}\end{pmatrix}^2}{2 \times \left[\begin{matrix}\text{Annual machine} \\ \text{capacity}\end{matrix} - \begin{pmatrix}\text{Annual average number} \\ \text{of orders for gears}\end{pmatrix} \times \begin{matrix}\text{Manufacturing} \\ \text{time per order for gears}\end{matrix}\right]}$$

$$= \frac{30 \times (100)^2}{2 \times [4{,}000 - (30 \times 100)]} = \frac{30 \times 10{,}000}{2 \times (4{,}000 - 3{,}000)} = \frac{300{,}000}{2 \times 1{,}000} = \frac{300{,}000}{2{,}000} = 150 \text{ hours per order (for gears)}$$

[3]The technical assumptions are (a) that customer orders for the product follow a Poisson distribution with a mean equal to the expected number of orders (30 in our example), and (b) that orders are processed on a first-in, first-out (FIFO) basis. The Poisson arrival pattern for customer orders has been found to be reasonable in many real-world settings. The FIFO assumption can be modified. Under the modified assumptions, the basic queuing and delay effects will still occur, but the precise formulas will be different.

CONCEPTS IN ACTION

Overcoming Bottlenecks on the Internet

In 2004, Intel's chief technology officer, Patrick Gelsinger, warned that the World Wide Web was becoming so overloaded with traffic that it might eventually collapse. Could this be true? Although the Internet's digital backbone will not collapse tomorrow, exponential growth in Web usage in recent years already causes many users to suffer from online bottlenecks. These bottlenecks are caused when too many people try to view the same information on a computer server at the same time. They affect all users, but these bottlenecks are most harmful to companies buying and selling their products and services over the Internet.

As companies become increasingly reliant on e-commerce and time-sensitive information sharing, the inability of a company to handle all the traffic on its Web site can become a serious problem. Oracle recently noted that although e-commerce companies generally set a target of 99.99% Web site availability, that still means that a company loses substantial amounts annually because users are unable to conduct their transactions during the 0.01% of bottleneck-related downtime. One study found that more than 40% of online shoppers abandon a transaction if the site they are on is responding too slowly. The costs can be much larger. A 22-hour site outage cost eBay over $5 million in auction fees. A three-day outage forced ESPN to compensate some of its 260,000 online fantasy baseball players. And site outages caused shares of E-Trade to lose 22% of their market value in one week.

To relieve these bottlenecks and avoid their negative consequences, companies—such as Microsoft, Akamai, EMC, Hitachi, and others—have developed technologies that use remote caching and remote mirroring. Storing, or caching, seldom-updated content on remote servers is one way to reduce network traffic. The Motley Fool Web site, for example, stores its static content on Akamai's third-party global network, which consists of over 2,000 servers. When someone accesses the Motley Fool Web site, the caching system routes each individual request for content to servers that are geographically closer to the user, so the request travels a shorter distance along the Internet for faster page loading and transaction processing.

Remote mirroring allows a company to copy (or "mirror") huge databases in many different geographically remote locations. Using redundant arrays of inexpensive disks (RAID) technology, backup databases are copied via the Internet on computer-storage devices. Each extra copy not only serves as a backup in the event of system crashes, but it also relieves traffic congestion on the Internet. Exodus Communications, which manages the Web sites of many companies, uses remote mirroring technology to instantly reroute Web traffic around trouble spots to data sites that have much less traffic and faster response times.

Remote caching and remote mirroring allow companies to efficiently relieve bottleneck constraints, increase capacity, and improve customer-response time. As Internet traffic increases exponentially in the coming years with voice-over IP (VoIP) telephone service and hundreds of millions of new users from developing countries logging on for the first time, these technologies will be critical to ensuring the stability, operability, and profitability of many of the Internet's most popular sites.

Sources: Risk Management (May 2001); *The Wall Street Journal* (March 20, 2001); *Business Wire* (October 4, 1999); and a poll conducted by **www.esearch.com** in 1999; "'Beware of the End of the World (Wide Web),' Says Intel," *Fortune.com*, September 10, 2004, **http://www.forbes.com/execpicks/feeds/general/2004/09/10/generalcomtex_2004_09_10_ir_0000-5884-KEYWORD.Missing.html**, accessed September 13, 2004; "Downtime and Lost Revenue," *NetSource America*, **http://www.netsourceamerica.com/networth1.html**, accessed September 17, 2004; D. Shand, "Banish Bottlenecks," *Computer World*, April 10, 2000, **http://www.computerworld.com/news/2000/story/0,11280,44371,00.html**, accessed September 17, 2004; T. Wilson, "The Cost of Downtime," NMSalert.com, April 23, 2004, **http://cms.nmsalert.com/website-monitoring-articles/downtime-costs-website**, accessed September 17, 2004.

Therefore, the average manufacturing lead time for an order is 250 hours (150 hours of average waiting time + 100 hours of manufacturing time). Note that manufacturing time per order is a squared term in the numerator. It indicates the disproportionately large impact manufacturing time has on waiting time. The longer the manufacturing time, the much greater the chance that the machine will be in use when an order arrives, leading to longer delays. The denominator in this formula is a measure of the unused capacity, or cushion. The smaller the unused capacity, the greater the chance that the machine is processing an earlier order, and the greater the delays.

Our formula describes only the *average* waiting time. A particular order might arrive when the machine is free, in which case manufacturing will start immediately. In another situation, FW may receive an order while two other orders are waiting to be processed, which means the delay will be longer than 150 hours.

Now suppose FW is considering whether to introduce a second product, a piston for pumps. FW expects to receive 10 orders for pistons, each order for 800 units, in the coming year. Each order will take 50 hours of manufacturing time, comprising 3 hours for setup and 47 hours of processing. Expected demand for FW's gears will be unaffected by whether FW introduces piston products.

Average waiting time *before* machine setup begins is determined using the following formula, which is an extension of the preceding formula for the single-product case.

$$\frac{\left[\begin{array}{c}\text{Annual average number}\\ \text{of orders for gears}\end{array} \times \left(\begin{array}{c}\text{Manufacturing}\\ \text{time per order}\\ \text{for gears}\end{array}\right)^2\right] + \left[\begin{array}{c}\text{Annual average number}\\ \text{of orders for pistons}\end{array} \times \left(\begin{array}{c}\text{Manufacturing}\\ \text{time per order}\\ \text{for pistons}\end{array}\right)^2\right]}{2 \times \left[\begin{array}{c}\text{Annual machine}\\ \text{capacity}\end{array} - \left(\begin{array}{c}\text{Annual average number}\\ \text{of orders for gears}\end{array} \times \begin{array}{c}\text{Manufacturing}\\ \text{time per order}\\ \text{for gears}\end{array}\right) - \left(\begin{array}{c}\text{Annual average number}\\ \text{of orders for pistons}\end{array} \times \begin{array}{c}\text{Manufacturing}\\ \text{time per order}\\ \text{for pistons}\end{array}\right)\right]}$$

$$= \frac{[30 \times (100)^2] + [10 \times 50^2]}{2 \times [4{,}000 - (30 \times 100) - (10 \times 50)]} = \frac{(30 \times 10{,}000) + (10 \times 2{,}500)}{2 \times (4{,}000 - 3{,}000 - 500)}$$

$$= \frac{300{,}000 + 25{,}000}{2 \times 500} = \frac{325{,}000}{1{,}000} = 325 \text{ hours per order (for gears } \textit{and} \text{ pistons)}$$

Introducing pistons causes average waiting time for an order to more than double, from 150 hours to 325 hours. That's because introducing pistons causes unused capacity to shrink, increasing the probability that, at any point in time, new orders will arrive while current orders are being manufactured or waiting to be manufactured. Average waiting time is very sensitive to the shrinking of unused capacity.

Introducing pistons (1) cuts the unused capacity cushion in half (from 1,000 to 500 hours), doubling the average waiting time by halving the denominator; and (2) increases the demands on the process (the numerator) by 25,000 hours, which further increases average waiting time. The total effect of introducing pistons is to increase average waiting time by 117% [(325 − 150) ÷ 150].

With the addition of another product, average manufacturing lead time for a gear order now is 425 hours (325 hours of average waiting time + 100 hours of manufacturing time), and for a piston order 375 hours (325 hours of average waiting time + 50 hours of manufacturing time). Note that a piston order spends 86.7% (325 ÷ 375) of its manufacturing lead time just waiting for manufacturing to start!

Given the anticipated effects on manufacturing lead time of adding pistons, should FW introduce pistons? The management accountant likely would be asked to evaluate the profitability of a new product, given capacity constraints. FW's management accountant needs to identify and analyze the relevant revenues and relevant costs of adding the piston product and, in particular, to evaluate the cost effects of the resulting delays on all products.

Relevant Revenues and Costs of Time

To determine the relevant revenues and costs of adding pistons, consider the following additional information:

Product	Annual Average Number of Orders	Average Selling Price per Order If Average Manufacturing Lead Time per Order Is: Less Than 300 Hours	More Than 300 Hours	Direct Material Cost per Order	Inventory Carrying Cost per Order per Hour
Gears	30	$22,000	$21,500	$16,000	$1.00
Pistons	10	10,000	9,600	8,000	0.50

Manufacturing lead times affect both revenues and costs in our example. Revenues are affected because customers are willing to pay a higher price for faster delivery. On the cost side, direct material costs and inventory carrying costs are the only costs that will be affected by introducing pistons (all other costs are unaffected, and hence irrelevant). Inventory carrying costs consist of the opportunity costs of investment tied up in inventory (see Chapter 11, pp. 390–391) and the relevant costs of storage, such as space rental, spoilage, deterioration, and materials handling. Companies usually calculate inventory carrying costs on a per-unit, per-year basis. To simplify calculations, we express inventory carrying costs on a per-order, per-hour basis. As in most companies, we assume FW acquires direct materials at the time the order is received by manufacturing, and, therefore, incurs inventory carrying costs for the duration of the manufacturing lead time.

FW acquires direct materials when it receives an order, rather than waiting until just before manufacturing is scheduled to start because of uncertainty about (1) how long it will take to obtain materials from suppliers and (2) when manufacturing will start.

Exhibit 19-8 presents relevant revenues and relevant costs for the "introduce pistons" and "do not introduce pistons" alternatives. Interestingly, the decision is to not introduce pistons, even though pistons have a positive contribution margin of $1,600 ($9,600 – $8,000) per order. Also, FW has the capacity to process pistons (even if it produces pistons, FW will, on average, use only 3,500 of the available 4,000 machine-hours). So why is FW better off to not introduce pistons? *Because of the negative effects that producing pistons will have on the existing product, gears.* The following table presents the *costs of time*—that is, the expected loss in revenues and expected increase in carrying costs as a result of delays caused by using machine capacity to manufacture pistons.

	Effect of Increasing Average Manufacturing Lead Time		
Product	**Expected Loss in Revenues for Gears (1)**	**Expected Increase in Carrying Costs for All Products (2)**	**Expected Loss in Revenues Plus Expected Increase in Carrying Costs of Introducing Pistons (3) = (1) + (2)**
Gears	$15,000[a]	$5,250[b]	$20,250
Pistons	—	1,875[c]	1,875
Total	$15,000	$7,125	$22,125

[a]($22,000 – $21,500) per order × 30 expected orders = $15,000.

[b](425 – 250) hours per order × $1.00 per hour × 30 expected orders = $5,250.

[c](375 – 0) hours per order × $0.50 per hour × 10 expected orders = $1,875.

Introducing pistons causes the average manufacturing lead time of gears to increase from 250 hours to 425 hours. The cost of longer manufacturing lead times is an increase in inventory carrying costs of gears and a decrease in gear revenues (caused by average manufacturing lead time for gears exceeding 300 hours). The expected costs of longer lead times from introducing pistons, $22,125, exceeds the expected contribution margin of $16,000

EXHIBIT 19-8

Determining Expected Relevant Revenues and Relevant Costs for Falcon Works' Decision to Introduce Pistons

Relevant Items	Alternative 1: Introduce Pistons (1)	Alternative 2: Do Not Introduce Pistons (2)	Difference (3) = (1) – (2)
Expected revenues	741,000[a]	$660,000[b]	$ 81,000
Expected variable costs	560,000[c]	480,000[d]	(80,000)
Expected inventory carrying costs	14,625[e]	7,500[f]	(7,125)
Expected total costs	574,625	487,500	(87,125)
Expected revenues minus expected costs	$166,375	$172,500	$ (6,125)

[a]($21,500 × 30) + ($9,600 × 10) = $741,000; average manufacturing lead time will be more than 300 hours.

[b]($22,000 × 30) = $660,000; average manufacturing lead time will be less than 300 hours.

[c]($16,000 × 30) + ($8,000 × 10) = $560,000.

[d]$16,000 × 30 = $480,000.

[e](Average manufacturing lead time for gears × Unit carrying cost per order for gears × Expected number of orders for gears) + (Average manufacturing lead time for pistons × Unit carrying cost per order for pistons × Expected number of orders for pistons) = (425 × $1.00 × 30) + (375 × $0.50 × 10) = $12,750 + $1,875 = $14,625.

[f]Average manufacturing lead time for gears × Unit carrying cost per order for gears × Expected number of orders for gears = 250 × $1.00 × 30 = $7,500.

($1,600 per order × 10 expected orders) from selling pistons by $6,125 (the difference calculated in Exhibit 19-8).

Our simple setting illustrates that when demand uncertainty is high, some unused capacity is desirable.[4] Increasing the capacity of a bottleneck resource reduces manufacturing lead times and delays. One way to increase capacity is to reduce the time required for setups and processing via more-efficient setups and processing. Another way to increase capacity is to invest in new equipment, such as flexible manufacturing systems that can be programmed to switch quickly from producing one product to producing another. Delays can also be reduced through careful scheduling of orders on machines—for example, by batching similar jobs together for processing.

When there is considerable variability in the arrival of orders at the bottleneck operation, unused capacity acts as a cushion to absorb some of that variability, reducing average waiting time.

Study Tip: To check your understanding of time as a competitive tool, see multiple-choice question 5 (*Student Guide*, p. 263). The fully explained answer is on page 266.

PART THREE: THEORY OF CONSTRAINTS AND THROUGHPUT-CONTRIBUTION ANALYSIS

7

Apply the three measures in the theory of constraints

. . . throughput contribution, investments, and operating costs

In this section, we consider products that are made from multiple parts and processed on multiple machines. With multiple parts and machines, dependencies arise among operations—that is, some operations cannot be started until parts from the preceding operation are available. Furthermore, some operations are bottlenecks (have limited capacity), and others are not.

Managing Bottlenecks

You may have studied the theory of constraints in operations management or production courses.

The **theory of constraints (TOC)** describes methods to maximize operating income when faced with some bottleneck and some nonbottleneck operations.[5] The TOC defines three measures:

1. **Throughput contribution** equals revenues minus the direct material costs of the goods sold.
2. *Investments* equal the sum of materials costs in direct materials, work-in-process, and finished goods inventories; R&D costs; and costs of equipment and buildings.
3. *Operating costs* equal all costs of operations (other than direct materials) incurred to earn throughput contribution. Operating costs include salaries and wages, rent, utilities, depreciation, and the like.

The objective of TOC is to increase throughput contribution while decreasing investments and operating costs. *TOC considers a short-run time horizon and assumes that operating costs are fixed costs.* The steps in managing bottleneck operations are:

8

Explain how to manage bottlenecks

. . . keep bottlenecks busy and increase their efficiency and capacity

Step 1: Recognize that the bottleneck operation determines throughput contribution of the entire system.

Step 2: Identify the bottleneck operation by identifying operations with large quantities of inventory waiting to be worked on.

Step 3: Keep the bottleneck operation busy and subordinate all nonbottleneck operations to the bottleneck operation. That is, the needs of the bottleneck operation determine the production schedule of the nonbottleneck operations.

Step 3 represents one of the concepts described in Chapter 11: To maximize operating income, the plant must maximize contribution margin (in this case, throughput contribution) of the constrained or bottleneck resource (see pp. 391–392). For this reason, step 3 suggests that the bottleneck machine must always be kept running. It should not be waiting for jobs. To achieve this objective, companies often maintain a small buffer

[4]Other complexities, such as analyzing a network of machines, priority scheduling, and allowing for uncertainty in processing times, are beyond the scope of this book. In these cases, the basic queuing and delay effects persist, but the precise formulas are more complex.

[5]See E. Goldratt and J. Cox, *The Goal* (New York: North River Press, 1986); E. Goldratt, *The Theory of Constraints* (New York: North River Press, 1990); E. Noreen, D. Smith, and J. Mackey, *The Theory of Constraints and Its Implications for Management Accounting* (New York: North River Press, 1995); and M. Woeppel, *Manufacturers' Guide to Implementing the Theory of Constraints* (Boca Raton, FL: Lewis Publishing, 2000).

inventory of jobs waiting for the bottleneck machine. The bottleneck machine sets the pace for all nonbottleneck machines. For example, production schedulers instruct workers at nonbottleneck machines to not produce more output than can be processed by the bottleneck machine. Producing more nonbottleneck output only creates excess inventory; it does not increase throughput contribution.

Step 4: Take actions to increase the efficiency and capacity of the bottleneck operation: The objective is to increase the difference between throughput contribution and the incremental costs of increasing efficiency and capacity. The management accountant's role in step 4 is calculating throughput contribution, identifying relevant and irrelevant costs, and preparing cost–benefit analyses of alternative actions.

We illustrate step 4 using data from Cardinal Industries (CI). CI manufactures car doors in two operations: stamping and pressing.

	Stamping	Pressing
Capacity per hour	20 units	15 units
Annual capacity (6,000 hours of capacity available in each operation; 6,000 hours × 20 units/hour; 6,000 hours × 15 units/hour)	120,000 units	90,000 units
Annual production and sales	90,000 units	90,000 units
Other fixed operating costs (excluding direct materials)	$720,000	$1,080,000
Other fixed operating costs per unit produced ($720,000 ÷ 90,000 units; $1,080,000 ÷ 90,000 units)	$8 per unit	$12 per unit

Each door sells for $100 and has a direct material cost of $40. Variable costs in other functions of the value chain—R&D, design of products and processes, marketing, distribution, and customer service—are negligible. CI's output is constrained by the capacity of 90,000 units in the pressing operation. What can CI do to relieve the bottleneck constraint of the pressing operation? Desirable actions include:

1. **Eliminate idle time (time when the pressing machine is neither being set up to process products nor actually processing products) at the bottleneck operation.** CI is considering permanently positioning two workers at the pressing operation to unload finished units as soon as one batch of units is processed and to set up the machine to process the next batch. Suppose the annual cost of this action is $48,000 and the effect is to increase bottleneck output by 1,000 doors per year. Should CI incur the additional costs? Yes, because CI's throughput contribution increases by $60,000 [(selling price per door, $100 – direct material cost per door, $40) × 1,000 doors], which exceeds the additional cost of $48,000. All other costs are irrelevant.
2. **Process only those parts or products that increase throughput contribution, not parts or products that will remain in finished goods or spare parts inventories.** Making products that remain in inventory does not increase throughput contribution.
3. **Shift products that do not have to be made on the bottleneck machine to nonbottleneck machines or to outside processing facilities.** Suppose Spartan Corporation, an outside contractor, offers to press 1,500 doors at $15 per door from stamped parts that CI supplies. Spartan's quoted price is greater than CI's own operating costs in the Pressing Department of $12 per door. Should CI accept the offer? Yes, because pressing is the bottleneck operation. Getting additional doors pressed by Spartan increases throughput contribution by $90,000 [($100 – $40) per door × 1,500 doors], while relevant costs increase by $22,500 ($15 per door × 1,500 doors). The fact that CI's unit cost is less than Spartan's quoted price is irrelevent in the analysis.

   Suppose Gemini Industries, another outside contractor, offers to stamp 2,000 doors from direct materials that CI supplies at $6 per door. Gemini's price is lower than CI's operating cost of $8 per door in the Stamping Department. Should CI accept the offer? No, because other operating costs are fixed costs. CI will not save any costs by subcontracting the stamping operations. Total costs will be greater by $12,000 ($6 per door × 2,000 doors) under the subcontracting alternative. Stamping more doors will not increase throughput contribution, which is constrained by pressing capacity.

4. **Reduce setup time and processing time at bottleneck operations (for example, by simplifying the design or reducing the number of parts in the product).** Suppose CI can reduce setup time at the pressing operation by incurring additional costs of $55,000 a year. Suppose further that reducing setup time enables CI to press 2,500 more doors a year. Should CI incur the costs to reduce setup time? Yes, because throughput contribution increases by $150,000 [($100 – $40 per door) × 2,500 doors], which exceeds the additional costs incurred of $55,000. Will CI find it worthwhile to incur costs to reduce machining time at the nonbottleneck stamping operation? No. Other operating costs will increase, but throughput contribution will remain unchanged because bottleneck capacity has not increased.
5. **Improve the quality of parts or products manufactured at the bottleneck operation.** Poor quality is often more costly at a bottleneck operation than it is at a nonbottleneck operation. The cost of poor quality at a nonbottleneck operation is the cost of materials wasted. If CI produces 1,000 defective doors at the stamping operation, the cost of poor quality is $40,000 (direct material cost per door, $40, × 1,000 doors). No throughput contribution is forgone because stamping has unused capacity. Despite the defective production, stamping can produce and transfer 90,000 good-quality doors to the pressing operation. At a bottleneck operation, the cost of poor quality is the cost of materials wasted *plus* the opportunity cost of lost throughput contribution. Bottleneck capacity not wasted in producing defective units could be used to generate additional throughput contribution. If CI produces 1,000 defective units at the pressing operation, the cost of poor quality is the lost revenue of $100,000, or alternatively stated, direct material costs of $40,000 (direct material cost per door, $40, × 1,000 doors) plus forgone throughput contribution of $60,000 [($100 – $40) per door × 1,000 doors].

   The high cost of poor quality at the bottleneck operation means that bottleneck time should not be wasted processing units that are defective. That is, inspection should be done before processing parts at the bottleneck operation to ensure that only good-quality units are transferred to the bottleneck operation. Furthermore, quality-improvement programs should place special emphasis on minimizing defects at bottleneck machines.

The opportunity cost of lost throughput contribution arising from quality problems at the bottleneck is an internal failure cost.

If the actions in step 4 are successful, the capacity of the pressing operation will increase and eventually exceed the capacity of the stamping operation. The bottleneck will then shift to the stamping operation. CI would then focus continuous-improvement actions on increasing stamping efficiency and capacity. For example, the contract with Gemini Industries to stamp 2,000 doors at $6 per door from direct material supplied by CI becomes attractive then. That's because throughput contribution will increase by ($100 – $40) per door × 2,000 doors = $120,000, while costs will increase by $12,000 ($6 per door × 2,000 doors).

The theory of constraints emphasizes management of bottleneck operations as the key to improving performance of production operations as a whole. It focuses on short-run maximization of throughput contribution—revenues minus direct material costs of goods sold. Because TOC regards operating costs as difficult to change in the short run, it does not identify individual activities and drivers of costs. TOC is, therefore, less useful for the long-run management of costs. Activity-based costing (ABC) systems, on the other hand, take a longer-run perspective when more costs can be managed; the focus is on improving processes by eliminating nonvalue-added activities and reducing the costs of performing value-added activities. ABC systems, therefore, are more useful for long-run pricing, long-run cost control and profit planning, and capacity management. The short-run TOC emphasis on maximizing throughput contribution by managing bottlenecks complements the long-run strategic-cost-management focus of ABC.[6]

Study Tip: To check your understanding of the theory of constraints, see multiple-choice questions 6 through 8 and Review Exercises 1 and 2 (*Student Guide*, beginning p. 263). Fully explained answers begin on page 266.

[6]For an excellent evaluation of TOC, operations management, cost accounting, and the relationship between TOC and activity-based costing, see A. Atkinson, *"Cost Accounting, the Theory of Constraints, and Costing,"* (Issue Paper, CMA Canada, December 2000).

Balanced Scorecard and Time-Related Measures

In this section, we use the balanced scorecard to summarize how financial and nonfinancial measures of time relate to one another. We classify these measures under the four perspectives of the balanced scorecard—financial, customer, internal business processes, and learning and growth. Managers use the balanced scorecard measures to reduce delays and to increase throughput of their bottleneck operations.

Financial measures
Revenue losses or price discounts attributable to delays
Carrying cost of inventories
Throughput contribution minus operating costs

Customer measures
Customer-response time (the time it takes to fulfill a customer order)
On-time performance (delivering a product or service by the scheduled time)

Internal-business-process measures
Average manufacturing time for key products
Idle time at bottleneck operations
Defective units produced at bottleneck operations
Average reduction in setup time and processing time at bottleneck operations

Learning-and-growth measures
Employee satisfaction
Number of employees trained in managing bottleneck operations

Note the cause-and-effect linkages across these measures. For example, better employee training leads to better management of bottleneck operations, which in turn leads to better customer-response times and higher revenues and throughput contributions. Managers use time-related measures in the balanced scorecard to help them identify actions that improve customer-response times and create long-run competitive advantage.

PROBLEM FOR SELF-STUDY

The Sloan Moving Corporation transports household goods from one city to another within the continental United States. It measures quality of service in terms of (a) time required to transport goods, (b) on-time delivery (within two days of agreed-upon delivery date), and (c) number of lost or damaged shipments. Sloan is considering investing in a new scheduling-and-tracking system costing $160,000 per year, which should help it improve performance with respect to items (b) and (c). The following information describes Sloan's current performance and the expected performance if the new system is implemented:

	Current Performance	Expected Future Performance
On-time delivery performance	85%	95%
Variable cost per carton lost or damaged	$60	$60
Fixed cost per carton lost or damaged	$40	$40
Number of cartons lost or damaged per year	3,000 cartons	1,000 cartons

Sloan expects each percentage point increase in on-time performance to increase revenue by $20,000 per year. Sloan's contribution margin percentage is 45%.

Required

1. Should Sloan acquire the new system? Show your calculations.
2. Sloan is very confident about the cost savings from fewer lost or damaged cartons as a result of introducing the new system. Calculate the minimum amount of increase in revenues needed for Sloan to invest in the new system.

SOLUTION

1. Additional costs of the new scheduling-and-tracking system are $160,000 per year. Additional annual benefits of the new scheduling-and-tracking system are:

Additional annual revenues from a 10% improvement in on-time performance, from 85% to 95%, $20,000 per 1% × 10 percentage points	$200,000
45% contribution margin from additional annual revenues (0.45 × $200,000)	$ 90,000
Decrease in costs per year from fewer cartons lost or damaged (only variable costs are relevant) [$60 per carton × (3,000 – 1,000) cartons]	120,000
Total additional benefits	$210,000

Because the benefits of $210,000 exceed the costs of $160,000, Sloan should invest in the new system.

2. As long as Sloan earns a contribution margin of $40,000 (to cover incremental costs of $160,000 minus relevant variable-cost savings of $120,000) from additional annual revenues, investing in the new system is beneficial. This contribution margin corresponds to additional revenues of $40,000 ÷ 0.45 = $88,889.

DECISION POINTS

The following question-and-answer format summarizes the chapter's learning objectives. Each decision presents a key question related to a learning objective. The guidelines are the answer to that question.

Decision	Guidelines
1. What are the four cost categories of a costs-of-quality program?	Four cost categories in a costs-of-quality program are prevention costs (costs incurred to preclude the production of products that do not conform to specifications), appraisal costs (costs incurred to detect which of the individual units of products do not conform to specifications), internal failure costs (costs incurred on defective products before they are shipped to customers), and external failure costs (costs incurred on defective products after they are shipped to customers).
2. What nonfinancial quality measures of customer satisfaction can managers use in their balanced scorecards?	Nonfinancial quality measures of customer satisfaction that managers can use in their balanced scorecards include number of customer complaints and percentage of defective units shipped to customers.
3. What methods can managers use to identify quality problems and improve quality?	Three methods to identify quality problems and to improve quality are (a) control charts, to distinguish random from nonrandom variations in an operating process; (b) Pareto diagrams, to indicate how frequently each type of failure occurs; and (c) cause-and-effect diagrams, to identify potential causes of failure.
4. How do managers identify the relevant costs and benefits of quality improvement programs?	The relevant costs of quality improvement programs are the incremental costs to implement the quality program. The relevant benefits are the cost savings and the estimated increase in contribution margin from the higher revenues that result from quality improvements.
5. Why should managers use both financial and nonfinancial measures of quality?	Financial measures are helpful to evaluate trade-offs among prevention costs, appraisal costs, and failure costs. Nonfinancial measures identify problem areas that need improvement and serve as indicators of future long-run performance.
6. What is customer-response time? What are the reasons for and the costs of delays?	Customer-response time is how long it takes from the time a customer places an order for a product or service to the time the product or service is delivered to the customer. Delays occur because of (a) uncertainty about when customers will order products or services and (b) bottlenecks due to limited capacity. Bottlenecks are operations at which the work to be performed approaches or exceeds available capacity. Costs of delays include lower revenues and increased inventory carrying costs.

7. What three measures do managers need to implement the theory of constraints?

The three measures in the theory of constraints are (a) throughput contribution (equal to revenues minus direct material costs of the goods sold); (b) investments (equal to the sum of materials costs in direct materials, work-in-process, and finished goods inventories along with R&D costs and costs of equipment and buildings); and (c) operating costs (equal to all operating costs, other than direct material costs, incurred to earn throughput contribution).

8. What are the steps managers can take to manage bottlenecks?

The four steps in managing bottlenecks are (a) recognize that the bottleneck operation determines throughput contribution, (b) identify the bottleneck, (c) keep the bottleneck busy and subordinate all nonbottleneck operations to the bottleneck operation, and (d) increase bottleneck efficiency and capacity.

TERMS TO LEARN

This chapter and the Glossary at the end of the book contain definitions of:

appraisal costs (p. 661)
average waiting time (p. 671)
bottleneck (p. 671)
cause-and-effect diagram (p. 665)
conformance quality (p. 661)
control chart (p. 664)
costs of quality (COQ) (p. 661)
customer-response time (p. 670)
design quality (p. 660)
external failure costs (p. 662)
internal failure costs (p. 662)
manufacturing cycle time (p. 670)
manufacturing lead time (p. 670)
on-time performance (p. 670)
Pareto diagram (p. 665)
prevention costs (p. 661)
quality (p. 660)
theory of constraints (TOC) (p. 675)
throughput contribution (p. 675)
time driver (p. 671)

PH Grade Assist

Prentice Hall Grade Assist (PHGA)
Your professor may ask you to complete selected exercises and problems in Prentice Hall Grade Assist (PHGA). PHGA is an online tool that can help you master the chapter's topics. It provides you with multiple variations of exercises and problems designated by the PHGA icon. You can rework these exercises and problems—each time with new data—as many times as you need. You also receive immediate feedback and grading.

ASSIGNMENT MATERIAL

Questions

19-1 Describe two benefits of improving quality.

19-2 How does conformance quality differ from design quality? Explain.

19-3 Name two items classified as prevention costs.

19-4 Distinguish between internal failure costs and external failure costs.

19-5 Describe three methods that companies use to identify quality problems.

19-6 "Companies should focus on financial measures of quality because these are the only measures of quality that can be linked to bottom-line performance." Do you agree? Explain.

19-7 Give two examples of nonfinancial measures of customer satisfaction relating to quality in a balanced scorecard.

19-8 Give two examples of nonfinancial measures of internal-business-process quality in a balanced scorecard.

19-9 Distinguish between customer-response time and manufacturing lead time.

19-10 "There is no trade-off between customer-response time and on-time performance." Do you agree? Explain.

19-11 Give two reasons why delays occur.

19-12 "Companies should always make and sell all products whose selling prices exceed variable costs." Assuming fixed costs are irrelevant, do you agree? Explain.

19-13 Describe the three main measures used in the theory of constraints.

19-14 Describe the four key steps in managing bottleneck operations.

19-15 Describe three ways to improve the performance of a bottleneck operation.

Exercises

Excel Lab
www.prenhall.com/horngren/cost12e

19-16 Costs of quality. (CMA, adapted) Costen, Inc., produces cell phone equipment. Jessica Tolmy, Costen's president, decided to devote more resources to the improvement of product quality after learning that her company had been ranked fourth in product quality in a 2005 survey of cell phone users. Costen's quality-improvement program has now been in operation for two years, and the cost report shown here has recently been issued.

	A	B	C	D	E
1	**Semi-annual COQ Report, Costen, Inc.**				
2	**(in thousands)**				
3		**6/30/2006**	**12/31/2006**	**6/30/2007**	**12/31/2007**
4	Prevention costs				
5	Machine maintenance	$ 440	$ 440	$ 390	$ 330
6	Supplier training	20	100	50	40
7	Design reviews	50	214	210	200
8	Total prevention costs	510	754	650	570
9	Appraisal costs				
10	Incoming inspection	108	123	90	63
11	Final testing	332	332	293	203
12	Total appraisal costs	440	455	383	266
13	Internal failure costs				
14	Rework	231	202	165	112
15	Scrap	124	116	71	67
16	Total internal failure costs	355	318	236	179
17	External failure costs				
18	Warranty repairs	165	85	72	68
19	Customer returns	570	547	264	188
20	Total external failure costs	735	632	336	256
21	Total quality costs	$2,040	$2,159	$1,605	$1,271
22	Total production and revenues	$8,240	$9,080	$9,300	$9,020

If you want to use Excel to solve this exercise, go to the Excel Lab at **www.prenhall.com/horngren/cost12e** and download the template for Exercise 19-16.

Required

1. For each period, calculate the ratio of each COQ category to revenues and to total quality costs.
2. Based on the results of requirement 1, would you conclude that Costen's quality program has been successful? Prepare a short report to present your case.
3. Based on the 2005 survey, Jessica Tolmy believed that Costen had to take steps to improve product quality. In making her case to Costen management, how might Tolmy have estimated the opportunity cost of not implementing the quality-improvement program?

19-17 Costs-of-quality analysis, nonfinancial quality measures. The Preston Corporation manufactures and sells industrial products. The following table presents financial information pertaining to quality in 2007 and 2008 (in thousands):

Excel Lab
www.prenhall.com/horngren/cost12e

	A	B	C
1		**2007**	**2008**
2	Revenues	$20,000	$25,000
3	Inspection of production	220	170
4	Design engineering	210	600
5	Cost of returned goods	120	300
6	Product-testing labor and equipment	530	250
7	Customer support	80	65
8	Scrap and rework costs	720	670
9	Preventive equipment maintenance	110	200
10	Incoming materials inspection	50	80
11	Breakdown maintenance	180	80
12	Warranty repair	1,000	635
13	Supplier evaluation	80	200

If you want to use Excel to solve this exercise, go to the Excel Lab at **www.prenhall.com/horngren/cost12e** and download the template for Exercise 19-17.

Required

1. Classify the items in the table into the categories of prevention costs, appraisal costs, internal failure costs, and external failure costs.

2. Calculate the ratio of each COQ category to revenues in 2007 and 2008. Comment on the trends in costs of quality between 2007 and 2008.
3. Give two examples of nonfinancial quality measures that Preston Corporation could monitor in its balanced scorecard as part of a total quality-control effort.

Excel Lab
www.prenhall.com/horngren/cost12e

19-18 Costs-of-quality analysis, nonfinancial quality measures. Ambrose Industries manufactures and sells two models of commercial air conditioners: Frostaire and Coolaire. Information on each model is as follows:

	A	B	C	D	E	F
1		**Frostaire**			**Coolaire**	
2	Units manufactured and sold	20,000	units		40,000	units
3	Selling price	$1,500			$500	
4	Variable costs per unit	$800			$300	
5	Hours spent on design	7,500			2,500	
6	Testing and inspection hours per unit	1.0			0.15	
7	Percentage of units reworked in plant	5%			10%	
8	Rework costs per air conditioner	$300			$120	
9	Percentage of units repaired at customer site	4%			8%	
10	Repair costs per air conditioner	$400			$180	
11	Estimated lost sales due to poor quality (units)	500	units		4,000	units

The labor rate for design is $80 per hour, and the rate for testing and inspection is $50 per hour.

If you want to use Excel to solve this exercise, go to the Excel Lab at **www.prenhall.com/horngren/cost12e** and download the template for Exercise 19-18.

Required

1. Calculate the costs of quality for Frostaire and Coolaire, classifying them into prevention costs, appraisal costs, internal failure costs, and external failure costs.
2. For each model of air conditioner, calculate the ratio of each COQ category as a percentage of revenues. Compare and comment on the costs of quality for Frostaire and Coolaire.
3. Give two examples of nonfinancial quality measures that Ambrose Industries could monitor in a balanced scorecard as part of a total-quality program.

Excel Lab
www.prenhall.com/horngren/cost12e

19-19 Nonfinancial measures of quality and time. (CMA, adapted) Eastern Switching Co. (ESC) produces telecommunications equipment. Charles Laurant, ESC's president, believes that product quality is the key to gaining competitive advantage. Laurant implemented a total quality management (TQM) program with an emphasis on customer satisfaction. The following information is available for the first year (2007) of the TQM program compared with the previous year.

	A	B	C	D	E
1		**2006**		**2007**	
2	Total number of units produced and sold	10,000		11,000	
3	Units delivered before or on scheduled delivery date	8,500		9,900	
4	Number of defective units shipped	400		330	
5	Number of customer complaints other than for defective units	500		517	
6	Average time from when customer places order for a unit to when unit is delivered to customer	30	days	25	days
7	Number of units reworked during production	600		627	
8	Manufacturing lead time	20	days	16	days
9	Direct and indirect manufacturing labor-hours	90,000		110,000	

If you want to use Excel to solve this exercise, go to the Excel Lab at **www.prenhall.com/horngren/cost12e** and download the template for Exercise 19-19.

Required

1. For each of the years 2006 and 2007, calculate:
   a. Percentage of defective units shipped
   b. On-time delivery rate
   c. Customer complaints as a percentage of units shipped
   d. Percentage of units reworked during production
2. On the basis of your calculations in requirement 1, has ESC's performance on quality and timeliness improved? Explain briefly.
3. Philip Larkin, a member of ESC's board of directors, comments that regardless of the effect that the program has had on quality, the output per labor-hour has declined between 2006 and 2007. Larkin believes that lower output per labor-hour will lead to an increase in costs and lower operating income.

a. How did Larkin conclude that output per labor-hour declined in 2007 relative to 2006?
b. Why might output per labor-hour decline in 2007?
c. Do you think that a lower output per labor-hour will decrease operating income in 2007? Explain briefly.

19-20 Quality improvement, relevant costs, and relevant revenues. The Photon Corporation manufactures and sells 20,000 copiers each year. The variable and fixed costs of rework and repair are as follows:

Excel Lab
www.prenhall.com/horngren/cost12e

	A	B	C	D
1		Variable Cost	Fixed Cost	Total Cost
2	Rework cost per hour	$ 40	$60	$100
3	Repair costs			
4	Customer support cost per hour	20	30	50
5	Transportation cost per load	180	60	240
6	Warranty repair cost per hour	45	65	110

Photon's current copiers have a quality problem: the copies they generate are either too light or too dark. Photon's engineers suggest changing the single lens in each copier. The new lens will cost $55 more than the old lens. In the next year, however, Photon expects that with the new lens it will (1) save 12,875 hours of rework, (2) save 900 hours of customer support, (3) move 200 fewer loads, (4) save 7,000 hours of warranty repairs, and (5) sell an additional 150 copiers, for a total contribution margin of $900,000. Photon believes that even as it improves quality, it will not be able to save any of the fixed costs of rework or repair. Photon uses a one-year time horizon for this decision, because it plans to introduce a new copier at the end of the year.

If you want to use Excel to solve this exercise, go to the Excel Lab at **www.prenhall.com/horngren/cost12e** and download the template for Exercise 19-20.

Required

1. Should Photon change to the new lens? Show your calculations.
2. Suppose the estimate of 150 additional copiers sold is uncertain. What is the minimum number of additional copiers that Photon needs to sell to justify adopting the new lens?

19-21 Customer-response time, on-time delivery. Pizzafest, Inc., makes and delivers pizzas to homes and offices in the Boston area. Fast, on-time delivery is one of Pizzafest's key strategies. Pizzafest provides the following information for 2007 about its customer-response time—the amount of time from when a customer calls to place an order to when the pizza is delivered.

Excel Lab
www.prenhall.com/horngren/cost12e

	A	B	C
1		January-June	July-December
2	Pizzas delivered in 30 minutes or less	150,000	198,000
3	Pizzas delivered in between 31 and 45 minutes	300,000	363,000
4	Pizzas delivered in between 46 and 60 minutes	120,000	66,000
5	Pizzas delivered in between 61 and 75 minutes	30,000	33,000
6	Total pizzas delivered	600,000	660,000

If you want to use Excel to solve this exercise, go to the Excel Lab at **www.prenhall.com/horngren/cost12e** and download the template for Exercise 19-21.

Required

1. For January–June and July–December 2007, calculate the percentage of pizzas delivered in each of the four time intervals (30 minutes or less, 31 to 45 minutes, 46 to 60 minutes, and 61 to 75 minutes). On the basis of these calculations, has customer-response time improved in July–December compared with January–June?
2. When customers call Pizzafest, they often ask how long it will take for the pizza to be delivered to their homes or offices. If Pizzafest quotes a long time interval, customers often will not place the order. If Pizzafest quotes too short a time interval and the pizza is not delivered on time, customers get upset and Pizzafest loses repeat business. Based on the January–June 2007 data, what customer-response time should Pizzafest quote to its customers if:
   a. It wants to have an on-time delivery performance of 75%?
   b. It wants to have an on-time delivery performance of 95%?
3. If Pizzafest had quoted the customer-response times you calculated in requirements 2a and 2b, would it have met its on-time delivery performance targets of 75% and 95%, respectively, for July–December 2007? Explain.
4. Pizzafest is considering giving an on-time guarantee for January–June 2008. If the pizza is not delivered within 60 minutes of placing the order, the customer gets the pizza free. Pizzafest estimates that

it will make additional sales of 20,000 pizzas and give away 15,000 pizzas as a result of this guarantee. The average price of a pizza is $13, and the variable cost of a pizza is $7.

a. What is the effect on Pizzafest's operating income of making this offer?

b. What nonfinancial and qualitative factors should Pizzafest consider before making this offer?

c. What actions can Pizzafest take to reduce customer-response time?

19-22 Waiting time, banks. Regal Bank has a small branch in Orillia, Canada. The counter is staffed by one teller. The counter is open for five hours (300 minutes) each day (the operating capacity). It takes 5 minutes to serve a customer (service time). The Orillia branch expects to serve 40 customers each day. (Note that the number of customers corresponds to the number of orders in the chapter discussion.)

Required

1. Using the formula on page 671, calculate how long, on average, a customer will wait in line before being served.
2. How long, on average, will a customer wait in line if the branch expects to serve 50 customers each day?
3. The bank is considering ways to reduce waiting time. How long will customers have to wait, on average, if the time to serve a customer is reduced to four minutes and the bank expects to serve 50 customers each day?

19-23 Waiting time, relevant costs, and relevant revenues. The Orillia branch of Regal Bank is planning a new promotion to attract more customers. Its counter is open for five hours (300 minutes) each day (the operating capacity). The bank expects to serve an average of 60 customers each day, instead of the 40 customers it currently averages. It will take 4 minutes to serve each customer (service time). (Note that the number of customers corresponds to the number of orders in the chapter discussion.)

Required

1. Using the formula on page 671, calculate how long, on average, a customer will wait in line before being served.
2. Regal Bank's policy is that the average waiting time in the line should not exceed 5 minutes. The bank cannot reduce the time to serve a customer below 4 minutes without negatively affecting quality. To reduce average waiting time for the 60 customers it expects to serve each day, the bank decides to keep the counter open for 336 minutes each day. Verify that by keeping the counter open for 336 minutes, the bank will be able to achieve its goal of an average waiting time of 5 minutes or less.
3. The bank expects to generate, on average, $30 in additional operating income each day as a result of the new promotion. The teller is paid $10 per hour and is employed in one-hour increments (that is, the teller can be employed for 5, 6, or 7 hours, and so on, but not for a fraction of an hour). If the bank wants average waiting time to be no more than 5 minutes, should the bank offer the new promotion?

PH Grade Assist

19-24 Theory of constraints, throughput contribution, relevant costs. The Mayfield Corporation manufactures filing cabinets in two operations: machining and finishing. It provides the following information.

	Machining	Finishing
Annual capacity	100,000 units	80,000 units
Annual production	80,000 units	80,000 units
Fixed operating costs (excluding direct materials)	$640,000	$400,000
Fixed operating costs per unit produced ($640,000 ÷ 80,000; $400,000 ÷ 80,000)	$8 per unit	$5 per unit

Each cabinet sells for $72 and has direct material costs of $32 incurred at the start of the machining operation. Mayfield has no other variable costs. Mayfield can sell whatever output it produces. The following requirements refer only to the preceding data. There is no connection between the requirements.

Required

1. Mayfield is considering using some modern jigs and tools in the finishing operation that would increase annual finishing output by 1,000 units. The annual cost of these jigs and tools is $30,000. Should Mayfield acquire these tools? Show your calculations.
2. The production manager of the Machining Department has submitted a proposal to do faster setups that would increase the annual capacity of the Machining Department by 10,000 units and cost $5,000 per year. Should Mayfield implement the change? Show your calculations.

PH Grade Assist

19-25 Theory of constraints, throughput contribution, relevant costs. Refer to the information in Exercise 19-24 in answering the following requirements. There is no connection between the requirements.

Required

1. An outside contractor offers to do the finishing operation for 12,000 units at $10 per unit, double the $5 per unit that it costs Mayfield to do the finishing in-house. Should Mayfield accept the subcontractor's offer? Show your calculations.

2. The Hunt Corporation offers to machine 4,000 units at $4 per unit, half the $8 per unit that it costs Mayfield to do the machining in-house. Should Mayfield accept Hunt's offer? Show your calculations.

PH Grade Assist

19-26 Theory of constraints, throughput contribution, quality. Refer to the information in Exercise 19-24 in answering the following requirements. There is no connection between the requirements.

Required

1. Mayfield produces 2,000 defective units at the machining operation. What is the cost to Mayfield of the defective items produced? Explain your answer briefly.
2. Mayfield produces 2,000 defective units at the finishing operation. What is the cost to Mayfield of the defective items produced? Explain your answer briefly.

Problems

19-27 Quality improvement, relevant costs, and relevant revenues. The Thomas Corporation sells 300,000 V262 valves to the automobile and truck industry. Thomas has a capacity of 110,000 machine-hours and can produce 3 valves per machine-hour. V262's contribution margin per unit is $8. Thomas sells only 300,000 valves because 30,000 valves (10% of the good valves) need to be reworked. It takes 1 machine-hour to rework 3 valves, so 10,000 hours of capacity are used in the rework process. Thomas's rework costs are $210,000. Rework costs consist of:

- Direct materials and direct rework labor (variable costs): $3 per unit
- Fixed costs of equipment, rent, and overhead allocation: $4 per unit

Thomas's process designers have developed a modification that would maintain the speed of the process and ensure 100% quality and no rework. The new process would cost $315,000 per year. The following additional information is available:

- The demand for Thomas's V262 valves is 370,000 per year.
- The Jackson Corporation has asked Thomas to supply 22,000 T971 valves (another product) if Thomas implements the new design. The contribution margin per T971 valve is $10. Thomas can make two T971 valves per machine-hour with 100% quality and no rework.

Required

1. Suppose Thomas's designers implement the new design. Should Thomas accept Jackson's order for 22,000 T971 valves? Show your calculations.
2. Should Thomas implement the new design? Show your calculations.
3. What nonfinancial and qualitative factors should Thomas consider in deciding whether to implement the new design?

19-28 Quality improvement, relevant costs, and relevant revenues. The Tan Corporation uses multicolor molding to make plastic lamps. The molding operation has a capacity of 200,000 units per year. The demand for lamps is very strong. Tan will be able to sell whatever output quantities it can produce at $40 per lamp.

Tan can start only 200,000 units into production in the Molding Department because of capacity constraints on the molding machines. If a defective unit is produced at the molding operation, it must be scrapped at a net disposal value of zero. Of the 200,000 units started at the molding operation, 30,000 defective units (15%) are produced. The cost of a defective unit, based on total (fixed and variable) manufacturing costs incurred up to the molding operation, equals $25 per unit, as follows:

Direct materials (variable)	$16 per unit
Direct manufacturing labor, setup labor, and materials-handling labor (variable)	3 per unit
Equipment, rent, and other allocated overhead, including inspection and testing costs on scrapped parts (fixed)	6 per unit
Total	$25 per unit

Tan's designers have determined that adding a different type of material to the existing direct materials would result in no defective units being produced, but it would increase the variable costs by $4 per lamp in the Molding Department.

Required

1. Should Tan use the new material? Show your calculations.
2. What nonfinancial and qualitative factors should Tan consider in making the decision?

19-29 Statistical quality control, airline operations. Jetrans Airlines operates daily round-trip flights on the London–Los Angeles route using a fleet of three 747s: the Spirit of Atlanta, the Spirit of Boston, and the Spirit of Sacramento. The budgeted quantity of fuel for each round-trip flight is the 12-month mean (average) round-trip fuel consumption of 200 gallon-units, with a standard deviation of 20 gallon-units. A gallon-unit is 1,000 gallons.

Excel Lab
www.prenhall.com/horngren/cost12e

Using a statistical quality control (SQC) approach, Shirley Watson, the Jetrans operations manager, investigates any round-trip with fuel consumption that is greater than two standard deviations from the mean. In October, Watson receives the following report for round-trip fuel consumption for the three planes on the London–Los Angeles route:

	A	B	C	D
1		**Spirit of**	**Spirit of**	**Spirit of**
2		**Atlanta**	**Boston**	**Sacramento**
3	**Flight**	**(gallon-units)**	**(gallon-units)**	**(gallon-units)**
4	1	208	206	194
5	2	187	188	208
6	3	194	192	221
7	4	202	214	208
8	5	211	184	242
9	6	215	226	234
10	7	216	198	249
11	8	218	212	227
12	9	221	202	232
13	10	232	186	244

If you want to use Excel to solve this problem, go to the Excel Lab at **www.prenhall.com/horngren/cost12e** and download the template for Problem 19-29.

Required

1. Using the $\pm 2\sigma$ rule, what variance-investigation decisions would be made?
2. Present SQC charts for round-trip fuel usage for each of the three 747s in October. What inferences can you draw from the charts?
3. Some managers propose that Jetrans Airlines present its SQC charts in monetary terms rather than in physical-quantity terms (gallon-units). What are the advantages and disadvantages of using monetary fuel costs rather than gallon-units in the SQC charts?

Excel Lab
www.prenhall.com/horngren/cost12e

19-30 Compensation linked with profitability, on-time delivery, and external quality-performance measures. Pacific-Dunlop supplies tires to major automotive companies. It has two tire plants in North America, in Detroit and Los Angeles. The semi-annual bonus plan for each plant manager has three components:

a. Profitability performance. Add 2% of operating income.
b. On-time delivery performance. Add $10,000 if on-time delivery performance to the 10 most important customers is 98% or better. If on-time delivery performance to these customers is below 98%, add nothing.
c. Product-quality performance. Deduct 50% of cost of sales returns from the 10 most important customers.

Semi-annual data for 2007 for the Detroit and Los Angeles plants are as follows:

	A	B	C
1		**January-June**	**July-December**
2	**Detroit**		
3	Operating income	$1,650,000	$1,600,000
4	On-time delivery rate[a]	98.4%	97.1%
5	Cost of sales returns[a]	$ 44,000	$ 35,000
6			
7	**Los Angeles**		
8	Operating income	$3,100,000	$3,700,000
9	On-time delivery rate[a]	96.3%	98.1%
10	Cost of sales returns[a]	$ 69,000	$ 50,000
11			
12	[a]**For the 10 most important customers**		

If you want to use Excel to solve this problem, go to the Excel Lab at **www.prenhall.com/horngren/cost12e** and download the template for Problem 19-30.

Required

1. Compute the bonuses paid in each half year of 2007 to the Detroit and Los Angeles plant managers.
2. Discuss the validity of the components of the bonus plan as measures of profitability, on-time delivery, and product quality. Suggest one shortcoming of each measure and how it might be overcome (by redesign of the plan or by another measure).
3. Why do you think Pacific-Dunlop includes measures of both operating income and on-time delivery in its bonus plan for plant managers? Give one example of what might happen if on-time delivery were dropped as a performance measure.

19-31 Waiting times, manufacturing lead times. The SRG Corporation uses an injection molding machine to make a plastic product, Z39. SRG makes products only after receiving firm orders from its customers. SRG estimates that it will receive 50 orders for Z39 (each order is for 1,000 units) during the coming year. Each order of Z39 will take 80 hours of machine time. The annual capacity of the machine is 5,000 hours.

Required

1. Calculate (a) the average amount of time that an order for Z39 will wait in line before it is processed and (b) the average manufacturing lead time per order for Z39.
2. SRG is considering introducing a new product, Y28. SRG expects it will receive 25 orders of Y28 (each order for 200 units) in the coming year. Each order of Y28 will take 20 hours of machine time. The average demand for Z39 will be unaffected by the introduction of Y28. Calculate (a) the average waiting time for an order received and (b) the average manufacturing lead time per order for each product, if SRG introduces Y28.

19-32 Waiting times, relevant revenues, and relevant costs (continuation of 19-31). SRG is still deciding whether it should introduce Y28. The following table provides information on selling prices, variable costs, and inventory carrying costs for Z39 and Y28. SRG will incur additional variable costs and inventory carrying costs for Y28 only if it introduces Y28. Fixed costs equal to 40% of variable costs are allocated to all products produced and sold during the year.

		Selling Price per Order If Average Manufacturing Lead Time per Order Is			
Product	**Annual Average Number of Orders**	**Less Than 320 Hours**	**More Than 320 Hours**	**Variable Cost per Order**	**Inventory Carrying Cost per Order per Hour**
Z39	50	$27,000	$26,500	$15,000	$0.75
Y28	25	8,400	8,000	5,000	0.25

Required

1. Should SRG manufacture and sell Y28? Show your calculations.
2. Should SRG manufacture and sell Y28 if the data in Problem 19-31 are changed as follows: Selling price per order is $6,400, instead of $8,400, if average manufacturing lead time per order is less than 320 hours; and $6,000, instead of $8,000, if average manufacturing lead time per order is more than 320 hours? All other data for Y28 are the same.

19-33 Manufacturing lead times, relevant revenues, and relevant costs. The Brandt Corporation makes wire harnesses for the aircraft industry. Brandt is uncertain about when and how many customer orders will be received. The company makes harnesses only after receiving firm orders from its customers. Brandt has recently purchased a new machine to make two types of wire harnesses, one for Boeing airplanes (B7) and the other for Airbus Industries airplanes (A3). The annual capacity of the new machine is 6,000 hours. The following information is available for next year:

			Selling Price per Order If Average Manufacturing Lead Time per Order Is			
Customer	**Annual Average Number of Orders**	**Manufacturing Time Required**	**Less Than 200 Hours**	**More Than 200 Hours**	**Variable Cost per Order**	**Inventory Carrying Cost per Order per Hour**
B7	125	40 hours	$15,000	$14,400	$10,000	$0.50
A3	10	50 hours	13,500	12,960	9,000	0.45

Required

1. Calculate the average manufacturing lead times per order (a) if Brandt manufactures only B7 and (b) if Brandt manufactures both B7 and A3.
2. Even though A3 has a positive contribution margin, Brandt's managers are evaluating whether Brandt should (a) make and sell only B7 or (b) make and sell both B7 and A3. Which alternative will maximize Brandt's operating income? Show your calculations.
3. What other factors should Brandt consider in choosing between the alternatives in requirement 2?

19-34 Theory of constraints, throughput contribution, relevant costs. Colorado Industries manufactures electronic testing equipment. Colorado also installs the equipment at customers' sites and ensures that it functions smoothly. Additional information on the Manufacturing and Installation Departments is as follows (capacities are expressed in terms of the number of units of electronic testing equipment):

	Equipment Manufactured	**Equipment Installed**
Annual capacity	400 units per year	300 units per year
Equipment manufactured and installed	300 units per year	300 units per year

Colorado manufactures only 300 units per year because the Installation Department has only enough capacity to install 300 units. The equipment sells for $40,000 per unit (installed) and has direct material costs of $15,000. All costs other than direct material costs are fixed. The following requirements refer only to the preceding data. There is no connection between the requirements.

Required

1. Colorado's engineers have found a way to reduce equipment manufacturing time. The new method would cost an additional $50 per unit and would allow Colorado to manufacture 20 additional units a year. Should Colorado implement the new method? Show your calculations.
2. Colorado's designers have proposed a change in direct materials that would increase direct material costs by $2,000 per unit. This change would enable Colorado to install 320 units of equipment each year. If Colorado makes the change, it will implement the new design on all equipment sold. Should Colorado use the new design? Show your calculations.
3. A new installation technique has been developed that will enable Colorado's engineers to install 10 additional units of equipment a year. The new method will increase installation costs by $50,000 each year. Should Colorado implement the new technique? Show your calculations.
4. Colorado is considering how to motivate workers to improve their productivity (output per hour). One proposal is to evaluate and compensate workers in the Manufacturing and Installation Departments on the basis of their productivities. Do you think the new proposal is a good idea? Explain briefly.

19-35 Theory of constraints, throughput contribution, quality, relevant costs. Aardee Industries manufactures pharmaceutical products in two departments: Mixing and Tablet-Making. Additional information on the two departments follows. Each tablet contains 0.5 gram of direct materials.

	Mixing	Tablet Making
Capacity per hour	150 grams	200 tablets
Monthly capacity (2,000 hours available in each department)	300,000 grams	400,000 tablets
Monthly production	200,000 grams	390,000 tablets
Fixed operating costs (excluding direct materials)	$16,000	$39,000
Fixed operating cost per tablet ($16,000 ÷ 200,000 grams; $39,000 ÷ 390,000 tablets)	$0.08 per gram	$0.10 per tablet

The Mixing Department makes 200,000 grams of direct materials mixture (enough to make 400,000 tablets) because the Tablet-Making Department has only enough capacity to process 400,000 tablets. All direct material costs are incurred in the Mixing Department. Aardee incurs $156,000 in direct material costs. The Tablet-Making Department manufactures only 390,000 tablets from the 200,000 grams of mixture processed; 2.5% of the direct materials mixture is lost in the tablet-making process. Each tablet sells for $1. All costs other than direct material costs are fixed costs. The following requirements refer only to the preceding data. There is no connection between the requirements.

Required

1. An outside contractor makes the following offer: If Aardee will supply the contractor with 10,000 grams of mixture, the contractor will manufacture 19,500 tablets for Aardee (allowing for the normal 2.5% loss of the mixture during the tablet-making process) at $0.12 per tablet. Should Aardee accept the contractor's offer? Show your calculations.
2. Another company offers to prepare 20,000 grams of mixture a month from direct materials Aardee supplies. The company will charge $0.07 per gram of mixture. Should Aardee accept the company's offer? Show your calculations.
3. Aardee's engineers have devised a method that would improve quality in the Tablet-Making Department. They estimate that the 10,000 tablets currently being lost would be saved. The modification would cost $7,000 a month. Should Aardee implement the new method? Show your calculations.
4. Suppose that Aardee also loses 10,000 grams of mixture in its Mixing Department. These losses can be reduced to zero if the company is willing to spend $9,000 per month in quality-improvement methods. Should Aardee adopt the quality-improvement method? Show your calculations.
5. What are the benefits of improving quality in the Mixing Department compared with improving quality in the Tablet-Making Department?

19-36 Quality improvement, Pareto diagram, cause-and-effect diagram. The Murray Corporation manufactures, sells, and installs photocopying machines. Murray has placed heavy emphasis on reducing defects and failures in its production operations. Murray wants to apply the same total quality management principles to manage its accounts receivable.

Required

1. On the basis of your knowledge and experience, what would you classify as failures in accounts receivable?
2. Give examples of prevention activities that could reduce failures in accounts receivable.
3. Draw a Pareto diagram of the types of failures in accounts receivable and a cause-and-effect diagram of possible causes of one type of failure in accounts receivable.

19-37 Ethics and quality. Information from a quality report for 2007 prepared by Lindsey Williams, assistant controller of Citocell, a manufacturer of electric motors, is as follows:

Revenues	$10,000,000
Inspection of production	$ 90,000
Warranty liability	$ 260,000
Product testing	$ 210,000
Scrap	$ 230,000
Design engineering	$ 200,000
Percentage of customer complaints	5%
On-time delivery rate	93%

Davey Evans, the plant manager of Citocell, is eligible for a bonus if the total costs of quality as a percentage of revenues are less than 10%, the percentage of customer complaints is less than 4%, and the on-time delivery rate exceeds 92%. Evans is unhappy about the customer complaints of 5% because, when preparing her report, Williams actually surveyed customers regarding customer satisfaction. Evans expected Williams to be less proactive and to wait for customers to complain. Evans's concern with Williams's approach is that it introduces subjectivity into the results and also fails to capture the seriousness of customers' concerns. "When you wait for a customer to complain, you know they are complaining because it is something important. When you do customer surveys, customers mention whatever is on their mind, even if it is not terribly important."

John Roche, the controller, asks Williams to see him. He tells her about Evans's concerns. "I think Davey has a point. See what you can do." Williams is confident that the customer complaints are genuine and that customers are concerned about quality and service. She believes it is important for Citocell to be proactive and obtain systematic and timely customer feedback, and then to use this information to make improvements. She is also well aware that Citocell has not done customer surveys in the past, and that, except for her surveys, Evans would probably be eligible for the bonus. She is confused about how to handle Roche's request.

Required

1. Calculate the ratio of each cost-of-quality category (prevention, appraisal, internal failure, and external failure) to revenues in 2007. Are the total costs of quality as a percentage of revenues less than 10%?
2. Would it be unethical for Williams to modify her analysis? What steps should Williams take to resolve this situation?

Collaborative Learning Problem

19-38 Quality improvement, theory of constraints. The Wellesley Corporation makes printed cloth in two departments: Weaving and Printing. Direct material costs are Wellesley's only variable costs. The demand for Wellesley's cloth is very strong. Wellesley can sell whatever output quantities it produces at $1,250 per roll to a distributor who markets, distributes, and provides customer service for the product. Wellesley provides the following information.

	Weaving	Printing
Monthly capacity	10,000 rolls	15,000 rolls
Monthly production	9,500 rolls	8,550 rolls
Direct material cost per roll of cloth processed at each operation	$500	$100
Fixed operating costs	$2,850,000	$427,500
Fixed operating cost per roll ($2,850,000 ÷ 9,500 rolls; $427,500 ÷ 8,550 rolls)	$300 per roll	$50 per roll

Wellesley can start only 10,000 rolls of cloth in the Weaving Department because of capacity constraints of the weaving machines. If the Weaving Department produces defective cloth, the cloth must be scrapped and yields zero net disposal value. Of the 10,000 rolls of cloth started in the Weaving Department, 500 (5%) defective rolls are produced. The cost of a defective roll, based on total (fixed and variable) manufacturing cost per roll incurred up to the end of the weaving operation, equals $785 per roll, as follows:

Direct material cost per roll (variable)	$500
Fixed operating cost per roll ($2,850,000 ÷ 10,000 rolls)	285
Total manufacturing cost per roll in Weaving Department	$785

The good rolls from the Weaving Department (called gray cloth) are sent to the Printing Department. Of the 9,500 good rolls started at the printing operation, 950 (10%) defective rolls are produced and scrapped at zero net disposal value. The cost of a defective roll based on total (fixed and variable) manufacturing cost per unit incurred up to the end of the printing operation, equals $930 per roll, calculated as follows:

Total manufacturing cost per roll in Weaving Department		$785
Printing Department manufacturing cost per roll		
Direct material cost per roll (variable)	$100	
Fixed operating cost per roll ($427,500 ÷ 9,500 rolls)	45	
Total manufacturing cost per roll in Printing Department		145
Total manufacturing cost per roll		$930

The Wellesley Corporation's total monthly sales of printed cloth equal the Printing Department's output.

Required Each requirement refers only to the preceding data. There is no connection between the requirements.

1. The Printing Department is considering buying 5,000 additional rolls of gray cloth from an outside supplier at $900 per roll. The Printing Department manager is concerned that the cost of purchasing the gray cloth is much higher than Wellesley's cost of manufacturing it. The quality of the gray cloth acquired from the outside supplier is very similar to that manufactured in-house. The Printing Department expects that 10% of the rolls obtained from the outside supplier will result in defective products. Should the Printing Department buy the gray cloth from the outside supplier? Show your calculations.
2. Wellesley's engineers have developed a method that would lower the Printing Department's rate of defective products to 6% at the printing operation. Implementing the new method would cost $350,000 per month. Should Wellesley implement the change? Show your calculations.
3. The design engineering team has proposed a modification that would lower the Weaving Department's rate of defective products to 3%. The modification would cost the company $175,000 per month. Should Wellesley implement the change? Show your calculations.

Get Connected: Cost Accounting in the News

Go to www.prenhall.com/horngren/cost12e for additional online exercise(s) that explore issues affecting the accounting world today. These exercises offer you the opportunity to analyze and reflect on how cost accounting helps managers make better decisions and handle the challenges of strategic planning and implementation.

CHAPTER 19 Video Case

RITZ-CARLTON HOTEL COMPANY: Managing Quality

If you have only heard or read the name "Ritz-Carlton," you are probably thinking of luxury and quality. That's what the managers at their 31 hotels and resorts want you to think. As managers at the first hotel company ever to win the Malcolm Baldrige National Quality Award, they see quality as a daily commitment to meeting customer expectations and making sure each hotel is free of any deficiency in fulfilling those expectations. In the hotel industry, quality can be hard to quantify. Ritz-Carlton guests do not purchase a product, they buy an experience. So creating the right combination of elements to make the experience outstanding to guests is the challenge and the goal of every employee, from maintenance to management.

Before applying for consideration for the Baldrige Award, company management undertook a rigorous self-examination of their operations in an attempt to measure and quantify quality. Nineteen processes were studied, including room service, guest reservation and registration, message delivery, and breakfast service. This period of self-study included statistical measurement of process work flows and cycle times for areas ranging from room-service delivery times and reservations to valet parking and housekeeping efficiency. Each hotel focused on one of the 19 areas for a year. The results were used to develop benchmarks against which future performance could be measured.

With specific, quantifiable targets in place, managers at the Ritz-Carlton now focus on continuous improvement. The goal is 100% customer satisfaction. Each hotel and resort property is run as an independent business, so the general manager at each location takes ownership for monitoring quality and taking action to prevent problems from arising or affecting a guest. Performance is reviewed at daily and weekly management meetings, and results are communicated back to employees. After all, if a guest's experience does not meet expectations, the company risks losing that guest to the competition.

One way the company has put more meaning behind its quality efforts is to organize its employees into "self-directed" work teams. The teams are formed within each functional area of the hotel, such as guest services, valet services, food and beverages, housekeeping, and maintenance. Managers no longer operate in command-and-control mode, in which orders are dictated and expected to be carried out. Instead, the employee teams determine employee work scheduling, what work needs to be done, and what to do about quality problems in their areas. Managers are expected to become facilitators and resources for helping the teams achieve their quality goals. Employees are also given the opportunity to take additional training on how the hotel is run, so they can see the relationship of their specific area's efforts to the overall goals of the hotel. Training topics range from budgets and purchasing to payroll and controllable costs. Employees are then tested and compensated for successful completion of training. The Ritz-Carlton expects that a more-educated and informed employee will be in a better position to make decisions that are in the best interest of guests and the organization as a whole.

QUESTIONS

1. In what ways could the Ritz-Carlton monitor its success at achieving quality?
2. Many companies say their goal is to provide quality products or services. What actions might you expect from a company that intends "quality" to be more than a slogan?
3. How does lack of quality, or missing a quality goal, affect Ritz-Carlton's contribution margin?
4. Why might it cost Ritz-Carlton less to "do things right" the first time?
5. How could control charts, Pareto diagrams, and cause-and-effect diagrams be used to identify quality problems?
6. What are some nonfinancial measures of customer satisfaction that might be used by Ritz-Carlton?

CHAPTER 20

INVENTORY MANAGEMENT, JUST-IN-TIME, AND BACKFLUSH COSTING

LEARNING OBJECTIVES

1. Identify five categories of costs associated with goods for sale
2. Balance ordering costs with carrying costs using the economic-order-quantity (EOQ) decision model
3. Identify and reduce conflicts that can arise between the EOQ decision model and models used for performance evaluation
4. Use a supply-chain approach to inventory management
5. Distinguish materials requirements planning (MRP) systems from just-in-time (JIT) systems for manufacturing
6. Identify the features of a just-in-time production system
7. Use backflush costing
8. Describe different ways backflush costing can simplify traditional inventory-costing systems

Elana Samel is the manager of Video Galore, an independent electronics store that sells blank videotapes. When a competitor moved into the area where Video Galore is located, many people predicted the store's quick closing. Elana wants to prove them wrong, but she knows that her business can't continue to thrive on past successes. Elana is meeting with Ervin Jackson, Video Galore's management accountant, to discuss the upcoming implementation of a just-in-time (JIT) purchasing plan for the videotapes.

Elana: Ervin, are you completely convinced about the benefits of moving to JIT purchasing? From the analysis you've prepared, it appears that the benefits we're going to see are lower inventory carrying costs, mostly in lower opportunity costs—costs that aren't recorded in the financial accounting system.

Ervin: You're right. They aren't in the system, but I am very confident about these savings. Opportunity costs are real economic costs even though we don't record them.

Elana: I also want to be sure that our supplier, Sontek, is in a position to make the many frequent deliveries that we are now requesting. I am concerned that we may not have tapes available when our customers want them.

Ervin: We've checked this out quite thoroughly. We'll place all orders over the Internet. Sontek is already supplying one of its other customers on a JIT basis, and from everything I know, they have done an outstanding job. We checked out another potential supplier, but Sontek was far superior in both reliability and quality.

Elana: Thank you. I think this is an exciting initiative for us. It is, of course, critical that we execute it flawlessly.

Inventory management is an important part of profit planning for manufacturing and merchandising companies such as Mitsubishi, Nestlé, Old Navy, CVS, and Home Depot, just as it is for Video Galore. Materials costs often account for more than 40% of total costs of manufacturing companies and more than 70% of total costs in merchandising companies. For each type of organization—merchandising and manufacturing—we follow the framework for cost accounting and cost management described in Chapter 2. We first describe how inventory costs are calculated, then how relevant costs of inventory are computed for different decisions, and finally how planning and control and performance evaluation are done when managing inventory.

Inventory Management in Retail Organizations

Inventory management includes planning, coordinating, and controlling activities related to the flow of inventory into, through, and out of an organization. Consider this breakdown of operations for three major retailers for which cost of goods sold constitutes their largest cost item.

	Kroger	Costco	Wal-Mart
Revenues	100.0%	100.0%	100.0%
Deduct costs:			
Cost of goods sold	73.7%	87.6%	77.5%
Selling and administration costs	19.2%	9.6%	17.5%
Other costs, interest, and taxes	6.5%	1.2%	1.5%
Total costs	99.4%	98.4%	96.5%
Net income	0.6%	1.6%	3.5%

The percentages of net income to revenues are very low. This means that improving the purchase and management of goods for sale can cause dramatic percentage increases in net income.

Costs Associated with Goods for Sale

1

Identify five categories of costs associated with goods for sale

. . . purchasing, ordering, carrying, stockout, and quality costs

Managing inventories to increase net income requires companies to effectively manage costs that fall into the following five categories:

1. **Purchasing costs**—the cost of goods acquired from suppliers, including incoming freight costs. These costs usually make up the largest cost category of goods for sale. Discounts for various purchase-order sizes and supplier credit terms affect purchasing costs.
2. **Ordering costs**—the costs of preparing and issuing purchase orders, receiving and inspecting the items included in the orders, and matching invoices received, purchase orders, and delivery records to make payments. Ordering costs include the cost of obtaining purchase approvals, as well as other special processing costs.
3. **Carrying costs**—the costs that arise while holding an inventory of goods for sale. Carrying costs include the opportunity cost of the investment tied up in inventory (see Chapter 11, pp. 390–391) and the costs associated with storage, such as space rental, insurance, obsolescence, spoilage, and shrinkage (resulting from theft).
4. **Stockout costs**—the costs that result when a company runs out of a particular item for which there is customer demand—a *stockout*—and the company must act quickly to meet that demand or suffer the costs of not meeting it. A company may respond to a stockout by expediting an order from a supplier, which can be expensive because of additional ordering costs plus any associated transportation costs. Or the company may lose sales due to the stockout. In this case, the opportunity cost of the stockout includes lost contribution margin on the sale not made plus any contribution margin lost on future sales due to customer ill will.
5. **Quality costs**—the costs that result when features and characteristics of a product or service are not in conformance with customer specifications. There are four categories of quality costs—prevention costs, appraisal costs, internal failure costs, and external failure costs—described in Chapter 19.

Toyota works with suppliers to reduce purchasing costs. It sends teams of experts to help suppliers streamline their production processes, which helps them meet Toyota's expected annual price reductions and its demands for high quality and on-time delivery.

Costs associated with goods for resale include opportunity costs that aren't recorded in the financial accounting system.

Note that not all inventory costs are available in financial accounting systems. For example, opportunity costs are not recorded in these systems and are a significant component in several of these cost categories.

Information-gathering technology increases the reliability and timeliness of inventory information and reduces costs in the five cost categories. For example, bar-coding technology allows a scanner to record purchases and sales of individual units. As soon as a unit is scanned, an instantaneous record of inventory movements is created that helps in the management of purchasing, carrying, and stockout costs. In the next several sections, we consider how relevant costs are computed for different inventory-related decisions in merchandising companies.

Economic-Order-Quantity Decision Model

2

Balance ordering costs with carrying costs using the economic-order-quantity (EOQ) decision model

. . . choose the inventory quantity per order to minimize costs

The first decision in managing goods for sale is *how much to order* of a given product. The **economic order quantity (EOQ)** is a decision model that, under a given set of assumptions, calculates the optimal quantity of inventory to order. The simplest version of an EOQ model assumes there are only ordering and carrying costs, and it also assumes:

- The same quantity is ordered at each reorder point.
- Demand, ordering costs, and carrying costs are known with certainty. The **purchase-order lead time**—the time between placing an order and its delivery—is also known with certainty.
- Purchasing cost per unit is unaffected by the quantity ordered. This assumption makes purchasing costs irrelevant to determining EOQ because purchasing costs of all units acquired will be the same, regardless of the order size in which the units are ordered.
- No stockouts occur. The basis for this assumption is that the costs of stockouts are so high that managers maintain adequate inventory to prevent them.
- In deciding on the size of a purchase order, managers consider costs of quality only to the extent that these costs affect ordering or carrying costs.

Given these assumptions, EOQ analysis ignores purchasing costs, stockout costs, and quality costs. EOQ is the order quantity that minimizes the relevant ordering and carrying costs (that is, the ordering and carrying costs affected by the quantity of inventory ordered):

$$\text{Relevant total costs} = \text{Relevant ordering costs} + \text{Relevant carrying costs}$$

Let's consider an example to see how EOQ analysis works. Video Galore, which was introduced at the beginning of the chapter, purchases blank videotapes from Sontek at \$14 a package (each package contains 10 tapes). Sontek pays for all incoming freight. No inspection is necessary at Video Galore because Sontek supplies quality merchandise. Video Galore's annual demand is 13,000 packages, at a rate of 250 packages per week. Video Galore requires a 15% annual rate of return on investment. The purchase-order lead time is two weeks. Relevant ordering cost per purchase order is \$200.

You may be familiar with calculating EOQ, reorder point, and safety stock from finance or production courses. In those courses, costs for the formulas are assumed. Here you will see that management accountants help (1) decide what costs to include in the formulas and (2) estimate the amounts of the costs.

Relevant carrying cost per package per year is:

Required annual return on investment, 0.15 × \$14	\$2.10
Relevant insurance, materials handling, breakage, shrinkage, and so on, per year	3.10
Total	\$5.20

Carrying costs are higher than you may think. In many companies, average annual carrying costs exceed 30% of purchasing costs. In the Video Galore example, annual carrying costs are 37% (\$5.20 ÷ \$14.00) of purchasing costs.

What is the EOQ of packages of videotapes? The formula for the EOQ model is:

$$EOQ = \sqrt{\frac{2DP}{C}}$$

where

D = Demand in units for a specified period (one year in this example)

P = Relevant ordering cost per purchase order

C = Relevant carrying cost of one unit in stock for the time period used for D (one year)

The formula indicates that EOQ increases with higher demand and/or higher ordering costs and decreases with higher carrying costs.

For Video Galore:

$$EOQ = \sqrt{\frac{2 \times 13{,}000 \times \$200}{\$5.20}} = \sqrt{1{,}000{,}000} = 1{,}000 \text{ packages}$$

Purchasing 1,000 packages per order minimizes total relevant ordering and carrying costs. Therefore, the number of deliveries each period (one year in this example) is:

$$\frac{D}{EOQ} = \frac{13{,}000}{1{,}000} = 13 \text{ deliveries}$$

The annual relevant total costs (RTC) for any order quantity, Q, can then be calculated as follows:

$$RTC = \text{Annual relevant ordering costs} + \text{Annual relevant carrying costs}$$

$$= \left(\begin{array}{c}\text{Number of}\\ \text{purchase orders}\\ \text{per year}\end{array} \times \begin{array}{c}\text{Relevant ordering}\\ \text{cost per}\\ \text{purchase order}\end{array}\right) + \left(\begin{array}{c}\text{Average inventory}\\ \text{in units}\end{array} \times \begin{array}{c}\text{Annual}\\ \text{relevant carrying}\\ \text{cost per unit}\end{array}\right)$$

$$= \left(\frac{D}{Q} \times P\right) + \left(\frac{Q}{2} \times C\right)$$

$$= \frac{DP}{Q} + \frac{QC}{2}$$

In this formula, Q can be any order quantity, not just the EOQ.
When Q = 1,000 units,

$$RTC = \frac{13{,}000 \times \$200}{1{,}000} + \frac{1{,}000 \times \$5.20}{2}$$

$$= \$2{,}600 + \$2{,}600 = \$5{,}200$$

Exhibit 20-1 graphs the annual relevant total costs of ordering (DP/Q) and carrying inventory ($QC/2$) under various order sizes (Q), and it illustrates the trade-off between these two types of costs. The larger the order quantity, the lower the annual relevant ordering costs, but the higher the annual relevant carrying costs. *Annual relevant total costs are at a minimum at the EOQ at which the relevant ordering and carrying costs are equal.*

When to Order, Assuming Certainty

The intuition for the reorder-point formula is that we need to reorder when the inventory on hand falls to the level at which it equals the amount needed for sales that will occur during the purchase-order lead time.

The second decision in managing goods for sale is *when to order* a given product. The **reorder point** is the quantity level of inventory on hand that triggers a new purchase order. The reorder point is simplest to compute when both demand and purchase-order lead time are known with certainty:

$$\text{Reorder point} = \begin{array}{c}\text{Number of units sold}\\ \text{per unit of time}\end{array} \times \begin{array}{c}\text{Purchase-order}\\ \text{lead time}\end{array}$$

EXHIBIT 20-1 Graphic Analysis of Ordering Costs and Carrying Costs for Videotape Packages at Video Galore

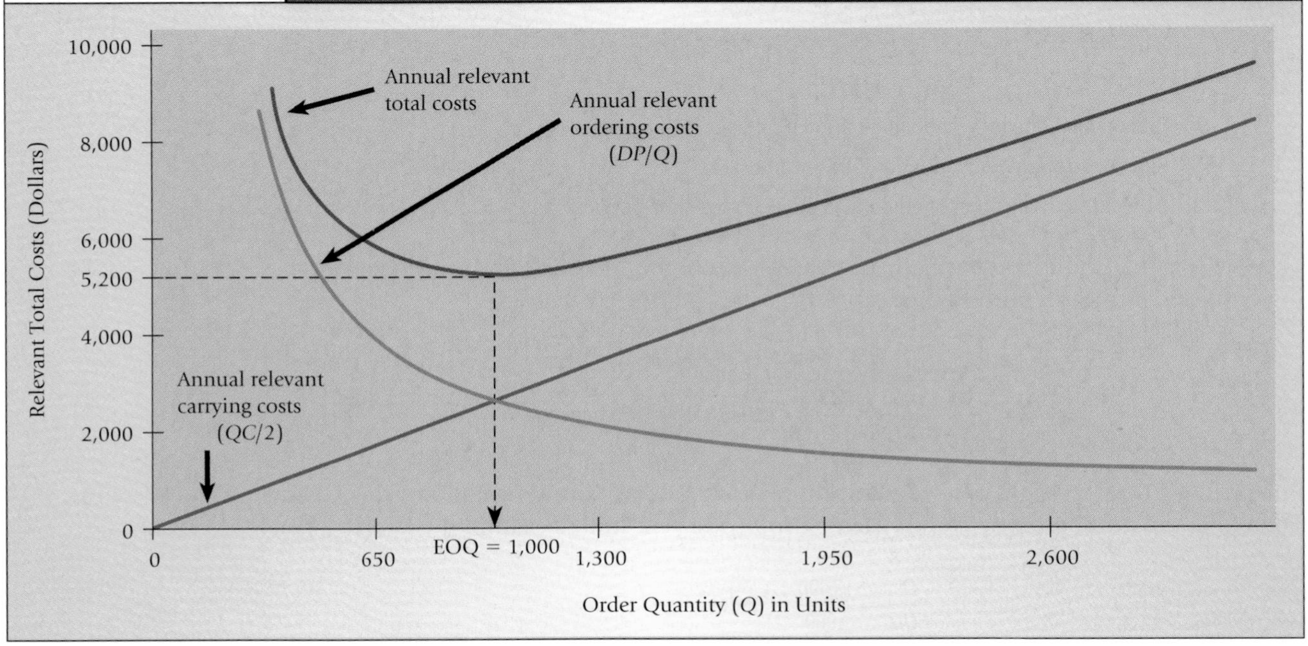

In our Video Galore example, we choose one week as the unit of time in the reorder-point formula:

Economic order quantity	1,000 packages
Number of units sold per week	250 packages per week
Purchase-order lead time	2 weeks

$$\text{Reorder point} = 250 \text{ packages per week} \times 2 \text{ weeks} = 500 \text{ packages}$$

Video Galore will order 1,000 packages each time inventory stock falls to 500 packages. The graph in Exhibit 20-2 shows the behavior of the inventory level of videotape packages, assuming demand occurs uniformly during each week.[1] If purchase-order lead time is two weeks, a new order will be placed when the inventory level falls to 500 packages, so the 1,000 packages ordered will be received at the precise time that inventory reaches zero.

Particularly for low-cost items, companies often use simple signals—such as stock falling below painted lines in bins—to indicate it's time to reorder.

Safety Stock

We have assumed that demand and purchase-order lead time are known with certainty. Retailers who are uncertain about demand, lead time, or the quantity that suppliers can provide, hold safety stock. **Safety stock** is inventory held at all times regardless of the quantity of inventory ordered using the EOQ model. Safety stock is used as a buffer against unexpected increases in demand, uncertainty about lead time, and unavailability of stock from suppliers. Video Galore's managers expect demand to be 250 packages per week, but they feel that a maximum demand of 400 packages per week may occur. If Video Galore's managers decide costs of stockouts are prohibitively high, they may decide to hold a safety stock of 300 packages. The 300 packages equal the maximum excess demand of 150 (400 − 250) packages per week times the two weeks of purchase-order lead time. The computation of safety stock hinges on demand forecasts. Managers will have some notion—usually based on experience—of the range of weekly demand.

EXHIBIT 20-2

Inventory Level of Videotape Packages at Video Galore[a]

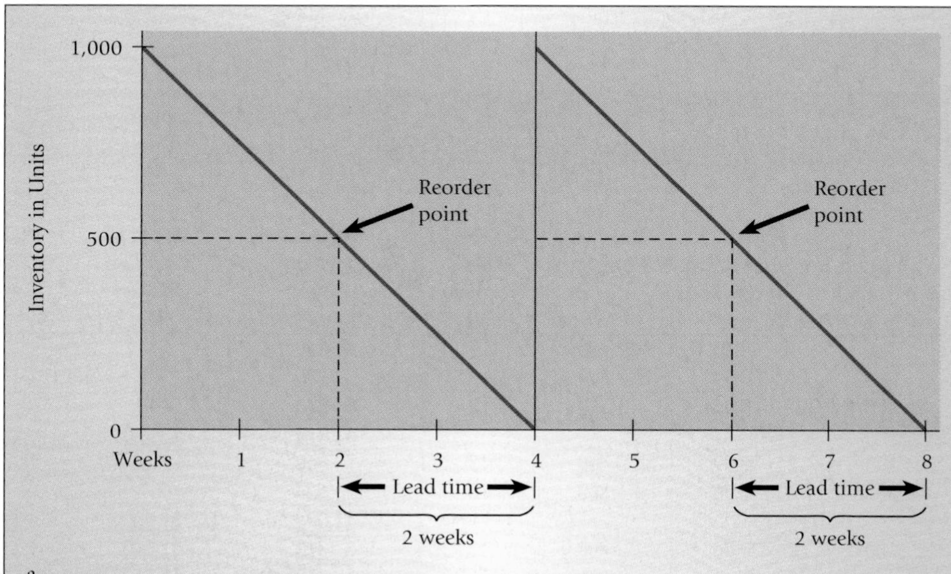

[a]This exhibit assumes that demand and purchase-order lead time are certain:
Demand = 250 tape packages per week
Purchase-order lead time = 2 weeks

[1]This handy but special formula does not apply when receipt of the order fails to increase inventory to the reorder-point quantity (for example, when lead time is three weeks and the order is a one-week supply). In these cases, orders will overlap.

A frequency distribution based on prior daily or weekly levels of demand forms the basis for computing safety-stock levels. Assume that one of the following levels of demand will occur over the two-week purchase-order lead time at Video Galore.

Total Demand for 2 Weeks	200 Units	300 Units	400 Units	500 Units	600 Units	700 Units	800 Units
Probability (sums to 1.00)	0.06	0.09	0.20	0.30	0.20	0.09	0.06

We see that 500 units is the most likely level of demand for two weeks because it has the highest probability of occurrence. We see also a 0.35 probability that demand will be 600, 700, or 800 packages (0.20 + 0.09 + 0.06 = 0.35).

In the Video Galore example, stockout costs include only the cost of rush orders, because rush orders are assumed to fully satisfy customer demand. However, stockouts can result in opportunity costs—lost contribution margin on lost current sales and lost future sales.

If a customer wants to buy videotapes and the store has none in stock, Video Galore can "rush" them to the customer at an additional cost to Video Galore of $4 per package. The relevant stockout costs in this case are $4 per package. The optimal safety-stock level is the quantity of safety stock that minimizes the sum of annual relevant stockout and carrying costs. Note that Video Galore will place 13 orders per year and will incur the same ordering costs whatever level of safety stock it chooses. Therefore, ordering costs are irrelevant for the safety-stock decision. Recall that the relevant carrying cost for Video Galore is $5.20 per unit per year.

Exhibit 20-3 tabulates annual relevant total stockout and carrying costs when the reorder point is 500 units. We need only consider safety-stock levels of 0, 100, 200, and 300 units, because demand will exceed the 500 units of stock available at reordering by 0 if demand is 500, by 100 if demand is 600, by 200 if demand is 700, and by 300 if demand is 800. As Exhibit 20-3 shows, annual relevant total stockout and carrying costs would be the lowest ($1,352) when a safety stock of 200 packages is maintained. Therefore, 200 units is the optimal safety-stock level. Consider the 200 units of safety stock as extra stock that Video Galore maintains. For example, Video Galore's total inventory of videotapes at the time of reordering its EOQ of 1,000 units would be 700 units (the reorder point of 500 units plus safety stock of 200 units).

When calculating safety stock, the trade-off is between stockout costs and carrying costs. Columns 7 and 8 in Exhibit 20-3 illustrate this trade-off.

EXHIBIT 20-3 **Computation of Safety Stock for Video Galore When Reorder Point Is 500 Units**

	A	B	C	D	E	F	G	H	I
1	Safety	Demand							
2	Stock	Levels			Relevant	Number of	Expected	Relevant	Relevant
3	Level	Resulting	Stockout	Probability	Stockout	Orders	Stockout	Carrying	Total
4	in Units	in Stockouts	in Units[a]	of Stockout	Costs[b]	per Year[c]	Costs[d]	Costs[e]	Costs
5	(1)	(2)	(3) = (2) - 500 - (1)	(4)	(5) = (3) x $4	(6)	(7) = (4) x (5) x (6)	(8) = (1) x $5.20	(9) = (7) + (8)
6	0	600	100	0.20	$ 400	13	$1,040		
7		700	200	0.09	800	13	936		
8		800	300	0.06	1,200	13	936		
9							$2,912	$ 0	$2,912
10	100	700	100	0.09	400	13	$ 468		
11		800	200	0.06	800	13	624		
12							$1,092	$ 520	$1,612
13	200	800	100	0.06	400	13	$ 312	$1,040	$1,352
14	300	-	-	-	-	-	$ 0[f]	$1,560	$1,560
15									
16	[a]Demand level resulting in stockouts – Inventory available during lead time (excluding safety stock), 500 units – Safety stock.								
17	[b]Stockout in units × Relevant stockout costs of $4.00 per unit.								
18	[c]Annual demand, 13,000 ÷ 1,000 EOQ = 13 orders per year.								
19	[d]Probability of stockout × Relevant stockout costs × Number of orders per year.								
20	[e]Safety stock × Annual relevant carrying costs of $5.20 per unit (assumes that safety stock is on hand at all times and that there is no overstocking								
21	caused by decreases in expected usage).								
22	[f]At a safety stock level of 300 units, no stockouts will occur and, hence, expected stockout costs = $0.								

Estimating Inventory-Related Relevant Costs and Their Effects

As in earlier chapters, we need to determine which costs are relevant when making and evaluating inventory-management decisions. We next describe the estimates that need to be made to calculate the annual relevant carrying costs of inventory, stockout costs, and ordering costs.

Considerations in Obtaining Estimates of Relevant Costs

Relevant inventory carrying costs consist of the *relevant incremental costs* plus the *relevant opportunity cost of capital*.

What are the *relevant incremental costs* of carrying inventory? Only those costs of the purchasing company—for example, warehouse rent, warehouse workers' salaries, costs of obsolescence, costs of shrinkage, and costs of breakage—that change with the quantity of inventory held. Salaries paid to clerks, stockkeepers, and materials handlers are irrelevant if they are unaffected by changes in inventory levels. Suppose, however, that as inventories increase (decrease), total salary costs increase (decrease) as clerks, stockkeepers, and materials handlers are added (transferred to other activities or laid off). In this case, salaries paid are relevant costs of carrying inventory. Similarly, costs of storage space owned that cannot be used for other profitable purposes when inventories decrease are irrelevant. But if the space has other profitable uses, or if total rental cost is tied to the amount of space occupied, storage costs are relevant costs of carrying inventory.

What is the *relevant opportunity cost of capital*? It is the return forgone by investing capital in inventory rather than elsewhere. It is calculated as the required rate of return multiplied by the per-unit costs that (a) vary with the number of units purchased and (b) are incurred at the time the units are received. (Examples of these per-unit costs are the price of units purchased, incoming freight, and incoming inspection.) Opportunity costs are not computed on investments (say, in buildings) if these investments are unaffected by changes in inventory levels.

Finance courses explain how to estimate the cost of capital.

In the case of stockouts, calculating the relevant opportunity cost requires an estimate of lost contribution margin on sales lost because of a stockout, as well as lost contribution margin on future sales lost because of customer ill will resulting from the stockout.

Relevant ordering costs are only those ordering costs that change with the number of orders placed (for example, costs of preparing and issuing purchase orders and receiving and inspecting materials).

Cost of a Prediction Error

Predicting relevant costs is difficult and seldom flawless, which raises the question, What is the cost when actual relevant costs differ from the estimated relevant costs used for decision making?

Let's revisit the Video Galore example. Suppose relevant ordering costs per purchase order are \$100, instead of the \$200 estimate we used earlier. We can calculate the cost of this "prediction" error using a three-step approach.

Step 1: Compute the Monetary Outcome from the Best Action That Could Be Taken, Given the *Actual* Amount of the Cost Input (Cost per Purchase Order). Using D = 13,000 packages, P = \$100, and C = \$5.20,

$$EOQ = \sqrt{\frac{2DP}{C}}$$

$$= \sqrt{\frac{2 \times 13{,}000 \times \$100}{\$5.20}} = \sqrt{500{,}000}$$

$$= 707 \text{ packages (rounded)}$$

Annual relevant total costs when EOQ = 707 packages are:

$$RTC = \frac{DP}{Q} + \frac{QC}{2}$$

$$= \frac{13{,}000 \times \$100}{707} + \frac{707 \times \$5.20}{2}$$

$$= \$1{,}839 + \$1{,}838 = \$3{,}677$$

Step 2: Compute the Monetary Outcome from the Best Action Based on the Incorrect Amount of the *Predicted* Cost Input (Cost per Purchase Order). When the relevant ordering cost per purchase order is predicted to be \$200, the best action is to purchase 1,000 packages in each order (p. 693). Annual relevant total costs using this order quantity when D = 13,000 packages, P = \$100, and C = \$5.20 are:

$$RTC = \frac{13{,}000 \times \$100}{1{,}000} + \frac{1{,}000 \times \$5.20}{2}$$

$$= \$1{,}300 + \$2{,}600 = \$3{,}900$$

Step 3: Compute the Difference Between the Monetary Outcomes from Step 1 and Step 2.

	Monetary Outcome
Step 1	\$3,677
Step 2	3,900
Difference	\$ (223)

The cost of the prediction error, \$223, is less than 7% of the relevant total costs of \$3,677. Note that the annual relevant-total-costs curve in Exhibit 20-1 is somewhat flat over the range of order quantities from 650 to 1,300 units. *The square root in the EOQ model reduces the sensitivity of the ordering decision to errors in predicting its parameters.*

In the next section, we consider a planning-and-control and performance-evaluation issue that frequently arises when managing inventory.

Conflict Between the EOQ Decision Model and Managers' Performance Evaluation

3

Identify and reduce conflicts that can arise between the EOQ decision model and models used for performance evaluation

. . . so managers can take actions that are in the best interest of the company as a whole

What happens if the order quantity calculated based on the EOQ decision model differs from the order quantity that managers making inventory-management decisions would choose to make their own performance look best? For example, because there are no opportunity costs recorded in financial accounting systems, conflicts may arise between the EOQ model's optimal order quantity and the order quantity that purchasing managers (who are evaluated on financial accounting numbers) will regard as optimal. As a result of ignoring some carrying costs (the opportunity costs), managers will be inclined to purchase larger lot sizes of materials than the lot sizes calculated according to the EOQ model. To achieve congruence between the EOQ decision model and managers' performance evaluations, companies such as Wal-Mart design performance-evaluation models that charge managers responsible for managing inventory levels with carrying costs that include a required return on investment.

Just-in-Time Purchasing

Just-in-time (JIT) purchasing is the purchase of materials (or goods) so that they are delivered just as needed for production (or sales). Consider JIT purchasing for Hewlett-Packard's (HP's) manufacture of computer printers. HP has long-term agreements with suppliers for the major components of its printers. Each supplier is required to make frequent deliveries of small orders directly to the production floor, based on the production schedule that HP gives its suppliers. Because HP holds very little inventory, a supplier who does not deliver components on time, or who delivers components that fail to meet agreed-upon quality standards, can cause an HP assembly plant not to meet its own scheduled deliveries for printers. Suppliers may sometimes fail to deliver products on time because of scheduling problems in their own plants, work stoppages, a strike, or contractual disputes. Generally, however, suppliers work hard to keep their commitments in order to build productive, long-term relationships with their customers.

JIT Purchasing and EOQ Model Parameters

Companies moving toward JIT purchasing to reduce their costs of carrying inventories (parameter C in the EOQ model) say that, in the past, carrying costs have actually been much greater than estimated because costs of warehousing, handling, shrinkage, and capital have not been fully identified. At the same time, the cost of placing a purchase order (parameter P in the EOQ model) is decreasing because:

- Companies are establishing long-term purchasing agreements that define price and quality terms over an extended period. Individual purchase orders covered by those agreements require no additional negotiation regarding price or quality.
- Companies are using electronic links, such as the Internet, to place purchase orders at a cost that is estimated to be a small fraction of the cost of placing orders by telephone or by mail.
- Companies are using purchase-order cards (similar to consumer credit cards such as VISA and MasterCard). As long as purchasing personnel stay within preset total and individual-transaction dollar limits, traditional labor-intensive procurement-approval procedures are not required.

Exhibit 20-4 tabulates the sensitivity of Video Galore's EOQ (p. 693) to changes in carrying and ordering costs. Exhibit 20-4 supports JIT purchasing because, as relevant carrying costs increase and relevant ordering costs per purchase order decrease, EOQ decreases and ordering frequency increases.

Relevant Costs of JIT Purchasing

JIT purchasing is not guided solely by the EOQ model. The EOQ model is designed only to emphasize the trade-off between relevant carrying and ordering costs. However, inventory management also includes purchasing costs, stockout costs, and quality costs. We next present the calculation of relevant costs in a JIT purchasing decision.

Video Galore has recently established an Internet business-to-business purchase-order link with Sontek. Video Galore triggers a purchase order for videotapes by a single computer entry. Payments are made electronically for batches of deliveries, rather than for each individual delivery. These changes reduce the ordering cost from $200 to only $2 per purchase order! Video Galore will use the Internet purchase-order link whether or not it shifts to JIT purchasing. Video Galore is negotiating to have Sontek deliver 100 packages of videotapes 130 times per year (5 times every 2 weeks), instead of delivering 1,000 packages 13 times per year, as shown in Exhibit 20-1. Sontek is willing to make these frequent deliveries, but it would add $0.02 to the price per videotape. Video Galore's required rate of return on investment remains at 15%. Assume the annual relevant carrying cost of insurance, materials handling, shrinkage, breakage, and the like remains at $3.10 per package per year.

EXHIBIT 20-4

Sensitivity of EOQ to Variations in Relevant Ordering and Carrying Costs for Video Galore

	A	B	C	D	E
1	**Relevant Carrying**	**Annual Demand (D) =**		**13,000**	**units**
2	**Costs per Package**	**Relevant Ordering Costs per Purchase Order (P)**			
3	**per Year (C)**	**$200**	**$150**	**$100**	**$30**
4	$ 5.20	EOQ = 1,000	EOQ = 866	EOQ = 707	EOQ = 387
5	7.00	862	746	609	334
6	10.00	721	624	510	279
7	15.00	589	510	416	228

EXHIBIT 20-5

Annual Relevant Costs
of Current Purchasing
Policy and JIT
Purchasing Policy for
Video Galore

	A	B	C
1		Relevant Costs Under	
2		Current	JIT
3		Purchasing	Purchasing
4	**Relevant Item**	**Policy**	**Policy**
5	Purchasing costs		
6	$14 per unit × 13,000 units per year	$182,000	
7	$14.02 per unit × 13,000 units per year		$182,260
8	Ordering costs		
9	$2 per order × 13 orders per year	26	
10	$2 per order × 130 orders per year		260
11	Opportunity carrying costs, required return on investment		
12	0.15 per year × $14 cost per unit × 500[a] units of average inventory per year	1,050	
13	0.15 per year × $14.02 cost per unit × 50[b] units of average inventory per year		105
14	Other carrying costs (insurance, materials handling, breakage, and so on)		
15	$3.10 per unit per year × 500[a] units of average inventory per year	1,550	
16	$3.10 per unit per year × 50[b] units of average inventory per year		155
17	Stockout costs		
18	No stockouts	0	
19	$4 per unit × 150 units per year		600
20	Total annual relevant costs	$184,626	$183,380
21	Annual difference in favor of JIT purchasing	▲ $1,246 ▲	
22			
23	[a]Order quantity ÷ 2 = 1,000 ÷ 2 = 500.		
24	[b]Order quantity ÷ 2 = 100 ÷ 2 = 50.		

Also assume that Video Galore incurs no stockout costs under its *current* purchasing policy, because demand and purchase-order lead times during each four-week period are known with certainty. Video Galore is concerned that lower inventory levels from implementing JIT purchasing will lead to more stockouts. That's because demand variations and delays in supplying videotapes are more likely in the short time intervals between orders delivered under JIT purchasing. Sontek has flexible manufacturing processes that enable it to respond rapidly to changing demand patterns. Nevertheless, Video Galore expects to incur stockout costs on 150 videotape packages per year under the JIT purchasing policy. When a stockout occurs, Video Galore must rush-order videotape packages from another supplier at an additional cost of $4 per package. Should Video Galore implement the JIT purchasing option of 130 deliveries per year? Exhibit 20-5 compares Video Galore's relevant costs under the current purchasing policy and the JIT policy, and it shows net cost savings of $1,246 per year by shifting to a JIT purchasing policy.

Supplier Evaluation and Relevant Costs of Quality and Timely Deliveries

When evaluating and choosing suppliers, quality and on-time delivery become increasingly important as the emphasis shifts away from minimizing purchasing costs to minimizing costs across the entire value chain.

Companies that implement JIT purchasing choose their suppliers carefully and develop long-run supplier relationships. Some suppliers are better positioned than others to support JIT purchasing. For example, Frito-Lay, a supplier of potato chips and other snack foods, makes more-frequent deliveries to retail outlets than many of its competitors. The company's corporate strategy emphasizes service, consistency, freshness, and quality of the delivered products.

What are the relevant costs when choosing suppliers? Consider again Video Galore. Denton Corporation, another supplier of videotapes, offers to supply all of Video Galore's videotape needs at a price of $13.80 per package—less than Sontek's price of $14.02—under the same JIT delivery terms that Sontek offers. Denton proposes an Internet purchase-order link identical to Sontek's link, making Video Galore's ordering cost $2 per purchase order. Video Galore's relevant cost of insurance, materials handling, breakage, and the like would be $3.00 per package per year if it purchases from Denton, versus $3.10 if it purchases from Sontek. Should Video Galore buy from Denton? To answer, we need to consider the relevant costs of quality and delivery performance.

EXHIBIT 20-6

Annual Relevant Costs of Purchasing from Sontek and Denton

	A	B	C
1		**Relevant Costs of Purchasing from**	
2	**Relevant Item**	**Sontek**	**Denton**
3	Purchasing costs		
4	$14.02 per unit × 13,000 units per year	$182,260	
5	$13.80 per unit × 13,000 units per year		$179,400
6	Ordering costs		
7	$2 per order × 130 orders per year	260	
8	$2 per order × 130 orders per year		260
9	Inspection costs		
10	No inspection necessary	0	
11	$0.05 per unit × 13,000 units		650
12	Opportunity carrying costs, required return on investment		
13	0.15 per year × $14.02 × 50[a] units of average inventory per year	105	
14	0.15 per year × $13.80 × 50[a] units of average inventory per year		103
15	Other carrying costs (insurance, materials handling, breakage, etc.)		
16	$3.10 per unit per year × 50[a] units of average inventory per year	155	
17	$3.00 per unit per year × 50[a] units of average inventory per year		150
18	Stockout costs		
19	$4 per unit × 150 units per year	600	
20	$4 per unit × 360 units per year		1,440
21	Customer returns costs		
22	No customer returns	0	
23	$10 per unit returned × 2.5% units returned × 13,000 units		3,250
24	Total annual relevant costs	$183,380	$185,253
25	Annual difference in favor of Sontek	↑ $1,873	↑
26			
27	[a]Order quantity ÷ 2 = 100 ÷ 2 = 50.		

Video Galore has used Sontek in the past and knows that Sontek will deliver quality videotapes on time. In fact, Video Galore does not even inspect the videotape packages that Sontek supplies and therefore incurs zero inspection costs. Denton, however, does not enjoy such a sterling reputation for quality. Video Galore anticipates the following negative aspects of using Denton:

- Inspection cost of $0.05 per package.
- Average stockouts of 360 packages per year requiring rush orders at an additional cost of $4 per package.
- Product returns of 2.5% of all packages sold due to poor videotape quality. Video Galore estimates an additional cost of $10 to handle each returned package.

Exhibit 20-6 shows the relevant costs of purchasing from Sontek and Denton. Even though Denton is offering a lower price per package, there is a net cost savings of $1,873 per year by purchasing videotapes from Sontek. Selling Sontek's high-quality videotapes also enhances Video Galore's reputation and increases customer goodwill, which could lead to higher sales and profitability in the future.

JIT Purchasing, Planning and Control, and Supply-Chain Analysis

4 **Use a supply-chain approach to inventory management**

. . . by coordinating the flow of inventory and information from initial sources of materials to delivery of products to consumers

The levels of inventories held by retailers are influenced by the demand patterns of their customers and supply relationships with their distributors and manufacturers, the suppliers to their manufacturers, and so on. *Supply chain* describes the flow of goods, services, and information from the initial sources of materials and services to the delivery of products to consumers, regardless of whether those activities occur in the same organization or in other organizations. Retailers should purchase inventories on a JIT basis only if activities throughout the supply chain are properly planned, coordinated, and controlled.

Procter and Gamble's (P&G) experience with its Pampers product illustrates the gains from supply-chain coordination. Retailers selling Pampers encountered variability in weekly demand because families purchased disposable diapers randomly.

Anticipating even more demand variability and lacking information about available inventory with P&G, retailers, orders to P&G became more variable. Trade promotions made the situation worse because retailers took advantage of lower prices to stock up for the future. Similarly, the high variability of orders at P&G translated into more variability of orders at P&G's suppliers. This resulted in high levels of inventory at all stages in the supply chain.

So how did P&G respond to these problems? By sharing information and planning and coordinating activities throughout the supply chain. The retailers began to share daily sales information about Pampers with P&G and P&G's suppliers. Sharing sales information reduced the level of uncertainty that P&G and its suppliers had about retail demand for Pampers. This reduction in demand uncertainty, combined with the sharing of inventory data throughout the supply chain, led to (1) fewer stockouts at the retail level, (2) reduced manufacture of Pampers not immediately needed by retailers, (3) fewer manufacturing orders that had to be "rushed" or "expedited," and (4) lower inventories held by each company in the supply-chain. The benefits of supply chain coordination at P&G have been so great that retailers such as Wal-Mart have contracted with P&G to manage Wal-Mart's retail inventories on a just-in-time basis. This practice is called *supplier- or vendor-managed inventory*. Supply-chain management, however, is not without its challenges (see Global Surveys of Company Practice, p. 703).

We now turn our attention to inventory management in manufacturing companies. Managers at manufacturing companies have also developed numerous systems to plan and implement production and inventory activities within their plants. We consider two widely used types of systems: materials requirements planning (MRP) and just-in-time (JIT) production.

Inventory Management and MRP

5

Distinguish materials requirements planning (MRP) systems

. . . manufacturing products based on demand forecasts

from just-in-time (JIT) systems for manufacturing

. . . manufacturing products only upon receiving customer orders

Materials requirements planning (MRP) is a "push-through" system that manufactures finished goods for inventory on the basis of demand forecasts. MRP uses (1) demand forecasts for final products; (2) a bill of materials detailing the materials, components, and subassemblies for each final product; and (3) the quantities of materials, components, and product inventories to determine the necessary outputs at each stage of production. Taking into account the lead time required to purchase materials and to manufacture components and finished products, a master production schedule specifies the quantity and timing of each item to be produced. Once production starts as scheduled, the output of each department is pushed through the production line whether or not it is needed. This "push through" can sometimes result in an accumulation of inventory when workstations receive work they are not yet ready to process.

Inventory management is a challenge in an MRP system. One reason for unsuccessful attempts to implement MRP systems has been a failure to collect and update inventory records. The management accountant aids in MRP by maintaining accurate records of inventory and its costs. For example, after becoming aware of the full costs of carrying finished goods inventory, National Semiconductor contracted with Federal Express to airfreight its microchips from a central location in Singapore to customer sites worldwide, instead of storing products at geographically dispersed warehouses. The change enabled National to move products from plant to customer in 4 days rather than 45 days and to reduce distribution costs from 2.6% to 1.9% of revenues. These benefits subsequently led National to outsource all its shipping activities to Federal Express, including shipments between its own plants in the United States, Scotland, and Malaysia.

The management accountant must also estimate setup costs and downtime costs for production runs. *Costs of setting up a production run are analogous to ordering costs in the EOQ model.* When the costs of setting up machines are high—as in the case of a blast furnace in a steel mill—processing larger batches of materials and incurring larger inventory carrying costs is cheaper because it reduces the number of setups that must be made. Similarly, when the downtime costs are high, there are sizable benefits from maintaining continuous production.

MRP is a push-through approach. We now consider JIT production, a "demand-pull" approach, which is used by companies such as Toyota in the automobile industry, Dell in the computer industry, and Braun in the appliance industry.

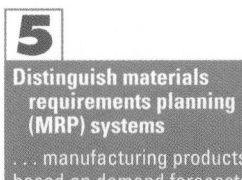

GLOBAL SURVEYS OF COMPANY PRACTICE

Challenges in Securing the Benefits of Supply-Chain Management

Supply-chain studies of inventory management reported in the business press frequently cite a wide range of benefits to both manufacturers and retailers. These benefits include fewer stockouts, reduced manufacture of items not subsequently demanded at the retail level, a reduction in rushed manufacturing orders, and lower inventory levels. One recent survey found that 78% of global managers identified the supply-chain function as "very important" or "somewhat important" to their organization's business strategy.[a]

Despite this critical role, many challenges plague effective supply-chain management. Principal among these challenges is receiving and sharing accurate, timely, and relevant information. When asked to rate the accuracy and timeliness of their supply chain's performance information, North American, European, and Asian companies responded as follows:

	North America	Europe	Asia
Exceeds expectations	1.5%	0.0%	9.7%
Meets expectations	43.9%	57.5%	67.7%
Below expectations	48.5%	32.5%	19.4%
Far below expectations	6.1%	10.0%	3.2%

Another survey of 220 retailers and manufacturers highlights some key issues that companies must address to benefit from adopting a supply-chain approach to inventory management.[b] Manufacturers gave the following rankings (in terms of importance) about the information they would like to receive from retailers stocking their products:

1. Retail sales forecasts for the products
2. Sales information on the products (such as daily sales at each retail outlet)
3. Pricing and advertising strategies of the retailer
4. Inventory levels at each retail outlet

A second issue is reducing the obstacles to manufacturers and retailers achieving the benefits of a supply-chain approach. Respondents cited the following obstacles:

1. Communication obstacles—including the unwillingness of some parties to share information
2. Trust obstacles—including the concern that all parties will not meet their agreed-upon commitments
3. Information-systems obstacles—including problems because of the information systems of different parties not being technically compatible
4. Limited resources—including problems related to the people and financial resources given to support a supply-chain initiative not being adequate

Adopting a supply-chain approach requires diverse organizations to cooperate and communicate on a broad set of issues. Respondents emphasized this challenge was not always successfully met. Not surprisingly, not all supply-chain initiatives have delivered the initially met projected financial and operating benefits.

[a] ITtoolbox/Oracle, "2004 ITtoolbox Supply."

[b] Research Incorporated, "Synchronizing the Supply Chain."

Full citations are in Appendix A at the end of the book.

Inventory Management and JIT Production

6

Identify the features of a just-in-time production system

. . . for example, organizing work in manufacturing cells, improving quality, reducing manufacturing lead time

Just-in-time (JIT) production, which is also called **lean production**, is a "demand-pull" manufacturing system that manufactures each component in a production line as soon as, and only when, needed by the next step in the production line. In a JIT production line, manufacturing activity at any particular workstation is prompted by the need for that workstation's output at the following workstation. Demand triggers each step of the production process, starting with customer demand for a finished product at the end of the process and working all the way back to the demand for direct materials at the beginning of the process. In this way, demand pulls an order through the production line. The demand-pull feature of JIT production systems achieves close coordination among workstations. It smooths the flow of goods, despite low quantities of inventory. JIT production systems aim to simultaneously (1) meet customer demand in a timely way (2) with high-quality products and (3) at the lowest possible total cost.

A JIT production system has these features:

- Production is organized in **manufacturing cells**, a grouping of all the different types of equipment used to make a given product. Materials move from one machine to another, and various operations are performed in sequence, minimizing materials-handling costs.
- Workers are hired and trained to be multiskilled and capable of performing a variety of operations and tasks, including minor repairs and routine maintenance of equipment.
- Defects are aggressively eliminated. Because of the tight links between workstations in the production line and the minimal inventories at each workstation, defects arising at one workstation quickly affect other workstations in the line. JIT creates an urgency for solving problems immediately and eliminating the root causes of defects as quickly as possible. Low levels of inventories allow workers to trace problems to and solve problems at earlier workstations in the production process, where the problems likely originated.
- *Setup time*—the time required to get equipment, tools, and materials ready to start the production of a component or product—is reduced. Simultaneously, *manufacturing lead time*—the time from when an order is received by manufacturing until it becomes a finished good—is also reduced. Reducing setup time makes production in smaller batches economical, which in turn reduces inventory levels. Reducing manufacturing lead time enables a company to respond faster to changes in customer demand (see Concepts in Action, p. 705).
- Suppliers are selected on the basis of their ability to deliver quality materials in a timely manner. Most companies implementing *JIT production* also implement *JIT purchasing*. JIT plants expect JIT suppliers to make timely deliveries of high-quality goods directly to the production floor.

Effect of JIT Systems on Product Costing

By reducing materials handling, warehousing, and inspection, JIT systems reduce overhead costs. JIT systems also aid in direct tracing of some costs usually classified as indirect. For example, the use of manufacturing cells makes it cost effective to trace materials handling and machine operating costs to specific products or product families made in these cells. These costs then become direct costs of those products. Also, the use of multiskilled workers in these cells allows the costs of setup, maintenance, and quality inspection to be traced as direct costs.

We next present a relevant-cost analysis for deciding whether to implement a JIT production system.

Financial Benefits of JIT and Relevant Costs

Early advocates saw the benefit of JIT production as lower carrying costs of inventory. But there are other benefits of lower inventories: heightened emphasis on improving quality by eliminating the specific causes of rework, scrap, and waste, and lower manufacturing lead times. In computing the relevant benefits and costs of reducing inventories in JIT production systems, the cost analyst should take into account all benefits and all costs.

Consider Hudson Corporation, a manufacturer of brass fittings. Hudson is considering implementing a JIT production system. To implement JIT production, Hudson must incur $100,000 in annual tooling costs to reduce setup times. Hudson expects that JIT will reduce average inventory by $500,000 and that relevant costs of insurance, storage, materials handling, and setup will decline by $30,000 per year. The company's required rate of return on inventory investments is 10% per year. Should Hudson implement a JIT production system? On the basis of the information provided, we would be tempted to say no. That's because annual relevant cost savings in carrying costs amount to $80,000 [(10% of $500,000) + $30,000)], which is less than the additional annual tooling costs of $100,000.

CONCEPTS IN ACTION

After the Encore: Just-in-Time Live Concert CDs

Each year, hundreds of thousands of rock music fans flock to Dave Matthews Band concerts. Although many of them stop by the merchandise stand to pick up a T-shirt or poster after the show ends, soon they will have another option . . . buying a multiple-CD set that contains a professional recording of the entire concert they just saw! Just-in-time production, enabled by recent advances in digital audio and CD-burning technology, now allows fans to relive the live concert experience, as soon as 10 minutes after the final chord is played!

Live concert recordings have long been hampered by production and distribution difficulties. Traditionally, fans could only hear these recordings via unofficial "bootleg" cassettes or CDs. Although some musical acts—ranging from John Mayer to U2—have at times allowed fans to tape their shows, amateur recording devices produced poor sound quality and copies that fans could acquire only through informal trading networks. Artists and record labels also received no compensation for their copyrighted work. Occasionally, artists would release official live albums between studio releases. But due to the remastering and album-production process, these recordings took months, if not years, to reach fans. Further, live albums typically sold few copies, and retail outlets that profit from volume-driven merchandise turnover were somewhat reluctant to carry them.

Enter instant concert recordings. Clear Channel Entertainment's *Instant Live* subsidiary, for example, employs a process consisting of microphones, recording and audio mixing hardware and software, and an army of high-speed CD burners to produce concert recordings during the show. As soon as each song is complete, *Instant Live* engineers burn that track onto hundreds of CDs. At the end of the show, they only have to burn one last song on each CD. Once completed, the CD sets are packaged and rushed to merchandise stands throughout the venue for instant sale. And sell they have! During *Instant Live's* initial testing, up to 20% of concertgoers bought these CDs, to the tune of $15 to $30 each. The artists got $6 to $8 from each CD sold, with the remaining money split between the record label, the concert venue, and the recording company. With a captive audience, Berklee College of Music professor Don Jordan notes, "It is almost an impulse buy. You had a great feeling coming out of it and . . . you can put it on again any time you want."

There are, of course, some limitations to this technology. With such a quick turnaround time, engineers cannot edit or remaster any aspect of the show. Therefore, any mistake during the show remains on the final CD. Also, although just-in-time live recordings work successfully in smaller venues, the logistics for arenas, amphitheatres, and stadiums are much more difficult. Dozens of additional employees and hundreds of costly, top-of-the-line CD burners are needed to meet the demands of larger crowds.

Despite these concerns, the benefits of this new technology include sound-quality assurance, near-immediate production turnaround, and low finished-goods carrying costs. Further, these recordings can also be distributed through retailers and artist Web sites. In 2001, Pearl Jam sold all 72 shows of its 2000 world tour through retail outlets, while the Vermont-based group Phish made every 2003 show available on its Web site for download, selling more than 150,000 recordings and grossing $1.2 million. With such an opportunity, it's no wonder that artists ranging from Incubus to Jimmy Buffett—and Dave Matthews Band—are planning to augment their existing CD sales with just-in-time recordings.

Sources: S. Chartland, "How to Take the Concert Home," *The New York Times*, May 3, 2004; S. Humphries, "Get Your Official 'Bootleg' Here," *Christian Science Monitor*, November 21, 2003; S. Knopper, "Live Discs a Hit with Fans," *Rolling Stone*, November 7, 2003; S. Galupo, "Death of the Live Concert Album?" *Washington Times*, July 9, 2004.

Our analysis, however, is incomplete. We have not considered the other benefits of lower inventories in JIT production. For example, Hudson estimates that implementing JIT will improve quality and reduce rework on 500 units each year, resulting in savings of $50 per unit. Also, better quality and faster delivery will allow Hudson to charge $2 more per unit on the 20,000 units that it sells each year. The annual relevant quality and delivery benefits from JIT and lower inventory levels equal $65,000 [(rework savings, $50/unit × 500 units) + (additional contribution margin, $2/unit × 20,000 units)]. Total annual relevant benefits and cost savings equal $145,000 ($80,000 + $65,000), which exceeds annual JIT implementation costs of $100,000. Therefore, Hudson should implement a

JIT production system. The Focus on Values and Behaviors feature on p. 707 describes some of the challenges management accountants face in valuing inventory and implementing JIT.

We next turn our attention to planning and control systems in JIT production.

Enterprise Resource Planning (ERP) Systems[2]

The success of a JIT production system hinges on the speed of information flows from customers to manufacturers to suppliers. Information flows are a problem for large companies that have fragmented information systems (for sales, manufacturing, and purchasing) spread over dozens of unlinked computer systems. The Enterprise Resource Planning (ERP) system comprises a single database that collects data and feeds it into software applications supporting all of a company's business activities. For example, using an ERP system, a salesperson can generate a contract for a customer in Germany, verify the customer's credit limits, and place a production order. The system schedules manufacturing in, say, Brazil, requisitions materials from inventory, orders components from suppliers, and schedules shipment. It also credits sales commissions to the salesperson and records all the costing and financial accounting information.

ERP systems give lower-level managers, workers, customers, and suppliers access to operating information. This benefit, coupled with tight coordination across business functions of the value chain, enables ERP systems to shift manufacturing and distribution plans rapidly in response to changes in supply and demand. Companies believe that an ERP system is essential to support JIT initiatives because of the effect it has on lead times. Using an ERP system, Autodesk, a maker of computer-aided design software, reduced order lead time from 2 weeks to 1 day; Fujitsu reduced lead time from 18 to 1.5 days. ERP systems also help in forecasting demand and in doing materials requirements planning as part of their operations and logistics modules.

Although the tight coupling of systems throughout a company streamlines administrative and financial processes and saves costs, it can also make a system large and unwieldy. Because of its complexity, suppliers of ERP systems such as SAP, Baan, Peoplesoft, and Oracle provide software packages that are standard, but that can be customized, although at considerable cost. Without some customization, unique and distinctive features that confer strategic advantage will not be available. The challenge when implementing ERP systems is to strike the right balance between standard systems and systems that for strategic reasons are designed to be unique.

Performance Measures and Control in JIT Production

Personal observation is often more effective in JIT plants than in traditional plants. That's because the production layout in a JIT plant is streamlined—for example, operations aren't obscured by piles of inventory or rework.

In addition to personal observation, the following list describes measures managers use to evaluate and control JIT production and how these measures are expected to be affected by JIT.

1. Financial performance measures, such as inventory turnover ratio (cost of goods sold ÷ average inventory), which is expected to decrease
2. Nonfinancial performance measures of time, inventory, and quality, such as:
   - Manufacturing lead time, expected to decrease
   - Units produced per hour, expected to increase
   - Number of days of inventory on hand, expected to decrease
   - $\frac{\text{Total setup time for machines}}{\text{Total manufacturing time}}$, expected to decrease
   - $\frac{\text{Number of units requiring rework or scrap}}{\text{Total number of units started and completed}}$, expected to decrease

Personal observation and nonfinancial performance measures provide the most timely, intuitive, and easy to understand measures of manufacturing performance. Rapid, meaningful feedback is critical because the lack of inventories in a demand-pull system makes it urgent to detect and solve problems quickly.

[2]For an excellent discussion, see T. H. Davenport, "Putting the Enterprise into the Enterprise System," *Harvard Business Review*, July–August 1998; Also see A. Cagilo, "Enterprise Resource Planning Systems and Accountants: Towards Hybridization?" *European Accounting Review*, May 2003.

FOCUS ON VALUES AND BEHAVIORS

CHALLENGES OF INVENTORY VALUATION AND JIT IMPLEMENTATION

Many companies have high inventory levels. Trouble erupts when companies seeking increases in income overstate inventories. El Paso Corporation, a leading provider of natural gas in North America, reported "that an outside investigation had found that some employees might have deliberately overstated oil and gas reserves and that it would need to restate five years of results . . . and take a $1 billion charge [to earnings] . . . The company said certain employees . . . provided reserve estimates that they knew, or should have known, were incorrect when they were reported." A recent survey by *CFO Magazine* found that since 2001, one-fifth of financial executives said they felt more pressure to use accounting methods to "make results appear more favorable" and that 47% have felt pressure from superiors to use aggressive accounting techniques. Recognizing the incentives managers may have to overstate inventory valuations, management accountants must pay careful attention to and correctly record both the physical quantity of inventories and values ascribed to them.

However, in other companies, such as Apple Computer, Volkswagen, Chrysler, Carrier, and IBM, inventory overstatement is not a danger because they use JIT systems and hold very little inventory. Moving to a JIT system brings on different challenges for management accountants.

To successfully implement JIT, management accountants must be comfortable working in a changing and ambiguous environment. They must also be able to balance the demands of different managers. For example, marketing managers may seek greater levels of customization and customer responsiveness that production and purchasing managers find burdensome. Management accountants must be able to recognize the diverse views and needs of a company, evaluate the economics of different options, communicate clearly, and work toward achieving a consensus.

Several of the rewards of moving to a JIT system—more-reliable deliveries to customers and greater customer responsiveness—may be difficult to quantify in the short run. Management accountants must therefore motivate their teams to focus on long-term successes. At Cessna, for example, it wasn't until its third year of using lean manufacturing for its single-engine aircraft and business jets that the company began to see productivity gains in the 40% to 60% range.

Source: *T. Damos, "CFO Pressure Cooker,"* Fortune, *June 28, 2004. H. Timmons, "El Paso Says Reserves May Have Been Falsified,"* The New York Times, *May 4, 2004, p. C14.*

The next section discusses backflush costing, which is a planning and control system that dovetails with JIT production and is less costly to operate than most traditional costing systems, which were described in Chapters 4, 7, 8, and 17.

Backflush Costing

7 **Use backflush costing**
. . . to delay recording some journal entries to later in the production and sales cycle

Organizing manufacturing in cells, reducing defects and manufacturing lead time, and ensuring timely delivery of materials, enables purchasing, production, and sales to occur in quick succession with minimal inventories. The absence of inventories makes choices about cost-flow assumptions (such as weighted-average or first-in, first-out) or inventory-costing methods (such as absorption or variable costing) unimportant: All manufacturing costs of the accounting period flow directly into cost of goods sold. The rapid conversion of direct materials into finished goods that are immediately sold greatly simplifies the costing system.

Simplified Normal or Standard Costing

Traditional normal and standard-costing systems (Chapters 4, 7, 8, and 17) use **sequential tracking**, which is a costing system in which recording of the journal entries occurs in the same order as actual purchases and progress in production. Costs are tracked sequentially as products pass through each of the following four stages:

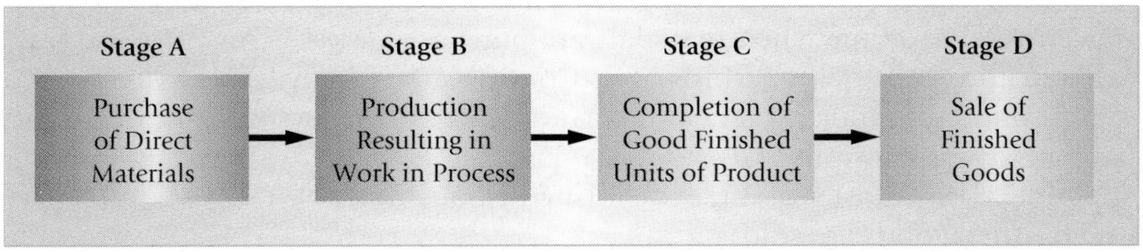

A sequential-tracking costing system has four *trigger points*, corresponding to stages A, B, C, and D. **Trigger point** refers to a stage in the cycle from purchase of direct materials (stage A) to sale of finished goods (stage D) at which journal entries are made in the accounting system.

An alternative approach to sequential tracking is backflush costing. **Backflush costing** is a costing system that omits recording some of the journal entries relating to the stages from purchase of direct materials to the sale of finished goods. When journal entries for one or more stages are omitted, the journal entries for a subsequent stage use normal or standard costs to work backward to "flush out" the costs in the cycle for which journal entries were *not* made. When inventories are minimal, as in JIT production systems, backflush costing simplifies the costing system without losing much information as a result of the simplification.

8

Describe different ways backflush costing can simplify traditional inventory-costing systems

. . . for example, by not recording journal entries for work in process, purchase of materials, or production of finished goods.

The following examples illustrate backflush costing. They differ in the number and placement of trigger points:

	Number of Journal-Entry Trigger Points	Location in Cycle When Journal Entries Are Made
Example 1	3	Stage A. Purchase of direct materials Stage C. Completion of good finished units of product Stage D. Sale of finished goods
Example 2	2	Stage A. Purchase of direct materials Stage D. Sale of finished goods
Example 3	2	Stage C. Completion of good finished units of product Stage D. Sale of finished goods

In all three examples, there are no journal entries in the accounting system for work in process (stage B) because JIT production results in minimal work in process.

We illustrate backflush costing using data from Silicon Valley Computer (SVC), which produces keyboards for personal computers. We assume the following information for SVC for the month of April.

- There are no beginning inventories of direct materials. Moreover, there is zero beginning and ending work in process.
- SVC has only one direct manufacturing cost category (direct materials) and one indirect manufacturing cost category (conversion costs). All manufacturing labor costs are included in conversion costs.
- From its bill of materials and an operations list (description of operations to be undergone), SVC determines that the standard direct material cost per keyboard unit is \$19 and the standard conversion cost is \$12.
- SVC purchases \$1,950,000 of direct materials. To focus on the basic concepts, we assume SVC has no direct materials variances. Actual conversion costs equal \$1,260,000. SVC produces 100,000 good keyboard units and sells 99,000 units.
- Any underallocated or overallocated conversion costs are written off to cost of goods sold at the end of April.

Example 1: Trigger points at purchase of direct materials (stage A), completion of good finished units of product (stage C), and sale of finished goods (stage D) In this example, SVC has two inventory accounts:

Type	Account Title
Combined materials inventory and materials in work in process	Inventory: Materials and In-Process Control
Finished goods	Finished Goods Control

Trigger point 1 occurs when materials are purchased. These costs increase (are debited to) Inventory: Materials and In-Process Control. Actual conversion costs are recorded as incurred under backflush costing, just as in other costing systems, and they increase (are debited to) Conversion Costs Control. Conversion costs are allocated to products at trigger point 2—the transfer of units to Finished Goods Control. Trigger point 3 occurs at the time finished goods are sold.

SVC uses the following steps to assign costs to units sold and to inventories.

Step 1: Record Direct Materials Purchased During the Accounting Period.

Entry (a)	Inventory: Materials and In-Process Control	1,950,000	
	Accounts Payable Control		1,950,000

This flow of costs is analogous to job costing in Chapter 4, except backflush costing bypasses the Work-in-Process Control account.

Step 2: Record Conversion Costs Incurred During the Accounting Period.

Entry (b)	Conversion Costs Control	1,260,000	
	Various accounts (such as Wages Payable Control)		1,260,000

Step 3: Determine the Number of Good Finished Units Manufactured During the Accounting Period. 100,000 good units were manufactured in April.

Step 4: Compute the Normal or Standard Cost per Finished Unit. The standard cost is \$31 (\$19 direct materials + \$12 conversion costs) per unit.

Step 5: Record the Cost of Good Finished Units Completed During the Accounting Period. 100,000 units × \$31 per unit = \$3,100,000.

Entry (c)	Finished Goods Control	3,100,000	
	Inventory: Materials and In-Process Control		1,900,000
	Conversion Costs Allocated		1,200,000

Step 5 gives backflush costing its name. Costs have not been recorded sequentially with the flow of product along its production route through work in process and finished goods. Instead, the output trigger point reaches back and pulls the standard direct material costs from Inventory: Materials and In-Process Control and the standard conversion costs for manufacturing the finished goods.

Step 6: Record the Standard Cost of Goods Sold During the Accounting Period. Standard cost of 99,000 units sold in April (99,000 units × \$31 per unit = \$3,069,000):

Entry (d)	Cost of Goods Sold	3,069,000	
	Finished Goods Control		3,069,000

Step 7: Record Underallocated or Overallocated Conversion Costs. Actual conversion costs may be underallocated or overallocated in an accounting period. Chapter 4 (pp. 119–121) discussed various ways to dispose of underallocated or overallocated manufacturing overhead costs. Companies that use backflush costing typically have low inventories, so proration of underallocated or overallocated conversion costs between finished goods and cost of goods sold is seldom necessary. Many companies write off underallocated or overallocated conversion costs to cost of goods sold only at the end of the fiscal year. Other companies, like SVC, make the write-off monthly. The journal entry to dispose of the difference between actual conversion costs incurred and standard conversion costs allocated is:

Entry (e)	Conversion Costs Allocated	1,200,000	
	Cost of Goods Sold	60,000	
	Conversion Costs Control		1,260,000

The April ending inventory balances are:

Inventory: Materials and In-Process Control (\$1,950,000 – \$1,900,000)	\$50,000
Finished Goods Control, 1,000 units × \$31/unit (\$3,100,000 – \$3,069,000)	31,000
Total	\$81,000

Exhibit 20-7, Panel A (p. 710), presents the journal entries for this example. Exhibit 20-8, Panel A (p. 711), provides a general-ledger overview of this version of backflush costing. The elimination of the typical Work-in-Process account reduces the amount of detail in the accounting system. Units on the production line may still be tracked in physical terms, but there is "no assignment of costs" to specific work orders while they are in the production cycle. In fact, there are no work orders or labor-time records in the accounting system. Champion International uses a method similar to Example 1 in its specialty papers plant.

The three trigger points to make journal entries in Example 1 will lead SVC's backflush costing system to report costs that are similar to the costs reported under sequential tracking when SVC has minimal work-in-process inventory. In Example 1, any inventories of direct materials or finished goods are recognized in SVC's backflush costing system when they first appear (as would be done in a costing system using sequential tracking).

EXHIBIT 20-7 Journal Entries in Backflush Costing

PANEL A, EXAMPLE 1: Three Trigger Points—Purchase of Direct Materials, Completion of Good Finished Units, and Sale of Finished Goods

Transactions			
(a) Purchase of direct materials[a]	Inventory: Materials and In-Process Control	1,950,000	
	Accounts Payable Control		1,950,000
(b) Incur conversion costs	Conversion Costs Control	1,260,000	
	Various Accounts		1,260,000
(c) Completion of good finished units[a]	Finished Goods Control	3,100,000	
	Inventory: Materials and In-Process Control		1,900,000
	Conversion Costs Allocated		1,200,000
(d) Sale of finished goods[a]	Cost of Goods Sold	3,069,000	
	Finished Goods Control		3,069,000
(e) Underallocated or overallocated conversion costs	Conversion Costs Allocated	1,200,000	
	Cost of Goods Sold	60,000	
	Conversion Costs Control		1,260,000

PANEL B, EXAMPLE 2: Two Trigger Points—Purchase of Direct Materials and Sale of Finished Goods

Transactions			
(a) Purchase of direct materials[a]	Inventory Control	1,950,000	
	Accounts Payable Control		1,950,000
(b) Incur conversion costs	Conversion Costs Control	1,260,000	
	Various Accounts		1,260,000
(c) Completion of good finished units	No entry		
(d) Sale of finished goods[a]	Cost of Goods Sold	3,069,000	
	Inventory Control		1,881,000
	Conversion Costs Allocated		1,188,000
(e) Underallocated or overallocated conversion costs	Conversion Costs Allocated	1,188,000	
	Cost of Goods Sold	72,000	
	Conversion Costs Control		1,260,000

PANEL C, EXAMPLE 3: Two Trigger Points—Completion of Good Finished Units and Sale of Finished Goods

Transactions			
(a) Purchase of direct materials	No entry		
(b) Incur conversion costs	Conversion Costs Control	1,260,000	
	Various Accounts		1,260,000
(c) Completion of good finished units[a]	Finished Goods Control	3,100,000	
	Accounts Payable Control		1,900,000
	Conversion Costs Allocated		1,200,000
(d) Sale of finished goods[a]	Cost of Goods Sold	3,069,000	
	Finished Goods Control		3,069,000
(e) Underallocated or overallocated conversion costs	Conversion Costs Allocated	1,200,000	
	Cost of Goods Sold	60,000	
	Conversion Costs Control		1,260,000

[a] A trigger point.

Accounting for Variances

Accounting for variances between actual and standard costs is basically the same under all standard-costing systems. The procedures are described in Chapters 7 and 8. Suppose that in Example 1, we now assume SVC had an unfavorable direct materials price variance of $42,000. Then entry (a) would be:

Inventory: Materials and In-Process Control	1,950,000	
Direct Materials Price Variance	42,000	
Accounts Payable Control		1,992,000

Direct material costs are often a large proportion of total manufacturing costs, sometimes well over 60%. Consequently, many companies will at least measure the direct materials efficiency variance in total by physically comparing what remains in direct materials

EXHIBIT 20-8 General-Ledger Overview of Backflush Costing

PANEL A, EXAMPLE 1: Three Trigger Points—Purchase of Direct Materials, Completion of Finished Goods, and Sale of Finished Goods

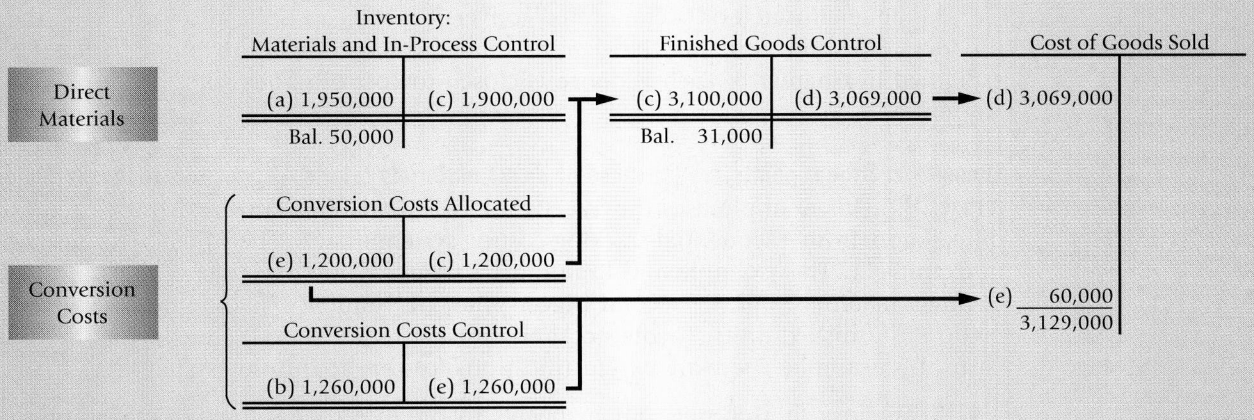

PANEL B, EXAMPLE 2: Two Trigger Points—Purchase of Direct Materials and Sale of Finished Goods

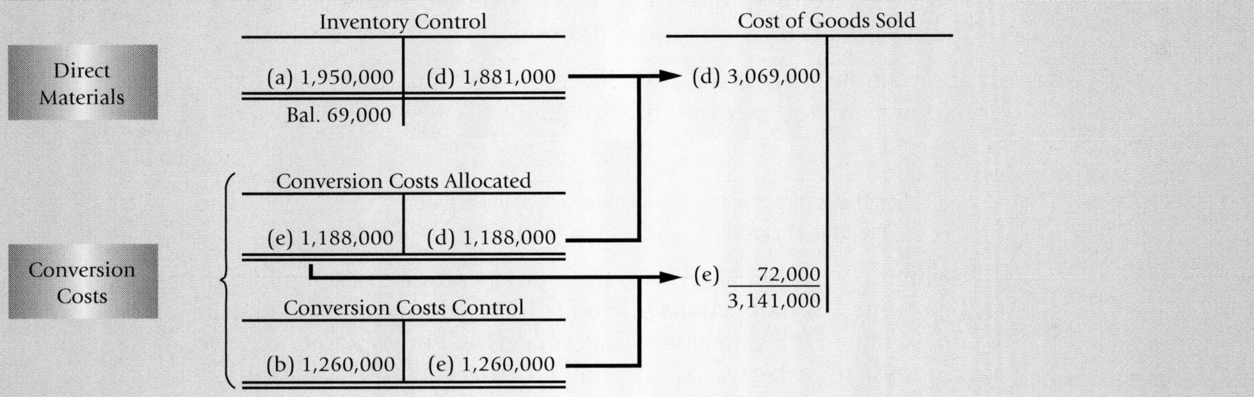

PANEL C, EXAMPLE 3: Two Trigger Points—Completion of Finished Goods and Sale of Finished Goods

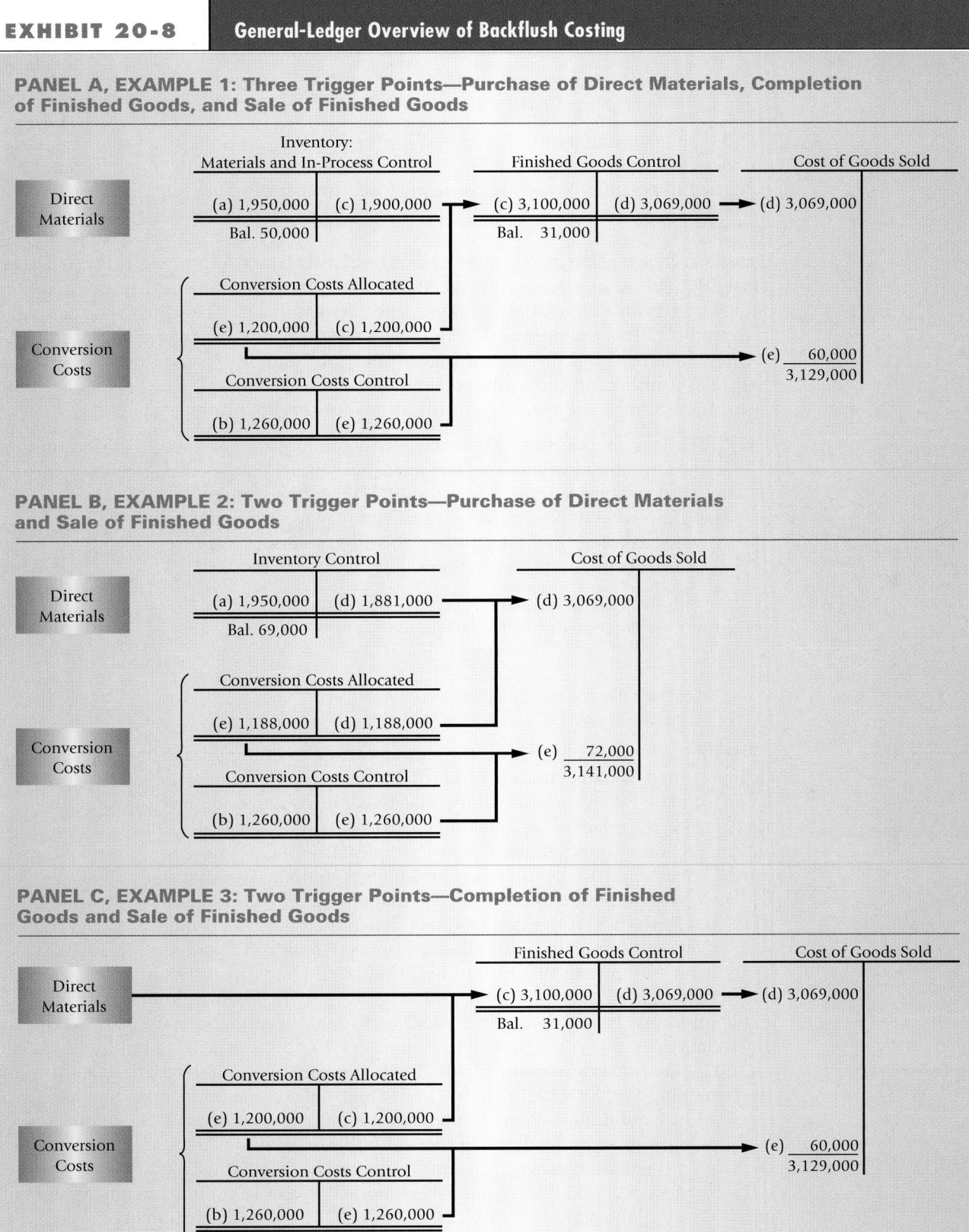

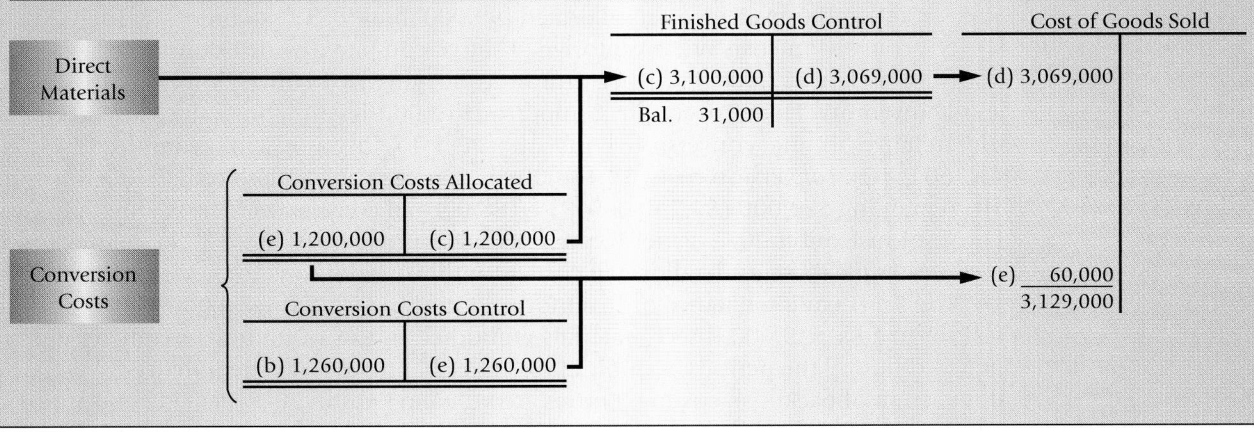

inventory against what should remain based on the output of finished goods for the accounting period. In our example, suppose that such a comparison showed an unfavorable materials efficiency variance of $30,000. The journal entry would be:

Direct Materials Efficiency Variance	30,000	
Inventory: Materials and In-Process Control		30,000

The underallocated or overallocated conversion costs are split into various overhead variances (spending variance, efficiency variance, and production-volume variance), as explained in Chapter 8. Each variance is closed to cost of goods sold, if immaterial in amount.

Example 2: Trigger points are purchase of direct materials (stage A) and sale of finished goods (stage D) This example uses the SVC data to illustrate a backflush costing system that differs more from a sequential-tracking costing system than the backflush costing system in Example 1. This example and Example 1 have the same first trigger point, purchase of direct materials. But the second trigger point in Example 2 is the sale, not the completion, of finished units. Toyota's cost accounting system at its Kentucky plant is similar to this example. There are two justifications for this accounting system:

1. To remove the incentive for managers to produce for inventory. Because finished goods inventory includes conversion costs, managers can increase operating income by producing more units than are sold. Having trigger point 2 as the sale instead of the completion of production eliminates a manager's incentive to produce for inventory by recording conversion costs as period costs instead of inventoriable costs.
2. To get managers more focused on selling units.

In this example, there is only one inventory account: direct materials, whether they are in storerooms, in process, or in finished goods.

Type	Account Title
Combines direct materials inventory and any direct materials in work-in-process and finished goods inventories	Inventory Control

Exhibit 20-7, Panel B, presents the journal entries for Example 2. The two trigger points are represented by transactions (a) and (d). Entry (a) is prompted by the same trigger point 1 as in Example 1, the purchase of direct materials. Entry (b) for the conversion costs incurred is recorded in the same way as in Example 1. Trigger point 2 is the sale of finished goods (not the completion of finished units, as in Example 1), so there is no entry corresponding to entry (c) of Example 1. The cost of finished units is computed only when finished goods are sold [which corresponds to entry (d) of Example 1]: 99,000 units sold × $31 per unit = $3,069,000, which is comprised of direct material costs (99,000 units × $19 per unit = $1,881,000) and conversion costs allocated (99,000 units × $12 per unit = $1,188,000).

No conversion costs are inventoried. That is, compared with Example 1, Example 2 does not assign $12,000 ($12 per unit × 1,000 units) of conversion costs to finished goods inventory. Hence, Example 2 allocates $12,000 less in conversion costs to inventory relative to the conversion costs allocated to inventory in Example 1. Of the $1,260,000 in conversion costs, $1,188,000 is allocated at standard cost to the units sold. The remaining $72,000 ($1,260,000 – $1,188,000) of conversion costs is underallocated. Entry (e) in Exhibit 20-7, Panel B, presents the journal entry if SVC, like many companies, writes off these underallocated costs monthly as additions to cost of goods sold.

The April ending balance of Inventory Control is $69,000 ($50,000 direct materials still on hand + $19,000 direct materials embodied in the 1,000 units manufactured but not sold during the period). Exhibit 20-8, Panel B, provides a general-ledger overview of this version of backflush costing. Entries are keyed to Exhibit 20-7, Panel B. The approach described in Example 2 closely approximates the costs computed using sequential tracking when a company holds minimal work-in-process and finished goods inventories.

Question: Are the only journal entries in backflush costing the ones for the trigger points?

Answer: No, in addition to the trigger-point entries, journal entries must be made for conversion costs incurred and for disposing of underallocated or overallocated conversion costs.

Example 3: Trigger points are completion of good finished units of product (stage C) and sale of finished goods (stage D) This example has two trigger points. Exhibit 20-7, Panel C, presents the journal entries. In contrast to Example 2, the first trigger point in Example 3 is delayed until stage C, SVC's completion of good finished units of product. It is represented by transaction (c). Because the purchase of direct materials is not a trigger point, there is no entry corresponding to transaction (a)—purchase of direct materials. Exhibit 20-8, Panel C, provides a general-ledger overview of this version of backflush costing. Entries are keyed to Exhibit 20-7, Panel C.

Compare entry (c) in Exhibit 20-7, Panel C, with entries (a) and (c) in Exhibit 20-7, Panel A. The simpler version in Example 3 ignores the $1,950,000 purchases of direct materials [shown in entry (a) of Example 1]. At the end of April, $50,000 of direct materials purchased have not yet been placed into production ($1,950,000 − $1,900,000 = $50,000), nor have the cost of those direct materials been entered into the inventory-costing system. The Example 3 version of backflush costing is suitable for a JIT production system in which both direct materials inventory and work-in-process inventory are minimal.

Example 3 doesn't record accounts payable for direct materials until the products being manufactured are completely through the production process! As a result, this version of backflush costing is feasible only if there's a short lag between receipt of direct materials and completion of production.

Extending Example 3, backflush costing systems could use the sale of finished goods as the only trigger point. This version of backflush costing is most suitable for a JIT production system with minimal direct materials, work-in-process, and finished goods inventories. That's because this backflush costing system maintains no inventory accounts.

Study Tip: To check your understanding of the material in this chapter, see the Featured Exercise, true–false statements 5 and 6, multiple-choice questions 2 and 5, and Review Exercises 2 and 3 (*Student Guide*, beginning p. 273). Fully explained answers begin on page 279.

Special Considerations in Backflush Costing

The accounting procedures illustrated in Examples 1, 2, and 3 do not strictly adhere to generally accepted accounting principles (GAAP). For example, work in process, which is an asset, exists although it is not recognized in the financial statements. Advocates of backflush costing, however, cite the generally accepted accounting principle of materiality in support of the various versions of backflush costing. As the three examples illustrate, backflush costing can approximate the costs that would be reported under sequential tracking by varying the number of trigger points and where they are located. If significant amounts of direct materials inventory or finished goods inventory exist, adjusting entries can be incorporated into backflush costing (as explained below).

Backflush costing is not restricted to companies adopting JIT production methods. Companies that have short manufacturing lead times, or those that have very stable inventory levels from period to period, may find that a version of backflush costing will report cost numbers similar to sequential tracking.

Suppose there are material differences in operating income and inventories based on a backflush costing system and a conventional standard-costing system. An adjusting entry can be recorded to make the backflush number satisfy GAAP. For example, the backflush entries in Example 2 would result in expensing all conversion costs to Cost of Goods Sold ($1,188,000 at standard costs + $72,000 write-off of underallocated conversion costs = $1,260,000). But suppose conversion costs were regarded as sufficiently material in amount to be included in Inventory Control. Then entry (e), closing the Conversion Costs accounts, would change as follows:

Original entry (e)	Conversion Costs Allocated	1,188,000	
	Cost of Goods Sold	72,000	
	Conversion Costs Control		1,260,000
Revised entry (e)	Conversion Costs Allocated	1,188,000	
	Inventory Control (1,000 units × $12)	12,000	
	Cost of Goods Sold	60,000	
	Conversion Costs Control		1,260,000

Critics say backflush costing leaves no audit trails—the ability of the accounting system to pinpoint the uses of resources at each step of the production process. However, the absence of large amounts of materials inventory and work-in-process inventory means managers can keep track of operations by personal observations, computer monitoring, and nonfinancial measures.

What are the implications of JIT and backflush costing systems for activity-based costing (ABC) systems? Simplifying the production process, as in a JIT system, makes more of the costs direct and reduces the extent of overhead cost allocations. Simple ABC systems are often adequate for companies implementing JIT. These simple ABC systems work well with backflush costing. Costs from ABC systems yield more-accurate budgeted conversion cost per unit for different products in the backflush costing system. The activity-based cost information is also useful for product costing, decision making, and cost management.

PROBLEMS FOR SELF-STUDY

PROBLEM 1

Lee Company has a Singapore plant that manufactures MP3 players. One component is an XT chip. Expected demand is for 5,200 of these chips in March 2006. Lee estimates the ordering cost per purchase order to be $250. The monthly carrying cost for one unit of XT in stock is $5.

Required

1. Compute the EOQ for the XT chip.
2. Compute the number of deliveries of XT in March 2006.

SOLUTION

1. $EOQ = \sqrt{\dfrac{2 \times 5{,}200 \times \$250}{\$5}}$

   $= 721$ chips (rounded)

2. Number of deliveries $= \dfrac{5{,}200}{721}$

   $= 8$ (rounded)

PROBLEM 2

Littlefield Company uses a backflush costing system with three trigger points:

- Purchase of direct materials
- Completion of good finished units of product
- Sale of finished goods

There are no beginning inventories. Information for April 2006 is:

Direct materials purchased	$880,000	Conversion costs allocated	$ 400,000
Direct materials used	$850,000	Costs transferred to finished goods	$1,250,000
Conversion costs incurred	$422,000	Cost of goods sold	$1,190,000

Required

1. Prepare journal entries for April (without disposing of underallocated or overallocated conversion costs). Assume there are no direct materials variances.
2. Under an ideal JIT production system, how would the amounts in your journal entries differ from the journal entries in requirement 1?

SOLUTION

1. Journal entries for April are:

Entry (a)	Inventory: Materials and In-Process Control	880,000	
	Accounts Payable Control		880,000
	(direct materials purchased)		
Entry (b)	Conversion Costs Control	422,000	
	Various accounts (such as Wages Payable Control)		422,000
	(conversion costs incurred)		
Entry (c)	Finished Goods Control	1,250,000	
	Inventory: Materials and In-Process Control		850,000
	Conversion Costs Allocated		400,000
	(standard cost of finished goods completed)		
Entry (d)	Cost of Goods Sold	1,190,000	
	Finished Goods Control		1,190,000
	(standard costs of finished goods sold)		

2. Under an ideal JIT production system, if the manufacturing lead time per unit is very short, there could be zero inventories at the end of each day. Entry (c) would be $1,190,000 finished goods production [to match finished goods sold in entry (d)], not $1,250,000. If the Marketing Department could only sell goods costing $1,190,000, the JIT production system would call for direct materials purchases and conversion costs of lower than $880,000 and $422,000, respectively, in entries (a) and (b).

DECISION POINTS

The following question-and-answer format summarizes the chapter's learning objectives. Each decision presents a key question related to a learning objective. The guidelines are the answer to that question.

Decision	Guidelines
1. What are the five categories of costs associated with goods for sale?	The five categories are purchasing costs (costs of goods acquired from suppliers), ordering costs (costs of preparing a purchase order and receiving goods), carrying costs (costs of holding inventory of goods for sale), stockout costs (costs arising when a customer demands a unit of product and that unit is not on hand), and quality costs (prevention, appraisal, internal failure, and external failure costs).
2. How do managers use the EOQ model?	The economic-order-quantity (EOQ) decision model calculates the optimal quantity of inventory to order by balancing ordering costs and carrying costs. The larger the order quantity, the higher the annual carrying costs and the lower the annual ordering costs. The EOQ model includes costs recorded in the financial accounting system as well as opportunity costs not recorded in the financial accounting system.
3. How can companies reduce the conflict between the EOQ decision model and models used for performance evaluation?	The opportunity cost of investment tied up in inventory is a key input in the EOQ decision model. Many companies include opportunity costs when evaluating managers so that the EOQ decision model is consistent with the performance-evaluation model.
4. What is a supply chain, and what is the benefit of supply-chain analysis?	The supply chain describes the flow of goods, services, and information from the initial sources of materials and services to the delivery of products to consumers, regardless of whether those activities occur in the same organization or in other organizations. Using supply-chain analysis allows companies to coordinate their activities and reduce inventories throughout the supply chain.
5. How do materials requirements planning (MRP) systems differ from just-in-time (JIT) production systems?	Materials requirements planning (MRP) systems use a "push-through" approach that manufactures finished goods for inventory on the basis of demand forecasts. Just-in-time (JIT) production systems use a "demand-pull" approach in which goods are manufactured only to satisfy customer orders.
6. What are the features of a JIT production system?	Five features of a JIT production system are (a) organizing production in manufacturing cells, (b) hiring and training multiskilled workers, (c) emphasizing total quality management, (d) reducing manufacturing lead time and setup time, and (e) building strong supplier relationships.
7. What is backflush costing?	Backflush costing delays recording some of the journal entries (and omits others) relating to the cycle from purchase of direct materials to the sale of finished goods.
8. How does backflush costing simplify inventory costing?	Traditional inventory-costing systems use sequential tracking, in which recording of the journal entries occurs in the same order as actual purchases and progress in production. Most backflush costing systems do not record journal entries for the work-in-process stage of production. Some backflush costing systems also do not record entries for either the purchase of direct materials or the completion of finished goods.

TERMS TO LEARN

This chapter and the Glossary at the end of the book contain definitions of:

backflush costing (p. 708)
carrying costs (p. 692)
economic order quantity (EOQ) (p. 692)
inventory management (p. 691)
just-in-time (JIT) production (p. 703)
just-in-time (JIT) purchasing (p. 698)
lean production (p. 703)
manufacturing cells (p. 704)
materials requirements planning (MRP) (p. 702)
ordering costs (p. 692)
purchasing costs (p. 692)
purchase-order lead time (p. 693)
quality costs (p. 692)
reorder point (p. 694)
safety stock (p. 695)
sequential tracking (p. 707)
stockout costs (p. 692)
trigger point (p. 708)

PH Grade Assist

Prentice Hall Grade Assist (PHGA)
Your professor may ask you to complete selected exercises and problems in Prentice Hall Grade Assist (PHGA). PHGA is an online tool that can help you master the chapter's topics. It provides you with multiple variations of exercises and problems designated by the PHGA icon. You can rework these exercises and problems—each time with new data—as many times as you need. You also receive immediate feedback and grading.

ASSIGNMENT MATERIAL

Questions

20-1 Why do better decisions regarding the purchasing and managing of goods for sale frequently cause dramatic percentage increases in net income?

20-2 Name five cost categories that are important in managing goods for sale in a retail company.

20-3 What assumptions are made when using the simplest version of the economic-order-quantity (EOQ) decision model?

20-4 Give examples of costs included in annual carrying costs of inventory when using the EOQ decision model.

20-5 Give three examples of opportunity costs that typically are not recorded in accounting systems, although they are relevant when using the EOQ model.

20-6 What are the steps in computing the cost of a prediction error when using the EOQ decision model?

20-7 Why might goal-congruence issues arise when an EOQ model is used to guide decisions on how much to order?

20-8 Describe JIT purchasing and its benefits.

20-9 What are three factors causing reductions in the cost to place purchase orders for materials?

20-10 "You should always choose the supplier who offers the lowest price per unit." Do you agree? Explain.

20-11 What is supply-chain analysis, and how can it benefit manufacturers and retailers?

20-12 What are some obstacles to companies adopting a supply-chain approach?

20-13 What are the main features of JIT production?

20-14 Distinguish inventory-costing systems using sequential tracking from those using backflush costing.

20-15 Describe three different versions of backflush costing.

Exercises

PH Grade Assist

20-16 Economic order quantity for retailer. Sports World (SW) operates a megastore featuring sports merchandise. It uses an EOQ decision model to make inventory decisions. It is now considering inventory decisions for its New England Patriots jerseys product line. This is a highly popular item. Data for 2005 are:

Expected annual demand for Patriots jerseys	10,000
Ordering cost per purchase order	$225
Carrying cost per year	$10 per jersey

Each jersey costs SW $40 and sells for $75. The $10 carrying cost per jersey per year comprises the required return on investment of $4.80 (12% × $40 purchase price) plus $5.20 in relevant insurance, handling, and theft-related costs. The purchasing lead time is 7 days. SW is open 365 days a year.

Required

1. Calculate the EOQ.
2. Calculate the number of orders that will be placed each year.
3. Calculate the reorder point.

20-17 Economic order quantity, effect of parameter changes (continuation of 20-16). Athletic Products (AP) manufactures the Patriots jerseys that Sports World (SW) sells to its customers. AP has recently installed computer software that enables its customers to conduct "one-stop" purchasing using state-of-the-art Web site technology developed by Cisco Systems. SW's ordering cost per purchase order will be $20 using this new technology.

Required

1. Calculate the EOQ for the Patriots jerseys using the revised ordering cost of $20 per purchase order. Assume all other data from Exercise 20-16 are the same. Comment on the result.
2. Suppose AP proposes to "assist" SW. AP will allow SW's customers to order directly from the AP Web site. AP would ship directly to these customers. AP would pay $10 to SW for every Patriots jersey purchased by one of SW's customers. Comment qualitatively on how this offer would affect inventory management at SW. What factors should SW consider in deciding whether to accept AP's proposal?

20-18 EOQ for a retailer. The Cloth Center sells fabrics to a wide range of industrial and consumer users. One of the products it carries is denim cloth, used in the manufacture of jeans and carrying bags. The supplier for the denim cloth pays all incoming freight. No incoming inspection of the denim is necessary because the supplier has a track record of delivering high-quality merchandise. The purchasing officer of the Cloth Center has collected the following information:

Annual demand for denim cloth	20,000 yards
Ordering cost per purchase order	$160
Carrying cost per year	20% of purchase costs
Safety-stock requirements	None
Cost of denim cloth	$8 per yard

The purchasing lead time is 2 weeks. The Cloth Center is open 250 days a year (50 weeks for 5 days a week).

Required

1. Calculate the EOQ for denim cloth.
2. Calculate the number of orders that will be placed each year.
3. Calculate the reorder point for denim cloth.

20-19 EOQ for manufacturer. Lakeland Company, which produces lawn mowers, purchases 18,000 units of a rotor blade part each year at a cost of $60 per unit. Lakeland requires a 15% annual rate of return on investment. In addition, the relevant carrying cost (for insurance, materials handling, breakage, and so on) is $6 per unit per year. The relevant ordering cost per purchase order is $150.

PH Grade Assist

Required

1. Calculate Lakeland's EOQ for the rotor blade part.
2. Calculate Lakeland's annual relevant ordering costs for the EOQ calculated in requirement 1.
3. Calculate Lakeland's annual relevant carrying costs for the EOQ calculated in requirement 1.
4. Assume that demand is uniform throughout the year and known with certainty so that there is no need for safety stocks. The purchase-order lead time is half a month. Calculate Lakeland's reorder point for the rotor blade part.

20-20 Sensitivity of EOQ to changes in relevant ordering and carrying costs. Alyia Company's annual demand for Model X253 is 10,000 units. Alyia is unsure about the relevant carrying cost per unit per year and the relevant ordering cost per purchase order. This table presents six possible combinations of carrying and ordering costs.

Relevant Carrying Cost per Unit per Year	Relevant Ordering Cost per Purchase Order
$10	$300
$10	$200
$15	$300
$15	$200
$20	$300
$20	$200

Required

1. Determine EOQ for Alyia for each of the relevant ordering and carrying-cost alternatives.
2. How does your answer to requirement 1 give insight into the impact on EOQ of changes in relevant ordering and carrying costs.

20-21 Purchase-order size for retailer, EOQ, just-in-time purchasing. The 24-Hour Mart operates a chain of supermarkets. Its best-selling soft drink is Fruitslice. Demand (*D*) in April for Fruitslice at its Memphis supermarket is estimated to be 6,000 cases (24 cans in each case). In early March, the Memphis supermarket estimated the ordering cost per purchase order (*P*) for Fruitslice to be $30. The carrying cost (*C*) of each case of Fruitslice in inventory for a month was estimated to be $1. At the end of March, the Memphis 24-Hour Mart reestimated its carrying cost to be $1.50 per case per month to take into account an increase in warehouse-related costs.

PH Grade Assist

During March, 24-Hour Mart restructured its relationship with suppliers. It reduced the number of suppliers from 600 to 180. Long-term contracts were signed only with those suppliers that agreed to make product-quality checks before shipping. Each purchase order will now be made by linking into the suppliers' computer network. The Memphis 24-Hour Mart estimated that these changes will reduce the ordering cost per purchase order to $5. The 24-Hour Mart is open 30 days in April.

Required

1. Calculate the EOQ in April for Fruitslice. Assume in turn:
   a. $D = 6,000$; $P = \$30$; $C = \$1$
   b. $D = 6,000$; $P = \$30$; $C = \$1.50$
   c. $D = 6,000$; $P = \$5$; $C = \$1.50$
2. How does your answer to requirement 1 give insight into the retailer's movement toward JIT purchasing policies?

PH Grade Assist

20-22 JIT production, relevant benefits, relevant costs. The Champion Hardware Company manufactures specialty brass door handles at its Lynchburg plant. Champion is considering implementing a JIT production system. The following are the estimated costs and benefits of JIT production.

a. Annual additional tooling costs would be $100,000.
b. Average inventory would decline by 80% from the current level of $1,000,000.
c. Insurance, space, materials-handling and setup costs, which currently total $300,000 annually, would decline by 25%.
d. The emphasis on quality inherent in JIT production would reduce rework costs by 30%. Champion currently incurs $200,000 in annual rework costs.
e. Improved product quality under JIT production would enable Champion to raise the price of its product by $4 per unit. Champion sells 40,000 units each year.

Champion's required rate of return on inventory investment is 15% per year.

Required

1. Calculate the net benefit or cost to Champion if it adopts JIT production at the Lynchburg plant.
2. What nonfinancial and qualitative factors should Champion consider when making the decision to adopt JIT production?
3. Suppose Champion implements JIT production at its Lynchburg plant. Give examples of performance measures Champion could use to evaluate and control JIT production. What would be the benefit of Champion implementing an enterprise resource planning (ERP) system?

20-23 Backflush costing and JIT production. Road Warrior Corporation assembles handheld computers that have scaled-down capabilities of laptop computers. Each handheld computer takes 6 hours to assemble. Road Warrior uses a JIT production system and a backflush costing system with three trigger points:

- Purchase of direct materials
- Completion of good finished units of product
- Sale of finished goods

There are no beginning inventories of materials or finished goods. The following data are for August 2005:

Direct materials purchased	$2,754,000	Conversion costs incurred	$723,600
Direct materials used	$2,733,600	Conversion costs allocated	$750,400

Road Warrior records direct materials purchased and conversion costs incurred at actual costs. When finished goods are sold, the backflush costing system "pulls through" standard direct material cost ($102 per unit) and standard conversion cost ($28 per unit). Road Warrior produced 26,800 finished units in August 2005 and sold 26,400 units. The actual direct material cost per unit in August 2005 was $102, and the actual conversion cost per unit was $27.

Required

1. Prepare summary journal entries for August 2005 (without disposing of under- or overallocated conversion costs).
2. Post the entries in requirement 1 to T-accounts for applicable Inventory: Materials and In-Process Control, Finished Goods Control, Conversion Costs Control, Conversion Costs Allocated, and Cost of Goods Sold.
3. Under an ideal JIT production system, how would the amounts in your journal entries differ from those in requirement 1?

20-24 Backflush costing, two trigger points, materials purchase and sale (continuation of 20-23). Assume the same facts as in Exercise 20-23, except that Road Warrior now uses a backflush costing system with the following two trigger points:

- Purchase of direct materials
- Sale of finished goods

The Inventory Control account will include direct materials purchased but not yet in production, materials in work in process, and materials in finished goods but not sold. No conversion costs are inventoried. Any under- or overallocated conversion costs are written off monthly to Cost of Goods Sold.

Required

1. Prepare summary journal entries for August, including the disposition of under- or overallocated conversion costs.
2. Post the entries in requirement 1 to T-accounts for Inventory Control, Conversion Costs Control, Conversion Costs Allocated, and Cost of Goods Sold.

20-25 Backflush costing, two trigger points, completion of production and sale (continuation of 20-23). Assume the same facts as in Exercise 20-23, except now Road Warrior uses only two trigger points, the completion of good finished units of product and the sale of finished goods. Any under- or overallocated conversion costs are written off monthly to Cost of Goods Sold.

Required

1. Prepare summary journal entries for August, including the disposition of under- or overallocated conversion costs.
2. Post the entries in requirement 1 to T-accounts for Finished Goods Control, Conversion Costs Control, Conversion Costs Allocated, and Cost of Goods Sold.

Problems

20-26 Effect of different order quantities on ordering costs and carrying costs, EOQ. Koala Blue, a retailer of bed and bath linen, sells 234,000 packages of Mona Lisa designer sheets each year. Koala Blue incurs an ordering cost of $81 per purchase order placed with Mona Lisa Enterprises and an annual carrying cost of $11.70 per package. Liv Carrol, purchasing manager at Koala Blue, seeks your help: She wants to understand how ordering and carrying costs vary with order quantity.

Excel Lab www.prenhall.com/horngren/cost12e

	A	B	C	D	E	F
1				Scenario		
2		1	2	3	4	5
3	Annual demand (packages)	234,000	234,000	234,000	234,000	234,000
4	Cost per purchase order	$ 81	$ 81	$ 81	$ 81	$ 81
5	Carrying cost per package per year	$11.70	$11.70	$11.70	$11.70	$11.70
6	Quantity (packages) per purchase order	900	1,500	1,800	2,100	2,700
7	Number of purchase orders per year					
8	Annual relevant ordering costs					
9	Annual relevant carrying costs					
10	Annual total relevant costs of ordering and carrying inventory					

If you want to use Excel to solve this problem, go to the Excel Lab at **www.prenhall.com/horngren/cost12e** and download the template for Problem 20-26.

Required

1. Complete the preceding table for Liv Carrol. What is the EOQ? Comment on your results.
2. Mona Lisa is about to introduce a Web-based ordering system for its customers. Liv Carrol estimates that Koala Blue's ordering costs will be reduced to $49 per purchase order. Calculate the new EOQ and the new annual relevant costs of ordering and carrying inventory.
3. Liv Carrol estimates that Koala Blue will incur a cost of $2,000 to train its two purchasing assistants to use the new Mona Lisa system. Help Liv Carrol present a case to upper management showing that Koala Blue will be able to recoup its training costs within the first year of adoption.

20-27 EOQ, uncertainty, safety stock, reorder point. (CMA adapted) The Starr Company distributes a wide range of electrical products. One of its best-selling items is a standard electric motor. The management of the Starr Company uses the EOQ decision model to determine the optimal number of motors to order. Management now wants to determine how much safety stock to hold.

The Starr Company estimates annual demand (300 working days) to be 30,000 electric motors. Using the EOQ decision model, the company orders 3,000 motors at a time. The lead time for an order is 5 days. The annual carrying cost of one motor in safety stock is $10. Management has also estimated that the additional stockout cost is $20 for each motor they are short.

The Starr Company has analyzed the demand during 200 past reorder periods. The records indicate the following patterns:

Demand During Lead Time	Number of Times Quantity Was Demanded
440	6
460	12
480	16
500	130
520	20
540	10
560	6
	200

Required

1. Determine the level of safety stock for electric motors that the Starr Company should maintain in order to minimize the sum of expected stockout costs and carrying costs. When computing carrying costs, assume that the safety stock is on hand at all times and that there is no overstocking caused by decreases in expected demand. (Consider safety-stock levels of 0, 20, 40, and 60 units.)
2. What would be the Starr Company's reorder point?
3. What factors should the Starr Company consider in estimating the stockout costs?

PH Grade Assist

20-28 EOQ, cost of prediction error. Ralph Menard is the owner of a truck repair shop. He uses an EOQ model for heavy-duty tires. He initially predicts the annual demand for heavy-duty tires to be 2,000. Each tire has a purchase price of $50. The ordering cost per purchase order is $40. The carrying cost per year is $4 per tire plus 10% of the purchase price per tire.

Required

1. Calculate the EOQ for tires, along with the sum of annual relevant ordering and carrying costs.
2. Suppose Menard is correct in all his predictions except the purchase price. If he had been a faultless predictor, he would have foreseen that the purchase price would drop to $30. What is the cost of the prediction error?

20-29 JIT purchasing, relevant benefits, relevant costs. (CMA adapted) The Margro Corporation is an automotive supplier that uses automatic turning machines to manufacture precision parts from steel bars. Margro's inventory of raw steel averages $600,000. John Oates, president of Margro, and Helen Gorman, Margro's controller, are concerned about the costs of carrying inventory. The steel supplier is willing to supply steel in smaller lots at no additional charge. Gorman identifies the following effects of adopting a JIT inventory program to virtually eliminate steel inventory:

- Without scheduling any overtime, lost sales due to stockouts would increase by 35,000 units per year. However, by incurring overtime premiums of $40,000 per year, the increase in lost sales could be reduced to 20,000 units per year. This would be the maximum amount of overtime that would be feasible for Margro.
- Two warehouses currently used for steel bar storage would no longer be needed. Margro rents one warehouse from another company under a cancelable leasing arrangement at an annual cost of $60,000. The other warehouse is owned by Margro and contains 12,000 square feet. Three-fourths of the space in the owned warehouse could be rented for $1.50 per square foot per year. Insurance and property tax costs totaling $14,000 per year would be eliminated.

Margro's required rate of return on investment is 20% per year. Margro's budgeted income statement for the year ending December 31, 2005 (in thousands) is as follows:

Revenues (900,000 units)		$10,800
Cost of goods sold		
Variable costs	$4,050	
Fixed costs	1,450	
Total costs of goods sold		5,500
Gross margin		5,300
Marketing and distribution costs		
Variable costs	$ 900	
Fixed costs	1,500	
Total marketing and distribution costs		2,400
Operating income		$ 2,900

Required

1. Calculate the estimated dollar savings (loss) for the Margro Corporation that would result in 2005 from the adoption of JIT purchasing.
2. Identify and explain other factors that Margro should consider before deciding whether to adopt JIT purchasing.

Excel Lab
www.prenhall.com/horngren/cost12e

20-30 Relevant benefits and costs of JIT purchasing, supply chain. Codleff Medical Instruments sells 25,000 units of RM-27, a surgical scalpel, each year, which it purchases from Slocombe Manufacturing. Slocombe's reputation for quality is the best in the industry. Codleff is now considering adopting JIT purchasing. The purchase price of each scalpel will increase by a small amount, and more-frequent, smaller orders will be placed with Slocombe. Also, Codleff anticipates that realistically, under JIT purchasing, there will be stockouts for about 50 units each year and each stockout will cost about $3 to handle. The anticipated relevant changes are summarized here:

	A	B	C
1		Current	JIT
2		Purchasing	Purchasing
3		Policy	Policy
4	Number of units ordered per year	25,000	25,000
5	Purchase price per unit	$18	$18.02
6	Ordering cost per purchase order	$ 2	$ 2
7	Number of purchase orders per year	50	500
8	Required annual rate of return on investment	20%	20%
9	Other carrying costs per unit per year	$ 6	$ 6
10	Expected number of stockout units per year	-	50
11	Cost per stockout unit	-	$ 3

If you want to use Excel to solve this problem, go to the Excel Lab at **www.prenhall.com/horngren/cost12e** and download the template for Problem 20-30.

Required

1. Calculate the estimated dollar savings (loss) for Codleff Medical Instruments from the adoption of JIT purchasing using the format of Exhibit 20-5.
2. Under what conditions would it be beneficial for Codleff to have Slocombe manage all inventories in the supply chain?

20-31 Supplier evaluation and relevant costs of quality and timely deliveries (continuation of 20-30). Codleff Medical Instruments adopted JIT purchasing in 2005 and selected Slocombe Manufacturing as its supplier. In 2006, Pruitt Steel, a Slocombe competitor, offers to supply all of Codleff's RM-27 needs at a lower price and under the same JIT delivery terms as Slocombe. Codleff anticipates that if it purchases from Pruitt, relevant carrying costs would be lower, but it would incur higher inspection costs, more stockouts, and more customer-support costs due to somewhat lower quality. The data for this decision are:

Excel Lab
www.prenhall.com/horngren/cost12e

	A	B	C
1		**Slocombe**	**Pruitt**
2	Number of units ordered and sold each year	25,000	25,000
3	Purchase price per unit	$18.02	$ 17.70
4	Ordering cost per purchase order	$ 2	$ 2
5	Order quantity per purchase order	50	50
6	Inspection cost per unit	$ 0	$ 0.08
7	Required annual rate of return on investment	20%	20%
8	Other carrying costs per unit per year	$ 6.00	$ 5.90
9	Expected number of stockout units per year	50	400
10	Cost per stockout unit	$ 3	$ 3
11	Customer support costs per year	$1,000	$10,000

If you want to use Excel to solve this problem, go to the Excel Lab at **www.prenhall.com/horngren/cost12e** and download the template for Problem 20-31.

Required

Calculate the relevant costs of purchasing (1) from Slocombe and (2) from Pruitt using the format of Exhibit 20-6. From which supplier should Codleff buy RM-27?

20-32 Supplier evaluation and relevant costs of quality and timely deliveries. Wayland Sporting Goods is evaluating two suppliers of footballs: Bigby and Kendall. Pertinent information about each potential supplier follows:

Excel Lab
www.prenhall.com/horngren/cost12e

	A	B	C
1		**Bigby**	**Kendall**
2	Number of units ordered per year	15,000	15,000
3	Purchase price per unit (case of two footballs)	$40.00	$41.00
4	Ordering cost per purchase order	$ 4	$ 4
5	Inspection cost per unit	$ 0.03	$ 0
6	Average inventory held during the year (units)	300	300
7	Required annual rate of return on investment	12%	12%
8	Other carrying costs per unit per year	$ 5.00	$ 4.50
9	Expected number of stockout units per year	400	100
10	Cost per stockout unit	$ 10	$ 8
11	Units returned by customers per year	300	50
12	Cost of handling each returned unit	$ 20	$ 20

If you want to use Excel to solve this problem, go to the Excel Lab at **www.prenhall.com/horngren/cost12e** and download the template for Problem 20-32.

Required

Calculate the relevant costs of purchasing (1) from Bigby and (2) from Kendall using the format of Exhibit 20-6. From which supplier should Wayland buy footballs?

20-33 Backflush costing and JIT production. The Acton Corporation manufactures electrical meters. For August, there were no beginning inventories of direct materials and no beginning or ending work in process. Acton uses a JIT production system and backflush costing with three trigger points for making entries in the accounting system:

- Purchase of direct materials—debited to Inventory: Materials and In-Process Control
- Completion of good finished units of product—debited to Finished Goods Control
- Sale of finished goods

Acton's August standard cost per meter is direct material, $25; and conversion cost, $20. The following data apply to August manufacturing:

Direct materials purchased	$550,000	Number of finished units manufactured	21,000
Conversion costs incurred	$440,000	Number of finished units sold	20,000

Required

1. Prepare summary journal entries for August (without disposing of under- or overallocated conversion costs). Assume no direct materials variances.
2. Post the entries in requirement 1 to T-accounts for Inventory: Materials and In-Process Control, Finished Goods Control, Conversion Costs Control, Conversion Costs Allocated, and Cost of Goods Sold.

20-34 Backflush, two trigger points, materials purchase and sale (continuation of 20-33). Assume that the second trigger point for Acton Corporation is the sale—rather than the completion—of finished goods. Also, the inventory account is confined solely to direct materials, whether these materials are in a storeroom, in work in process, or in finished goods. No conversion costs are inventoried. They are allocated to the units sold at standard costs. Any under- or overallocated conversion costs are written off monthly to Cost of Goods Sold.

Required

1. Prepare summary journal entries for August, including the disposition of under- or overallocated conversion costs. Assume no direct materials variances.
2. Post the entries in requirement 1 to T-accounts for Inventory Control, Conversion Costs Control, Conversion Costs Allocated, and Cost of Goods Sold.

20-35 Backflush, two trigger points, completion of production and sale (continuation of 20-33). Assume the same facts as in Problem 20-33 except now there are only two trigger points: the completion of good finished units of product and the sale of finished goods.

Required

1. Prepare summary journal entries for August, including the disposition of under- or overallocated conversion costs. Assume no direct materials variances.
2. Post the entries in requirement 1 to T-accounts for Finished Goods Control, Conversion Costs Control, Conversion Costs Allocated, and Cost of Goods Sold.

20-36 Backflush costing, income manipulation, ethics. Carol Brown, the chief financial officer of Silicon Valley Computer, is an enthusiastic advocate of JIT production. The SVC Keyboard Division, which produces keyboards for personal computers, has made dramatic improvements in its operations with a highly successful JIT implementation. The Keyboard Division president now wants to adopt backflush costing.

Brown discusses the backflush-costing proposal with Ralph Strong, the controller of SVC. Strong is totally opposed to backflush costing. He argues that it will open up "a Pandora's box," by allowing division managers to manipulate reported division operating income. A member of Strong's group outlines the three possible versions of backflush costing shown in Exhibit 20-8 (p. 711). Strong notes that none of these methods tracks work in process. He asserts that this omission would allow managers to "artificially change" reported operating income by manipulating work-in-process levels. He is especially scathing about the versions of backflush costing in which no entries are made until a sale occurs.

"Suppose the division has already met its target operating income and wants to shift some of this year's income to next year," he says. "Under backflush costing with sale of finished goods as the trigger point, the division will have an incentive this year to not sell goods produced this year. This is a bizzare incentive. I rest my case about why we should stay with a job-costing system using sequential tracking."

Strong concludes that as long as reported accounting numbers are central to SVC's performance and bonus reviews, backflush costing should never be adopted.

Required

1. What factors should SVC consider in deciding whether to adopt a version of backflush costing?
2. Are Strong's concerns about income manipulation sufficiently important for SVC to not adopt backflush costing?
3. What other ways does SVC have to motivate managers to not "artificially change" reported income?

Collaborative Learning Problem

20-37 Backflushing. The following conversation occurred between Brian Richardson, plant manager at Glendale Engineering, and Charles Cheng, plant controller. Glendale manufactures automotive component parts, such as gears and crankshafts, for automobile manufacturers. Richardson has been very enthusiastic about implementing JIT and about simplifying and streamlining production and other business processes.

"Charles," Richardson began, "I would like to substantially simplify our accounting in the new JIT environment. Can't we just record one journal entry at the time we ship products to our customers? I don't want to have our staff spending time tracking inventory from one stage to the next, when we have as little inventory as we do."

"Brian," Cheng said, "I think you are right about simplifying the accounting, but we still have a fair amount of direct materials and finished goods inventory that varies from period to period, depending on the demand for specific products. Doing away with all inventory accounting may be a problem."

"Well," Richardson replied, "you know my desire to simplify, simplify, simplify. I know that there are some costs of oversimplifying, but I believe that, in the long run, simplification pays dividends. Why don't you and your staff study the issues involved, and I will put it on the agenda for our next management meeting."

Required

1. What version of backflush costing would you recommend that Cheng adopt? Remember Richardson's desire to simplify the accounting as much as possible. Develop support for your recommendation.
2. Think about the three versions of backflush costing shown in Exhibit 20-8 (p. 711). These versions differ with respect to the number and types of trigger points used. Suppose your goal of implementing backflush costing is to simplify the accounting, but only if it closely matches the sequential-tracking approach. Which version of backflush costing would you propose if:
   a. Glendale had no direct materials and no work-in-process inventories but did have finished goods inventory?
   b. Glendale had no work in process and no finished goods inventories but did have direct materials inventory?
   c. Glendale had no direct materials, no work-in-process, and no finished goods inventories?
3. Backflush costing has its critics. In an article in the magazine *Management Accounting* titled "Beware of the New Accounting Myths," R. Calvasina, E. Calvasina, and G. Calvasina state:

   > The periodic (backflush) system has never been reflective of the reporting needs of a manufacturing system. In the highly standardized operating environments of the present JIT era, the appropriate system to be used is a perpetual accounting system based on an up-to-date, realistic set of standard costs. For management accountants to backflush on an actual cost basis is to return to the days of the outdoor privy (toilet).

   Comment on this statement.

Get Connected: Cost Accounting in the News

Go to www.prenhall.com/horngren/cost12e for additional online exercise(s) that explore issues affecting the accounting world today. These exercises offer you the opportunity to analyze and reflect on how cost accounting helps managers make better decisions and handle the challenges of strategic planning and implementation.

CHAPTER 20 Video Case

REGAL MARINE: Supply-Chain Management

Like most manufacturers, a big portion of Regal Marine's costs is tied up in the purchase of the materials used in the production of its various luxury-boat models. Regal Marine is trying to reduce its direct material costs by implementing a supply-chain management approach.

Supply-chain management is more than just seeking the lowest-cost provider of materials. Regal Marine is working closely with suppliers to promote innovation, quality, and timely delivery of component parts.

The manufacture of a power boat starts with the fiberglass-and-gelcoat-covered hull and deck. Separate fabrication units off to the side of the main assembly floor produce the upholstered seats, cabinetry, and wiring panels for instrumentation. As boats move through the assembly process, each specially fabricated component is installed. The boats are then shrink-wrapped and loaded onto delivery trucks for shipment to distributors and showrooms.

To strengthen its upstream supply-chain relationship, Regal Marine is partnering with major suppliers of materials, such as windshields, engines, and gelcoatings, to drive innovation at reasonable costs. Key vendors are invited to participate in the product-design process so that new materials may be tested and designed into future boat models.

The company also has joined with about 15 other boat manufacturers to form a purchasing association. The association helps members to negotiate better price discounts with materials suppliers. Association members also share noncompetitive information about industrywide materials changes.

For some components, such as snaps and fasteners, Regal Marine is working with local suppliers to provide direct replenishment on the assembly floor on a just-in-time basis. Suppliers are responsible for maintaining the inventory, and Regal Marine benefits by not having to place orders for restocking. Suppliers make sure no stockouts occur, and they don't charge Regal Marine for the components stocked until they are used in production. This helps Regal Marine reduce its inventory costs.

QUESTIONS

1. Comment on the supply-chain management approaches that Regal Marine uses.
2. What role might Regal Marine's retail distributors play in the company's supply-chain management efforts? What obstacles might Regal Marine and its retail partners face?

CHAPTER 21

CAPITAL BUDGETING AND COST ANALYSIS

LEARNING OBJECTIVES

1. **Recognize the multiyear focus of capital budgeting**
2. **Understand the six stages of capital budgeting for a project**
3. **Use and evaluate the two main discounted cash flow (DCF) methods: the net present value (NPV) method and the internal rate-of-return (IRR) method**
4. **Use and evaluate the payback method**
5. **Use and evaluate the accrual accounting rate-of-return (AARR) method**
6. **Identify and reduce conflicts from using DCF for capital budgeting decisions and accrual accounting for performance evaluation**
7. **Identify relevant cash inflows and outflows for capital budgeting decisions**

Stacey Murray, executive director of Lifetime Care Hospital, was reviewing a proposal for a new X-ray machine with Jared Kim, the CFO of Lifetime Care. Lifetime Care, a for-profit hospital, had enjoyed strong financial performance over the years, but recently, several new upscale hospitals had begun operating in the area. The competition from these hospitals had reduced Lifetime Care's operating income in the past two years. Murray had concluded from patient surveys that, to be more competitive and attract patients, Lifetime needed to modernize its equipment, improve the quality of patient care, and reduce costs.

Stacey: At our last staff meeting, the doctors made it clear that we need to modernize our equipment or we will continue to lose patients. I told the radiologists we were evaluating a new X-ray machine, but I need to know if the one under consideration is state of the art.

Jared: Well, from the independent research reports I've received, the XCAM8 is one of the best on the market. It was introduced last year and has a solid service record to date. It's a bit expensive, though.

Stacey: I can see that from your proposal. Do the potential increase in revenues and the savings in costs from greater efficiency justify this level of investment?

Jared: We haven't assumed higher revenues because I don't think we'll get more patients or be able to charge higher rates than we are allowed right now. But the significant cash savings in operating costs justify the investment.

Stacey: How certain are you about achieving these savings? I'd be hesitant to spend this money if there is significant risk that the cash savings will not materialize.

Jared: We've done some sensitivity analysis and are quite confident that even if the cash savings are somewhat lower than predicted, this investment is a good one.

Stacey: Okay, let's go ahead and schedule the sales representative to come in and demonstrate the equipment to our radiologists. After that, let's revisit the proposal once more to make sure we haven't missed anything.

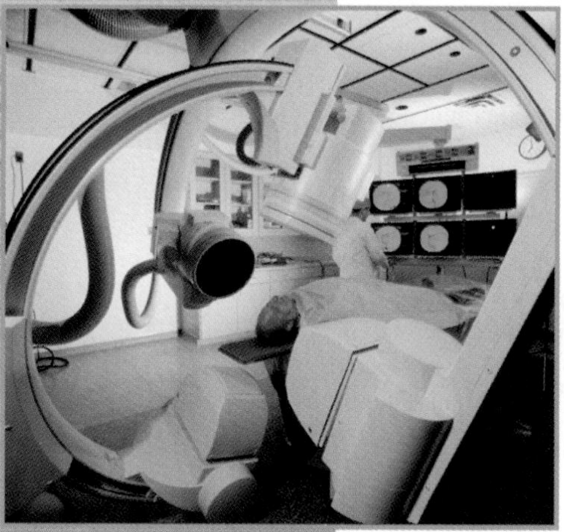

Managers at companies such as Palm, Electronic Arts, Best Buy, Orbitz, and Vodafone continually face challenging investment decisions. In this chapter, we introduce capital budgeting methods, which deal with how an organization selects projects that are intended to increase the "capital" (the monetary value) of the organization. These methods help managers analyze projects that span multiple years.

Two Dimensions of Cost Analysis

Before we describe specific capital budgeting methods, we highlight how cost analysis for the *project-by-project dimension* of capital budgeting differs from cost analysis for the *period-by-period dimension* found in much of accounting.

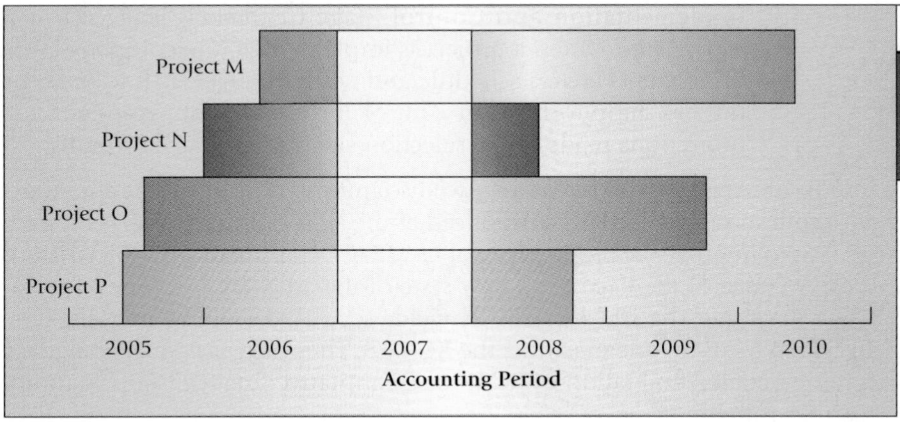

EXHIBIT 21-1

The Project and Time Dimensions of Capital Budgeting

Exhibit 21-1 illustrates two different dimensions of cost analysis: (1) horizontally across, as the project dimension, and (2) vertically upward, as the accounting-period dimension. Each project is represented as a horizontal rectangle starting and ending at different times and stretching over time spans longer than one year. Capital budgeting analyzes each project over its entire lifespan by considering *all* the cash flows from investing in it. The vertical rectangle for the 2007 accounting period represents the dimension of income determination and routine annual planning and control that cuts across all projects.

1

Recognize the multiyear focus of capital budgeting

. . . capital budgeting decisions consider revenues and costs over long periods

The accounting system that corresponds to the project dimension in Exhibit 21-1 considers life-cycle revenues and costs (Chapter 12, pp. 436–438). For example, a life-cycle analysis for a new-car project at Volvo could encompass a 10-year period. It would accumulate revenues from the new car as well as costs incurred on the project for all business functions in the value chain, from R&D to customer service.

Stages of Capital Budgeting

2

Understand the six stages of capital budgeting for a project

. . . identification, search, information-acquisition, selection, financing, and implementation and control

Capital budgeting is making long-run planning decisions for investments in projects. Capital budgeting is a decision-making and control tool. There are six stages:

Stage 1: **Identification Stage** *Determine which types of capital investments are necessary to accomplish organization objectives and strategies.* For example, a strategy of product differentiation to increase profitability could be promoted by projects that develop new products, new customers, or new markets. Or, a strategy of cost leadership could be promoted by projects that improve productivity and efficiency. Identifying which types of capital projects to invest in is largely the responsibility of line management.

Stage 2: **Search Stage** *Explore alternative capital investments that will achieve organization objectives.* Cross-functional teams from all parts of the value chain evaluate alternative projects. Some alternatives are rejected early. Others are thoroughly evaluated in the next stage, the information-acquisition stage.

Stage 3: **Information-Acquisition Stage** *Consider the expected costs and benefits of alternative capital investments.* These costs and benefits can be quantitative or qualitative. Capital budgeting emphasizes quantitative financial factors, but nonfinancial quantitative and qualitative factors are also considered.

Stage 4: **Selection Stage** *Choose projects for implementation.* Organizations choose projects whose expected benefits exceed expected costs by the greatest amounts. Managers evaluate the conclusions reached on the basis of the formal quantitative analysis, using their judgment and intuition to take into account nonfinancial factors.

Stage 5: **Financing Stage** *Obtain project funding.* Sources of financing include internally generated cash flow as well as equity and debt securities sold in the capital markets. Financing is the responsibility of the treasury function, which is overseen by the chief financial officer of the organization.

Stage 6: Implementation and Control Stage *Get projects under way and monitor their performance.* When a project is implemented, the company evaluates if capital investments are on schedule and within budget. As the project generates cash inflows, monitoring and control include a postinvestment audit comparing projections made at the selection stage against actual results.

To illustrate capital budgeting, we use information from Lifetime Care Hospital, the for-profit, taxable company introduced at the start of this chapter. One of Lifetime Care's goals is to improve the productivity of its X-Ray Department. To achieve this goal, managers *identify* (stage 1) the need for a new state-of-the-art X-ray machine to replace the existing X-ray machine. The *search* (stage 2) yields several alternative models, but the managers decide to focus on one machine: the XCAM8. They next *acquire information* (stage 3) to do a more-detailed evaluation of XCAM8. Quantitative financial information for the formal analysis follows:

Lifetime Care's revenues will be unchanged regardless of whether the new X-ray machine is acquired. The only relevant financial benefit in purchasing the new X-ray machine is the cash savings in operating costs.

The existing X-ray machine can operate for five more years and will have no terminal disposal value at the end of that time. The required net after-tax initial investment for the new machine is $379,100, which is calculated as follows:

Most capital budgeting projects require an increase in working capital—a cash outlay (usually at the beginning of the project) that will be recovered at the end of the project.

Cost of new machine	$390,000
Investment in working capital	
(supplies and spare parts for new machine)	9,000
Cash flow from disposing of existing machine (after-tax)	(19,900)
Net initial investment for new machine	$379,100

Managers expect the new machine to have a five-year useful life and no terminal disposal value at the end of that time. The new machine is faster and easier to operate and can X-ray a larger area. These improvements will decrease labor, power, and utilities costs. Managers expect the investment to result in annual cash savings in operating costs (after-tax) of $100,000 for each of the first four years and $91,000 in year 5. These savings generally occur uniformly throughout the year. To simplify computations, all operating cash flows are assumed to occur at the end of the year. The additional working-capital investment of $9,000 is expected to be recovered in full at the end of year 5.

Managers at Lifetime Care also identify the following nonfinancial qualitative benefits of investing in the new X-ray machine:

- Higher quality of X-rays, which would lead to improved diagnoses and better patient treatment.
- Improved safety of technicians and patients. The greater efficiency of the new machine would mean that X-ray technicians and patients would have less exposure to the possible harmful effects of radiation.

These nonfinancial qualitative benefits are not considered in the formal financial analysis because their effects are difficult to quantify in financial terms.

To make the *selection* (stage 4), the manager decides whether to purchase the new X-ray machine. This chapter discusses four capital budgeting methods to analyze financial information:

1. Net present value (NPV)
2. Internal rate of return (IRR)
3. Payback
4. Accrual accounting rate of return (AARR)

Both the NPV and IRR methods use discounted cash flows.

3

Use and evaluate the two main discounted cash flow (DCF) methods: the net present value (NPV) method and the internal rate-of-return (IRR) method

. . . to explicitly consider all project cash flows and the time value of money

Discounted Cash Flow

Discounted cash flow (DCF) methods measure all expected future cash inflows and outflows of a project as if they occurred at a single point in time. The key feature of DCF methods is the **time value of money**, which means that a dollar (or any other monetary unit) received today is worth more than a dollar received at any future time. The reason is that $1 received today can be invested at, say, 10% per year so that it grows to $1.10 at the end of one year. The time value of money is the opportunity cost (the return of $0.10 forgone per year) from not having the money today. In this example, $1 received one year from now is worth $1 ÷ 1.10 = $0.9091 today. In this way, discounted cash flow methods explicitly weight cash flows by the time value of money. So in our example, $100 received one year from now will be weighted by 0.9091 to yield a discounted cash flow of $90.91, which is today's value of that $100 next year. DCF focuses on cash inflows and outflows rather than on operating income as determined by accrual accounting.

Management accountants usually ignore the time value of money in short-run analyses because the amount of interest forgone is insignificant.

The compound interest tables and formulas used in DCF analysis are in Appendix C, pages 833–839. If you are unfamiliar with compound interest, do not proceed until you have studied Appendix C. The tables in Appendix C will be used frequently in this chapter.

The two DCF methods we describe are the net present value (NPV) method and the internal rate-of-return (IRR) method. DCF methods use the **required rate of return (RRR)**, which is the minimum acceptable annual rate of return on an investment. RRR is the return that an organization could expect to receive elsewhere for an investment of comparable risk. The RRR is also called the **discount rate, hurdle rate, cost of capital**, or **opportunity cost of capital**. Assume that the required rate of return for Lifetime Care's X-ray machine project is 8% per year.

Net Present Value Method

The **net present value (NPV) method** calculates the expected monetary gain or loss from a project by discounting all expected future cash inflows and outflows to the present point in time, using the required rate of return. Based on financial factors alone, only projects with a zero or positive NPV are acceptable. That's because the return from these projects equals or exceeds the cost of capital—the return available by investing the capital elsewhere. If all other things are equal, the higher the NPV, the better. To use the NPV method, apply the following three steps:

Step 1: Draw a Sketch of Relevant Cash Inflows and Outflows. The right side of Exhibit 21-2 shows arrows that depict the cash flows of the new X-ray machine. *Note that parentheses denote relevant cash outflows throughout all exhibits in*

EXHIBIT 21-2 Net Present Value Method: Lifetime Care Hospital's New X-Ray Machine

	A	B	C	D	E	F	G	H	I
1			Net initial investment	$379,100					
2			Useful life	5 years					
3			Annual cash inflow	$100,000					
4			Required rate of return	8%					
5									
6		Present Value	Present Value of	Sketch of Relevant Cash Flows at End of Each Year					
7		of Cash Flow	$1 Discounted at 8%	0	1	2	3	4	5
8	**Approach 1: Discounting Each Year's Cash Flow Separately**[a]								
9	Net initial investment	$(379,100)	1.000	$(379,100)					
10		92,600	0.926		$100,000				
11		85,700	0.857			$100,000			
12	Annual cash inflow	79,400	0.794				$100,000		
13		73,500	0.735					$100,000	
14		68,100	0.681						$100,000
15	NPV if new machine purchased	$ 20,200							
16									
17	**Approach 2: Using Annuity Table**[b]								
18	Net initial investment	$(379,100)	1.000	$(379,100)					
19					$100,000	$100,000	$100,000	$100,000	$100,000
20									
21	Annual cash inflow	399,300	3.993						
22	NPV if new machine purchased	$ 20,200							
23									
24	*Note:* Parentheses denote relevant cash outflows throughout all exhibits in Chapter 21.								
25	[a] Present values from Table 2, Appendix C at the end of the book. For example, 0.857 = 1÷(1.08)².								
26	[b] Annuity present value from Table 4, Appendix C. The annuity table value of 3.993 is the sum of the individual discount rates								
27	0.926 + 0.857 + 0.794 + 0.735 + 0.681, subject to rounding.								

Chapter 21. The sketch helps the decision maker visualize and organize the data in a systematic way. Note, Exhibit 21-2 includes the outflow for the acquisition of the new machine at the start of year 1 (also referred to as end of year 0). The NPV method specifies cash flows regardless of the source of the cash flows, such as from operations, purchase or sale of equipment, or investment in or recovery of working capital. *Do not* inject accrual-accounting concepts such as sales made on credit or noncash expenses into the determination of cash inflows and outflows.

Step 2: Choose the Correct Compound Interest Table from Appendix C. In our example, we can discount each year's cash flow separately using Table 2, or we can compute the present value of an annuity, a series of equal cash flows at equal time intervals, using Table 4. Both tables are in Appendix C. If we use Table 2, we find the discount factors for periods 1 through 5 under the 8% column. Approach 1 in Exhibit 21-2 uses the five discount factors. Because the investment in the new machine produces an annuity, we may also use Table 4. We find the discount factor for five periods under the 8% column. Approach 2 shows that this discount factor is 3.993, which is the sum of the five discount factors used in approach 1. To obtain the present value amount, multiply each discount factor by the amount represented by each arrow on the right in Exhibit 21-2 (–$379,100 × 1.000; $100,000 × 0.926; and so on to $100,000 × 3.993).

Step 3: Sum the Present Value Figures to Determine NPV. If NPV is zero or positive, financial considerations suggest that the project should be accepted; its expected rate of return equals or exceeds the required rate of return. If NPV is negative, the project should be rejected; its expected rate of return is below the required rate of return.

Exhibit 21-2 calculates an NPV of $20,200 at the required rate of return of 8% per year. The project is acceptable based on financial information. The cash flows from the project are adequate (1) to recover the net initial investment in the project and (2) to earn a return greater than 8% per year on the investment tied up in the project over its useful life.

> If you use a calculator or computer to determine NPV, you will typically get a slightly different answer than you would by using the tables in Appendix C. That's because (1) the factors in the tables have only three decimal places versus eight (or more) for calculators, and (2) the tables assume cash flow occurs at the end of the period, whereas some calculators assume cash flows are continuous.

Managers must also weigh nonfinancial factors such as reduced health risks to patients and technicians from X-rays and better diagnoses and treatments for patients. If NPV had been negative, the manager would need to decide whether these positive nonfinancial benefits outweighed the negative NPV.

Pause here. Do not proceed until you understand what you see in Exhibit 21-2. Compare approach 1 with approach 2 in Exhibit 21-2 to see how Table 4 in Appendix C merely aggregates the present value factors of Table 2. That is, the fundamental table is Table 2. Table 4 simply reduces calculations when there is an annuity.

Internal Rate-of-Return Method

The **internal rate-of-return (IRR) method** calculates the discount rate at which the present value of expected cash inflows from a project equals the present value of its expected cash outflows. That is, IRR is the discount rate that makes NPV = $0. Exhibit 21-3 presents the cash flows and shows the calculation of NPV using a 10% annual discount rate for Lifetime Care's X-ray machine project. At a 10% discount rate, NPV of the project is $0. Therefore, IRR is 10% per year.

How does an analyst determine the discount rate that yields NPV = $0? In most cases, analysts solving capital budgeting problems use a calculator or computer program to provide the internal rate of return. The following trial-and-error approach can also provide the answer.

Step 1: Use a discount rate and calculate the project's NPV.

Step 2: If the calculated NPV is less than zero, use a lower discount rate. (A *lower* discount rate will *increase* NPV. Remember that we are trying to find a discount rate for which NPV = $0.) If NPV is greater than zero, use a higher discount rate to lower NPV. Keep adjusting the discount rate until NPV = $0. In the Lifetime Care example, a discount rate of 8% yields an NPV of +$20,200 (see Exhibit 21-2). A discount rate of 12% yields an NPV of –$18,600 (3.605, the present value annuity factor from Table 4, × $100,000 minus $379,100).

EXHIBIT 21-3 **Internal Rate-of-Return Method: Lifetime Care Hospital's New X-Ray Machine[a]**

	A	B	C	D	E	F	G	H	I
1			Net initial investment	$379,100					
2			Useful life	5 years					
3			Annual cash inflow	$100,000					
4			Annual discount rate	10%					
5									
6		**Present Value**	**Present Value of**	**Sketch of Relevant Cash Flows at End of Each Year**					
7		**of Cash Flow**	**$1 Discounted at 10%**	**0**	**1**	**2**	**3**	**4**	**5**
8	**Approach 1: Discounting Each Year's Cash Flow Separately[b]**								
9	Net initial investment	$(379,100) ←	1.000 ←	$(379,100)					
10		90,900 ←	0.909 ←		$100,000				
11		82,600 ←	0.826 ←			$100,000			
12	Annual cash inflow	75,100 ←	0.751 ←				$100,000		
13		68,300 ←	0.683 ←					$100,000	
14		62,100 ←	0.621 ←						$100,000
15	NPV if new machine purchased[c]	$ 0							
16	(the zero difference proves that								
17	the internal rate of return is 10%)								
18									
19	**Approach 2: Using Annuity Table**								
20	Net initial investment	$(379,100) ←	1.000 ←	$(379,100)					
21					$100,000	$100,000	$100,000	$100,000	$100,000
22									
23	Annual cash inflow	379,100 ←	3.791[d] ←						
24	NPV if new machine purchased	$ 0							
25									
26	*Note:* Parentheses denote relevant cash outflows throughout all exhibits in Chapter 21.								
27	[a] The internal rate of return is computed by methods explained on pp. 728-729.								
28	[b] Present values from Table 2, Appendix C, at the end of the book.								
29	[c] Sum is $(100) due to rounding. We round to $0.								
30	[d] Annuity present value from Table 4, Appendix C. The annuity table value of 3.791 is the sum of the individual discount rates								
31	0.909 + 0.826 + 0.751 + 0.683 + 0.621, subject to rounding.								

Therefore, the discount rate that makes NPV = $0 must lie between 8% and 12%. We use 10% and get NPV = $0. Hence, the IRR is 10% per year.

The step-by-step computations of internal rate of return are easier when the cash inflows are equal, as in our example. Information from Exhibit 21-3 can be expressed by:

$$\$379{,}100 = \text{Present value of annuity of } \$100{,}000 \text{ at } X\% \text{ per year for 5 years}$$

Or, what factor F in Table 4 (Appendix C) will satisfy this equation?

$$\$379{,}100 = \$100{,}000F$$

$$F = \$379{,}100 \div \$100{,}000 = 3.791$$

On the five-period line of Table 4, find the percentage column that is closest to 3.791. It is exactly 10%. If the factor (F) falls between the factors in two columns, straight-line interpolation is used to approximate IRR. This interpolation is illustrated in the Problem for Self-Study (p. 743).

A project is accepted only if IRR equals or exceeds required rate of return (RRR). In the Lifetime Care example, the X-ray machine has an IRR of 10%, which is greater than the RRR of 8%. On the basis of financial factors, Lifetime Care should invest in the new machine. In general, the NPV and IRR decision rules result in consistent project acceptance or rejection decisions. If IRR exceeds RRR, then the project has a positive NPV (favoring acceptance). If IRR equals RRR, NPV = $0. If IRR is less than RRR, NPV is negative (favoring rejection). Obviously, managers prefer projects with higher IRRs to projects with lower IRRs, if all other things are equal. The IRR of 10% means the cash inflows from the project are adequate to (1) recover the net initial investment in the project and (2) earn a return of exactly 10% on the investment tied up in the project over its useful life.

Comparison of Net Present Value and Internal Rate-of-Return Methods

One advantage of the NPV method is that it expresses computations in dollars, not in percentages. Therefore, we can sum NPVs of individual projects to calculate an NPV of a combination of projects. In contrast, IRRs of individual projects cannot be added or averaged to represent the IRR of a combination of projects.

Managers using the IRR method assume that the discount rate is equal to the rate of return earned on the project. Such investment opportunities may not be available. Managers using the NPV method assume that the funds obtainable from competing projects can be reinvested at the company's RRR. The NPV method is generally regarded as a better method than the IRR method. Refer to corporate finance texts for more details on these issues.

Another advantage of the NPV method is that it can be used when the RRR varies over the life of a project. Suppose the X-ray machine considered by Lifetime Care has a RRR of 9% per year in years 1 and 2 and 12% per year in years 3, 4, and 5. Total present value of the cash inflows can be calculated as $378,100 (computations not shown).

Given the net initial investment of $379,100, NPV calculations indicate that the project is undesirable: NPV is –$1,000 ($378,100 – $379,100). It is not possible to use the IRR method in this case. That's because different RRRs in different years (9% annually for years 1 and 2 versus 12% annually for years 3, 4, and 5) mean there is not a single RRR that the IRR (a single figure) can be compared against to decide if the project should be accepted or rejected.

Despite these limitations of the IRR method, surveys report widespread use of the IRR method. Why? Probably because managers find the IRR method easier to understand and because, in most instances, their decisions would be unaffected by using IRR or NPV. In some cases, however, as when comparing two projects with unequal lives or unequal investments, the two methods will not indicate the same decision.

Sensitivity Analysis

To present the basics of the NPV and IRR methods, we have assumed that the expected values of cash flows will occur *for certain*. Obviously, such predictions are not certain. To examine how a result will change if the predicted financial outcomes are not achieved or if an underlying assumption changes, managers can use *sensitivity analysis*, a "what-if" technique introduced in Chapter 3.

Sensitivity analysis can take various forms. Suppose the manager at Lifetime Care believes forecasted savings are difficult to predict. She asks, "What are the minimum annual cash savings that make investment in the new X-ray machine acceptable—that is, lead to NPV = $0?" For the data in Exhibit 21-2, let *A* = Annual cash flow and let NPV = $0. Net initial investment is $379,100, and the present value factor at the 8% required annual rate of return for a five-year annuity of $1 is 3.993. Then:

$$\begin{aligned} NPV &= \$0 \\ 3.993A - \$379{,}100 &= \$0 \\ 3.993A &= \$379{,}100 \\ A &= \$94{,}941 \end{aligned}$$

At the discount rate of 8% per year, annual cash flow can decrease to $94,941 (a decline of $100,000 – $94,941 = $5,059) before the NPV falls to $0. If the manager believes she can attain annual cash savings of at least $94,941, she can justify investing in the new X-ray machine on financial grounds.

Exhibit 21-4 shows that variations in the annual cash inflows or RRR significantly affect NPV of the X-ray machine project. NPVs can also vary with different useful lives of a project. Sensitivity analysis helps managers to focus on decisions that are most sensitive to different assumptions and to worry less about decisions that are not so sensitive.

Given the rapid pace of technological change, estimating the useful life of a project can be one of the most challenging aspects of capital budgeting.

EXHIBIT 21-4 **Net Present Value Calculations for Lifetime Care Hospital Under Different Assumptions of Annual Cash Flows and Required Rates of Return[a]**

	A	B	C	D	E	F
1	Required	Annual Cash Flows				
2	Rate of Return	$80,000	$90,000	$100,000	$110,000	$120,000
3	6%	$(42,140)	$ (20)	$42,100	$84,220	$126,340
4	8%	$(59,660)	$(19,730)	$20,200	$60,130	$100,060
5	10%	$(75,820)	$(37,910)	$ 0	$37,910	$ 75,820
6						
7	[a]All calculated amounts assume the project's useful life is five years.					

Payback Method

4 **Use and evaluate the payback method** . . . to calculate the time it takes to recoup the investment

We now consider the third method for analyzing the financial aspects of projects. The **payback method** measures the time it will take to recoup, in the form of expected future cash flows, the net initial investment in a project. As in NPV and IRR, payback (also called payback period) does not distinguish among the sources of cash flows, such as from operations, purchase or sale of equipment, or investment or recovery of working capital. Payback is simplest to calculate when a project has uniform cash flows. We consider this case first.

Uniform Cash Flows

In the Lifetime Care example, the X-ray machine costs $379,100, has a five-year expected useful life, and generates a $100,000 *uniform* cash flow each year. The payback period is:

$$\text{Payback period} = \frac{\text{Net initial investment}}{\text{Uniform increase in annual future cash flows}}$$

$$= \frac{\$379{,}100}{\$100{,}000} = 3.8 \text{ years}^1$$

The payback method highlights liquidity, a factor that often plays a role in capital budgeting decisions. Managers prefer projects with shorter payback periods (projects that are more liquid) to projects with longer payback periods, if all other things are equal. Projects with shorter payback periods give an organization more flexibility because funds for other projects become available sooner. Also, managers are less confident about cash flow predictions that stretch far into the future.

Under the payback method, organizations choose a cutoff period for a project. The greater the risks of a project, the shorter the cutoff period. Japanese companies favor the payback method over other methods and use cutoff periods ranging from three to five years. Projects with a payback period that is less than the cutoff period are considered acceptable, and those with a payback period that is longer than the cutoff period are rejected. If Lifetime Care's cutoff period under the payback method is three years, it will reject the new machine.

The payback method is easy to understand. As in DCF methods, the payback method is not affected by accrual accounting conventions such as depreciation. Payback is a useful measure when (1) preliminary screening of many proposals is necessary, (2) interest rates are high, and (3) the expected cash flows in later years of a project are highly uncertain. That's because, under these conditions, companies give much more weight to cash flows in early periods of a capital budgeting project and to recovering the investments they have made.

Companies often use the payback method in conjunction with DCF analyses to select positive NPV projects that have an acceptably short payback period.

Two weaknesses of the payback method are that (1) it fails to incorporate the time value of money and (2) it does not consider a project's cash flows after the payback period. Consider an alternative to the $379,100 X-ray machine. Another X-ray machine, with a three-year useful life and no terminal disposal value, requires only a $300,000 net

[1]Cash savings from the new X-ray machine occur uniformly *throughout* the year, but for simplicity in calculating NPV and IRR, we assume they occur at the *end* of each year. A literal interpretation of this assumption would imply a payback of 4 years because Lifetime Care will only recover its investment when cash inflows occur at the end of year 4. The calculations shown in the chapter, however, better approximate Lifetime Care's payback on the basis of uniform cash flows throughout the year.

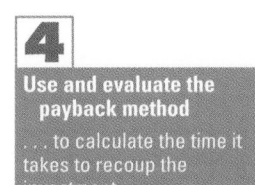

initial investment and will also result in cash inflows of $100,000 per year. First, compare the payback periods:

$$\text{Machine 1} = \frac{\$379{,}100}{\$100{,}000} = 3.8 \text{ years}$$

$$\text{Machine 2} = \frac{\$300{,}000}{\$100{,}000} = 3.0 \text{ years}$$

The payback criterion favors machine 2, with the shorter payback. If the cutoff period were three years, machine 1 would fail to meet the payback criterion.

Consider next the NPV of the two investment options using Lifetime Care's 8% required rate of return for the X-ray machine investment. At a discount rate of 8%, NPV of machine 2 is −$42,300 (2.577, the present value annuity factor for three years at 8% per year from Table 4, times $100,000 = $257,700 minus net initial investment of $300,000). Machine 1, as we know, has a positive NPV of $20,200 (from Exhibit 21-2). The NPV criterion suggests Lifetime Care should acquire machine 1. Machine 2, with a negative NPV, would fail to meet the NPV criterion.

The payback method gives a different answer than the NPV method in this example because the payback method ignores cash flows after the payback period and ignores the time value of money. Another problem with the payback method is that choosing too short a cutoff period for project acceptance may promote the selection of only short-lived projects. An organization will tend to reject long-run, positive-NPV projects. Despite these differences, companies find it useful to look at both NPV and payback when making capital investment decisions.

Nonuniform Cash Flows

When cash flows are not uniform, the payback computation takes a cumulative form: The cash flows over successive years are accumulated until the amount of net initial investment is recovered. Assume that Venture Law Group is considering the purchase of videoconferencing equipment for $150,000. The equipment is expected to provide a total cash savings of $380,000 over the next five years, due to reduced travel costs and more-effective use of associates' time. The cash savings occur uniformly throughout each year, but nonuniformly across years. Payback occurs during the third year:

Year	Cash Savings	Cumulative Cash Savings	Net Initial Investment Unrecovered at End of Year
0	—	—	$150,000
1	$ 50,000	$ 50,000	100,000
2	60,000	110,000	40,000
3	80,000	190,000	—
4	90,000	280,000	—
5	100,000	380,000	—

Straight-line interpolation within the third year reveals that the final $40,000 needed to recover the $150,000 investment (that is, $150,000 − $110,000 recovered by the end of year 2) will be achieved halfway through year 3 (in which $80,000 of cash savings occur):

$$\text{Payback period} = 2 \text{ years} + \left(\frac{\$40{,}000}{\$80{,}000} \times 1 \text{ year}\right) = 2.5 \text{ years}$$

The videoconferencing example has a single cash outflow of $150,000 in year 0. When a project has multiple cash outflows occurring at different points in time, these outflows are added to obtain a total cash-outflow figure for the project. No adjustment is made for the time value of money when adding these cash outflows in computing the payback period.

5 **Use and evaluate the accrual accounting rate-of-return (AARR) method**
... after-tax operating income divided by investment

Accrual Accounting Rate-of-Return Method

We now consider a fourth method for analyzing the financial aspects of capital budgeting projects. **Accrual accounting rate of return (AARR)** divides an accrual accounting measure of average annual income of a project by an accrual accounting measure of its investment. It is also called **accounting rate of return**. We illustrate AARR for the Lifetime Care example using the project's net initial investment as the amount in the denominator:

$$\text{Accrual accounting rate of return} = \frac{\text{Increase in expected average annual after-tax operating income}}{\text{Net initial investment}}$$

Variations of this formula exist in practice. Some companies use "increase in expected average annual operating income" in the numerator and/or "average investment per year" in the denominator.

NPV, IRR, and payback are all based on *cash flows*; AARR is based on *accrual accounting*.

If Lifetime Care purchases the new X-ray machine, the increase in expected average after-tax annual savings in operating costs will be \$98,200. This amount is the expected after-tax total operating savings of \$491,000 (\$100,000 for four years and \$91,000 in year 5) ÷ 5 years. The new machine results in additional depreciation deductions of \$70,000 per year (\$78,000 – \$8,000, see p. 735). The net initial investment is \$379,100. The AARR on net initial investment is:

$$AARR = \frac{\$98{,}200 - \$70{,}000}{\$379{,}100} = \frac{\$28{,}200 \text{ per year}}{\$379{,}100} = 0.074, \text{ or } 7.4\% \text{ per year}$$

AARR of 7.4% per year indicates the rate at which a dollar of investment generates after-tax operating income. AARR on the new X-ray machine is low for two reasons: (1) using net initial investment makes the denominator larger than it would be using average level of investment, and (2) annual depreciation must be deducted from annual operating income in the numerator. Many companies calculate AARR using an average level of investment to recognize that the book value of the investment declines over time. In its simplest form, average investment for Lifetime Care (with terminal disposal value of machine equal to \$0 and terminal recovery of working capital equal to \$9,000) is

$$\text{Average investment over five years} = \frac{\text{Net initial investment} + \text{Disposal value}}{2} = \frac{\$379{,}100 + \$9{,}000}{2} = \$194{,}050$$

$$AARR = \frac{\$28{,}200}{\$194{,}050} = 0.145, \text{ or } 14.5\% \text{ per year}$$

Our point here is that companies vary in how they calculate AARR. There is no uniformly preferred approach. Be sure you understand how AARR is defined in each individual situation. Projects whose AARR exceeds a specified accrual accounting required rate of return are regarded as acceptable (the higher the AARR, the better the project is considered to be).

The AARR method is similar to the IRR method in that both methods calculate a rate-of-return percentage. The AARR method calculates return using operating-income numbers after considering accruals and taxes, whereas the IRR method calculates return on the basis of after-tax cash flows and the time value of money. Because cash flows and time value of money are central to capital budgeting decisions, the IRR method is regarded as better than the AARR method.

AARR computations are easy to understand, and they use numbers reported in the financial statements. AARR gives managers an idea of how the accounting numbers they will report in the future will be affected if a project is accepted. Unlike the payback method, which ignores cash flows after the payback period, the AARR method considers income earned throughout a project's expected useful life. Unlike the NPV method, the AARR method uses accrual accounting income numbers. It does not track cash flows, and it ignores the time value of money. Critics cite these arguments as drawbacks of the AARR method.

Evaluating Managers and Goal-Congruence Issues

6

Identify and reduce conflicts from using DCF for capital budgeting decisions and accrual accounting for performance evaluation

. . . an acceptable project can decrease operating income in its early years

As the Global Surveys of Company Practice (p. 735) indicate, companies frequently report NPV, IRR, payback, and AARR on the forms they use for evaluating capital investment decisions. When different methods lead to different rankings of projects, finance theory suggests that more weight be given to the NPV method. That's because the assumptions made by the NPV method are most consistent with making decisions that maximize company value. Corporate finance texts discuss these issues in more detail.

Capital budgeting decisions made using the NPV method might not be consistent with decisions that would be made if AARR were used for performance evaluation. Consider the manager of the X-Ray Department at Lifetime Care. The NPV method indicates that the manager should purchase the new X-ray machine because it has a positive NPV of $20,200. But suppose top management of Lifetime Care uses AARR for judging performance. The manager of the X-Ray Department may then reject purchasing the new X-ray machine if the AARR of 7.4% on the net initial investment reduces the AARR of the entire X-Ray Department and negatively affects the department's reported performance.

There is an inconsistency between using the NPV method as best for capital budgeting decisions and then using a different method to evaluate performance over short time horizons. This inconsistency means managers are tempted to make capital budgeting decisions on the basis of short-run accrual accounting results, even though these decisions, in terms of DCF, are not in the best long-run interest of the organization as a whole. Such temptations become more pronounced if managers are frequently transferred (or promoted), or if their bonuses are affected by the level of year-to-year accrual income.[2] This conflict can be reduced by evaluating managers on a project-by-project basis and by looking at how well managers achieve the amounts and timing of forecasted cash flows.

Note that the conflict between decision making and performance evaluation persists even if a company uses AARR for both purposes. If the AARR on the X-ray machine exceeds the minimum required AARR but is below the current AARR of the X-Ray Department, the manager may still be tempted to reject purchasing the X-ray machine. That's because the lower AARR of the X-ray machine will reduce the AARR of the entire X-Ray Department and hurt the manager's reported performance. Chapter 23 describes how performance evaluation models such as economic value added (EVA®) help achieve greater congruency with decision making models.

Relevant Cash Flows in Discounted Cash Flow Analysis

7

Identify relevant cash inflows and outflows for capital budgeting decisions

. . . the differences in expected future cash flows resulting from the investment

One of the biggest challenges in capital budgeting, particularly DCF analysis, is determining which cash flows are relevant in making an investment selection. Relevant cash flows are the differences in expected future cash flows as a result of making the investment. In the Lifetime Care example, the relevant cash flows are the differences in expected future cash flows between continuing to use the old machine and purchasing the new one. *When reading this section, focus on identifying expected future cash flows and the differences in expected future cash flows.*

To illustrate relevant cash flow analysis, consider the Lifetime Care example and these additional assumptions:

There are entire courses dealing with income tax laws; this chapter illustrates a general approach for incorporating income taxes into capital budgeting decisions.

- Lifetime Care is a profitable company. The income tax rate is 40% of operating income each year.
- The before-tax operating cash savings from the new X-ray machine are $120,000 in years 1 through 4 and $105,000 in year 5.
- For tax purposes, Lifetime Care uses the straight-line depreciation method and assumes no terminal disposal value, which results in an equal amount of depreciation each year.
- Gains or losses on the sale of depreciable assets are taxed at the same rate as ordinary income.
- The tax effects of cash inflows and outflows occur at the same time that the cash inflows and outflows occur.
- Lifetime Care uses an 8% required rate of return for discounting after-tax cash flows.

[2]Managers are often interested in how accepting a project will affect a bonus plan that is based on reported annual accrual accounting numbers. Do not assume that the AARR computed by the formula on page 733 is the appropriate number to use in examining the effect that adoption of a project will have on a manager's bonus plan. It is necessary to examine on a year-by-year basis how the AARR is computed when determining bonuses. For example, the numerator in the formula is the "increase in expected average annual after-tax operating income." This average increase need not be the same each year during a project. Assume the president of Lifetime Care receives an annual $50,000 lump-sum bonus if the AARR on assets exceeds 8% in that year. Project A has an AARR over its five-year life of 10% and an NPV of $20,000. Project B has an AARR over its five-year life of 9% and an NPV of $18,000. Project A has cash inflows in years 1 and 5 but zero cash inflows in years 2, 3, and 4. Project B has equal cash inflows in years 1 through 5. It could well be that the president would receive higher bonuses with project B—the project with a lower NPV.

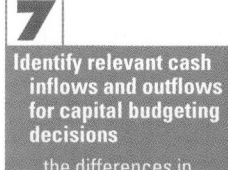

GLOBAL SURVEYS OF COMPANY PRACTICE

Comparison of Capital Budgeting Methods

What methods do companies around the world use for analyzing capital investment decisions? The percentages in the following table indicate how frequently particular capital budgeting methods are used in eight countries. The reported percentages exceed 100% because many companies surveyed use more than one method.

	United States[a]	Australia[b]	Canada[c]	Cyprus[d]	Japan	Poland[e]	Scotland[f]	United Kingdom[g]
Payback	35%	61%	50%	37%	52%	40%	78%	70%
IRR	45%	37%	62%	9%	4%	25%	58%	81%
NPV	50%	45%	41%	11%	6%	30%	48%	80%
AARR	5%	24%	17%	4%	36%	—	31%	56%
Other	8%	7 %	8%	49%	5%	50%	—	31%

Some observations about these surveys:

1. Companies in the United States, Australia, Canada, Poland, Scotland, and the United Kingdom tend to use more than one method to evaluate capital investments. (The sum of the capital budgeting percentages in the columns for each of these countries ranges from approximately 150% to 300%.)
2. Japanese and Cypriot companies tend to use one method. (The sum of the capital budgeting percentages for Japan and Cyprus are approximately 100%.)
3. The payback method is popular in all countries. Japanese companies use the payback method as their primary method of analysis in their capital budgeting decisions. Companies in the United States, Australia, Canada, Poland, Scotland, and the United Kingdom use discounted cash flow (DCF) methods (IRR and NPV) extensively.
4. In addition to Canada and the United Kingdom, IRR is the most-used capital-budgeting method in Singapore and Thailand.[h,i]
5. The AARR method lags behind DCF methods in all surveyed countries except Japan, where it is preferred over IRR and NPV.

[a] P. Ryan and G. Ryan, "Capital Budgeting."
[b] P. Blayney and I. Yokohama, "Comparative Analysis."
[c] V. Jog and A. Srivastava, "Corporate Financial Decision Making."
[d] I. Lazaridis, "Capital Budgeting Practices."
[e] A. Szychta, "The Scope and Application."
[f] A. Sangster, "Capital Investment Appraisal."
[g] G. Arnold and P. Hatzopoulos, "The Theory-Practice Gap."
[h] G. Kester and T. Chong, "Capital Budgeting Practices."
[i] O. Arsiraphongphisit, G. Kester, and T. Skully, "Financial Policies."
Full citations are in Appendix A at the end of the book.

Summary data for the X-ray machines are:

	Old X-Ray Machine	New X-Ray Machine
Purchase price	—	$390,000
Current book value	$40,000	—
Current disposal value	6,500	Not applicable
Terminal disposal value 5 years from now	0	0
Annual depreciation	8,000[a]	78,000[b]
Working capital required	6,000	15,000

[a] $40,000 ÷ 5 years = $8,000 annual depreciation.
[b] $390,000 ÷ 5 years = $78,000 annual depreciation.

Relevant After-Tax Flows

We use the *differential approach* to decision making introduced in Chapter 11. We compare (1) the after-tax cash outflows as a result of replacing the old machine with (2) the savings in future after-tax cash outflows by using the new machine rather than the old machine.

It is important first to understand how income taxes affect cash flows in each year. Income taxes are a fact of life for most corporations and individuals. As Benjamin Franklin said, "Two things in life are certain: death and taxes." Exhibit 21-5 shows how investing in the new machine will affect Lifetime Care's cash flow from operations and its income taxes in year 1. Recall that Lifetime Care will save $120,000 in before-tax cash operating outflows by investing in the new machine (p. 734), but it will record additional depreciation of $70,000 ($78,000 – $8,000) for tax purposes.

Panel A shows that the year 1 cash flow from operations, net of income taxes, equals $100,000, using two methods based on the income statement. The first method focuses on cash items only, the $120,000 cash savings minus income taxes of $20,000. The second method starts with the $30,000 increase in net income (calculated after subtracting the $70,000 additional depreciation deductions for income tax purposes) and adds back that $70,000, because depreciation is an operating cost that reduces net income but is a noncash item itself.

Panel B of Exhibit 21-5 describes a third method that we will use frequently to compute cash flow from operations, net of income taxes. The easiest way to interpret the third method is to think of the government as a 40% (equal to the tax rate) partner in Lifetime Care. Each time Lifetime Care obtains cost savings, S, (or cash revenues in excess of cash costs), its income is higher by S, so it will pay 40% of the cash savings ($0.40S$) in taxes. This results in after-tax cash operating flows of $S - 0.40S$, which in this example is $120,000 – (0.40 × $120,000) = $72,000, or $120,000 × (1 – 0.40) = $72,000.

To achieve the higher cash savings, S, Lifetime Care incurs higher depreciation charges, D, from investing in the new machine. Depreciation cost does not directly affect cash flow because depreciation is a noncash cost, but higher depreciation cost *lowers* Lifetime Care's taxable income by D, saving income tax cash outflows of $0.40D$, which in this example is 0.40 × $70,000 = $28,000.

Letting t = tax rate, cash flow from operations, net of income taxes, in this example equals the cash savings, S, minus the tax payments on these savings, $t \times S$, plus the tax

EXHIBIT 21-5

Effect on Cash Flow from Operations, Net of Income Taxes, in Year 1 for Lifetime Care's Investment in the New X-Ray Machine

PANEL A: Two Methods Based on the Income Statement

S	Savings in cash costs	$120,000
D	Additional depreciation deduction	70,000
OI	Increase in operating income	50,000
T	Income taxes (Income tax rate $t \times OI$) = 40% × $50,000	20,000
NI	Increase in net income	$ 30,000
	Increase in cash flow from operations, net of income taxes	
	Method 1: $S - T$ = $120,000 – $20,000 = $100,000 or	
	Method 2: $NI + D$ = $30,000 + $70,000 = $100,000	

PANEL B: Item-by-Item Method

	Effect of cash operating flows	
S	Savings in cash costs	$120,000
$t \times S$	Deduct income tax cash outflow at 40%	48,000
$S - (t \times S) = (1 - t) \times S$	After-tax cash flow from operations (excluding the depreciation effect)	72,000
	Effect of depreciation	
D	Additional depreciation deduction, $70,000	
$t \times D$	Income tax cash savings from additional depreciation deduction at 40% × $70,000	28,000
$(1 - t) \times S + (t \times D) = S - (t \times S) + (t \times D)$	Cash flow from operations, net of income taxes	$100,000

savings on depreciation deductions, $t \times D$: \$120,000 − (0.40 × \$120,000) + (0.40 × \$70,000) = \$120,000 − \$48,000 + \$28,000 = \$100,000.

By the same logic, each time Lifetime Care has a gain on the sale of assets, G, it will show tax outflows, $t \times G$; and each time Lifetime Care has a loss on the sale of assets, L, it will show tax benefits or savings, $t \times L$.

Categories of Cash Flows

A capital investment project typically has three categories of cash flows: (1) net initial investment in the project, which includes the acquisition of a new asset and needed additions to working capital, minus the after-tax cash flow from current disposal of an existing asset; (2) after-tax cash flow from operations (including income tax cash savings from annual depreciation deductions); and (3) after-tax cash flow from terminal disposal of an asset and recovery of working capital. We use the Lifetime Care example to discuss these three categories.

Study Tip: See the useful road map for this important section (the box on *Student Guide*, p. 285).

As you work through the cash flows in each category, refer to Exhibit 21-6. This exhibit sketches the relevant cash inflows and outflows for Lifetime Care's decision to purchase the new machine as described in items 1 through 3 here. Note that the total relevant cash flows for each year equal the relevant cash flows used in Exhibits 21-2 and 21-3 to illustrate the NPV and IRR methods.

1. Net Initial Investment Three components of net-initial-investment cash flows are (a) cash outflow to purchase the machine, (b) cash outflow for working capital, and (c) after-cash cash inflow from current disposal of the old machine.

1a. *Initial machine investment.* These outflows, made for purchasing plant and equipment, occur at the beginning of the project's life and include cash outflows for transporting and installing the equipment. In the Lifetime Care example, the \$390,000 cost (including transportation and installation) of the X-ray machine is an outflow in year 0. These cash flows are relevant to the capital budgeting decision because they will be incurred only if Lifetime decides to purchase the new machine.

1b. *Initial working-capital investment.* Initial investments in plant and equipment are usually accompanied by additional investments in working capital. These additional investments take the form of current assets, such as accounts receivable and inventories, minus current liabilities, such as accounts payable. Working-capital investments are similar to plant and equipment investments in that they require cash.

The Lifetime Care example assumes a \$9,000 additional investment in working capital (for supplies and spare-parts inventory) if the new machine is acquired.

EXHIBIT 21-6 Relevant Cash Inflows and Outflows for Lifetime Care Hospital's New X-Ray Machine

	A	B	C	D	E	F	G	H
1			Sketch of Relevant Cash Flows at End of Year					
2			0	1	2	3	4	5
3	1a.	Initial machine investment	\$(390,000)					
4	1b.	Initial working-capital investment	(9,000)					
5	1c.	After-tax cash flow from current disposal						
6		of old machine	19,900					
7	Net initial investment		(379,100)					
8	2a.	Annual after-tax cash flow from operations						
9		(excluding the depreciation effect)		\$ 72,000	\$ 72,000	\$ 72,000	\$ 72,000	\$ 63,000
10	2b.	Income tax cash savings from annual						
11		depreciation deductions		28,000	28,000	28,000	28,000	28,000
12	3a.	After-tax cash flow from terminal disposal						
13		of machine						0
14	3b.	After-tax cash flow from recovery of						
15		working capital						9,000
16	Total relevant cash flows,							
17		as shown in Exhibits 21-2 and 21-3	\$(379,100)	\$100,000	\$100,000	\$100,000	\$100,000	\$100,000
18								

The additional working-capital investment is the difference between working capital required to operate the new machine ($15,000) and working capital required to operate the old machine ($6,000). The $9,000 additional investment in working capital is a cash outflow in year 0.

1c. *After-tax cash flow from current disposal of old machine.* Any cash received from disposal of the old machine is a relevant cash inflow (in year 0). That's because it is an expected future cash flow that differs between the alternatives of investing and not investing in the new machine. Only if Lifetime Care invests in the new X-ray machine, will it dispose of the old machine for $6,500. Recall that the book value (which is original cost minus accumulated depreciation) of the old equipment is irrelevant to the decision (Chapter 11, p. 396). It is a past, or sunk, cost. Nothing can change what has already been spent.

To calculate the tax consequences of disposing of the old machine, we compute the gain or loss on disposal:

Current disposal value of old machine (given, p. 735)	$ 6,500
Deduct current book value of old machine (given, p. 735)	40,000
Loss on disposal of machine	$(33,500)

Any loss on the sale of assets lowers taxable income and results in tax savings. The after-tax cash flow from disposal of the old machine equals:

Current disposal value of old machine	$ 6,500
Tax savings on loss (0.40 × $33,500)	13,400
After-tax cash inflow from current disposal of old machine	$ 19,900

The sum of items **1a, 1b,** and **1c** appears in Exhibit 21-6 as the year 0 net initial investment for the new X-ray machine equal to $379,100 (initial machine investment, $390,000, plus additional working-capital investment, $9,000, minus after-tax cash inflow from current disposal of the old machine, $19,900).

2. Cash Flow from Operations This category includes the difference between each year's cash flow from operations under the two alternatives. Organizations make capital investments to generate cash inflows in the future. These inflows may result from producing and selling additional goods or services, or, as for Lifetime Care, from savings in cash operating costs. Annual cash flow from operations can be net outflows in some years. For example, oil production may require large expenditures every, say, five years to improve oil-extraction rates. Always focus on cash flow from operations, not on revenues and expenses under accrual accounting.

The savings in operating cash flows (for labor and materials)—$120,000 in each of the first four years and $105,000 in the fifth year—are relevant because they are expected future cash flows that will differ between the alternatives of investing and not investing in the new machine. The after-tax effects of these cash flows follow.

2a. *Annual after-tax cash flow from operations (excluding the depreciation effect).* The 40% tax rate reduces the benefit of the $120,000 operating cash flow savings for years 1 through 4 with the new X-ray machine. After-tax cash flow (excluding the depreciation effect) is:

Annual cash flow from operations with new machine	$120,000
Deduct income tax payments (0.40 × $120,000)	48,000
Annual after-tax cash flow from operations	$ 72,000

For year 5, the after-tax cash flow (excluding the depreciation effect) is:

Annual cash flow from operations with new machine	$105,000
Deduct income tax payments (0.40 × $105,000)	42,000
Annual after-tax cash flow from operations	$ 63,000

Exhibit 21-6, item **2a**, shows the $72,000 amounts for each of the years 1 through 4 and $63,000 for year 5.

To reinforce the idea about focusing on cash flows, consider the following additional fact about the Lifetime Care example. Suppose total X-Ray Department overhead costs will not change whether the new machine is purchased or the old machine is kept. X-Ray Department overhead costs are allocated to individual X-ray machines—Lifetime Care has several—on the basis of

Question: Why is book value of old equipment *always* irrelevant in capital budgeting decisions?

Answer: Book value is not associated with any current cash flows. It's the difference between the equipment's original cost and its accumulated depreciation under accrual accounting.

We assume Lifetime Care has sufficient positive taxable income so that the full amount of the loss on disposal of the old machine is a tax deduction in year 0.

If Lifetime Care were a nonprofit organization, not subject to income taxes, there would be no tax consequences from disposing of the machine.

the labor costs for operating each machine. Because the new X-ray machine would have lower labor costs, overhead costs allocated to it would be $30,000 less than the amount allocated to the machine it would replace. How should Lifetime Care incorporate the decrease in allocated overhead costs of $30,000 in the relevant cash flow analysis?

To answer that question, we need to ask, "Do *total* overhead costs of the X-Ray Department decrease as a result of acquiring the new machine?" In our example, they do not. Total overhead costs of the X-Ray Department remain the same whether or not the new machine is acquired. *Only the overhead costs allocated to individual machines change.* The overhead costs allocated to the new machine are $30,000 less than the amount allocated to the machine it would replace. This $30,000 difference in overhead would be allocated to *other* machines in the department. That is, no cash flow savings in total overhead would occur. Therefore, the $30,000 should not be included as part of annual cash savings from operations.

Next consider the effects of depreciation. *The depreciation line item is itself irrelevant in DCF analysis.* That's because it's a noncash allocation of costs, whereas DCF is based on inflows and outflows of *cash*. In DCF methods, the initial cost of equipment is regarded as a *lump-sum* outflow of cash in year 0. Deducting depreciation expenses from operating cash inflows would result in counting the lump-sum amount twice. *However, depreciation results in income tax cash savings. These tax savings are a relevant cash flow.*

2b. *Income tax cash savings from annual depreciation deductions.* Tax deductions for depreciation, in effect, partially offset the cost of acquiring the new X-ray machine. The following table calculates the income tax cash savings from the additional depreciation deductions each year as a result of acquiring the new machine.

Year	Depreciation Deduction on New X-Ray Machine (p. 735)	Depreciation Deduction on Old X-Ray Machine (p. 735)	Difference in Depreciation Deduction	Income Tax Rate	Increase in Income Tax Cash Savings from Depreciation Deductions with New X-Ray Machine
1	$78,000	$8,000	$70,000	40%	$28,000
2	78,000	8,000	70,000	40%	28,000
3	78,000	8,000	70,000	40%	28,000
4	78,000	8,000	70,000	40%	28,000
5	78,000	8,000	70,000	40%	28,000

Be sure to understand how depreciation affects cash flow. Depreciation expense is deductible for income tax purposes, so it reduces the company's tax payment, *increasing* the company's net cash flows.

Exhibit 21-6, item **2b**, shows these $28,000 amounts for years 1 through 5.[3]

For economic-policy reasons, usually to encourage (or in some cases, discourage) investments, government tax laws specify which depreciation methods and which depreciable lives will be allowed. Suppose the government, under U.S. income tax laws, permitted accelerated depreciation to be used. This provision would result in higher depreciation deductions in earlier years. If allowable, should Lifetime Care use accelerated depreciation? Yes, because there is a general rule in tax planning for profitable companies such as Lifetime Care: When there is a legal choice, take the depreciation (or any other deduction) sooner rather than later. That causes the income tax savings to occur earlier, increasing NPVs.

3. Terminal Disposal of Investment The disposal of the new investment generally increases cash inflow when the project terminates. Errors in forecasting terminal disposal value are seldom critical for long-duration projects because the present value of amounts to be received in the distant future is usually small. Two components of the terminal disposal value of an investment are (a) after-tax cash flow from terminal disposal of machines and (b) after-tax cash flow from recovery of working capital.

[3]If Lifetime Care were a nonprofit hospital not subject to income taxes, cash flow from operations would equal $120,000 in years 1 through 4 and $105,000 in year 5. The operating cash savings would not be reduced by 40%, and there would also be no income tax cash savings from the depreciation deduction.

3a. *After-tax cash flow from terminal disposal of machines.* At the end of the useful life of the project, the machine's terminal disposal value may be $0 or an amount considerably less than the net initial investment. The relevant cash inflow is the difference in expected after-tax cash inflow from terminal disposal at the end of five years under the two alternatives of purchasing the new machine or keeping the old machine.

Both the existing and the new X-ray machines have zero after-tax cash inflow from terminal disposal in year 5. Hence, the difference in after-tax cash inflow from terminal disposal is also $0. The general approach for computing the relevant amounts (illustrated for the new machine) is:

Terminal disposal value of new machine at end of year 5	$0
Deduct book value of new machine at end of year 5	0
Gain (or loss) on disposal of new machine	$0
Terminal disposal value of new machine at end of year 5	$0
Deduct taxes paid on gain (add taxes saved on loss), $0.40 \times \$0$	0
After-tax cash inflow from terminal disposal of new machine	$0

3b. *After-tax cash flow from terminal recovery of working-capital investment.* The initial investment in working capital is usually fully recouped when the project is terminated. At that time, inventories and accounts receivable necessary to support the project are no longer needed. Lifetime Care receives cash equal to the book value of its working capital. Thus, there is no gain or loss on working capital and, hence, no tax consequences. The relevant cash inflow is the difference in the expected working capital recovered under the two alternatives. At the end of year 5, Lifetime recovers $15,000 cash from working capital if it invests in the new X-ray machine versus $6,000 if it continues to use the old machine. The relevant cash inflow in year 5 if Lifetime invests in the new machine is $9,000 ($15,000 – $6,000).

Some capital investment projects *reduce* working capital. Assume that a computer-integrated manufacturing (CIM) project with a seven-year life will reduce inventories and, hence, working capital by $20 million from, say, $50 million to $30 million. This reduction will be represented as a $20 million cash *inflow* for the project in year 0. At the end of seven years, the recovery of working capital will show a relevant incremental cash *outflow* of $20 million. That's because, at the end of year 7, the company recovers only $30 million of working capital under CIM, rather than the $50 million of working capital it would have recovered had it not implemented CIM.

In this example, the relevant working capital (WC) cash flows are the differences between the WC needs of the new machine and the WC needs of the old machine at the beginning and end of the project.

Study Tip: To check your understanding of the material in this chapter, see the Featured Exercise, true–false statements 3 and 7, multiple-choice questions 1 through 7, and Review Exercises 1 and 2 (*Student Guide*, beginning p. 287). Fully explained answers begin on page 293.

Exhibit 21-6 shows items **3a** and **3b** in the year 5 column. The relevant cash flows in Exhibit 21-6 serve as inputs for the four capital budgeting methods described earlier in the chapter.

Managing the Project

Stage 6 of capital budgeting—*implementation and control*—is managing the project. There are two aspects of managing a project: management control of the investment activity itself and management control of the project as a whole.

Capital budgeting projects, such as purchasing an X-ray machine or videoconferencing equipment, are easier to implement than projects such as building shopping malls or manufacturing plants. The building projects are more complex, so monitoring and controlling the investment schedules and budgets are critical to successfully completing the investment activity.

A postinvestment audit provides management with feedback about the performance of a project, so management can compare actual results to the costs and benefits expected at the time the project was selected. Suppose actual outcomes (such as operating cash savings from the new X-ray machine in the Lifetime Care example) are much lower than expected. Management must then investigate to determine if this result occurred because the original estimates were overly optimistic or because of implementation problems. Either of these explanations is a concern.

Optimistic estimates may result in the acceptance of a project that should have been rejected. To discourage optimistic estimates, companies such as DuPont maintain records

FOCUS ON VALUES AND BEHAVIORS

LONG-TERM CONTRACTS AND PERFORMANCE EVALUATION AT ENRON

A basic tenet in finance is that when managers make positive NPV decisions and communicate these decisions to financial markets, the stock prices of their companies rise in response. So when Enron entered into a long-term contract to sell gas to the Chicago-based Peoples Gas, Light & Coke Co., Enron's stock price rose to represent the financial market's assessment of the deal. Stock prices change in anticipation of future cash flows. In contrast, accounting income numbers generally measure performance achieved—revenues, expenses, and cash flows that have already occurred during the past year.

Enron, however, recorded the present value of the future cash flows from the contract as income in the year the contract was signed. Enron also compensated managers who brought in these deals on the basis of the NPV of the contract, which required highly subjective judgments based on future prices of natural gas that were very difficult to predict when a contract was signed. Enron's chief risk officer was responsible for challenging and validating these future prices. Enron also sought external verification of price estimates whenever possible. Nevertheless, the absence of established public market prices and postcontract audits created incentives for managers to assume high prices of natural gas in the future, report higher operating income, and claim higher rewards.

Pressure is part of every business, but employees at Enron were under severe scrutiny. Its performance management system ranked all employees within a business group from the best to the worst performers. Employees in the bottom 20% were warned about their performance and were terminated if they showed no significant improvement. This pressure to perform coupled with the opportunity to report higher operating income created a strong temptation to inflate estimates of future cash flows. Enron's culture and lack of values and controls encouraged unethical behavior. At the time of Enron's collapse in 2001, many managers had been rewarded for anticipated future performance that did not materialize. The important message here for management accountants: Be aware of control-system weaknesses when making capital investment decisions and act with the highest integrity.

Source: *M. Salter, L. Levesque, and M. Ciampa, "The Rise and Fall of Enron," Harvard Business School working paper, 2002.*

comparing actual results to the estimates made by individual managers when seeking approval for capital investments. Postinvestment audits discourage unrealistic forecasts. The Focus on Values and Behaviors feature above describes how the incentive systems at Enron and the absence of postinvestment audits led managers to overstate project cash inflows and to accept projects that should never have been undertaken. Implementation problems, such as not achieving budgeted revenues or exceeding budgeted costs, are a concern because the returns from the project will then be inadequate. Postinvestment audits can point to areas of implementation that need improvement (such as better quality-control processes).

Postinvestment audits of capital projects require information on the costs and benefits attributable to the project. It can be costly, however, to untangle those cash flows from the company's overall cash flows.

Postinvestment audits require thoughtfulness and care. They should be done only after project outcomes have stabilized because performing audits too early may yield misleading feedback. Obtaining actual results to compare against estimates is often not easy. For example, actual labor-cost savings from the new X-ray machine may not be comparable to the estimated savings because the actual number and types of X-rays taken may be different from the quantities assumed during the selection stage. Other benefits, such as the impact on patient treatment, may be difficult to quantify.

Strategic Considerations in Capital Budgeting

A company's strategy is the source of its strategic capital budgeting decisions. Strategic decisions by United Airlines, Westin Hotels, Federal Express, and Pizza Hut to expand in Europe and Asia required capital investments to be made in several countries (see also Concepts in Action feature, p. 742). The strategic decision by Barnes & Noble to support book sales over the Internet required capital investments creating barnesandnoble.com and an Internet infrastructure. General Electric's decision to enter the television industry resulted in a big investment to acquire NBC. Pfizer's decision to develop its cholesterol-reducing drug Lipitor led to major investments in R&D and marketing. General Motors' decision to build a new line of cars led to major investments in its Saturn project.

Some strategic investments are made to avoid putting a company at a competitive disadvantage. For example, cellular telephone companies such as Motorola, Nokia, and Samsung have added features providing customers Internet access and e-mail capabilities; companies not providing these features will suffer a decline in market share. The benefit of capital investments in this case isn't higher revenues but the prevention of a decline in revenues and profits. Such benefits may be difficult to quantify.

CONCEPTS IN ACTION

Globalizing Capital Budgeting at AES Corporation

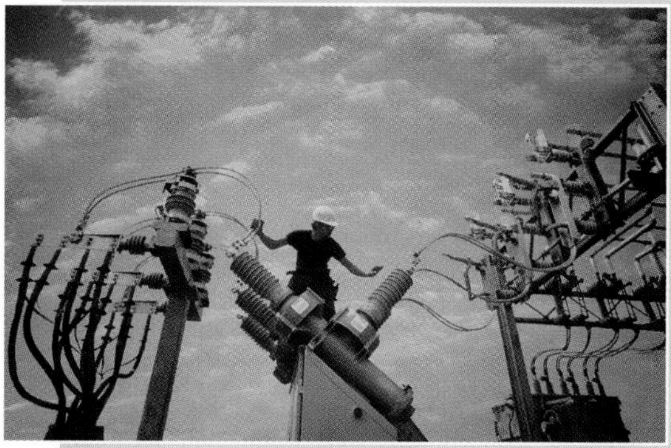

AES Corporation, a Fortune 500 company, is a leading global electricity producer with more than $30 billion in assets stretched across 30 countries and five continents. Despite impressive international growth throughout the company's 20-year history, the global economic downturn that began in late 2000 devastated AES. The devaluation of key South American currencies, adverse changes in energy regulatory environments, and declines in energy prices weakened AES's cash flow and ability to service debt. As a result, AES stock collapsed and its market capitalization fell nearly 95%, from $28 billion in December 2000 to $1.6 billion just two years later.

In response, the AES board of directors asked Rob Venerus, director of the company's new Corporate Analysis & Planning Group, to develop a new methodology for evaluating capital budgeting projects. Historically, capital budgeting at AES was fairly straightforward. Early in the company's history, a relatively simple model was developed, and a 12% discount rate was applied to all projects, regardless of geographic location. This model remained unchanged through the years, despite rapid expansion into new international markets that required advanced financial-analysis methods. For example, when AES entered countries such as Brazil and Argentina, the model failed to properly adjust the required rate of return to account for higher risk, such as regulatory and currency risk. Another factor that created fundamental difficulties for applying this model overseas was an ever-increasing complexity in the financing of international operations.

To overhaul the capital budgeting process so that managers could evaluate each international investment as a distinct opportunity with unique risks, Venerus knew he would have to calculate a cost of capital for each of the many diverse AES businesses. These businesses included power plant construction, energy generation, and power distribution. As a starting point, he considered 15 representative projects from various countries and derived a weighted average cost of capital (WACC) for each project. This involved measuring all of the constituent parts for the projects: the cost of debt, the target capital structure, the local-country tax rates, and an appropriate cost of equity.

During this process Venerus knew he had to find a way to capture the country-specific risks in foreign markets. He developed an approach with two parts. First, he calculated a cost of debt and a cost of equity for each of the 15 projects using U.S. market data. Second, he added the difference between the yield on local government bonds and the yield on corresponding U.S. Treasury bonds to both the cost of debt and the cost of equity. Venerus and his team believed that this difference, or "sovereign spread," approximated the incremental borrowing costs (and market risk) in the local country.

These efforts provided AES with a more sophisticated way to think about capital budgeting risk and its cost of capital around the world. As a global company with operations in countries that were significantly different from the United States, this framework helped AES more accurately evaluate capital projects and protect against overleveraging its assets, which almost imploded the company in 2002. Although subsequent changes to the model's calculations and methodology were made, this process helped AES regain its financial footing through the reevaluation and restructuring of existing capital projects while ensuring that the company only selected new capital projects that met these revised criteria. So far, the company has been successful! By 2004, AES was projecting long-term financial stability and double-digit earnings per share growth through 2008.

Sources: Based on "Globalizing the Cost of Capital and Capital Budgeting at AES," Harvard Business School Case No. 9-204-109, AES Corporation 2003 annual report, and discussions with the case writer and company management.

Capital investment decisions that are strategic in nature require managers to consider a broad range of factors that may be difficult to estimate. Consider some of the difficulties of justifying investments in computer-integrated manufacturing (CIM) technology made by companies such as Mitsubishi, Sony, and Audi. In CIM, computers give instructions that quickly and automatically set up and run equipment to manufacture many different products. Quantifying these benefits requires some notion of consumer-demand changes that may occur many years in the future. CIM technology also increases worker knowledge of and experience with automation; however, the benefit of this knowledge and experience is difficult to measure. Managers need to develop judgment and intuition to make these decisions.

Customer Value and Capital Budgeting

Consider Potato Supreme, which makes potato products for sale to retail outlets. It is currently analyzing two of its customers: Shine Stores and Always Open. Potato Supreme predicts the following cash flow from operations, net of income taxes (in thousands), from each customer account for the next five years:

	2006	2007	2008	2009	2010
Shine Stores	$1,450	$1,305	$1,175	$1,058	$ 950
Always Open	690	1,160	1,900	2,950	4,160

To remain viable, companies must keep profitable customers (and gain new ones).

Which customer is more valuable to Potato Supreme? Looking at only the current period, 2006, Shine Stores provides more than double the cash flow compared to Always Open ($1,450 versus $690). A different picture emerges, however, when looking over the entire five-year horizon. Using Potato Supreme's 10% RRR, the NPV of the Always Open customer is $7,610, compared to $4,591 for Shine Stores (computations not shown). Note how NPV captures in its estimate of customer value the future growth of Always Open. Potato Supreme uses this information to allocate more resources and salespersons to service the Always Open account. Potato Supreme can also use NPV calculations to examine the effects of alternative ways of increasing customer loyalty and retention, such as introducing frequent-purchaser cards.

These NPV amounts are calculated using the 10% present value discount factors in Table 2 of Appendix C. For example, year 1 has a present value of $1,318 ($1,450 × 0.909) for Shine Stores and $627 ($690 × 0.909) for Always Open.

A comparison of year-to-year changes in customer NPV estimates highlights whether managers have been successful in maintaining long-run profitable relationships with their customers. Suppose the NPV of Potato Supreme's customer base declines 15% in one year. Management can then examine the reasons for the decline, such as aggressive pricing by competitors, and devise new-product development and marketing strategies for the future.

Capital One, a financial-services company, uses NPV to estimate the value of different credit-card customers. Cellular telephone companies such as Cellular One and Verizon attempt to sign up customers for multiple years of service. The objective is to prevent "customer churn," customers switching frequently from one company to another. The higher the probability of customer churn, the lower the NPV of the customer to the telecommunications company.

Investment in Research and Development

Companies such as GlaxoSmithKline in the pharmaceutical industry and Intel in the semiconductor industry regard R&D projects as important strategic investments. The payoffs from R&D investments, however, are far into the future and are more uncertain than other investments such as new equipment. On the positive side, R&D investments are often staged—that is, at different points in time, companies have the option to increase or decrease the resources committed to a project based on how successful it has been up to that time. This option feature of R&D investments—called real options—is an important aspect of R&D investments and increases the NPV of these investments. That's because a company can limit its losses when things are going badly and take advantage of new opportunities when things are going well.

PROBLEM FOR SELF-STUDY

PART A

Returning to the Lifetime Care X-ray machine project, assume that Lifetime is a *nonprofit organization* and that the expected annual cash inflows from the operating-cost savings are $130,000 in years 1 through 4 and $121,000 in year 5. Using data from page 735, the net initial investment is $392,500 (new machine, $390,000 plus additional working capital, $9,000 minus terminal disposal value of old machine, $6,500). All other facts are unchanged: a five-year useful life, no terminal disposal value, and an 8% RRR. Year 5 cash inflows are $130,000, which includes a $9,000 recovery of working capital.

Required

Calculate the following:

1. Net present value
2. Internal rate of return
3. Payback
4. Accrual accounting rate of return on net initial investment

SOLUTION

1. $NPV = (\$130{,}000 \times 3.993) - \$392{,}500$

$$= \$519{,}090 - \$392{,}500 = \$126{,}590$$

2. There are several approaches to computing IRR. One is to use a calculator with an IRR function. This approach gives an IRR of 19.6%. Another approach is to use Table 4 in Appendix C at the end of the text:

$$\$392{,}500 = \$130{,}000F$$

$$F = \frac{\$392{,}500}{\$130{,}000} = 3.019$$

On the five-period line of Table 4, the column closest to 3.019 is 20%. To obtain a more-accurate number, use straight-line interpolation:

	Present Value Factors	
18%	3.127	3.127
IRR	—	3.019
20%	2.991	—
Difference	0.136	0.108

$$IRR = 18\% + \frac{0.108}{0.136}(2\%) = 19.6\% \text{ per year}$$

3.
$$\text{Payback period} = \frac{\text{Net initial investment}}{\text{Uniform increase in annual future cash flows}}$$
$$= \$392{,}500 \div \$130{,}000 = 3.0 \text{ years}$$

4.
$$AARR = \frac{\text{Increase in expected average annual operating income}}{\text{Net initial investment}}$$

$$\text{Increase in expected average annual cash operating savings} = [(\$130{,}000 \times 4) + \$121{,}000] \div 5 \text{ years}$$
$$= \$641{,}000 \div 5 = \$128{,}200$$

$$\text{Increase in annual depreciation} = \$70{,}000\ (\$78{,}000 - \$8{,}000,\ \text{see p. 735})$$

$$\text{Increase in expected average annual operating income} = \$128{,}200 - \$70{,}000 = \$58{,}200$$

$$AARR = \frac{\$58{,}200}{\$392{,}500} = 14.8\% \text{ per year}$$

PART B

Assume that Lifetime Care is subject to income tax at a 40% rate. All other information from Part A is unchanged. Compute the NPV of the new X-ray machine project.

SOLUTION

To save space, Exhibit 21-7 shows the calculations using a format slightly different from the format used in this chapter. Item **2a** is where the new $130,000 cash flow assumption affects the NPV analysis (compared to Exhibit 21-6). All other amounts in Exhibit 21-7 are identical to the corresponding amounts in Exhibit 21-6. For years 1 through 4, after-tax cash flow (excluding the depreciation effect) is:

Annual cash flow from operations with new machine	$130,000
Deduct income tax payments (0.40 × $130,000)	52,000
Annual after-tax cash flow from operations	$ 78,000

EXHIBIT 21-7 **Net Present Value Method Incorporating Income Taxes: Lifetime Care Hospital's New X-Ray Machine with Revised Annual Cash Flow from Operations**

	A	B	C	D	E	F	G	H	I	J
1			**Present**	**Present Value of**						
2			**Value of**	**$1 Discounted at**	**Sketch of Relevant Cash Flows at End of Each Year**					
3			**Cash Flow**	**8%**	**0**	**1**	**2**	**3**	**4**	**5**
4	**1a.**	Initial machine investment	$(390,000)	1.000	$(390,000)					
5										
6	**1b.**	Initial working-capital investment	(9,000)	1.000	(9,000)					
7	**1c.**	After-tax cash flow from current								
8		disposal of old machine	19,900	1.000	19,900					
9	Net initial investment		(379,100)							
10	**2a.**	Annual after-tax cash flow from								
11		operations (excluding the depreciation effect)								
12		Year 1	72,228	0.926		$78,000				
13		Year 2	66,846	0.857			$78,000			
14		Year 3	61,932	0.794				$78,000		
15		Year 4	57,330	0.735					$78,000	
16		Year 5	49,441	0.681						$72,600
17	**2b.**	Income tax cash savings from annual								
18		depreciation deductions								
19		Year 1	25,928	0.926		$28,000				
20		Year 2	23,996	0.857			$28,000			
21		Year 3	22,232	0.794				$28,000		
22		Year 4	20,580	0.735					$28,000	
23		Year 5	19,068	0.681						$28,000
24	**3.**	After-tax cash flow from								
25		a. Terminal disposal of machine	0	0.681						$ 0
26		b. Recovery of working capital	6,129	0.681						$ 9,000
27	NPV if new machine purchased		$ 46,610							
28										

For year 5, after-tax cash flow (excluding the depreciation effect) is:

Annual cash flow from operations with new machine	$121,000
Deduct income tax payments (0.40 × $121,000)	48,400
Annual after-tax cash flow from operations	$ 72,600

NPV in Exhibit 21-7 is $46,610. As computed in Part A, NPV when there are no income taxes is $126,590. The difference in these two NPVs illustrates the impact of income taxes in capital budgeting analysis.

DECISION POINTS

The following question-and-answer format summarizes the chapter's learning objectives. Each decision presents a key question related to a learning objective. The guidelines are the answer to that question.

Decision	**Guidelines**
1. Over what time horizon is capital budgeting done?	Capital budgeting is long-run planning for proposed investment projects. The life of a project is usually longer than one year, so capital budgeting decisions consider cash inflows and outflows over long periods. In contrast, accrual accounting measures income on a year-by-year basis.
2. What are the six stages of capital budgeting?	The six stages of capital budgeting are (a) the identification stage, (b) the search stage, (c) the information-acquisition stage, (d) the selection stage, (e) the financing stage, and (f) the implementation and control stage.
3. What are the two main discounted cash flow (DCF) methods? What are their advantages?	The two main DCF methods are the net present value (NPV) method and the internal rate-of-return (IRR) method. The NPV method calculates the expected net monetary gain or loss from a project by discounting to the present all expected future cash inflows and outflows, using the required rate of return. A project is acceptable in financial terms if it has a

positive NPV. The IRR method computes the rate of return (also called the discount rate) at which the present value of expected cash inflows from a project equals the present value of expected cash outflows from the project. A project is acceptable in financial terms if its IRR exceeds the required rate of return. DCF is the best approach to capital budgeting. It explicitly includes all project cash flows and recognizes the time value of money. The NPV method is the preferred DCF method.

4. What is the payback method? What are its two main weaknesses?

The payback method measures the time it will take to recoup, in the form of cash inflows, the total cash amount invested in a project. The payback method neglects both cash flows after the payback period and the time value of money.

5. What is the accrual accounting rate-of-return (AARR) method? What is its limitation?

The accrual accounting rate of return (AARR) divides an accrual accounting measure of average annual income from a project by an accrual accounting measure of its investment. AARR considers profitability but does not consider the time value of money.

6. What conflicts can arise between using DCF methods for capital budgeting decisions and accrual accounting for performance evaluation? How can these conflicts be reduced?

Using accrual accounting to evaluate the performance of a manager may create conflicts with using DCF methods for capital budgeting. Frequently, the decision made using a DCF method will not report good "operating income" results in the project's early years under accrual accounting. For this reason, managers are tempted to not use DCF methods even though the decisions based on them would be in the best interests of the company as a whole over the long run. This conflict can be reduced by evaluating managers on a project-by-project basis and by looking at their ability to achieve the amounts and timing of forecasted cash flows.

7. What are the relevant cash inflows and outflows for capital budgeting decisions? How should accrual accounting concepts be considered?

Relevant cash inflows and outflows in DCF analysis are the differences in expected future cash flows as a result of making the investment. Only cash inflows and outflows matter; accrual accounting concepts are irrelevant for DCF methods. For example, the income taxes saved as a result of depreciation deductions are relevant because they decrease cash outflows, but the depreciation itself is a noncash item.

APPENDIX: CAPITAL BUDGETING AND INFLATION

Because of inflation, the cash inflows for future periods will be measured in dollars that have less value than the dollars invested in the project in year 0. Failure to account for inflation will make the project appear more attractive than it really is.

The Lifetime Care example (Exhibits 21-2 to 21-6) does not include adjustments for inflation in the relevant revenues and costs. **Inflation** is the decline in the general purchasing power of the monetary unit, such as dollars. An inflation rate of 10% per year means that an item bought for $100 at the beginning of the year will cost $110 at the end of the year.

Why is it important to account for inflation in capital budgeting? Because declines in the general purchasing power of the monetary unit will inflate future cash flows above what they would have been in the absence of inflation. These inflated cash flows will cause the project to look better than it really is unless the analyst recognizes that the inflated cash flows are measured in dollars that have less purchasing power than the dollars that were initially invested. When analyzing inflation, distinguish real rate of return from nominal rate of return:

Real rate of return is the rate of return demanded to cover investment risk if there is no inflation. The real rate is made up of two elements: (a) a risk-free element (that's the pure rate of return on risk-free long-term government bonds when there is no expected inflation) and (b) a business-risk element (that's the risk premium demanded for bearing risk).

Nominal rate of return is the rate of return demanded to cover investment risk and the decline in general purchasing power of the monetary unit as a result of expected inflation. The nominal rate is made up of three elements: (a) a risk-free element when there is no expected inflation, (b) a business-risk element, and (c) an inflation element. Items (a) and (b) make up the real rate of return to cover investment risk. The inflation element is the premium above the real rate. The rates of return earned in the financial markets are nominal rates, because investors want to be compensated both for the investment risks they take and for the expected decline in the general purchasing power, as a result of inflation, of the money they get back.

Assume that the real rate of return for investments in high-risk cellular data-transmission equipment at Network Communications is 20% per year and that the expected inflation rate is 10% per year. Nominal rate of return is:

$$\begin{aligned}\text{Nominal rate} &= (1 + \text{Real rate})(1 + \text{Inflation rate}) - 1\\ &= (1 + 0.20)(1 + 0.10) - 1\\ &= (1.20 \times 1.10) - 1 = 1.32 - 1 = 0.32, \text{ or } 32\%\end{aligned}$$

Nominal rate of return is related to the real rate of return and the inflation rate:

Real rate of return	0.20
Inflation rate	0.10
Combination (0.20 × 0.10)	0.02
Nominal rate of return	0.32

Note the nominal rate, 0.32, is slightly higher than 0.30, the real rate (0.20) plus the inflation rate (0.10). That's because the nominal rate recognizes that inflation of 10% also decreases the purchasing power of the real rate of return of 20% earned during the year. The combination component represents the additional compensation investors seek for the decrease in the purchasing power of the real return earned during the year because of inflation.[4]

Net Present Value Method and Inflation

When incorporating inflation into the NPV method, the key is *internal consistency*. There are two internally consistent approaches:

1. **Nominal approach**—predicts cash inflows and outflows in nominal monetary units *and* uses a nominal rate as the required rate of return
2. **Real approach**—predicts cash inflows and outflows in real monetary units *and* uses a real rate as the required rate of return

We will limit our discussion to the simpler nominal approach. Consider an investment that is expected to generate sales of 100 units and a net cash inflow of \$1,000 (\$10 per unit) each year for two years *absent inflation*. Assume cash flows occur at the end of each year. If inflation of 10% is expected each year, net cash inflows from the sale of each unit would be \$11 (\$10 × 1.10) in year 1 and \$12.10 (\$11 × 1.10, or \$10 × $(1.10)^2$) in year 2, resulting in net cash inflows of \$1,100 in year 1 and \$1,210 in year 2. The net cash inflows of \$1,100 and \$1,210 are nominal cash inflows because they include the effects of inflation. *Nominal cash flows are the cash flows that are recorded in the accounting system.* The cash inflows of \$1,000 each year are real cash flows. The accounting system does not record these cash flows. The nominal approach is easier to understand and apply because it uses nominal cash flows from accounting systems and nominal rates of return from financial markets.

Assume that Network Communications can purchase equipment to make and sell a cellular data-transmission product at a net initial investment of \$750,000. It is expected to have a four-year useful life and no terminal disposal value. An annual inflation rate of 10% is expected over this four-year period. Network Communications requires an after-tax nominal rate of return of 32% (see p. 746). The following table presents the predicted amounts of real (that's assuming no inflation) and nominal (that's after considering cumulative inflation) net cash inflows from the equipment over the next four years (excluding the \$750,000 investment in the equipment and before any income tax payments):

Under the nominal approach, first express all amounts in terms of *future-year dollars* (using cumulative inflation-rate factors), then discount the resulting amounts to their present value using *nominal discount-rate factors.*

Year (1)	Before-Tax Cash Inflows in Real Dollars (2)	Cumulative Inflation Rate Factor[a] (3)	Before-Tax Cash Inflows in Nominal Dollars (4) = (2) × (3)
1	\$500,000	$(1.10)^1 = 1.1000$	\$550,000
2	600,000	$(1.10)^2 = 1.2100$	726,000
3	600,000	$(1.10)^3 = 1.3310$	798,600
4	300,000	$(1.10)^4 = 1.4641$	439,230

[a]1.10 = 1.00 + 0.10 inflation rate.

We continue to make the simplifying assumption that cash flows occur at the end of each year. The income tax rate is 40%. For tax purposes, the cost of the equipment will be depreciated using the straight-line method.

Exhibit 21-8 shows the calculation of NPV using cash flows in nominal dollars and using a nominal discount rate. The calculations in Exhibit 21-8 include the net initial machine investment, annual after-tax cash flows from operations (excluding the depreciation effect), and income tax cash savings from annual depreciation deductions. The NPV is \$202,513 and, based on financial considerations alone, Network Communications should purchase the equipment.

[4]The real rate of return can be expressed in terms of the nominal rate of return as follows:

$$\text{Real rate} = \frac{1 + \text{Nominal rate}}{1 + \text{Inflation rate}} - 1 = \frac{1 + 0.32}{1 + 0.10} - 1 = 0.20, \text{ or } 20\%$$

EXHIBIT 21-8 Net Present Value Method Using Nominal Approach to Inflation for Network Communication's New Equipment

	A	B	C	D	E	F	G	H	I	J	K	L
1						Present	Present Value					
2						Value of	Discount Factor[a] at	Sketch of Relevant Cash Flows at End of Each Year				
3						Cash Flow	32%	0	1	2	3	4
4	1.	Net initial investment										
5		Year	Investment Outflows									
6		0	$(750,000)			$(750,000) ←	1.000 ←	$(750,000)				
7	2a.	Annual after-tax cash flow from										
8		operations (excluding the depreciation effect)										
9			Annual		Annual							
10			Before-Tax	Income	After-Tax							
11			Cash Flow	Tax	Cash Flow							
12		Year	from Operations	Outflows	from Operations							
13		(1)	(2)	(3) = 0.40 x (2)	(4) = (2) - (3)							
14		1	$550,000	$220,000	$330,000	250,140 ←	0.758 ←		$330,000			
15		2	726,000	290,400	435,600	250,034 ←	0.574 ←			$435,600		
16		3	798,600	319,440	479,160	208,435 ←	0.435 ←				$479,160	
17		4	439,230	175,692	263,538	86,704 ←	0.329 ←					$263,538
18						795,313						
19	2b.	Income tax cash savings from annual										
20		depreciation deductions										
21		Year	Depreciation	Tax Cash Savings								
22		(1)	(2)	(3) = 0.40 x (2)								
23		1	$187,500[b]	$75,000		56,850 ←	0.758 ←		$ 75,000			
24		2	187,500	75,000		43,050 ←	0.574 ←			$ 75,000		
25		3	187,500	75,000		32,625 ←	0.435 ←				$ 75,000	
26		4	187,500	75,000		24,675 ←	0.329 ←					$ 75,000
27						157,200						
28	NPV if new equipment purchased					$ 202,513						
29												
30												
31	[a]The nominal discount rate of 32% is made up of the real rate of return of 20% and the inflation rate of 10% [(1 + 0.20) (1 + 0.10)] − 1 = 0.32.											
32	[b]$750,000 ÷ 4 = $187,500											

TERMS TO LEARN

This chapter and the Glossary at the end of the book contain definitions of:

accounting rate of return (p. 733)
accrual accounting rate of return (AARR) (p. 732)
capital budgeting (p. 725)
cost of capital (p. 727)
discount rate (p. 727)
discounted cash flow (DCF) methods (p. 726)
hurdle rate (p. 727)
inflation (p. 746)
internal rate-of-return (IRR) method (p. 728)
net present value (NPV) method (p. 727)
nominal rate of return (p. 746)
opportunity cost of capital (p. 727)
payback method (p. 731)
real rate of return (p. 746)
required rate of return (RRR) (p. 727)
time value of money (p. 726)

PH Grade Assist

Prentice Hall Grade Assist (PHGA)
Your professor may ask you to complete selected exercises and problems in Prentice Hall Grade Assist (PHGA). PHGA is an online tool that can help you master the chapter's topics. It provides you with multiple variations of exercises and problems designated by the PHGA icon. You can rework these exercises and problems—each time with new data—as many times as you need. You also receive immediate feedback and grading.

ASSIGNMENT MATERIAL

Questions

21-1 "Capital budgeting has the same focus as accrual accounting." Do you agree? Explain.

21-2 List and briefly describe each of the six stages in capital budgeting.

21-3 What is the essence of the discounted cash flow methods?

21-4 "Only quantitative outcomes are relevant in capital budgeting analyses." Do you agree? Explain.

21-5 How can sensitivity analysis be incorporated in DCF analysis?

21-6 What is the payback method? What are its main strengths and weaknesses?

21-7 Describe the accrual accounting rate-of-return method. What are its main strengths and weaknesses?

21-8 "The trouble with discounted cash flow methods is that they ignore depreciation." Do you agree? Explain.

21-9 "Let's be more practical. DCF is not the gospel. Managers should not become so enchanted with DCF that strategic considerations are overlooked." Do you agree? Explain.

21-10 "All overhead costs are relevant in NPV analysis." Do you agree? Explain.

21-11 Bill Watts, president of Western Publications, accepts a capital budgeting project proposed by Division X. This is the division in which the president spent his first 10 years with the company. On the same day, the president rejects a capital budgeting project proposal from Division Y. The manager of Division Y is incensed. She believes that the Division Y project has an internal rate of return at least 10 percentage points higher than the Division X project. She comments, "What is the point of all our detailed DCF analysis? If Watts is panting over a project, he can arrange to have the proponents of that project massage the numbers so that it looks like a winner." What advice would you give the manager of Division Y?

21-12 Distinguish different categories of cash flows to be considered in an equipment-replacement decision by a taxpaying company.

21-13 Describe three ways income taxes can affect the cash inflows or outflows in a motor-vehicle-replacement decision by a taxpaying company.

21-14 How can capital budgeting tools assist in evaluating a manager who is responsible for retaining customers of a cellular telephone company?

21-15 Distinguish the nominal rate of return from the real rate of return.

Exercises

21-16 **Exercises in compound interest, no income taxes.** To be sure that you understand how to use the tables in Appendix C at the end of this book, solve the following exercises. Ignore income tax considerations. The correct answers, rounded to the nearest dollar, appear on pages 757–758.

Required

1. You have just won $5,000. How much money will you accumulate at the end of 10 years if you invest it at 6% compounded annually? At 14%?
2. Ten years from now, the unpaid principal of the mortgage on your house will be $89,550. How much do you need to invest today at 6% interest compounded annually to accumulate the $89,550 in 10 years?
3. If the unpaid mortgage on your house in 10 years will be $89,550, how much money do you need to invest at the end of each year at 6% to accumulate exactly this amount at the end of the tenth year?
4. You plan to save $5,000 of your earnings at the end of each year for the next 10 years. How much money will you accumulate at the end of the tenth year if you invest your savings compounded at 12% per year?
5. You have just turned 65 and an endowment insurance policy has paid you a lump sum of $200,000. If you invest the sum at 6%, how much money can you withdraw from your account in equal amounts at the end of each year so that at the end of 10 years (age 75) there will be nothing left?
6. You have estimated that for the first 10 years after you retire you will need a cash inflow of $50,000 at the end of each year. How much money do you need to invest at 6% at your retirement age to obtain this annual cash inflow? At 20%?
7. The following table shows two schedules of prospective operating cash inflows, each of which requires the same net initial investment of $10,000 now:

	Annual Cash Inflows	
Year	**Plan A**	**Plan B**
1	$ 1,000	$ 5,000
2	2,000	4,000
3	3,000	3,000
4	4,000	2,000
5	5,000	1,000
Total	$15,000	$15,000

The required rate of return is 6% compounded annually. All cash inflows occur at the end of each year. In terms of net present value, which plan is more desirable? Show your computations.

21-17 Capital budgeting methods, no income taxes. Riverbend Company runs hardware stores in a tri-state area. Riverbend's management estimates that if it invests $160,000 in a new computer system, it can save $60,000 in annual cash operating costs. The system has an expected useful life of 5 years and no terminal disposal value. The required rate of return is 12%. Ignore income tax issues in your answers. Assume all cash flows occur at year-end except for initial investment amounts.

Required

1. Calculate the following for the new computer system:
   a. Net present value
   b. Payback period
   c. Internal rate of return
   d. Accrual accounting rate of return based on the net initial investment (assume straight-line depreciation)
2. What other factors should Riverbend consider in deciding whether to purchase the new computer system?

PH Grade Assist

21-18 Capital budgeting methods, no income taxes. City Hospital, a non-profit organization, estimates that it can save $28,000 a year in cash operating costs for the next 10 years if it buys a special-purpose eye-testing machine at a cost of $110,000. No terminal disposal value is expected. City Hospital's required rate of return is 14%. Assume all cash flows occur at year-end except for initial investment amounts.

Required

1. Calculate the following for the special-purpose eye-testing machine:
   a. Net present value
   b. Payback period
   c. Internal rate of return
   d. Accrual accounting rate of return based on net initial investment (Assume straight-line depreciation.)
2. What other factors should City Hospital consider in deciding whether to purchase the special-purpose eye-testing machine?

PH Grade Assist

21-19 Capital budgeting, income taxes. Assume the same facts as in Exercise 21-18 except that City Hospital is a taxpaying entity. The income tax rate is 30% for all transactions that affect income taxes.

Required

1. Do requirement 1 of Exercise 21-18.
2. How would your computations in requirement 1 be affected if the special-purpose machine had a $10,000 terminal disposal value at the end of 10 years? Assume depreciation deductions are based on the $110,000 purchase cost and zero terminal disposal value using the straight-line method. Answer briefly in words without further calculations.

21-20 Capital budgeting with uneven cash flows, no income taxes. Southern Cola is considering the purchase of a special-purpose bottling machine for $23,000. It is expected to have a useful life of 4 years with no terminal disposal value. The plant manager estimates the following savings in cash operating costs:

Year	Amount
1	$10,000
2	8,000
3	6,000
4	5,000
Total	$29,000

Southern Cola uses a required rate of return of 16% in its capital budgeting decisions. Ignore income taxes in your analysis. Assume all cash flows occur at year-end except for initial investment amounts.

Required

Calculate the following for the special-purpose bottling machine:

1. Net present value
2. Payback period
3. Internal rate of return
4. Accrual accounting rate of return based on net initial investment (Assume straight-line depreciation. Use the average annual savings in cash operating costs when computing the numerator of the accrual accounting rate of return.)

21-21 Comparison of projects, no income taxes. (CMA, adapted) Fox Valley Healthcare, Inc., is a non-profit organization. Jim Ruffalo, president of Fox Valley, has developed a plan to add a new building. He has selected a building contractor, Vukacek Construction Co. Vukacek is ready to start as soon as the contract is signed and will complete the work in two years.

The building contractor has offered Fox Valley a choice of three payment plans, as follows:

- **Plan I** Payment of $200,000 at the time of signing the contract and $3,000,000 upon completion of the building. The end of the second year is the completion date.
- **Plan II** Payment of $1,000,000 at the time of signing the contract and $1,000,000 at the end of each of the two succeeding years.

- **Plan III** Payment of $100,000 at the time of signing the contract and $1,000,000 at the end of each of the three succeeding years.

Ruffalo has asked the treasurer, Lisa Monroe, for her assessment of the three payment plans. Fox Valley has a required rate of return of 12%.

Required

1. Using the net present value method, calculate the comparative cost of each of the three payment plans being considered by Fox Valley Healthcare.
2. Which payment plan should the treasurer recommend? Explain.
3. Discuss the financial factors, other than the cost of the plan, and the nonfinancial factors that Monroe should consider in selecting an appropriate payment plan.

21-22 Payback and NPV methods, no income taxes. (CMA, adapted) Andrews Construction is analyzing its capital expenditure proposals for the purchase of equipment in the coming year. The capital budget is limited to $6,000,000 for the year. Lori Bart, staff analyst at Andrews, is preparing an analysis of the three projects under consideration by Corey Andrews, the company's owner.

Excel Lab
www.prenhall.com/horngren/cost12e

	A	B	C	D
1		**Project A**	**Project B**	**Project C**
2	**Projected cash outflow**			
3	Net initial investment	$3,000,000	$1,500,000	$4,000,000
4				
5	**Projected cash inflows**			
6	Year 1	$1,000,000	$ 400,000	$2,000,000
7	Year 2	1,000,000	900,000	2,000,000
8	Year 3	1,000,000	800,000	200,000
9	Year 4	1,000,000		100,000

If you want to use Excel to solve this exercise, go to the Excel Lab at **www.prenhall.com/horngren/cost12e** and download the template for Exercise 21-22.

Required

1. Because the company's cash is limited, Andrews thinks the payback method should be used to choose between the capital budgeting projects.
   a. What are the benefits and limitations of using the payback method to choose between projects?
   b. Calculate the payback period for each of the three projects. Ignore income taxes. Using the payback method, which projects should Andrews choose?
2. Bart thinks that projects should be selected based on their NPVs. The required rate of return is 10%. Assume all cash flows occur at the end of the year except for initial investment amounts. Calculate the NPV for each project. Ignore income taxes.
3. Which projects, if any, would you recommend funding? Briefly explain why.

21-23 DCF, accrual accounting rate of return, working capital, evaluation of performance, no income taxes. Hammerlink Company has been offered a special-purpose metal-cutting machine for $110,000. The machine is expected to have a useful life of eight years, with a terminal disposal value of $30,000. Savings in cash operating costs are expected to be $25,000 per year. However, additional working capital is needed to keep the machine running efficiently without stoppages. Working capital includes such items as filters, lubricants, bearings, abrasives, flexible exhaust pipes, and belts. These items must continually be replaced, so an investment of $8,000 needs to be maintained in them at all times, but this investment is fully recoverable (will be "cashed in") at the end of the useful life. Hammerlink's required rate of return is 14%. Ignore income taxes in your analysis. Assume all cash flows occur at year-end except for initial investment amounts.

PH Grade Assist

Required

1. Calculate net present value.
2. Calculate internal rate of return.
3. Calculate accrual accounting rate of return based on net initial investment. Assume straight-line depreciation.
4. You have the authority to make the purchase decision. Why might you be reluctant to base your decision on the DCF methods?

21-24 New equipment purchase, income taxes. National College Publishing, Inc., is considering the purchase of PR2020, a new printing machine, with an estimated useful life of 4 years. It estimates pretax cash flows for the machine as shown on page 752, with no anticipated change in working capital. National has a 12% after-tax required rate of return, and its income tax rate is 40%. Assume depreciation is calculated on a

PH Grade Assist

Excel Lab
www.prenhall.com/horngren/cost12e

straight-line basis for tax purposes using the initial machine investment and estimated terminal disposal value of the machine. Assume all cash flows occur at year-end except for initial investment amounts.

	A	B	C	D	E	F
1		Relevant Cash Flows at End of Each Year				
2		0	1	2	3	4
3	Initial machine investment	$(220,000)				
4	Annual cash flow from operations (excluding the depreciation effect)		$90,000	$90,000	$90,000	$90,000
5	Cash flow from terminal disposal of machine					$20,000

If you want to use Excel to solve this exercise, go to the Excel Lab at **www.prenhall.com/horngren/cost12e** and download the template for Exercise 21-24.

Required

1. Calculate (a) net present value, (b) payback period, and (c) internal rate of return.
2. Compare and contrast the capital budgeting methods in requirement 1.

Excel Lab
www.prenhall.com/horngren/cost12e

21-25 New equipment purchase, income taxes. Presentation Graphics (PG) prepares slides and other aids for professional presentations. PG is considering the purchase of a special-purpose workstation with an estimated useful life of 5 years. PG estimates pretax cash flows for the workstation as shown below, with no anticipated change in working capital. PG has a 12% after-tax required rate of return, and its income tax rate is 40%. PG uses straight-line depreciation for tax purposes. Assume all cash flows occur at year-end except for initial investment amounts.

	A	B	C	D	E	F	G
1		Relevant Cash Flows at End of Each Year					
2		0	1	2	3	4	5
3	Initial workstation investment	$(50,000)					
4	Annual cash flow from operations (excluding the depreciation effect)		$25,000	$25,000	$25,000	$25,000	$25,000
5	Cash flow from terminal disposal of machine						$ 0

If you want to use Excel to solve this exercise, go to the Excel Lab at **www.prenhall.com/horngren/cost12e** and download the template for Exercise 21-25.

Required

1. Calculate (a) net present value, (b) payback period, and (c) internal rate of return.
2. Compare and contrast the capital budgeting methods in requirement 1.

21-26 Selling a plant, income taxes. (CMA, adapted) Waterford Corporation, a clothing manufacturer, has a plant that will become idle on December 31, 2005. John Landry, corporate controller, has been asked to look at three options regarding the plant.

- **Option 1:** The plant, which has been fully depreciated for tax purposes, can be sold immediately for $9,000,000.
- **Option 2:** The plant can be leased to Auburn Mills, one of Waterford's suppliers, for four years. Under the lease terms, Auburn would pay Waterford $2,400,000 rent per year (payable at year-end) and would grant Waterford a $474,000 annual discount off the normal price of fabric purchased by Waterford (assume discount received at year-end for each of the four years). Auburn would bear all of the plant's ownership costs. Waterford expects to sell this plant for $2,000,000 at the end of the four-year lease.
- **Option 3:** The plant could be used for four years to make souvenir jackets for the Olympics. Fixed overhead costs (a cash outflow) before any equipment upgrades are estimated to be $200,000 annually for the four-year period. The jackets are expected to sell for $42 each. Variable cost per unit is expected to be $33. The following production and sales of jackets are expected: 2006, 200,000 units; 2007, 300,000 units; 2008, 400,000 units; 2009, 100,000 units. In order to manufacture the jackets, some of the plant equipment would need to be upgraded at an immediate cost of $1,500,000. The equipment would be depreciated using the straight-line depreciation method and zero terminal disposal value over the four years it would be in use. Because of the equipment upgrades, Waterford could sell the plant for $3,000,000 at the end of four years. No change in working capital would be required.

Waterford treats all cash flows as if they occur at the end of the year, and it uses an after-tax required rate of return of 12%. Waterford is subject to a 40% income tax rate.

Required

1. Calculate net present value of each of the options and determine which option Waterford should select using the NPV criterion.
2. What nonfinancial factors should Waterford consider before making its choice?

Problems

21-27 Equipment replacement, no income taxes. Superfast Chips manufactures and delivers prototype chips to customers. The production plant was set up when the company began operations in Dublin, Ireland, in 2000. It is outdated and constrains future growth. Next year, in 2007, Superfast expects to deliver 460 prototype chips at an average price of $80,000 per prototype. Superfast's marketing vice president forecasts growth of 50 prototype chips per year through 2013. That is, demand will be 460 in 2007, 510 in 2008, 560 in 2009, and so on.

The plant cannot produce more than 450 prototypes annually. To meet future demand, Superfast must either modernize the plant or replace it. The old equipment is fully depreciated and can be sold for $3,000,000 if the plant is replaced. If the plant is modernized, the costs to modernize it are to be capitalized and depreciated over the useful life of the updated plant. The old equipment is retained as part of the modernize alternative. The following data on the two options are available:

	Modernize	Replace
Initial investment in 2007	$28,000,000	$49,000,000
Terminal disposal value in 2013	$5,000,000	$12,000,000
Useful life	7 years	7 years
Total annual cash operating costs per prototype	$62,000	$56,000

Superfast uses straight-line depreciation for income reporting, assuming zero terminal disposal value. For simplicity, we assume no change in prices or costs in future years. The investment will be made at the beginning of 2007, and all transactions thereafter occur on the last day of the year. Superfast's required rate of return is 12%.

There is no difference between the modernize and replace alternatives in terms of required working capital. Superfast Chips has a special waiver on income taxes until 2013.

Required

1. Sketch the cash inflows and outflows of the modernize and replace alternatives over the 2007 to 2013 period.
2. Calculate payback period for the modernize and replace alternatives.
3. Calculate net present value of the modernize and replace alternatives.
4. What factors should Superfast Chips consider in choosing between the alternatives?

21-28 Equipment replacement, income taxes (continuation of 21-27). Assume the same facts as in Problem 21-27, except that the plant is located in Austin, Texas. Superfast has no special waiver on income taxes. It pays a 30% tax rate on all income. Proceeds from sales of equipment above book value are taxed at the same 30% rate.

Required

1. Sketch the after-tax cash inflows and outflows of the modernize and replace alternatives over the 2007 to 2013 period.
2. Calculate net present value of the modernize and replace alternatives.
3. Suppose Superfast is planning to build several more plants. It wants to have the most advantageous tax position possible. Superfast has been approached by Spain, Malaysia, and Australia to construct plants in their countries. Use the data in Problem 21-27 and this problem to briefly describe in qualitative terms the income tax features that would be advantageous to Superfast.

21-29 DCF, sensitivity analysis, no income taxes. (CMA, adapted) Bristol Engineering, Inc., manufactures electronic components. The company has developed a device that management believes could be modified and marketed as an electronic game.

PH Grade Assist

The following information for the new product was developed from the best estimates of the marketing and production managers:

Annual sales (all for cash)	1,000,000 units
Selling price	$10 per unit
Cash variable cost	$4 per unit
Cash fixed costs	$2,000,000 per year
Investment required	$12,000,000
Project life	5 years

At the end of the five-year useful life, there will be no terminal disposal value. Assume all cash flows occur at year-end except for initial investment amounts.

The electronic game industry is a new market for Bristol, and management is concerned about the reliability of the estimates. The controller has proposed applying sensitivity analysis to selected factors.

Ignore income taxes in your computations. Bristol Engineering's required rate of return on this project is 14%.

Required

1. Calculate the net present value of this investment proposal.
2. Calculate the effect on the net present value of the following two changes in assumptions. (Treat each item independently of the other.)
   a. 10% reduction in the selling price
   b. 10% increase in the variable cost per unit
3. Discuss how management would use the data developed in requirements 1 and 2 in its consideration of the proposed capital investment.

Excel Lab
www.prenhall.com/horngren/cost12e

21-30 NPV and customer profitability, no income taxes. Stone Art Company sells granite and marble countertops. The following table provides revenue and cost data for two of Stone Art's customers: Harvey Builders and Kestle Constructors. It shows the results for the year ended 2006 and also the expected future annual percentage increase in each category, by customer.

	A	B	C	D	E	F
1		Future Annual Percentage Increase			2006	
2		Harvey	Kestle		Harvey	Kestle
3		Builders	Constructors		Builders	Constructors
4	Revenues	6%	5%		$94,500	$585,000
5	Costs	5%	4%		60,800	510,000
6	Cash flow from operations				$33,700	$ 75,000

Assume that (a) all transactions occur at year-end, (b) all revenues are cash inflows, and (c) all costs are cash outflows. Ignore income taxes. Stone Art's required rate of return is 12%.

If you want to use Excel to solve this problem, go to the Excel Lab at **www.prenhall.com/horngren/cost12e** and download the template for Problem 21-30.

Required

1. Calculate the cash flow from operations for each customer for 2007, 2008, and 2009.
2. Stone Art estimates the value of each customer using the net present value of the cash flow from operations over the next three years. Calculate the value of Harvey Builders and Kestle Constructors to Stone Art at the end of 2006. Which customer is more valuable?
3. Kestle Constructors threatens to switch to another supplier unless Stone Art gives a 10% price reduction on all sales to Kestle Constructors starting in 2007. Calculate the three-year NPV of Kestle Constructors to Stone Art after incorporating the 10% discount. Should Stone Art continue to sell to Kestle Constructors? What other factors should Stone Art consider before making its final decision?

PH Grade Assist

21-31 NPV of JIT, income taxes. (CMA, adapted) Hathaway Door Company produces door and window systems for sale to large construction companies. Hathaway's management is considering installing a JIT system (computer system and materials-handling equipment) to better serve its customers. The facts to be considered in the decision are:

- The system will cost $1,500,000 and will have a five-year useful life. It is assumed to have zero terminal value for tax reporting of straight-line depreciation. At the end of five years, Hathaway expects to sell the system for $100,000.
- Service improvements related to the system will result in a $1,000,000 increase in revenues during the first year, and this increase will grow by 5% each year thereafter. Hathaway's contribution margin is 60%.
- Smaller, more-frequent purchase orders will result in a $150,000 increase in annual materials-handling costs and an $80,000 reduction in the current annual cost of renting the warehouse.
- Working-capital needs will decrease by $200,000.
- Hathaway is subject to an income tax rate of 30% on all taxable transactions and requires an after-tax rate of return of 12%.

Assume that all cash flows occur at year-end except for initial investment amounts.

Required

1. If the JIT system is installed at Hathaway, calculate the expected incremental after-tax cash flow from operations during each of the five years.
2. Calculate the expected NPV of installing the JIT system at Hathaway.
3. Based on your analysis in requirement 2, would you recommend installing the JIT system? Identify nonfinancial factors you would consider in making your recommendation.

Excel Lab
www.prenhall.com/horngren/cost12e

21-32 Replacement of a machine, income taxes, sensitivity. (CMA, adapted) WRL Company operates a snack food center at the Hartsfield Airport. On January 1, 2003, WRL purchased a special cookie-cutting machine, which has been used for three years. It is January 1, 2006, and WRL is considering whether it should purchase a new, more-efficient cookie-cutting machine. WRL has two options: (1) continue using the old machine or (2) sell the old machine and purchase a new machine. The seller of the new machine isn't offering a trade-in. The following information has been obtained:

	A	B	C
1		Old Machine	New Machine
2	Initial purchase cost of machines	$80,000	$120,000
3	Useful life from acquisition date (years)	7	4
4	Terminal disposal value at the end of useful life on Dec. 31, 2009, assumed for depreciation purposes	$10,000	$ 20,000
5	Expected annual cash operating costs:		
6	Variable cost per cookie	$ 0.20	$ 0.14
7	Total fixed costs	$15,000	$ 14,000
8	Depreciation method for tax purposes	Straight line	Straight line
9	Estimated disposal value of machines:		
10	January 1, 2006	$40,000	$120,000
11	December 31, 2009	$ 7,000	$ 20,000
12	Expected number of cookies made and sold each year	300,000	300,000

WRL is subject to a 40% income tax rate. Assume that any gain or loss on the sale of machines is treated as an ordinary tax item and will affect the taxes paid by WRL in the year in which it occurs. WRL's after-tax required rate of return is 16%. Assume all cash flows occur at year-end except for initial investment amounts.

If you want to use Excel to solve this problem, go to the Excel Lab at **www.prenhall.com/horngren/cost12e** and download the template for Problem 21-32.

Required

1. You have been asked whether WRL should buy the new machine. To help in your analysis, calculate the following:
   a. One-time after-tax cash effect of disposing of the old machine
   b. Annual recurring after-tax cash operating savings from using the new machine (variable and fixed)
   c. Cash tax savings due to differences in annual depreciation of the old machine and the new machine
   d. Difference in after-tax cash flow from terminal disposal of new machine and old machine.
2. Use your calculations in requirement 1 and the net present value method to determine whether WRL should use the old machine or acquire the new machine.
3. How much more or less would the recurring after-tax cash operating savings of the new machine need to be for WRL to earn exactly the 16% after-tax required rate of return? Assume that all other data about the investment do not change.

21-33 Capital budgeting, inflation, income taxes, appendix. (J. Fellingham, adapted) Abbie Young is manager of the customer-service division of an electrical appliance store. Abbie is considering buying a machine at a cost of $10,000 on December 31, 2005. The machine will last five years. Abbie estimates that the incremental before-tax cash savings from using the machine will be $3,000 annually. The $3,000 is measured at current prices and will be received at the end of each year. For tax purposes, she will depreciate the machine using the straight-line method, assuming no terminal disposal value. Abbie requires a 10% after-tax real rate of return (that is, the rate of return is 10% when all cash flows are denominated in December 31, 2005, dollars).

Required

Treat each of the following cases independently.

1. There are no income taxes, but the annual inflation rate is 20%. Calculate the net present value of the machine. The cash savings each year will be increased by a factor equal to the cumulative inflation rate. Use the nominal discount rate in your calculations.
2. The annual inflation rate is 20%, and the income tax rate is 40%. Calculate the net present value of the machine. Use the same nominal discount rate as in requirement 1 in your calculations.

21-34 Ethics, capital budgeting. (CMA, adapted) Evans Company plans to expand its manufacturing capabilities to meet the growing demand for its products. The first alternative is to expand its current manufacturing facility, which is located next to a vacant lot in the heart of St. Louis. The second alternative is to convert a warehouse, already owned by Evans, that is located 20 miles outside St. Louis. Evans's controller, George Watson, directs Helen Dodge, assistant controller, to use net present value computations to evaluate both proposals. On completing her analysis, Dodge reports to Watson that the proposal to expand the current manufacturing facility has a slightly positive net present value. The proposal to convert the warehouse has a large negative net present value.

Watson is upset over Dodge's conclusions. He returns the proposal to her with the comment, "You must have made an error. The warehouse proposal should look better and have a positive net present value. Work on the projections and estimates."

Dodge suspects that Watson is anxious to have the warehouse proposal selected because this location would eliminate his long commute into St. Louis. Feeling some pressure, she checks her calculations but finds no errors. Dodge reviews her projections and estimates. These, too, are quite reasonable. Even so, she replaces some of her original estimates with new estimates that are more favorable to the warehouse proposal, although these new estimates are less likely to occur. The revised proposal has a smaller negative net present value. Dodge is confused about what she should do.

Required

1. Referring to the "Standards of Ethical Conduct for Management Accountants" described in Chapter 1 (p. 16), explain:
   a. Whether George Watson's conduct was unethical when he gave Helen Dodge specific instructions on reviewing the proposal
   b. Whether Helen Dodge's revised proposal for converting the warehouse is unethical
2. Identify the steps that Helen Dodge should take in attempting to resolve this situation.

21-35 Capital budgeting estimates, ethics. (R. Madison and C. Verschoor, adapted from *Strategic Finance*, December 2000) Amy Kimbell was recently promoted to assistant corporate controller at Hi-Quality Productions, Inc. (Hi-Q), a manufacturer of automotive components. As part of its capital budgeting process, Hi-Q does postinvestment audits comparing projections made at the time projects are selected to actual results. Kimbell participates in these reviews as a member of the capital budget committee.

The committee is meeting to review a $4 million investment Hi-Q made in automated process technology a year ago. Kimbell was not a member of the committee at that time. During the review, Kimbell notes that several of the projections in the original investment proposal were very aggressive, including a very high disposal value for equipment and an excessively long useful life over which cost savings were projected to occur. If more realistic projections had been used, Kimbell doubts that the board would have approved the investment.

Kimbell also notes that substantial amounts of incremental service-department operating costs directly caused by the new investment are not being directly charged. Instead, these costs are being allocated as part of general overhead. As a result, only a portion of the costs are allocated to the new investment. Finally, she notes that the estimated rate for spoiled and defective work contained in the proposal is being used in the review rather than the actual rate, which is considerably higher.

When Kimbell questions these points she is told that, as a new committee member, she should observe rather than participate. When she continues to express her concerns, Kimbell is firmly informed that the committee unanimously recommended approval of the proposal because it was in the company's best interest in the long run. Given this consensus, certain "adjustments and exceptions" to the postinvestment audit process were justified to ensure the overall long-run well-being of the company.

Required

1. As a management accountant, should Kimbell take the position that the capital budget committee's behavior and stance are unethical? Refer to the Standards of Ethical Conduct for Management Accountants described in Chapter 1 (p. 16).
2. What action, if any, should Kimbell take?

Collaborative Learning Problem

21-36 Relevant costs, outsourcing, capital budgeting, no income taxes. The Strubel Company currently makes as many units of Part No. 789 as it needs. David Lin, general manager of the Strubel Company, has received a bid from the Gabriella Company for supplying Part No. 789. Current plans call for Gabriella to supply 1,000 units of Part No. 789 per year at $50 a unit. Gabriella can begin supplying on January 1, 2006, and continue for five years, after which time Strubel will not need the part. Gabriella can accommodate any change in Strubel's demand for the part and will supply it for $50 a unit, regardless of quantity.

Jack Tyson, controller of the Strubel Company, reports the following costs for manufacturing 1,000 units of Part No. 789:

Direct materials	$22,000
Direct manufacturing labor	11,000
Variable manufacturing overhead	7,000
Depreciation on machine	10,000
Product and process engineering	4,000
Rent	2,000
Allocation of general plant overhead costs	5,000
Total costs	$61,000

The following additional information is available:

a. Part No. 789 is made on a machine used exclusively for the manufacture of Part No. 789. The machine was acquired on January 1, 2005, at a cost of $60,000. The machine has a useful life of six years and no terminal disposal value. Depreciation is calculated on the straight-line method.

b. The machine could be sold on January 1, 2006, for $15,000.

c. Product and process engineering costs are incurred to ensure that the manufacturing process for Part No. 789 works smoothly. Although these costs are fixed in the short run with respect to units of Part No. 789 produced, they can be saved in the long run if this part is no longer produced. If Part No. 789 is outsourced, product and process engineering costs of $4,000 will be incurred for 2006 but not thereafter.

d. Rent costs of $2,000 are allocated to products on the basis of the floor space used for manufacturing the product. If Part No. 789 is discontinued, the space currently used to manufacture it would become available. The company could then use the space for storage and save $1,000 currently paid for outside storage.

e. General plant overhead costs are allocated to each department on the basis of direct manufacturing labor dollars. These costs will not change in total, but no general plant overhead will be allocated to Part No. 789 if the part is outsourced.

Assume all cash flows other than disposal of machine occur at the end of each year. Ignore income taxes. Strubel has a 12% required rate of return for this project.

Required

1. Use the NPV method to determine whether David Lin should outsource Part No. 789.
2. Describe any sensitivity analysis that seems advisable, but you need not perform any sensitivity calculations.
3. What other factors should Lin consider in making the decision?
4. Lin is particularly concerned about his bonus for 2006. The bonus is based on Strubel's accounting income. What decision will Lin make if he wants to maximize his bonus in 2006?

Answers to Exercises in Compound Interest (Exercise 21-16)

The general approach to these exercises centers on a key question: Which of the four basic tables in Appendix C should be used? No computations should be made until this basic question has been answered with confidence.

1. **From Table 1.** The $5,000 is the present value P of your winnings. Their future value S in 10 years will be:

$$S = P(1 + r)^n$$

The conversion factor, $(1 + r)^n$, is on line 10 of Table 1.

$$\text{Substituting at 6\%: } S = 5{,}000(1.791) = \$8{,}955$$

$$\text{Substituting at 14\%: } S = 5{,}000(3.707) = \$18{,}535$$

2. **From Table 2.** The $89,550 is a future value. You want the present value of that amount. $P = S \div (1 + r)^n$. The conversion factor, $1 \div (1 + r)^n$, is on line 10 of Table 2. Substituting,

$$P = \$89{,}550\ (0.558) = \$49{,}969$$

3. **From Table 3.** The $89,550 is a future value. You are seeking the uniform amount (annuity) to set aside annually. Note that $1 invested each year for 10 years at 6% has a future value of $13.181 after 10 years, from line 10 of Table 3.

$$S_n = \text{Annual deposit } (F)$$

$$\$89{,}550 = \text{Annual deposit } (13.181)$$

$$\text{Annual deposit} = \frac{\$89{,}550}{13.181} = \$6{,}794$$

4. **From Table 3.** You need to find the future value of an annuity of $5,000 per year. Note that $1 invested each year for 10 years at 12% has a future value of $17.549 after 10 years.

$$S_n = \$5{,}000F, \text{ where } F \text{ is the conversion factor}$$

$$S_n = \$5{,}000(17.549) = \$87{,}745$$

5. **From Table 4.** When you reach age 65, you will get $200,000, a present value at that time. You need to find the annuity that will exactly exhaust the invested principal in 10 years. To pay yourself $1 each year for 10 years when the interest rate is 6% requires you to have $7.360 today, from line 10 of Table 4.

$$P_n = \text{Annual withdrawal } (F)$$

$$\$200{,}000 = \text{Annual withdrawal } (7.360)$$

$$\text{Annual withdrawal} = \frac{\$200{,}000}{7.360} = \$27{,}174$$

6. **From Table 4.** You need to find the present value of an annuity for 10 years.

$$\text{At 6\%:} \quad P_n = \text{Annual withdrawal } (F)$$

$$P_n = \$50{,}000(7.360)$$

$$P_n = \$368{,}000$$

$$\text{At 20\%:} \quad P_n = \$50{,}000(4.192)$$

$$P_n = \$209{,}600, \text{ a much lower figure}$$

7. Plan B is preferable. The NPV of plan B exceeds that of plan A by $980 ($3,126 – $2,146):

		Plan A		Plan B	
Year	PV Factor at 6%	Cash Inflows	PV of Cash Inflows	Cash Inflows	PV of Cash Inflows
0	1.000	$(10,000)	$(10,000)	$(10,000)	$(10,000)
1	0.943	1,000	943	5,000	4,715
2	0.890	2,000	1,780	4,000	3,560
3	0.840	3,000	2,520	3,000	2,520
4	0.792	4,000	3,168	2,000	1,584
5	0.747	5,000	3,735	1,000	747
			$ 2,146		$ 3,126

Even though plans A and B have the same total cash inflows over the five years, plan B is preferred because it has greater cash inflows occurring earlier.

Get Connected: Cost Accounting in the News

Go to www.prenhall.com/horngren/cost12e for additional online exercise(s) that explore issues affecting the accounting world today. These exercises offer you the opportunity to analyze and reflect on how cost accounting helps managers to make better decisions and handle the challenges of strategic planning and implementation.

CHAPTER 21 Video Case

Capital Budgeting at Pearson Education

How does a division know when it's time to expand its operations and build new facilities? For Pearson's Higher Education Group, located in Upper Saddle River, NJ, it wasn't hard to identify the need. Its four existing distribution centers were bursting at the seams, with no room for expansion. With forecasts indicating continued growth, something had to be done.

But identifying a need and getting the project approved by top management are two different issues. The Higher Education Group had to demonstrate a clear link between the capital budgeting project and the Group's overall strategy. For Pearson's Higher Education Group, the ability to turn around customer orders quickly and accurately is critical. So the Group's senior management embarked on a capital budgeting project to lease an 890,000 square-foot building in Cranbury, New Jersey, and equip it with $25 million in warehouse distribution equipment such as shelving, conveyers, shrink-wrap machines, and transport vehicles. As part of the proposal, one of the old distribution center buildings was to be sold for $17 million.

In justifying the project, managers projected significant improvements in productivity and efficiency. For example, in the shipping department, the old facility had just 22 shipping doors and barely enough space to move around. The new facility was designed to have 37 shipping docks, allowing for more efficient customer-order staging. Managers also expected to reduce the number of times workers handled orders, leading to faster turnarounds. For example, in the carton-making area, automated equipment used to fabricate boxes reduced headcount from 16 workers to 4. And in the preparation of value packs (a package containing multiple items shrink-wrapped together) managers predicted the new facility would save hundreds of thousands of dollars in labor costs alone.

For each area of the new facility—from receiving and quality assurance, to shipping and returns processing—costs of equipment, labor savings, and waste reduction were calculated. Formal quantitative analysis techniques such as net present value and payback were used to analyze each element of the proposal. Pearson Education expected a payback of five years or less on the overall project.

Pearson Education's Management Committee in London approved the request. The team that worked on the project was now responsible for managing the construction of the new distribution center.

The state-of-the-art distribution center became operational on February 3, 2003, right on budget and schedule. Many of the gains management anticipated in its initial request for funding have been achieved. Average daily inventory is over $127 million, and close to 88% of Pearson Higher Education sales ship from the Cranbury location.

QUESTIONS

1. What risks did Pearson Higher Education face with the Cranbury distribution center project?
2. As part of the capital budgeting request, Pearson Higher Education included numerous material-handling machines. Assume that an automated shrink-wrap machine costs $240,000. No change in working capital is expected. The machine is estimated to save $80,000 a year in cash operating costs for the next five years. The machine has no terminal disposal value at the end of year 5. The after-tax required rate of return is 12%. The company uses straight-line depreciation for tax purposes, and its income tax rate is 40%. Compute net present value and payback period for this machine. Should Pearson Education have invested in this machine? Why or why not?
3. If you were conducting the postinvestment audit on this project, what would you look for, and why?

CHAPTER 22

MANAGEMENT CONTROL SYSTEMS, TRANSFER PRICING, AND MULTINATIONAL CONSIDERATIONS

LEARNING OBJECTIVES

1. Describe a management control system and its three key properties
2. Describe the benefits and costs of decentralization
3. Explain transfer prices and four criteria used to evaluate them
4. Calculate transfer prices using three methods
5. Illustrate how market-based transfer prices promote goal congruence in perfectly competitive markets
6. Understand how to avoid making suboptimal decisions when transfer prices are based on full cost plus a markup
7. Describe the range over which two divisions negotiate the transfer price when there is unused capacity
8. Apply a general guideline for determining a minimum transfer price
9. Incorporate income tax considerations in multinational transfer pricing

Transfer pricing—the price one subunit in a company charges for the services it provides to another subunit—is both fascinating and contentious. Fascinating because top managers use transfer prices (1) to focus managers' attention on their own subunits and (2) to plan and coordinate actions across different subunits to maximize operating income for the company as a whole. Contentious because managers of different subunits often have very different preferences about how transfer prices should be set. For example, some managers may prefer transfer prices to be based on market prices. Others may prefer transfer prices based on costs.

Consider Horizon Petroleum. Horizon has two divisions: the Transportation Division and the Refining Division. Horizon evaluates managers on the basis of division operating income. The Transportation Division purchases crude oil in Matamoros, Mexico, and it operates a pipeline that transports crude oil from Matamoros to Houston, Texas. The Refining Division manages a refinery in Houston that processes crude oil into gasoline. Patricia Jennings, the president of Horizon, has called a meeting with the division managers and Jessica Hamm, controller, to review the company's transfer-pricing policies.

Patricia: I have asked Jessica to lead a review of our transfer-pricing policies to learn about any concerns you might have.

Carl Gramm (manager of the Refining Division): If we want to be sure that we are always making the right decisions, we should transfer product at the variable cost of the Transportation Division. Of course, to motivate employees, I know Anthony wants the Transportation Division to show operating income, so perhaps we can compromise and use a transfer price that is 110% of the full cost of the Transportation Division. To reduce the tax burden of Horizon Petroleum as a whole, we want to keep the transfer price as low as possible. As a result, the higher income in the U.S. would be taxed at the U.S.'s lower tax rates.

Anthony Closz (manager of the Transportation Division): I have a very different view from Carl's. I think we need to set the transfer price at the market prices prevailing for delivering crude oil to the Houston refinery. After all, this is what it would cost Carl to buy crude oil if we did not have our own Transportation Division. I know that this transfer price is much higher than the transfer price based on full cost plus 10%, but it seems to me that using market prices would help us make the best decisions. The tax argument also has problems. The Mexican tax authorities are unlikely to accept a low transfer price because it would reduce the Transportation Division's operating income and, therefore, reduce tax revenues for Mexico.

Carl: My problem with Anthony's analysis is that market prices are very unstable and, at least in the last few years, different crude oil producers have offered very different prices. If Anthony offers me a market price and I can buy crude oil at a better price from an external supplier, Anthony will be stuck with idle capacity, high fixed costs, and no revenues. This would not be good for Horizon because the company as a whole would incur higher costs. Anthony has excess capacity so, instead of producing crude oil at variable cost, we would be buying crude oil at a much higher price. This is why I believe the transfer price should be set at variable cost.

Jessica: Patricia, both Anthony and Carl make good points. I will work with them over the next couple of months and then make a proposal to you.

Patricia: That sounds terrific. Thank you all for your comments.

The transfer-pricing issues at Horizon Petroleum are common to many companies, such as Astra Zeneca, Cummins Engines, and Panasonic. But in each of these companies, transfer pricing is only part of the larger management control system. This chapter develops the links between strategy, organization structure, management control systems, and accounting information. We'll examine the benefits and costs of centralized and decentralized organization structures, and we'll look at the pricing of products or services transferred between subunits of the same company. We emphasize how accounting information, such as costs, budgets, and prices, helps in planning and coordinating actions of subunits. Some of the material in the chapter is "softer" than material in other chapters—that is, it includes relatively few numbers. Nevertheless, the concepts are important for management accountants to understand.

Management Control Systems

1

Describe a management control system

. . . gathers information for planning and control decisions

and its three key properties

. . . aligns with strategy, fits with organization structure, and motivates employees

A **management control system** is a means of gathering and using information to aid and coordinate the planning and control decisions throughout an organization and to guide the behavior of its managers and other employees. Some companies design their management control system around the concept of the balanced scorecard (see Chapter 13 for details). Consider British Petroleum (BP). Its management control system contains financial and nonfinancial information in each of the four perspectives of the balanced scorecard.

1. **Financial perspective**—for example, stock price, net income, return on investment, cash flow from operations, and cost per gallon of gasoline.
2. **Customer perspective**—for example, customer satisfaction, time taken to respond to customer requests for products, customers' repeat purchases, and market share in key market segments.
3. **Internal-business-process perspective**—for example, on-time delivery of gasoline from refineries to retail stations, gasoline quality, refinery downtime, number of days lost due to accidents and environmental problems, speed of service at retail stations, friendliness of employees, and stocking of convenience stores.
4. **Learning-and-growth perspective**—for example, employee satisfaction, absenteeism, information systems capabilities, and number of processes with real-time feedback.

The target performance levels are based on competitor benchmarks, which indicate the performance levels necessary to meet customer needs, compete effectively, and achieve financial goals. Well-designed management control systems use information both from within the company, such as net income and employee satisfaction, and from outside the company, such as stock price and customer satisfaction.

Management accountants must have the interpersonal and analytical skills necessary to evaluate and implement management control systems, as well as the ability to interpret outputs of these systems. The behavioral issues in this chapter and throughout this book are very important to accountants' careers.

Management control systems consist of formal and informal control systems. The formal management control system of a company includes explicit rules, procedures, performance measures, and incentive plans that guide the behavior of its managers and other employees. The formal control system is comprised of several systems. For example, the management accounting system provides information regarding costs, revenues, and income. The human resources systems provide information on recruiting, training, absenteeism, and accidents; and quality systems provide information on yield, defective products, and late deliveries to customers.

The informal management control system includes shared values, loyalties, and mutual commitments among members of the company, company culture, and the unwritten norms about acceptable behavior for managers and other employees. Examples of company slogans that reinforce values and loyalties are "At Ford, Quality Is Job 1," and "At Home Depot, Low Prices Are Just the Beginning."

Evaluating Management Control Systems

To be effective, management control systems should be closely aligned to the company's strategies and goals. Two examples of strategies at BP are providing innovative products and services to increase market share in key customer segments (perhaps by targeting customers who are willing to pay more for faster service, better facilities, and well-stocked convenience stores) and reducing costs and targeting price-sensitive customers. Suppose BP decides, wisely or unwisely, to provide innovative products and services. The management control system must then reinforce this goal, and BP should tie managers' rewards to achieving the targeted measures.

BP's balanced scorecard-based management control system can help managers determine if their strategy is working. For example, if BP achieves its targets in the learning-and-growth and internal-business-process perspectives, it is implementing its strategy well. However, if after achieving these targets, BP does not see improvements in the customer and financial perspectives, it means its strategy is not working. BP's managers would then have to consider different ways of pursuing the strategy of providing innovative products and services (perhaps by improving the facilities and service at its gas stations), or they could consider changing the strategy to become a low-cost, low-price gasoline supplier.

Management control systems should be designed to fit the company's organization structure and the decision-making responsibility of individual managers. Different levels of management at BP need different kinds of information to perform their tasks. For example, top management needs stock-price information to evaluate how much shareholder value the company has created. Stock price, however, is less important for line managers supervising individual refineries. They are more concerned with obtaining information about on-time delivery of gasoline, equipment downtime, product quality, number of days lost to accidents and environmental problems, cost per gallon of gasoline, and employee satisfaction.

Now consider the marketing manager at BP. The company's management control system should provide this manager with information about service at the gas stations, customer satisfaction, and market share—information that helps the manager in the planning and control of operations. The marketing manager requires very different information from that required by the refinery manager. But, in both cases, the management control system provides information to aid each manager's decision making and to align their actions.

Effective management control systems should also motivate managers and other employees. **Motivation** is the desire to attain a selected goal (the *goal-congruence* aspect) combined with the resulting pursuit of that goal (the *effort* aspect).

Goal congruence exists when individuals and groups work toward achieving the organization's goals—that is, managers working in their own best interest take actions that align with the overall goals of top management. Suppose the goal of BP's top management is to maximize operating income. If the management control system evaluates the refinery manager *only* on the basis of costs, the manager may be tempted to make decisions that minimize cost but overlook product quality or timely delivery to retail stations, which will likely not maximize operating income of the company as a whole. In this case, the management control system will not achieve goal congruence.

Effort is exertion toward achieving a goal. Effort goes beyond physical exertion, such as a worker producing at a faster rate, to include both physical and mental actions. Management control systems motivate managers and other employees to exert effort through a variety of rewards tied to the achievement of goals. These rewards can be monetary (such as cash, shares of company stock, use of a company car, or membership in a club) or nonmonetary (such as power or pride in working for a successful company).

Organization Structure and Decentralization

2

Describe the benefits of decentralization

. . . responsiveness to customers, faster decision making, management development

and the costs of decentralization

. . . loss of control, duplication of activities

Management control systems must fit an organization's structure. An organization whose structure is decentralized has additional issues to consider for its management control system to be effective.

Decentralization is the freedom for managers at lower levels of the organization to make decisions. **Autonomy** refers to the degree of freedom to make decisions. The greater the freedom, the greater the autonomy. As we discuss the issues of decentralization and autonomy, we use subunit to refer to any part of an organization. A subunit may be a large division, such as the Refining Division of BP, or a small group, such as a two-person advertising department of a local clothing chain. Decentralization empowers managers and other employees of subunits to take decisive actions.

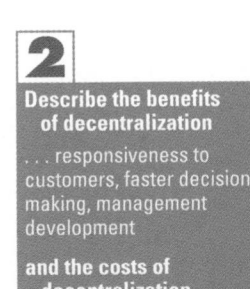

Total decentralization means minimum constraints and maximum freedom for managers at the lowest levels of an organization to make decisions. Total centralization means maximum constraints and minimum freedom for managers at the lowest levels of an organization to make decisions. Companies' organization structures fall somewhere in between these two extremes because there are both benefits and costs of decentralization.

Benefits of Decentralization

How much decentralization is optimal? Managers try to choose the degree of decentralization that maximizes benefits over costs. From a practical standpoint, top management can seldom quantify either the benefits or the costs of decentralization. Still, the cost-benefit approach helps them focus on the issues.

Supporters of decentralizing decision making and granting responsibilities to managers of subunits advocate the following benefits:

1. **Creates greater responsiveness to local needs.** Good decisions cannot be made without good information. Compared with top managers, subunit managers are better informed about their customers, competitors, suppliers, and employees, as well as about local factors that affect performance, such as ways to decrease costs, improve quality, and be responsive to customers. Eastman Kodak reports that two advantages of decentralization are an "increase in the company's knowledge of the marketplace and improved service to customers."
2. **Leads to gains from faster decision making.** Decentralization speeds decision making, creating a competitive advantage over centralized organizations. Centralization slows decision making as responsibility for decisions creeps upward through layer after layer of management. Interlake, a manufacturer of materials-handling equipment, cites this benefit of decentralization: "We have distributed decision-making powers more broadly to the cutting edge of product and market opportunity." Interlake's materials-handling equipment must often be customized to fit customers' needs. Delegating decision making to the sales force allows Interlake to respond faster to changing customer requirements.
3. **Increases motivation of subunit managers.** Subunit managers are more motivated when they can exercise initiative. Johnson & Johnson, a highly decentralized company, maintains that "Decentralization = Creativity = Productivity."
4. **Assists management development and learning.** Giving managers more responsibility helps develop an experienced pool of management talent to fill higher-level management positions. The company also learns which people are not management material. According to Tektronix, an electronics instruments company: "Decentralized units provide a training ground for general managers and a visible field of combat where product champions can fight for their ideas."
5. **Sharpens the focus of subunit managers.** In a decentralized setting, the manager of a small subunit has a concentrated focus. A small subunit is more flexible and nimble than a larger subunit and can adapt quickly to changing market opportunities. Also, top management, relieved of the burden of day-to-day operating decisions, can spend more time and effort on strategic planning for the entire organization.

Costs of Decentralization

Advocates of more-centralized decision making point to the following costs of decentralizing decision making:

1. **Leads to suboptimal decision making, which arises when a decision's benefit to one subunit is more than offset by the costs or loss of benefits to the organization as a whole.** This cost arises because top management has given up control over decision making.

Suboptimal decision making—also called **incongruent decision making** or **dysfunctional decision making**—is most likely to occur when the subunits in the company are highly interdependent, such as when the end product of one subunit is used or sold by another subunit. For example, a manufacturing manager evaluated on the basis of manufacturing costs may be unresponsive to requests from marketing to schedule a rush order for a customer if altering production schedules will increase manufacturing costs. From the company's viewpoint, however, supplying the product to the customer may be preferred both because the customer is willing to pay a premium price and because the company expects the customer to place many orders in the future. Suboptimal decision making also occurs when subunit managers do not have the necessary skills to do their jobs.

2. **Focuses manager's attention on the subunit rather than the company as a whole.** Individual subunit managers may regard themselves as competing with managers of other subunits in the same company as if they were external rivals. Consequently, managers may be unwilling to share information or to assist when another subunit faces an emergency. Also, subunit managers may use information they have about local conditions to further their own self-interest rather than to help achieve the company's goals. For example, they may not disclose the full potential for sales for fear of missing their goal or so they can reduce the effort they need to exert.

3. **Increases costs of gathering information.** Managers may spend too much time obtaining information about different subunits of the company needed to coordinate their actions.

4. **Results in duplication of activities.** Several individual subunits of the company may undertake the same activity separately. For example, there may be a duplication of staff functions (accounting, human resources, and legal) if a company is highly decentralized. Centralizing these functions helps to consolidate, streamline, and use fewer resources for these activities.

Comparison of Benefits and Costs

To choose an organization structure that will implement a company's strategy, top managers must compare the benefits and costs of decentralization, often on a function-by-function basis. For example, the controller's function may be highly decentralized for many problem-solving and attention-directing purposes (such as preparing operating budgets and performance reports) but highly centralized for other purposes (such as processing accounts receivables and developing income tax strategies). Decentralizing budgeting and reporting enables the manager of a subunit, for example, to tailor a report to focus on information that she needs to make better decisions and increase income. At the same time, management control systems such as the balanced scorecard align and coordinate actions of decentralized subunits. Centralizing income tax strategies allows the organization to trade off income in a subunit with losses in other subunits to evaluate the impact on the organization as a whole.

Surveys of U.S. and European companies report that the decisions made most frequently at the decentralized level and least frequently at the corporate level are related to product mix and product advertising. In these areas, subunit managers must make faster decisions based on local information. Decisions related to the type and source of long-term financing are made least frequently at the decentralized level and most frequently at the corporate level. In these cases, corporate managers have better information about financing terms in different markets and can obtain the best terms. The benefits of decentralization are generally greater when companies face uncertainties in their environments, require detailed local knowledge for performing various jobs, and have few interdependencies among divisions.

Decentralization in Multinational Companies

Multinational companies—companies that operate in multiple countries—are often decentralized because centralized control of a company with subunits around the world is often physically and practically impossible. Also, language, customs, cultures, business practices, rules, laws, and regulations vary significantly across countries. Decentralization enables managers in different countries to make decisions that exploit their knowledge of local business and political conditions and to deal with uncertainties in their individual environments. For example, Philips, a global electronics company headquartered in the Netherlands, delegates marketing and pricing decisions for its television business in the Indian and Singaporean markets to the managers in those countries. Multinational corporations often rotate managers between foreign locations and corporate headquarters.

Job rotation combined with decentralization helps develop managers' abilities to operate in the global environment.

There are drawbacks to decentralizing multinational companies. One of the most important is the lack of control. Barings PLC, a British investment banking firm, went bankrupt and had to be sold when one of its traders in Singapore caused the firm to lose more than £1 billion on unauthorized trades that were not detected until after the trades were made. Similarly, a trader at Sumitomo Corporation racked up $2.6 billion in copper-trading losses because poor controls failed to detect the magnitude of the trader's activities. Multinational corporations that implement decentralized decision making usually design their management control systems to measure and monitor division performance. Information and communications technology helps the flow of information for reporting and control.

Choices About Responsibility Centers

To measure the performance of subunits in centralized or decentralized companies, the management control system uses one or a mix of the four types of responsibility centers presented in Chapter 6:

1. *Cost center*—the manager is accountable for costs only.
2. *Revenue center*—the manager is accountable for revenues only.
3. *Profit center*—the manager is accountable for revenues and costs.
4. *Investment center*—the manager is accountable for investments, revenues, and costs.

Centralization or decentralization is not mentioned in the descriptions of these centers because each type of responsibility center can be found in either centralized or decentralized companies.

A common misconception is that *profit center*—and, in some cases, *investment center*—is a synonym for a decentralized subunit and *cost center* is a synonym for a centralized subunit. *Profit centers can be coupled with a highly centralized organization, and cost centers can be coupled with a highly decentralized organization.* For example, managers in a division organized as a profit center may have little freedom in making decisions. They may need to obtain approval from corporate headquarters for every expenditure over, say, $10,000 and may be forced to do what the central staff wants. In another company, divisions may be organized as cost centers, but their managers may have great latitude on capital expenditures and on where to purchase materials and services. In short, the labels "profit center" and "cost center" are independent of the degree of centralization or decentralization in a company.

Transfer Pricing

3

Explain transfer prices
... price one subunit charges another for product

and four criteria used to evaluate them
... goal congruence, management effort, subunit performance evaluation, and subunit autonomy

In decentralized organizations, much of the decision-making power resides in its individual subunits. In these cases, the management control system often uses *transfer prices* to coordinate the actions of the subunits and to evaluate their performance.

A **transfer price** is the price one subunit (department or division) charges for a product or service supplied to another subunit of the same organization. If, for example, a car manufacturer has a separate division that manufactures engines, the transfer price is the price the engine division charges when it transfers engines to the car assembly division. The transfer price creates revenues for the selling subunit (the engine division in our example) and purchase costs for the buying subunit (the assembly division in our example), affecting each subunit's operating income. These operating incomes can be used to evaluate subunits' performances and to motivate their managers. The product or service transferred between subunits of an organization is called an **intermediate product**. This product may either be further worked on by the receiving subunit or, if transferred from production to marketing, sold to an external customer.

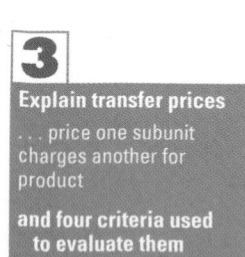

In one sense, transfer pricing is a curious phenomenon. Activities within an organization are clearly nonmarket in nature; products and services are not bought and sold as they are in open-market transactions. Yet, establishing prices for transfers among subunits of a company has a distinctly market flavor. The rationale for transfer prices is that subunit managers (such as the manager of the engine division), when making decisions, need only focus on how their decisions will affect their subunit's performance, without evaluating their impact on companywide performance. In this sense, transfer prices ease the subunit managers' information-processing and decision-making tasks. In a well-designed transfer-pricing system, optimizing subunit performance (the performance of the engine division) leads to optimizing the performance of the company as a whole.

As in all management control systems, transfer prices should help achieve a company's strategies and goals and fit its organization structure. In particular, transfer prices should promote goal congruence and a sustained high level of management effort. Subunits selling a product or service should be motivated to hold down their costs; subunits buying the product or service should be motivated to acquire and use inputs efficiently. The transfer price should also help top management evaluate the performance of individual subunits and their managers. If top management favors a high degree of decentralization, transfer prices should also promote a high degree of subunit autonomy in decision making. That is, a subunit manager seeking to maximize the operating income of his or her subunit should have the freedom to transact with other subunits of the company (on the basis of transfer prices) or to transact with external parties.

4

Calculate transfer prices using three methods

. . . market-based, cost-based, negotiated

There are three methods for determining transfer prices:

1. **Market-based transfer prices.** Top management may choose to use the price of a similar product or service publicly listed in, say, a trade association Web site. Also, top management may select, for the internal price, the external price that a subunit charges to outside customers.
2. **Cost-based transfer prices.** Top management may choose a transfer price based on the cost of producing the product in question. Examples include variable production cost, variable and fixed production costs, and full cost of the product. Full cost of the product includes all production costs plus costs from other business functions (R&D, design, marketing, distribution, and customer service). The cost used in cost-based transfer prices can be actual cost or budgeted cost. Sometimes, the cost-based transfer price includes a markup or profit margin that represents a return on subunit investment.
3. **Negotiated transfer prices.** In some cases, the subunits of a company are free to negotiate the transfer price between themselves and then to decide whether to buy and sell internally or deal with external parties. Subunits may use information about costs and market prices in these negotiations, but there is no requirement that the chosen transfer price bear any specific relationship to either cost or market-price data. Negotiated transfer prices are often employed when market prices are volatile and change constantly. The negotiated transfer price is the outcome of a bargaining process between selling and buying subunits.

To see how each of the three transfer-pricing methods works and to see the differences among them, we examine transfer pricing at Horizon Petroleum against the four criteria of goal congruence, management effort, subunit performance evaluation, and subunit autonomy (if desired).

An Illustration of Transfer Pricing

As described in the introduction of this chapter, Horizon Petroleum has two divisions, each operating as a profit center. The Transportation Division purchases crude oil in Matamoros, Mexico, and transports it from Matamoros to Houston, Texas. The Refining Division processes crude oil into gasoline. For simplicity, let's assume gasoline is the only salable product the Houston refinery makes and that it takes two barrels of crude oil to yield one barrel of gasoline.

Variable costs in each division are variable with respect to a single cost driver: barrels of crude oil transported by the Transportation Division, and barrels of gasoline produced by the Refining Division. The fixed cost per unit is based on the budgeted annual fixed costs and practical capacity of crude oil that can be transported by Transportation, and the budgeted fixed costs and practical capacity of gasoline that can be produced by Refining. Horizon Petroleum reports all costs and revenues of its non-U.S. operations in U.S. dollars using the prevailing exchange rate.

In dealing with transfer-pricing issues, top management must address two questions. One is a policy question: Should divisions be permitted to buy from external suppliers when the same goods are available internally? The other is an operational question: What will the transfer price be? Answering this question involves deciding (1) which of the three transfer-pricing methods will be used and (2) how disputes are to be resolved (negotiations, arbitration, or top-management directives).

- The Transportation Division has obtained rights to certain oil fields in the Matamoros area. It has a long-term contract to purchase crude oil produced from these fields at $12 per barrel. The division transports the oil to Houston and then "sells" it to the Refining Division. The pipeline from Matamoros to Houston has the capacity to carry 40,000 barrels of crude oil per day.
- The Refining Division has been operating at capacity (30,000 barrels of crude oil a day), using oil supplied by Horizon's Transportation Division (an average of 10,000 barrels per day) and oil bought from other producers and delivered to the Houston refinery (an average of 20,000 barrels per day at $21 per barrel).
- The Refining Division sells the gasoline it produces at $58 per barrel.

Exhibit 22-1 summarizes Horizon Petroleum's variable and fixed costs per barrel of crude oil in the Transportation Division and variable and fixed costs per barrel of gasoline in the Refining Division, the external market prices of buying crude oil, and the external market price of selling gasoline. What's missing in the exhibit is the actual transfer price from the Transportation Division to the Refining Division. This transfer price will vary depending on the transfer-pricing method used. Transfer prices from the Transportation Division to the Refining Division under each of the three methods are:

1. Market-based transfer price of $21 per barrel of crude oil based on the competitive market price in Houston.
2. Cost-based transfer prices at, say, 110% of full cost, where full cost is the cost of the crude oil purchased plus the Transportation Division's own variable and fixed costs: $1.10 \times (\$12 + \$1 + \$3) = \$17.60$.
3. Negotiated transfer price of $19.25 per barrel of crude oil, which is between the market-based and cost-based transfer prices.

Exhibit 22-2 presents division operating incomes per 100 barrels of crude oil purchased under each transfer-pricing method. Transfer prices create income for the selling division and corresponding costs for the buying division that cancel out when division results are consolidated for the company as a whole. The exhibit assumes all three transfer-pricing methods yield transfer prices that are in a range that does not cause division managers to change the business relationships shown in Exhibit 22-1. That is, Horizon Petroleum's total operating income from purchasing, transporting, and refining the 100 barrels of crude oil and selling the 50 barrels of gasoline is the same, $600, *regardless of the internal transfer prices used.*

$$\text{Operating income} = \text{Revenues} - \text{Cost of crude oil purchases} - \text{Transportation costs} - \text{Refining costs}$$

$$= \$58 \times 50 \text{ barrels of gasoline} - \$12 \times 100 \text{ barrels of crude oil}$$
$$- \$4 \times 100 \text{ barrels of crude oil} - \$14 \times 50 \text{ barrels of gasoline}$$
$$= \$2{,}900 - \$1{,}200 - \$400 - \$700 = \$600$$

EXHIBIT 22-1 **Operating Data for Horizon Petroleum**

	A	B	C	D	E	F	G	H
1								
2				**Transportation Division**				
3	Contract price per barrel of crude			Variable cost per barrel of crude oil	$1			
4	oil supplied in Matamoros	=	$12 →	Fixed cost per barrel of crude oil	3			
5				Full cost per barrel of crude oil	$4			
6				↓				
7								
8				Barrels of crude oil transferred				
9								
10				↓				
11				**Refining Division**				
12	Market price per barrel of crude			Variable cost per barrel of gasoline	$ 8		Market price per barrel of	
13	oil supplied to Houston refinery	=	$21 →	Fixed cost per barrel of gasoline	6	→	gasoline sold to external parties =	$58
14				Full cost per barrel of gasoline	$14			
15								

Division Operating Income of Horizon Petroleum for 100 Barrels of Crude Oil Under Alternative Transfer-Pricing Methods							
EXHIBIT 22-2									

	A	B	C	D	E	F	G	H
1	**Production and Sales Data**							
2	Barrels of crude transferred = 100							
3	Barrels of gasoline sold = 50							
4								
5		Internal Transfers			Internal Transfers at		Internal Transfers at	
6		at Market Price of			110% of Full Cost =		Negotiated Price of	
7		$21			$17.60		$19.25	
8		per barrel			per barrel		per barrel	
9	**Transportation Division**							
10	Revenues, $21, $17.60, $19.25 × 100 barrels of crude oil	$2,100			$1,760		$1,925	
11	Costs							
12	Crude oil purchase costs,							
13	$12 × 100 barrels of crude oil	1,200			1,200		1,200	
14	Division variable costs,							
15	$1 × 100 barrels of crude oil	100			100		100	
16	Division fixed costs,							
17	$3 × 100 barrels of crude oil	300			300		300	
18	Total division costs	1,600			1,600		1,600	
19	Division operating income	$ 500			$ 160		$ 325	
20								
21	**Refining Division**							
22	Revenues, $58 × 50 barrels of gasoline	$2,900			$2,900		$2,900	
23	Costs							
24	Transferred-in costs, $21, $17.60, $19.25							
25	× 100 barrels of crude oil	2,100			1,760		1,925	
26	Division variable costs,							
27	$8 × 50 barrels of gasoline	400			400		400	
28	Division fixed costs,							
29	$6 × 50 barrels of gasoline	300			300		300	
30	Total division costs	2,800			2,460		2,625	
31	Division operating income	$ 100			$ 440		$ 275	
32								
33	Operating income of both divisions together	$ 600			$ 600		$ 600	

Note further that under all three methods, summing the two division operating incomes equals Horizon Petroleum's total operating income of $600. By keeping total operating income the same, we focus attention on the effects of different transfer-pricing methods on the operating income of each division. Subsequent sections of this chapter show that different transfer-pricing methods can cause managers to take different actions leading to different total operating incomes.

Consider the two methods in the first two columns of Exhibit 22-2. The operating income of the Transportation Division is $340 more ($500 – $160) if transfer prices are based on market prices rather than on 110% of full cost. The operating income of the Refining Division is $340 more ($440 – $100) if transfer prices are based on 110% of full cost rather than market prices. If the Transportation Division's sole criterion were to maximize its own division operating income, it would favor transfer prices at market prices. In contrast, the Refining Division would prefer transfer prices at 110% of full cost to maximize its own division operating income. Little wonder that subunit managers take considerable interest in setting transfer prices, especially those managers whose compensation or promotion directly depends on subunit operating income. To reduce the excessive focus of subunit managers on their own subunits, many companies compensate subunit managers on the basis of both subunit and companywide operating incomes.

If market prices of crude oil in the Houston area fluctuated in response to local supply-and-demand conditions, then under the market-based method, the operating incomes of the Transportation and Refining divisions would fluctuate as well. The Transportation and Refining divisions may instead prefer to negotiate a more stable, long-run transfer price. In our example, the negotiated transfer price of $19.25 is between the

110% of full cost and market-based transfer prices and splits the $600 of operating income almost equally between the divisions ($325 for the Transportation Division and $275 for the Refining Division). Note that setting the transfer price at 110% of full cost also has the effect of shielding both divisions from fluctuations in crude oil prices in Houston. As Exhibit 22-2 shows, the $17.60 transfer price depends only on 110% of full cost of the Transportation Division. The market price of crude oil in Houston is irrelevant in this calculation.

We next examine market-based, cost-based, and negotiated transfer prices in more detail. We show how the choice of transfer-pricing method combined with managers' sourcing decisions can determine the size of the companywide operating-income pie itself.

5

Illustrate how market-based transfer prices promote goal congruence in perfectly competitive markets

. . . division managers transacting internally are motivated to take the same actions as if they were transacting externally

Market-Based Transfer Prices

Transferring products or services at market prices generally leads to optimal decisions when three conditions are satisfied: (1) The market for the intermediate product is perfectly competitive, (2) interdependencies of subunits are minimal, and (3) there are no additional costs or benefits to the company as a whole from buying or selling in the external market instead of transacting internally.

Perfectly-Competitive-Market Case

A **perfectly competitive market** exists when there is a homogeneous product with buying prices equal to selling prices and no individual buyers or sellers can affect those prices by their own actions. By using market-based transfer prices in perfectly competitive markets, a company can achieve (1) goal congruence, (2) management effort, (3) subunit performance evaluation, and (4) subunit autonomy.

In perfectly competitive markets, the minimum price the selling division is willing to accept from the buying division is the market price, because the selling division can always sell its output in the external market at that price. The maximum price the buying division is willing to pay to the selling division is the market price, because the buying division can always buy its input in the external market at that price.

Reconsider Horizon Petroleum. Assume there is a perfectly competitive market for crude oil in the Houston area. As a result, the Transportation Division can sell and the Refining Division can buy as much crude oil as each wants at $21 per barrel. Horizon would prefer its managers to buy or sell crude oil internally. Think about the decisions that Horizon's division managers would make if each had the option to sell or buy crude oil externally. If the transfer price between Horizon's Transportation and Refining Divisions is set below $21, the manager of the Transportation Division will be motivated to sell all crude oil to external buyers in the Houston area at $21 per barrel. If the transfer price is set above $21, the manager of the Refining Division will be motivated to purchase all crude oil requirements from external suppliers. Only a $21 transfer price will motivate the Transportation Division and the Refining Division to buy and sell internally. That's because neither division profits by buying or selling in the external market.

Suppose Horizon evaluates division managers on the basis of their individual division's operating income. The Transportation Division will sell, either internally or externally, as much crude oil as it can profitably transport, and the Refining Division will buy, either internally or externally, as much crude oil as it can profitably refine. At a $21-per-barrel transfer price, the actions that maximize each division's operating income are also the actions that maximize operating income of Horizon Petroleum as a whole. Furthermore, external market-based transfer prices motivate division managers to exert management effort to maximize their own division's operating income. Market prices also serve to evaluate the economic viability and profitability of each division individually. For example, if under market-based transfer prices, the Refining Division consistently shows small or negative profits, Horizon may decide to shut down the Refining Division and simply transport and sell the oil to other refineries in the Houston area.

Distress Prices

When supply outstrips demand, market prices may drop well below their historical averages. If the drop in prices is expected to be temporary, these low market prices are sometimes called "distress prices." Deciding whether a current market price is a distress price is often difficult. The market prices of several agricultural commodities, such as wheat and oats, have stayed for many years at what many people initially believed were temporary distress levels!

Which transfer price should be used for judging performance if distress prices prevail? Some companies use the distress prices themselves, but others use long-run average prices, or "normal" market prices. In the short run, the manager of the selling subunit should meet the distress price as long as it exceeds the incremental costs of supplying the product or service. If not, the selling division should stop selling the product or service to the buying division; the buying division should buy the product or service from an external supplier. These actions would increase division and companywide operating income. If the long-run average market price is used, forcing the manager to buy internally at a price above the current market price will hurt the buying division's short-run operating income. Using the long-run average market price, however, provides a better measure of the long-run viability of the supplier division. If the price remains low in the long run, though, the company should use the low market price as the transfer price. If the distress price is lower than the variable and fixed costs that can be saved if manufacturing facilities are shut down, the production facilities of the selling subunit should be sold, and the buying subunit should purchase the product from an external supplier.

Be aware of the conflict distress prices can cause. Because the selling division receives very low revenues from distress prices, managers may decide to produce other products that would not be in the company's best interest in the long run. Alternatively, if the transfer price is based on the long-run average market price, the buying division will prefer to buy externally. If top management *requires* buying internally (at the long-run average market price), autonomy is violated.

Cost-Based Transfer Prices

6

Understand how to avoid making suboptimal decisions when transfer prices are based on full cost plus a markup

. . . in situations when buying divisions regard the fixed costs and the markup as variable costs

Cost-based transfer prices are helpful when market prices are unavailable, inappropriate, or too costly to obtain—for example, when the product is specialized or when the internal product is different from the products available externally in terms of quality and customer service.

Full-Cost Bases

In practice, many companies use transfer prices based on full cost. To approximate market prices, cost-based transfer prices are sometimes set at full cost plus a margin. These transfer prices, however, can lead to suboptimal decisions. Suppose Horizon Petroleum makes internal transfers at 110% of full cost. Recall that the Refining Division purchases, on average, 20,000 barrels of crude oil per day from a local Houston supplier, who delivers the crude oil to the refinery at a price of $21 per barrel. To reduce crude oil costs, the Refining Division has located an independent producer in Matamoros—Gulfmex Corporation—that is willing to sell 20,000 barrels of crude oil per day at $16 per barrel, delivered to Horizon's pipeline in Matamoros. Given Horizon's organization structure, the Transportation Division would purchase the 20,000 barrels of crude oil in Matamoros from Gulfmex, transport it to Houston, and then sell it to the Refining Division. The pipeline has unused capacity and can ship the 20,000 barrels per day at its variable cost of $1 per barrel without affecting the shipment of the 10,000 barrels of crude oil per day acquired under its existing long-term contract arrangement. Will Horizon Petroleum incur lower costs by purchasing crude oil from Gulfmex in Matamoros or by purchasing crude oil from the Houston supplier? Will the Refining Division show lower crude oil purchasing costs by acquiring oil from Gulfmex or by acquiring oil from its current Houston supplier?

The following analysis shows that Horizon Petroleum's operating income would be maximized by purchasing oil from Gulfmex. The analysis compares the incremental costs in both divisions under the two alternatives. The analysis assumes the fixed costs of the Transportation Division will be the same regardless of the alternative chosen. That is, the Transportation Division cannot save any of its fixed costs if it does not transport Gulfmex's 20,000 barrels of crude oil per day.

- **Alternative 1:** Buy 20,000 barrels from the Houston supplier at $21 per barrel. Total costs to Horizon Petroleum are 20,000 barrels × $21 per barrel = $420,000.
- **Alternative 2:** Buy 20,000 barrels in Matamoros at $16 per barrel and transport them to Houston at a variable cost of $1 per barrel. Total costs to Horizon Petroleum are 20,000 barrels × ($16 + $1) per barrel = $340,000.

There is a reduction in total costs to Horizon Petroleum of $80,000 ($420,000 – $340,000) by acquiring oil from Gulfmex.

Suppose the Transportation Division's transfer price to the Refining Division is 110% of full cost. The Refining Division will see its reported division costs increase if the crude oil is purchased from Gulfmex:

$$\text{Transfer price} = 1.10 \times \begin{pmatrix} \text{Purchase price} & & \text{Variable cost per unit} & & \text{Fixed cost per unit} \\ \text{from} & + & \text{of Transportation} & + & \text{of Transportation} \\ \text{Gulfmex} & & \text{Division} & & \text{Division} \end{pmatrix}$$

$$= 1.10 \times (\$16 + \$1 + \$3) = 1.10 \times \$20 = \$22$$

- **Alternative 1:** Buy 20,000 barrels from Houston supplier at \$21 per barrel. Total costs to Refining Division are 20,000 barrels × \$21 per barrel = \$420,000.
- **Alternative 2:** Buy 20,000 barrels from the Transportation Division of Horizon Petroleum that were purchased from Gulfmex. Total costs to Refining Division are 20,000 barrels × \$22 per barrel = \$440,000.

As a profit center, the Refining Division can maximize its short-run division operating income by purchasing from the Houston supplier at \$420,000.

The transfer-pricing method has led the Refining Division to regard the fixed cost (and the 10% markup) of the Transportation Division as a variable cost. That's because the Refining Division looks at each barrel that it obtains from the Transportation Division as a variable cost of \$22 per barrel; if 10 barrels are transferred, it costs the Refining Division \$220; if 100 barrels are transferred, it costs \$2,200. From the viewpoint of Horizon Petroleum as a whole, its variable cost per barrel is \$17 (\$16 to purchase the oil from Gulfmex plus \$1 to transport it to Houston). The remaining \$5 (\$22 − \$17) per barrel is the Transportation Division's fixed cost and markup. Buying crude oil in Houston costs Horizon Petroleum an additional \$21 per barrel. For the company, it is cheaper to buy from Gulfmex in Matamoros. But the Refining Division sees the problem differently. From its perspective, it prefers buying from the Houston supplier at a cost of \$420,000 (20,000 barrels × \$21 per barrel) because buying from Gulfmex costs the division \$440,000 (20,000 barrels × \$22 per barrel). In this example, the transfer price based on full cost plus a markup does not achieve goal congruence.

Should Horizon's top management interfere and force the Refining Division to buy from the Transportation Division? Top management interference would undercut the philosophy of decentralization, so Horizon's top management would probably view the decision by the Refining Division to purchase crude oil from external suppliers as an inevitable cost of decentralization and not interfere. Of course, some interference may occasionally be necessary to prevent costly blunders. But recurring interference and constraints would simply transform Horizon from a decentralized company into a centralized company.

What transfer price will promote goal congruence for both the Transportation and Refining divisions? The minimum transfer price is \$17 per barrel. A transfer price below \$17 does not provide the Transportation Division with an incentive to purchase crude oil from Gulfmex in Matamoros, whereas a transfer price above \$17 generates contribution margin to cover its fixed costs. The maximum transfer price is \$21 per barrel. A transfer price above \$21 will cause the Refining Division to purchase crude oil from the external market rather than from the Transportation Division. A transfer price between the minimum and maximum transfer prices of \$17 and \$21 will promote goal congruence: Each division will increase its own reported operating income while increasing Horizon Petroleum's operating income if the Refining Division purchases crude oil from Gulfmex in Matamoros. For example, a transfer price based on the full costs of \$20 without a markup will achieve goal congruence; the Transportation Division will show no operating income and will be evaluated as a cost center.

In the absence of a market-based transfer price, senior management at Horizon Petroleum cannot easily determine the profitability of the investment made in the Transportation Division and hence whether Horizon should keep or sell the pipeline. Furthermore, if the transfer price had been based on the actual costs of the Transportation Division, it would provide the division with no incentive to control costs. That's because all cost inefficiencies of the Transportation Division would get passed along as part of the actual full-cost transfer price. However, surveys indicate (see p. 774) that, despite the limitations, managers generally prefer to use full-cost-based transfer prices. That's because these transfer prices represent relevant costs for long-run decisions, they facilitate external pricing based on variable and fixed costs, and they are the least costly to administer.

Using full-cost-based transfer prices requires an allocation of each subunit's fixed costs to products. Full-cost transfer pricing raises many issues. How are indirect costs allocated to products? Have the correct activities, cost pools, and cost-allocation bases been identified? Should the chosen fixed-cost rates be actual or budgeted? The issues here are similar to the issues that arise in allocating fixed costs, which were introduced in Chapter 14. Calculations of full-cost-based transfer prices using activity-based cost drivers can provide more-refined allocation of costs to products. Using budgeted costs and budgeted rates lets both divisions know the transfer price in advance. Some companies calculate budgeted rates based on practical capacity rather than master-budget capacity utilization levels. Using budgeted rates and practical capacity overcomes the problem of inefficiencies in actual costs and costs of unused capacity getting passed along to the buying division. That's because transfer prices are based on budgeted (efficient) costs, not what the actual cost or capacity utilization turns out to be. Also, variations in the total quantity of units produced by the selling division do not affect the transfer price.

Constant cost-based transfer prices create an incentive for managers of selling divisions to decrease their costs.

Variable-Cost Bases

Transferring 20,000 barrels of crude oil from the Transportation Division to the Refining Division at the variable cost of $17 per barrel achieves goal congruence, as shown in the preceding section. The Refining Division would buy from the Transportation Division because the Transportation Division's variable cost (which is also the relevant incremental cost for Horizon Petroleum as a whole) is less than the $21 price charged by external suppliers. However, at the $17-per-barrel transfer price, the Transportation Division would record an operating loss, and the Refining Division would show large profits because it would be charged only for the variable costs of the Transportation Division. One approach to addressing this problem is to have the Refining Division make a lump-sum transfer payment to cover fixed costs and generate some operating income for the Transportation Division while the Transportation Division continues to make transfers at variable cost. The fixed payment is the price the Refining Division pays for using the capacity of the Transportation Division. The income earned by each division can then be used to evaluate the performance of each division and its manager.

Prorating the Difference Between Maximum and Minimum Transfer Prices

An alternative cost-based approach is for Horizon Petroleum to choose a transfer price that splits, on some fair basis, the $4 difference between the $21-per-barrel maximum transfer price the Refining Division is willing to pay and the $17-per-barrel minimum transfer price the Transportation Division wants to receive. Suppose Horizon Petroleum allocates the $4 difference on the basis of the budgeted variable costs of the Transportation Division and the Refining Division for a given quantity of crude oil. Using the data in Exhibit 22-2 (p. 767), the variable costs are as follows:

Transportation Division's variable costs to transport 100 barrels of crude oil ($1 × 100)	$100
Refining Division's variable costs to refine 100 barrels of crude oil and produce 50 barrels of gasoline ($8 × 50)	400
Total variable costs	$500

Of the $4 difference in transfer prices ($21 − $17), the Transportation Division gets to keep ($100 ÷ $500) × $4.00 = $0.80, and the Refining Division gets to keep ($400 ÷ $500) × $4.00 = $3.20. That is, the transfer price between the Transportation Division and the Refining Division would be $17.80 per barrel of crude oil ($16 purchase cost + $1 variable cost + $0.80 that the Transportation Division gets to keep). This approach is a budgeted variable-cost-plus transfer price. The "plus" indicates the setting of a transfer price above variable cost.

To decide on the $0.80 and $3.20 allocations of the $4.00 contribution to total company operating income per barrel, the divisions must share information about their variable costs. In effect, each division does not operate (at least for this transaction) in a

Because transfer pricing allocates operating income across divisions, division managers often view each other as competitors; this attitude could limit their willingness to share information.

totally decentralized manner. Because most organizations are hybrids of centralization and decentralization anyway, this approach deserves serious consideration when transfers are significant. Note, however, that each division has an incentive to overstate its variable costs to receive a more-favorable transfer price.

Dual Pricing

There is seldom a single cost-based transfer price that simultaneously meets the criteria of goal congruence, management effort, subunit performance evaluation, and subunit autonomy. As a result, some companies choose **dual pricing**, using two separate transfer-pricing methods to price each transfer from one subunit to another. An example of dual pricing arises when the selling division receives a full-cost-based price and the buying division pays the market price for the internally transferred products. Assume Horizon Petroleum purchases crude oil from Gulfmex in Matamoros at $16 per barrel. One way of recording the journal entry for the transfer between the Transportation Division and the Refining Division is:

1. Debit the Refining Division (the buying division) with the market-based transfer price of $21 per barrel of crude oil.
2. Credit the Transportation Division (the selling division) with the 110%-of-full-cost transfer price of $22 per barrel of crude oil.
3. Debit a corporate cost account for the $1 ($22 – $21) per barrel difference between the two transfer prices.

The dual-pricing system promotes goal congruence because it makes the Refining Division no worse off if it purchases the crude oil from the Transportation Division rather than from the external supplier at $21 per barrel. The dual-pricing system gives the Transportation Division a corporate subsidy. The effect of dual pricing is that the operating income for Horizon Petroleum as a whole is less than the sum of the operating incomes of the divisions.

Dual pricing is not widely used in practice even though it reduces the goal incongruence associated with a pure cost-based transfer-pricing method. One concern with dual pricing is that it leads to problems in computing the taxable income of subunits located in different tax jurisdictions, such as in our example, where the Transportation Division is taxed in Mexico while the Refining Division is taxed in the United States. A second concern is that the manager of the supplying subunit does not have sufficient incentive to control costs with a dual-pricing system because the supplying division records revenues based on actual costs. A third concern is that dual pricing insulates managers from the frictions of the marketplace because costs, not market prices, affect the revenues of the supplying division.

Negotiated Transfer Prices

7

Describe the range over which two divisions negotiate the transfer price when there is unused capacity

. . . from variable cost to market price of the product transferred

Negotiated transfer prices result from a bargaining process between selling and buying subunits. Consider again a transfer price between the Transportation and Refining Divisions of Horizon Petroleum. The Transportation Division has unused capacity it can use to transport oil from Matamoros to Houston. As we have seen earlier, the Transportation Division will only purchase oil from Gulfmex and sell oil to the Refining Division if the transfer price equals or exceeds $17 per barrel of crude oil—that's its variable cost. The Refining Division will only buy crude oil from the Transportation Division if the price does not exceed $21 per barrel—that's the price at which the Refining Division can buy crude oil in Houston.

Given the Transportation Division's unused capacity, Horizon Petroleum as a whole maximizes operating income if the Refining Division purchases crude oil from the Transportation Division rather than from the Houston market (incremental cost per barrel of $17 versus $21). Both divisions would be interested in transacting with each other (thereby achieving goal congruence) if the transfer price is set between $17 and $21. For example, a transfer price of $19.25 per barrel will increase the Transportation Division's operating income by $19.25 – $17 = $2.25 per barrel. It will increase the Refining

Division's operating income by $21 − $19.25 = $1.75 per barrel because the Refining Division can now buy the crude oil for $19.25 internally rather than for $21 in the external market.

Where between $17 and $21 will the transfer price per barrel be set? Under a negotiated transfer price, the answer depends on several things: the bargaining strengths of the two divisions; information the Transportation Division has about the price minus incremental marketing costs of supplying crude oil to outside refineries; and the information the Refining Division has about its other available sources of crude oil. Negotiations become particularly sensitive because Horizon Petroleum can now evaluate each division's performance on the basis of division operating income. The price negotiated by the two divisions will, in general, have no specific relationship to either costs or market price. But cost and price information is often the starting point in the negotiation process. A negotiated transfer price strongly preserves division autonomy because the transfer price is the outcome of negotiations between division managers. It also has the advantage that each division manager is motivated to put forth effort to increase division operating income. Its disadvantage is the time and energy spent on the negotiations.

The Global Surveys of Company Practice (p. 774) indicates that the full-cost-based transfer price is generally the most frequently used transfer-pricing method around the world, followed by market-based transfer price and negotiated transfer price.

A General Guideline for Transfer-Pricing Situations

8

Apply a general guideline for determining a minimum transfer price

. . . incremental cost plus opportunity cost of supplying division

Exhibit 22-3 summarizes the properties of the different transfer-pricing methods using the criteria described in this chapter. As the exhibit indicates, there is no transfer-pricing method that meets all criteria. Market conditions, the goal of the transfer-pricing system, and the criteria of goal congruence, management effort, subunit performance evaluation, and subunit autonomy (if desired) must all be considered simultaneously. The transfer price a company will eventually choose depends on the economic circumstances and the decision at hand. The following general guideline (formula) is a helpful first step in setting a minimum transfer price in many situations:

$$\text{Minimum transfer price} = \begin{array}{c}\text{Incremental cost}\\ \text{per unit}\\ \text{incurred up}\\ \text{to the point of transfer}\end{array} + \begin{array}{c}\text{Opportunity cost}\\ \text{per unit}\\ \text{to the selling subunit}\end{array}$$

EXHIBIT 22-3

Comparison of Different Transfer-Pricing Methods

Criteria	Market-Based	Cost-Based	Negotiated
Achieves goal congruence	Yes, when markets are competitive	Often, but not always	Yes
Useful for evaluating subunit performance	Yes, when markets are competitive	Difficult unless transfer price exceeds full cost and even then is somewhat arbitrary	Yes, but transfer prices are affected by bargaining strengths of the buying and selling divisions
Motivates management effort	Yes	Yes, when based on budgeted costs; less incentive to control costs if transfers are based on actual costs	Yes
Preserves subunit autonomy	Yes, when markets are competitive	No, because it is rule-based	Yes, because it is based on negotiations between subunits
Other factors	Market may not exist, or markets may be imperfect or in distress	Useful for determining full cost of products and services; easy to implement	Bargaining and negotiations take time and may need to be reviewed repeatedly as conditions change

Domestic and Multinational Transfer-Pricing Practices

Transfer pricing remains an important accounting priority for managers around the world. A recent survey of managers in 22 countries, including the United States, Australia, Canada, and Japan found that 86% of all respondents believed transfer pricing was important to their group's operations.[a]

What transfer-pricing methods are used around the world? The following tables indicate how extensively particular transfer-pricing methods are used in different countries.

A. Domestic Transfer-Pricing Methods

Methods	United States[b]	Australia[c]	Canada[d]	Japan[b]	New Zealand[e]	United Kingdom[f]
Market-based	26%	13%	34%	34%	18%	26%
Cost-based:						
Variable cost	3	—	6	2	10	10
Absorption or full cost	49	—	37	44	61	38
Other	1	—	3	—	—	1
Total	53%	65%	46%	46%	71%	49%
Negotiated	17%	11%	18%	19%	11%	24%
Other	4%	11%	2%	1%	—	1%
	100%	100%	100%	100%	100%	100%

B. Multinational Transfer-Pricing Methods

Methods	United States[b]	Australia	Canada[d]	Japan[b]	New Zealand	United Kingdom
Market-based	35%	—	37%	37%	—	—
Cost-based:						
Variable cost	0	—	5	3	—	—
Absorption or full cost	42	—	26	38	—	—
Other	1	—	2	—	—	—
Total	43%	—	33%	41%	—	—
Negotiated	14%	—	26%	22%	—	—
Other	8%	—	4%	—	—	—
	100%	—	100%	100%	—	—

Note: Dashes indicate information was not disclosed in survey.

The surveys indicate that for domestic transfer pricing, managers in all countries use cost-based transfer prices more frequently than market-based transfer prices. For multinational transfer pricing, managers use cost-based methods only slightly more often than market-based methods. Many companies have market-based transfer prices in some divisions and cost-based transfer prices in others.

Survey evidence indicates that managers consider the following factors important when making domestic transfer-pricing decisions (in order of importance): (1) maximizing consolidated after-tax profits, (2) performance evaluation, and (3) management motivation. Factors cited as important for multinational transfer-pricing decisions include (in order of importance): (1) income tax rate and other tax differences among countries, (2) total income of the company, and (3) income- or dividend-repatriation restrictions.[b,g]

[a] Ernst & Young, *Transfer Pricing 2003 Global Survey.*

[b] R. Tang, *Transfer Pricing Systems.*

[c] M. Joye and P. Blayney, "Cost and Management."

[d] R. Tang, "Canadian Transfer Pricing."

[e] Z. Hoque, and M. Alam, "Organization Size."

[f] C. Drury, S. Braund, P. Osborne, and M. Tayles, *A Survey.*

[g] J. Elliott, "International Transfer Pricing."

Full citations are in Appendix A at the end of the book.

Incremental cost in this context means the additional cost of producing and transferring the product or service. Opportunity cost here is the maximum contribution margin forgone by the selling subunit if the product or service is transferred internally. For example, if the selling subunit is operating at capacity, the opportunity cost of transferring a unit internally rather than selling it externally is equal to the market price minus variable cost. That's because by transferring a unit internally, the subunit forgoes the contribution margin it could have obtained by selling the unit in the external market. We distinguish incremental cost from opportunity cost because the financial accounting system typically records incremental cost but not opportunity cost. The guideline measures a *minimum* transfer price because the selling subunit will be motivated to sell the product to the buying subunit only if the transfer price covers the incremental cost the selling subunit incurs to produce the product and the opportunity cost it forgoes by selling the product internally rather than in the external market. We illustrate the general guideline in some specific situations using data from Horizon Petroleum.

In transfer-pricing situations, opportunity cost is the profit the selling division (SD) forgoes by selling internally rather than externally. Assume the SD has no idle capacity for a particular product and can sell all it produces at $4 per unit. Incremental cost is $1 per unit. If the SD sells internally, the opportunity cost is $3 per unit ($4 revenue per unit − $1 incremental cost per unit). In contrast, if the SD has unused capacity with no alternative use, no profit is forgone by selling internally (opportunity cost is $0).

1. A perfectly competitive market for the intermediate product exists, and the selling division has no unused capacity. If the market for crude oil in Houston is perfectly competitive, the Transportation Division can sell all the crude oil it transports to the external market at $21 per barrel, and it will have no unused capacity. The Transportation Division's incremental cost (as shown in Exhibit 22-1, p. 766) is $13 per barrel (purchase cost of $12 per barrel plus variable transportation cost of $1 per barrel) for oil purchased under the long-term contract or $17 per barrel (purchase cost of $16 plus variable transportation cost of $1) for oil purchased at current market prices from Gulfmex. The Transportation Division's opportunity cost per barrel of transferring the oil internally is the contribution margin per barrel forgone by not selling the crude oil in the external market: $8 for oil purchased under the long-term contract (market price, $21, minus variable cost, $13) and $4 for oil purchased from Gulfmex (market price, $21, minus variable cost, $17). In either case,

$$\frac{\text{Minimum transfer price}}{\text{per barrel}} = \frac{\text{Incremental cost}}{\text{per barrel}} + \frac{\text{Opportunity cost}}{\text{per barrel}}$$

$$= \$13 + \$8 = \$21$$

or

$$= \$17 + \$4 = \$21$$

The minimum transfer price per barrel is the market price of $21. Market-based transfer prices are ideal in perfectly competitive markets when there is no unused capacity in the selling division.

2. An intermediate market exists that is not perfectly competitive, and the selling division has unused capacity. In markets that are not perfectly competitive, capacity utilization can only be increased by decreasing prices. Unused capacity exists because decreasing prices is often not worthwhile—it decreases operating income.

If the Transportation Division has unused capacity, its opportunity cost of transferring the oil internally is zero because the division does not forgo any external sales or contribution margin from internal transfers. In this case,

$$\frac{\text{Minimum transfer price}}{\text{per barrel}} = \frac{\text{Incremental cost}}{\text{per barrel}} = \begin{array}{c}\text{\$13 per barrel for oil purchased under the}\\ \text{long-term contract, or \$17 per barrel for}\\ \text{oil purchased from Gulfmex in Matamoros}\end{array}$$

Any transfer price above incremental cost but below $21—the price at which the Refining Division can buy crude oil in Houston—motivates the Transportation Division to transport crude oil to the Refining Division and the Refining Division to buy crude oil from the Transportation Division. In this situation, the company could either use a cost-based transfer price or allow the two divisions to negotiate a transfer price between themselves.

In general, when markets are not perfectly competitive, the potential to influence demand and operating income through prices complicates the measurement of opportunity costs. The transfer price depends on constantly changing levels of supply and demand. There is not just one transfer price. Rather, the transfer prices for various quantities supplied and demanded depend on the incremental costs and opportunity costs of the units transferred. Consider the following situation: Suppose the Refining Division receives an order to supply specially processed gasoline. The Refining Division will only profit from this order if the Transportation Division can supply crude oil at a price not exceeding $19 per barrel. Suppose the incremental cost to purchase and supply crude oil is $17 per barrel. In this case, the transfer price that would benefit both divisions must be greater than $17 but less than $19 (rather than $21).

3. **No market exists for the intermediate product.** This situation would occur for the Horizon Petroleum case if the crude oil transported by the Transportation Division could be used only by the Houston refinery (due to, say, its high tar content) and would not be wanted by external parties. Here, the opportunity cost of supplying crude oil internally is zero because the inability to sell crude oil externally means no contribution margin is forgone. For the Transportation Division of Horizon Petroleum, the minimum transfer price under the general guideline is the incremental cost per barrel (either $13 or $17). As in the previous case, any transfer price between the incremental cost and $21 will achieve goal congruence. Note, however, that knowledge of the incremental cost per barrel of crude oil would be helpful to the Refining Division for many decisions, such as short-run pricing.

Multinational Transfer Pricing and Tax Considerations

9

Incorporate income tax considerations in multinational transfer pricing

. . . set transfer prices to minimize tax payments to the extent permitted by tax laws

Transfer prices often have tax implications. Tax factors include not only income taxes, but also payroll taxes, customs duties, tariffs, sales taxes, value-added taxes, environment-related taxes, and other government levies. Our aim here is to highlight tax factors, and in particular income taxes, as important considerations in determining transfer prices.

Consider the Horizon Petroleum data in Exhibit 22-2 (p. 767). Assume that the Transportation Division based in Mexico pays Mexican income taxes at 30% of operating income and that the Refining Division based in the United States pays income taxes at 20% of operating income. Horizon Petroleum would minimize its total income tax payments with the 110%-of-full-cost transfer-pricing method, as shown in the following table, because this method minimizes income reported in Mexico, where income is taxed at a higher rate than in the United States.

	Operating Income for 100 Barrels of Crude Oil			Income Tax on 100 Barrels of Crude Oil		
Transfer-Pricing Method	Transportation Division (Mexico) (1)	Refining Division (U.S.) (2)	Total (3) = (1) + (2)	Transportation Division (Mexico) (4) = 0.30 × (1)	Refining Division (U.S.) (5) = 0.20 × (2)	Total (6) = (4) + (5)
Market price	$500	$100	$600	$150.00	$20	$170.00
110% of full costs	160	440	600	48.00	88	136.00
Negotiated price	325	275	600	97.50	55	152.50

Income tax considerations raise additional issues. Tax issues may conflict with other objectives of transfer pricing. Suppose the market for crude oil in Houston is perfectly competitive. In this case, the market-based transfer price achieves goal congruence and provides incentives for management effort. It also helps Horizon to evaluate the economic profitability of the Transportation Division. But it is costly from the perspective of income taxes. To minimize income taxes, Horizon would favor using 110% of full cost for tax reporting. Tax laws in the United States and Mexico, however, constrain this option. In particular, the Mexican tax authorities, aware of Horizon's incentives to minimize income taxes by reducing the income reported in Mexico, would challenge any attempts to shift income to the Refining Division through an unreasonably low transfer price (see also Concepts in Action, p. 777).

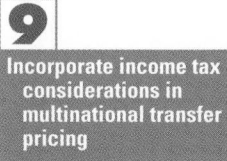

CONCEPTS IN ACTION

U.S. Internal Revenue Service, Japanese National Tax Agency, and Transfer-Pricing Games

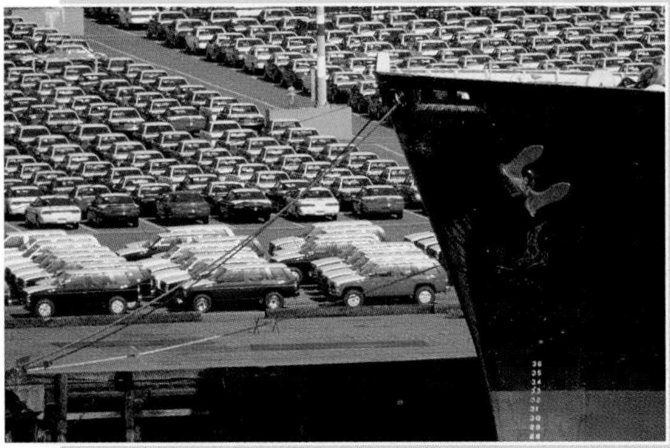

Tax authorities and government officials around the world pay close attention to taxes paid by multinational companies operating within their boundaries. At the heart of the issue are the transfer prices that companies use to transfer products from one country to another. The U.S. Internal Revenue Service (IRS) and the Japanese National Tax Agency (NTA) have been among the most active agencies pursuing international transfer-pricing disputes.

For example, in 1993, the IRS investigated and concluded that Nissan Motor Company had understated U.S. taxes by setting transfer prices on passenger cars and trucks imported from Japan at "unrealistically" high levels. Nissan argued that it had maintained low margins in the United States to increase long-run market share in a very competitive market. Eventually, Nissan agreed to pay the IRS $170 million, but the company suffered no loss. That's because the Japanese NTA refunded Nissan the full amount of the IRS payment.

Conversely, in May 1994, Japan's NTA alleged that Coca-Cola Corporation had underreported its taxable income in Japan by charging "excessive" transfer prices to its local subsidiary for materials and concentrate imported from the parent company and by levying "excessive" royalty payments on its Japanese subsidiary for use of its brand name and sales and marketing expertise. The NTA pointed out that the royalties paid by Coca-Cola's Japanese subsidiary were higher than those paid by other companies in the same industry. It also said that the Japanese subsidiary paid royalties even for products it had developed on its own. The NTA imposed taxes and penalties of $150 million. Coca-Cola filed a complaint with the IRS, charging that the levying of the Japanese tax resulted in the same income being taxed twice, because Coca-Cola had already paid tax on this income in the United States. This complaint led to negotiations between Japanese and U.S. tax authorities to decide which country gets to tax Coca-Cola's Japanese income. In a 1998 compromise settlement, Japan's NTA reduced its tax levy against Coca-Cola from $150 million to $50 million.

In 2000, Japan's NTA and the IRS had to settle another dispute regarding transfer prices. This time Coca-Cola's Japanese subsidiary had to record an additional $450 million in taxable income from 1993 through 1999, which meant that it owed approximately $170 million in back taxes and penalties. To avoid double taxation, the IRS refunded Coca-Cola the tax it had already paid to the United States.

Historically, disputes arose between governments over what constituted a "fair" transfer price because of the absence of an easily observable market price for the transferred product. In 2003, the U.S. and Japan signed a new tax treaty that, among other things, stipulates that future transfer-pricing disputes be addressed in accordance with the Organization for Economic Cooperation and Development's *Transfer Pricing Guidelines*, which advocates the use of a more-transparent "arm's length" transfer-pricing protocol.

Although this development has eased disputes between the United States and Japan, the IRS and NTA remain actively engaged in transfer-pricing conflicts with other nations. In 2004, the IRS fined U.K.-based pharmaceutical manufacturer GlaxoSmithKline $5.2 billion in back taxes and interest, stemming from a transfer-pricing dispute regarding profits from 1989 through 1996. Meanwhile, the Japanese NTA brought action against Honda Motor Company in 2004 for understating technology royalties paid to the company from 1997 through 2002 by its Brazilian subsidiary. The NTA is seeking over $100 million in back taxes. Both cases remain under review.

Sources: Adapted from C. Pass, "Transfer Pricing in Multinational Companies," *Management Accounting* (September 1994); "Coca-Cola Gets 10 Billion Yen Reprieve in Back Taxes," *Yomiuri Shimbun* (February 24, 1998); *Financial Times* (September 3, 1999); and *Daily Yomiuri* (February 24, 1998, and April 30, 2000). Morrison & Foster, LLP, *New United States–Japan Tax Treaty Enters into Force: New Withholding Rates Take Effect on July 1, 2004*, April 2004; S. Vollmer and C. Serres, "IRS Fines GlaxoSmithKline $5.2 Billion in Audit of North Carolina Drug Giant," *News & Observer* (Raleigh, NC), January 8, 2004; "Honda's ¥25.4 Billion Transfer Pricing Adjustment," *Transfer Pricing Times* (July 20, 2004).

Study Tip: To check your understanding of the material in this chapter, see the Featured Exercise, true–false statements 9 and 10, multiple-choice questions 1 through 7, and Review Exercise 2 (*Student Guide*, beginning p. 301). Fully explained answers begin on page 307.

Section 482 of the U.S. Internal Revenue Code governs taxation of multinational transfer pricing. Section 482 requires that transfer prices between a company and its foreign division or subsidiary, for both tangible and intangible property, equal the price that would be charged by an unrelated third party in a comparable transaction. Regulations related to Section 482 recognize that transfer prices can be market-based or cost-plus-based, where the plus represents margins on comparable transactions.[1]

If the market for crude oil in Houston is perfectly competitive, Horizon would be required to use the market price for transfers from the Transportation Division to the Refining Division. Horizon might successfully argue that the transfer price should be set below the market price because the Transportation Division incurs no marketing and distribution costs when selling crude oil to the Refining Division. For example, suppose the market price for supplying crude oil to external parties in Houston is $21 per barrel and marketing and distribution costs equal $1.50 per barrel. Horizon could set the transfer price at $19.50 ($21 – $1.50) per barrel, the selling price net of marketing and distribution costs. Under the U.S. Internal Revenue Code, Horizon could obtain advanced approval of the transfer-pricing arrangements from the tax authorities, called an *advanced pricing agreement* (*APA*). The APA is a binding agreement for a specified number of years. The goal of the APA program is to avoid costly transfer-pricing disputes between taxpayers and tax authorities.

To meet multiple transfer-pricing objectives, such as minimizing income taxes, achieving goal congruence, and motivating management effort, a company may choose to keep one set of accounting records for tax reporting and a second set for internal management reporting. The difficulty here is that tax authorities may interpret two sets of books as meaning the company manipulated its reported taxable income to avoid tax payments. To avoid the problems caused by maintaining two sets of books, companies that choose tax-minimizing transfer-pricing strategies often use other management control techniques.

Consider a U.S. company that makes high-end data storage machines that it sells through its own sales organization in different countries. To minimize taxes, suppose the U.S. company sets a very high transfer price. Setting a high transfer price lowers the operating income of the sales organization in each country, even though the country sales organization has no say or control in determining the transfer price. To neutralize this negative effect on income, the company evaluates sales managers only on revenues minus marketing costs incurred in their respective countries. That is, the transfer prices incurred to acquire the product by the sales organizations in the countries are added back to the operating income of the sales organizations for performance-evaluation purposes. The difficulty with this approach is that it creates incentives for the sales organization in each country to maximize revenue rather than profit per dollar of marketing costs. Corporate managers must then step in and specify product priorities based on the full product-profitability information available to them.

Additional factors that arise in multinational transfer pricing include tariffs and customs duties levied on imports of products into a country. The issues here are similar to income tax considerations; companies will have incentives to lower transfer prices for products imported into a country to reduce tariffs and customs duties charged on those products.

In addition to the motivations for choosing transfer prices already described, multinational transfer prices are sometimes influenced by restrictions that some countries place on dividend- or income-related payments to parties outside their national borders. By increasing the prices of goods or services transferred into divisions in these countries, companies can seek to increase the cash paid out of these countries without violating dividend- or income-related restrictions. (See the Focus on Values and Behaviors feature, p. 779.)

[1]R. Feinschreiber (Ed.), *Transfer Pricing Handbook,* 3rd ed. (New York: John Wiley & Sons, 2002); L. Eden, *Taxing Multinationals: Transfer Pricing and Corporate Income Taxation in North America* (Toronto: University of Toronto Press, 1998); M. Levey, "Transfer Pricing—What Next?" *International Financial Law Review* (June 2001); J. Henshall, S. Wrappe, and K. Chung, "Transfer Pricing," *International Tax Review* (April 2001).

FOCUS ON VALUES AND BEHAVIORS

TRANSFER PRICING PRESSURES

Transfer pricing requires one subunit manager to earn revenues and another subunit manager to incur costs. Managers are frequently evaluated on the basis of subunit profits. Little wonder then, that subunit managers care deeply about how transfer prices are set. It is natural for subunit managers to argue for transfer prices that make their own performance look good. Management accountants must ensure that the transfer prices set are in the best interests of the company as a whole. This requires management accountants to understand business issues and the external market environment within which the businesses function. They must also never cave in to pressure from managers that will make a subunit's performance look good while hurting the corporation as a whole.

Transfer prices also have tax implications, particularly when products are transferred across country borders. Setting transfer prices is almost always a matter of judgment. At no time, however, should management accountants choose transfer prices that do not adhere to the tax codes of different countries. The time and cost to resolve transfer pricing disputes can be very high.

Consider Motorola, the electronics products manufacturer. In 2004, the Internal Revenue Service (IRS) notified the company that it was disputing the way Motorola calculated earnings from 1996 to 2000, resulting in an additional tax liability of $500 million. The underlying issue was related to transfer pricing involving Motorola's 67 tax entities around the world. The IRS claimed too much profit was left in the company's tax entities abroad and that not enough income was recognized in the United States, resulting in lower tax payments. Company officials vigorously defended their accounting practices and now must convince the IRS that its practices are within the law.

Source: *R. Crockett, "Motorola's Taxing Dispute,"* Business Week Online, *August 12, 2004, <http://www.businessweek.com/bwdaily/dnflash/aug2004/nj20040812_8175_db016.htm>, accessed September 17, 2004.*

PROBLEM FOR SELF-STUDY

The Pillercat Corporation is a highly decentralized company. Each division manager has full authority for sourcing decisions and selling decisions. The Machining Division of Pillercat has been the major supplier of the 2,000 crankshafts that the Tractor Division needs each year.

The Tractor Division, however, has just announced that it plans to purchase all its crankshafts in the forthcoming year from two external suppliers at $200 per crankshaft. The Machining Division of Pillercat recently increased its selling price for the forthcoming year to $220 per unit (from $200 per unit in the current year).

Juan Gomez, manager of the Machining Division, feels that the 10% price increase is justified. It results from a higher depreciation charge on some new specialized equipment used to manufacture crankshafts and an increase in labor costs. Gomez wants the president of Pillercat Corporation to force the Tractor Division to buy all its crankshafts from the Machining Division at the price of $220. The following table summarizes the key data.

	A	B
1	Number of crankshafts purchased by Tractor Division	2,000
2	External supplier's market price per crankshaft	$200
3	Variable cost per crankshaft in Machining Division	$190
4	Fixed cost per crankshaft in Machining Division	$ 20

Required

1. Compute the advantage or disadvantage in terms of annual operating income to the Pillercat Corporation as a whole if the Tractor Division buys crankshafts internally from the Machining Division under each of the following cases:
   a. The Machining Division has no alternative use for the facilities used to manufacture crankshafts.
   b. The Machining Division can use the facilities for other production operations, which will result in annual cash operating savings of $29,000.
   c. The Machining Division has no alternative use for its facilities, and the external supplier drops the price to $185 per crankshaft.

2. As the president of Pillercat, how would you respond to Juan Gomez's request that you force the Tractor Division to purchase all of its crankshafts from the Machining Division? Would your response differ according to the three cases described in requirement 1? Explain.

SOLUTION

1. Computations for the Tractor Division buying crankshafts internally for one year under cases **a**, **b**, and **c** are:

	A	B	C	D
1			**Case**	
2		**a**	**b**	**c**
3	Number of crankshafts purchased by Tractor Division	2,000	2,000	2,000
4	External supplier's market price per crankshaft	$ 200	$ 200	$ 185
5	Incremental cost per crankshaft in Machining Division	$ 190	$ 190	$ 190
6	Opportunity costs of the Machining Division supplying	-	$ 29,000	-
7	crankshafts to the Tractor Division			
8				
9	Total purchase costs if buying from an external supplier			
10	(2,000 shafts x $200, $200, $185 per shaft)	$400,000	$400,000	$370,000
11	Incremental costs of buying from the Machining Division			
12	(2,000 shafts x $190 per shaft)	380,000	380,000	380,000
13	Total opportunity costs of the Machining Division	-	29,000	-
14	Total relevant costs	380,000	409,000	380,000
15	Annual operating income advantage (disadvantage) to			
16	Pillercat of buying from the Machining Division	$ 20,000	$ (9,000)	$ (10,000)
17				

The general guideline that was introduced in the chapter (p. 773) as a first step in setting a transfer price can be used to highlight the alternatives:

	A	B	C	D	E	F	G
1	**Case**	**Incremental Cost per Unit Incurred to Point of Transfer**	+	**Opportunity Cost per Unit to the Supplying Division**	=	**Transfer Price**	**External Market Price**
2	**a**	$190	+	$ 0	=	$190.00	$200
3	**b**	$190	+	$14.50[a]	=	$204.50	$200
4	**c**	$190	+	$ 0	=	$190.00	$185
5							
6	[a] Opportunity cost per unit	=	Total opportunity costs	÷	Number of crankshafts	= $29,000 ÷ 2,000 = $14.50	
7							

Comparing transfer price to external-market price, the Tractor Division will maximize annual operating income of Pillercat Corporation as a whole by purchasing from the Machining Division in case **a** and by purchasing from the external supplier in cases **b** and **c**.

2. Pillercat Corporation is a highly decentralized company. If no forced transfer were made, the Tractor Division would use an external supplier, a decision that would be in the best interest of the company as a whole in cases **b** and **c** of requirement 1 but not in case **a**.

Suppose in case **a**, the Machining Division refuses to meet the price of $200. This decision means that the company will be $20,000 worse off in the short run. Should top management interfere and force a transfer at $200? This interference would undercut the philosophy of decentralization. Many top managements would not interfere because they would view the $20,000 as an inevitable cost of a suboptimal decision that can occur under decentralization. But how high must this cost be before the temptation to interfere would be irresistible? $30,000? $40,000?

Any top management interference with lower-level decision making weakens decentralization. Of course, Pillercat's management may occasionally interfere to prevent costly mistakes. But recurring interference and constraints would hurt Pillercat's attempts to operate as a decentralized company.

DECISION POINTS

The following question-and-answer format summarizes the chapter's learning objectives. Each decision presents a key question related to a learning objective. The guidelines are the answer to that question.

Decision	Guidelines
1. What is a management control system and how should it be designed?	A management control system is a means of gathering and using information to aid and coordinate the planning and control decisions throughout the organization and to guide the behavior of managers and other employees. Effective management control systems are (a) closely aligned to the organization's strategy, (b) fit the organization's structure, and (c) motivate managers and other employees to give effort to achieve the organization's goals.
2. What are the benefits and costs of decentralization?	The benefits of decentralization include (a) greater responsiveness to local needs, (b) gains from faster decision making, (c) increased motivation of subunit managers, (d) greater management development and learning, and (e) sharpened focus of subunit managers. The costs of decentralization include (a) suboptimal decision making, (b) decreased loyalty toward the organization, (c) increased costs of information gathering, and (d) duplication of activities.
3. What is a transfer price, and what is it intended to achieve?	A transfer price is the price one subunit charges for a product or service supplied to another subunit of the same organization. Transfer prices seek to achieve (a) goal congruence, (b) management effort, (c) subunit performance evaluation, and (d) subunit autonomy (if desired).
4. What methods can be used to calculate transfer prices?	Transfer prices can be (a) market-based, (b) cost-based, or (c) negotiated. Different transfer-pricing methods produce different revenues and costs for individual subunits, and hence, different operating incomes for the subunits.
5. What transfer price should be used if the market for the product to be transferred is perfectly competitive?	In perfectly competitive markets, there is no unused capacity, and division managers can buy and sell as much of a product or service as they want at the market price. Setting the transfer price at the market price motivates division managers to transact internally and to take exactly the same actions as they would if they were transacting in the external market.
6. What problems can arise when full cost plus a markup is used as a transfer price?	A transfer price based on full cost plus a markup may lead to suboptimal decisions because it leads the buying division to regard the fixed costs and the markup of the selling division as a variable cost. The buying division may then purchase products from an external supplier expecting savings in costs that, in fact, will not occur.
7. What is the range over which two divisions will negotiate a transfer price when there is unused capacity?	When there is unused capacity, the transfer-price range for negotiations generally lies between the minimum price at which the selling division is willing to sell (its variable cost per unit) and the maximum price the buying division is willing to pay (the price at which the product is available from external suppliers).
8. What is the general guideline for determining a minimum transfer price?	The general guideline states that the minimum transfer price equals the incremental cost per unit incurred up to the point of transfer plus the opportunity cost per unit to the selling division resulting from transferring products or services internally.
9. What are the income tax considerations when determining transfer prices?	Transfer prices can reduce income tax payments by reporting more income in low-tax-rate countries and less income in high-tax-rate countries. However, tax regulations of different countries restrict the transfer prices that companies can use.

TERMS TO LEARN

This chapter and the Glossary at the end of this book contain definitions of:

autonomy (p. 761)
decentralization (p. 761)
dual pricing (p. 772)
dysfunctional decision making (p. 762)
effort (p. 761)
goal congruence (p. 761)
incongruent decision making (p. 762)
intermediate product (p. 764)
management control system (p. 760)
motivation (p. 761)
perfectly competitive market (p. 768)
suboptimal decision making (p. 762)
transfer price (p. 764)

PH Grade Assist	**Prentice Hall Grade Assist (PHGA)** Your professor may ask you to complete selected exercises and problems in Prentice Hall Grade Assist (PHGA). PHGA is an online tool that can help you master the chapter's topics. It provides you with multiple variations of exercises and problems designated by the PHGA icon. You can rework these exercises and problems—each time with new data—as many times as you need. You also receive immediate feedback and grading.

ASSIGNMENT MATERIAL

Questions

22-1 What is a management control system?

22-2 Describe three criteria you would use to evaluate whether a management control system is effective.

22-3 What is the relationship among motivation, goal congruence, and effort?

22-4 Name three benefits and two costs of decentralization.

22-5 "Organizations typically adopt a consistent decentralization or centralization philosophy across all their business functions." Do you agree? Explain.

22-6 "Transfer pricing is confined to profit centers." Do you agree? Explain.

22-7 What are the three methods for determining transfer prices?

22-8 What properties should transfer-pricing systems have?

22-9 "All transfer-pricing methods give the same division operating income." Do you agree? Explain.

22-10 Under what conditions is a market-based transfer price optimal?

22-11 What is one potential limitation of full-cost-based transfer prices?

22-12 Give two reasons why the dual-pricing system of transfer pricing is not widely used.

22-13 "Cost and price information play no role in negotiated transfer prices." Do you agree? Explain.

22-14 "Under the general guideline for transfer pricing, the minimum transfer price will vary depending on whether the supplying division has unused capacity or not." Do you agree? Explain.

22-15 How should managers consider income tax issues when choosing a transfer-pricing method?

Exercises

22-16 **Management control systems, balanced scorecard.** Durham Corporation makes exclusive furniture. Each piece of handcrafted furniture is sturdy, has a unique design, and is of superb quality.

Required

Describe the financial and nonfinancial measures that you would include in Durham's balanced-scorecard-based management control system.

22-17 **Decentralization, responsibility centers.** Quinn Corporation manufactures and sells lighting products. Quinn's Marketing Divisions are organized along product lines: wall sconces, recessed lights, track lights, and so on. The Manufacturing Division produces lighting products for all the marketing divisions.

During the planning process, each Marketing Division specifies the quantity of each style of light to be manufactured. Senior management then assigns the task of manufacturing the lights to different plants in the Manufacturing Division. Because manufacturing capacity is limited, some of the production is also outsourced. Senior management determines the manufacturing schedule for different plants on the basis of detailed studies that have been done to measure the time and cost of manufacturing different types of lighting products at the different plants. Manufacturing managers are evaluated based on achieving target output within budgeted costs.

Required

1. Is the Manufacturing Division a cost center or a profit center? Explain.
2. Quinn Corporation is considering decentralizing its marketing and manufacturing decision making by letting the Manufacturing Division and the Marketing Divisions directly negotiate the prices for manufacturing various products.
   a. How should Quinn evaluate the Manufacturing Division under this proposal?
   b. Would you recommend that Quinn Corporation decentralize its marketing and manufacturing decision making? Explain.

22-18 Decentralization, goal congruence, responsibility centers. Hexton Chemicals consists of seven independent operating divisions. The operating divisions are assisted by a number of support groups, such as R&D, human resources, and environmental management. The environmental-management group consists of 20 environmental engineers. These engineers must seek business from the operating divisions—that is, the projects they work on must be mutually agreed to and paid for by one of the operating divisions. Under Hexton's rules, the environmental group is required to charge the operating divisions for environmental services at cost.

Required

1. Is the environmental-management group centralized or decentralized?
2. What type of responsibility center is the environmental-management group?
3. What benefits and problems do you see in structuring the environmental-management group in this way? Does it lead to goal congruence and motivation? Explain.

22-19 Multinational transfer pricing, effect of alternative transfer-pricing methods, global income tax minimization. User Friendly Computer, Inc., with headquarters in San Francisco, manufactures and sells a desktop computer. User Friendly has three divisions, each of which is located in a different country:

a. China Division—manufactures memory devices and keyboards
b. South Korea Division—assembles desktop computers using internally manufactured parts and memory devices and keyboards from the China Division
c. U.S. Division—packages and distributes desktop computers

Each division is run as a profit center. The costs for the work done in each division for a single desktop computer are as follows:

China Division:	Variable cost = 1,000 yuan
	Fixed cost = 1,800 yuan
South Korea Division:	Variable cost = 360,000 won
	Fixed cost = 480,000 won
U.S. Division:	Variable cost = \$100
	Fixed cost = \$200

- Chinese income tax rate on China Division's operating income: 40%
- South Korean income tax rate on South Korea Division's operating income: 20%
- U.S. income tax rate on U.S. Division's operating income: 30%

Each desktop computer is sold to retail outlets in the United States for \$3,200. Assume that the current foreign exchange rates are:

8 yuan = \$1 U.S.

1,200 won = \$1 U.S.

Both the China and the South Korea divisions sell part of their production under a private label. The China Division sells the comparable memory/keyboard package used in each User Friendly desktop computer to a Chinese manufacturer for 3,600 yuan. The South Korea Division sells the comparable desktop computer to a South Korean distributor for 1,560,000 won.

Required

1. Calculate the after-tax operating income per unit earned by each division under the following transfer-pricing methods: (a) market price, (b) 200% of full cost, and (c) 300% of variable cost. (Income taxes are not included in the computation of the cost-based transfer prices.)
2. Which transfer-pricing method(s) will maximize the after-tax operating income per unit of User Friendly Computer?

22-20 Transfer-pricing methods, goal congruence. British Columbia Lumber has a Raw Lumber Division and a Finished Lumber Division. The variable costs are:

PH Grade Assist

- Raw Lumber Division: \$100 per 100 board-feet of raw lumber
- Finished Lumber Division: \$125 per 100 board-feet of finished lumber

Assume that there is no board-feet loss in processing raw lumber into finished lumber. Raw lumber can be sold at \$200 per 100 board-feet. Finished lumber can be sold at \$275 per 100 board-feet.

Required

1. Should British Columbia Lumber process raw lumber into its finished form? Show your calculations.
2. Assume that internal transfers are made at 110% of variable cost. Will each division maximize its division operating-income contribution by adopting the action that is in the best interest of British Columbia Lumber as a whole? Explain.
3. Assume that internal transfers are made at market prices. Will each division maximize its division operating-income contribution by adopting the action that is in the best interest of British Columbia Lumber as a whole? Explain.

22-21 Effect of alternative transfer-pricing methods on division operating income. (CMA, adapted) Ajax Corporation has two divisions. The Mining Division makes toldine, which is then transferred to the Metals

PH Grade Assist

Division. The toldine is further processed by the Metals Division and is sold to customers at a price of $150 per unit. The Mining Division is currently required by Ajax to transfer its total yearly output of 400,000 units of toldine to the Metals Division at 110% of full manufacturing cost. Unlimited quantities of toldine can be purchased and sold on the outside market at $90 per unit.

The following table gives the manufacturing cost per unit in the Mining and Metals divisions for 2007:

	Mining Division	Metals Division
Direct material cost	$12	$ 6
Direct manufacturing labor cost	16	20
Manufacturing overhead cost	32[a]	25[b]
Total manufacturing cost per unit	$60	$51

[a]Manufacturing overhead costs in the Mining Division are 25% fixed and 75% variable.

[b]Manufacturing overhead costs in the Metals Division are 60% fixed and 40% variable.

Required

1. Calculate the operating incomes for the Mining and Metals divisions for the 400,000 units of toldine transferred under the following transfer-pricing methods: (a) market price and (b) 110% of full manufacturing cost.
2. Suppose Ajax rewards each division manager with a bonus, calculated as 1% of division operating income (if positive). What is the amount of bonus that will be paid to each division manager under the transfer-pricing methods in requirement 1? Which transfer-pricing method will each division manager prefer to use?
3. What arguments would Brian Jones, manager of the Mining Division, make to support the transfer-pricing method that he prefers?

22-22 Transfer pricing, general guideline, goal congruence. (CMA, adapted). Quest Motors, Inc., operates as a decentralized multidivision company. The Tivo Division of Quest Motors purchases most of its airbags from the Airbag Division. The Airbag Division's incremental cost for manufacturing the airbags is $90 per unit. The Airbag Division is currently working at 80% of capacity. The current market price of the airbags is $125 per unit.

Required

1. Using the general guideline presented in the chapter, what is the minimum price at which the Airbag Division would sell airbags to the Tivo Division?
2. Suppose that Quest Motors requires that whenever divisions with unused capacity sell products internally, they must do so at the incremental cost. Evaluate this transfer-pricing policy using the criteria of goal congruence, evaluating division performance, motivating management effort, and preserving division autonomy.
3. If the two divisions were to negotiate a transfer price, what is the range of possible transfer prices? Evaluate this negotiated transfer-pricing policy using the criteria of goal congruence, evaluating division performance, motivating management effort, and preserving division autonomy.
4. Do you prefer the transfer-pricing policy in requirement 2 or requirement 3? Explain your answer briefly.

22-23 Multinational transfer pricing, global tax minimization. The Mornay Company manufactures telecommunications equipment at its plant in Toledo, Ohio. The company has marketing divisions throughout the world. A Mornay marketing division in Vienna, Austria, imports 1,000 units of Product 4A36 from the United States. The following information is available:

U.S. income tax rate on the U.S. division's operating income	40%
Austrian income tax rate on the Austrian division's operating income	44%
Austrian import duty	10%
Variable manufacturing cost per unit of Product 4A36	$350
Full manufacturing cost per unit of Product 4A36	$500
Selling price (net of marketing and distribution costs) in Austria	$750

Suppose the U.S. and Austrian tax authorities only allow transfer prices that are between the full manufacturing cost per unit of $500 and a market price of $650, based on comparable imports into Austria. The Austrian import duty is charged on the price at which the product is transferred into Austria. Any import duty paid to the Austrian authorities is a deductible expense for calculating Austrian income taxes due.

Required

1. Calculate the after-tax operating income earned by the U.S. and Austrian divisions from transferring 1,000 units of Product 4A36 (a) at full manufacturing cost per unit and (b) at market price of comparable imports. (Income taxes are not included in the computation of the cost-based transfer prices.)
2. Which transfer price should the Mornay Company select to minimize the total of company import duties and income taxes? Remember that the transfer price must be between the full manufacturing cost per unit of $500 and the market price of $650 of comparable imports into Austria. Explain your reasoning.

22-24 Multinational transfer pricing, goal congruence (continuation of 22-23). Suppose that the U.S. division could sell as many units of Product 4A36 as it makes at $600 per unit in the U.S. market, net of all marketing and distribution costs.

Required

1. From the viewpoint of the Mornay Company as a whole, would after-tax operating income be maximized if it sold the 1,000 units of Product 4A36 in the United States or in Austria? Show your computations.
2. Suppose division managers act autonomously to maximize their division's after-tax operating income. Will the transfer price calculated in requirement 2 of Exercise 22-23 result in the U.S. division manager taking the actions determined to be optimal in requirement 1 of this exercise? Explain.
3. What is the minimum transfer price that the U.S. division manager would agree to? Does this transfer price result in the Mornay Company as a whole paying more import duty and taxes than the answer to requirement 2 of Exercise 22-23? If so, by how much?

22-25 Transfer-pricing dispute. The Allison-Chambers Corporation, manufacturer of tractors and other heavy farm equipment, is organized along decentralized product lines, with each manufacturing division operating as a separate profit center. Each division manager has been delegated full authority on all decisions involving the sale of that division's output both to outsiders and to other divisions of Allison-Chambers. Division C has in the past always purchased its requirement of a particular tractor-engine component from Division A. However, when informed that Division A is increasing its selling price to $150, Division C's manager decides to purchase the engine component from external suppliers.

Division C can purchase the component for $135 per unit in the open market. Division A insists that, because of the recent installation of some highly specialized equipment and the resulting high depreciation charges, it will not be able to earn an adequate return on its investment unless it raises its price. Division A's manager appeals to top management of Allison-Chambers for support in the dispute with Division C and supplies the following operating data:

C's annual purchases of the tractor-engine component	1,000 units
A's variable cost per unit of the tractor-engine component	$120
A's fixed cost per unit of the tractor-engine component	$20

Required

1. Assume that there are no alternative uses for internal facilities. Determine whether the company as a whole will benefit if Division C purchases the component from external suppliers for $135 per unit. What should the transfer price for the component be set at so that division managers acting in their own divisions' best interests take actions that are in the best interest of the company as a whole?
2. Assume that internal facilities of Division A would not otherwise be idle. By not producing the 1,000 units for Division C, Division A's equipment and other facilities would be used for other production operations that would result in annual cash-operating savings of $18,000. Should Division C purchase from external suppliers? Show your computations.
3. Assume that there are no alternative uses for Division A's internal facilities and that the price from outsiders drops $20. Should Division C purchase from external suppliers? What should the transfer price for the component be set at so that division managers acting in their own divisions' best interests take actions that are in the best interest of the company as a whole?

22-26 Transfer-pricing problem (continuation of 22-25). Refer to Exercise 22-25. Assume that Division A can sell the 1,000 units to other customers at $155 per unit, with variable marketing cost of $5 per unit.

Required

Determine whether Allison-Chambers will benefit if Division C purchases the 1,000 units from external suppliers at $135 per unit. Show your computations.

Problems

22-27 General guideline, transfer pricing. The Shamrock Company manufactures and sells television sets. Its Assembly Division (AD) buys television screens from the Screen Division (SD) and assembles the TV sets. The SD, which is operating at capacity, incurs an incremental manufacturing cost of $80 per screen. The SD can sell all its output to the outside market at a price of $120 per screen, after incurring a variable marketing and distribution cost of $5 per screen. If the AD purchases screens from outside suppliers at a price of $120 per screen, it will incur a variable purchasing cost of $3 per screen. Shamrock's division managers can act autonomously to maximize their own division's operating income.

Required

1. What is the minimum transfer price at which the SD manager would be willing to sell screens to the AD?
2. What is the maximum transfer price at which the AD manager would be willing to purchase screens from the SD?
3. Now suppose that the SD can sell only 80% of its output capacity of 10,000 screens per month on the open market. Capacity cannot be reduced in the short run. The AD can assemble and sell more than 10,000 TV sets per month.
   a. What is the minimum transfer price at which the SD manager would be willing to sell screens to the AD?
   b. From the point of view of Shamrock's management, how much of the SD output should be transferred to the AD?
   c. What transfer-pricing policy will achieve the outcome desired in part 3b?

22-28 Pertinent transfer price. Europa, Inc., has two divisions, A and B, which manufacture expensive bicycles. Division A produces the bicycle frame, and Division B assembles the rest of the bicycle onto the frame. There is a market for both the subassembly and the final product. Each division has been designated as a profit center. The transfer price for the subassembly has been set at the long-run average market price. The following data are available for each division:

Selling price for final product	$300
Long-run average selling price for intermediate product	200
Incremental cost per unit for completion in Division B	150
Incremental cost per unit in Division A	120

The manager of Division B has made the following calculation:

Selling price for final product		$300
Transferred-in cost per unit (market)	$200	
Incremental cost per unit for completion	150	350
Contribution (loss) on product		$ (50)

Required

1. Should transfers be made to Division B if there is no unused capacity in Division A? Is the market price the correct transfer price? Show your computations.
2. Assume that Division A's maximum capacity for this product is 1,000 units per month and sales to the intermediate market are now 800 units. Should 200 units be transferred to Division B? At what transfer price? Assume that for a variety of reasons, Division A will maintain the $200 selling price indefinitely. That is, Division A is not considering lowering the price to outsiders even if idle capacity exists.
3. Suppose Division A quoted a transfer price of $150 for up to 200 units. What would be the contribution to the company as a whole if a transfer were made? As manager of Division B, would you be inclined to buy at $150? Explain.

22-29 Pricing in imperfect markets (continuation of 22-28). Refer to Problem 22-28.

Required

1. Suppose the manager of Division A has the option of (a) cutting the external price to $195, with the certainty that sales will rise to 1,000 units, or (b) maintaining the external price of $200 for the 800 units and transferring the 200 units to Division B at a price that would produce the same operating income for Division A. What transfer price would produce the same operating income for Division A? Is that price consistent with that recommended by the general guideline in the chapter so that the desirable decision for the company as a whole would result?
2. Suppose that if the selling price for the intermediate product were dropped to $195, sales to external parties could be increased to 900 units. Division B wants to acquire as many as 200 units if the transfer price is acceptable. For simplicity, assume that there is no external market for the final 100 units of Division A's capacity.
   a. Using the general guideline, what is (are) the minimum transfer price(s) that should lead to the correct economic decision? Ignore performance-evaluation considerations.
   b. Compare the total contributions under the alternatives to show why the transfer price(s) recommended lead(s) to the optimal economic decision.

Excel Lab
www.prenhall.com/horngren/cost12e

22-30 Effect of alternative transfer-pricing methods on division operating income. Crango Products is a cranberry cooperative that operates two divisions: a Harvesting Division and a Processing Division. Currently, all of Harvesting's output is converted into cranberry juice by the Processing Division, and the juice is sold to large beverage companies that produce cranberry juice blends. The Processing Division has a yield of 500 gallons of juice per 1,000 pounds of cranberries. Cost and market price data for the two divisions are as follows:

	A	B	C	D	E
1	**Harvesting Division**			**Processing Division**	
2	Variable cost per pound of cranberries	$0.10		Variable processing cost per gallon of juice produced	$0.20
3	Fixed cost per pound of cranberries	$0.25		Fixed cost per gallon of juice produced	$0.40
4	Selling price per pound of cranberries in outside market	$0.60		Selling price per gallon of juice	$2.10

If you want to use Excel to solve this problem, go to the Excel Lab at **www.prenhall.com/horngren/cost12e** and download the template for Problem 22-30.

Required

1. Compute Crango's operating income from harvesting 500,000 pounds of cranberries during June 2006 and processing them into juice.
2. Crango rewards its division managers with a bonus equal to 5% of operating income. Compute the bonus earned by each division manager in June 2006 for each of the following transfer pricing methods:
   a. 200% of full cost
   b. Market price
3. Which transfer-pricing method will each division manager prefer? How might Crango resolve any conflicts that may arise on the issue of transfer pricing?

22-31 Goal-congruence problems with cost-plus transfer-pricing methods, dual-pricing system (continuation of 22-30). Assume that Pat Borges, CEO of Crango, had mandated a transfer price equal to 200% of full cost. Now he decides to decentralize some management decisions and sends around a memo that states: "Effective immediately, each division of Crango is free to make its own decisions regarding the purchase of direct materials and the sale of finished products."

Excel Lab www.prenhall.com/horngren/cost12e

If you want to use Excel to solve this problem, go to the Excel Lab at **www.prenhall.com/horngren/cost12e** and download the template for Problem 22-30.

Required

1. Give an example of a goal-congruence problem that will arise if Crango continues to use a transfer price of 200% of full cost and Borges' decentralization policy is adopted.
2. Borges feels that a dual transfer-pricing policy will improve goal congruence. He suggests that transfers out of the Harvesting Division be made at 200% of full cost and transfers into the Processing Division be made at market price. Compute the operating income of each division under this dual transfer-pricing method when 500,000 pounds of cranberries are harvested during June 2006 and processed into juice.
3. Why is the sum of the division operating incomes computed in requirement 2 different from Crango's operating income from harvesting and processing 500,000 pounds of cranberries?
4. Suggest two problems that may arise if Crango implements the dual transfer prices described in requirement 2.

22-32 Multinational transfer pricing, global tax minimization. Industrial Diamonds, Inc., based in Los Angeles, has two divisions:

- South African Mining Division, which mines a rich diamond vein in South Africa
- U.S Processing Division, which polishes raw diamonds for use in industrial cutting tools

Excel Lab www.prenhall.com/horngren/cost12e

The Processing Division's yield is 50%: It takes 2 pounds of raw diamonds to produce 1 pound of top-quality polished industrial diamonds. Although all of the Mining Division's annual output of 2,000 pounds of raw diamonds is sent for processing in the United States, there is also an active market for raw diamonds in South Africa. The foreign exchange rate is 7 ZAR (South African Rand) = $1 U.S. The following information is known about the two divisions:

	A	B	C
1	**South African Mining Division**		
2	Variable cost per pound of raw diamonds	560	ZAR
3	Fixed cost per pound of raw diamonds	1,540	ZAR
4	Market price per pound of raw diamonds	3,150	ZAR
5	Tax rate	18%	
6			
7	**U.S. Processing Division**		
8	Variable cost per pound of polished diamonds	150	U.S. dollars
9	Fixed cost per pound of polished diamonds	700	U.S. dollars
10	Market price per pound of polished diamonds	5,000	U.S. dollars
11	Tax rate	30%	

If you want to use Excel to solve this problem, go to the Excel Lab at **www.prenhall.com/horngren/cost12e** and download the template for Problem 22-32.

Required

1. Compute the annual pre-tax operating income, in U.S. dollars, of each division under the following transfer-pricing methods: (a) 200% of full cost and (b) market price.
2. Compute the after-tax operating income, in U.S. dollars, for each division under the transfer-pricing methods in requirement 1. (Income taxes are not included in the computation of cost-based transfer price, and Industrial Diamonds does not pay U.S. income tax on income already taxed in South Africa.)
3. If the two division managers are compensated based on after-tax division operating income, which transfer-pricing method will each prefer? Which transfer-pricing method will maximize the total after-tax operating income of Industrial Diamonds?
4. In addition to tax minimization, what other factors might Industrial Diamonds consider in choosing a transfer-pricing method?

22-33 Multinational transfer pricing and taxation. (Richard Lambert, adapted) Anita Corporation, headquartered in the United States, manufactures state-of-the-art milling machines in the United States. It has two marketing subsidiaries, one in Brazil and one in Switzerland, that sell its products. Anita is building one new machine, at a cost of $500,000. There is no market for the equipment in the United States, but the equipment can be sold in Brazil for $1,000,000. The Brazilian subsidiary, however, would incur transportation and modification costs of $200,000. Alternatively, the equipment can be sold in Switzerland for $950,000, but the Swiss subsidiary would incur transportation and modification costs of $250,000. The U.S. company can sell the equipment to either its Brazilian or its Swiss subsidiary, but not to both. The Anita

Corporation and its subsidiary companies operate in a highly decentralized manner. Managers in each company have considerable autonomy and are interested in maximizing their own company's income.

Required

1. From the viewpoint of Anita Corporation and its subsidiaries, should Anita manufacture the equipment? If it does, where should it sell the equipment to maximize total operating income? What would the operating income for Anita and its subsidiaries be from the sale? Ignore any income tax effects.
2. What range of transfer prices will result in achieving the actions determined to be optimal in requirement 1? Explain your answer.
3. The effective income tax rates are as follows: 40% in the United States, 60% in Brazil, and 15% in Switzerland. The tax authorities in the three countries are uncertain about the cost of the intermediate product and will allow any transfer price between $500,000 and $700,000. If Anita and its subsidiaries want to maximize after-tax operating income, (a) should the equipment be manufactured, and (b) where and at what price should it be transferred and sold? Show your computations.
4. Now suppose managers act autonomously to maximize their own subsidiary's after-tax operating income. The tax authorities will allow transfer prices only between $500,000 and $700,000. Which subsidiary will get the product and at what price? Is your answer the same as your answer in requirement 3? Explain why or why not.

22-34 Transfer pricing, goal congruence. The Orsilo Corporation makes and sells 10,000 boom boxes each year. Its Assembly Division purchases components from other divisions of Orsilo or from external suppliers and assembles the boom boxes. In particular, the Assembly Division can purchase the tape player from the Cassette Division of Orsilo or from Johnson Corporation. Johnson agrees to meet all of Orsilo's quality requirements and is currently negotiating with the Assembly Division to supply 10,000 tape players at a price between $38 and $45 per tape player.

A critical component of the tape player is the head mechanism that reads the tape. To ensure the quality of its boom boxes, Orsilo requires that if Johnson wins the contract to supply tape players, it must purchase the head mechanism from Orsilo's Cassette Division for $20 each.

The Cassette Division can manufacture at most 12,000 cassette decks annually. It also manufactures as many additional head mechanisms as can be sold. The incremental cost of manufacturing the head mechanism is $15 per unit. The incremental cost of manufacturing a tape player (including the cost of the head mechanism) is $25 per unit, and any number of tape players can be sold for $35 each in the external market.

Required

1. What are the incremental costs minus revenues from sale to external buyers for the company as a whole if the Cassette Division transfers 10,000 tape players to the Assembly Division and sells the remaining 2,000 tape players on the external market?
2. What are the incremental costs minus revenues from sale to external buyers for the company as a whole if the Cassette Division sells 12,000 tape players on the external market and the Assembly Division accepts Johnson's offer at (a) $38 per tape player or (b) $45 per tape player?
3. What is the minimum transfer price per tape player at which the Cassette Division would be willing to transfer 10,000 tape players to the Assembly Division?
4. Suppose that the transfer price is set to the minimum computed in requirement 3 plus $1, and the division managers at Orsilo are free to make their own profit-maximizing sourcing and selling decisions. Now, Johnson offers 10,000 tape players for $40.50 each.
   a. What decisions will the managers of the Cassette Division and Assembly Division make?
   b. Are these decisions optimal for Orsilo as a whole?
   c. Based on this exercise, at what price would you recommend the transfer price be set?

22-35 Transfer pricing, utilization of capacity. (J. Patell, adapted) The California Instrument Company (CIC) consists of the Semiconductor Division and the Process-Control Division, each of which operates as an independent profit center. The Semiconductor Division employs craftsmen who produce two different electronic components: the new high-performance Super-chip and an older product called Okay-chip. These two products have the following cost characteristics:

	Super-chip	Okay-chip
Direct materials	$2	$1
Direct manufacturing labor, 2 hours × $14; 0.5 hour × $14	28	7

Annual overhead in the Semiconductor Division totals $400,000, all fixed. Due to the high skill level necessary for the craftsmen, the Semiconductor Division's capacity is set at 50,000 hours per year.

One customer orders a maximum of 15,000 Super-chips per year, at a price of $60 per chip. If CIC cannot meet this entire demand, the customer curtails its own production. The rest of the Semiconductor Division's capacity is devoted to the Okay-chip, for which there is unlimited demand at $12 per chip.

The Process-Control Division produces only one product, a process-control unit, with the following cost structure:

- Direct materials (circuit board): $60
- Direct manufacturing labor (5 hours × $10): $50

Fixed overhead costs of the Process-Control Division are $80,000 per year. The current market price for the control unit is $132 per unit.

A joint research project has just revealed that a single Super-chip could be substituted for the circuit board currently used to make the process-control unit. Using Super-chip would require an extra one hour of labor per control unit for a new total of six hours per control unit.

Required

1. Calculate the contribution margin per hour of selling Super-chip and Okay-chip. If no transfers of Super-chip are made to the Process-Control Division, how many Super-chips and Okay-chips should the Semiconductor Division sell? Show your computations.
2. The Process-Control Division expects to sell 5,000 control units this year. From the viewpoint of California Instruments as a whole, should 5,000 Super-chips be transferred to the Process-Control Division to replace circuit boards? Show your computations.
3. If demand for the control unit is certain to be 5,000 units but its *price is uncertain*, what should the transfer price of Super-chip be to ensure that the division managers' actions maximize operating income for CIC as a whole? (All other data are unchanged.)
4. If demand for the control unit is certain to be 12,000 units, but its *price is uncertain*, what should the transfer price of Super-chip be to ensure that the division managers' actions maximize operating income for CIC as a whole? (All other data are unchanged.)

22-36 Ethics, transfer pricing. The Belmont Division of Durham Industries manufactures component R47, which it transfers to the Alston Division at 200% of variable cost. The variable cost of R47 is $14 per unit. Joe Lasker, the management accountant of the Belmont Division, calls Hal Tanner, his assistant, into his office. Lasker says, "I am not sure about the fixed- and variable-cost distinctions you are making. I think the variable cost is higher than $14 per unit."

Tanner knows that showing a higher variable cost will increase the Belmont Division's profits and lead to higher bonuses for the division employees. However, Tanner is uncomfortable about making any changes because he has used the same method to classify costs as either variable or fixed over the last few years. Nevertheless, Tanner recognizes that fixed- and variable-cost distinctions are not always clear-cut.

Required

1. Calculate Belmont Division's contribution margin from transferring 10,000 units of R47 (a) if the variable cost is $14 per unit, and (b) if the variable cost is $16 per unit.
2. Evaluate whether Lasker's suggestion to Tanner regarding variable costs is ethical. Would it be ethical for Tanner to revise the variable cost per unit? What steps should Tanner take to resolve this situation?

Collaborative Learning Problem

22-37 Goal congruence, income taxes, different market conditions. The San Ramon Corporation makes water pumps. The Engine Division makes the engines and supplies them to the Assembly Division, where the pumps are assembled. San Ramon is a successful and profitable corporation that attributes much of its success to its decentralized operating style. Each division manager is compensated on the basis of division operating income.

The Assembly Division currently acquires all its engines from the Engine Division. The Assembly Division manager could purchase similar engines in the market for $400 each. The Engine Division is currently operating at 80% of its capacity of 4,000 units and has the following costs:

Direct materials ($125 per unit × 3,200 units)	$400,000
Direct manufacturing labor ($50 per unit × 3,200 units)	160,000
Variable manufacturing overhead costs ($25 per unit × 3,200 units)	80,000
Fixed manufacturing overhead costs	520,000

All the Engine Division's 3,200 units are currently transferred to the Assembly Division. No engines are sold in the external market.

The Engine Division has just received an order for 2,000 units at $375 per engine that would utilize half the capacity of the plant. The order must either be taken in full or rejected. The order is for a slightly different engine than what the Engine Division currently makes, but it takes the same amount of manufacturing time. To produce the new engine would require direct material cost per unit of $100, direct manufacturing labor cost per unit of $40, and variable manufacturing overhead cost per unit of $25.

Required

1. From the viewpoint of the San Ramon Corporation as a whole, should the Engine Division accept the order for the 2,000 units? Show your computations.
2. What range of transfer prices will result in achieving the actions determined to be optimal in requirement 1 if division managers act in a decentralized manner?
3. The manager of the Assembly Division has proposed a transfer price for the engines equal to the full cost of the engines, including an allocation of overhead cost. The Engine Division allocates overhead cost to engines on the basis of the total capacity of the plant used to manufacture the engines.
   a. Calculate the transfer price for the engines transferred to the Assembly Division under this arrangement.
   b. Do you think that the transfer price calculated in requirement 3a will result in achieving the actions determined to be optimal in requirement 1 if division managers act in a decentralized manner?
   c. Comment in general on one advantage and one disadvantage of using full cost of the producing division as the basis for setting transfer prices.

4. Now consider the effect of income taxes.
   a. Suppose the Assembly Division is located in a state that imposes a 10% tax on income earned within its boundaries and the Engine Division is located in a state that imposes no tax on income earned within its boundaries. What transfer price would be chosen by the San Ramon Corporation to minimize state income tax payments for the corporation as a whole? Assume that only transfer prices that are greater than or equal to full manufacturing cost and less than or equal to the market price of "substantially similar" engines are acceptable to the tax authorities.
   b. Suppose that the San Ramon Corporation announces the transfer price computed in requirement 4a to price all transfers between the Engine and Assembly Divisions. Each division manager then acts autonomously to maximize division operating income. Will division managers acting in a decentralized manner achieve the actions determined to be optimal in requirement 1? Explain.
5. Consider your responses to requirements 1 through 4 and assume the Engine Division will continue to have opportunities for outside business as described in requirement 1. What transfer-pricing policy would you recommend San Ramon use, and why? Would you continue to evaluate division performance on the basis of division operating incomes? Explain.

WWW

Get Connected: Cost Accounting in the News

Go to www.prenhall.com/horngren/cost12e for additional online exercise(s) that explore issues affecting the accounting world today. These exercises offer you the opportunity to analyze and reflect on how cost accounting helps managers make better decisions and handle the challenges of strategic planning and implementation.

CHAPTER 22 Case

INFORMATION SYSTEMS CORPORATION: Transfer Prices and Goal Congruence

Information Systems Corporation makes computer systems and has high interdependence among its profit centers. Interdivisional transfers are made at full cost plus a profit margin.

The Semiconductor Division produces random access memories (RAMs) for ultimate consumption by several product divisions. Approximately 75% to 80% of the plant's total annual output consists of standard RAMs that product divisions can purchase either from the Semiconductor Division or from external suppliers in the United States and abroad. Unique, proprietary RAMs used in selected products comprise 20–25% of the plant's annual output. These RAMs can only be purchased from the Semiconductor Division.

Until five years ago, the Semiconductor Division supplied all the company's requirements for RAMs. But five years ago it was necessary, despite continued plant expansion, to purchase RAMs from external suppliers to meet demand. Non-U.S. companies entered the U.S. market with high-quality products and aggressive pricing. In a short time, market prices for many RAMs were at or below the Semiconductor Division's costs.

The manager of each product division is evaluated as a profit center. Product-division managers have considerable autonomy in choosing where to buy the components they use in their products. Not surprisingly, these managers began purchasing components from external suppliers rather than pay more for the higher-cost RAMs produced internally by the Semiconductor Division.

The Semiconductor Division has unused capacity. Manufacturing costs are primarily fixed. As production decreased, these fixed costs were spread over fewer production units, resulting in higher costs and transfer prices for RAMs. In response, more product-division managers sought external suppliers, and so it went.

The Semiconductor Division began to focus on cutting its fixed costs to remain cost competitive. It began to increase productivity significantly, to reduce indirect human resources, and to control spending. The plan was to reduce its cost of RAMs from $25 to around $10 over a three-year period.

This plan would be difficult to achieve if the demand for RAMs produced by the Semiconductor Division declined or if the planned cuts in fixed costs were not made. In this case, the higher cost per RAM would be passed along to the product divisions when the RAMs were transferred at actual cost. In committing to buy RAMs from the Semiconductor Division, a product-division manager did not have any guarantee that the cost and price would not increase later if planned volumes did not materialize or if the plant was unable to meet its cost objectives.

The Semiconductor Division manager, recognizing this dilemma, asked the financial staff to recommend a different system for interdivisional transfers. He wanted this new system, at a minimum, to convey to its internal customers the steps the division was taking on cost control and productivity and to indicate a commitment to lower prices.

The financial staff noted that many external suppliers did forward pricing—that is, they set prices not on the basis of current costs but rather on the basis of what they expected future costs to be. The prices that vendors offered were firm commitments, regardless of their own costs to produce RAMs. The prices and margins did, of course, vary with the type of RAM (lower for standard products and higher for specialized products).

QUESTIONS

1. Why are the plant's costs for semiconductors higher than competitors' market prices?
2. What alternatives could the controller recommend to the general manager for interdivisional transfers?
3. What would you recommend as an appropriate transfer-pricing method?

CHAPTER 23

PERFORMANCE MEASUREMENT, COMPENSATION, AND MULTINATIONAL CONSIDERATIONS

LEARNING OBJECTIVES

1. **Select financial and nonfinancial performance measures to use in a balanced scorecard**
2. **Design an accounting-based performance measure**
3. **Analyze return on investment (ROI) using the DuPont method**
4. **Use the residual-income (RI) measure and understand its advantages**
5. **Describe the economic value added (EVA®) method**
6. **Contrast current-cost and historical-cost asset-measurement methods**
7. **Indicate the difficulties that occur when the performance of divisions operating in different countries is compared**
8. **Understand the roles of salaries and incentives when rewarding managers**
9. **Describe the four levers of control and why they are necessary**

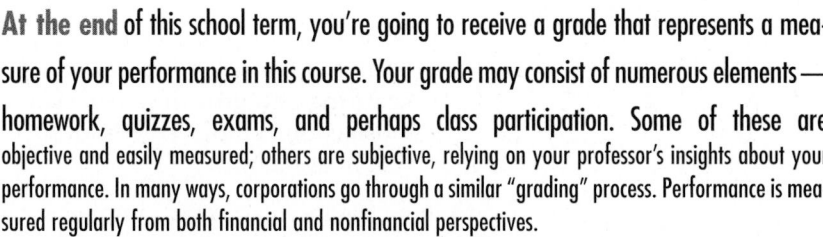

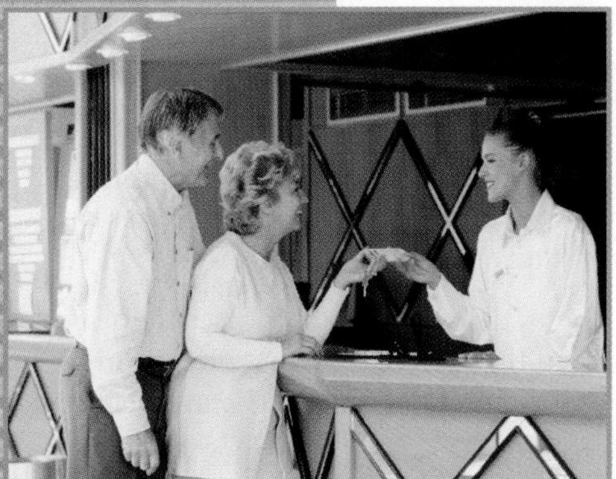

At the end of this school term, you're going to receive a grade that represents a measure of your performance in this course. Your grade may consist of numerous elements—homework, quizzes, exams, and perhaps class participation. Some of these are objective and easily measured; others are subjective, relying on your professor's insights about your performance. In many ways, corporations go through a similar "grading" process. Performance is measured regularly from both financial and nonfinancial perspectives.

Sally Fonda, the owner and CEO of Hospitality Inns, has just received the annual performance reports for Hospitality's three hotels. She is meeting with Jeff Lewis, the CFO, to discuss the reports.

Sally: I was accustomed to seeing the return-on-investment and return-on-sales numbers for each of our hotel properties, but over the past couple of years we have added this new measure: economic value added (EVA®). Some hotels do better on our traditional measures and some do better on EVA, so I am wondering how we should evaluate the performance of each hotel.

Jeff: Each method examines a different aspect of performance. For example, return on sales tells us how well each hotel manager is managing margins. Return on investment is a measure that tells us whether the return we are generating exceeds the cost of the investment. We introduced EVA to overcome some of the problems we faced with the return-on-investment measure.

Sally: How are we using these performance measures to reward managers? Do we have the right balance between the salary we pay and performance-based bonuses? Should we make more use of nonfinancial measures in evaluating our managers' performance? Should we make more use of team incentives?

Jeff: At its most basic level, the trade-off is between creating incentives and imposing risk. As you know, managers sometimes complain when their bonuses are low, claiming that factors beyond their control led to poor performance. This is the risk part. On the other hand, putting more of managers' compensation at risk creates the incentive for them to work harder. Using nonfinancial measures, in addition to financial measures, focuses managers on a broader range of factors, and team-based measures encourage individuals to work together.

Sally: Thanks, Jeff. I know we went over these issues when we designed our new compensation system, but it is important to continually review the system to make sure that it's working like we want it to and that it's not creating unintended consequences. What gets measured and rewarded is exactly what gets done, so getting incentives and compensation right is important. At the same time, we must pay attention to our core values and our code of conduct.

Measuring performance is an integral part of any management control system. Making strategic planning and control decisions requires information about the performance of different subunits of the organization. To be effective, performance measures (both financial and nonfinancial) and rewards must motivate managers and other employees at all levels to strive to achieve company strategies and goals. This chapter discusses the general design, implementation, and uses of performance measures.

Financial and Nonfinancial Performance Measures

1

Select financial performance measures

. . . such as return on investment, residual income

and nonfinancial performance measures to use in a balanced scorecard

. . . such as customer-satisfaction, number of defects

Top management at McDonald's designs the performance-evaluation system on the basis of QSVC (quality, service, cleanliness, and value).

Many organizations are increasingly presenting financial and nonfinancial performance measures for their subunits in a single report called the *balanced scorecard* (Chapter 13, p. 457).[1] Different organizations stress different measures in their scorecards, but the measures are always derived from a company's strategy. Hospitality Inns' strategy is to provide excellent customer service and to charge a higher room rate than its competitors. Hospitality Inns uses the following measures in its balanced scorecard:

1. **Financial perspective**—stock price, net income, return on sales, return on investment, economic value added
2. **Customer perspective**—market share in different geographic locations, customer satisfaction, average number of repeat visits
3. **Internal-business-process perspective**—Customer-service time for making reservations, for check-in, and in restaurants; cleanliness of hotel and room, quality of room service; time taken to clean rooms; quality of restaurant experience; number of new services provided to customers (fax, wireless Internet, video games); time taken to plan and build new hotels
4. **Learning-and-growth perspective**—employee education and skill levels, employee satisfaction, employee turnover, hours of employee training, and information-system availability

As in all balanced scorecard implementations, the goal is to make improvements in the learning-and-growth perspective that will lead to improvements in the internal-business-process perspective that, in turn, will result in improvements in the customer and financial perspectives. Hospitality Inns also uses balanced scorecard measures to evaluate and reward the performance of its managers.

Some performance measures, such as the time it takes to plan and build new hotels, have a long time horizon. Other measures, such as time taken to check in or quality of room service, have a short time horizon. In this chapter, we focus on organization subunits' most widely used performance measures that cover an intermediate-to-long time horizon. These are internal financial measures based on accounting numbers routinely reported by organizations. In later sections, we describe why companies use both financial and nonfinancial measures to evaluate performance.

2

Design an accounting-based performance measure

. . . to achieve top management's goals, measure subunit performance, and motivate managers

Designing accounting-based performance measures requires six steps:

Step 1: Choose Performance Measures That Align with Top Management's Financial Goals. For example, is operating income, net income, return on assets, or revenues the best measure of a subunit's financial performance?

Step 2: Choose the Time Horizon of Each Performance Measure in Step 1. For example, should performance measures, such as return on assets, be calculated for one year or for a multiyear period?

Step 3: Choose a Definition of the Components in Each Performance Measure in Step 1. For example, should assets be defined as total assets or net assets (total assets minus total liabilities)?

Step 4: Choose a Measurement Alternative for Each Performance Measure in Step 1. For example, should assets be measured at historical cost or current cost?

Step 5: Choose a Target Level of Performance. For example, should all subunits have identical targets, such as the same required rate of return on assets?

Step 6: Choose the Timing of Feedback. For example, should manufacturing performance reports be sent to top management daily, weekly, or monthly?

These six steps need not be done sequentially. The issues considered in each step are interdependent, and top management will often proceed through these steps several times before deciding on one or more accounting-based performance measures. The answers to

[1]See R. Kaplan and D. Norton, *The Balanced Scorecard* (Boston: Harvard Business School Press, 1996); R. S. Kaplan and D. P. Norton, *The Strategy-Focused Organization: How Balanced Scorecard Companies Thrive in the New Business Environment* (Boston: Harvard Business School Press, 2001); and R. S. Kaplan and D. P. Norton, *Strategy Maps: Converting Intangible Assets into Tangible Outcomes* (Boston: Harvard Business School Press, 2004).

the questions raised at each step depend on top management's beliefs about how well each alternative measure fulfills the behavioral criteria discussed in Chapter 22: goal congruence, management effort, subunit performance evaluation, and subunit autonomy.

Choosing Among Different Performance Measures: Step 1

Four measures are commonly used to evaluate the economic performance of company subunits. We illustrate these measures for Hospitality Inns.

Hospitality Inns owns and operates three hotels—one each in San Francisco, Chicago, and New Orleans. Exhibit 23-1 summarizes data for each hotel for the most recent year, 2006. At present, Hospitality Inns does not allocate the total long-term debt of the company to the three separate hotels. The exhibit indicates that the New Orleans hotel generates the highest operating income, $510,000, compared with Chicago's $300,000 and San Francisco's $240,000. But does this comparison mean the New Orleans hotel is the most "successful"? The main weakness of comparing operating incomes alone is that differences in *the size of the investment* in each hotel are ignored. **Investment** refers to the resources or assets used to generate income. The question is not, How large is operating income? Rather, it is, How large is operating income in relation to the investment made to earn it?

Three of the approaches to measuring performance include a measure of investment: return on investment, residual income, and economic value added. A fourth approach, return on sales, does not measure investment.

Return on Investment

3

Analyze return on investment (ROI) using the DuPont method

. . . calculate return on sales and investment turnover

Return on investment (ROI) is an accounting measure of income divided by an accounting measure of investment.

$$\text{Return on investment (ROI)} = \frac{\text{Income}}{\text{Investment}}$$

Return on investment is the most popular approach to measure performance. ROI is popular for two reasons: it blends all the ingredients of profitability—revenues, costs, and investment—into a single percentage; and it can be compared with the rate of return on opportunities elsewhere, inside or outside the company. Like any single performance measure, however, ROI should be used cautiously and in conjunction with other measures.

EXHIBIT 23-1

Financial Data for Hospitality Inns for 2006 (in Thousands)

	A	B	C	D	E
1		**San Francisco Hotel**	**Chicago Hotel**	**New Orleans Hotel**	**Total**
2	Hotel revenues	$1,200,000	$1,400,000	$3,185,000	$5,785,000
3	Hotel variable costs	310,000	375,000	995,000	1,680,000
4	Hotel fixed costs	650,000	725,000	1,680,000	3,055,000
5	Hotel operating income	$ 240,000	$ 300,000	$ 510,000	$1,050,000
6	Interest costs on long-term debt at 10%				450,000
7	Income before income taxes				600,000
8	Income taxes at 30%				180,000
9	Net income				420,000
10	Net book values at the end of 2006:				
11	Current assets	$ 400,000	$ 500,000	$ 660,000	$1,560,000
12	Long-term assets	600,000	1,500,000	2,340,000	4,440,000
13	Total assets	$1,000,000	$2,000,000	$3,000,000	$6,000,000
14	Current liabilities	$ 50,000	$ 150,000	$ 300,000	$ 500,000
15	Long-term debt				4,500,000
16	Stockholders' equity				1,000,000
17	Total liabilities and stockholders' equity				$6,000,000
18					

ROI is also called the *accounting rate of return* or the *accrual accounting rate of return* (Chapter 21, pp. 732–733). Managers usually use the term ROI when evaluating the performance of an organization subunit such as a division and the term accrual accounting rate of return when an ROI measure is used to evaluate a project. Companies vary in the way they define income in the numerator and investment in the denominator of the ROI calculation. Some companies use operating income for the numerator; others prefer to calculate ROI on an after-tax basis and use net income. Some companies use total assets in the denominator; others prefer to focus only on those assets financed by long-term debt and stockholders' equity and use total assets minus current liabilities.

Consider the ROIs of each of the three Hospitality hotels in Exhibit 23-1. For our calculations, we use the operating income of each hotel for the numerator and total assets of each hotel for the denominator.

	A	B	C	D	E	F
1	**Hotel**	**Operating Income**	÷	**Total Assets**	=	**ROI**
2	San Francisco	$240,000	÷	$1,000,000	=	24%
3	Chicago	300,000	÷	2,000,000	=	15%
4	New Orleans	510,000	÷	3,000,000	=	17%

Using these ROI figures, the San Francisco hotel appears to make the best use of its total assets.

Each hotel manager can increase ROI, for example, by increasing revenues or decreasing costs (each of which increases the numerator), or by decreasing investment (which decreases the denominator). A hotel manager can increase ROI even when operating income decreases by reducing total assets by a greater percentage. Suppose, for example, that operating income of the Chicago hotel decreases by 4% from \$300,000 to \$288,000 [\$300,000 × (1 – 0.04)] and total assets decrease by 10% from \$2,000,000 to \$1,800,000 [\$2,000,000 × (1 – 0.10)]. The ROI of the Chicago hotel would then increase from 15% to 16% (\$288,000 ÷ \$1,800,000).

ROI can provide more insight into performance when it is represented as two components:

$$\frac{\text{Income}}{\text{Investment}} = \frac{\text{Income}}{\text{Revenues}} \times \frac{\text{Revenues}}{\text{Investment}}$$

ROI tells how much income each dollar of investment generates. Here is the intuition for the two ROI components: (1) Income ÷ Revenues (*return on sales*) tells how much of each revenue dollar becomes income; the goal is to get higher income per revenue dollar. (2) Revenues ÷ Investment (*investment turnover*) tells how many revenue dollars are generated by each dollar of investment; the goal is to make each investment dollar "work harder" to generate more revenues.

which is also written as,

$$ROI = \text{Return on sales} \times \text{Investment turnover}$$

This approach is known as the *DuPont method of profitability analysis*. The DuPont method recognizes the two basic ingredients in profit-making: increasing income per dollar of revenues and using assets to generate more revenues. An improvement in either ingredient without changing the other increases ROI.

Assume that top management at Hospitality Inns adopts a 30% target ROI for the San Francisco hotel. How can this return be attained? We illustrate the DuPont method for the San Francisco hotel and show how this method can be used to describe three alternative ways in which the San Francisco hotel can increase its ROI from 24% to 30%.

	A	B	C	D	E	F	G	H	I	J
1			**Operating Income**	**Revenues**	**Total Assets**	**Operating Income / Revenues**	**x**	**Revenues / Total Assets**	=	**Operating Income / Total Assets**
2			**(1)**	**(2)**	**(3)**	**(4) = (1) ÷ (2)**		**(5) = (2) ÷ (3)**		**(6) = (4) x (5)**
3	**Current ROI**		$240,000	$1,200,000	$1,000,000	20%	×	1.2	=	24%
4	**Alternatives**									
5	**A.**	Decrease assets (such as receivables), keeping revenues and operating income per dollar of revenue constant	240,000	1,200,000	800,000	20%	×	1.5	=	30%
6	**B.**	Increase revenues (via higher occupancy rate), keeping assets and operating income per dollar of revenue constant	300,000	1,500,000	1,000,000	20%	×	1.5	=	30%
7	**C.**	Decrease costs (via, say, efficient maintenance) to increase operating income per dollar of revenue, keeping revenues and assets constant.	300,000	1,200,000	1,000,000	25%	×	1.2	=	30%

Other alternatives, such as increasing the selling price per room, could increase both the revenues per dollar of total assets and the operating income per dollar of revenues. ROI makes clear the benefits that managers can obtain by reducing their investment in current or long-term assets. Some managers are conscious of the need to boost revenues or to control costs, but they pay less attention to reducing their investment base. Reducing the investment base means decreasing idle cash, managing credit judiciously, determining proper inventory levels, and spending carefully on long-term assets.

Residual Income

Residual income (RI) is an accounting measure of income minus a dollar amount for required return on an accounting measure of investment.

$$\text{Residual income }(RI) = \text{Income} - (\text{Required rate of return} \times \text{Investment})$$

Required rate of return multiplied by the investment is the *imputed cost of the investment*. **Imputed costs** are costs recognized in particular situations but not incorporated in financial accounting records.

Suppose Hospitality Inns' investments are financed 50% by long-term debt and 50% by stockholders' equity. Long-term debt has an interest cost of 10% per year, which is booked in Hospitality Inn's financial accounting records under accrual accounting procedures. Hospitality Inns' stockholders' equity has a cost of 14% per year. This 14% represents the opportunity cost to equity investors of investing in Hospitality Inns—the return forgone by not investing in other equity securities of similar risk. The cost of equity, like all opportunity costs, is not booked in Hospitality Inns' financial accounting records. It is an imputed cost that is, nevertheless, a real economic cost of the amount of investment financed by equity. The weighted-average cost of capital for investments in Hospitality Inns is (50% × cost of debt) + (50% × cost of equity) = (0.50 × 10%) + (0.50 × 14%) = 5% + 7% = 12%. This is the required rate of return used when calculating RI for Hospitality Inns. A large component of this required rate of return is an imputed cost.

Assume each hotel faces similar risks. Hospitality Inns defines residual income for each hotel as operating income minus the required rate of return of 12% of total assets:

	A	B	C	D	E	F	G	H
1	**Hotel**	**Operating Income**	-	**Required Rate of Return**	×	**Investment**	=	**Residual Income**
2	San Francisco	$240,000	-	(12%	×	$1,000,000)	=	$120,000
3	Chicago	$300,000	-	(12%	×	$2,000,000)	=	$ 60,000
4	New Orleans	$510,000	-	(12%	×	$3,000,000)	=	$150,000

Given the 12% required annual rate of return, the New Orleans hotel has the best RI.

Some companies favor the RI measure because managers will concentrate on maximizing an absolute amount, such as dollars of RI, rather than a percentage, such as ROI. The objective of maximizing RI means that as long as a subunit earns a return in excess of the required return for investments, that subunit should continue to invest.

The objective of maximizing ROI may induce managers of highly profitable subunits to reject projects that, from the viewpoint of the company as a whole, should be accepted. Suppose Hospitality Inns is considering upgrading room features and furnishings at the San Francisco hotel. The upgrade will increase operating income of the San Francisco hotel by $70,000 and increase its total assets by $400,000. The ROI for the expansion is 17.5% ($70,000 ÷ $400,000), which is attractive to Hospitality Inns because it exceeds the required rate of return of 12%. By making this expansion, however, the San Francisco hotel's ROI will decrease:

$$\text{Preupgrade } ROI = \frac{\$240,000}{\$1,000,000} = 0.24, \text{ or } 24\%$$

$$\text{Postupgrade } ROI = \frac{\$240,000 + \$70,000}{\$1,000,000 + \$400,000} = \frac{\$310,000}{\$1,400,000} = 0.221, \text{ or } 22.1\%$$

Use the residual-income (RI) measure

. . . income minus a dollar amount for required return on investment

and understand its advantages

. . . motivates managers to act in the best interest of the company as a whole.

Question: What required rate of return should management use to calculate residual income?

Answer: The company's weighted-average cost of capital. Conceptually, it would be better to use the cost of capital based on each division's risk level. For example, an oil-exploration division would warrant a higher required rate of return than an oil-refining division. Generally, the cost of capital based on each division's risk level is not available.

Companies using RI vary in the way they define income (for example, operating income or net income) and investment (for example, total assets employed or total assets employed minus current liabilities).

Generally, RI is more likely than ROI to induce goal congruence. This preference for RI over ROI parallels the preference for net present value over internal rate of return in capital budgeting.

The annual bonus paid to the San Francisco manager may decrease if ROI affects the bonus calculation and the upgrading option is selected. Consequently, the manager may not look upon the expansion favorably. In contrast, if the annual bonus is a function of RI, the San Francisco manager will view the expansion favorably:

$$\text{Preupgrade } RI = \$240{,}000 - (0.12 \times \$1{,}000{,}000) = \$120{,}000$$

$$\text{Postupgrade } RI = \$310{,}000 - (0.12 \times \$1{,}400{,}000) = \$142{,}000$$

Goal congruence (ensuring that subunit managers work toward achieving the company's goals) is more likely to be achieved by using RI rather than ROI as a measure of the subunit manager's performance.

5

Describe the economic value added (EVA®) method

. . . a variation of residual income using after-tax amounts

Economic Value Added[2]

Economic value added is a specific type of RI calculation that has recently attracted considerable attention. **Economic value added (EVA®)** equals after-tax operating income *minus* the (after-tax) weighted-average cost of capital *multiplied* by total assets minus current liabilities.

$$\begin{matrix}\text{Economic value} \\ \text{added (EVA)}\end{matrix} = \begin{matrix}\text{After-tax} \\ \text{operating income}\end{matrix} - \left[\begin{matrix}\text{Weighted-} \\ \text{average} \\ \text{cost of capital}\end{matrix} \times \left(\begin{matrix}\text{Total} \\ \text{assets}\end{matrix} - \begin{matrix}\text{Current} \\ \text{liabilities}\end{matrix}\right)\right]$$

EVA substitutes the following numbers in the RI calculations: (1) Income equal to after-tax operating income, (2) a required rate of return equal to the (after-tax) weighted-average cost of capital, and (3) investment equal to total assets minus current liabilities.[3]

We use the Hospitality Inns data in Exhibit 23-1 to illustrate the basic EVA calculations. The weighted-average cost of capital (WACC) equals the *after-tax* average cost of all the long-term funds used by Hospitality Inns. The company has two sources of long-term funds: (a) long-term debt with a market value and book value of \$4.5 million issued at an interest rate of 10%, and (b) equity capital that also has a market value of \$4.5 million (but a book value of \$1 million).[4] Because interest costs are tax-deductible and the income tax rate is 30%, the after-tax cost of debt financing is 0.10 × (1 – Tax rate) = 0.10 × (1 – 0.30) = 0.10 × 0.70 = 0.07, or 7%. The cost of equity capital is the opportunity cost to investors of not investing their capital in another investment that is similar in risk to Hospitality Inns. Hospitality's cost of equity capital is 14%.[5] The WACC computation, which uses market values of debt and equity, is:

Finance courses explain the calculation of WACC in greater detail.

$$WACC = \frac{(7\% \times \text{Market value of debt}) + (14\% \times \text{Market value of equity})}{\text{Market value of debt} + \text{Market value of equity}}$$

$$= \frac{(0.07 \times \$4{,}500{,}000) + (0.14 \times \$4{,}500{,}000)}{\$4{,}500{,}000 + \$4{,}500{,}000}$$

$$= \frac{\$945{,}000}{\$9{,}000{,}000} = 0.105, \text{ or } 10.5\%$$

The company applies the same WACC to all its hotels because each hotel faces similar risks.

[2]S. O'Byrne and D. Young, *EVA and Value-Based Management: A Practical Guide to Implementation* (New York: McGraw-Hill, 2000); J. Stein, J. Shiely, and I. Ross, *The EVA Challenge: Implementing Value Added Change in an Organization* (New York: John Wiley and Sons, 2001).

[3]When implementing EVA, companies make several adjustments to the operating income and asset numbers reported under generally accepted accounting principles (GAAP). For example, when calculating EVA, costs such as R&D, restructuring costs, and leases that have long-run benefits are recorded as assets (which are then amortized), rather than as current operating costs. The goal of these adjustments is to obtain a better representation of the economic assets, particularly intangible assets, used to earn income. Of course, the specific adjustments applicable to a company will depend on its individual circumstances.

[4]The market value of Hospitality Inns' equity exceeds book value because book value, based on historical cost, does not measure the current value of the company's assets and because various intangible assets, such as the company's brand name, are not shown at current value in the balance sheet under GAAP.

[5]For details on calculating cost of equity capital adjusted for risk, see J. Van Horne, *Financial Management and Policy*, 12th ed. (Upper Saddle River, NJ: Prentice Hall, 2002).

Total assets minus current liabilities (see Exhibit 23-1) can also be computed as:

$$\text{Total assets} - \text{Current liabilities} = \text{Long-term assets} + \text{Current assets} - \text{Current liabilities}$$
$$= \text{Long-term assets} + \text{Working capital}$$

where

$$\text{Working capital} = \text{Current assets} - \text{Current liabilities}$$

After-tax hotel operating income is:

$$\text{Hotel operating income} \times (1 - \text{Tax rate}) = \text{Hotel operating income} \times (1 - 0.30) = \text{Hotel operating income} \times 0.70$$

EVA calculations for Hospitality Inns are as follows:

	A	B	C	D	E	F	G	H	I	J	K	L	M	N	O	P	Q
1	**Hotel**	**After-Tax Operating Income**			-	**(Weighted-Average Cost of Capital**	**x**	**[Total Assets**	-	**Current Liabilities)**		=					**EVA**
2	San Francisco	$240,000	×	0.7	-	[10.50%	×	($1,000,000	-	$ 50,000)	]	=	$168,000	-	$ 99,750	=	$68,250
3	Chicago	$300,000	×	0.7	-	[10.50%	×	($2,000,000	-	$150,000)	]	=	$210,000	-	$194,250	=	$15,750
4	New Orleans	$510,000	×	0.7	-	[10.50%	×	($3,000,000	-	$300,000)	]	=	$357,000	-	$283,500	=	$73,500

The New Orleans hotel has the highest EVA. Economic value added, like residual income, charges managers for the cost of their investments in long-term assets and working capital. Value is created only if after-tax operating income exceeds the cost of investing the capital. To improve EVA, managers can, for example, (a) earn more after-tax operating income with the same capital, (b) use less capital to earn the same after-tax operating income, or (c) invest capital in high-return projects.

Managers in companies such as Briggs and Stratton, Coca-Cola, CSX, Equifax, and FMC use the estimated impact on EVA to guide their decisions. Division managers find EVA helpful because it allows them to incorporate into decisions at the division level the cost of capital, which is generally only available at the companywide level. Comparing the actual EVA achieved to the estimated EVA is useful for evaluating performance and providing feedback to managers about performance. CSX, a railroad company, credits EVA for decisions such as to run trains with three locomotives instead of four and to schedule arrivals just in time for unloading rather than having trains arrive at their destination several hours in advance. The result? Higher income because of lower fuel costs and lower capital investments in locomotives.

Return on Sales

The income-to-revenues ratio (or sales ratio)—often called *return on sales* (*ROS*)—is a frequently used financial performance measure. ROS is one component of ROI in the DuPont method of profitability analysis. To calculate ROS for each of Hospitality's hotels, we divide operating income by revenues:

	A	B	C	D	E	F
1	**Hotel**	**Operating Income**	÷	**Revenues (Sales)**	=	**Return on Sales (ROS)**
2	San Francisco	$240,000	÷	$1,200,000	=	20.0%
3	Chicago	$300,000	÷	$1,400,000	=	21.4%
4	New Orleans	$510,000	÷	$3,185,000	=	16.0%

The Chicago hotel has the highest ROS, but its performance is rated worse than the other hotels using measures such as ROI, RI, and EVA.

Comparing Performance Measures

The following table summarizes the performance of each hotel and ranks it (in parentheses) under each of the four performance measures:

	A	B	C	D	E	F	G	H	I
1	**Hotel**	**ROI**		**RI**		**EVA**		**ROS**	
2	San Francisco	24%	(1)	$120,000	(2)	$68,250	(2)	20.0%	(2)
3	Chicago	15%	(3)	$ 60,000	(3)	$15,750	(3)	21.4%	(1)
4	New Orleans	17%	(2)	$150,000	(1)	$73,500	(1)	16.0%	(3)

The RI and EVA rankings are the same. They differ from the ROI and ROS rankings. Consider the ROI and RI rankings for the San Francisco and New Orleans hotels. The New Orleans hotel has a smaller ROI. Although its operating income is only slightly more than twice the operating income of the San Francisco hotel—$510,000 versus $240,000—its total assets are three times as large—$3 million versus $1 million. The New Orleans hotel has a higher RI because it earns a higher income after covering the required rate of return on investment of 12%. The high ROI of the San Francisco hotel indicates that its assets are being used efficiently. Even though each dollar invested in the New Orleans hotel does not give the same return as the San Francisco hotel, this large investment creates considerable value because its return exceeds the required rate of return. The Chicago hotel has the highest ROS but the lowest ROI. The high ROS indicates that the Chicago hotel has the lowest cost structure per dollar of revenues of all of Hospitality Inns' hotels. The reason for Chicago's low ROI is that it generates very low revenues per dollar of assets invested. Is any one method better than the others for measuring performance? No, because each evaluates a different aspect of performance.

ROS measures how effectively costs are managed. To evaluate overall aggregate performance, ROI, RI, or EVA measures are more appropriate than ROS because they consider both income and investments. ROI indicates which investment yields the highest return. RI and EVA measures overcome some of the goal-congruence problems of ROI. Some managers favor EVA because it explicitly considers tax effects while (pretax) RI measures do not. Other managers favor (pretax) RI because it is easier to calculate and because, in most cases, it leads to the same conclusions as EVA. The Global Surveys of Company Practice (p. 799) indicate that, generally, companies use multiple financial measures to evaluate performance.

Choosing the Time Horizon of the Performance Measures: Step 2

Step 2 of designing accounting-based performance measures is choosing the time horizon of the performance measures. The ROI, RI, EVA, and ROS calculations represent the results for a single period, one year in our example. Managers could take actions that cause short-run increases in these measures but conflict with the long-run interest of the company. For example, managers may curtail R&D and plant maintenance in the last three months of a fiscal year to achieve a target level of annual operating income. For this reason, many companies evaluate subunits on the basis of ROI, RI, EVA, and ROS over multiple years.

Another reason to evaluate subunits over multiple years is that the benefits of actions taken in the current period may not show up in short-run performance measures, such as the current year's ROI or RI. For example, an investment in a new hotel may adversely affect ROI and RI in the short run but benefit ROI and RI in the long-run.

A multiyear analysis highlights another advantage of the RI measure: Net present value of all cash flows over the life of an investment equals net present value of

GLOBAL SURVEYS OF COMPANY PRACTICE

Key Financial Performance Measures Used Around the Globe

Multiple global surveys indicate extensive use of financial performance measures. The percentage of the largest U.S. companies that view specific financial performance measures as most important are income in comparison with budget, 49%; return on investment (ROI), 29%; economic value added (EVA), 14%; return on sales (ROS), 3%; and other measures, 5%.[a] Similar to many U.S. companies, Australian, Indian, and Dutch corporations also focus on ROI and income.[b,c,d] In contrast, 82% of Japanese companies use return on sales (ROS), whereas only 37% use ROI in measuring financial performance.[e] Some researchers argue that Japanese managers favor ROS because it is easier to calculate, lessens the emphasis on short-term profitability, and is a market-oriented measure that provides more-useful insights for making pricing and target costing decisions. The following table presents the key financial performance measures (in order of importance) used by companies in seven different countries.

Country	Key Financial Performance Measures
United States	Income, ROI, EVA
Australia	ROI, income
Germany[f]	Revenue, contribution margin (on a per-unit basis)
India	ROI, income
Japan	ROS, ROI
Netherlands	ROI, cash flow, income
Singapore[g]	ROI

[a]R. Tang, *Transfer Pricing.*
[b]R. Crehnall and K. Smith, "Adoption and Benefits."
[c]P. Joshi, "The International Diffusion."
[d]T. Groot, "Managing Costs."
[e]H. Wijewardena and A. De Zoysa, "A Comparative Analysis."
[f]G. Scherrer, "Management Accounting."
[g]B. Ghosh and Y. Chan, "Management Accounting."
Full citations are in Appendix A at the end of the book.

the RIs.[6] This characteristic means that if managers use the net present value method to make investment decisions (as advocated in Chapter 21), then using multiyear RI to evaluate managers' performances achieves goal congruence.

Another way to motivate managers to take a long-run perspective is by compensating them on the basis of changes in the market price of the company's stock. That's because stock prices incorporate the expected future effects of current decisions.

[6]We are grateful to S. Reichelstein for pointing out this equality. To see the equivalence, suppose the $400,000 investment in the San Francisco hotel increases operating income by $70,000 per year as follows: Increase in operating cash flows of $150,000 each year for five years minus depreciation of $80,000 ($400,000 ÷ 5) per year, assuming straight-line depreciation and $0 terminal disposal value. Depreciation reduces the investment amount by $80,000 each year. Assuming a required rate of return of 12%, net present values of cash flows and residual incomes are as follows:

Year	0	1	2	3	4	5	Net Present Value
(1) Cash flow	–$400,000	$150,000	$150,000	$150,000	$150,000	$150,000	
(2) Present value of $1 discounted at 12%	1	0.89286	0.79719	0.71178	0.63552	0.56743	
(3) Present value: (1) × (2)	–$400,000	$133,929	$119,578	$106,767	$ 95,328	$ 85,114	$140,716
(4) Operating income		$ 70,000	$ 70,000	$ 70,000	$ 70,000	$ 70,000	
(5) Assets at start of year		$400,000	$320,000	$240,000	$160,000	$ 80,000	
(6) Capital charge: (5) × 12%		$ 48,000	$ 38,400	$ 28,800	$ 19,200	$ 9,600	
(7) Residual income: (4) – (6)		$ 22,000	$ 31,600	$ 41,200	$ 50,800	$ 60,400	
(8) Present value of RI: (7) × (2)		$ 19,643	$ 25,191	$ 29,325	$ 32,284	$ 34,273	$140,716

Choosing Alternative Definitions for Performance Measures: Step 3

To illustrate step 3 of designing accounting-based performance measures, we consider four alternative definitions of investment that companies use:

1. **Total assets available**—includes all assets, regardless of their intended purpose.
2. **Total assets employed**—total assets available minus the sum of idle assets and assets purchased for future expansion. For example, if the New Orleans hotel in Exhibit 23-1 has unused land set aside for potential expansion, total assets employed by the hotel would exclude the cost of that land.
3. **Total assets employed minus current liabilities**—total assets excluding assets financed by short-term creditors. One negative feature of defining investment in this way is that it may encourage subunit managers to use an excessive amount of short-term debt because short-term debt reduces the amount of investment.
4. **Stockholders' equity**—calculated by assigning liabilities among subunits and deducting these amounts from the total assets of each subunit. One drawback of this method is that it combines operating decisions made by hotel managers with financing decisions made by top management.

Companies that use ROI or RI generally define investment as the total assets available. When top management directs a subunit manager to carry extra or idle assets, total assets employed can be more informative than total assets available. Companies that adopt EVA define investment as total assets employed minus current liabilities. The most common rationale for using total assets employed minus current liabilities is that the subunit manager often influences decisions on current liabilities of the subunit.

Choosing Measurement Alternatives for Performance Measures: Step 4

6

Contrast current-cost

. . . cost today of purchasing an asset

and historical-cost asset-measurement methods

. . . original cost of an asset minus accumulated depreciation

Distinguish step 3 from step 4. Step 3 requires managers to define the components of the performance measure chosen in step 1. For example, managers may define "investment" as total assets employed minus current liabilities. After choosing the definition in step 3, managers choose the basis for measuring dollar values in the definition in step 4 (for example, historical cost or current cost).

To design accounting-based performance measures, we need to consider different ways to measure assets included in the investment calculations. Should assets be measured at historical cost or current cost? Should gross book value (that is, original cost) or net book value (original cost minus accumulated depreciation) be used for depreciable assets?

Current Cost

Current cost is the cost of purchasing an asset today identical to the one currently held, or the cost of purchasing an asset that provides services like the one currently held if an identical asset cannot be purchased. Of course, measuring assets at current costs will result in different ROIs than the ROIs calculated on the basis of historical costs.

We illustrate the current-cost ROI calculations using the data for Hospitality Inns (Exhibit 23-1) and then compare current-cost-based ROIs and historical-cost-based ROIs. Assume the following information about the long-term assets of each hotel:

	A	B	C	D
1		**San Francisco**	**Chicago**	**New Orleans**
2	Age of facility in years (at end of 2006)	8	4	2
3	Gross book value (original cost)	$1,400,000	$2,100,000	$2,730,000
4	Accumulated depreciation	$ 800,000	$ 600,000	$ 390,000
5	Net book value (at end of 2006)	$ 600,000	$1,500,000	$2,340,000
6	Depreciation for 2006	$ 100,000	$ 150,000	$ 195,000

Hospitality Inns assumes a 14-year estimated useful life, zero terminal disposal value for the physical facilities, and straight-line depreciation.

An index of construction costs indicating how the cost of construction has changed over the eight-year period that Hospitality Inns has been operating (1998 year-end = 100) is:

When a specific cost index (such as the construction cost index) is not available, companies often use a general index (such as the consumer price index) to calculate an approximation of current costs.

	A	B	C	D	E	F	G	H	I
1	**Year**	**1999**	**2000**	**2001**	**2002**	**2003**	**2004**	**2005**	**2006**
2	Construction cost index	110	122	136	144	152	160	174	180

Earlier in this chapter, we computed an ROI of 24% for San Francisco, 15% for Chicago, and 17% for New Orleans (p. 794). One possible explanation of the high ROI for the San Francisco hotel is that its long-term assets are expressed in 1998 construction-price levels—prices that prevailed eight years ago—and the long-term assets for the Chicago and New Orleans hotels are expressed in terms of higher, more-recent construction-price levels, which depress ROIs for these two hotels.

Exhibit 23-2 illustrates a step-by-step approach for incorporating current-cost estimates of long-term assets and depreciation expense into the ROI calculation. We make these calculations to approximate what it would cost today to obtain assets that would produce the same expected operating income that the subunits currently earn. (Similar adjustments to represent the current costs of capital employed and depreciation expense can also be made in the RI and EVA calculations.) The current-cost adjustment reduces by more than half the ROI of the San Francisco hotel.

	A	B	C
1		**Historical Cost ROI**	**Current Cost ROI**
2	San Francisco	24%	10.8%
3	Chicago	15%	11.1%
4	New Orleans	17%	14.7%

Adjusting assets to recognize current costs negates differences in the investment base caused solely by differences in construction-price levels. Compared with historical-cost ROI, current-cost ROI is a better measure of the current economic returns from the investment. If Hospitality Inns were to invest in a new hotel today, investing in one like the New Orleans hotel offers the best ROI.

A drawback of using current costs is that it can be difficult to obtain current-cost estimates for some assets. That's because the estimate requires a company to consider, in addition to increases in price levels, technological advances such as in computers and in processes that could reduce the current cost of assets needed to earn today's operating income.

Long-Term Assets: Gross or Net Book Value?

Because the historical cost of assets is often used to calculate ROI, there has been much discussion about whether gross book value or net book value of assets should be used. Using the data in Exhibit 23-1 (p. 793), we calculate ROI using net and gross book values of plant and equipment as follows:

	A	B	C	D	E	F	G
1		**Operating Income (from Exhibit 23-1)**	**Net Book Value of Total Assets (from Exhibit 23-1)**	**Accumulated Depreciation (from p. 800)**	**Gross Book Value of Total Assets**	**2006 ROI Using Net Book Value of Total Assets (calculated earlier)**	**2006 ROI Using Gross Book Value of Total Assets**
2		(1)	(2)	(3)	(4) = (2) + (3)	(5) = (1) ÷ (2)	(6) = (1) ÷ (4)
3	San Francisco	$240,000	$1,000,000	$800,000	$1,800,000	$\frac{\$240,000}{\$1,000,000} = 24\%$	$\frac{\$240,000}{\$1,800,000} = 13.3\%$
4	Chicago	$300,000	$2,000,000	$600,000	$2,600,000	$\frac{\$300,000}{\$2,000,000} = 15\%$	$\frac{\$300,000}{\$2,600,000} = 11.5\%$
5	New Orleans	$510,000	$3,000,000	$390,000	$3,390,000	$\frac{\$510,000}{\$3,000,000} = 17\%$	$\frac{\$510,000}{\$3,390,000} = 15.0\%$

EXHIBIT 23-2 **ROI for Hospitality Inns: Computed Using Current-Cost Estimates as of the End of 2006 for Depreciation Expense and Long-Term Assets**

	A	B	C	D	E	F	G	H	I	J	K	L	M
1	**Step 1:** Restate long-term assets from gross book value at historical cost to gross book value at current cost as of the end of 2006.												
2		**Gross book value of long-term assets at historical cost**	**x**		**(Construction cost index in 2006**	÷	**Construction cost index in year of construction)**	=		**Gross book value of long-term assets at current cost at end of 2006**			
3	San Francisco	$1,400,000	x		(180	÷	100)	=		$2,520,000			
4	Chicago	$2,100,000	x		(180	÷	144)	=		$2,625,000			
5	New Orleans	$2,730,000	x		(180	÷	160)	=		$3,071,250			
6													
7	**Step 2:** Derive net book value of long-term assets at current cost as of the end of 2006. (Assume estimated useful life of each hotel is 14 years.)												
8		**Gross book value of long-term assets at current cost at end of 2006**	**x**		**(Estimated remaining useful life**	÷	**Estimated total useful life)**	=		**Net book value of long-term assets at current cost at end of 2006**			
9	San Francisco	$2,520,000	x		(6	÷	14)	=		$1,080,000			
10	Chicago	$2,625,000	x		(10	÷	14)	=		$1,875,000			
11	New Orleans	$3,071,250	x		(12	÷	14)	=		$2,632,500			
12													
13	**Step 3:** Compute current cost of total assets in 2006. (Assume current assets of each hotel are expressed in 2006 dollars.)												
14		**Current assets at end of 2006 (from Exhibit 23-1)**	+		**Long-term assets from Step 2 above**	=	**Current cost of total assets at end of 2006**						
15	San Francisco	$400,000	+		$1,080,000	=	$1,480,000						
16	Chicago	$500,000	+		$1,875,000	=	$2,375,000						
17	New Orleans	$660,000	+		$2,632,500	=	$3,292,500						
18													
19	**Step 4:** Compute current-cost depreciation expense in 2006 dollars.												
20		**Gross book value of long-term assets at current cost at end of 2006 (from Step 1)**	÷		**Estimated total useful life**	=	**Current-cost depreciation expense in 2006 dollars**						
21	San Francisco	$2,520,000	÷		14	=	$180,000						
22	Chicago	$2,625,000	÷		14	=	$187,500						
23	New Orleans	$3,071,250	÷		14	=	$219,375						
24													
25	**Step 5:** Compute 2006 operating income using 2006 current-cost depreciation expense.												
26		**Historical-cost operating income**	-		**(Current-cost depreciation expense in 2006 dollars (from Step 4)**	-	**Historical-cost depreciation expense)**	=		**Operating income for 2006 using current-cost depreciation expense in 2006 dollars**			
27	San Francisco	$240,000	-		($180,000	-	$100,000)	=		$160,000			
28	Chicago	$300,000	-		($187,500	-	$150,000)	=		$262,500			
29	New Orleans	$510,000	-		($219,375	-	$195,000)	=		$485,625			
30													
31	**Step 6:** Compute ROI using current-cost estimates for long-term assets and depreciation expense.												
32		**Operating income for 2006 using current-cost depreciation expense in 2006 dollars (from Step 5)**	÷		**Current cost of total assets at end of 2006 (from step 3)**	=	**ROI using current-cost estimate**						
33	San Francisco	$160,000	÷		$1,480,000	=	10.8%						
34	Chicago	$262,500	÷		$2,375,000	=	11.1%						
35	New Orleans	$485,625	÷		$3,292,500	=	14.7%						

Using gross book value, the 13.3% ROI of the older San Francisco hotel is lower than the 15.0% ROI of the newer New Orleans hotel. Those who favor using gross book value claim it enables more-accurate comparisons of ROI across subunits. For example, using gross-book-value calculations, the return on the original plant-and-equipment investment is higher for the newer New Orleans hotel than for the older San Francisco hotel. This difference probably reflects the decline in earning power of the San Francisco hotel. Using the net book value masks this decline in earning power because the constantly decreasing investment base results in a higher ROI for the San Francisco hotel—24% in this example. This higher rate may mislead decision makers into thinking that the earning power of the San Francisco hotel has not decreased.

The proponents of using net book value as an investment base maintain it is less confusing because (1) it is consistent with the amount of total assets shown in the conventional balance sheet, and (2) it is consistent with income computations that include deductions for depreciation expense. Surveys report net book value to be the dominant measure of assets used by companies for internal performance evaluation.

When using net book value, the declining denominator increases ROI as an asset ages, all other things equal. Evaluating managers based on assets at net book value rather than at gross book value increases the incentive for retaining old property, plant, and equipment.

Choosing Target Levels of Performance: Step 5

We next consider target-setting for accounting-based measures of performance against which actual performance can be compared. Historical-cost-based accounting measures are usually inadequate for evaluating economic returns on new investments, and in some cases, they create disincentives for expansion. Despite these problems, historical-cost ROIs can be used to evaluate current performance by establishing *target* ROIs. For Hospitality Inns, we need to recognize that the hotels were built in different years, which means they were built at different construction-price levels. Top management could adjust the target historical-cost-based ROIs accordingly, say, by setting San Francisco's ROI at 26%, Chicago's at 18%, and New Orleans' at 19%.

This useful alternative of comparing actual results with target or budgeted performance is frequently overlooked. The budget should be carefully negotiated with full knowledge of historical-cost accounting pitfalls. *Companies should tailor a budget to a particular subunit, a particular accounting system, and a particular performance measure.* For example, many problems of asset valuation and income measurement can be resolved if top management can get subunit managers to focus on what is attainable in the forthcoming budget period—whether ROI, RI, or EVA is used and whether the financial measures are based on historical cost or some other measure, such as current cost.

Because older assets valued at historical cost inflate ROI (particularly if investment is defined as net book value rather than gross book value), top management may set higher target ROIs for divisions with older assets.

A popular way to establish targets is to set continuous improvement targets. If a company is using EVA as a performance measure, top management can evaluate operations on year-to-year changes in EVA, rather than on absolute measures of EVA. Evaluating performance on the basis of *improvements* in EVA makes the initial method of calculating EVA less important.

In establishing targets for financial performance measures, companies using the balanced scorecard simultaneously determine targets in the customer, internal-business-process, and learning-and-growth perspectives. For example, Hospitality Inns will establish targets for employee training and employee satisfaction, customer service time for reservations and check-in, quality of room service, and customer satisfaction that each hotel must reach to achieve its ROI and EVA targets.

Choosing the Timing of Feedback: Step 6

The final step in designing accounting-based performance measures is the timing of feedback. Timing of feedback depends largely on (a) how critical the information is for the success of the organization, (b) the specific level of management receiving the feedback, and (c) the sophistication of the organization's information technology. For example, hotel managers responsible for room sales want information on the number of rooms sold (rented) on a daily or weekly basis. That's because a large percentage of hotel costs are fixed costs, so achieving high room sales and taking quick action to reverse any declining sales trends are critical to the financial success of each hotel. Supplying managers with daily information about room sales is much easier if Hospitality Inns has a computerized room-reservation and check-in system. Top management, however, may look at information about daily room sales only on a monthly basis. In some instances, for example because of concern about the low sales-to-total-assets ratio of the Chicago hotel, they may want the information weekly.

For example, managers who are responsible for day-to-day operations usually require more-frequent feedback than top management.

The timing of feedback for measures in the balanced scorecard varies. For example, human resources managers at each hotel measure employee satisfaction annually because satisfaction is best measured over a longer horizon. However, housekeeping-department managers measure the quality of room service over much shorter time horizons, such as a week. That's because poor levels of performance in these areas for even a short period of time can harm a hotel's reputation for a long period. Moreover, housekeeping problems can be detected and resolved over a short time period.

Performance Measurement in Multinational Companies

7

Indicate the difficulties that occur when the performance of divisions operating in different countries is compared

... adjustments needed for differences in inflation rates and changes in exchange rates

Our discussion so far has focused on performance evaluation of different divisions of a company operating within a single country. We next discuss the additional difficulties created when the performance of divisions of a company operating in different countries is compared. Several issues arise.[7]

- The economic, legal, political, social, and cultural environments differ significantly across countries.
- Governments in some countries may limit selling prices of, and impose controls on, a company's products. For example, some countries in Asia, Latin America, and Eastern Europe impose tariffs and custom duties to restrict imports of certain goods. Starting in 2005, the General Agreement on Trade and Tariffs (GATT) seeks to reduce and eliminate tariffs and duties imposed by countries.
- Availability of materials and skilled labor, as well as costs of materials, labor, and infrastructure (power, transportation, and communication), may also differ significantly across countries.
- Divisions operating in different countries account for their performance in different currencies. Issues of inflation and fluctuations in foreign-currency exchange rates affect performance measures.

As a result of these differences, adjustments need to be made to compare performance measures across countries.

Calculating the Foreign Division's ROI in the Foreign Currency

Suppose Hospitality Inns invests in a hotel in Mexico City. The investment consists mainly of the costs of buildings and furnishings. Also assume:

- The exchange rate at the time of Hospitality's investment on December 31, 2004, is 10 pesos = $1.
- During 2005, the Mexican peso suffers a steady decline in its value. The exchange rate on December 31, 2005, is 15 pesos = $1.
- The average exchange rate during 2005 is [(10 + 15) ÷ 2] = 12.5 pesos = $1.
- The investment (total assets) in the Mexico City hotel is 30,000,000 pesos.
- The operating income of the Mexico City hotel in 2005 is 6,000,000 pesos.

What is the historical-cost-based ROI for the Mexico City hotel in 2005?

To answer, Hospitality Inns' managers first have to determine: Should they calculate the ROI in pesos or in dollars? If they calculate the ROI in dollars, what exchange rate should they use? The managers may also be interested in how the ROI of Hospitality Inns Mexico City (HIMC) compares with the ROI of Hospitality Inns New Orleans (HINO), which is also a relatively new hotel of approximately the same size. The answers to these questions yield information that will be helpful when making future investment decisions.

$$\text{HIMC's } ROI \text{ (calculated using pesos)} = \frac{\text{Operating income}}{\text{Total assets}} = \frac{6{,}000{,}000 \text{ pesos}}{30{,}000{,}000 \text{ pesos}} = 0.20, \text{ or } 20\%$$

HIMC's ROI of 20% is higher than HINO's ROI of 17% (p. 794). Does this mean that HIMC outperformed HINO based on the ROI criterion? Not necessarily. That's because HIMC operates in a very different economic environment than HINO.

---

[7]See M. Z. Iqbal, *International Accounting—A Global Perspective* (Cincinnati: South-Western College Publishing, 2002).

The peso has declined in value relative to the dollar in 2005. Research shows that the peso's decline is correlated with correspondingly higher inflation in Mexico than in the United States.[8] As a result of the higher inflation in Mexico, HIMC will charge higher prices for its hotel rooms, which will increase HIMC's operating income and lead to a higher ROI. Inflation clouds the real economic returns on an asset and makes historical-cost-based ROI higher. Differences in inflation rates between the two countries make a direct comparison of HIMC's peso-denominated ROI with HINO's dollar-denominated ROI misleading.

Calculating the Foreign Division's ROI in U.S. Dollars

One way to make a comparison of historical-cost-based ROIs more meaningful is to restate HIMC's performance in U.S. dollars. But what exchange rate should be used to make the comparison meaningful? Assume operating income was earned evenly throughout 2005. Hospitality Inns' managers should use the average exchange rate of 12.5 pesos = $1 to convert operating income from pesos to dollars: 6,000,000 pesos ÷ 12.5 pesos per dollar = $480,000. The effect of dividing the operating income in pesos by the higher pesos-to-dollar exchange rate prevailing during 2005, rather than the 10 pesos = $1 exchange rate prevailing on December 31, 2004, is that any increase in operating income in pesos as a result of inflation during 2005 is eliminated when converting back to dollars.

At what rate should HIMC's total assets of 30,000,000 pesos be converted? The 10 pesos = $1 exchange rate prevailing when the assets were acquired on December 31, 2004. That's because HIMC's assets are recorded in pesos at the December 31, 2004, cost, and they are not revalued as a result of inflation in Mexico in 2005. Because the cost of assets in HIMC's financial accounting records is unaffected by subsequent inflation, the exchange rate prevailing when the assets were acquired should be used to convert the assets into dollars. Using exchange rates after December 31, 2004, would be incorrect because these exchange rates incorporate the higher inflation in Mexico in 2005. Total assets are converted to 30,000,000 pesos ÷ 10 pesos per dollar = $3,000,000.

Then,

$$\text{HIMC's } ROI \text{ (calculated using dollars)} = \frac{\text{Operating income}}{\text{Total assets}} = \frac{\$480{,}000}{\$3{,}000{,}000} = 0.16, \text{ or } 16\%$$

As we have discussed, these adjustments make the historical-cost-based ROIs of the Mexico City and New Orleans hotels comparable because they negate the effects of any differences in inflation rates between the two countries. HIMC's ROI of 16% is less than HINO's ROI of 17%.

Residual income calculated in pesos suffers from the same problems as ROI calculated using pesos. Calculating HIMC's RI in dollars adjusts for changes in exchange rates and makes for more-meaningful comparisons with Hospitality's other hotels:

$$\begin{aligned}\text{HIMC's } RI &= \$480{,}000 - (0.12 \times \$3{,}000{,}000)\\ &= \$480{,}000 - \$360{,}000 = \$120{,}000\end{aligned}$$

which is also less than HINO's RI of $150,000. In interpreting HIMC's and HINO's ROI and RI, keep in mind that they are historical-cost-based calculations. They do, however, pertain to relatively new hotels.

Distinction Between Managers and Organization Units[9]

Our focus thus far has been on methods we can use to evaluate the performance of a subunit of a company, such as a division. However, is evaluating the performance of a subunit manager the same as evaluating the performance of the subunit—that is, if the subunit performed well, does it mean the manager performed well, and if the subunit did not perform well, does it mean the manager did not perform well? In this section, we argue that the performance evaluation of a *manager* should be distinguished from the performance evaluation

[8]F. D. S. Choi, "Resolving the Inflation/Currency Translation Dilemma," *Management International Review* (Vol. 34, Special Issue, 1994); H. Louis, "The Value Relevance of the Foreign Translation Adjustment," *The Accounting Review* (October 2003).

[9]The presentations here draw (in part) from teaching notes prepared by S. Huddart, N. Melumad, and S. Reichelstein.

of that manager's *subunit*. For example, companies often put the most skillful division manager in charge of the division producing the poorest economic return in an attempt to improve it. The division may take years to show improvement. Furthermore, the manager's efforts may result merely in bringing the division up to a minimum acceptable ROI. The division may continue to be a poor performer in comparison with other divisions, but it would be a mistake to conclude from the poor performance of the division that the manager is performing poorly. The division's performance may be adversely affected by economic conditions over which the manager has no control.

As another example, consider again the Hospitality Inn Mexico City (HIMC) hotel. Suppose, despite the high inflation in Mexico, HIMC could not increase room prices because of price-control regulations imposed by the government. HIMC's performance in dollar terms would be very poor because of the decline in the value of the peso. But should top management conclude from HIMC's poor performance that the HIMC manager performed poorly? Probably not. That's because most likely the poor performance of HIMC is largely the result of regulatory factors beyond the manager's control.

In the following sections, we show the basic principles for evaluating the performance of an individual subunit manager, although these principles apply to managers at all organization levels. Later sections consider examples at the individual-worker level and the top-management level. We illustrate these principles using the RI performance measure.

8

Understand the roles of salaries and incentives when rewarding managers

... balancing risk and performance-based rewards

The Basic Trade-Off: Creating Incentives versus Imposing Risk

How the performance of managers and other employees is measured and evaluated affects their rewards. Compensation arrangements range from a flat salary with no direct performance-based incentive (or bonus), as in the case of many government employees, to rewards based only on performance, as in the case of real estate agents who get no salary and are compensated via commissions paid on the properties they sell. Most managers' total compensation includes some combination of salary and performance-based incentive. In designing compensation arrangements, we need to consider the *trade-off between creating incentives and imposing risk*. We illustrate this trade-off in the context of our Hospitality Inns example.

Recall from the conversation at the beginning of the chapter that Sally Fonda owns the Hospitality Inns chain of hotels. Roger Brett manages the Hospitality Inns San Francisco (HISF) hotel. Assume Fonda uses RI to measure performance. To improve RI, Fonda would like Brett to increase sales, control costs, provide prompt and courteous customer service, and reduce working capital. But even if Brett did all those things, high RI is not guaranteed. That's because HISF's RI is affected by many factors beyond Fonda's and Brett's control, such as a recession in the San Francisco economy or an earthquake that might negatively affect HISF. Or, there could be other uncontrollable factors, such as road construction near competing hotels, that might have a positive effect on HISF's RI. The bottom line: Uncontrollable factors make HISF's profitability uncertain and, therefore, risky.

People who decide to become entrepreneurs (owners) are generally more risk-tolerant than those who decide to work for others (managers). It is more efficient for owners to bear risk than managers, because managers demand a premium (extra compensation) for bearing risk. The objective of many compensation plans is to provide managers with incentives to work hard while minimizing the risk placed on them.

As an entrepreneur, Fonda expects to bear risk. But Brett does not like being subject to risk. One way of "insuring" Brett against risk is to pay Brett a flat salary, regardless of the actual amount of RI earned. All the risk would then be borne by Fonda. This arrangement creates a problem, however, because Brett's effort is difficult to monitor. The absence of performance-based compensation means that Brett has no direct incentive to work harder or to undertake extra physical and mental effort beyond what is necessary to retain his job or to uphold his own personal values.

Moral hazard describes situations in which an employee prefers to exert less effort (or to report distorted information) compared with the effort (or accurate information) desired by the owner because the employee's effort (or validity of the reported information) cannot be accurately monitored and enforced.[10] In some repetitive jobs, such as in

[10]The term *moral hazard* originated in insurance contracts to represent situations in which insurance coverage caused insured parties to take less care of their properties than they might otherwise. One response to moral hazard in insurance contracts is the system of deductibles (that is, the insured pays for damages below a specified amount).

electronic assembly, a supervisor can monitor the workers' actions, and the moral-hazard problem may not arise. However, a manager's job is to gather and interpret information and to exercise judgment on the basis of the information obtained. Monitoring a manager's effort is more difficult.

Paying no salary and rewarding Brett *only* on the basis of some performance measure—RI in our example—raises different concerns. In this case, Brett would be motivated to strive to increase RI because his rewards would increase with increases in RI. But compensating Brett on RI also subjects him to risk. That's because HISF's RI depends not only on Brett's effort, but also on factors such as local economic conditions over which Brett has no control.

Brett does not like being subject to risk. To compensate Brett for taking risk, Fonda must pay him extra compensation. That is, using performance-based bonuses will cost Fonda more money, *on average*, than paying Brett a flat salary. Why "on average"? Because Fonda's compensation payment to Brett will vary with RI outcomes. When averaged over these outcomes, the RI-based compensation will cost Fonda more than paying Brett a flat salary. The motivation for having some salary and some performance-based bonus in compensation arrangements is to balance the benefit of incentives against the extra cost of imposing risk on the manager.

Intensity of Incentives and Financial and Nonfinancial Measurements

What affects the intensity of incentives? That is, how large should the incentive component of a manager's compensation be relative to the salary component? To answer these questions, we need to understand how much the performance measure is affected by actions the manager takes to further the owner's objectives.

Preferred performance measures are those that are sensitive to or that change significantly with the manager's performance. They do not change much with changes in factors that are beyond the manager's control. Sensitive performance measures motivate the manager as well as limit the manager's exposure to risk, reducing the cost of providing incentives. Less-sensitive performance measures are not affected by the manager's performance and fail to induce the manager to improve. The more that owners have sensitive performance measures available to them, the more they can rely on incentive compensation for their managers.

When possible, owners use performance-evaluation measures that are tightly linked to managers' efforts. Managers are evaluated based on things they can affect, even if they are not completely controllable. For example, salespersons often earn commissions based on the amount of sales revenues they generate. Salespersons can affect the amount of sales they generate by working harder, but they cannot control other factors (such as the economy and competitors' products) that also affect the amount of their sales.

The salary component of compensation dominates when performance measures that are sensitive to managers' actions are not available. This is the case, for example, for some corporate staff and government employees. A high salary component, however, does not mean incentives are completely absent. Promotions and salary increases do depend on some overall measure of performance, but the incentives are less direct. The incentive component of compensation is high when sensitive performance measures are available and when monitoring the employee's effort is difficult, such as in real estate agencies.

In evaluating Brett, Fonda uses measures from multiple perspectives of the balanced scorecard because nonfinancial measures on the balanced scorecard—employee satisfaction and the time taken for check-in, cleaning rooms, and providing room service—are more sensitive to Brett's actions. Financial measures such as RI are less sensitive to Brett's actions because they are affected by external factors such as local economic conditions that are beyond Brett's control. Residual income may be a very good measure of the economic viability of the hotel, but it is only a partial measure of Brett's performance.

Study Tip: To check your understanding of the material in this chapter, see the Featured Exercise, true–false statement 7, multiple-choice questions 1 through 6, and Review Exercises 1 through 3 (*Student Guide*, beginning p. 316). Fully explained answers begin on page 321.

Another reason for using nonfinancial measures in the balanced scorecard is that these measures follow Hospitality Inns' strategy and are drivers of future performance. Evaluating managers on these nonfinancial measures motivates them to take actions that will sustain long-run performance. Therefore, evaluating performance in all four perspectives of the balanced scorecard promotes both short- and long-run actions.

Benchmarks and Relative Performance Evaluation

Owners often use financial and nonfinancial benchmarks to evaluate performance. Benchmarks representing "best practice" may be available inside or outside an organization. For HISF, benchmarks could be from similar hotels, either within or outside the Hospitality Inns chain. Suppose Brett has responsibility for revenues, costs, and investments. In evaluating Brett's performance, Fonda would want to use as a benchmark a hotel of a similar size influenced by the same uncontrollable factors—for example, location, demographic trends, and economic conditions—that affect HISF. If all these factors were the same, *differences* in performances of the two hotels would occur only because of differences in the two managers' performances. Benchmarking, which is also called *relative performance evaluation*, filters out the effects of the common uncontrollable factors.

Can the performance of two managers responsible for running similar operations within a company be benchmarked against one another? Yes, but this approach could create a problem: The use of these benchmarks may reduce incentives for these managers to help one another. That's because a manager's performance-evaluation measure improves either by doing a better job or as a result of the other manager doing poorly. When managers do not cooperate and work together, the company suffers. In this case, using internal benchmarks for performance evaluation may not lead to goal congruence.

Performance Measures at the Individual Activity Level

There are two issues when evaluating performance at the individual-activity level:

1. Designing performance measures for activities that require multiple tasks
2. Designing performance measures for activities done in teams

Performing Multiple Tasks

Most employees perform more than one task as part of their jobs. Marketing representatives sell products, provide customer support, and gather market information. Manufacturing workers are responsible for both the quantity and quality of their output. Employers want employees to allocate their time and effort intelligently among various tasks or aspects of their jobs.

Consider mechanics at an auto repair shop. Their jobs have two distinct aspects: repair work—performing more repair work generates more revenues for the shop—and customer satisfaction—the higher the quality of the job, the more likely the customer will be pleased. If the employer wants an employee to focus on both aspects, then the employer must measure and compensate performance on both aspects.

If managers are evaluated on a single performance measure, they will treat other measures as secondary to that single measure. For example, managers might curtail advertising and maintenance to increase the current year's ROI. This is why performance evaluation needs to be based on a variety of factors, as in the balanced scorecard.

Suppose the employer can easily measure the quantity, but not the quality, of auto repairs. If the employer rewards workers on a by-the-job rate, which pays workers only on the basis of the number of repairs actually performed, mechanics will likely increase the number of repairs they make and quality will likely suffer. Sears, Roebuck and Co. experienced this problem when it introduced by-the-job rates for its mechanics. To resolve the problem, Sears' managers took three steps to motivate workers to balance both quantity and quality. (1) They dropped the by-the-job rate system and paid mechanics an hourly salary, a step that deemphasized the quantity of repairs. Management determined mechanics' bonuses, promotions, and pay increases on the basis of an assessment of each mechanic's overall performance regarding quantity and quality of repairs. (2) Sears evaluated employees, in part, using data such as customer-satisfaction surveys, the number of dissatisfied customers, and the number of customer complaints. (3) Finally, Sears used staff from an independent outside agency to randomly monitor whether the repairs performed were of high quality.

Team-Based Compensation Arrangements

Team-based incentive compensation encourages employees to work together to achieve common goals. Individual-based incentive compensation rewards employees for their own performance, consistent with responsibility accounting. A mix of both types of incentives encourages employees to maximize their own performance while working together in the best interest of the company as a whole.

Many manufacturing, marketing, and design problems can be resolved when employees with multiple skills, knowledge, experiences, and perceptions pool their talents. A team achieves better results than individual employees acting alone.[11] Companies reward individuals on a team based on team performance. Such team-based incentives encourage individuals to help one another as they strive toward a common goal.

The specific forms of team-based compensation vary across companies. Colgate Palmolive rewards teams on the basis of each team's performance. Novartis, the Swiss pharmaceutical company, rewards teams on companywide performance—a certain amount of team-based bonuses are paid only if the company reaches certain goals. To

[11] *Teams That Click: The Results-Driven Manager Series* (Boston: Harvard Business School Press, 2004).

encourage the development of team skills, Tennessee Eastman, a chemical manufacturer, rewards team members using a checklist of team skills, such as communication and willingness to help one another. Whether team-based compensation is desirable depends, to a large extent, on the culture and management style of a particular organization. For example, one criticism of team-based compensation, especially in the United States, is that incentives for individual employees to excel are diminished, harming overall performance. Another problem is how to manage team members who are not productive contributors to the team's success but who, nevertheless, share in the team's rewards.

Executive Performance Measures and Compensation

The principles of performance evaluation described in the previous sections also apply to executive compensation plans. These plans are based on both financial and nonfinancial performance measures and consist of a mix of (1) base salary; (2) annual incentives, such as a cash bonus based on achieving a target annual RI; (3) long-run incentives, such as stock options (described later in this section) based on stock performance over, say, a five-year period; and (4) other benefits, such as medical benefits, pensions plans, and life insurance.[12]

Well-designed plans use a compensation mix that balances risk (the effect of uncontrollable factors on the performance measure and hence compensation) with short-run and long-run incentives to achieve the organization's goals. For example, evaluating performance on the basis of annual EVA sharpens an executive's short-run focus. And using EVA and stock option plans over, say, five years motivates the executive to take a long-run view as well.

Stock options give executives the right to buy company stock at a specified price (called the exercise price) within a specified period. Suppose that on September 16, 2004, Marriott International gave its CEO the option to buy 200,000 shares of Marriott stock at any time before June 30, 2012, at the September 16, 2004, market price of $49 per share. Let's say Marriott's stock price rises to $69 per share on March 24, 2010, and the CEO exercises his options on all 200,000 shares. The CEO would earn $20 ($69 – $49) per share on 200,000 shares, or $4 million. If Marriott's stock price stays below $49 during the entire period, the CEO will simply forgo his right to buy the shares. By linking CEO compensation to increases in the company's stock price, the stock option plan motivates the CEO to improve the company's long-run performance and stock price. (See also the Concepts in Action feature, p. 810.)

Accounting rules in force at the time this book was written require U.S. companies to, at the very least, disclose in a note to the financial statements the effect on net income and earnings per share if the company had recognized an expense equal to the estimated fair market value of the options on the grant date.[13] Many companies, however, such as Coca-Cola, have chosen to recognize stock option expense in their income statements. Accounting regulators in the United States are currently debating whether to require all companies to recognize stock option expense in their income statements.

The Securities and Exchange Commission (SEC) requires detailed disclosures of the compensation arrangements of top-level executives. In complying with these rules in 2004, Marriott International, for example, disclosed a compensation table showing the salaries, bonuses, stock options, other stock awards, and other compensation earned by its top five executives during the 2001, 2002, and 2003 fiscal years. Marriott also disclosed how well its stock performed relative to a measure of the broad market (S&P 500 Index) and stocks of other motels and hotels (the S&P Lodging Hotel Index). Investors use this information to evaluate the relationship between compensation and performance across companies generally, across companies of similar sizes, and across companies operating in similar industries.

---

[12] *The Wall Street Journal*/Mercer Human Resource Consulting, *2003 CEO Compensation Survey and Trends* (New York: Mercer Human Resource Consulting, May 2004).

[13] If the exercise price is less than the market price of the stock on the date the options are granted, the company must recognize compensation cost equal to the difference between the two prices. This difference is less than the fair market value of the options. The company can choose either to recognize the full fair market value as a cost or to disclose in a note to the financial statements the effect on net income and earnings per share.

CONCEPTS IN ACTION

CEO Compensation and Company Performance

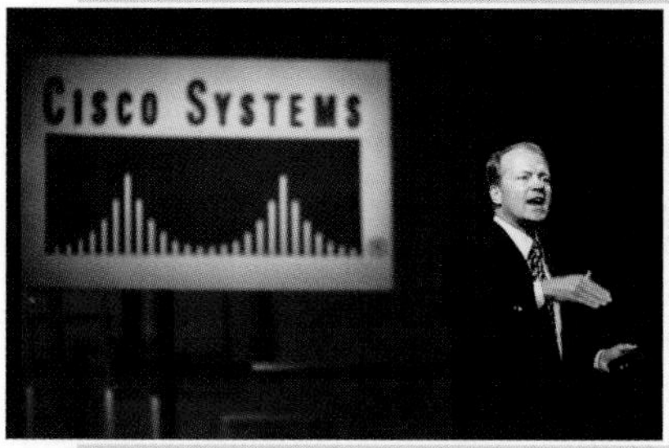

Over the years, CEO compensation has been a hot-button issue for many publicly-traded companies, their shareholders, the general public, and the government. The recent wave of corporate scandals has only intensified the scrutiny placed on the large salaries, stock-option grants, and other executive perks given to corporate heads. The following table summarizes the 2003 compensation packages for the highest-paid CEOs of Fortune 500 companies:

CEO	Company	Return to Shareholders in 2003	Total Compensation	Salary & Bonus	Value of Stock Options Granted in 2003	Value of Restricted Stock Granted in 2003	Other
Larry Culp, Jr.	Danaher	39.8%	$53,000,000	6%	41%	52%	1%
Chuck Cawley	MBNA	32.9%	$52,100,000	14%	32%	53%	1%
John Chambers	Cisco Systems	85.0%	$47,700,000	0%	100%	0%	0%
James Cayne	Bear Stearns	36.1%	$42,400,000	26%	20%	25%	29%
Larry Glasscock	Anthem	19.2%	$32,900,000	10%	24%	0%	66%

These packages are generally characterized by substantial stock-option grants, which are directly linked to a company's stock-price performance. CEOs with stock-option-heavy packages, such as John Chambers of Cisco, earn very high compensation if their companies perform well. In contrast, the following table outlines the 2003 compensation packages for the lowest-paid Fortune 500 CEOs.

CEO	Company	Return to Shareholders in 2003	Total Compensation	Salary & Bonus	Value of Stock Options Granted in 2003	Value of Restricted Stock Granted in 2003	Other
Richard Kinder	Kinder Morgan	50.3%	$1	100%	0%	0%	0%
Warren Buffett	Berkshire Hathaway	15.8%	$308,000	32%	0%	0%	68%
Charles Jenkins, Jr.	Publix Supermarkets	N/A	$564,000	96%	0%	0%	4%
Donald Anderson	TransMontaigne	39.0%	$595,000	70%	0%	29%	1%
Glenn Tilton	UAL	13.4%	$777,000	96%	0%	0%	4%

The lowest-paid Fortune 500 CEOs are characterized by the absence of stock options in their compensation arrangements, though Richard Kinder owns 19.5% of Kinder Morgan stock and Warren Buffett has a net worth of over $36 billion, mostly in Berkshire Hathaway stock. These compensation packages lack a strong, direct link to company performance.

This raises an interesting question: Does a company's performance differ depending on how a CEO is compensated? Most shareholders, analysts, and boards of directors believe that linking compensation to performance motivates CEOs, attracts talent, and is seen as fair. But changes are coming. As a result of external pressures and strengthened demand for results, boards of directors and their compensation committees are making modifications in the structure of CEO compensation packages. Many companies, such as General Electric and Microsoft, are moving away from granting stock options, rebalancing the long-term incentive mix, and reigning in overall pay while strengthening the link between pay and performance.

Source: Adapted from M. Boyle, "When Will They Stop?" *Fortune* (May 3, 2004) and *The Wall Street Journal*/Mercer Human Resource Consulting, *2003 CEO Compensation Survey and Trends* (New York: Mercer Human Resource Consulting, May 2004).

The SEC rules also require companies to disclose the principles underlying their executive compensation plans and the performance criteria—such as profitability, revenue growth, and market share—used in determining compensation. In its annual report, Marriott International described these principles as "building a strong correlation between stockholder return and executive compensation, offering incentives that encourage attainment of short-run and long-run business goals, and providing a total level of pay that is commensurate with performance." Marriott uses cash flow, earnings per share, and guest satisfaction as performance criteria to determine annual incentives for its executives.

Strategy and Levers of Control[14]

9

Describe the four levers of control and why they are necessary

. . . boundary, belief, and interactive control systems counterbalance diagnostic control systems

Given the management accounting focus of this book, this chapter has emphasized the role of quantitative financial and nonfinancial performance-evaluation measures that companies use to implement their strategies. These measures—such as ROI, RI, EVA, customer satisfaction, and employee satisfaction—monitor critical performance variables that help managers track progress toward achieving a company's strategic goals. Because these measures help diagnose whether a company is performing to expectations, they are collectively called **diagnostic control systems**. Companies motivate managers to achieve these goals by holding managers accountable for and by rewarding them for meeting these goals. The concern, however, is that the pressure to perform may cause managers to cut corners and misreport numbers to make their performance look better than it is, as happened at companies such as Enron, WorldCom, Tyco, and Health South (see also the Focus on Values and Behaviors feature below). To avoid unethical behavior, companies need to balance the push for performance resulting from diagnostic control systems, the first of four levers of control, with three other levers: *boundary systems, belief systems,* and *interactive control systems*.

Boundary systems describe standards of behavior and codes of conduct expected of all employees, especially actions that are off-limits. Ethical behavior on the part of managers is paramount. In particular, numbers that subunit managers report should not be tainted by "cooking the books." They should be free of, for example, overstated assets, understated liabilities, fictitious revenues, and understated costs.

FOCUS ON VALUES AND BEHAVIORS

THE COURAGE TO SAY NO

Managers often face intense performance pressures. Sometimes these pressures cause them to search for ways—sometimes unethical and illegal—to book profit that makes their performance look better and helps them earn higher rewards. Management and financial accountants must never participate in these illegal actions, as the case of Betty Vinson illustrates.

Vinson joined WorldCom as a staff accountant in 1996 and was soon promoted to a senior accounting position responsible for compiling quarterly results. As the telecommunications industry revenues dried up in 2000, WorldCom faced immense pressure to reduce expenses and remain profitable. When expense reduction failed, CFO Scott Sullivan and Controller David Myers asked Vinson and her accounting colleagues to draw down $828 million from a reserve account instead of recording expenses. Convinced the transaction was wrong, she nonetheless participated when told it was a one-time solution. From late 2000 to early 2002 Vinson was continually pressured into making illegal transfers, including re-entering "line costs" as capital expenditures rather than operating leases in clear violation of SEC rules.

Though Vinson resolved to resign, she faced personal financial pressures as the provider of income and health insurance for her family. Vinson remained at WorldCom and continued the fraudulent accounting practices. In 2002, Vinson decided she had had enough. Unfortunately, it was too late. The SEC had already begun an inquiry into WorldCom's accounting practices and on June 26, 2002, announced that it had found $3.8 billion in fraudulent accounting entries at WorldCom.

Vinson cooperated with federal regulators and prosecutors and initially believed she would not be prosecuted. But U.S. attorneys had other ideas: Because Vinson had made her own decisions about the capital expenditure accounts into which line costs were transferred, she bore responsibility for WorldCom's accounting fraud. Vinson was named as an unindicted co-conspirator. She pleaded guilty to two criminal counts of conspiracy and securities fraud in October 2002. Vinson is awaiting final sentencing and could serve a maximum term of up to 15 years in prison.

Source: *Pulliam, S., "Over the Line: A Staffer Ordered to Commit Fraud Balked, Then Caved,"* The Wall Street Journal, *June 23, 2003, p. A1*

[14]For a more-detailed discussion see R. Simons, "Control in an Age of Empowerment," *Harvard Business Review* (March-April 1995).

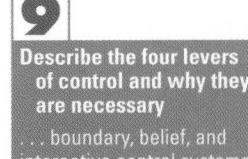

Codes of business conduct signal appropriate and inappropriate individual behaviors. The following is from Caterpillar Tractor's "Code of Worldwide Business Conduct and Operating Principles":

> *The law is a floor. Ethical business conduct should normally exist at a level well above the minimum required by law. Caterpillar employees shall not accept costly entertainment or gifts (excepting mementos and novelties of nominal value) from dealers, suppliers and others with whom we do business. And we won't tolerate circumstances that produce, or reasonably appear to produce, conflict between personal interests of an employee and interests of the company.*

Division managers often cite enormous pressure from top management "to make the budget" as excuses or rationalizations for not adhering to ethical accounting policies and procedures. A healthy amount of motivational pressure is desirable, as long as the "tone from the top" and the code of conduct simultaneously communicate the absolute need for all managers to behave ethically at all times. Managers should train employees to behave ethically. They should promptly and severely reprimand unethical conduct, regardless of the benefits that might accrue to the company from unethical actions. Some companies, such as Lockheed-Martin, emphasize ethical behavior by routinely evaluating employees against a business code of ethics.

Many organizations also set explicit boundaries precluding actions that harm the environment. Environmental violations (such as water and air pollution) carry heavy fines and are prison offenses under the laws of the United States and other countries. But in many companies, environmental responsibilities extend beyond legal requirements.

Socially responsible companies, such as BP, set aggressive environmental goals and measure and report their performance against them. German, Swiss, Dutch, and Scandinavian companies report on environmental performance as part of a larger set of social responsibility disclosures (such as employee welfare and community development activities). Some companies, such as DuPont, make environmental performance a line item on every employee's salary appraisal report. Duke Power Company appraises employees on their performance in reducing solid waste, cutting emissions and discharges, and implementing environmental plans. The result? Duke Power has met all its environmental goals.

Belief systems articulate the mission, purpose, and core values of a company. They describe the accepted norms and patterns of behavior expected of all managers and employees with respect to each other, shareholders, customers, and communities. Johnson & Johnson describes its values and norms in its credo statement:

> *We believe our first responsibility is to the doctors, nurses and patients, to mothers and fathers and all others who use our products and services. . . . Everything we do must be of high quality.*
>
> *We are responsible to our employees. . . . We must respect their dignity and recognize their merit. They must have a sense of security in their jobs. . . . We must be mindful of ways to help our employees fulfill their family responsibilities and provide opportunity for development and advancement. . . . Our actions must be just and ethical.*
>
> *We are responsible to the communities in which we live. . . . We must support good works and charities and bear our fair share of taxes. . . . We must encourage better health and education.*
>
> *Our final responsibility is to our stockholders. Business must make a sound profit. . . . We must experiment with new ideas . . . develop innovative programs and pay for mistakes.*

Johnson & Johnson's credo is intended to inspire all managers and other employees to do their best. Belief systems play to employees' intrinsic motivations.

Intrinsic motivation is the desire to achieve self-satisfaction from good performance regardless of external rewards such as bonuses or promotion. Intrinsic motivation comes from being given greater responsibility, doing interesting and creative work, having pride in doing that work, establishing commitment to the organization, and developing personal bonds with coworkers. High intrinsic motivation enhances performance because managers and workers have a sense of achievement in doing something important, feel satisfied with their jobs, and see opportunities for personal growth.

Interactive control systems are formal information systems that managers use to focus organization attention and learning on key strategic issues. An excessive focus on diagnostic control systems and critical performance variables can cause an organization to ignore emerging threats and opportunities—changes in technology, customer preferences, regulations, and industry competition that can undercut a business.

Interactive control systems track strategic uncertainties that businesses face, such as the emergence of digital imaging in the case of Kodak and Fujifilm, airline deregulation in the case of American Airlines and Southwest Airlines, and the shift in customer preferences for mini- and microcomputers in the case of IBM. The result is ongoing discussion and debate about assumptions and action plans. New strategies emerge from the dialogue and debate surrounding the interactive process. Interactive control systems force busy managers to step back from the actions needed to manage the business today and to shift their focus forward to positioning the organization for the opportunities and threats of tomorrow.

Measuring and rewarding managers for achieving critical performance variables is an important driver of corporate performance. But these diagnostic control systems must be counterbalanced by the other levers of control—boundary systems, belief systems, and interactive control systems—to ensure that proper business ethics, inspirational values, and attention to future threats and opportunities are not sacrificed while achieving business results.

PROBLEM FOR SELF-STUDY

The Baseball Division of Home Run Sports manufactures and sells baseballs. Assume production equals sales. Budgeted data for February 2006 are:

Current assets	\$ 400,000
Long-term assets	600,000
Total assets	\$1,000,000
Production output	200,000 baseballs per month
Target ROI (Operating income ÷ Total assets)	30%
Fixed costs	\$ 400,000 per month
Variable cost	\$4 per baseball

Required

1. Compute the minimum selling price per baseball necessary to achieve the target ROI of 30%.
2. Using the selling price from requirement 1, separate the target ROI into its two components using the DuPont method.
3. Compute the RI of the Baseball Division for February 2006, using the selling price from requirement 1. Home Run Sports uses a required rate of return of 12% on total division assets when computing division RI.
4. In addition to her salary, Pamela Stephenson, the division manager, receives 3% of the monthly RI of the Baseball Division as a bonus. Compute Stephenson's bonus. Why do you think Stephenson is rewarded using both salary and a performance-based bonus? Stephenson does not like bearing risk.

SOLUTION

1.

$$\text{Target operating income} = 30\% \text{ of } \$1,000,000 \text{ of total assets}$$
$$= \$300,000$$
$$\text{Let } P = \text{Selling price}$$
$$\text{Revenues} - \text{Variable costs} - \text{Fixed costs} = \text{Operating income}$$
$$200,000P - (200,000 \times \$4) - \$400,000 = \$300,000$$
$$200,000P = \$300,000 + \$800,000 + \$400,000$$
$$= \$1,500,000$$
$$P = \$7.50 \text{ per baseball}$$

Proof:		
	Revenues, 200,000 baseballs × \$7.50/baseball	\$1,500,000
	Variable costs, 200,000 baseballs × \$4/baseball	800,000
	Contribution margin	700,000
	Fixed costs	400,000
	Operating income	\$ 300,000

2. The DuPont method describes ROI as the product of two components: return on sales (income ÷ revenues) and investment turnover (revenues ÷ investment).

$$\frac{\text{Income}}{\text{Revenues}} \times \frac{\text{Revenues}}{\text{Investment}} = \frac{\text{Income}}{\text{Investment}}$$

$$\frac{\$300{,}000}{\$1{,}500{,}000} \times \frac{\$1{,}500{,}000}{\$1{,}000{,}000} = \frac{\$300{,}000}{\$1{,}000{,}000}$$

$$0.2 \times 1.5 = 0.30, \text{ or } 30\%$$

3. $$\begin{aligned} RI &= \text{Operating income} - \text{Required return on investment} \\ &= \$300{,}000 - (0.12 \times \$1{,}000{,}000) \\ &= \$300{,}000 - \$120{,}000 \\ &= \$180{,}000 \end{aligned}$$

4. $$\begin{aligned} \text{Stephenson's bonus} &= 3\% \text{ of } RI \\ &= 0.03 \times \$180{,}000 = \$5{,}400 \end{aligned}$$

The Baseball Division's RI is affected by many factors, such as general economic conditions, beyond Stephenson's control. These uncontrollable factors make the Baseball Division's profitability uncertain and risky. Because Stephenson does not like bearing risk, paying her a flat salary, regardless of RI, would shield Stephenson from this risk. But there is a moral-hazard problem with this compensation arrangement. Because Stephenson's effort is difficult to monitor, the absence of performance-based compensation will provide Stephenson with no incentive to undertake extra physical and mental effort beyond what is necessary to retain her job or to uphold her personal values.

Paying no salary and rewarding Stephenson only on the basis of RI provides Stephenson with incentives to work hard but also subjects her to excessive risk because of uncontrollable factors that will affect RI and hence Stephenson's compensation. A compensation arrangement based only on RI would be more costly for Home Run Sports because it would have to compensate Stephenson for taking on uncontrollable risk. A compensation arrangement that consists of both a salary and an RI-based performance bonus balances the benefits of incentives against the extra costs of imposing uncontrollable risk.

DECISION POINTS

The following question-and-answer format summarizes the chapter's learning objectives. Each decision presents a key question related to a learning objective. The guidelines are the answer to that question.

Decision	**Guidelines**
1. What financial and nonfinancial performance measures do companies use in their balanced scorecards?	Financial measures such as return on investment and residual income measure aspects of both manager performance and organization-subunit performance. In many cases, financial measures are supplemented with nonfinancial measures of performance from the customer, internal-business-process, and learning-and-growth perspectives of the balanced scorecard—for example, customer-satisfaction, quality of products and services, and employee satisfaction.
2. What are the steps in designing an accounting-based performance measure?	The steps are (a) choose performance measures that align with top management's financial goals, (b) choose the time horizon of each performance measure, (c) choose a definition of the components in each performance measure, (d) choose a measurement alternative for each performance measure, (e) choose a target level of performance, and (f) choose the timing of feedback.
3. How does the DuPont method analyze return on investment?	The DuPont method describes return on investment (ROI) as the product of two components: income divided by revenues (return on sales) and revenues divided by investment (investment turnover). For example, ROI can be increased by increasing revenues, decreasing costs, and decreasing investment.

4. What is residual income and what are its advantages?	Residual income (RI) is income minus a dollar amount of required return on investment. RI is designed to overcome some of the limitations of ROI. For example, RI is more likely than ROI to promote goal congruence. ROI may induce managers of highly profitable divisions to reject projects (because accepting the project reduces ROI) even though the project should be accepted from the perspective of the company as a whole.
5. What is economic value added?	Economic value added (EVA) is a variation of the RI calculation. It equals after-tax operating income minus the product of (after-tax) weighted-average cost of capital and total assets minus current liabilities.
6. Should companies use the current cost or the historical cost of assets to measure performance?	Current cost of an asset is the cost now of purchasing an asset identical to the one currently held. Historical-cost asset-measurement methods generally consider net book value of the assets, which is original cost minus accumulated depreciation. Historical-cost measures are often inadequate for measuring economic returns. Current-cost measures are better. More generally, however, problems in any performance measure can be overcome by emphasizing budgets and targets that stress continuous improvement.
7. How can companies compare the performance of divisions operating in different countries?	Comparing the performance of divisions operating in different countries is difficult because of legal, political, social, economic, and currency differences. ROI and RI calculations for subunits operating in different countries need to be adjusted for differences in inflation between the two countries and changes in exchange rates.
8. Why are managers compensated based on a mix of salary and incentives?	Companies create incentives by rewarding managers on the basis of performance. But managers face risks because factors beyond their control may also affect their performance. Owners choose a mix of salary and incentive compensation to trade off the incentive benefit against the cost of imposing risk.
9. What are the four levers of control, and why does a company need to implement them?	The four levers of control are diagnostic control systems, boundary systems, belief systems, and interactive control systems. Implementing the four levers of control helps a company simultaneously strive for performance, behave ethically, inspire employees, and respond to strategic threats and opportunities.

TERMS TO LEARN

This chapter and the Glossary at the end of this book contain definitions of:

belief systems (p. 812)
boundary systems (p. 811)
current cost (p. 800)
diagnostic control systems (p. 811)
economic value added (EVA®) (p. 796)
imputed costs (p. 795)
interactive control systems (p. 812)
investment (p. 793)
moral hazard (p. 806)
residual income (RI) (p. 795)
return on investment (ROI) (p. 793)

PH Grade Assist

Prentice Hall Grade Assist (PHGA)
Your professor may ask you to complete selected exercises and problems in Prentice Hall Grade Assist (PHGA). PHGA is an online tool that can help you master the chapter's topics. It provides you with multiple variations of exercises and problems designated by the PHGA icon. You can rework these exercises and problems—each time with new data—as many times as you need. You also receive immediate feedback and grading.

ASSIGNMENT MATERIAL

Questions

23-1 Give examples of financial and nonfinancial performance measures that can be found in each of the four perspectives of the balanced scorecard.

23-2 What are the six steps in designing accounting-based performance measures?

23-3 What factors affecting ROI does the DuPont method of profitability analysis highlight?

23-4 "RI is not identical to ROI, although both measures incorporate income and investment into their computations." Do you agree? Explain.

23-5 Describe EVA.

23-6 Give three definitions of investment used in practice when computing ROI.

23-7 Distinguish between measuring assets based on current cost and historical cost.

23-8 What special problems arise when evaluating performance in multinational companies?

23-9 Why is it important to distinguish between the performance of a manager and the performance of the organization subunit for which the manager is responsible? Give an example.

23-10 Describe moral hazard.

23-11 "Managers should be rewarded only on the basis of their performance measures. They should be paid no salary." Do you agree? Explain.

23-12 Explain the role of benchmarking in evaluating managers.

23-13 Explain the incentive problems that can arise when employees must perform multiple tasks as part of their jobs.

23-14 Describe two disclosures required by the SEC with respect to executive compensation.

23-15 Describe the four levers of control.

Exercises

23-16 ROI, comparisons of three companies. (CMA, adapted) Return on investment (ROI) is often expressed as follows:

$$\frac{\text{Income}}{\text{Investment}} = \frac{\text{Income}}{\text{Revenues}} \times \frac{\text{Revenues}}{\text{Investment}}$$

Required

1. What advantages are there in the breakdown of the computation into two separate components?
2. Fill in the following blanks:

	Companies in Same Industry		
	A	**B**	**C**
Revenues	$1,000,000	$500,000	?
Income	$ 100,000	$ 50,000	?
Investment	$ 500,000	?	$5,000,000
Income as a percentage of revenues	?	?	0.5%
Investment turnover	?	?	2
ROI	?	1%	?

After filling in the blanks, comment on the relative performance of these companies as thoroughly as the data permit.

Excel Lab
www.prenhall.com/horngren/cost12e

23-17 Analysis of return on invested assets, comparison of two divisions, DuPont method. Infotech Systems, Inc., has two divisions: Software and Services. Results (in millions) for the past three years are partially displayed here:

	A	B	C	D	E	F	G
1		**Operating Income**	**Operating Revenues**	**Total Assets**	**Operating Income / Operating Revenues**	**Operating Revenues / Total Assets**	**Operating Income / Total Assets**
2	**Software Division**						
3	**2006**	$340	$3,980	$ 960	?	?	?
4	**2007**	420	?	?	10%	?	42%
5	**2008**	580	?	?	11%	5	?
6	**Services Division**						
7	**2006**	$310	$1,180	$ 640	?	?	?
8	**2007**	?	1,500	900	22%	?	?
9	**2008**	?	?	1,170	?	2	25%
10	**Infotech Systems, Inc.**						
11	**2006**	$650	$5,160	$1,600	?	?	?
12	**2007**	?	?	?	?	?	?
13	**2008**	?	?	?	?	?	?

If you want to use Excel to solve this exercise, go to the Excel Lab at **www.prenhall.com/horngren/cost12e** and download the template for Exercise 23-17.

Required

1. Complete the table by filling in the blanks.
2. Use the DuPont method of profitability analysis to explain changes in the operating-income-to-total-assets ratios over the 2006 through 2008 period for each division and for Infotech Systems Inc. as a whole. Comment on the results.

PH Grade Assist

23-18 ROI and RI. (D. Kleespie, adapted) The Black Diamond Ski Company produces and distributes a wide variety of winter sports equipment. Its newest division, Nature Trails, manufactures and sells a single product:

Terrapin, a snowshoe made with high-tech materials. The demand for Terrapins is relatively insensitive to price changes. The following data are available for Nature Trails, which is an investment center for Black Diamond:

Total annual fixed costs	$15,000,000
Variable cost per pair of Terrapins	$ 250
Number of Terrapin pairs sold each year	150,000
Average operating assets invested in the division	$24,000,000

Required

1. Compute Nature Trails' ROI if the selling price of Terrapins is $360 per pair.
2. If management requires an ROI of at least 25% from the division, what is the minimum selling price that the Nature Trails Division should charge per pair of Terrapins?
3. Assume that Black Diamond judges the performance of its investment centers on the basis of RI rather than ROI. What is the minimum selling price that Nature Trails should charge per pair of Terrapins if the company's required rate of return is 20%?

23-19 Pricing, ROI, performance evaluation. Hardy, Inc.'s motorcycle division assembles motorcycles and uses long-run average demand to set the budgeted production level and budgeted costs for pricing purposes. The following information is available for the coming year:

PH Grade Assist

- Variable cost: $1,600 per unit
- Fixed costs: $24,000,000
- Investment (total assets): $80,000,000

Required

1. What level of operating income is required to attain an ROI (operating income as a percentage of total assets) of 20%? What level of revenues will be needed to achieve that operating income if Hardy assembles and sells 100,000 motorcycles? What will be the selling price of each motorcycle?
2. Using the selling price calculated in requirement 1, what ROI will Hardy earn if it sells 150,000 motorcycles? 50,000 motorcycles?
3. Lauren Snyder, the motorcycle division manager, is paid an annual bonus based on how much the actual ROI exceeds the target ROI of 20%. Last year, with the same cost structure and selling price, her division assembled and sold 150,000 motorcycles, compared with 100,000 motorcycles this year. How will she feel about the bonus plan this year? Suggest some reasons why she may feel that this bonus plan is not a fair measure of performance.

23-20 Financial and nonfinancial performance measures, goal congruence. (CMA, adapted) Summit Equipment specializes in the manufacture of medical equipment, a field that has become increasingly competitive. Approximately two years ago, Ben Harrington, president of Summit, decided to revise the bonus plan (based, at the time, entirely on operating income) to encourage division managers to focus on areas that were important to customers and that added value without increasing cost. In addition to a profitability incentive, the revised plan includes incentives for reduced rework costs, reduced sales returns, and on-time deliveries. Bonuses are calculated and awarded semiannually on the following basis: A base bonus is calculated at 2% of operating income; this amount is then adjusted as follows:

a. **(i)** Reduced by excess of rework costs over and above 2% of operating income
(ii) No adjustment if rework costs are less than or equal to 2% of operating income

b. **(i)** Increased by $5,000 if more than 98% of deliveries are on time, and by $2,000 if 96% to 98% of deliveries are on time
(ii) No adjustment if on-time deliveries are below 96%

c. **(i)** Increased by $3,000 if sales returns are less than or equal to 1.5% of sales
(ii) Decreased by 50% of excess of sales returns over 1.5% of sales

Note: If the calculation of the bonus results in a negative amount for a particular period, the manager simply receives no bonus, and the negative amount is not carried forward to the next period.

Results for Summit's Charter Division and Mesa Division for 2006, the first year under the new bonus plan, follow. In 2005, under the old bonus plan, the Charter Division manager earned a bonus of $27,060 and the Mesa Division manager, a bonus of $22,440.

	Charter Division		Mesa Division	
	January 1, 2006 to June 30, 2006	July 1, 2006 to Dec. 31, 2006	January 1, 2006 to June 30, 2006	July 1, 2006 to Dec. 31, 2006
Revenues	$4,200,000	$4,400,000	$2,850,000	$2,900,000
Operating income	$462,000	$440,000	$342,000	$406,000
On-time delivery	95.4%	97.3%	98.2%	94.6%
Rework costs	$11,500	$11,000	$6,000	$8,000
Sales returns	$84,000	$70,000	$44,750	$42,500

Required

1. Why did Harrington need to introduce these new performance measures? That is, why does Harrington need to use these performance measures in addition to the operating-income numbers for the period?

2. Calculate the bonus earned by each manager for each six-month period and for 2006.
3. What effect did the change in the bonus plan have on each manager's behavior? Did the new bonus plan achieve what Harrington desired? What changes, if any, would you make to the new bonus plan?

PH Grade Assist

23-21 ROI, RI, EVA. (D. Solomons, adapted) Consider the following data for the two geographical divisions of the Potomac Electric Company that operate as profit centers:

	Atlantic Division	Pacific Division
Total assets	$1,000,000	$5,000,000
Current liabilities	250,000	1,500,000
Operating income	200,000	750,000

Required

1. Calculate the ROI for each division using operating income as the measure of income and total assets as the measure of investment.
2. Potomac Electric has used RI as a measure of management performance, the variable it wants a manager to maximize. Using this criterion, what is the RI for each division using operating income and total assets, if the required rate of return on investment is 12%?
3. Potomac Electric has two sources of funds: long-term debt with a market value of $3,500,000 and an interest rate of 10%, and equity capital with a market value of $3,500,000 at a cost of equity of 14%. Potomac's income tax rate is 40%. Potomac applies the same weighted-average cost of capital to both divisions, because each division faces similar risks. Calculate the EVA for each division. Which of the measures calculated in requirements 1, 2, and 3 would you recommend Potomac Electric use? Why? Explain briefly.

Excel Lab
www.prenhall.com/horngren/cost12e

23-22 ROI, RI, EVA. The Burlingame Transport Company operates a Truck Rental Division (that rents trucks to individuals) and a Transportation Division (that transports goods from one city to another). Some division financial measures for 2006 are as follows:

	A	B	C
1		Truck Rental Division	Transportation Division
2	Total assets	$11,000,000	$9,500,000
3	Current liabilities	$ 2,200,000	$2,800,000
4	Operating income	$ 825,000	$ 855,000
5	Required rate of return	12%	12%

If you want to use Excel to solve this exercise, go to the Excel Lab at **www.prenhall.com/horngren/cost12e** and download the template for Exercise 23-22.

Required

1. Calculate return on investment (ROI) for each division using operating income as a measure of income and total assets as a measure of investment.
2. Calculate residual income (RI) for each division using operating income as a measure of income and total assets minus current liabilities as a measure of investment.
3. Tony Bratch, the Truck Rental Division manager, argues that the Transportation Division has "loaded up on a lot of short-term debt" to boost its RI. Calculate an alternative RI for each division that is not sensitive to the amount of short-term debt taken on by the Transportation Division. Comment on the result.
4. Burlingame, whose tax rate is 40%, has two sources of funds: long-term debt with a market value of $9,000,000 at an interest rate of 10%, and equity capital with a market value of $6,000,000 and a cost of equity of 15%. Applying the same weighted-average cost of capital (WACC) to each division, calculate EVA for each division.
5. Use your preceding calculations to comment on the relative performance of each division.

23-23 ROI, RI, measurement of assets. (CMA, adapted) Ashton Corporation recently announced a bonus plan to be awarded to the manager of the most profitable division. The three division managers are to choose whether ROI or RI will be used to measure profitability. In addition, they must decide whether investment will be measured using gross book value or net book value of assets. Ashton defines income as operating income and investment as total assets. The following information is available for the year just ended:

Division	Gross Book Value of Assets	Accumulated Depreciation	Operating Income
Bristol	$800,000	$430,000	$94,700
Darden	760,000	410,000	91,700
Gregory	500,000	280,000	61,400

Ashton uses a required rate of return of 10% on investment to calculate RI.

Each division manager has selected a method of bonus calculation that ranks his or her division Number 1. Identify the method for calculating profitability that each manager selected, supporting your answer with appropriate calculations. Comment on the strengths and weaknesses of the methods chosen by each manager.

Required

23-24 Multinational performance measurement, ROI, RI. The Sandvik Corporation manufactures electric motors in the United States and Sweden. The U.S. and Swedish operations are organized as decentralized divisions. The following information is available for 2006; ROI is calculated as operating income divided by total assets:

PH Grade Assist

	U.S. Division	Swedish Division
Operating income	?	8,100,000 kronas
Total assets	$8,000,000	52,500,000 kronas
ROI	15%	?

Both investments were made on December 31, 2005. The exchange rate at the time of Sandvik's investment in Sweden on December 31, 2005, was 7 kronas = $1. During 2006, the Swedish krona declined steadily in value so that the exchange rate on December 31, 2006, is 8 kronas = $1. The average exchange rate during 2006 is [(7 + 8) ÷ 2] = 7.5 kronas = $1.

Required

1. **a.** Calculate the U.S. division's operating income for 2006.
   b. Calculate the Swedish division's ROI for 2006 in kronas.
2. Top management wants to know which division earned a better ROI in 2006. What would you tell them? Explain your answer.
3. Which division do you think had the better RI performance? Explain your answer. The required rate of return on investment (calculated in U.S. dollars) is 12%.

23-25 Multinational performance measurement, ROI, RI. Loren Press has two printing presses that operate as separate divisions, one located in Durham, North Carolina, and the other in Nyon, Switzerland. The following information is available for 2007. The required rate of return on investments (calculated in U.S. dollars) is 15%.

	Durham Division	Nyon Division
Operating income	$ 765,000	1,040,000 Swiss francs
Total assets	$4,500,000	5,750,000 Swiss francs

Both investments were made on December 31, 2006. The exchange rate at the time of Loren's investment in Switzerland on December 31, 2006, was 1.15 Swiss francs = $1. During 2007, the Swiss franc declined steadily in value, reaching an exchange rate on December 31, 2007, of 1.45 Swiss francs = $1. The average exchange rate during 2007 is [(1.15 + 1.45) ÷ 2] = 1.30 Swiss francs = $1.

Required

1. **(a)** Calculate Durham Division's ROI for 2007. **(b)** Calculate Nyon Division's ROI for 2007 in Swiss francs. **(c)** Which division earned a better ROI in 2007? Explain.
2. Top management wants to compare the performance of the two divisions using RI. Which division do you think had the better RI performance? Explain your answer.
3. On the basis of your answers to requirements 1 and 2, which division is performing better? If you had to promote one of the division managers to vice president, which manager would you choose? Explain.

23-26 Risk sharing, incentives, benchmarking, multiple tasks. The Dexter Division of AMCO sells car batteries. AMCO's corporate management gives Dexter management considerable operating and investment autonomy in running the division. AMCO is considering how it should compensate Jim Marks, the general manager of the Dexter Division. Proposal 1 calls for paying Marks a fixed salary. Proposal 2 calls for paying Marks no salary and compensating him only on the basis of the division's ROI, calculated based on operating income before any bonus payments. Proposal 3 calls for paying Marks some salary and some bonus based on ROI. Assume that Marks does not like bearing risk.

Required

1. Evaluate the three proposals, specifying the advantages and disadvantages of each.
2. Suppose that AMCO competes against Tiara Industries in the car battery business. Tiara is approximately the same size and operates in a business environment that is similar to Dexter's. The top management of AMCO is considering evaluating Marks on the basis of Dexter's ROI minus Tiara's ROI. Marks complains that this approach is unfair because the performance of another company, over which he has no control, is included in his performance-evaluation measure. Is Marks's complaint valid? Why or why not?
3. Now suppose that Marks has no authority for making capital-investment decisions. Corporate management makes these decisions. Is ROI a good performance measure to use to evaluate Marks? Is ROI a good measure to evaluate the economic viability of the Dexter Division? Explain.
4. Dexter's salespersons are responsible for selling and providing customer service and support. Sales are easy to measure. Although customer service is important to Dexter in the long run, it has not yet implemented customer-service measures. Marks wants to compensate his sales force only

on the basis of sales commissions paid for each unit of product sold. He cites two advantages to this plan: (a) It creates strong incentives for the sales force to work hard, and (b) the company pays salespersons only when the company itself is earning revenues. Do you like his plan? Why or why not?

Problems

23-27 Relevant costs, performance evaluation, goal congruence. (N. Melumad, adapted) Pike Enterprises has three operating divisions. The managers of these divisions are evaluated on their division operating income, a figure that includes an allocation of corporate overhead proportional to the revenues of each division. The income statements (in thousands) for the first quarter of 2007 are as follows:

	Andorian Division	Orion Division	Tribble Division	Pike Enterprises
Revenues	$2,000	$1,200	$1,600	$4,800
Cost of goods sold	1,050	540	640	2,230
Gross margin	950	660	960	2,570
Division overhead	250	125	160	535
Corporate overhead	400	240	320	960
Division operating income	$ 300	$ 295	$ 480	$1,075

John Moore, the manager of the Andorian Division, is unhappy that his profitability is about the same as the Orion Division's and is much less than the Tribble Division's, even though his revenues are much higher than either of these divisions. Moore also knows that he is carrying one line of products with low profitability. He was going to replace this line of business as soon as more-profitable product opportunities became available, but he has kept it because the line is marginally profitable and uses facilities that would otherwise be idle. Moore now realizes, however, that the revenues from this product line are attracting a large amount of corporate overhead because of the allocation procedure in use. This low-margin line of products had the following characteristics (in thousands) for the most recent quarter:

- Revenues: $800
- Cost of goods sold: $600
- Avoidable division overhead: $100

Required

1. Prepare the income statement for Pike Enterprises for the second quarter of 2007. Assume that revenues and operating results are identical to the first quarter except that Moore has discontinued the low-margin product line.
2. Is Pike Enterprises better off from discontinuing the low-margin product line?
3. Is Moore better off from discontinuing the low-margin product line?
4. Suggest changes for Pike's system of division reporting and evaluation that will motivate division managers to make decisions that are in the best interest of Pike Enterprises as a whole. Discuss any potential disadvantages of your proposal.

23-28 ROI performance measures based on historical cost and current cost. Mineral Waters Ltd. operates three divisions that process and bottle sparkling mineral water. The historical-cost accounting system reports the following information for 2007:

	Calistoga Division	Alpine Springs Division	Rocky Mountains Division
Revenues	$500,000	$ 700,000	$1,100,000
Operating costs			
(excluding plant depreciation)	300,000	380,000	600,000
Plant depreciation	70,000	100,000	120,000
Operating income	$130,000	$ 220,000	$ 380,000
Current assets	$200,000	$ 250,000	$ 300,000
Long-term assets—plant	140,000	900,000	1,320,000
Total assets	$340,000	$1,150,000	$1,620,000

Mineral Waters estimates the useful life of each plant to be 12 years, with no terminal disposal value. The straight-line depreciation method is used. At the end of 2007, the Calistoga plant is 10 years old, the Alpine Springs plant is 3 years old, and the Rocky Mountains plant is 1 year old. An index of construction costs over the 10-year period that Mineral Waters has been operating (1997 year-end = 100) is:

1997	2004	2006	2007
100	136	160	170

Given the high turnover of current assets, management believes that the historical-cost and current-cost measures of current assets are approximately the same.

1. Compute the ROI ratio (operating income to total assets) of each division using historical-cost measures. Comment on the results.
2. Use the approach in Exhibit 23-2 (p. 802) to compute the ROI of each division, incorporating current-cost estimates as of 2007 for depreciation expense and long-term assets. Comment on the results.
3. What advantages might arise from using current-cost asset measures as compared with historical-cost measures for evaluating the performance of the managers of the three divisions?

Required

23-29 Evaluating managers, ROI, DuPont method, value-chain analysis of cost structure. Peach Computer Corporation is the largest personal computer company in the world. The CEO of Peach is retiring, and the board of directors is considering external candidates to fill the position. The board's top two choices are CEOs Peter Diamond (current CEO of NetPro) and Norma Provan (current CEO of On Point). As a board member on the search committee, you collect the following information (in millions):

Excel Lab
www.prenhall.com/horngren/cost12e

	A	B	C	D	E
1		NetPro		On Point	
2		2005	2006	2005	2006
3	Revenues	$600.0	$480.0	$300.0	$525.0
4	Costs				
5	R&D	71.2	40.2	35.9	76.1
6	Production	132.6	145.6	107.6	128.2
7	Marketing and distribution	173.2	193.7	96.4	153.8
8	Customer service	65.5	40.0	30.4	67.6
9	Total costs	442.5	419.5	270.3	425.7
10	Operating income	$157.5	$ 60.5	$ 29.7	$ 99.3
11	Total assets	$540.0	$510.0	$240.0	$360.0

In early 2007, a leading computer magazine gave On Point's main product five stars, its highest rating. NetPro's main product received three stars, down from five stars a year earlier. In the same article, On Point's new products received praise; NetPro's new products were judged as "mediocre."

If you want to use Excel to solve this problem, go to the Excel Lab at **www.prenhall.com/horngren/cost12e** and download the template for Problem 23-29.

Required

1. Use the DuPont method to calculate NetPro's and On Point's ROIs in 2005 and 2006. Comment on the results. What can you tell from the DuPont analysis that you might have missed from calculating ROI itself?
2. Compute the percentage of costs in each of the four business-function cost categories for NetPro and On Point in 2005 and 2006. Comment on the results.
3. Relate the results of requirements 1 and 2 to the comments made by the computer magazine. Of Diamond and Provan, whom would you suggest to be the new CEO of Peach?

23-30 ROI, RI, ROS, management incentives. (CMA, adapted) The Jump-Start Division (JSD) of Mason Industries manufactures go-carts and other recreational vehicles. JSD is considering building a new plant in 2007. The investment will cost $2.5 million. The expected revenues and costs for the new plant in 2007 are:

Revenues	$2,400,000
Variable costs	800,000
Fixed costs	1,120,000
Operating income	$ 480,000

JSD's ROI in 2006 is 24%, and its return on sales (ROS) is 19%. ROI is defined as operating income divided by total assets. The bonus of Maureen Grieco, the division manager of JSD, is based on division ROI.

Required

1. Explain why Grieco would be reluctant to build the new plant. Show your calculations.
2. Suppose Mason Industries uses RI to determine Grieco's bonus and the required rate of return on investment is 15%. Will Grieco be more willing to build the new plant? Explain.
3. Suppose Mason Industries uses ROS to determine Grieco's bonus. Will Grieco be more willing to build the new plant? What are the advantages and disadvantages of using ROS to determine Grieco's bonus?

23-31 Division manager's compensation, risk sharing, incentives (continuation of 23-30). The top management of Mason Industries is considering the following alternative compensation arrangements for Maureen Grieco, the division manager of JSD:

- Make Grieco's compensation a fixed salary without any bonus. Mason's top management believes that one advantage of this arrangement is that Grieco will be less inclined to reject future investments just because of their impact on ROI or RI.

- Make all of Grieco's compensation depend on the division's RI. The benefit of this arrangement is that it creates incentives for Grieco to aggressively seek and accept all proposals that increase JSD's RI.
- Evaluate Grieco's performance using benchmarking by comparing JSD's RI against the RI achieved by managers of other companies that also manufacture and sell go-carts and recreational vehicles and have comparable levels of investment. Mason's top management believes that the advantage of benchmarking is that it focuses attention on Grieco's performance relative to peers, rather than on the division's absolute performance.

Required

1. Assume Grieco does not like bearing risk. Using concepts of performance evaluation described in this chapter, evaluate the three proposals that Mason's top management is considering. Indicate the positive and negative features of each proposal.
2. What compensation arrangement would you recommend? Explain briefly.

23-32 ROI, RI, DuPont method, investment decisions, balanced scorecard. Media Group has two major divisions: Newspapers and Television. Summary financial data (in millions) for 2005 and 2006 are as follows:

Excel Lab
www.prenhall.com/horngren/cost12e

	A	B	C	D	E	F	G	H	I
1		Operating Income			Revenues			Total Assets	
2		2005	2006		2005	2006		2005	2006
3	Newspapers	1,890	2,310		9,450	9,660		9,240	10,290
4	Television	273	336		12,600	13,440		5,670	6,300

The two division managers' annual bonuses are based on division ROI (defined as operating income divided by total assets). If a division reports an increase in ROI from the prior year, its management is automatically eligible for a bonus; however, the management of a division reporting a decline in ROI has to present an explanation to the Media Group board and is unlikely to get any bonus.

Ken Kearney, manager of the Newspapers Division, is considering a proposal to invest $400 million in a high-speed color printing press. It is estimated that the new press's special color effects and the division's ability to cover late-breaking news will increase 2007 division operating income by $60 million. Media Group uses a 12% required rate of return on investment for each division.

If you want to use Excel to solve this problem, go to the Excel Lab at **www.prenhall.com/horngren/cost12e** and download the template for Problem 23-32.

Required

1. Use the DuPont method of profitability analysis to explain differences in 2006 ROIs between the two divisions. Use 2006 total assets as the investment base.
2. Why might Kearney be less than enthusiastic about accepting the investment proposal for the high-speed color printing press, despite his belief in the benefits of the new printing technology?
3. Rupert Bronson, CEO of Media Group, is considering a proposal to base division executive compensation on division RI.
   a. Compute the 2006 RI of each division.
   b. Would adoption of an RI measure reduce Kearney's reluctance to adopt the high-speed color printing press investment proposal?
4. Bronson is concerned that the focus on annual ROI could have an adverse long-run effect on Media Group's customers. What other measurements, if any, do you recommend that Bronson use? Explain briefly.

23-33 Division managers' compensation, levers of control (continuation of 23-32). Rupert Bronson seeks your advice on revising the existing bonus plan for division managers of Media Group. Assume division managers do not like bearing risk. He is considering three ideas:

- Make each division manager's compensation depend on division RI.
- Make each division manager's compensation depend on companywide RI.
- Use benchmarking, and compensate division managers on the basis of their division's RI minus the RI of the other division.

Required

1. Evaluate the three ideas Bronson has put forth using performance-evaluation concepts described in this chapter. Indicate the positive and negative features of each proposal.
2. Bronson is concerned that the pressure for short-run performance may cause managers to cut corners. What systems might Bronson introduce to avoid this problem? Explain briefly.
3. Bronson is also concerned that the pressure for short-run performance might cause managers to ignore emerging threats and opportunities. What system might Bronson introduce to avoid this problem? Explain briefly.

23-34 Ethics, manager's performance evaluation. (A. Spero, adapted) Hamilton Semiconductors manufactures specialized chips that sell for $20 each. Hamilton's manufacturing costs consist of variable cost of $2 per chip and fixed costs of $9,000,000. Hamilton also incurs $400,000 in fixed marketing costs each year.

Hamilton calculates operating income using absorption costing—that is, Hamilton calculates manufacturing cost per unit by dividing total manufacturing costs by actual production. Hamilton costs all units in inventory at this rate and expenses the costs in the income statement at the time when the units in inventory are sold. Next year, 2007, appears to be a difficult year for Hamilton. It expects to sell only 500,000 units. The demand for these chips fluctuates considerably, so Hamilton usually holds minimal inventory.

Required

1. Calculate Hamilton's operating income in 2007 (a) if Hamilton manufactures 500,000 units and (b) if Hamilton manufactures 600,000 units.
2. Would it be unethical for Randy Jones, the general manager of Hamilton Semiconductors, to produce more units than can be sold in order to show better operating results? Jones's compensation has a bonus component based on operating income. Explain your answer.
3. Would it be unethical for Jones to ask distributors to buy more product than they need? Hamilton follows the industry practice of booking sales when products are shipped to distributors. Explain your answer.

23-35 Ethics, levers of control. (R. Madison, adapted, *Strategic Finance*, January 2000). United Forest Products (UFP) is a large timber and wood processing plant. UFP's performance-evaluation system pays its managers substantial bonuses if the company achieves annual budgeted profit numbers. In the last quarter of 2005, Amy Kimbell, UFP's controller, noted a slight increase in output and a significant decrease in the purchase cost of raw timber.

One day when Kimbell was at the log yard where timber is received and scaled (weighed and checked for quality) to determine what UFP pays for it, she noted that a timber contractor was quite aggravated when he was given the scale report (board feet and quality). When she asked one of the scale employees what was bothering the contractor, he revealed that the scalers had received instructions from their supervisors to deliberately "lowball" evaluations of timber quantity and quality. This reduced the price paid to timber suppliers, which also reduced direct material costs, helping UFP to meet its profit target.

Required

1. What should Kimbell do? You may want to refer to *Standards of Ethical Conduct for Management Accountants and Resolution of Ethical Conflict*, pp. 16–17.
2. Which lever of control is UFP emphasizing? What changes, if any, should be made?

Collaborative Learning Problem

23-36 ROI, RI, division manager's compensation, balanced scorecard. Key information for the Peoria Division (PD) of Barrington Industries for 2006 follows.

Revenues	$15,000,000
Operating income	$ 1,800,000
Total assets	$10,000,000

PD's managers are evaluated and rewarded on the basis of ROI defined as operating income divided by total assets. Barrington Industries expects its divisions to increase ROI each year.

Next year, 2007, appears to be a difficult year for PD. PD had planned a new investment to improve quality but, in view of poor economic conditions, has postponed the investment. ROI for 2007 was certain to decrease if PD had made the investment.

Management is now considering ways to meet its target ROI of 20% for next year. It anticipates revenues to be steady at $15,000,000 in 2007.

Required

1. Calculate PD's return on sales (ROS) and ROI for 2006.
2. **a.** By how much would PD need to cut costs in 2007 to achieve its target ROI of 20%, assuming no change in total assets between 2006 and 2007?
   b. By how much would PD need to decrease total assets in 2007 to achieve its target ROI of 20%, assuming no change in operating income between 2006 and 2007?
3. Calculate PD's RI in 2006 assuming a required rate of return on investment of 15%.
4. PD wants to increase RI by 50% in 2007. Assuming it could cut costs by $45,000 in 2007, by how much would PD need to decrease total assets in 2007?
5. Barrington Industries is concerned that the focus on cost cutting, asset sales, and no new investments will have an adverse long-run effect on PD's customers. Yet Barrington wants PD to meet its financial goals. What other measurements, if any, do you recommend that Barrington use? Explain briefly.

Get Connected: Cost Accounting in the News

Go to www.prenhall.com/horngren/cost12e for additional online exercise(s) that explore issues affecting the accounting world today. These exercises offer you the opportunity to analyze and reflect on how cost accounting helps managers to make better decisions and handle the challenges of strategic planning and implementation.

CHAPTER 23 Video Case

McDONALD'S CORPORATION: Performance Measurement and Compensation

Not long ago, McDonald's top management wanted to revise the compensation package for managers in all 1,800 of its U.S.-based company-owned restaurants. The revision was intended to make sure the company continued to offer a competitive compensation package to managers. Top management also was interested in improving the linkage between its corporate vision and management incentives. The question facing management was: What was the best structure for the new plan?

McDonald's was founded in 1955 by Ray Kroc, a milkshake-machine salesman of great personal ambition. On a chance visit to a restaurant in Southern California, he noted the long line of customers waiting to buy a milkshake. If customers would come and wait at one restaurant for shakes, he reasoned, certainly they would come if there were other locations. The restaurant was owned by the McDonald brothers. Ray Kroc approached the brothers about expanding to multiple locations—the rest is history.

Ray Kroc built McDonald's around a new food-production system that applied precise procedures that not only helped streamline operations for efficient service, but also created a pleasant family atmosphere for dining. Standards were established for food portions, and equipment was designed to prepare meals quickly. The words "quality, service, cleanliness, and value," or QSCV, stood behind every meal, every customer interaction, every day. Ray Kroc wanted each customer's restaurant experience to be the best.

The vision of being the best is still alive today at McDonald's. Managers are trained in all aspects of operations at the company's central training center in Oak Brook, Illinois. Called Hamburger University, the facility provides intensive courses of study to help managers understand how to deliver QSCV. Managers are loyal to McDonald's, but the job market is competitive. McDonald's knows that its compensation scheme and incentives must meet the expectations of its managers or they risk losing them. So, what should be rewarded and how?

For many managers at company-owned restaurants, McDonald's has chosen incentives tied to performance in four areas: operational excellence, customer satisfaction, people, and profitability. These areas are all linked to the corporate vision of offering the best quick-service restaurant experience, and they are reported to the restaurants on a monthly report called a "scorecard."

Restaurant managers are evaluated on the elements of the four areas that are within their control. For example, McDonald's believes that taking care of its people is key to success, so managers are given incentives to reduce employee turnover and increase employee commitment. For profitability, sales are important, but they can't always be controlled by restaurant managers. For example, a restaurant located near roadway construction may see a decline in sales due to limited access. Weather also affects business. Instead, restaurant managers may be compensated more heavily for achieving adjusted "bottom line" targets or cost-control targets, or for operational excellence as measured by mystery shoppers or restaurant performance grading.

The key is linking incentive payments to actual results. If goals are not achieved, incentive payments are not made. Rewards are tied to the effort necessary to achieve desired results, so managers feel they are fairly compensated. By giving rewards frequently and in a timely manner, McDonald's reinforces the actions that resulted in good performance initially, thereby increasing the likelihood of the actions being repeated.

QUESTIONS

1. Of the 28,000-plus restaurants that McDonald's operates around the globe, 1,800 are company-owned. Does it make sense to devise a single compensation plan for use in all 1,800 locations? Why or why not?
2. Return on investment has been used in the past as part of a restaurant manager's performance evaluation. For company-owned restaurants, is this a viable measure of performance for restaurant managers? Why or why not?
3. Put yourself in the position of a restaurant manager at McDonald's. Because the restaurants operate with the same vision, should McDonald's use benchmarking and relative performance evaluation to compensate restaurant managers? What are the benefits? Costs?

APPENDIX A

Global Surveys of Company Practice

American Electronics Association, *Operating Ratios Survey 1993–94* (Santa Clara, CA: American Electronics Association, 1993)—Cited in Chapter 18

Anderson, S. and W. Lanen, "Economic Transition, Strategy and the Evolution of Management Accounting Practices: The Case of India," *Accounting, Organizations and Society* (1999)—Cited in Chapters 5 and 7

APQC/CAM-I, *Activity Based Management Consortium Study* (American Productivity and Quality Center/CAM-I, 1995)—Cited in Chapter 5

Arnold, G. and P. Hatzopoulos, "The Theory-Practice Gap in Capital Budgeting: Evidence from the United Kingdom," *Journal of Business Finance & Accounting* (2000)—Cited in Chapter 21

Arsiraphongphisit, O., G. Kester, and T. Skully, "Financial Policies and Practices of Listed Firms in Thailand: Capital Structure, Capital Budgeting, Cost of Capital, and Dividends," *Journal of Business Administration* (2000)—Cited in Chapter 21

Asada, T., J. Bailes, and M. Amano, "An Empirical Study of Japanese and American Budget Planning and Control Systems" (Working Paper, Tsukuba University and Oregon State University, 1989)—Cited in Chapter 6

Ask, U., C. Ax, and S. Jönsson, "Cost Management in Sweden: From Modern to Post-Modern," in Bhimani, A. (ed.) *Management Accounting: European Perspectives* (Oxford: Oxford University Press, 1996)—Cited in Chapter 14

Ax, C. and T. Bjornenak, "The Building and Diffusion of Management Accounting Innovations—The Case of the Balanced Scorecard," (Munich: European Accounting Association Congress, 2000)—Cited in Chapter 13

Ballas, A. and G. Venieris, "A Survey of Management Accounting Practice in Greek Firms," in Bhimani, A. (ed.) *Management Accounting: European Perspectives* (Oxford: Oxford University Press, 1996)—Cited in Chapter 6

Bjornenak, T., "Conventional Wisdom and Costing Practices," *Management Accounting Research* (1997)—Cited in Chapter 9

Blayney, P. and I. Yokohama, "Comparative Analysis of Japanese and Australian Cost Accounting and Management Practices," (Working Paper, The University of Sydney, Australia, 1991)—Cited in Chapters 15 and 21

Burns, J. and H. Yazdifar, "Tricks or Treats?" *Financial Management* (2001)—Cited in Chapter 1

Chia, A. and H. Hoon, "Adopting and Creating Balanced Scorecards in Singapore-Based Companies," *Singapore Management Review* (2000)—Cited in Chapter 13

Chun, L., N. Kassim, and B. Minai, "Are Management Accounting Systems in Malaysia Outmoded?" *Singapore Management Review* (1996)—Cited in Chapter 9

Clarke, P., "Management Accounting Practices in Large Irish Manufacturing Firms," *Irish Journal of Management* (1997)—Cited in Chapters 4, 7, and 12

Clarke, P., N. Hill, and K. Stevens, "Activity-Based Costing in Ireland: Barrier to, and Opportunities for, Change," *Critical Perspectives on Accounting* (1999)—Cited in Chapter 5

Clarke, P. and T. Mullins, "Activity-Based Costing in the Non-Manufacturing Sector in Ireland: A Preliminary Investigation," *Irish Journal of Management* (2001)—Cited in Chapter 5

Cohen, J. and L. Paquette, "Management Accounting Practices: Perceptions of Controllers," *Journal of Cost Management* (1991)—Cited in Chapter 4

Coopers & Lybrand, *Survey of Accounting Practices in the European Oil and Gas Industry* (Denton, TX: Coopers & Lybrand/University of North Texas, February 1997)—Cited in Chapter 16

Cotton, W., S. Jackman, and R. Brown, "Note on a New Zealand Replication of the Innes et al. UK Activity-Based Costing Survey," *Management Accounting Research* (2003)—Cited in Chapter 5

Crenhall, R. and K. Smith, "Adoption and Benefits of Management Accounting Practices: An Australian Study," *Management Accounting Research* (1998)—Cited in Chapters 6, 12, and 23

Dean, G., M. Joye, and P. Blayney, *Strategic Management Accounting Survey* (Sydney: The University of Sydney, 1991)—Cited in Chapter 14

Drury, C., S. Braund, P. Osborne, and M. Tayles, A Survey of Management Accounting Practices in UK Manufacturing Companies, (London: Chartered Association of Certified Accountants, 1993)—Cited in Chapter 8 and 22

Drury, C. and M. Tayles, "Product Costing in U.K. Manufacturing Organizations," *The European Accounting Review* (1994)—Cited in Chapter 14

Ekholm, B. and J. Wallin, "Is the Annual Budget Really Dead?" *The European Accounting Review* (2000)—Cited in Chapter 6

Elliott, J., "International Transfer Pricing, A Survey of U.K. and Non-U.K. Groups," *Management Accounting* (1998)—Cited in Chapter 22

Ernst & Young, *2003 Survey of Management Accounting* (New York: Ernst & Young, March 2003)—Cited in Chapters 1, 7, 9, 12, and 13

Ernst & Young, *Transfer Pricing 2003 Global Survey* (New York: Ernst & Young, November 2003)—Cited in Chapter 22

Firth, M., "The Diffusion of Managerial Accounting Procedures in the People's Republic of China and the Influence of Foreign Partnered Joint Ventures," *Accounting, Organizations and Society* (1996)—Cited in Chapters 7, 9, and 12

Frigo, M., "2001 CMG Survey of Performance Management Trends and Challenges in Performance Management," *Cost Management Update* (Montvale, NJ: Institute of Management Accountants, 2001)—Cited in Chapter 13

Garg, A., D. Ghosh, J. Hudick, and C. Nowacki, "Roles and Practices in Management Accounting Today: Results from the 2003 IMA—E&Y Survey," *Strategic Finance* (2003)—Cited in Chapter 2

Ghosh, B. and Y. Chan, "Management Accounting in Singapore—Well in Place?" *Managerial Auditing Journal* (1997)—Cited in Chapters 5, 6, 7, and 23

Glader, M., "Ekonomistyrning i Svenska Börsföretag," Rapport från Sektionen för Redovisning och Finansiering," (Stockholm: Stockholm School of Economics, 1996)—Cited in Chapter 6

Grant Thornton, *Survey of American Manufacturers* (New York: Grant Thornton, 1992)—Cited in Chapter 12

Groot, T., "Activity Based Costing in U.S. and Dutch Food Companies," *Advances in Management Accounting* (1999)—Cited in Chapters 4 and 5

Groot, T., "Managing Costs in The Netherlands: Past Theory and Current Practice," in Bhimani, A. (ed.) *Management Accounting: European Perspectives* (Oxford: Oxford University Press, 1996)—Cited in Chapter 23

Guilding, C., D. Lamminmaki, and C. Drury, "Budgeting and Standard Costing Practices in New Zealand and the United Kingdom," *The International Journal of Accounting* (1998)—Cited in Chapters 2, 6, and 8

Haldma, T. and K. Lääts, "Contingencies Influencing the Management Accounting Practices of Estonian Manufacturing Companies," *Management Accounting Research* (2002)—Cited in Chapters 2, 9, and 17

"Hong Kong Strikes a Perfect Balance," *Australian CPA* (2003)—Cited in Chapter 13

Hoque, Z. and M. Alam, "Organization Size, Business Objectives, Managerial Autonomy, Industry Conditions, and Management's Choice of Transfer Pricing Methods: A Contextual Analysis of New Zealand Companies" (Working Paper, Victoria University of Wellington, New Zealand, 1998)—Cited in Chapter 22

Innes, J., F. Mitchell, and D. Sinclair, "Activity-Based Costing in the U.K.'s Largest Companies: A Comparison of 1994 and 1999 Survey Results," *Management Accounting Research* (2000)—Cited in Chapter 5

Israelsen, P., M. Andersen, C. Rohde, and P. Sorensen, "Management Accounting in Denmark: Theory and Practice," in Bhimani, A. (ed.) *Management Accounting: European Perspectives* (Oxford: Oxford University Press, 1996)—Cited in Chapter 12

ITtoolbox/Oracle, "2004 ITtoolbox Supply Chain Survey," (Scottsdale, Arizona, 2004)—Cited in Chapter 20

Jog, V. and A. Srivastava, "Corporate Financial Decision Making in Canada," *Revue Canadienne des Sciences de l'Administration* (1994)—Cited in Chapter 21

Joshi, P., "The International Diffusion of New Management Accounting Practices: The Case of India," *Journal of International Accounting, Auditing & Taxation* (2001)—Cited in Chapters 6, 9, 12, and 23

Joye, M. and P. Blayney, "Cost and Management Accounting Practices in Australian Manufacturing Companies: Survey Results" (Accounting Research Centre, The University of Sydney, 1991)—Cited in Chapter 10, 17, and 22

Kester, G. and T. Chong, "Capital Budgeting Practices of Listed Firms in Singapore," *Singapore Management Review* (1998)—Cited in Chapter 21

Koester, R. and D. Barnett, "Petroleum Refinery Joint Cost Allocation" (Working Paper, California State University, Dominguez Hills, 1996)—Cited in Chapter 16

Lamminmaki, D. and C. Drury, "A Comparison of New Zealand and British Product-Costing Practices," *International Journal of Accounting* (2001)—Cited in Chapters 4, 7, and 12

Lazere, C., "All Together Now," *CFO* (February 1998)—Cited in Chapter 6

Lazaridis, I., "Capital Budgeting Practices: A Survey in Firms in Cyprus," *Journal of Small Business Management* (2004)

Lukka, K. and M. Granlund, "Cost Accounting in Finland: Current Practice and Trends of Development," *The European Accounting Review* (1996)—Cited in Chapter 9

Malmi, T., "Balanced Scorecard in Finnish Companies: A Research Note," *Management Accounting Research* (2001)—Cited in Chapter 13

Mouritsen, J., "Five Aspects of Accounting Departments' Work," *Management Accounting Research* (1996)—Cited in Chapter 8

NAA Tokyo Affiliate, "Management Accounting in the Advanced Manufacturing: Comparative Study on Survey in Japan and U.S.A.," (Tokyo: NAA, 1988)—Cited in Chapter 10

Obara, L. and N. Ukpai, "Cost Accounting Practice in the Information Sector of Nigeria: A Survey of Eastern Business Zone." (Tangier, Morocco: African Training and Research Centre in Administration for Development, 2001)—Cited in Chapter 17

Ogunmokun, G., L. Chan, and L. Li, "An Exploratory Study of the Pricing Practices of Canadian and Hong Kong Businesses," *International Journal of Management* (1997)—Cited in Chapter 12

Pierce, B., "Management Accounting Without Accountants?" *Accountancy Ireland* (2001)—Cited in Chapter 1

Research Incorporated, "Synchronizing the Supply Chain Through Collaborative Design," (Alpharetta, Georgia, 1998)—Cited in Chapter 20

Rodrigues, L. and G. Sousa, "The Use of the Balanced Scorecard in Portugal," *Journal for Management Theory and Practice* (2002)—Cited in Chapter 13

Ryan, P. and G. Ryan, "Capital Budgeting Practices of the Fortune 1000: How Have Things Changed?" *Journal of Business and Management* (2002)—Cited in Chapter 21

Sangster, A., "Capital Investment Appraisal Techniques: A Survey of Current Usage," *Journal of Business, Finance, & Accounting* (April 1993)—cited in Chapter 21

Scherrer, G., "Management Accounting: A German Perspective," in Bhimani, A. (ed.) *Management Accounting: European Perspectives* (Oxford: Oxford University Press, 1996)—Cited in Chapter 23

Sharman, P., "The Case for Management Accounting," *Strategic Finance* (2003)—Cited in Chapter 5

Siegel, G. and J. Sorensen, "The Practice Analysis of Management Accounting," *Management Accounting* (1999)—Cited in Chapter 1

Speckbacher, S., J. Bischof, and T. Pfeiffer, "A Descriptive Analysis of the Implementation of Balanced Scorecards in German-Speaking Countries," *Management Accounting Research* (2003)—Cited in Chapter 13

Szychta, A., "The Scope and Application of Management Accounting Methods in Polish Enterprises," *Management Accounting Research* (2002)—Cited in Chapters 15 and 21

Tang, R., "Canadian Transfer Pricing in the 1990s," *Management Accounting* (1992)—Cited in Chapter 22

Tang, R., *Transfer Pricing Systems Management: Practical Issues and Cases* (Montvale, NJ: Institute of Management Accountants, 2001)—Cited in Chapter 22 and 23

Towers Perrin, "CompScan Report: Inside the Balanced Scorecard," (New York: Towers Perrin, January 1996)—Cited in Chapter 13

Wijewardena, H. and A. De Zoysa, "A Comparative Analysis of Management Accounting Practices in Australia and Japan: An Empirical Investigation," *International Journal of Accounting* (1999)—Cited in Chapters 4, 7, 17, and 23

APPENDIX B

Recommended Readings

The literature of cost accounting and related areas is vast and varies. The following books illustrate recent publications that capture current developments:

Ansari, S., J. Bell, and CAM-I Target Cost Core Group. *Target Costing: The Next Frontier in Strategic Cost Management.* Homewood, IL: Irwin McGraw-Hill, 1997.

Brimson, J., *Activity Accounting: An Activity-Based Costing Approach.* New York: John Wiley & Sons, 1997.

Connell, R., *Measuring Customer and Service Profitability in the Finance Sector.* London, U.K.: Chapman & Hall, 1996.

Cooper, R., and R. Kaplan, *The Design of Cost Management Systems.* Upper Saddle River, NJ: Prentice Hall, 1999.

Duska, R., and B. Duska, *Accounting Ethics.* Malden, MA: Blackwell Publishing, 2003.

Gray, R., and J. Bebbington, *Accounting for the Environment, 2nd Edition.* Thousand Oaks, CA: Sage Publications, 2002.

Johnson, H., *Relevance Regained.* New York: Free Press, 1992.

Miller, J., *Implementing Activity-Based Management.* New York: John Wiley & Sons, 1996.

Oliver, L., *Designing Strategic Cost Systems.* New York: John Wiley & Sons, 2004.

Player, S., and D. Keys, *Activity-Based Management.* New York: MasterMedia Limited, 1995.

Shank. J., and V. Govindarajan, *Strategic Management Accounting.* New York: Free Press, 1993.

Simons, R., *Performance Measurement and Control Systems for Implementing Strategy.* Upper Saddle River, NJ: Prentice Hall, 2000.

Young, S., and S. O'Byrne, *EVA and Value-Based Management.* Columbus, OH: McGraw-Hill, 2000.

Books of readings related to cost or management accounting include:

Aly, I., ed., *Readings in Management Accounting.* Dubuque, Iowa: Kendall/Hunt, 1995.

Bhimani, A., ed., *Management Accounting in the Digital Economy.* New York: Oxford University Press, 2003.

Brinker, B., ed., *Emerging Practices in Cost Management.* Boston: Warren, Gorham, and Lamont, 1995.

Ratnatunga, J., J. Miller, N. Mudalige, and A. Sohalled, eds., *Issues in Strategic Management Accounting.* Sydney, Australia: Harcourt Brace Jovanovich, 1993.

Young, M., ed., *Readings in Management Accounting, 4th Edition.* Upper Saddle River, NJ: Prentice Hall, 2003.

The Harvard Business School series in accounting and control offers important contributions to the cost accounting literature, including:

Anthony, R., *The Management Control Function.* Boston: Harvard Business School Press, 1998.

Berliner, C., and J. Brimson, eds., *Cost Management for Today's Advanced Manufacturing: The CAMI Conceptual Design.* Boston: Harvard Business School Press, 1988.

Bruns, W., ed., *Performance Measurement, Evaluation, and Incentives.* Boston: Harvard Business School Press, 1992.

Cooper, R., *When Lean Enterprises Collide.* Boston: Harvard Business School Press, 1995.

Hope, J., and R. Fraser, *Beyond Budgeting: How Managers Can Break Free from the Annual Performance Trap.* Boston: Harvard Business School Press, 2003.

Johnson, H., and R. Kaplan, *Relevance Lost: The Rise and Fall of Management Accounting.* Boston: Harvard Business School Press, 1987.

Kaplan, R., ed., *Measures for Manufacturing Excellence.* Boston: Harvard Business School Press, 1990.

Kaplan, R., and R. Cooper, *Cost and Effect.* Boston: Harvard Business School Press, 1998.

Kaplan, R., and D. Norton, *The Balanced Scorecard.* Boston: Harvard Business School Press, 1996.

Kaplan, R., and D. Norton, *The Strategy-Focused Organization: How Balanced Scorecard Companies Thrive in the New Business Environment.* Boston: Harvard Business School Press, 2001.

Kaplan, R., and D. Norton, *Strategy Maps: Converting Intangible Assets into Tangible Outcomes.* Boston: Harvard Business School Press, 2004.

Simons, R., *Levers of Control.* Boston: Harvard Business School Press, 1995.

Productivity Press publishes many books with a global focus on cost and management accounting, including:

Cooper, R., and R. Slagmulder, *Target Costing and Value Engineering.* Portland, OR: Productivity Press, 1997.

Maskall, B., and B. Baggaley, *Practical Lean Accounting: A Proven System for Measuring and Managing the Lean Enterprise.* Portland, OR: Productivity Press, 2003.

Monden, Y., *Cost Reduction Systems: Target Costing and Kaizen Costing.* Portland, OR: Productivity Press, 2003.

Sakurai, M. *Integrated Cost Management.* Portland, OR: Productivity Press, 1996.

The Institute of Management Accountants publishes monographs and books covering cost accounting topics, such as:

Atkinson, A., J. Hamburg, and C. Ittner, *Linking Quality to Profits.* Montvale, NJ: Institute of Management Accountants and Milwaukee, WI: ASQC Quality Press, 1994.

Cooper, R., R. Kaplan, L. Maisel, E. Morrissey, and R. Oehm, *Implementing Activity-Based Cost Management: Moving from Analysis to Action.* Montvale, NJ: Institute of Management Accountants, 1993.

Epstein, M., *Measuring Corporate Environmental Performance.* Montvale, NJ: Institute of Management Accountants, 1995.

Klammer, T., *Managing Strategic and Capital Investment Decisions.* Burr Ridge, IL: Irwin and Montvale, NJ: Institute of Management Accountants, 1994.

Martinson, O., *Cost Accounting in the Service Industry.* Montvale, NJ: Institute of Management Accountants, 1994.

Noreen, E., D. Smith, and J. Mackey, *The Theory of Constraints and Its Implications for Management Accounting.* Great Barrington, MA: North River Press, 1995.

The Financial Executives Research Foundation publishes monographs and books concerning topics of interest to financial executives, such as:

de Mesa Graziano, C., *Enron and the Powers Report: An Examination of Business and Accounting Failures.* Morristown, NJ: Financial Executives Research Foundation, 2002.

Jablonski, S., *Changing Roles of Financial Management.* Morristown, NJ: Financial Executives Research Foundation, 2004.

The Chartered Institute of Management Accountants, London, U.K., publishes monographs and books, including:

Burns, J., M. Ezzamel, and R. Scapens, *Challenge of Management Accounting Change.* London, U.K.: Chartered Institute of Management Accountants, 2003.

Doyle, D., *Cost Control: A Strategic Guide.* London, U.K.: Chartered Institute of Management Accountants, 2002.

Drury, C., ed., *Management Accounting Handbook.* London, U.K.: Butterworth Heinemann and Chartered Institute of Management Accountants, 1997.

Drury, C., and M. Tayles, *Cost System Design and Profitability Analysis in UK Companies.* London, U.K.: Chartered Institute of Management Accountants, 2000.
Ezzamel, M., C. Green, S. Lilley, and H. Willmott, *Changing Managers and Managing Change.* London, U.K.: Chartered Institute of Management Accountants, 1995.
Friedman, A., and S. Lylne, *Activity Based Techniques: The Real Life Consequences.* London, U.K.: Chartered Institute of Management Accountants, 1995.
Murphy, C., J. Currie, M. Fahy, and W. Golden, *Deciding the Future: Management Accountants as Decision Support Personnel.* London, U.K.: Chartered Institute of Management Accountants, 1995.
Elsevier B.V. publishes *Advances in Management Accounting* on an annual basis. It is edited by M. Epstein and J. Lee and includes a broad cross-section of research articles and case studies.

Case books on cost and management accounting include:

Allen, B., E. Brownlee, M. Haskins, L. Lynch, J. Rotch, *Cases in Management Accounting and Control Systems*, 4th Edition. Upper Saddle River, NJ: Prentice Hall, 2004.
Shank, J., *Cases in Cost Management: A Strategic Emphasis*, 2nd Edition. Mason, OH: South-Western College Publishing, 2000.

The following are detailed annotated bibliographies of the cost management and accounting research literatures:

Bentley, H., *Bibliography of Works on Accounting by American Authors.* Mansfield Centre, CT: Martino Publishing, 1998.
Brown, L., J. Gardner, and M. Vasarhelyi, *Accounting Research Directory: Database of Accounting Literature.* Princeton, NJ: Markus Wiener Publishers, 1994.
Clancy, D., *Annotated Management Accounting Readings.* Management Accounting Section of the American Accounting Association, 1986.
Klemstine, C., and M. Maher, *Management Accounting Research: 1926-1983.* New York: Garland Publishing, 1984.

Two journals bearing on management accounting are published by sections of the American Accounting Association, 7171 Bessie Drive, Sarasota, FL 34233: *Journal of Management Accounting Research* and *Behavioral Research in Accounting.*

Professional associations that specialize in serving members with cost and management accounting interests include:

- *Institute of Management Accountants*, 10 Paragon Drive, Montvale, NJ 07645. Publishes the *Strategic Finance* and *Management Accounting Quarterly* journals.
- *Financial Executives International*, 200 Campus Drive, Florham Park, NJ 07932. Publishes *Financial Executive.*
- *Society of Cost Estimating and Analysis*, 101 South Whiting Street, Suite 201, Alexandria, VA 22304. Publishes the *Journal of Cost Analysis* and monographs on topics related to cost estimation and price analysis in government and industry.
- *The Institute of Internal Auditors*, 249 Maitland Avenue, Altamonte Springs, FL 32701. Publishes *The Internal Auditor* journal. Also publishes monographs on topics related to internal control.
- *Society of Management Accountants of Canada*, One Robert Speck Parkway, Suite 1400, Mississauga, Ontario L4Z 3M3. Publishes the *CMA Magazine.*
- *The Chartered Institute of Management Accountants*, 26 Chapter Street, London, SW1P 4NP. Publishes the *Financial Management* journal. Also publishes monographs covering cost and management accounting topics.

In many countries, individuals with cost and management accounting interests belong to professional bodies that serve members with financial reporting and taxation, as well as cost and management accounting, interests.

APPENDIX C

Notes on Compound Interest and Interest Tables

Interest is the cost of using money. It is the rental charge for funds, just as renting a building and equipment entails a rental charge. When the funds are used for a period of time, it is necessary to recognize interest as a cost of using the borrowed ("rented") funds. This requirement applies even if the funds represent ownership capital and if interest does not entail an outlay of cash. Why must interest be considered? Because the selection of one alternative automatically commits a given amount of funds that could otherwise be invested in some other alternative.

Interest is generally important, even when short-term projects are under consideration. Interest looms correspondingly larger when long-run plans are studied. The rate of interest has significant enough impact to influence decisions regarding borrowing and investing funds. For example, $100,000 invested now and compounded annually for 10 years at 8% will accumulate to $215,900; at 20%, the $100,000 will accumulate to $619,200.

Interest Tables

Many computer programs and pocket calculators are available that handle computations involving the time value of money. You may also turn to the following four basic tables to compute interest.

Table 1—Future Amount of $1

Table 1 shows how much $1 invested now will accumulate in a given number of periods at a given compounded interest rate per period. Consider investing $1,000 now for three years at 8% compound interest. A tabular presentation of how this $1,000 would accumulate to $1,259.70 follows:

Year	Interest per Year	Cumulative Interest Called Compound Interest	Total at End of Year
0	$ —	$ —	$1,000.00
1	80.00 (0.08 × $1,000)	80.00	1,080.00
2	86.40 (0.08 × $1,080)	166.40	1,166.40
3	93.30 (0.08 × $1,166.40)	259.70	1,259.70

This tabular presentation is a series of computations that could appear as follows, where S is the future amount and the subscripts 1, 2, and 3 indicate the number of time periods.

$$S_1 = \$1{,}000(1.08)^1 = \$1.080$$

$$S_2 = \$1{,}080(1.08) = \$1{,}000(1.08)^2 = \$1{,}166.40$$

$$S_3 = \$1{,}166.40 \times (1.08) = \$1{,}000(1.08)^3 = \$1{,}259.70$$

The formula for the "amount of 1," often called the "future value of $1" or "future amount of $1," can be written

$$S = P(1 + r)^n$$

$$S = \$1{,}000(1 + .08)^3 = \$1{,}259.70$$

S is the future value amount; P is the present value, $1,000 in this case; r is the rate of interest; and n is the number of time periods.

Fortunately, tables make key computations readily available. A facility in selecting the *proper* table will minimize computations. Check the accuracy of the preceding answer using Table 1, p. 836.

Table 2—Present Value of $1

In the previous example, if $1,000 compounded at 8% per year will accumulate to $1,259.70 in 3 years, then $1,000 must be the present value of $1,259.70 due at the end of 3 years. The formula for the present value can be derived by reversing the process of *accumulation* (finding the future amount) that we just finished.

If
$$S = P(1+r)^n$$

then
$$P = \frac{S}{(1+r)^n}$$

$$P = \frac{\$1{,}259.70}{(1.08)^3} = \$1{,}000$$

Use Table 2, p. 837, to check this calculation.

When accumulating, we advance or roll forward in time. The difference between our original amount and our accumulated amount is called *compound interest*. When discounting, we retreat or roll back in time. The difference between the future amount and the present value is called *compound discount*. Note the following formulas (where P = $1,000):

$$\text{Compound interest} = P[(1+r)^n - 1] = \$259.70$$

$$\text{Compound discount} = S\left[1 - \frac{1}{(1+r)^n}\right] = \$259.70$$

Table 3—Amount of Annuity of $1

An (ordinary) *annuity* is a series of equal payments (receipts) to be paid (or received) at the end of successive periods of equal length. Assume that $1,000 is invested at the end of each of 3 years at 8%:

End of Year		Amount
1st payment	$1,000.00 ➤ $1,080.00 ➤	$1,166.40, which is $1,000(1.08)^2
2nd payment	$1,000.00 ➤	1,080.00, which is $1,000(1.08)^1
3rd payment		1,000.00
Accumulation (future amount)		$3,246.40

The preceding arithmetic may be expressed algebraically as the amount of an ordinary annuity of $1,000 for 3 years = $\$1{,}000(1+r)^2 + \$1{,}000(1+r)^1 + \$1{,}000$.

We can develop the general formula for S_n, the amount of an ordinary annuity of $1, by using the example above as a basis:

1. $S_n = 1 + (1+r)^1 + (1+r)^2$
2. Substitute: $S_n = 1 + (1.08)^1 + (1.08)^2$
3. Multiply (2) by $(1 + r)$: $(1.08)S_n = (1.08)^1 + (1.08)^2 + (1.08)^3$
4. Subtract (2) from (3): Note that all terms on the right-hand side are removed except $(1.08)^3$ in equation (3) and 1 in equation (2). $1.08S_n - S_n = (1.08)^3 - 1$
5. Factor (4): $S_n(1.08 - 1) = (1.08)^3 - 1$

6. Divide (5) by (1.08 – 1): $S_n = \frac{(1.08)^3 - 1}{1.08 - 1} = \frac{(1.08)^3 - 1}{.08}$

7. The general formula for the amount of an ordinary annuity of $1 becomes: $S_n = \frac{(1 + r)^n - 1}{r}$ or $\frac{\text{Compound interest}}{\text{Rate}}$

This formula is the basis for Table 3, p. 838. Look at Table 3 or use the formula itself to check the calculations.

Table 4—Present Value of an Ordinary Annuity of $1

Using the same example as for Table 3, we can show how the formula of P_n, *the present value of an ordinary annuity*, is developed.

End of Year			0	1	2	3
1st payment	$\frac{1{,}000}{(1.08)^1}$ =	$926.14 ←		$1,000		
2nd payment	$\frac{1{,}000}{(1.08)^2}$ =	$857.52 ←			$1,000	
3rd payment	$\frac{1{,}000}{(1.08)^3}$ =	$794.00 ←				$1,000
Total present value		$2,577.66				

For the general case, the present value of an ordinary annuity of $1 may be expressed as:

1. $$P_n = \frac{1}{1 + r} + \frac{1}{(1 + r)^2} + \frac{1}{(1 + r)^3}$$

2. Substitute $$P_n = \frac{1}{1.08} + \frac{1}{(1.08)^2} + \frac{1}{(1.08)^3}$$

3. Multiply by $\frac{1}{1.08}$: $$P_n \frac{1}{1.08} = \frac{1}{(1.08)^2} + \frac{1}{(1.08)^3} + \frac{1}{(1.08)^4}$$

4. Subtract (3) from (2): $$P_n - P_n \frac{1}{1.08} = \frac{1}{1.08} - \frac{1}{(1.08)^4}$$

5. Factor: $$P_n\left(1 - \frac{1}{(1.08)}\right) = \frac{1}{1.08}\left[1 - \frac{1}{(1.08)^3}\right]$$

6. or $$P_n\left(\frac{.08}{1.08}\right) = \frac{1}{1.08}\left[1 - \frac{1}{(1.08)^3}\right]$$

7. Multiply by $\frac{1.08}{.08}$: $$P_n = \frac{1}{.08}\left[1 - \frac{1}{(1.08)^3}\right]$$

The general formula for the present value of an annuity of $1.00 is:

$$P_n = \frac{1}{r}\left[1 - \frac{1}{(1 + r)^n}\right] = \frac{\text{Compound discount}}{\text{Rate}}$$

Solving, $$P_n = \frac{.2062}{.08} = 2.577$$

The formula is the basis for Table 4, p. 839. Check the answer in the table. The present value tables, Tables 2 and 4, are used most frequently in capital budgeting.

The tables for annuities are not essential. With Tables 1 and 2, compound interest and compound discount can readily be computed. It is simply a matter of dividing either of these by the rate to get values equivalent to those shown in Tables 3 and 4.

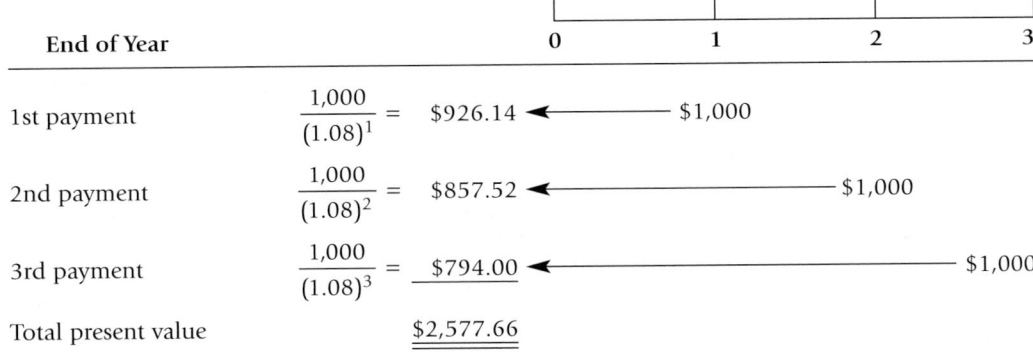

TABLE 1

Compound Amount of $1.00 (The Future Value of $1.00)

$S = P(1 + r)^n$. In this table P = $1.00

Periods	2%	4%	6%	8%	10%	12%	14%	16%	18%	20%	22%	24%	26%	28%	30%	32%	40%	Periods
1	1.020	1.040	1.060	1.080	1.100	1.120	1.140	1.160	1.180	1.200	1.220	1.240	1.260	1.280	1.300	1.320	1.400	1
2	1.040	1.082	1.124	1.166	1.210	1.254	1.300	1.346	1.392	1.440	1.488	1.538	1.588	1.638	1.690	1.742	1.960	2
3	1.061	1.125	1.191	1.260	1.331	1.405	1.482	1.561	1.643	1.728	1.816	1.907	2.000	2.097	2.197	2.300	2.744	3
4	1.082	1.170	1.262	1.360	1.464	1.574	1.689	1.811	1.939	2.074	2.215	2.364	2.520	2.684	2.856	3.036	3.842	4
5	1.104	1.217	1.338	1.469	1.611	1.762	1.925	2.100	2.288	2.488	2.703	2.932	3.176	3.436	3.713	4.007	5.378	5
6	1.126	1.265	1.419	1.587	1.772	1.974	2.195	2.436	2.700	2.986	3.297	3.635	4.002	4.398	4.827	5.290	7.530	6
7	1.149	1.316	1.504	1.714	1.949	2.211	2.502	2.826	3.185	3.583	4.023	4.508	5.042	5.629	6.275	6.983	10.541	7
8	1.172	1.369	1.594	1.851	2.144	2.476	2.853	3.278	3.759	4.300	4.908	5.590	6.353	7.206	8.157	9.217	14.758	8
9	1.195	1.423	1.689	1.999	2.358	2.773	3.252	3.803	4.435	5.160	5.987	6.931	8.005	9.223	10.604	12.166	20.661	9
10	1.219	1.480	1.791	2.159	2.594	3.106	3.707	4.411	5.234	6.192	7.305	8.594	10.086	11.806	13.786	16.060	28.925	10
11	1.243	1.539	1.898	2.332	2.853	3.479	4.226	5.117	6.176	7.430	8.912	10.657	12.708	15.112	17.922	21.199	40.496	11
12	1.268	1.601	2.012	2.518	3.138	3.896	4.818	5.936	7.288	8.916	10.872	13.215	16.012	19.343	23.298	27.983	56.694	12
13	1.294	1.665	2.133	2.720	3.452	4.363	5.492	6.886	8.599	10.699	13.264	16.386	20.175	24.759	30.288	36.937	79.371	13
14	1.319	1.732	2.261	2.937	3.797	4.887	6.261	7.988	10.147	12.839	16.182	20.319	25.421	31.691	39.374	48.757	111.120	14
15	1.346	1.801	2.397	3.172	4.177	5.474	7.138	9.266	11.974	15.407	19.742	25.196	32.030	40.565	51.186	64.359	155.568	15
16	1.373	1.873	2.540	3.426	4.595	6.130	8.137	10.748	14.129	18.488	24.086	31.243	40.358	51.923	66.542	84.954	217.795	16
17	1.400	1.948	2.693	3.700	5.054	6.866	9.276	12.468	16.672	22.186	29.384	38.741	50.851	66.461	86.504	112.139	304.913	17
18	1.428	2.026	2.854	3.996	5.560	7.690	10.575	14.463	19.673	26.623	35.849	48.039	64.072	85.071	112.455	148.024	426.879	18
19	1.457	2.107	3.026	4.316	6.116	8.613	12.056	16.777	23.214	31.948	43.736	59.568	80.731	108.890	146.192	195.391	597.630	19
20	1.486	2.191	3.207	4.661	6.727	9.646	13.743	19.461	27.393	38.338	53.358	73.864	101.721	139.380	190.050	257.916	836.683	20
21	1.516	2.279	3.400	5.034	7.400	10.804	15.668	22.574	32.324	46.005	65.096	91.592	128.169	178.406	247.065	340.449	1171.356	21
22	1.546	2.370	3.604	5.437	8.140	12.100	17.861	26.186	38.142	55.206	79.418	113.574	161.492	228.360	321.184	449.393	1639.898	22
23	1.577	2.465	3.820	5.871	8.954	13.552	20.362	30.376	45.008	66.247	96.889	140.831	203.480	292.300	417.539	593.199	2295.857	23
24	1.608	2.563	4.049	6.341	9.850	15.179	23.212	35.236	53.109	79.497	118.205	174.631	256.385	374.144	542.801	783.023	3214.200	24
25	1.641	2.666	4.292	6.848	10.835	17.000	26.462	40.874	62.669	95.396	144.210	216.542	323.045	478.905	705.641	1033.590	4499.880	25
26	1.673	2.772	4.549	7.396	11.918	19.040	30.167	47.414	73.949	114.475	175.936	268.512	407.037	612.998	917.333	1364.339	6299.831	26
27	1.707	2.883	4.822	7.988	13.110	21.325	34.390	55.000	87.260	137.371	214.642	332.955	512.867	784.638	1192.533	1800.927	8819.764	27
28	1.741	2.999	5.112	8.627	14.421	23.884	39.204	63.800	102.967	164.845	261.864	412.864	646.212	1004.336	1550.293	2377.224	12347.670	28
29	1.776	3.119	5.418	9.317	15.863	26.750	44.693	74.009	121.501	197.814	319.474	511.952	814.228	1285.550	2015.381	3137.935	17286.737	29
30	1.811	3.243	5.743	10.063	17.449	29.960	50.950	85.850	143.371	237.376	389.758	634.820	1025.927	1645.505	2619.996	4142.075	24201.432	30
35	2.000	3.946	7.686	14.785	28.102	52.800	98.100	180.314	327.997	590.668	1053.402	1861.054	3258.135	5653.911	9727.860	16599.217	130161.112	35
40	2.208	4.801	10.286	21.725	45.259	93.051	188.884	378.721	750.378	1469.772	2847.038	5455.913	10347.175	19426.689	36118.865	66520.767	700037.697	40

TABLE 2 *(Place a clip on this page for easy reference.)*

Present Value of $1.00

$P = \frac{S}{(1+r)^n}$. In this table $S = \$1.00$.

Periods	2%	4%	6%	8%	10%	12%	14%	16%	18%	20%	22%	24%	26%	28%	30%	32%	40%	Periods
1	0.980	0.962	0.943	0.926	0.909	0.893	0.877	0.862	0.847	0.833	0.820	0.806	0.794	0.781	0.769	0.758	0.714	1
2	0.961	0.925	0.890	0.857	0.826	0.797	0.769	0.743	0.718	0.694	0.672	0.650	0.630	0.610	0.592	0.574	0.510	2
3	0.942	0.889	0.840	0.794	0.751	0.712	0.675	0.641	0.609	0.579	0.551	0.524	0.500	0.477	0.455	0.435	0.364	3
4	0.924	0.855	0.792	0.735	0.683	0.636	0.592	0.552	0.516	0.482	0.451	0.423	0.397	0.373	0.350	0.329	0.260	4
5	0.906	0.822	0.747	0.681	0.621	0.567	0.519	0.476	0.437	0.402	0.370	0.341	0.315	0.291	0.269	0.250	0.186	5
6	0.888	0.790	0.705	0.630	0.564	0.507	0.456	0.410	0.370	0.335	0.303	0.275	0.250	0.227	0.207	0.189	0.133	6
7	0.871	0.760	0.665	0.583	0.513	0.452	0.400	0.354	0.314	0.279	0.249	0.222	0.198	0.178	0.159	0.143	0.095	7
8	0.853	0.731	0.627	0.540	0.467	0.404	0.351	0.305	0.266	0.233	0.204	0.179	0.157	0.139	0.123	0.108	0.068	8
9	0.837	0.703	0.592	0.500	0.424	0.361	0.308	0.263	0.225	0.194	0.167	0.144	0.125	0.108	0.094	0.082	0.048	9
10	0.820	0.676	0.558	0.463	0.386	0.322	0.270	0.227	0.191	0.162	0.137	0.116	0.099	0.085	0.073	0.062	0.035	10
11	0.804	0.650	0.527	0.429	0.350	0.287	0.237	0.195	0.162	0.135	0.112	0.094	0.079	0.066	0.056	0.047	0.025	11
12	0.788	0.625	0.497	0.397	0.319	0.257	0.208	0.168	0.137	0.112	0.092	0.076	0.062	0.052	0.043	0.036	0.018	12
13	0.773	0.601	0.469	0.368	0.290	0.229	0.182	0.145	0.116	0.093	0.075	0.061	0.050	0.040	0.033	0.027	0.013	13
14	0.758	0.577	0.442	0.340	0.263	0.205	0.160	0.125	0.099	0.078	0.062	0.049	0.039	0.032	0.025	0.021	0.009	14
15	0.743	0.555	0.417	0.315	0.239	0.183	0.140	0.108	0.084	0.065	0.051	0.040	0.031	0.025	0.020	0.016	0.006	15
16	0.728	0.534	0.394	0.292	0.218	0.163	0.123	0.093	0.071	0.054	0.042	0.032	0.025	0.019	0.015	0.012	0.005	16
17	0.714	0.513	0.371	0.270	0.198	0.146	0.108	0.080	0.060	0.045	0.034	0.026	0.020	0.015	0.012	0.009	0.003	17
18	0.700	0.494	0.350	0.250	0.180	0.130	0.095	0.069	0.051	0.038	0.028	0.021	0.016	0.012	0.009	0.007	0.002	18
19	0.686	0.475	0.331	0.232	0.164	0.116	0.083	0.060	0.043	0.031	0.023	0.017	0.012	0.009	0.007	0.005	0.002	19
20	0.673	0.456	0.312	0.215	0.149	0.104	0.073	0.051	0.037	0.026	0.019	0.014	0.010	0.007	0.005	0.004	0.001	20
21	0.660	0.439	0.294	0.199	0.135	0.093	0.064	0.044	0.031	0.022	0.015	0.011	0.008	0.006	0.004	0.003	0.001	21
22	0.647	0.422	0.278	0.184	0.123	0.083	0.056	0.038	0.026	0.018	0.013	0.009	0.006	0.004	0.003	0.002	0.001	22
23	0.634	0.406	0.262	0.170	0.112	0.074	0.049	0.033	0.022	0.015	0.010	0.007	0.005	0.003	0.002	0.002	0.000	23
24	0.622	0.390	0.247	0.158	0.102	0.066	0.043	0.028	0.019	0.013	0.008	0.006	0.004	0.003	0.002	0.001	0.000	24
25	0.610	0.375	0.233	0.146	0.092	0.059	0.038	0.024	0.016	0.010	0.007	0.005	0.003	0.002	0.001	0.001	0.000	25
26	0.598	0.361	0.220	0.135	0.084	0.053	0.033	0.021	0.014	0.009	0.006	0.004	0.002	0.002	0.001	0.001	0.000	26
27	0.586	0.347	0.207	0.125	0.076	0.047	0.029	0.018	0.011	0.007	0.005	0.003	0.002	0.001	0.001	0.001	0.000	27
28	0.574	0.333	0.196	0.116	0.069	0.042	0.026	0.016	0.010	0.006	0.004	0.002	0.002	0.001	0.001	0.000	0.000	28
29	0.563	0.321	0.185	0.107	0.063	0.037	0.022	0.014	0.008	0.005	0.003	0.002	0.001	0.001	0.000	0.000	0.000	29
30	0.552	0.308	0.174	0.099	0.057	0.033	0.020	0.012	0.007	0.004	0.003	0.002	0.001	0.001	0.000	0.000	0.000	30
35	0.500	0.253	0.130	0.068	0.036	0.019	0.010	0.006	0.003	0.002	0.001	0.001	0.000	0.000	0.000	0.000	0.000	35
40	0.453	0.208	0.097	0.046	0.022	0.011	0.005	0.003	0.001	0.001	0.000	0.000	0.000	0.000	0.000	0.000	0.000	40

TABLE 3
Compound Amount of Annuity of $1.00 in Arrears* (Future Value of Annuity)

$$S_n = \frac{(1+r)^n - 1}{r}$$

Periods	2%	4%	6%	8%	10%	12%	14%	16%	18%	20%	22%	24%	26%	28%	30%	32%	40%	Periods
1	1.000	1.000	1.000	1.000	1.000	1.000	1.000	1.000	1.000	1.000	1.000	1.000	1.000	1.000	1.000	1.000	1.000	1
2	2.020	2.040	2.060	2.080	2.100	2.120	2.140	2.160	2.180	2.200	2.220	2.240	2.260	2.280	2.300	2.320	2.400	2
3	3.060	3.122	3.184	3.246	3.310	3.374	3.440	3.506	3.572	3.640	3.708	3.778	3.848	3.918	3.990	4.062	4.360	3
4	4.122	4.246	4.375	4.506	4.641	4.779	4.921	5.066	5.215	5.368	5.524	5.684	5.848	6.016	6.187	6.362	7.104	4
5	5.204	5.416	5.637	5.867	6.105	6.353	6.610	6.877	7.154	7.442	7.740	8.048	8.368	8.700	9.043	9.398	10.946	5
6	6.308	6.633	6.975	7.336	7.716	8.115	8.536	8.977	9.442	9.930	10.442	10.980	11.544	12.136	12.756	13.406	16.324	6
7	7.434	7.898	8.394	8.923	9.487	10.089	10.730	11.414	12.142	12.916	13.740	14.615	15.546	16.534	17.583	18.696	23.853	7
8	8.583	9.214	9.897	10.637	11.436	12.300	13.233	14.240	15.327	16.499	17.762	19.123	20.588	22.163	23.858	25.678	34.395	8
9	9.755	10.583	11.491	12.488	13.579	14.776	16.085	17.519	19.086	20.799	22.670	24.712	26.940	29.369	32.015	34.895	49.153	9
10	10.950	12.006	13.181	14.487	15.937	17.549	19.337	21.321	23.521	25.959	28.657	31.643	34.945	38.593	42.619	47.062	69.814	10
11	12.169	13.486	14.972	16.645	18.531	20.655	23.045	25.733	28.755	32.150	35.962	40.238	45.031	50.398	56.405	63.122	98.739	11
12	13.412	15.026	16.870	18.977	21.384	24.133	27.271	30.850	34.931	39.581	44.874	50.895	57.739	65.510	74.327	84.320	139.235	12
13	14.680	16.627	18.882	21.495	24.523	28.029	32.089	36.786	42.219	48.497	55.746	64.110	73.751	84.853	97.625	112.303	195.929	13
14	15.974	18.292	21.015	24.215	27.975	32.393	37.581	43.672	50.818	59.196	69.010	80.496	93.926	109.612	127.913	149.240	275.300	14
15	17.293	20.024	23.276	27.152	31.772	37.280	43.842	51.660	60.965	72.035	85.192	100.815	119.347	141.303	167.286	197.997	386.420	15
16	18.639	21.825	25.673	30.324	35.950	42.753	50.980	60.925	72.939	87.442	104.935	126.011	151.377	181.868	218.472	262.356	541.988	16
17	20.012	23.698	28.213	33.750	40.545	48.884	59.118	71.673	87.068	105.931	129.020	157.253	191.735	233.791	285.014	347.309	759.784	17
18	21.412	25.645	30.906	37.450	45.599	55.750	68.394	84.141	103.740	128.117	158.405	195.994	242.585	300.252	371.518	459.449	1064.697	18
19	22.841	27.671	33.760	41.446	51.159	63.440	78.969	98.603	123.414	154.740	194.254	244.033	306.658	385.323	483.973	607.472	1491.576	19
20	24.297	29.778	36.786	45.762	57.275	72.052	91.025	115.380	146.628	186.688	237.989	303.601	387.389	494.213	630.165	802.863	2089.206	20
21	25.783	31.969	39.993	50.423	64.002	81.699	104.768	134.841	174.021	225.026	291.347	377.465	489.110	633.593	820.215	1060.779	2925.889	21
22	27.299	34.248	43.392	55.457	71.403	92.503	120.436	157.415	206.345	271.031	356.443	469.056	617.278	811.999	1067.280	1401.229	4097.245	22
23	28.845	36.618	46.996	60.893	79.543	104.603	138.297	183.601	244.487	326.237	435.861	582.630	778.771	1040.358	1388.464	1850.622	5737.142	23
24	30.422	39.083	50.816	66.765	88.497	118.155	158.659	213.978	289.494	392.484	532.750	723.461	982.251	1332.659	1806.003	2443.821	8032.999	24
25	32.030	41.646	54.865	73.106	98.347	133.334	181.871	249.214	342.603	471.981	650.955	898.092	1238.636	1706.803	2348.803	3226.844	11247.199	25
26	33.671	44.312	59.156	79.954	109.182	150.334	208.333	290.088	405.272	567.377	795.165	1114.634	1561.682	2185.708	3054.444	4260.434	15747.079	26
27	35.344	47.084	63.706	87.351	121.100	169.374	238.499	337.502	479.221	681.853	971.102	1383.146	1968.719	2798.706	3971.778	5624.772	22046.910	27
28	37.051	49.968	68.528	95.339	134.210	190.699	272.889	392.503	566.481	819.223	1185.744	1716.101	2481.586	3583.344	5164.311	7425.699	30866.674	28
29	38.792	52.966	73.640	103.966	148.631	214.583	312.094	456.303	669.447	984.068	1447.608	2128.965	3127.798	4587.680	6714.604	9802.923	43214.343	29
30	40.568	56.085	79.058	113.263	164.494	241.333	356.787	530.312	790.948	1181.882	1767.081	2640.916	3942.026	5873.231	8729.985	12940.859	60501.081	30
35	49.994	73.652	111.435	172.317	271.024	431.663	693.573	1120.713	1816.652	2948.341	4783.645	7750.225	12527.442	20188.966	32422.868	51869.427	325400.279	35
40	60.402	95.026	154.762	259.057	442.593	767.091	1342.025	2360.757	4163.213	7343.858	12936.535	22728.803	39792.982	69377.460	120392.883	207874.272	1750091.741	40

*Payments (or receipts) at the end of each period.

TABLE 4 *(Place a clip on this page for easy reference.)*

Present Value of Annuity $1.00 in Arrears*

$$P_n = \frac{1}{r}\left[1 - \frac{1}{(1+r)^n}\right]$$

Periods	2%	4%	6%	8%	10%	12%	14%	16%	18%	20%	22%	24%	26%	28%	30%	32%	40%	Periods
1	0.980	0.962	0.943	0.926	0.909	0.893	0.877	0.862	0.847	0.833	0.820	0.806	0.794	0.781	0.769	0.758	0.714	1
2	1.942	1.886	1.833	1.783	1.736	1.690	1.647	1.605	1.566	1.528	1.492	1.457	1.424	1.392	1.361	1.331	1.224	2
3	2.884	2.775	2.673	2.577	2.487	2.402	2.322	2.246	2.174	2.106	2.042	1.981	1.923	1.868	1.816	1.766	1.589	3
4	3.808	3.630	3.465	3.312	3.170	3.037	2.914	2.798	2.690	2.589	2.494	2.404	2.320	2.241	2.166	2.096	1.849	4
5	4.713	4.452	4.212	3.993	3.791	3.605	3.433	3.274	3.127	2.991	2.864	2.745	2.635	2.532	2.436	2.345	2.035	5
6	5.601	5.242	4.917	4.623	4.355	4.111	3.889	3.685	3.498	3.326	3.167	3.020	2.885	2.759	2.643	2.534	2.168	6
7	6.472	6.002	5.582	5.206	4.868	4.564	4.288	4.039	3.812	3.605	3.416	3.242	3.083	2.937	2.802	2.677	2.263	7
8	7.325	6.733	6.210	5.747	5.335	4.968	4.639	4.344	4.078	3.837	3.619	3.421	3.241	3.076	2.925	2.786	2.331	8
9	8.162	7.435	6.802	6.247	5.759	5.328	4.946	4.607	4.303	4.031	3.786	3.566	3.366	3.184	3.019	2.868	2.379	9
10	8.983	8.111	7.360	6.710	6.145	5.650	5.216	4.833	4.494	4.192	3.923	3.682	3.465	3.269	3.092	2.930	2.414	10
11	9.787	8.760	7.887	7.139	6.495	5.938	5.453	5.029	4.656	4.327	4.035	3.776	3.543	3.335	3.147	2.978	2.438	11
12	10.575	9.385	8.384	7.536	6.814	6.194	5.660	5.197	4.793	4.439	4.127	3.851	3.606	3.387	3.190	3.013	2.456	12
13	11.348	9.986	8.853	7.904	7.103	6.424	5.842	5.342	4.910	4.533	4.203	3.912	3.656	3.427	3.223	3.040	2.469	13
14	12.106	10.563	9.295	8.244	7.367	6.628	6.002	5.468	5.008	4.611	4.265	3.962	3.695	3.459	3.249	3.061	2.478	14
15	12.849	11.118	9.712	8.559	7.606	6.811	6.142	5.575	5.092	4.675	4.315	4.001	3.726	3.483	3.268	3.076	2.484	15
16	13.578	11.652	10.106	8.851	7.824	6.974	6.265	5.668	5.162	4.730	4.357	4.033	3.751	3.503	3.283	3.088	2.489	16
17	14.292	12.166	10.477	9.122	8.022	7.120	6.373	5.749	5.222	4.775	4.391	4.059	3.771	3.518	3.295	3.097	2.492	17
18	14.992	12.659	10.828	9.372	8.201	7.250	6.467	5.818	5.273	4.812	4.419	4.080	3.786	3.529	3.304	3.104	2.494	18
19	15.678	13.134	11.158	9.604	8.365	7.366	6.550	5.877	5.316	4.843	4.442	4.097	3.799	3.539	3.311	3.109	2.496	19
20	16.351	13.590	11.470	9.818	8.514	7.469	6.623	5.929	5.353	4.870	4.460	4.110	3.808	3.546	3.316	3.113	2.497	20
21	17.011	14.029	11.764	10.017	8.649	7.562	6.687	5.973	5.384	4.891	4.476	4.121	3.816	3.551	3.320	3.116	2.498	21
22	17.658	14.451	12.042	10.201	8.772	7.645	6.743	6.011	5.410	4.909	4.488	4.130	3.822	3.556	3.323	3.118	2.498	22
23	18.292	14.857	12.303	10.371	8.883	7.718	6.792	6.044	5.432	4.925	4.499	4.137	3.827	3.559	3.325	3.120	2.499	23
24	18.914	15.247	12.550	10.529	8.985	7.784	6.835	6.073	5.451	4.937	4.507	4.143	3.831	3.562	3.327	3.121	2.499	24
25	19.523	15.622	12.783	10.675	9.077	7.843	6.873	6.097	5.467	4.948	4.514	4.147	3.834	3.564	3.329	3.122	2.499	25
26	20.121	15.983	13.003	10.810	9.161	7.896	6.906	6.118	5.480	4.956	4.520	4.151	3.837	3.566	3.330	3.123	2.500	26
27	20.707	16.330	13.211	10.935	9.237	7.943	6.935	6.136	5.492	4.964	4.524	4.154	3.839	3.567	3.331	3.123	2.500	27
28	21.281	16.663	13.406	11.051	9.307	7.984	6.961	6.152	5.502	4.970	4.528	4.157	3.840	3.568	3.331	3.124	2.500	28
29	21.844	16.984	13.591	11.158	9.370	8.022	6.983	6.166	5.510	4.975	4.531	4.159	3.841	3.569	3.332	3.124	2.500	29
30	22.396	17.292	13.765	11.258	9.427	8.055	7.003	6.177	5.517	4.979	4.534	4.160	3.842	3.569	3.332	3.124	2.500	30
35	24.999	18.665	14.498	11.655	9.644	8.176	7.070	6.215	5.539	4.992	4.541	4.164	3.845	3.571	3.333	3.125	2.500	35
40	27.355	19.793	15.046	11.925	9.779	8.244	7.105	6.233	5.548	4.997	4.544	4.166	3.846	3.571	3.333	3.125	2.500	40

*Payments (or receipts) at the end of each period.

APPENDIX D

Cost Accounting in Professional Examinations

This appendix describes the role of cost accounting in professional examinations. We use professional examinations in the United States, Canada, Australia, Japan, and the United Kingdom to illustrate the role.[1] A conscientious reader who has solved a representative sample of the problems at the end of the chapters will be well prepared for the professional examination questions dealing with cost accounting. This appendix aims to provide perspective, instill confidence, and encourage readers to take the examination.

American Professional Examinations

CPA and CMA Designations

Many American readers may eventually take the Certified Public Accountant (CPA) examination, the Certified Management Accountant (CMA) examination, or the CFM (Certified Financial Manager) examination. Certification is important to professional accountants for many reasons, such as:

1. Recognition of achievement and technical competence by fellow accountants and by users of accounting services
2. Increased self-confidence in one's professional abilities
3. Membership in professional organizations offering programs of career-long education
4. Enhancement of career opportunities
5. Personal satisfaction

The CPA certificate is issued by individual states; it is necessary to obtain a state's license to practice as a Certified Public Accountant. A prominent feature of public accounting is the use of independent (external) auditors to give assurance about the reliability of the financial statements supplied by managers. These auditors are called Certified Public Accountants in the United States and Chartered Accountants in many other English-speaking nations. The major U.S. professional association in the private sector that regulates the quality of external auditing is the American Institute of Certified Public Accountants (AICPA).

The CMA and CFM designations are offered by the Institute of Management Accountants (IMA). The IMA is the largest association of management accountants in the world.[2] The major objective of the CMA and CFM certifications is to enhance the development of the management accounting profession. In particular, focus is placed on the modern role of the management accountant as an active contributor to, and a participant in management. The CMA and CFM designations are gaining increased stature in the business community as a credential parallel to the CPA designation.

The CMA and CFM examinations are given in a computer-based format and have four parts. The questions are carefully constructed multiple-choice and written-response questions that test all levels of cognitive skills. The CMA exam consists of:

Part 1: Business Analysis

- Global Business
- Quantitative Methods
- Business Economics
- Internal Controls
- Financial Statement Analysis

[1]We appreciate the help from Tom Craven (United States), Bill Langdon (Canada), John Goodwin (Australia), Michi Sakurai (Japan), and Louise Drysdale and Andrea Jefferies (U.K.).

[2] The IMA has a wide range of activities driven by many committees. For example, the Management Accounting Practices Committee issues statements on both financial accounting and management accounting. The IMA also has an extensive continuing-education program.

Part 2: Management Accounting and Reporting

- Budget Preparation
- Cost Management
- Information Management
- Performance Measurement
- External Financial Reporting

Part 3: Strategic Management

- Strategic Planning
- Strategic Marketing
- Corporate Finance
- Decision Analysis
- Investment Decisions

Part 4: Business Application

- All topics from Parts 1, 2, and 3, plus:
  - Organizational Management
  - Organizational Communication
  - Behavioral issues
  - Ethical Considerations

A person who has successfully completed the U.S. CPA examination is exempt from Part 1. The CFM exam content is currently being reviewed, but it has traditionally been similar to the CMA examination with topics on corporate financial management replacing topics on financial accounting, reporting, and analysis. For more information, visit the IMA website at **http://www.imanet.org**.

Cost/management accounting questions are prominent in the CMA examination. The CPA examinations also include such questions, although they are less extensive than questions regarding financial accounting, auditing, and business law. This book includes many questions and problems used in past CMA and CPA examinations. In addition, a supplement to this book, *Student Guide and Review Manual* [John K. Harris (Upper Saddle River, NJ: Prentice Hall, 2006)], contains over 100 CMA and CPA questions and explanatory answers. Careful study of appropriate topics in this book will give candidates sufficient background for succeeding in the cost accounting portions of the professional examinations.

The IMA publishes *Strategic Finance* monthly. Each issue includes advertisements for courses that help students prepare for the CMA examination.[3]

Canadian Professional Examinations

Three professional accounting designations are available in Canada

Designation	Sponsoring Organization
Certified Management Accountant (CMA)	Society of Management Accountants (SMA)
Certified General Accountant (CGA)	Certified General Accountants' Association (CGA)
Chartered Accountant (CA)	Canadian Institute of Chartered Accountants (CICA)

The SMA represents over 37,000 certified management accountants employed throughout Canadian business, industry, and government.

The CMA Entrance Examination is a one-day examination covering eleven topics: management accounting, corporate finance, operations management, information technology, strategic management, international business, human resources, marketing, financial accounting, taxation, and internal control. These topics are tested in roughly

[3]Other U.S. professional associations also require detailed knowledge of cost accounting. For example, the Certified Cost Estimator/Analyst (CCEA) program is administered by the Society of Cost Estimating and Analysis, 101 South Whiting Street, Suite 201, Alexandria, VA, 22304. The society's primary purpose is to improve the effectiveness of cost estimation, especially contract cost estimation and price analysis.

equal proportions, although management accounting and financial accounting may be tested to a somewhat greater extent.

Multiple-choice questions comprise 50% and a comprehensive case study the other 50% of the exam. Topics covered on recent examinations in the management accounting area include relevant costing, transfer pricing, capital budgeting, performance measures, activity-based costing, cost allocation, and productivity.

The Society of Management Accountants publishes *CMA Management* monthly. This magazine includes details of courses that assist students in preparing for the CMA exam.

Australian Professional Examinations

CPA Australia in the largest body representing accountants in Australia. Their professional designation is termed a CPA (Certified Practicing Accountant). The basic entry requirement for Associate membership in the Society is having an approved Bachelors degree. Associates of the Society can advance to CPA status by passing the CPA program and having the required amount of work experience. There are three compulsory core segments in the program: Reporting and Professional Practice, Corporate Governance and Accountability, and Business Strategy and Leadership. Candidates must also take three of nine elective subjects. These subjects are assurance services and auditing, financial accounting, financial reporting and disclosure, financial risk management, insolvency and reconstruction, knowledge management, personal financial planning and superannuation, strategic management accounting, and taxation.

The strategic management accounting segment topics include:

1. Management accounting in the contemporary business environment
2. Principles of strategic management
3. Strategy formulation, evaluation, and choice
4. Strategy implementation
5. Performance measurement and reward systems

INTHEBLACK, published monthly, includes advertisements for courses that help students prepare for the CPA examination.

The Institute of Chartered Accountants in Australia (ICAA) offers the Chartered Accountant (CA) certification that has membership requirements including passing five modules: CA Foundations (a general business overview), Financial Reporting and Assurance, Taxation and Financial Reporting, Strategic Business Management, and CA Integrative (an integrated capstone experience). Management-accounting-related topics are incorporated throughout the modules. These include:

- purpose and perspective (including strategic and operational management, organizations, goals, ethics, operational environments, and cost concepts);
- strategic management accounting (including strategic applications, project evaluation, and capital budgeting); and
- operational management accounting (including decisions analysis, financial planning and management, product and service costing, control, and performance evaluation)

Japanese Professional Examinations

There are two major management accounting organizations—Japanese Industrial Management and Accounting Association (JIMMA) and Enterprise Management Association. The JIMMA is the oldest, largest, and most authoritative accounting organization of its kind in Japan. It directs a School of Cost Control and a School of Corporate Tax Accounting. There are two courses in the School of Cost Control—Preparatory Course and Cost Control Course. These courses are taught by university professors and executives from member corporations. The Enterprise Management Association is the Japanese chapter of the U.S.-based Institute of Management Accountants.

The Japanese Institute of Certified Public Accountants (JICPA) is the organization of the CPA profession in Japan. The CPA exam, conducted by the Certified Public Accountants Board, consists of three stages. The second stage covers cost accounting.

United Kingdom Professional Examinations

The Chartered Institute of Management Accountants (CIMA) is the largest professional management accounting body in the United Kingdom. CIMA provides a wide range of services to members in commerce, education, government, and the accounting profession.

The syllabus for the CIMA examination consists of three pillars:

- *Business Management:* includes papers on organizational management and information systems; integrated management; and business strategy
- *Management Accounting:* includes papers on performance evaluation; decision making; and risk control and strategy
- *Financial Management:* includes papers on financial accounting and tax principles; financial analysis; and financial strategy.

Management Accounting, published monthly by CIMA, includes details of courses assisting students in preparing for their examinations.

Management accounting topics are also covered by several other professional bodies. The syllabus for the examinations of the Chartered Association of Certified Accountants (ACCA) has three distinct parts. Skills examined include information for control, decision making, management, strategy, reporting, taxation, and overall strategic financial management. Other accounting bodies include the Institute of Chartered Accountants in England and Wales (ICAEW) and the Institute for Chartered Accountants of Scotland (ICAS). Both Institutes have requirements that cover proficiency in "general management" topics as well as professional accounting topics.

GLOSSARY

Abnormal spoilage. Spoilage that would not arise under efficient operating conditions; it is not inherent in a particular production process. (634)

Absorption costing. Method of inventory costing in which all variable manufacturing costs and all fixed manufacturing costs are included as inventoriable costs. (296)

Account analysis method. Approach to cost function estimation that classifies various cost accounts as variable, fixed, or mixed with respect to the identified level of activity. Typically, qualitative rather than quantitative analysis is used when making these cost-classification decisions. (338)

Accounting rate of return. See *accrual accounting rate-of-return (AARR)*.

Accrual accounting rate of return (AARR). Divides an accrual accounting measure of average annual income of a project by an accrual accounting measure of its investment. Also called *accounting rate of return* or *return on investment (ROI)*. (732)

Activity. An event, task, or unit of work with a specified purpose. (144)

Activity-based budgeting (ABB). Budgeting approach that focuses on the budgeted cost of the activities necessary to produce and sell products and services. (196)

Activity-based costing (ABC). Approach to costing that focuses on individual activities as the fundamental cost objects. It uses the costs of these activities as the basis for assigning costs to other cost objects such as products or services. (144)

Activity-based management (ABM). Method of management decision-making that uses activity-based costing information to improve customer satisfaction and profitability. (152)

Actual cost. Cost incurred (a historical or past cost), as distinguished from a budgeted or forecasted cost. (27)

Actual costing. A costing system that traces direct costs to a cost object by using the actual direct-cost rates times the actual quantities of the direct-cost inputs and allocates indirect costs based on the actual indirect-cost rates times the actual quantities of the cost allocation bases. (100)

Adjusted allocation-rate approach. Restates all overhead entries in the general ledger and subsidiary ledgers using actual cost rates rather than budgeted cost rates. (119)

Allowable cost. Cost that parties to a contract agree to include in the costs to be reimbursed. (547)

Appraisal costs. Costs incurred to detect which of the individual units of products do not conform to specifications. (661)

Artificial costs. See *complete reciprocated costs*.

Attention directing. Role of management accounting that helps managers focus on opportunities and problems. (10)

Autonomy. The degree of freedom to make decisions. (761)

Average cost. See *unit cost*.

Average waiting time. The average amount of time that an order will wait in line before machine is set up and order is processed. (671)

Backflush costing. Costing system that omits recording some of the journal entries relating to the stages from purchase of direct material to the sale of finished goods. (708)

Balanced scorecard. A framework for implementing strategy that translates an organization's mission and strategy into a set of performance measures. (457)

Batch-level costs. The costs of activities related to a group of units of products or services rather than to each individual unit of product or service. (147)

Belief systems. Lever of control that articulates the mission, purpose, norms of behaviors, and core values of a company intended to inspire managers and other employers to do their best. (812)

Benchmarking. The continuous process of comparing the levels of performance in producing products and services and executing activities against the best levels of performance in competing companies or in companies having similar processes. (241)

Book value. The original cost minus accumulated depreciation of an asset. (396)

Bottleneck. An operation where the work to be performed approaches or exceeds the capacity available to do it. (671)

Boundary systems. Lever of control that describes standards of behavior and codes of conduct expected of all employees, especially actions that are off-limits. (811)

Breakeven point. Quantity of output sold at which total revenues equal total costs, that is where the operating income is zero. (65)

Budget. Quantitative expression of a proposed plan of action by management for a specified period and is an aid to coordinating what needs to be done to implement that plan. (7)

Budgeted cost. Predicted or forecasted cost (future cost) as distinguished from an actual or historical cost. (27)

Budgetary slack. The practice of underestimating budgeted revenues, or overestimating budgeted costs, to make budgeted targets more easily achievable. (199)

Budgeted indirect-cost rate. Budgeted annual indirect costs in a cost pool divided by the budgeted annual quantity of the cost allocation base. (108)

Bundled product. A package of two or more products (or services) that is sold for a single price, but whose individual components may be sold as separate items at their own "stand-alone" prices. (547)

Business function costs. The sum of all costs (variable and fixed) in a particular business function of the value chain. (382)

Byproducts. Products from a joint production process that have low total sales values compared with the total sales value of the main product or of joint products. (567)

Capital budgeting. The making of long-run planning decisions for investments in projects. (725)

Carrying costs. Costs that arise while holding inventory of goods for sale. (692)

Cash budget. Schedule of expected cash receipts and disbursements. (205)

Cause-and-effect diagram. Diagram that identifies potential causes of defects. Four categories of potential causes of failure are human factors, methods and design factors, machine-related factors, and materials and components factors. Also called a *fishbone diagram*. (665)

Certified in Financial Management (CFM). Certifies that the holder has met the admission criteria and demonstrated the competency of technical knowledge in financial management required by the *Institute of Management Accountants*. (16)

Certified Management Accountant (CMA). Certifies that the holder has met the admission criteria and demonstrated the competency of technical knowledge in management accounting required by the *Institute of Management Accountants*. (16)

Chief financial officer (CFO). Executive responsible for overseeing the financial operations of an organization. Also called *finance director*. (13)

Choice criterion. Objective that can be quantified in a decision model. (81)

Coefficient of determination (r^2). Measures the percentage of variation in a dependent variable explained by one or more independent variables. (357)

Collusive pricing. Companies in an industry conspire in their pricing and production decisions to achieve a price above the competitive price and so restrain trade. (440)

Common cost. Cost of operating a facility, activity, or like cost object that is shared by two or more users. (544)

Complete reciprocated costs. The support department's own costs plus any interdepartmental cost allocations. Also called the *artificial costs* of the support department. (541)

Composite unit. Hypothetical unit with weights based on the mix of individual units. (511)

Conference method. Approach to cost function estimation on the basis of analysis and opinions about costs and their drivers gathered from various departments of a company (purchasing, process engineering, manufacturing, employee relations, and so on). (337)

Conformance quality. Refers to the performance of a product or service relative to its design and product specifications. (661)

Constant. The component of total cost that, within the relevant range, does not vary with changes in the level of the activity. Also called *intercept*. (333)

Constant gross-margin percentage NRV method. Method that allocates joint costs to joint products in such a way that the overall gross-margin percentage is identical for the individual products. (572)

Constraint. A mathematical inequality or equality that must be satisfied by the variables in a mathematical model. (402)

Continuous Budget. See *rolling budget*.

Contribution income statement. Income statement that groups costs into variable costs and fixed costs to highlight the contribution margin. (63)

Contribution margin. Total revenues minus total variable costs. (62)

Contribution margin per unit. Selling price minus the variable cost per unit. (62)

Contribution margin percentage. Contribution margin per unit divided by selling price. Also called *contribution margin ratio*. (63)

Contribution margin ratio. See *contribution margin percentage*.

Control. Taking actions that implement the planning decisions, deciding how to evaluate performance, and providing feedback that will help future decision making. (7)

Control chart. Graph of a series of successive observations of a particular step, procedure, or operation taken at regular intervals of time. Each observation is plotted relative to specified ranges that represent the limits within which observations are expected to fall. (664)

Controllability. Degree of influence that a specific manager has over costs, revenues, or related items for which he or she is responsible. (198)

Controllable cost. Any cost that is primarily subject to the influence of a given responsibility center manager for a given period. (198)

Controller. The financial executive primarily responsible for management accounting and financial accounting. Also called *chief accounting officer*. (14)

Conversion costs. All manufacturing costs other than direct material costs. (42)

Cost. Resource sacrificed or forgone to achieve a specific objective. (27)

Cost accounting. Measures, analyzes, and reports financial and nonfinancial information relating to the cost of acquiring or using resources in an organization. It provides information for both management accounting and financial accounting. (2)

Cost Accounting Standards Board (CASB). Government agency that has the exclusive authority to make, put into effect, amend, and rescind cost accounting standards and interpretations thereof designed to achieve uniformity and consistency in regard to measurement, assignment, and allocation of costs to contracts within the United States. (546)

Cost accumulation. Collection of cost data in some organized way by means of an accounting system. (27)

Cost allocation. Assignment of indirect costs to a particular cost object. (27)

Cost-allocation base. A factor that links in a systematic way an indirect cost or group of indirect costs to a cost object. (98)

Cost-application base. Cost-allocation base when the cost object is a job, product or customer. (98)

Cost assignment. General term that encompasses both (1) tracing accumulated costs that have a direct relationship to a cost object and (2) allocating accumulated costs that have an indirect relationship to a cost object. (27)

Cost-benefit approach. Approach to decision-making and resource allocation based on a comparison of the expected benefits from attaining company goals and the expected costs. (11)

Cost center. Responsibility center where the manager is accountable for costs only. (197)

Cost driver. A variable, such as the level of activity or volume, that causally affects costs over a given time span. (32)

Cost estimation. The attempt to measure a past relationship based on data from past costs and the related level of an activity. (330)

Cost function. Mathematical description of how a cost changes with changes in the level of an activity relating to that cost. (333)

Cost hierarchy. Categorization of indirect costs into different cost pools on the basis of the different types of cost drivers, or cost-allocation bases, or different degrees of difficulty in determining cause-and-effect (or benefits received) relationships. (147)

Cost incurrence. Describes when a resource is consumed (or benefit forgone) to meet a specific objective. (427)

Cost leadership. Organization's ability to achieve lower costs relative to competitors through productivity and efficiency improvements, elimination of waste, and tight cost control. (457)

Cost management. The approaches and activities of managers in short-run and long-run planning and control decisions that increase value for customers and lower costs of products and services. (2)

Cost object. Anything for which a measurement of costs is desired. (27)

Cost of capital. See *required rate of return (RRR)*.

Cost of goods manufactured. Cost of goods brought to completion, whether they were started before or during the current accounting period. (39)

Cost pool. A grouping of individual cost items. (98)

Cost predictions. Forecasts about future costs. (336)

Cost tracing. Describes the assignment of direct costs to a particular cost object. (27)

Costs of quality (COQ). Costs incurred to prevent, or the costs arising as a result of, the production of a low-quality product. (661)

Cost-volume-profit (CVP) analysis. Examines the behavior of total revenues, total costs, and operating income as changes occur in the output level, the selling price, the variable cost per unit, or the fixed costs of a product. (60)

Cumulative average-time learning model. Learning curve model in which the cumulative average time per unit declines by a constant percentage each time the cumulative quantity of units produced doubles. (350)

Current cost. Asset measure based on the cost of purchasing an asset today identical to the one currently held, or the cost of purchasing an asset that provides services like the one currently held if an identical asset cannot be purchased. (800)

Customer cost hierarchy. Hierarchy that categorizes costs related to customers into different cost pools on the basis of different types of cost drivers, or cost-allocation bases, or different degrees of difficulty in determining cause-and-effect or benefits-received relationships. (502)

Customer life-cycle costs. Focuses on the total costs incurred by a customer to acquire, use, maintain, and dispose of a product or service. (438)

Customer-profitability analysis. The reporting and analysis of revenues earned from customers and the costs incurred to earn those revenues. (501)

Customer-response time. Duration from the time a customer places an order for a product or service to the time the product or service is delivered to the customer. (670)

Customer service. Providing after-sale support to customers. (5)

Decentralization. The freedom for managers at lower levels of the organization to make decisions. (761)

Decision model. Formal method for making a choice, often involving both quantitative and qualitative analyses. (379)

Decision table. Summary of the alternative actions, events, outcomes, and probabilities of events in a decision. (82)

Degree of operating leverage. Contribution margin divided by operating income at any given level of sales. (72)

Denominator level. The denominator in the budgeted fixed overhead rate computation. (264)

Denominator-level variance. See *production-volume variance*.

Dependent variable. The cost to be predicted. (339)

Design of products, services, or processes. The detailed planning and engineering of products, services, or processes. (4)

Design quality. Refers to how closely the characteristics of a product of service meet the needs and wants of customers. (660)

Designed-in costs. See *locked-in costs*.

Diagnostic control systems. Lever of control that monitors critical performance variables that help managers track progress toward achieving a company's strategic goals. Managers are held accountable for meeting these goals. (811)

Differential cost. Difference in total cost between two alternatives. (386)

Differential revenue. Difference in total revenue between two alternatives. (386)

Direct allocation method. Cost allocation method that allocates each support department's costs to operating departments only. Also called *direct method*. (538)

Direct costing. See *variable costing*.

Direct costs of a cost object. Costs related to the particular cost object that can be traced to that object in an economically feasible (cost-effective) way. (27)

Direct manufacturing labor costs. Include the compensation of all manufacturing labor that can be traced to the cost object (work in process and then finished goods) in an economically feasible way. (37)

Direct material costs. Acquisition costs of all materials that eventually become part of the cost object (work in process and then finished goods), and that can be traced to the cost object in an economically feasible way. (37)

Direct materials inventory. Direct materials in stock and awaiting use in the manufacturing process. (37)

Direct materials mix variance. The difference between (1) budgeted cost for actual mix of the actual total quantity of direct materials used and (2) budgeted cost of budgeted mix of the actual total quantity of direct materials used. (517)

Direct materials yield variance. The difference between (1) budgeted cost of direct materials based on the actual total quantity of direct materials used and (2) flexible-budget cost of direct materials based on the budgeted total quantity of direct materials allowed for the actual output produced. (517)

Direct method. See *direct allocation method.*

Discount rate. See *required rate of return (RRR).*

Discounted cash flow (DCF) methods. Capital budgeting methods that measure all expected future cash inflows and outflows of a project as if they occurred at a single point in time. (726)

Discretionary costs. Arise from periodic (usually annual) decisions regarding the maximum amount to be incurred and have no measurable cause-and-effect relationship between output and resources used. (473)

Distribution. Delivering products or services to customers. (5)

Downsizing. An integrated approach of configuring processes, products, and people to match costs to the activities that need to be performed to operate effectively and efficiently in the present and future. Also called *rightsizing.* (475)

Downward demand spiral. Pricing context where prices are raised to spread capacity costs over a smaller number of output units. Continuing reduction in the demand for products that occurs when the prices of competitors' products are not met and, as demand drops further, higher and higher unit costs result in more and more reluctance to meet competitors' prices. (312)

Dual pricing. Approach to transfer pricing using two separate transfer-pricing methods to price each transfer from one subunit to another. (772)

Dual-rate cost-allocation method. *See dual-rate method.*

Dual-rate method. Allocation method that classifies costs in each cost pool into two pools (a variable-cost pool and a fixed-cost pool) with each pool using a different cost-allocation base. Also called *dual-rate cost-allocation method.* (532)

Dumping. Under U.S. laws, occurs when a non-U.S. company sells a product in the United States at a price below the market value in the country where it is produced, and this lower price materially injures or threatens to materially injure an industry in the United States. (440)

Dysfunctional decision making. See *suboptimal decision making.*

Economic order quantity (EOQ). Decision model that calculates the optimal quantity of inventory to order under a set of assumptions. (692)

Economic value added (EVA®). After-tax operating income minus the (after-tax) weighted average cost of capital multiplied by total assets minus current liabilities. (796)

Effectiveness. The degree to which a predetermined objective or target is met. (236)

Efficiency. The relative amount of inputs used to achieve a given output level. (236)

Efficiency variance. The difference between actual input quantity used and budgeted input quantity allowed for actual output, multiplied by budgeted price. Also called *usage variance.* (230)

Effort. Exertion toward achieving a goal. (761)

Engineered costs. Costs that result from a cause-and-effect relationship between the cost driver, output, and the (direct or indirect) resources used to produce that output. (472)

Equivalent units. Derived amount of output units that (a) takes the quantity of each input (factor of production) in units completed and in incomplete units of work in process and (b) converts the quantity of input into the amount of completed output units that could be produced with that quantity of input. (598)

Event. A possible relevant occurrence in a decision model. (81)

Expected monetary value. See *expected value.*

Expected value. Weighted average of the outcomes of a decision with the probability of each outcome serving as the weight. Also called *expected monetary value.* (83)

Experience curve. Function that measures the decline in cost per unit in various business functions of the value chain, such as manufacturing, marketing, distribution, and so on, as the amount of these activities increases. (349)

External failure costs. Costs incurred on defective products after they are shipped to customers. (662)

Facility-sustaining costs. The costs of activities that cannot be traced to individual products or services but support the organization as a whole. (148)

Factory overhead costs. See *indirect manufacturing costs.*

Favorable variance. Variance that has the effect of increasing operating income relative to the budgeted amount. Denoted F. (223)

Feedback. Involves managers examining past performance and systematically exploring alternative ways to make better informed decisions and plans in the future. (7)

Finance director. See *chief financial officer (CFO).*

Financial accounting. Measures and records business transactions and provides financial statements that are based on generally accepted accounting principles. It focuses on reporting to external parties such as investors and banks. (2)

Financial budget. Part of the master budget that focuses on how operations and planned capital outlays affect cash. It is made up of the capital expenditures budget, the cash budget, the budgeted balance sheet, and the budgeted statement of cash flows. (186)

Financial planning models. Mathematical representations of the relationships among operating activities, financial activities, and other factors that affect the master budget. (193)

Finished goods inventory. Goods completed but not yet sold. (37)

First-in, first-out (FIFO) process-costing method. Method of process costing that assigns the cost of the previous accounting period's equivalent units in beginning work-in-process inventory to the first units completed and transferred out of the process, and assigns the cost of equivalent units worked on during the current period first to complete beginning inventory, next to start and complete new units, and finally to units in ending work-in-process inventory. (604)

Fixed cost. Cost that remains unchanged in total for a given time period, despite wide changes in the related level of total activity or volume. (30)

Fixed overhead flexible-budget variance. The difference between actual fixed overhead costs and fixed overhead costs in the flexible budget. (265)

Fixed overhead spending variance. Same as the fixed overhead flexible-budget variance. The difference between actual fixed overhead costs and fixed overhead costs in the flexible budget. (265)

Flexible budget. Budget developed using budgeted revenues and budgeted costs based on the actual output in the budget period. (224)

Flexible-budget variance. The difference between an actual result and the corresponding flexible-budget amount based on the actual output level in the budget period. (225)

Full costs of the product. The sum of all variable and fixed costs in all business functions of the value chain (R&D, design, production, marketing, distribution, and customer service). (382)

Goal congruence. Exists when individuals and groups work toward achieving the organization's goals. Managers working in their own best interest take actions that align with the overall goals of top management. (761)

Gross margin percentage. Gross margin divided by revenues. (79)

Growth component. Change in operating income attributable solely to the change in the quantity of output sold between one period and the next. (467)

High-low method. Method used to estimate a cost function that uses only the highest and lowest observed values of the cost driver within the relevant range and their respective costs. (341)

Homogeneous cost pool. Cost pool in which all the costs have the same or a similar cause-and-effect or benefits-received relationship with the cost-allocation base. (499)

Hurdle rate. See *required rate of return (RRR)*.

Hybrid costing system. Costing system that blends characteristics from both job-costing systems and process-costing systems. (617)

Idle time. Wages paid for unproductive time caused by lack of orders, machine breakdowns, material shortages, poor scheduling, and the like. (43)

Imputed costs. Costs recognized in particular situations but not incorporated in financial accounting records. (795)

Incongruent decision making. See *suboptimal decision making*.

Incremental cost. Additional total cost incurred for an activity. (386)

Incremental cost-allocation method. Method that ranks the individual users of a cost object in the order of users most responsible for the common cost and then uses this ranking to allocate cost among those users. (545)

Incremental revenue. Additional total revenue from an activity. (386)

Incremental revenue-allocation method. Method that ranks individual products in a bundle according to criteria determined by management (for example, sales), and then uses this ranking to allocate bundled revenues to the individual products. (549)

Incremental unit-time learning model. Learning curve model in which the incremental time needed to produce the last unit declines by a constant percentage each time the cumulative quantity of units produced doubles. (350)

Independent variable. Level of activity or cost driver used to predict the dependent variable (costs) in a cost estimation or prediction model. (339)

Indirect costs of a cost object. Costs related to the particular cost object that cannot be traced to that object in an economically feasible (cost-effective) way. (27)

Indirect-cost rate. Total indirect costs in a cost pool divided by the total quantity of the cost-allocation base for that cost pool. (104)

Indirect manufacturing costs. All manufacturing costs that are related to the cost object (work in process and then finished goods) but that cannot be traced to that cost object in an economically feasible way. Also called *manufacturing overhead costs* and *factory overhead costs*. (37)

Industrial engineering method. Approach to cost function estimation that analyzes the relationship between inputs and outputs in physical terms. Also called *work measurement method*. (337)

Inflation. The decline in the general purchasing power of the monetary unit, such as dollars. (746)

Input-price variance. See *price variance*.

Insourcing. Process of producing goods or providing services within the organization rather than purchasing those same goods or services from outside vendors. (384)

Inspection point. Stage of the production process at which products are examined to determine whether they are acceptable or unacceptable units. (634)

Institute of Management Accountants (IMA). A professional accounting organization. It is the largest association of management accountants in the United States. (16)

Interactive control systems. Formal information systems that managers use to focus organization attention and learning on key strategic issues. (812)

Intercept. See *constant*.

Intermediate product. Product transferred from one subunit to another subunit of an organization. This product may either be further worked on by the receiving subunit or sold to an external customer. (764)

Internal failure costs. Costs incurred on defective products before they are shipped to customers. (662)

Internal rate-of-return (IRR) method. Capital budgeting discounted cash flow (DCF) method that calculates the discount rate at which the present value of expected cash inflows from a project equals the present value of its expected cash outflows. (728)

Inventoriable costs. All costs of a product that are considered as assets in the balance sheet when they are incurred and that become cost of goods sold only when the product is sold. (37)

Inventory management. The planning, coordinating, and controlling activities related to the flow of inventory into, through, and out of an organization. (691)

Investment. Resources or assets used to generate income. (793)

Investment center. Responsibility center where the manager is accountable for investments, revenues, and costs. (197)

Job. A unit or multiple units of a distinct product or service. (99)

Job-cost record. Source document that records and accumulates all the costs assigned to a specific job, starting when work begins. Also called *job-cost sheet.* (101)

Job-cost sheet. See *job-cost record.*

Job-costing system. Costing system in which the cost object is a unit or multiple units of a distinct product or service called a job. (99)

Joint costs. Costs of a production process that yields multiple products simultaneously. (566)

Joint products. Two or more products that have high total sales values compared with the total sales values of other products yielded by a joint production process. (567)

Just-in-time (JIT) production. Demand-pull manufacturing system in which each component in a production line is produced as soon as, and only when, needed by the next step in the production line. Also called *lean production.* (703)

Just-in-time (JIT) purchasing. The purchase of materials (or goods) so that they are delivered just as needed for production (or sales). (698)

Kaizen budgeting. Budgetary approach that explicitly incorporates continuous improvement anticipated during the budget period into the budget numbers. (195)

Labor-time record. Source document that contains information about the amount of labor time used for a specific job and in a specific department. (102)

Lean production. See *just-in-time (JIT) production.*

Learning curve. Function that measures how labor-hours per unit decline as units of production increase because workers are learning and becoming better at their jobs. (349)

Life-cycle budgeting. Budget that estimates the revenues and business function costs of the value chain attributable to each product from initial R&D to final customer service and support. (436)

Life-cycle costing. System that tracks and accumulates business function costs of the value chain attributable to each product from initial R&D to final customer service and support. (436)

Line management. Managers (for example, in production, marketing, or distribution) who are directly responsible for attaining the goals of the organization. (13)

Linear cost function. Cost function in which the graph of total costs versus the level of a single activity related to that cost is a straight line within the relevant range. (333)

Linear programming (LP). Optimization technique used to maximize an objective function (for example, contribution margin of a mix of products), when there are multiple constraints. (402)

Locked-in costs. Costs that have not yet been incurred but, based on decisions that have already been made, will be incurred in the future. Also called *designed-in costs.* (428)

Main product. Product from a joint production process that has a high total sales value compared with the total sales values of all other products of the joint production process. (567)

Make-or-buy decisions. Decisions about whether a producer of goods or services will insource (produce goods or services within the firm) or outsource (purchase them from outside vendors). (384)

Management accounting. Measures, analyzes, and reports financial and nonfinancial information that helps managers make decisions to fulfill the goals of an organization. It focuses on internal reporting. (2)

Management by exception. Practice of concentrating on areas not operating as expected and giving less attention to areas operating as expected. (222)

Management control system. Means of gathering and using information to aid and coordinate the planning and control decisions throughout an organization and to guide the behavior of its managers and employees. (760)

Manufacturing cells. Grouping of all the different types of equipment used to make a given product. (704)

Manufacturing cycle time. See *manufacturing lead time.* (670)

Manufacturing lead time. Duration between the time an order is received by manufacturing to the time a finished good is produced. Also called *manufacturing cycle time.* (670)

Manufacturing overhead allocated. Amount of manufacturing overhead costs allocated to individual jobs, products, or services based on the budgeted rate multiplied by the actual quantity used of the cost-allocation base. Also called *manufacturing overhead applied.* (115)

Manufacturing overhead applied. See *manufacturing overhead allocated.*

Manufacturing overhead costs. See *indirect manufacturing costs.*

Manufacturing-sector companies. Companies that purchase materials and components and convert them into various finished goods. (36)

Margin of safety. Amount by which budgeted (or actual) revenues exceed breakeven revenues. (70)

Marketing. Promoting and selling products or services to customers or prospective customers. (5)

Market-share variance. The difference in budgeted contribution margin for actual market size in units caused solely by actual market share being different from budgeted market share. (512)

Market-size variance. The difference in budgeted contribution margin at the budgeted market share caused solely by actual market size in units being different from budgeted market size in units.(513)

Master budget. Expression of management's operating and financial plans for a specified period (usually a fiscal year) and includes a set of budgeted financial statements. Also called *pro forma statements.* (182)

Master-budget capacity utilization. The expected level of capacity utilization for the current budget period (typically one year). (310)

Materials requirements planning (MRP). Pushthrough system that manufactures finished goods for inventory on the basis of demand forecasts. (702)

Materials-requisition record. Source document that contains information about the cost of direct materials used on a specific job and in a specific department. (101)

Merchandising-sector companies. Companies that purchase and then sell tangible products without changing their basic form. (36)

Mixed cost. A cost that has both fixed and variable elements. Also called a *semivariable cost.* (334)

Moral hazard. Describes situations in which an employee prefers to exert less effort (or to report distorted information) compared with the effort (or accurate information) desired by the owner because the employee's effort (or validity of the reported information) cannot be accurately monitored and enforced. (806)

Motivation. The desire to attain a selected goal (the goal-congruence aspect) combined with the resulting pursuit of that goal (the effort aspect). (761)

Multicollinearity. Exists when two or more independent variables in a multiple regression model are highly correlated with each other. (363)

Multiple regression. Regression model that estimates the relationship between the dependent variable and two or more independent variables. (342)

Net income. Operating income plus nonoperating revenues (such as interest revenue) minus nonoperating costs (such as interest cost) minus income taxes. (62)

Net present value (NPV) method. Capital budgeting discounted cash flow (DCF) method that calculates the expected monetary gain or loss from a project by discounting all expected future cash inflows and outflows to the present point in time, using the required rate of return. (727)

Net realizable value (NRV) method. Method that allocates joint costs to joint products on the basis of final sales value minus separable costs of total production of the joint products during the accounting period. (572)

Nominal rate of return. Made up of three elements: (a) a risk-free element when there is no expected inflation, (b) a business-risk element, and (c) and an inflation element. (746)

Nonlinear cost function. Cost function in which the graph of total costs based on the level of a single activity is not a straight line within the relevant range. (347)

Nonvalue-added cost. A cost that, if eliminated, would not reduce the actual or perceived value or utility (usefulness) customers obtain from using the product or service. (426)

Normal capacity utilization. The level of capacity utilization that satisfies average customer demand over a period (say, 2–3 years) that includes seasonal, cyclical, and trend factors. (310)

Normal costing. A costing system that traces direct costs to a cost object by using the actual direct-cost rates times the actual quantities of the direct-cost inputs and that allocates indirect costs based on the budgeted indirect-cost rates times the actual quantities of the cost-allocation bases. (108)

Normal spoilage. Spoilage inherent in a particular production process that arises even under efficient operating conditions. (633)

Objective function. Expresses the objective to be maximized (for example, operating income) or minimized (for example, operating costs) in a decision model (for example, a linear programming model). (402)

On-time performance. Delivering a product or service by the time it is scheduled to be delivered. (670)

One-time-only special order. Orders that have no long-run implications. (381)

Operating budget. Budgeted income statement and its supporting budget schedules. (186)

Operating department. Department that directly adds value to a product or service. Also called a *production department* in manufacturing companies. (532)

Operating income. Total revenues from operations minus cost of goods sold and operating costs (excluding interest expense and income taxes). (40)

Operating leverage. Effects that fixed costs have on changes in operating income as changes occur in units sold and hence in contribution margin. (72)

Operation. A standardized method or technique that is performed repetitively, often on different materials, resulting in different finished goods. (620)

Operation-costing system. Hybrid-costing system applied to batches of similar, but not identical, products. Each batch of products is often a variation of a single design, and it proceeds through a sequence of operations, but each batch does not necessarily move through the same operations as other batches. Within each operation, all product units use identical amounts of the operation's resources. (620)

Opportunity cost. The contribution to operating income that is forgone or rejected by not using a limited resource in its next-best alternative use. (388)

Opportunity cost of capital. See *required rate of return (RRR).*

Ordering costs. Costs of preparing, issuing, and paying purchase orders, plus receiving and inspecting the items included in the orders. (692)

Organization structure. Arrangement of lines of responsibility within the organization. (197)

Outcomes. Predicted economic results of the various possible combinations of actions and events in a decision model. (82)

Output unit-level costs. The costs of activities performed on each individual unit of a product or service. (147)

Output-level overhead variance. See *production-volume variance.*

Outsourcing. Process of purchasing goods and services from outside vendors rather than producing the same goods or providing the same services within the organization. (384)

Overabsorbed indirect costs. See *overallocated indirect costs.*

Overallocated indirect costs. Allocated amount of indirect costs in an accounting period is greater than the actual (incurred) amount in that period. Also called *overapplied indirect costs* and *overabsorbed indirect costs.* (118)

Overapplied indirect costs. See *overallocated indirect costs.*

Overtime premium. Wage rate paid to workers (for both direct labor and indirect labor) in excess of their straighttime wage rates. (43)

Pareto diagram. Chart that indicates how frequently each type of defect occurs, ordered from the most frequent to the least frequent. (665)

Partial productivity. Measures the quantity of output produced divided by the quantity of an individual input used. (480)

Payback method. Capital budgeting method that measures the time it will take to recoup, in the form of expected future cash flows, the net initial investment in a project. (731)

Peak-load pricing. Practice of charging a higher price for the same product or service when the demand for it approaches the physical limit of the capacity to produce that product or service. (438)

Perfectly competitive market. Exists when there is a homogeneous product with buying prices equal to selling prices and no individual buyers or sellers can affect those prices by their own actions. (768)

Period costs. All costs in the income statement other than cost of goods sold. (38)

Physical measure method. Method that allocates joint costs to joint products on the basis of the relative weight, volume, or other physical measure at the splitoff point of total production of these products during the accounting period. (570)

Planning. Selecting organization goals, predicting results under various alternative ways of achieving those goals, deciding how to attain the desired goals, and communicating the goals and how to attain them to the entire organization. (7)

Practical capacity. The level of capacity that reduces theoretical capacity by unavoidable operating interruptions such as scheduled maintenance time, shutdowns for holidays, and so on. (310)

Predatory pricing. Company deliberately prices below its costs in an effort to drive out competitors and restrict supply and then raises prices rather than enlarge demand. (439)

Prevention costs. Costs incurred to preclude the production of products that do not conform to specifications. (661)

Previous department costs. See *transferred-in costs.*

Price discount. Reduction in selling price below list selling price to encourage increases in customer purchases. (502)

Price discrimination. Practice of charging different customers different prices for the same product or service. (438)

Price-recovery component. Change in operating income attributable solely to changes in prices of inputs and outputs between one period and the next. (467)

Price variance. The difference between actual price and the budgeted price multiplied by actual quantity of input. Also called *input-price variance* or *rate variance.* (230)

Prime costs. All direct manufacturing costs. (42)

Pro forma statements. Budgeted financial statements. (182)

Probability. Likelihood or chance that an event will occur. (82)

Probability distribution. Describes the likelihood (or the probability) that each of the mutually exclusive and collectively exhaustive set of events will occur. (82)

Problem solving. Role of management accounting that focuses on comparative analysis for decision making. (10)

Process-costing system. Costing system in which the cost object is masses of identical or similar units of a product or service. (99)

Product. Any output that has a positive total sales value (or an output that enables an organization to avoid incurring costs). (566)

Product cost. Sum of the costs assigned to a product for a specific purpose. (44)

Product-cost cross-subsidization. Costing outcome where one undercosted (overcosted) product results in at least one other product being overcosted (undercosted). (140)

Product differentiation. Organization's ability to offer products or services perceived by its customers to be superior and unique relative to the products or services of its competitors. (457)

Product life cycle. Spans the time from initial R&D on a product to when customer service and support is no longer offered for that product. (436)

Product-mix decisions. Decisions about which products to sell and in what quantities. (391)

Product overcosting. A product consumes a low level of resources but is reported to have a high cost per unit. (140)

Product-sustaining costs. The costs of activities undertaken to support individual products regardless of the number of units or batches in which the units are produced. (148)

Product undercosting. A product consumes a high level of resources but is reported to have a low cost per unit. (140)

Production. Acquiring, coordinating, and assembling resources to produce a product or deliver a service. (14)

Production department. See *operating department.*

Production-denominator level. The denominator in the budgeted manufacturing fixed overhead rate computation. (264)

Production-volume variance. The difference between budgeted fixed overhead and fixed overhead allocated on the basis of actual output produced. Also called *denominator-level variance* and *output-level overhead variance.* (266)

Productivity. Measures the relationship between actual inputs used (both quantities and costs) and actual outputs produced; the lower the inputs for a given quantity of outputs or the higher the outputs for a given quantity of inputs, the higher the productivity. (480)

Productivity component. Change in costs attributable to a change in the quantity of inputs used in the current period relative to the quantity of inputs that would have been used in the prior period to produce the quantity of current period output. (467)

Profit center. Responsibility center where the manager is accountable for revenues and costs. (197)

Proration. The spreading of underallocated manufacturing overhead or overallocated manufacturing overhead among ending work in process, finished goods, and cost of goods sold. (119)

Purchase-order lead time. The time between placing an order and its delivery. (693)

Purchasing costs. Cost of goods acquired from suppliers including incoming freight or transportation costs. (692)

PV graph. Shows how changes in the quantity of units sold affect operating income. (66)

Qualitative factors. Outcomes that are difficult to measure accurately in numerical terms. (381)

Quality. The total features and characteristics of a product made or a service performed according to specifications to satisfy customers at the time of purchase and during use. (660)

Quality costs. See *costs of quality (COQ).*

Quantitative factors. Outcomes that are measured in numerical terms. (381)

Rate variance. See *price variance.*

Real rate of return. The rate of return demanded to cover investment risk (with no inflation). It has a risk-free element and a business-risk element. (746)

Reciprocal allocation method. See *reciprocal method.*

Reciprocal method. Cost allocation method that fully recognizes the mutual services provided among all support departments. Also called *reciprocal allocation method.* (540)

Reengineering. The fundamental rethinking and redesign of business processes to achieve improvements in critical measures of performance, such as cost, quality, service, speed, and customer satisfaction. (458)

Refined costing system. Costing system that reduces the use of broad averages for assigning the cost of resources to cost objects (jobs, products, services) and provides better measurement of the costs of indirect resources used by different cost objects—no matter how differently the different cost objects use indirect resources. (143)

Regression analysis. Statistical method that measures the average amount of change in the dependent variable associated with a unit change in one or more independent variables. (342)

Relevant costs. Expected future costs that differ among alternative courses of action being considered. (380)

Relevant range. Band of normal activity level or volume in which there is a specific relationship between the level of activity or volume and the cost in question. (33)

Relevant revenues. Expected future revenues that differ among alternative courses of action being considered. (380)

Reorder point. The quantity level of inventory on hand that triggers a new purchase order. (694)

Required rate of return (RRR). The minimum acceptable annual rate of return on an investment. Also called the *discount rate, hurdle rate, cost of capital,* or *opportunity cost of capital.* (727)

Research and development. Generating and experimenting with ideas related to new products, services, or processes. (4)

Residual income (RI). Accounting measure of income minus a dollar amount for required return on an accounting measure of investment. (795)

Residual term. The vertical difference or distance between actual cost and estimated cost for each observation in a regression model. (343)

Responsibility accounting. System that measures the plans, budgets, actions, and actual results of each responsibility center. (197)

Responsibility center. Part, segment, or subunit of an organization whose manager is accountable for a specified set of activities. (197)

Return on investment (ROI). An accounting measure of income divided by an accounting measure of investment. See also *accrual accounting rate of return.* (793)

Revenue allocation. The allocation of revenues that are related to a particular revenue object but cannot be traced to it in an economically feasible (cost-effective) way. (547)

Revenue center. Responsibility center where the manager is accountable for revenues only. (197)

Revenue driver. A variable, such as volume, that causally affects revenues. (61)

Revenue object. Anything for which a separate measurement of revenue is desired. (547)

Revenues. Inflows of assets (usually cash or accounts receivable) received for products or services provided to customers. (38)

Rework. Units of production that do not meet the specifications required by customers for finished units that are subsequently repaired and sold as good finished units. (633)

Rightsizing. See *downsizing.*

Rolling budget. Budget or plan that is always available for a specified future period by adding a period (month, quarter or year) to the period that just ended. Also called *continuous budget.* (184)

Safety stock. Inventory held at all times regardless of the quantity of inventory ordered using the EOQ model. (695)

Sales mix. Quantities of various products or services that constitute total unit sales. (74)

Sales-mix variance. The difference between (1) budgeted contribution margin for the actual sales mix, and (2) budgeted contribution margin for the budgeted sales mix. (510)

Sales-quantity variance. The difference between (1) budgeted contribution margin based on actual units sold of all products at the budgeted-mix and (2) contribution margin in the static budget (which is based on the budgeted units of all products to be sold at the budgeted mix). (511)

Sales value at splitoff method. Method that allocates joint costs to joint products on the basis of the relative total sales value at the splitoff point of the total production of these products during the accounting period. (569)

Sales-volume variance. The difference between a flexible-budget amount and the corresponding static-budget amount. (225)

Scorekeeping. Role of management accounting that focuses on accumulating data and reporting results to management describing how the organization is doing and how well it is implementing its strategies. (10)

Scrap. Residual material leftover when making a product. (633)

Selling-price variance. The difference between the actual selling price and the budgeted selling price multiplied by the actual units sold. (227)

Semivariable cost. See *mixed cost.*

Sensitivity analysis. A what-if technique that managers use to examine how an outcome will change if the original predicted data are not achieved or if an underlying assumption changes. (69)

Separable costs. All costs (manufacturing, marketing, distribution, and so on) incurred beyond the splitoff point that are assignable to each of the specific products identified at the splitoff point. (566)

Sequential allocation method. See *step-down method.*

Sequential tracking. Approach in a product-costing system in which recording of the journal entries occurs in the same order as actual purchases and progress in production. (707)

Service department. See *support department.*

Service-sector companies. Companies that provide services or intangible products to their customers. (36)

Service-sustaining costs. The costs of activities undertaken to support individual services. (148)

Simple regression. Regression model that estimates the relationship between the dependent variable and one independent variable. (342)

Single-rate cost-allocation method. See *single-rate method.*

Single-rate method. Allocation method that allocates costs in each cost pool to cost objects using the same rate per unit of a single allocation base. Also called *single-rate cost-allocation method.* (532)

Slope coefficient. Coefficient term in a cost estimation model that indicates the amount by which total cost changes when a one-unit change occurs in the level of activity within the relevant range. (333)

Source document. An original record that supports journal entries in an accounting system. (101)

Specification analysis. Testing of the assumptions of regression analysis. (358)

Splitoff point. The juncture in a joint-production process when two or more products become separately identifiable. (566)

Spoilage. Units of production that do not meet the specifications required by customers for good units and that are discarded or sold at reduced prices. (633)

Staff management. Staff (such as management accountants and human resources managers) who provide advice and assistance to line management. (13)

Stand-alone cost-allocation method. Method that uses information pertaining to each user of a cost object as a separate entity to determine the cost-allocation weights. (544)

Stand-alone revenue-allocation method. Method that uses product-specific information on the products in the bundle as weights for allocating the bundled revenues to the individual products. (549)

Standard. A carefully predetermined price, cost, or quantity. It is usually expressed on a per unit basis. (228)

Standard cost. A carefully determined cost of a unit of output. (228)

Standard costing. Costing system that traces direct costs to output produced by multiplying the standard prices or rates by the standard quantities of inputs allowed for actual outputs produced and allocates overhead costs on the basis of the standard overhead-cost rates times the standard quantities of the allocation bases allowed for the actual outputs produced. (257)

Standard error of the estimated coefficient. Regression statistic that indicates how much the estimated value of the coefficient is likely to be affected by random factors. (358)

Standard input. A carefully determined quantity of input required for one unit of output. (228)

Standard price. A carefully determined price that a company expects to pay for a unit of input. (228)

Static budget. Budget based on the level of output planned at the start of the budget period. (223)

Static-budget variance. Difference between an actual result and the corresponding budgeted amount in the static budget. (223)

Step cost function. A cost function in which the cost remains the same over various ranges of the level of activity, but the cost increases by discrete amounts (that is, increases in steps) as the level of activity changes from one range to the next. (348)

Step-down allocation method. See *step-down method.*

Step-down method. Cost allocation method that partially recognizes the mutual services provided among all support departments. Also called *sequential allocation method* or *step-down allocation method.* (528)

Stockout costs. Costs that result when a company runs out of a particular item for which there is customer demand. The company must act to meet that demand or suffer the costs of not meeting it. (692)

Strategic cost management describes cost management that specifically focuses on strategic issues. (4)

Strategy. Specifies how an organization matches its own capabilities with the opportunities in the marketplace to accomplish its objectives. (3)

Suboptimal decision making. Decisions in which the benefit to one subunit is more than offset by the costs or loss of benefits to the organization as a whole. Also called *incongruent decision making* or *dysfunctional decision making.* (762)

Sunk costs. Past costs that are unavoidable because they cannot be changed no matter what action is taken. (380)

Super-variable costing. See *throughput costing.*

Supply chain. Describes the flow of goods, services, and information from the initial sources of materials and services to the delivery of products to consumers, regardless of whether those activities occur in the same organization or in other organizations. (5)

Support department. Department that provides the services that assist other internal departments (operating departments and other support departments) in the company. Also called a *service department.* (532)

Target cost per unit. Estimated long-run cost per unit of a product or service that enables the company to achieve its target operating income per unit when selling at the target price. Target cost per unit is derived by subtracting the target operating income per unit from the target price. (425)

Target operating income per unit. Operating income that a company aims to earn per unit of a product or service sold. (425)

Target price. Estimated price for a product or service that potential customers will pay. (425)

Target rate of return on investment. The target annual operating income that an organization aims to achieve divided by invested capital. (432)

Theoretical capacity. The level of capacity based on producing at full efficiency all the time. (309)

Theory of constraints (TOC). Describes methods to maximize operating income when faced with some bottleneck and some nonbottleneck operations. (675)

Throughput contribution. Revenues minus the direct material costs of the goods sold. (675)

Throughput costing. Method of inventory costing in which only variable direct material costs are included as inventoriable costs. Also called *super-variable costing.* (306)

Time driver. Any factor in which a change in the factor causes a change in the speed of an activity. (671)

Time value of money. Takes into account that a dollar (or any other monetary unit) received today is worth more than a dollar received at any future time. (726)

Total factor productivity (TFP). The ratio of the quantity of output produced to the costs of all inputs used, based on current period prices. (481)

Total-overhead variance. The sum of the flexible-budget variance and the production-volume variance. (273)

Transfer price. Price one subunit (department or division) charges for a product or service supplied to another subunit of the same organization. (764)

Transferred-in costs. Costs incurred in previous departments that are carried forward as the product's costs when it moves to a subsequent process in the production cycle. Also called *previous department costs.* (612)

Trigger point. Refers to a stage in the cycle from purchase of direct materials to sale of finished goods at which journal entries are made in the accounting system. (708)

Uncertainty. The possibility that an actual amount will deviate from an expected amount. (71)

Underabsorbed indirect costs. See *underallocated indirect costs.*

Underallocated indirect costs. Allocated amount of indirect costs in an accounting period is less than the actual (incurred) amount in that period. Also called *underapplied indirect costs* or *underabsorbed indirect costs.* (118)

Underapplied indirect costs. See *underallocated indirect costs.*

Unfavorable variance. Variance that has the effect of decreasing operating income relative to the budgeted amount. Denoted U. (223)

Unit cost. Cost computed by dividing total cost by the number of units. Also called *average cost.* (35)

Unused capacity. The amount of productive capacity available over and above the productive capacity employed to meet consumer demand in the current period. (472)

Usage variance. See *efficiency variance.*

Value-added cost. A cost that, if eliminated, would reduce the actual or perceived value or utility (usefulness) customers obtain from using the product or service. (426)

Value chain. The sequence of business functions in which customer usefulness is added to products or services of a company. (4)

Value engineering. Systematic evaluation of all aspects of the value chain, with the objective of reducing costs while improving quality and satisfying customer needs. (426)

Variable cost. Cost that changes in total in proportion to changes in the related level of total activity or volume. (30)

Variable costing. Method of inventory costing in which only all variable manufacturing costs are included as inventoriable costs. Also called *direct costing.* (296)

Variable overhead efficiency variance. The difference between the actual quantity of variable overhead cost-allocation base used and budgeted quantity of variable overhead cost-allocation base that should have been used to produce actual output, multiplied by budgeted variable overhead cost per unit of cost-allocation base. (260)

Variable overhead flexible-budget variance. The difference between actual variable overhead costs incurred and flexible-budget variable overhead amounts. (259)

Variable overhead spending variance. The difference between actual variable overhead cost per unit and budgeted variable overhead cost per unit of the cost-allocation base, multiplied by actual quantity of variable overhead cost-allocation base used for actual output. (261)

Variance. The difference between an amount based on an actual result and the corresponding budgeted amount. (222)

Weighted-average process-costing method. Method of process costing that assigns the equivalent-unit cost of the work done to date (regardless of when it was done) to equivalent units completed and transferred out of the process and to equivalent units in ending work-in-process inventory. (602)

Work-in-process inventory. Goods partially worked on but not yet completed. Also called *work in progress.* (37)

Work in progress. See *work-in-process inventory.*

Work-measurement method. See *industrial-engineering method.*

AUTHOR INDEX

COMPANY INDEX

SUBJECT INDEX

D

E

F

Q

R

S

T

U

V

W

X

Y